FEDERICO GARCÍA LORCA: A LIFE

LORCA'S GRANADA

FIRE IN THE BLOOD: THE NEW SPAIN

IAN GIBSON

W · W · NORTON & Company
NEW YORK · London

THE Shameful Life OF SALVADOR DALÍ

The author and publishers are grateful to the institutions and individuals for permission to reproduce the drawings, paintings and photographs cited on pages 11–19. Although every effort has been
made to trace the owners and copyright holders of individual illustrations, the author and publishers
apologize for any errors or omissions and would be grateful to be notified of any corrections that
should be incorporated in the next edition or reprint of this volume.

For information about permission to reproduce selections from this book, write to Permissions,
W. W. Norton & Company, Inc., 500 Fifth Avenue, New York, NY 10110.

The text of this book is composed in Monotype Bell
with the display set in Belucian and Avant Garde Demi Oblique
Desktop composition by Gina Webster
Manufacturing by The Courier Companies, Inc.
Book design by Antonina Krass

Library of Congress Cataloging-in-Publication Data

Gibson, Ian.
The shameful life of Salvador Dalí / Ian Gibson. — 1st American ed.
p.   cm.
Originally published: London : Faber and Faber, 1997.
Includes bibliographical references and index.
ISBN 0-393-04624-9
Dalí, Salvador, 1904– . 2. Artists—Spain—Biography.
I. Title.
N7113.D3G53   1998
709'.2—dc21
[B]   97–46707
            CIP

W. W. Norton & Company, Inc., 500 Fifth Avenue, New York, N.Y. 10110
http://www.wwnorton.com

W. W. Norton & Company Ltd., 10 Coptic Street, London WC1A 1PU

1 2 3 4 5 6 7 8 9 0

For Rafael and Maite Santos Torroella,
guiding lights of this biography.

As always, for Carole.

And in loving memory of
my cousin, Rosy Gibb

Contents

Black and White Illustrations

work, which left its mark on his own. Miró, moreover, paved the way for him in Paris. (ADAGP, Paris and DACS, London)

175 Joan Miró, *The Harlequin's Carnaval*, 1924–5, reproduced in *La Révolution Surréaliste*, Paris, no. 8, 1 December 1926. A clear precedent for Dalí's beaches in paintings such as *Honey is Sweeter than Blood*. (ADAGP, Paris and DACS, London)

177 The last known picture of Lorca, Dalí and Buñuel together, accompanied by José Moreno Villa and José Rubio Sacristan. Madrid, in a park by the River Manzanares, 1926. (Don Juan Luis Buñuel Collection, Paris)

179 Lorca playing dead on the Dalís' terrace at Es Llané, Cadaqués, 1925 or 1927 (see colour plate VIII). Published in the New York little magazine, *Alhambra*, 1929.

180 Dalí, *La playa* ('The Beach'), 1927. Original and dimensions unknown. Published in *Verso y Prosa*, Murcia, April 1927. The fused heads of Dalí and Lorca lie on the beach. Note the exposed vein on the severed hand and wrist, which recurs in many of the paintings and drawings of Dalí's 'Lorca Period.'

187 Dalí, *Saint Sebastian with a sole's head*, 1927. Original, title and dimensions unknown. Published in *L'Amic de les Arts*, Sitges, 31 July 1927. A further allusion to Lorca.

189 Pablo Picasso, *Studio with Plaster Head*, 1925. Dalí saw this painting when he visited Picasso in Paris in 1926. Its influence is obvious in works such as *Composition with Three Figures* (*Neo-Cubist Academy*; colour plate IX). (Succession Picasso/DACS)

190 Dalí, *El poeta en la platja d'Empúries* ('The Poet on the Beach at Empúries'), 1927. Original and dimensions unknown. The poet is Lorca, who first visited the Greek and Roman remains at Empúries (Ampurias) with Dalí in 1925. Note the Dalínian flotsam and jetsam that relates the drawing to Dalí's great *Honey is Sweeter than Blood* (photograph on p. 210).

194 Dalí, *Autorretrat* ('Self-portrait'), 1926. Original and dimensions uknown. Published in *L'Amic de les Arts*, Sitges, 31 January 1927. Again, the fused heads of Dalí and Lorca.

196 Yves Tanguy, *Ring of Invisibility*, 1925. Published in *La Révolution Surréaliste*, Paris, no. 7, 15 June 1926, where Dalí certainly saw it. The skyscape and mysterious figures influenced Dalí's study for *Honey is Sweeter than Blood*. (ARS, NY and DACS, London/Giuseppe Nahmad Collection, Geneva)

197 Yves Tanguy, *Lost Animals*, 1926, reproduced in *La Révolution Surréaliste*, Paris, no. 8, 1 December 1926. The fish-head of the figure on the left probably inspired that of Dalí's Saint Sebastian (illustration on p. 187). (ARS, NY and DACS, London)

203 Dalí, *The Bather*, 1927. Ink, 37.3 x 49.1 cm. Federico García Lorca almost certainly collaborated on the drawing during his stay with Dalí that summer in Cadaqués. (The Salvador Dali Museum, St. Petersburg, Florida)

210 Dalí, *Honey is Sweeter than Blood*, 1927. Dimensions unknown. The painting has

apparently been lost. One of the key works of Dalí's 'Lorca Period', it shows the poet's severed head lying not far from Dalí's and what appears to be the mummified corpse of Luis Buñuel.

211   Yves Tanguy, *He Did What He Wanted*, 1927. 'I've stolen everything from Uncle Yves', Dalí once exaggerated, although the borrowings are considerable. To Tanguy's beaches or seabeds Dalí added the scintillating luminosity of the Empordà and a technique of extreme precision. (ARS, NY and DACS, London/Richard S. Zeisler Collection, New York)

212   Yves Tanguy, *Extinction of Useless Lights*, 1927. Dalí probably took note of the severed hand and the stark shadow projected by the object in the foreground. (ARS, NY and DACS, London/Museum of Modern Art, New York)

213   A Catalan cartoonist pokes fun at Dalí's *Honey is Sweeter than Blood* (see illustration on p. 210). The caption reads: 'And what is your opinion of these pictures?' 'They show that cars are on the increase—more road accidents every day.' (*La Veu de Catalunya*, Barcelona, 20 October 1927).

217   Buñuel with his portrait by Dalí. (Don Juan Buñuel Collection, Paris)

226   Jean Arp, *Mountain, Table, Anchor, Navel*, 1925. Dalí admired Arp's work, which he knew from photographs, and was struck by Breton's introduction to his 1927 catalogue. (Museum of Modern Art, New York)

233   Dalí, *Male Figure and Female Figure on Beach*, 1928. Dimensions and whereabouts unknown. Reproduced in *La Gaceta Literaria*, Madrid, 1 February 1929. More insinuating fingers.

253   At Le Havre in 1929 during a break from shooting the beach scene in *Un Chien andalou*. From left to right: Dalí, Buñuel, Simone Mareuil (the female protagonist), Buñuel's fiancée Jeanne Rucard and the actor who played the young man at the end of the film, Robert Hommet. (Don Juan Luis Buñuel Collection, Paris)

257   Dalí and Buñuel on the rocks at Cape Creus, 1929. (Don Juan Luis Buñuel Collection, Paris)

264   Marie-Laure and Charles de Noailles, 1929. (M. Edmond de la Haye Jousselin)

270   Gala stripping in the garden, *c.* 1924. (Fundació Gala–Salvador Dalí, Figueres)

271   Gala's wall-penetrating eyes photographed and touched up by Max Ernst, 1925. (ADAGP, Paris and DACS, London)

274   Gala as Harpie by Max Ernst. Page of drawings published in Paul Éluard's *Au Défaut du silence*, 1924. (ADAGP, Paris and DACS, London)

277   The very picture of elegance: Dalí and Gala with two unidentified acquaintances and behind them, sporting a bow tie, René Crevel, Barcelona, *c.* 1931. (Fundació Gala–Salvador Dalí, Figueres)

279   Dalí, *Portrait of Paul Éluard*, 1929. Oil on cardboard. 35 x 25 cm. Dalí began the portrait within days of meeting Éluard's wife, Gala, in Cadaqués. (private collection)

ACKNOWLEDGEMENTS

My first thanks must go to Faber and Faber who, in the shape of Matthew Evans, Robert McCrum and Julian Loose, believed in me sufficiently to guarantee the basic wherewithal to make this book possible. It took longer than planned, and I am grateful to Fabers for their forbearance.

At the top of this list, too, must go Antoni Pitxot, head of Dalí's Theatre-Museum in Figueres, without whose generous complicity I would never have received Dalí's confidences in 1986. While I worked on the biography he was consistently helpful.

The book is dedicated to the great authority on Dalí, Rafael Santos Torroella, and his wife Maite. It could not have been otherwise: for Santos Torroella not only suggested that I follow my biography on Lorca with one on Dalí but, as I struggled to do so, was always at the ready with his vast knowledge of the painter and his world. Maite, too, never failed me, her clarity of mind, her excellent memory and her shrewd appraisal of people proving vital time and again. It is impossible for me to thank these friends enough. As for my wife Carole, to whom the book is also dedicated, once again she has borne the brunt of my biographical ups and downs with fortitude, and has confirmed her status as my best critic. I promise her that I will never again embark on a work of this magnitude.

Special thanks must go to my literary agent, Ute Körner, and her assistant Guenny Rodewald: their encouragement has been of inestimable value to me throughout.

To Dalí's ex-secretary and 'military adviser', Captain Peter Moore, and his wife Catherine I owe a huge debt of gratitude. They have been generosity personified and with great patience have put up with endless questioning, demands for documents and other requests.

Nanita Kalaschnikoff, the woman who after Gala meant most to Dalí, has been a marvellous collaborator. Endless discussions with her over the years in Marbella, London, Figueres, Cadaqués and Paris, and an infinity of telephone calls, have helped me to understand many facets of Dalí's personality that would otherwise have escaped me.

The book would have been infinitely poorer without the unstinting collaboration of

Reynolds and Eleanor Morse and the staff at the Salvador Dali Museum in St Petersburg, Florida, where Marshall Rousseau, Joan Knopf, Peter Tush and Carol Butler were unfailingly helpful. At the museum Reynolds Morse allowed me the rare privilege of perusing his monumental Dalí journal, which, when published, will prove to be our leading source of first-hand information on the artist and his complicated world. The Morses' library and collection of newspaper cuttings also proved invaluable.

So, too, did the help and encouragement provided at the Museo Nacional Centro de Arte Reina Sofía in Madrid (MNCARS) by Miguel del Valle Inclán and Antonio Majado, who answered my constant enquiries and requests for photocopies with faultless efficiency and generosity. It is collaborators such as these who make the biographer's at times agonising life worthwhile.

Other friends helped in Madrid. José Bello, his memory astonishing at ninety-three, continued to be a fount of information about Dalí, Lorca, Buñuel and the Residencia de Estudiantes days (the Residencia's current director, José García Velasco, was the perfect host on numerous occasions, and thanks, too, to Ana Gutiérrez). Angeles Vian Herrero, librarian of the Faculty of Fine Arts at the Universidad Complutense, showed me files relating to Dalí's years at the Special School of San Fernando. The Hemeroteca Municipal (Municipal Newspaper Library) came up trumps as usual, and I am particularly grateful to Matilde López Adán. Alberto and Conchita Reig Tapia helped in more ways than one. José Gómez de la Serna put his experience as a notary public at my disposal and told me how to go about locating Dalí's wills, and the then Minister of Culture, Carmen Alborch, earned my deep gratitude by instructing the relevant authorities to make them available to me.

I am beholden to Miguel Domenech Martínez, Dalí's lawyer, who in a long interview helped me to understand better different aspects of the legal tangle surrounding the Dalís when they returned to Spain full-time in the early 1980s.

Moving to Spain's east coast, I must thank the Gala-Salvador Dalí Foundation in Figueres, in particular Fèlix Fanés, director of the Institute of Dalinian Studies, who allowed me to work in the archive before it was officially opened to researchers, and his colleague Montserrat Aguer. I am also grateful to Ramón Boixadós, Ana Beristain, Margarita Ruiz Combalía and Luis Peñuelas. Antoni Pitxot I have already mentioned

Also in Figueres much help was forthcoming at the Biblioteca Municipal Fages de Climent, where Mari Angels Vayreda and Maria Luïsa Vidal looked after my every research need with a solicitiousness that went far beyond professional efficiency. Narcís Oliveras i Terradas and his wife made up for one notable deficiency at the library by allowing me most kindly to work with their complete and unique file of *Empordà Federal*.

Erika Serna i Coba, librarian of the Arxiu Històric Comarcal, did me many favours. So, too, did Eva Astarloa, of the Arxiu Històric Municipal. Maria Asunció Trayter led me to the stereoscope belonging to her forebear Esteban Trayter and which so impressed Dalí as a child. Alicia Viñas showed me round the Museu de l'Empordà and took me to meet her aunt Carme Roget, Dalí's adolescent girlfriend. Josep Maria Joan Rosa accompanied me to the Pichots' Torre del Molí. Alfons Romero was a mine of information about Dalí's home town. Durán's Hotel, Dalí's HQ in Figueres, provided the relaxation, and I am grateful to Lluís Durán, his wife and staff for many pleasant hours of conversation about Dalí, Figueres, the tramuntana and related topics, not least the wines of the region. The historian Antoni Egea Codina kindly helped with information about the first Dalís in Llers. In Cadaqués, Rosa Maria Salleras provided fascinating information about the young Dalí, not least about his horror of locusts. Carlos Lozano's first-hand experience of Dalí's court in Paris and Cadaqués was invaluable. Pere Vehí shared his wide knowledge of Dalí, and his remarkable archive, most liberally (I will never forget the hours spent in the Bar Boyà, where something akin to Dalinian madness can take hold of the unwary researcher). Among other favours, it was he who enabled me to establish contact with Enric Sabater, Dalí's second secretary and one of the most elusive men I have ever met. My thanks to him for our long conversation on that occasion, and for subsequent favours.

As regards the geological structure of Cape Creus, with its micaschist metamorphoses which so influenced Dalí, I am indebted to Miguel Angel Casares López, who went to considerable trouble to put together a reading list for me.

Around the corner at Roses, Kiko Fransoy Molina, of the Land Registry Office, never flinched when I asked him for yet more photocopies of deeds relating to Dalí's properties.

Barcelona, of course, was another centre of operations. The contribution to my research by the late Montserrat Dalí, Dalí's favourite cousin, was immense. She provided not just the small print of family history but helped me to understand the Dalís' feelings about Catalunya and Spain. I remember her with intense pleasure, not least a prolonged and fruitful lunch at the Tres Portes. Later, Eulalia Maria Bas i Dalí, her daughter, was generous in putting family documents at my disposal. Dalí's relative Gonzalo Serraclara de la Pompa, too, was an invaluable source of family information. Without him I would never have understood the Barcelona years of the painter's father. As regards the mother's side of the family, the knowledge, archive and generosity of Felipe Domènech Biosca were fundamental.

Still in Barcelona, the publisher Eduard Fornés was a vital ally. At the Diocesan

Archive, Father Leandre Niqui Puigvert was instrumental in helping me to trace the ecclesiastical papers relating to Don Salvador Dalí's second marriage (thanks also to Father Josep Maria Martí Bonet). The staff of the Arxiu Històric de la Ciutat (Casa de l'Ardiaca) were courteous and efficient despite working in painfully restricted conditions. Maria Lluïsa Bachs Benítez was assiduous in searching out the wedding certificate of Salvador Dalí Cusí and Felipa Domènech, as well as other documents, and Víctor Fernández Puertas was consistently helpful to me, sending copies of his latest discoveries in the field of Dalinian studies. I am grateful to him, too, for guiding me in the direction of the Joan Abelló Museum in Mollet del Vallès, whose Dalí papers, then mainly unpublished, were to prove of great interest to my research. My sincere thanks to both Joan Abelló Prat and his secretary, Victoria Pérez. Also to Lluís Permanyer, who provided me with useful information and a tape-recording of his vital interview with Dalí, and to Josep Playà i Maset, author of an excellent small book on Dalí and the Empordà and himself an *empordaneso*, who was always at hand to put me right on small details. At the Biblioteca de Catalunya, the director, Manuel Jorba, and his staff were charming and efficient.

South from Barcelona, at Sitges, erstwhile home of *L'Amic de les Arts*, María Saborit was a charming hostess at the Biblioteca Popular Santiago Rusiñol. I recall with nostalgia working in the Miquel Utrillo room, with its complete collection of *Destino*.

To Dalí's 'Italian family', Giuseppe and Mara Albaretto and their daughter Cristiana, I owe a deeper understanding not only of Dalí but of Gala's relationship with William Rotlein. It was a privilege to be welcomed to their Turin mansion and be shown part of their collection.

A very special word of thanks must go to Michael Dibb and Louise Allen, whose encouragement has been invaluable as we worked together on the two *Omnibus* films on Dalí made while the book was being written. Interviewing for the *Omnibus* project brought me closer to key figures in Dalí's world than would otherwise have been the case, and Mike and Louise's comments on these people, many of whom we came to like, were always helpful and pertinent. So, too, were those of our film editor, Chris Swain.

During these five years of research my old friend Eutimio Martín in Aix en Provence was always a present help, keeping an eye on new publications in France, faxing reviews and coming up with frequent research suggestions. Eutimio engineered the location of Dalí and Gala's marriage certificate in Paris and then obtained a copy, a highly difficult operation which required the assistance of Gérard Dufour, of the University of Aix en Provence, and Antonio Portanet. My grateful thanks to all three of them. I could not have believed that so much red tape still existed in France.

My account of the collaboration of Dalí and Buñuel would have been much less satisfactory without the outstanding books and collaboration of Agustín Sánchez Vidal, undoubtedly the world authority on the director.

At the Edward James Foundation, in West Dean, Sussex, the archivist, Sharon-Michi Kusunoki, was courtesy itself.

In Paris, Didier Schulmann and Nathalie Schoeller arranged for me to see surrealist catalogues at the Pompidou Centre, and Yves Péret, director of the Bibliothèque Littéraire Jacques Doucet, and his assistant M. Bertonnier, were helpful as I worked my way through Dalí's letters to Breton. At the National Gallery of Scotland in Edinburgh I was treated with similar courtesy as I perused the other half of the correspondence: my thanks particularly to Patrick Elliott.

In New York, Michael Stout gave me and the *Omnibus* team generously of his time and insights into Dalí's last years.

It is a pleasure to thank Dawn Ades, David and Judy Gascoyne, Michael Raeburn and Marilyn McCully for their ready sharing of information.

Donald S. Lamm, my American publisher, made some extremely helpful comments at proof stage.

I hope that the following, all of whom assisted me in one way or another, will forgive me for not explaining what I owe to each of them. My thanks to all and every one—and to anyone whom I may inadvertently have overlooked:

Bernard Adams, Conxa Alvarez (library of the Universidad de Barcelona), John Anderson, Narcís-Jordi Aragó, Manuel Arroyo, Benjamí Artigas, April Ashley, Henriette Babeanu, Francisco Badia, Àngel Baró i Noguer, Joella Bayer, the late Isidor Bea, Blanca Berasátegui, Josep Maria Bernils, Jesús Blázquez, Juan Manuel Bonet, Juan and Michèle Borrás, Domingo Bóveda (La Salle College, Figueres), Juan Luis Buñuel, Humphrey Burton, Pere Buxeda, José Luis Caño, Juan Cano Areche, Màrius Carol, Narcís Castella Calzada, Cate Arries, Elizabeth and David Challen, François Chapon, William Chislett, Louis Adrean (The Cleveland Museum of Art), Carmina Virgili (Colegio de España, Paris), Cathy Coleman, Miguel and Carola Condé, Jesús Conte, Xavier Corberó, Fleur Cowles, Peter Crookston, the late Anna Maria Dalí Domènech, Andrew Dempsey, José Díaz, James Dickie, the late Felipe Domènech Vilanova, Carlos Dorado, Luis Durán, Cécile Éluard, Isidre Escofet, Ramón and Sra Estalella, Alberto Estrada Vilarasa, Duncan Fallowell, José Fernández Berchí, Luis Ignacio Fernández Posada, Firmo Ferrer, Mosén Xabier Ferrer, Albert Field, Miquel Figueras i Xuclà, Dolores Devesa (Filmoteca Nacional, Madrid), Joan Florensa, Raimundo Fortuny Marqués, José Luis Franco Grande, Paul Funge, Fundación Federico García Lorca,

Madrid, Tomás García García, Pere Garriga Camps, Daniel Giralt-Miracle, Montserrat Gómez, Thomas Glick, Emilio Gómez G. Mallo, the late Maruja Gómez G. Mallo, Carlos Gonzales, María Luisa González, Eric Green, Julien Green, David and Marie-Jeanne Harley, Linda Ashton (Harry Ransom Humanities Research Center, University of Texas at Austin), L. P. Harvey, Edmond de la Haye Jousselin, Miguel Hernández, Michael D. Higgins, Miquel Horta, Frank Hunter, Rafael Inglada, Enric Jardí, Xavier Jiménez, the late Paz Jiménez Encina de Marquina, Allen Josephs, Richard Kidwell, Marc Lacroix, Carlton Lake, Michael Lambert, Donald Lamm, John Liddy, Mark Little, Tomás Llorens, Bernabé and Cecilia López García, Ana-Galicia López López, Anja Louis, Juan de Loxa, the late Peter Luddington, Rosa Maria Malet, Sr and Sra Marín Asensio, Josep Maria Marques (Archivo Diocesano, Girona), José María Martínez Palmer, the late Juan Ramón Masoliver, George Melly, Quim Miró, César Antonio Molina, Sean and Rosemary Mulcahy, Billy O Hanluain, Helen Oppenheimer, Karl Orend, Enrique and María Dolores Orio Trayter, Guillermo de Osma, Inés Padrosa Gorgot, Pandora, Juan Pérez de Ayala, José Pierre, Justo Polo, Emilia Pomés Palomer, Jaume Pont Ibáñez, Fernando Pérez Puente, María Carmen García-Redondo Pasual (Radio Televisión Española), Luis Revenga, Edward C. Riley, Luis Romero, Robert Royal, Sr. Romeu (Casa del Libro 'Catalònia', Barcelona). Francesc Ros, Luis Saiz, Christopher Sawyer-Lauçanno, Teresa Serraclara Pla, Norio Shimizu, Beatrice and Georges de la Taille, Xavier Tarraubella, Andréu Teixidor de Ventós, Joan Tharrats, Hugh Thomas, Clifford Thurlow and Iris Gioia, Javier Tomeo, Mosén Pedro Travesa, Joan Trayter, Gillian Varley (Victoria and Albert Museum Library), Chelsea E. Vaughn, Dr Manuel Vergara, Jaume Vidal Oliveras, Joan Vives, Robert Whitaker, Marian White (Tate Gallery Library), Phil Wickham (British Film Institute), Jordi Xargayño Teixidor, Joaquim and Dolors Xicot, Carlos A. Rodriguez Zapater.

The author would also like to acknowledge Compañia General Fabril Editora, Buenos Aires, for *La arboleda perdida. Libros I y II de memorias*, by Rafael Alberti; Change International/Equivalences, Paris, for *Dali: inédits de Belgrade*, by Branko Aleksie; Éditions Gallimard, Paris for 'Angelus'; Paidos, Buenos Aires, for *Dalí desnudado*, by Alain Bosquet; Éditions Gallimard for *Le Surréalisme et la peinture, nouvelle èdition revue et corrigèe 1928–1965* and *Oeuvres complètes, 2 volumes*, by André Breton; Editions Robert Laffont, Paris, for *Mon Dernier Soupir*, by Luis Buñuel; The Ecco Press, New York, for *The Passionate Years*, by Caresse Crosby; Dasa Edicions, F. L. for *The Secret Life of Salvador Dali*; Quartet Books, London, for *The Unspeakable Confessions of Salvador Dalí*, by Salvador Dalí; Random House UK Ltd for *The Diary of a Genius*, by Salvador Dalí, translated by Richard Howard; Editions Gallimard for *Lettres à Gala* and *Oeuvres com-*

plètes, 2 volumes, by Paul Éluard; The Museum of Modern Art, New York, for *Fantastic Art, Dada, Surrealism*, edited by Alfred H. Barr Jr, essays by Georges Hugnet; Paragon House, New York, for *In Quest of Dalí*, by Carlton Lake; Herederos de Federico García Lorca for extracts from Lorca's work, and translations by Ian Gibson. *Oda a Salvador Dalí*; 'Thamar y Amnón' (*Romancero gitano*); 'Muerto de amor' (*Romancero gitano*); *Oda a Walt Whitman*; and '*Panorama ciego de Nueva York*' (*Poeta en Nueva York*) by Federico García Lorca from *Obras Completa*, and extract from *Epistolaria completo*, copyright © by Herederos de Federico Garcia Lorca. Ian Gibson's English-language translations copyright © by Ian Gibson and Herederos de Federico García Lorca. All rights reserved. For information regarding rights and permissions for works by Federico García Lorca, please contact William Peter Kosmas, Esq., 77 Rodney Court, 6/8 Maida Vale, London W9 1TJ. Black Sparrow Press for 'Explosion of the Swan, Salvador Dalí on Federico García Lorca', by Gerard Malanga, from *Sparrow*, 35; Editorial Juventud, arcelona, for *Vivencias con Salvador Dalí*, by Emilio Puignau; Editorial Planeta, Barcelona, for *Lorca–Dalí. Una amistad traicionada*, by Antonina Rodrigo; Editorial Juventud for *El mundo de ayer*, by Stefan Zweig; British Broadcasting Corporation for Dalí interview with Malcolm Muggeridge, on *Panorama*; London Weekend Television for 'Hello Dalí!', on *Aquarius*.

The author and publishers regret any inadvertent omission or inaccuracies, and would be pleased to rectify these at the earliest opportunity.

Salvador Dalí is not a trustworthy source of information about himself. From his adolescence he set out consciously to become a myth, and he continued to work at being Dalí even after he had achieved his goal. A vital stage in the process was his *The Secret Life of Salvador Dalí*, written in French and published in English translation, for American consumption, in 1942, when he was thirty-eight. Whatever its other qualities, the *Secret Life* is not concerned with rigorous autobiographical truth. On the contrary, it goes out of its way to distort it, becoming, in the process, a biographical minefield. Dalí never published a sequel, and his boastful diary, *Journal d'un génie* (1964), which purports to prove that the daily life of a genius is different in kind from that of other mortals, is a very poor substitute. He did, however, continue on his myth-making path by encouraging other writers, in particular Louis Pauwels and André Parinaud, to publish accounts of his verbal reminiscences. Pauwels's *Les Passions selon Dalí* (1968) and Parinaud's *Comment on devient Dalí* (1973)—the latter was published in English as *The Unspeakable Confessions of Salvador Dalí*—are in their way even less reliable than the *Secret Life* as sources, since it is never made clear how the texts were put together or to what extent their respective editors intervened in shaping them. While no biography of Dalí can avoid using these four books, particularly the *Secret Life*—which despite its distortions contains significant clues between the lines—they ought to be treated with ever-vigilant scepticism. This I have tried to do.

Dalí, understandably, did not like biographers (beginning with his sister), and if his reaction to Françoise Gilot and Carlton Lake's *My Life with Picasso* is anything to go by, almost certainly feared them. Perhaps the *Secret Life* was an early attempt to forestall such meddlers? Perhaps Dalí hoped that, if he himself displayed his alleged 'secrets' in public, nobody else would bother to enquire further? If so, he was mistaken. We badly want to know the real secrets of an artist who, at his best, stirred and challenged the imagination of his age. Moreover, towards the end of his life, the ailing Dalí gave signs of wanting to set the biographical record straight, at least in one regard.

In January 1986, thanks to Dalí's friend Antoni Pitxot, the painter summoned me to meet him in Figueres—at once. I was in Madrid and caught the next plane. Dalí, it transpired, desperately wanted to convince me that his great friend Federico García Lorca had loved him sexually, not merely 'platonically', and to ensure that I made this clear in the second volume of my biography of the poet. Despite his appalling physical condition, his difficulty in articulating and his evident despair, he provided me with some astonishing details about that relationship which I was able to include only partially in the volume in question, and which appear in the present book for the first time. I could hardly believe my ears.

I was angry with myself for not having got to Dalí sooner, while he was still in reasonable health, and promised to return. But, with Lorca to finish and the painter in rapid decline, I never did. Three years later Dalí was dead. I then realised that, since that January afternoon in 1986, I had been pondering without fully realising it on the possibility of writing a biography of the painter. It was another two years before the project crystallized. Now the task is done, with what success only others can judge.

Whether my view of Dalí as a shame-driven personality is accepted generally remains to be seen. What is certain is that, seven years after his death, the man, his work and his world urgently need reassessment. My hope is that this book will be seen as a useful contribution to such a reconsideration.

Ian Gibson
Restábal (Granada)
22 June 1997

The Witches of Llers

The remains of the little Catalan town of Llers stand on a hill overlooking the plain of the Upper Empordà region in north-east Spain. They are a gaunt reminder of the ferocious civil war that unleashed itself in July 1936 and raged for almost three years. In February 1939 Llers was bursting at the seams with Republican soldiers and thousands of refugees fleeing from General Franco. When it became obvious that all was lost, the military ordered the civilians out and fused the magazine, installed in the parish church, before hurrying off to cross the French frontier at Le Perthus, an hour's march away. Behind them, the terrific explosion blew most of the town sky-high.[1]

Llers was once reputed to be infested with witches. Perhaps, some locals today will hint ironically, their malign influence was responsible for the place's terrible fate, hardly mitigated by the construction, after the war, of a new quarter further down the hill. Today the town is only a shadow of its former self.

Salvador Dalí's ancestors on his father's side were agricultural labourers from Llers, although the painter never mentions the fact in his misleadingly titled autobiography, *The Secret Life of Salvador Dalí*, or anywhere else in his work. That he knew about his background there can be no doubt, however; and in 1925 he illustrated a book called *The Witches of Llers* by his friend, the Empordanese poet Carles Fages de Climent.

The Llers parish registers, which fortunately survived the civil war, enable us to trace these Dalí forbears back step-by-step to the late seventeenth century, but no further.[2] Some earlier documentation has come to light in the Historical Archive at Girona, the provincial capital. It shows that, while a census carried out in 1497 mentions no Dalís in Llers, a notarial protocol dated 12 April 1558 lists among its inhabitants a certain

Chapter ONE

Pere Dalí. This man may have been the father of the Joan Dalí who, according to a seventeenth-century Latin document preserved in the same archive, bought an inner courtyard in Llers in 1591 which was in turn inherited by his son, Gregori, and then by his grandson of the same name. The latter, who sold the courtyard in 1699, is the first Dalí to appear in the surviving Llers records.[3]

Dalí is neither a Spanish nor a Catalan name, and has almost completely disappeared throughout the Iberian Peninsula. The painter repeatedly claimed that his forbears, and accordingly his surname, were of Arab origin. 'In my family tree my Arab lineage going back to the time of Cervantes has been almost definitely established,' he boasts in the *Secret Life*.[4] Other remarks of his show that he had in mind the notorious Dalí Mamí, a sixteenth-century pirate who fought for the Turks and was responsible, among other dubious achievements, for Miguel de Cervantes's period of captivity in Algeria. But there is not a shred of evidence to suggest that the artist was related to that adventurer.[5]

Insisting on his 'Arab lineage', Dalí once pushed the date of the connection back much further than the sixteenth century, claiming that his ancestors descended from the Moors who invaded Spain in AD 711. 'From these origins,' he added, 'comes my love of everything that is gilded and excessive, my passion for luxury and my love of oriental clothes.'[6] Again and again we find him referring to such 'atavisms'. On one occasion a burning summer thirst is ascribed to this origin;[7] on another, the 'African desert' featured in his painting *Perspectives* (1936–7).[8] A later picture gave rise to the commentary: 'I always paint those vast sandy expanses that go as far as the eye can see. I don't know why; I have never been in North Africa. I suppose it's an atavism of the Arab blood.'[9] Dalí even liked to think that the readiness of his skin to go almost black in the sun was another Arab trait.[10]

It seems that Dalí was right to claim Arab blood—or, at least, Moorish. The surname occurs regularly throughout the Muslim world, and there are several Dalís in the Tunisian, Moroccan and Algerian telephone guides (rendered indifferently Dalí, Dallagi, Dallai, Dallaia, Dallaji and, particularly, Daly).[11] Oddly, though, the painter never seems to have delved further into his background. Had he done so, he might have discovered that in the local Catalan of the River Ebro region there used to be an interesting trace of Spain's Muslim past in the noun *dalí*, from the Arabic for 'guide' or 'leader', which designated a kind of strong staff wielded by the *daliner*, or boss, of the men employed to tow boats from the riverbank.[12] It might also have dawned on him that from the same Arabic root comes the Catalan *adalil* and Spanish *adalid*, a not-too-common term in both languages for 'leader' (and which has given rise to the Arab surname Dalil, also quite frequent in North Africa). Dalí enjoyed saying that the fact of being called Salvador showed that he was destined to be the 'Saviour' of Spanish art. Had he realized that his highly unusual surname coincided with the word for 'guide' or 'leader' in Arabic, he would no doubt have informed the world, just as he liked to tell people that it corresponded phonetically to the Catalan *delit*, 'delight'. As it was, he hugely enjoyed its extreme rarity, emphasizing its palatal 'l' by energetically pressing his tongue against the roof of his mouth, and coming down hard on the accented 'í'. Salvador Dalí simply could not have had a rarer, or more colourful, surname, and it gave him endless pleasure.[13]

It may be, in view of what has been said, that the first Dalís to settle in Llers in the fifteenth century were *moriscos*, the pejorative term for the Spanish Muslims who opted for forced conversion to Christianity rather than expulsion after the fall of Granada in 1492 to Ferdinand and Isabella, the event that marked the end of the so-called Christian 'Reconquest' of Spain and inaugurated centuries of harsh religious and racial repression. But if so we do not know from where they came. In the extant parish registers of Llers the first reference to the family occurs in 1688 when Gregori Dalí, described in the Girona Latin document already mentioned as 'laborator Castri de Llers' ('labourer of the stronghold of Llers') and here, in Catalan, as a 'young labourer' ('jove trebellador'), married Sabina Rottlens, daughter of a carpenter from the nearby and much larger town of Figueres, today capital of the Upper Empordà.[14] Like Gregori Dalí and his father before him, the subsequent generations of Dalí menfolk are classified in the records almost invariably as 'labourers', although a few were blacksmiths, including the painter's great-great-grandfather, Pere Dalí Raguer, born at Llers in the 1780s.[15] Among the ruins of the town there is a wall with a bricked-up doorway which the locals claim was the entrance to the Dalí forge, 'Can Dagué' ('The House of the Dagger-Maker'). They also point out the site of a solid stone house erected by another Dalí forbear: only the site, though, because 'Can Dalí' ('Dalí's House') was blown to pieces in the 1939 explosion.[16]

At the beginning of the nineteenth century, for reasons unknown, Silvestre Dalí Raguer, the elder brother of Pere, the blacksmith, moved from Llers to the isolated fishing village of Cadaqués, forty miles away on the other side of the mountains flanking the sea. The first reference to him in the Cadaqués parish records comes in 1804, when the baptism of his son Felipe is registered.[17] Silvestre's profession is not stated. After losing his first wife in Llers, Pere Dalí followed his brother to Cadaqués where, in 1817, he married a local girl, Maria Cruanyes.[18] Several entries in the parish registers describe him as 'blacksmith', so it seems safe to assume that on arrival in

Cadaqués he continued the profession he had practised in Llers.[19] Pere Dalí and Maria Cruanyes had three sons: Pere, Cayetano and, in 1822, Salvador, the future painter's great-grandfather.[20] In 1843 the latter married Francisca Viñas, whose father, according to the wedding certificate, was a 'labourer',[21] although in another document he is described as a sailor.[22] According to gossip transmitted years later to the Catalan writer Josep Pla, Salvador Dalí Cruanyes and his wife led a turbulent life together and petitioned, unsuccessfully, for a divorce.[23]

Cadaqués

Cadaqués, famous thanks to the work of Salvador Dalí, is severed from the plain of the Upper Empordà by a coastal range dominated by the forbidding, maquis-clothed hump of the Pení Mountain, which rises to 613 metres. Despite the twists and turns, and the narrowness of the road, today it only takes about forty minutes to drive here leisurely from Figueres. In the 1800s it was a very different matter and the return journey could not be done in a day. An adequate road connecting the village to Roses, and thence to Figueres, was not built until early in the twentieth century. For Cadaqués, the Land's End of eastern Spain, the sea was not only its livelihood but its highway in and out. The inhabitants did not feel Empordanese, had little time for the *sardana* (the national dance of Catalunya), spoke their own peculiar version of Catalan, known as *salat*, and, unlike the denizens of the Empordà plain, enjoyed dressing in lively colours. In essence, as Josep Pla maintained, the place was an island.[24]

The south-east-facing bay of Cadaqués is the deepest on the hazardous Costa Brava and the most protected from the elements. Here, when the sea outside is lashed into a fury, boats can lie peacefully at anchor. Thanks to this fine natural harbour, Cadaqués boasted a sizeable merchant fleet until the early years of the twentieth century and maintained an active Mediterranean and South American trade. Many Cadaqués men had been to Cuba or Africa but never to Figueres, and the sailors were often away from home for months on end.

Over the centuries Cadaqués supplied fighters as well as mariners, and whenever the Crown of Aragon (which from AD 1137 incorporated Catalunya) embarked on a new Mediterranean enterprise, the *cadaquesencs* were sure to be there, as happened in 1228–9, when King Jaume I seized Majorca from the Moors. As a result of this conquest, the Majorcan variety of Catalan is deeply influenced by *salat*.

Desperately exposed to attack from the sea, unable to depend on assistance from the

Cadaqués today.

hinterland, Cadaqués was early fortified by the counts of Empúries, lords of the region, against Moorish and Turkish incursions. Its massive ramparts did not prevent it from being often sacked, though: by the Moors in 1444, when its archives were destroyed; by Barbarossa in 1534; and several times more over the next few hundred years. Even in the early eighteenth century, when Spain was still a power to be reckoned with, Moorish raiders continued to threaten the coast. All of this, added to the hazards attending fishing in the area, meant that the people of Cadaqués developed a tough, independent character. For Josep Pla, their fabled tenacity can best be appreciated in the patiently constructed dry slate walls (*parets seques*)—almost two thousand kilometres of them, it has been calculated[25]—with which they have terraced the hillsides, protecting them from erosion: only a people of immense determination, held Pla, could have succeeded in taming such a hostile environment and making it productive.[26]

In the nineteenth century Cadaqués earned its living principally from wine and salted fish. Among the latter, its anchovies were famous and much in demand at Rome. Coral culled by divers from nearby Cape Creus was also exported profitably. From Civitavecchia and Genoa the boats brought back wood for making wine and fish barrels, and by mid-century the population was reasonably prosperous. But then disaster struck when, in 1883, the phylloxera epidemic that had already ravaged France, and, the previous year, the Empordà plain, reached Cadaqués, and the carefully terraced hillsides lost their vines. The devastation spelt poverty and exile for many families, and reduced the population from 2,500 to 1,500 souls.[27]

Another consequence of the phylloxera was an increase in smuggling. Cadaqués had always done a strong line in contraband, a profession encouraged by the Costa Brava's innumerable inlets and caves, ideal for hiding booty. Now the proclivity received a new impetus, and the village, cut off from the rest of the country by its mountain barrier but only a few miles by sea from the French frontier, became an Empordanese version of Gibraltar. Salt, much in demand in Cadaqués for curing fish, was the prime objective, since great savings could be made by avoiding the government tax on the commodity. Before long, however, the authorities discovered the reason for the sharp decline in revenue from that quarter and began to take repressive action.[28] Silk, coffee, essence of perfume and tobacco leaves were also landed in huge quantities. The latter were furtively rolled into cigars and cigarettes and then re-exported. *Cadaqués, tabaquers, contrabandistes, bons mariners i lladres* ran the saying, attributed to the nearby, and rival, seaside village of Port de la Selva: 'Cadaqués, tobacco hawkers, smugglers, good sailors and thieves'. It was a neatly comprehensive description of how these people made their living.

A Paranoiac in the Family

Salvador Dalí Cruanyes and Francisca Viñas had two children, Aniceto Raimundo Salvador, born in 1846,[29] and Gal Josep Salvador, on 1 July 1849.[30] Gal, who was thus named in honour of Saint Gall (whose feast day is 1 July), was living by the age of twenty with a married woman from Roses, Teresa Cusí Marcó, five years his senior, and the latter's daughter, Catalina Berta Cusí, born in 1863.[31] On 25 July 1871 Teresa gave birth to Gal's daughter Aniceta Francisca Ana, who died the following year.[32] Then, on 25 October 1872, she produced a son, Salvador Rafael Aniceto, the future painter's father,[33] and, on 23 January 1874, her last child, Rafael Narciso Jacinto.[34] Two months later, her estranged husband Pedro Berta having died, she married Gal.[35] The fact that Salvador and Rafael were born out of wedlock was hidden from future members of the family: the Dalís tended to be secretive.[36]

About their lives during those early years we know hardly anything. Salvador Dalí's father was born, he told him in 1921, 'in a white house beside the church'. On the same occasion he recalled happy days before the phylloxera struck the vines and, it seems, misled him into believing that his paternal grandfather, Gal Dalí, had been a doctor.[37] In fact, as a document in the Roses Land Registry office shows, he was a *taponero*, that is, a maker of wooden or cork stoppers for casks: a relatively lucrative profession in Cadaqués, given the lively export trade in fish, olives and, until the phylloxera outbreak, wine. The same document details the small, one-storey house that Gal inherited on the death of his mother in 1870. Situated at 321 Calle del Call, it is described as being in a lamentable state of repair. This, presumably, was the 'white house beside the church' in which Dalí's father and uncle were born.[38]

Gal Dalí later got into the transport business, running a horsedrawn 'bus' between Cadaqués and Figueres. According to a vaguely remembered anecdote in Figueres, he painted a large 'G' and 'T' on the back of the carriage. They stood for Gal and Teresa, his wife, but also meant 'Gràcies i Torneu', 'Thanks and Please Come Again'. He was something of a character.[39]

Around 1881 Gal Dalí moved to Barcelona. According to family tradition the main reason for this decision was that he found he could no longer stand the tramuntana. This fierce north wind, as integral a part of life in the Upper Empordà as the rain in London, has to be experienced to be believed. Dry and bitterly cold in winter, it roars and blasts its way down through the passes of the Pyrenees (hence tramuntana, 'from across the mountains'), sweeping the sky clear of clouds, and, hitting the Empordà, forces the cypresses almost to their knees, smashes flowerpots, snaps television masts and coats the cliffs of Cape Creus white with salt lashed from the waves. The tramuntana blows regularly at over 130 kilometres an hour, and has been known to overturn railway carriages and hurl cars into the sea. At Port-Bou, on the French frontier, it can be so violent that the paramilitary Civil Guard used to enjoy a special dispensation allowing them to climb to their quarters upstairs on all-fours: a position that would normally have been considered undignified in the extreme for a force of law and order famed for its *machismo*.[40]

Along the coast of the Upper Empordà the tramuntana often collides head-on with the *llebeig* (or *garbí*), a south-wester that blows in from Africa. In the words of a local historian, the region is 'an impressive metereological laboratory', an 'incessant battle-field' between two great winds.[41]

The tramuntana can affect the emotions as brutally as it does the sea and countryside, and is a constant topic of conversation in this region. The Empordanese are known for their intransigence (the Dalís were no exception), and one authority on the area has attributed this to their having to push constantly against the wind.[42] Anyone a little dotty in these parts, or with a tendency suddenly to flare up, is likely to be labelled *atramuntanat* ('touched by the tramuntana'), and in the past *crimes passionnels* committed when the wind was raging were half-way to being condoned. As for depressives, they can be driven to absolute despair by a prolonged bout of the wind—and the bouts may last for eight or ten days, especially in winter. It is even alleged that the tramuntana is responsible for suicides, especially in Cadaqués. The protagonist of Gabriel García Márquez's short story, 'Tramuntana', is such a victim.[43] It may well be that Gal Dalí feared that, if he stayed on in the village, he was in mortal danger.

For more normally constituted people, however, the tramuntana can be exhilarating, and for a long time it was believed to be a disinfectant. In 1612 the disappearance of a severe epidemic of fever in Figueres coincided with a particularly energetic visitation of the wind. The thankful citizens organized a pilgrimage to the village church of Our Lady of Requesens, considered appropriate because it lies due north of the town among the foothills of the Alberes Mountains, from where the wind sweeps down onto the plain. The procession became an annual event, setting out on the first Sunday of June and returning a few days later. It only died out in the early years of the twentieth century, when improved medicine had made the wind's allegedly prophylactic ministrations less necessary.[44]

When the tramuntana holds sway, the sky of the Empordà acquires the scintillating luminosity, and its landscape the sharply defined contours, that Salvador Dalí so often captured in his paintings. They are the qualities which the artist's friend Carles Fages de Climent evoked in his 'Prayer to the Christ of the Tramuntana':

> Arms stretched on the holy wood
> Lord! Protect the sheep-fold and the sown field.
> Give the exact green to our meadows
> and measure out the precise tramuntana
> to dry the grass but not spoil our wheat.
>
> Braços en creu damunt la pia fusta
> Senyor! Empareu la cleda i el sembrat.
> Doneu el verd exacte a nostre prat
> i mesureu la tramuntana justa
> que exugui l'herba i no ens espolsi el blat.[45]

If the tramuntana had become a very real threat to his sanity, Gal had another good reason for moving himself and his family to Barcelona for, in September 1882, it would be time for his son Salvador, ten that year, to begin his *bachillerato* (*baccalauréat*) course, only possible where there was an official Instituto, or State secondary school. In theory he could have moved the family to Figueres, which had one of the oldest Institutos in Spain; but the capital of the Upper Empordà suffers as much from the tramuntana as does Cadaqués, and Gal may have felt that it was better to make a clean break and get to wind-free Barcelona. Perhaps, more importantly, he felt he would have more opportunities for making money in the capital.

Montserrat Dalí, Gal's granddaughter, was told as a child how, swearing never to return to Cadaqués, their forbear had gathered his family and belongings together and set off for the railway station at Figueres, taking with him a sack full of gold coins and, to protect the latter, two hired guards equipped with blunderbusses. Might the loot have proceeded from some supplementary activity in the smuggling line, an activity in which so many *cadaquesencs* were involved in one way or another? Montserrat Dalí (who did not know about Gal's 'bus') inclined to this view, but there is no proof. The source of Gal's treasure trove remains a mystery.[46]

Barcelona

When Gal Dalí Viñas arrived with his family in Barcelona around 1881 the city had approximately 250,000 inhabitants out of a total of some 1,700,000 for Catalunya as a whole. In 1865 the destruction of the restricting walls of the medieval city had finally been achieved, the enterprising, grid-system *Eixample*, or Extension to Barcelona, was now nearing completion, and the population was rocketing (thirteen years later more than half the Catalan population would be living in the city). Barcelona's cotton mills, which had so much impressed the great English hispanist Richard Ford forty years earlier, were enjoying a boom; thanks to the phylloxera plague that had devastated the French vineyards, and soon would strike south of the Pyrenees, the value of Catalan wines and brandy had soared; and many rich Catalans had returned from Cuba and elsewhere in South America and were pouring their wealth into industry and the construction of extravagant houses. For seven years now the city had been indulging in an unprecedented credit binge, known popularly as the *febre d'or*, 'gold fever'. Sixteen new banks opened in 1881–2, the peak years of the fever, and huge fortunes were made on the stock exchange. Greed for easy money had gripped the Catalans, who are habitually pilloried in the rest of Spain for their tight-fistedness and hoarding instinct (there are more savings banks in Catalunya than in the rest of the country put together). 'People opened their savings and poured them into the Llotja [stock exchange],' writes Robert Hughes in his marvellous book on Barcelona. 'Schemes rose like thistledown, like bubbles, like balloons. The destiny of everything was to rise. For several years, the

Catalans lost whatever claim they might have to their supposed cardinal virtue of *seny*.'[47]

Seny (common sense, caution) did indeed seem to have been put aside—and the impetuous Gal Dalí was no exception. The siren-song of quick gain was soft music to his ears and he decided to invest his cache of gold in the stock exchange. Gal was still sensible enough to ensure, first, that his sons were launched on a good education. In September 1882 Salvador entered one of the best private schools in the city, the College of San Antonio, run by the Piarist fathers (*escolapios*) on the Ronda de San Antonio, and was also enrolled at the Instituto for the first year of his *bachillerato*, gateway to university and the professions.[48] Two years later his brother Rafael followed in his footsteps. They both worked hard, although Rafael proved the better student.[49]

Gal Dalí was a litigious man and, according to his granddaughter, Montserrat, forever in and out of the courts.[50] His lawyer, Gonçal Serraclara Costa, enjoyed a high reputation in the city and was one of the increasingly vociferous band of Catalans who, sick of their region's political subservience to far-off Madrid, wanted Spain restructured as a federal republic. In the 1860s Serraclara had represented Barcelona in the central Madrid parliament, but in 1869, unjustly accused of anti-monarchist rabble-raising, he had been forced into exile in France. When allowed home in 1872 he had opted out of active politics, playing no part in the short-lived Federal Republic (1873–4)—largely engineered by the Catalans—and devoting himself to the family law office, which under his direction acquired considerable prestige in the city.[51]

Josep Maria Serraclara, Gonçal's youngest brother, worked with him in the office and was every bit as passionate a Catalan nationalist. He became celebrated as a defence lawyer in political trials and, later, was deputy mayor of Barcelona. In 1883 he married Catalina Berta, the daughter of Gal Dalí's wife Teresa by her first husband. Gal was now not only well connected but could count on free legal advice. He needed it, having developed a paranoid tendency to slap injunctions on people in high places whom he felt were persecuting him.[52]

The Barcelona stock exchange now took a turn for the worse—the boom was over—and Gal Dalí suddenly lost a considerable sum of money, some of it not his own. He was already suffering from a form of persecution mania and the reversal of his fortunes came as a terrible blow. In the early hours of 10 April 1886 he appeared on the balcony of his third-floor rented apartment on the Rambla de Catalunya, screaming that thieves were trying to steal his money and kill him. But there were no thieves. That afternoon he almost succeeded in hurling himself into the street, but was prevented by the police. Six days later, however, he did the job properly, landing on his head in an inner patio and dying instantly. According to one newspaper, the 'unhappy madman' was to have been interned that day in a lunatic asylum. He was only thirty-six years old.[53]

The suicide was hushed up (Gal's name did not appear in the newspaper reports), and the official death certificate, based on a statement by his lawyer son-in-law, Josep Maria Serraclara, stated euphemistically that Dalí Viñas died of a 'cerebral traumatism'. Gal, despite his suicide, received a Catholic burial in the East Cemetery.[54]

Josep Maria Serraclara (then twenty-three) and his wife Catalina Berta took in the bereaved family. Teresa Cusí, Gal's widow, lived with them until her death in 1912, and Salvador and Rafael until they finished their university careers.

The subject of Gal's suicide became taboo in the family, and the form of the grandfather's demise was carefully hidden from the next generation. 'In England you say that every family has "a skeleton in the cupboard", well, in our family it was our grandfather's suicide,' Montserrat Dalí, the painter's cousin and exact contemporary, recalled in 1992, shortly before her death. 'When I found out what had happened I was already grown up and it came as a most terrible shock. It was Catalina Berta who told me, and she said, "Don't breathe a word of this to your father." Salvador found out at about the same time.'[55] We may assume that the revelation deeply affected the painter, who neither mentions the suicide in his extant adolescent diaries or his published work, nor, so far as it has been possible to ascertain, ever breathed a word about it to his close friends.[56] During his childhood Dalí must have heard stories of people committing suicide in Cadaqués under the influence of the tramuntana; now he had discovered that his own grandfather, who had fled from Cadaqués because he dreaded the dire wind, had been unable to escape his fate. Little wonder, then, that years later, without mentioning any names, he said that the *cadaquesencs* were 'the greatest paranoiacs produced by the Mediterranean': once touched by the tramuntana, always touched.[57] In view of this unacknowledged family trauma, surely we are justified in assuming a connection between Dalí's stubborn silence about Gal, his famous insistence that he himself was sane ('the only difference between a madman and me is that I am not mad') and the elaboration, in the 1930s, of his 'paranoiac-critical method'. Moreover, the concern in the Dalí family about inherited paranoia (and depression) was justified: years later Montserrat's father, Rafael, tried to kill himself in exactly the same way as his father, and was only prevented by the sudden appearance of a servant.[58]

It is possible that the rise and fall of Gal Dalí may have partly inspired a famous novel, Narcís Oller's *La febre d'or* (*Gold Fever*), set during the last great flourish of the credit boom in 1880–1 and published ten years later when it was all over. Oller, a disciple of Zola who believed that a good novel must be based on the scrupulous reporting of real life, told Spain's most celebrated contemporary novelist, Benito Pérez Galdós, that he had gone to considerable lengths to mask the identity of the characters in the book, whose protagonist, an ex-carpenter turned stock-exchange speculator, is called Gil Foix. The similarity of the names Gil and Gal catches the eye. There are other striking coincidences, not least Gil's reaction to his spectacular bankruptcy. It is true that unlike Gal he does not jump off a balcony. But he commits mental suicide, retreating into what his doctors term 'neurasthenia' and suffering, as Gal did, from the delusion that people are trying to rob him. Nobody knowing the sad case of the Cadaqués stopper-maker who tried to make the big time in Barcelona could have failed to notice the parallel. But there is no record of any awareness of, or reaction to, the novel on the part of Gal Dalí's two sons, or of anyone else in the family.[59]

The Dalí Brothers and Catalunya

Salvador Dalí Cusí, the artist's father, finished his bachillerato successfully in October 1888 and entered the Law Faculty at Barcelona University that same winter.[60] His brother Rafael enrolled in the Medical Faculty two years later.[61] The two were similar in personality and physique: corpulent, passionate men who enjoyed arguing about religion and politics and could suddenly flare up violently in a bout of ferocious temper. Salvador, in particular, was known for this latter tendency, a characteristic he never lost.[62] No doubt influenced by the Serraclaras, Salvador and Rafael were soon converts to the Catalan federalist cause (they disliked the centralist Bourbon monarchy intensely) and stout defenders of the Catalan language which, since the eighteenth century, had been systematically excluded by Madrid from public life. Indeed, so convinced a supporter of Catalan federalism was Salvador that, shortly after graduating, he gave a series of lectures on the subject to a working-class audience in Barcelona's Federalist-Republican Centre.[63] Both he and Rafael were vehement, anti-clerical atheists, and Salvador was to remain so for forty years—until, that is, the excesses of the 1936–9 civil war drove him to reconsider his position, whereupon he became as aggressive a Catholic as previously he had been a free-thinker. Salvador Dalí Cusí argued his case, whatever it was, with missionary zeal ('a permanent militant', Josep

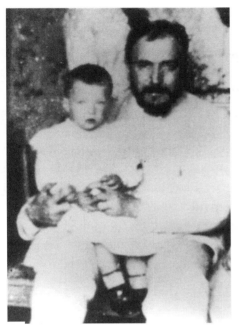

Salvador Dalí Cusí with the first Salvador.

Pla called him), and he passed on his ability for a rapid but carefully argued volte-face to his son.[64]

The Dalí brothers transmitted their Catalanist fervour to their offspring: Rafael to his only child Montserrat and Salvador to the future painter and his sister Anna Maria. Right up to her death in 1993, aged almost ninety, Montserrat Dalí's eloquence on the subject of the wrongs done to Catalunya by Madrid never waned. Her obsession, above all, was the 'Nueva Planta': the 'New Order' imposed on Catalunya by Spain's first Bourbon king, Philip V, in 1714, after the Catalans had made the mistake of supporting the Hapsburg pretender, Archduke Charles, in the War of the Spanish Succession (Spain's last Hapsburg king had died in 1700 without a direct successor).

It is true that 11 September 1714, the day on which Barcelona surrendered to the Bourbon troops, marks a watershed in the history of Catalunya. One third of the city was razed to the ground in reprisal, and there were mass executions; under the 'New Order' the Catalan institutions, including the parliament (Gen-eralitat) and the universities, were closed down; while, most offensive of all, Spanish was imposed as the language of the administration. The latter provision meant that official documents such as death or birth certificates, previously couched in Catalan, must perforce now be made out in Spanish, with the changes in the forms of Christian names that this implied: Spanish Pedro for Catalan Pere, for example, or Narciso for Narcís. But although concerted efforts were made to undermine the use of Catalan in other areas, the people, rich and poor alike, never stopped speaking their native tongue. It was their main way of resisting the oppressor. The Catalans' subservience to distant Madrid was symbolically expressed in the unassailable citadel the hated Philip V ordered to be erected just outside the city walls. How, Montserrat Dalí would ask again and again, could you expect Catalans to feel anything but repugnance for Madrid, the Spanish language and the centralist monarchy? Was it not a fact that, when she and her cousin Salvador, the painter, were at school, Catalan was still not taught? That even today the ignorant believe that Catalan is 'a dialect of Spanish', as if it were not a language in its own right, with a fine literature? Was it not true that the enemies of Catalunya used always to sneer that the Catalans 'bark' their language rather than speak it? Just think, she would add, that Catalunya, which formerly stretched into France and was once co-partner in the Kingdom of Aragon, with a Mediterranean empire, had been reduced by the Bourbons to mere provincial status, despite the fact that its capital was as populous as Madrid, richer and more civilized! Compare the two cities, she would say: in Barcelona there was civic pride, life was well ordered, people cared passionately about their city, the buildings of Gaudí, the Extension; Madrid was chaotic, dirty, noisy. Montserrat Dalí's fine nostrils would flare as she spoke, her eyes flash fire. 'In Catalunya we call it the *fet diferencial*,' she would exclaim. 'We're different, we're not like other Spaniards.' And naturally, she insisted, her cousin Salvador felt exactly as she did about being Catalan. In their families they never spoke Spanish, because Spanish was associated with school, with repression. It was an imposed language, and they and their parents before them had come to resent it deeply; so whenever they could they all avoided using it. And that was that.[65]

The Budding Notary Public

Salvador Dalí Cusí, the painter's father, had a solid but not outstanding university career, taking his law degree in 1893.[66] For the next few years he prepared deeds in a land registry office and worked part-time for the Serraclaras.[67]

For one brief moment he was in the public eye. On 7 June 1896 a bomb was thrown at the tail-end of a Corpus Christi procession in Barcelona, killing twelve workers. The attack was attributed to the anarchists, who were then proliferating in the Catalan capital. It may, however, have been perpetrated by an 'agent provocateur' in the pay of the police (which would explain why no notabilities were killed). The authorities, at all events, reacted with great brutality. Anarchist suspects were rounded up, taken to the infamous military prison on the slopes of Montjuïc, the mountain outside Barcelona overlooking the sea, and, in many cases, subjected to appalling tortures to make them confess. Several suspects died and one went mad. Five men, almost certainly innocent, were garrotted; and, of those acquitted, sixty-five were sent to the harsh penal settlement in Río de Oro, in the Spanish Sahara. The Montjuïc trials, held in December 1896, showed the other face of a country that eight years earlier, with the Barcelona International Exposition, had sought to impress the world by its modernity.[68]

Among the anarchist suspects thrown into gaol after the bombing was a young lawyer called Pere Coromines. Although in fact he was a moderate Republican, Coromines was tried as an anarchist accomplice. Called as one of the defence witnesses, Salvador Dalí Cusí, described in court as an intimate friend of the accused, insisted that the latter was known for his patriotism and had been praised in that capacity by *El Diario de Barcelona*, the most conservative, and rabidly anti-anarchist, newspaper in town. There was no possibility that he could have been involved in the bombing outrage.[69] Coromines, ably defended by a military lawyer, was acquitted, and went on to become a famous newspaper editor, writer and political commentator.[70] Grateful for the support of his friend Dalí, he rarely failed henceforth to pay him an annual visit.[71]

By the time of the Montjuïc trials, and now wanting to be his own master, Salvador Dalí Cusí had decided to bend his efforts towards becoming a *notario*, or notary, a public servant authorized to draw up contracts, deeds and wills and to witness signatures, all for a good fee. To become a *notario* you had to learn the subject by yourself after finishing your law studies (there was no professional degree) and apply to take the Ministry of Justice public examination when a vacancy presented itself. Once you were awarded a *notaría*, and provided you behaved impeccably, you had security for life. The system remains very much the same today. It is significant that both Salvador Dalí Cusí and his brother went for professions guaranteed to provide a steady income and a solid position in society (the Serraclaras used their influence to have Rafael appointed as doctor to the Barcelona Fire Brigade, and he never changed jobs). After what had happened to their father, as few risks as possible for *them*. This despite their enthusiasm for progressive causes.

In 1898 Salvador Dalí Cusí began to apply unsuccessfully for various *notarías*, deciding the following year to concentrate his efforts on the town of Figueres. In this decision he was encouraged by a close friend he had made at the Instituto in Barcelona, Josep ('Pepito') Pichot Gironés. The friendship had continued at Barcelona University, where Pichot abandoned his law studies in 1892 after two years without having passed a single examination;[72] and it seems likely that Dalí Cusí frequented the Pichot family's first-floor apartment at Carrer de Montcada, 21, a cavernous mansion set in the heart of old Barcelona and only a few metres from the city's most beautiful church, Santa Maria del Mar, a soaring Gothic miracle of symmetry and grace. Josep Pichot's father, Ramon Pichot Mateu, had worked his way up to a senior position in the firm of Vidal i Ribas (which specialized in drugs and chemical products), and his wealthy and well-related mother Antonia Gironès Bofill, a woman passionately interested in the arts, was the daughter of a Cadaqués man made good, Antonio Gironès. The latter circumstance cannot have been indifferent to her son's friend Dalí Cusí, given the fact that he was himself a *cadaquesenc*.[73]

At a moment when Barcelona had become one of Europe's most exciting centres of avant-garde art and architecture in the wake of the 1888 International Exposition, which gave the city a new confidence, the Pichots' salon was celebrated for its hospitality, style and verve. In the same rambling building, on the second floor, lived the young writer Eduardo Marquina, whose father, like the Pichots', worked for Vidal i Ribas. Marquina, who became a famous dramatist but today is almost forgotten, married Mercedes, the youngest of the seven Pichot children, in 1903.[74] One of these, Ramon, was a painter, and by the late 1890s had struck up a close relationship with Pablo Picasso, nine years his junior. It is just possible that Salvador Dalí Cusí may have met Picasso at the Pichot family's apartment in Carrer Montcada or, failing that, at the café Els Quatre Gats ('The Four Cats'), founded by the painters Santiago Rusiñol and Ramon Casas in 1897, and immortalized in Picasso's illustration for the menu. But even if no such encounter took place, Dalí Cusí must surely have been well informed about Picasso and Ramon Pichot's bohemian life in Barcelona and, immediately afterwards, in turn-of-the-century Paris.

One of the most original feats of Dalí Cusí's friend Josep Pichot was to marry his aunt Angela, his mother's sister, known in the family as Angeleta. He did so early in 1900, when he was thirty and she twenty-eight. Angela Gironès had inherited a house in Figueres, presumably from her father, who seems to have had interests there (her sister, Antonia, was born in Figueres[75]), and the couple decided to settle in the town.[76] According to both Pichot and Dalí family tradition, Josep was instrumental in convincing Salvador Dalí Cusí that he must persevere in trying for the Figueres *notaría*. That way the two friends could continue to see each other regularly. Moreover, did not Figueres have the nearest *notaría* to Cadaqués?[77] Salvador needed little encouragement. Unlike his brother Rafael, who had inherited his father's loathing of the tramuntana, he remembered his birthplace with great affection and was excited at the prospect of being able to revisit it often.[78] He failed to obtain the Figueres *notaría* in 1899 but succeeded when it fell vacant again in April 1900, being appointed by the Ministry of Justice, after the usual *oposición*, or public examination, on 27 April 1900. He received his credentials from the College of Notaries in Barcelona on 31 May 1900, after Josep Maria Serraclara had advanced him funds for the sizeable deposit, and took formal possession of the post on 7 June.[79] Dalí Cusí lost no time in starting work, and from 24 June until 30 August

1900 we find him advertising his practice prominently on the front page of a local newspaper, *El Regional.*[80]

Felipa Domènech

Having secured his desired post, Salvador Dalí Cusí, now aged twenty-eight, was in a position to marry his fiancée, Felipa Domènech Ferrés, a demure and pretty Barcelona girl two years younger than himself (she was born in 1874). They had met in Cabrils, a charming village some thirty kilometres north of the city in the hills behind the seaside resort of Vilassar-de-Mar, while Salvador was holidaying there at the Serraclaras' summer villa.[81] Anselm Domènech Serra, Felipa's father, had died in 1887, aged forty-seven, when she was thirteen. A haberdashery importer, he had travelled extensively in France.[82] Her mother, Maria Anna Ferrés Sadurní, who unlike her husband would live to a ripe old age, was a quiet, sensitive soul with an artistic temperament inherited from her father, Jaume Ferrés. The latter, a considerable craftsman, ran a long-standing family establishment that specialized in making *objets d'art* and Maria Anna Ferrés told Anna Maria Dalí, the painter's sister, that her father had been the first person in Catalunya to work with tortoiseshell. Several Domènech objects, original or embellished, 'all done artistically, with exquisite taste and simplicity', became Dalí family heirlooms: boxes, walking sticks, fans, an urn, combs for fixing the mantilla in Holy Week processions, even a book with a tortoiseshell cover. Maria Anna made skilful paper cut-outs which were later to delight her grandchildren. Her artistic sensibility was further shown by the fact that, shortly before her death, she suddenly began to recite, with faultless memory, compositions by the seventeenth-century poet Luis de Góngora. No one had suspected such familiarity with the intricate verse of the author of the *Soledades.*[83]

Grandmother Maria Anna was a good talker, and loved recounting that as a small child she had travelled with her father on Spain's first railway—from Barcelona to Mataró, fifty kilometres up the coast—and that they had been able to drink a glass of water without, miracle of miracles, spilling a single drop.[84]

On her father's death, Maria Anna Ferrés had inherited the business. It was located in the Call, formerly Barcelona's ghetto, just off the Plaça de Sant Jaume. Her descendants are convinced that the Ferrés family was of Jewish origin.[85]

Felipa Domènech, Maria Anna's first child, helped her mother in the workshop and developed considerable skill as a designer of 'artistic objects'. She was deft with her fingers, and drew well. The delicate wax figurines she enjoyed fashioning out of coloured candles would delight the future painter as a child.[86]

Felipa was followed by Anselm (1877) who, while still a lad, began to work in Barcelona's most famous bookshop, the Llibreria Verdaguer, which was also a publishing house. Founded in 1835 by Joaquim Verdaguer, it had passed to his son, Àlvar, Anselm's uncle and godfather, and been a leading force in the 'Renaixença', the Catalan literary revival. Àlvar Verdaguer's son died when still a child, and his three daughters showed little interest in the establishment. It was natural, therefore, that Anselm should eventually become a partner in the business. This happened in 1915.[87]

The Llibreria Verdaguer stood almost directly opposite the Liceu opera house on Barcelona's famous boulevard, the Rambla, and was a favourite meeting place for writers and artists. Anselm was in his element in this setting, and before he was twenty had become deeply involved in the artistic and literary life of Barcelona. In particular he loved music, and was to found the Barcelona Wagner Association and, with Amadeu

The Llibreria Verdaguer, in the Ramblas, Barcelona, owned by Dalí's uncle Anselm Doménech.

Vives and Lluís Millet, the Orfeo Catalá (a musical society devoted especially to Catalan folk tradition). Anselm Domènech was destined to play an important role in the artistic development of his nephew Salvador Dalí.[88]

As for Felipa and Anselm's sister Catalina (born 1884), Maria Anna Ferrés's last child, she became a hatmaker of some talent, working from home.[89]

On 29 December 1900 Salvador Dalí Cusí and Felipa Domènech were married in Barcelona in the church of Nuestra Señora de la Merced. The witnesses were Àlvar Verdaguer, the bookseller, and a celebrated lawyer friend of the groom, Amadeu Hurtado.[90] We do not know where the couple spent their honeymoon, only that Felipa, within a few weeks of her marriage and now settled into her new home in Figueres, was already pregnant.

Figueres

In 1900, when Salvador Dalí Cusí arrived to take over the *notaría*, Figueres was a flourishing town of almost 11,000 inhabitants (today the population has tripled). Situated on the edge of the beautiful and fertile Upper Empordà plain, five kilometres from the Dalí homeland of Llers, it was the region's unchallenged capital, a position it had gradually wrested over the centuries from nearby Castelló d'Empúries, seat of the counts of Empúries in the Middle Ages.

Until the signing of the Peace of the Pyrenees in 1659, Figueres had lain well back from the French frontier. Under the new agreement, however, when Spain lost the Roussillon and Perpignan to France, the town woke up to discover that the border was a mere twenty-three kilometres away (where it remains). Such proximity, and the continuing hostilities between France and Spain, turned the Empordà plain into a sensitive frontier area, and led to the construction, in the middle of the eighteenth century, of a massive sunken fortress just behind Figueres. The Castle of Saint Ferdinand was Spain's rejoinder to that of Bellegarde on the French side of the border at Le Perthus. It was also a reminder that Catalunya was under the thumb of the central government in Madrid. Garrisoned by the fittingly designated Regiment of San Quintín (Philip II defeated the French at Saint Quentin in 1557), the fortress played a vital role in the social and economic development of Figueres. It provided jobs for hundreds of masons and workmen, stimulated local trade and created a vigorous demand for entertainment, from prostitution to opera.[1]

From the castle's three-kilometre perimeter there are striking views of the eastern

Chapter Two

Pyrenees, dominated by the snow-covered bulk of the Canigó (2,784 metres). Situated just on the other side of the border, the Canigó is one of Catalunya's two Holy Mountains (the other is Montserrat) and an object of veneration to French and Spanish Catalans alike. Directly north, another peak, the Neulós (1,263 metres), is the highest point of the Alberes range that separates the Upper Empordà from France. Beneath the hill, a stone's throw from the fortress, the A-7 motorway now speeds the traffic to and from the frontier at Le Perthus, clearly visible on the horizon. At the seawards edge of the plain lies the town of Roses, one of the Costa Brava's most famous summer resorts (and birthplace of Gal Dalí's wife, Teresa Cusí), while just out of sight at the southern rim of the broad bay are the extensive remains of Empúries, which gives the region its name.

Every Spanish schoolchild has heard of Empúries (spelt Ampurias in Castilian) and knows that it was a Greek trading post (emporium) and later, in 218 BC, the spot where the Romans first landed in the Iberian Peninsula. The latter had come to ward off the Carthaginian threat, and, having done it successfully, decided to stay on. As a result, Spaniards (with the notable exception of the Basques) speak modern versions of Latin.

By the turn of the nineteenth century, Figueres had become one of the most politically lively towns in Catalunya and was a veritable hotbed of republican and federalist sentiment (top-dressed with anti-clericalism). Intense, if minority, opposition came from the monarchist and voluble Catholic supporters of the Madrid-directed status quo. The town had its own periodicals, both conservative and progressive; several clubs and social centres; a bullring, inaugurated in 1894; musical societies; a theatre visited regularly by Spain's leading dramatic and operatic companies; and a Thursday market, rich in produce from the surrounding countryside and enlivened by the colourful traditional costumes of the peasants. Since 1877 Figueres had been linked by railway to Barcelona, since 1896 lit by electric light. And in August 1898 the first motorcar had made its appearance, puttering down from France.[2] The modernist movement in architecture was just beginning to make an impression, and some good Art Nouveau buildings were going up. On Sundays the regimental band gave concerts in the Rambla—occasions for much ogling between the military and the local girls. As for its achievements in the field of human endeavour, Figueres could boast a respectable artistic, literary and scientific tradition, and was especially proud of Narcís Monturiol (1819–85), socialist champion of women's and workers' rights and, most memorably, pioneer of the submarine (Spain, characteristically, had failed to exploit the prototype's commercial potential). Pep Ventura (1817–75), the creator of the modern version of the *sardana*, the national dance of Catalunya, was another famous local figure, although in fact he had been born in Andalusia. Figueres had also produced some notable politicians, including the prophet of Spanish federalism, Abdó Terrades (1812–56), and, during the ill-fated Federal Republic of 1873–4, no fewer than three ministers: Francesc Sunyer i Capdevila, Joan Tutau and General Ramon Nouviles. After the Bourbon Restoration (1874) the town had consistently returned republican MPs to Madrid. Far from being a provincial backwater, it was civilized, prosperous and strongly influenced by French culture and the proximity of Europe.

It is not to be wondered at, then, that the gregarious Salvador Dalí Cusí quickly felt at home here, nor that before long he had become a prominent member of the Sport Figuerense, the town's most liberal club and centre of political debate. Here in the evening he would join Pepito Pichot and his many new friends to discuss the issues of the day. Soon Dalí Cusí became notorious for the vehemence with which he defended the cause of Catalan federalism, so dear to the hearts of many *figuerencs*.[3]

The Two Salvadors

The chambers taken by the fledgling notary were on the ground floor of a handsome building in Calle Monturiol, 20, in the very heart of the town, fifty metres from the fashionable, plane-lined Rambla and almost opposite the 'Sport'. Above them, on the first floor, Dalí Cusí rented a spacious flat.

Salvador and Felipa's first child was born on 12 October 1901. The birth certificate, couched in Spanish, not Catalan, as the law required, states that the child was named Salvador Galo Anselmo: Salvador after his father, paternal great-grandfather and other Dalí forbears; Galo as a tribute to his ill-fated paternal grandfather; and Anselmo in deference to his maternal grandfather, Anselm Domènech, and the latter's son.[4] We know hardly anything about this first Salvador, who died twenty-two months later, on 1 August 1903, victim, according to his death certificate, of 'an infectious gastro-enteritic cold'[5]. Whether the diagnosis was correct it is impossible to say. The local press expressed conventional condolences to the child's parents, who buried him in a hurriedly acquired niche in Figueres cemetery.[6]

Years later Dalí told his American patron Reynolds Morse that his mother was so depressed at the loss of her first child that his father took her on a visit to the lake at Requesens. This was the isolated spot, some twenty-five kilometres due north of

The Dalí family tomb in Figueres cemetery, purchased for the burial of the first Salvador.

Figueres among the foothills of the Pyrenees, to which the citizens used to make an annual pilgrimage to implore the tramuntana to continue its good work of blowing the Empordà plain free of illness and disease. Perhaps Señora Dalí wanted to pray at the little church there for the perfect health of her next child; or perhaps she wanted to take the ferruginous waters for which the place was noted. Whatever the truth of the matter, Dalí told Morse that she was so moved by the beauty of the spot (which he himself visited later) that she burst into tears. Dalí seems to recall this episode in his painting *Mountain Lake*, also known as *Beach with Telephone* (1938), where the lake acquires the form of a stranded whale, possibly an allusion to the impression of a giant cetacean snout given by the rounded wooded hill and its reflection in the glassy water.[7]

Nine months and ten days after the death of his brother, as if conceived in the urgency of grief, the 'real' Salvador Dalí came into the world, the signal event occurring in the family apartment at 8.45 p.m. on 11 May 1904.[8] On 20 May he was baptized Salvador Felipe Jacinto in the parish church of Saint Peter. His godparents were

The lake at Requesens, with the mirror image of a sea monster or whale, that seems to have inspired Dalí's Mountain Lake *(also known as* Beach with Telephone*), 1938.*

his uncle Anselm Domènech, the Barcelona bookseller, and Teresa Cusí, his maternal grandmother.[9] The child was not named Salvador in memory of his dead brother, as has often been asserted, but for the same reason as had been the latter—family tradition (in Catalunya, as in the rest of Spain, it was common for the same Christian names to be regularly handed down from generation to generation, Anselm Domènech, Dalí's uncle and now godfather, being another case in point). It would have been unheard of, certainly, to burden the new son with the second and third names of his deceased brother, and of course the Dalís did not do this. Felipe was no doubt chosen as the male form of Felipa, the child's mother, while Jacinto was a gesture in the direction of Rafael Dalí Cusí, Don Salvador's brother, whose full name was Rafael Narciso Jacinto.

In Dalí's extant adolescent diaries there is no mention of his dead brother, although of course there may have been in those that are missing. The references to him occurring in his subsequent writings are shot through with misinformation and fantasy, in what proportion deliberately or unconsciously it is imposssible to say. In the *Secret Life*

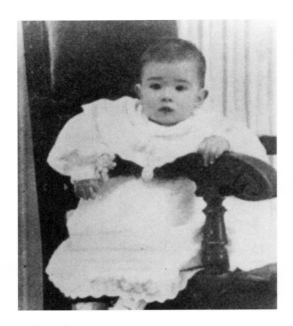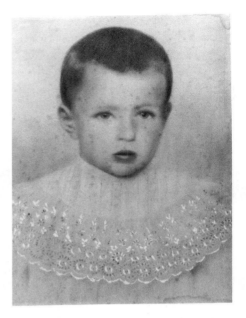

Dalí aged one.

Dalí's brother, Salvador Galo Anselmo, who died at the age of twenty-two months in 1903, nine months before the birth of the future painter.

Dalí states that his brother was seven years old, not twenty-two months, when he died, and that his demise (from meningitis, he alleges, in blatant disagreement with the death certificate) occurred three years before his own birth, not nine months; he also says that his brother had 'the unmistakeable facial morphology of a genius', showing signs of 'alarming precocity'.[10] Later, in *The Unspeakable Confessions*, Dalí claimed that his parents had committed 'a subconscious crime' by giving him the same name as his brother and thereby forcing him to live up to an impossible ideal, a crime aggravated by the fact that they kept a photograph of the dead child on a cupboard in their bedroom in, as Dalí would have us believe, significant juxtaposition with a reproduction of Velázquez's *Christ*.[11] This photograph is probably the one left among Anna Maria Dalí's effects at her death. While the child is pretty (prettier, certainly, than Salvador II, indeed almost angelic in appearance), nothing about its mien suggests 'the unmistakeable facial morphology of a genius' or the 'alarming precocity' to which the painter refers. Nor does another picture of the child, sitting with a somewhat dazed expression on the knee of his proud father. As for Dalí's *Portrait of My Dead Brother*, executed in 1963, it is based on a photograph of another child, considerably older than the defunct twenty-two-month-old.[12]

Most of what Dalí has to say about his brother appears to be make-believe masquerading as true history and intended to supply the curious with an arresting but spurious justification for the artist's eccentric behaviour. It is also, perhaps, a red herring designed to put biographers, whom arguably Dalí feared, firmly off the track. In the latter respect, it must be said, he succeeded only too well.[13]

Monturiol, 20

In his *Secret Life* and elsewhere in his autobiographical writings Dalí offers only the scantest evocation of the spacious apartment in Monturiol, 20, where he spent the first ten years of his life in Figueres. It is fortunate, therefore, that this gap has been partially filled by his sister Anna Maria's recollections of their first home, abandoned by the family in 1912 when she was only four.

The house still stands, at today's number 6, hemmed in on both sides by modern blocks. The Dalís' first-floor apartment looked north onto Carrer Monturiol itself (where the main entrance is situated), south onto the parallel Carrer Caamaño and west over a delightful garden belonging to a local aristocrat, the Marquesa de la Torre, whose palatial home at the far end of the grounds gave on to the Rambla. The ample communal terrace on top of Monturiol, 20, where the washing was done, afforded bet-

The Marquesa de la Torre's garden seen from Carrer Caamaño.

ter views then than it does today, and from it the Dalís could see a broad swathe of the Empordà plain, with the mountains of the coastal range of Sant Pere de Roda at its edge.

Running the full length of the apartment on the side facing the garden was a long *galeria*, or balcony, which Anna Maria recalled in later life with deep nostalgia. It was embellished with pots of lilies and sweet-smelling spikenard (the latter would always be Salvador's favourite flower as a result), and Felipa Domènech, an ardent bird fancier, had installed at one end of it an aviary where she reared canaries and doves (Dalí briefly mentions the canaries on the first page of the *Secret Life*).[14] The chestnut trees in the garden almost brushed against the balcony, affording it great privacy. In an adolescent text, written after the family had moved, Dalí evoked the Marquesa de la Torres's 'palace' bathed in moonlight, with a nightingale singing among the branches of the huge eucalyptus and the croaking of frogs in the pond.[15] If by night the balcony was magic, by day, according to Anna Maria Dalí, it was 'pure Impressionism' (birds,

Carrer Monturiol 20, the Dalís' first house in Figueres, viewed from the Marquesa de la Torre's garden before it was built on.

shadows, flowers, long dresses), a 'Flemish' touch being added by the serene presence of grandmother Maria Anna Ferrés, draped in her widow's weeds and quietly knitting.[16]

Maria Anna Ferrés and her twenty-seven-year-old daughter Catalina had moved in with the Dalís in 1910, when Salvador was six and Anna Maria two, occupying a small apartment on the top floor of the building. Their arrival was to have important consequences for the whole family.[17]

The apartment beneath the Dalís, on the mezzanine floor (not above them, as Salvador writes in the *Secret Life*), was occupied by the Matas family. The parents, Pedro and Maria, were from the province of Barcelona, and had emigrated to Buenos Aires. They returned to Spain with three children, Ursula, Antonia and Dionisio, and settled in Figueres where, in the 1906 census, Pedro is described as a businessman.[18] The two families became very friendly, and Anna Maria claims to remember the laughter of the Matas girls and her mother and Aunt Catalina bubbling up from the downstairs balcony while they drank *mate* (Paraguay tea) and gossiped.[19] This balcony, today dismally curtailed by the new adjoining building, was wider than the Dalís' and flanked by an imposing stone balustrade, no longer extant. Dalí told Amanda Lear many years later that as a child he had been jealous of the balustrade, so much more distinguished and 'high bourgeois', he felt, than the wrought-iron railing running the length of *their* balcony.[20] Salvador was much impressed by the life-style of the Matas family, and records that Ursula, who was fourteen years his senior, seemed to him the very epitome of elegance, 'the 1900 archetype of beauty'. As for the family's comfortable drawing-room, with its stuffed stork, accumulated bric-à-brac and *mate* keg with a picture of Napoleon (Salvador's idol), it expressed, he tells us, his deepest social longings. He was often entertained there, drinking quantites of *mate* served from a silver sipper passed from mouth to mouth, and such assiduity gave him a life-long taste for the frequentation of 'the most important apartments'. Alas, it all came to an end in 1911, when the Matas family departed for Barcelona.[21]

Dalí's first drawings, according to Anna Maria, were done on the balcony at Monturiol, 20: tiny swans and ducks obtained by scratching the red paint off the top of the table to reveal the white surface underneath. Felipa Domènech's delight with her son's efforts was expressed in a much-repeated phrase that became part of the collective memory of the family: 'When he says he'll draw a swan, he draws a swan; and when he says he'll do a duck, it's a duck', she would say happily.[22] She may well have felt a very personal satisfaction at the revelation of Salvador's artistic talent, for this woman of 'angelic tenderness' was capable, by Dalí's account, of drawing 'astonishing pictures of fantastic animals on a long strip of paper with coloured pencils' which, carefully folded, 'could be reduced to a small book which unfolded like an accordion'.[23]

A strong influence on the lives of both Salvador and Anna Maria was that of their nurse, Llúcia Gispert de Montcanut, who is lovingly evoked in both the *Secret Life* and in Anna Maria's memoirs. Dalí recalls that Llúcia and his grandmother, Maria Anna Ferrés, were 'two of the neatest old women, with the whitest hair and the most delicate and wrinkled skin, that I have ever seen'.[24] While Anna Maria concentrates on Llúcia's kindness, endless patience and bulbous nose, the object of much affection and constant teasing,[25] it is the nurse's yarns that Salvador remembers best. Llúcia would sing him to sleep with traditional Catalan lullabies, and told him many stories, two of which are incorporated into the narrative of the *Secret Life*.[26] Dalí did an appreciative early portrait of Llúcia in 1917 or 1918, and remembered her songs and anecdotes until the end of his days.[27]

If Llúcia had Catalan folklore in the blood, for Doña Felipa and her sister Catalina, city girls, it had been conscientiously acquired in Barcelona, where both of them frequented the Orfeu Català which their brother Anselm had helped to found. They built up an ample repertoire of folksongs and these they loved to sing as they went about the house and, more importantly, when it was time to coax Salvador to sleep. Anna Maria provides the words of a charming Catalan lullaby, addressed to the Angel of Slumber, which was used on these occasions and had perhaps been transmitted by Llúcia.[28] The father, too, enjoyed his music, and Anna Maria remembers him sprawled in his rocking chair listening to Gounod's *Ave Maria* or passages from *Lohengrin* on a gramophone with a huge trumpet. Don Salvador passionately admired the *sardana*, Catalunya's national dance, and its great revitalizer, Pep Ventura, and was the proud possessor of the latter's *tenora*, a Catalan version of the oboe. Sometimes he would organize a *sardanas* session in the Rambla, which was always hosed down first. A characteristic fragrance of damp flowerbeds would then fill the air.[29]

Cock of the Roost

Salvador Dalí was a chronic case of what in England, France or the United States would be termed the spoilt child, a category hardly recognized in Spain. His parents, perhaps blaming themselves to a certain extent for the death of their first son, were over-protective with the second, and seem habitually to have given him his own way, encouraging a pattern that was to persist all his life. From the day he came into the world his every whim was catered to, and he quickly learnt that, by exercising what his sister Anna Maria termed his 'terrible temper', he could invariably bend his parents to his will. According to her, the family discovered that the only way to keep Salvador quiet was never to deny him what he wanted but, rather, to coax him surreptitiously into demanding something more reasonable.[30] Dalí himself recalled that every morning, when he woke up, his mother would look lovingly into his eyes and recite the traditional formula: *Cor què vols? Cor què desitges* ('Sweet heart, what do you want? Sweet heart, what do you desire?'). Often, as he grew older, he would reply that what he wanted was to be taken to the cinema.[31]

Salvador's love of the cinema had first been stimulated by the home sessions provided by his mother, who worked the handle-operated projector. He remembered two of the titles: *The Fall of Port Arthur* (a short documentary on the Russo-Japanese war) and a film called *The Enamoured Student*. According to Anna Maria, her mother also showed them films starring Charlie Chaplin and Max Linder. And there were magic lantern shows, too. Once the Sala Edison, Figueres's first proper cinema, was opened in 1914, Salvador was able to see as many films as he wanted.[32]

The appeasement policy employed with Salvador by his parents had disastrous consequences for his development. Stubborn as a mule in the pursuit of his own interests, worshipped, cajoled, cosseted, spruced, petted and polished, he was the unchallenged cock of the roost until the arrival of Anna Maria in January 1908. Neither in the *Secret Life* nor in any of his other autobiographical writings does Dalí stop to analyse the possible impact of Anna Maria's appearance on his sense of supremacy. His telling of the Halley's Comet episode, however, suggests that there was great resentment at this unexpected competition. Dalí may not have kicked Anna Maria on the head that evening, when she was two and he six, but he probably badly wanted to.[33]

Dalí's account of how he used his excretory functions to manipulate his parents is uproariously funny, but did he *really* deposit turds around the house in the most inaccessible, or unexpected, places, in order to extract the maximum benefits from the household's anxiety about his bowel movements?[34] Or, when eight, still wet his bed in order to humiliate his father, who had promised him a red tricycle if he desisted?[35] Dalí's allegiance to Freud's views on anality is so overt that we cannot afford full credence to the account of his potty-time excesses. Nonetheless, no one looking at his Surrealist paintings could fail to notice his obsession with excrement.

First School—and Intimations of Shame

'When I was seven years old my father decided to take me to school,' Dalí begins the witty fourth chapter of his *Secret Life*. The chapter is entitled 'False Memories', a warning to the wary. In it Dalí recalls, and partially fabulates, his experience at the Figueres Municipal Primary School, which was run at that time by an eccentric and innovative teacher called Esteban Trayter Colomer (1851–1920). Dalí reproduces a school photograph, with the date 15 September 1908 clearly stamped on it, which proves conclusively how little he cares about chronological accuracy. It shows Trayter, sporting a truly astonishing cleft beard that practically reaches down to his waist, standing proudly beside his charges, some eighty of them, at the beginning of the academic year. There in the fourth row, almost at the master's elbow, is Salvador Dalí: but aged four, not seven. It is a very timid looking little Salvador Dalí indeed.

Dalí states categorically in the *Secret Life* that he only attended the school run by Trayter for a year.[36] He may have believed this when he sat down to write his autobiography three decades later, but the evidence suggests strongly that he remained with Trayter for a further year; until, that is, the summer of 1910, the Halley's Comet summer, after which, aged six, he entered his next school.

Esteban Trayter with his class in 1908. Dalí, aged four, stands close to the teacher and is marked with a cross.

Why, Dalí asks, did his father, a respected and worthy notary, send his son to the Municipal Primary School, intended for poorer children, when he could have put him into a private institution, more appropriate for people of their station? Anwering his own question Dalí explains that, as a free-thinker with anarchist sympathies, his father could not possibly contemplate patronizing any of the alternative schools, all of them Catholic.[37] It is also likely that Don Salvador was impressed by Trayter's personality and reputation. A man of wide interests, the teacher drew beautifully, collected Romanesque capitals and Gothic sculpture (a proclivity to which Dalí refers in the _Secret Life_) and was an ardent francophile, frequently visiting Paris and bringing back such marvellous presents for his numerous children that they nicknamed him 'Mr Lafayette', after the famous store in which he habitually made his purchases. His only failing, apparently, was that he had frequent bad tempers.[38]

In 1952 Dalí returned to the theme of Trayter, portraying him as a militant atheist:

> My first teacher, Trayter, when I was very young, only made me learn that 'God does not exist', and that 'religion was something for women'. This idea appealed to me enormously from the beginning. At the same time I found an empirical confirmation of this in the bosom of my family in which the women went to church but my father, who was a free-thinker, never. Besides, he [Dalí's father] embellished his succulently picturesque conversation with an uninterrupted series of the richest blasphemies.[39]

Trayter's proselytizing in favour of atheism is not attested by more reliable sources, and indeed seems extremely unlikely in view both of the many official honours heaped on him during his long career as a primary school teacher, and of his close friendship with a well-known Figueres priest, Father Callis.[40] However, that he was an unorthodox thinker from a Catholic point of view is shown by the fact that he was so fervent a disciple of Darwin that he named one of his four daughters Darwina.[41] But even if Trayter had really recommended atheism to his charges, such pleading would only have served to reinforce the relentless anti-Catholic indoctrination Salvador was receiving at home from his father, and which continued throughout his childhood and adolescence.[42]

Dalí's claim that at the Municipal Primary School his acute awareness of being better-off than the other pupils increased his 'natural tendencies to megalomania' probably ought to be taken seriously. Immaculately turned out by his indulgent mother, his appearance must have made a striking contrast indeed with that of the other, less-favoured boys.[43]

Two or three of Dalí's evocations of Trayter stand out in particularly sharp relief. The first concerns those occasions on which the teacher would invite him home after class to show him his treasures (Trayter and his large family lived only a few metres from the Dalís in a building later replaced by the Museum of the Empordà, on the corner of the Rambla). The master's den was a magic cave, 'for me the most mysterious of all the places that still crowd my memory. Such must have been the room where Faust worked.' The premises were dominated by a monster bookcase where great dusty volumes jostled with an assortment of 'incongruous and heterogeneous objects', some of them half concealed under covers that made them doubly fascinating. Trayter would produce an outsize rosary purchased in Jerusalem for his wife, the beads fashioned out of genuine olive-wood from the Mount of Olives, or take out a statuette of Mephistopheles with a moveable arm which waved a devil's trident that lit up. A desiccated frog, infallible guide to the weather, dangled from a string; and there were sundry instruments, 'probably medical paraphernalia', whose unknown use 'tormented me by the scabrous ambiguity of their explicit shapes'.[44]

Europe had been swept with a wave of enthusiasm for stereoscopic pictures at the turn of the century. Hardly a middle-class family escaped the craze, and the Trayters were no exception. The *pièce de résistance* of the teacher's collection of marvels was a gadget Dalí recalled as a large square box containing a kind of 'optical theatre':

> I have never been able to determine or reconstruct in my mind exactly what it was like. As I remember it one saw everything as if at the bottom of and through a very limpid and stereoscopic water, which became successively and continually coloured with the most varied iridescences. The pictures themselves were edged and dotted with coloured holes lighted from behind and were transformed one into another in an incomprehensible way that could be compared only to the metamorphoses of the so-called 'hypnagogic' images which appear to us in the state of 'half-slumber'. It was in this marvellous theatre of Senor Trayter that I saw the images which were to stir me most deeply for the rest of my life.[45]

This may have been the French stereoscope that has been preserved by Trayter's descendants along with some boxes of double slides manufactured in Paris by the firm B.K. Photographie. Perhaps the eccentric teacher bought them at Lafayette's during one of his frequent visits to the French capital. The slides correspond almost exactly to Dalí's recollection of them: the tiny holes perforating their edges are filled with celluloid plaques of different colours, and when lit from behind do indeed illuminate scenes thrown into relief with the most 'varied iridescences'.[46]

Dalí tells us that in Trayter's 'optical theatre' his attention was particularly riveted by a series of coloured views of snow-bound Russian landscapes studded with cupolas, and, among these, by a sequence of a pretty little Russian girl in a sledge, enveloped in white furs and pursued by wolves with phosphorescent eyes:

> This girl would look at me fixedly and her expression, awe-inspiringly proud, oppressed my heart; her little nostrils were as lively as her glance, which gave her something of the wild look of a small forest animal. This extreme vivacity provided a moving contrast to the infinite sweetness and serenity conveyed by an oval face and a combination of features as miraculously harmonious as those of a Madonna of Raphael. Was it Gala? I am certain it was.[47]

Did Dalí really see a little Russian girl in Trayter's stereoscope, or was this a 'false memory' invented later to please Gala, his Russian wife, and lend weight to the myth that their union was predestined? No such scene is recorded in the slides preserved by the teacher's descendants, which proves nothing, but the fact that among them there are others of Russia suggests that we would do well not to dismiss Dalí's claim, or doubt that in his eccentric teacher's 'optical theatre' he saw the images that were to stir him deeply for the rest of his life. Moreover, whether Gala was foreshadowed there or not, it is a fact that the revelation of that magic world laid the basis for the fascination with stereoscopic vision and optical illusions of different kinds that was to characterize Dalí all his life.

In Dalí's evocation of his time at Trayter's school, the description of his relationship with a boy called Butchaques takes up a lot of space. Fair-haired, blue-eyed and considerably taller than Salvador, the latter had long noticed that he was the most handsome of all his companions. He watched him furtively, he assures us, and, when their eyes met, felt the blood congeal in his veins. One day Butchaques came up behind him, we are told, and put his hands gently on Dalí's shoulders: 'I jumped, swallowing my saliva the wrong way, which made me cough convulsively. I welcomed this cough, for it excused my agitation and made it less noticeable. I had in fact just blushed crimson on identifying the child who was touching me as Butchaques.'[48]

Shame is a rare emotion in Spain, where children have been allowed to express aggression and tenderness more freely than in Britain, and encouraged to show off. As a result the vocabulary of shame is much less subtle than in English. Spanish makes no clear distinction between blushing from shame and flushing with anger, for example, and a book such as Christopher Ricks's *Keats and Embarrassment* would be difficult to translate into Spanish with anything approaching fidelity. There are very few descriptions of shame in Spanish nineteenth-century novels or poetry (they abound, of course, in English literature), and Dalí's *Secret Life*, where the theme of the author's feelings of shame as a child is developed in detail, is unique in the annals of Spanish autobiography.

Later in this same chapter Dalí recounts how, after a freak snowstorm in Figueres, he meets the local version of the Russian girl he has seen in Trayter's 'magic theatre'. Suddenly, sitting beside a fountain just outside the town, there she is! Overcome with 'mortal shame', he is too frightened to make a direct approach to the child, whom for the purposes of his narrative he calls Galuchka (since he insists she prefigured Gala).[49] When he sees her again, this time in Figueres, he is seized with 'insurmountable shame' and decides to wait till nightfall before making an advance: 'At twilight and in the growing darkness I would no longer feel ashamed. I could then look Galuchka in the eye, and she would not see me blush.'[50] The experience of sudden shame is that of *exposure* to the critical scrutiny or ridicule of others, as many writers on shame have pointed out.[51] It is not surprising, therefore, that Dalí should use the word in his depiction of this painful emotion. Galuchka's gaze is so piercing that it seems to penetrate the body of a nurse behind whom Salvador hides to escape it, 'leaving me more and more in the open and gradually and irremissibly exposing me to the devouring activity of that adored though mortally anguishing glance'; her stare throws him into 'the new situation of feeling myself exposed, looked at by Galuchka'.[52]

At several other points in the *Secret Life* Dalí hints, rather than states explicitly, that fear of blushing (ereutophobia) and his shame about being ashamed were major components in the fashioning of his personality, alienating him from his companions and driving him into solitude. In *On Shame and the Search for Identity*, probably the most penetrating work on the subject of shame ever written, Helen Merrell Lynd has devoted memorable pages to the 'incommunicability' of shame, on shame as an emotion which it is literally impossible to acknowledge verbally when it happens because 'the experience of shame is itself isolating, alienating, incommunicable'.[53] As Lynd explains, a person experiencing shame is incapable of communicating to anyone else what is taking place because the adrenalin released into the bloodstream is urging him or her to escape or hide. All that can be done is to 'put on a brave face'; to disguise the discomfiture as best as possible; to pretend it is not happening. On the evidence of the *Secret Life* it seems that perhaps as early as seven or eight Dalí developed a phobia about blushing that made it extremely difficult for him to maintain normal relations with the people around him, including his companions at school, and forced him to find ways to disguise his mortification.

It is worth noticing that, in telling us of his crush on the fair-haired and blue-eyed Butchaques, Dalí stresses that his fascination was centred on the boy's buttocks:

> Butchaques appeared to me beautiful as a little girl, yet his excessively chunky knees gave me a feeling of uneasiness, as did also his buttocks too tightly squeezed into pants that were too excruciatingly narrow. Yet in spite of my embarrassment an invincible curiosity impelled me to look at these tight pants each time a violent movement threatened to split them wide open.[54]

Butchaques's buttocks are mentioned again some pages later as the hallmark of this precocious love-object.[55] All of this would be merely anecdotal were it not for the fact that Dalí's painting confirms him as a man absolutely obsessed with bottoms. In one of his most disturbing works, *The Lugubrious Game* (1929), whose explicit anality shocked even the Surrealists, the tight short pants and knobbly knees of the youth remind one unavoidably of Dalí's description of his schoolfriend.

XV

Dalí asks us to believe that he and Butchaques were constantly caressing each other and that each time they separated they exchanged a long kiss on the mouth. This must be a gross exaggeration, for had their affection been expressed so blatantly one imagines that strong repressive action would have been taken by Trayter. Unfortunately Joan Butchaques, who became a plumber by trade, never gave his view of the matter. In his seventies he said that someone had told him he was in a book by Dalí. But he took his recollections of the artist to the grave.[56]

Barcelona Again

Salvador Dalí Cusí had stayed in close touch with the Serraclara household after settling in Figueres, and wrote regularly to his mother, Teresa Cusí, to keep her abreast of family news.[57]

It soon became customary for the Dalís to spend Christmas and New Year with the Serraclaras. The annual reunion meant an exciting train ride for Salvador, a guaranteed shower of affection and presents at the other end, the bustle of a great city, wonderful entertainment and the thrill of being taken to Gaudí's Parc Güell, that extravaza of brilliantly coloured mosaics, undulating lines and crooked columns whose artificial trees made of stone, Dalí wrote later (recalling a visit with Ursula Matas), gave him 'a sense of unforgettable anguish'.[58] Salvador looked forward to Christmas with wild impatience and, as might be expected, the occasion provided an ideal opportunity for tantrums. During the visits to Barcelona he 'got so worked up he never stopped crying and raging,' Anna Maria reports, presumably from hearsay since the visits came to an end in 1912, four years after her birth. 'They gave him so many presents,' she goes on, 'that he used to go quite beserk.' Receiving presents was to prove one of Dalí's life-long addictions. He usually abstained from giving them.[59]

One day Salvador wanted a string of sugar garlic hanging up in the window of a shop that happened to be closed. The ensuing tantrum proved so excessive, according to Anna Maria, that Felipa Domènech, by all accounts a woman of sweet temperament, was driven almost to distraction.[60]

As well as the annual Christmas gathering in Barcelona, the Dalís often spent some weeks during the summer at the Serraclaras' charming villa in Cabrils, the village north of the capital near Vilassar de Mar where Don Salvador had first met Felipa

Dalí with his favourite cousin, Montserrat.

Domènech.[61] Rafael Dalí and his family were also visitors, and there is a delightful photograph of Salvador and his cousin Montserrat holding hands there at the age of three or four.

Two scenes in the *Secret Life* are set in Cabrils, when Dalí says he was five. The first involves the alleged pushing of a smaller child off a low bridge, just for the fun of it.[62] The second is more interesting. In it Dalí recounts how he spies on a beautiful woman urinating in the countryside. Caught out, he continues to stare, transfixed, at the bubbling cascade, while 'a mortal shame welled into my face with the ebb and flow of my crazed blood'.[63] This 'mortal shame' reminds us of the scenes with Butchaques and Galuchka and is a further indication of the extent to which, in the early Dalí, sexual staring soon became the object of painful repression.

Cadaqués and the Pichots

Pepito and Angeleta Pichot's house in Figueres stood in the Carreró de la Barceloneta, a cul-de-sac not far from the notorious Garrigal quarter, famous for its prostitutes and gypsies. It was just the sort of area to appeal to a bohemian, and the jovial Pepito made great friends with its denizens, particularly the gypsies; their strong presence in Figueres since the eighteenth century was a consequence of the erection of the huge fortress of Saint Ferdinand, whose hundreds of horses needed constant attention. The Pichot house was a spacious, rambling pile, almost English in character, with a large garden and an inner walled patio. Giving free rein to his vocation as a floriculturist, Pepito did wonders. The patio became an orchard, a Figueres version of the biblical *hortus conclusus*, and the garden a riot of roses. The young Dalí was a frequent visitor. 'It was one of the most marvellous places of my childhood,' he wrote.[64]

The Pichots were frustrated in their

A contented Dalí, aged about six, in Pepito Pichot's magic garden in Figueres.

The Pichots' house at Es Sortell before the garden grew.

attempts to produce a family (Angeleta had numerous miscarriages) and finally adopted a girl, Julia, who was to play a part in the adolescent Dalí's sexual fantasies.[65] Pepito adored and was fascinated by Salvador, and Dalí is deeply appreciative of him in the *Secret Life*. If the Pichots were all gifted, 'Pepito was, perhaps, the most artistic of all without, however, having cultivated any of the fine arts in particular'.[66]

The mother of the numerous Pichot clan, Antonia Gironès, was highly enterprising, a characteristic she passed on to her seven children, not least Pepito. Early in the century she rented summer accommodation in Cadaqués at the Punta d'en Pampa, a few metres from the tiny beach of Sa Cueta.[67] The family found Cadaqués so congenial that before long Antonia decided to buy property there, acquiring a low-lying, barren promontory on the south-east rim of the bay called Es Sortell, which was described in the Land Registry as a *yermo*, or wasteland.[68] It was an inspired choice, despite the local sceptics. Pepito, the failed law student now turned horticulture fiend, was detailed to convert the promontory into an exotic garden, and succeeded brilliantly against all the odds. The original L-shaped house, built to designs by Ramon Pichot's friend the painter Miquel Utrillo, was a modest, ground-floor affair that gradually expanded over the following years.[69]

There is a engaging group picture of the Pichots taken at Es Sortell, allegedly in

The Pichot clan photographed at Es Sortell in 1908 by the family's horticulturist, Pepito.

1908 although it may be slightly later. Only Pepito, the photographer, is missing. Standing by the door is the painter, Ramon, Picasso's friend, whom Gertrude Stein met in Paris in 1907 ('rather a wonderful creature, he was long and thin like one of those primitive Christs in Spanish churches and when he did a Spanish dance which he did later at the famous banquet to Rousseau, he was awe-inspiringly religious'[70]). Next to Pichot is his wife, Laure Gargallo, known to her friends as Germaine. This is the beauty for whom Picasso's impotent friend Casagemas committed suicide in 1901, and with whom the insatiable artist may well have had a more successful sexual fling.[71] Striking, too, is the writer Eduardo Marquina, Mercedes Pichot's husband, who stares confidently at the camera from his wicker chair, his four-year-old-son Lluís at his elbow. Marquina's literary career was then looking up, and soon he would enjoy his first successes in the theatre. Three of the Pichots were in the process of becoming professional musicians when the picture was taken. Behind Marquina, with the dazzling smile, is Ricard, who at the age of seventeen had won first prize for the 'cello at the Paris Conservatoire and was a favourite pupil of Pau Casals. Twelve years later, by which time Ricard was a well-known musician, Dalí was to paint an Impressionist portrait of him practising at Es Sortell.[72] Ricard's brother Lluís, the violinist, is the dapper fellow on the right of the picture with the pipe and white, Cadaqués-style fisherman's hat. A few years later, he, Ricard and the Figueres pianist Lluís Bonaterra founded the Trio Hispania, performing successfully in Europe and throughout Spain. Finally, beside Marquina and looking up at her brother Ricard, is Maria. Known professionally as Maria Gay (after her husband, the pianist Joan Gay), and in the family as 'Niní', Maria was a distinguished opera singer and destined for fame as one of the finest Carmens of all time.[73]

By 1908 the potential of Es Sortell as a summer retreat was plain to see. Doña Antonia Gironès was delighted by the success of her venture, and soon Cadaqués became a mecca for the Pichots' wide assortment of bohemian friends, who would arrive in Figueres by train and take a *tartana*, or covered buggy, to Cadaqués. It was a bone-shaking, nine hours journey, but at the journey's end lay one of the prettiest villages on the Mediterranean, a village where there were no taps in the houses and the women still carried the well-water home on their heads in pitchers.[74]

Given Don Salvador Dalí's intimate friendship with Pepito Pichot, he and his wife were soon guests at Es Sortell. Before long the notary felt the urge to possess or rent a property in the village where he had spent the first nine years of his life. He discussed the matter with Pepito, who agreed to rent him a converted stable, owned by his sister Maria, that stood by the water's edge at the little beach of Es Llané (or Llaner), a few hundred metres from Es Sortell on the Cadaqués side.[75] Next door was a fanciful, low villa painted pink and nicknamed by the villagers Es Tortell ('The Pastry House')

Es Llané c.1910, showing the Dalís' house and, just along the shore, the Art Nouveau building nicknamed by the locals 'Es Tortell' ('The Cake').

because it looked as if you could eat it. On the other side of the converted stable, a little further along the beach, Pepito Pichot rented another house to his friend Juan
Salleras, from Figueres, whose daughter Rosa Maria, six years younger than Salvador,
was to be 'adopted' by the latter at birth after he had tried in vain to buy her from her
mother with his piggy-bank savings. For several years these were the only properties
at Es Llané.[76]

Behind the beach were orchards and olive groves enclosed within the dry slate walls
for which Cadaqués is famous, and traversed by tiny lanes picking their way up the hill,
while on the other side of Es Sortell came a profusion of coves bounded, at Cala Nans,
by the lighthouse. This was Salvador Dalí's childhood paradise, which later grew to
embrace all of Cadaqués and its immediate surroundings. He came to love the village
with a fanatical intensity, and during the school year in Figueres never ceased to dream
of the forthcoming holidays at Es Llané.

Among the wonders of Cadaqués which Salvador began to explore as a child, Cape
Creus, lying just around the corner to the north-east, reigned supreme. This massive
headland, as Dalí reminds us in the *Secret Life*, is 'exactly the spot where the mountains
of the Pyrenees come down into the sea, in a grandiose geological delirium'.[77]

*Dalí called Cape Creus, which lies just around the corner from Port Lligat, 'a grandiose geological deliri-
um'. Over the centuries the mica-schist has been sculpted into weird shapes by the wind, rain and salt lashed
from the sea.*

Grandiose the delirium certainly is; grim and forbidding, too, for this is a place of deadly currents and countless shipwrecks—and in spring, briefly, a botanist's paradise. Dalí liked to remind people that Creus is the most easterly point of the Iberian Peninsula, and that the island that stands just off the cape welcomes Spain's first sunbeams of the day. Aptly called Massa d'Oros ('Mass of Golds'), it is known more familiarly as La Rateta ('The Mouse').

Indented with innumerable creeks, even the smallest with its evocative name, the cliffs and escarpments of Creus are composed fundamentally of slaty-textured mica-schist, a metamorphic rock resulting from tremendous compression and which consists of alternate folia of mica and quartz. Often the dark mica-schist is juxtaposed with thick seams of pure quartz, and locals will assure you that from the billions of tiny silver plaques embedded in the rock the sun strikes a sparkling radiance visible to ships far out at sea. Over the centuries the rains and the tramuntana, the latter laden with corrosive cargoes of sand and salt, have sculpted the easily eroded mica-schist into weird shapes: 'The Eagle', 'The Camel', 'The Dead Woman', 'The Rhinoceros', 'The Monk' and so forth. At Creus even the casual visitor will soon begin to see strange things, to perceive weird images which no sooner assume the

Walking at Creus one never knows what to expect next. Dalí's 'mental landscape', he once said, resembled the cape's 'protean and fantastic rocks'. Lorca and Buñuel were deeply impressed by them.

form of, say, a phantasmagoric bird or animal than they turn into a wrinkled human profile, a fairy palace or a clump of tropical vegetation as one moves among them or approaches them from the sea. Creus is a vast natural theatre of optical illusions, and the prolonged contemplation of its metamorphoses reinforced Dalí's lifelong obsession with visual tricks, notably the double image. His 'mental landscape', he once said, resembled 'the protean and fantastic rocks of Cape Creus', the rocks which some etymologists think gave Cadaqués its name (*cap*, 'cape' + *quer*, 'rock').[78] On another occasion Dalí explained that he felt he was a human incarnation of this primitive landscape, that he embodied its 'living nucleus'.[79] He was not the first artist to have been deeply moved by the place, moreover, and was impressed to learn that, as he had suspected, 'the sublime Gaudí', architect of the great unfinished church of the Sagrada Familia in Barcelona, had visited Creus as an adolescent and been 'nourished by the soft and baroque, hard and Gothic rocks of this divine spot'.[80] Little wonder, then, that eventually Dalí made his home in the tiny fishing village of Port Lligat, at the foot of the cape, or that Creus was to become one of the key settings of his paintings.

Salvador was soon close friends with Lluís, the son of Eduardo Marquina and

The rock at Creus that partly inspired Dalí's The Great Masturbator *(colour plate XIV).*

Mercedes Pichot, a fortnight younger than himself, and with Pepito, the son of
Maria and Joan Gay. The children were in and out of each other's houses all summer long.[81] At Es Sortell Salvador was exposed daily to Ramon Pichot's paintings,
and would often have heard Ricard, Lluís and Maria practising. Sometimes the family organized nocturnal concerts that were Surrealist *avant la lettre*, taking advantage of the phenomenon known locally as *calma blanca*, when Cadaqués Bay goes
dead calm and mirrors the village with a ghostly precision. On such occasions, particularly when there was a full moon to illuminate the proceedings, a grand piano
would be placed in the Pichots' boat with a specially wide bottom, and moored off
Es Sortell beach. The musicians, attired in evening dress, would install themselves
on the floating platform and begin to play, the magical atmosphere being heightened by a pair of tame swans floating by as if on a lake. When the news spread that

The Dalís on the beach at Es Llané, c.1909.

there was to be a concert, the people of Cadaqués would gather silently on the beach and wait in suspense for the siren-music to come wafting in across the still water.[82]

The Pichots were not only creative artists but flamboyant, well-travelled bohemians. The summer-by-summer contact with such people, and their international friends, must have been thrilling as Salvador advanced from childhood to adolescence. It is even possible that at Es Sortell the six-year-old Dalí coincided with his future rival Picasso when, in the summer of 1910, inveigled into visiting Cadaqués by Ramon Pichot, the artist descended on the village with his current girlfriend, Fernande Olivier. Certainly the young Dalí often heard later about that sojourn, never repeated, and became aware that Picasso (whose Cubism was then attaining its moment of maximum abstraction) had produced important paintings of Cadaqués during his stay. Dalí liked to recall an anecdote from that summer. Maria Pichot, the opera singer, was being importuned at the time by an insistent tenor who, in despair, broke into her bedroom one day. She was seen by Picasso fleeing through her window and shouting *En juliol, ni dona ni cargol* ('In July, neither women nor snails')—a popular local saying. In later life Dalí enjoyed reminding Picasso of the incident by sending him a telegram each July with this colourful piece of enigmatic Empordanese advice.[83]

Felipa Doménech, Dalí's mother, with her younger sister Catalina, known in the family as 'La Tieta'.

There is a fine photograph of the Dalí family in Cadaqués at about the time of Picasso's visit in 1910, grouped on the beach in front of their house at Es Llané with 'El Beti', a fisherman who used to take them for trips around the bay, resting on his oars just offshore behind them. The picture was almost certainly taken by Pepito Pichot. The Dalís had just been joined in Figueres by Felipa Domènech's mother, Maria Anna Ferrés, and by her sister Catalina, who accompany them here. The latter, flanked by Salvador and Anna Maria, looks happiness personified. The children adored her and soon she was known by the affectionate Catalan tag of 'la tieta', 'Auntie'. The name stuck to her for the rest of her life.

The Christian Brothers

In 1910, at the end of Salvador Dalí's second year with Esteban Trayter, his father took a decision that was greatly to affect the boy's future: he enrolled him for that autumn at the college inaugurated in Figueres the previous year by the Christian Brothers, the French teaching order founded in the eighteenth century by Jean-Baptiste de la Salle. In 1904 a new law had banned the Order from running schools in France (where the Jesuits had already been proscribed), with the result that the Christian Brothers stepped up their operations abroad. Catalunya was one of their first objectives.[84]

The Figueres college was a Spanish extension of the Institut des Frères des Ecoles Chrétiennes in Béziers, a boarding establishment of considerable prestige. At the beginning almost all the teachers in Figueres were from the parent school, as well as the majority of the 120 pupils. Instruction was entirely in French, and this appealed greatly to the francophile in Don Salvador Dalí. An excellent opportunity had now presented itself for enabling his son to learn French, one that made the waiving of anti-clerical prejudices seem justified, and he decided to go ahead. In this respect Don Salvador was no less pragmatic than his brother Rafael, who, shelving his hostility to the Church, placed his daughter Montserrat in the hands of French nuns in Barcelona for the same linguistic reason. Both men had done well at French when they were with the Piarist Fathers, and it may be that their love of the language was not unconnected to their admiration for the French Revolution.[85]

The splendid complex erected by the Christian Brothers in 1909 on the outskirts of Figueres, next to the railway line, was officially named 'Collège Hispano-Français de l'Immaculée Conception Béziers-Figueras' but soon became known popularly as 'Els Fossos' ('The Holes') because of the dips characterizing the wasteland surrounding the school.

Such was the insistence in 'Els Fossos' on speaking French that local pupils heard chatting in their own language during recreation were liable to punishment, albeit not too severe.[86] To ease the transition for these boys, a Spanish brother versed in French provided special classes.[87]

As a result of the six years he spent in the school, Dalí fulfilled his father's aspirations by acquiring excellent spoken French, although with a thick Catalan accent. The language's unphonetic spelling was beyond him, however, and he never mastered it. Nor did he ever learn to spell Catalan and Spanish correctly. Like most Spanish children he had difficulties with b's and v's, which are pronounced the same, and with the h (unaspirated in standard Spanish and often inserted or omitted incorrectly); and the fact that the written o in Catalan is pronounced u, and the e as an a, made matters worse. French, Catalan and Spanish between them combined to make Salvador a hopeless speller in all three.

A further reflection imposes itself: if at the Municipal School run by Esteban Trayter instruction was imparted only in Spanish (the legal requirement in all official institutions in Catalunya, where the native tongue was still the object of repression by Madrid), between the ages of six and twelve Dalí spoke and heard French much more often than Spanish, which he hardly used at all given that at home, as with his friends outside school, conversation was habitually conducted in Catalan. When he left 'Els Fossos' to begin his secondary education, the balance was to tilt in favour of Spanish, but by then French was deeply rooted in his unconscious. This circumstance helps to explain the pleasure which the adolescent Dalí was to take in French literature. But it is a circumstance never once mentioned amongst the 'true memories' of the college included in the *Secret Life*, where Dalí gives the impression that he spent only two years, not six, with the Christian Brothers (who are not even identified as French), learnt absolutely nothing and never moved up a class.

There are no detailed school records to help us to assess the accuracy of Dalí's account of his time at 'Els Fossos'. True, for his first four years he was in 'huitième', but this in itself does not mean that he did not make annual progress, since the class catered for children from six to ten. His last two years were spent in 'septième', but, again, the one surviving document tells us nothing about what he studied, or with what success or lack of it. All we can be certain of is that, during these six years, the Christian Brothers would have striven to give him a broad general education.[88]

That the curriculum included art is proved by a brief article published by Dalí in 1927 in which he praised the 'common sense' of one of his teachers at 'Els Fossos'. This man, whose name is not recorded, liked to issue his pupils with simple drawings done by himself with a ruler, and then require them to block them in carefully with watercolours. His advice was simple: 'To paint them well, to paint well in general, consists in not going over the line.' Dalí, whose best painting is remarkable for its careful attention to tiny detail, may have owed a real debt to these early lessons, and he remembered the brother's advice later in *50 Secrets of Magic Craftsmanship*. It is a pity that we do not know more about that 'simple master' who, no student of aesthetic theory, nonetheless observed a 'norm of conduct' capable of inspiring an ethic of artistic probity.[89]

Dalí begins the fifth chapter of the *Secret Life*, entitled 'True Childhood Memories' (as distinct from the 'false' ones of the previous chapter), with an evocation of the view in winter from Classroom One of the college, a view dominated by two cypress trees whose changing lights at sundown, he tells us, riveted his attention as the shadow of the 'rectilinear architecture' of the building moved upwards. Seconds later, as the Angelus chimed, the whole class would rise to its feet 'and we would repeat in chorus the prayer recited with bowed head and folded hands by the superior'.[90]

The classroom today is almost unchanged but, though a group of cypresses can still be seen from its large windows arrowing upwards at the edge of the playing field, modern buildings now slice off the previously unbroken panorama of the Empordà plain. In Dalí's day the passageway outside the classroom was lined with cabinets containing a splendid collection of minerals, tropical butterflies, birds and fossils and, above them, a row of some sixty religious pictures, brought from Béziers and now dispersed.[91] If Dalí forgets the cabinets in the *Secret Life*, he distinctly remembers some of the paintings and reproductions. One represented 'a fox's head emerging from a cavern, carrying a dead goose dangling from its jaws'. The other was a copy of Millet's *Angelus*, a work destined to exert a strong influence on his own production.[92]

XVII

Monturiol, 24

At the beginning of July 1912, coinciding with the end of his son's second year with the Christian Brothers, Don Salvador Dalí Cusí began to announce prominently on the front page of a local newspaper, *La Veu de l'Empordà*, that he had moved his office and home to new premises at Monturiol, 24, the boxed advertisements recalling those inserted in the local press when he set up his practice twelve years earlier, in 1900.[93]

There is no mention of the move in the *Secret Life*, where Dalí writes as if for the first twenty-five years of his existence he lived in the new apartment. Anna Maria, however, is eloquent on the loss of her childhood paradise. Gone for ever the magic balcony with its birds and games and spikenard, gone the prospect over the Marquesa de la Torre's gardens, the destruction of which, for urban development, was the main reason for decamping.[94]

The Dalís' second home was on the top floor of a fanciful new building, the work of the most celebrated architect in Figueres at the time, Josep Azemar i Pont. It over-

The Dalís' second home in Figueres at Carrer Monturiol 24, to which they moved in 1912. Dalí improvised his first studio in a wash-house on the roof terrace, which looked out across the plain of the Emporda to the mountains flanking the Mediterranean.

looked the Plaça de la Palmera, where the Thursday market and the annual spring fair were held; and, as befitted the now thriving notary, the premises were more spacious and luxurious than the family's previous apartment (his office, as before, was downstairs). The building, today numbered Monturiol, 10, is a listed monument and has undergone no significant changes since 1912. It faces almost due east and has a wide central staircase-cum-light-well which leads up to a rooftop terrace similar to that at Monturiol, 20, but with a far more extensive view. Dalí's painting *Girl from Figueres*, done towards 1925, recreates accurately part of the townscape as it then appeared from here, with the mauve hills of the coastal range of Sant Pere de Roda, on the edge of the Empordà plain, rising on the horizon and, in the foreground, the College of the French Dominican Sisters, with its characteristic belfry. Though not shown in the painting, a glimpse could also be caught from the terrace of the lovely Bay of Roses, sixteen kilometres away.

The rooftop terrace of Monturiol, 24 is one of the key childhood environments recalled in the *Secret Life*. Then as now there were two abandoned laundry rooms up here, used mainly for storage, and Dalí assures us that one of them was soon made available to him as a studio. No date is provided for the cession, but internal evidence in the narrative suggests that it took place when he was nine or ten. It was a tiny space, with room only for a cement trough on the floor and the servant who used to pummel the dirty linen. But it was more than enough for a budding artist's first atelier. Salvador placed a chair inside the trough, he tells us, the scrubbing board laid across the top served as a table for working on and, when it was hot, he would strip off, turn on the tap and sit in water up to his waist as he drew. 'It was something like Marat's bathtub,' he remarks (a rather indifferent drawing of the child artist in his trough, presumably done specially for the *Secret Life*, accompanies this account).[95]

Apart from Anna Maria there were no other children in the house (the Viñas family downstairs had none), and she herself does not seem to have been permitted access to her brother's preserve. Salvador had the space entirely to himself. At this age, he says, he loved to dress up as a boy king, decking himself out in the ermine cape, crown and sceptre that had been given to him as a present by one of his uncles in Barcelona. Whether the uncle responsible was Rafael Dalí or Anselm Domènech has not been recorded. But whoever it was he catered thereby, perhaps unwittingly, to a fascination for disguise that was one of Salvador's 'strongest passions' as a child. Attired thus, he recalls, he enjoyed strutting around his terrace, improvising ardent speeches to his imagined subjects. Later he claimed that his desire to scale the heights—and stay there—sprang from these early days as sole ruler of a lofty kingdom perched on top of one of the best modern buildings in Figueres.[96]

One important item installed by Dalí in his first studio was a complete collection of Gowans's Art Books, which began to be issued in 1905 by Gowans and Gray, Ltd, of London and Glasgow, in a French as well as an English edition. Each volume comprised sixty black-and-white illustrations of the Great Masters born before 1800, 'affording', reads the standard title page, 'examples of the different characteristics of the Artist's work'. The series soon became immensely popular, and it is still possible to pick up odd volumes in second-hand bookshops. It seems probable that Salvador's father started acquiring the collection as soon as it began to be issued, or shortly afterwards. Perhaps he even took out a standing order. At all events, Salvador could not have possessed the full complement until 1913, when the final volume, number 52 (Lawrence) appeared. The coincidence between this date and the Dalís' move to their second home means that, aged nine, Salvador could well have been in a position to install the whole series (3,120 black-and-white reproductions) in his newly acquired laundry-room studio on the roof of Monturiol, 24. In the *Secret Life* he refers with gratitude to the collection:

> These little monographs which my father had so prematurely given me as a present produced an effect on me that was one of the most decisive in my life. I came to know by heart all those pictures of the history of art, which have been familiar to me since my earliest childhood, for I would spend entire days contemplating them. The nudes attracted me above all else, and Ingres's Golden Age appeared to me the most beautiful picture in the world, and I fell in love with the naked girl symbolizing the fountain.[97]

In an adolescent manuscript Dalí had already expressed his debt to these little books more graphically:

> The Gowans's collection is closely linked to my childhood. From a very early age I remember the collection in our home and I used to look at the reproductions with positive delight. I adored Rubens's sensual nudes and the Flemish domestic scenes.
>
> Today I sometimes have to make an effort to separate out a real lived incident from one of these reproductions. Many times, lived events and pictures fuse in my memory. When I leaf through these pages again, I feel that I've really *seen* all this and that I've known these people for ages and very intimately. I feel sure that I picnicked once in that shady Watteau glade or that, when I was small, my nurse was that giggling cuddly girl by Teniers; I've walked at twilight by a fountain in a garden with a Renaissance building, through one of those landscapes used by Titian as backdrops for his Venuses of golden flesh stretched on folds of fine and costly dresses, etc. But all these reproductions are so mixed up with other memories that often it is extremely difficult for me to be sure where the truth begins and where the farce [sic] begins. Thus, for example, the Claudes and Watteaus are confused with my first walks to 'La Forêt' with the 'Brothers'. Titian's Renaissance building merges completely with that of the Marquesa de la Torre, also in Renaissance style, which was in front of our apartment.[98]

If the format of the Gowans's Art Books was tiny, the range covered was triumphantly comprehensive.[99] Accustomed as we are nowadays to colour reproductions, it requires some readjustment of the imagination to appreciate how these small-scale, black-and-white plates could have made such a great impact on the young Dalí. Yet, once one tries to relinquish one's prejudices, their fascination becomes immediately apparent. Slim as well as minute (15 x 10 cm), these eminently transportable monographs fitted the narrowest pocket. They were the sort of little volumes with which one could make friends, and Dalí most probably enjoyed them not only in the seclusion of his house-top preserve but took them with him on his walks into the lush countryside around Figueres. Thus by the age of ten or so the future artist was acquainted with work by almost all the Great Masters of European painting.

The move to Monturiol, 24, coinciding with the near completion of Salvador's collection of Gowans's Art Books, was followed almost immediately by a bereavement that changed the pattern of the Dalís' family life: on 5 October 1912 Don Salvador's long-widowed mother, Teresa Cusí, died in Barcelona. She was buried in a newly acquired niche in the Poble Nou cemetery, and the remains of her unfortunate husband, the suicide Gal, were brought from their first resting place in another part of the precinct to lie beside her.[100] Teresa Cusí's death spelt the end of the Christmas and New Year visits to the Serraclaras' flat in Barcelona: the end, as far as Salvador and Anna Maria were concerned, of an era.[101]

First Steps in Painting

If Don Salvador Dalí Cusí's best friend was Pepito Pichot, there is no record of any particular intimacy with the latter's brother Ramon, the painter, who spent most of his time in Paris. He knew and admired his work, however; and when the artist exhibited some forty watercolours, pastels and oils at the rooms of the Cine Edison in Figueres in May 1913, he bought a still-life entitled *Magranes* ('Pomegranates'). It is hard to believe that Salvador did not see this exhibition, which included numerous works inspired by Cadaqués.[102]

Ramon Pichot was not the only contemporary artist with whom the Dalí family were on friendly terms. Anna Maria Dalí claimed that her brother's first box of oil paints was given to him by a German painter called Siegfried Bürmann (1890–1980), who turned up in Cadaques in 1914, fleeing from French Morocco after the First World War broke out.[103] According to Dalí, Bürmann 'spent the whole period of the war in Cadaqués teaching ladies the steps of the Argentine tango and singing German songs to the accompaniment of the guitar'.[104] Bürmann had studied with Max Reinhardt at the Deutsches Theater in Berlin, specializing in stage design, and was a talented artist.[105] If he gave the young Dalí a box of oils, which is possible, this could not have been before August 1914, the month the war started, by which time it seems that Salvador had already begun to paint. It is also possible that Anna Maria Dalí got the story wrong, confusing Bürmann with their next-door neighbour in Es Llané, Juan Salleras, whose daughter Rosa Maria had been 'adopted' by the six-year-old Salvador. An English-style weekend artist, working in both oils and watercolours, Salleras loved to paint Cadaqués during his holidays in the village. According to Rosa Maria, Salvador was allowed to help her father carry his equipment, and would spend hours watching him at work and bombarding him with questions about what he was doing. One day, according to this version, Salleras, touched by the boy's enthusiasm, bought him a box of paints and encouraged him to try for himself.[106]

Perhaps both Bürmann and Salleras were important to Dalí. There can be little doubt, however, that the major initial influence on his artistic development was Ramon Pichot, the full revelation of whose work was to come a few years later.

Dalí's earliest known paintings, a series of five tiny undated landscapes, appear to have been done when he was ten or eleven, shortly after the move to Monturiol, 24. Which came first is a matter of dispute. Dalí authority Albert Field, owner of the oil-on-cardboard entitled *Landscape*, insists that the artist always maintained it was his first painting.[107] It can hardly have been executed as early as 1910, though, as is often claimed, and 1913 or 1914 seems a much more likely bet. The picture shows a path leading through a green field to a group of buildings sheltered behind a screen of cypress trees. One of them has a tall, industrial-looking chimney. Behind them two mountain peaks soar to dizzy heights, their altitude emphasized by the presence (against the narrow band of sky in the top right-hand corner) of a couple of large birds of prey, the upward sweep of their broad wings suggesting they are vultures rather than eagles. One of the mountains is covered in snow and must surely be the giant Canigó. If this really is Dalí's first painting, it is touching to find him initiating his career in the lee, as it were, of the mountain that, after Montserrat, Catalans hold most sacred.[108]

Another painting from the group, done in gouache on a postcard, is entitled *Vilabertran*. According to its owner, Captain Peter Moore, it dates from 1913. It shows a path leading through fields with poppies to a house set among dark trees at sunset.[109] Vilabertran, a tiny hamlet two kilometres north-east of Figueres, clusters around a fine Romanesque church, Saint Mary of Vilabertran, whose twelfth-century, three-storied belltower was visible from Dalí's classroom at the Christian Brothers. The village, with its church and tree-encircled pond (euphemistically known as 'The Lake'), was one of the family's favourite walks. Half-way there was a spring, the Font del Soc ('Tree-stump Fountain'), a shady spot ideal for a halt. For good measure the place had suitably revolutionary overtones. For here, in 1843, Abdó Terrades, the Catalan federalist, whom Don Salvador Dalí must have greatly admired, had held a much remembered open-air meeting.[110]

The Approach of Adolescence

The life of Salvador Dalí from 1912 to 1916, which alternated between Figueres and Cadaqués, is poorly documented. No records of relevance are preserved in the archives of the Christian Brothers, apart from the one mentioned. None of his teachers seems to have set down any recollections of the future world celebrity, and it has not been possible to trace any of Dalí's contemporaries at the school, the majority of whom were French. As for the Dalí family archive, inherited at Anna Maria's death by her life-long housekeeper and companion, its contents, with some exceptions, are still being withheld. Dalí's own later account of these years in the *Secret Life* is so chaotic, incomplete and inaccurate as to make it virtually useless for biographical purposes, while Anna Maria's portrayal of her brother at the time, when she was aged four to eight, is vitiated by her reading of the *Secret Life* (in the 1944 Argentinian edition), which colonized her mind with 'false memories', by a complete lack of research and by a disregard for chronology almost as glaring as her brother's.

The situation on the Domènech side of the family is no more heartening, for many papers and much correspondence was lost during the civil war. This is a tragedy, for the young Dalí was tremendously fond of his bookseller uncle and godfather, Anselm Domènech, who, delighted with the child's artistic promise, went out of his way to encourage him during his visits to Barcelona. While none of Anselm's letters to his nephew seems to be extant, an early one from Salvador to him and his wife, dated 12 April 1915, survived the holocaust. In it he thanks them for sending some Easter cakes. The letter shows that Anselm's daughter, Carmen, was staying with the Dalís at the time—a further indication of the friendship uniting the two families. Contrary to what one might have expected, given the chaos of Dalí's later handwriting, the calligraphy of the brief missive is immaculate (if not the spelling), tending to confirm Salvador's claim that he once won a prize at 'Els Fossos' for this subject.[111]

On his mother's side Dalí had a distant older 'cousin' (in fact aunt) whom he seems to have liked very much. This was Carolina Barnadas Ferrés, the daughter of grandmother Maria Anna's sister Carolina. Carolineta, as she was known affectionately in the family, died from meningitis on 22 December 1914 in Barcelona. She was thirty-four, and a spinster. Dalí was ten at the time. Years later he told his patron Edward James about the arrival of the fateful blue telegram as they were finishing dinner. When the notary opened it and announced that Carolineta was dead, grandmother Maria Anna had emitted a terrible scream of anguish, whereupon the entire family began to wail. The death made its mark on Dalí, who was to conjure up the delicate, almost pre-Raphaelesque spectre of Carolineta in two paintings set on the strand at Roses and in many drawings.[112]

The rather fuzzy picture of Salvador that emerges from the scant documentation of these early years is that of a highly suggestible, dreamy, extremely timid and hopelessly unpractical child for whom the most simple mechanical operations posed insurmountable difficulties, and for whom fantasy and reality were inextricably fused. Dalí recalled that his father used to say he was like the 'the boy from Tonyà', a legendary dullard from this village at the edge of the Empordà plain. One receives the strong impression that the notary was a distant and fearsome, if deeply admired, figure who allotted his son little time, fully occupied as he was in attending during the day to his practice and in perorating each evening across the street at his club, the 'Sport'.[113]

If Dalí greatly admired his powerful and irascible father, on one occasion the latter failed him so badly that he provided the future painter with an obsessive theme. As a public servant, Don Salvador was not able to spend the whole summer in Cadaqués with his family. When obliged to work he would join them at weekends, and his arrival was awaited with intense impatience by the children, not least because sometimes he came with presents. One day he was late, so their impatience was even greater than usual. Finally a taxi pulled up outside the house and the family rushed out. 'I've crapped,' the pillar of Figueres society announced loudly to all and sundry as he hurried indoors, not only making no attempt to hide what had happened but, it appeared to Salvador, positively revelling in it. Dalí recounted later that he had felt utterly humiliated by his father's insistence on turning what had happened into a 'Greek tragedy', when he could easily have slipped indoors without saying anything. The incident, which he believed occurred when he was ten or twelve, had 'changed him completely', marking a 'turning point' in his life. To a child already self-conscious and ashamed, with deep-rooted excremental obsessions, his father's public, and brazen, revelation of his reason for being late came with all the force of an authentic trauma. The incident was to be recalled in *The Lugubrious Game* (1929).[114]

XV

It was not the only time that the notary made his son feel ashamed. One day, according to Rosa Maria Salleras, he scolded Salvador publicly from the balcony of Es Llané, 'just like Mussolini talking to the crowd'. Rosa Maria soon decided that she disliked this violent, domineering, unpredictable and at times uncouth man, a person capable of throwing a client out of the door. Dalí said he once saw his father, wearing only his pyjamas and underpants, fighting in the street outside their house with an importunate landowner. When the opponents fell to the ground the notary's penis popped out, bumping on the sidewalk 'like a sausage'. 'When my father used to get angry,' Dalí recalled, 'the whole Rambla of Figueres would hold its breath; his voice issued from his throat like a hurricane that carried away everything in its path'.[115]

Salvador was fortunate indeed in having virtually a second father in Pepito Pichot. The failed law student turned amateur horticulturalist, local politician and *bon viveur* continued to take a deep interest in him and was always at hand for excursions and visits to places of entertainment. Typically, when the French pilot Henri Tixier visited Figueres in the summer of 1912 to give a display of aerobatics, it was with Pepito that a sailor-suited Salvador was photographed at the improvised airfield outside the town at the Camp dels Enginyers.[116] By 1912 Pichot and Salvador were almost inseparable, and the friendship deepened during Dalí's years with the Christian Brothers.

Dalí with Pepito Pichot at an air display in Figueres in May 1912.

Those years were now drawing to a close. The Brothers did not prepare boys for the State *bachillerato*, the six-year course taught throughout Spain at the official Institutos and normally begun at ten. Without the *bachillerato* it was impossible to enter university and hence the liberal professions, so it was natural that Don Salvador Dalí Cusí, very ambitious for his son, should be adamant that he now begin the course (had he not been hopeless at mathematics, he would probably have done so two years earlier[117]). As the summer of 1916 approached, therefore, Salvador knew that soon he would have to sit the entrance examination to Figueres Instituto. The prospect of having to leave the Christian Brothers may well have filled him with foreboding, for the indications are that he had been happy and unpressurized at 'Els Fossos'. All that was now to change.

In June 1916, just turned twelve, Salvador succeeded in passing the entrance examination to the Instituto, despite almost having a nervous collapse in the process. He then went for a much-needed holiday with Pepito Pichot.[118]

El Molí de la Torre

Pepito Pichot could satisfy his love of flowers by tending the walled garden of his home in Figueres and looking after Es Sortell in Cadaqués, but he needed a bigger tract of land in order to put his agricultural plans into effect. The opportunity came when, in 1911, his well-off sister María, the opera singer, purchased an interest in a splendid country house and estate on the banks of the River Manol, just outside Figueres, called the Molí de la Torre ('Tower Mill').[1] Pepito was detailed to administer the new acquisition, and three years later, in 1914, we find him advertising in *Empordà Federal* for a miller, an indication of his desire to make the Molí profitable.[2]

The outward appearance of the elegant and rambling pile, built in 1853, is little changed today. Part of the interior has been modernized, however, and the mill-race no longer works the wheel.

It was to this delightful retreat that Salvador Dalí, just turned twelve, was driven in a horse-drawn conveyance by Pepito Pichot at the beginning of June 1916 to convalesce from the strains of sitting his entrance examination to the Instituto, and of having to face up to the harsh reality of his immediate scholastic future. Dalí devotes many pages of his *Secret Life* and later writings to his time at the Tower, but they are shot through with fantasy, inaccuracies and a determination to impress the reader. An earlier, and more trustworthy account of his month-long sojourn, written ten years after the event in 1922, is interpolated in one of his adolescent diaries. It is entitled *Songs of When I Was Twelve: Verse with Prose and Colours.*[3]

These pages evoke a young Dalí much affected by the presence at the Molí de la

Chapter THREE

El Molí de la Torre, the Pichots' property just outside Figueres.

Torre of the Pichots' adopted daughter, Julia, aged about sixteen, whose blossoming body rivets his attention. One afternoon, on an impulse, he grabs her breasts as she wakes from her siesta in the garden. Julia laughs. Another day he, Julia and a girl-friend of hers go to pick linden-blossom, propping ladders against the heavily laden trees. A flash of white underwear and bare thighs sets him on fire. When one evening, pestered by Salvador to reveal the name of her beau, Julia finally blurts it out, he blushes 'scarlet in the shadows'. The detail confirms that the numerous instances of childhood shame recalled later in the *Secret Life* are no mere narrative invention.

But even more than Julia's enticing body it is the work of Ramon Pichot that comes as a revelation during Salvador's stay at the Molí de la Torre. 'Sometimes, in the diffuse light that penetrates the cracks in the shutter', he writes in the same account, 'I look at the big *pointilliste* painting by Ramon Pichot and marvel at the colours of the water in the creek.' The painting in question may have been *Cala Nans*, a spot later painted by Dalí himself. Or perhaps it was Pichot's rendering of another cove, near Creus this time, Cala Jugadora, a painting whose whereabouts is not known today. Dalí later said that Pichot had been so impressed by the rocks at Jugadora that he had incrusted slivers of mica in the picture. These scintillated in the early morning sunlight, dazzling Dalí almost literally as well as figuratively.[4] The epiphany of Pichot's work is evoked in greater detail in the *Secret Life*:

These breakfasts were my discovery of French Impressionism, the school of painting which has in fact made the deepest impression on me in my life because it represented my first contact with an anti-academic and revolutionary aesthetic theory. I did not have eyes enough to see all that I wanted to see in those thick and formless daubs of paint, which seemed to splash the canvas as if by chance, in the most capricious and nonchalant fashion. Yet as one looked at them from a certain distance and squinting one's eyes, suddenly there occurred that incomprehensible miracle of vision by virtue of which this musically coloured medley became organized, transformed into pure reality. The air, the distances, the instantaneous luminous moment, the entire world of phenomena sprang from the chaos! R. Pichot's oldest painting recalled the stylistic and iconographic formulae characteristic of Toulouse-Lautrec. I squeezed from these pictures all the literary residue of 1900, the eroticism of which burned deep in my throat like a drop of Armagnac swallowed the wrong way. I remember especially a dancer at the Bal Tabarin dressing. Her face was perversely naive and she had red hairs under her arms.

But the paintings that filled me with the greatest wonder were the most recent ones, in which deliquescent impressionism ended in certain canvases by frankly adopting in an almost uniform manner the *pointilliste* formula. The systematic juxtaposition of orange and violet produced in me a kind of illusion and sentimental joy like that which I had always experienced in looking at objects through a prism, which edged them with the colours of the rainbow. There happened to be in the dining room a crystal carafe stopper, through which everything became 'impressionistic'. Often I would carry this stopper in my pocket to observe the scene through the crystal and see it 'impressionistically'.[5]

Salvador had taken his box of oil paints to the Molí de la Torre, and under the impact of Pichot's recent paintings now applied himself with ferocious energy to the business of becoming an Impressionist. His 1922 account shows that sundown (already a favourite subject) seemed to lend itself particularly well to his new experiments:

This morning I painted the geese, under the cherry-tree, and I've learnt quite a lot about how to do trees, but what I like best are the sunsets, that's when I really like to paint, using the cadmium straight from the tube to edge the mauve and blue clouds, this way they have a thick layer of paint, necessary because it's so difficult to avoid making a sunset look like a tinted print!

A few lines further on the assurance grows:

I now know what you have to do to be an Impressionist. You have to use cadmium for the spots where the sun touches. For the shadow, mauve and blue, without using turpentine and with a thick layer of paint; the brushstrokes should be up and down, and sideways for the sky; it's also important to paint the sun glancing on the sand and, above all, not to use black, because black isn't a colour.

'Why aren't you using turpentine?' asked a perplexed Pepito Pichot. 'Because I'm an Impressionist,' Dalí says he replied firmly.[6]

Given his love of high places, Salvador spent much of his time at the Pichots on top of the squat tower that gives the property its name, telling us in the *Secret Life* about the games and fantasies in which he indulged there. He unwittingly exaggerates the height of the tower, however (the distorting mirror of time has done its work) and forgets to mention that one of his earliest oil paintings, presumably executed that summer, was an attempt to catch the magnificent view it affords over the lush Empordà plain, with the coastal range of Sant Pere de Roda and the Bay of Roses at its edge—and the promise of Cadaqués beyond.[7] In the *Secret Life* Dalí recalls an imaginative painting of cherries, done on the panel of an old door at the Molí de la Torre, in which he incorporated real cherry-stems and live worms. That Pepito Pitchot exclaimed 'That shows real genius!' when he saw the work is confirmed by family tradition.[8]

The month at the Molí affected the twelve-year-old deeply, inspiring not only his first Impressionist works but, in 1920 or so, a projected novel, *Summer Afternoons*, whose protagonist, Lluís, is a romantic young painter who bears an unmistakable resemblance to Salvador.[9] As for Julia, known in the family affectionately as Julieta, she reappeared under the barely disguised name of Dulita in 'Rêverie' (1930), a blatantly frank masturbatory fantasy that outraged the puritans in the French Communist Party when it was published in André Breton's review, *Le Surréalisme au Service de la Révolution*.

No record has been found of Salvador's annual holiday that summer in Cadaqués after his stay with Pichot, but we can be sure that once back in his beloved hideaway by the sea he continued to apply himself to the serious business of becoming an Impressionist painter.

Instituto, Marist Brothers and Municipal Drawing School

Not content with having had his son accepted by Figueres Instituto for the autumn of 1916, Salvador Dalí Cusí enrolled him simultaneously at the Marist Brothers' College

Dalí looking camera-shy (in the front row) on an excursion from the Figueres Instituto.

on the Rambla (whose site is today occupied by the Banco Hispano-Americano at no. 21).[10] Founded in 1906, the college supplemented the *enseñanza oficial*, or official teaching, imparted at the Instituto. Lessons were gone over, difficulties addressed; and there was some religious instruction, with early morning masses, the rosary and improving homilies. Such double attendance at State and private school was a practice widely adopted throughout Spain by middle-class parents determined that their sons get to university.

Dalí's parents must have been pleased with his progress at the Instituto. He settled down well to his work and in May 1917 passed all his first-year examinations with flying colours (it is impossible to gauge how much the extra coaching from the Marist Brothers helped). The subjects were Spanish Language ('Good'), General and European Geography ('Excellent'), Notions of Arithmetic and Geometry ('Good'), Religion First Year ('Excellent') and Calligraphy ('Excellent').[11]

The Instituto was fortunate in having an excellent drawing teacher in Juan Núñez Fernández (1877–1963), an Andalusian from Estepona, near Málaga. Núñez was a graduate of the Royal Academy Special School in Madrid, better known as the

Academy of San Fernando, where he specialized in engraving and won two prizes. In 1899 he went to Rome to continue his studies at the Spanish Academy of Fine Arts,

moving on to Paris in 1903. He took up his position in Figueres in 1906. A tall, handsome, self-effacing man with a rather military manner inherited from his father, a lieutenant-colonel in the Spanish army, Núñez was by all accounts a charismatic, no-nonsense teacher with a true vocation for his profession.

Of the Great Masters, Núñez most admired Ribera, Rembrandt and, above all, Velázquez.[12] A superb engraver, in 1919 he won a medal at the National Exhibition for his fine etching of Van Dyck's *The Kiss of Judas*, now in the Royal Academy of Fine Arts in Madrid along with an original engraving of King Alfonso XIII.[13] He also had a flair for charcoal and pencil drawing, his teaching speciality, and occasionally (but not so successfully) worked in oils. His landscapes, influenced by the Impressionists and by the Catalan Joaquim Mir, his favourite

Juan Nuñez Fernández, Dalí's revered art teacher in Figueres.

modern, have considerable charm but he never exhibited them, perhaps fearing adverse criticism. Núñez, it transpired at his death, was a secret writer, numerous unpublished poems and short stories being found among his papers.[14]

Núñez not only taught at the Instituto but soon after his arrival in Figueres was appointed director of the Municipal Drawing School, which ran evening classes. Here also Salvador was enrolled by his eager father in the autumn of 1916, three years before he began Núñez's *bachillerato* course at the Instituto.

Núñez immediately realized that in the notary's son he had been entrusted with an outstanding pupil; while Salvador seems to have grasped equally quickly that here was just the teacher he needed. The two hit it off perfectly. One wonders if Dalí told Núñez about the priest at the de la Salle college who had insisted that his charges be careful 'not to go over the line' when colouring in drawings. It was advice of which Núñez, himself a stickler for precision, would no doubt have approved. Such was

Salvador's progress that at the end of his first year, coinciding with the successful termination of his inaugural session at the Instituto and with his thirteenth birthday, he received a Special Merit certificate (*diploma de honor*) for his performance at the Municipal Drawing School. The document, dated 1 June 1917, was signed by Núñez and the popular mayor of Figueres, Marià Pujolà, a close friend of Dalí's father and Pepito Pichot.[15]

According to Anna Maria, their father was so delighted with Salvador's progress that he organized an exhibition of all his recent work in the family apartment. The guests were invited to partake of a *garotada*, or feast of sea-urchins, the Dalís' favourite special-occasion dish, on the terrace overlooking the Plaça de la Palmera.[16]

Núñez was Dalí's art teacher for six years, at the Municipal School and the Instituto, and exerted a wholly beneficial influence on his pupil. Dalí himself admits as much in his *Secret Life* (suitably exaggerating the number of students with whom he had to compete):

> He was truly devoured by an authentic passion for the Fine Arts. From the beginning he singled me out among the hundred students in the class, and invited me to his house, where he would explain to me the 'savage strokes' (this was his expression) of an original engraving by Rembrandt which he owned; he had a very special manner of holding this engraving, almost without touching it, which showed the profound veneration with which it inspired him. I would always come away from Señor Núñez's home stimulated to the highest degree, my cheeks flushed with the greatest artistic ambitions.[17]

Thirty years later Dalí went even further in his praise, saying that, of all his teachers, Núñez was the one he most respected and the one from whom he learnt most.[18]

It seems likely that Núñez discussed with his charges the collection of fifteen paintings from the Prado that had been housed in Figueres Instituto since the late nineteenth century (and today are in the Museu de l'Empordà). They included some commendable canvases by Mengs and Juan de Arellano, a selection of fairly minor Flemish works and others from the school of Ribera. The very fact of having paintings on loan from the Prado gave a fillip to art teaching at the Instituto, and was a permanent reminder that Spain possessed one of the greatest art galleries in the world.[19]

At the Municipal Drawing School and the Instituto, Dalí became friends with another budding artist, Ramon Reig Corominas (1903–63), a year older than himself. Today considered one of Catalunya's finest watercolourists, he wrote a moving obituary when Núñez died. In it he expressed veneration for his teacher and recalled that, 'when he corrected our work, pencil in hand, he would allow himself some witty commentary on our mistakes while, with unerring aim, making the necessary changes on the sheet . . . With one stroke, without any hesitation, rapidly, he used to introduce an angle or line on which it would have been impossible to improve.' Reig went on to say that Núñez left an indelible mark on his pupils by imposing the discipline of careful attention to detail.[20]

Núñez was such a good teacher that it could almost be said that he created a 'school' of Figueres painters, a difficult achievement in view of the anarchic temperament of the Empurdanese. Another pupil who came under his influence was Marià Baig, two years younger than Dalí, whose promising career was cut short when he lost his sight at the age of forty. Baig did some still-lifes of loaves of bread so similar to Dalí's that the only possible explanation lies in Núñez's coaching.[21]

In the *Secret Life*, Dalí jumbles together his recollections of the three teaching establishments he attended during the six years from 1916 to 1922 (Marists, Municipal Drawing School and Instituto), often making it impossible to know which detail fits where. Not only that, he sometimes attributes an episode that occurred after 1916 to an earlier period of his development, perhaps with the aim of impressing us by his precocity. A case in point is his much-quoted account of 'seeing things' on the ceiling of Esteban Trayter's infant school, which he had attended between the ages of four and six:

> The great vaulted ceiling which sheltered the four sordid walls of the class was discoloured by large brown moisture stains, whose irregular contours for some time constituted my whole consolation. In the course of my interminable and exhausting reveries, my eyes would untiringly follow the vague irregularities of these mouldy silhouettes and I saw rising from this chaos which was as formless as clouds progressively concrete images which by degrees became endowed with an increasingly precise, detailed and realistic personality.
>
> From day to day, after a certain effort, I succeeded in recovering each of the images which I had seen the day before and I would then continue to perfect my hallucinatory work; when by dint of habit one of the discovered images became too familiar, it would gradually lose its emotive interest and would instantaneously become metamorphosed into 'something else', so that the same formal pretext would lend itself just as readily to being interpreted successively by the most diverse and contradictory figurations, and this would go on to infinity.

The astonishing thing about this phenomenon (which was to become the keystone of my future aesthetic) was that having once seen one of the images I could always thereafter see it again at the mere dictate of my will, and not only in its original form but almost always further corrected and augmented in such a manner that its improvement was instantaneous and automatic.[22]

The infant Dalí may well have seen images in the stains on Trayter's ceiling, but they can hardly have been subjected at such an early age to the process of interpretation just described. An entry in Dalí's diary for 21 January 1920 suggests that, in the *Secret Life*, he attributed to Trayter's school recollections of a later classroom at the Marist Brothers college: 'Leaning on the varnished table I stared at the scratches on the bare walls, composing imaginatively with the fingers of my left hand allegorical pictures and scribbles. There beneath the table was one looking just like a ballerina. Higher up there was a Roman soldier.'[23] There is no evidence that by 1920 Dalí had read Leonardo da Vinci's *Treatise on Painting*, in which the artist discusses the varied images of landscapes, people and even battle-scenes that can be conjured up by contemplating a spot on a wall, ashes in the fireplace, clouds or streams.[24] When Dalí later did so he was no doubt reminded of his own experiences in the same line as a schoolboy, hindsight finding in them the 'keystone' of his 'future aesthetic', a precedent, that is, of the 'paranoiac' double image. Another precedent, of course, was the discovery of the rocky metamorphoses of Cape Creus.[25]

An early and striking instance of the double image occurs among the hundreds of drawings and doodles with which Dalí extra-illustrated his schoolbooks and which include racing-cars, naked girls (one of them participating in the Saturnalia), workers on strike, Roman soldiers, bullfighters, caricatures of teachers and schoolmates, weird animals and Dalí himself in the company of gloriously elegant, slim-legged women. In the image in question Dalí has converted the picture of a parrot on its perch into the nose of a monstrous, Arcimboldi-type head, imitating so exactly the style of the original that the ink-work is indistinguishable from the lines of the printed drawing. The effort suggests that Dalí, fascinated by optical tricks since he first peered into Esteben Trayter's stereoscope, had recently been impressed not only by the images appearing on walls but by reproductions of the fifteenth-century Italian's astonishing fantasies.[26]

The official records of Dalí's studies at Figueres Instituto show that, despite what he liked to claim later had been a mediocre school career, he did well there. Even allowing for the possibility that some of his teachers were excessively indulgent, or pressurized by his father (who was on familiar terms with several of them), the marks as a whole can hardly have been trumped up. Having passed his first year (1916–17) successfully, Dalí turned in the following results:

> 1917–18. Latin First Year ('Excellent'), Spanish Geography ('Excellent'), Arithmetic ('Pass'), Religion Second Year ('Excellent'), Gymnastics First Year ('Pass').

> 1918–19. Latin Second Year ('Pass'), Spanish History ('Good'), Geometry ('Pass'), French First Year ('Excellent'), Religion Third Year ('Excellent'), Gymnastics Second Year ('Pass').

> 1919–20. Literary Theory ('Excellent'), Universal History ('Excellent'), Algebra and Trigonometry ('Pass'), French Second Year ('Good'), Drawing First Year ('Good').

> 1920–1. Psychology and Logic ('Excellent'), History of Literature ('Good'), Physics ('Good'), Physiology and Hygiene ('Excellent'), Drawing Second Year ('Excellent').

> 1921–2. Ethics and Law ('Good'), Natural History ('Pass'), General Chemistry ('Pass'), Agriculture and Agrarian Technology ('Pass').

Among Dalí's fourteen 'Excellents' were five *matrículas de honor*, or remissions of registration fees for the following year. It was a commendable performance.[27]

The 'Passes' Dalí got for arithmetic, geometry, algebra and trigonometry had only been achieved after an immense effort and, perhaps, some understanding from his teachers. He found these subjects absolutely beyond his capabilities, as his diaries record with painful insistence, and dreaded being questioned on them in class.[28] Jaume Miravitlles, one of Dalí's best friends at both the Marist Brothers and the Instituto, had been his coach, at Don Salvador Dalí Cusí's instigation, in arithmetic, geometry, physics and chemistry, subjects at which 'Met', as he was known familiarly, excelled. It was a hopeless task. Miravitlles, probably exaggerating somewhat, said later that he finally succeeded in teaching Dalí to add and subtract, but that he never learned to cope with division and multiplication.[29]

Leaps and Locusts

As adolescence approached, Dalí's self-consciousness increased, with correspondingly frantic efforts to conceal it. 'I was at this time extremely timid,' he writes in the *Secret*

Life, 'and the slightest attention made me blush to the ears; I spent my time hiding, and remained solitary.'[30] Ten years later, in a 1953 entry in *The Diary of A Genius*, Dalí reflected further on the feelings of shame that mortified him in his youth:

> I've enjoyed every minute of today, engrossed in the following subject: I'm the same person as the adolescent who was afraid to cross the street or the terrace of his parents' house, to such an extent was he ruled by shame! I used to blush so furiously in the presence of men or women I considered elegant that, with great frequency, I felt completely befuddled and on the point of collapsing.[31]

When public appearances were unavoidable, Salvador would put on one of the compensatory performances at which he was now a master. Asked a question in class, he would feign a paroxysm in order to mask his embarrassment, shielding himself with his arms as if warding off some danger, or collapsing on his table.[32] The most spectacular ploy involved hurling himself off staircases from a considerable height while being watched by his peers—and surviving intact.[33]

If, understandably, Dalí's contemporaries often had difficulty in deciding when he was being 'serious' and when 'acting', they were in no doubt about one thing: his terror of locusts was genuine.

According to the artist, in an article published in 1929, he had loved capturing these creatures up to the age of seven or eight, admiring their wings before setting them free. *Llagostas de camp* ('country locusts'), he terms them. (Another local term for the creature is *llagosta de rostoll* ('stubble locust').) Dalí used the word *sauterelle* in the original French manuscript of the *Secret Life*, but it was the wrong term: no French grasshopper, or English, could be mistaken for a Catalan *llagosta de camp*, which can attain a length of several centimetres and whose scientific name is *Anacridium aegyptium*, the Egyptian tree locust. Moreover grasshoppers hop, as their name correctly indicates; locusts crawl.[34]

One day, Dalí tells us, he caught a tiny fish in a rockpool in front of their house at Es Llané. To his horror he discovered that it had a face like that of a locust. It was the beginning of a lifelong phobia. 'Since then I have an absolute terror of locusts,' he wrote, 'a terror which recurs with the same intensity every time I see one of the creatures; even to think about them produces an impression of extreme anguish.'[35] In the *Secret Life* Dalí adds that the small viscous fish with the locust-face that gave him such a shock as a child is common in Cadaqués and known as a *babosa* ('slug').[36] Rosa Maria Salleras, the Dalís' neighbour in Cadaqués, has a particularly vivid memory of the painter's locust phobia. 'When we wanted to tease him we would send one of the younger children to him with a locust, telling him Salvador had asked for it,' she recalled. 'He used to go berserk. It was sheer, total panic. When we were children we would let them walk over our faces, and it was a funny tickling feeling. But he grew to loathe them, particularly their feet.'[37]

Jaume Miravitlles witnessed the phobia in action at the Marist Brothers college in Figueres, where Dalí's companions used to enjoy suddenly producing one of the insects for his delectation. Once, 'Met' remembered, Dalí threw himself from a first-floor window to avoid one, almost killing himself in the process.[38] Other contemporary witnesses have recalled similar scenes,[39] and Dalí himself refers to them briefly in one of his adolescent diaries.[40] The *Secret Life* confirms that Dalí's schoolmates were merciless in their exploitation of his terror, being assisted in their sadism by the circumstance that the locusts were bigger and more terrifying in Figueres than in Cadaqués, with heavy, horse-like heads. To escape from such baiting, Dalí tells us, he invented a 'counter-locust', persuading his tormentors that what he *really* feared was paper birds. So effective was his simulation of terror as these substitutes were liberally showered on him that before long the schoolboy Torquemadas had forgotten all about locusts.[41]

But not Dalí, and it is little wonder, in view of the strength of his phobia, that *Anacridium aegyptium* proliferates in the paintings of his early Surrealist period, along with the embodiments of his other fears and obsessions.

First Artistic Initiatives

The Fires i Festes de la Santa Creu ('Fairs and Fiestas of the Holy Cross'), Figueres's annual spring festivity, began each third of May after months of excited preparation. They lasted for a week and were an occasion not merely for revelling, fraternization, going to bullfights, fixing up marriages and dancing *sardanas* on the Rambla, but for the sale and exchange of all kinds of produce and animals. The peasants flocked in from throughout the region, colourfully dressed; the hotels and boarding houses were packed; citizens and countryfolk mixed freely; and children had the time of their lives, with entertainments catering for every taste, from the Bearded Woman and the Flea-Circus to the Magic Lantern and the Dancing Skull. Gradually, however, with the arrival of modern gadgetry (including the motorcar), the Fires i Festes began to lose their character, and today they bear little resemblance to those of Dalí's youth and adolescence.[42]

The 1918 Fires were particularly memorable because to the usual bustle was added the inauguration, on the refurbished Rambla, of an impressive monument to that famous son of Figueres, Narcís Monturiol, pioneer of the submarine and utopian Socialist. For years there had been talk of the monument: a popular subscription had been opened, and there were frequent articles in the press. Now at last the dream had become a reality. The sculpture surmounting the elaborate plinth was by Enric Casanovas and represented a full-bodied female, with naked breasts and wide hips, rising from the sea with a sprig of olive leaves in her hand. Coinciding with the auspicious occasion a local writer, Josep Puig Pujadas, owner-editor of the newspaper *Empordà Federal*, published a book on Monturiol, *Life of the Hero* (*Vida d'Heroi*), which was launched at a banquet attended by, among other worthies, Dalí's father.[43]

Dalí was so impressed by Casanovas's sculpture that it modified the way he represented the human form in his work at this time, complementing the influence currently being exerted on him by reproductions of the frescoes of Puvis de Chavannes.[44]

The Fires saw another important event this year. Organized by the newly founded Societat de Concerts at its premises in the Teatre Principal, an exhibition of Empordanese artists brought together, for the first time, the work of contemporary local painters. Dalí was not among them. The art critic of *Empordà Federal* expressed some disappointment at the traditional cast of most of the exhibits, only a few of which showed any awareness of contemporary European trends. Among the exceptions was Ramon Reig, Dalí's schoolfriend, whose four paintings pleasantly surprised the critic, who predicted a splendid future for the young painter.[45]

Perhaps the praise reaped by his friend Reig acted as a stimulus to Dalí, making him determined to exhibit his work at the earliest opportunity. Meanwhile, during the autumn of 1918, flushed with optimism at the ending of the Great War and the possibilities for a new international order based on peace and co-operation, Dalí and four fellow-students at the Instituto prepared to launch a little school magazine, *Studium*. The editor and moving spirit behind the initiative was the fifteen-year-old Joan Xirau Palau, the youngest of four brothers from a Figueres family much involved in left-wing politics. It was Xirau's father who put up the money for the venture.[46] Xirau was enthusiastically supported by Dalí, a boy called Joan Turró (later a celebrated doctor), Ramón Reig and the politically precocious Jaume Miravitlles, already a true-blood revolutionary.[47]

In December 1918, just before the appearance of the magazine, Dalí exhibited officially for the first time, sharing the occasion with two other Figueres painters, Josep Bonaterra Gras and Josep Montoriol Puig. The show was held in the rooms of the

Societat de Concerts, in the Teatre Principal, where, the previous spring, both Bonaterra and Montoriol had participated in the exhibition of Empordanese painters. Bonaterra, twenty years older than Dalí, went on to become quite a well-known painter in Catalunya if not further afield; Montoriol did not fulfil his promise and is today almost forgotten. The art critic of *Empordà Federal*, the pseudonymous 'Puvis' (almost certainly the paper's owner-editor, Josep Puig Pujadas) was emphatic in his praise of the notary's son. 'Salvador Dalí will be a revelation for many people,' he wrote:

> The person who has inside him what the pictures on exhibit at the Concerts Society reveal is already *something big* in the artistic sense . . . We have no right to talk of the boy Dalí because the said boy is already a man . . . We have no right to say that he *shows promise*. Rather, we should say that he is already *giving*.
>
> The person who experiences light as Dalí Domènech does, who thrills in the presence of a fisherman's innate elegance, who dares at sixteen to risk the sugary, warm brush-strokes of *The Drinker*, who has as refined a decorative sense as the charcoal drawings reveal (and, among these, especially that of Es Baluard) is already the sort of artist who will make a real mark and who will paint excellent pictures even though he insists on producing such inartistic things as *The Debtor*, for example.
>
> We salute the novel artist and are quite certain that in the future our words (humble words, as is our wont) will have the value of a prophecy: Salvador Dalí will be a great painter.[48]

The charcoal drawing of Es Baluard ('The Bastion'), the fortified prow of Cadaqués, is almost certainly that belonging today to the Salvador Dali Museum in Florida.[49] 'Puvis' did well to single it out, and Dalí himself wrote in 1922 that it seemed to him 'brilliant' (*genial*).[50]

'Puvis' also did well to mark the originality of The Drinker, arguably the painting entitled by Dalí *Man with a Porró*,[51] a 50 x 32 cm gouache dated 1918 and notable for its bold use of colour and almost Expressionist technique in the depiction of the drinker's joyous face as he raises his glass wine-dispenser—the *porró* (Spanish *porrón*) habitually used in Catalunya for communal drinking.[52]

The accolade from 'Puvis' must have pleased Dalí greatly. But even more, perhaps, the gesture by his father's great friend, Joaquim Cusí Fortunet, proprietor of the booming Laboratorios del Norte de España ('North of Spain Laboratories'), which specialized in ophthalmic products. Cusí, who before long would be a millionaire, hailed from Llers, the Dalí homeland, and was an enlightened capitalist, a type more commonly found in Catalunya than in the rest of Spain. According to Anna Maria Dalí, Cusí bought two of her brother's paintings, 'the first he ever sold'.[53] The circumstance is worth underlining: from the outset of his career Salvador Dalí was cosseted by the local press, fully supported by his family and encouraged by a rich family friend. Endowed with an impressive natural talent and a remarkable capacity for hard work, it seemed clear that artistic success could not elude him. All he had to do was to keep on painting.

On 1 January 1919, just as the exhibition drew to a close, *Studium*, the little magazine edited by Dalí and his friends, made its first appearance. It was a modest affair, only six pages printed on grey rag paper, but had flair. It comes as a surprise to find that the articles are in Spanish, not Catalan, with a few exceptions. The reason for this was a commendable urge to reach out to the student community in the rest of the State. The Catalanist fervour was there between the lines, however, and a poem in the fifth issue is dedicated among others 'to the enthusiastic Catalanist and faithful lover of Catalan letters, Salvador Dalí Domènech'.

We can safely assume that the contents of the little magazine were the result of much debate. Dalí took it upon himself to write an article each month on a great painter, to provide the occasional more literary piece, and to contribute illustrations; Xirau piled in with a long essay, split up into monthly chunks, on 'The Empordà Down the Ages'; while Miravitlles guaranteed a series on his current obsession: scientific inventions in the service of mankind. As for outside contributors, it was decided to run in each issue a selection of verse by 'Iberian poets': not Spanish poets, not Catalan poets, but 'Iberian' poets. It was a further indication of the outward-looking idealism inspiring the enterprise. The poets were the Catalan Joan Maragall, the Nicaraguan Rubén Darío, the Portuguese Guerra Junqueiro, the Andalusian Antonio Machado, another Catalan, Jacint Verdaguer, and, finally, the Castilian Enrique de Mesa. The notes to the poetry selections were by Ramon Reig, whose comments on Rubén Darío are perhaps the most interesting. 'His works are impregnated with a cosmopolitan spirit that can be found in nobody as in Rubén Darío,' he wrote.[54]

Darío (1867–1916) had revolutionized Spanish poetry in the early 1900s, deeply marking the sensibilities of a new generation of readers. With its incorporation of the themes and innovations of French *fin de siècle* poetry, its refined sexuality, its musicality, its pantheism and its exoticism, his work had irrupted with the power of a religious revival into a Spain where poetry had become stiflingly academic, trite and irrelevant. Little wonder, then, that Dalí and his companions greatly admired him.

Dalí's six notes on famous artists (each of about 450 words) appeared in successive issues under the heading 'The Great Masters of Painting'. The masters adduced were Goya, El Greco, Dürer, Leonardo da Vinci, Michelangelo and Velázquez. In each case two black-and-white tipped-in reproductions were provided, the majority almost certainly copied from Dalí's collection of Gowans's Art Books. Dalí's notes confirm yet again, moreover, that he had spent years poring over the latter, revelling in their every detail. In 1919 he had not seen the originals of the works he reproduces in *Studium*, and there were as yet no colour reproductions; but he gives the impression of knowing them intimately.

The tiny pieces, written in a prose much superior to that of his colleagues, express the young Dalí's deep respect for the painters in question. It is worth noting what he finds to praise in each.

Goya attracts him for his curiosity about every aspect of life, for his openness to the world around him, and Dalí underlines the sharp contrast between the tapestries and festive canvasses (with their disporting *majas* and bullfighters) and the works of the 'black' period done at the Quinta del Sordo. He approves of the fact that Goya expresses 'the desires and aspirations of his people'. Art should be useful.

If Goya is the man of the earth, its joys and its torments, El Greco is pure spirituality. Dalí has no time for those who think that the artist's elongated forms are the result of an optical defect. Absolutely not! They express exactly what El Greco felt, which is what they should do: true art does not abide by rules, but by the faithful expression of feeling.

Dürer, like Goya, expresses the beliefs and customs of his people, and Dalí finds his art notable for the depth of its thought. It is interesting to find the sixteen-year-old schoolboy stressing, as in the case of El Greco, Dürer's 'tireless life' and 'incessant work'. Dalí's ability for sticking at it was to amaze everyone who knew him.

As for Leonardo, Salvador reminds the reader that he was the prototype of the 'Renaissance Man'. As such he commands the young Dalí's unquestioning allegiance: 'Above all he was a passionate soul, in love with life; he studied and analysed everything with the same ardour and the same pleasure; in life everything appeared to him positive and attractive.' Da Vinci's paintings are exemplary in the 'reflective, constant, "loving" work' that has gone into them. Leonardo ' strove incessantly, with love, with the fever of the creator, resolving extremely difficult problems that gave a tremendous impetus to art'.

The note on Michelangelo is shorter than the others, the eulogy lacking conviction and giving the impression of having been dashed off to meet a deadline.

For Velázquez, on the other hand, Dalí's admiration is clearly genuine. He is 'one of the greatest, perhaps the greatest, Spanish painter and one of the greatest in the world', and Dalí finds that, in the distribution and placing of his colours, he seems at times an 'Impressionist' *avant la lettre*. This fervour for Velázquez would remain with Dalí throughout his life.

As well as his commentaries on great painters, Dalí also contributed several illustrations to the magazine, including the vignette for the title, and two literary texts, the first he had published: a tiny piece of poetic prose entitled 'Twilight' and a poem similarly crepuscular in theme. Both efforts remind us that Dalí admired the sundowns of Modest Urgell; they suggest, too, that he had been dipping into the early poetry of Juan Ramón Jiménez and Antonio Machado and, plausibly, the French symbolists who inspired them, particularly Paul Verlaine. In 'Twilight', as two lovers pass before him and are enveloped by the night, the narrator feels his loneliness and wishes he could 'smile like them'. In the poem the lovers recur:

Cuan els sorolls s'adormen	When the sounds fall silent
Els reflectes d'un llac . . .	Reflections in a lake . . .
Un cloquer romanic . . .	A Romanesque belfry . . .
La quietud de la tarda	The peace of the dying
morenta . . . El misteri	Afternoon . . . The mystery
de la nit propera . . . tot	Of oncoming night . . . everything
es dorm i difumina . . . i	Is falling asleep, losing its outline . . .
es allavors que baix la pálida	Now, under the pale
claror de'una estrella,	Light of a star
bora el portal d'una casa	At the door of a venerable
antigua essen enraonar	House they are speaking in
baix i tot seguit els sorolls	Low voices and then all the sounds
s'adormen i el fresc	Stop and the fresh
aureix de la nit gronxant	Night breeze, moving
les acacias del jardí	The acacias in the garden,
fa caura d'amun dels	Makes a shower of white flowers
anamurats una pluja	Fall on the lovers . . .[55]
de flors blancas . . .	

Love of art, the passionate urge to be something in life, the call of erotic desire: it's all there in *Studium*, overtly or between the lines. But what strikes one most is the concern these adolescents feel for society. They want to change the world.

The Rebel

Anna Maria Dalí has recalled that, while Salvador was studying for his *bachiller-ato*, her father and brother would never stop arguing during mealtimes, the wom-enfolk listening in awe without daring to intervene. Sometimes the debate became so heated that Don Salvador even forgot to make his nightly trip across the street to the 'Sport', where he was awaited by his habitual group of cronies.[56] Dalí's father was a book-lover and had a 'voluminous library' which made its mark on Salvador from an early age, not least because it contained bound volumes of one of Spain's finest illustrated magazines of the late nineteenth century, *La Ilustración Catalana*, whose plates fascinated the child.[57] Later Dalí ransacked, or said he did, the philosophical and political section of the library, which reflected the radical tastes of the notary's early years. The work that most affected him, according to the *Secret Life*, was Voltaire's *Philosophical Dictionary*, on account of its fierce and closely reasoned anti-clericalism.[58] *Thus Spake Zarathustra* also impressed Dalí, appealing to his urge to be an artistic Superman and also making him question his father's atheism:

> When I opened Nietzsche for the first time I was profoundly shocked, for, as if it were a simple question of black and white, he had the nerve to say: 'God is dead!' What! I had only just learnt that there was no God and now someone was telling me he had died! I grew suspicious immediately. Zarathustra appeared to me a grandiose hero, with a strength of spirit I admired, but at the same time he betrayed himself with puerilities that I had already left behind me. One day I would be greater than he.[59]

Dalí also enjoyed dipping into Kant, although he says he understood not a word, and Spinoza, 'for whose way of thinking I nourished a real passion at the time'.[60] No doubt these and other books were energetically discussed by father and son, the daily onus of having to keep his end up sharpening Dalí's tendency to dogmatize, which later became part of his public persona.

Don Salvador Dalí Cusí, while maintaining his support for the Catalan federalist cause, had gradually become less virulent politically as his practice thrived, channelling his former quasi-anarchist leanings into the promotion of Esperanto, which had begun to interest him soon after his arrival in Figueres. But his radical leanings had already been successfully transmitted to his son, who by now was a fervent advocate of the Red Revolution.[61]

A few months after *Studium* ran its course Dalí began to keep a diary in Catalan entitled *My Impressions and Intimate Memories*. The only volumes that have turned up so far are numbers 2 (10–20 November 1919), 3 (21 November–6 December 1919), 6 (7 January–1 February 1920), 9 (11 April–5 June 1920), 10 (5 June–autumn 1920) and 11 (10 October–December 1920). With the exception of volume 6, the property of the Salvador Dalí Museum in Florida, these diaries are preserved at the Fundación Gala–Salvador Dalí in Figueres, along with a further volume entitled *My Life in this World* (an account of events in Dalí's life between 1920 and 1921); a slim notebook with ten pages of impressions jotted down in October 1921; and a volume, dating from 1922, with recollections of Dalí's early life and schooldays. To these can be added an incomplete sixteen-page unpublished manuscript entitled *Doodles. Essays on Painting. A Catalogue of my Paintings with Notes (Ninots. Ensatjos sobre pintura. Catalec dels cuadrus em notes)*, written in 1922, which contains invaluable information on Dalí's progress as an artist.[62]

Despite the gaps occasioned by the five missing volumes, the journals provide a detailed account of Dalí's life in Figueres between the ages of fifteen and seventeen. But not of his long holidays in Cadaqués, where each summer, after yearning for the village throughout the year, the writer gives way to the painter and diary-keeping is forgotten. In Figueres and Barcelona Dalí feels poignant nostalgia for Cadaqués, referring to it in the feminine (*l'hermosa Cadaqués*, 'beautiful Cadaqués') and sometimes falling to sleep dreaming about it. While he struggles with his school subjects, particularly 'hateful and stupid' algebra, his thoughts constantly revert to the blissful summer days spent in the studio in Cadaqués he has inherited from the painter Ramon Pichot.[63] A letter he wrote to his uncle Anselm Domènech after the summer of 1919, and transcribed later in his diary, sets the scene:

I spent a delicious summer, as always, in the ideal and dreamy village of *Cadaqués*. There, beside the Latin sea, I gorged myself on light and colour. I spent the fiery days of summer painting frenetically and trying to capture the incomparable beauty of the sea and of the sun-drenched beach.

I'm growing more and more aware all the time of the difficulty of art; but I'm also growing to enjoy it and love it increasingly. I still admire the great French Impressionists, *Manet, Degas and Renoir*, the ones who direct my path most firmly. My technique has changed almost completely and my colours are much clearer than before, having abandoned the dark blues and reds which previously contrasted (inharmoniously) with the clarity and luminosity of the others.

I still hardly pay any attention to preparatory drawing, which I manage to do without almost completely. It's colour and feeling that command my efforts. I don't care at all whether one house is higher or lower than another. It's the colour and the range that give life and harmony.

I believe that drawing is a very secondary part of painting, and is picked up automatically, through habit, and that therefore it doesn't need any detailed study or particular effort.

Every day I'm more interested in portraiture, although from the point of technique I treat it like landscape or still-life.

I got the book you sent. Many thanks. It's extremely interesting and very beautifully printed.

I wish you'd come here, even if only for a day. We could exchange views and you could see my modest things.

I'm sending you something I dashed off quickly, *Afternoon Sun*.[64]

The letter can be set beside an entry in Dalí's essay *Doodles* (*Ninots*), written in 1922. Looking back to the work he had produced in the summer of 1919, he wrote that at that time he was possessed by 'an uncontrollable Impressionism'. If, in 1918, he had greatly liked the painters José Mongrell, Eugenio Chicharro and Eduardo Hermoso (today almost forgotten), now he found the first two 'intolerable' and the latter merely 'passable'. All his current enthusiasm was for the French Impressionists.[65]

The young Dalí portrayed in the pages of his adolescent diary scrutinizes two daily newspapers (the Barcelona *La Publicitat*, published in Catalan, and the Madrid *El Sol*, the most widely read liberal paper in Spain), as well as keeping an eye on Madrid illustrated weeklies such as *Mundo Gráfico* and *Blanco y Negro*. In them he follows with rapt attention the debates in the central Parliament, the vagaries of labour unrest in Madrid, Paris and Barcelona and of a protracted lockout in the Catalan capital, the hunger strike of the mayor of Cork, the danger signals being transmitted from a Germany hell-bent on rearmament and revenge, the question of the Allies' recognition of Soviet Russia and, above all, the advance of the Red Army. Dalí thinks of himself as a Communist, identifies fully with the workers, loathes capitalism and is an entrenched enemy of the Spanish status quo, with its press censorship and an army likely, at any moment, to stage a military coup. As for King Alfonso XIII, Dalí comments that he is only interested in hunting and regattas.[66]

Dalí's bitter disappointment with Spain, which verges at times on scorn, had been fuelled by reading a pessimistic novel, *The Way of the World (Ansí es el mundo)*, by Pío Baroja, a leading representative of the so-called Generation of 1898, thus labelled because in that year Spain had lost the last of its American colonies, Cuba and Puerto Rico, as well as the Philippines, in an ignominious confrontation with the United States.[67] For the Generation of 1898, Spain was suffering a breakdown in confidence and identity. Who are we? Where have we gone wrong? How have we managed to lose one of the largest empires the world has ever seen? How can we become strong again, and, anyway, how do we understand the word 'strong'? Where the Dalí of these diaries is concerned there is only one remedy for the country's ills: a full-blooded revolution. On 12 November 1919 we find him writing that he awaits it 'with open arms and with the cry of "Long live the Soviet Republic!" at the ready. And if to achieve a true democracy and a truly social republic a tyranny is necessary first, well, long live tyranny!'[68] A few days later, commenting on a formidable row that has just taken place in the Madrid Cortes, he exclaims: 'It makes you want to throw a bomb into the Parliament to destroy once and for all such a farce, so many lies, so much hypocrisy!'[69] In the Catalan capital, where the lockout continues, violence is on the increase. On 24 November 1919 we read: 'In Barcelona they've thrown another bomb. Terrorism once more! All the better.'[70] The young Dalí is convinced that his longed-for Spanish revolution is just around the corner. Has not Trotsky, the saviour of the Revolution, said that Spain will follow the example of Russia?[71] If even in friendly Figueres the class struggle is gathering momentum, he writes on 6 December 1919, imagine what it's going to be like in the big cities![72]

While there is no evidence that the adolescent Dalí sought to join the Spanish Communist Party, he was certainly prepared to assert his revolutionary ideals in public and, when necessary, to stand up against authority. In November 1919 the headmaster of Figueres Instituto suddenly decided to separate the boys from the handful of girls attending the school, shutting up the latter in the library. Dalí led a protest, persuaded the girls to break out of their confinement, and succeeded in having the previous situation restored. What did the headmaster think, that co-education was immoral?[73]

Dalí and his friends used the word *putrefactes*, 'putrescent', to write off people like the headmaster. A judge appointed to investigate the behaviour of one of the teachers, for example, is immediately proclaimed a *putrefacte*; and the group often engage in *putrefacte*-spotting sessions in the Rambla, alternating them with discussions about Communism. The word became all the rage.[74]

In his revolutionary fervour Dalí was seconded by his erstwhile colleague on

Studium, 'Met' Miravitlles, whose father, Joan Miravitlles Sutrá, had been involved in the anarchist troubles in Barcelona in the 1890s, at the time when Salvador Dalí Cusí's friend Pere Coromines was tried. On 7 January 1920 Dalí had a conversation with Miravitlles senior at a funeral in Figueres: 'He was in Montjuïc gaol. He fought the police twice, knocking them to the ground with bottles. Such things honour the person who experiences them (*because nowadays anyone with a reputation for intellectual integrity is in gaol*) and I must say I was impressed. Also he told me about trades union activity then . . . Met's father's eyes blazed with hatred as he told me about the despotism of the bourgeoisie.'[75]

The precocious Jaume Miravitlle's adherence to Marxism was not only a result of his father's example but of his friendship with a passionate Communist called Martí Vilanova, who also influenced Dalí although there is no reference to him in the extant diaries.[76] Martí belonged to a group of older intellectuals who met at premises owned by Josep Soler Grau, one of Dalí's teachers at the Instituto, at 4, Carrer Muralla. Among the members were Pelai Martínez Paricio, who became one of Spain's youngest qualified architects, and the writer Antoni Papell Garbí. Out of the friends' endless discussions about art and politics came a satirical magazine called *El Sanyó Pancraci* (Mr Pancraci), named after a well-known local eccentric. While it was originally intended that this should be a fortnightly journal, only three sporadic issues appeared. Today they are such rare collector's items that nobody seems to have a copy of the second. The first issue appeared on 15 August 1919, the last on 15 February 1920.

Shortly after the magazine fizzled out, Dalí rented the premises at 4, Carrer Muralla for a studio. The place was daubed with graffiti and in an appalling state of disrepair. He cleaned it up and decorated it with murals, painted jars and plates and an imaginary, mock-Goya portrait of Pancraci. One of Dalí's painted jars has survived, but only photographs of the murals, which were later rubbed off.[77]

Also influential on Dalí at this time was the Majorcan poet and philosopher Gabriel Alomar (1873–1941), head of the Department of Literature at the Instituto since 1912 and headmaster, briefly, in 1918.[78] Alomar was a fascinating and enigmatic personality. In 1904 he had assured himself an obscure niche in art and literary history by coining the term Futurism, which was appropriated, redefined and launched worldwide shortly afterwards (without acknowledgement) by F. T. Marinetti, when he founded his movement of the same name.[79] Two years later, in 1906, Alomar met the great Nicaraguan poet Rubén Darío (celebrated, as we have seen, in *Studium*) and invited him to visit Majorca. They became close friends, and Alomar is one of the characters in Darío's unfinished novel *The Island of Gold,* inspired by George Sand's Majorcan idyll with Chopin, where he appears under the thin disguise of 'the Futurist'.[80] A passionate federalist republican, Alomar was soon popular in Figueres, which returned him to the Madrid parliament in June 1919,[81] and his books and lectures were frequently discussed in the pages of *Empordà Federal.* Dalí, like Jaume Miravitlles, was undoubtedly influenced by this remarkable individual, with whom he studied Spanish Language during his first year in the Instituto. According to 'Met' it was Alomar who first perceived Dalí's literary talent, and this may well have been the case.[82] Alomar struck up a friendly relationship with Pepito Pichot and Dalí's father, who, according to the painter, liked to quote one of the Majorcan's dicta to justify his own love of swearing: 'Blasphemy constitutes the finest ornament of the Catalan language.'[83] It seems, though, that Alomar and Salvador Dalí Cusí fell out. And the latter was offended when, in 1931, the ex-teacher recalled that, if Salvador had been a 'donkey' (*ruc*) in his class at Figueres Instituto, now that he was a Surrealist he had become a hundred per cent more so.[84]

Nature and Art

Along with Dalí's deep scorn for the philistines, and his identification with the proletariat, goes a feeling for nature of such intensity that it verges on the pantheistic. His descriptions of the sea-edged Empordà plain, particularly as the sun goes down, are of an extreme sensitivity and reveal a gift for close observation. It is this empathy with nature, he records, that he is seeking to express in his paintings. One passage in particular stands out. The dreaded examinations are successfully over (this is May 1920) and he is about to begin to paint. Before long will come the annual holiday in Cadaqués:

> As soon as I was ready I opened the cupboard in my room and carefully took out some boxes. I opened them. They had the tubes of paint. Those clean and shiny tubes represented for me a whole world of aspirations, and I looked at them and caressed them with hands trembling with emotion, just as I imagine lovers do. My thoughts raced away. A whole future full of hopes and happiness seemed to emanate from those colours. It was as though I was already painting, and I was carried away, quite carried away thinking about the joyous day when, after a year of demands, emotions and lies, I could begin the conscious work, the sacred work, of the creator. And I saw my tubes emptying their pure colours onto the palette, and my brushes catching them up lovingly. I saw my work progressing. The suffering in creation. My ecstasy as I lost myself in the mystery of light, of

colour, of life. My soul merging with that of Nature ... Always searching for more, always further ... More light, more blue ... more sun ... losing myself in Nature, being her submissive disciple ... Oh, I could go mad! How happy I'll be the day I can externalize all that I've imagined, felt and thought in a whole year of thinking, of seeing, of having to withhold and repress my creative urges![85]

Concurrently with his diary and his painting Dalí did some work on his novel, *Summer Afternoons*, of which only about twenty pages are known. Briefly mentioned earlier in connection with his sojourn, when he was twelve, in the Molí de la Torre, *Summer Afternoons* concerns a young painter, Lluís, an exact calque of the Dalí portrayed in the adolescent journals:

> His passionate temperament made him paint with his heart more than with his intelligence, and dazzled by the sublimity of Nature he spent hours and hours searching for the right light, looking now for one colour, now for another. Lluís put into this effort all his feeling, all his soul. He enjoyed the suffering of creation.
>
> He revelled in the suffering of creation. He made every effort to express the movements of his heart, what Nature whispered to him, what the splendid sun-drenched cherry-tree told him. And indefatigably athirst for art, drunk on beauty, he looked with his clear eyes at smiling Nature, impregnated with sun and joy, and would fall into a brief ecstasy.[86]

Summer Afternoons draws on Dalí's love of Vilabertran, the village outside Figueres to which he had often walked with his parents as a child and where the family of his friend from the Municipal Drawing School, Ramon Reig, had inherited a charming house. It appears under the name of Horta Fresca, an allusion to the market gardens, or *hortas*, for which the village and its surrounding countryside are celebrated in Figueres. A romantic place, favourite haunt of lovers, the 'lake' of Vilabertran had a rowing boat, and was just the spot for picnics. The reflections of a Romanesque belfry in a lake, evoked in Dalí's first published poem, 'When the Sounds Fall Silent', quoted earlier, undoubtedly allude to this *locus amoenus*; while Dalí's oils, *Vilabertran Bell-Tower* (1918–19) and *The Lake at Vilabertran* (1920), provide visual equivalents. Like Dalí, Ramon Reig enjoyed painting the pond and its surroundings.[87] So did their teacher, Juan Núñez: a painting of the spot done by him in 1919, inferior to Dalí's two works on the same subject, shows the rowing boat in the foreground.[88]

Years later Dalí set here one of the scenes of his projected film *The Wheel-Barrow of Flesh*. Indeed he even tried to buy the 'lake' and its surroundings, with no luck; and in

1973, when Amanda Lear accompanied him to Vilabertran, he told her he was planning to build an imitation of the pond beside his home at Port Lligat. The spot's melancholy, he added, reminded him of a canvas by Modest Urgell, *The Same as Always*.[89] The title was a self-teasing allusion to Urgell's recurrent obsession with dusk, cemeteries and ruins, a theme, dear to the heart of the adolescent Dalí, on which the painting in question rang yet another change.

Today the rowing boat has gone and the pond, smothered in vegetation, is hidden behind an impenetrable fence. It looks more like the quagmire in *Psycho* than a component of Dalí's lost paradise.

Dalí's 1919–20 diary shows that as an adolescent he was far from indifferent to music, whatever scorn he might profess for it later, and derived intense pleasure from the concerts that were often held in Figueres. Mozart he particularly admired.[90] It is also likely that in Figueres he enjoyed his first *zarzuelas*, the characteristic comic operettas of Spain, which were put on in the Teatre Principal by the leading companies touring the country.[91]

In mid-April 1920, as the school year drew to a close, Don Salvador Dalí decided, in his usual authoritative fashion, that when his son finished his *bachillerato* he would proceed to the Royal Academy Special School of Painting, Sculpture and Engraving in Madrid. The diary records Dalí's reaction. He is sure it has been the most important decision yet taken concerning his future. In Madrid, he promises himself, he will work 'like mad' for three years before winning a prize that will enable him to study in Rome for a further four, after which he will return to Spain in triumph and: 'I'll be a genius, and the world will admire me. Perhaps I'll be despised and misunderstood, but I'll be a genius, a great genius, I'm certain of it.'[92] It comes as a shock to find that, by the age of sixteen, over two years before he arrived in Madrid, Dalí had worked out his plan for the next decade with such precision, and that he was already thinking of himself in such exalted terms.

Other passages in the diary reveal that, by 1920, Dalí's every movement and gesture was carefully gauged to make the maximum effect on the public at large, as were the clothes and hairstyle over which he took infinite pains. Dalí at sixteen was a dandy, and would remain so all his life ('How you dress is vital for success,' he wrote in 1952. 'I've rarely sunk to the level of dressing in civilian clothes. I always go in Dalí uniform'[93]). In imitation of the self-portrait of his idolized Raphael (reproduced in the frontispiece of the Gowans's Art Books selection of the master) he grew his hair as long as a girl's, supplementing it with flamboyant sideburns. He wore a black wide-brimmed hat, sported an ample flowing necktie and was in the habit of slinging his overcoat around his shoulders like a cape (still today a Spanish macho practice intended to impress).[94] 'As soon as possible,' he recalls in the *Secret Life*, 'I wanted to make myself "look unusual", to compose a masterpiece with my head.'[95]

Luckily for Dalí that head was impressive. The adolescent future genius was bronzed, with straight, jet-black hair and a fine nose and blue eyes, the only irregular feature being the little, sticky-out ears which perhaps his long hair was designed to cover. At 1.70m (5ft 7in), Dalí was of more than average height for a Spaniard at the time.[96] He was slim, almost athletic-looking, and the diaries show that neither he nor the girls had any doubt that he was strikingly handsome (they are always giving him the glad eye). The awareness of his attractiveness must, one imagines, have helped to compensate in some measure for his 'habitual timidity'.[97]

'It' and 'Them'

In the *Secret Life* Dalí is extremely witty on the subject of 'it', which began to concern him not long after he entered Figueres Instituto. 'It' was masturbation:

> I was utterly backward in the matter of 'solitary pleasure', which my friends practised as a regular habit. I heard their conversations sprinkled with allusions, euphemisms and hidden meanings, but in spite of the efforts of my imagination I was unable to understand whereof 'it' consisted: I would have died of shame rather than dare to ask how one went about doing 'it', or even to broach the matter indirectly, for I was afraid it might be found out that I did not know all about 'it'. One day I reached the conclusion that one could do 'it' all by oneself, and that 'it' could also be done mutually, even by several at a time, to see who could do 'it' fastest.[98]

'It' finally happened—in the lavatories of the Instituto, as Dalí's adolescent diary records. By 1920 the masturbatory habit was not only inveterate but imbued with anxiety. An entry for 17 January 1920 reads: 'In the afternoon I struggled between my appetites and my determination. The former won, leaving me depressed and sad (*abatut i trist*). I've taken a firm decision.'[99] The following May he writes: 'I felt sexually aroused. I went to the lavatories. I experienced tremendous pleasure. On leaving, I felt depressed (*abatut*) and disgusted with myself. As usual I've decided not to do it again. But this time I'm really serious. I believe that all this makes you lose blood (*Crec que amb tot això es perd sang*). Not what I need, exactly.'[100]

One wonders what Dalí meant, or thought he meant, by 'loss of blood'? Perhaps he had been taught, or had gleaned, that repeated masturbation, as well as morally disgusting, would make him weak, impotent, homosexual or even insane. This was the orthodox medical view in the nineteenth century (William Acton, Krafft-Ebing) and it survived well into the twentieth, as Alex Comfort has shown with deadly sarcasm in *The Anxiety Makers*.[101] But whatever Dalí's fears about the habit, it never left him. By his own admission, and that of many people who knew him well, it was virtually his only means to orgasm throughout his entire life. He was never prepared to concede that this was a tragedy, however; and he became the only painter in the history of art to make masturbation a major theme of his work. He is also the only Spanish autobiographer ever to have admitted openly that masturbation dominated his life. In a country noted until recently for its machismo, this was a considerable achievement.

Dalí said later that his onanistic fantasies were habitually enacted in superimposed belfries, the reason being that as an adolescent he used to masturbate on his rooftop terrace in Figueres while watching the setting sun lighting the tower of Sant Pere, the church where he had been baptized. He then discovered that the tower resembled that of Sant Narcís, in Girona, and one in Delft figured in a painting by his beloved Vermeer (plausibly *View of Delft*, included in the relevant Gowans's Art Books volume).[102] 'He had a fixation about towers,' according to one of the closest friends of his life, Nanita Kalaschnikoff. 'He would juxtapose the three belfries in his imagination and when everything was exactly right, all the details correct, he'd ejaculate.' Towers with erotic connotations were to figure frequently in Dalí's paintings from his Surrealist period onwards.[103]

Dalí was reading foreign novels at this time, recommending Anatole France and 'the Russians' to Jaume Miravitlles along with his admired Pío Baroja.[104] He was also dipping into French erotica (much superior, it must be said, to its Spanish counterpart). In December 1919 he recorded in his diary that he had just read Alfred de Musset's anonymous novelette *Gamiani*. 'More than anything else,' he commented, 'this sensual work has awakened in me a great aversion to the gross and stupid sensuality that the French erotic author portrays with such acuteness and naturalness.'[105]

That Dalí was having difficulty in coming to terms with his sexuality is evident from many other remarks scattered throughout the diary and his published memoirs. In *The Unspeakable Confessions* he describes his adolescent quandary in the following terms:

> At the time I was suffering from two obsessions that paralysed me. A panic fear of venereal disease. My father had inculcated into me a horror of the microbe. This deep anxiety has never left me, and has even driven me to bouts of madness.
>
> But, above all, for a long time I experienced the misery of believing that I was impotent.

Naked, and comparing myself to my schoolfriends, I discovered that my penis was small, pitiful and soft. I can recall a pornographic novel whose Don Juan machine-gunned female genitals with ferocious glee, saying that he enjoyed hearing women creak like watermelons. I convinced myself that I would never be able to make a woman creak like a watermelon. And this feeling of weakness ate away at me. I tried to hide the anomaly, but often I was the victim of inextinguishable attacks of laughter, hysterical, even, which were a sort of proof of the disturbances that agitated me profoundly.[106]

Dalí's anxiety about the small size of his penis was no exaggeration and, as a friend of his has confirmed, continued into later life.[107] As for his account of how he tried 'to hide the anomaly', it reads like a clinical case history. 'The kind of perception human beings have of their bodies, the image they hold of them, is peculiarly involved in shame,' Helen Merrell Lynd writes in *On Shame and the Search for Identity*. 'Certain features of one's own body are unalterable, uncontrollable; in a unique way they are oneself. Sudden exposure of them . . . or lack of control of them . . . or awareness of the difference between the way one sees his own body and the way others may see it—all these are experiences of shame deeply associated with the quick of oneself, with one's own identity.' Lynd might almost have had Dalí in mind.[108]

Dalí added some years later that the author of the book with the rampant Don Juan was 'El Caballero Audaz' (the pseudonym of José María Carretero), a well-known writer of semi-pornographic novels, and that it had come as a relief to discover that the erotic scene in question involved not fornication, but sodomy. Dalí also made another revelation about his sexuality: 'That seemed easier, although you have to have a very strong erection to be able to penetrate. And my problem is that I've always been a premature ejaculator. So much so, that sometimes it's enough for me just to look in order to have an orgasm'.[109]

How did Salvador Dalí Cusí succeed in filling his son with such a panic fear of venereal disease? Dalí claimed later that his father, considering it was time for him to become acquainted with the facts of life, left a medical book on permanent display on top of the piano. In it there were photographs illustrating 'the terrible consequences' of the disease. His father maintained, the painter added, that such a volume should be on show in all well-ordered homes as a warning to the young. On the face of it it seems unlikely that Dalí Cusí would have had recourse to such a crude and insensitive method for keeping his son on the straight and narrow. But perhaps he did. Or maybe the episode of the book was a defensive 'false memory' devised later by Dalí as a rational explanation for his fear of attempting copulation, or for his impotence.[110]

The diaries show that Dalí was by now much interested in girls. The first to appear in these pages, in November 1919, is a certain Estela ('the beautiful Estela'), whom Dalí got to know at the Municipal Drawing School. There are *billets doux*, amorous glances and a conventional love poem from the painter; brief encounters on the Rambla under the vigilant eye of the girl's grandmother; and jealousy when it transpires that Estela is being courted by an officer from Barcelona.[111]

Soon afterwards Dalí's attentions became centred on another girl, Carme Roget Pumerola, whose father owned one of the most popular cafés on the Rambla, the

Carme Roget, Dalí's adolescent girlfriend, in September 1920.

Emporium, which still thrives today. Carme was two years older than Salvador (she was born in 1902) and a pupil at the private college run by French Dominican nuns just off the Plaça de la Palmera, visible from the Dalís' balcony. She told Salvador that she remembered him as a child playing with Anna Maria on the beach at Es Llané: a further link between them.[112] She was tall, handsome, blonde and progressive, with large eyes that Salvador greatly admired, and a good swimmer. Like Dalí she attended evening class at the Municipal Drawing School.[113]

Carme had a close friend and confidante called Maria Dolors Carré, known to everyone as Lola, who was in Dalí's year at the Instituto. Soon Salvador and some of his companions, especially two boys called Sala and Peix and his painter friend Ramon Reig, were seeing the girls often. Maria Dolors had a complex about her large nose ('Lolita's nose is returning from Barcelona this afternoon and she's coming tomorrow,' her friends would joke behind her back), but this did not stop her from being good fun. There were escapades to spots outside the town, visits to the cinema (appreciated not least for the opportunities the darkness provided for 'amorous initiations'[114]), endless talk and much horseplay. Notes and missives were exchanged. They invented names for each other—'the Countess', 'the Marquess', 'the Baron'—supplied themselves with the requisite visiting cards, pretended they were rich and on one occasion announced that they were about to set off on a trip to Italy. Reig put it about that personally he would be embarking for Venice at the 'lake' of Vilabertran. Dalí, more realistically, thought it would be wonderful to sail on one of the small schooners that in those days still plied beween Cadaqués and Italy, and make for Rome. For reading, they would take Rubén Darío. Dalí even had a fantasy, which he jotted down with an accompanying drawing, about visiting Washington to collect an inheritance from a rich uncle: in the midst of intense excitement the Baron of the Eight Broken Candles is welcomed by a group of American millionaires who hold a great reception in his honour at the palace of the Princess Ragadora.[115]

Since according to the strict conventions of the day Carme Roget could not receive letters from an admirer at home, even though in this case he was the son of the local notary, Maria Dolors Carré acted as go-between. Gradually the friendship deepened, and by May 1920 Carme was in love with Salvador and proud of his growing celebrity. Dalí, however, was playing games, studying Carme's every gesture and mood (and his own) in a detached, literary sort of way, and writing up the progress of the affair in his diary. In mid-May 1920, under the heading 'Of How All is Lies and Deceit', he comments: 'I realize what a cynic I am. I'm not in love with Carme but nonetheless I've been pretending to be and have told Sala that I am.'[116] When he sees her again, he 'feigns admirably' to be in love. One evening they go for a twilight walk. 'I watch the sunset in Carme's eyes, which are quite moist with emotion,' he jots down in his diary.[117]

When Dalí visited Barcelona to stay with his uncles, he would write to Carme regularly, sending the letters to her friend Lola Carré, and sometimes directing his missives to both of them. Often, as he himself admits in his diary, these communications are ludicrously insincere and overblown. On 1 June 1920 he wrote a spoof letter pretending that he was already in the city:

> Dear Friends:
>
>   I'm taking this opportunity of asking you to forgive me for not having said goodbye to you, but it was impossible.
>
>   Here I'm so far away from you that it's terrible . . . I'm greatly missing those twilights full of poetry . . . Up the Passeig Nou . . . the reds of the sunset tinged the clouds with fine colours, and in the sky the constellations were agonizing [sic] and beginning to twinkle . . . there, beneath a canopy of leaves, we stayed until it was dark . . . in the reedbeds the frogs were croaking . . . further away, a cricket . . . In your eyes the stars were reflected . . .
>
>   And in the vagueness of the twilight I was dreaming about things that are always impossible! . . .

> Please don't laugh at all this . . . Here in Barcelona, where everything is mere prose, I love to remember you, the memory of you is poetry . . .[118]

In September of the same year the two girls received a letter in similar tone. Salvador apologized for having interrupted their conversation in the Rambla, and added his habitual complaints about not being able to find love:

> Everything changes, even your way of thinking, when at last you believe in love . . . I, too, once believed in love . . . But for me it was very cruel . . . I've always been in love with the impossible . . . I'm in love with art and art is impossible for me because I have to study. I'm in love with a girl more beautiful than art, but also more impossible.
>
> And the leaves are beginning to fall . . . and life is sad, living without faith, without hope, loving uselessly, in silence . . .[119]

In the midst of these amorous games, Dalí won first prize at the Municipal Drawing School, jotting down an account of the prize-giving ceremony in his diary:

> 'Salvador Dalí!'
>
> 'Here!' and, opening my way, I proceeded up to the platform. Then the mayor said solemnly: 'It is my great pleasure to give you the first prize. It does much credit, first, to the Dalí family and, second, to the School, from which it will be said a famous artist has emerged.'
>
> 'Thank you very much.'
>
> I took the prize, the *first prize*, controlling my urge to break out laughing because it was all very funny. Then out to the Rambla and afterwards home, where the family were smiling with satisfaction to have a son who, according to the exact words of a real, genuine mayor, was a credit to it and to his school![120]

Carme Roget, who was present on the occasion, as the same entry shows, must have taken great pride in Salvador's achievement. Their relationship continued, and one of her replies to the painter's letters has survived. Dalí had been plaguing her to tell him why she loved him and she answered on 28 December 1920:

> Dearest Salvador:
>
> Your long letter has made me immensely happy because you tell me why you love me and other things that I badly needed to hear. How happy I'd be if I were close to you, very close, with nobody listening to us, this stupid society that surrounds us and spies on us and listens to us . . . and criticizes us, when all we want is to pass unnoticed, to be left alone and for them to forget about us!

You want me to tell you why I love you and I can't because even I don't know, all I can tell you is that I love you very, very much, more than any human being has ever loved. We have the same ideals, you think the way I do, you like to be different to other people, just as I do.

I don't know how to convince you that I love you, perhaps some day my way of thinking won't be so foolish as it is now, when I don't know how to describe what my heart's saying, my poor heart enchained by love of you, and which thumps like mad when I see you and when I'm with you, looking at you.

How happy I'd always be at your side and, if our dream could become reality, at the sea, in a pretty house just for us, our little love-nest, near the waves, you painting and I sitting on the floor beside you watching, with my eyes ever so wide open, the masterpiece which would bring you fame, fame the world would give you but which for me would be terrible—for your Carme, who wants you to be an artist, not from pride at being an artist's beloved, no, no, but so that you can succeed in carrying out your plan, so that your artistic dream can become reality—because, frankly, for me, the less successful you are the more I could believe that you would be mine, because I'm frightened that if you become a great artist you'll forget the person who will always love you and who loves you very, very much.

I know you don't want me to tell you this but don't be angry with me, I've said it without meaning to or perhaps because of some remaining doubts that I've now cast aside for good.

Tell me why you want me, and if when I'm older I'll love you as much as I do now. You want me to tell you that I'll always love you, isn't that it? And if other boys want my love I'll say that I don't believe in love and I'll laugh at them and I'll love the love that for me will be you. Don't be jealous of anyone if you see him talking to me because, although I'm talking to him, my thoughts and my heart are with you as they always were before you loved me and I always prayed to the Virgin that you would love me and my request has been granted.

Write me a long reply and when you're not with me think a lot about me and paint a lot and study a lot and from time to time have a rest, put down the brushes or the book to think about your beloved who's always thinking about her Salvador and drops off to sleep at night thinking about you and wakes up with the same thought, and take this kiss that far from your side your Carme sends you.

Forgive my handwriting. I've written very fast. Try to be with me on Saturday and Sunday because I'm missing you a great deal and without you I feel I'm dying of longing.[121]

'One can never forget one's first love affair,' Carme Roget mused in 1993, not long before her death, insisting that it had also been the first time for Salvador:

I was his only girlfriend, and we continued together until he left for Madrid. We were only children! In those days love was different, we had a romantic relationship, now people fall in love in a few seconds, jump into bed straightaway and have two or three affairs every year. We were so innocent! Our love was romantic, romantic. Once, when he kissed me, I hardly knew what was happening and ran to tell my friends! Salvador was handsome, he had long sideburns and above all he was very affectionate and very funny. When I was with him I used to kill myself laughing![122]

The version of the affair given in the *Secret Life*, where Carme, not mentioned by name, is the girlfriend of the 'five-year romance', suggests that indeed no overt sex was involved (sex was restricted to 'it'). Dalí portrays himself as an insatiable sadist, tormenting his mistress with his coldness and refusal to love her and enjoying reducing her to a position of abject subservience: 'I knew and she knew that I did not love her; I knew that she knew I did not love her; she knew that I knew that she knew that I did not love her. Not loving her, I kept my solitude intact, being free to exercise my "principles of sentimental action" on a very beautiful creature.'[123]

Carme's father did not think much of the painter, and there are still people in Figueres who remember that one evening he slapped her face in the Rambla for associating with such a disreputable individual. Carme, too, came to see that Salvador was not her ideal mate. After he moved to Madrid in 1922 she broke off the relationship ('he expected me to write to him every day, but how could I possibly do that? I told him we couldn't continue'), and soon found another suitor in the shape of a handsome businessman called Prat, a good footballer, whom Dalí despised heartily—and told her so. Characteristically, having lost the girl he could not love, Dalí became rabidly jealous, following the couple everywhere and spying on them. Carme Roget eventually married her businessman in 1928.[124]

Dalí and the Avant-Garde

On 4 December 1919 Dalí had recorded in his diary the death of Renoir, 'without doubt the best, or one of the best, of the French Impressionists', adding: 'Today should be a day of mourning for all artists, for all those who love art and love themselves'.125 The diary, as well as the paintings, show that up to at least the end of 1920 Dalí's allegiance to Impressionism remained unshaken. Indeed, it had been reinforced during a spell in Barcelona in the summer of 1920, when he visited the Palacio de Bellas Artes for the first time with his family and relatives and was so dazzled by the landscapes of Joaquim Mir (1873–1940), the painter admired by his teacher Juan Fernández Núñez, that it appears he did not notice the Cubist works of André Llote.[126] At the turn of the century Mir had belonged, with Ramon Pichot, Isidre Nonell and others, to the Colla del Safrá, or 'Saffron Group', so named for the predominantly yellowish tones of their work at the time. His later paintings were much more lurid, though, and it was these that now caught Dalí's eye: 'Room after room and finally one which is a spiritual refuge, a place in which to spend hours and hours. Mir! Mir! . . . Still waters with diabolic transparencies, gilded trees, skies scintillating with dreamy colour . . . But, more than stagnant waters, golden sunsets, shady gardens, colour, colour, colour, colour! . . . Mir is a genius with colour and light, and can stand beside the great French Impressionists, of whom he's a fervent disciple.'[127] At least one of the paintings Dalí executed in Cadaqués after this encounter showed the undoubted impact of Mir's extravagant palette, as he himself recognized.[128]

But change was on the way. It was probably early in 1921 that Pepito Pichot brought a present for Salvador from his brother Ramon in Paris, handing it to him with words along the lines of 'this is to show you that there isn't much steam left in Impressionism'. The present was a lavishly illustrated Futurist publication that spelt out the demise of Impressionism with great energy. Published in Milan in 1914, it comprised the Futurist Manifesto, other inflammatory Futurist texts and a profuse anthology of reproductions of Futurist works by Boccioni, Carrà, Russolo, Balla, Severini and Soffici.129 In 1927 or thereabouts Dalí told Sebastià Gasch, the Catalan art critic, that the book had provoked his wild enthusiasm and convinced him that Futurism was the true successor to Impressionism.[130] Thus, Ramon Pichot, the artist who had inspired the young Dalí to become an Impressionist painter, was also the person responsible for weaning him off that movement and showing him which way he must now go. To prove that he had taken the point, Dalí essayed a Futurist drawing opposite one of the Carrà reproductions in the book. Forty years later he recalled that for four months he had painted under the influence of Boccioni, who was 'not only the most important sculptor of Futurism but also the most important painter.'[131]

In his move away from Impressionism Dalí was also encouraged by two slightly older friends, Joan Subias Galter and Jaume Maurici Soler, who were mines of information about contemporary painting and literature.

Subias Galter (1897–1984), who later became a distinguished professor of art and history and published more than forty books, often appears in Dalí's adolescent diaries as one of the group of friends frequenting Carme Roget and her chum

Lola. Like Dalí and Juan Núñez, he was an admirer of Joaquim Mir.[132] In an article published in Figueres in May 1921, Subias praised the gouache posters that
Dalí had done for the recent Santa Creu festivities. Several critics had pointed out
that they and other works in the same vein owed an evident debt to the painter
Xavier Nogués Casas (1873–1941), famous for his celebration of Catalan country
life; Dalí's brilliant colours, however, as he himself wrote in 1922, distinguished
him from the older man. Subias appreciated this originality and deemed the
posters excellent.[133] *Fair of the Holy Cross* (1921) gives a good idea of what they   *II*
looked like.

Maurici Soler (1898–1981), a talented poet, had, at the age of only nineteen, founded the Figueres weekly *Alt Empordà*, each issue of which ran a first-rate literary page
(edited by Maurici himself) and another on art. The paper was intensely pro-Catalan in
spirit.[134] In early 1920 Maurici devoted one of his literary pages to new European poetry. It included an excerpt from Apollinaire's lecture 'L'Esprit Nouveau et les poètes'
(given in 1917), Catalan translations from Pierre Reverdy, Philippe Soupault, Albert-
Birot, Paul Dermée and Marinetti, and an interesting 'Futurist Poem' (in fact a 'calligramme') by one of Catalunya's great literary rebels of the moment, Joan Salvat-
Papasseit, a poet who for several years had been among Dalí's favourites.[135] There were
also some irreverent recommendations from the Futurist Manifesto, one of which may
have caught Dalí's eye: the exaltation of 'perilous jumps'.[136] Maurici and Dalí became
good friends, and in 1921 Salvador produced charming designs for the covers of several of his books.[137]

As for Barcelona, Dalí had a splendid ally there, as we know, in his uncle Anselm
Domènech, owner of the Llibreria Verdaguer, who supplied him with new books and
magazines and kept him closely informed about the contemporary art scene in the
Catalan capital. The *sanctus sanctorum* of modern art in the city was the gallery run by
one of Domènech's friends, Josep Dalmau (1867–1937), a native of the industrial town
of Manresa. Himself a painter, he had been deeply influenced by Art Nouveau as a
young man, holding a successful exhibition (his first and only as an artist) at the Els
Quatre Gats café in Barcelona in 1898. Like most of his fellow-*modernistes*, Dalmau
was a lover of France, and spent the years 1901 to 1906 in Paris. Realizing that he was
not cut out to be a professional painter, he returned to Barcelona and set himself up
as an antiquarian and art dealer. He began in the Carrer del Pi; then, in 1911, moved
to more spacious premises at 18, Carrer Portaferrissa, just off the Rambla. Here, in
1912, he mounted an exhibition of Cubist art, the first in Spain. It included works by
Marie Laurencin, Albert Gleizes, Jean Metzinger, Juan Gris, Le Fauconier and Marcel

Duchamp, whose *Nu descendant un escalier, numéro 2* ('Naked Figure Descending a Staircase, Number 2') was the hit of the show.[138]

During the Great War Dalmau befriended and exhibited several foreign artists who had taken refuge in neutral Spain. In 1916 he staged one of the first exhibitions of abstract art in the world, with Serge Charchoune as star turn, and that same year put on a one-man show by Albert Gleizes. In 1917 he patronized the publication of an avant-garde magazine, *391*, whose editor was the Franco-Cuban painter Francis Picabia. In 1918 he held an exhibition by Joan Miró (who had been much influenced by the 1912 Cubist show) and, in October–November 1920, mounted a comprehensive exhibition of (mainly) French avant-garde art which included, among the forty-five artists represented, works by Braque, Gris, Lipchitz, Léger, Metzinger, Miró, Gleizes, Derain, Lhote, Matisse, Picasso, Van Dongen, Diego Rivera and Severini.[139] Dalmau's energy in promoting contemporary art was boundless. 'If Barcelona has a place in the history of the Avant Garde,' the critic Jaume Vidal Oliveras has written, 'it is thanks to his solitary mission.'[140]

It seems unlikely that the young Dalí saw any of Dalmau's pre-war, or wartime, exhibitions, while his diaries for October and November 1920 do not mention the French avant-garde show then running at the gallery. On 17 October 1920, however, he had a passionate conversation with Joan Subias, who had just returned from Barcelona. 'We talked about El Greco, the Russian Revolution and Picasso,' he recorded in his diary, 'and later discussed metaphysics and Cubism.' Since Dalmau's avant-garde exhibition had just opened, it is hard to imagine that Subias, art lover that he was, had not visited it. He may even have shown Dalí the luxurious exhibition catalogue, which contained numerous illustrations.[141]

There are no further references in the extant adolescent diaries to Picasso until the summer of 1922, when Dalí, elated to have finished his schooldays, records that the great artist is now one of his 'likes'.[142] That this was so is demonstrated by the works on which Dalí was now busily occupied, having put his Impressionist period firmly behind him.

A Family Tragedy. Madrid Beckons

One Sunday morning at the beginning of February 1921, Carme Roget met Salvador, Anna Maria and Catalina Domènech on her way to mass. She was numbed to hear that the painter's mother had just been rushed to a clinic in Barcelona, where she was to undergo a serious operation. The family were in consternation and about to take early communion to pray for her recovery. But Felipa Domènech did not recover, dying of cancer of the uterus on 6 February 1921, aged forty-seven, after an operation performed at the Ribas i Ribas clinic in the Catalan capital (Calle Valencia, 390). Although Anna Maria Dalí later wrote that the tragedy had struck suddenly, one newspaper obituary said that the death came after 'a long and painful illness', which seems more likely. Felipa Domènech was buried in the Poble Nou cemetery, in the same niche as Gal Dalí and Teresa Cusí.[143]

Such was the impact of Felipa's death that her sister Catalina, 'la tieta', had a severe nervous breakdown and was sent by Salvador Dalí Cusí to convalesce at the Barcelona home of his friend Joaquim Cusí Fortunet, pharmaceutical tycoon. It was almost a year before she recovered sufficiently to return to Figueres.[144]

Dalí says in the *Secret Life* that the death of his mother was the greatest blow he had ever experienced, the loss making him determined to achieve fame at whatever cost: 'With my teeth clenched with weeping, I swore to myself that I would snatch my mother from death and destiny with the swords of light that some day would savagely gleam around my glorious name!'[145]

No sooner had Dalí's mother died than he suffered another loss. Nothing had suggested that Pepito Pichot was unwell. But in July 1921, at the age of fifty-two, he suddenly died. Dalí's diary for this month is missing, but we cannot doubt that he felt keenly the disappearance of his great friend and ally.[146]

Dalí's ten-page diary entry for October 1921 confirms that, once he assimilated the shock of his mother's death, he did indeed get to work with renewed vigour on the construction of his public image and of his fame. In this he was helped by reading Ramón del Valle-Inclán's novel *Summer Sonata*, the extravagant individualism of whose protagonist could not fail to fascinate him. 'At last I know the Marquess of Bradomín,' he writes. 'I find him really attractive'. In a section headed 'Thoughts About Myself', Dalí confesses: 'There's no doubt that I'm a completely theatrical type who only lives in order to "pose" . . . I'm a "poseur" in my manner of dressing, in my manner of talking and even in my manner of painting, in certain cases.' Indeed, perhaps even the fact of having admitted that he is a *poseur* is itself a pose! His studio is untidy—but deceptively so: in order that people will see that he's reading Pío Baroja, the novels are left in a suitably visible position, along with *The Quixote* and volumes on Futurism and Cubism. As well as a *poseur*, Dalí now considers himself a 'refined egotist', but 'this may not be apparent', for 'as well as an egotist I'm naive at certain times, which is what I imagine people notice most'. One of his main preoccupations ('as well as other artistic ones, completely romantic and noble') is that people should find him interesting, different: 'This is why I've let my hair grow long, and have sideburns.' To prove to himself and everyone else that he is indeed different, he is busily courting the favours of a gypsy girl he terms 'the Queen'. 'In a short time I've made important advances along the path of farce and deceit,' he writes, adding that he is fast growing accustomed to being 'a great actor in this even greater comedy that is life, the farcical life of our society'. Despite the fact that he is constantly acting, even when he is by himself, his major ambition remains art, 'and this is more important than anything else'. The last sentence of the self-assessment reads: 'I ammadly in love with myself.'[147]

These pages from October 1921 also show that, since the death of Felipa Domènech, Dalí has become not just more of a Narcissus but more of a Marxist rebel. He has just taken out a subscription to the French Marxist paper *L'Humanité* because, he explains, 'I'm now more Communist than ever.' But there is a suggestion that he is beginning to lose his faith in the capacity of Spaniards to achieve the hoped-for revolution. In 1920 he had written that Spain was a country in which everything moved so slowly that there was no hurry even to start something as vital as the revolution.[148] Now, a year later, he has come to the conclusion that 'Spain is shit, both the Government and the people,' the latter because they continue to put up with 'one of the most shameful tyrannies of humanity'. The tyrannous Government in question has been handling Spanish military operations in Morocco with disastrous results (to Dalí's delight). When news comes on 10 October 1921 that the Spanish Army has retaken the Gurugú hill, near Melilla, from Abd el Krim, he comments: 'They've taken the Gurugú back from us, but what a difference between our withdrawal and that of the Spaniards!' In a footnote he explains: 'I consider myself completely Moorish.'[149]

During the autumn of 1921 Dalí, Martí Vilanova, Rafael Ramis and Jaume Miravitlles set up what the latter termed ten years afterwards 'the first "soviet" in Spain', a group called Social Renovation ('Renovació Social') with a short-lived periodical of the same name.[150]

The first and, it seems, only issue of *Social Renovation* appeared on 26 December 1921, preceded by a manifesto addressed to 'Figueres public opinion'. Subtitled *Fortnightly Mouthpiece of a Group of Socialists of this Town*, all the contributors to these four pages wrote under pseudonyms, perhaps wisely, as it turned out, since the local representative of the Madrid Government refused to allow the group to register as a political party. The articles are ardently Marxist, in favour of the class struggle and the dictatorship of the proletariat, and one of them, signed by 'Jak', has the stamp of the bitterly ironic Dalí we know from his diaries: the Soviets are barbarians, the

Bolsheviks kill women, old people and eat babies; Lenin is a tyrant and sadist; and the writers who support the regime (Wells, Anatole France, Gorki) are morally degenerate. How strange, therefore, that the Russians, despite the revolutionary turmoil and the shortage of food, are currently engaged in setting up, in Moscow, of all things, a museum of Impressionist paintings, expropriated from their millionaire owners![151]

Dalí was painting as hard as he was preaching. In January 1922, his work was seen for the first time in Barcelona when he sent eight pictures to an ambitious exhibition mounted in Josep Dalmau's prestigious gallery by the Catalan Students' Association. Since his friend Ramon Reig also took part, it was probably their teacher, Juan Núñez, who encouraged them to participate in the event.

On show were 124 works by forty students. Dalí's exhibits were *Smiling Venus* (*Venus que somriu*), *Olive Trees, Cadaqués, Lunch on the Grass* (*El berenar sur l'herbe*), *Outing to the Hermitage* (*La festa a l'ermita*), *Market, Twilight* (*Crepuscle*) and *Salomé*. A close friend of the Dalí family, Carlos Costa, editor of the Barcelona daily *La Tribuna*, praised these works on the front page of the newspaper, singling out *Twilight* and *Market*. He reminded his readers that a year earlier he had predicted the young artist's rise to fame, a prediction now vindicated.[152] Other Barcelona newspapers also spoke highly of Dalí,[153] and an illustrated magazine, *Catalunya Gráfica*, published a black-and-white reproduction of *Market*. The work, whose whereabouts are today unknown, was executed in tempera and almost certainly represented the Figueres Thursday market of which Dalí was so fond. According to Rafael Santos Torroella, it clearly showed the influence of Ramon Pichot.[154] A distinguished jury awarded Dalí the Barcelona University Rector's Prize for the painting. Back home in Figueres, *Empordà Federal*, proudly reporting the good news, noted that all Dalí's exhibits had been sold.[155]

Salvador's triumph in Barcelona, and its repercussions in the press, must have greatly pleased his bereaved father. The success was repeated when, in July, Dalí took part in the Exhibition of Empordanese Artists, now an annual event in Figueres, held that year in the Casino Menestral, the Artisans' Club. Dalí, wrote 'Puvis' (who a year and a half earlier had augured his greatness as a painter) 'is a powder store of the fieriest energies and solidest qualities'.[156] It was now widely accepted, in both Barcelona and Figueres, that Dalí had outstanding artistic potential and was destined for fame.[157]

By April 1920, as we have seen, Dalí Cusí had decided that when Salvador finished his *bachillerato* he was to go on to study for an art degree at Madrid's Royal Academy Special School of Painting, Sculpture and Engraving. June 1922, the date of Salvador's final examination in Figueres Instituto, was fast approaching, and given his good record there seemed no reason to doubt that he would pass. The way to Madrid, then, was almost open.

When the decision was taken to send Salvador to the Special School, the recommendation of Juan Núñez had probably been vital, given that he himself was a graduate of the establishment. More pro-Madrid counsel came from Eduardo Marquina, the dramatist married to Mercedes Pichot, who was on good terms with Alberto Jiménez Fraud, director of the capital's hugely successful Residencia de Estudiantes, the most enlightened university hall of residence in Spain. At the Residencia, Marquina probably reasoned, Salvador would not only benefit from congenial company and a cosmopolitan atmosphere but be inspired to apply himself fully to his career. The arguments in favour of Madrid seemed conclusive to all parties, and when, as expected, Salvador passed his *bachillerato*, an interview was arranged with Alberto Jiménez Fraud for early September.

At about this time Dalí had a discussion with the painter Marià Llavanera, fourteen years his senior. Llavanera told him that his aesthetic ideal was to fuse the best in classical art with the best in modern painting: the draftsmanship and rigour of the Renaissance with the light, colour and atmospheric effects of Impressionism—Michelangelo and Cézanne merged in a new synthesis. Dalí disagreed strongly. 'I believe that painting, and all the arts, are almost instinctive,' he wrote in *Doodles* (*Ninots*) a few days later under the heading 'Anarchic Doctrine':

> To have to follow a preconceived path is pure torture . . . I believe that one has to paint without any aesthetic doctrine, paint for the sake of painting, accept no restrictions, follow the impulses of one's most liberated sensibility, paint romantically without thinking that what one is painting is reasonable. What has logic got to do with painting? Painting is a sensual matter, the essential thing in a painter is the lack of dogmas, doctrines and methods, a painter cannot map out his map without doing violence to his sensibility.[158]

In such an 'anarchic' frame of mind Dalí settled down in Cadaqués for the summer months, writing later in his diary that, despite his attempts to be disagreeable, he had found favour with the ladies. He conjectured that they had read something about him in the newspapers and been duly impressed.[159] Before leaving, he penned a suitably high-flown valediction, alluding to a local girl, Andrea, who had caught his fancy:

> Farewell, Cadaqués, farewell olive groves and paths full of tranquillity. Farewell sailors, masters of ease and life, I'm going far away to attend to things of which I've no need. To study, to see the Prado.
>
> And you, with a gaze like a Gothic statue, you who are young, with two breasts like two

fruits under your white dress, you who perhaps realize that you please me and that I love you, farewell also, girl![160]

Dalí may have wished to affect an attitude of jaded indifference concerning his forthcoming attendance at the Royal Academy of San Fernando. It befitted the image of the Romantic painter with no time for mundane considerations. Nonetheless we can be sure that he thought constantly that summer about his move to the Spanish capital. After all, as he had foreseen in his diary two years earlier, it was to be the next vital step on the road to his supreme goal: international fame.

First Steps at the 'Resi' and the Special School

The Residencia de Estudiantes was the offspring of the Institución Libre de Enseñanza, or Free Teaching Institution, a progressive secondary school opened in Madrid in 1876 by Francisco Giner de los Ríos and other forward-looking university teachers. 'Free' meant freedom, first, from the Church interference that had strangled education in the country for centuries—and, now that the Bourbons had just been restored, threatened to go on doing so. And, second, freedom from State meddling. From the outset the Free Teaching Institution had many enemies, but against all the odds it survived. Seeking to produce well-rounded individuals devoted to the construction of a 'European' Spain, its impact on the intellectual, political and moral life of the nation was to be enormous.[1]

Alberto Jiménez Fraud (1883–1964), the young warden of the Residencia de Estudiantes, had taught for three years at the Free Teaching Institution and been deeply affected by the liberal ethos that pervaded the school. Giner de los Ríos's obsession with the advancement of Spain, his humanity and his conviction that only the creation of a select minority of cultured men and women of European outlook could bring about a change in Spain's dismal fortunes—all exerted a profound influence on Jiménez. Between 1907 and 1909 he spent several months in England, where he admired the Oxbridge tutorial system. And when, in 1910, Giner de los Ríos invited him to become warden of an experimental students' hostel in Madrid, he accepted the challenge with alacrity. He was then twenty-six.[2]

The first Residencia de Estudiantes had only fifteen bedrooms and seventeen students: an inauspicious beginning for one of the most exciting educational experiments

Chapter FOUR

in the history of modern Spain. At the time there was nothing in the country corresponding to a British residential college or university hall of residence, and students from the provinces normally had no option but to live in squalid digs. The new hostel set out on a tiny scale to correct this tendency. The plan was to provide a combination of comfortable lodgings, unofficial tutorial advice and an inter-disciplinary atmosphere, and from the beginning Jiménez Fraud selected the students carefully to ensure that there was a balance between the 'two cultures'. Stress was laid on the importance of communal effort and personal responsibility, and a marked austerity was apparent in the running—and decoration—of the house. The warden and his collaborators were what V.S. Pritchett, who visited them in 1924, called 'puritans of a sunny kind'. They felt themselves to be missionaries in the service of a new Spain. Frivolity was taboo, and when there was fun it had to be the good, clean variety.[3]

The Residencia proved an immediate success, and a huge demand for places soon forced it to move to more spacious premises. A new complex was begun in 1915 on a group of hillocks at the northern end of the Paseo de la Castellana, the great rectilinear avenue that bisects Madrid and which at that time fizzled out at today's Plaza de San Juan de la Cruz. The site, on the east flank of the avenue and almost in open countryside, afforded a stunning view of the Sierra de Guadarrama, snow-capped in winter, and was twenty minutes by tram from the centre of the capital, then a small city of some 600,000 inhabitants.

The new Residencia's brick pavilions were conceived in the style known as *neomudéjar*, inspired by the architecture produced by Spanish Muslim builders working centuries earlier under the Christians. Slim, light and airy, they were eminently practical and endowed with a generous provision of showers and baths. The poet Juan Ramón Jiménez helped to design the gardens, and by the time Dalí arrived in the autumn of 1922 the poplars planted along the little canal running in front of the buildings were thriving. The place was a veritable oasis on the outskirts of the city where Madrid merged into the parched Castilian plain.

Inside, the buildings were austere, as befitted the somewhat spartan spirit of the house. Pinewood furniture was the rule (with the exception of the rather uncomfortable cane chairs), and the only touches of colour came in paintings, glazed tiles and traditional pottery. The bedrooms had a slightly monastic air, and to facilitate the students' concentration there was a strict ban on late-night noise. The place was kept spotless; and woe betide anyone who dropped a cigarette-butt on the floor.

Once its five pavilions had been completed, the Residencia was in a position to accommodate 150 students, a figure that remained practically constant until 1936 and made it possible for all the occupants to know each other by sight if not always by name. It was a community of ideal proportions.[4]

The majority of the residents were students of medicine, attracted by the laboratories and by the free supplementary instruction given in these as part of Jiménez Fraud's 'support system' for undergraduates. The medics were followed in numbers by the industrial engineers, whose School was situated in a wing of the nearby Natural History Museum. As for the accusation of social elitism sometimes levelled at the Residencia, it is true that the overwhelming majority of students came from middle-class backgrounds, inevitably so given that secondary education was almost entirely limited to the comfortably off. But the Board was acutely aware of this circumstance, and strove to make places available to the less privileged.[5]

One of Alberto Jiménez Fraud's principal endeavours was to persuade distinguished men and women, both Spanish and foreign, to lecture to his community. To this end two organizations were set up: the Hispano-English Committee, in 1923, and, the following year, the Society for Courses and Lectures. The latter was backed by a committee of aristocratic blue-stockings, the *crème de la crème* of Madrid female society, and proved an enormous success. Among those who gave talks were H.G. Wells, G.K. Chesterton, Albert Einstein, Louis Aragon, Paul Valéry, the Egyptologist Howard Carter, Max Jacob, José Ortega y Gasset, Salvador de Madariaga, Roger Martin du Gard, Hilaire Belloc, Leo Frobenius and, on several occasions, the Catalan writer and art critic Eugenio d'Ors, who was to be one of the early Dalí's staunchest supporters. Another Catalan who lectured at the Residencia, a few years before Dalí's arrival, was his father's old friend Pere Coromines.

There was music-making, too, at the Residencia, and of a high quality. Manuel de Falla and the guitarist Andrés Segovia came often, and there were visits by the harpsichordist Wanda Landowska, the pianist Ricardo Viñes and the composers Darius Milhaud, Igor Stravinsky, Francis Poulenc and Maurice Ravel.

In a country woefully short on modern libraries, the Residencia had an excellent and constantly expanding one, with numerous foreign journals and magazines. It stayed open late, browsing was encouraged and students could take books to their rooms. Not content with this, the Residencia also turned its hand to publishing, and produced books that today are much-prized collector's pieces, among them the first edition of Antonio Machado's complete poetry (1917) and seven volumes of essays by the philosopher Miguel de Unamuno, a frequent visitor.

For its emblem the 'Resi', as it was known affectionately, designed a medallion based on the head of a fifth-century BC Athenian sculpture known as the *Blond Athlete*, which represents a handsome, Apollonian youth with curly hair. No doubt the head was felt by Don Alberto and his collaborators to express the ideal of the 'perfect citizen'. *Mens sana in corpore sano,* if not explicitly the motto of the house, was virtually so in practice. Football, tennis, running, sunbathing, hockey—the Residencia balanced its intellectual seriousness with a devotion to sport mainly inspired by what Don Alberto had seen in England. It almost comes as a surprise that they did not run a cricket team. As for the vast quantities of tea consumed in the rooms (alcohol was forbidden and, unheard of in Spain, wine was not served with meals), it was another indication of British influence.[6]

John Brande Trend, later Professor of Spanish at Cambridge, was delighted by the atmosphere he found at the Residencia, and in his book *A Picture of Modern Spain* (1921) stressed the tremendous influence exerted on the thinking of Alberto Jiménez Fraud and his colleagues by the English tutorial system. 'Oxford and Cambridge in Madrid', Trend termed the experiment, explaining that the Residencia's main concern was 'to awaken curiosity (a faculty lacking in many Spaniards)' and to arouse both the desire to learn and 'the power to form personal judgements instead of accepting what other people say'. Trend forgot to mention it, but the Residencia did not have a chapel: an absence that its Catholic detractors found offensive but which symbolized its determination to remain as free as possible from outside interference of any kind.[7]

When Dalí turned up at the Residencia in September 1922, with his father and sister in tow, the hostel was just embarking on the most brilliant period of its history.

Anna Maria evoked their arrival years later in her book *Salvador Dalí Seen by his Sister,* recalling the impact made on the *madrileños* by her brother's eccentric appearance: hair almost down to his shoulders, outlandishly long sideburns, cape brushing the ground, gilded cane. The threesome must have made an unusual group, certainly, as they explored the capital, chatting animatedly to each other in their Ampurdanese Catalan, Salvador's flamboyance complemented by the good looks of his buxom, fourteen-year-old sister and by the swaying, corpulent form of the notary, his massive bald head fringed with tufts of the purest white hair.[8]

The San Fernando Royal Academy of Fine Arts, which one imagines the Dalís hurried at once to inspect, was founded in 1742 by Felipe V, Spain's first Bourbon monarch, and opened in 1752. Similar institutions were established later in Valencia, Seville and Zaragoza, but not Barcelona. 'The idea was to improve the standard of architects and artists,' one authority has written, 'and to raise the arts in Spain to the level of other European countries.'[9] The Academies were both teaching and norm-shaping corporations, and the underlying assumption was that in Spain the French-inspired neo-classical aesthetic should be imposed as a matter of course. Politics, that is to say, were involved: the Academies were to be a further expression of Bourbon power, orderliness and enlightenment; an instrument for educating barbarous Spain in matters of good taste.

The Special School of Painting, Sculpture and Engraving, the teaching department of the Royal Academy, was housed with the latter in a fine building at the beginning of the Calle de Alcalá, just off the Puerta del Sol, the Piccadilly Circus of Madrid. Inevitably, given the standing of the Academy, this was the art school of most prestige in the country. Which does not mean that it was particularly good. According to Eugenio d'Ors, writing in 1924, it had decayed to such an extent by that time that all respect for tradition and discipline had been lost. The School was 'a mawkish, flabby, disjointed farce'. But this was perhaps an excessively harsh judgement.[10]

We need not be surprised that Don Salvador Dalí Cusí, rather than send his son to one of the provincial Schools of Fine Art, should have decided to enrol him at the venerable institution in the capital whose degrees provided the best guarantee of a steady teaching job. He must also have felt certain that the nearby Prado would prove an invaluable university for his son, irrespective of his progress at the Special School.

On 11 September 1922 Dalí applied to sit the entrance examination.[11] The *Secret Life* provides an uproariously funny account of what happened, but it is impossible to check its accuracy from external sources. If we can believe Dalí, the test that September consisted in making a drawing from a cast of Jacopo Sansovino's *Bacchus*. The candidates were allowed six two-hour sessions (one per day) to complete their drawing, which had to conform to exact measurements. Dalí being Dalí, his drawing stubbornly refused to meet the dimensional requirements, and half-way through the examination was far too small. After much rubbing out and restarting, the finished product was even tinier.[12]

Dalí wrote excitedly to his Uncle Anselm Domènech in Barcelona while waiting for the results, telling him that he was thrilled with Madrid. His most moving experience to date had been seeing the Velázquezes in the Prado. Certain that he would be admitted to the Special School (where he had already noted how low the standards were), he asked Anselm to switch his subscription to the French Communist paper *L'Humanité to* Madrid. He also asked him to take out a subscription on his behalf to the Parisian art journal *L'Esprit Nouveau*, the mouthpiece of Amédée Ozenfant and Le Corbusier's Purism.[13] Domènech complied, as usual, and true to character Dalí made sure that in Madrid people saw him with *L'Esprit Nouveau* and another avant-garde publication, the Milan journal *Valori Plastici*, under his arm. In 1928 he said that *L'Esprit Nouveau* had opened his eyes to 'the simple and emotive beauty of the miraculous mechanical-industrial world', with its standardized objects free of all artistic pretensions.[14]

Dalí with his class at the Royal Academy School of San Fernando, Madrid, c.1922–4.

As Dalí had foreseen, he passed his entrance test to San Fernando despite the small size of his drawing; and Don Salvador and Anna Maria, who had been sick with anxiety, departed with a deep sigh of relief for Figueres after commending him to the good offices of a Catalan student at the school, Josep Rigol Formaguera.[15]

On 30 September Salvador signed up for the subjects he wanted to study during his first session at the School: 'Perspective', 'Modelling', 'Anatomy', 'History of Art (Antiquity and the Middle Ages)' and 'Statue Drawing'.[16]

Dalí seems hardly to have communicated with the other students in the Residencia de Estudiantes during his first weeks in Madrid. Driven by the ambition recorded in his adolescent diaries, and feeling his timidity keenly, he applied himself with unswerving dedication to his classes in the Academy, shutting himself up in his room at the 'Resi' when he got back, spending no money and devoting Sunday mornings to the Prado.[17]

But gradually he began to come out of his shell. In this he was encouraged by one of the Residencia's most engaging denizens, José ('Pepín') Bello Lasierra, whom Dalí, in the *Secret Life*, claims was responsible for 'discovering' him:

> One day, when I was out, the chamber maid had left my door open, and Pepín Bello, happening to pass by, saw my two Cubist paintings. He could not wait to divulge the discovery to the members of the group. These knew me by sight, and I was even the butt of

their caustic humour. They called me 'the musician', or 'the artist', or 'the Pole'. My anti-European way of dressing made them judge me unfavourably, as a rather commonplace, more or less hairy romantic residue. My serious, studious air, totally lacking in humour, made me appear to their sarcastic eyes a lamentable being, stigmatized with mental deficiency, and at best picturesque. Nothing indeed could contrast more violently with their British-style tailored suits and golf jackets than my velvet jackets and my flowing neckties; nothing could be more diametrically opposed to them than my long tangled hair, falling down to my shoulders, and their smartly trimmed hair, regularly worked over by the barbers of the Ritz or the Palace Hotel. At the time I became acquainted with the group, particularly, they were all possessed by a complex of dandyism combined with cynicism, which they displayed with accomplished worldliness. They inspired me at first with such great awe that each time they came to see me in my room I thought I would faint.[18]

This account seems to be pretty accurate. José Bello insisted years later that what most struck him about Dalí was his extreme timidity. The Salvador of those early days at the 'Resi', he recalled, was 'literally sick with timidity', the most self-conscious person he had ever met. He blushed frequently and appeared totally uninterested in girls.[19] One of Dalí's contemporaries at the Special School, the sculptor Cristino Mallo, was similarly impressed: 'At that time the amazing thing about Dalí, who later did such scandalous things, was that above all he was extremely bashful.'[20] 'The Dalí of that period looked like Buster Keaton,' another friend, Rafael Sánchez Ventura, recalled. 'He was morbidly shy—just the opposite of what he was like later on.'[21]

José Bello himself was anything but timid. He was born on 9 May 1904, two days before Dalí, in the Aragonese town of Huesca, where his father, a distinguished civil engineer, was building a reservoir, and had entered the Residencia in 1915 just before before it moved to its new premises. In 1921, when he joined the medical faculty of Madrid University, he settled back into the hostel after a short absence, priding himself on being one of its longest inmates. 'Pepín', as he was always known to the Residencia set, had what Spaniards call *don de gentes*, a winning way with people. He was *muy simpático*, very easy-going, a night bird (from childhood he suffered from insomnia), and, unlike most Spaniards, a very good listener, with a profound curiosity about other people. Despite his interest in medicine, he never became a doctor; despite his artistic and literary ability, never produced more than a handful of sketches or poems; but he had an extraordinary gift for whimsy, for inventiveness and, above all, for friendship.[22]

By the time Dalí arrived at the 'Resi' that autumn, Pepín Bello had struck up what was to be a lifetime's friendship with another student from Aragon: the future film director

Luis Buñuel. Born in 1900 in the little town of Calanda, not far from Teruel in the province of Zaragoza, Buñuel was the son of a rich entrepreneur who, on returning in middle age from Cuba, had married the prettiest girl in the locality, twenty years younger than himself, and settled down to a quiet life. Like Dalí, Luis, the eldest of five children, was cock of the domestic roost, and enjoyed the unconditional indulgence of his young, adoring and beautiful mother. The latter was hugely relieved when, after carefully vetting Madrid's sordid boarding houses, she was directed to the hall of residence presided over by Alberto Jiménez Fraud: here, she had decided immediately, her darling boy would be in safe hands.[23]

Dalí, Lorca and Pepín Bello in an affectionate mood at the Residencia de Estudiantes. Dated 1926 by Luis Buñuel.

Her darling boy, who entered the Residencia in the autumn of 1917, was a born rebel. Luis Buñuel conformed more than Pepín Bello to the notion other Spaniards hold of the Aragonese—that is, he was aggressively stubborn and self-reliant. Tough, proud of his good looks and fine physique, Buñuel was a manic keep-fit fiend. Each morning at the 'Resi', irrespective of weather conditions, he could be seen running, jumping, doing press-ups, pummelling a punchball or hurling his javelin. He liked to go barefoot while about these activities. The strength of his arm and stomach muscles afforded him endless satisfaction (he was always lying down and asking people to jump on his tummy), and he fancied himself particularly as a boxer although, despite the combative image he worked so hard to project, he was, as he himself admitted later, a bit short on physical courage. Buñuel's determination to prove his ability on the sports field and in the ring was matched, if we can believe his memoirs, by his assiduous patronage of Madrid's leading whorehouses, at that time, or so he tells us, the best in the world. Faced with such a disconcerting example of male prowess and apparent self confidence, Buñuel's fellow residents came up with a good nickname for him: Tarquin the Proud.[24]

Buñuel had begun his chequered academic career by enrolling in the Department of Agricultural Engineering at Madrid University, changing almost immediately to Industrial Engineering. This subject also failed to rouse his enthusiasm, so he switched to the Natural Sciences, and for a year devoted himself to the study of Entomology, in which pursuit he was engrossed when Dalí made his appearance at the Residencia (insects would always fascinate Buñuel, and his spider phobia was almost as acute as Dalí's panic fear of locusts). Finally, in 1924, he graduated in History.[25]

Luis Buñuel, like Pepín Bello, was a great talker and noctambulist, and Madrid, the most friendly and loquacious of late-night cities, offered him the opportunity to indulge both proclivities to his heart's content. By the time Dalí arrived at the 'Resi' Buñuel knew the Spanish capital backwards. He made it his immediate business to initiate Salvador, and in his memoirs, admittedly almost as untrustworthy as Dalí's, maintained that it was he, not Bello, who 'discovered' him.[26]

The sociable Buñuel belonged to several of the city's literary *tertulias*, or cenacles. The *tertulia*, a regular gathering of like-minded friends for the primary purpose of conversational self-affirmation, was a thriving Madrid institution. There were hundreds of them, their members meeting at the same time each day or night in the same café around the same table. Most of the famous cafés were grouped along the section of the Calle de Alcalá lying between the Puerta del Sol and the Plaza de la Cibeles, and only a few paces away from the San Fernando Special School. Politicians, poets, bullfighters, doctors, actors, lawyers—they all had their favourite haunts, and well-informed visitors to Madrid knew that by stepping of an evening into, say, the Granja del Henar, they could be sure of seeing a selection of the capital's brightest literary and political pundits hard at it. The almost complete absence of women at these sessions did not then strike anyone as unusual, for women in Spain had not even begun to come into their own (that would happen on the advent of the Second Republic in 1931). This was essentially a man's world, and the only females who trespassed on it were the occasional demimondaine or curious foreigner.

Buñuel had literary aspirations and considered himself an anarchist. Two years after his arrival in Madrid he was associating with the avant-garde writers and artists who, in 1919, grouped themselves under the banner of a new movement, Ultra, inspired by the latest trends in Europe. Among the contributors to the group's typographically innovative magazine of the same name were the poet Guillermo de Torre (born, like Buñuel, in 1900), who was fast becoming an authority on contemporary art and literature (Dalí termed him 'our equivalent of Marinetti');[27] the Argentinian poet Jorge Luis

Borges (born in 1899) and his artist sister Norah; the prolific Madrid writer Ramón Gómez de la Serna; and, in February 1922, Buñuel himself.[28]

Ultra's heroes were people like Apollinaire, Pierre Reverdy, Jean Cocteau, Pablo Picasso, Juan Gris, Diaghilev (who had visited the country with his Ballets Russes in 1916 and 1917), Marinetti (whose Futurist Manifesto Ramón Goméz de la Serna had been the first to publish in Spain) and the Chilean, Paris-based poet Vicente Huidobro, who had spent five months in Madrid in 1918.

The *ultraístas* devoured the French literary magazines of the day, despised sentimentality (taboo after the horror of the Great War) and believed that art should now express the spirit of an age represented by the Eiffel Tower, machines, skating rinks, dynamos, ragtime and foxtrots, streamlined motor cars, radio and cinema, aeroplanes, telegraphy, transatlantic steamers, svelte girls on beaches and Kodaks. Ultra gives the lie to the textbook cliché that, where Spain was concerned, only Barcelona could boast an avant-garde scene at the time. In fact, while Madrid was much more cut-off physically from Paris than Barcelona, and had no contemporary art gallery to match Dalmau, it was more in touch with Europe than might be suspected. Dalí soon became aware of this, writing to his friend, Juan Xirau, with whom he had collaborated on the school magazine *Studium*:

> In Madrid, as distinct from Barcelona, modern avant-garde painting has not only had no repercussions but it's not even known, except by the group of poets and writers I'm going to tell you about. Nonetheless, where literature and poetry are concerned, there's a whole generation who have followed every new development, with all its joys and preoccupations, from Rimbaud to Prévert.[29]

The acknowledged guru of that generation was the indefatigable Ramón Gómez de la Serna (1883–1964). Novelist, poet, compulsive founder of small magazines, essayist, wit and man-about-town, Gómez de la Serna ran Madrid's most famous literary *tertulia*, known as Pombo, which met every Saturday night in the basement of a café just off the Puerta del Sol. Much-travelled and highly sociable, 'Ramón' (as he was universally known in pre-civil-war Madrid) kept a very close eye on what was happening in Europe. During the war he had been in Switzerland and France; he knew Tristan Tzara and other members of the Dada movement personally, and could tell engaging stories about them; he was on friendly terms with Picasso, who had dropped in on Pombo in 1917 when visiting Madrid with Diaghilev and the Ballets Russes; and he had invented the *greguería*, a pithy definition or comparison that used metaphorical shock tactics to make its point and had become quite a rage. This sort of thing:

Lecture: the longest leave-taking known to man.

The woman looked at me as if I were an empty taxi.

The rainbow is the ribbon Nature puts on after washing her hair.[30]

'Ramón,' Luis G. de Candamo has written, 'foreshadowed Futurist modes of expression, stressing dream intuitions and the meanderings of the unconscious (the logic of the absurd, in a word) before anyone else.'[31] Before anyone else in Madrid, that is to say. Ramón's was the light touch missing in the somewhat puritanical Residencia de Estudiantes, and it is not surprising that Luis Buñuel soon became a regular of Pombo, a personal friend of Ramón and an adept at *greguerías*:

> We would arrive, say hello, sit down, ask for a drink—almost always coffee and a lot of water (the waiters never stopped bringing water)—and begin a desultory conversation, mainly literary, about the most recent publications, what we'd been reading, the political news. We lent each other books and foreign magazines. We criticized those who weren't there. Sometimes a writer would read a poem or article and Ramón would give his opinion, which we always listened to and sometimes disagreed with. The time flew. More than one night some of us would go on talking while we strolled through the streets.[32]

It is likely that Dalí, before returning that Christmas to Figueres for the holidays, made some visits to Pombo.[33] At all events he was certainly accompanying Buñuel by then on the latter's forays through nocturnal Madrid. One proof, in the absence of *IV* diaries and correspondence, is *Night-Walking Dreams* (*Sueños noctámbulos*), a remarkable watercolour-and-ink painting done by Dalí at this time. The art critic and leading Dalí authority, Rafael Santos Torroella, has demonstrated that the painting shows the clear influence of the Uruguayan painter Rafael Pérez Barradas, a close friend of Dalí, Buñuel, Pepín Bello and other members of their group, and a habitual contributor to *Ultra* and similar publications of the moment.[34] In 1913, at the age of twenty-three, Barradas had left his native Montevideo and sailed to Italy, where he came into contact with Futurism. He had then moved on to Paris and frequented the Cubists. A year later he was in Barcelona, where he struck up a close friendship with Josep Dalmau who, in 1917, staged an exhibition of his work which it is unlikely Dalí saw but which he might have heard about. Then, in 1918, disappointed by the lack of public response to his painting in the Catalan capital, Barradas had moved to Madrid, where his fortunes began to improve, though not for long (he then returned to Barcelona and died back home in Montevideo in 1929).[35] Barradas was fascinated by café and street life and, in tune with his *ultraísta* friends, loved the mechanical paraphernalia of contemporary urban society. The style in which he attempted to express this dynamism he termed 'vibrationist'. It derived from both Cubism and Futurism, but the use of brilliant colour and the sense of movement were very much Barradas's own. Dalí was impressed.

Night-Walking Dreams is made up of a series of simultaneous vignettes evoking a dimly-lit, small-hours perambulation through Old Madrid. Dalí's debt to Barradas's art is not only manifest but the Uruguayan is arguably the hatted, left-hand figure of the group of four standing in the pool of light cast by a street lamp at the bottom-centre of the picture. Barradas, wearing an overcoat, is flanked, as Santos Torroella has demonstrated conclusively, by the broad-shouldered Buñuel, looking like a Chicago gangster; on his right are an unmistakable Dalí and a companion of his at the Special School, the painter Maruja Mallo, a liberated female student in the woman-excluding society of the time. Since Barradas does not appear in any of the other nocturnal scenes recorded in the painting, Santos Torroella deduces that the journey begins here with the Uruguayan taking leave of his friends.[36] Higher up, slightly to right-of-centre, we find the group at another moment in their excursion, with Buñuel on the left, Dalí to the right and Maruja Mallo below; while, at top-left, we see Dalí and Maruja Mallo walking towards a stark cross (perhaps they have entered a church). And there is Dalí again in the bottom left-hand corner, with Maruja's head resting on his shoulder. Behind them, or so it appears, is Buñuel, accompanied by a bevy of marauding cats.

Night-Walking Dreams is the masterwork of a series of watercolours begun in Figueres shortly before Dalí's arrival in Madrid.[37] They show his new interest in urban night-life and, not least, in prostitutes and brothels. We meet drunks reeling under the moon, couples hurrying urgently homewards, men slinking up narrow stairs, a portly client stripping off in front of a whore waiting for him in naked readiness on a bed, a man caressing a girl's breasts in a cabaret and, in a painting entitled *The First Days of Spring*, Dalí himself spying from behind a tree at a pair of lovers sitting together on a bench in Figueres. Clearly, love and the flesh were much on Dalí's mind.[38]

A Marriage in the Family

On 9 October 1922, only a few weeks after he had settled in at the Residencia de Estudiantes, Dalí's maternal grandmother, Maria Anna Ferrés, died in Figueres at the age of eighty. She was buried in the niche that contained the remains of the first Salvador.[39] According to Anna Maria Dalí her last words were: 'My grandson is in Madrid. My grandson will be a great painter. The best painter in Catalunya.'[40] Her death served another blow to her daughter Catalina, 'la tieta', who had still not fully recovered from the shock of losing her sister Felipa the previous year.

Salvador Dalí Cusí now decided that it would be appropriate for him and Catalina to marry. Presumably she was in agreement. The canon law of the time made it impossible for them to do so without a special dispensation from the Pope, however, given that Catalina was the sister of Don Salvador's dead wife (an impediment termed by the Church 'first degree of affinity in the collateral line'). On 15 November, in a document addressed through the parish priest of Figueres to the ecclesiastical authorities at Girona, seat of the bishop, Dalí Cusí set out the reasons why he and Catalina felt they should be joined in matrimony. These were (1) that they were already living under the same roof; (2) their shared love of the children; (3) the fact that they both proceeded from honourable families; and (4) that Catalina was free to do so. The Church machinery worked quickly and the papal dispensation was granted on 29 November 1922. On 22 December the couple were married in the parish church of San Jaime Apóstol in Barcelona. The notary was fifty, Catalina thirty-nine.[41]

According to Montserrat Dalí, Anna Maria and Salvador gave their approval to the marriage, given Catalina's place in the family as their 'second mother', although Salvador said he could not understand why it was really necessary ('Papá, no hi veig la necessitat!').[42] One biographer has alleged that he discovered that his father was having sex with Catalina before Felipa Domènech's death, and never forgave him as a result.[43] But there is not a shred of evidence to support such a claim. Given Dalí Cusí's profession and status in Figueres, where everyone knew everyone else's business, Catalina's presence in the home once her mother was dead would certainly have given rise to gossip. And gossip the increasingly conservative notary public could well do without. Montserrat Dalí, who was not present at the wedding herself, felt that it had been held away from Figueres in order to avoid publicity.[44] The Domènech side of the family must also have approved of the union, for Catalina's brother Anselm, owner of the Llibreria Verdaguer, was one of the witnesses.[45] Had Dalí felt that his father, in marrying Catalina, was betraying the memory of his first wife, or that he had been having an affair with her before the latter's death, he would surely have made this clear sooner or later in his autobiographical writings. But he never did so. It was a marriage based on affection, social necessity and perhaps, in the face of the recent deaths and unhappiness, on an emotional need to affirm the cohesion of the group.

It may be that the wedding was held in late December in order to enable Salvador to be present at the ceremony after finishing his first term at the Special School. But there is no proof that he, or his sister Anna Maria for that matter, attended. All we know is that by the end of the month Dalí was back home in Figueres for the Christmas holidays, his return being duly recorded in the local press, which also announced that he was on the jury which would award prizes for the best floats and children's lamps (*fanalets*) at the Three Wise Men procession on 6 January, the day on which Spanish children traditionally receive their presents.[46]

In Figueres Dalí flaunted the latest copy of *L'Esprit Nouveau*, writing in his diary that Carme Roget, suitably impressed, 'would humbly bow her forehead in an attentive attitude over the Cubist paintings'.[47]

Breton and Picabia in Barcelona

In Figueres, if not in Madrid, Dalí must surely have heard about the visit by André Breton to Barcelona that November to lecture to the Ateneu, hub of the city's intellectual life, and attend the opening of an exhibition by his friend Francis Picabia at the Dalmau Gallery. Both Breton's preface to the exhibition catalogue and his lecture were in French (in the former he confessed that he knew no Spanish and was utterly ignorant of Spanish culture). The lecture, 'Caractères de l'évolution moderne et ce qui en participe', was delivered on 17 November 1922. Couched in a complex style more suited to an essay than a talk, particularly to a non-French audience, it nonetheless made a considerable impact.[48]

The main propositions of the lecture were simple enough: Cubism, Futurism and Dada all expressed aspects of 'a more general movement' which it was still impossible to define precisely; Dada (to which Breton himself had contributed so signally) had run its course; and a new, revolutionary movement was at hand. Two years afterwards Breton was to appropriate the term 'Surrealism', coined by Apollinaire in 1917, for the movement still 'latent' in 1922.[49]

Dalí may have seen or even possessed a copy of the Picabia catalogue with Breton's preface, perhaps through the good offices of his uncle, Anselm Domènech. And he must surely have been aware already of Picabia's machine paintings, much in evidence at his Dalmau exhibition, several of which had been reproduced in the four issues of the magazine *391* published by Picabia during his stay in Barcelona in 1917.[50] He would probably have been struck by Breton's scorn for Cézanne, vented in the preface to the catalogue as well as in his lecture, and was to echo it a few years later when Cézanne became one of his *bêtes noires*. For Breton, the merit of Picabia's machine paintings was precisely that, unlike Cézanne's, they were 'pure of all representational intention'. Dalí would also have noted Breton's assertion that Picasso was the artist 'to whom we owe the most'.[51] The 'we' meant the new wave of young writers and painters in Paris associated with the magazine *Littérature*, founded by Breton, Philippe Soupault and Louis Aragon in 1919. It was there that the first two had published, in 1920, excerpts from their *Les Champs magnétiques*, the inaugural text of what was soon to become the Surrealist movement. One of the subliminal messages of Breton's utterances in Barcelona was that in Paris, and Paris alone, was the 'modern spirit' being courageously forged. It was a conviction to which Breton and his friends were soon to give real substance.

Federico García Lorca

During his first three months at the Residencia, Dalí must have been affected by what he heard about the hostel's most charismatic, if sporadic, inmate, who at that time was back home in Andalusia.

Federico García Lorca, six years older than Dalí, was born in the village of Fuente Vaqueros, near Granada, in 1898. In 1918 his gentleman-farmer father had financed his first book, *Impressions and Landscapes*, mainly an account of trips through Castile and northern Spain; in 1919 he had entered the 'Resi', two years after Buñuel, ostensibly to continue his studies at Madrid University; in 1920 he had staged his first play, *The Butterfly's Evil Spell*, which had fallen foul of a Madrid audience; in 1921 his first collection of verse, *Book of Poems*, had appeared in the capital, receiving an appreciative review on the front page of Spain's leading progressive newspaper, *El Sol* (where Dalí, an avid reader of the paper, might have seen it); in the summer of 1922 he had helped his friend Manuel de Falla organize a flamenco festival in the Alhambra; and by that autumn his return was eagerly awaited at the 'Resi'.

Dalí, with his driving urge to shine, may have quailed at the prospect of having to compete with Lorca, for the *granadino* was not only a hugely promising poet and dramatist but an excellent pianist, a spell-binding conversationist, a compelling raconteur and, perhaps above all, a modern jongleur, at his happiest when reciting his work to a live public, or singing folksongs to his own accompaniment. To make matters worse Lorca even drew well and had a tremendous *don de gentes*.

But there was one drawback: he was homosexual, a fact which even in Spain today some of his few surviving friends still refuse to accept. José Moreno Villa, Alberto

Jiménez Fraud's right-hand man at the Residencia, was aware of the truth—a truth the poet had to keep to himself as much as possible because even in the Residencia, Spain's most liberal centre of culture, homosexuality was taboo. A poet, painter and art critic of considerable talent who became friends with Dalí, Buñuel and Lorca, Moreno Villa (1887–1955) was one of the few contemporaries to allude, after Lorca's assassination by the Fascists in 1936, to the 'unmentionable' aspect of his multiple personality. In his autobiography, *Vida en claro* (published in Mexico in 1944), Moreno Villa evoked the magic days at the Residencia, and commented on Lorca: 'Not all the students liked him. Some of them sniffed out his defect [sic] and distanced themselves. Nonetheless, when he opened the piano and began to sing, they all lowered their defences.'[52]

This was the dazzling young Andalusian Dalí met early in 1923 when Lorca returned to the 'Resi' after his long absence. The two had a lot in common: a shared love of the poetry of Rubén Darío and of France (both had been Germanophobes during the war); a childhood in which music, and particularly folksong, had played an important role; a passionate concern with social injustice; and an uneasy relationship with their sexuality. It seems that they warmed to each other immediately. Three years later Dalí told the Barcelona art critic, Sebastià Gasch, that their 'great friendship' was characterized by the violent opposition between the poet's 'eminently religious spirit' and his own, equally eminent, anti-religious animus, which led to constant, late-night discussions.[53] This may well have been the case. At all events, Dalí was greatly affected, as he recorded in the *Secret Life*:

> Although I realized at once that my new friends were going to take everything from me without being able to give me anything in return—for in reality of truth they possessed nothing of which I did not possess twice, three times, a hundred times as much—on the other hand, the personality of Federico García Lorca produced an immense impression on me. The poetic phenomenon in its entirety and 'in the raw' presented itself before me suddenly in flesh and bone, confused, blood-red, viscous and sublime, quivering with a thousand fires of darkness and of subterranean biology, like all matter endowed with the originality of its own form.[54]

Later in his narrative Dalí makes a confession unique in Spanish autobiography:

> During this time I knew several elegant women on whom my hateful cynicism desperately grazed for moral and erotic fodder. I avoided Lorca and the group, which grew to be his group more and more. This was the culminating moment of his irresistible personal influ-

ence—and the only moment in my life when I thought I glimpsed the torture that envy can be. Sometimes we would be walking, the whole group of us, along El Paseo de la Castellana on our way to the café where we held our usual literary meetings, and where I knew Lorca would shine like a mad and fiery diamond. Suddenly I would set off at a run, and no one would see me for three days.[55]

Knowing Dalí's difficulty in handling his feelings of shame, it was not surprising that Lorca's fabulous social success should have made him keenly aware of his comparative inadequacy. One afternoon Pepín Bello, Lorca and Dalí were in a café where an animated discussion on art was taking place. Both Bello and Lorca joined in energetically, but Dalí remained silent. 'Say something, for God's sake,' Bello urged, 'or they'll think you're stupid.' Finally Dalí got to his feet, mumbled with lowered eyes 'I'm a fine painter, too,' and sat down to the general bemusement of the company. Bello burst out laughing when he recounted this incident.[56]

Dalí must have been present on many occasions when Lorca gave one of his impromptu folklore sessions at the 'Resi'. Sometimes, as the poet Rafael Alberti, another Andalusian, has recalled in his memoirs, Federico would hold competitions:

'Where's this one from? Let's see if anyone knows,' the poet would ask, singing and accompanying himself:

> The lads from Monleón
> Went off early to plough,
> Alas! alas!
> Went off early to plough.

In those days, when there was growing research into, and a new fervour for, the old songs and ballads, it was not difficult to pinpoint their place of origin.

'From the Salamanca area,' someone would reply, no sooner had the tragic bull-fighting ballad got under way.

'Correct, well done,' Federico would agree, at once serious and burlesque, adding, with a pedagogical intonation: 'And it was included in his songbook by the priest Don Dámaso Ledesma.'[57]

One of Lorca's favourites was a gypsy folksong from Granada called 'El zorongo gitano', which, before he harmonized and adapted it for his performances, had already been quoted by Albéniz and by Manuel de Falla (who weaves it into *Nights in the Gardens of Spain*). Dalí never forgot Lorca's renderings of the song. In December 1966, thirty years after the poet's assassination, the BBC made a documentary about Dalí in New York. At one point he walks down the street singing to himself. It is the 'zorongo'. Suddenly, turning to the camera, he recites the song's most arresting verse:

La luna es un pozo chico,	The moon? Only a tiny round well!
las flores no valen nada,	Flowers? They count for nothing!
lo que valen son tus brazos	What counts are your arms
cuando de noche me abrazas.	when you hug me at night.

'García Lorca!' explains Dalí as he plunges through a doorway.[58]

Dada may have been defunct in Paris by 1922, as Breton asserted in his Barcelona lecture, but Dada-type games were all the rage among the more jocose elements at the 'Resi', with Lorca to the fore. Soon even Dalí, usually averse to group activity, was joining in as best he could. At one gathering it was recalled that the previous evening, in the gardens of the hostel, some moonstruck romantic had recited Verlaine. At this point Guillermo de Torre, one of the leading lights in the Ultra movement, burst into the room and, according to an entry in Dalí's diary, exclaimed:

'Universal hatred of the moon!' says Marinetti. What's this I've just heard? A snatch of Verlaine? Unworthy sons of the year 1923! What has it served you to be born beneath the wings of aircraft? And you still dare to call yourself avant-gardists, when you don't even know that the combustion engine sounds better than any hendecasyllable? I'm leaving! I'm leaving immediately because I'm afraid my contact with you will turn me into an antediluvian being, and particularly because my sensibility won't allow me to stay still. I need the constant reflection of colours, of mutifarious images; your ridiculous sentimentalism is understandable because you spend whole days talking and talking in this room without moving. Avant-garde *tertulias* should have a dynamic quality, they only make sense when they're linked to speed! The plush sofás of the Café Platerías are turning us into old men. This very evening I'm going to make enquires about buying a bus for our meetings.[59]

Torre did his best to enlist Lorca and Dalí in the *ultraísta* ranks, where, like himself, Buñuel was a militant. He met with little success, although the poet was certainly influenced by the movement's insistence on the primacy of the image. As for Dalí, the iconoclastic message of Torre and his friends made its mark, and his already well-established rebelliousness was further fuelled by his contact with the group.

Dalí's and Buñuel's published accounts of their years at the Residencia are very incomplete and often inaccurate, while Lorca was murdered before he could write one. We have some of the correspondence exchanged between the three friends, but there are yawning gaps (neither Buñuel nor Dalí were document-hoarders). Most of Dalí's letters to Lorca, beginning in 1925, have been preserved, but of Lorca's to Dalí only two or three have come to light—and there were dozens. As regards the Residencia's records, which must have contained information about the rooms the friends inhabited at different times, as well as other details of interest, the civil war saw to it that these were mainly lost. The result is that it is almost impossible to reconstruct the development of the passionate relationship uniting three of Spain's most creative geniuses of the twentieth century. It was a relationship lived with extraordinary intensity and at high speed. Reading the accounts by Buñuel and Dalí one can see how, in retrospect, linear time was blotted out, leaving in the memory only a chronologically jumbled mosaic of luminous incidents. One is reminded of a remark made by Picasso to Gertrude Stein: 'You forget that when we were young an awful lot happened in a year.'[60]

A Visit from King Alfonso XIII and Other Entertainments

The young Dalí felt intense scorn for Alfonso XIII, as his adolescent diaries show. So when it was announced that on 3 March 1923 the King was to visit the Special School of Painting, Sculpture and Engraving to inaugurate the new library he decided to act. His fellow-student Josep Rigol was roped in, and wrote later:

> Dalí, who was very anti-monarchist, said to me quite seriously: 'We're going to put a bomb under him.' Since I was used to his ways I replied: 'Right, let's do it. But how do we make it?' 'Very simple,' Salvador explained. 'We get an empty milk tin, fill it with powder, push in a wick—and that's it.' 'And where do we get the powder?' I insisted. 'That's easy,' he replied. 'I'll buy some cartridges in a gun shop, because it's going to be a protest bomb, not a killer.'
>
> The king had to go up a big staircase. Along the bannister there were some stone urns, and we put the bomb in one of them. At the right moment we lit the fuse, but the contraption didn't go off. No one ever knew a thing about our failed attempt; it was a great secret between Dalí and me. If the bomb had been discovered, he and I, 'the Catalans', would immediately have been accused, because we were the ones who organized all the protests. In the assembly room Dalí ended up fighting a monarchist student, who criticized him for mocking the king.[61]

How accurate this account is we cannot say, although there is some independent corroboration from another student, Cristino Mallo, one of Dalí's best friends at the time. He claimed sixty years later that Salvador and Rigol had flaunted red ribbons in their buttonholes during the visit (emblem of Marxism) and addressed each other across the hall in vociferous Catalan.[62]

In Dalí's lengthy re-elaboration of the King's visit in the *Secret Life* there is no mention of the bomb attempt. He recalls one incident in particular:

> When the inspection was over preparations were made for taking group pictures with the King. An armchair was ordered for the King to sit in, but instead he seated himself on the floor with the most irresistibly natural movement. Thereupon he took the butt of the cigarette he had been smoking, wedged it between his thumb and forefinger and gave it a flick, making it describe a perfect curve and fall exactly into the hole of a spittoon standing more than two metres away. An outburst of friendly laughter greeted this gesture, a peculiar and characteristic stunt of the 'Chulos'—that is, the common people of Madrid. It was a graceful way of flattering the feelings of the students, and especially of the domestics who were present. They had seen executed to perfection a 'feat' which was familiar to them and which they would not have dared to perform in the presence of the professors or of the well-bred young gentlemen.[63]

Alfonso XIII was renowned for this sort of gesture, so it may well be that the 'chulo' exploit recorded by Dalí really occurred. But what are we to make of the commentary that follows?:

> It was at this precise moment that I had proof that the King had singled me out among all the others. No sooner had the cigarette dropped into the hole of the spittoon than the King cast a quick glance at me, with the obvious idea of observing my reaction. But there was something more in this incisive glance; there was something like the fear lest someone discovered the flattery he had just proffered to the people—and this someone could be none other than I. I blushed, and when the King looked at me again he must necessarily have noticed it.
>
> After the picture-taking, the King bade each one of us goodbye. I was the last to shake his hand, but I was also the only one who bowed with respect in doing so, even going to the extent of placing one knee on the ground. When I raised my head I perceived a faint quiver of emotion pass across his famous Bourbon lower lip. There could be no doubt that we recognized each other![64]

There is *every* doubt about whether Alfonso XIII 'recognized' Dalí. But none about the impact he made that afternoon on the student who for days had been plotting to scare him with a makeshift bomb. March 23, 1923 marks the beginning of Dalí's gradual conversion to monarchism, and he would never tire in later life of recalling the King's visit and, in particular, his impressive 'feat' with the cigarette butt.[65]

It was at about this time that Luis Buñuel (who loathed Alfonso XIII) founded his 'Noble Order of Toledo', a city for which he had developed an overriding passion. Buñuel insisted that the idea of the Order had come to him in a vision, and was determined that his friends should enrol. Among the co-founders were Lorca, his brother Francisco and Pepín Bello. Buñuel appointed himself Grand Master, naturally. The other members were assigned to categories ranging from Knights to Squires and, most menial of all, the 'Guests of the Guests of the Squires'. Dalí was a Knight; the painter Manuel Angeles Ortiz and the poet José María Hinojosa were Squires; and Buñuel named José Moreno Villa 'Head of the Guests of the Squires'. The qualifications for admission to the Order were minimal: one simply had to love Toledo unconditionally and get drunk there for at least one whole night, wandering up and down the steep, narrow streets celebrated in so many works of Spanish literature. Anyone with the pathetic habit of going to bed early could never hope to rise above the level of abject squiredom.[66]

Buñuel had been fascinated since childhood by disguises, as had Lorca and Dalí, and his and their enthusiasm was contagious. The members of the Order would appear in Toledo in the most varied and at times outrageous garb. Buñuel indulged to the full his compulsive need to masquerade as a priest (a need that never abandoned him entirely), and Dalí could always be relied on to cut a flamboyant figure on their visits to the ancient city. There are some amusing photographs of these expeditions, which continued over several years. One, taken on 18 January 1925, just before Buñuel left for Paris, shows Dalí with his habitual pipe (which he never lit) and the smart haircut he now favoured, his shoulder-length bohemian locks and sideburns having been discarded not long after his arrival in Madrid. In the picture with Dalí and Buñuel are Pepín Bello, José Moreno Villa, José María Hinojosa, Juan Vicéns and his effervescent fiancée, María Luisa González. María Luisa, who was training to be a librarian, had become extremely friendly, through Vicéns, with Buñuel, Dalí and Lorca, and was a frequent visitor to the 'Resi'. She recalled years later that the historian Américo Castro often lent them his house in Toledo for weekends. Dalí, she said, was always tremendously entertaining on these outings.[67]

The poet Rafael Alberti, who also belonged to the Order, has recalled that in the inn they frequented at Toledo, the Venta del Aire (which still exists today), Dalí did a mural of the principal members which, according to one version, was removed after the civil war by a group of Americans, perhaps on the painter's instructions. It has never been heard of since.[68]

If Dalí was entertaining in Toledo, he was also in his element when he, Lorca, Buñuel and José Bello dropped in on the smart Rector's Club at the Palace Hotel, which had become all the rage thanks to the arrival in Madrid of The Jackson Brothers, a black jazzband from New York.[69] Dalí was soon a fervent jazz fan, and part of his allowance, like Buñuel's, went on the latest records. In the *Secret Life* he recalls the mad nights at the Palace, the copious libations, the beautiful women. Their friendship with the members of the band became so close that Dalí designed a backdrop for the group repre-

José María Hinojosa, Dalí, Luis Buñuel, María Luisa González, José Moreno Villa and Pepín Bello in Toledo, probably 1924.

senting, he told his family, 'The Paradise of the Blacks' (*El paraíso de los negros*), a title Lorca later appropriated for one of his New York poems.[70]

Dalí got swept up in the Charleston craze, too, and became a considerable performer, taking lessons in Cadaqués. He also mastered the difficult art of the tango. Such was the friends' passion for jazz that Buñuel tried to persuade Alberto Jiménez Fraud, head of the Residencia, to allow the Jacksons to give a concert in the hostel. But Jiménez refused: the music was incompatible with the spirit of a house where not even dogs were allowed lest they barked at night and disturbed the scholars at their books.[71]

Jiménez Fraud was right to be on his guard, for the Madrid version of the Roaring Twenties was something to be reckoned with. Dalí, Lorca and Buñuel enjoyed it to the full and one gets the impression that they spent few nights studying. As Dalí wrote later, they squandered the money earned by their fathers' labours with a 'limitless magnificence and generosity'.[72] A lot of it went on cafés, the establishment most frequented by the threesome being the Oriente, near Atocha station, south of the Prado. More went on the-atres, and not least on *zarzuelas*, the popular Spanish operettas for which Madrid, partic-ularly, is celebrated. One of these, *Pharaoh's Court*, a witty reworking of the story of Joseph and Potiphar's wife, greatly amused Dalí and Lorca. Potiphar has just returned from a victorious campaign in Syria and, unknown to everyone, has been badly wounded in the testicles by an arrow. He is understandably horrified when the Pharaoh insists on marrying him there and then to the beautiful and passionate Lota ('Just what I need!' he mumbles in an aside). After a wedding night spent listening to Potiphar's stories about the war and nothing else, Lota decides that he's not the man for her and turns her attentions to Joseph. The latter, true to the Biblical source, is sexy but honourable, and refuses to succumb. His *double-entendre* song about tumescence and detumescence always sends audiences into fits of laughter:

Cuando te miro el cogote,	When I look at the nape of your neck,
el nacimiento del pelo,	where your hair begins to grow,
se me sube, se me sube, se me baja	my blood rushes up, up, and then down
la sangre por todo el cuerpo . . .	throughout my whole body . . .

Decades later Dalí promised to take Amanda Lear to see *Pharaoh's Court* in Barcelona, recalling with nostalgia his student days in Madrid; and in 1979 he performed a rendering of Joseph's song during an interview on Spanish television. Lorca, he said, considered it 'sublime'.[73]

Rustication Unwarranted

Dalí, despite the fun and games in Toledo and his discovery of nocturnal Madrid, worked hard during his first year at the Special School, so hard that he did not even concoct an excuse for returning to Figueres in May 1923 to take part in the annual spring festival, the Fires i Festes. Instead he sent a lyrical piece to *Empordà Federal* in which he evoked the delights of an event that he was now missing for the first time. The imagery owed an obvious debt to Ramón Gómez de la Serna's *greguerías*.[74]

A month or so later Dalí passed his end-of-session examinations in 'Perspective', 'Anatomy' and 'Statue Drawing', won a prize in 'History of Art (Antiquity and the Middle Ages)' and only fluffed in 'Modelling'. Considering that he was also engaged in his own personal struggle as a creative artist, the results were more than acceptable. During the year, both in Madrid and at home for the Christmas and Easter holidays, he had painted as assiduously as usual, his work developing along two simultaneous, but quite different, lines. On the one hand he had continued to experiment with Cubism and its derivations, influenced principally by Juan Gris and the Italian 'Metaphysicals' (the latter he knew from the review *Valori Plastici*); on the other, he had produced paintings and drawings in a more 'realistic' mode inspired mainly by his sister Anna Maria, who was to be the subject of more than twelve portraits done between 1923 and 1926.[75] When he settled back into his studio at Cadaqués in the summer of 1923, Dalí must have felt that his first year in Madrid had gone according to plan. But his academic career was about to suffer a temporary setback.

The summer holidays over, Dalí returned to Madrid to retake the examination in 'Modelling', and passed.[76] On 29 September, installed again at the Residencia, he signed up for the subjects he wanted to study during his second year at the Special School: 'Preparatory Colour Studies', 'History of Art (Modern and Contemporary Periods)', 'Still-Life Drawing' and 'Engraving on Copper' (*Grabado Calcográfico*).[77] Then something unexpected happened. The beginning of the academic year coincided with arrangements for the election of a new Professor of Open-Air Painting to succeed the previous incumbent, Joaquín Sorolla, who had died that August. There were four candidates: three virtually unknown artists called Lloréns, Zaragoza and Labrada and one, Daniel Vázquez Díaz, who had a European reputation. The works submitted by the four in support of their applications were on exhibition to the public for several weeks before the election. The press showed interest in the matter, and the students were in no doubt that only Vázquez Díaz deserved the appointment. In this they were strongly supported by *El Sol*, where, on 10 October, the art critic Francisco Alcántara said that Vázquez Díaz represented the new versus the old and should already have been appointed on his merits.[78]

The jury was composed of five members of the San Fernando Royal Academy: art historian Elías Tormo, the painters Cecilio Pla and José Moreno Carbonero, Rafael Domènech Gallissà and Enrique Simonet Lombardo. They had one vote each, so the successful candidate needed three. The election took place publicly on the evening of 17 October 1923 in the assembly hall of the Academy, packed for the occasion with journalists, the artists' friends and families, other painters and a full complement of Special School students.

The following day's newspapers reported on the uproar when the results were announced.[79] The most graphic eye-witness account, however, is Dalí's. It came, soon after the event, in a long letter to his fellow-student Josep Rigol, temporarily absent from Madrid:

> The members of the tribunal arrive. Silence, expectation. The voting by name begins. Domènech: 'I abstain!' Murmurs of disapproval. Cecilio Pla: 'Señor Vázquez Díaz!' Applause, a great ovation. Elías Tormo, the *presidente* of the tribunal: 'Señor Vázquez

Díaz!' Huge ovation. Moreno Carbonero: 'I abstain!' Uproar. Simonet: 'I abstain!' Another uproar. And Tormo announces: 'The Chair remains vacant!' A vast tumult, sticks thrown in the air, shouts, insults hurled at the tribunal, 'Long live so-and-so', 'Down with the other', din, confusion (and all the other necessary ingredients).

Tormo and Cecilio Pla received more ovations while the others fled into the Still-Life classroom and called the police, who arrived on the scene at once. I played no part in the hubbub at all because I'm a friend of Vázquez Díaz and was with him the whole time, talking about the injustice that had been done to him. If it hadn't been for this I would certainly have been among those who shouted most.

According to Dalí's account, a crowd of inquisitive *madrileños*, attracted by the din, now pushed their way in from the Calle de Alcalá to see what was up. The police were booed, and only when they threatened to charge did the throng disperse. After the fracas the students went to the offices of several newspapers to give their version of what had happened and to hand in an explanatory note, which was published the following morning.[80]

In his letter to Rigol, Dalí says that the students voiced their protest as a body, spontaneously, with no question of there having been any particular ringleaders or preconceived plan of action. But this was not the view of the Special School authorities. The following day Dalí and other students were summoned before a disciplinary committee solely because, Dalí informed Rigol, 'our ideas had always been known to them'. Dalí was interrogated by the director, Miguel Blay, who told him that there were rumours that he had been one of the principal participants in the protest. Dalí denied the charge, adducing his reasons, and said that, if they could come up with proof he would abide by the results. But there was no proof. Blay then asked Dalí to give the names of the main ringleaders. Dalí said he did not know who they were and that, even if he did, he would not split on his companions. He was not a common informer. The latter remark caused 'great irritation to all of them'. Finally, according to Dalí, Blay asked him if he had any personal interest in the outcome of the election and he replied: 'In my view nobody is entitled to interfere with my opinions. But in this instance, yes, I was in favour of Vázquez Díaz, and to my credit.' He was then asked to leave.

That evening, Salvador continued informing Rigol, he learnt that he and five other companions had been sent down for a year. The promised support was not forthcoming next morning from the students as a whole, cowed into submission by Blay's threat that if they failed to return to class there would be reprisals. Outside the School, one of the rusticated victims, Calatayud Sanjuan, punched Rafael Domènech, who had abstained in the voting. 'It was the only thing to do,' writes Dalí. Later he and his fellow-victims

went to lodge a formal complaint at the Ministry of Public Education, the body ultimately responsible for the School.[81]

Dalí's suspension was confirmed in an official communication to him dated 22
October 1923. Not only was he sent down for a year but the letter stated explicitly that
he could not present himself for the end-of-session examinations in the subjects for
which he had enrolled in September. This meant that he would have to repeat the entire
year in 1924–5 if he wished to continue at the School. It was a harsh and unjust sentence.[82]

Dalí's father, convinced that his son was innocent of the charges laid against him, took
advantage of a trip to Madrid for other purposes to carry out his own enquiry. The
director, Miguel Blay, told him that Salvador was 'a Bolchevik in art'. Dalí *père* also
talked to a selection of students, teachers and even janitors. Cristino Mallo recalled Don
Salvador's visit clearly. True to his irascible temperament, the notary had grasped one
of the teachers by the lapels and nearly hit him.[83] He reached the conclusion that the person most to blame for what had happened was Rafael Domènech, whom he considered
was suffering from a persecution mania.[84] He then drew up a petition attributed to
Salvador which was sent to the Ministry of Public Education. It was dated Figueres, 21
November 1923, and read:

> The undersigned student at the Special School of Painting, Sculpture and Painting has
> been punished arbitrarily and unjustly by a disciplinary committee.
>
> My excellent behaviour, both at Figueres Instituto during my *bachillerato* and at the
> Special School itself, could enable me to obtain, in accordance with the Royal Order of 3
> June 1909, a remission or modification of the punishment imposed on me if the latter were
> fair. But since the punishment is unjust I am not allowed to benefit from the Order's dis-
> positions because Article 10 requires as an indispensable condition for the granting of
> such a remission by the Ministry that, in asking for it, one should frankly admit the jus-
> tice of the punishment imposed upon one, something I am utterly unable to do since such
> acceptance is incompatible with my conviction of absolute innocence.
>
> From what I have said it is clear that the Royal Order in question gives guilty parties
> the necessary machinery to enable them to have their punishment reduced and even
> waived, whereas it does not provide the innocent with any means of voicing their claims.
> It is for this reason that, since the law does not give me the necessary means of defence,
> I have no option but to accept with resignation a punishment imposed arbitrarily. It is
> my wish that what has happened to me may serve to bring about the modification of the
> said Royal Order so that in future the innocent may not have fewer rights than the
> guilty.[85]

Dalí's father included a copy of this eminently reasonable document with a curt letter, dated 23 November 1923, addressed to Miguel Blay:

> Dear Sir. Having spoken to the students, teachers and other employees at the School I have arrived at a conclusion completely favourable to my son. Since we cannot possibly agree with the decision of the Disciplinary Committee we have no option but to accept the punishment with resignation and wait until next September in order to re-enrol our son. The latter's behaviour and application will be so impeccable from that moment until the end of his degree course that you will have cause to regret having punished him so severely.[86]

As for Dalí's later versions of what happened during the election furore, he claimed in the *Secret Life* that when the verdict was announced he simply rose and left the hall discreetly before the president of the jury had finished his speech. According to Dalí, the student outcry occurred after he had left and was in no way inspired by his departure. This account seems less accurate than the one he gave in his letter to Josep Rigol shortly after the event.[87]

We know from the letter that immediately Dalí's rustication was confirmed he returned to Figueres. We are largely in the dark about his activities back home, however, because both *Alt Empordà* and *Empordà Federal*, our main sources of information for the cultural and political life of the town, had been shut down after General Primo de Rivera's successful *coup d'état* that September (a *coup* accepted by King Alfonso XIII, which initiated seven years of moderate military dictatorship), while there seems to be no complete extant file of the conservative paper *La Veu de l'Empordà*, which might have provided some insights. We do know, however, that during these months Dalí re-established contact with his art teacher at the Instituto, Juan Núñez, and asked him to coach him in engraving, a procedure which now fascinated him. His father bought him a press, which was installed in the apartment, and Núñez would come round in the afternoons. Dalí claimed later that thanks to Núñez he was soon 'familiar with all the techniques and had even devised some of my own'. There is only one documented survivor of these experiments: the etching of the head of a young woman, signed and printed by Dalí in 1924.[88]

It appears that at some point during his rustication Salvador travelled back to Madrid where, according to one source, he enrolled at a private art school, the Academia Libre, run by the Catalan painter Julio Moisés Fernández. But no information about this period has come to light.[89]

Whatever Dalí Cusí's assurances to Miguel Blay about his son's future conduct, Salvador was now determined to take his revenge on the Special School and its teachers, for whom his scorn was boundless. In this he knew he was supported by many friends and admirers including the influential theatre director and critic Cipriano Rivas Cherif, who in March 1924 published an article called 'The Case of Salvador Dalí' in one of the country's leading intellectual journals, *España* (which Dalí had been reading since at least October 1919).[90] Dalí, he wrote, had played no part in the disturbances at the School. But he was an 'undesirable' and, as such, had attracted the ire of his conventional teachers. 'Perhaps with their harsh treatment they will help to test the tenacity of an artist whose vocation is to create free of impediments,' suggested Rivas Cherif. In this he was right on target.[91]

A Spell in Prison

On 15 May 1924 King Alfonso XIII paid an official visit to Girona and, after lunch, suddenly decided to inspect the large garrison at nearby Figueres. According to a note in *Abc*, the Madrid monarchist daily, Figueres, despite its reputation as 'the cradle of federalism', produced a mass turnout and gave the King the warmest welcome he had so far received in Catalunya.[92]

This is hardly likely to have been the case. Alfonso XIII had never been popular in the town and was even less so now that he was supporting the Primo de Rivera dictatorship. The authorities had been thrown into consternation by the announcement of the King's imminent arrival, and, fearing disturbances, had hurriedly consulted their lists of potential trouble-makers, some of whom were taken into custody.

After the King's visit the round-up continued. Among those arrested were Dalí, who was placed in solitary confinement in Figueres on 21 May,[93] and two of his closest friends, the militant Communists Martí Vilanova and Jaume Miravitlles.[94] Dalí was transferred to Girona gaol on 30 May and held there until 11 June, when he was released by the military judge without charges being preferred.[95]

The prison records do not state the reason for Dalí's arrest.[96] It appears that it was mainly intended to intimidate his father, who in April 1923, a few months before the Primo de Rivera coup, had initiated legal proceedings in connection with an electoral fraud perpetrated by the Right in Figueres.[97] Not easily put off, the stubborn notary had continued to press charges under the dictatorship, to the great irritation of the latter's representatives in the province. On the return of democracy in 1931 Dalí Cusí was to swear that, when subjected to an interrogation in Figueres police station, he had seen a list of the names of people 'intensely liable to cause public disorder' prominently displayed on a cupboard door. It was headed by his son. According to the notary, before Salvador was arrested the Civil Guard (Spain's paramilitary rural police force) had searched his rooms in the family apartment, finding nothing incriminating. Dalí Cusí also asserted that the Civil Governor of Girona, maximum provincial representative of the Madrid Government, had told him that if he dropped his electoral fraud charges his son would be freed. That the Right had decided to punish the father through the son seems beyond doubt, therefore, although Dalí's Marxist and anti-monarchist history were well known to the local authorities, who may have remembered that, while at the Instituto, he had been accused of participating in the burning of a Spanish flag (unjustly, according to Dalí's account in the *Secret Life*).[98]

Dalí exploited to the maximum the honour of having been a prisoner of the Primo de Rivera dictatorship, notorious for its hostility towards Catalunya, and until the end of his days would enjoy recalling his time behind bars. In his version of events the three weeks soon became a month, and the restrictions of prison life were remembered as an agreeable stimulus to the imagination. In Girona he had been fêted by the genuine political prisoners and their friends; when he made fun of the military authorities they had shaved off his hair (which Martí Vilanova kept so that one day he could make those responsible swallow it); and when he was let out he was received as a hero and given 'a veritable ovation' in the streets of Figueres (given the press censorship it is impossible to know if this was true or not).[99] Dalí must have revelled in his growing fame that summer in Cadaqués. And even more so in the prospect of returning in triumph to Madrid and re-enrolling at the Special School. He did so in September 1924, signing up for the four subjects that his unfair rustication had prevented him from studying the previous academic year.[100]

Dalí was now beginning to shed some of his timidity, enough at any rate to enable him to take part in a send-up Residencia de Estudiantes production, by Luis Buñuel, of Zorrilla's *Don Juan Tenorio*, a play traditionally performed throughout Spain on All Souls Night. Buñuel's version was called *The Profanation of Don Juan*. He himself played the protagonist, characteristically, and Dalí that of his rival, Don Luis. No contemporary account of the evening seems to have survived, but there is a photograph. Thirty years later Dalí was to design the sets for an important commercial production of *Don Juan Tenorio* in Madrid, and all his life he would enjoy reciting lines from the famous play; as for Buñuel, there are poignant allusions to *Don Juan* in his filmography. Since Lorca had taken part in an earlier version of Buñuel's production, there was that complicity, too. Zorrilla's play was yet another strand in the dense fabric of the threesome's complex relationship.[101]

The Epiphany of Freud and the Shadow of Maldoror

In the spring of 1922, some four months before Dalí's arrival in Madrid, the publishing house Biblioteca Nueva had begun to bring out the Complete Works of Freud in Spanish translation, thanks in no small measure to the interest and support of the philosopher José Ortega y Gasset, one of the country's few readers of Freud in the original German. Such was the impact of the first volumes that Ortega's *Revista de Occidente* (Spain's leading intellectual journal, radically European in outlook as its name implied) was able to refer in October 1923 to the 'greed' with which Freud was currently being 'devoured' in Spain.[102] Freud himself expressed surprise that a Madrid publisher should be the first in the world to embark on the difficult enterprise of producing his complete works in another language. On 7 May 1923 he wrote to the translator, Luis López-Ballesteros y de Torres, explaining that he had taught himself Spanish as a young student because he wanted to read Don Quixote in the tongue of Cervantes. Thus he felt competent to judge these versions. He thought them excellent: the interpretation of his thinking was extremely accurate, the style elegant. The feat seemed to him all the more admirable as López Ballesteros was neither a doctor nor a psychiatrist.[103]

By the time Dalí enrolled at the Special School in September 1922, Biblioteca Nueva had brought out the first two volumes of the *Complete Works: The Psychopathology of Everyday Life*, published in May 1922,[104] and, shortly afterwards, a volume entitled *A Sexual Theory and Other Essays*, which contained *Three Essays on Sexuality, Five Lectures on Psycho-Analysis*, 'On Dreams' and 'Beyond the Pleasure Principle'.

José Ruiz-Castillo Franco, the owner of Biblioteca Nueva, was a good friend of the Residencia de Estudiantes. But even had this not been the case these volumes would soon have been read closely by that civilized and enquiring community, defined above all by its intellectual curiosity, and one of whose members, Gonzalo R. Lafora, was perhaps Spain's first practising psychoanalyst.[105]

Luis Buñuel was among those who 'devoured' Freud at this time, and in his memoirs he refers to the impression made on him by *The Psychopathology of Everyday Life*. 'Freud and the discovery of the unconscious meant a great deal to me when I was young,' he concedes laconically.[106] It may be that Buñuel had read the book before Dalí arrived at the Residencia, and that he talked to him about it and encouraged him to read it for himself. At all events, Dalí had no sooner set foot in Madrid than he immersed himself in Freud, as José Moreno Villa recalled in 1944.[107]

The second volume in the series made an even greater impact at the Residencia, particularly *Three Essays on Sexuality*, the work which, in the opinion of James Strachey, translator of the Standard Edition of Freud in English, stands with *The Interpretation of Dreams* as Freud's 'most important contribution to human knowledge'.[108] Since their appearance in 1905, the three essays had gradually been convincing the West not only to acknowledge the existence of infantile sexuality but its survival in the so-called sexual perversions. And there was growing readiness to accept Freud's thesis that mental illness in general has sexual roots that reach back to childhood. It is not surprising, therefore, given the intellectual vitality of Madrid at the time, that the essays' publication in Spanish was perceived as an event of major cultural importance.

This second volume of the *Complete Works* included 'On Dreams', and put into Spanish circulation a series of Freudian concepts commonplace today but then extremely novel: the distinction between *latent* and *manifest* content; the role of *repression* (*censorship*) in transforming disturbing material into symbols; the mechanisms of *displacement* and *condensation*; and, above all, Freud's cogently argued conviction that dreams, whatever their appearance to the contrary, are almost always an expression of wish-fulfilment, of our (mainly unconfessed) desires.

The addition to the volume of 'Beyond the Pleasure Principle', first published in German only two years earlier, gave Spanish readers an early opportunity to assess the reasoning on which Freud based another conviction, namely that the psyche always struggles to affirm the 'pleasure principle' in the face of the 'reality principle' (the postponement of pleasure in the interests of conservation, safety, duty and so forth).

In his autobiographical writings Dalí gives the impression that at the Residencia he only read *The Interpretation of Dreams*, which was not published until 1924.[109] The work, he writes in the *Secret Life*, 'presented itself to me as one of the capital discoveries in my life, and I was seized with a real vice of self-interpretation, not only of my dreams but of everything that happened to me, however accidental it might seem at first glance'.[110] Since we know that Dalí acquired the Biblioteca Nueva volumes immediately on their appearance, or soon afterwards, it seems highly likely that by 1924 he was familiar with the first two. Perhaps he had also read, or at least dipped into, the volumes that followed hard on their heels in 1923: *Jokes and their Relation to the Unconscious* and *Introductory Lectures on Psycho-Analysis*.[111] During the 1920s Dalí read and re-read Freud incessantly, and many passages in his copy of *The Interpretation of Dreams* are underlined. If Ramon Pichot's Impressionism had dazzled him in 1916 with the force of a revelation, changing his way of looking at nature, Freud revolutionized his attitude to himself and to society.[112]

The Biblioteca Nueva's edition of *The Interpretation of Dreams* appeared not long before the publication, in October 1924, of André Breton's *Manifesto of Surrealism*.[113] In December this was intelligently analysed in the *Revista de Occidente*, where its indebtedness to Freud was heavily underscored.[114] Dalí must surely have seen the article, given the extent to which Ortega y Gasset's journal was read and discussed at the Residencia, and probably read the manifesto itself soon afterwards. By early 1925, at all events, he was both indulging in an orgy of Freud-orientated self-analysis (with therapeutic aspirations, one assumes) and beginning to become aware of the movement initiated by André Breton. It would be several years before the full impact of either Freud or Breton became apparent in his work, however; and the realization that his peculiar gifts as a painter could be enlisted in the service of the unconscious came only gradually.

At about this time another author affected Dalí almost deeply as Freud, and stimulated him in his search for inner liberation: Isidore Ducasse, self-styled Comte de Lautréamont, whose *The Songs of Maldoror* (*Les Chants de Maldoror*) was one of Surrealism's most revered sources. Born in Montevideo in 1846, Ducasse had died sick and impoverished in Paris in 1870 at the age of thirty-four, a year after the publication of his book.[115] The latter made no mark on the reading public and was only rescued from oblivion fifty years later when, in 1920, it was reprinted with a preface by Rémy de Gourmont.[116] As for Ducasse's *Poésies*, the only known copy of which was the one preserved in the Bibliothèque Nationale, Breton reprinted it in the journal *Littérature* in 1919, and in 1920 it too was reissued in book form.[117] Overnight Lautréamont became an avant-garde cult figure in Paris, and Breton referred to him in his 1922 lecture in Barcelona as perhaps the most liberating force on the contemporary poetic imagination.[118] 'For us, from the outset', he ratified thirty years later, 'there was no genius that could hold a candle to Lautréamont. We felt that a great sign of the times resided in the fact that his hour still hadn't come, whereas for us it was indisputably here.'[119]

The 'rediscovery' of Lautréamont was noted in Madrid, where once again it was Biblioteca Nueva that took the initiative, bringing out a translation of *The Songs of Maldoror* by Julio Gómez de la Serna with an enthusiastic and well-informed introduction by the latter's famous brother, Ramón, who, in 1909, had been the first person to publish extracts from the book in Spain.[120] The prologue reveals Gómez de la Serna's deep reverence for Ducasse: for his courage, his dignity, his radical scepticism, his rebellion against the Old Testament God and his horror at man's inhumanity to man; also for the extraordinary originality of his literary style and inventiveness. Ramón's apostrophe to Lautréamont gives us the measure of his admiration:

We need to let the immense energy of your songs make us capable of a scepticism preg-nant with that dignity which is your hallmark. Your terrible, insistent pride—this is the quality that can bring peace and order to mankind. We all need to be as proud as you: it would mean that no one would take anything from anyone else, that everyone would live as independently as possible, discovering the means, without servility or conspiration, of living out of his own resources. This way, even if people's station was humble, it would be *their* station, prepared by them, and they too could be proud.

Your song, so verbally profuse, so personal, holds no dangers. On the contrary, it pre-pares the way for a personal ethic that despises evil, laziness, hypocrisy and stupid vanity, and promotes the maturity of the decent individual, conscious of his aim in life, who never interferes with his neighbour, does not despise him gratuitously and does not steal from him. Out of scorn for such a proceeding you refused to take anything from anyone. You respected their possessions and for this reason despised the thought of appropriating them. This made you original in a world where the proud man actually betrays pride, that is, lives at the expense of others or by stealing.

In his prologue Gómez de la Serna refers to an enthusiastic appraisal of Lautréamont by the great Nicaraguan poet Rubén Darío, so much admired by Dalí and his friends at Figueres Instituto. The piece was included in Darío's book *Los raros* (*The Characters* or *The Odd Ones*), published in 1896, a collection of pen-portraits of bohemian and 'deca-dent' French writers, mainly late nineteenth-century, that included Camille Mauclair, Leconte de Lisle, Paul Verlaine, Villiers de l'Isle Adam, Jean Richepin, Rachilde and, for good measure, a couple of foreigners: Edgar Allan Poe and the Portuguese Eugenio de Castro. Thirty years before the Surrealists discovered Ducasse's remarkable similes, Darío had been struck by his comparison of an adolescent boy's beauty to that of 'the fortuitous meeting on a dissecting table of a sewing machine and an umbrella', and of that of a beetle's to 'the trembling of an alcoholic's hands'.

Federico García Lorca, who like Dalí had been a fervent Darío enthusiast during his youth, possessed a copy of *Los raros* and had drawn on its Lautréamont piece in his first book, *Impressions and Landscapes* (1918), evoking at second-hand the weird barking of dogs at the moon described by Ducasse.[121] It may be that Dalí, too, knew *Los raros* and had come across Lautréamont there. If not, perhaps Lorca told him about the book. But what seems certain is that he read Julio Gómez de la Serna's translation of *The Songs of Maldoror* while at the Residencia de Estudiantes (where José Bello, encouraged by the poet Rafael Alberti, borrowed José Moreno Villa's copy),[122] and that in his mind Lorca, the tempter, came to be inseparably associated with the book's eponymous and rebel-lious hero. 'The shadow of Maldoror was then hovering over my life,' Dalí writes enigmatically in the *Secret Life*, 'and it was just at this period that for the duration of an eclipse precisely another shadow, that of Federico García Lorca, came and darkened the virginal originality of my spirit and my flesh.'[123]

By early 1925 Lorca was becoming increasingly fascinated by the painter. Dalí must have found himself in a quandary, for, if he was hugely flattered by his attentions, he had a ferocious resistence to admitting the possibility that he, too, might be homosexual, or might have homosexual leanings, and may have felt that if their friendship went any further he was in danger of succumbing. For the moment, however, there was no question of cutting Maldoror-Lorca off. On the contrary, Dalí positively encouraged the poet by inviting him to accompany him during Holy Week to Cadaqués. A fortnight before they set off, Salvador touched Eduardo Marquina, his 'protector' in Madrid, for the loan of a hundred pesetas to enable him, Federico and other friends to make the season's 'last visit' to the snow peaks of the Guadarrama mountains, north of Madrid. That rite duly celebrated, he and Lorca boarded a train for Catalunya.[124]

With Lorca in Cadaqués

In 1925 Holy Week began on 5 April. A few days earlier, Salvador Dalí Cusí, his wife Catalina and Anna Maria travelled down to Cadaqués to prepare the house at Es Llané, shut up since the previous summer, for the arrival of their special guest. The sun shone and the Pení Mountain and the shoreline were an explosion of aromatic herbs and wild flowers. The taxi bringing Salvador and Lorca from Figueres puttered down into Cadaqués at midday and within minutes Anna Maria, now seventeen, was intrigued by the poet, who was at his most voluble and charismatic. Lunch was served on the eucalyptus-shaded terrace at the edge of the beach, a few yards from the sea. 'By the time we got to the dessert,' Anna Maria recalled, 'we were such good friends that it was as though we had always known one another.'[125]

Lorca was delighted with Cadaqués, the Holy Week processions and confectionery, the fabulous Baroque retable of the parish church, Dalí's family and the local people. Among the latter there was a remarkable crackpot called Lídia Noguer, whose mother, Dolors Sabà (known as 'la Sab-ana'), was reputed to have been a witch.[126] Lídia had inherited her mother's talent for oracular pronouncements, had a very expressive face with protruding eyeballs that, according to Anna Maria, gave her the appearance of a crab, and spiced her conversation with strange metaphors.[127] Like Don Quixote, Lídia appeared perfectly sane when discussing most subjects but would suddenly become lunatic if anyone touched on

Lorca with Dalí at Es Llané, Cadaqués, 1927.

Another photograph with Lorca from the same summer.

one of her obsessions. Of indeterminate age but probably about fifty when Lorca met her, she had kept a boarding house as a young woman in Cadaqués. It was there that Picasso and Fernande had stayed in 1910 when they visited Ramon Pichot. A slightly earlier guest had been the writer and art critic Eugenio d'Ors, then an adolescent, for whom Lídia conceived a passion that remained with her until her death in 1946. When her mind went, perhaps as a result of losing her fisherman husband, Nando, who was drowned in a storm, her always vivid imagination, freed from the constraints of reason, blossomed extravagantly, and she convinced herself that she was none other than Teresa, the stately Catalan protagonist of a famous book by d'Ors, *La ben plantada* (*The Well-Planted One*), published in 1911. Lídia came to believe, moreover, that d'Ors communicated with her regularly, between the lines, in his column in a Barcelona newspaper, which she perused avidly and glossed in the letters with which she bombarded the famous writer.[128] Dalí, for whom Cadaqués was the most paranoiac-intensive spot on the Mediterranean[129] and who by 1925 had probably discovered that his grandfather Gal had committed suicide under the influence of paranoiac delusions, could not fail to be fascinated:

Lídia possessed the most marvellously paranoiac brain aside from my own that I have ever known. She was capable of establishing completely coherent relations between any subject whatsoever and her obsession of the moment, with sublime disregard of everything else, and with a choice of detail and a play of wit so subtle and so calculatingly resourceful that it was often difficult not to agree with her on questions which one knew to be utterly absurd. She would interpret d'Ors's articles as she went along with such felicitous discoveries of coincidence and plays on words that one could not fail to wonder at the bewildering imaginative violence with which the paranoiac spirit can project the image of our inner world upon the outer world, no matter where or in what form or on what pretext. The most unbelievable coincidences would arise in the course of this amorous correspondence, which I have several times used as a model for my own writings.[130]

The passage suggests strongly that Dalí's famous 'paranoiac-critical method', developed after he had committed himself to Surrealism, owed more than a little to Lídia Noguer; and there is a photograph confirming the pleasure with which he would listen to her elucubrations on the terrace at Es Llané. Another photograph, a portrait of Lídia, is even more interesting, for on the back she has written: 'This woman is the the witch responsible for the whole business of Dalí and a lot more besides.'[131] As for Lorca, he was so enthralled by the strange creature that Dalí later dedicated a poem, 'Fish Pursued by a Bunch of Grapes', to 'a conversation between Federico and Lídia'.[132]

Lorca, needing little encouragement, read his as yet unstaged play *Mariana Pineda* to the Dalís and some selected friends. Anna Maria records that she was in tears when he finished and her father radiant with enthusiasm. As for Salvador, he wore a triumphant look on his face which meant 'What did you expect?'[133]

Utterly at home with his hosts and by now hopelessly involved with Salvador, Lorca unfolded during his brief stay the rich tapestry of his many and varied tal-

Dalí with Lídia in Cadaqués, c.1927.

ents. There were impromptu poetry recitals, anecdotes, mimicry, tricks, turns on the piano at the Pichots' summer quarters around the corner, Es Sortell, and even the occasional bout of sulks for good measure. Dalí's family were soon unconditional fans.[134]

Salvador badly wanted Lorca to see Cape Creus, and arranged a boat trip. It produced in the poet, terrified as he was of drowning, a mixture of delight and apprehension, and later, writing to Anna Maria, he recalled 'the very real danger of shipwreck' they had run, and the delicious rabbit, seasoned with salt and *sand*, they had consumed on the beach at Tudela beneath the rock known as the Eagle.[135]

Lorca enjoyed Cadaqués's Holy Week festivities, guzzling the delicious traditional sweetmeats produced for the occasion and following the processions. On one of the days Dalí took him to Girona to see the Easter ceremonies for which the cathedral is renowned. As for the lush landscape of the Upper Empordà, Lorca said that, after his native plain of Granada, he had seen no more beautiful place in all Spain. Dalí also took him to the famous Greek and Roman ruins at Empúries, the ancient trading port that gives the region its name. These Lorca found fascinating, especially a large mosaic representing the sacrifice of Iphigenia, which immediately inspired him to write something on the subject.

At the end of Holy Week the Dalís returned to Figueres, where the notary arranged for Lorca to give a second reading of *Mariana Pineda* and a poetry recital. Both were a great hit. As a last gesture of appreciation, Don Salvador hosted a performance of *sardanas* in the Rambla for the poet's benefit. It was the first time Lorca had seen Catalunya's national dance, and he was impressed. Then, the festivities over, Federico and Dalí set off for Barcelona, where they stayed for a couple of days with Anselm Domènech before returning to Madrid.[136]

Surrealism in Madrid and 'The Ibéricos'

Lorca and Dalí just missed the lecture on Surrealism given by Louis Aragon at the Residencia de Estudiantes on 18 April 1925. They must have received a full account of it from their friends there, however, perhaps from Alberto Jiménez Fraud himself, and may even have read it, for it was normal practice for visiting speakers to present a copy of their talks to the warden. At all events, key excerpts from the lecture were published shortly afterwards, in the June 1925 issue of *La Révolution Surréaliste*, which almost certainly reached the Residencia.

Aragon, using the 'insolent tone', which, as he explained to his audience, he enjoyed

employing on such occasions, had launched a ferocious attack against contemporary
Western society, against 'the great intellectual powers (universities, religions, governments) which divide out the world among themselves and separate the individual from
himself at infancy, in accordance with a sinister, pre-established plan'. He assured his listeners that 'the old Christian era' was over, and that he had come to Madrid to preach
the good news of the advent of Surrealism, 'the arrival of a new spirit of rebellion, a spirit determined to attack everything':

> We shall awaken everywhere the germs of confusion and unease. We are the agitators of
> the spirit. All barricades are valid, all barriers against your accursed pleasures. Jews, leave
> your ghettos! Starve the people, so that they know at last the taste of the bread of hunger!
> Move yourself, India of the thousand arms, great legendary Brahma! It is your turn,
> Egypt! And let the drug traffickers hurl themselves at our terrified countries. Let far-off
> America crumble under the weight of her buildings amidst her absurd prohibitions.
> Rebel, world! Look how dry the ground is, how ready for the fire! Like straw, one might
> say.[137]

It seems that no Madrid newspaper reported on, or reproduced extracts from,
Aragon's lecture, which had been delivered in French (as had Breton's a few years earlier in Barcelona). Nonetheless, the fact could not be denied: Surrealism, in the person
of one of its fiercest advocates, had made its debut in the Spanish capital—and a fittingly provocative one at that (for good measure, according to Buñuel, Aragon
shocked Alberto Jiménez Fraud by enquiring if there were any interesting urinals in
town).[138] The fact that the event had taken place at the Residencia de Estudiantes
proved once again that the hostel was the leading centre of contemporary culture in
Spain.

Aragon's visit coincided with the setting up in Madrid of a new association called the
Sociedad Ibérica de Artistas, the word 'Ibérica' pointing to the inclusion of Portugal. In
their manifesto, signed among others by Manuel de Falla, Daniel Vázquez Díaz, the
music critic Adolfo Salazar, Lorca and Guillermo de Torre, the 'Ibéricos' explained that
the main drive behind the founding of the Society was the lack of a modern art forum
in the Spanish capital where painters of different tendencies could show their work and
feel themselves accepted.[139]

On 27 May 1925 the association's inaugural exhibition opened at the Palacio de
Velázquez, in Madrid's Retiro Park. In the photograph of the occasion published on the
front cover of *Abc*, a coy Dalí stands beside Eugenio d'Ors, Eduardo Marquina, the

Minister of Education and Fine Arts and the sculptor Victorio Macho. Marquina's attendance in what appears to have been an official capacity can probably be best explained by the fact that the show included two rooms dedicated to the work of his brother-in-law Ramon Pichot, who had just died in Paris, to the consternation of his great friend Picasso.[140]

Before the exhibition opened, some of the more loudly iconoclastic 'Ibéricos' distributed leaflets setting out their objectives.[141] In view of its scathing attack on the Royal Academy of San Fernando and its School, one of these has been attributed to Dalí:

> The undersigned artists, all of us currently exhibiting at the Artistas Ibéricos Salon, wish to state:
> 1. That we are stimulated by effort and deadened by the good will of the public.
> 2. That we loathe official painting.
> 3. And understand it perfectly.
> 4. That we consider Valencian painting horrible.
> 5. That we respect and find marvellous the paintings of the great masters: Raphael, Rembrandt, Ingres, etc.
> 6. That it would appear that those who show most disrespect towards classical art are precisely the people in the Academy of San Fernando, since they are beginning to get all worked up about their discovery of the early French Impressionists, falsified by the incomprehension of the Valencian painters who, like Muñoz Degrain, now amaze the Academy. For our part we believe that few people have done more damage to the young than Sorolla and those who followed him.
> 7. That we admire our own age and the painters of our age and wish our works to be an expression of our admiration for: Derain, Picasso, Matisse, Braque, Juan Gris, Severini, Picabia, Chirico, Soffici, Lhote, Kisling, Gleizes, Léger, Ozenfant, Togores, Friesz, etc.[142]

José Moreno Villa was one of the more than forty 'Ibéricos' on show, and wrote profusely in the press about the exhibition. While this was eclectic, Moreno Villa noted that the vocabulary used by his fellow-artists to refer to their work was extremely homogeneous. There was much talk of 'dense, stable colour' or 'dumb, compact colour', of 'well-worked material', of 'plasticity' (or 'plastic value'), of 'weight', 'volume', 'clarity', 'carefully calculated rhythms' and 'lineal sensibility'. Nobody apparently even considered the possibility of paintings *meaning* anything: paintings did not *mean*, they were solidly constructed objects in their own right, and that was that. Spanish art, Moreno Villa felt sure, had entered a new era.[143]

The show launched Dalí triumphantly in Madrid. He exhibited eleven works, seven in his Cubist mode and four—*Bather* (1924), *Portrait of Luis Buñuel* (1924), *Seated Girl Seen from Behind* (1924) and *Female Nude* (1925)—in his more 'realistic'.[144] Of the Cubist paintings, one in particular, *Still Life* (1924)—also known as *Syphon and Bottle of Rum*—riveted the attention of public and critics alike. It owed an obvious debt to the Italian 'Metaphysicals', particularly Morandi, whose work Salvador had first admired in *Valori Plastici*.[145] Not everyone approved of the painting, though. 'It represents a meal after it's been eaten,' observed the satirical review *Buen Humor*. 'The pears left over were too green to be consumed—consult the painting; and if there's only half a bottle left it's because they drank the rest.' Lorca sent the cutting to Dalí, who had returned to Catalunya, with the comment: 'My impression is that the author is Manuel Abril. It's not the least bit funny.'[146]

Lorca sitting proudly under Dalí's Still Life *(Syphon and Bottle of Rum). See colour plate V.*

Another of the Cubist paintings on exhibition, *Portrait* (1923–4), almost certainly marks the first appearance of Lorca in Dalí's work, and shows him giving a reading at the Residencia de Estudiantes. Since Lorca was arguably the person who was following Dalí's Cubist adventure most closely at the time, the painting can be viewed not only as a tribute to the poet but to the understanding critic.[147] Some months later Dalí went a step further and gave Lorca *Female Nude* and *Syphon and Bottle of Rum*, and there is a splendid photograph of the poet sitting proudly under the latter.

José Moreno Villa knew Dalí, the man and his work, better than any other critic in Madrid, thanks to the fact that they both lived at the Residencia de Estudiantes, and he left his readers in no doubt that the Catalan was the most original artist in the entire exhibition. More than a Figueres man, he wrote, Dalí was a product of Cadaqués, where before him Picasso and Derain had executed Cubist works. Given this circumstance,

Dalí could not escape being 'a partisan of the architectonic, constructivist and formal tendency in painting'.[148]

Several other leading critics praised Dalí's work. Manuel Abril, to whom Lorca attributed the satirical article in *Buen Humor*, probably incorrectly, noted Dalí's two tendencies (his alternation of Cubist and more 'realistic' modes), pointing out that they were strictly contemporaneous. In *Syphon and Bottle of Rum*, he wrote, 'painting's musical construction achieves all its limpid exactitude and its triumphant harmony'.[149] Dalí must have been delighted with the accolade from Eugenio d'Ors, probably the most celebrated authority on art in the country; and, where international reaction was concerned, by a brief mention from the Hispanist Jean Cassou in the *Mercure de France*, who termed him and Benjamín Palencia 'esprits clairs, bons géomètres'.[150]

Salvador's success in Madrid was duly reported by the Barcelona, Girona and Figueres papers.[151] His father was pleased, but it did not stop him from writing at about this time to one of his son's teachers at the Special School, the painter Cecilio Pla, to enquire about his academic progress. Pla replied that Salvador was a good pupil, adding euphemistically 'but he tends not always to turn up at class'.[152]

Such non-attendance did not seem to matter. Dalí sailed through his end-of-year examinations, doing excellently in 'Preparatory Colour Studies' and 'History of Art (Modern and Contemporary Periods)' and passing in 'Still-Life Drawing' and 'Engraving'.[153]

Dalmau

During the summer, Lorca and Dalí corresponded profusely, and the poet, now busily at work on an ode to his friend, tried desperately to persuade him to visit Granada. To no avail. Dalí had been invited by Josep Dalmau to hold a one-man exhibition in his famous gallery that autumn, and was painting in a frenzy. Nothing could be allowed to stand in the way, not even the *Book of Putrid Pigs* he and Lorca were planning.[154]

Dalí and his friends in Figueres had applied the term *putrefacte* to the town's philistines. The word also existed in Spanish (*putrefacto*), and, probably due to Dalí's influence, now became current at the Residencia to designate whatever was considered conventional, bourgeois, out-of-date or artistically fetid. Dalí depicted *putrefactos* in a wide variety of shapes and sizes, his witty drawings of the species being much celebrated at the 'Resi'. 'Some wore scarfs, coughed a lot and sat alone on street benches,' the poet Rafael Alberti recalled:

Others were elegant, with a flower in their buttonholes, carried a stick and were accompanied by a little *beasty*. There were Academy-member *putrefactos*, and *putrefactos* who were putrid without being in the Academy. They came in all genders—masculine, feminine, neuter and epicene. And were of all ages.[155]

With rare exceptions, the teachers at the Royal Academy of San Fernando were undoubtedly *putrefactos*, and by this stage Dalí was heartily sick of them. His forthcoming exhibition at Dalmau seemed like a good excuse for not returning to the Special School for the 1925–6 session. His father agreed on the condition that Salvador use the year to get his compulsory military service out of the way. In September, just before the autumn term began, Dalí Cusí informed the School why his son would not be re-enrolling for the forthcoming session. Salvador, he explained, would be a 'free student' during the year, preparing himself privately in Figueres and registering again in the spring of 1926 in order to take his examinations.[156]

As things turned out Dalí did not begin his military service that autumn as planned. Nonetheless he made no effort to return to Madrid for the 1925–6 session. Free of the Special School, he first devoted the tremendous energy at his command to the business of ensuring that his exhibition at the Dalmau Gallery was a huge success. In this he was stimulated by the encouraging postcards he was receiving from friends in Paris, including Buñuel, José María Hinojosa and Juan Vicéns, who, with his wife María Luisa González, was in the process of setting up a Spanish bookshop in the French capital.[157]

Dalí's Dalmau exhibition ran from 14 to 27 November. Twenty-two works (seventeen paintings and five drawings) were on show, one from 1917, three from 1924 and eighteen from 1925. That the young artist had been working very hard indeed was evident. Anna Maria Dalí, of whom there were eight portraits, was a dominant presence in the exhibition, while Don Salvador,

Un àpet en aquestos temps?

Dalí, Un àpet en aquestos temps? *('An Appetite at Times Like These?'). Original and dimensions unknown. Dalí cartoon of a 'putrescent' family, done in the mid-1920s. Published anonymously in* L'hora, *Barcelona, 6 November 1931.*

with his massive bulk, also confronted the visitor. The exquisitely printed catalogue included three strategically placed quotations from Ingres, whom Dalí had admired since first encountering his work in Gowans's Art Books as a child.[158] The quotations, extracted from the French painter's *Pensées*—at this time one of Dalí's bedside books[159]—elevated Ingres to the status of tutelary genius of the exhibition. The first, perhaps chosen to justify the influences visible in the show (Picasso, Morandi, Ingres himself), was: 'Whoever only wants to draw on his own inner world will soon be reduced to the most miserable of all imitations, that of his own works'. The second, adduced perhaps as a disguised tribute to Dalí's drawing teacher at the Christian Brothers, who had insisted on his pupils 'not going over the line', read: 'Drawing is the probity of art'. The third, which can certainly be applied to the

Dalí's ally Josep Dalmau, of Galeries Dalmau fame, by the cartoonist Luis Bagaría, c.1910–20.

portraits of Anna Maria, was similarly dogmatic: 'Beautiful forms are flat planes with curves. Beautiful forms are those which have firmness and plenitude, where small detail does not conflict with large masses.'[160]

The exhibition was a triumph both critically and commercially, as Dalí hastened to inform Lorca, sending him the only adverse review he had seen with the remark 'the others are so unconditionally enthusiastic that they're of no interest', and adding that he'd even been given a celebratory banquet (held at the Hotel España in Barcelona on 21 November and followed on 5 December by another in Figueres).[161] Among the most admired paintings were *Syphon and Bottle of Rum*, first exhibited at the 'Ibéricos' show in Madrid a few months earlier and which Dalí was soon to give to Lorca, the splendid *Venus and Sailor (Homage to Salvat-Papasseit)*, and *Figure at a Window*, in which Anna Maria, seen from behind, contemplates from the dining-room window at Es Llané the waves rippling the surface of Cadaqués Bay. As yet there was no trace of Surrealism.[162]

V
VI

In the *Secret Life* and his later autobiographical writings Dalí claimed that Picasso had dropped in on the show and been much taken with 'the painting of the girl's back' (presumably *Figure at a Window*), praising it when he returned to Paris.[163] But there is no proof that Picasso saw the exhibition, or was even in the city that fortnight. Moreover, since Dalí, if not physically on the premises for the duration of the show, was readily to hand, it is inconceivable that, had Picasso put in an appearance and expressed approval, he would not immediately have rushed to meet him, extracting the maximum publicity from the occasion and recalling it profusely afterwards.

The flood of reviews provoked by the exhibition made Dalí's father decide to stick all the cuttings about Salvador's blossoming career into a book, so that a full record of his progress would remain for posterity. On the last day of the year Dalí Cusí wrote an elaborate preface to the album. It tells us a great deal about the notary's strengths and weaknesses—and shows what a formidable problem he constituted for his son:

Salvador Dalí Domènech, Apprentice Painter

After twenty-one years of cares, anxieties and great efforts I am at last able to see my son almost in a position to face life's necessities and to provide for himself. A father's duties are not so easy as is sometimes believed. He is constantly called upon to make certain concessions, and there are moments when these concessions and compromises sweep away almost entirely the plans he has formed and the illusions he has nourished. We, his parents, did not wish our son to dedicate himself to art, a calling for which he seems to have shown great aptitude since his childhood.

I continue to believe that art should not be a means of earning a livelihood, that it should be solely a relaxation for the spirit to which one may devote oneself when the leisure moments of one's manner of life allow one to do so. Moreover we, his parents, were convinced of the difficulty of his reaching the preeminent place in art which is achieved only by true heroes conquering all obstacles and reverses. We knew the bitterness, the sorrows and the despair of those who fail. And it was for these reasons that we did all we could to urge our son to exercise a liberal, scientific or even literary profession. At the moment when our son finished his baccalaureate studies, we were already convinced of the futility of turning him to any other profession than that of a painter, the only one which he has genuinely and steadfastly felt to be his vocation. I do not believe that I have the right to oppose such a decided vocation, especially as it was necessary to take into consideration that my boy would have wasted his time in any other discipline or study, because of the 'intellectual laziness' from which he suffered as soon as he was drawn out of the circle of his predilections.

When this point was reached, I proposed to my son a compromise: that he should attend the Special School of Painting, Sculpture and Engraving in Madrid, that he should take all the courses that would be necessary for him to obtain the official title of professor of art, and that once he had completed his studies he should take the competitive examination in order to be able to use his title of professor in an official pedagogical centre, thus securing an income that would provide him with all the indispensable necessities of life and at the same time permit him to devote himself to art as much as he liked during the free hours which his teaching duties left him. In this way I would have the assurance that he would never lack the means of subsistence, while at the same time the door that would enable him to exercise his artist's gifts would not be closed to him. On the contrary, he would be able to do this without risking the economic disaster which makes the life of the unsuccessful man even more bitter.

This is the point we have now reached! *I* have kept my word, making assurance for my son that he shall not lack anything that might be needed for his artistic and professional education. The effort which this has implied for me is very great, if it be considered that I do not possess a personal fortune, either great or small, and that I have to meet all my obligations with the sole honourable and honest gain of my profession, which is that of a notary, and that this gain, like that of all notaryships in Figueres, is a modest one. For the moment my son continues to perform his duties at the School, meeting a few obstacles for which I hold the pupil less responsible than the detestable organization of our centres of culture. But the official progress of his work is good. My son has already finished two complete courses and won two prizes, one for History of Art and the other for General Apprenticeship in Colour Painting. I say his 'official progress', for the boy might do better than he does as a 'student of the School', but the passion which he feels for painting distracts him from his official studies more than it should. He spends most of his hours painting pictures of his own which he sends to exhibitions after careful selection. The success he has won by his paintings is much greater than I myself could ever have believed possible. But, as I have already mentioned, I should prefer such success to come later, after he had finished his studies and found a position as a professor. For then there would no longer be any danger that my son's promise would not be fulfilled.

In spite of all that I have said, I should not be telling the truth if I were to deny that my boy's present successes please me, for if it should happen that my son would not be able to win an appointment to a professorship, I am told that the artistic orientation he is following is not completely erroneous, and that however badly all this should turn out, whatever else he might take up would definitely be an even greater disaster, since my son has a gift for painting, and only for painting.

This album contains the collection of all I have seen published in the press about my son's works during the time of his apprenticeship as a painter. It also contains other documents relating to incidents that have occurred in the School, and to his imprisonment, which might have an interest as enabling one to judge my son as a citizen, that is to say, as a man. I am collecting, and shall continue to collect, everything that mentions him, whether it be good or bad, as long as I have knowledge of it. From the reading of all the contents something may be learned of my son's value as an artist and a citizen. Let him who has the patience to read everything judge him with impartiality.[164]

On the face of it, Don Salvador Dalí Cusí's preference for his son's academic success over his precocious fame as a freelance artist seemed reasonable enough. Events, however, were soon to overtake all such considerations.

Paris at Last

In January 1926 one of Spain's most progressive newspapers, the *Heraldo de Madrid*, mounted an exhibition of modern Catalan art in the newly inaugurated Fine Arts Club (Círculo de Bellas Artes) in the Calle de Alcalá, just off the Puerta del Sol. Dalí sent two pictures, both of which had been seen for the first time a few months earlier at his Dalmau Gallery one-man show in Barcelona: *Figure at a Window*, featuring his sister Anna Maria and *Venus and Sailor*. The latter excited great interest, provoked a telegram of congratulation from Lorca and was bought by the painter Daniel Vázquez Díaz (the inadvertent cause of Dalí's rustication in 1923).[165] Cipriano Rivas Cherif, who had supported Dalí against the Special School in the journal *España* in 1924, made much of *Venus and Sailor* in an article. 'Salvador Dalí knows what he is doing,' he ended his piece. 'And he knows his classics. God protect his sight and preserve him.'[166]

There is no evidence that Dalí travelled across from Figueres for the exhibition. His mind was firmly set these days on Barcelona and Paris, particularly the latter, not least because Luis Buñuel, now taking his first steps in the film world, was urging him to visit.[167] Salvador needed little encouragement. In mid-March he was immersed in Raymond Radiguet's novel, *Count Orgel's Ball*, and communicated his excitement to Lorca. Set against the backdrop of Dalí's subsequent life, and his obsession with the aristocracy, there seems little doubt that the coruscating *roman à clef* stimulated his growing determination to conquer Paris and penetrate the upper reaches of French society.[168]

By this time, moreover, Dalí had put the case for a Parisian trip successfully to his father, for on 14 March 1926 Josep Dalmau gave him two letters of recommendation:

VI

one for Max Jacob and the other for no less a personage than André Breton. The letters confirm the great importance of Dalmau as a link between the Parisian avant-garde and Barcelona.[169]

There could be no question of the notary public's allowing his son to travel alone to France: he might get lost, he might mislay his money, he might get run over crossing the street—anything could happen, since Salvador, as everyone knew, had no practical sense whatsoever. It seemed a very good idea for him to see the Louvre, however: this Dalí Cusí could not deny; and with his customary decisiveness he now ordained that, during the Easter holidays, his wife and Anna Maria should accompany Salvador on a brief visit to the French capital.

The excited little band boarded their train in Figueres on 11 April 1926. To meet them at the station in Paris was Luis Buñuel, probably accompanied by the painter Manuel Ángeles Ortiz, Lorca's close friend from Granada, who had been in the French capital since 1922.[170] Aware that Ortiz enjoyed privileged access to Picasso, whose Cubist work he followed closely—too closely, in Dalí's opinion[171]—the latter had persuaded Lorca to write to him in advance of the trip and ask him to arrange an audience with the great man. Ortiz had duly obliged.[172] When Dali arrived at the artist's apartment in the Rue de la Boëtie, with *Girl from Figueres*, of which he was extremely proud,[173] under his arm, he was as deeply moved, he tells us in the *Secret Life*, as if about to be received by the Pope:

Dalí with his uncle Anselm Domènech in front of Large Harlequin and Small Bottle of Rum. *Dated Cadaqués 1925 by Luis Buñuel.*

VII

> 'I have come to see you,' I said, 'before visiting the Louvre.'
> 'You're quite right,' he answered.[174]

Dali's awe was understandable, given his vast admiration for Picasso and his desire to emulate him. In the same, all too brief, account he claims that the latter examined _Girl from Figueres_ carefully, but with no comment, for fifteen minutes.[175]

Once Picasso had completed his scrutiny, he devoted two hours, according to Dalí, to hauling out his own canvasses, 'going to enormous trouble'.[176] We don't know which pictures these were, but, thanks to an article published in June 1926, shortly after Dalí's visit, by Christian Zervos, editor of _Cahiers d'Art_, we can at least identify some of the paintings prominently on view in Picasso's studio at the time.[177] They included, as well as recent collages, examples of two tendencies that characterized his production from 1923 to 1926: works of classical inspiration, such as _The Three Graces_, and a host of still-lifes deriving from his Cubist period. From the work Dalí produced immediately after his visit to Paris, we can deduce that the latter deeply impressed him, in particular _Studio with Plaster Head_, now in the Museum of Modern Art, New York.

Did Picasso show Dalí _The Three Dancers_ (1925), in which, as he later explained to Roland Penrose, the gloomy face darkly outlined is that of his great friend and counsellor Ramon Pichot, who had just died?[178] Given Picasso's sorrow at the loss of Pichot, his memories of his visit to Cadaqués in 1910 and Pichot's decisive influence on Dalí, it is unlikely that the two did not refer to the dead man.

If Picasso seems soon to have forgotten all about Dalí's visit to his studio, for Salvador it was an experience of crucial and lasting importance.[179] He had now met one of his two contemporary idols—Freud would have to wait—and could boast, and did, not only that he knew Picasso personally but that the great artist approved of his work. March 1926 marks a key moment in his life.

Anna Maria Dalí, forgetting all about Picasso, later recalled that, since their 'only purpose' in Paris was to visit the Louvre, they spent hours and hours in the gallery. Leonardo da Vinci, Raphael and Ingres were the painters who most enthused her brother, she tells us: he was 'literally in ecstasy'.[180] Anna Maria forgot, too, that they also visited the Musée Grévin in the Boulevard Montmartre (Dalí's interest in the celebrated waxworks had been stimulated by a Cocteau poem, 'Tour du secteur calme'[181]) and Versailles; and overlooks the fact that Salvador's introduction to Parisian café life was almost as stimulating as his meeting with Picasso.

That life, as far as the sizeable group of Spanish artists resident in Paris was concerned, centred on the famous Montparnasse cafés La Rotonde, Le Sélect and Le Dôme, then at the pinnacle of their fame (this was the Kiki de Montparnasse era). Dalí had no sooner arrived in town than Ortiz and Buñuel took him to La Rotonde and introduced him to some of the members of the Spanish painting community. They included Hernando Viñes, Apeles Fenosa, Francisco Bores, Joaquín Peinado and another friend of

Lorca's from Granada, Ismael González de la Serna, who had done the cover design for his first book, *Impressions and Landscapes*. All of them were working under the influence of Cubism and had so far been little affected by Surrealism.[182]

This was not the case for another Paris resident, Joan Miró, Dalí's fellow Catalan, who had been closely associated with the Surrealists since 1924, when Breton's first manifesto affected him deeply. 'It changed me in the sense that I wanted to emulate its spirit,' he recalled in 1977.[183] Thus 'changed', Miró had abandoned his realistic style and begun to paint under the influence of hallucinations brought on by hunger (he was extremely poor) and by his obsessive reading of the new poetry to which the Surrealists introduced him.[184] In June 1925 he had exhibited at his dealer Pierre Loeb's Galerie Pierre, and at the end of the year took part in a collective exhibition, *La Peinture Surréaliste*, organized in the same locale.[185] By then Miró was highly considered by Breton, who wrote later that his 'tumultuous entrance' into the movement in 1924 had 'marked an important stage in the development of Surrealist art'.[186] Dalí did not meet Miró during his brief stay in Paris, but he may have seen some of his work. Only

Joan Miró, The Hunter, *1923–4, reproduced in* La Révolution Surréaliste, *Paris, no. 4, 15 July 1925. In the mid-1920s Dalí greatly admired his fellow Catalan's work, which left its mark on his own. Miró, moreover, paved the way for him in Paris.*

a month earlier, on 10 March 1926, the Galerie Surréaliste had opened at the move-ment's headquarters, 16, Rue Jacques-Callot, a tiny street at the heart of the Latin Quarter linking the Rue de Seine and Rue Mazarine and still, today, an art mecca.[187] Miró was one of the gallery's artists along with Masson, Tanguy, Chirico, Man Ray, Marcel Duchamp, Picabia, Malkine, Picasso and Ernst.[188] According to Roland Penrose, Miró's most recent paintings were always on view at this time in the Galerie Surréaliste and the Galerie Pierre (near by at 13, Rue Bonaparte).[189]

There is no proof that Dalí visited either gallery during his few days in Paris, but it is almost inconceivable, given his passionate interest in what was going on in the French capital, that he would have failed to do so. At all events, Miró must have been frequent-ly discussed in his presence by the members of the Spanish colony; and if Picasso was Dalí's great obsession, Miró, eleven rather than twenty-three years his senior, would probably have seemed like a more attainable model to emulate at this juncture. Dalí must also have been aware that Miró, a rebel like himself, had fled to Paris in 1919 after an

Joan Miró, The Harlequin's Carnaval, *1924–5, reproduced in* La Révolution Surréaliste, *Paris, no. 8, 1 December 1926. A clear precedent for Dalí's beaches in paintings such as* Honey is Sweeter than Blood.

exhibition held at Dalmau had failed to arouse the enthusiasm of the Barcelona public. And surely he must also have known of Miró's passionate attachment to his parents' farm at Montroig, near Tarragona, an attachment matched in intensity only by Dalí's obsessive love for Cadaqués. They had, then, a lot in common. Moreover, Dalí could hardly have failed to notice the four Mirós reproduced by this time in *La Révolution Surréaliste: Maternity* and *The Hunter* (more often known as *Catalan Landscape*) in the fourth issue (15 July 1925; *Tilled Land* and *The Trap* in the fifth (15 October 1925). Very shortly afterwards the influence of the Surrealist Miró would begin to make itself felt in Dalí's work, as would that of the Picassos he had seen at Rue de la Boëtie.

During his hectic visit to Paris Dalí renewed contact with his friends from Madrid, Juan Vicéns and María Luisa González, who, now married, had recently taken over the running of the León Sánchez Cuesta Spanish Bookshop, an offshoot of the parent house in Madrid. Situated at 10, Rue Gay Lussac, a few yards from the Luxembourg Garden, it became one of the main haunts of the Spanish community in the capital and in 1930 Buñuel was to immortalize its window in *L'Age d'or*. The vivacious María Luisa González was delighted to find Dalí as impractical as ever, and quite incapable of crossing the Paris streets without clinging to his stepmother's arm (a detail also recalled by Buñuel, whose recollections of Dalí's visit are disappointingly sketchy).[190]

It is likely that in Paris Dalí also saw his friend the Malaga poet José María Hinojosa, like Vicéns and María Luisa González a member of Buñuel's Order of Toledo, for whose *Poema del campo* he had provided a cover design and two illustrations the previous year. Hinojosa had just published his second book of verse, *Poesía de perfil*, illustrated by Manuel Angeles Ortiz. Whereas the earlier collection had been sprinkled with dedications to members of the 'Resi' group in Madrid, now it was the Spaniards in Paris who were singled out. The shift is indicative of the magnetic attraction that mid-twenties Paris was exerting on young Spanish writers and artists.

After their four or five days in the French capital, Dalí, Anna Maria and Catalina Domènech took a train to Brussels so that Salvador could admire the Flemish painters whose reproductions in the Gowans's Art Books series had so fired his imagination as a child. Almost certainly they also made a quick dash to Bruges. Oddly enough, there is no reference to the Belgian visit in the *Secret Life*. Anna Maria, however, remembers it in her book. The main objective, she says, was Vermeer. A few months later Dalí assured Lorca that Vermeer was 'the greatest painter there's ever been'.[191]

It was only the briefest of visits to Belgium: Pepín Bello received a card from Dalí postmarked in Brussels on 26 April and Lorca one sent two days later from Cadaqués (even in those days French trains were remarkably efficient).[192] No sooner back home,

Dalí wrote a note to his uncle Anselm in Barcelona. The trip, he reported, had been 'a success in every sense, both spiritual and material', and he had lots of things to tell him when they met again.[193]

Farewell to Madrid

Shortly afterwards Dalí was back in Madrid to re-enrol at the Special School, where in June he would have to present himself for examination in the four subjects he had been mugging up by himself as an 'unofficial student'. In the capital he coincided with Buñuel, who was on a brief visit from Paris, and Lorca. The three were photographed together in the pleasure gardens beside the River Manzanares, accompanied by José Moreno Villa and another friend from the Residencia, José Rubio Sacristán.

Ever since his visit to Cadaqués in 1925 Lorca had been at work on his 'Ode to Salvador Dalí', sending the painter excerpts with such reluctance that he was always

The last known picture of Lorca, Dalí and Buñuel together, accompanied by José Moreno Villa and José Rubio Sacristan. Madrid, in a park by the River Manzanares, 1926.

complaining.[194] The poem was published at last in the April issue of José Ortega y Gasset's *Revista de Occidente*, and was immediately recognized as an achievement of major importance.

One of the finest paeans to friendship in the Spanish language, the ode celebrates Dalí's asepsis in both art and life, praising his 'desire for an eternity with boundaries' and noting the determination of this 'hygienic soul' to flee from the 'impressionist mist' and 'the dark forest of incredible forms'. Lorca, more emotional than Dalí, was well aware of the painter's compulsive need for precision and order, of his 'love of whatever can be explained', of his 'fear of the emotion' that awaited him 'in the street':

> On taking your palette, with its bullet hole in one wing,
> you ask for the light that animates the top of the olive.
> The broad light of Minerva, the constructor of scaffolds,
> where there's no room for dreams or their inexact flora.
>
> You ask for the ancient light that lodges in the brain
> without descending to the mouth or heart.
> The light feared by Bacchus's impassioned vines
> and the uncontrolled strength of the curved water.[195]

Dalí was hugely flattered by the poem, and all the more so when that July, in *the Mercure de France*, the Hispanist Jean Cassou singled it out as an extraordinary example of what he called 'a sensibility absolutely new in Spain', resulting from the influence of contemporary French art and first registered collectively at the Salón de los Ibéricos exhibition in Madrid. As we saw, Cassou had reviewed that show enthusiastically for the same journal, singling out Dalí and Benjamín Palencia as 'esprits clairs, bons géomètres'.[196]

It was probably during May of this year that Lorca attempted to seduce Dalí, who may have been a little more complaisant now that the ode had appeared—and in such a distinguished publication. In 1955 Dalí told Alain Bosquet that the poet had tried on two occasions to sodomize him, but that nothing had happened because he, Dalí, was not a 'pederast', and, moreover, 'it hurt':

> But I was very flattered from the point of view of my personal prestige. Deep down I said to myself that he was a very great poet and that I owed him a little bit of the Divine Dalí's ar—! He ended up by using a girl, and she replaced me in the sacrifice. Not having succeeded in persuading me to put my ar— at his disposal, he swore to me that the sacrifice

exacted from the girl was compensated by his own: it was the first time he'd had intercourse with a woman.[197]

The girl, Dalí revealed in an interview in 1986, was Margarita Manso, a fellow student at the Special School. She was very slim, he said, very boyish ('with no breasts'),
very sexually liberated and fascinated by both him and Lorca.[198] Other contemporaries
were struck by the girl's attractiveness and sexual insouciance, among them Lorca's
friend, the painter and set designer Santiago Ontañón. 'She was both very pretty and
very modern,' he recalled in 1987, 'and in those days that made her doubly interesting.'[199]

Margarita Manso's file at the Special School shows that she was born in Valladolid in
1908 and lived with her parents in Madrid, where her mother was a dressmaker. She
entered the School in the autumn of 1925, aged fifteen, and stayed until the end of the
1926–7 session, passing all her subjects with no great distinction. When Dalí met her
is not clear, but May 1926 is the most likely date since, as we know, he was not in Madrid

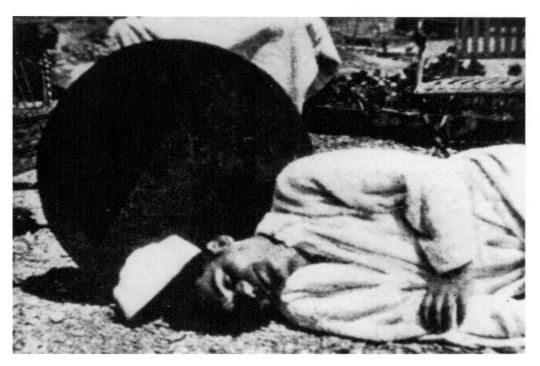

*Lorca playing dead on the Dalís' terrace at Es Llané, Cadaqués, 1925 or 1927 (see colour plate VIII).
Published in the New York little magazine,* Alhambra, *1929.*

during the earlier part of the session when Margarita Manso first started to attend classes.[200]

Margarita had got to know Lorca soon after beginning at the School, perhaps through the poet's exotic boyfriend, the sculptor Emilio Aladrén, who was also a student there. With Lorca and Dalí's companion at the School, Maruja Mallo, she was involved in the launching of a new fashion 'by default', which soon caught on in Madrid. It consisted, simply, in not wearing hats (at a time when everyone did so, scrupulously). They baptized the movement *sinsombrerismo* ('nohattism'). 'People thought we were positively immoral, as if we had no clothes on, and almost attacked us in the street,' Maruja Mallo recalled in 1979, adding that she, Lorca and Margarita were always together at that time.[201]

When Dalí returned to Madrid he immediately joined forces with the *sinsombrerista* group, despite his proclivity for elegant hats. One day they decided to visit the Benedictine monastery of Santo Domingo de Silos, in Old Castile, famous for its Gregorian chant and its double Romanesque cloister. When the girls tried to enter the church, the monks intervened forcibly. 'No skirts here!' they were informed briskly. Maruja Mallo and Margarita Manso solved the problem by donning Lorca and Dalí's jackets as trousers (how this contortion was achieved the former never quite managed to explain satisfactorily) and tucking their hair under caps. Thus attired they managed to slip in without being discovered. 'It must have been the first time that transvestites-in-reverse entered Santo Domingo de Silos,' Maruja Mallo chuckled years later, wondering at the same time what had become of Margarita Manso after the civil war: she had disappeared into thin air.[202]

BOLETIN DE LA JOVEN LITERATURA

MURCIA - 1927 - ABRIL

SALVADOR DALÍ La playa

Dalí, La playa ('The Beach'), 1927. Original and dimensions unknown. Published in Verso y Prosa, Murcia, April 1927. The fused heads of Dalí and Lorca lie on the beach. Note the exposed vein on the severed hand and wrist, which recurs in many of the paintings and drawings of Dalí's 'Lorca Period'.

It seems that Dalí had the sexually charged scene with Lorca and Margarita Manso in mind when, in a letter to the poet in the summer of 1926, he wrote: 'I haven't been able to understand Margarita at all either. Was she stupid? Mad?'[203] The allusion suggests that Lorca had expressed his own bemusement in his last letter. He may have been referring to the same episode, moreover, when he framed a poem he wrote at this time, 'Backwaters' ('Remansos'), within the enigmatic, bracketed and italicized question: '(*Margarita, who am I?*)'. It appeared on the front page of the Murcia magazine *Verso y Prosa* in April 1927, accompanied, surely not accidentally, by a superb pen drawing by Dalí of his and Lorca's heads lying side by side on the shore at Cadaqués. Nor, one feels, can the relation of the poem's title, 'Remansos', to Margarita's surname, Manso, have been fortuitous.

In May 1927 Dalí alluded to Margarita Manso in a letter to Lorca, who at that time was passing through Madrid. 'Remember me to Margarita,' he wrote. 'By now she must be a big girl.'[204] A year later, when Lorca published the *Gypsy Ballads*, Dalí told him that in his opinion the poem 'Thamar and Amnon', with its 'bits of incest' and the line 'murmur of imprisoned rose', was one of the best things in the book.[205] The comment was a further allusion to their shared scene with Margarita Manso, for, as Dalí explained years later, after Lorca had made love to her he rocked her in his arms whispering in her ear the quatrain containing the line quoted—the quatrain, that is, in which Amnon, about to rape his sister, exclaims:

Thamar, en tus pechos altos	Thamar, in your firm breasts
hay dos peces que me llaman,	Are two fishes which call me,
y en la yema de tus dedos	And in the tips of your fingers
rumor de rosa encerrada.	murmur of imprisoned rose.[206]

The scene with Margarita Manso had impressed Dalí deeply. He must have noticed, moreover, that Lorca's ballad 'Muerto de amor' ('Dead from Love') was dedicated to her. In future years Dalí was to enjoy quoting the lines from this poem that evoke the weird, transforming light of the crescent moon:

Ajo de agónica plata	Garlic-clove of deathly silver,
la luna menguante, pone	The dying moon wreathes
cabelleras amarillas	yellow tresses around
a las amarillas torres.	the yellow towers.[207]

In June 1926 Dalí began his end-of-year examination at the Special School. His official progress-sheet shows that he was failed in 'Colour and Composition' and 'Moving Objects Drawn from the Natural', and did not present himself for 'Theory of the Fine Arts' or 'Study of Architectural Forms'.[208] Dalí failed in 'Colour and Composition' and 'Moving Objects Drawn from the Natural'? It seemed impossible. But behind the results starkly recorded on the form there lay an event which before long acquired mythical status.

Dalí had been summoned to appear before the examining board on 11 June to demonstrate his knowledge of 'Theory of the Fine Arts'. According to the Special School authorities, he failed to turn up, telephoning to ask permission to be examined at a 'second session'. His request was granted, the date being set for the morning of 14 June.[209] Salvador Dalí Cusí did not accept this version of events. He came to the conclusion that his son had indeed turned up on 11 June and that it was the examining board that had not materialized.[210]

The School had a hit-or-miss system of oral examinations, which were held in public. The student was required to pick out of a drum one or more numbered balls, each designating a theme relating to the subjects he had studied during the session. He was then asked to elaborate on whichever of these themes he preferred. Dalí refused to pull out the balls. According to the minutes, drawn up immediately afterwards, he said: 'No. Since all the teachers at the San Fernando School are incompetent to judge me, I'm withdrawing.' The board, understandably, was outraged.[211]

Dalí's gesture appears to have been fully premeditated, despite the account he gave later in the *Secret Life* and elsewhere.[212] His friend Josep Rigol remembered that he decked himself out for the showdown in a loud jacket with a gardenia sprouting from its buttonhole, and knocked back a large absinthe before entering the hall—for inspiration, he said, although it is more likely that he needed to generate some Dutch courage.[213] On 23 June 1926 an extraordinary meeting of the professors was convened to pronounce judgement on Dalí's behaviour. His record since entering the School was reviewed by the Director, Miguel Blay, who recalled his rustication in 1923–4 and alluded to some rumours Dalí had allegedly spread in Barcelona about being victimized by one of his teachers, Rafael Domènech. The professors quickly took the unanimous decision to expel Dalí for good. He, or in default his father, was to be informed immediately, and the expulsion order posted prominently on the School's notice-board.[214]

A letter written by Dalí to his family shortly after he had insulted not only his examiners but the entire staff at the Special School claimed that it was his outrage at having been failed in the other two subjects that had driven him to behave as he did: 'It was the only way to react with *dignity* to their rotten treatment, anything less would have been to accept an injustice, and it's completely wrong that absolutely ignorant people should dare to examine me.' The following afternoon, Salvador said, he was leaving for Barcelona. The good news was that Count Edgar Neville (a well-known Spanish writer) had commissioned a painting of the Madonna and had told him to name his price. 'So I'm rich!' Salvador ended. 'As soon as I arrive in Cadaqués I'll begin to paint.'[215] The promise cannot have been much consolation to his father, whom Dalí managed to convince over the summer, nonetheless, that once again he had been unfairly treated by the authorities.

There is a paternal postscript to Dalí's removal from the Special School. On 12 November 1926 the expulsion was confirmed officially in the *Bulletin of the Ministry of Public Education and Fine Arts*. Don Salvador pasted the decree into his album, and in seven angry pages expatiated on 'the detestable Special School of Painting, Sculpture and Engraving, of which one could well say that it is a fitting representative of our unhappy Spain'. Lack of knowledge of their own rules; gross absenteeism on the part of the teachers; fails and passes awarded arbitrarily; History of Art taught by that man Domènech, 'one of the most inept pedagogues in the whole of Spain'. As for engraving, where that art was concerned it was fortunate indeed that his son had had the excellent Juan Núñez as his teacher at the Figueres Instituto . . . in short, a disaster. Little wonder that Salvador had fallen foul of such a corrupt and detestable institution.[216]

Sixteen years later Dalí came nearer to telling the truth about his expulsion, tacitly admitting in the process that he had misled his father in the interests of his career as a painter:

> Any committee of professors, in any country in the world, would have done the same on feeling themselves insulted. The motives for my action were simple: I wanted to have done with the School of Fine Arts and with the orgiastic life of Madrid once and for all; I wanted to be forced to escape all that and come back to Figueres to work for a year, after which I would try to convince my father that my studies should be continued in Paris. Once there, with the work that I would bring, I would definitely seize power![217]

One wonders if, at this point, Dalí remembered the entry he had made in his diary in April 1920, when his father announced that after his *bachillerato* he would proceed to the Royal Academy School in Madrid. Elated at the prospect, he had foreseen that, after working 'like a madman' at the School for three years, he would continue his studies in Rome for a further four and then return to Spain a genius.[218] It had not quite worked out like that, but nor had things gone so badly. With his recent brief experience of Paris acting as a powerful stimulus, and the Special School safely behind him, Dalí now set about producing the works that would enable him to make his definitive escape to the French capital. He had the vision, the talent and the energy. But it was to require three years of intense effort to turn the dream into reality.

As for Madrid, Dalí said in 1970 that it was the city in Europe that meant most to him. 'The places Velázquez painted and the most important memories of my life—the years with Lorca, Buñuel, the *ultraístas*. For me that's Madrid,' he told a reporter.

It was perhaps one of the most sincere statements he ever made.[219]

Lorca and Saint Sebastian

In July 1926, only a few weeks after his definitive expulsion from the Royal Academy Special School, Dalí was visited by the theatre critic Melchor Fernández Almagro, a great friend of Lorca's. Fernández Almagro was surprised to find Cadaqués so isolated (it had taken him two hours to get there by car from Figueres), and much impressed by the beauty of the village and its dramatic surroundings. With Ramon Pichot dead, Dalí was now the 'official' painter of the locality, he told his readers, describing his house by the sea at Es Llané and pointing out that the girl in *Figure at a Window*, which *madrileños* had been able to admire a few months earlier, was the painter's sister. She had the 'dusky beauty of an incipient Empordanese Venus'.[1]

What Fernández Almagro could not have realized was that Anna Maria, of whom Dalí had painted at least twelve portraits since 1923, was currently being supplanted in his work by the obsessive presence of Lorca.[2] During the poet's action-crammed visit to Cadaqués in the spring of 1925 Dalí had begun some preliminary sketches for a portrait of him enacting his own death and putrefaction. This was a macabre performance Lorca used to stage in his bedroom at the Residencia de Estudiantes after, Dalí recalled, 'the most transcendental conversations on poetry that have yet taken place this century'.[3] Dalí described the ceremony in French on at least two occasions,[4] but the English of his description to the poet Gerard Malanga is more lively:

> Something completely sure about Lorca is his obsession with death. He talked about death all the time, about the death of himself—for instance, every night it was impossible for Lorca to sleep before each of his friends came to his room. I remember one morning Lorca

VI

Chapter FIVE

played dead. He said, 'This is the second day of my death,' and described 'my coffin coming in the streets of Granada', and the 'Ballet of the Death inside the Coffin'. Everybody
came and everybody is completely anguished about this mimic representation—and Lorca
laughed because of the look of terror in the face of the people and became relaxed, and very
happy, and slept very well. This was necessary every night to make a representation of his
death.[5]

VIII

On the basis of his drawings of Lorca's weird ritual, and of a photograph by Anna
Maria of the poet[6] 'acting dead' on their terrace at Es Llané in 1925, Dalí began the
painting entitled *Still Life* (*Invitation to Sleep*). Finished in 1926, it seems to have been
the first work of what Rafael Santos Torroella has termed Dalí's 'Lorca period'. The outline of Lorca's head is unmistakable, and in both the painting and photograph we find
the round table that was a permanent fixture on the terrace. Beside Lorca's head Dalí
has placed one of the *aparells*, or gadgets, which appear with frequency in his paintings
from 1926 onwards. With their central round orifice and spindly legs, suggestive of tottering, perhaps these gadgets are intended to represent the female sexuality feared by
both Lorca and Dalí. In the background, behind the poet's head and between two parallel railings that lead to a vista over the sea, there is an aeroplane—an allusion to the
precision and asepticism of the machine age, now as dear to the heart of Dalí as it had
been to the Marinetti of the Futurist Manifesto.

In the substantial series of paintings and drawings belonging to the 'Lorca period', the
poet's head is habitually fused with that of Dalí and almost always, as in this picture,
lying on a stylized version of the terrace by the sea at Es Llané.

IX

The greatest painting of Dalí's 'Lorca period' is undoubtedly *Neo-Cubist Academy*, subsequently entitled *Composition with Three Figures* (*Neo-Cubist Academy*). Acquired by the
Dalís' close friend Joaquim Cusí Fortunet when it was first exhibited in early 1927, and
still in the family, it has never again been seen in public and is not available even to
researchers. Yet this masterpiece, apart from its intrinsic beauty, is vital to an understanding of Dalí's development as an artist and of his relationship with the poet.

In Spanish art terminology the word 'academy' corresponds roughly to 'academy figure' in English and refers to a painting or drawing of a nude figure done more for the
sake of practice or instruction than as a work of art. In the case of the present work the
term probably alludes ironically to the staid Royal Academy School in Madrid from
which Dalí had just been ousted and where Cubism, 'neo' or otherwise, was still virtually unacknowledged.

Rafael Santos Torroella has shown that the composition's central figure, seen from a window of the house at Es Llané, is a sailor-version of Saint Sebastian, patron of Cadaqués. That this is so is indicated by the branch lying on the becalmed sea at his left flank (symbol of the tree to which, in some representations, he was bound by his executioners); by the fact that his right arm appears to be tied behind his back; and by the exposed vein on his left wrist, which occurs in various drawings of Saint Sebastian done by Dalí at this time.[7]

Lorca and Dalí had begun to develop a shared fascination for Saint Sebastian before Salvador was expelled from the Special School. During the summer of 1926 the poet worked on a series of three lectures on the martyr, to be illustrated with slides, and collected reproductions of paintings and sculptures that featured him. In particular, Lorca begged his friend, the poet Jorge Guillén, then in Valladolid, to get him a photograph of Pedro Berruguete's tiny sculpture of Sebastian preserved in the city's famous museum. It portrays the saint as a beautiful, languid youth uncannily like Oscar Wilde's Lord Alfred Douglas.[8] One cannot doubt that Lorca and Dalí were perfectly aware of the well-established artistic tradition which has elevated Saint Sebastian to the status of unofficial tutelar of homosexuals and sado-masochists, from the Renaissance up to our own times. In this tradition, as Cécile Beurdeley has written, it is often impossible to tell which is greater: the saint's 'sexual ambiguity' or his 'ecstatic masochism'.[9]

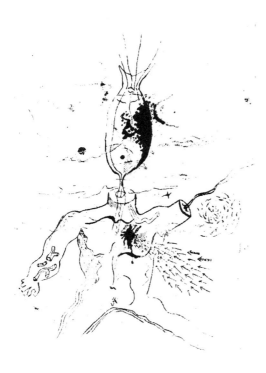

Dalí, Saint Sebastian with a sole's head, 1927. Original, title and dimensions unknown. Published in L'Amic de les Arts, Sitges, *31 July 1927. A further allusion to Lorca.*

Pondering on this predilection for Saint Sebastian on the part of homosexuals and sado-masochists, Alberto Savinio, brother of Giorgio de Chirico and an essayist admired by Dalí, concludes that, as well as the saint's youth and 'ephebe's body', there is an added lure. 'The reason why inverts are so attracted to Saint Sebastian,' he writes, 'can be found in the analogy between certain sexual details and the arrows which lacerate the naked body of the young relative of Diocletian.' The arrows, in other words, are phallic symbols.[10]

Dalí would have agreed, and so, as he probably knew, would Freud.[11] In a letter apparently written in September 1926, Dalí reminded Lorca that Saint Sebastian was the patron of Cadaqués and asked him if he had noticed that, in the representations of the martyr, there is never any suggestion that the arrows pierce his *buttocks*—a teasing allusion, surely, to anal intercourse and to the poet's attempts to possess him.[12]

The same letter shows that at this time Dalí viewed Saint Sebastian above all as an embodiment of the objectivity to which he had come to believe contemporary art should aspire. The saint's impassivity, serenity and detachment as the arrows sear his flesh are the qualities the painter was now seeking to express in his own life and work:

> Let me tell you again about Saint Objectivity, who now goes under the name of Saint Sebastian.
>
> Cadaqués is a 'sufficient fact', any attempt at transcendence would be excessive, a venial sin; excessive profundity could be even worse, it could be ecstasy. Personally I don't enjoy anything intensely, I shun whatever could send me into ecstasy, like motorcars. Ecstasy's a threat to the intelligence.
>
> Seven o'clock, when I finish painting, is when the sky performs its amazing and dangerous feats and when, instead of contemplating nature's almost always insufferable spectacle, I go for my Charleston lesson at the Salisachs; it's a most appropriate dance, impoverishing the spirit to perfection.
>
> How wonderful I feel! I'm undergoing a complete resurrection! It's marvellous no longer to feel the necessity of indulging in everything, the nightmare of being submerged in *nature*, that is, in mystery, in the imprecise, in what cannot be grasped; marvellous to be centred at last, limited to a few simple truths and preferences, clear, ordered, sufficient for my spiritual sensuality.
>
> Your professor, of course, will say: but nature also has its order, its laws, its *superior* proportions.
>
> 'Superior', dangerous word that; it means superior to *us*, an order we can't grasp, mysterious laws and proportions, and the next thing, of course, you've got religion and we're into the principles of faith and the occult and Papini fasting and wanting to write an encyclopaedia.
>
> But thank God today it's clear where art begins and where 'naturism' begins.
>
> Goethe, who was so clear-thinking, said that nature and art are two different things. Le Corbusier also knows about this—and about love, too.[13]

Lorca did not have to be reminded of the painter's terror of losing control: he was all too aware of it, as his 'Ode to Salvador Dalí' had already shown.

The painting *Composition with Three Figures (Neo-Cubist Academy)* owes a huge debt to Picasso's *Studio with Plaster Head*, which Dalí had seen when he visited the artist in Paris.[14] Many elements in Picasso's still-life—perhaps itself a gloss on Chardin's *Attributes of the Arts*[15]—passed directly into Dalí's canvas. The branch by the saint's left flank is almost identical to Picasso's; Dalí has borrowed the plaster-cast head, and the shadow it projects is so similar to Picasso's that it could almost be substituted for it; the framework around the window echoes Picasso's; both works feature pointed, elongated clouds; both, an open book; and the scroll, firmly grasped by the hand of the severed arm in the Picasso, reappears in the left hand of Dalí's Sebastian.

The scroll, though, is no longer *just* a scroll. Santos Torroella proposes a staff or scep-

Pablo Picasso, Studio with Plaster Head, *1925. Dalí saw this painting when he visited Picasso in Paris in 1926. Its influence is obvious in works such as* Composition with Three Figures *(Neo-Cubist Academy; colour plate IX).*

tre, sensing a reference to Polykleitos' *Doryphoros.*[16] But this does not explain the elliptical hole, which reminds one of an object appearing in a painting done by Dalí the previous year, *Large Harlequin and Small Bottle of Rum,* interpreted by the same critic as a portrait of Lorca. In this work, which, like *Composition with Three Figures (Neo-Cubist Academy),* is set in the Dalís's house at Es Llané and features similar, Mantegna-style clouds, the instrument lying on the floor next to the ace of hearts has the look of a simple rustic flute.[17] Perhaps Sebastian is carrying this selfsame instrument, emblem of music and poetry? And it may be significant, too, that, to the right of his head as we look at the picture, Dalí has introduced what appears to be a tuning peg. This can be read as a further allusion to Lorca who, in the earlier picture, is playing a guitar with two such pegs.

EL POETA EN LA PLATJA D'EMPÚRIES VIST PER SALVADOR DALÍ

Dalí, El poeta en la platja d'Empúries (*'The Poet on the Beach at Empúries'), 1927. Original and dimensions unknown. The poet is Lorca, who first visited the Greek and Roman remains at Empúries (Ampurias) with Dalí in 1925. Note the Dalínian flotsam and jetsam that relates the drawing to Dalí's great* Honey is Sweeter than Blood *(photograph p. 210).*

Lorca's presence in the picture becomes explicit in the plaster-cast head borrowed from Picasso, which Santos Torroella has shown represents his and Dalí's fused faces, with Dalí's in the centre and Lorca's chunkier features on the right.*

The two female figures who dominate the foreground of the painting are further evidence of the impact of Picasso's work on Dalí's art at this time, as a comparison with the substantial ladies appearing in such 'neo-classical' works of the older artist as *The Source* (1921), *Large Bather* (1921), *Women by the Sea* (1921) and *Two Women Running on the Beach* (1922) makes abundantly clear. So impressed was Dalí by the latter that he had a colour reproduction of it pinned to the wall of his studio, along with other tokens of his allegiance to Picasso.[18]

---

*Anyone sceptical about such an identification should consult Santos Torroella's seminal monograph, *La miel es más dulce que la sangre (Honey is Sweeter than Blood),* which traces the presence of the conflated heads of artist and poet in some fifty paintings and drawings of this period.

The female in the bottom-left corner of *Composition with Three Figures (Neo-Cubist Academy)* recurs in other Dalís of this period, such as *Figure on the Rocks,*[19] and belongs to the category the painter baptized crudely as trossos de cony ('bits of cunt'). The figure's see-through shift has run up to reveal the naked lower part of her ample body, the shadow that envelops the genital area heightening an eroticism further signalled by her erect nipples. It is little wonder that Santos Torroella interprets her as 'Venus, or perhaps Lust'.[20] She is gazing in the direction of the saint, her clenched fist perhaps signalling her emotion at his unexpected appearance. The head casts a dark shadow which parallels that thrown by the placid seated female immersed in her book on the right, whom Santos Torroella sees as 'Virtue, or Reflection, somewhat hieratic but very human in her self-absorption'.[21]

No analysis by Dalí of his intentions in *Composition with Three Figures (Neo-Cubist Academy)* has come to light. All we know is that he was ecstatic about the canvas, sending a photograph of it to Lorca for publication in the avant-garde Granada magazine *gallo* ('cockerel') with the comment: 'Neo-cubist academy (if you saw the real thing!) (it measures two metres by two).'[22]

The Assault on Barcelona

In October 1926 Dalí exhibited two paintings at the annual Barcelona Autumn Salon, held at the Establiments Maragall (Sala Parés): *Girl Sewing* (1925?)[23] and the recently executed *Figure on the Rocks,* which shows Anna Maria, at her most monumental and neo-classically Picassian, dozing in the sun astride the beetling cliffs of Cape Creus, her profile shadowed on her right arm and the sea glinting far below.[24]

Coinciding with the Autumn Salon, Josep Dalmau opened an ambitious show at his new premises on the Passeig de Gràcia. It was laboriously entitled Exhibition of Catalan Pictorial Modernism Compared with a Selection of Works by Foreign Avant-Garde Artists. Dalí was represented by three paintings straight from his easel: *Still Life by Moonlight, Barcelona Mannequin*—both relating to his obsession with Lorca—and an unidentified work entitled *Figure.*[25]

Dalí's paintings had been catching the eye of an up-and-coming art critic, Sebastià Gasch, a highly combative advocate of the tenets of Purism and Cubism, imbibed from Ozenfant and Jeanneret's now defunct journal, *L'Esprit Nouveau.*[26] Seven years older than Dalí (he was born in Barcelona in 1897), Gasch had published his first piece of art criticism in December 1925. In May 1926 he began a regular column in an exquisitely designed new magazine, *L'Amic de les Arts* ('The Friend of the Arts'), produced, entirely in Catalan, in the charming little town of Sitges, just south of Barcelona. In his inaugural contribution, Gasch reported the presence of a small Dalí hanging unobtrusively in a corner of Galeries Dalmau. His enthusiasm for the painting (which unfortunately he does not identify) knew no bounds:

> Salvador Dalí's picture succeeds fully in satisfying our eyes, our intelligence and our sensibility. This little masterpiece, sculptural, architectural and of classical structure, where nothing is the result of caprice, chance or intuition, whose every element is carefully organized, can only increase the solid reputation of this pure artist, now undoubtedly one of our foremost painters.[27]

Gasch had a very low opinion indeed of contemporary Catalan painting, referring in one of his articles to 'the putrescent state of our art scene'.[28] Dalí, though, was a glorious exception, and Gasch now took it upon himself to keep the public informed about his progress. In the November 1926 issue of *L'Amic de les Arts* he published a critique of the Autumn Salon at the Sala Parés, which he considered feeble in the extreme, a 'putrescent concourse'. Dalí was in another category, the star turn of the show, and Gasch enthused about *Girl Sewing*, reproducing a preparatory drawing, presumably supplied by the artist, which revealed the rigidly geometrical structure responsible for what he termed the work's 'definitive eurhythmy, its clear harmony, its perfect unity'.[29] Gasch had also dropped in on the Dalmau exhibition, finding it much superior to the Autumn Salon. The three paintings exhibited by Dalí he considered an advance on his earlier Cubism. No longer 'cold, reasoned and implacably methodized', this had given way, Gasch felt, to 'a more sensitive Cubism where instinct plays as important a role as reason, or a more important one, even; the Cubism currently being cultivated by Picasso'.[30]

In another leading art magazine, *La Gaseta de les Arts*, Gasch essayed a startling comparison between the pictorial rhythm he identified in Dalí's current production and a recent record by the Southern Syncopated Orchestra, a black American jazzband.[31] Dalí was delighted. He wrote to Gasch, whom he had not yet met in person:

> Your article in the *Gaseta de les Arts* has interested me greatly for the relationship it establishes between my painting and one of my greatest loves, jazz, that fantastic, anti-artistic music. 'Artistic'—horrible word that only serves to indicate things totally lacking in art. Artistic performance, artistic photography, artistic advertisement, artistic furniture. Horror! Horror! What we all like, on the other hand, is the *purely industrial* object, dancehalls and the quintessential poetry of Buster Keaton's hat.[32]

The letter led to the beginning of a close friendship that was to last for five years and give rise to a dense correspondence on contemporary art. Gasch's militant espousal of Cubism and Purism matched Dalí's, as did his insistence that the business of art is not to imitate nature, while his determination to *épater le bourgeois* spurred the painter to an ever greater provocativeness. His Catalan prose style, too—agile, incisive, ironic—appealed greatly to Dalí. Before long Gasch became the person who, after Lorca, meant most to Dalí—not least for the professional coverage of the painter's activities that he was only too happy to provide.

Years later, after the friendship had come to a brusque end, Gasch recalled the Dalí he had first met in 1926:

> Dalí had all the look of a 'sportsman'. He wore a jacket of brown 'homespun'—a rough, warm material—and beige trousers. The ensemble was roomy and allowed ample space for the movements of his neat body, with its muscles of steel, fibrous and flexible. It was a sort of uniform, really. Dalí never took it off when he was in Barcelona, and it emitted the stale whiff of a provincial bazaar. His hair was jet-black, very straight, stuck down with a copious dose of brillantine. The face, its skin as tightly stretched as that of a drum, as brilliant as enamelled porcelain, was brown and looked as if it had just been attended to by the make-up man in a theatre or film studio. A tiny moustache—the finest line, imperceptible at first glance, as if traced by a surgeon's knife—protected the upper lip. In that waxen child's face, hard, inexpressive and stiff, there shone, with extraordinary intensity, two minuscule, febrile, terrible, menacing eyes. Terrifying eyes, the eyes of a madman.
>
> The tone of his voice was rough and hoarse. Indeed, you would have thought he suffered from chronic hoarseness. He was loquacious in the extreme. The words gushed from a mouth which, when it smiled its sinister smile—Dalí never laughed outright, loudly—revealed little teeth sharp as cutting implements. He spoke in a hectic rush of words, but in fact what he was saying had the implacability of logic. His arguments were always solid. Everything he said was carefully articulated, coherent, cogent. He gave the impression of being a man who, after resolving with great effort a series of moral and aesthetic problems, had succeeded in evolving a very clear view indeed of things both human and divine, and was able to exteriorize them with complete clarity.

Looking back over his friendship with Dalí, Gasch went on to stress the painter's innate irony—Empordanese in origin, he believed—claiming it had appalled him by its 'incredible cruelty', at once glacial, impassive and utterly tranquil:

> The fact is that everything that Dalí said and did revealed a complete lack of heart. In him sensitivity was totally absent. He had, on the other hand, a privileged and devastatingly

lucid intelligence. In all his actions, in everything he said, and naturally in his painting, the cerebral man is the one we find to the fore.[33]

Gasch, however accurate his description of the surface Dalí, did not attempt to plumb the depths of the painter's apparent cruelty, to probe into its causes, to get to the bedrock of his personality. If he had done so, drawing more fully on the hundreds of letters he received from the artist, the biographer's task would be greatly assisted. But Gasch died without publishing more than a smattering of this correspondence, and his widow consistently refused access to researchers. When, if ever, these letters become available, they will undoubtedly greatly enhance our knowledge of the Dalí of this period.

Dalí's presence in the two Barcelona collectives held that autumn was a prelude to his second one-man exhibition at Dalmau, which ran from 31 December 1926 to 14 January 1927. Twenty-three paintings and seven drawings were on show, distributed in two sections of the gallery according to whether they belonged to the artist's 'Cubist' or 'objective' tendency.[34] The first item in the catalogue was *Composition with Three Figures (Neo-Cubist Academy)*, hung in the most prominent position and clearly intended to stand as the exhibition's *pièce de résistance*. At least three of the other works rang the changes on the fused head motif: *Still Life (Invitation to Sleep)*, *Table by the Sea* (later renamed *Homage to Eric Satie*) and *Harlequin* (subsequently known as *Amoeba Head*). It is likely that one of the three paintings entitled *Natura morta (Still-Life)*, impossible to identify with certainty, was the Lorca-inspired picture later called *Still Life by Moonlight* (1926). The inclusion of these pictures in the show is an eloquent indication of the extent to which Lorca was on Dalí's mind at the time. 'I spent a month in Barcelona for the exhibition,' he wrote to the poet in the middle of January, 'and now

SALVADOR DALÍ
AUTORRETRAT

Dalí, Autorretrat *('Self-Portrait'), 1926. Original and dimensions unknown. Published in* L'Amic de les Arts, *Sitges, 31 January 1927. Again, the fused heads of Dalí and Lorca.*

I'm happily back in Figueres with a new stock of gramophone records and an infinity of old and new things to read. And with lots of pictures *at the tips of my fingers*, not in my head.'[35]

Meanwhile, at *L'Amic de les Arts*, Sebastià Gasch had become a permanent member of staff and was busily promoting Dalí, two of whose drawings illustrated a 'Christmas Story' by J.V. Foix—soon another important ally of Dali—in the December 1926 issue. Dalí knew that he could count on Gasch to report glowingly on his Dalmau exhibition. At the end of January the magazine carried a reproduction of *Composition with Three Figures (Neo-Cubist Academy)* on its front page, announced forthcoming articles on Dalí by Gasch and another critic, Magí Cassanyes, and published an imaginative 'Introduction to Salvador Dalí' by Foix. The latter was illustrated by a drawing of the fused heads of Dalí and Lorca significantly entitled *Self-Portrait* by the painter. Foix had been much impressed by the exhibition. 'I had the absolute certainty of witnessing the exact moment of the birth of a painter,' he wrote, implying the adjective 'great'.[36]

The February issue of *L'Amic* contained Gasch's review of Dalí's show, illustrated by reproductions of *Barcelona Mannequin* and *Figures Lying on the Sand*. The whereabouts of the latter are unknown today, but, to judge from the black-and-white reproductions, the four Anna Marias prostrate on the beach made this canvas one of Dalí's most remarkable 'bits of cunt'.[37] Gasch's article was an expanded version of the comments on Dalí he had published in earlier issues of the magazine. He noted the meticulous composition of the pictures, exemplified by the triangular organization of the personages in *Composition with Three Figures (Neo-Cubist Academy)*; maintained, as he had done earlier, that Dalí's most recent work showed more feeling than had previously been the case; and suggested that perhaps Dalí was allowing himself to be too influenced by the 'neo-classical' Picasso—God, Gasch felt, had failed to provide Dalí with the profound inner life and rich instinctual nature of Picasso and Joan Miró. We do not know what Dalí made of this last, debatable, remark, although one imagines it must have irritated him.[38]

The general response of the critics to the exhibition delighted Dalí, as it did his father, who eagerly pasted the reviews into his book of cuttings, which was now swelling considerably. By the time the show closed Dalí must have felt confident that his conquest of Paris, the supreme aim of his life, was closer at hand.

Intimations of Tanguy and Miró

Meanwhile, in Paris, a remarkable young painter was giving new prestige to the Surrealist movement. Born in 1900 of Breton parents, Yves Tanguy had unexpectedly found his vocation when in 1923, peering out of a bus in the Rue de La Boëtie, he saw De Chirico's *The Child's Brain* in the window of the Paul Guillaume Gallery. At the risk of breaking his neck he had jumped off the moving vehicle and gone back to scrutinize the canvas. The painting had been loaned by its owner, André Breton, who by an extraordinary coincidence had also seen it in the same window from a bus a few years earlier. Like Tanguy, Breton had been so disturbed by the apparition that he had alighted in order to have a closer look, deciding there and then that he must own the work. If the discovery of *The Child's Brain* deeply affected Breton, it positively transformed Tanguy, who had apparently never held a paintbrush in his life. He now set to work feverishly to make up for lost time, and by 1926 was becoming one of the leading artists of the Surrealist movement.[39]

What knowledge can Dalí have possessed of Tanguy's production before painting, probably towards the end of 1926, the study for the great work so engimatically entitled *Honey is Sweeter than Blood*, done the following summer? There is no evidence that Dalí met Tanguy during the high-speed week he spent in Paris in April 1926. If, however, he visited the newly inaugurated Galerie Surréaliste, which he probably did, he would almost certainly have seen some of his work. Shortly afterwards, at all events, *The Ring of Invisibility* (1925) was reproduced in *La Révolution Surréal-iste* (no. 7, 15 June 1926), and, six months later, *Lost Animals* (no. 8, 1 December 1926).

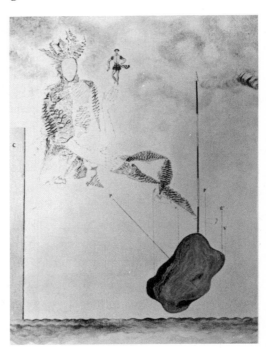

The Ring of Invisibility made a particular impact on Dalí, despite the fact that the reproduction does little justice to the original. The immense sky-scape conjured up by this picture, linked to the sea by the De Chirico-style vertical ruler on the left, may well have suggested the possibility of executing a Cadaqués version of the scene. And certainly the mysterious figures and objects populating Tanguy's sky can be related to those appearing in the study for *Honey is Sweeter than Blood*.[40]

Yves Tanguy, Ring of Invisibility, *1925. Published in* La Révolution Surréaliste, *Paris, no. 7, 15 June 1926, where Dalí certainly saw it. The skyscape and mysterious figures influenced Dalí's study for* Honey is Sweeter than Blood.

As for Tanguy's *Lost Animals*, it is difficult not to relate the stark beach (or is it a
desert?), with its clear division between
land and sky, to the spectral shore featured
in the same Dalí study. Moreover the fish
forming the head of the weird figure on
the left is strikingly similar to the one for
which the donkey reaches up in Dalí's
Gadget and Hand, finished in the summer
of 1927, and one may also be tempted to
see a connection between it and the fish-
head of Saint Sebastian in a drawing done
at this time.

Santos Torroella has argued that, in the
study for *Honey is Sweeter than Blood*, the
recumbent head lying on the line between
shore and sky is an idealized version of
Lorca's. It is difficult not to agree, given
that in the finished picture the poet's features are unmistakable.[41] As for the stark
black shadows cast by Dalí's gadgets and
assorted objects, a nod in the direction of

X

Yves Tanguy, Lost Animals, *1926, reproduced
in* La Révolution Surréaliste, *Paris, no. 8, 1
December 1926. The fish-head of the figure on
the left probably inspired that of Dalí's Saint
Sebastian (illustration on p. 187).*

De Chirico, several of whose paintings had been reproduced by this time in *La
Révolution Surréaliste*, seems undeniable: such shadows were to be one of the hallmarks
of Dalí's work from now on. Then there is the rotting donkey, the first of many to
appear in Dalí's work. It apparently derived from some childhood memories of Buñuel
and Pepín Bello that were much discussed in the Residencia de Estudiantes.[42] A few
years later Georges Bataille maintained that Dalí's putrescent donkey expressed the
painter's feeling of sexual inadequacy, the animal, 'symbol of a grotesque and powerful
sexuality', being deliberately represented as 'dead and decomposed'.[43]

The study for *Honey is Sweeter than Blood* is also of great interest for inaugurating the
presence of an object that was to recur again and again in Dalí's paintings of this period, namely the strange cylinder that lies in front of Lorca's head. Dalí claimed in *The
Tragic Myth of Millet's 'Angelus'* (1933) that it was a 'delirious image', the first that had
presented itself to him spontaneously, and that it had produced an anguish inexplicably
linked to Millet's famous painting. The apparition occurred, he wrote, when he was row-

ing furiously in Cadaqués. The image consisted of 'a white, sunlit, elongated, cylindrical form with rounded ends and several irregularities. The form was lying on the brown-violet ground. On all its circumference it bristled with little black rods suspended in every possible position, like flying walking-sticks.' Dalí, never to be trusted where dates are concerned, situated the incident in 1929; but the presence of the hallucinatory image in the study for *Honey is Sweeter than Blood* shows that it must have come to him at least three years earlier.[44]

If Tanguy's influence on the study is palpable, so too is that of Joan Miró, some of whose paintings Dalí may have seen at the Galerie Surréaliste, and five of which had been reproduced in *La Révolution Surréaliste* by December 1926, the last being *The Harlequin's Carnaval*, the product of hallucinations brought on, according to Miró, by hunger.[45] It is also possible that by this time Dalí may have seen the occasional Miró at the Dalmau Gallery in Barcelona, and his friend and ally Sebastià Gasch, who knew Miró personally, must have provided him with information about the artist. What is clear is that Miró's landscapes, with their sharp divisions between sky and earth, their meticulous detail and their crystalline light, much brighter than that of Tanguy's, greatly appealed to Dalí. Miró enjoyed painting beaches, and, like Tanguy, tended to populate both them and the sky above with a wealth of objects and creatures. Those appearing in such paintings as *The Hunter* (*Catalan Landscape*) and *The Harlequin's Carnaval* have several points in common with the study for *Honey is Sweeter than Blood*—Dalí's cones, for example, are modelled on Miró's—and even more so with the densely thronged finished picture. The disquieting sexuality and nightmarish atmosphere of both the study and the final painting, however, are all Dalí's own.

Castor and Pollux

'Today, 1 February 1927, at six in the morning, the boy went up the hill to the Castle in Figueres to begin his military service': thus an entry in Salvador Dalí Cusí's book of cuttings devoted to recording the progress of his son's career. On the face of it, nobody could have been more temperamentally unsuited to military service than 'the boy' (*el noi*), as his father was still calling him. The fact is, however, that Dalí was spared the rigours of the system: there is no record of his having had to drill, learn to fire a gun, drive a lorry or submit himself to any similar indignities. Presumably he sat around most of the day entertaining his fellow conscripts until the time came for him to go home for the night. He seems quite to have enjoyed the experience, not least, given his anal obsessions, cleaning the latrines.[46] According to one of his accounts, he even staged fits in order to be allowed off guard duty at night: 'The ruse worked, I was exempted, even when I volunteered. *My skill at deception was proving itself once again*'.[47]

At the beginning of March Dalí sent Lorca a drawing of a cockerel for the cover of the poet's projected review *Gallo*, and informed him that he was now, of all things, a soldier. 'No trips for the moment,' he wrote, 'but this summer we must spend at least three months together in Cadaqués.' Dalí was writing an 'article' on Saint Sebastian, he said, and enclosed some teasing considerations on the saint, emblem of their relationship. The letter ended (before continuing in a postscript): 'Mon cher! I want a very long letter from you . . . In my "Saint Sebastian" I think of you a lot and sometimes I think it's you . . . Let's see if it turns out that you're Saint Sebastian! . . . But for the moment let me use his name to sign this. A big hug from your SAINT SEBASTIAN.' Part of the letter is written on a kitsch greetings card of amorous intention in which a winged mermaid, the upper part of her body discreetly clothed, proffers a large bowl of fruits. Beneath the drawing are printed some lines of doggerel:

To My Beloved

If I didn't give you a sign
of my love and friendship,
in truth, my love,
I'd hardly seem attentive.
Have the goodness, therefore,
to accept my offer:
soul, life and heart.
With an unequalled affection
love wide and without end,
I only feel happy
when I can be by your side.

Dalí had modified the line 'love wide and without end', underlining 'wide' and 'without' and adding to the latter a footnote reading 'instead of *without* read *with*, signed Saint Sebastian'. These personal additions must have perplexed, and perhaps disturbed, Lorca. Was Dalí expressing his rejection of the romantic notion of love beyond death while, at the same time, suggesting that sooner or later, and perhaps sooner, their relationship would have to end since he could not submit to the poet's demands? We cannot be sure, although it seems likely that Dalí's additions, together with the bantering tone of the letter in general, were intended as a warning to Lorca not to press his claims too insistently.[48]

A second visit by the poet was now imminent. After struggling in vain for years to get his *Mariana Pineda* performed, he had finally convinced the great Catalan actress, Margarita Xirgu, to take it on. The première was to be in Barcelona that June, and Lorca immediately reminded Dalí that he had promised to design the sets. Dalí replied with some general indications and expressed the hope that he would have time to do proper drawings. He did.[49]

Lorca arrived in Barcelona at the end of April or beginning of May, and travelled up to Figueres almost at once to spend a few days with Dalí. It was the first time they had seen each other since Salvador's expulsion from the Special School almost a year before, and one can imagine the explosive energies released. Dalí, now aggressively astride his New Objectivity hobby horse, seems to have hurt Lorca somewhat with some comments about his book of poems, *Canciones* (Songs), just published. After Lorca had gone back to Barcelona to see to *Mariana Pineda*, Dalí tried to explain himself in a letter:

> Here is what I think. No previous era has ever known such perfection as ours. Until the invention of the machine there were no perfect things, and mankind had never seen anything so *beautiful* or *poetic* as a nickel-plated engine. The machine has changed everything. Our epoch, compared to others, is MORE different than the Greece of the Parthenon from Gothic. You've only got to think of the badly made and highly ugly objects produced before mechanization. We are surrounded by a new, perfect beauty, productive of new poetic states.
>
> We read Petrarch and we can see that he is the product of his period—mandolines, trees full of birds, antique curtains. He has recourse to the materials of his time. I read your 'orange and lemon' and can't sense the painted mouths of tailors' dummies.[50] I read Petrarch and, yes, I can sense those full breasts cushioned in lace.
>
> I look at Fernand Léger, Picasso, Miró, etc., and I know that there are machines and new discoveries in Natural History.
>
> Your poems are Granada without trams, with no aeroplanes yet; an antique Granada with natural elements, far removed from today, purely traditional and *constant*. Constant, of course!, I know you'll say, but the constant, or the eternal as you all call it, takes on in each period a flavour which is the flavour preferred by those of us who draw on those same constants but in a new way.

To drive his point home, Dalí, now turned poetry critic, added a postscript:

Another clarification. The epoch of the troubadours was for songs accompanied on the mandoline. Nowadays songs have to be composed for jazz and to be listened to on the *best* of all instruments: the gramophone. Our age has its own song, the only one possible in our age.[51]

How Lorca reacted to this badgering we do not know, since, with a few exceptions, his letters to Dalí have not been found. But he can hardly fail to have been impressed by the painter's critical acumen.

Shortly afterwards, Dalí, now on three months' summer leave, joined Lorca in Barcelona, where Margarita Xirgu was preparing the première of *Mariana Pineda* at the Teatro Goya. Dalí handed over his drawings for the scenery and costumes, and when he and Lorca were not supervising the sets, or attending rehearsals, they frequented the city's lively cafés with other young artists and writers.

One of these, the journalist Rafael Moragas, dropped in on the dress rehearsal of *Mariana Pineda*, and was much impressed by Dalí's contribution, which he predicted would cause a sensation.[52] In the event the scenery and costumes provoked little more than a stir of admiration when the play opened on 24 June, and a feeling, on the part of at least one critic, that their stark modernity was somewhat in conflict with the romantic tone of the work.[53] The production was successful enough to constitute a major breakthrough for Lorca, however. Margarita Xirgu undertook to perform the play around Spain during her imminent summer tour, and to open her autumn season with it in Madrid. The poet's euphoria was understandable. Dalí was delighted, too, and not just on Lorca's behalf: *Mariana Pineda* was good publicity for him as well.[54]

Lorca's elation was increased when he found he was being taken seriously as an artist by Sebastià Gasch. 'Fiery, vehement, intensely passionate, a flaming torch, Lorca makes a tremendous impression,' Gasch wrote in *L'Amic de les Arts*.[55] Like everyone who met Lorca, Gasch was amazed that any one individual could be so richly talented. Poet, playwright, raconteur, pianist and actor—it seemed impossible. But when Lorca pressed a portfolio of coloured drawings into his hands, Gasch discovered that there was still more come. He could hardly believe his eyes.[56] Gasch discovered that Lorca badly wanted to exhibit his work. Where better than at Dalmau? Given both Gasch's and Dalí's friendship with the famous gallery-owner and promoter of modern art, it seemed to Lorca that they could perhaps sound him out on his behalf. Dalmau looked at the portfolio—and gave the go-ahead. The show, composed of twenty-four coloured drawings, hardly rippled the surface of the art scene in Barcelona, but Lorca was satisfied. The exhibition served among other things as a demonstration of his friendship with Dalí, whose influence, moreover, was clearly visible in several of the drawings on display. One of them, *The Kiss*, alludes to Dalí's 'Lorca series' and is a burlesque self-portrait on which the outline of Salvador's head has been superimposed, the lips of both meeting in the kiss of the title. The shadow of Lorca's head, in red, is a direct quotation from Dalí's *Barcelona Lady* and *Still Life by Moonlight*, in both of which the painter's and Federico's heads merge; and Lorca was probably amused that the significance of the drawing must have been lost on everyone except himself and Salvador.[57] The exhibition also included at least one portrait of Dalí by Lorca. In another such portrait, almost certainly from this summer and possibly also included in the exhibition, Lorca portrayed Dalí sitting at the foot of a high tower, beneath a yellow crescent moon, wearing a white, egg-shaped cap and a white robe, his palette in his right hand (a very obviously phallic finger emerging from the hole), a little red fish affixed to the end of each finger of the other hand and, in the centre of his chest, pointing upwards, a large, red, vertical fish. 'Lorca saw me as the incarnation of life, with a hat like that of the Dioscuri. Each finger of my right hand has been converted into a fish-chromosome,' Dalí was to comment. The idea that Dalí and Lorca were twin souls, like Castor and Pollux, had evidently occurred to them.[58]

Not surprisingly, Dalí and Lorca even did some drawings together during the summer. An example is *The Bather*, now in the Salvador Dali Museum in Florida, which, although signed by Dalí, shows the obvious intervention of Lorca. Dalí was about to start writing in *L'Amic de les Arts*, and one day he and Gasch went down to Sitges with Lorca so that the poet could meet the team responsible for the magazine. In an historic group photograph taken at the station, Dalí, dressed in the loose-fitting jacket and trousers that, according to Gasch, he then wore habitually, is nonchalantly holding a magazine which, on inspection, turns out to be the June 1927 issue of the New York journal *Science and Invention*. Dalí was fascinated by the advances of technology and the increasing perfection of modern machinery, so the choice of reading matter made sense. Reading matter? Dalí had no English as yet, but the publication was liberally illustrated, and anyway it needed little effort to make out the titles of the articles: 'Television Perfected at Last' (in 1927!), ' "Metropolis"—a Movie Based on Science', 'The Month's Scientific News Illustrated', 'New Inventions in the Camera's Eye', 'Motor Hints', 'New Phonograph Pick-up', 'One-tube Radio and Cabinet' and so on. It was in character for Dalí, whose interest in science was to grow with the years, to flaunt the magazine (as he had done earlier with *L'Esprit Nouveau*). Carrying it under his arm gave him the air of a cosmopolitan dilettante and was all part of the game.

Lorca made an indelible impression in Sitges, where, at the house of the publisher and

Dalí, The Bather, *1927. Ink, 37.3 x 49.1 cm. Federico García Lorca almost certainly collaborated on the drawing during his stay with Dalí that summer in Cadaqués.*

editor of *L'Amic de les Arts*, Josep Carbonell, he improvised one of the folklore sessions for which he had become famous at the Residencia de Estudiantes, accompanying himself at the piano.[59] Among the company that day was Lluís Montanyà. Born in Barcelona in 1903, Montanyà, a self-made authority on contemporary French literature, wrote regularly for *L'Amic de les Arts*. Given his knowledge of things French, he and Dalí must have had much to talk about, not least the Surrealists, of whom Montanyà was basically dismissive, disapproving vehemently of Crevel's novel *Difficult Death* on the dubious grounds that it was overtly homosexual.[60] Montanyà, who seems not to have suspected that Lorca was gay, was as stunned by the Andalusian poet as Gasch had been shortly before him. 'Everything about him equals "South",' he rapturized in *L'Amic*, 'with his dark brown skin, his sparkling, intensely alive eyes, his thick black hair and his manner, at once cordial, vehement and energetic.'[61]

Dalí was proud of the impact that Lorca's personality and multiple gifts made on everyone he met in Catalunya, an impact celebrated in an article by Gasch in *L'Amic*. The piece went on to lament the mentality of the Little Catalaners for whom the rest of

Spain, let alone Andalusia, was a closed book, anything coming from beyond the Ebro (Catalunya's southern boundary) being considered anathema.[62] Fittingly, the same page carried a snippet about Diaghilev's production of *Romeo and Juliet*, for which Max Ernst and Joan Miró had painted the sets. When the production was put on in Barcelona, both audiences and critics had shown complete indifference.[63] It seems likely that Dalí saw it, and even met Diaghilev, for elsewhere in the review we learn that, following in Miró's footsteps, he had just been invited to design the scenery for a Ballets Russes version of *Carmen*. The project never got off the ground, but the invitation must have served as a further stimulus to Dalí's desire to achieve international fame.[64]

'Saint Sebastian'

Lorca's exhibition at Dalmau coincided with the short run of *Mariana Pineda*. When the excitement of these intense days and nights was over he settled in with the Dalís at Cadaqués, staying for the whole month of July. There were excursions, as in 1925; music, poetry and jazz records on the terrace overlooking the sea; fool-acting on the beach beyond; and, so far as Dalí at least was concerned, some hard work. Work that meant, in the first place, quickly putting the finishing touches to his prose piece 'Saint Sebastian', about which he had told Lorca back in March, saying that as he was writing it he often thought of him and even wondered if he and the saint were the same person. 'Saint Sebastian', which signalled Dalí's full arrival on the Catalan literary scene, is an imaginative exposition of his current aesthetic of Holy Objectivity and asepsia; of the rigorous avoidance of sentimentality and 'putrescence'. It owed a strong (and unacknowledged) debt to the descriptions of gadgets by one of the writers he most admired, Raymond Roussel, in *Impressions of Africa*. Not surprisingly, Dalí dedicated 'Saint Sebastian' to Lorca when it appeared in the July issue of *L'Amic de les Arts*, for the poet, as Dalí had intimated in March, appears obliquely in the text as the 'someone very well known' whose head is reminiscent of part of the saint's. A further, and equally recondite, allusion to Lorca comes in Dalí's illustration of Sebastian that accompanied the piece. It had been done recently, and showed the saint's head in the form of a flatfish. Since Dalí had referred to Lorca as a sole (*lenguado*) in recent correspondence touching on Sebastian, the implication of the flatfish head seems obvious enough.[65]

'Saint Sebastian' is such an important landmark in Dalí's life and career that no apology need be made for incorporating it in full in this narrative:

Saint Sebastian

Irony

Heraclitus, in a fragment quoted by Themistius, tells us that Nature likes to hide herself. Alberto Savinio believes that her hiding of herself is an expression of modesty. It is an ethical matter, he tells us, since this modesty derives from the relationship between Nature and Man. And in this he discovers the prime cause that engenders irony.[66]

Enriquet, the Cadaqués fisherman, told me these same things in his own language one day when, looking at a painting of mine that represented the sea, he said: 'You've caught it exactly. But it's better in the painting because one can count the waves.'[67]

Irony could also begin in such a preference, if Enriquet were capable of moving from physics to metaphysics.

Irony, as I have said, is nakedness;[68] it is the gymnast who hides behind the pain of Saint Sebastian. And it is also this pain, because it can be counted.[69]

Patience

There is a patience in Enriquet's rowing which is a wise form of inaction; but there is also a patience which is a form of passion, the humble patience in the maturation of the paintings of Vermeer of Delft, which is the same patience as that of the ripening of fruit trees.

And there is yet another form: a form between inaction and passion, between Enriquet's rowing and Van der Meer's painting, which is a form of elegance. I refer to the patience and exquisite death-throes of Saint Sebastian.

Description of the figure of Saint Sebastian

I realized that I was in Italy because of the black and white marble flagstones of the flight of stairs. I climbed them. At the end was Saint Sebastian, tied to the trunk of an old cherry tree. His feet rested on a broken capital.[70]

The more I observed his face, the odder it appeared. Nonetheless I had the impression that I had known him all my life, and the aseptic light of the morning revealed the smallest details with such clarity and purity that it was impossible for me to be uneasy.

The saint's head was divided into two parts: one was formed of a matter similar to that of a jellyfish and sustained by an extremely delicate circle of nickel; the other was occupied by half a face which reminded me of someone very well known; from the latter circle there emerged a support of very white plaster which seemed to be the dorsal column of the figure. All the arrows bore an indication of their temperature and a little inscription engraved on steel which read: *Invitation to the Coagulation of the Blood.* In certain parts of the body the veins appeared on the surface with their deep, Patinir-storm blue,[71] and effected curves of a painful voluptuousness on the pink coral of the skin.

When they arrived against the shoulders of the saint, the movements of the breeze were imprinted as if on a sensitive plate.

Trade-winds and counter-trade-winds

On touching his knees, the tenuous breezes stopped short. The martyr's halo appeared to be made of rock crystal, in whose solidified whisky there flowered a rough and bleeding starfish.

On the sand covered with shells and mica, precise instruments belonging to an unknown physics projected their explicative shadows, and offered their crystals and aluminiums to the disinfected light. A few letters drawn by Giorgio Morandi indicated: *Distilled Gadgets.*

The sea breeze

Every minute there came the smell of the sea, constructed and anatomical like the bits of a crab.

I breathed in. Nothing was mysterious any longer. The pain of Saint Sebastian was a mere pretext for an aesthetics of objectivity. I breathed in again, and this time I shut my eyes, not out of mysticism, not in order to see more clearly my inner I—as one might say, platonically—but for the simple sensuality of the physiology of my eyelids.

Later I read slowly the names of the gadgets, and the terse indications on them; each annotation was the point of departure for a whole series of intellectual delectations, and a new scale of precisions for hitherto unknown normalities.

With no previous explanations I understood intuitively the use of each of them and the joy of each of their sufficient exactitudes.

Heliometer for the deaf and dumb

One of the gadgets was labelled *Heliometer for the Deaf-and-Dumb.* The name was already an indication of its connection with astronomy, but it was above all its constitution that evidenced this. It was an instrument of high physical poetry formed by distances and by the relationships between these distances; these relationships were expressed geometrically in some of the parts, and arithmetically in others; in the centre, a simple indicating mechanism served to measure the saint's death-throes. The mechanism was composed of a small dial of graduated plaster, in the middle of which a red blood-clot, pressed between two crystals, acted as a sensitive barometer for each new wound.

In the upper part of the heliometer was Saint Sebastian's magnifying glass.

This was at once concave, convex and flat. Engraved on the platinum frame of its clean, precise crystals could be read *Invitation to Astronomy*; and beneath, in letters standing out as if in relief: *Holy Objectivity.* On a numbered crystal rod one could read further: *Measurement of the Apparent Distances between Pure Aesthetic Values* and, to one side, on a highly fragile test-tube, this subtle announcement: *Apparent Distances and Arithmetical Measurements between Pure Sensual Values.* The test-tube was half full of sea-water.

Saint Sebastian's heliometer had neither music nor voice and, in some parts, was blind. These blind spots of the gadget were those corresponding to its sensitive algebra and those intended to make concrete that which is most insubstantial and miraculous.

Invitation to astronomy

I put my eye to the magnifying glass, the product of a slow distillation at once numerical and intuitive.

Each drop of water, a number. Each drop of blood, a geometry.

I began to look. In the first place, the caress of my eyelids against the wise surface. Then I saw a succession of clear sights, perceived in such a necessary arrangement of measurements and proportions that each detail was shown to me like a simple and eurhythmic architectural organism.

On the deck of the white packet-boat a girl with no breasts was teaching sailors drenched in the south wind to dance the *black bottom*. Aboard other liners, the *Charleston* and *blues* dancers were finding Venus each morning in the bottom of their *gin cocktails*, at pre-aperitifs time.

All this was the exact opposite of vagueness, everything could be seen clearly, with a magnifying glass's clarity. When I fixed my eyes on any detail, this detail grew bigger, like a close-up in the cinema, and acquired its sharpest plastic quality.

I see the girl playing *polo* in the nickel-plated headlamp of the *Isotta Fraschini.* I direct my curiosity solely to her eye, which now occupies the maximum visual area. This one eye, suddenly enlarged and now the sole spectacle, is the whole depths and the whole surface of an ocean, in which all poetic suggestions navigate and all plastic possibilities are stabilized. Each eyelash is a new direction and a new quietude; the *mascara*, oily and sweet, forms, in its microscopic increase, precise spheres through which can be seen the Virgin of Lourdes or Giorgio de Chirico's painting *Evangelical Still-Life* (1926).[72]

When I read the tender letters of the biscuit

Supérieur
Petit Beurre
Biscuit

my eyes fill with tears.

An indicating arrow, and beneath: *Address Chirico; Towards the Limit of a Metaphysics.*

The thin line of blood is a dumb and ample plan of the underground. I don't want to continue until I reach the life of the radiant *leucocyte*. The red ramifications turn into a little stain, passing speedily through all the stages of their decrease. I see the eye restored to its original size in the depths of the concave mirror of the headlamp, like a singular organism in which swim the reflections' precise fish in their watery, lachrymal medium.

Before continuing to look, I paused again to study the details of the saint. Saint Sebastian, free of symbolisms, was a *fact* in his unique and simple presence. Only with such objectivity is it possible to observe a stellar system with calm. I renewed my heliometric viewing. I was perfectly aware that I was moving within the anti-artistic and astronomical orbit of *Movietone Fox*.

The spectacles succeed each another, simple facts giving rise to new lyrical states.

The girl in the bar plays 'Dinah'[73] on her little gramophone, while she prepares gin for the motorists: inventors of subtle mixtures of games of chance and black superstition in the mathematics of their engines.

At Portland autodrome, the racing blue Bugattis, seen from the aeroplane, acquire the dreamlike movement of hydroids which descend spiralling to the bottom of the aquarium with open parachutes.

The rhythm of Josephine Baker in slow motion coincides with the purest and slowest growth of a flower produced by the cinematographic accelerator.

Cinematographic breeze again. White gloves and black keys of Tom Mix,[74] pure as the last amorous embraces of fish; crystals and stars of Marcoussis.[75]

Adolphe Menjou,[76] in an anti-transcendental atmosphere, provides us with a new dimension of the *dinner-jacket* and of ingenuity (now only acceptable with cynicism).

Buster Keaton—here's true Pure Poetry, Paul Valéry!—post-machine-age avenues, Florida, Le Corbusier, Los Angeles. The Pulchritude and eurhythmics of the standardized implement, aseptic, anti-artistic variety shows, concrete, humble, lively, joyous, comforting clarities, to oppose to a sublime, deliquescent, bitter, putrescent art . . .

Laboratory, clinic.

The white clinic falls silent around the pure chromolithography of a lung.

Within the crystals of the glass case the chloroformed scalpel sleeps like a Sleeping Beauty in the wood of nickels and enamel, where embraces are impossible.

The American magazines offer to our eyes *Girls, Girls, Girls,*[77] and, under the sun of Antibes, Man Ray obtains the clear portrait of a magnolia, more efficacious for our flesh than the tactile creations of the Futurists.[78]

A glass case with shoes in the Grand Hotel.

Tailors' dummies. Dummies quiescent in the electric splendour of the shop windows, with their neutral mechanical sensualities and disturbing articulations. Living dummies, sweetly stupid, who walk with the alternative and senseless rhythm of hips and shoulders, and carry in their arteries the new, reinvented physiologies of their costumes.

The dummies' mouths. Saint Sebastian's wounds.[79]

Putrefaction

The other side of Saint Sebastian's magnifying glass corresponded to putrefaction. Everything, seen through it, was anguish, obscurity and even tenderness—tenderness because of the exquisite absence of spirit and naturalness.

Preceded by I am not sure what lines from Dante, I saw the whole world of the putrescent philistines: the lachrymose and transcendental artists, far removed from all clarity, cultivators of all germs, ignorant of the precision of the double, graduated decimetre; the family who buy 'objets d'art' to put on top of the piano; the public-works employee; the associate committee member; the professor of psychology . . . I did not want to continue. The delicate moustache of a ticket-box clerk moved me. I felt in my heart all its exquisite, Franciscan and intensely delicate poetry. My lips smiled despite my urge to cry. I stretched myself on the sand. The waves approached the shore with the quiet murmur of Henri Rousseau's *Bohémienne endormie*.

'Saint Sebastian' came as a revelation to those who, unlike Lorca and Gasch, were as unaware of Dalí's fanatical allegiance to the cult of Holy Objectivity and rejection of sentimentality as they were of his literary ability. Only Lorca was in a position to interpret the hidden message of the piece, which must have seemed to him, at one level, like a reply, or rejoinder, to his by-now famous ode to the painter, in which he had identified Dalí's terror of emotional involvement. Dalí's justification of his allegiance to a cult of objectivity and asepsia must have seemed to Lorca a confirmation of his determination to remain aloof, sufficiently, at least, to avoid sexual entanglement with the poet.

The editor of *L'Amic de les Arts*, Josep Carbonell, was so impressed by 'Saint Sebastian' that he threw the columns of the magazine open to Dalí, who wrote regularly from the next issue onwards. In later years, true to type, Dalí was to deprecate the contribution of *L'Amic de les Arts* to contemporary culture, claiming that he had only used it for his own self-promotion.[80] The truth is, however, that he took his relationship with the magazine extremely seriously and, thanks to the stimulus it provided, published in its elegant pages some of his most valuable critical writings.

Dalí, as usual, was bursting with ideas and plans. Some months earlier he and Gasch had decided that the time was ripe for launching a manifesto attacking the stagnation, pretentiousness and *putrescence*, as they saw it, of the Catalan art scene. The two friends, who were soon joined by Lluís Montanyà, decided to call their projected document *The Anti-Art Manifesto*. Lorca now piled in with suggestions, and Anna Maria, ever ready with her Kodak, photographed him and Dalí engaged in thought-transmission on the terrace at Es Llané. Their foreheads are linked by the cord of the poet's white beachrobe, which is connected to a precarious Eiffel Tower of wine glasses erected on the round table between them. Their pens are at the ready. Lorca was so proud of the photograph that, two years later, he handed it over to a small New York magazine, *Alhambra*, for publication, along with others taken in Cadaqués at the same time. The caption read: 'Writing a Manifesto with the painter Dalí'.

Honey is Sweeter than Blood

At about this time Dalí told Gasch that he had begun two new paintings, *The Wood of Gadgets* and *The Birth of Venus*.[81] The first of these was re-named *Honey is Sweeter than Blood* shortly afterwards. The second was soon designated *Sterile Efforts* and, finally, *Little Ashes (Cenicitas)*. The whereabouts, and dimensions, of *Honey is Sweeter than Blood* are unknown. It has never been reproduced in colour and our knowledge of it derives

XI

Dalí, Honey is Sweeter than Blood, *1927. Dimensions unknown. The painting has apparently been lost. One of the key works of Dalí's 'Lorca Period', it shows the poet's severed head lying not far from Dalí's and what appears to be the mummified corpse of Luis Buñuel.*

from a contemporary black-and-white photograph. *Little Ashes* fared better and today is one of the stars of the Dalí collection in Madrid's Queen Sofía Art Centre.

During the summer of 1927 *L'Amic de les Arts* informed its readers that Dalí was hard at work on the two paintings and expressed the view that they would 'give rise to heated discussion'.[82] On 12 August Dalí told Josep Maria Junoy, editor of the *Nova Revista*, that *Honey is Sweeter than Blood* inaugurated 'a new orbit, equidistant between Cubism and Surrealism on the one hand and a primitive art such as the Brueghels' on the other'.[83]

Both paintings, as well as *Gadget and Hand*, also painted at this time, make it almost certain that during the summer someone showed Dalí, or gave him, the catalogue of the exhibition Yves Tanguy et Objets d'Amérique, held at the Galerie Surréaliste in Paris from 27 May to 15 June. The catalogue, which has a preface by Breton and a text by Éluard, reproduced two of the twenty-three paintings on show: *He Did What He Wanted* (1927) and *Extinction of Useless Lights* (1927), as well as a detail from *Hurry! Hurry*! Dalí would have been amused by the zanily arbitrary titles, and by Tanguy's indication that the alternative *When They Shoot Me* (*Quand on me fusillera*) could equally well be applied to all of them.[84]

Yves Tanguy, He Did What He Wanted, 1927. 'I've stolen everything from Uncle Yves', Dalí once exaggerated, although the borrowings are considerable. To Tanguy's beaches or seabeds Dalí added the scintillating luminosity of the Empordà and a technique of extreme precision.

Dawn Ades, for whom the influence of Tanguy on the Dalí of this period is 'paramount' (she finds lesser appropriations from Ernst and Miró), is convinced that *Honey is Sweeter than Blood* and *Gadget and Hand* show that Dalí was familiar with *He Did What He Wanted*, which 'has the same kind of figures scattered ambiguously through earth and sky and Dalí borrows the ghostly configurations in the sky, which in Tanguy's case are actually scratched through the paint'. It is impossible to disagree with her.[85] José Pierre, author of the introduction to the catalogue of the Tanguy retrospective held in

Yves Tanguy, Extinction of Useless Lights, *1927. Dalí probably took note of the severed hand and the stark shadow projected by the object in the foreground.*

Paris in 1982, has referred, not without scorn, to what he terms Dalí's 'systematic hypertanguysation' from 1926 onwards, and lists the elements in his view 'appropriated' and 'confiscated' from Tanguy by the Catalan. They include 'levitated' figures, the use of numbers and letters (as in *Gadget and Hand* and *Little Ashes*), ectoplasmic forms, phallic fingers and wisps of smoke ('fumées').[86] That Dalí did indeed borrow these elements, as well as several others (including the severed hand and shadows of *Extinction of Useless Lights*), is evident enough, although he added many of his own to swell the repertory, such as pairs of flying breasts, lopped arms and heads, decapitated dummies, putrescent donkeys and, of course, the 'gadgets' themselves (*aparells* in Catalan). Above all, though, it is the *light* of Dalí's Tanguy-inspired paintings that distinguishes them from the Frenchman's: in place of the muted tones of Tanguy's 'mental beaches',

as Pierre calls them, which perhaps derived from his childhood holidays in Brittany, Dalí's are drenched in the brilliant, high-precision light of the tramuntana-scoured Empordà, which in turn gives rise to shadows of Chiricoesque starkness that Dalí was soon exploiting.[87]

In later life, Dalí was to make no bones about how much he owed to Tanguy. According to Merlye Secrest, he once said to Agnes Tanguy, the painter's niece: 'I pinched everything from your Uncle Yves' ('J'ai tout piqué de Tonton Yves'). Whether these were his exact words we shall never know, but the admission of debt seems clear enough.[88]

Lorca, present while Dalí worked on *Honey is Sweeter than Blood*, was fascinated by the painting's steeply angled, spectral beach, with its rows of 'gadgets' and assorted flotsam and jetsam, all depicted with nightmarish precision. In his study for the painting, as we have seen, Dalí had included a stylized version of Lorca's head among the debris litter-

— I què n'hi sembla d'aquestes pintures?
— Que es nota l'increment que van prenent els autos, perquè cada dia hi ha més desgràcies.

A Catalan cartoonist pokes fun at Dalí's Honey is Sweeter than Blood *(illustration on p. 210). The caption reads: 'And what is your opinion of these pictures?' 'They show that cars are on the increase—more road accidents every day.'*

ing the beach. Now he made it more realistic, along the lines of that appearing in the drawing *The Beach*, published the previous April, and perhaps in response to the poet's demands, for according to the caption to the reproduction of *Honey is Sweeter than Blood* included in the *Secret Life*, Lorca wrote to Dalí: 'Inscribe my name in this canvas, so that my name may amount to something in the world.'[89] The poet's head casts the shadow of Dalí's, in accordance with other works of the 'Lorca period', and lies half-buried in the sand between a decapitated female dummy reclining beside a pool of its own spilt blood and a rotting, fly-infested donkey. Near by we find another severed head, almost certainly Dalí's, separated from the poet's by an attenuated, disembodied arm; while at the dummy's feet is stretched a dark corpse, as infested by flies as the donkey. It has been suggested that the latter may well represent Luis Buñuel, with whom Dalí was corresponding regularly at this time and who was trying busily to separate him from Lorca. From both Dalí's and the poet's mouths issues a thin line of blood.[90]

At the end of the month, on his way home to Granada, Lorca wrote an emotional letter to Dalí from Barcelona in which he alluded to *Honey is Sweeter than Blood* and 'Saint Sebastian':

> From where I am I can hear (how sad it makes me, dearest chap!) the soft trickle of blood from the Sleeping Beauty of the Wood of Gadgets and the crackling of two little beasties like the sound of a pistachio nut cracked between one's fingers. The decapitated woman is the finest imaginable poem on the theme of blood, and has more blood than all that spilt in the Great War, which was *hot* blood with no other purpose than to *irrigate* the earth and appease a symbolic thirst for eroticism and youth. Your pictorial blood, and in general the whole tactile concept of your physiological aesthetic, has such a concrete, well-balanced air, such a logical and true quality of pure poetry that it attains the category *of that which we need absolutely in order to live.*

One can say: 'I was tired and I sat down in the shade and freshness of that blood', or: 'I came down from the hill and ran all along the beach until I found the melancholy head in the spot where the delicious little crackling beasties, so useful for the digestion, gathered.' Now I realize how much I am losing by leaving you.

The 'melancholy head' was, presumably, the poet's own. At the end of the letter Lorca suddenly made an admission: 'I behaved towards you like an indecent ass, you who are the best thing I've got. With every minute I see it more clearly and I'm dreadfully sorry. But it only increases my affection for you and my identification with your ideas and your human integrity.'[91] Rafael Santos Torroella believes that the reference was to a second, and presumably very recent, attempt on the part of the poet to have anal intercourse with Dalí. It seems certain, at all events, that by the end of Lorca's holiday in Cadaqués the painter had become seriously disturbed by the growing intensity of their relationship. Desperate to prove his masculinity and to assert his independence, Dalí may have felt that he was now in danger of succumbing to homosexual impulses.

If it was Lorca who proposed for *Honey is Sweeter than Blood* the neatly descriptive, but short-lived, alternative title *The Wood of Gadgets*,[92] the definitive name of the painting appropriated a favourite and sybilline expression of Lídia Noguer, which she was wont to proclaim on occasions of particular solemnity.[93] Dalí was still a virgin, and, as we know from the *Secret Life* and his later autobiographical writings and statements to the media, a compulsive masturbator. It may be that in the title *Honey is Sweeter than Blood* there is also an allusion to the theme of masturbation, soon to become a leitmotif of Dalí's paintings. The clue comes in the *Secret Life*, where Dalí recounts yet another act of masturbation: 'Once more I wrenched from my body that familiar solitary pleasure, sweeter than honey, while biting into the corner of my pillow lighted by a moonbeam, sinking my teeth into it till they cut through the saliva-drenched fabric.'[94] If masturbation is a pleasure sweeter than honey, and honey is sweeter than blood, one wonders if blood, in the context of this painting, might not stand for sexual intercourse (and the fear of it), the statement 'honey is sweeter than blood' thereby being equivalent to 'masturbation is sweeter than fucking'. In Lorca's 'Ode to Walt Whitman', written two years later in New York, there is a stanza which lends weight to this interpretation, and which may even contain an allusion, conscious or not, to *Honey is Sweeter than Blood*—a picture which, as we know, meant a great deal to the poet:

Porque es justo que el hombre no busque su deleite
en la selva de sangre de la mañana próxima.

El cielo tiene playas donde evitar la vida
y hay cuerpos que no deben repetirse en la aurora.

Because it's legitimate for a man not to seek his pleasure
in the early morning's jungle of blood.
The sky has beaches where we can escape from life
and there are bodies which ought not to repeat themselves in the dawn.[95]

Dalí's loathing of the female genitalia and the 'jungle of blood' (Lorca's metaphor for intercourse) was as strong as the poet's, and would remain so all his life; and masturbation would always be his principal mode of sexual satisfaction.

In 1950 Dalí said he considered *Honey is Sweeter than Blood* one of his most important paintings, explaining that it contained 'all the obsessions of my entry into Surrealism'.[96] These obsessions also appeared in the other painting on which he was at work in the summer of 1927, *The Birth of Venus* (later *Sterile Efforts* and finally *Little Ashes*). As a result of Santos Torroella's dedicated researches, it is now generally accepted that the two heads in *The Birth of Venus* represent those of Lorca (on the shoreline) and Dalí (in the foreground). The work displays one of Dalí's most alluring female nudes, seen from behind and, as in *Honey is Sweeter than Blood*, suitably decapitated. Dalí, a self-confessed worshipper of the female posterior, always insisted that he loathed large breasts as much as women's genitals, stating his preference, among the body's orifices, for the anus.[97] In *The Birth of Venus*, Lorca's head is represented, yet again, with the eyes shut. Is he enacting his own death? Dreaming? Or do the closed eyes suggest, perhaps, the poet's blissful unconcern at the torment unleashed in Dalí's brain by the contemplation of the shapely female buttocks? All we can say is that the painting, as suggested by its second title, *Sterile Efforts*, seems to be yet another expression of the sexual and emotional conflicts that were then afflicting both friends.

One other painting from the summer of 1927 must be mentioned briefly. *Gadget and Hand* goes further than the pictures we have been discussing in its exposition of Dalí's sexual problems at the time. The setting of the painting, as in *Still Life* (*Invitation to Sleep*), is a stylized version of the terrace in front of the Dalís' house at Cadaqués. But what are we to make of the tottering, anthropomorphic 'gadget' standing on the terrace, crowned by a pustulating red hand bearing the vein motif that appears in other paintings of this summer? For Paul Moorhouse, the 'gadget' is a self-portrait that shows Dalí as 'an automaton in the grip of onanistic obsession', with a tumescent, masturbating hand in the place of a brain. Around the figure are the causes of the obsession: an ele-

X

VIII

gant, twenties bather in a see-through costume, a pair of flying breasts, a decapitated naked female torso, various ghostly female forms, one of Dalí's rotting donkeys with a fishbone inside its head and, we might add, apparently being sodomized by the point of a hexagon while it tries to nibble a fish (symbol of the female genitalia, in the view of the same critic).[98]

It is difficult to disagree with Moorhouse's pin-pointing of the theme of the painting. The *redness* of the hand (which he does not mention) must surely relate to the shame, guilt and anxiety involved in Dalí's compulsive masturbation, and perhaps to the fear of being caught at it 'red-handed'. Incapacitated by shame from experiencing sexual satisfaction in the external world, anxious about his indulgence in what English dictionaries were calling 'self-abuse' up to the 1960s, Dalí was in a painful quandary. *Gadget and Hand* is the first in a long series of paintings, drawings and texts which treat of masturbation. Among his other achievements, Dalí was the first serious artist in history ever to make onanism one of the principal themes of his work.

'The Nefarious García'

Luis Buñuel, meanwhile, alarmed at the growing intimacy between Lorca and Dalí, was writing nasty things to that easy-going mutual friend of all three, Pepín Bello. Buñuel did not admit to it, of course, but reading between the lines his jealousy seems obvious enough. 'I've had a disgusting letter from Federico and his acolyte Dalí,' he wrote from Brittany on 27 July 1927. 'He's got him [Dalí] completely enslaved.'[99] The Spanish adjective used by Buñuel to describe the letter was *asquerosa*, which to his great amusement, as he commented in another letter to Pepín on 5 August, coincided with the name of a village in Granada where the poet's father had a house. The jocular tone cannot disguise the venom:

> Dalí me escribe cartas asquerosas.
> Es un asqueroso.
> Y Federico dos asquerosos,
> Uno por ser de Asquerosa y otro porque es un asqueroso.

> Dalí is writing me disgusting letters.
> He's disgusting.
> Federico is doubly disgusting,
> First because he's *from* Disgusting and second because he *is* disgusting.[100]

None of Buñuel's letters to Dalí at this time have come to light, nor Dalí's replies. Presumably Buñuel did all he could in them to undermine Dalí's feelings for Lorca. On 5 September 1927, writing again to José Bello, he returned to the charge:

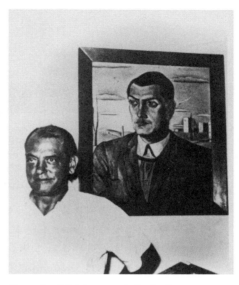

Buñuel with his portrait by Dalí.

> Federico sticks in my craw incredibly. I thought that the boyfriend [Dalí] was putrescent, but now I see that the other is even worse. It's his awful aestheticism that has distanced him from us. His extreme narcissism was already enough to make a pure friendship with him impossible. Anyway, it's his problem. The trouble is that his work may suffer as a result.
>
> Dalí is deeply under his influence. He believes himself to be a genius, thanks to the love Federico professes for him. He's written to me saying: 'Federico is better than ever. He's *the* great man, his drawings have genius. I'm producing amazing work, etc.' And then, of course, his successes in Barcelona are so easily achieved. How I'd love to see him arrive here and renew himself far from the influence of the nefarious García! Because, and it's a fact, Dalí is a real male and very talented.[101]

The letter gives us the measure of Buñuel at this time. Knowing, as he did, how worried Dalí was about his virility, it was an easy task for him to work on the painter's anxiety over Lorca. Despite his efforts, however, Dalí and the poet continued writing to each other until 1929 (they met again only in 1934), and followed each other's burgeoning careers with fascination and pride. Dalí was not given to sentimentality. When, years later, he said that Lorca had been the greatest friend of his youth, we can be sure that he was not exaggerating.

A Visit from Joan Miró

Joan Miró was as fanatical a Catalan as Dalí and every summer returned from Paris to his beloved Montroig, near Tarragona. On 21 August 1927 he wrote from there to Sebastià Gasch to tell him that his dealer, Pierre Loeb, would be visiting him at the beginning of September. Miró explained that he would like Loeb to see Dalí's work, as well as that of Francesc Domingo and any other other young Catalan painter the critic cared to recommend. It was all to be very secret. 'I'll write to Dalí,' he said, 'asking him for permission to take this friend of mine to see him (it mustn't be known that it's Pierre!) and to enable him to make sure that he has enough things to show us to give us an idea of his production.'[1]

Miró had not yet met Dalí, nor, it appears, seen any of his paintings. Gasch sent him Dalí's address in Figueres and Miró, as promised, got in touch. Dalí replied with deference on 1 September 1927. He would be delighted to see Miró and his friend, he wrote, adding that he had just finished two paintings that seemed to him to inaugurate a new phase that was 'much more representative of my way of being than anything I've produced up to now'.[2]

Miró and Loeb arrived in Figueres in mid-September. After they had gone Dalí wrote to Gasch:

> The day before yesterday your friend Miró and his companion came to see me. They didn't stay long. Miró made a great impression on me as a person, and I need hardly say that we scarcely spoke a word to one another. What most interested him were my two most recent canvasses: *The Wood of Gadgets* [*Honey is Sweeter than Blood*] and *Gadget and*

Chapter Six

Hand. They both felt that some bits of the pictures are reminiscent of Yves Tanguy, but with a much better technique, with much more *naturalness* and infinitely more plasticity. As for the paintings in the New Objectivity line, they looked at the portrait of Anna Maria and said it was better than Severini. The only thing Miró's friend told me was that he wanted to keep closely in touch with me.[3]

The last remark shows that, despite Miró's secretiveness, he had revealed Loeb's identity; and suggests that Dalí was disappointed that the dealer did not sign him up there and then. Dalí wrote excitedly to Lorca to tell him about Miró's visit, the letter hinting that the two had talked about the painter during the summer:

I'm really pleased that you like Miró. Miró has said things that go beyond Picasso.[4] I don't know if I told you that I'm now in touch with Miró and that he came to Figueres and will return soon to Cadaqués to see my latest things; he's a creature of enormous Purity, with a big heart. He thinks that I'm much better than all the young painters in Paris put together, and he's written to me telling me that I've got everything set up for me there in order to make a great hit. As you must be aware, *he's* had great financial success there.

Dalí appended an explanatory footnote to the word 'Purity': 'I use the term in exactly the opposite sense given to it by Juan Ramón [Jiménez], Benjamín Palencia and the other great PIGS. Miró paints chickens with hairs and pricks, etc.'[5] The presence of explicitly sexual elements in Miró's work was soon acting as a liberating force on Dalí, and many of his 1927–8 paintings and drawings owe an undeniable debt in this respect to the older artist.

Shortly after Miró's visit Dalí sent him photographs of his work, informing him that he had also remitted a selection to Pierre Loeb. Miró replied warmly on 31 October, promising to notify him in good time of his departure for Paris so that Dalí could send him more material to show to people there.[6]

From the moment the considerate Miró took him under his wing, Dalí lost no opportunity to praise the painter in the critical articles he was now beginning to send regularly to *L'Amic de les Arts.* His piece 'Photography, Pure Creation of the Spirit', published in the 30 September 1927 issue, was an important statement. In line with his views on Holy Objectivity, Dalí expressed his appreciation of the camera's potential for the accurate recording of the external world, which had definitively relieved painting of that onerous burden. Henceforth, he wrote, if anyone wanted to paint a jellyfish it would be 'absolutely necessary to represent a guitar or a harlequin playing a clarinet'.[7]

Dawn Ades has pointed out that Dalí's views at this time on photography owed a debt to Lazlo Moholy-Nagy's Bauhaus book *Painting, Photography, Film* (1925), and that he soon grasped the implications for his painting of 'the distortions or enlargements of reality' made possible by the camera (close-ups, slow motion, superimpositions, fades, dissolves, montage, X-ray and so forth), several of these techniques being hinted at in *Honey is Sweeter than Blood* and *Little Ashes.*[8]

Is Dalí a Surrealist?

Meanwhile, encouraged by Miró's positive reaction to *Honey is Sweeter than Blood* and *Gadget and Hand*, Dalí had sent the two works to the annual Autumn Salon in Barcelona. The show ran at the Sala Parés from 8 to 21 October 1927 and the paintings, as *L'Amic de les Arts* had predicted during the summer, provoked much discussion, sparking off a debate about whether Dalí was now a Surrealist or not.[9]

Rafael Benet was foremost among the critics who insisted that Dalí had indeed joined the Surrealist ranks, while the painter's friends and colleagues on *L'Amic de les Arts*, Gasch and Montanyà, firmly maintained the opposite. Gasch had been hostile to Surrealism for over a year, terming the movement, in October 1926, 'a minuscule, sterile group of sinister lovers of scandal for the sake of scandal'.[10] In September 1927 he stated that his attitude to Surrealism 'was frankly one of condemnation',[11] adding in October, with a snide reference to Freud, that he was totally opposed to the sexual 'immorality' of some Surrealist paintings.[12] Gasch was predisposed, therefore, to interpret Dalí's hesitations about the movement as rejection. In the October issue of *L'Amic de les Arts*, coinciding with the Sala Parés exhibition, he even went so far as to maintain that Dalí was 'the archetypal anti-Surrealist'. 'Nobody loathes Surrealism so thoroughly as Dalí,' he pontificated, adding: 'The fraternal friendship that unites us enables me to say this with confidence.' This was far from an accurate statement of the case.[13]

Soon, with no explanation, Gasch changed his tune momentarily, preaching that contemporary painting should, ideally, be a combination of Purism and Surrealism along the lines (he now perceived) being practised by Dalí. But only momentarily. His hostility to the basic tenets of the movement was to take on a new vehemence during 1928.[14]

While the critics squabbled about whether Dalí was or was not a Surrealist, his two paintings at the Autumn Salon provoked much dismay and amusement. A witty cartoon published in *La Veu de Catalunya* offered an imaginative explanation for the proliferation of severed limbs in *Honey is Sweeter than Blood*: motorcar accidents were on the increase.

Dalí set out his view of the matter in a special sheet inserted into the October issue of *L'Amic de les Arts*. The burden of his argument was that, while 'artistic' painting can only make sense to the *cognoscenti*, his current production appealed directly to the unconscious and could be understood instantaneously by the simple at heart (children, say, or the fishermen of Cadaqués), but certainly not by that obtuse breed, the art critics. People had lost the ability to see the objective world clearly, Dalí argued: they were not using their eyes, they found 'ordinary' things ordinary when, in fact, they are miraculous. 'To see is to invent,' he stated emphatically, quoting what he had just written in his article on photography. Was he, then, as some critics seemed to think, a Surrealist? Dalí hedged his bets:

> What I have said should be more than sufficient to make clear the distance that separates me from Surrealism, despite the intervention, in what we might call the phenomenon of 'poetic transposition', of the subconscious at its purest and of instinct at its freest. But this would lead me off too far now, and anyway these are considerations that it's up to the critics to analyse and clarify.[15]

This is not the voice of someone who 'loathes' Surrealism. It shows, rather, that Dalí was becoming increasingly aware of its relevance for his life and work. All this time, from different sources, it was being constantly borne in on him that Surrealism, unlike Impressionism or Cubism, was not simply a new art tendency but a revolutionary, subversive movement that aimed at changing the world by tapping, and liberating, the forces latent in the psyche. Given Dalí's temperament, given his reading of Freud, indeed given his personal problems, how could he be indifferent? Years later, reflecting on *Honey is Sweeter than Blood*, he stated categorically that it expressed 'all the obsessions of my entry into Surrealism'.[16]

If Gasch and Montanyà were critics, not creative writers, Dalí had another colleague on *L'Amic de les Arts* who combined with sophistication the varied callings of poet, essayist, novelist, critic and journalist. Born in Barcelona in 1893 (the same year as Miró), Josep Vicenç Foix had published his first verse in 1917 and soon became deeply involved in the Barcelona avant-garde, editing the revue *Trossos* in the latter months of its ephemeral existence. Foix was not only sympathetic to Surrealism, but, in the view of both Gasch and Montanyà, a genuine Surrealist himself.[17] Certainly, to judge from the extremely inventive, quasi-Surrealist pieces he had been publishing in *L'Amic de les Arts* since its inception in 1926, his proximity to the positions of Breton and his group was undeniable. Dalí greatly admired this drily witty *littérateur*, whose family owned a cake shop in Barcelona's Sarrià quarter, and he illustrated several of his pieces in *L'Amic*. It seems impossible that he and Foix did not discuss Surrealism together. Either way

Foix's support was important at this stage in Dalí's career, not least for the enthusiastic backing he gave the painter in the Barcelona newspaper La *Publicitat*, to which he was a regular contributor. Always with an eye on the main chance, Dalí tended increasingly to choose friends who were useful to him. Foix was an excellent case in point.

The Painter as Poet

Since his first efforts in verse, published as an adolescent in the school magazine *Studium,* Dalí seemed to have lost the urge to write poetry. But in the autumn of 1927 he believed he had recovered it, writing that October to Lorca: 'Don't you agree that the only poets, the only ones who are producing genuinely new poetry, are we painters? Yes!' To prove it he included a Spanish translation of a composition he had just dashed off in Catalan:

Poem of the Little Objects

There's a sweet little object looking at us, smiling.
I'm happy, I'm happy, I'm happy, I'm happy.
The sewing needles nail themselves gently to the small, tender nickels.
My girlfriend's hand is made of cork full of Parisian lace.
My girlfriend's knees are of smoke.
The sugar dissolves in the water, is tinged red with the blood *and jumps like a flea.*
My girlfriend has a wristwatch made of putty.
My girlfriend's breasts: one a madly buzzing wasps' nest, the other a tranquil sea
    urchin.
The little sea urchins, the little sea urchins, the little sea urchins, the little sea
    urchins, the little sea urchins sting.
The partridge's eye is bright red.
Little objects, little objects, little objects, little objects, little objects,
Little objects, little objects, little objects, little objects, little objects,
There are little still objects, *like a loaf of bread.*

Dalí asked Lorca if he liked it, clearly expecting him to say yes. And he asked him again in his next letter. The poet's reaction is unknown. Maybe he never gave Dalí his opinion, but it seems fair to assume that he can hardly have considered the composition a masterpiece of modern verse—although modern it undoubtedly was and interesting for elements later incorporated in Dalí's painting, not least the putty wristwatch, which looks forward to his famous soft watches of the 1930s.[18]

Dalí also sent the piece to Pepín Bello, asking for his judgement and, just in case, supplying his own. 'How different it is,' he exclaimed, 'from the imbecilic, sentimental and anti-poetic ecstacy of Juan Ramón Jiménez, for example! Juan Ramón, Head of the Putrescent Philistines of Spain.'[19]

In another letter to Bello, dated 24 October 1927, Dalí announced that he was about to bring out an article on the cinema in *La Gaceta Literaria*, Spain's most ambitious and widely distributed cultural review, published fortnightly in Madrid by the writer Ernesto Giménez Caballero, later the principal theorist of Spanish Fascism.

Unlike *L'Amic de les Arts*, which only printed articles in Catalan, the large-format *La Gaceta Literaria* reached out to the entire 'Iberian' world, as its full title proudly proclaimed: *La Gaceta Literaria ibérica:americana: internacional.* During its first six months of publication (the inaugural issue appeared on 1 January 1927), the review made its mark on both sides of the Atlantic. Dalí had met the dynamic Giménez Caballero in Madrid, and was on close terms with the review's assistant editor and secretary, Guillermo de Torre, one of the leading lights of the Ultra movement in the early 1920s, as we have seen. By the autumn of 1927 Lorca, Gasch and Montanyà were all contributors to the *Gaceta*, while Buñuel had been signed up as the magazine's film correspondent in Paris. It was little wonder, then, that Dalí, now playing the fame-game for all he was worth, turned to Giménez Caballero's review for additional self-promotion, his first contribution being a drawing of the Figueres philosopher Joaquim Xirau, reproduced on 1 December 1927.

Dalí's promised article on the cinema, 'Artistic Film, Anti-Artistic Film', appeared in *La Gaceta Literaria* a fortnight later, dedicated to Buñuel. As might have been expected by anyone who had been following his recent thinking, Dalí attacked all those films that had a conventional story-line, films such as Fritz Lang's famous *Metropolis*, which the painter claimed to despise. 'The possibilities of photography and the cinema reside in the unlimited fantasy born of things themselves,' Dalí insisted (it was the thesis he had sought to illustrate in his 'Poem of the Little Objects'). 'The anonymous anti-artistic film-maker films a white cake, an anodyne and simple room, the driver's cabin of a train, the policeman's star, a kiss inside a taxi. When the film is shown it turns out that a whole, fairytale world of unmistakable poetry has been recorded.' By the same token, given the possibilities of the camera, a lump of sugar can loom larger than the most grandiose cityscape—and be more fascinating.[20]

Before long it would occur to Dalí that the documentary was the ideal vehicle for capturing the reality of the external world, since to the virtues of still photography it added that of movement. In particular, Dalí was fascinated by film's ability to express metamorphosis, the merging of one thing into another. While nowadays this surprises no one, in the 1920s it seemed little short of miraculous. Surrealism, determined as it was to draw on the unconscious, soon realized the extraordinary potential of film for the simulation of those transformations, and shiftings of perspective, often staggering in their unexpectedness and originality, that characterize dream language. Out of this realization was to come Buñuel and Dalí's *Un Chien andalou*.

Meanwhile, Miró was continuing to make efforts on Dalí's behalf in Paris, showing people photographs of the artist's work, talking to dealers, stimulating interest and, presumably, trying to persuade Pierre Loeb to sign him up. On 7 December the latter thanked Dalí for the photographs he had sent, encouraged him to dispatch more and said, guardedly, that he now 'envisaged the possibility' of taking him on board—when, that was, Dalí stopped jumping from tendency to tendency and developed a strong personality of his own. 'I'm certain you'll soon find *a direction*', wrote Loeb, 'and with your gifts I'm convinced you're going to have an excellent career as a painter.' Coming from Pierre Loeb this was praise indeed.[21]

A week later Dalí heard from Paul Rosenberg, Picasso's dealer, who reminded him that he had been in touch after the artist's exhibition at Dalmau (in January 1927). He expressed his surprise that Dalí had not replied. Rosenberg had seen photographs of Dalí's recent work and asked him to visit him when he arrived in Paris. Considering Rosenberg's importance in the art world, this, too, was excellent news.[22]

Then came a letter from Miró, dated 17 December 1927, which shows how vital a role he was now playing in the furtherance of Dalí's career. He was getting ready to set off for Paris:

> Dear Dalí,
>
> Delighted to receive your drawings.
>
> Without doubt you're a very talented man with a brilliant career ahead of you *in Paris*. Pierre has also written to me, very impressed and, it appears, well disposed towards you.
>
> He wrote to me earlier telling me he had given some of your photographs to Christian Zervos, at *Cahiers d'Art*.
>
> I think we've got everything set up, all that's necessary now is to *hammer away* constantly.
>
> Have you sent your latest drawings to Pierre? I'd like you to do so. I'd rather hang on to my own of yours so that I can show them personally to other people.
>
> Before I leave I'll ask you to send photographs of other things from different periods or

expressing other states of mind. I think it's very important for these to be known, too. Finally, keep on pushing yourself but without any impatience. Hoping you're well, I'm delighted to be your friend and companion. Yours ever, Miró.[23]

Over these months, while letters came and went between Dalí and Miró, and *L'Amic de les Arts* reported that Dalí was in contact 'with two of the most famous Parisian dealers',[24] the disloyal and envious Luis Buñuel followed with cynical fascination Salvador's efforts to achieve a breakthrough in the French capital. In a long letter to Pepín Bello on 8 November 1927 he wrote that he had only published Dalí's article on the cinema in *La Gaceta Literaria* out of pity, since it said nothing that he, Buñuel, had not already written in *Cahiers d'Art*. 'Dalí's falling behind,' he went on gleefully. 'I know for a fact that he's sending photographs of his work to the dealers here. Rosenberg has said that he doesn't draw badly and Pierre—you know, the Surrealist dealer—says that he's influenced by Miró. They haven't bought a thing from him and that's the sum of his achievement. On the other hand in Spain everyone says "he's got genius!", "he's really modern!" He's falling behind, I tell you. And it's Federico's fault.' Buñuel went on to say how pleased he was by the 'failure' of Lorca's *Mariana Pineda* in Madrid that October.[25] The play had not, in fact, been the critical disaster in Madrid that Buñuel fondly imagined; nor was Lorca in any sense responsible for anything retrograde in Dalí's current production. But the poet was homosexual and, for Buñuel, that made him fair game for sneers.

Dalí had written to Lorca shortly after the Madrid production of *Mariana Pineda*. The letter showed the increasing hold that Surrealism was now exerting on him, despite his public utterances to the contrary. After describing enthusiastically the paintings on which he was then working, and which were 'killing him with joy', he expressed particular satisfaction with the invention of some 'lost breasts' (*pechos extraviados*), not to be confused, he insisted, with the *flying* variety that had already appeared in his pictures. Then the tone became more intimate. 'Hola Señor,' he teased the poet,

> You must be rich now, if I were with you I'd be your little prostitute to move you and steal your banknotes which I'd then soak (this time in donkey's water). I'm tempted to send you a bit of my lobster-coloured pyjamas, or rather 'lobster's-dream-coloured', to see if you take pity on me from your position of opulence and send me money.

Dalí then proceeded to attack Margarita Xirgu, who had so far paid him nothing for the sets of *Mariana Pineda*, pointing out that with 500 pesetas he and Lorca would be in a position to launch their *Anti-Art Manifesto* and begin an all-out campaign against the 'putrescent' values they detested.[26]

It is easy to imagine that Dalí's libidinous bantering in this letter served to heighten the poet's unhappiness at being separated from him. Perhaps this was the intention. Meanwhile, behind the scenes, Buñuel doubled his efforts to ensure that the separation became as definitive as possible.

Arp, Breton

Dalí admired the German artist Jean (or Hans) Arp, although he only knew his work from photographs. On 21 November 1927 a major exhibition of Arp's recent production opened in Paris at the Galerie Surréaliste. Dalí obtained, or was shown, a copy of the catalogue. In it he found a preface by André Breton which greatly impressed him. The exhibition coincided, moreover, with the publication in *La Révolution Surréaliste* of a substantial extract from Breton's long essay *Surrealism and Painting*, which had been appearing sporadically in the magazine since 1925.[27] Proof that Dalí read this extract as well as Breton's preface to the Arp catalogue comes in a long article he now wrote for *L'Amic de les Arts*, 'The New Limits of Painting', the first part of which was published on 29 February 1928. A fortnight earlier, Salvador Dalí Cusí had jotted down in his album the good tidings that his son had just finished his military service.[28]

The main theme of 'The New Limits of Painting' is that, thanks to Surrealism, painting and poetry have now been definitively released from the obligation of representing the conventional nature of objects in the external world. A 'change of sensibility' is taking place, Dalí assures his readers. Art based on sensations is no longer valid. The artist now looks inwards. The article shows that Dalí had been much struck by the following paragraph on Arp's *Mountain, Table, Anchor, Navel* in Breton's preface to the exhibition catalogue:

Jean Arp, Mountain, Table, Anchor, Navel, *1925. Dalí admired Arp's work, which he knew from photographs, and was struck by Breton's introduction to his 1927 catalogue.*

With Arp, the days of *distribution* are over. Previously the word 'table' was a begging word [*parole mendiante*]: it wanted us to eat, to lean on it or not, to write. The word 'mountain' was a begging word: it wanted us to contemplate, to climb it or not, to breathe deeply. The word 'anchors' was a begging word: it wanted us to pause, it wanted something to turn rusty or not, then for us to set off again. *In reality* (if we now know what we mean by reality) a nose can be perfectly at home beside an armchair, it can even adopt the form of an armchair. What difference is there *basically* between a couple dancing and the cover of a beehive? The birds have never sung better than in this aquarium.[29]

Dalí glossed Breton's paragraph thus in 'The New Limits of Painting':

To us, a nose's place, far from having necessarily to be on a face, seems more appropriate on the edge of an arm-chair; nor is there any problem about the same nose's being sustained on top of a little puff of smoke. Yves Tanguy did not launch his delicate *messages* in vain . . . All of this is so obvious that it is not necessary to insist on it since the day (the day belongs by right to Surrealism) when the poetic autonomy of things and words began and the latter stopped being (in André Breton's term) *paroles mendiantes*.[30]

Tanguy's painting, *Second Message*, had recently been reproduced in *La Révolution Surréaliste* (nos 9–10, 1 October 1927), but Dalí was clearly alluding also to the 'messages' contained in his earlier paintings, messages to which he, Dalí, had not been indifferent.[31]

Under the impact of Breton's piece on Arp, the notion of 'the poetic autonomy of things and words', already being elaborated by Dalí in his own theoretical writings, quickly became a new article of faith for him and was to be brandished with typical fanaticism in letters and articles throughout 1928, not always with due credit to Breton. Thus we find the latter's dancing couple and bees, as well as his underlined phrase 'in reality', turning up without acknowledgement in Dalí's article 'Reality and Surreality'.[32] And Dalí had this to say in a letter to Lorca: 'In reality, there's no relation between two dancers and a honeycomb, unless it's the relation between Saturn and the little grub that sleeps in the chrysalis, or at least unless in reality there isn't any difference between the dancing couple and a honeycomb.'[33]

Similarly, from Breton's comments on Ernst in *Surrealism and Painting* Dalí took the notion of an object's being allowed to change the course of its shadow—if it felt thus inclined.[34] But not all his examples were filched. In 'New Limits of Painting' he allows autonomy to the eye (why should eyes have to be dependent on heads?), and insists that the hands of a clock be allowed a life of their own. To this last notion he returned in the letter to Lorca just quoted:

The hands of a clock (don't worry about my examples, I'm not trying to find specially poetic ones) begin to have real value the moment they stop telling the time and, losing the *circular* rhythm and arbitrary mission to which our intelligence has subjected them (to tell the time), they escape from the clock to occupy the spot that corresponds to the sex organs of little crumbs of bread.[35]

To make sure that his admiration for Breton did not go unnoticed, Dalí quoted in the second part of 'New Limits of Painting' (published on 30 April 1928) another paragraph from the Arp preface. 'Everything I love, everything I think and feel, inclines me to a private philosophy of immanence according to which surreality would be included in reality itself and neither superior nor external to it,' wrote Breton:

> And reciprocally, too, for the container would also be the content. It would be a question, almost, of a communicating vessel between the container and the content. This is to say that I reject with all my strength the attempts which, in both painting and writing, could have the effect of removing thought from life, or of placing life under the control of thought. What one hides is worth neither more nor less than what one discovers. And what one hides from oneself, neither more nor less than what one allows others to discover. A rupture, properly ascertained and suffered, testifies at one and the same time to our beginning and to our end.

'Naturally,' commented Dalí immediately after the quotation. 'The New Limits of Painting', with appreciative nods in the direction of Tanguy and Ernst as well as its explicit admiration for Breton, shows that in early 1928 Dalí was drawing ever closer to Surrealism. He still maintained, though, that his attitude to it was one of independence. In the third part of the essay, published in *L'Amic de les Arts* on 31 May 1928, he glossed Miró's recent recommendation that the time had now come for 'the assassination of art':

> The assassination of art, what a perfect compliment! The Surrealists are dedicated, in all sincerity, to this mission. I'm far from sharing their thinking, but can we still doubt that only those who give everything to this purpose will experience the full joy of the new intelligence that is dawning? Surrealism lays its neck on the block while everyone else is still playing the coquette and many people are keeping an apple in their pockets in case of sudden thirst.[36]

The impact on Dalí of Breton's Arp preface may have been strengthened by the inclusion of the text at the end of *Surrealism and Painting*, issued by Gallimard in

February 1928.[37] It seems likely that Dalí soon obtained a copy of the profusely illustrated *plaquette*, perhaps from his uncle Anselm Domènech in Barcelona,[38] perhaps from Miró. Alternatively he could have had access to Sebastià Gasch's copy.[39] No doubt he would have been struck by the title page, where the painters singled out for discussion were prominently listed: Ernst, De Chirico, Miró, Braque, Arp, Picabia, Picasso, Man Ray, Masson and Tanguy. Dalí, on the threshold of pronouncing himself unconditionally a Surrealist, may have decided that he would make certain of being included in later editions of the book. If so, he was absolutely right. But he would have to wait until 1945.

The Anti-Art Manifesto

The Anti-Art Manifesto, on which Dalí was already working in the summer of 1927 when Lorca stayed with him in Cadaqués, had undergone endless transformations since then and was now entering the final straight. Lorca had dropped out, or been dropped (this was to be a strictly Catalan affair), and Dalí had told Pepín Bello in October that the manifesto would be signed by 'tailors, motorists, dancers, bankers, film directors, music-hall artistes, airmen and rotten donkeys'.[40] Now the sole co-signatories were to be Sebastià Gasch and Lluís Montanyà. In the months leading up to the completion of his military service, Dalí sent the latter 'vastly long letters' every day about the manifesto, suggesting, or insisting upon, tiny changes, chopping, rewriting, revamping. Gasch and Montanyà visited him frequently in Figueres, where there were endless discussions; and sometimes breathless telegrams would arrive in Barcelona with yet another last-minute alteration.[41]

The manifesto was directed mainly against the stagnation of the Catalan art establishment, the trio being particularly revolted, according to Gasch, by what they termed the 'false Hellenism' of certain Catalan writers. In one of his letters to Gasch, Dalí launched a furious attack on a dancer called Aurea:

> Aurea! Aurea! A pure question of stomach; one can only react against all this by being *openly insulting*. What's the use of the Bernat Metxe Foundation if they can't distinguish between Greece and Aurea?[42] For us, Greece is in the antiseptic creases of the female golfer's pullover; for them, in the repugnant folds draping Aurea's body, pestilent with gauzes and tinsel! We've got to DENOUNCE all these things, undoubtedly. If not, it won't be clear that we have absolutely NOTHING in common with the hairy pigs and intellectuals of Catalunya . . . When will the day come when we can print publicly 'THE GREAT HAIRY PUTRESCENT PIG ANGEL GUIMERÀ'?[43]

The dramatist Àngel Guimerà (1845–1924), best known for his rural drama *Tierra baixa* (1897), was one of the sacred cows of Catalan culture, and Gasch and Montanyà, more restrained than Dalí, had to dissuade him from using this phrase in the manifesto, which after all was to be signed by them as well. The two felt obliged again and again to curb Dalí's 'impetuosity' at this time, no easy task.[44] Dalí reserved his anti-Guimerà onslaught for a later occasion. As for Aurea, General Primo de Rivera's censors in Barcelona (the dictator was to remain in power for another two years) saw to it that her name was removed from the document, the innocuous expression 'pseudo-classical dancers' being substituted.[45]

The Anti-Art Manifesto appeared in March 1928 and soon received the nickname of *The Yellow Paper* from the colour of the broadsheets on which it was printed. Gasch saw to the distribution, making sure that anyone who was anything in Catalan literature, art, commerce or journalism received a copy. The document, in this its final and public metamorphosis, expressed outrage at what Dalí, Gasch and Montanyà termed 'the grotesque and pathetic spectacle of contemporary intellectual life in Catalunya, shut in upon itself in an enclosed and putrescent atmosphere'. The signatories insisted, as the Madrid *ultraístas* had done eight years earlier, that society had definitively entered the post-machine era and that a new state of mind now predominated, symbolized by the aeroplane, the cinema, jazz, the gramophone, transatlantic steamers and the like. It was the artist's duty to express this state of mind and none other. At the end of the manifesto was appended a list of the artists, writers and poets of whom the authors approved: Picasso, Gris, Ozenfant, De Chirico, Miró, Lipchitz, Brancusi, Arp, Le Corbusier, Reverdy, Tzara, Éluard, Aragon, Desnos, Maritain, Maurice Raynal (the critic), Christian Zervos (editor of *Cahiers d'Art*), Breton and, his name figuring between those of Cocteau and Stravinsky, García Lorca, no less. No doubt there had been much haggling over this eclectic selection of notables. Lorca, miles away in Granada, must have felt flattered by his inclusion, but when he reprinted the manifesto in his review *Gallo* he made sure, modestly, that his name was silently omitted. There wasn't a newspaper or magazine in Barcelona, or rag in the suburbs and provinces, according to Gasch, which did not comment on *The Anti-Art Manifesto*, the reactions ranging from the indulgent to the scornful. The truth of this statement is borne out by Salvador Dalí Cusí's album, where the cuttings fill several pages.[46]

The most negative appraisal came from the art critic Rafael Benet in a private letter to Gasch which infuriated Dalí. The manifesto, he said, was merely a Futurist rehash—and snobbish at that. Worst of all, it had offended no one.[47] With hindsight it can be seen that the rehash charge, though largely true, missed the point, which was to challenge

Catalan artists to relinquish local colour and take a hard look at the modern world. It may not have fulfilled this purpose—but it certainly helped to increase Dalí's fame.

Lectures and Painting

On 13 May 1928 Dalí and two other colleagues on *L'Amic de les Arts*, Josep Carbonell, the editor, and J.V. Foix, lectured to the Sitges Ateneu, 'El Centaure', on 'the most recent artistic and literary trends'.[48] Dalí's short talk was a model of clarity and dry wit. Following the precedent of *The Anti-Art Manifesto*, he attacked the 'patina' of contemporary Catalan art, wondered why Barcelona's Gothic Quarter had not yet been demolished, reminded his listeners that the Parthenon was a glistening novelty, not a ruin, when it was built, and addressed to 'those who cared about civilization' a programme of ten recommendations:

1. The abolition of the *sardana*.[49]
2. The rejection, in other words, of all that is regional, typical, local, etc.
3. Scorn for buildings more than twenty years old.
4. The propagation of the realization that we live in a post-machine age.
5. The propagation of the realization that stressed concrete really exists.
6. That there's also something called electricity.
7. The necessity, as a matter of hygiene, for baths and clean underwear.
8. The necessity for having a clean face, that is, free from patina.
9. The use of the most modern objects of our age.
10. The recognition that artists are an obstacle to civilization.

Dalí ended his speech with a fine swagger:

'Gentlemen: Out of respect for art, for the Parthenon, Raphael, Homer, the Egyptian Pyramids and Giotto, let us pronounce ourselves against art. When our artists take a daily bath, practise a sport, live without patina, then it will be time to worry again about art. That's all.'[50]

By coincidence, a series of lectures on art was also being held at this time in Figueres, at the Casino Menestral, to accompany an exhibition of local painting to which Dalí had contributed nine works, four of them from his 'Lorca period': *Still Life (Invitation to Sleep)*, *Gadget and Hand*, *Honey is Sweeter than Blood* and *Harlequin*. Among the speakers were two controversial art critics, Joan Sacs and Rafael Benet, with both of whom Dalí had taken issue on several occasions. Dalí was billed to close the cycle on 21 May with a talk on the latest artistic trends, and the rooms were packed with *figuerencs* eager to hear their controversial painter. The text of Dalí's lecture is unknown, but a newspaper report shows that he was on his best behaviour: no scandal this time (with his family in the audience). Clearly and precisely, with the aid of numerous slides, Dalí summarized the development of modern painting from Cubism to Surrealism, expressed his sympathy for the latter movement and glossed with approval Freud's theory of the unconscious, 'which obeys laws totally at variance with those of the waking mind'. The audience appears greatly to have enjoyed the lecture, which was followed by Dalí's friend Puig Pujades reading extracts from J.V. Foix's recent book of quasi-Surrealist prose, *Gertrudis*.[51]

The popular mayor of Figueres, Ramon Bassols, then rose to give a short speech. During it several members of the packed audience noticed his increasing pallor, attributing this to the emotion of the moment. When Bassols left the platform he staggered— and dropped stone dead into the arms of Puig Pujades. The event received widespread press-coverage, both locally and in Barcelona.[52] 'The comic papers claimed that the enormities expressed in the course of my lecture had killed him,' Dalí recalled in the *Secret Life*. Though no such enormities had in fact been expressed, the incident served to enhance Dalí's growing reputation as a public speaker with a dangerous tongue.[53]

Having brought his lecture campaign to a successful close, Dalí now retired to Cadaqués to concentrate on his painting. Among the works he produced this summer were a series of beachscapes incorporating real sand (or shingle), shells and bits of fishermen's cork floats washed up at Es Llané or around the corner at Es Sortell.[54] It was a technique with which he had begun to experiment towards the end of 1927 under the influence of André Masson and Picasso.[55] In these works the collaged elements are generally affixed to an almost colourless ground, and often serve as the setting for activities so blatantly erotic that only the very obtuse, the hypocritical or the very repressed could fail to miss the point. As in the previous summer's *Honey is Sweeter than Blood* there is also the occasional putrescent donkey, while the birds and spectral cows show that Dalí has been looking closely at Max Ernst.

XII

One of the most sexually provocative of the summer's paintings was *Dialogue on the Beach*, whose much later title, *Unsatisfied Desires*, clarifies its theme. The hand on the left, with its rampantly phallic finger, is that of Dalí the compulsive masturbator, and had been adumbrated a year earlier in *Little Ashes*. But it is also the male sexual apparatus itself: the first finger representing an erect penis, testicles the third and fourth. As for the red-edged, hairy black orifice located between the thumb and first finger, it inescapably suggests a vagina. The phallic finger points in the direction of the other party to the dialogue, clearly female, from which the hand is separated by an anodyne grey space, as if the figures were located on islands and attempting to communicate, in vain, over an insurmountable expanse of sea. The red, ribbon-like form at the female's orifice echoes the one juxtaposed with a thumb at the pinnacle of the wraith-like, Tanguyesque shape spiralling against the sky, which Santos Torroella interprets as representing the unsatisfied desires of the picture's second title;[56] both draw the eye back to the space, picked out in the same red, at the centre of the masturbatory hand. *Dialogue on the Beach*, which shows the formal influence of Miró, can be read as the expression of Dalí's despair at the sexual loneliness to which his inability to find a partner was driving him, and for which shame-ridden masturbation was the only outlet.

Dalí, Male Figure and Female Figure on Beach, *1928. Dimensions and whereabouts unknown. Reproduced in* La Gaceta Literaria, *Madrid, 1 February 1929. More insinuating fingers.*

The masturbatory hand appears in several other paintings done this summer, notably in *Beigneuse* (sic), also entitled *Female Nude*, and *The Bather*, where the influence of Miró is again unmistakable.[57] In another work of similar theme, *Male Figure and Female Figure on a Beach*, only known today from a contemporary black-and-white photograph, the hand is juxtaposed with ideograms of breasts owing an obvious debt to Arp. Dalí greatly admired the German artist, as we have seen, and other paintings from these months, notably the group representing fishermen and women on the beach at Cadaqués, are undisguisedly Arpian.

Gypsy Ballads

Meanwhile, at the end of July 1928, Lorca's *Gypsy Ballads* was published in Madrid. Its success was instantaneous and staggering. One distinguished critic stated that Lorca had forged 'the most personal and singular instrument of poetic expression in Spanish since the great innovations of Rubén Darío'.[58] No greater praise could have been lavished on the poet. Other critics were equally appreciative. The ballads, with their highly original fusion of traditional and modern elements, appealed not only to the critics but to the general public, and before long the first edition had sold out. At thirty, Lorca, almost overnight, became the most famous and admired young poet in Spain: a living classic.

The publication of *Gypsy Ballads* coincided with a personal crisis in Lorca's life to which he alluded cryptically in letters to various friends. Dalí was aware of the poet's tormented relationship with the young sculptor Emilio Aladrén, who had been in his class at the Royal Academy of San Fernando, and in his reply to an unhappy communication from Lorca wrote to him what seems, on the basis of the sole fragment that has come to light, to have been one of his most feeling letters. We only know it because it was quoted by Lorca himself in a letter to a young Colombian friend, Jorge Zalamea. Dalí had counselled the poet:

> You're a Christian hurricane and you need my paganism. During your last stay in Madrid you gave in to something to which you should never have given in. I'm going to go and see you and take you a sea-cure. It'll be winter and we'll light the fire. The poor animals will be frozen with cold. You'll remember that you're an inventor of marvellous things and we'll live together with a camera for taking our pictures.[59]

Lorca told Zalamea excitedly that Dalí would be going to see him in Granada that

September. But the longed-for visit never took place. Probably, once again, Dalí claimed that he was too busy with his work.

That August Dalí sat down with the *Gypsy Ballads* and subjected the eighteen poems (many of which he must already have known by heart) to searing scrutiny. At the beginning of September he wrote a long letter to Lorca in which he formulated his objections to the ballads while at the same time affirming that they contained 'the most fabulous poetic substance that has ever existed'. As Lorca must have expected, in view of *The Anti-Art Manifesto* and Dalí's recent articles, the painter thought them too traditional, too immersed in local colour, too anecdotal, too tied to 'the lyrical norms of the past' despite their pretensions to modernity. Even Lorca's most arresting metaphors Dalí judged stereotyped and conformist. His main gripe, however, was that the poet had not abandoned himself to the dictates of the unconscious. In other words, that Lorca was not yet a Surrealist. Most of the ballads had in fact been composed some years earlier.

Dalí could not refrain from lecturing his friend in terms that once again recall his gloss on André Breton's preface to the Arp catalogue:

> You're moving among threadbare, anti-poetic clichés. You mention a rider and you assume that he's on a horse and that the horse is galloping; *that's going a long way* because *in reality* it would be *useful to ascertain* if really it's the rider who's on top, if the reins aren't actually an organic continuation of the very hands themselves, if in reality it doesn't turn out that the hairs on the rider's balls aren't travelling faster than the horse, and that the horse, in fact, is something immobile stuck to the ground by vigorous roots, etc. . . . We need to leave things *free* of the conventional ideas to which our intelligence has subjected them. Then these sweet little things will behave automatically in accordance with their true, *consubstantial* natures. Let them decide for themselves the direction in which their shadows are projected!

Dalí informed Lorca that he would be enlarging on these notions in an article, dedicated to him, for *La Gaceta Literaria*. Entitled 'Reality and Surreality', it appeared on 15 October 1928 without the promised dedication but repeating almost word for word the ideas contained in the letter to the poet.[60]

The letter showed geniune concern over an aspect of Lorca's poetic personality that, in fact, he himself now considered obsolete. Dalí had rarely shown himself so appreciative of his friend, so tender almost:

> I love you for what your book reveals you to be, which is quite the opposite of the idea the putrescent philistines have spread about you, that is, Lorca the bronzed gypsy with black

hair, childlike heart, etc. etc . . . You, little beastie, with your little fingernails, with your body sometimes half possessed by death, or in which death wells up from your nails to your shoulders in the most sterile of efforts! I've drunk death against your shoulder in those moments when you abandoned your great arms, which had become like two crumpled empty sheaths of the insensitive and useless folds of the tapestries ironed at the Residencia. The day you lose your fear, and shit on the Salinases[61] of the world, give up Rhyme—in short, art as understood by the pigs—you'll produce witty, horrifying, intense, poetic things such as no other poet ever could.

The letter ended with a direct exposition of Dalí's current attitude to Surrealism:

Surrealism is one of the means of Evasion. But it's Evasion itself that's the important thing. I'm beginning to have my own modes apart from Surrealism, but the latter is something alive. As you can see, I no longer talk about it as I used to do, and am delighted to say that my views have changed considerably since last summer. Not bad, eh?[62]

Lorca needed little prompting to embark on the adventure proposed by Dalí, an adventure that was to bring him to the very threshold of Surrealism. The work he produced immediately after the reception of the letter, which he told Sebastià Gasch was 'intelligent and arbitrary',[63] bore witness to the respect in which he held the painter's critical acumen, as would do *Poet in New York* and *The Public*. It is difficult to believe that Lorca failed to reply to Dalí's letter, but his answer is unknown.

The Great Autumn Salon Scandal

Early in August 1928 Dalí accepted an offer to exhibit at the Barcelona Autumn Salon, held annually in Joan Maragall's Sala Parés, and undertook at the same time to give another lecture. A few weeks later, when his old friend and ally Josep Dalmau invited him to take part in a forthcoming collective show at his famous gallery, Dalí told him of the previous engagement and said he hoped his presence in both exhibitions would not prove incompatible.[64]

The two works Dalí sent to Maragall were the scandalous *Dialogue on the Beach* and *Thumb, Beach, Moon and Putrescent Bird*, a beach scene, complete with collaged sand, that no one could have found reprehensible.[65] Maragall was appalled by *Dialogue on the Beach* and wrote to Dalí at the beginning of September to tell him, as diplomatically as he could, that he was unable to exhibit the painting. If he did so, he said, it would damage the reputation of the gallery and give grave offence to the public. Moreover, it would do nothing to enhance Dalí's prestige either. He begged him to withdraw the picture voluntarily.[66] In his angry reply, dated 4 September 1928, Dalí said that the painting was the product of inspiration, of 'the purest and truest elements in his soul'. Moreoever, if, as people were always saying, works of this kind were 'unintelligible', how could the public be offended? Anyway, in view of Maragall's attitude he had decided to withdraw *both* paintings. He hoped that Maragall knew what he was doing. Not quite closing the door, Dalí finished by saying that, unless the dealer changed his mind *immediately*, the two works would be shown elsewhere.[67]

That same day Dalí wrote to Dalmau, enclosing copies of Maragall's letter and his reply. He told the dealer that in fact he was delighted by Maragall's objections, since they proved that painting could still possess 'the subversive value of horrifying and traumatizing the public'; he asked for Dalmau's honest opinion of the matter and whether he would be prepared to exhibit the works, adding in a postscript that, if Dalmau showed *Dialogue on the Beach*, it would be worth pointing out in the catalogue that it had been rejected by the Autumn Salon. Clearly Dalí intended to extract the maximum publicity from the developing situation.[68]

Dalmau did not reply until 6 October (perhaps he was away at the time). In the interim, Dalí reached a compromise with Maragall. He sold him *Thumb, Beach, Moon and Putrescent Bird*, accepted that the dealer could show it on his own initiative at the Autumn Salon, and ratified his promise to give a lecture during the exhibition.[69]

When Dalmau received Dalí's letter the Autumn Salon had just opened. He had seen the catalogue, which listed *Thumb, Beach, Moon and Putrescent Bird*. It would have given him extreme pleasure to exhibit both works, he assured Dalí, but now it was too late. To show the rejected painting by itself would be unprofessional.[70]

On 6 October 1928, the same day that Dalmau wrote to Dalí, the Barcelona press published a note from the Sala Parés hanging committee explaining that they had found them themselves obliged to reject one of Dalí's paintings which, despite its artistic merits, 'was not fit to be exhibited in any gallery habitually visited by a numerous public little prepared for certain surprises'. There was no indication as to the nature of the latter. Beneath this note the papers carried Dalí's rejoinder: owing to the non-admission of the offensive painting, he had decided to withdraw both works. The fact that the second was on show had nothing to do with him: it now belonged to a private collection.[71]

In order to accommodate Dalí, Dalmau decided to put off the opening of his own exhibition until the day after the Autumn Salon finished, that is, 28 October, asking him to send not only *Dialogue on the Beach* but two other paintings of his choice.[72] Meanwhile, on 16 October, Dalí delivered his promised talk to a large and expectant audience that, attracted by the controversy and by the artist's blossoming reputation as an incendiary lecturer, had begun to throng the narrow Carrer Petritxol, seat of the Sala Parés, long before the doors opened. The two rooms were filled to bursting point. It had been anounced that the audience would be encouraged to contradict Dalí's views, so the evening promised well. When the painter appeared on the dais, accompanied by Joan Maragall, he was dressed, as always, for the occasion, a 'magnificent' woollen jacket, suitably 'sporting', setting off his meticulously smoothed-down, jet-black hair and the dark brown of his sunburnt face.[73]

Entitled 'Catalan Art Today in Relation to the Most Recent Expressions of Youthful Intelligence', the drift of the twenty-five minute lecture, as might have been expected, was that most of contemporary Catalan art was rubbish, 'putrescent', a mere prolongation of Impressionism, as if Picasso and high-precision machinery did not exist. Only Miró, 'one of the purest values of our age', was spared the holocaust. Repeating, at times almost word for word, the burden of what he had written to Lorca a month and a half earlier and just regurgitated in *La Gaceta Literaria*, Dalí argued with concision, wit and his habitual exaggeration that the only viable art now was that which expressed the 'instinct and intuition of the artist'; which dared to venture down the 'unexplored roads of the spirit, of surreality'. Over and again he used the word 'real' in the sense given to it in Breton's *Surrealist Manifesto* ('the real function of thought'), his thesis resting explicitly on the Freudian assumption that what is ultimately 'real' about a human being is his or her subliminal thought processes, those 'deepest elements in the human spirit'. The short lecture ended with an impassioned anti-art diatribe.[74]

One of Dalí's great talents was the ability to overstate his position, whatever it might be, with such a Buster Keaton straight face, such intensity and such apparent logic that his would-be opponents were often reduced to silence or bumbling incoherence. So it was once he finished his lecture and Maragall asked for objections. Some timid complaints were voiced, to be sure, but, as Dalí himself pointed out a few days later, 'the artists and intellectuals didn't enter the ring', preferring to attack him from a safe distance in the press.[75]

The lecture, which was printed by *La Publicitat*, generated a considerable amount of newspaper comment, adverse and favourable. Dalí probably appreciated particularly the observations by Josep Pla, one of the most famous and popular writers in Catalunya and, like Dalí, from the Empordà. Pla insisted that the lecture had been perfectly cogent, and expressed satisfaction that Dalí was fulfilling the mission of every true son of the Empordà, a region known for its eccentrics, when visiting Barcelona: to leave people with their mouths open.[76]

A few days after his lecture Dalí asked Dalmau to collect *Dialogue on the Beach* from the Sala Parés, sending him *Feminine Nude* and *Male Figure and Female Figure on a Beach* to accompany it in the forthcoming exhibition.[77] Meanwhile, behind Dalí's back, his father had decided to intervene, writing to Dalmau on 21 October to ask him to find some way of dissuading Salvador (perhaps by stressing the risk of police intervention?) from his determination to exhibit the objectionable work.[78] From this moment the situation became increasingly farcical, Dalmau, now almost as sick with apprehension as Maragall had been before him, suggesting to Dalí on 26 October, without mentioning the notary's letter, that they cover over the offensive bits of the painting. If not, he said, his establishment was in danger of being closed down by the authorities, with the consequent damage to his business.[79] Dalmau probably foresaw Dalí's reaction. The reply arrived that same day. To alter the painting in any way would be to behave worse than Maragall, Dalí said. It was unthinkable. 'Convinced now that it is impossible for me to exhibit in Barcelona, I give in,' Dalí ended.[80] *Dialogue on the Beach* was not shown at Dalmau, *Male Figure and Female Figure on a Beach* taking its place. As we have seen, the painting was similar in theme to the rejected one but not nearly so blatant in its sexuality.

In none of this correspondence did Dalí concede that *Dialogue on the Beach* could be considered obscene. Yet this was the nub of the issue. It is difficult not to agree with Santos Torroella when he writes that the episode illustrates well Dalí's inbred proclivity for double dealing.[81]

If Dalí was now the talk of Barcelona there had been little press-coverage in Madrid of his progress since he left the city in 1926. As a result of the Sala Parés scandal, however, this situation began to change. On 6 November 1928, one of the capital's most popular illustrated weeklies, *Estampa*, published an interview with the painter. In it Dalí branded all contemporary Spanish artists, with the exception of Picasso and Miró, as 'putrescent'; expressed his admiration for Ernst, Tanguy and Arp; and, for the first time, explicitly proclaimed himself a Surrealist. The most interesting moment of the interview came at the end, when the reporter asked him three pertinent questions: 'Finally, what is the moral aim of your work? What is your deepest purpose in art? What is the main aspiration of your life?' Dalí replied:

> I'll tell you, methodically. First, the only moral aim is to be true to the reality of my inner life; second, my deepest purpose in art is to contribute to the extinction of the artistic phenomenon and to acquire international prestige; third, my definitive aspiration is always to express an alive state of mind. I hate philistine putrescence.[82]

The photograph of Dalí that accompanied the interview, taken in Barcelona's Plaça de Catalunya, shows the painter at his most determined. Dressed in his habitual sports jacket, he stares at the camera with fanatical eyes. All that remained now was the conquest of Paris. A happy circumstance was just about to bring the realization of this supreme aim closer than even Dalí could have hoped.

Un Chien andalou

On 29 December 1928 Dalí wrote to Pepín Bello from Figueres to tell him that he was about to launch a Surrealist magazine, with contributions from Luis Buñuel as well as 'our Catalan group'. He was sending Pepín some questions. These he must answer with 'the most brutal sincerity'. The replies would be published in the new review. The 'questions' ran:

> I like above all the legs of . . . (examples) hens, donkeys, caterpillars
> The music of . . .
> The books of . . .
> The landscapes of . . .
> The clothes of . . .
> The moustaches of . . .
> The buttocks of . . .
> The paintings of . . .
> The motorcars of . . .
> The chairs of . . .[1]

Pepín obliged immediately. Dalí was pleased with his efforts, especially 'I like the buttocks of the holychrists' (*Me gustan los culos de los santocristos*), and delighted by his unsolicited calligramme on the subject of Madrid's liberal, but now rather staid, club, the Ateneo.[2]

The projected Surrealist magazine did not materialize. Instead, Dalí appropriated what was to be the last issue of *L'Amic de les Arts*. But before this appeared another, even more exciting, enterprise got under way.

Chapter SEVEN

Luis Buñuel, as we have seen, greatly admired Ramón Gómez de la Serna, whose literary cenacle, Pombo, he had attended assiduously while at the Residencia de Estudiantes. In the autumn of 1928 Buñuel was preparing a film based on a series of short stories by Gómez de la Serna about city life. 'To link them,' he recalled, 'it occurred to me to show, in the form of a documentary, the different stages in the production of a daily newspaper':

> A man buys a newspaper in the street and sits down on a bench to read it. Then Gómez
> de la Serna's short stories appear, one by one, in the different sections of the paper: an accident or crime report, a political event, a piece of sports news, etc. I think that at the end
> the man got up, folded up the paper and threw it away.[3]

Buñuel persuaded his mother to finance the film, which was to be to be called *Caprichos*, but Gómez de la Serna failed to come up with the promised screenplay.[4] Buñuel then communicated the outline to Dalí, who, finding it 'extremely mediocre', informed him that he himself had just produced a very short scenario 'which had the touch of genius, and which went completely counter to the contemporary cinema'.[5] Dalí later said that he had jotted down the scenario as it came to him (presumably in Catalan) on the lid of a shoebox.[6]

Buñuel was impressed by Dalí's outline, and in the middle of January 1929 we find him writing to Pepín Bello from Paris to tell him that he is about to set off for a fortnight in Figueres, where he and Dalí are going to work together on 'some very cinematographic ideas they have in common'. Even if the world collapses around them, Buñuel says, shooting will begin that April. The letter shows that he and Dalí had already discussed the project at length. But unfortunately there is no record of their conversations, and no correspondence seems to have survived.[7] Nor has Dalí's original scenario come to light, although there is no doubt that it existed, for in a letter to the painter written shortly after the screening of *Un Chien andalou* six months later, Buñuel recognized his 'protagonism in the *conception* of the film'.[8]

Buñuel travelled to Figueres as planned, and after a week's work the script was ready. One afternoon the two friends bumped into the local newspaperman and author, Josep Puig Pujades, one of Dalí's strongest supporters in the town, and invited him to hear it. Buñuel, who conducted the reading, told Puig Pujades that the title of the film was *Dangereux de se pencher en dedans* ('Dangerous to Lean Inside')—a facetious revamping of the famous admonition affixed beneath the windows of French train compartments (his and Dalí's first idea had been *The Marist Sister with the Crossbow*).[9] Puig Pujades reported in a local newspaper:

> The entire film is a series of normal events which give an impression of abnormality. They are not arbitrary events, since each has its *raison d'être*, but the way in which they are linked and cut is deeply disturbing . . . You realize that either you must be amazed by everything, no matter how run-of-the mill or commonplace, or by nothing at all.

What were Buñuel and Dalí hoping to achieve? 'The aim is to produce something absolutely new in the history of the cinema,' Buñuel told Puig Pujades, adding: 'We hope to make visible certain subconscious states which we believe can only be expressed by the cinema.' The film was unclassifiable, without precedents, 'as different from the film of objects as from that of dreams or the "absolute film"'. It would have some sound; and rather than the mere pooling of his and Dalí's feelings, it was the outcome of 'a certain number of violent coincidences' which had been occupying them for some time. Confirming his letter to Pepín Bello, Buñuel said he expected to finish shooting by May. The film would be premiered in the Studio des Ursulines, in Paris, before moving on to the Cineclub in Madrid and 'specialized cinemas' in Berlin, Geneva, Prague, London and New York.

As regards the elaboration of the script, Buñuel told Puig Pujades that he and Dalí had worked together in complete harmony. 'You'd imagine such intimate and total collaboration impossible,' he admitted, 'but as we rejected each other's ideas, or suggested other ideas and concepts, it was exactly as if we were practising self-criticism.'[10]

Fifty years later Buñuel was more explicit about their work on the script:

> We were so attuned to each other that there was no argument. We wrote accepting the first images that occurred to us, systematically rejecting those deriving from culture or education. They had to be images which surprised us, and which we both accepted without discussion. Only that. For example: the woman grasps a tennis racket to protect herself from the man who wants to attack her. Then he looks around for something with which to counter-attack and (now I'm talking to Dalí) 'What does he see?' 'A flying toad.' 'Bad!' 'A bottle of brandy.' 'Bad!' 'Well then, two ropes.' 'Good, but after the ropes, what?' 'He pulls them and falls, because they're tied to something very heavy.' 'Ah, then it's good for him to fall.' 'With the ropes come two big dry marrows.' 'What else?' 'Two Marist Brothers.' 'That's it, two Marist Brothers!' 'Next?' 'A cannon.' 'Bad!' 'A luxurious armchair.' 'No, a grand piano.' 'Terrific, and on top of the grand piano a donkey . . . no, two rotting donkeys. Fantastic!' That's to say, we encouraged irrational images to well up, unexplained.[11]

The method, as evoked by Buñuel, bore a striking resemblance to the practice of automatic writing, first developed by Breton and Soupault in *The Magnetic Fields*. Little wonder, then, that when he published the screenplay in *La Révolution Surréaliste* at the end of 1929, Buñuel felt able to state: '*Un Chien andalou* would not exist if Surrealism did not exist.'[12]

Buñuel, unlike Dalí, knew how to use a typewriter, and had been careful to bring his with him to Figueres. Whether he typed out their ideas the moment they were agreed on we do not know, since the drafts of the script have not appeared. It is more likely, however, that they were jotted down by hand as they arose, and that after each session Buñuel made a typewritten fair copy of what they had produced, discussing with Dalí the new possibilities that occurred to him as he worked.[13]

Which images in the final version were suggested by Dalí, which by Buñuel? The latter informed Pepín Bello on 10 February 1929, shortly after his visit to Figueres, that 'all their things' at the Residencia de Estudiantes were in the film.[14] He was scarcely exaggerating: he, Dalí, Bello, Lorca and other friends at the 'Resi' shared a common fund of imagery assimilated and elaborated during their years together in Madrid, and it is usually impossible to identify the ultimate sources of this material. The matter is made more complicated by the absence of drafts, of information about the editorial process of the film (all we have is the final French version of the script published by Buñuel in 1929) and by the conflicting claims made later by both authors.

Take the famous opening sequence of the severed eye. In 1929, shortly after the film was made, Buñuel told Georges Bataille that it had been Dalí's idea: the painter had seen a long, narrow cloud slice the moon in two, and been duly disturbed.[15] In Dalí's 1924 portrait of Buñuel, which places the latter in the setting of the Residencia de Estudiantes, a similar cloud is featured in proximity to Buñuel's right eye;[16] and in a 1926 prose piece Dalí mentions a girl's eye threatened by a razor—the instrument with which the eye is severed in the film.[17] All in all, then, it seems likely that Buñuel was accurately reported by Bataille, yet by the 1960s he was claiming the scene for himself.[18] The issue is further complicated by the fact that José Moreno Villa, Buñuel and Dalí's friend at the Residencia, apparently announced one morning over breakfast that he had just had a dream in which he accidentally cut his eye with a razor while shaving.[19] If to all this we add the fact that the eye-slitting cloud also echoes the ones in a painting in the Prado greatly admired by Buñuel, Dalí and Lorca, Mantegna's *Death of the Virgin*, we can see that here, at least, is one Residencia 'thing' in the film.[20]

In the 1960s Buñuel also claimed authorship of the severed hand which is poked by a distracted androgyne in the street, and of the ants that issue from a hole in the male protagonist's palm. In 1982 he contradicted himself as regards the latter: the ants were Dalí's idea.[21] As for the chopped-off hand, one must again question Buñuel's memory, for severed hands and arms first appeared in Dalí's work in 1926 (the study for *Honey is Sweeter than Blood*) and pullulated in them over the next three years. They had also appeared in Lorca's poetry and drawing, and, in fact, were virtually a topos in European art and literature at the time, which by then had also come up with the occasional slit eye.[22]

Buñuel told Bataille that the rotting donkeys placed on the grand pianos were his and Dalí's 'shared obsession'.[23] This was true. As we saw earlier, Buñuel claimed to have seen one as a child, and to have been much affected. So did Pepín Bello. But, again, it was Dalí who first incorporated them in his work, in the study for *Honey is Sweeter than Blood*.[24]

If the Residencia de Estudiantes is one of the clues that helps us to understand *Un Chien andalou*, the cinema itself is another. Dalí was as passionate a film-goer as Buñuel, and, to judge from what they both wrote about the cinema, they must have discussed energetically their likes and dislikes among the latest productions. To such an extent is the film shot through with allusions to Chaplin, Keaton, Harold Lloyd and so forth that Agustín Sánchez Vidal, the leading authority on Buñuel, has remarked that there is hardly an image in it that could not be traced to a cinematographic precedent.[25]

Given Buñuel and Dalí's passionate interest in Freudian theory, there can be little doubt that the brutal opening sequence of *Un Chien andalou*, with an athletic Buñuel in the role of sadistic barber, is intended to illustrate Freud's formulation in *The Interpretation of Dreams*, according to which 'the blinding in the legend of Oedipus, as well as elsewhere, stands for castration'[26] (Buñuel conceded in 1947, moreover, that the only possible method of interpreting the film's symbols would be, 'perhaps', psycho-analysis[27]). Termed 'prologue' in the script, the eye-slitting sequence, which still has the power to make the unprepared faint, introduces a nightmare narrative whose male pro-tagonist, strongly effeminate in character, is racked by sexual anguish and alienation. Lorca came to the conclusion that he was the model for this personage, telling a friend in New York in 1930 (if we can believe Buñuel): 'Buñuel has made a tiny little shit of a film called *Un Chien andalou*—and I'm the Dog.'[28] Although Buñuel denied the charge,[29] the poet's indignation was not unjustified: southerners at the Residencia were some-times referred to jokingly as 'Andalusian dogs';[30] Lorca, their leading representative, was the most famous Andalusian poet of the day; Buñuel and Dalí disapproved of his Andalusian poetry; Lorca was all too aware that Buñuel found his homosexuality unpalatable; while the scene in which the male protagonist of the film suddenly materi-alizes on the bed and then 'comes to life' resembles the poet's enactments at the

Residencia of his death and resurrection. How could Lorca possibly fail to miss the innuendoes?

The poet may have been particularly struck by the scene, attributed by Buñuel to Dalí,[31] in which the male protagonist cycles precariously down a Parisian street, adorned in chambermaid gear, and falls off into the gutter. 'The feminine atmosphere of his frills suggests that he's been castrated,' one Buñuel authority has commented, 'a *quid pro quo*, maybe, for the infantile sadism indulged in the prologue.'[32] This episode, Lorca must have realized at once, alludes directly to his minuscule 'dialogue', *Buster Keaton's Outing*, written in July 1925 shortly after his first visit to Cadaqués.[33] Dalí admired the piece so much that he had suggested, early in 1926, that the poet include it in their projected *Book of Putrescent Pigs*.[34] It was first published in Lorca's review *Gallo* in the spring of 1928, where Dalí, as a contributor, may well have re-read it. In this tiny work, shot through with allusions to the cinema, an effeminate Buster Keaton not only falls off his bicycle, as does the male protagonist of *Un Chien andalou*, but fails miserably in two heterosexual encounters. He is, in a word, impotent—as Buñuel said Lorca was.[35] The connection beween the two works is further suggested by the fact that both the mysterious box that the male protagonist of *Un Chien andalou* carries on his chest, and his tie, are decorated with the same zebra pattern as the stockings worn by one of the girls in Lorca's text. Dalí must have been perfectly aware that Lorca's Keaton embodied the poet's sexual difficulties. To quote from *Buster Keaton's Outing* in the film was, therefore, particularly malicious on his and Buñuel's part.[36]

Lorca may have suspected another wink in his direction in the extraordinary, and highly erotic, opening seconds of the male protagonist's attempted seduction of the girl, described thus in the shooting script:

> Close-up of lecherous hands on her breasts. These emerge from under the jersey. Now one sees an expression of terrible, almost mortal anguish, cross his face. Bloody saliva drools from his mouth onto the naked bosom of the girl.
>
> The breasts disappear to become thighs which the character continues to feel. His expression has changed. His eyes shine with cruelty and lust. His mouth, before wide open, now shuts and becomes minuscule, as if tightened by a sphincter.[37]

The anguish on the male protagonist's face at the appearance of the naked breasts may reflect Lorca's loathing of bosoms, recalled many years afterwards by Dalí;[38] while the lust he experiences in caressing the girl's buttocks (not thighs) must surely be intended as a further allusion to the homosexuality suggested by the sphincter-tight mouth indicated in the script. As for the blood, it issues from the corner of the protagonist's mouth almost exactly as it does from that of the poet's severed head in Dalí's *Honey is Sweeter than Blood*, the eyes of both heads, moreover, having a similar fixed stare. Buñuel never forgot this sequence, saying that it expressed the 'secret but constant link' between copulation and death that had been impressed on him during his childhood in primitive Aragon.[39]

All in all, it seems impossible to doubt that in creating their male protagonist Buñuel and Dalí really had Lorca in mind. That this was so is a further token of the extent to which their three lives were enmeshed and of how each was influenced by the work and the personality of the other.

Dalí was fascinated by the possibilities afforded by film to animate, by means of dissolves and montage, the weird metamorphoses that are the natural language of the dream and which he had been trying to express in his paintings since 1927. Among the film's more successful essays in this genre are the transformation of a woman's armpit into a sea urchin ('a woman's armpit hairs dissolve to sea-urchin spines', reads the script). Such techniques, as the artist said later, gave him the opportunity to produce 'an animated Dalí painting'.[40]

Dalí's excitement about his and Buñuel's project, which still had not received its definitive title, was intense, not least because he hoped it would bring him notoriety where he most badly needed it: in the French capital. Over the following weeks, as Buñuel worked on the shooting script in Paris, he and Dalí must have been in constant contact. But once again there is no record of their correspondence.

Both Buñuel and Dalí wanted the maximum publicity for their joint venture. Not content with the reproduction in a Barcelona paper of the Puig Pujades interview,[41] they decided to spread the good news in the most influential Spanish arts magazine of the day, the Madrid-based *La Gaceta Literaria*, to which both were contributors. On 1 February the editor, Ernest Giménez Caballero, himself a film fan (and maker), obligingly reproduced the essence of what Buñuel had told Puig Pujades. Soon everyone in the Spanish intellectual world knew about the projected film.[42] Back in Paris, Buñuel wrote to Pepín Bello on 10 February 1929 to keep him up to date. He and Dalí were 'closer than ever', he said, and had worked in 'intimate collaboration' on the script. The film would be 'something really big'. The letter shows that Buñuel had a book of poems ready to go to press. When he and Dalí hit on its title, *Le Chien andalou*, he told Bello, they had 'pissed themselves laughing'. 'I have to tell you,' Buñuel added, 'that there isn't an Andalusian dog in the whole book.'[43]

But despite boasting that his book of poetry was about to appear, Buñuel did not publish it then or later. Shortly afterwards he appropriated its title for the film, presumably with Dalí's approval and another laughing session (this time at Lorca's expense), changing the definite article to the indefinite along the way.

André Breton, Benjamin Péret

While Buñuel made frantic preparations to begin shooting *Un Chien andalou*, Dalí, assisted by Sebastià Gasch and Lluís Montanyà, busied himself with the last, 'Surrealist' issue of *L'Amic de les Arts*. According to *La Gaceta Literaria* on 1 February, this 'violent issue' of the Sitges magazine would attack art in general (Chaplin, painting, music, architecture, imagination, 'etc. etc.'), defend anti-artistic activities (Surrealist objects, engineering, idiotic films, Surrealist texts, photography, the gramophone) and include contributions from Pepín Bello, Sebastià Gasch, Buñuel, J.V. Foix and Dalí. Illustrated by photographs and reproductions of recent work by Picasso, Miró and Dalí, there would also be an excerpt from a letter (presumably to Dalí) from Lorca.[44]

The issue appeared in the middle of March and Dalí immediately sent a copy to Buñuel, who pronounced it 'fantastic',[45] Apart from the absence of Picasso and of the promised excerpt from Lorca's letter, the contents were pretty much as *La Gaceta Literaria* had announced. Nine-tenths of the issue was the work of Dalí, whose alignment with the postulates of Surrealism was explicit throughout, several approving references to Breton lending weight to a comment by Jaume Miravitlles in Paris in November 1928 to the effect that he was the only author who now interested Dalí.[46]

Dalí was not only following Breton's work with rapt attention as it appeared in *La Révolution Surréaliste* but obtaining copies of his books, among them *Introduction to the Discourse on the Scarcity of Reality*, published by Gallimard in 1927 and glossed approvingly by Dalí in this last issue of *L'Amic de les Arts*. It was an exaggeration to say that Breton was the only French author occupying Dalí's attention at the time, however. So, too, was Benjamin Péret, whose *Le Grand Jeu* he now recommended to the readers of *L'Amic*, calling him 'the most authentic French poet of our time'. A poem by Péret, from *Dormir, dormir dans les pierres*, was included in the issue, in the original French, introduced rapturously by 'D.G.M.' (Dalí, Gasch, Montanyà): 'We oppose Benjamin Péret, one of the most authentic representatives of the poetry of our age and one of the most SCANDALOUS figures of our epoch, to our indigenous poetry [?] and conventionality.' The reference to scandal was probably an allusion to the celebrated photograph that had appeared in 1926 in *La Révolution Surréaliste*, in which the French poet, sporting a dark vest, is seen addressing a soutaned and hatted cleric. The caption reads 'Our contributor Benjamin Péret insulting a priest'.[47] According to Buñuel, the photograph made a great impression on him, and it is likely that it did so on Dalí, too.[48]

Buñuel was as much a fan of Péret's poetry as Dalí, and may indeed have introduced the latter to his work. In a long letter to Pepín Bello dated 17 February 1929 he told him that Péret was his and Dalí's 'idol' and that he was preparing an essay on him, with quotations, for *La Gaceta Literaria*. He proposed that it should be signed by Dalí, Pepín and himself. For Bello's delectation, he was enclosing his own Spanish renderings of three poems included in *Le Grand Jeu*: 'J'irai veux-tu', 'Les Morts et leurs enfants' and 'Testament de Parmentier'.[49] In his memoirs Buñuel recalled:

> Benjamin Péret was for me the Surrealist poet par excellence: total freedom, a limpid inspiration, like a clear fountain, without any cultural effort and immediately recreating another world. In 1929, Dalí and I used to read aloud some of the poems from *Le Grand Jeu* and sometimes we ended up on the floor killing ourselves laughing.[50]

Jazz, foxtrots and modern music in general are praised by this last issue of *L'Amic de les Arts* (the record reviewer particularly likes 'Show Me the Way to Go Home' and 'What! No Spinach?'), and, where the cinema is concerned, Dalí's attention is firmly focused on the potential of the documentary, with its capacity for the objective representation of reality. He imagines a film narrating 'the long life of the hairs in an ear', or providing a 'slow-motion account of the life of a draught', and pronounces that between this sort of film and Surrealism there is no essential conflict. On the contrary, they complement each other.

The magazine included Buñuel's answers to a questionnaire on the cinema drawn up by Dalí. Buñuel expressed his dislike of Chaplin, who in his opinion had now sold out to the artists and intellectuals, declared his affinity with the Surrealists and, in an aside, revealed that Breton's novel *Nadja*, which had appeared in the summer of 1928, was one of Dalí's favourites.[51] From Dalí's article 'The Photographic Donnée', published a month earlier, we know that he had enjoyed the photographs accompanying the novel, which in his view gave it a 'testimonial value' that would have been impossible from paintings. One imagines that these photographs must have whetted his appetite to visit the Paris of the Surrealists.[52]

Dalí had read from cover to cover the latest issue of *La Révolution Surréaliste* (no. 11, March 1928), which he now recommended to the readers of *L'Amic de les Arts*, particularly its 'Investigations on Sex' report. The result of two evenings of intense mutual questioning among the Surrealists, the exchanges had been marked by an extraordinary frankness, and ranged from fellatio, the 69 position and the desirability or not of simultaneous orgasm, to anal intercourse (homosexual and heterosexual), mutual masturbation, fantasies during coitus, first sexual experiences and prostitution. Buñuel recalls in his memoirs how deeply fascinated he was by the report—despite having already been for three years in Paris, where he had quickly discovered that, in matters of love and sex, the French ordered things differently and were extremely uninhibited about public displays of amorous affection.[53] Publication of such a document would have been as unthinkable in the Spain of those days (still under the yoke of General Primo de Rivera, though not for much longer) as in England, and it is not difficult to imagine Dalí's enthusiasm.

Dalí had also warmed to the issue's celebration of the 'centenary' of hysteria. And he must have been excited, too, by Aragon's poem 'Angelus', which launches a ferocious attack on bourgeois fathers—the sort for whom a bit of tawdry sex on the side is compatible with rejection of their sons:

> These are our fathers, gentlemen, our fathers
> Who find that we're not at all like them,
> Decent folk who've
> Never once got themselves sucked off except when away from their wives . . .[54]

The burden of the last, 'violent' issue of *L'Amic de les Arts* was that only Surrealism could express fully the sensibility of the age that had discovered the unconscious. Its publication showed that Dalí now considered himself an adept of the revolutionary movement that had declared war on Family, Religion and Fatherland. He could not have taken a better passport with him to Paris, where presumably it was his intention to submit it to the scrutiny of Breton.

It appears, moreover, that by this time Dalí and Buñuel had an ambitious project to publish their own Surrealist magazine in the French capital. Coinciding with Dalí's departure to join Buñuel, *La Gaceta Literaria* wrote:

> There is insistent talk about the immediate appearance of a review of high spiritual tension. It will be published in Paris by Salvador Dalí and Luis Buñuel. This review will be the organ of a very restricted group, more or less akin to the Surrealist one. But with a sense of absolute clarity, precision and exactitude. Healthy. Nothing pathological. And frankly anti-French in spirit. To the 'charme' of the Ile de France the review will appose the racial intensity of Cadaqués, of Montroig[55] and Aragon . . . By its vigour, its vitality and its asepsia, the review will be situated in the Antipodes of the delicacy, the fragrance, the lyricism of a Paul Éluard, for example.[56]

The review never appeared, its projected 'anti-French spirit' finding an alternative out-let in *Un Chien andalou*, which Buñuel was now almost ready to begin shooting.

A Catalan in Paris

While Dalí prepared to join Buñuel, a major Exhibition of Painting and Sculptures by Spaniards Resident in Paris opened in Madrid. Significantly, the organizers (the Society for Courses and Lectures at the Residencia de Estudiantes) included Dalí in the line-up, along with two other Spanish artists not based in France: Benjamín Palencia and the sculptor Alberto. The threesome's presence, the exhibition catalogue explained, was justified by 'the intimate ideological and technical, as well as fraternal, relationship linking them to the others'.[57] Perhaps the organizers were also aware of Dalí's imminent departure for Paris.

Two of Dalí's five paintings on show had strong Lorca connections: *Sterile Efforts* (later called *Little Ashes*) and *Honey is Sweeter than Blood*, which was acquired by the Duchess of Lerma and never seen again.[58] The work entitled *Naked Woman* shocked the more staid critics: a piece of cork, vaguely fashioned into the shape of a torso, with a prominent slit in the centre, was affixed with string to a board on which, in the manner of Hans Arp, Dalí had painted a curved outline in oil.[59] *Male Figure and Female Figure on a Beach* contained phallic allusions along the lines of the picture rejected by the Sala Parés in 1928 and, like *Honey is Sweeter than Blood*, was acquired by a female aristocrat, the Duchess of Peñaranda.[60] *Gadget and Hand*, with its masturbatory theme, completed Dalí's contribution to the show.

It was a dazzling contribution, as the critics realized, and Dalí's father duly pasted the reviews into his book of cuttings. Both notary and son must have been particularly pleased by the one that appeared in Spain's leading high-society magazine, *Blanco y Negro*, which said that Dalí, 'the well-known iconoclast', was the main 'surprise' in the show, and reproduced *Sterile Efforts*, *Gadget and Hand* and *Honey is Sweeter than Blood*.[61]

Meanwhile, on 22 March, Buñuel wrote to Dalí to tell him that he was going to begin shooting on 2 April. He asked him to bring some ants, which were proving impossible to find in Paris. 'Make sure you catch them the same day you come here,' he admonished. 'The moment you arrive in Paris take them to me at the studio and I'll film them straightaway. You've plenty of time to locate them and can come as late as 9 April. After that it'll be too late. It depends on you whether I'll have to use caterpillars, flies or rab-bits in the hole in the hand.' Buñuel added precise instructions as to how the ants should be kept alive and transported.[62]

XI

Three days later Buñuel wrote to Pepín Bello, regretting that the latter could not make it to Paris to play a part in the film and, at the same time, 'to fuck the star, who's randy, full-bodied with big tits, imbecilic and not ugly'.[63] Simone Mareuil was alluring, certainly, and had the body the script required. As for the male protagonist, Buñuel had chosen Pierre Batcheff, whom he had met and liked while working with Jean Epstein on the latter's *La Tropique des Sirènes*, starring Joséphine Baker.[64] Batcheff, who died a few years later, was perfect for the part: Dalí recalled in the *Secret Life* that he had 'exactly the physical appearance of the adolescent I had dreamed of for the hero'.[65] Batcheff's wife, Denise Tual, recalled years later that Buñuel and Dalí had made numerous emendations to the script in consultation with her husband, with much coming and going, door-slamming and excited discussion from which she was excluded, despite the fact that all this was going on in her own home.[66]

Shooting seems to have begun as planned on 2 April, at the Billancourt studios outside Paris. Buñuel's cameraman was Albert Duverger, whom, like Pierre Batcheff, he had met and admired while working with Jean Epstein. Dalí arrived a few days later and stayed for some two months, financed, presumably, by his father, although his two sales at the Madrid exhibition may have helped. He lived, he tells us, in an 'immeasurably prosaic hotel room' in the Rue Vivienne, the street running from the National Library to the Boulevard Montmartre which had harboured his hero Isidore Ducasse, author of *The Songs of Maldoror*.[67]

A journalist from Barcelona, Pere Artigas, dropped in on the set towards the end of the filming of the interiors, which lasted for a week, and interviewed Dalí (Buñuel was too busy directing to talk to him). Dalí, confident of the success of the venture, told Artigas that it was the first 'Surrealist transposition effected in the cinema', Man Ray and Robert Desnos's *The Starfish* being 'no more than "another" artistic conception having nothing to do with Surrealism'—which was true. *Un Chien andalou*, Dalí said, 'belongs to the pure, automatic tendency of Benjamin Péret'.

Artigas saw Buñuel shoot the scene in which Dalí and Jaume Miravitlles play two Marist Brothers dragged across the floor by a manic Pierre Batcheff along with a couple of grand pianos topped by rotting donkeys. The dead animals had been meticulously arranged by putrescent-donkey-expert Dalí, who applied runny glue to their eye-sockets to give the impression of trickling blood. According to one witness, the stench of the carcasses was pestilential.[68] The presence of the Marists was a hilarious allusion to the fact that Dalí, Miravitlles and Buñuel had all studied with the Brothers. Dalí, showing the whites of his eyes in simulated terror, was particularly effective in his abject role. 'We'd gone to Billancourt ready for anything,' Artigas ended his account, 'but the spectacle surpassed all our expectations. My God! My God! Whatever will Dalí and Buñuel's *Un Chien andalou* be like?'[69]

It would not be long before the world found out. Buñuel worked fast, setting the pattern for his later films. Dalí, who wrote that he had been able 'to take part in the directing through conversations we held every evening',[70] accompanied Buñuel to Le Havre for the beach sequence at the end of the film, looking positively radiant in a group photograph which shows him in his favourite V-necked jersey, his hair cropped short.

In the absence of letters to his family or friends at this time, our only source of strictly contemporary information about Dalí's sojourn in the French capital comes in the series of six articles he had been commissioned to write before leaving Barcelona by the newspaper *La Publicitat*, presumably through the good offices of his friend J.V. Foix. Entitled 'Documentary-Paris-1929' (in the last issue of *L'Amic de les Arts* Dalí had pronounced himself in favour of 'literary documentaries'), these articles appeared sporadi-

At Le Havre in 1929 during a break from shooting the beach scene in Un Chien andalou. *From left to right: Dalí, Buñuel, Simone Mareuil (the female protagonist), Buñuel's fiancée Jeanne Rucard and the actor who played the young man at the end of the film, Robert Hommet.*

cally between 26 April and 28 June and contain, despite Dalí's declared intention not to report in any conventional sense on what he was doing in Paris, an invaluable insight into his state of mind at the time.

Convinced as he was by Freud's dogma that what normally pass for insignificant details are in fact the relevant ones, Dalí's six-part 'literary documentary' focuses on such apparent trifles as the moustaches and dinner jackets currently fashionable in Paris; reports 'faits divers' chosen allegedly at random from the newspapers, including weather conditions and the number of deaths and births registered in the metropolis; captures exactly what he sees on the tables at the cafés Coupole, Perruquet or Select Américain; and records, among other minutiae, the recipes for new cocktails. Where the arts are concerned, Benjamin Péret is proclaimed, once again, the great literary hero of the moment, and the documentary notes (the word 'notes' occurs again and again) that René Magritte has just produced a painting of a pipe with the title *This Isn't a Pipe*—in fact the title was *The Betrayal of Images*—another called *Flowers of the Abyss* and a third work which is probably *The Living Mirror*. Dalí has a coffee in the Dôme with the Russian-born director Eugène Deslaw, whose film *The Electric Night* he had perhaps seen in Madrid. (Deslaw, who always carried a camera with him, was then making a documentary on Montparnasse.) Buñuel is having difficulties in finding ants in Paris for *Un Chien andalou* (which suggests that Dalí failed to take them from Cadaqués, or, if he did so, to keep them alive en route). There is an oblique reference to Dalí's friend from the Residencia days, Juan Vicéns, who runs the Librairie Espagnole with his wife María Luisa González. Is the bookseller interested in Surrealism? Certainly, 'in the sense that it's the only living movement of the spirit'. Dalí goes to see Joan Miró boxing; visits jazz clubs; and at Robert Desnos's flat listens to records of tangos and rumbas the poet has just brought back from Cuba. In the bedroom, placed next to a 'Surrealist object' by De Chirico, a starfish floats in alcohol, a reminder that it was Desnos who supplied the scenario for Man Ray's *The Starfish*. Dalí also has a chance to see Joan Miró's bedroom, where a bird fashioned from a bit of a chair made by Max Ernst dangles from the ceiling on a thread. René Clair, begetter in 1924 of the remarkable avant-garde film *Entr'acte*, is now making a documentary about a beauty contest. Dalí has seen W.S. Van Dyke and Robert Flaherty's *White Shadows of the South Seas*, the first talkie shown in Europe: you can hear the sound of the sea breaking over a coral reef and palm trees rustling in the breeze. We are informed that he and his friends think that sound films have great potential, particularly for documentaries. In short, whatever Dalí's pretensions to objectivity, his enthusiasm for Paris, the fabulous Paris of the late 1920s, pervades these articles.

By the time they began to be published in Barcelona, *Un Chien andalou* was almost ready for screening. Buñuel had told Puig Pujades in Figueres that the film would be shown first at the Studio des Ursulines, Paris's leading experimental cinema, so he must already have had that guarantee before the scenario was even finished. The version given later in his memoirs is somewhat different. One day, according to this, he met the art critic E. Tériade, who was on friendly terms with the Spanish painters resident in Paris, at the offices of Christian Zervos's *Cahiers d'Art*. Tériade introduced him to Man Ray, who had recently completed a short film called *The Mysteries of the Château du Dé* for the Vicomte Charles de Noailles, the art patron. Ray badly needed another film to flesh out the bill of fare at the première, and asked Buñuel to show him *Un Chien andalou*. Buñuel ran it for him and Louis Aragon a few days later at the Studio des Ursulines. They were astounded by the film and spread the news among their fellow Surrealists. Not long afterwards Buñuel was summoned to meet the group at the Cyrano, in the Place Blanche, just a few metres away from Breton's apartment at 42, Rue Fontaine. Present, he tells us, were Ernst, Breton, Éluard, Tzara, René Char, Pierre Unik, Yves Tanguy, Jean Arp, Maxime Alexandre and René Magritte. The encounter marked a turning-point in his life. Thus far Buñuel's undocumented account in *My Last Sigh*, which contains no suggestion that Dalí was present.[71] Thirty years later Dali stated that he had been introduced to Breton by Miró during his second visit to Paris, and been profoundly affected. 'In my eyes he immediately became a second father,' he is quoted as saying. 'I felt at the time that I had been granted a second birth. The Surrealist group was for me a sort of nourishing placenta and I believed in Surrealism as if it constituted the Tables of the Law. I assimilated totally, with an incredible and insatiable appetite, both the letter and the spirit of the movement, which moreover coresponded so exactly to my deepest self that I incorporated it with the greatest naturalness.' Never again would Dalí acknowledge so honourably the near veneration which he felt for Breton in the early days of their relationship.'[72]

The Surrealists' recollections of their first meeting with Dalí are extremely vague as regards chronology but agree on the painter's shyness. Maxime Alexandre claimed to remember Joan Miró arriving one day at the Cyrano with 'a timid little young man, very self-effacing, wearing a suit and a hard collar like a shop-assistant and the only one of us with a moustache'.[73] Louis Aragon also noticed Dalí's social unease.[74] So did Georges Sadoul, then fast becoming a leading authority on the cinema. Dalí, he recalled, 'had the big eyes, the grace and the timidity of a gazelle'.[75] Such references remind one of the surprise Dalí's manner had caused among his new companions at the Residencia de Estudiantes seven years earlier, and tie in with the harrowing account of this visit to

Paris given in the *Secret Life*, where the painter remembers how ashamed he felt in the presence of so much sophistication, weeping as he spied on the lovers in the Luxembourg Garden and masturbating violently in his hotel bedroom while he fantasized miserably about the sexual orgies taking place all around him. Dalí was such an exhibitionist that at times he could not even wank without watching himself:

> Mortification at not having been able to attain the inaccessible beings whom I had grazed with my glance filled my imagination. With my hand, before my wardrobe mirror, I accomplished the rhythmic and solitary sacrifice in which I was going to prolong for as long as possible the incipient pleasure looked forward to and contained in all those feminine forms I had looked at longingly that afternoon.[76]

The *Secret Life* adds one or two colourful details to our picture of the painter's two months in the French capital. We learn, for example, that Dalí had with him his recently finished *The First Days of Spring*, done in oil and collage, 'in which libidinous pleasure was described in symbols of a surprising objectivity', and that Robert Desnos, with whom he seems to have become quite friendly, was frustrated at not being able to buy it ('it's like nothing that's being done in Paris'!).[77] Dalí said later that he painted the picture, 'a veritable erotic delirium', to spite the organizers of the Barcelona Autumn Salon for their puritanical treatment of him a few months earlier.[78]

The First Days of Spring inaugurated a series of works in which, determined to be more Surrealist than the Surrealists themselves, Dalí elaborated a symbolic language for delineating, with microscopic precision, his erotic obsessions. It deserves, therefore, careful scrutiny. One of the clues to the picture comes on the right, where a soberly dressed old man with a white beard is rejecting the offer of what appears to be a purse from a little girl in a smock (although the shadow of his hand on the beach looks surprisingly like an erection). It has generally been accepted that this personage is Freud, and that his presence justifies a psychoanalytic interpretation of the painting.[79] A further hint that this is Dalí's intention comes in the collaged photograph of himself as a child, which he has placed strategically on the steps in the centre of the picture. Steps, stairs and ladders, as Dalí must have known, are consistently classified by Freud as symbols of sexual intercourse. The child's gaze is intent, alert, and he looks suitably bemused— which is presumably why Dalí selected the snapshot.[80]

To the right of the photograph we find the first appearance of an icon soon to proliferate in Dalí's work: a waxy-complexioned head with closed eyes, long eyelashes, prominent nose and a giant locust glued to the spot where there should be a mouth. The shape

XIII

of the head, which represents Dalí as compulsive masturbator, was inspired by a rock in the inlet of Cullaró at Cape Creus[81] and was soon to find its maximum expression in *The* *XIV*
Great Masturbator, begun in the summer of 1929. As regards the locust, we already know that Dalí was terrified of these creatures. Their obsessive presence in the paintings of this period perhaps alludes to the painter's fear of sexual contact and of impotence, while the closed eyes indicate that the masturbator, oblivious to external reality, is only concerned with the erotic fantasies being played out in the theatre of his mind. One of these fantasies probably concerns the chubby-cheeked child of oriental aspect whose face peers out at us from within the masturbator's skull. A flash-back to the reveries occasioned by Esteban Trayter's stereoscope, in which Dalí had seen a little Russian girl on a sleigh? Perhaps. And has the face been painted or is it a collage? Even at close range it is impossibe to be sure (and even less so in a reproduction). The con-fusion, of course, is deliberate.

Dalí and Buñuel on the rocks at Cape Creus, 1929.

The infantile nature of the masturbator's fantasies is indicated by the images contained within a sort of balloon that issues from his head. The deer refers to the transfers which delighted Dalí as a child.[82] So, too, may the bird motif repeated below, while the pencil can be related to the schoolroom flash-back in *Un Chien andalou*. And the debonair man casting the stark shadow? Perhaps he is the confident male the masturbator dreams of becoming.

To the right of the masturbator's head, gripping the latter's skin by its teeth, we find the first appearance of another image soon to become a celebrated Dalinian icon: the painter's head in the guise of a jug, Freudian symbol, by dint of its receptibility, of feminine sexuality.[83] Its proliferation in the paintings Dalí did at this time perhaps indicates that the artist, obsessed by his impotence, feared increasingly that he might be homosexual. The jug motif is repeated less explicitly in the centre-foreground, linked to the red fish-head which appeared in earlier paintings and, if Moorhouse is right, symbolizes for Dalí the female genitalia.[84]

The most blatantly erotic imagery in the painting comes in the left-of-centre fore-ground where, against a collaged scene of (springtime?) high jinks on board a pleasure cruiser, Dalí has set the activity of a grotesque couple. Flies emerge from a vortex, sug-gestive of genitalia, at the centre of the female's red face. The man leaning abjectly on her shoulder is gagged and apparently having an emission into a bucket from which emerges a phallic finger. The latter (in case we should miss the point) is located above a hole and a pair of balls, and is about to enter a double-image vagina fashioned between the personage's hands and echoing that painted on the female's tie.

Two men with a sledge-like wheeled conveyance are to the right of the steps, one of whom is practically astride the other's back. The homosexuality implied in the posture seems obvious enough. Coming towards them from the far distance are a father and child (another motif about to become obsessive in Dalí's painting) while, on the other side of the steps, a lone seated figure looks towards the horizon with his back to the springtime activities we have been contemplating, as if he had opted out. He is the only figure in the picture who does not cast a shadow. Is he collaged or painted, or both? It is impossible to tell. Once again, as in the head of the little girl, Dalí is deliberately con-fusing our perceptions.

It is not surprising that Robert Desnos admired this intensely disquieting variation on the theme of spring as aphrodisiac. It was now clear to Dalí that by combining Freudian and personal symbols he had hit on an original formula, at once subjective and objective, for the expression of his deepest anxieties and longings. The discovery led directly to one of the most fruitful periods in his career.

Meanwhile Joan Miró was proving untiring in his efforts to introduce Dalí into polite society. One evening he escorted him to dinner at the apartment of the Duquesa de Dato, widow of the Spanish prime minister, Eduardo Dato, who had been gunned down in 1921 by anarchists in Madrid. A distinguished patroness of the arts, Isabel Dato lived habitu-ally in Paris but also ran a salon in Madrid. Carlos Morla Lynch, a Chilean diplomat, thought that, decked out in one of her favourite three-cornered hats, she looked like the Chevalier des Grieux in *Manon Lescaut*.[85] She must have known about Dalí before meet-ing him, for she had been one of the aristocratic purchasers at the Exhibition of Spanish Painters Resident in Paris, staged in Madrid a few months earlier.[86] Among the guests at Isabel Dato's table the night Miró took Dalí was the Countess 'Toto' Cuevas de Vera, another art-loving Madrid aristocrat and woman-about-town, who became a close friend of the painter some years later.[87] Meeting these blue-blooded high-flyers Dalí must have felt that he was being levered into the right social groove at last, although for the moment his extreme bashfulness prevented him from shining in conversation.[88]

Miró's services did not stop at taking Dalí to dinner at the luxurious apartments of noble Spanish ladies. An even greater favour was to introduce him to the Belgian art dealer Camille Goemans, who lived in the same block as himself in the Rue Tourlaque, a few metres from Montmartre cemetery.[89]

Camille Goemans was born at Louvain in 1900. Ex-civil servant, writer and Surrealist poet, in early 1927 he had moved from Brussels to Paris, where for two years he ran the Galerie Jacques-Callot, located just a few doors away from the Galerie Surréaliste. Goemans was a close friend of René Magritte, who followed him to Paris, and became the painter's leading promoter in the French capital. When Miró introduced Dalí to Goemans the latter had just set up his own premises, the Galerie Goemans, at 49, Rue de Seine, opening with an exhibition of collages by Picasso, Arp, Ernst and Magritte.[90] Goemans liked Dalí's work and, on 14 May, signed him up in a contract which stipulated that between 15 May and 15 November 1929 the Catalan's entire production was to be handled by him. In return, Dalí would receive 1,000 francs a month from the date of the contract. Goemans undertook to organize an exhibition of his work during the 1929–30 season.

It seems that Dalí discussed the terms of this breakthrough contract with his father by telephone, for two days after the agreement was signed Dalí Cusí wrote to Miró, asking him for his sincere opinion of his son's chances. The painter, with his habitual caution, replied on 20 May that he was doing everything in his power personally to further Salvador's career and that, while the going would not be easy, he was confident that things would work out now that he had been taken on board by Goemans.[91] On 22 May one of the leading Catalan-language Barcelona newspapers, *La Veu de Catalunya*, reported the signing of the contract. The notary pasted the clipping into his album, where it was joined soon afterwards by the contract itself. Don Salvador Dalí Cusí had every cause for satisfaction: his son's conquest of Paris was proceeding as planned.

At Goemans's apartment Dalí met René Magritte, whose recent work he referred to appreciatively in his 'documentary' series for *La Publicitat*. David Sylvester, Magritte's biographer, states that Dalí did not visit the latter's studio outside Paris during his stay, and that he probably only knew his work through photographs.[92] But Magritte must surely have been in the habit of taking paintings to Goemans, and it seems fair to surmise that Dalí would have seen some of these on his visits to Rue Tourlaque. A further reference to Magritte in the *La Publicitat* series, moreover, suggests that Dalí had inside information about the older artist's progress, perhaps proceeding from Magritte himself. 'The Belgian Surrealist painter,' he wrote, 'has just imagined a wide city street full of a multitude of people of all kinds, all riding horses, but horses not going anywhere and moving within a tiny radius.'[93] It seems likely, moreover, that Dalí showed Magritte some of his own work during these weeks and that the Belgian was impressed. How, otherwise, can one explain his decision to visit Dalí in Cadaqués that summer along with Goemans, Buñuel and Paul Éluard?

According to the *Secret Life*, Dalí had been introduced to Éluard by Goemans one evening at the Bal Tabarin. As always the handsome poet was in female company, this time 'a lady dressed in black spangles'. 'That's Paul Éluard, the Surrealist poet,' Dalí tells us Goemans confided when the couple entered. 'He's very important, and what's more he buys paintings. His wife is in Switzerland, and the woman with him is a girlfriend of his.'[94] This meeting must have taken place in April 1929, since Éluard, always on the move, left Paris at the end of the month and did not return until after Dalí had gone back to Spain.[95] 'Éluard struck me as a legendary being,' Dalí recalls in the *Secret Life*. 'He drank calmly, and appeared completely absorbed in looking at the beautiful women. Before we took leave of each other, he promised to come and see me the next summer in Cadaqués.'[96]

It is difficult to believe that Éluard made such a promise to Dalí on their first meeting; probably they saw each other again during the month. At all events, Dalí was soon a fervent admirer of Éluard's poetry, quoting enthusiastically in his *La Publicitat* series from Éluard and Péret's joint *152 Proverbes mis au goût du jour*.

An Andalusian Dog in Paris

Dalí returned to Figueres before the première of *Un Chien andalou*, paying a brief visit to Cadaqués with his family on 2 June.[97] In his autobiographical writings the painter does not mention the editorial process of the film, or having visited the cutting room to see Buñuel at work. It is surely inconceivable, however, that he would have abandoned Paris before viewing the finished product.[98] What Dalí does tell us, in the *Secret Life*, is that he was unwell towards the end of his stay in Paris, developing 'a violent inflammation of the tonsils' followed by angina.[99] That he did indeed catch something is confirmed by a doctor's prescription pasted into Salvador Dalí Cusí's album. Dated 23 May 1929, it prescribes abundant water and a selection of powders including aspirin, bromohydrate and caffeine citrate. Perhaps Dalí was in a state of nervous exhaustion.[100]

On 6 June 1929 the première of *Un Chien andalou* took place at the Studio des Ursulines, Buñuel having taken up Man Ray's invitation to share the bill with his *The Mysteries of the Château du Dé*, which was shown first.[101] It was a memorable evening so far as Buñuel's film was concerned. The would-be pugilist had apparently filled his pockets with stones in case the reaction of the audience was hostile. But he need not have worried. Man Ray's film was not appreciated by the gathering, who considered it conventionally avant-garde, whereas the Spaniards' seventeen-minute-long *tour de force* electrified those present, many of whom were violently affected by the opening scene of the severed eye.[102] According to Buñuel, the 'fine flower' of Parisian society was in the cinema: 'a handful of aristocrats, some writers or painters already famous (Picasso, Le Corbusier, Cocteau, Christian Bérard, the composer Georges Auric) and of course the Surrealist group in full'.[103] Buñuel's memory is never too trustworthy. It is fortunate, therefore, that we have the contemporary account of a Catalan journalist who was present that historic evening. He reported shortly afterwards, agog, that among the audience, along with Man Ray's patron, the Vicomte de Noailles, and Man Ray himself, were Fernand Léger, Constantin Brancusi, Robert Desnos, Hans Arp, Max Ernst, Tristan Tzara, Joan Miró, Christian Zervos, Jacques Lipchitz, Roger Vildrac, André Breton, Louis Aragon, Le Corbusier, René Clair and E. Tériade.[104]

The critics, by and large, were intrigued. One of them, André Delons, wrote a few weeks later in the Brussels review *Variétés* that 'it is the first time, and I mean first time, that images, penetrated with our terrible human gestures, carry their desires through to the very end, cut their way to their final goal through their predestined obstacles . . . One has the impression of being present at some genuine return of truth, of truth skinned alive . . . It is quite clear, for example, for whoever has eyes to see, that a *divertissement* such as *Entr'acte*, after this, is no longer valid today.'[105] For J. Bernard Brunius, of *Cahiers d'Art*, Buñuel had destroyed with one razor-slash the pretensions of those for whom art was a matter of pleasant sensations. He had captured brilliantly 'the absurd but implacable logic of the dream'. An authentic Spaniard, he had demonstrated that he was driven by that 'living force that draws true men to the most anguishing problems'.[106] There was generous praise, too, from Robert Desnos, who wrote:

> I do not know any film which works so directly on the spectator, any film which is made so specifically for him, which engages him in conversation, in intimate rapport. But whether it's the eye sliced by a razor, and whose crystalline liquid trickles viscously, or the assemblage of Spanish priests and grand pianos bearing its load of dead donkeys, there is nothing in it that does not partake of humour and poetry, intimately linked.[107]

The most dazzling review of all, however, came from one of Buñuel and Dalí's friends from their Residencia de Estudiantes days, the writer Eugenio Montes, who had been sent to Paris for the occasion by *La Gaceta Literaria*. After the screening Montes heard Fernand Léger, Tristan Tzara and Tériade, among many others, agree that the film was a landmark in the history of the cinema. Dalí was so excited by the review, which appeared on the front page of the *Gaceta* on 15 June 1929, that he later reproduced part of it in the *Secret Life*.[108] Montes had emphasized the essentially Spanish quality of the film, alluding (for the initiated, and inverting the terms) to Dalí's painting *Honey is Sweeter than Blood*, and cocking more than one snook at the French:

> The elemental, barbarous beauty of the desert—moon, earth—where 'blood is sweeter than honey', reappears before the world. No! Do not look here for the roses of France. Spain is not a garden, nor are Spaniards gardeners. Spain is a planet. In a desert the roses are rotting donkeys. No 'esprit', therefore. Nothing decorative. Spain goes for the essential, not the refined. Spain does not refine. Nor falsify. Spain does not know how to paint tortoises or to cover donkeys with glass instead of hair. In Spain the statues of Christ bleed. And when they are taken out into the street for processions, the Civil Guard escorts them.[109]

All in all, Dalí's later claim that *Un Chien andalou* 'ruined in a single evening ten years of pseudo-intellectual post-war advance-guardism' was not without justification.[110]

On 24 June Buñuel wrote to Dalí. All was going well with the film, and Mauclair, the head of Studio 28, was fixing things so that the censorship would not intervene when public showings began in his cinema that autumn (he hoped to run the film for two months). Meanwhile, it was to be screened for three days at a luxury seaside resort. Art patron Charles de Noailles was expressing great interest in the film, and had rented it for a special session at his private cinema at the beginning of July, offering the premises to Buñuel for his own guests the following day (Picasso had said he wanted to attend). Buñuel had now met 'all' the Surrealists, who had expressed their admiration for the film, especially Queneau, Prévert, Morise and Naville. Artaud and Vitrac had just shown it again in Studio 28 along with one by Eugène Deslaw. *Un Chien andalou* was received with enthusiasm; Deslaw's effort was booed. All the magazines were asking for stills, and Buñuel was telling anyone who cared to listen to bear in mind Dalí's 'protagonism in the *conception* of the film':

> As you know, up to now there's been a tendency in the cinema only to mention the director or the actors. Auriol, Desnos, Brunius, etc., will place our names side by side, which is important so that we appear as a team. Montes's article isn't bad, but I'm sorry he men-

tioned the vile *jota** and the disgusting River Ebro. Every day they introduce me to people who want to know us.[111]

Charles and Marie-Laure de Noailles had been positively bowled over by *Un Chien andalou*—and by Luis Buñuel, to whom it seems they were introduced by Christian Zervos, editor of *Cahiers d'Art*, probably on the night of the première.[112] Before long Buñuel was being invited to dinner.[113] The Noailles offered to help in whatever way they could to ensure that the film received a licence for public screening, which it did at the end of June,[114] and on 3 July they showed the film in Buñuel's presence in their private cinema. The most sophisticated in Paris, it already had provision for sound.[115] The canny Aragonese, at first wary of dealing with aristocrats, was soon won over by the charming and enlightened couple. Many years later he told Max Aub: 'I've never met art patrons as generous as them. They had exemplary discretion, grace, good taste and consideration.'[116] Over the following weeks the Noailles held several further viewings for their friends, critics and, as the Vicomte put it, 'useful people'. Among the guests were Jean Hugo, Cocteau, François Poulenc, Comte Étienne de Beaumont, the Danish film director Carl Theodor Dreyer, René Crevel and the poet Léon-Paul Fargue.[117] Noailles, the perfect gentleman, made sure that Buñuel was properly recompensed for these screenings.[118]

Thanks largely to Noailles, the fame of *Un Chien andalou* was now spreading rapidly. That July it was seen, at a festival of shorts in Paris, by the English critic Oswell Blakeston. He found it difficult 'to follow threads consciously which are meant to appeal to our subconscious', noticed that the film touched on homosexuality, and felt sure that it 'means something individually'. He hoped that he would be able see it again—and again.[119]

Charles de Noailles (1891–1981) was the son of the Prince de Poix, the scion of an ancient and wealthy family who counted Chateaubriand and Saint-Simon among their ancestors and who for generations had been art lovers and collectors. Noailles was particularly interested in architecture, and later in life became an international authority on botany and gardening. His wife Marie-Laure was the daughter of a hugely rich Jewish-American banker, Maurice Bischoffsheim, and a Frenchwoman of some distinction, Madame de Croisset, who descended from the Marquis de Sade and whose mother, the Comtesse Joselle de Chevigné, was one of the models for the Princesse de Guermantes in Proust's *A la recherche du temps perdu*.[120] Marie-Laure was brought up surrounded by

---

*The *jota* is the 'national' dance of Aragon. The Ebro flows through Saragossa, the region's capital.

books and interesting people, early developed a taste for poetry and painting and, while still an adolescent, became a friend and passionate admirer of Jean Cocteau. By the time she married Noailles in 1923, aged twenty, she had inherited her father's huge fortune.

A striking figure with a large, beaky nose that made her look a bit like Louis XIV, she was to prove 'as autocratic as he with friends and lovers'.[121]

Charles and Marie-Laure de Noailles, when Buñuel met them, were the leading patrons of art and literature in France. They had a Renaissance aura. 'Their wealth was so vast as to be secure from the fluctuations of national economies or the panic of international crises,' James Lord, the biographer of Giacometti (another of their protégés), has written. 'There was no limitation to their role but that of their taste, which proved to be as catholic as it was clairvoyant.'[122] In Paris the couple lived and entertained at 11, Place des États Unis, the palatial mansion that Marie-Laure had inherited from her banker father. Here she and her husband put together a fabulous collection of contemporary art, including representative works by all the Paris-based painters of consequence.[123] Count Jean-Louis de Faucigny-Lucinge, who knew the Noailles intimately, recalled that Marie-Laure had 'a very good eye indeed for painting', her innate good taste hav-

Marie-Laure and Charles de Noailles, 1929.

ing been warmly praised by no less a connoisseur than Bernard Berenson.[124] Soon she took the place of a declining Misia Sert as the French capital's most exciting hostess (if you didn't attend Marie-Laure's evenings you didn't exist), and became the talk of the town in the process.

The Noailles' social whirl in Paris was complemented by the fun-and-games at their Mediterranean villa on the heights above Hyères, whose atmosphere was captured for posterity in the film they commissioned in 1928 from Jacques Manuel, *Biceps and Jewels*, and in Man Ray's *The Mysteries of the Château du Dé*. The villa, begun in 1924, had been

entrusted to the architect Robert Mallet Stevens, after consultations with Gropius and
Le Corbusier. Beginning as 'a small modern house, pleasant to live in', it grew into a
Cubist folly occupying almost 2,000 square metres of ground space, with endless corri-
dors and rooms, all designed to receive maximum sunlight, an indoors swimming pool,
a gymnasium, a solarium and squash court (the Noailles were athletics-mad), a Cubist
garden (whose terraces were duly embellished with sculptures by Giacometti, Laurens,
Lipchitz and Zadkine), ultra-modern furniture and, everywhere, pictures: De Chirico,
Klee, Picasso, Braque, Miró, Chagall, Masson, Ernst . . .

The building and extensive grounds were bought by the Hyères town council on
Marie-Laure de Noailles's death in 1970, and today are undergoing restoration.
Although the atmosphere of the place is now spoiled by the roar of jets from the airport
below, it is not difficult, strolling around the premises, to understand why people clam-
oured to be invited here in the twenties and thirties.

The Noailles enjoyed surrounding themselves by the creative men and women to
whom their immense wealth, as well as their own charm and talent, gave them access,
and the list of those who enjoyed their patronage, and their hospitality, in Paris and
Hyères would run to pages. According to one person who knew them well, Pierre Bergé,
the couple had a taste for subversion, and 'found their own equilibrium in exerting a
destabilizing influence on other people'.[125]

The initiative to commission Buñuel and Dalí's next film came from Marie-Laure,
who had been struck by how superior *Un Chien andalou* was to Man Ray's *The Mysteries
of the Château du Dé*.[126] Buñuel was promised that he would have complete freedom to do
what he wanted, and accepted at once.[127] Dalí was by then in Spain, but in the last article of his *La Publicitat* series, written before he left Paris, he announced that Buñuel's
forthcoming project was a documentary about Cadaqués and its coast, 'with coverage
ranging from the big toes of the local fishermen to the tops of the cliffs of Cape Creus,
via the waving of all kinds of plants and all kinds of submarine seaweed'.[128] Since it had
already been agreed that Buñuel would visit Dalí in Cadaqués that summer, along with
the Éluards, the Magrittes and Camille Goemans, it seems fair to assume that Buñuel
now suggested to Dalí that they work together there in August on the script of the new
film.

Not long after his return to Catalunya, and installed once again in Cadaqués, Dalí
underwent a sort of regression to his childhood, or so he tells us, nurturing his irrational side, suffering from fits of uncontrollable laughter and seeing 'infinite images
which I could not localize precisely but which I knew with certainty that I had seen
when I was little'. One of these images was a deer deriving from the transfers with

which he and his sister had so much enjoyed playing (and which had already made an appearance in *The First Days of Spring*). As for the others:

> I also saw more complicated and condensed images: the profile of a rabbit's head, whose eye also served as the eye of a parrot, which was larger and vividly coloured. And the eye served still another head, that of a fish enfolding the other two. This fish I sometimes saw with a grasshopper clinging to its mouth. Another image which often came into my head, especially when I was rowing, was that of a multitude of little parasols of all the colours in the world.[129]

Dalí decided to incorporate these and other similar images into a painting, following only the promptings of his subconscious as to their arrangement. The result was *The Lugubrious Game (Le Jeu lugubre)*.[130]

XV   *The Lugubrious Game* contains a veritable anthology of the sexual obsessions for which only compulsive masturbation and painting itself were providing Dalí with an outlet at the time. Into this picture, he tells us, he poured his 'body and soul'.[131] The little painting (44.4 x 30.3 cm) rewards close scrutiny. The gaudily coloured parrot's head, to which Dalí refers in the passage just quoted, is easily located at its centre and, merging with it from below, the deer. It may take a while for the rabbit's head within which the parrot's is enclosed to come into view: when it suddenly does so, some people have the experience of a minor revelation. The front of the rabbit's head, as Dalí indicates, is also intended to be that of a fish—a resemblance more apparent if one turns the picture around. The dark interior of the rabbit's ear seems incongruous, an infallible indication that one is in the presence of a double image. Sure enough: as Paul Moorhouse has pointed out, the ear is also a vulva.[132]

A dizzy whirl of these fantasies, or, as Georges Bataille termed them, 'objects of desire', emanates from the masturbator's head.[133] For Dawn Ades, the device is 'an image borrowed directly from a certain type of medium's drawing which similarly shows the medium's "vision" rising from her own forehead'.[134] The right arm and bare breasts of the girl with the collaged head are at the same time an ithyphallic finger and testicles. The former is about to insert itself between two chubby buttocks into an anus whose edge is milling with ants (which call up *Un Chien andalou*). To the right of her left breast, the tip of a phallic cigarette is placed at the entrance to another orifice, paralleling the activity of a finger busily at work on the masturbator's head.

At this time Dalí was obsessed by the subject of anal penetration, whether by phallus or finger. While working on the painting he wrote to Pepín Bello, saying he was still tired after his spell in Paris and inviting him to Cadaqués. 'So, I'm waiting for you,' he ended; 'I'll be delighted when you come, and will have my finger (as always) stuck into that famous hole, which is the arsehole and none other.'[135]

To the left of the phallic finger Dalí has placed a chalice surmounted by an upright host, in an arrangement common in Roman Catholic iconography (and which Dalí may have seen first, as a child, in Ingres's *The Virgin with the Host*, included in the relevant volume of his Gowans's Art Books collection).[136] The juxtaposition of the chalice and host with an *anus*, and an anus about to be digitally penetrated at that, shows to what an extent Dalí was now determined not only to comply to the letter with Surrealism's proscription of religion, but to attack it for all he was worth. In this game he had a willing partner in Buñuel, who had told Pepín Bello in February that he and Dalí planned to write a book of poems together that summer in Cadaqués. Some of their proposed titles were 'Mules Fleeing from a Consecrated Host', 'Battle between Consecrated Hosts and Ants', 'Consecrated Host with Moustache and Penis' and 'Consecrated Hosts Issuing from the Arse of a Nightingale and Saluting'.[137] Blasphemy, challenging God to do His worst, vastly appealed at this time to both Dalí and Buñuel; and the host was one of their principal targets. In this connection we should bear in mind Spaniards' proclivity to mix the sacred and the profane in their swearing, as Ernest Hemingway discovered to his delight. A common expression of irritation is 'I shit on the Host!' (¡*Me cago en la hostia*!); and one not infrequently hears 'I shit in the Chalice!' (¡*Me cago en el copón*!). Such phrases, one need hardly say, are found deeply shocking by Catholics from other countries.

Vaginas, for Dalí the most terrifying of orifices, abound in the picture. Merging with the girl's head is that of a man whose mouth has been transformed into a blood-red female organ. The hats have vulva-like clefts, and above the anus, at the centre of the whirling vortex, another vagina echoes the dark interior of the rabbit's ear below.[138]

These are some of the small details. If we stand back, as it were, to get an overall view of the action-packed painting, other elements become more prominent. It can be seen, for example, that the masturbator's head and the magma of elements beneath it, stretching down to the severed legs of the figure with the pink buttocks, form together the outline of a donkey's head (yet another donkey!), one of whose ears sprouts from the back of the masturbator's.

As for the couple in the lower right-hand corner, we saw earlier that they relate to a traumatic afternoon in Cadaqués when Dalí's father arrived home and announced that he had crapped in his pants, deeply shaming Salvador but showing no apparent concern himself (see p. 83). The father figure here is staring fixedly and delightedly at something, perhaps the (presumably female) buttocks, and holding in his right hand what appears to be a sharp implement wrapped in a bloodstained cloth. The figure leaning pathetically on his shoulder is naked and clearly in some sort of agony. What has happened? Almost certainly the bearded man represents 'parental authority' and has imposed castration (condign penalty for masturbation) on the personage, arguably his son, who clings to him while one of his fingers is inserted into a vagina-shaped orifice in his head. One is reminded that shame cuts like a knife and is a form of emotional castration.[139]

And the figure on top of the monument, hiding its face and extending a grossly magnified hand? For Ades the face-hiding is a further indication of shame, the grotesque hand denoting the cause of the latter: masturbation.[140] I think we must agree with this reading, for the hand is very similar to those appearing in Dalí's other works of masturbatory theme. A youthful, seated figure, perhaps representing Dalí himself, is handing something up to the statue. Ades is probably right again in identifying it as 'an enlarged sex organ'.[141] It is significant, too, that the old man with the stick looking up at the gigantic monument is very like the figure of Don Salvador Dalí Cusí which we find in other paintings done this summer and autumn, notably *The Great Masturbator*.

Lions in Dalí's paintings of this period tend to symbolize raging and terrifying desires. Here the one with its foot on a cannonball is, moreover, a direct allusion to those guarding the entrance to the Spanish Parliament in Madrid. Parliaments, like strict fathers, legislate, lay down the law. And masturbation is a forbidden and shameful activity. We saw earlier that, in an adolescent diary, Dalí recorded his attempts to stop masturbating, fearing that the practice might make him 'lose blood', that is, potency (see p. 110). This danger is probably indicated here by the object placed near the left-hand lower corner of the painting, identified by Ades as a 'softened dripping candle', a Freudian dream symbol for impotence.[142] This interpretation is strengthened by the presence of the staircase, which, for the same critic, expresses, by its 'oppressive size', a fear of sexual intercourse.[143]

Ultimately, what is the theme of this painting in which, as Georges Bataille was the first to point out, castration has been inflicted?[144] What is the crime that has merited such terrible retribution? A pencil study for the painting increases the likelihood that the root sin is not just the practice of masturbation but voyeurism: sexual staring, curiosity. The parental figure wears long trousers in the prototype, his face seems older. A hand holds a revolver, and naked figures are seen indulging in a variety of sexual activities (including female mutual masturbation) from which the ashamed younger figure, unlike the man, is hiding his face.[145] By 1929 Dalí was all too well aware that, no matter what course his life took, no matter how successful a ruse his exhibitionism, he would never belong to the happy band of the sexually uninhibited. The shame that slays desire, in Swinburne's outburst against 'the supreme evil, God', had done its work well.[146] He was an impotent outsider, desperate to join in but unable to do so. And no painting of his shows it more clearly than *The Lugubrious Game*. Dalí's family, understandably, did not warm to this painting as it took shape before their eyes. Anna Maria wrote twenty years later that the works Dalí executed that summer were 'horribly disturbing', veritable nightmares—and blamed her brother's new Surrealist friends. *The Lugubrious Game*, she said, was the picture most representative of the dire change they had wrought on Salvador's spirit.[147]

Gala, Éluard

At the beginning of August 1929 the Magrittes, Camille Goemans and his girlfriend, Yvonne Bernard, arrived as promised in Cadaqués, where they had rented an apartment for the month.[148] A few days later they were joined by Éluard, his wife Gala and their daughter, Cécile, who put up on the front at the Hotel Miramar (today Residencia de la Academia). The presence of such an unusual group of visitors could not fail to pass unnoticed. On 15 August the local fortnightly paper, *Sol Ixent*, announced that spending the summer in Cadaqués were the 'well-known' Paris art dealer Goemans, 'the highly distinguished' Belgian painter Magritte and the 'great' French poet Éluard, 'accompanied by their respective families'. There was no mention of Buñuel, which suggests that he arrived after the periodical went to press.[149]

Paul Éluard liked flashing photographs of Gala naked, and may well have shown some of them to Dalí in Paris, with pertinent observations.[150] Dalí heard a great deal about Gala from other people during his stay, too, so that before he returned to Spain he was already beginning to think of her as the woman he had been waiting for.[151] The partner of such a consummate Don Juan as Éluard had to be very special indeed, certainly. But when Dalí saw Gala in her swimsuit on the beach at Es Llané the reality outstripped what he had imagined; the *petite* Russian turned exotic Parisienne was his dream body personified, the one (albeit decapitated) that two years earlier he had painted from behind in *Little Ashes*, with its perfectly contoured thighs and legs and delicately curved buttocks set off by a wasp waist. In the picture the headless woman's breasts, hidden from sight, are by implication of modest dimensions, in proportion with the rest of the body. Breasts for Dalí had to be small to be beautiful, and full bosoms repelled him. Gala's were just right, 'so sweet', Éluard once wrote to her, 'that you could eat them'.[152] Dalí would never fail to tell anyone who asked that he was really a bottoms man him-

XI

III

self. Six years before meeting Gala he had painted a *pointilliste* scene of naked female bathers, stressing their buttocks as they hauled themselves into boats or disported in the water. Now, after so much agonized waiting, a real-life Venus Callipygia had materialized before his eyes in the setting he most loved in the world: the beach at Es Llané which he had discovered as a child, on which in 1925 and 1927 he had frolicked with

IX

Lorca and where, in *Composition with Three Figures (Neo-Cubist Academy)*, he had visualized Saint Sebastian, patron of Cadaqués, striding confidently ashore. The setting was ideal; the physique perfect. It was passion at first sight:

> Her body still had the build of a child's. Her shoulder blades and the sub-renal muscles had that somewhat sudden athletic tension of an adolescent's. But the small of her back, on the other hand, was extremely feminine and pronounced, and served as an infinitely svelte hyphen between the wilful, energetic and proud leanness of her torso and her very delicate buttocks which the exaggerated slenderness of her waist enhanced and rendered greatly more desirable.[153]

Among Gala's other physical charms were lovely arms, shapely legs and trim ankles. She walked purposefully, with a spring, and people would turn to look back at her when she strode past them in the street.[154] Not long after meeting her, Dalí read Jensen's *Gradiva* and Freud's analysis of the remarkable short story. He decided at once that Gala was a reincarnation of Gradiva, the enigmatic, high-stepping heroine whose Latin name means 'the girl splendid in walking' and who brings the deluded archaeologist, Norbert Hanold, back to his senses and marries him. Henceforth Gala would be Dalí's very own 'Gradiva Rediviva', sometimes termed 'Celle qui avance'.

Gala's face could hardly have been considered beautiful but it was certainly compelling and, when she decided to

Gala stripping in the garden, c. 1924.

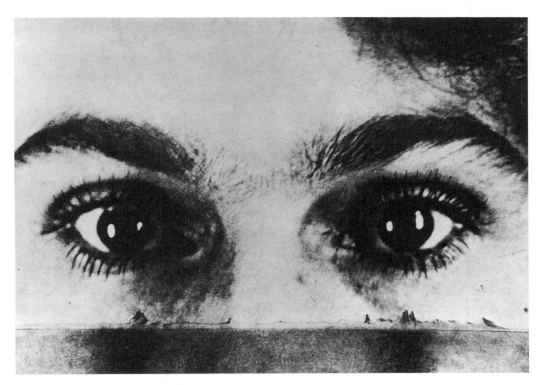

Gala's wall-penetrating eyes photographed and touched up by Max Ernst, 1925.

turn on the charm, even pretty. Because it was olive-shaped, Dalí later nicknamed her *Oliva* or the Catalan diminutive *Oliveta* (probably with the small and delicious olives of Cadaqués in mind). Gala had a fine mouth and a flashing smile. Her long straight nose was a bit too long, though, and it and her close-set black eyes could make her look like a bird of prey when she was in a bad mood, which she often was. Dalí once said that he liked her 'aggressive and disagreeable face'.[155] Really the animal Gala most resembled was the cat: she was slinky, graceful and potentially vicious. Her gaze, particularly when fixed on other women, had a fierce intensity capable, Éluard once wrote, of piercing defensive walls ('regard perceur de murailles').[156] For Dalí's friend from the Residencia days, María Luisa González, they were narrow rat's eyes that could see into your soul.[157]

When Gala was on her best behaviour she radiated personality, however, and her eyes seemed to open wider, as in Max Ernst's photo-portrait of her, done in 1925. Another picture, showing her at Port Lligat in the early 1930s, does justice to her alluring physique. All in all, there could be no doubt about it: Gala *avait du chien*, a quality much admired by the French.[158]

Helena Diakanoff Devulina (Gala was her pet name at home in Russia) was not as young as her lithe appearance suggested, having been born in Kazan on 26 August 1894.

She was, that is, exactly thirty-five when she met Dalí, ten years her junior.[159] Very little indeed is known about her childhood. Her father, Ivan, was a high-ranking Moscow civil servant; her mother, Antonina, a cultured woman who moved in a circle of writers and artists and published a collection of children's stories. Dalí always insisted that Gala had Jewish blood; if so, it probably derived from her mother.[160]

Antonina and Ivan's apartment was full of books. As a child Gala devoured the stories of the Comtesse de Ségur, then immensely popular throughout Europe, identifying in her imagination with little French girls dressed in crinolines, and began to learn the language from a French governess when she was seven.[161] This early exposure to things Gallic was similar to Dalí's, and from the moment they met they communicated in French—and would continue to do so. At home Gala also learnt German, a language she brushed up in the 1920s by attending an adult education institution in Paris.[162]

When Gala was about ten she lost her father. One version has it that he died in Siberia, gold-prospecting for the Tsar;[163] another that he abandoned Antonina, presumably for someone else. Whatever the truth of the matter, the latter was left in straitened circumstances to bring up four children—Gala had a sister, Lidia, seven years younger than herself, and two teenage brothers, Nikolai and Vadim.[164] A resourceful and unconventional woman, Antonina set up house before long with a wealthy lawyer called Gomberg. This unofficial stepfather was apparently disliked by all the children except Gala.[165]

From childhood Gala suffered from poor health (perhaps a disorder of the neck glands), spending much time in Moscow sanatoriums,[166] and at school her peers teased her for being hopelessly unathletic.[167] She was passionately interested in literature and read voraciously, a habit that remained with her all her life. Banned as a female from Moscow University, she attended the M.G. Brukhonendo Feminine Institute, did well and received a special permit from the authorities allowing her to teach children at home.[168]

In 1912, when Gala was eighteen, her doctors, fearing she was in danger of contracting tuberculosis, recommended a spell at the famous Clavadel Sanatorium near Davos, in Switzerland. She stayed there for two years, and it was at Clavadel that she met and fell in love with the young French poet Eugène Grindel, who adopted the pen-name of Paul Éluard soon afterwards. A year and a half younger than Gala, he was suffering from mild tuberculosis. In 1914, just before the outbreak of war, Gala returned to Russia and Éluard to Paris, where he was mobilized. They corresponded regularly and, in 1916, Gala made her way across Europe to rejoin and marry her lover.

Some thirty of Gala's early letters to Éluard, written during the war while living with

the poet's domineering mother in Paris, have been preserved. They reveal a passionately erotic temperament which at times verged on the hysterical. Éluard always maintained that he and Gala were virgins when they married in 1917, and this seems to have
been the case. The letters show that Gala was religious, obsessed with purity (she had
been brought up in the Russian Orthodox Church but became a Catholic to marry Éluard) and struggling to curb her 'whorish tendencies' (*qualités putainesques*), as she termed
them:[169] tendencies which upset Éluard, who in some of his early letters refers to her
saleté, shocked, it appears, by the frankness of her caresses. The correspondence makes
it clear that Gala had been much sought after by men back home (she is already fully
aware of her sexual charisma), and shows that she was absolutely determined to get her
own way in life, even to the extent of ordering Éluard to keep away from the front for
her sake, and of making him feel a coward as a result (this is the 'delicate question' that
recurs throughout these letters).[170] A typical recommendation: 'Do the dressings well,
you're very tender, very good and very capable, you can help the unfortunate creatures
better where you are than in the accursed trenches. Don't do anything to harm me.
Remain on good terms with the doctor so that he'll keep you with him.'[171] Another: 'Do
everything you can to be made an auxiliary and *never* get near to the firing, in the
trenches. I assure you the war will be over in a year. You must make every possible effort
to escape alive from this nightmare.'[172] While waiting for his return, Gala read hungri-
ly, as she always would, attended French classes (she had decided to obtain her *brevet*,
which would qualify her to teach the language), proved useless at household chores and
told Éluard about the seductive clothes she had acquired 'only for him'.[173] Her letters end
habitually with a variation on the phrase 'I kiss you on the mouth and everywhere'. One
day she wrote: 'I kiss you everywhere with the sweetest and strongest "violence".'[174]
Gala, quite clearly, was an erotic volcano on the point of eruption:

> Don't think I'm a coquette by nature, really, believe me. It's only for you. I feel that when
> a man returns from the filthy front he wants to find his wife prettily dressed and perfumed
> (because, don't get angry, I've also bought perfume but I promise you not to put it on until
> you're here, you'll see that the bottle is still full). Don't be sad and angry. Believe me, it's
> all for you.[175]

The course of Gala's life with Éluard up to the time she met Dalí in 1929 can be traced
briefly. Their only child, Cécile, was born in May 1918, six months before the Armistice,
and was almost certainly unplanned (in her extant letters to Éluard during the war, Gala
at no time mentions the desire to have a baby once they marry). Gala was to prove less

than a loving mother, and soon decided that Cécile was an intolerable encumbrance, virtually dumping her on Éluard's mother. Éluard, luckily for his daughter, proved himself a kind and appreciative father. As he became an increasingly well-known poet, Gala was drawn with him into the pulsating literary and artistic world of avant-garde Paris, heralded by the foundation, in 1919, of Breton, Aragon and Soupault's review *Littérature*, on which Éluard was soon collaborating. Dada and its spirit of violent rebellion had just hit Paris, and out of the ensuing experiments, manifestos and ferment came Breton and Soupault's first attempt at automatic writing, *The Magnetic Fields*—and Surrealism. The intensely superstitious Gala was at the thick of it, her interest in the occult matching that of the Surrealists in such phenomena as hypnotism, dreams and thought transference.

If Gala had been a virgin up to her marriage, up to, that is, the age of twenty-three, she soon compensated for her lack of sexual experience and, as Éluard's letters to her show, learnt to give free rein to her *qualités putainesques*. Her appetite for sex, in fact, was so overwhelming that it verged on the nymphomaniac. Soon she needed lovers. This posed no problem: the couple, as they became increasingly aware of their attractiveness, and of the abundance of willing partners, embarked on a life-style in which free love was the rule and possessiveness taboo. One of Gala's first post-marital conquests was Max Ernst, whom she and Éluard met, and immediately adored, in Cologne in 1921. In 1922, when Ernst, one of Dada's most dazzling stars, arrived in Paris, hot on the heels of Tristan Tzara, he moved in with the Éluards, who were then living outside

Gala as Harpie by Max Ernst. Page of drawings published in Paul Éluard's Au Défaut du silence, *1924.*

the city at Eaubonne. Before long the handsome and fabulously inventive German painter was sharing their bed. Years afterwards, remembering this remarkable *ménage à trois*, Gala apparently expressed regret that some 'anatomical problem' had prevented her from being simultaneously sodomized and fucked by the two men.[176]

Ernst soon began to produce compulsive drawings of Gala. She is also one of the 'friends' who appears in his painting *Au Rendez-vous des Amis* (1922), standing at the extreme right of the last row, her back to the company and pointing in another direction with her right hand—an indication, perhaps, of her fierce independence and complete lack of team spirit.[177] Ernst featured her nude in another canvas from the same period, *La Belle Jardinière*, which was exhibited in 1923 and reproduced in 1925 in *La Révolution Surréaliste*.[178] A series of over a hundred drawings of Gala's face done to illustrate a tiny book of poems by Éluard, *Au Défaut du silence*, published anonymously in 1925, shows the muse in a less flattering light: in the overwhelming majority she looks not only ugly but positively evil. We are reminded of Philippe Soupault's cruel nickname for her, 'Gala la Gale' ('Gala the Scabies'), with its attendant suggestion, albeit not etymological, of *galle*, gall, bitterness.[179]

The many photographs of Gala in the 1920s (at balls, visiting spas, lounging on beaches . . .) testify to her growing seductiveness throughout the decade. She was, certainly, formidably sexy—and all too happy to reveal her naked body to the eye of the camera.[180] At this time Éluard was making a good living by working with his father in real estate and speculating in art. He could afford to give Gala the elegant life for which she had always craved, and even more so when his father died in 1927. According to Éluard's biographer, Jean-Charles Gateau, the couple, leaving the poet's mother to bring up Cécile, splashed between then and the summer of 1929 the equivalent, in 1988 terms, of two million francs. By the time Gala met Dalí, however, Éluard's inheritance had not only shrunk considerably but he was seriously worried about money.[181] Gala was anxious, too, the decline in their fortunes re-igniting intense childhood fears of poverty and insecurity.[182]

In 1946 Éluard was to destroy Gala's letters (only her pre-marital ones survived the holocaust), asking her to do the same with his, the aim being to deprive posterity of all trace of their '*vie intime*'.[183] Luckily for us Gala did not comply with his wishes, keeping Éluard's letters intact. His outpourings and reactions to what she has told him, or failed to tell him, are a source of priceless information about their lives, providing many insights into the personality of this highly enigmatic woman whom the early Surrealists called 'the Tower' (because of her secretiveness) and whom Patrick Waldberg once nicknamed memorably as 'the Sibyl of the Steppes'.[184]

With the luxury, the trips, the fabulous hotels and the self-congratulation of these years went extreme promiscuity, as if Éluard and Gala felt obliged to prove over and over again their sexual appeal and their independence. A considerable degree of voyeurism was also involved, particularly on the part of Éluard, and they followed each other's conquests with amused complicity (on one occasion Éluard writes: 'Understand, and make him understand, that I want us to have you together some time, as was agreed').[185] Gala detested physical ugliness or deformities of any kind, so her lovers had invariably to be handsome. This obsession with being surrounded by the beautiful she was to share with Dalí.[186] Éluard often comes across in these letters as vanity personified, taking himself with fearsome seriousness (there are no laughs here, and little in the way of thought for other people): 'Dear Gala, I'm making love here far too much, far too much. But what wouldn't I give to spend a night with you. Everything';[187] 'Here I'm very elegant, very good-looking. Everyone adores me';[188] 'My book's in all the shops and I've ordered a handsome grey suit.'[189] Women are picked up and cast aside; a wonderful new toothpaste enables him to have teeth 'like snow';[190] and, where making love to Gala is concerned, she's asked repeatedly not to come back when she's having a period: the messiness would spoil the fun.[191]

The fun included mutual masturbation, and the fact that Gala had no hang-ups about this practice must have been a huge relief to Dalí, the Great Masturbator in person. What also transpires from Éluard's letters is that by the summer of 1929 Gala was going for what she wanted with such brutal determination that even he was appalled. She had just been visiting the Parksanatorium clinic at Arosa, in Switzerland, where she had acquired yet another lover, one Baer, with whom she figures in dozens of photographs preserved in the Fundació Gala–Salvador Dalí in Figueres. Éluard, despite his liaison with an attractive Berliner called Alice Apfel ('La Pomme') was, he said, missing her desperately. Money was much on his mind (the bottom had dropped out of the art market), he had had to sell more shares, and for the first time in years it seemed that they could only afford an economical summer holiday. 'I now realize that nothing can stop you, that you're pitiless', Éluard wrote to Gala on 30 July, fearing that he was losing his grip on her. A few days later they met up at Leysin, the health resort near Montreux where René Crevel, one of Gala's closest friends, was being treated for tuberculosis. Then they set off with their daughter to see Dalí.[192]

Gala, Dalí

What happened in Cadaqués proved that Éluard's fears about Gala were all too justified. Since his adolescent relationship with Carme Roget, there is no evidence that Dalí had had even the slightest fling with anyone of the other sex. By his own account he lived in a state of permanent erotic deprivation, relieved only by masturbation. Having now met the woman of his fantasies, as sexually shameless as he was ashamed, he found himself in a terrible quandary. How could he possibly interest her? There is no way of corroborating the antics to which, according to the *Secret Life*, he resorted manically in his endeavours to enamour the thrilling Russian (goat-manure perfume, garish outfit, bloodied armpits, pearl necklace, red geranium behind the ear, outbursts of crazed laughter . . .):[193] Gala, highly secretive about her private life, never told her side of the story, and Anna Maria Dalí's books on her brother contain no information whatsoever about the bizarre courtship.

It is just possible that before arriving in Cadaqués Gala was already curious about the painter. 'Éluard kept telling me about his handsome Dalí. I felt he was almost pushing me into his arms before I even saw him,' it appears she once commented.[194] On her side too, then, there may have been a predisposition. At all events, encouraged by Éluard or not, she was soon flirting with the painter.[195]

Buñuel, who had now arrived in Cadaqués and was staying at Es Llané with Dalí and his family, saw it happen. 'Overnight Dalí changed beyond recognition,' he recalls in his memoirs. The projected work on the script of their next film was, suddenly, impossible.

The very picture of elegance: Dalí and Gala with two unidentified acquaintances and behind them, sporting a bow tie, René Crevel, Barcelona, c. 1931.

'All he did was talk about Gala, repeating everything she said. A total transformation.'[196] Buñuel later used the words 'transfigured', 'unhinged', 'bewitched' to describe Dalí's state.[197] For once, Dalí's account tallies with Buñuel's: Luis was 'terribly disappointed, for he had come to Cadaqués with the idea of collaborating with me on the scenario for a new film, whereas I was more and more absorbed in nursing my personal madness, and had thoughts only for this and for Gala'.[198]

Things weren't helped by the fact that Buñuel, scrutinizing Gala on the beach, discovered that she suffered from what in his eyes was a repugnant defect: there was a pronounced gap between her thighs. As he put it later to Max Aub: 'I hated women whose genitals were in a sort of wedge between two separated legs.'[199] Photographs taken at this time, however, show that, whatever he may have felt later, at the beginning Buñuel was quite happy to pose smilingly with the incipient lovers.

How did the rest of the group react to what was going on? Goemans's observations are not known, but years later Georgette Magritte recalled that Éluard did not seem to be jealous, only worrying that the couple might have an accident during their long walks together. Perhaps the poet felt they were in danger of falling over a cliff in their absorption.[200]

While Dalí and Gala became increasingly engrossed in each other, the rest of the company explored Cadaqués and its surroundings. No doubt they talked about Picasso's visit to the village in 1910 with Fernande Olivier, and it is hard to imagine that Dalí would have failed to introduce them to the Pichots and their bohemian world at Es Sortell. Magritte produced some paintings, the most memorable being *Threatening Weather*, in which a naked female torso, a French horn and a Catalan country chair hang spectrally juxtaposed over the bay of Cadaqués and the indented coastline that stretches south in a series of blue headlands towards Cape Norfeu. In the painting's 'metallically bright palette' David Sylvester finds 'a testimony to the fact that Dalí was working at the same time on *The Lugubrious Game*'.[201] For Rafael Santos Torroella, *Threatening Weather* attempts to catch the moment when the tramuntana unleashes itself on the bay, the wind's rushing voice being symbolized by the French horn.[202] Magritte's waves can also be read as a tribute to those in Dalí's by then celebrated portrait of Anna Maria at the window of Es Llané, which he must have seen when he visited the family. Magritte was much taken by Anna Maria, and gave her a painting, *The Birth of Flowers*, in which Sylvester also finds the influence of Dalí's 'polished technique' in *The Lugubrious Game*.[203]

If that technique impressed Magritte during his visit to Cadaqués, it was the painting's content that most affected the other members of the group, not least its anal and scatological elements. Dalí records that Gala was detailed to ask him if he was 'coprophagic', which they suspected. Had they enquired if he was coprophiliac, he could certainly not have denied the charge so easily. 'I swear to you that I am not "coprophagic", he claims he told Gala. 'I consciously loathe that type of aberration as much as you can possibly loathe it. But I consider scatology as a terrorizing element, just as I do blood, or my phobia for grasshoppers.' The explanation was accepted.[204]

According to Dalí, it was Éluard who provided the title for *The Lugubrious Game*.[206] From this, and the fact that Dalí now embarked on a portrait of Éluard, we can deduce that the two saw much of each other during the poet's brief stay in Cadaqués. The portrait repeats several of the motifs of *The Lugubrious Game*: the head of the masturbator; the fearsome locust, with an onanistic finger entering a hole in its stomach; a maelstrom of ants infesting what may be a consecrated wafer at the masturbator's non-existent mouth; shells and jagged rocks that indicate Cadaqués (accompanied this time, for good measure, by a segment of mica-schist that forms the base of the bust).

Dalí, Portrait of Paul Éluard, *1929. Oil on cardboard. 35 x 25 cm. Dalí began the portrait within days of meeting Éluard's wife, Gala, in Cadaqués.*

It is impossible to resist the temptation to look for allusions to Gala. Perhaps relevant is the fact that the locust has lost its arms and legs and that the former are pushing up through the fingers of the delicate female hand on Éluard's forehead, which presumably are crushing the dreaded insect along with the moth. Might the suggestion be that Dalí senses that Gala could help to allay his sexual fears? One notes, also, the two hands clasping each other, affectionately it would seem, at the bottom of the portrait, linked by a mane of flowing tresses to the rocks of Cape Creus. Beside them a mop of hair suggests a maidenhead. An allusion, perhaps, to Dalí's seaside walks with Gala, to their growing intimacy, to his hopes for sexual potency and liberation.

The figures on the beach also transmit a poignant message. Near the horizon a man walks with a small child, as in *The First Days of Spring*, their backs turned to the apparition of Éluard that hovers over the beach. Their far-off presence may be an indication that Dalí feels that a break with his dependence on his father is imminent. On the other side of the picture a group of three people stand by one of the elongated white objects, surmounted by a jostle of airborne sticks, that appeared in the study for *Honey is Sweeter than Blood* and thereafter proliferated. As was noted earlier, Dalí explained that this was the first 'delirious image' to come to him, occurring while he was rowing in Cadaqués, and that it produced a sensation of anguish somehow relating to Millet's *Angelus.*[206] Certainly it has produced anguish here. One of the men hides his face with his hands, and another leans on the shoulder of a personage with highlighted genitals. Meanwhile, closer to hand, a couple of bearded individuals bear away two of the triangular 'gadgets' (*aparells*) frequent in Dalí's work from 1927 onwards, and which almost certainly symbolize the female genitalia.

Éluard, increasingly anxious about his financial situation, left Cadaqués before the others in order to continue his art world wheeler-dealing. Gala and Cécile stayed on at the Miramar and remained there after the Magrittes, Goemans and his girlfriend took their leave at the beginning of September. Éluard met the latter at the station in Paris, where they gave him a letter from Gala. In his reply he explained that he was busy preparing their new flat in Montmartre, just below the Sacré-Coeur at 7, Rue Becquerel, which he hoped would be ready by the beginning of October. Paris was stiflingly hot and she need not hurry home. Two more letters followed in quick succession. Éluard told Gala that he had bought back Dalí's 'beautiful painting' from the dealer Charles Ratton (which painting is not clear) and that he was thinking about her the whole time. He wanted her to be 'supremely elegant' in Paris; asked her to write a 'really nice' letter to Goemans; raved on about her sexual attractions; and entreated her to do the impossible—to bring *The Lugubrious Game* with her to Paris, also Dalí's portrait of him and two other unspecified works. The request casts Gala in the role of commercial go-between, and one wonders if this, in fact, was not her initial role: to seduce Dalí, as she had probably seduced De Chirico, with a view to gaining access to his work.[207]

One day, Buñuel said decades later, he, Dalí and Gala went on a boat trip with La Lídia, Dalí's paranoiac friend, to Cape Creus. There Buñuel, who knew nothing about painting, observed that the grandiose scene reminded him of the Valencian painter Sorolla, one of Dalí's pet hates. Salvador, given his passionate identification with Creus, was incensed, for the remark could not have been more inappropriate. 'What? Why? Are you blind? This is Nature. What's it got to do with . . . ?' Gala then remarked: 'There you two go again, like dogs on heat.' According to Buñuel, Gala, jealous of their friendship, continued to needle them during the picnic, to such an extent that he finally leapt to his feet and pretended to throttle her while Dalí, on his knees, begged him to desist.[208]

The scene, not mentioned by Dalí in his memoirs, seems to have occurred more or less as Buñuel describes it. Years later Cécile Éluard recalled that she had always had a vague memory of Buñuel as a huge man with bulging eyes who was choking her mother. She thought it was the recollection of a nightmare but, when Buñuel's autobiography appeared, realized in conversation with Jean-Claude Carrière that the assault had really taken place.[209]

If Gala was jealous of Buñuel, it seems fair to assume that the Aragonese, deeply sensitive despite his bluff exterior, was devastated to discover that this woman was now not only coming between him and Salvador but interrupting their work together.

In the *Secret Life* Dalí provides a gripping account of a crucial love scene with Gala, enacted 'in one of the most truculently deserted and mineral spots of Cadaqués'. According to Dalí, he asked Gala insistently on this occasion, as their passion mounted, 'What do you want me to do to you?' Finally she answered: 'I want you to kill me!' (in Dalí's original French, 'ge veux que vous me fesiez crever!').[210] Dalí interpreted the request literally, and tells us that Gala now revealed that since her childhood she had suffered from an 'insurmountable horror' of the

Gala and Dalí in 1930.

moment of death, wanting it to take her by surprise. He does not suggest that, by her use of the word *crever*, what Gala may really have been suggesting as a fitting climax to their love scene among the rocks was some energetic copulation. In the event she was neither killed nor penetrated. The pity is that we don't have her version of what happened.[211]

Dalí was struck by the similarity between Gala's name and that of his paranoiac grandfather Galo (Gal in Catalan), the suicide in the family cupboard, the more so given her own tendency to move 'between the poles of lucidity and madness'. The coincidence is not mentioned in his published work; but years later, in conversation, he interpreted the onomastic equivalence retrospectively as one of the 'premonitory signs' that Gala was his predestined partner.[212] He may also have been impressed by the fact that her real name was Helen, particularly when he realized that he was about to steal this wonderful creature from her husband in an act of epic daring.

Dalí's infatuation with Gala sowed immediate war in the ranks of his family. In those days, in the conservative Empordà, to go out with a Frenchwoman was considered tantamount to frequenting a prostitute. This particular Frenchwoman, to make matters worse, was married as well as sexy and shameless, and the village tongues were soon wagging (they would wag even more when they discovered she was in fact Russian). Nothing more appalling could have befallen the increasingly reactionary Don Salvador Dalí Cusí, who was soon referring to Gala as 'la madame'. His immediate instinct was to change his will, which he did on 26 September 1929. The estate now went to Anna Maria, not equally to both children as had previously been the case, and Salvador received the absolute minimum required by law, which the notary quantified as 15,000 pesetas (about a million and half pesetas today). In an astonishing gesture, he was exonerated from repaying the money spent on his education. Not a stone of the family house at Es Llané could be his unless Anna Maria died first, and it was laid down that, if his sister was unable to inherit for whatever reason, Salvador was to be prevented from enjoying full rights to the house until his stepmother, Catalina ('la tieta'), had died. The will also radically altered the situation of the latter, which suggests that, unlike Anna Maria, hostile to Gala from the outset, Catalina Domènech had sided with Salvador, or at least shown some understanding: she would have the right to inhabit a room in Es Llané until her death, but no more. The main intention of the will, in tune with Dalí Cusí's violent character, was clearly to humiliate his son to the utmost extent permitted by the law. In practice, if not technically, the painter was as good as disinherited.[213]

It seems likely, in view of the new will, that Dalí Cusí and Salvador had had a tremendous row about Gala. The family must have breathed a sigh of relief when she and Cécile left Cadaqués, probably in late September, boarding a train for Paris in Figueres. With her Gala took *The Lugubrious Game*, as Éluard had begged her to, and perhaps some other paintings.[214]

Without Gala, Dalí now concentrated with ferocious energy on preparing work for his Goemans exhibition, and soon finished the *Portrait of Paul Éluard*, *The Great Masturbator* and *The Accommodations of Desire*.[215]

The head featured in *The Great Masturbator*, inspired by the rock at Cullaró, had made its inaugural appearance in *The First Days of Spring*. To its representation in this much larger painting Dalí added, along with the lion, locust and other elements present in so many paintings of the period, an allusion to fellatio, another of his secret desires. According to the artist, the face placed beside the prominent genitals of the male figure with bloodied knees was inspired by the print of a woman smelling a lily, and is 'mixed with memories of Cadaqués, of summer, of the rocks of Cape Creus'.[216] The intense eroticism of the scene is heightened by the noticeably phallic aspect of the arum lily's spathe and of the lion's tongue. The theme of fellatio was to recur frequently in the paintings done over the following months, and one cannot but deduce that, in this respect, Gala gave Dalí what he wanted, or promised to do so.

The journey's end signalled by the arrival of Gala in Dalí's life, and alluded to in the couple embracing among the rocks of Cape Creus in *The Great Masturbator* (beneath the belly of the fearful locust) did not mean that the painter was able, or even tried, to give up his auto-eroticism. On the contrary, he said in 1979, Gala had helped him to refine his masturbatory technique, to make it easier for him to achieve good emissions! As for the picture, it reflected 'the guilt of a face completely extinguished vitally by so much masturbation: the nose touches the ground and has a horrible boil. Every time I lose a bit of sperm I have the conviction that I've wasted it. I feel guilty.' Inhibited by the force of Dalí's personality, few interviewers ever dared to question him closely about his relationship with Gala. But on this occasion the Catalan writer and journalist Lluís Permanyer was an exception. Did Dalí make love to Gala during their first weeks together in Cadaqués? No, Dalí replied, it took about three months.[217]

In the *Secret Life*, Dalí explains that *The Accommodations of Desire* expressed his anxiety about sex with Gala: 'Never in my life had I yet "made love", and I represented this act to myself as terribly violent and disproportionate to my physical vigour—"this was not for me".'[218] But Dalí is rationalizing. Later, in his *Unspeakable Confessions*, he came closer to telling the truth. In the painting, he said, 'lion's jaws express my terror at the revelation of the possession of a woman's cunt, which is going to lead to a revelation of my impotence. I was getting ready for the recoil of my shame.'[219]

The shame-ridden Dalí, then, solicited by the uninhibited Gala, feared that, when the moment came, he would not get, or be able to sustain, an erection. In this respect, the group at the top of the painting is relevant. Here once again we find an adult male on whose shoulder an anguished youth of effeminate aspect is leaning, as in *The Lugubrious Game*, with a lion in attendance. The adult is chewing the youth's delicate hand with apparent delight. Below, we find the recurrent motif of an individual with his head in his hands. For Moorhouse this figure is Dalí hiding his face 'in shame and guilt'.[220] In shame, certainly. To the left of the group we find a tiny vignette of Dalí Cusí, portly and white-haired, waving goodbye: an indication, surely, that the artist now knew that a break with his family was inevitable.

Dalí finished at this time, or executed from scratch, three other paintings for his forthcoming Goemans show: *The Enigma of Desire*, *The Illumined Pleasures* and *Man with an Unhealthy Complexion Listening to the Sound of the Sea*. They continue the exploration of his sexual anxieties and share many elements in common with the other paintings just discussed: collage so skilfully deployed that it is impossible to tell whether one is looking at something affixed or at a further proof of Dalí's skill as a miniaturist; and a profusion of lions, jugs with idiotic faces, probing fingers, ashamed heads, locusts and 'great masturbators' set on a spectral beach with allusions to the cliffs and rocks of Creus.

The Enigma of Desire rings a particularly significant change on the masturbator motif. All the habitual details of the onanist's head are present, but this time, instead of a whirl of erotic fantasies issuing from his nape, we find a typical mica-schist rock from Creus in whose holes, or alveoli, like niches in a Spanish cemetery, the painter has inscribed the obsessive legend 'Ma Merè'. Through a gap in the rock we see, in the distance, a naked female torso. The paucity of references to Dalí's dead mother is an interesting feature of his work. Here is an exception to the rule. Why does she make such a poignant appearance at this moment in Dalí's life? Perhaps the artist senses that Gala is now about to take the place of Felipa Domènech, to become the mother he lost eight years earlier.

Max Ernst, Pietà or Revolution by Night, *1923. Dalí knew this painting well, and in* Illumined Pleasures *(colour plate XVI) arguably borrowed Ernst's rendering of Freud (on the wall at right of picture).*

Referring to the group at the left of the painting, Dalí told Robert Descharnes that it shows him 'embracing his father'.[221] Since the scene also comprises an obvious reference to castration, in the form of the knife, with the ubiquitous fish, locust and lion in terrifying attendance, the suggestion of oedipal guilt and its punishment is surely indicated.[222]

Illumined Pleasures is one of Dalí's works that most lends itself to Freudian analysis. Indeed, it even appears that the elderly gentleman exquisitely assisting the frenzied female with bloodied hands in the foreground is none other than Freud himself, his representation here deriving from Max Ernst's depiction of the founder of psychoanalysis in *Pietà or Revolution by Night*, which, since it belonged to Éluard, Dalí may well have admired in Paris.[223]

With its borrowings from De Chirico (the

picture-within-a-picture boxes, the threatening shadows, the 'cephalic biomorph' with a toupée near the horizon),[224] *Illumined Pleasures* would need a monograph to itself. Here we can only consider it briefly.

Who is the woman being helped by the Freud-figure in the foreground? It seems obvious that there is an allusion to Gala as Venus rising from the waves—the face, with its long nose, calls her to mind immediately. The body, however, with its full breasts, is much heavier than hers. Perhaps the figure is a fusion of Dalí's mother and Gala. Her bloodied hands show that she has just committed a terrible act, presumably with the knife represented on the left, held by a female hand which a male one is restraining. Again, from the Freudian point of view there can be no doubt about what act has been perpetrated: castration.[225] The supposition is reinforced by the fact that, as Dawn Ades has pointed out, the shadow in the centre foreground of the picture, cast by a person out of frame, is identical to that thrown by the father figure on whose shoulder the castrated son is leaning in *The Lugubrious Game*.[226] The scene reminds one, finally, of Dalí's affirmation, in *The Tragic Myth of Millet's Angelus*, to the effect that, in the early stages of their relationship, Gala took the place of the threatening mother and enabled him gradually to overcome his panic fear of sexual intercourse.[227]

Further allusions to the family come in the group on top of the central panel, where we find Dalí, once again in the guise of a jug, accompanied this time by his sister similarly depicted. The lion, habitually a symbol of sexual desire in the paintings of these months, here probably also represents Dalí Cusí, the angry father. It is hardly the snapshot of a happy family group.

And what of the personage, distinctly effeminate in appearance, who stands with his head against the right of the central panel? He appears to be a combination of Peeping Tom and the ubiquitous ashamed figure of the paintings of this period, Dalí having cleverly arranged a double image so that the shadow of his head is also a hole in the wall. The hand seems to be lightly spattered with blood, the emblematic colour of guilt as of blushful shame. The hint, once again, is surely that the figure is engaged in masturbatory activity.

As for the bevy of cyclists in the box on the right, the stones they are are carrying on their heads, according to Dalí, represent magnified versions of the pebbles he used to enjoy gathering on the little beach of Confitera, across the bay from their house in Cadaqués. Confitera means 'Confectionist' (female variety), and the pebbles, which presumably gave the beach its name, looked like sugared almonds. They recur in other paintings of the period, and Dalí said that for him they symbolized 'solidified desire'. Perhaps, therefore, the cyclists are pedalling in search of sexual fulfilment.[228]

Illumined Pleasures, like most of the paintings of this period, with the exception of *The Great Masturbator* and *The Enigma of Desire*, packs an amazing amount of precise detail into a canvas of minute proportions (it measures only 24 x 34.5 cm). So does Dalí's last painting for the Goemans exhibition, *Man with an Unhealthy Complexion Listening to the Sound of the Sea*, which, like *Illumined Pleasures*, owes a very obvious debt to De Chirico and features, yet again, the distraught youth leaning on the shoulder of the adult male with the manic grin, represented here as a jug.[229]

While Dalí worked feverishly on these paintings in Figueres, back in Paris *Un Chien andalou* opened commercially at Jean Mauclaire's Studio 28 (10, Rue Tholozé, Montmartre), a 400-seat experimental cinema. Studio 28's eighth session ran from 1 October to 23 December 1929, and *Un Chien andalou* shared the bill with a thriller by Donald Crisp, *14–101*, starring William Boyd, Alain Hale and Robert Armstrong. The two films alternated with another double bill, so it would be misleading to say that *Un Chien andalou* 'ran for months'. Nonetheless it undoubtedly made its mark, ensuring that the names of Buñuel and Dalí were firmly linked in the minds of people interested in the avant-garde cinema.[230]

There could have been no better curtain-raiser for Dalí's imminent re-appearance in the French capital; but, characteristically, neither he nor Buñuel were pleased with the public success of *Un Chien andalou*. How could a film intended to be subversive, to attack the very foundations of bourgeois society, have wide appeal? It was outrageous! In an article published by the Barcelona magazine *Mirador* to coincide with the first showing of the film, on 24 October, in the Catalan capital (*Mirador*, in imitation of *La Gaceta Literaria* in Madrid, ran a cinema club), Dalí wrote that the audiences in Paris who professed to enjoy it were merely demonstrating their snobbery, their pathetic worship of the new for the sake of the new. 'The public haven't grasped the moral point of the film,' he insisted, 'which is directed at *them* with total cruelty and violence.' Dalí ended by saying that the only success he acknowledged was the praise lavished on the film by Eisenstein at the recent Congress of Independent Cinema, held at La Sarraz in Switzerland, and the fact that a contract had been signed for its distribution in the Soviet Union.[231]

Un Chien andalou was much discussed in the Barcelona press, and greatly enhanced Dalí's fame in the city. Even the Catalan opponents of Surrealism, headed by Sebastià Gasch, were forced to admit that the film was overwhelming in its emotional impact. For weeks afterwards its disturbing images had haunted him.[232] A few days after the showing, which it seems Dalí did not attend, the painter boarded a train for Paris, his exhibits for Goemans having been packed to demanding instructions by a long-suffering Figueres cabinet-maker.[233]

Success in Paris

Back in Paris Dalí saw Buñuel and, picking up from their frustrated efforts the previous summer, they got down to some work together on the screenplay of the new film commissioned by Charles and Marie-Laure de Noailles. Buñuel's correspondence with the Vicomte shows that the project was soon developing into a full-blooded continuation of *Un Chien andalou*, a connection indicated by its first title, *La Bête andalouse* (*The Andalusian Beast*)—the animal is feminine now—which would only be replaced by *L'Age d'or* (*The Golden Age*) late during shooting.[234] Our knowledge of the script and its elaboration is lamentably incomplete since, as in the case of *Un Chien andalou*, the early drafts are unknown and neither Buñuel nor Dalí later provided a detailed account of their collaboration. It is clear, however, that they were in complete agreement about the theme of the sequel to their first joint effort—the battle to the death between the sexual instinct and the repressive forces of bourgeois society (Church, Family, Fatherland)—and that they had been reading the Marquis de Sade.

Marie-Laure de Noailles was not only a descendant of Sade but had purchased the manuscript of The *120 Days of Sodom*, one of the most persecuted books in Europe, from the great authority on the Divine Marquis, Maurice Heine[235]. María Luisa González, Dalí and Buñuel's bookseller friend in Paris, has recalled the fascination that Marie-Laure's Sade connection, and her manuscript (a long scroll written in a tiny hand), held for all the Spanish group in the French capital, not least Buñuel.[236] Buñuel read *The 120 Days of Sodom* avidly, not in the manuscript, though, but in Roland Tual's copy of the rare Berlin edition which Proust had also borrowed.[237] The book, probably the most complete catalogue of sexual practices ever compiled, deeply impressed Buñuel, 'more even than Darwin'. He immediately bent his efforts to procuring other key works by Sade, all unavailable on the open market: *Justine, Juliette, Philosophy in the Boudoir, Dialogue between a Priest and a Dying Man*. These readings constituted for him, he said, a veritable 'cultural revolution'. And we can be sure that he discussed them with Dalí.[238]

In his memoirs Dalí does not recall his first meeting with Charles and Marie-Laure de Noailles, but it is likely, given his collaboration on the script of Buñuel's new film, that by the autumn of 1929 he was already frequenting their splendid mansion in the Place des États Unis. As for Marie-Laure's manuscript of *The 120 Days of Sodom*, he must have heard about it from Buñuel if not from its owner. And it is hard to believe that he failed to dip into Buñuel's borrowed copy of the book at this time, not least because the latter had decided to end the film with a scene which shows the Duc de Blangis and his three partners in lechery emerging from the Château de Seligny after completing the longest sexual orgy in the annals of world literature.

These were exciting times for Dalí, not only because of the continuing success of *Un Chien andalou* at Studio 28 and the progress of the new film but because it was apparent that the Goemans show was going to be a sell-out: before the exhibition got under way the Vicomte de Noailles bought *The Lugubrious Game* (presumably the deal was promoted by Éluard) and André Breton *The Accommodations of Desire*. Other paintings were also sold prior to the vernissage.[239] To crown Dalí's elation, his reunion with Gala was a success and she promised to accompany him to Spain for a brief holiday once the paintings had been hung to his satisfaction. Dalí must have felt that the tide was turning at last in his favour: not only was his work selling but he had found the woman he yearned for.[240]

The catalogue of the Goemans exhibition, which ran from 20 November to 5 December, listed eleven works, all but the last two from 1929. There were also some unspecified graphics. *The Lugubrious Game*, in pride of place at no. 1, was followed by *The Accommodations of Desire, The Illumined Pleasures, The Sacred Heart, The Image of Desire* [also called *The Enigma of Desire*], *Face of the Great Masturbator* [i.e. *The Great Masturbator*], *The First Days of Spring, Man with an Unhealthy Complexion Listening to the Sound of the Sea* and *Portrait of Paul Éluard*. Then, to round off the show, came two of Dalí's best works from 1927: *Sterile Efforts* (later called *Little Ashes*) and *Gadget and Hand*, the latter having been bought previously by Éluard.

The Sacred Heart, done in ink on canvas, was almost certainly executed by Dalí after he returned to Paris. A few months earlier, in *La Gaceta Literaria*, he had published a 'poem' entitled 'I Can't See Anything in the Landscape, Anything'. The jumble of elements which in fact the author *did* see in the landscape were inoffensive enough. But then came a view through an anus, of all things, onto a series of images similar to those contained within the masturbator's head in *The Lugubrious Game*. Among these we find 'a very clear photograph of a well-dressed young man spitting for pleasure on the portrait of his mother'.[241] It was not suggested that Dalí was the young man in question. But now, in what looked like the most deliberate of provocations, he incorporated the phrase in *The Sacred Heart*, this time ascribing it blatantly to himself: 'Sometimes I spit for PLEASURE on the portrait of my mother'. Was the gesture intended to demonstrate that Dalí was as fiercely opposed to religion and the family as was Breton? Soon afterwards he claimed that he had simply followed the dictates of his subconscious,

Dalí, Sometimes I Spit for Pleasure on the Portrait of my Mother *(also known as* The Sacred Heart*), 1929. Indian ink on lawn stuck on canvas, 68.3 x 50.1 cm. The picture that got Dalí thrown out of his family.*

pointing out that in dreams we sometimes treat horribly the people we love best—even when they are dead.[242]

The fact that André Breton had not only bought *The Accommodations of Desire* before the exhibition opened but written the preface to the catalogue was an indication of how seriously the founder of Surrealism was now taking Dalí, eight years his junior. 'Dalí,' he begins, 'appears here like a man hesitating (and whom the future will show was not hesitating) between talent and genius, or, as one might have said in the past, between vice and virtue.' For Breton, Dalí's current work is making a devastating contribution to the Surrealist attack on the values of contemporary society and on conventional reality. Dalí is a liberator: 'With Dalí it is perhaps the first time that our mental windows have opened completely and that we are going to feel ourselves slipping upwards towards the trapdoor to the fulvous sky.' Dalí's work has the virtue of helping us to see what lies behind the appearances of things, of helping us to develop our ability for what Breton calls 'voluntary hallucination'. There can be no doubt: 'Dalí's art, the most hallucinatory that has been produced up to now, constitutes a veritable threat. Absolutely new creatures, visibly mal-intentioned, are suddenly on the move.'[243]

If the exhibition proved a financial success, the critical reception was less unanimously appreciative than might have been expected from Breton's initial accolade, and in general the reviews were short. Dalí must have been particularly irritated by E. Tériade's dismissive comments in *L'Intransigeant*. Noting that Dalí had come from Catalunya with the agenda of conquering the French capital, Tériade found the exhibition worse than provincial—it expressed 'provincial despair trying to be up-to-date'. Two years earlier, perhaps, it might have had some interest. He advised Dalí, who clearly possessed talent, to distrust all the qualities he displayed in this exhibition. Reading between the lines one senses that the review was as much directed against Surrealism in general as against the Spaniard in particular.[244]

Other critics were more indulgent. 'Le Rapin', in *Comoedia*, found Dalí's paintings 'strange, Bruegelesque, extremely interesting'.[245] The most sensitive review came from 'Flouquet', in Henri Barbusse's weekly, *Monde*, who enthused about the 'astonishing power' of these works, their assault on logic and on 'good taste'. Dalí was more adept at minute detail than a Persian, more sure of his means than a Japanese. A 'sower of unease', the Catalan, 'Flouquet' concluded, 'expresses all the poetry, both terrible and sweet, of Freudianism'. Dalí sent the cutting, and an invitation card to the vernissage, to his Barcelona friend J.V. Foix, who reproduced both in *La Publicitat*. He also sent the snippet, along with other reviews, to his father, who duly pasted them into his album.[246]

Banishment

Sure in the knowledge that the Goemans exhibition was going to be a financial success, Dalí and Gala left Paris just before the opening, bound for Spain 'on a voyage of love'.[247] They went first to Barcelona; after which they spent an idyllic few days just down the coast at the summer resort of Sitges (home of the defunct *L'Amic de les Arts*), which offered them 'the desolation of its beaches attenuated by the sparkling Mediterranean winter sun.'[248] On 24 November a local periodical informed its readers that Dalí was staying at the Parc-Hotel Terramar, a splendid new establishment at the end of the promenade set amidst luxuriant gardens and providing absolute tranquillity. There was no reference to his companion, one assumes out of discretion.[249]

Their 'voyage of love' over, Gala returned to Paris while Dalí betook himself to Figueres. There, according to the *Secret Life*, his father quizzed him about Goemans and his contract.[250] Later he said that Dalí Cusí also pried into his relationship with Gala: he had concluded that she was on drugs and had turned Salvador into a peddler. How else could the artist's substantial earnings be accounted for?[251]

At the end of November Buñuel travelled down to Figueres to continue working with Dalí on their new scenario. In his memoirs, dictated decades later, he tells us that he arrived to bellows of rage:

> The father opened the door violently, with indignation, and pushed his son out into the street, calling him a wretch. Dalí retorted and stood up for himself. I went up to them. The father, pointing at his son, told me he never wanted to see his pig of a son again in his house. The cause (quite justified) of the paternal fury was as follows: in an exhibition held in Barcelona Dalí had written on one of his paintings, in black ink and bad writing: 'I spit for pleasure on the portrait of my mother'.[252]

Buñuel's recollections are often untrustworthy, but, in essence, this account is accurate enough, apart from the confusion of Paris and Barcelona. It seems clear that, by late November, Don Salvador had already got wind of his son's inscription on *The Sacred Heart*, which he, his daughter and his second wife interpreted as an outrageous insult to the memory of the painter's mother, Felipa Domènech. 'Salvador had publicly disowned the fundamental basis of his life,' wrote Anna Maria in her book on her brother.[253] The damage was compounded when, on 15 December, Eugenio d'Ors published an article in *La Gaceta Literaria* in which he reproduced *The Lugubrious Game* and, while recognizing that Dalí's vocation was 'one of the most genuine, clear and felicitous known to our modern painting', criticized him for his obscenity, his desire to shock and, above all, his offensive inscription, misquoted as 'I have spat on my Mother' ('J'ai craché sur ma Mère').[254]

Popular tradition in Figueres has it that, when the expulsion took place, the notary was heard to roar a prophecy along the lines of 'For not obeying your father you'll always be a poor wretch! You'll end up in poverty, eaten by fleas, without a friend . . . ! And you'll be lucky if your sister takes you a bowl of soup!' Such a dire omen, bordering on a curse, would not have been out of character for Salvador Dalí Cusí, but the painter himself never alluded to it in his published work or, so far as we know, in conversation.[255]

Dalí senior gave his own version of events a year later in a letter to Lorca:

> I do not know if you are aware that I had to throw my son out of the house. It has been extremely painful for all of us, but for dignity's sake it was essential to take such a tremendous decision. In one of the paintings of his Paris exhibition he committed the vile act of writing these insolent words: 'I spit on my mother'. Imagining that he was drunk when he wrote it, I asked him to explain himself. But he would not do so, and insulted all of us again. No comment.
>
> He is pathetic, ignorant and an incomparable pedant, as well as being totally shameless. He thinks he knows it all but he can't even read or write. Anyway, you know him better than I do.
>
> He has even sunk to the level of accepting the money and food given to him by a married woman who, with the consent and approval of her husband, is keeping him well fed until she finds something better.
>
> You can imagine what unhappiness all this filth is causing us.[256]

When Dalí Cusí threw Salvador out he allowed him to go with Buñuel to the family house in Cadaqués, perhaps hoping that he would recant—which he didn't. From the village Buñuel wrote excitedly to Noailles on 29 November 1929, telling him that the script of the new film would be even better than that of *Un Chien andalou,* and that he wouldn't be leaving until it was fully elaborated, in eight or ten days. Despite what Buñuel wrote later, and despite what had just happened in Figueres, there is no contemporary indication that he and Dalí failed to work harmoniously on their second joint venture.[257]

Before Buñuel's departure, on about 6 December,[258] Dalí received a letter from his father sentencing him to 'irrevocable banishment' from the family home and, one imagines, informing him that he had already been virtually disinherited in the notary's new will.[259] In view of the success of his exhibition in Paris and of his burgeoning relationship with Gala, and perhaps remembering the positive results of his self-induced ejection from the San Fernando Special School three years earlier, Dalí may have seen the new turn of events, at least initially, as more positive than negative—as a necessary stimulus to success and personal liberation. The arrival of the letter moved him to cut off his hair and bury it on the beach at Es Llané: a symbolic assertion, not of contrition, one assumes, but of the fact that he was about to embark on a new life. Not satisfied with this gesture, he had his head shaved and got Buñuel to photograph him with a sea urchin on his head, the first allusion to the legend of William Tell that was soon to become a leitmotif in his work.

Dalí cropped his hair after being repudiated by his father. Photograph by Luis Buñuel, Cadaqués, 1929.

On 14 December Buñuel wrote to Noailles from Zaragoza. He told him that the new script was completely finished and that, as he had predicted, it was much superior to that of the earlier film.[260]

Dalí remained in Cadaqués by himself for a few days after Buñuel left. Then, suitably gorged with sea urchins, he took a taxi to the station, bound for Paris—and Gala. It was a departure he never forgot:

> The road that goes from Cadaqués and leads towards the mountain pass of Peni makes a
> series of twists and turns, from each of which the village of Cadaqués can be seen, reced-

ing farther into the distance. One of these turns is the last from which one can still see Cadaqués, which has become a tiny speck. The traveller who loves this village then involuntarily looks back, to cast upon it a last friendly glance of leave-taking filled with a sober and effusive promise of return. Never had I neglected to turn around for this last glance at Cadaqués. But on this day, when the taxi came to the bend in the road, instead of turning my head I continued to look straight before me.[261]

In the family apartment at Figueres Dalí left behind most of his private possessions, including dozens of paintings, probably hundreds of drawings, many books (including his beloved Gowans's Art Books and his Biblioteca Nueva volumes of Freud) and reams of correspondence. It was five years before he spoke to his father again, and much of this invaluable material was never returned to him. The failure to do so was to be one of the major causes of future conflict between the painter and his family.

The *Second Surrealist Manifesto*

When Luis Buñuel arrived back in Paris on 30 December 1929 he found Dalí already there, 'as the result of some events,' Buñuel wrote to Charles de Noailles, 'about which I'll tell you when we meet'. With Dalí in Paris, work could now go ahead quickly on the shooting script of the new film which, Buñuel assured his genial patron, was making rapid progress.[1]

Dalí's return coincided with the publication of what was to be the last issue of *La Révolution Surréaliste*, which marked his and Buñuel's official entry into the movement. The packed number led off with Breton's *Second Surrealist Manifesto* and included reproductions of Dalí's *The Accommodations of Desire* and *Illumined Pleasures* as well as the screenplay of *Un Chien andalou*, for which Buñuel had written a short and mordant introduction:

> The publication of this screenplay in '*La Révolution Surréaliste*' is the only one I authorize.[2] It expresses, unconditionally, my complete identification with Surrealist thought and activity. *Un Chien andalou* would not exist if Surrealism did not exist.
>
> A successful film—that's what the people who've seen it think. But what can I do against those who adore everything that's new, even when the novelty in question outrages their deepest convictions? What can I do against a gagged or insincere press? Against the imbecilic mob which finds *beautiful* or *poetic* that which, in reality, is nothing but a despairing, passionate incitement to murder?[3]

Dalí entered Surrealism at a time of crisis for the movement, and Breton greatly appreciated the invigorating enthusiasm, even fanaticism, of the new adept. 'For three

Chapter EIGHT

or four years,' he recalled in 1952, 'Dalí was an incarnation of the Surrealist spirit and made it shine with all its brilliance as only someone could who had not played any part in the episodes, sometimes thankless, of its gestation.'[4] Recently there had been defections and expulsions; and, in particular, the subject of Surrealism's relations with the Communist Party was causing much agony. The manifesto addressed the latter question with precision. Breton argued that dialectical materialism and Surrealism were not only compatible but should be complementary, and expressed regret that the Communist Party, as he had had occasion to learn from his own painful experience of membership, was failing stubbornly to understand the aims of the movement. Surrealism, he insisted, was indissolubly wedded to 'the process of Marxist thought'. But:

> Why should we accept that the dialectical method can only be applied correctly to solving social problems? It is the whole of us Surrealists' ambition to supply it with possibilities of application that in no way conflict with its immediate, practical concerns. I really cannot see why, whatever a few short-sighted revolutionaries may think, we should abstain from raising the problems of love, of dreaming, of madness, of art, of religion—provided, that is, we consider these issues from the same angle from which they (and we too) envisage the Revolution.[5]

But where did Surrealism stand on an issue currently dividing the leadership of the International, the position of Trotsky and the other dissidents within the Party? Although Breton, diplomatically, allows that the differences being aired are merely 'tactical', the document leaves us in no doubt of his allegiance to Trotsky. Given Breton's commitment to human freedom and his horror of the closed mind, it could not have been otherwise.

The manifesto reveals its author, once again, as a severe moralist, now committed to 'the rigorous discipline of the spirit to which we are determined to submit everything'. Nothing but a total revolution of that spirit will satisfy Surrealism. Art, literature, poetry—all are secondary to the supreme aim of provoking a general 'crisis of consciousness'. Surrealism, five years after its inception, is still only in its initial stages, Breton reminds his readers before stating, with an unmistakably Biblical echo, that 'very few of those who present themselves can measure up to Surrealism's purpose'. The method for achieving that purpose was, as before, the harnessing of the subconscious:

> Let us remember that the point of Surrealism is simply the total recovery of the powers of the mind by a means none other than a vertiginous inner descent, the systematic lighting up of our hidden places, and the progressive shading off of the others. A ceaseless promenade in full forbidden zone.[6]

Breton's *Second Manifesto* greatly impressed Dalí, who did a frontispiece for its publi-cation in book form at the end of June and signed a joint statement by fifteen Surrealists in support of the movement's founder, then under heavy fire from the dissidents.[7]

Not long after he joined the Surrealist ranks, and inspired by Breton's insistence on the importance of group activity, Dalí produced a scenario for a five-minute documen-tary whose purpose was to explain Surrealism to a wide audience. The admirably clear commentary owes an explicit debt to Breton, and stresses that Freud's explorations of the subconscious are at the very basis of the movement's thinking. The film begins by showing a girl engaged in automatic writing. Then an animated drawing of a tree illus-trates the interrelationship of the conscious mind (trunk, branches, fruit) and the uncon-scious (roots, tubers), an interrelationship conditioned, as the commentary explains, by the Freudian tension between the pleasure principle (the depths of the mind, dreams, fantasies, etc.) and the reality principle (waking life, logic, practicality, morality, etc.). The Surrealists are seen engaged in an experiment with a sleeping collaborator, going down into the Paris Métro (image of the unconscious), executing a *cadavre exquis*,[8] using collage to transform banal images into vehicles of enigma and 'poetic disorientation', and making Surrealist objects. By showing a diagram illustrating the different readings of his painting *Invisible Sleeping Woman, Horse, Lion, etc.*, Dalí seeks to demonstrate how 'paranoiac delirium', which he considers a normal activity of the dreaming mind, can be simulated by images in the waking world. The film ends with some optimistic words from André Breton about the huge potential of Surrealism.

While the scenario quotes from the murder scene in *Un Chien andalou*, there is no ref-erence to *L'Age d'or*, which suggests that it was written before the filming of the latter had begun. Perhaps Dalí hoped to make the documentary after he had finished working with Buñuel on their second project. If so, his hopes were dashed. No further references to it have come to light.[9]

Dalí and Gala's reunion in Paris must have gone well, for three weeks later the cou-ple fled the city together, Dalí recalling in the *Secret Life* that he felt the urgent need to get away in order to concentrate on a painting that had occurred to him during his recent visit to Cadaqués: the portrait of an 'invisible man'.[10] Gala had chosen the place for their escapade, the Hôtel du Château at Carry-le-Rouet, a small spa some twenty-five kilometres from Marseille overlooking the sea near Martigny. There the lovers were installed by 11 January 1930.

Éluard immediately decided that he could not do without Gala, and promised to join her in Marseille the following week—if, that was, an envisaged art sale went ahead suc-cessfully.[11] It didn't, and his letters became increasingly filled with misery:

I need you so much. It's driving me mad. I die at the idea of being with you again, of see-
ing you, of kissing you. I want your hands, your mouth, your sex joined to mine, con-
stantly. We'll masturbate each other in the street, in the cinemas, with the window open.
This morning I masturbated wonderfully thinking about you. My imagination never stops.
I see you everywhere, in everything, on everything. I love you so much I could die of it.
Your cunt covers my face, eats it, covers me with your beauty, with your genius.
Everything about you is beautiful: your eyes, your mouth, your hair, your breasts, your
body hair, your buttocks, your cunt, your hands which never let go what they're mastur-
bating, the space between your thighs, near your cunt, your shoulders. I go crazy when I
think about each part of your body.[12]

Dalí and Gala stayed at Carry-le-Rouet until March. Dalí wrote later that they were
months of marvellous sexual initiation.[13] A drawing of their room, done later for the
Secret Life, shows the couple embracing on the floor surrounded by piles of firewood,
and perhaps it was at this time that Dalí wrote Buñuel a six-page letter on the joys of
physical love.[14] Dalí also claimed that for two months he and Gala did not once leave the
hotel. While he worked on his painting *The Invisible Man*, whose progress was painfully slow, Gala scrutinized her Tarot cards which, according to Dalí, kept announcing 'a
letter from a dark man, and money', and replied from time to time to Éluard's frenzied
communications.[15]

The letter augured by the cards duly arrived. Its author was not a dark man but the
pale-complexioned (and rapidly balding) Vicomte de Noailles. The account provided in
the *Secret Life* of this episode is slightly inaccurate.[16] What really occurred is that
Noailles, informed by Buñuel on 8 February that Camille Goemans's gallery was about
to fold (his wife had left him for another man), asked him to tell Dalí that he was prepared to take the place of the gallery provisionally, making good the monthly payments
which the artist would now lose. Buñuel passed on the good news to Dalí.[17]

It happened that at this time Salvador was receiving regular messages from Lídia, his
cracked friend in Cadaqués, which he kept and analysed as 'paranoiac documents of the
first order'. On the shore at the tiny village of Port Lligat, around the corner from
Cadaqués at the foot of Cape Creus, Lídia's sons owned a crumbling shack with a collapsed
roof where they kept their fishing gear. 'With the capriciousness which always characterizes my decisions,' Dalí writes in the *Secret Life*, 'it became in a moment the only spot
where I would, where I could, live. Gala wanted only what I wished.' A letter was dispatched to Lídia, who replied saying that her sons agreed to let him have the cottage.[18]
Thus encouraged, and sure in the knowledge that Noailles was willing to help, Dalí now
wrote to him. He explained that he had just heard from Paris that the Goemans gallery

was about to reopen—reassuring news, with its promise of more sales. Then, reminding Noailles that he had recently offered his assistance if needed, Dalí made bold to ask him if he would be prepared to forward the money necessary to enable him to set himself up in Cadaqués. With 20,000 francs, he said, he could both buy the shack and make it habitable. In exchange, his patron would receive a painting, of whatever dimensions he wished, from Dalí's forthcoming production. So, would he help?[19] On 3 March Noailles wrote enclosing the cheque for 20,000 francs and reporting excitedly that Buñuel had begun shooting the interiors for his new film in Paris (at the Billancourt Studios) on 24 February.[20]

Despite what he tells us in the *Secret Life*, Dalí did not visit Noailles in Hyères. On receiving the cheque he wrote effusively:

> Thank you infinitely for the cheque for 20,000 francs, which I've just received. I owe you, therefore, a picture, which you can choose among all the things I'll do next year. I'm absolutely thrilled to have this house in Cadaqués, which clearly resolves in the best way possible the practical aspect of my life.
>
> I'll keep you abreast of what I'm doing and send you photos of the cabin.
>
> I've already booked my reservation on the boat leaving for Barcelona next Saturday.
>
> I've tried, in vain, to cash the cheque but hope to be able to do so rapidly next Monday in Marseille. If I fail I'll return the cheque to you by express registered mail and ask you to let me have a money order instead, if that's possible and easy for you.
>
> My sincere thanks once again, dear Monsieur Noailles, and please remember me fondly to Madame Noailles.[21]

Noailles was eventually to receive *The Old Age of William Tell* for his generosity.

L'Age d'or

From Carry-le-Rouet Dalí had been bombarding Buñuel with last-minute suggestions for the shooting script of *La Bête andalouse*, as the film was still called.[22] He was particularly obsessed by the love scene (which takes place in the garden while the guests listen to an orchestra playing *Tristan and Isolde*), and his proposals for its improvement were accompanied by detailed drawings:

> In the love scene he could kiss the tips of her fingers and rip out one of her nails with his teeth [drawing indicated by arrow], we'll be able to appreciate the horrible tearing out by using a dummy's hand with a paper fingernail stuck on, this way we could see the tearing-

out taking place [drawing indicated by arrow], at this point she can emit a short, high, spine-chilling shriek, afterwards everything will continue normally as before—this element of horror *I think terrific*, much stronger than the severed eye [in *Un Chien andalou*], I didn't really want to use a horror element but, now that we have this one which is *superior* to the previous one, we must use it (something we never would have done had it only turned out to be merely equal or inferior in intensity) and above all in *this* love scene it's really apposite!

Buñuel was as obsessed as Dalí with the scene in question, telling Noailles that, if successful, it alone would be 'far stronger that the whole of *Un Chien andalou*,'[23] and decided to incorporate Dalí's suggested improvement in a modified form: in the film the lovers suck each other's fingers greedily, then the man caresses the girl's face with a hand revealed in close-up to be missing all its fingers (the mutilated hand of a cripple was used for this shot).[24]

In the same letter, Dalí went on to supply Buñuel with hints on how to film 'the cunt you're always dreaming about showing in the cinema':

In the love scene she has her head bent like this for a moment [drawing indicated by arrow] (this moment I see like Lady Windermere's fan[25]). He looks at her and you can see her lips trembling—here there are two solutions—1. the face recedes slightly and the lips are lightly superimposed [drawing indicated by arrow] until we almost see two real lips of a cunt *shaved* so that they look more like the previous ones, or else 2. the lips are in close-up surrounded by the white background of the face. Against this background of facial skin and *around the lips* begins to appear vaguely the superimpression of some shots of a feather boa (cunt hairs) framing the cleavage (white, same background as the previous face which served as background to the mouth); the superimpression continues until we see the image in close-up (her head and mouth disappear from view in the process), her chest heaving in accelerated rhythm like this [indicated by arrow]. The feathers are moved softly by the breeze [indicated by arrow]. Breasts moving [indicated by arrow].

That it's a cunt-mouth hole etc. will be obvious and impossible to cut, since of the two pictures one is a real mouth and the other a cleavage surrounded by real feathers [drawing, indicated by an arrow, beneath which comes the following explanation also indicated by an arrow]. At the moment of the superimpression, the mouth, *damp* and drooling, should be half open, with the tongue, not the *teeth*, visible . . . In the love scene *she's* almost naked, we've got to see a lot of her breasts and a lot of her *arse*, I visualize her cleavage like this and her shoulders absolutely bare [indicated by arrow].

Buñuel did not take up Dalí's ingenious 'cunt-mouth', suggestions which are a further indication of his obsession at this time with the double and multiple image. Nor did he respond to Dalí's plea for the near nakedness of the female lead, probably because he knew that any such overtness would fall foul of the censors.

Dalí ended with a list of further suggestions:

> A train with its windows *full of Frenchmen* flashes past, very quickly. But this is for another film—
>
> Someone can have his fly slightly *unbuttoned* (only a little!), the shirt is visible so little that people think it was done *unintentionally* and without meaning to cause embarrassment. This personage appears quite a bit, and even comes up close to the camera from time to time –
>
> [In the left margin] If you film this scene well it could be incredibly erotic, don't you think, I really love it.
>
> VERY GOOD
>
> In the love scene and before the light is turned out we must *hear* someone pissing and the noise of the bidet, one long stream then two or three short ones, *after this* you hear the kiss, etc., all of this with a beautiful, exciting woman and the garden etc. etc. will have a tremendously randy poetry.
>
>   [In the left margin] a very *characteristic* noise that not a person will miss, before it she can say something in order that it should be totally obvious, 'wait a moment I'll be back in a minute', or 'I'll be with you in a jiffy'.[26]

Buñuel incorporated the man with his fly-button undone (one of the images that later attracted the ire of the censors) and greatly appreciated Dalí's suggestions concerning the bidet-cum-urinal, which, adding a personal touch of scatology, he used in another scene.

Dalí was now in a state of high, and inventive, excitement about the film. In another letter to Buñuel he came up with more drawings and ideas, this time for the incorporation of tactile sensations. The first sheet is headed by the illustration of a Dalinian gadget that would transmit the relevant sensations to the members of the audience. An arrow points to hairs, another to the hot water that would spray onto the audience's fingers when a bidet is heard running. Dalí explains:

> I'm doing a lot of thinking about tactile cinema, it would be easy and fantastic if we could apply it to our film as a simple illustration. The audience rest their hands on a table on

which different materials appear in synchronization with the film. On the screen a personage caresses someone's skin and on the table there's skin etc., there'd be effects that are absolutely Surrealist and spine-chilling. A personage touches a corpse and on the table the fingers sink into putty!, if we could use six or seven tactile synchronizations well chosen ...

We should think about this at least, for later on if not for now. The audience would go berserk.

At the bottom of the page, in case Buñuel should miss the point, Dalí adds a drawing of members of the audience in a state of blatant erection as they watch a 'tit' (*teta*) being caressed on the screen, and finger lecherously the artifical breasts that have materialized on the tables in front of them.[27]

A last page of suggestions was taken into consideration by Buñuel as he finalized the shooting script:

> Just as there's the man covered in dust there can be a man horribly bloodied who strolls unconcernedly among the passers-by—or, just as they [the protagonists] grow older or younger, he can have a horribly bloodied face for a second (very good, this).
>
> *
>
> Somehow we must add to the love dialogue, as if they were talking about something they both know, that bit 'I always desired the death of my children' (the 'my love' bit), at this point he can say 'my love' with his face all bloodied.
>
> *
>
> When they're in the mud *she* screams *as if they were slitting her throat*. Before the things begin to be thrown out of the window, inside the room we hear a piano playing the waltz of the waves very slowly, as if a nostalgic, slow and sentimental scene were about to begin. And above all, insist on the donkeys and pianos!
>
> *
>
> A small detail, at the party: a woman gets up from her chair with a bloodied bottom. We hardly notice—in a corner of the room somewhere.
>
> In the street documentary bit, a little chap, I mean a lame little chap, falls, gets up and carries on, but lost among a lot of others.
>
> *
>
> A small detail for the male personage in the love scene, a shot of his hand contracting, etc., identical, the same, as the shot a moment later of the conductor before he begins to cry.[28]

Buñuel rejected Dalí's recommendation about the woman with the bloody bottom, and no donkeys or pianos accompany, to the music of a waltz, the burning pine, giraffe, archbishop and other assorted bric-à-brac hurled out of the window by the infuriated male protagonist. But he incorporated the love dialogue, spoken in off, and saw to it that Gaston Modot's handsome features were liberally clotted with blood:

> She: I'd been waiting for you for so long! What joy! What joy to have assassinated our children!
> He: My love, my love, my love, my love, my love, my love.[29]

In his memoirs, Buñuel played down Dalí's contribution to the screenplay of *L'Age d'or*, giving the reader to understand that he only accepted one of the painter's suggestions: the scene in which a man walks in a public garden with a stone on his head and passes a statue similarly hatted.[30] The letters quoted, however, as well as Buñuel's pencilled-in modifications to the script, show that Dalí worked in close collaboration with him right up to the beginning of shooting in early March and that Buñuel carefully weighed each of his proposals. This is confirmed, moreover, in a letter that Buñuel wrote to Pepín Bello on 11 May 1930, where we find him saying: 'As in *Un Chien andalou*, I worked out the plot with Dalí.'[31] It can be seen once again, therefore, that Buñuel, intentionally or unconsciously, failed to do retrospective justice to Dalí.

Buñuel had dutifully kept Noailles abreast of his preparations to begin filming *L'Age d'or*, telling him excitedly on 28 February that Sergei Eisenstein, no less, had begged for a small part in the film. 'C'est vraiment la gloire,' the Vicomte replied.[32] Shooting commenced on 3 March 1930, the same day that the generous Noailles posted Dalí the cheque with which to acquire his longed-for fisherman's shack in Port Lligat.[33]

Port Lligat and Paranoia

Dalí had been invited to give a lecture on Surrealism to the Ateneu Club in Barcelona, and now informed Breton of his immediate departure for Catalunya. The postcard, a photograph of the beach at Carry-le-Rouet, had been transformed by the painter into a gloss on Seurat's study for *A Sunday Afternoon at the Island of the Grande Jatte*. For one critic, this 'objet trouvé' is proof of the closeness already existing between Breton and his volcanic new acolyte.[34]

Dalí and Gala travelled to Barcelona by sea, embarking at Marseille on 10 March.[35] From the Catalan capital they made their way to Cadaqués to clinch the deal with Lídia. There, acting on instructions from Dalí's father, who was outraged to discover his son's plans for setting up home in Port Lligat, the Hotel Miramar refused to put them up. As

Port Lligat means 'Tied-in Harbour' in Catalan. Dalí's home on the edge of the bay looks across the still water to the jagged, black island of Sa Farnera. The place can be depressing on a grey day.

a result they had to stay in a small boarding house where one of the Dalís' former maids at Es Llané did her best to make them comfortable. Lídia, too, was supportive.[36]

The one-storied shack on the shore at Port Lligat that had been sold to Dalí by Lídia's fisherman son, Bienvenido Costa Noguer, had twenty-one square metres of floor space.[37] Whatever the state of the property it was certainly primitive in the extreme, with no electricity and no running water, and it is hard to imagine that Gala, accustomed to the good life in Paris, was thrilled with the acquisition, which had cost the painter 250 pesetas. But perhaps she saw its potential.[38]

If Cadaqués was still isolated in 1930, Port Lligat, twenty minutes or so away on foot by a rough track that passed in front of the cemetery, could fairly be considered land's end. More accessible by boat than by any other means of transport, its sole inhabitants were a dozen or so taciturn fishermen, who plied their trade in the treacherous waters of Cape Creus.

But Dalí had returned home, to the spot he repeatedly said he loved best in the world, and he was never to regret the decision. Port Lligat, at once Ithaca and Omphalos, immediately became the very centre of his universe, and he was delighted to discover that in the bay that reached almost to his doorstep, bounded by the black and jagged island of Sa Farnera, the fleet of the Holy Roman Emperor, Charles V, had anchored early in the sixteenth century. It seemed to him an illustrious omen. Port Lligat means 'tied-in port', and in truth the bay is more like an enclosed lake than a tract of sea. This, too, pleased Dalí. Here, he felt, he would be secure. Here he would make his home, expanding the property as his fortunes improved. And so it worked out.

After a week making arrangements for some refurbishing of the shack, Dalí and Gala returned to Barcelona where, on 22 March 1930, the painter delivered his lecture 'The Moral Position of Surrealism' to the Ateneu Club, a fitting title for a talk in what his friend Jaume Miravitlles described as Catalunya's 'most prestigious moral tribune'.[39] It was the first time that Dalí had undertaken to speak as an official member of Breton's movement—and it shows in the text. The reader of biographies does not expect to have to sit through a lecture. The excuse for inviting him or her to do so now is that the talk gives us the very essence of Dalí at this crucial moment in his development. The moral seriousness of Breton's *Second Manifesto* pervades the document, and it is clear, too, that Dalí has been looking again at *The Interpretation of Dreams*, re-reading *Beyond the Pleasure Principle* and perusing, maybe for the first time, *Totem and Taboo*:

> First of all, allow me to condemn the eminently vile act of giving a lecture and, even more so, of listening to one. It's only with the most sincere apologies that I once again do such a thing, without any doubt the furthest removed from that purest of all Surrealist acts, which, as Breton has said in his *Second Manifesto*, consists in going down into the street with a revolver and opening fire indiscriminately on the crowd.
>
> Nevertheless, on a certain plane of relativity, the ignoble act of giving a lecture can be used for highly demoralizing and confusion-creating purposes. Confusion-creating because, alongside the procedures [of demoralization][40] (which should be considered good whenever they serve the purpose of definitively destroying the ideas of family, fatherland and religion), we are interested equally in everything that can contribute to the ruin and discredit of the world of the senses and of the intellect, which, in the lawsuit we have brought against reason, can be condensed in the rabidly paranoiac determination to systematize confusion, the confusion that is taboo to Western thought (which has ended up by being cretinously reduced to the 'no-thing' of speculation, vagueness and idiocy).
>
> An ignoble snobbery has trivialized the discoveries of modern psychology, adulterating them to the unheard-of level of using them to decorate mundane salon-conversations, or to lend a fatuous appearance of novelty to the immense cloacum of the modern novel and

theatre. The truth is, of course, that the mechanisms identified by Freud are pretty unsavoury and, above all, hardly apt for the amusement of contemporary society.

Really, these mechanisms have thrown a harsh, dazzling light on human behaviour.

Take a look at domestic affection.

Take self-abnegation: a wife much in love with her husband looks after him for two years during a long and cruel illness; she tends him day and night with an abnegation that exceeds all the limits of tenderness and sacrifice. Naturally, as a recompense for so much love, the husband in question gets better; and at once the woman has a serious nervous breakdown. People believe, of course, that her illness is a consequence of nervous exhaustion. But nothing could be further from the truth. Happy people don't suffer from nervous exhaustion. Psychoanalysis and the careful interpretation of the patient's dreams confirm the highly intense but unconscious (and, as such, unknown to the patient) desire to get rid of her husband. This is why his restoration to health motivates her neurosis. The death wish turns against her. Her extreme abnegation is used as a defence against the unconscious wish.[41]

A widow throws herself on her husband's tomb. Who understands this? The Hindus do, and try to preempt the evil desires of their women with the law that orders widows to be burnt.

Then, abnegation again—the highly disinterested abnegation you find among relatives [?].[42] During the Great War it was shown statistically that there was a very high level of sadism amongst the nurses of the Red Cross. And particularly amongst the most self-abnegating of them who, abandoning good and privileged bourgeois homes, betook themselves en masse to the battlefields—where they were often caught with their scissors cutting unnecessarily long centimetres [of flesh], for sheer pleasure, numerous cases of veritable martyrdom being registered. There must have been intense pleasure involved to justify such harshness. Unless, as is very probable, the mental mechanism of the charming nurses was complicated further by the attractions of masochistic virtue.

The revision of the so-called elevated human sentiments would be interminable in the light of the new psychology. But really such an exhaustive revision is not altogether necessary for us to indicate how, on the moral plane which the Surrealist crisis of consciousness believes before all else it should provoke, a figure like that of the Marquis de Sade appears today with the purity of a diamond, whereas, for example—to refer to one of our local Catalan writers—nothing could appear to us lower, more ignoble, more worthy of opprobrium than the 'fine sentiments' of that great pig, that great pederast, that immense hairy putrefaction, Angel Guimerà.[43]

Not long ago I inscribed on a painting of mine representing the Sacred Heart the phrase 'J'ai craché sur ma mère'.[44] Eugeni d'Ors (whom I consider an absolute *con*) saw in the said inscription simply a private insult, simply a manifestation of cynicism. I need hardly say that the interpretation is incorrect and removes all the really subversive sense from the inscription. The whole point, on the contrary, centres on a moral conflict very similar to the one we find in dreams, when we assassinate a beloved person; and this is a very common dream. The fact that subconscious impulses often appear extremely cruel to our consciousness is a further reason for lovers of truth not to hide them.

The crisis of the world of the senses, the error and systematic confusion which Surrealism has provoked in the sphere of images and reality, are other potent recourses for demoralizing people. And if today I can say that Art Nouveau, which in Barcelona is exceptionally well represented, is the one closest to what we can love sincerely at the moment, this is proof of our repugnance for and total indifference to art, the same repugnance that leads us to consider the postcard as the most vital document of modern popular thought, a thought often so profound that it defies psychoanalysis (I am thinking specially of pornographic postcards) . . .

* * *

The birth of the new Surrealist images should be considered first and foremost as the birth of images of demoralization. It is necessary to insist on the extreme perceptiveness, recognized by every psychologist, of paranoia, a form of mental illness which consists in organizing reality in such a way as to make it serve for the control of an imaginative construct. A paranoiac who thinks he's been poisoned discovers in everything around him, down to the most imperceptible and subtle details, the preparations for his death. Recently, by a completely paranoiac process, I have obtained the visual image of a woman, the position, shadows and morphology of whom, without altering or deforming in the least her real appearance, are at the same time those of a horse.[45] One imagines that it is only a question of a more violent paranoiac intensity to obtain the appearance of a third image, and a fifth and a thirtieth. In this case it would be interesting to know what it is that the image really represents, which is the truth, and then the question arises as to whether the images we have of reality are in fact a product of our paranoiac faculty.

But this is just a small example. There remain the great systems, states more widespread and better-known: hallucinations, the power of voluntary hallucination, pre-sleep, illumination [?], daytime dreaming (for we dream without interruption), mental alienation and many other states no less meaningful and important than the so-called normal state of the enormously normal putrid pig drinking coffee.

Notwithstanding the 'normality' of the people who fill the streets, their actions of a practical order betray a painful automatism. Everyone is painfully twisted and agitated by systems they believe normal and logical; nevertheless all their actions, all their gestures, are guided unconsciously by the world of irrationality and conventions [?], the images half-seen in dreams and then lost; this is why, when they come across images that resemble the latter, they believe that it's love and say that the very sight of them makes them dream.

Pleasure is the most legitimate aspiration of mankind. In human life the reality principle rises up against the pleasure principle. It is the duty of our intelligence to embark on a rabid defence of all that which—despite the abominably mechanical nature of practical life, despite ignoble humanitarian sentiments, despite the pretty phrases (love of work, etc. etc.) which we [Surrealists] all heap with shit—can lead to masturbation, exhibitionism, crime, love.

The reality principle versus the pleasure principle: the true position of true intellectual despair is precisely the defence of all that which, via the path of pleasure and mental prisons [?] of all kinds, can destroy reality, reality every day more subject, more humiliatingly subject, to the violent reality of our spirit.

The Surrealist revolution is above all a revolution of a moral order; this revolution is alive, it's the only one with a spiritual content in contemporary Western thought.

The Surrealist revolution has defended: automatic writing, the Surrealist text, pre-sleep images,[46] dreams, mental alienation, hysteria, the intervention of chance, opinion polls about sex, the insult, anti-religious aggression, Communism, the hypnotic trance, primitive objects, Surrealist objects, the postcard.

The Surrealist revolution has defended the names of the Comte de Lautréamont, Trotsky, Freud, the Marquis de Sade, Heraclitus, Uccello, etc.

The Surrealist group has provoked bloody frays in the Brasserie des Lilas, the Cabaret Maldoror, theatres and the street.

The Surrealist group has published various manifestos insulting Anatole France, Paul Claudel, Maréchal Foch, Paul Valéry, Cardinal Dubois, Serge Diaghilev and others.

I address myself to the new generation in Catalunya and announce that a moral crisis of the highest order has been provoked, that those who persist in the amorality of decent and reasonable ideas have their faces covered in my spit.[47]

The lecture greatly offended some members of the audience, and according to Jaume Miravitlles led to the enforced resignation of the Ateneu's president, Pere Coromines, the old friend of Dalí's father.[48] One of those most outraged was Sebastià Gasch, who recalled, decades afterwards, that Dalí's words and manner that evening had upset him deeply, attacking 'in the most violent way my most intimate convictions'. Given Gasch's declared animus against Surrealism, such a reaction was no doubt inevitable.[49]

Dalí's lecture was hardly covered in the newspapers because it coincided with the arrival in Barcelona of a high-powered contingent of Madrid intellectuals that included the philosopher José Ortega y Gasset, the historian Américo Castro, the philologist Ramón Menéndez Pidal and the writer Manuel Azaña (future President of the Second Republic). They had come to express their support for Catalan culture and, as a result, took the lion's share of space in the press. Dalí's lecture could not have been worse timed. In fact, all it achieved seems to have been a laconic note in *La Publicitat*: 'He extended himself in considerations on the war waged by Surrealism against morality, the fatherland, religion and the family. He spoke about domestic and private issues and insulted the memory of an illustrious dead Catalan. There were no incidents.'[50]

Dalí must have been infuriated not only by the lack of press coverage but by the failure of the Ateneu audience to react aggressively to his provocation. Twelve years later he was to rewrite history, claiming that the lecture had come to an end when, after he insulted Angel Guimerà, chairs were thrown at him and he was escorted from the hall by the police.[51]

One of the most intriguing aspects of Dalí's lecture is the interest it reveals in paranoia, already adumbrated in his unpublished film scenario. In a theoretical text, 'The Rotten Donkey', published that July in Breton's new journal, *Le Surréalisme au Service de la Révolution*, he explored the subject further, arguing that paranoia held great potential for Surrealism:

> I believe that the moment is at hand when, by harnessing the paranoiac and active component of our thinking processes, it will be possible (simultaneously with automatic procedures and other passive states) to systematize confusion and contribute to the total discrediting of the world of reality.

Harnessing, systematization: the concession in the direction of 'automatic procedures and other passive states' only serves to underline the point that Dalí now favours the ordering of the unconscious over the freewheeling autonomy recommended by Breton in his first manifesto.

Dalí's interest in paranoia, as the lecture shows and 'The Rotten Donkey' confirms, is inseparable from his interest in double and multiple images. By the time he wrote 'The Rotten Donkey' he had added a third image, that of the lion, to the picture mentioned in the lecture. Finally entitled *Invisible Sleeping Woman, Horse, Lion, etc.*, this work, he stated later, was inspired by his contemplation of the rocks of Cape Creus, whose fantastic shapes and metamorphoses had fascinated him since childhood.[52] Dalí's efforts to induce in the viewer a state akin to paranoiac delirium as he studies the picture are not entirely successful, however, and the limbs of both horse and woman undergo considerable distortions in the process of accommodating them to the scheme of the double image. In the contemporaneous *The Invisible Man* the man's head and the general outline of his seated figure are far more immediately visible than Dalí intended (he doesn't suddenly 'appear', as does the rabbit in *The Lugubrious Game*), and his right arm, for example, cannot be read as such but only as a naked female seen from behind (in a posture identical

Dalí, The Invisible Man, *1930. Oil on canvas, 140 x 80 cm. In this unfinished work the man's head and the general outline of his seated figure are more immediately visible than Dalí intended.*

to that of the woman at the end of *Un Chien andalou*), just as his left hand can only be interpreted as a hand. The right hand, however, does have a more hallucinatory quality, as does the woman-horse, quoted from *Invisible Sleeping Woman, Horse, Lion, etc.*, in the left background, behind the by now ubiquitous jug motif representing an idiotic Dalí and his sister Anna Maria (the angry lion appearing in the forefront of the painting is presumably an allusion to Dalí's father).

By the summer of 1930 Dalí had invented what he called 'paranoiac-critical thought', in which the double image played an integral part.[53] The word 'method' was not substituted for 'thought' until, probably, 1932.[54] It was a brilliant *trouvaille*, suggesting as it did that there was a technique for provoking and experiencing the sort of paranoiac phenomena with which Dalí was concerned. But if the term 'paranoiac-critical method' was soon famous (Dalí made sure of that), the 'method' itself remained elusive in the extreme—so elusive, indeed, that Dalí said in later life 'I don't know what it consists of but . . . it works very well!'[55]

The *purpose* of the 'method' was another matter, however, as Dalí was to explain in *Diary of a Genius*. 'In general terms,' he wrote, 'it's an attempt to achieve the most rigorous systematization possible of the most delirious phenomena and materials, with the intention of making tangibly creative my most obsessively dangerous ideas.'[56]

Dalí never identified these obsessively dangerous ideas, nor did he ever suggest that if, from 1930 onwards, he was increasingly fascinated by paranoia it was in part because of the revelation that his paternal grandfather, Gal, had suffered from such serious paranoiac delusions that they had driven him to suicide. It is difficult to believe that that discovery, attested as we have seen by his cousin Montserrat, did not shake him profoundly, not merely because an unsuspected skeleton had suddenly appeared in the family cupboard but because, pondering on the behaviour of his father and of his Uncle Rafael, at times as seemingly crazy as that of their unstable progenitor, he must have wondered if he himself had not inherited a paranoiac tendency. It can be argued that it was in order to reduce this possibility, to defuse this fear, that Dalí elaborated a 'method' which, by confronting paranoia through its simulation, sought to bring the potential incidence of the illness under control.

How much did Dalí really know by 1930 about paranoia (meaning 'disordered mind' in Classical Greek, the word had been appropriated by psychiatry in the nineteenth century to designate delusional insanity and, in particular, persecution mania of the kind apparently suffered by Dalí's grandfather)?[57] Certainly he would have come across several passing references to the phenomenon in *The Interpretation of Dreams*, but, more importantly, he may have read, or had his attention drawn to, *Introductory Lectures on Psychoanalysis*, in which Freud reiterates his conviction that paranoia 'regularly arises from an attempt to fend off excessively strong homosexual impulses.'[58] Knowing Dalí's fear of being homosexual, one can easily imagine that this sentence stopped him in his tracks. Perhaps his 'paranoiac-critical method', as well as being a bid to preclude paranoia and harness the unconscious, was designed as a deliberate defence against a sexual temptation that racked him with anxiety.

'The Rotten Donkey' was read with fascination by a young French psychoanalyst who was writing a thesis on paranoia at this time, Jacques Lacan. It seemed to Lacan that Dalí was right in seeking to harness the energy of paranoia for creative purposes, for active intervention in the external world, and he contacted the painter.[59] Lacan does not appear to have described the encounter, and Dalí's amusing account in the *Secret Life* may be somewhat exaggerated;[60] but there is no doubt that 'The Rotten Donkey' and the meeting with its author influenced the development of Lacan's thinking on paranoia, even though he never acknowledged it,[61] while Dalí was encouraged to proceed in the way that he was going.

Dalí Cusí again

Dalí's father had not been idle since he discovered to his horror that Salvador had purchased a shack at Port Lligat and was planning to live there in sin with the adulterous Russian wife of Paul Éluard. When Dalí and Gala arrived back in Cadaqués after the lecture in Barcelona to see how work was progressing on their tiny property, they were harassed by the Civil Guard, that traditional embodiment of Spanish repression, at the instigation of the fearsome notary. Dalí recalled in 1972 that his father made his and Gala's existence a nightmare on that occasion. 'To see the Pichots,' he said, 'we had to

Port Lligat before Dalí bought his fisherman's hut.

go by boat so as not to pass in front of my parents' house at Es Llané', which for him had become 'a lump of sugar soaked in gall'.[62]

Dalí and Gala only spent a short time at Port Lligat on this occasion. A letter from Don Salvador Dalí Cusí to Buñuel written shortly after their departure gives us the true measure of the father with whom the painter had to contend:

> My Good Friend: I suppose you have now received the letter I wrote to you last Saturday.
>
> If you retain your friendship with my son you could do something for me. I am not writing to him directly because I have not got his address.
>
> Yesterday he passed through Figueres, they told me, and went on to Cadaqués with the 'madame'. He was only able to stay a few hours in Cadaqués because in the evening the Civil Guard, obeying orders, visited him. He was saved a scare because if he had stayed to sleep in Cadaqués he would have had a bad time.
>
> He left yesterday afternoon or night for Paris where I gather he is going to spend eight days. You must know where the 'madame' lives and could tell her to inform him that he need not try to return to Cadaqués, for the simple reason that he will not be allowed to remain in the said village for even two or three hours. Then things will get so complicated for him that he will not be able to return to France.

Whatever legal costs become necessary will have to be paid by my son as I expect you will warn him.

My son has no right to embitter my life. Cadaqués is my spiritual refuge, and my peace of mind is disturbed by the presence of my son in the village in question. Moreover this is my wife's place of repose and will be destroyed if my son, with his indecent conduct, befouls it.

I am not prepared to suffer more. That is why I have gone to all these lengths to ensure that he does not trouble me during the summer.

For the moment the measure I have taken is sufficient to prevent my son from sullying us this summer and next. When the measure is no longer adequate, I will have recourse to whatever I have at hand, including physical violence. My son will not come to Cadaqués, he must not come, he cannot come.

Either this summer or next, because I have other measures to prevent him from disturbing me; but when the measures I dispose of at the moment are no longer sufficient, let us fight each other and then we will see who wins and I can tell you that since I wish to win whatever the cost I will do all I can to make sure I win, getting people to help me to beat him up, or seeking the opportunity to bestow the blows myself without receiving any in return. This is in no way vile because I am warning the victim in advance of my intentions and therefore, if he wishes to come to Cadaqués, he can take all the precautions he wants to defend or protect himself (as he desires).

His theories have convinced me completely. He believes that in the world the thing is to do as much evil as possible and now I too believe this. Spiritual evil no one can cause him because he is a completely debased person, but I can cause him physical damage because he *still* has flesh and bones.

Best wishes from your friend, Salvador Dalí.[63]

Back in Paris, safe for the moment from paternal violence, it seems unlikely that Dalí did not rush to see Buñuel, who finished shooting the last interiors of the film on 24–26 March 1930 and, on 31 March–1 April, the spoken exteriors. On 4 April Buñuel and his team arrived in Cape Creus to shoot the bandit scenes, the arrival of the 'Majorcans' (the 'putrescent' Catholic hierarchy, represented by the mumbling archbishops who turn into fossilized skeletons) and the founding of Imperial Rome. Max Ernst was head of the bandits, who included members of the Spanish colony in Paris and the English Surrealist Roland Penrose.[64]

Dalí had decided not to accompany Buñuel to Cadaqués, probably in order to avoid his father but, more importantly, because he was worried about Gala's health. Before leaving Paris with her for a restorative visit to Malaga, where they had been invited to stay by the poet José María Hinojosa, he must surely have visited the exhibition of collages staged by Camille Goemans, who had managed to get his gallery going again temporarily. It opened on 28 March 1930 and comprised works by Arp, Braque, Duchamp, Ernst, Gris, Miró, Magritte, Man Ray, Picabia, Picasso, Tanguy and Dalí, who was represented by *The First Days of Spring.* This was Goemans's last show, and soon afterwards the gallery closed down definitively.[65]

News would soon have reached Dalí about Buñuel's shoot in Cadaqués. When the team arrived the weather was vile, but next day it cleared up and filming got under way successfully at Tudela, the isolated Cape Creus creek to whose weird mica-schist formations Dalí had introduced Buñuel the previous summer and where, in 1925, Lorca had enjoyed munching his sandwiches after the imaginary terrors of their boat trip from Cadaqués.[66] Excitement in Cadaqués had run high as Buñuel recruited extras among the villagers. When it was all over, the local paper *Sol Ixent* commented on 3 May:

> Our readers can imagine what it was like to see old grandfather Firmo, Enriquet de la Maula, Mario Coll and a few others playing the part of bishops, dressed with mitres on the beach at Tudela. Manel de la Maula and Enriquet's daughters as nuns. Josep Albert as a Cardinal, etc. etc. Our readers will tell us if we're not right when we say that Cadaqués is a sort of small-scale Hollywood, full of film stars capable of rivalling John Gilbert, Chaney, the Barrymores, Mary Pickford, etc.[67]

Before leaving, Buñuel shot a few tiny, silent sequences of Dalí Cusí and his second wife Catalina, 'la tieta', at Es Llané. We see the massive figure of the notary guzzling sea-urchins with huge relish, watering the garden he had weaned so patiently from the rocky hillside behind the house, smoking his inseparable pipe, swaying to and fro in his rocking chair . . . and looking confidently into the lens. So this is how the notary appeared to the world at the age of fifty-eight! This is the awe-inspiring figure who, in Dalí's portraits, gives the impression that he owns Cadaqués! Seeing these images rescued sixty years later it requires little effort to grasp the problem Dalí Cusí posed for his son, which is conceivably why Buñuel shot them. Fussing around the notary, catering to his needs, 'la tieta', who is twelve years younger, has more the appearance of a submissive servant than of a wife. No beauty, certainly. Dalí Cusí was so pleased with Buñuel's camerawork that he had the film shown at the local cinema.[68]

Meanwhile, Dalí had painted the first major work in which he alluded directly to the relationship with Gala that was partially to blame for his estrangement from his father. *XIX* *Imperial Monument to the Child-Woman* is habitually assigned to 1929 but was almost certainly executed in Paris in early 1930. The child-woman of the title, Dalí explained later, is Gala. The 'monument' is based on the mica-schist phantasmagoria of Cape Creus among which their love affair had begun, and expresses 'all the puerile terrors' of his childhood and adolescence, which he now offered up to her as a sacrifice. 'I wanted this painting to be a daybreak in the style of Claude Lorrain,' he went on (alluding to the Prado's *Embarkation of Saint Paula at Ostia*), 'with the morphology of the "modern style" corresponding to the height of Barcelona bad taste'.[69]

While the painting may not express *all* Dalí's 'puerile terrors' (there is no sign of the dreaded locust, for example), it certainly contains a pretty comprehensive anthology of his obsessive motifs at the time. Here again are the roaring lions, the idiotic jug-faces of Dalí and his sister Anna Maria (whose shared eye makes it impossible to take them both in together), a tiny head of the Great Masturbator, this time wearing a crown (at bottom left-centre), the staring manic eyes of the aggressive father figure, a masturbatory finger and hand holding a cigarette (as in *The Lugubrious Game*) and, twice, two faces hiding themselves in shame or terror. One of the latter, significantly, crowns the whole edifice. There are some new elements, however. The painting contains the first reference to the couple at prayer in Millet's *Angelus*, soon to become another Dalinian obsession; Napoleon, Dalí's childhood hero, occupies a niche in the monument, along with Mona Lisa; and there is a remarkable cameo in the bottom left corner of the picture of an adult couple being brutally ejected from their bed by a plank pushed by a car whose head-lamps bathe the scene in an eerie green light (an attack on conventional marriage?).

As for Gala, who has inspired the monument and is duly acknowledged by the kneeling figure in the lower right corner, she is suggested both by the shapely female buttocks figuring at the very centre of the painting and by the bust at the left. Here the woman, while beautiful, looks exhausted—an allusion, perhaps, to the pleurisy from which Gala was suffering at the time and which was making both Dalí and Éluard extremely anxious (the latter told her that his hair was turning white as a result).[70] 'Her illness had given her such a fragile look,' Dalí recalled, 'that when one saw her in her tea-rose pink nightgown she looked like one of those fairies drawn by Raphael Kishner that seemed on the point of dying from the mere effort of smelling one of the decorative gardenias twice as large and heavy as their heads.'[71] Clearly what Gala needed was a holiday—but well out of the reach of the atrabilious notary of Figueres. The latter is probably the figure who, holding a child by the hand, stands down below the monument to the right and can be seen pointing to a notably phallic rock bathed in the light of the Claude Lorrain sunrise. The crevices in the rock, as in so many of Dalí's paintings of this period, hold a collection of keys and ants, suggestive of fearful sexuality.

Interlude in Malaga

The Malaga review *Litoral*, which ran sporadically from November 1926 to June 1929, was one of Spain's most handsomely produced and influential literary magazines. Among its regular contributors *Litoral* counted the poets Manuel Altolaguirre, Emilio Prados (its begetters), Luis Cernuda, Rafael Alberti, Vicente Aleixandre and Lorca, the latter's friend Manuel Angeles Ortiz (the painter who had arranged for Dalí to meet Picasso in Paris), the painter-poet José Moreno Villa (right-hand man of Alberto Jiménez Fraud at the Residencia de Estudiantes) and another Malaga poet, José María Hinojosa, for whose *Poema del campo* (1925) Dalí had provided a cover and frontispiece. Dalí himself had sent a drawing for the special Góngora tercentenary issue, published in October 1927, and the magazine was often mentioned appreciatively by *L'Amic de les Arts*.[72]

Hinojosa, who had joined the editorial board of *Litoral* in May 1929, enjoyed private means and was the magazine's principal financial supporter. In March 1930 he was in Paris, and when he saw Dalí and Gala there after their return from Barcelona he invited them to spend a few weeks in Malaga at his expense that Easter. In return he was to get a painting. Since it seemed that a few weeks by the sea might help Gala to convalesce from her pleurisy, she and Dalí accepted the invitation, setting off for Spain early in April.[73]

First the couple spent a few days in Barcelona, where Éluard deluged Gala with letters and telegrams.[74] Then they set off by train on a three-day, fly-infested, third-class haul down the coast to Malaga where, on 15 April, a local newspaper reported that Dalí, 'the great Catalan painter', was staying in Torremolinos, then a tiny fishing village with hardly a tourist.[75] Hinojosa installed the lovers in 'the Englishman's Castle' (El Castillo del Inglés), which stood on a low cliff overlooking the little cove of La Carihuela. The charming property used to belong to an eccentric English philanthropist and had just been converted into what has been described as the 'first hotel on the Costa del Sol', the Santa Clara.[76] In the *Secret Life* the hotel, which had an annexe, becomes the 'fisherman's cottage which overlooked a field of carnations on the edge of a cliff falling abruptly into the sea'.[77]

Easter began that year on 14 April, and Dalí and Gala went into Malaga for the processions. It was the first time the painter had visited Picasso's home town, and he imagined that he saw physical types resembling his great rival on all sides.[78]

Life in pre-boom Torremolinos was fit for a lotus-eater. 'Gala, with a build like a boy's, burned by the sun, would walk about the village with her breasts bare,' Dalí recalled eleven years later. The fisherfolk, very free in their customs (they were anarchists) showed no disapproval of the nonchalant Russian's semi-nudity. More affected was the poet José Luis Cano, then only twenty, whom Emilio Prados took out to meet the flamboyant couple. 'Gala's stare struck me forcibly,' Cano recalled. 'Her eyes blazed intensely as if they wished to scorch whatever they looked at. For clothes she wore only a small red skirt, and her naked breasts, very brown and pointed, were exposed with complete naturalness to the sun.'[79] Another young Malaga poet, Tomás García, also remembered Gala's bare breasts—and his shock when she said she was missing her husband and jumped up to send him a telegram which read 'Paul, my love, I love you.'[80] José Luis Barrionuevo, a friend of Hinojosa, has said that Gala was forever telegraphing Éluard 'extremely affectionately.'[81]

Gala, topless again, in Port Lligat, c.1931.

The *Litoral* group could not help noticing how passionately involved Dalí was with Gala. The latter, more Parisian than the Parisians themselves, had no inhibitions about kissing in public, a practice unheard of in Spain, and made no attempt to restrain herself in Malaga. Such attentions greatly bolstered Dalí's ego and he responded as ardently as he could, given his self-consciousness, attracting the wrath of a participant in one of the Easter processions who hissed a recommendation that he 'wait' until he got back to *Madrid* (in the provinces the Spanish capital, although tame by Paris standards, was considerd a hotbed of libertinism).[82] Manuel Altolaguirre also recalled the endless embracing, guaranteed to cause offence when it didn't arouse jealousy or anger. Altolaguirre worked in a tourist office, and told enquirers that the garishly dressed couple he was showing around Malaga were Egyptians. On a visit to Torremolinos he found Dalí and Gala bathing stark naked and disapointed that they seemed to be attracting no voyeurs.[83]

One afternoon—it was 18 May 1930—Emilio Prados proposed that together they execute a Surrealist *cadavre exquis*. Dalí and Gala agreed. Gala drew the head, Dalí the neck, Darío Carmona (another member of the *Litoral* group) the arms and chest, José Luis Cano the belly and genitals, Prados the legs. The result was charming.[84]

Years later Darío Carmona recalled Dalí's shyness on their visits to Torremolinos ('it may sound absurd, but Dalí was a bit timid'), and his horror of grasshoppers (he would go back to the house if there was one on the path to the beach). One day he saw Dalí and Gala in Malaga. They were both very sunburnt. Dalí, in pre-hippy guise, was wearing an open jacket to reveal his smooth dark skin and the necklace of green glass beads which he sported throughout his stay. His long hair was jet-black. 'Mohamed, one penny, Mohamed, one penny,' the beggar children chanted in English.[85]

Prados and Altolaguirre asked Dalí to join them in setting up a Surrealist magazine to act as the Spanish mouthpiece of the movement. Dalí expressed enthusiasm. The Malaga-born Surrealist poet Vicente Aleixandre, who was to win the Nobel Prize for Literature, also lent his support.[86] But Hinojosa, who apparently had suggested the idea in the first place, was rapidly becoming more Catholic and right-wing and, disturbed by the 'revolutionary aspect' that Dalí and Prados proposed giving to the publication, withdrew his offer of financial assistance. The project was abandoned.[87]

During the five weeks the couple spent in Torremolinos, Dalí worked tirelessly on *The Invisible Man.*[88] It was probably at this juncture that he added the female figures whose stomachs seem to be exploding in an efflorescence of roses on the steps of the arcaded building on the right. This was almost certainly an allusion to a painful gynaecological problem that was beginning to affect Gala and which was only resolved by an operation that rendered her sterile the following summer. Dalí, desperately anxious about Gala, did another painting this year, *The Bleeding Roses*, in which the female figure was now the protagonist. Tied to a column like Saint Sebastian, she writhes in agony while the blood from the roses on her belly trickles down her thighs.[89]

Éluard was as worried about Gala as Dalí. He was missing her desperately (only consoled by his collection of photographs of her naked), sensed that he was losing her, and was burdened with financial problems. The last thing Gala wanted to hear about was the latter, obsessed as she was with money and security. All her efforts were now directed towards making Dalí successful.[90]

Dalí's departure from Malaga was announced in the local press on 22 May 1930.[91] The couple returned to Paris via Madrid, where they spent a few days and were filmed by the dynamic Ernesto Giménez Caballero, editor-owner of *La Gaceta Literaria*, on the roof of his printing-house. The surviving sequence, only a few seconds long, shows Gala at her most radiant and seductive. When she blows a cheeky kiss at the camera one can see why so many men found her irresistible. Dalí, standing in a daze beside her, looks as if he simply cannot believe his luck. Later Giménez Caballero said that he found Gala, whom he had not met before, 'tense and arachnid'. Perhaps he intimidated her (Giménez Caballero could be very intimidating indeed), but there is no sign of either tension or spider-woman in these priceless images of felicity.[92]

The sculptor Cristino Mallo, who had been at the Special School with Dalí, found him changed. 'He was very different and had a little moustache. I remember he spied me in the street. He was with Gala in a cab; he called me over and introduced me to her.'[93] Dalí took Gala to see the Residencia de Estudiantes, where it's hard to imagine they didn't talk about Lorca (who had just arrived in Cuba after eight months in New York). Natalía Jiménez de Cossío, wife of Alberto Jiménez Fraud, remembered their visit and that José Moreno Villa was persuaded by Gala to make her a present of a painting by Dalí given to him by the artist a few years earlier. Dalí promised to send him another to replace it—but never did.[94]

A few days later Dalí and Gala were back in Paris, where Buñuel was putting the finishing touches to his film which, he now told Pepín Bello, he had renamed *Down with the Constitution*! although, naturally, it had nothing to do with any constitution past or present.[95] It is not known who thought up the definitive title, *L'Age d'or*, which the film received shortly afterwards and which probably contains an ironic illusion to the famous scene in *Don Quixote* in which the knight errant harangues a group of goatherds on the joys of the simple life.[96] Nor is it known if Dalí visited the cutting room or made any last-minute suggestions. Buñuel says in his memoirs that Dalí 'really loved' *L'Age d'or* when he saw it for the first time, exclaiming that 'it was like an American film'. This may well have been so, but there is no contemporary documentation to prove it.[97]

Meanwhile, on 21 June, with Camille Goemans definitively out of business, Dalí had signed up with a new dealer, Pierre Colle, recommended to him by the ever-helpful Charles de Noailles.[98]

On 30 June 1930 the final, sonorized version of *L'Age d'or* was screened for the first time in the Noailles' private cinema. Owing to some technical difficulties the première was not a complete success. Over the following ten days, with no hitches, the Noailles provided screenings for select groups of friends and critics. The Vicomte was delighted. 'I get the impression that at the moment nothing else is being talked about in Paris,' he wrote on 10 July to Buñuel, who, like Dalí, had returned to Spain at the beginning of the month.[99]

The skeletal archbishops in L'Age d'or, *Cape Creus, 1930.*

Summer in Port Lligat

In Port Lligat Dalí and Gala found that their fisherman's cabin had made splendid progress. Salvador hurried off photographs to Noailles, who quipped in reply that, if the Catalan ever gave up painting, he could turn his energies profitably to architecture.[100]

The couple's return to Port Lligat, where they stayed until the autumn, coincided with the publication of the first issue of *Le Surréalisme au Service de la Révolution*, which Éluard immediately dispatched to Dalí, telling Gala to make sure they read it carefully, all of it.[101] One imagines that the first thing Dalí did was to check that 'The Rotten Donkey', dedicated proudly to 'Gala Éluard', had been printed satisfactorily.

Le Surréalisme au Service de la Révolution was even more soberly printed than its predecessor, *La Révolution Surréaliste*, and bore on its green cover an enigmatic emblem which, as Éluard explained to Gala, symbolized the conjunction of Saturn and Uranus (which, strangely, had presided over his, Breton's and Aragon's births).[102] The inaugural issue of the new journal spelt out clearly in what ways Surrealism now felt that it could serve the cause of the Revolution, and expressed its loathing for French colonialism (in Indo-China) as vehemently as it did for the French flag, the French army, the Marseillaise, Christianity in general and the Catholic Church in particular. But where the work of the creative artist was concerned, Breton insisted on maintaining his distance from the Communist Party: above all the artist must be true to his inspiration. This attitude was to lead before long to friction with the Party and eventually to the breakdown of relations.

The issue carried a 'Declaration' in which Breton's faithful of the moment swore allegiance to their leader:

An older André Breton in front of Dalí's William Tell, *which he owned and continued greatly to admire (see colour plate xx).*

Determined to use, indeed abuse, at all times the authority conferred on us by the conscious and systematic practice of written or other modes of expression, and being in agreement with André Breton in all respects and resolved to *apply* the conclusions which derive from a reading of the SECOND SURREALIST MANIFESTO, the undersigned, under no illusions about the efficacy of 'artistic and literary' reviews, have decided to lend their support to the periodical which, under the title:

SURREALISM IN THE SERVICE OF THE REVOLUTION

will not only permit them to reply instantaneously to the scum who profess to think, but will prepare the definitive turning of the intellectual energies alive today to the profit of inevitable revolution.

Buñuel and Dalí signed the document with Maxime Alexandre, Louis Aragon, Joë Bousquet, René Char, René Crevel, Paul Éluard, Max Ernst, Marcel Fournier, Camille Goemans, Georges Malkine, Paul Nougé, Benjamin Péret, Francis Ponge, Marco Ristic, Georges Sadoul (in trouble with the authorities for writing an insulting letter to a military cadet), Yves Tanguy, André Thirion, Tristan Tzara and Albert Valentin.

The first issue of the new review did both Dalí and Buñuel proud, publishing, as well as Dalí's 'The Rotten Donkey', three full-page stills from *L'Age d'or*, each showing the female protagonist, Lya Lys, on the point of orgasm, a photograph, attributed to Buñuel, of a gloved archbishop caressing a beautiful woman over the caption 'Are you feeling cold?' and two reproductions of Dalí's unfinished *The Invisible Man*.

The whole issue, like Breton's *Second Manifesto* itself, exhaled a high seriousness, and any humour it contained was directed, with bitter scorn, at bourgeois society—and anyone who happened to disagree with Surrealism. The group that had now ranged itself alongside Breton, after the expulsion of the dissidents, was determined to play its part in the destruction of what it considered a disgusting system and the creation of a new order. That Dalí was determined to participate wholeheartedly in this venture is beyond any doubt.

Meanwhile he settled down to his first summer of work and pleasure in Port Lligat. Despite his father's threats there was nothing he could do to prevent his son from setting up home around the corner, and there is no record of any further attempts at intimidation. The summer's delights, meaning first and foremost the miracle of Gala, included waiting for the promised visit by René Char, Éluard and the latter's latest conquest. Maria Benz, alias Nusch, was a beautiful, fragile, leggy girl the poet had seen that June on the Boulevard Haussmann and had immediately approached. Nusch quickly succumbed, and soon afterwards Éluard had written to Gala and asked if he could take her with him to Cadaqués.[103] Gala put up no objections, and was perhaps relieved to learn that her husband had found someone else. But Éluard still believed that nothing had changed between them, writing from Cannes, where he was staying with Nusch, that he dreamt of her every night: 'I've got the same room you and I had last year. I'm not like you, I'm moved by the memories of us together. I see you naked in this room and I weep for those three so happy weeks I spent here with you.'[104] Gala's replies are unknown but the poet found them reassuring, being particularly pleased with her lively descriptions ('authentic Gala') of paintings, presumably Dalí's.[105]

On 13 August, Éluard, Nusch and René Char embarked at Marseille on an Italian cargo ship, the MN *Catalani*, bound for Barcelona. From there they made their way to Dalí and Gala, putting up at the Hotel Miramar, as Éluard, Gala and their daughter Cécile had done exactly a year earlier.[106] It seems they only stayed for a few days. One imagines that Dalí Cusí must have been outraged to learn that Éluard, abandoned by Gala for his son, had dared to come back to Cadaqués with another woman, as if nothing had happened. At Port Lligat Char took a memorable photograph of the two couples, both radiant. One wonders if he felt something of a gooseberry in the midst of such amorous self-absorption.[107]

During the summer Dalí continued to grapple with the technical problems posed by *The Invisible Man*, and produced two texts, 'The Sanitary Nannygoat' and 'The Great Masturbator', which were included at the end of the year in his little book, *The Visible Woman*, which Gala helped to edit. The first of these (dated 13 August 1930) constitutes an almost impenetrable excursus, heralded by its arbitrary title, on the crisis of 'contemporary poetic thought'. The latter, Dalí argued, could only be invigorated by an injection of his own 'paranoiac-critical thought', his 'delirium of paranoiac interpretation'. As for 'The Great Masturbator', it describes in precise detail a setting, perhaps inspired by Raymond Roussel's *Locus Solus*, in which two heads of the Great Masturbator are accompanied, in a fountain-lined alley, by sculptures of William Tell, by now one of Dalí's compulsive figurations of his father. In the shadow of the two largest sculptures of Tell, a couple are trying to make love but only succeed in urinating on each other. Scatological images pullulate, which suggests that, despite the epiphany of Gala, Dalí is still obsessed by excrement; and there is a long list of attendant creatures in a state of putrefaction, including, of course, donkeys. In other alleys of this unlikely garden are assembled heterogeneous mountains of bric-à-brac that includes consecrated wafers, dried snots, Art Nouveau artefacts and 'numerous sorts of animals in heat', among them a statue of a couple engaged in coprophagy.[108]

Dalí was still smarting over the lack of public response to the lecture he had given to the Ateneu in March, largely due, as we saw, to the fact that it had coincided with the arrival in Barcelona of a group of leading Madrid intellectuals. He vented his rage in a note published in the October issue of *La Surrealisme au Service de la Révolution*:

> I believe that it is absolutely impossible that there exists on earth (with the exception, naturally, of the vile region of Valencia) a place that has produced anything as abominable as what are commonly known as Castilian and Catalan intellectuals; the latter are real pigs; their moustaches are habitually full of real, authentic shit, and most of them, moreover, wipe their arses with paper instead of soaping their holes *comme il faut*, as is done in other countries, while the hair of their balls and armpits is totally filled with a festering infinity of tiny and furious 'Master Millets' and 'Àngel Guimeràs'. Sometimes these intellectuals affect polite and mutual gatherings in honour of each other, conceding, mutually, that their respective languages are very beautiful, and dancing really fabulous dances such as the *sardana*, for example, which in itself would suffice to cover with shame and opprobrium an entire country were it not impossible, as occurs in the Catalan region, to add one more

shameful aspect to those already constituted by the landscape, the towns, the climate, etc., of this ignoble country.[109]

Dalí and Gala returned to Paris in October to be at the première of *L'Age d'or*, settling back into the flat Éluard had rented at Rue Becquerel and where his place had now been usurped by 'le petit Daris' for whom, notwithstanding, he continued to entertain deep affection.[110]

The scandal of *L'Age d'or*

On the morning of 22 October 1930 Charles and Marie-Laure de Noailles staged a private screening of *L'Age d'or* at the Cinéma du Panthéon to which they invited the *crème de la crème* of Parisian society. A plan of the seating arrangements shows that among the 300 guests invited were Cocteau, Pierre Colle, Gertrude Stein, Nancy Cunard, Picasso, Julien Green, André Gide, Brancusi, André Malraux, Darius Milhaud, Paul Morand, Giacometti, Georges Bataille, Robert Desnos, Blaise Cendrars, Carl Dreyer, Duchamp, Pierre Batcheff (of *Un Chien andalou* fame) and Fernand Léger. The Surrealists were there in force, naturally. Dalí and Gala were placed in front of Yves Tanguy and Maurice Heine, a few seats away from Éluard and Breton.[111]

The great absentee was Buñuel, who arrived back in Paris a few days later. There he received a full account of the session from his friend Juan Vicéns, manager of the León Sánchez Cuesta Spanish Bookshop, who told him that many of the aristocratic guests were so shocked by the film that they had left the cinema without saying a word to their hosts and had refused to attend the reception the Noailles held afterwards at the Place des États Unis.[112] The following day *Paris-Soir* described the private viewing under the heading 'Vicomtesse Noailles patronizes "L'Age d'or"'. Since Marie-Laure was known to be of Jewish extraction, her gesture, in the eyes of the French extreme Right, was tantamount to financing 'bolshevist' subversion.[113] Marie-Laure's great friend Cocteau sprang to her support a few weeks later in *Le Figaro*, which published a glowing review of his film *The Life of a Poet*, also financed by the Noailles: the latter, he said, were being mocked, ridiculed and insulted by those of their own class for the unparalleled generosity with which they were prepared to support new ventures in art. Cocteau was also full of praise for Buñuel's new film:

> Scenes like that of the cow or of the conductor in *L'Age d'or* can be considered as events of capital importance, the appearance of the *tragic gag*. I do not doubt that they will receive

sneers. Nonetheless the fact remains that they exist and that nothing can now hold back the dark river of which they are the spring.[114]

Meanwhile Buñuel had been invited to Hollywood by talent-scouts at Metro-Goldwyn-Mayer. With *L'Age d'or* the talk of Paris, on 28 October he embarked at Le Havre for New York on board the *Leviathan*, arriving on 3 November.[115] Before continuing to Los Angeles he saw Angel del Río, Lorca's friend at Columbia University, who told him that the poet was convinced that the 'Andalusian dog' of Buñuel's first film was none other than himself. In this, as we saw, Lorca was not far off the mark, despite Buñuel's later disclaimers.[116]

Lorca by then was back in Spain after his visit to New York and Cuba, and was astounded to learn that Dalí had found the woman in his life. 'It's impossible!' he exclaimed to the poet Rafael Alberti. 'He can only get an erection when someone sticks a finger up his anus!' Lorca knew his man—but he didn't know Gala.[117]

L'Age d'or had now received its exhibition certificate from the censorship authorities and was scheduled to open at Studio 28 in early November. The première was held up by technical difficulties and tookplace on 28 November 1930. On display in the foyer were paintings by Arp, Dalí, Ernst, Tanguy and Man Ray, along with photographs andother documents. The Dalís were *The Host in a Ring*, *The Birth of the Day*, *The Widow* and *Invisible Sleeping Woman, Horse, Lion, etc.*[118]

In the absence of Buñuel, Dalí had provided Studio 28 with a hastily compiled programme note and a synopsis of the film, which were on sale to the public:[119]

L'Age d'or

My general idea in writing the screenplay of 'L'Age d'or' with Buñuel[120] *was to show the straight and pure line of 'behaviour' of an individual who pursues love in the face of ignoble humanitarian and patriotic ideals and other miserable mechanisms of reality.*

Salvador Dalí.

The screenplay

Scorpions live amongst the boulders. Perched on one of these boulders, a bandit is watching a group of archbishops who are singing seated in a mineral landscape. The bandit runs to tell his friends about the nearby presence of the Majorcans (the archbishops).[121] Arriving at the cabin he finds his friends in a strange state of weakness and depression.

They pick up their weapons and all leave with the exception of the youngest, who cannot even get up. They set off among the boulders; but, one after the other, exhausted, they fall to the ground. Then the bandits' leader collapses too, all hope lost. From where he lies, he hears the noise of the sea and sees the Majorcans who are now skeletons scattered among the rocks.

A great sea-borne concourse puts in at this rugged and lonely spot. The concourse comprises priests, military men, nuns, cabinet ministers and various civilians. All make their way to the spot where the remains of the Majorcans lie. Like the authorities leading the funeral cortège, the crowd take off their hats.

The purpose is the founding of Imperial Rome. The first stone is placed when penetrating cries distract people's attention. In the mud, two steps away, a man and a woman are engaged in amorous fray. They are pulled apart. The man is struck and policemen drag him away.

This man and this woman will be the protagonists of the film. The man, thanks to a document which reveals his importance and the high humanitarian and patriotic mission which the Government has entrusted to him, is soon set free. From this moment all his efforts are directed towards love. In the course of an unconsummated love scene presided over by the violence of frustrated acts, the male protagonist is called to the telephone by the high-up authority who confided to him the mission in question. This minister accuses him. Because he has abandoned his task, thousands of old people and innocent children have perished. The male protagonist of the film greets this accusation with insults and, refusing to listen any more, returns to the beloved woman just when an inexplicable coincidence succeeds even more definitively in separating her from him. After this we see him throwing a flaming pine tree out of a window, followed by a huge agricultural instrument, an archbishop, a giraffe and feathers. All this at the precise moment in which the survivors of the Château of Selligny leave by the snow-covered drawbridge. The Count of Blangis is clearly Jesus Christ. This last episode is accompanied by a pasodoble.[122]

The self-appointed guardians of the bourgeois society so viciously pilloried in *L'Age d'or* were not slow to perceive the intensely subversive nature of the film, Dalí's programme notes providing them with all the additional ammunition they could have desired. By the autumn of 1930 Fascism was gathering impetus in Paris, and several violent incidents had already occurred. No sooner did the film open than there began to be rumours that right-wing activists were planning an attack on Studio 28. It came on the evening of 3 December, when members of two extremist groups, the Patriotic League and the Anti-Semitic League, interrupted the performance at the precise moment when a monstrance is removed from a taxi to facilitate the descent of an elegant woman with shapely silk-clad legs, and dumped in the street (both Dalí and Buñuel were going out of their way at this time to ridicule the Host). Chanting 'We'll show you that there are still Christians in France!' and 'Death to the Jews!', the thugs hurled violet ink at the screen and intimidated the audience with clubs. They then lit smoke and stink bombs to force the spectators into the street, and, as a final flourish, wrecked whatever they could lay their hands on in the foyer, slashing the paintings, ripping apart (or stealing) the Surrealist books and magazines on display and cutting the telephone. Dalí's *Sleeping Woman, Horse, Lion, etc.* was almost completely destroyed (he soon produced two new versions), but his other three paintings escaped almost unscathed. It was half an hour before the police intervened—the delay, as it transpired, perhaps being intentional. Some two dozen token arrests were effected. Once the screen had been patched up, the projection got under way again to the applause of the audience, more than sixty of whom signed a collective protest before leaving.[123]

The following day Dalí wrote to Charles de Noailles in Hyères. Above all he wanted to clear up a point concerning the programme notes:

> After my last visit to you I learnt that in a letter to M. Mauclaire[124] you had said that you were disturbed by the fact that, in the programme notes for *L'Age d'or*, Count Blangis is explicitly identified with Christ. Since it was I who wrote the synopsis of the screenplay I feel myself obliged to offer you an explanation with the greatest possible frankness, an explanation which I deeply regret not having been able to give to you in person because of the always incomplete, and terribly uncommunicative, nature of letters.
>
> The synopsis of the screenplay was requested of me (as always happens in such cases) in a great rush and hurry. This would not have prevented me from consulting with you if I had not been convinced of your total approval, given that in this synopsis of *L'Age d'or* all I do is to describe the scenes accepted in the film, where, naturally, they take on an even more directly subversive value.
>
> It is true that I could have avoided insisting on certain scenes in the film given that the public can grasp the sense of these scenes perfectly while watching the film itself, but this would have created a serious problem since the programme notes are not aimed only at the spectators but at a great number of people who may never see the film. It is for this reason that we took the decision of sending many copies of the programme notes abroad and to Spain (for example) where Buñuel's and my position have a certain prominence. If I had suppressed the reference to Christ I would have betrayed, clearly, Buñuel's idea (for it was Buñuel who suggested the entire scene to me when I was in Carry-le-Rouet, and I was in complete agreement, too—Buñuel was determined to include this sequence).
>
> In short, on the one hand I knew that Buñuel would have been very upset by such a mutilation of the scenario, on the other I didn't think that you would be worried since all

of this is already in the film and much more powerfully and violently so with the detail of the girl who is sacrificed, etc.

I hope, dear sir, that you will now be in a position to appreciate the precise nature of my role in the preparation of the programme notes in question, which I deeply regret have seemed to you excessive, but at all events I tried to act correctly in every respect.[125]

Over the next days and weeks there was not a newspaper or periodical in Paris that failed to review, comment on, attack or praise *L'Age d'or* which, if *Un Chien andalou* had first brought the names of Buñuel and Dalí to the attention of the French capital, now catapulted them to fame. News of the scandal also reached Spain, Britain and the United States. The Noailles sent Buñuel packets of cuttings and these, along with those proceeding from other sources, he pasted into an album preserved today in the Noailles archives at the Centre Georges Pompidou in Paris. They make fascinating reading.

The reviews appearing in the right-wing press left no doubt of the ferocity of the repressors in a city where, if literature and theatre were (for the moment) free from censorship, films were subjected to inquisitorial scrutiny by the municipal authorities, particularly those suspected of displaying Marxist tendencies. Earlier in the year the police had prevented Eisenstein, no less, from screening his *The General Line* at the Sorbonne after a lecture on the contemporary Russian cinema, and there had been other cases of blatant violation of the right to freedom of expression in the cinema.[126] Of the leading conservative newspapers, *Le Figaro* was the most vehement in its condemnation of *L'Age d'or*, and openly supported the groups who had protested violently against a 'bolshevist' film that not only attacked Religion, Family and Fatherland but was revolting and pornographic to boot. The aim of *L'Age d'or* was to corrupt, and it must be suppressed! Paul Ginisty, head of the censorhip section of the Ministry of Fine Arts, was called upon to axe the film, despite the fact that it had been passed by the Censorship Commission on 1 October; and Dalí, whose programme notes scandalized the Right almost as much as the film itself, was given to understand that France could do without him.[127]

L'Ami du Peuple (a more populist version of *Le Figaro*) also launched furious diatribes against the film, punning wittily, in one of its attacks, that a more apt title for it would be *L'Age d'ordure*. Without naming Buñuel and Dalí, the paper labelled as 'métèques' ('dagos') those responsible for the production of such excremental filth. Fascism *à la française* was showing its face.[128]

Meanwhile the capital's leading film critics were unanimous in their praise of *L'Age d'or*. For Jean-Paul Dreyfus, of *La Revue du Cinéma*, the film aimed at ramming home the message implicit in *Un Chien andalou*, namely that Buñuel and Dalí despised the bourgeoisie and its determination to repress the life of the instincts. Moreover, since the sub-title of *L'Age d'or* proclaimed this a Surrealist film, it should be judged as such—and not as something else. With great perception, Dreyfus found in the blasphemous content of the film proof that Buñuel was obsessed by the religion he claimed to loathe: it showed that he had spent too long under the yoke of the Marist Brothers. He also thought the film deployed a sense of subtle, anguished humour unlike anything previously achieved in the cinema. *L'Age d'or*, he felt certain, would shake hundreds and hundreds of spectators out of their complacency.[129]

A few days later, in the Communist daily *L'Humanité*, Leon Moussinac wrote that never in the history of the cinema had the bourgeoisie and its 'accessories'—the police, religion, the army, morality, the family, the State—received such a volley of hard kicks in the pants. There could be no doubt that the film served the cause of the Revolution. The attack on the bourgeoisie, though, was inflicted with consummate artistry:

> Although this is an intellectual film, full of literature, we experience without difficulty the direct violence of most of the images, images which cannot be paraphrased. If one says, for example, that they show a blind man being thrown to the ground, an old woman slapped in the face, an archbishop being thrown through a window, a son killed by his father, Jesus Christ as if returning from an orgy, one fails to convey their true significance.[130]

Another perceptive critic, Louis Chavance, noted Buñuel's innovative use of documentary sequences (the scorpions at the beginning of the film and the heaving lava inserted into the toilet sequence): it was an attempt to translate collage into cinematographic terms. Chavance had been struck by the fact that, unlike *Un Chien andalou*, *L'Age d'or* did not move in a dream atmosphere. The reason was that this time Buñuel wanted to allow the audience no escape and to force it to confront the miseries of emotional repression as it exists in the real world.[131]

The campaign mounted by the right-wing press against *L'Age d'or* was gathering momentum by the hour, and now received powerful support from the Italian Embassy, which protested that the film contained an insulting parody of the minute King Victor Emmanuel and his much taller queen, and that its very title was intended as a satirical allusion to Mussolini's Fascist regime. The Embassy had not failed to notice that the hilarious ceremony at the beginning of the film, the founding of Imperial Rome, is explicitly dated 1930, and complained that 'the purely revolting character of certain passages . . . makes the fact that many of the film's scenes take place in Rome all the more painful for Italians'.[132]

The Paris police chief, Préfet Jean Chiappe, whom the Surrealists detested and an American critic later termed 'the French equivalent of J. Edgar Hoover', found himself inundated with requests to ban the film. He needed no encouragement. On 5 December 1930 Studio 28 was ordered to cut out the two archbishop sequences; on the 8th to remove the phrase 'The Count of Blangis is clearly Jesus Christ' from the programme notes; on the 9th to take the film to the Censorship Office, where its pass was to be reviewed. On 10 December the film was prohibited; on the 11th legal action was initiated against Jean-Placide Mauclaire, owner of Studio 28; and on the 12th the police seized two copies of the film, one in the cinema and the other at Mauclaire's home.[133]

Le Figaro was delighted by the success of its campaign and lavish in praise of Préfet Chiappe, who was quoted as saying that he saw it as his duty to preserve 'the atmosphere, not puritanical, certainly, but elegant and vigorous, that constitutes the charm of Paris'.[134]

Charles de Noailles, who had put up the money for the film, was expelled from the snobbish Jockey Club, shunned by the aristocratic circles to which he belonged by birth and even, it seems, threatened with excommunication. His letters to Buñuel in Hollywood show that all he wanted now was to withdraw into the wings. Please, he begged, do everything you can to keep my name out of the scandal. Buñuel, whose admiration for Noailles and his wife was profound, promised to take all the blame.[135]

The Surrealists, outraged by what had happened and seeing it as manifest proof that Fascism was gaining strength in France, went into immediate action, printing a four-page brochure, 'L'Affaire de "L'Age d'or"', in which they provided a full account of events, including quotations from the newspapers, and a detailed 'Revue-programme' in which they made high claims for the revolutionary content of *L'Age d'or*, the theme of which they interpreted as the struggle between the sexual and death instincts raging in the psyche of modern man at a time when 'putrescent' capitalist society, on the verge of collapse, was 'trying to survive by having recourse to priests and policemen as its only props'.[136]

Buñuel never forgave police chief Chiappe for spearheading the suppression of his film, which was not shown again publicly for half a century. So much for the commercial success on which he had counted! Over thirty years later he took some revenge in *Le Journal d'une femme de chambre* (1964), where a group of extreme right-wingers run through the streets of Paris shouting 'Long live Chiappe! Down with the Jews!'[137]

The Visible Woman

News of the scandal surrounding *L'Age d'or* immediately reached Spain, where the Madrid monarchist daily *Abc* spread the rumour that Buñuel was now despised by the Surrealists because he had 'fled' to the United States before the première in order to avoid trouble.[138] Intrigued and disbelieving, the ever-alert Ernesto Giménez Caballero betook himself post-haste to Paris to interview Dalí. There he satisfied himself that there had been no question of Buñuel's running away. Gimenez Caballero was impressed by the Rue Becquerel apartment ('magnificent and overwhelming'), the door to which was opened by a suitably elegant maid, and by the fact that Dalí was still co-habiting with 'Madame Éluard'. Giménez Caballero was beginning to formulate at this time the guiding lines of Spanish Fascism, and expressed his delight at the 'direct action' of the thugs who had smashed up Studio 28, an action which he chose to consider highly Surrealist and subversive. He now advised Dalí and his friends to come to terms with the rowdies: that way they could pool their subversive energies! As regards the 'dissensions' within Surrealism, Dalí denied these. Aligning himself closely with Breton's *Second Manifesto* he explained to Giménez Caballero that, for reasons of 'hygiene', there had been *expulsions*, not discrepancies, and expressed his complete loyalty to the mainstream Surrealist movement, 'the only genuinely subversive and vital group in contemporary thinking'.[139]

On 15 December 1930 Editions Surréalistes published Dalí's luxurious plaquette *The Visible Woman*. The 'visible woman' was Gala, who's wall-penetrating gaze assails us from both the cover and the pre-frontispiece of the book, which reproduce Max Ernst's photograph-and-pencil portrait of the same title, done in 1925. Gala's presence pervades Dalí's first book, which contains three texts already mentioned—'The Rotten Donkey', 'The Sanitary Nanny Goat' and 'The Great Masturbator'—and a crucial fourth piece, 'Love'. Three crudely erotic drawings illustrate passages in the texts (one of them, the frontispiece, is reproduced in heliogravure), and there is a black-and-white reproduction of *Invisible Sleeping Woman, Horse, Lion, etc.* Two photographs corroborate Dalí's admiration for Catalan Art Nouveau architecture: they show a Domènech i Muntaner building in Barcelona and a house in Figueres.

'Love', the most coherent of the four pieces, explores the relationship between dreams, sexuality and the death wish. 'The bloody osmoses between dream and love occupy the entire life of man,' the painter asserts in a memorable phrase. 'Love' proves, once again, that Dalí is a Freudian adept. Repugnance, for example, he reads as a defence against desire, and true love (here Dalí goes beyond his master) would be to eat one's partner's excrement, as he had already suggested in the earlier piece, 'The Great Masturbator'. Since the urge to sleep can be interpreted as a death wish, Dalí is interested in the postures people assume when dormant. A documentary could usefully be made on the subject, he proposes, and lovers should ideally drop off in the 69 position or in that of the ceremony in which, after intercourse, the female praying mantis devours the male. Dalí had read about this ceremony, enthralled, in Fabre's *The Life of Insects* (which also inspired Buñuel to include the scorpion sequence at the beginning of *L'Age d'or*).

Dalí had provided a suitably shocking front cover illustration and frontispiece for Breton and Éluard's *The Immaculate Conception*, published in November, and an appreciative blurb in which he said that the texts, in their simulation of different states of madness, expressed the 'latent content' of the Surrealist dream.[140] He was now on very close terms with both men, who reciprocated by providing a blurb for *The Visible Woman* in which they stressed the importance of the contribution that Dalí had already made to Surrealism:

> In 1930 the task, and Dalí's more than anyone else's, is to extract man from the cavern of lies which, with the complicity of innumerable public authorities, he erects around himself . . .
>
> On Dalí's great abilities (abilities defined on the artistic level) depends today the liquidation of a threadbare formula which, let us be clear about it, is that of the bourgeois world reduced to using, as its only defence, the weapon of censorship, increasingly well-sharpened and therefore all the more easily broken.
>
> Dialectical thought fused with psychoanalytic thought, the one and the other crowned by what Dalí terms, strikingly, paranoiac-critical thought, is the most admirable instrument yet proposed for consigning to the ruins of immortality the phantom-woman with the verdigris face, smiling eyes and hard curls who is not simply the spirit of our birth, that is to say, of Art Nouveau, but also the even more attractive phantom of *the future*.[141]

In Figueres Dalí's father was shown a copy of *The Visible Woman* by Josep Puig Pujadas, to whom the painter had presumably sent it, and was so disgusted that he immediately drew up a new will completely disinheriting his son. In it, as justification for his action, he referred to the painting on which the artist had written in 1929 'I have spat on my mother' (the misquote derived from Eugenio d'Ors's report in *La Gaceta Literaria*), and reproduced (slightly inaccurately) the phrase from 'Love' which referred to 'parental bedrooms, not ventilated in the morning, giving off the vile smell of uric acid, bad tobacco, good sentiments and shit'. We do not know if the notary informed his son of his disinheritance, but it would certainly have been in character for him to do so.[142]

The year ended on a positive note for Dalí, despite his troubles with his father. The same could hardly be said for the Surrealist movement, although Breton appreciated the injection of new energy and ideas provided by the painter. Political tension, centred on the movement's relations with the Communist Party, was on the increase. The Second International Conference of Revolutionary Writers, held at Kharkov from 6 to 11 November 1930, had taken a hard line on Freud and Trotsky that deeply upset Breton, who on 28 November, with André Thirion, floated the idea of setting up an alternative 'Association des Artistes et Écrivains Révolutionnaires' (AEAR), whose aim would be to work for the 'rapprochement' of psychoanalyis and Marxism. A few days later, on 1 December, Aragon and Georges Sadoul, who had attended the Kharkov conference with orders from Breton to defend the Surrealist position, signed an 'autocritical' letter denouncing the Surrealists' 'Freudism' and 'Trotskyism', Aragon expressing his disagreement with the *Second Manifesto* and agreeing to toe the party line. The document presaged the forthcoming rupture.[143]

Dalí, for his part, was happy at this time to collaborate with the Communists, designing, at the instigation of Thirion, two posters for the celebration of the tenth anniversary of the founding of the party in France. One of these, reminiscent of some pro-Soviet sketches he had done ten years earlier in Figueres, shows a red flag bearing the letters URSS floating over a bonfire on which the symbols of the hated bourgeoisie, including communion-cups, have been heaped. Beneath the sketch Dalí indicated, with unusual modesty: 'I think that the motif of the flames and also the movement of the flag is something that Tanguy could do particularly well, no doubt much better than me.'[144]

The New Régime in Spain

In 1930 General Primo de Rivera had gone into exile in Paris after seven years in power. Since then a succession of caretaker governments, still largely militaristic in composition, had been promising to hold general elections—but dragging their feet. On 12 April 1931 municipal polls were held in Spain for the first time since Primo de Rivera had abolished them in 1923. The results showed that the majority of voters were not prepared to forgive Alfonso XIII for supporting the dictatorship, and that they wanted a Republic. Following the example of Primo de Rivera, the King left unmolested for Paris, perhaps hoping thereby to prevent the outbreak of civil war, but he did not abdicate. Not even leading monarchists were now prepared to speak a good word on his behalf, and it was widely felt that he should not have been allowed out of the country. On 14 April 1931, two days after the municipal elections, the Second Republic was proclaimed. Its advent was greeted with joy by democratically minded Spaniards, and with predictable hostility by the Catholic Church. Only a few weeks later, on 7 May, Cardinal Segura, Primate of All Spain, attacked in a fierce pastoral letter the provisional government's proposed reforms, which included the legalization of divorce and prostitution, fairer land distribution and the secularization of education. On 11 May, six convents and a Jesuit building were set on fire in Madrid. There were similar incidents elsewhere, and soon Catholic opposition to the incipient Republic was hardening fast.[1]

The Surrealists, and not least Dalí, followed the developments in Spain with fascination and deep concern. Shortly after the convent-burning in Madrid they issued a tract of extraordinary virulence, *Fire! (Au feu!)* in which, losing all sense of proportion, they expressed their support for the incendiaries and said that the Republic had already

Chapter NINE

become a bourgeois farce orchestrated by the Church and the landowners. The provisional government was betraying the people. Nothing short of full-blooded Marxist revolution would do for Spain: burning chapels were to revenge the bonfires of human flesh previously set alight by the Spanish clergy; the church treasures should be seized to finance the weapons necessary for transforming the 'bourgeois Revolution' into a proletarian one. As for the priests, they must be hunted down in their lairs and their buildings and symbols destroyed. 'Whatever is not violence, when it is a question of religion, of God the scarecrow, of the prayer parasites,' the document thundered, 'is tantamount to compromising with the unnameable vermin of christianity, which must be exterminated.' The Surrealists were disgusted that Alfonso XIII had been granted asylum in Paris, where he was receiving accolades from the French Right, and even more so by the arrival in France of Spanish priests fleeing from 'the magnificent spray of sparks visible over the top of the Pyrenees'. The King should be returned to Spain to be judged by the people, and French atheists, revolutionaries and workers continue to fight for the day when God would be swept from the surface of the world. The tract was signed by Benjamin Péret, René Char, Yves Tanguy, Louis Aragon, Georges Sadoul, Georges Malkine, André Breton, René Crevel, André Thirion, Paul Éluard, Pierre Unik, Maxime Alexandre and ten unnamed 'foreign comrades'. The latter, one assumes, included Dalí and Buñuel.[2]

Colle and Levy

All this was happening on the eve of Dalí's important exhibition at the Pierre Colle Gallery, situated just off the Rue de la Boëtie at 29, Rue Cambacérès, which ran from 3 to 15 June 1931. The sixteen paintings on show (eleven from private collections) were the unfinished *The Invisible Man* (1929–31), *Sterile Efforts* (*Little Ashes*) (1927), *Crepuscular Personage* (1928), *The Lugubrious Game* (1929), *The Accommodations of Desires* (1929), *Portrait of Paul Éluard* (1929), *Invisible Sleeping Woman, Horse, Lion,* (1930), *Daybreak* (1930), *Sleeping Woman, Horse, Lion, etc.* (1930), *William Tell* (1930), *Memory of the Child-Woman* (1931), *The Persistence of Memory* (1931), *Masochist Ensemble* (1931) and three recent works undated in the catalogue: *The Moment of Transitions, The Profanation of the Host* and *Funereal Sentiment.* Also exhibited were seven pastels and a sculpture in copper, *Gradiva,* all executed in 1930, and 'three "modern-style" objects' glossed in the catalogue notes by a Dalí for whom 'the delirious and all-beautiful Art Nouveau ornamentation' of the Paris Métro entrances now seemed 'the perfect symbol of spiritual dignity'.[3]

The picture that excited most interest at the exhibition was *The Persistence of Memory* (1931), in which the 'soft watch' made its début. Dalí describes the epiphany of this unique timepiece in the *Secret Life*, suggesting that its appearance was not unrelated to the ingestion of a particularly strong piece of Camembert cheese:

> I got up and went into the studio, where I lit the light in order to cast a final glance, as is *XXIII*
> my habit, at the picture I was in the midst of painting. This picture represented a land-
> scape near Port Lligat, whose rocks were lighted by a transparent and melancholy twi-
> light; in the foreground an olive tree with its branches cut, and without leaves. I knew that
> the atmosphere which I had succeeded in creating with this landscape was to serve as a
> setting for some idea, for some surprising image, but I did not in the least know what it
> was going to be. I was about to turn out the light, when instantaneously I 'saw' the solu-
> tion. I saw two soft watches, one of them hanging lamentably on the branch of the olive
> tree.[4]

Dalí had immediately gone to work with renewed energy. When Gala returned from the cinema she was amazed by his latest invention. 'No one could forget it after seeing it,' he says she exclaimed.[5] Dalí had produced one of his most enigmatic images, and soon the soft watch was proliferating in his work almost as much as the head of the Great Masturbator had been doing since 1929.

Several of the paintings in the exhibition referred to Dalí's repudiation by his father *XX* and to the latter's continuing opposition to his relationship with Gala. *William Tell* is a particularly strong statement, and seems to hinge fundamentally on the feelings of shame engendered by comparison with the authoritative, sensuous and at times vio-lent Dalí Cusí, feelings now greatly exacerbated by the painter's banishment from the family home. It is one of the most sexually crude paintings Dalí ever executed, the depiction of Tell's huge and repugnant penis (echoed in that of the horse) having the power to make people turn away in embarrassment or disgust when the work is exhib-ited. As Paul Moorhouse has written, it is impossible to miss the allusions to castra-tion:

> The hero has become a bearded father figure wielding a pair of scissors, his intent made
> apparent by the obsessive repetition of phallic references in the painting. His own penis
> and that of the horse are fully exposed and are echoed in the egg-cup motif on the plinth
> and the eggs in the nest. The youth's genitals are concealed by a leaf, so that it is unclear
> whether castration is impending or has happened. The water gushing from the hole in the
> wall is, however, suggestive of mutilation.[6]

The presence of the grand piano with its rotting donkey is an obvious allusion to *Un Chien andalou*, and a reminder, perhaps, of Dalí's view that his father was to blame for his impotence by having placed on the family piano, when he was a child, a book on venereal disease which turned him off the female genitals for life.[7] The pianist's head is also that of William Tell, as we can see from other paintings in the series. He has crapped in his pants as nonchalantly as the father figure in *The Lugubrious Game*, the presence of the recurrent symbol of the lion strengthening the paternal association. The huge size of his penis, underlined in other works of the Tell series, may be a reminiscence of seeing Dalí Cusí's well-endowed member pop out, sausage-like, as he rolled on the ground battering a client who had infuriated him in Figueres.[8]

Another painting on show at Colle's, *Memory of the Child-Woman*, done after *William Tell*, recalls *Imperial Monument to the Child-Woman*, the title indicating that Gala is again the protagonist. The bust situated in the middle of the centrepiece (yet another variation on the rocks of Cape Creus) undoubtedly represents Tell, since the head is exactly equivalent to that of the pianist in *William Tell*. Now, however, he is bleeding from both eyes, suggesting an intensification of castration anxiety. One of the most interesting aspects of the painting is that Tell has sprouted the breasts attributed to Gala in *The Bleeding Roses* (the allusion being strengthened by the presence of the same red flowers). Is Dalí suggesting that his father, who had seen Gala on the beach at Es Llané in the summer of 1929 and had witnessed the initiation of their relationship, was not indifferent to her body? Later paintings in the series leave one with the growing suspicion that this is so and that Dalí, humiliated as he was by his father's strength, and by extension virility, had begun to fantasize about his being the better able of the two for Gala.

The inscriptions in the rock's alveoli (not usually legible in reproductions) throw some light on the painting's theme. The left-hand hole contains the ubiquitous key, which, in tune with Freud, Dalí uses obsessively as a phallic symbol. Its constant presence in the paintings and drawings of the period suggests extreme anxiety about impotence and his ability to penetrate Gala. In the top-right hole he has written, ten times, the expression 'Ma Mère' ('My Mother'), repeating the motif that had taken full stage in *The Enigma of Desire*. The suggestion is perhaps that Gala has become for him the mother he lost when he was sixteen. The middle hole contains the words 'Fantaisie diurne' ('Diurnal Fantasy'), the title of another painting in the same series. In the bottom one Dalí has written 'Le gran chienalie chanasie', 'Le gran masturbateur', 'Guillaume Tell', 'Olivette Olivette Olivette' and 'concretion nostalgique d'un clé' ('nostalgic materialization of a key'). The first legend, which looks like mere nonsense, may contain a reference to Lorca, via *Un Chien andalou*, and Olivette was one of Dalí's pet names for Gala. The allusions, then, are to Dalí's loves and anxieties. There is also one that suggests an interest in sado-masochism: at the left of the medallion covering Tell's midriff, and again not clearly visible in even the best reproductions, two naked women, juxtaposed with ants, a Great Masturbator, the jug motif and a key, are engaged in flagellation.[9]

The Profanation of the Host, on show at Colle's for the first time, is one of Dalí's most sacrilegious paintings (although later he tried to exonerate himself by saying that it was a work 'of Catholic essence').[10] While it may have been begun in 1929, the date habitually ascribed to it, the painting was almost certainly not finished until 1930, after Dalí had been thrown out by his father. The picture develops a motif that had made its first appearance in *The Lugubrious Game*, where the Host's profanation consisted in being placed next to an anus about to be penetrated by a finger. In the present work, the Host and communion cup are positioned in front of the mouth of the Great Masturbator, from which a blood-imbued liquid is flowing into the Cup. Santos Torroella has suggested that the liquid is sperm symbolized by saliva, this possibility being reinforced by the presence in it of blood, which for Dalí is often associated with masturbation (in his adolescent diary, as we saw, he had feared that too much wanking would make him 'lose blood').[11] The same critic has drawn our attention to another possible source for the motif, an anecdote included in Ernesto Giménez Caballero's book *I, Inspector of Drains* (1928), in which an old Jesuit recalls how a schoolfriend of his used to boast that he had ejaculated into the Chalice, exclaiming: 'I sully myself over God and the Virgin, His Mother, and in the Holy Cup.' Dalí had been close to Giménez Caballero in 1928, publishing regularly in his *La Gaceta Literaria*, and he may well have been struck by this piece of daring. Indeed, his boast in the painting of the Sacred Heart of Jesus that got him thrown out of his home ('Sometimes I spit for pleasure on the portrait of my mother') might conceivably have been calqued on the same phrase.[12]

Dalí may also have had in mind Paolo Uccello's altarpiece, similarly titled *The Profanation of the Host*, one panel of which shows a Host bleeding after some Jews have attempted in vain to destroy it by fire.[13] And it is possible, too, that he was aware that, in Bouvier's *The Secret Manual of the Confessor* (a compilation reviled by Max Ernst in his article 'Danger of Pollution', published in the December 1931 issue of *Le Surréalisme au Service de la Révolution*), ejaculation into the Holy Cup was singled out as a particularly heinous sin.[14]

The swirling construction occupying the middle ground of the work, with Art Nouveau elements relating it to *The Great Masturbator*, contains four other onanists' heads, each with a locust at its mouth. To increase the terror, ants are in attendance.

XVIII

From the beach, far below, a statuesque woman of apparently huge dimensions stares haughtily in the direction of the masturbators, oblivious to the other figures around her (notably a naked male directly behind). But it is in the dark foreground, out of the sun, that most of the action is taking place. Here again is the lion's head, suggestive of the angry father, juxtaposed with the crazily staring, lascivious adult male figure, now equipped with a huge penis, whom we know from *The Lugubrious Game*. A young person leans in shame and surrender on his shoulder, as he does in that painting, and a girl is seen in a similar posture to his right. The glinting white of a woman's eye suggests wild excitement. Naked buttocks and breasts gleam voluptuously in the half-light. This is where it's happening, whatever exactly *it* is.

Once he got a good pictorial idea, Dalí tended to go for over-kill. Having devised his head of the Great Masturbator, he produced hundreds of them; the Soft Watch was soon hanging from, or draped over, innumerable props; and now his Profaned Host and Chalice, with the Great Masturbator officiating, began to take off, recurring in dozens of paintings and drawings done over the following months and years.[15]

The Colle exhibition signalled the appearance in Dalí's life of an ebullient young New Yorker, Julien Levy, who was just about to open a contemporary art gallery on Madison Avenue. Levy, whose wife Joella was the daughter of the English poet and painter Mina Loy, spoke good French, was interested in photography, dabbled in film-making and was a close friend of Marcel Duchamp, who had introduced him to Paris in 1927. There he met many expatriate artists and writers and, through Duchamp, Man Ray and the Surrealists. Two years later, in 1929, he saw his first Dalí, *Illumined Pleasures*, in the window of Camille Goemans's gallery. Now, in 1931, he was in Paris again, on the lookout for Surrealist paintings for his gallery, and had just met Pierre Colle, 'a younger man than I, dark, magnetic and burning with enthusiasm'. They became immediate friends.[16]

Levy was intrigued by the Dalí exhibition (although he had slight misgivings about what he considered the Catalan's versatility) and bought *The Persistence of Memory* for the trade price of $250, more than he had ever paid for a painting. He showed it to his father, who was passing through Paris. He approved (although he thought its title should be changed to *The Limp Watches*), and Levy felt sure that, this being so, America would too. He was right. America was to love it.[17]

It is not clear from Levy's dazzling autobiography, *Memoir of an Art Gallery*, whether he met Dalí in person that summer. But if not then it must have been soon afterwards:

> Dalí, when I first met him, offered no confirmation of my preconceived notion that he might be slick or pandering. He was disquieting to me. He has never ceased to be so, not

because of ambiguity but rather by his singleminded intensity and frankness. He fixed his piercing black eyes on me,* he crowded against me, his restless hands alternately picking at my sleeve or suit lapel or fluttering emphatically as he described his newest, his most revolutionary of all Dalinian theories, his most recent work as yet unseen, perhaps as yet unaccomplished and now being enacted in the mind's eye.[18]

Levy and Colle got on so well that it was agreed between them that the former should be the first dealer to put on a show by Dalí in New York. The city was not then the great art centre it was to become, and there was very little awareness of contemporary European painting. Levy discovered with delight and astonishment that it was to fall to him to change this situation. The Dalí show would have to wait for two years, however. Meanwhile Levy sailed back to New York with *The Persistence of Memory* ('10 by 14 inches of Dalí dynamite'), which was shown for the first time in public the following December at the Wadsworth Athenaeum in Hartford, Connecticut, to which the generous young dealer lent his group exhibition *Surrealism: Paintings, Drawings and Photographs* before it opened at his own gallery that January.

Accompanying *The Persistence of Memory* at Levy's were two other Dalís from private collections: *Solitude* and *By the Seaside* (*Bord de la mer*). Alongside these hung works by Picasso, Max Ernst, Pierre Roy, Duchamp, Man Ray, Jean Cocteau, Joseph Cornell and a selection of photographs by Eugène Atget, Man Ray, Moholy-Nagy and others. The exhibition was a huge success. 'A pleasant madness prevails at Julien Levy's new and interesting gallery,' wrote *Art News*, 'with its miscellany of surrealistic paintings, drawings, prints and what-not. Mr Levy has been at considerable pains to inform us what these ultra-modern men are up to, and he is to be congratulated on the well-rounded line-up of the surrealistic camp.'[19] 'Contemporary art historians,' Levy himself mused later, 'will never convince me that the first American Surrealist show was not mine.' *The Persistence of Memory* was widely discussed and reproduced. 'Cartoons of it were in the more lurid tabloids,' recalled Levy. 'Journalists from coast to coast wrote stories about "Limp Watches".'[20]

Reports must have reached Dalí that there was an avid public waiting for his work in New York. Levy, for his part, was now convinced that he could successfully promote Dalí's work in America, and shortly afterwards bought *Illumined Pleasures* from Paul Éluard (the first Dalí he had seen) and, from André Breton, *The Accommodations of Desire*.[21]

*Dalí's eyes were in fact greenish-grey, not black.

Levy was not the only American art buff who had appreciated Dalí's exhibition at Pierre Colle's in the summer of 1931. It was also seen by Alfred Barr, first director of New York's Museum of Modern Art, which had opened in 1929, and one of Levy's fine arts tutors at Harvard. Barr and Dalí now met at a dinner party given by Charles and Marie-Laure de Noailles. The MOMA's director, Dalí recalled, 'was young, pale, and very sickly-looking; he had stiff and rectilinear gestures like those of pecking birds—in reality he was pecking at contemporary values, and one felt that he had the knack of picking just the full grains, never the chaff. His information on the subject of modern art was enormous.' Barr's wife prophesied that Dalí would have dazzling success in America, and encouraged him to go there. From 1931 onwards, in fact, New York would never be far from Dalí's thoughts.[22]

The Sterile Woman, Crevel and Communism

Meanwhile Gala's gynaecological problem, which had begun to worry her the previous summer, had grown worse. She now discovered with horror that she had developed a cyst. Although the clinical records have not come to light, it seems that the specialist consulted, Doctor René Jacquemaire, decided the growth should be removed without delay. When Ernesto Giménez Caballero saw Dalí in Paris around 20 July 1931 the painter told him that Gala had just undergone 'a terrible operation' and that he was about to take her to convalesce in the French Pyrenees. Dalí added that Gala would not now be able to have children. It may be, therefore, that the operation was a hysterectomy. 'Gala is the sterile woman of salt who fertilizes and sweetens the art of Dalí,' Giménez wrote a few weeks later in *La Gaceta Literaria*. 'Dalí believes that his love is perverse, because she is the wife of a friend and because she is sterile and violent.' Dalí's definition of Gala as the sterile and violent woman was to be consecrated by Éluard and Breton in their *Abridged Dictionary of Surrealism*, published in 1938.

Dalí told Giménez Caballero about the plans that were afoot to hold an exhibition of Surrealist Objects, and announced that he was planning a Surrealist Pleasure Park which would include a hollow globe providing visitors with the illusion of re-entering their mother's womb. Giménez Caballero deduced correctly that the project (never carried out) was for Charles and Marie-Laure de Noailles.[23]

The spot chosen for Gala's convalescence was Vernet-les-Bains, a charming spa in the eastern Pyrenees overlooked by the Canigó, the soaring mountain revered by Catalans on both sides of the frontier. She arrived there on 21 July, accompanied by René Crevel, now one of Dalí's best friends as well as hers. Dalí, who had been held up in Paris, fol-

lowed them two days later and they were also joined, briefly, by Éluard.[24] Dalí succeeded in cheering up the neurotic Crevel, and, when he was not painting, the two had long
discussions. 'My conversations with Dalí hinge on the absence of contemporary philosophy, on the desire, the determination of everyone to fashion such a philosophy,' Crevel
wrote to Marie-Laure de Noailles.[25]

On 30 July the threesome (Éluard had left) travelled down to Port Lligat, the Figueres
paper *Empordà Federal* announcing on 15 August that Dalí, 'the formidable artist and
great Communist', had just arrived from Vernet and was installed in his house by the
sea.[26] Crevel was blissfully happy with the pair, and much impressed by the landscape of
Cape Creus. 'At last I know Cadaqués, I'm living here and writing here,' he told Marie-
Laure. 'Dalí's painting and writing surprise us all the time. He's composing a poem on
William Tell and working on *The Invisible Man*' (the poem, announced a few months
later in *Love and Memory*, was never published). The fisherman's shack, which had now
been much improved, he deemed 'comfortable in the doll's house line'. As for Cadaqués,
Crevel found it 'incredibly backward', with poverty and illiteracy the order of the day.
The locals stared at them in amazement, particularly when Gala appeared wearing her
pijama and Dalí a red Lacoste pullover and shorts. Salvador was working on a portrait
of Marie-Laure begun in Paris. 'How lucky you are to inspire artists,' Crevel observed.[27]

During his stay, Crevel worked on *Dalí or Anti-Obscurantism*, an essay published the
following November (the most intelligent assessment of Dalí's work to date), frolicked
with Gala in the garden, marvelled with Dalí at the mica-schist metamorphoses of Cape
Creus and participated in the trick photography sessions with a sheet that Dalí quoted
in *The Old Age of William Tell*. André Thirion was deeply struck by this and other paintings done at the time, which he read as a passionate homage to the Gala whom Dalí had
feared might not survive her operation.[28] It seems that the painter explained later that
The Old Age of William Tell expressed his and Gala's repudiation by Dalí Cusí.[29] But this   *XXII*
is only part of the story. Behind the sheet, 'unmentionable things', as one of Dalí's biographers has put it, are being done to Tell by two females (presumably involving masturbation or fellatio or both), while the couple representing Dalí and Gala walk away in
shame or disgust.[30] Tell is Wearing breasts as in *Memory of the Child-Woman*. One of the
females is looking at his genitals with ravenous lust. The scene is watched by the ubiquitous lion, whose threatening shadow falls across the sheet. Against the column on the
left leans a figure reminiscent of the vulnerable Gala who appears in *Imperial Monument*   *XIX*
to the Child-Woman, while in the right background a naked couple are embracing, breasts
with grotesquely erect nipples, droplets of blood and the same red blooms that adorned
the Muse in *The Invisible Man* and *The Bleeding Roses*, making this look like another

expression of Dalí's anxiety about his father's sexual interest in Gala.

Crevel's *Dalí or Anti-Obscurantism* shows how deeply he had been impressed by *The Visible Woman*, by Dalí's theories of paranoia and, particularly, by the painter's advocation of Art Nouveau. Crevel wanted to see for himself the buildings by Gaudí that had fired his friend's imagination as a child, those 'realizations of solidified desires' whose genius Dalí was now proclaiming in Paris. Dalí accompanied him to Barcelona, and Crevel wrote enthusiastically to Marie-Laure de Noailles and Prince Jean-Louis de Faucigny-Lucinge about the city's riotous panoply of 'unbelievable' Art Nouveau architecture.[31]

Crevel also told them about the excitement and miseries of Barcelona's famous red-light quarter near the port, the Barrio Chino (to which Dalí had also introduced Lorca a few years earlier), and said he was much struck by the political fervour of the young left-wing militants he was meeting in the city.[32] Among the latter was Dalí's old school-friend from Figueres, Jaume Miravitlles, now one of the leading lights in a fledgling non-Stalinist Communist party, the Bloc Obrer i Camperol (Workers' and Peasants' Front), the fusion of two groups that had split away from the Second International.[33] 'Met', who until his death would enjoy remembering that he was one of the Marist Brothers dragged across the floor in *Un Chien andalou*, was currently throwing himself with his customary vigour into the fight to prevent the Republic from losing its revolutionary thrust, and was interested in the relations between Surrealism and Communism. Out of his discussions with Dalí and Crevel came an invitation to them to lecture in Barcelona at a specially convened meeting of the Workers' and Peasants' Front.

The event was held on 18 September 1931. Miravitlles was in the chair, and opened the meeting by telling the packed audience of workers and students (leavened with a sprinkling of middle-class intellectuals) that, just after the Russian Revolution, he, Dalí, Martí Vilanova and Rafael Ramis had set up in Figueres what amounted to the first Soviet in Spain. Dalí could be trusted, therefore: his history as a revolutionary stretched back to his adolescence. Nonetheless, Miravitlles insisted, there were fundamental differences between Surrealism and Communism, mainly the relative importance given to the economic question: the Surrealists wanted a revolution from within, a radical change in the inner man, whereas Communism was convinced that only a new economic structure could alter society. Despite this divergence, however, there was a potent common denominator: hatred of the bourgeoisie and the determination to destroy it.[34]

Crevel spoke first, in French with a translator. To judge from the Catalan synopsis it must have been difficult for the audience to follow his thinking. He pointed out that Surrealism was a movement, not a school, and that it gave primacy to collective over individual action. It had opposed the French war in the Rif against Abd-el-Krim. It supported revolution in Spain. Crevel attacked the intellectual establishment, which he saw as a complacent instrument of the bourgeoisie, extended himself on the question of racial prejudice and anti-semitism, and voiced his loathing for the Catholic Church. He ended by quoting Breton's famous definition of Surrealism: 'Pure mental automatism, by means of which it is proposed to express, either in speech, in writing or in any other manner, the true functioning of thought. Dictation by thought without any rational, aesthetic or moral control.' Crevel felt the talk had gone well.[35]

Then it was Dalí's turn. His lecture was entitled 'Surrealism in the Service of the Revolution', like the movement's current periodical. He began by attacking the Catalan cultural establishment, as he had done at the Ateneu in 1930, and asked the 'bourgeois' journalists in the audience to leave. Some did. He then proceeded to argue that Surrealism had developed a method for penetrating what he called the 'subterranean and proletarian zone of the mind'. 'Surreality' was in open opposition to capitalist 'reality', to the conventions of capitalist thinking. It aimed at demoralizing bourgeois society. That it was succeeding in this objective was clear from the attacks to which it was now being subjected. Dalí went on to say that, while the Surrealists were Communists, the need for the conciliation of Marx and Freud often came up against 'the cretinism of the official representatives of proletarian literature'. Henri Barbusse was a case in point. Dalí explained that he was not arguing that Surrealism would be the 'state of mind' of the proletariat in the future, but said he believed it was the only vital contemporary movement compatible with Communism. At a time when the Spanish provisional government was giving every indication of being anti-revolutionary in intention, he recommended the Communists to undertake the *moral* revolution. The synopsis ends:

> He invited the audience, in the name of the Surrealists, to descend to the subversive world of Surrealism. 'Damn all the 25,000 projected schools, the Ortega y Gassets and the Marañóns of Spain. These people retain the ignoble ideas of the fatherland and the family. At a time when prisoners are being shot in the back, the silence of the intellectuals makes them accomplices' . . . He recommended the putting aside of sentimentalism, spitting on the flag of the fatherland, threatening parents with revolvers and descending to the world of subversion. He said that the political group most suited to Catalan youth was the Communists, and the only example worth following that of the lives of the trades unionists who had fought in this very street [the Carrer Mercaders]. He ended with a 'Long live the Construction Trades Union!'[36]

Dalí's close identification with the Workers' and Peasants' Front was ratified in the following issues of the party's journal, *L'hora*, which reproduced several anti-bourgeois cartoons he had done in the 1920s. These were later included, with one exception, in Miravitlles's book *The Rhythm of the Revolution* (1933).

So far as *L'hora* was concerned, Dalí was now a full-blown member of the Workers' and Peasants' Front. But some adherents of the organization were not convinced of his full commitment to the cause. Even Miravitlles had his doubts, as can be seen from his pamphlet *Against Bourgeois Culture*, published shortly afterwards. 'Met' appreciated the efficacy of Dalí's subversive attacks on bourgeois values, and of Surrealism's in general. But this did not mean that Surrealism was the answer to the problems of the proletariat. No worker worthy of the name could possibly follow Dalí's advice to 'return to the pristine sources of crime, exhibitionism and masturbation,' 'Met' wrote testily, since crime, exhibitionism and masturbation 'are no more than elements of decadence incrusted in capitalism.'[37]

No further information has come to light concerning Dalí's relationship with Miravitlles and the Workers' and Peasants' Front, due largely to the destruction, or dispersal, of archives during the Spanish Civil War. To follow the development of the artist's political involvement and thinking at this time our main source is his incomplete correspondence with André Breton, split today between Paris and, surprisingly, Edinburgh.

Dalí and the Surrealist Object

The Surrealist Object was one of the movement's most original creations and the end result of experiments dating back to analytic Cubism. By revealing the hidden or secret structures of familiar objects such as guitars, newspapers, bottles, tables, houses and so forth, the experiments had initiated a fresh, revolutionary way of looking at the external world. Soon the need had been felt to liberate the object from the strictures imposed upon it by painting on a flat surface, and in this respect the Surrealists had no hesitation in recognizing Marcel Duchamp as their direct predecessor with his 'invention' of what he termed the *objet tout fait*, the first example of which was a bicycle wheel mounted on a stool (1913). Two years later, in New York, Duchamp had substituted the American word 'readymade' for the original French term. His most famous essay in the genre remains *Fountain*, exhibited in 1917: a porcelain urinal with an undisguisedly phallic spout.[38]

Duchamp's readymades appealed strongly to Dada, with its determination to shock post-war society out of its lethargy and conventionality, and Man Ray's *Gift* (1921)—a smoothing iron with a jagged vertical line of metal teeth that rendered it useless for service in the linen room—was a brilliant and witty link in the chain leading to the Surrealist Object. Surrealism inherited Dada's fascination for the readymade, and embarked on more rigorous experimentation, quickly sensing the genre's potential for the expression of unconscious promptings. The first issue of *La Révolution Surréaliste* (1 December 1924) pointed the way by illustrating its preface with a Man Ray photograph of a disturbing unidentified object wrapped in sackcloth and tied up with string.[39]

That same year, in a dream, Breton saw and handled an unusual book. Its spine consisted of a wooden gnome with a long, Assyrian beard hanging down to its feet, and its pages were made of thick black wool. 'I would like to put some objects such as this into circulation', he wrote in his *Introduction to the Discourse on the Scarcity of Reality*, a *plaquette* published by Gallimard in 1927; 'their future seems to me eminently problematic and disturbing'.[40] Soon he and other members of the group were busily producing dream-inspired artefacts. In 1928 Breton published in *La Révolution Surréaliste* a photograph of an object made by him and Aragon. Called *Here Lies Giorgio de Chirico*, it consisted of a box containing a weird assemblage of miniature objects that included the Leaning Tower of Pisa and a sewing machine.[41]

An article published by Dalí in the last, 'Surrealist' issue of *L'Amic de les Arts* (31 March 1929), just before his second visit to Paris, showed that he had read Breton's *Introduction to the Discourse on the Scarcity of Reality* and been much impressed. Under the heading 'Surrealist Objects. Oneiric Objects' Dalí wrote:

> Alongside the *Surrealist Objects* already invented and defined, Breton has proposed the fabrication of new objects which, responding also to the needs of human fetishism, represent a special lyricism which stands in relation to the lyricism of the Surrealist Object as the Surrealist text does to the oneiric text.
>
> These new objects, which could be considered *oneiric objects*, would satisfy, as Breton says, the perpetual desire for verification; it would be necessary, he adds, to construct as far as possible some objects to which we could only attain in dreams and which appear equally indefensible whether considered from the point of view of utility or of pleasure.[42]

In his paintings of the late 1920s, Dalí had littered his beach scenes with two-dimensional representations of objects that deserved the name of Surrealist, the spindly *aparells*, or gadgets, that proliferate in *Honey is Sweeter than Blood* being the most obvious example. And it could be argued that the box in which the severed hand is placed in *Un*

Chien andalou was the first Surrealist Object to appear in a film. It was natural, therefore, that Dalí took to the production of three-dimensional objects with intense enthusiasm.

XXI

One of his earliest ventures was *Board of Demented Associations*, or *Fireworks* (1930–1), in which he appropriated an exquisitely worked box of Roman candles, rockets, bangers, Bengal-lights, crackers, squibs and attendant pyrotechnical gadgetry. Each object was meticulously labelled, as if the whole box were a museum piece, Dalí adding to the fireworks tiny, meticulous paintings of his obsessive icons of the moment: ladies' high-heeled shoes (one of them with a glass of milk standing inside it, another rubbing a clitoris), William Tell with bleeding eyes, a swarm of ants, Great Masturbators (one with the dreaded locust stuck to its mouth), the jug motif of Dalí as idiot, an imaginative copulation (woman on top), the horribly leering male adult, and, on the largest firework in the whole explosive collection, labelled 'Whistling Volcano', a lady in black stockings who raises a leg to show off her genitals.

Some time in 1931 Breton asked Dalí and André Thirion to come up with proposals for intensifying Surrealist group activity. Thirion, encouraged by Aragon, plumped for anti-clerical action; Dalí for the proliferation of Surrealist Objects.[43] Both proposals were accepted. Anti-clericalism became virulent in the pages of *Le Surréalisme au Service de la Révolution*, with Georges Sadoul as its principal exponent, and Breton announced there in December 1931 that he was asking all his friends to implement Dalí's suggestion for making 'animatable objects, openly erotic, I mean destined to procure, by indirect means, a particular sexual emotion'.[44]

In the same issue of the review Dalí published an article, 'Surrealist Objects', which contained a 'general catalogue' of the genre's variants: *Symbolically Functioning Objects* (automatic origin); *Transubstantiated Objects* (affective origin); *Objects for Hurling* (dream origin); *Enveloped Objects* (daytime fantasies); *Machine Objects* (experimental fantasies); and *Mould Objects* (hypnagogic origin). He then proceeded to analyse the first category, hinting that in successive articles he would devote himself to the other five (which he never did). 'Symbolically Functioning Objects', he explained, lend themselves to a modicum of mechanical operation and are based on 'fantasies and representations prone to arise from the carrying out of unconscious actions'. These unconscious actions, Dalí had no doubt, were erotic fantasies of an essentially perverse nature. Dalí acknowledged that his immediate point of departure for the Symbolically Functioning Object was Giacometti's *Suspended Ball* (1930–1), reproduced in the same issue of *Le Surréalisme au Service de la Révolution*. He described it thus: 'A wooden ball with a feminine cleft hangs on a thin violin string over a crescent shape whose sharp edge almost touches the cavity. The spectator is moved instinctively to make the ball slide onto the sharp edge, but the length of the string only allows him partially to achieve this.'

Dalí's only objection to Giacometti's object was that it still owed an excessive debt to sculpture (it was, as Crevel said in the same issue, an 'animated sculpture').[45] The true Surrealist Object should be completely free of formal preoccupations on the part of the artist. The examples of the Symbolically Functioning Object described by Dalí, and illustrated in the same issue of the magazine, are Valentine Hugo's subtly erotic *Gloved Hand and Red Hand*,[46] Breton's *Bicycle Saddle, Sphere and Foliage*,[47] an object by Gala, *Sponges and Bowl of Flour*, which shows that she was not without creative flair, and Dalí's *Shoe and Glass of Milk* (later called *Symbolically Functioning Scatological Object*). He described the latter as follows:

Alberto Giacometti, Suspended Ball, *1930–1, reproduced in* Le Surréalisme au Service de la Révolution, *Paris, no. 3, December 1931. Dalí acknowledged that Giacometti's ball was his point of departure for the* Symbolically Functioning Scatological Object.

A woman's shoe, inside which a glass of warm milk has been placed in the centre of a paste ductile in form and excremental in colour.

The mechanism is designed to plunge a lump of sugar, on which an image of a shoe has been painted, into the milk, in order to observe the dissolving of the sugar and consequently of the image of the shoe. Several accessories (pubic hairs stuck to a lump of sugar, a little erotic photograph) complete the object, which is accompanied by a box with spare lumps of sugar and a special spoon with which to stir grains of lead placed inside the shoe.

Following Breton's musings on the city of the future in *Introduction to the Discourse on the Scarcity of Reality*, Dalí envisaged a world about to be inundated with revolutionary objects that would radically alter its perceptions:

The museums will fast fill with objects whose uselessness, size and crowding will necessitate the construction, in deserts, of special towers to contain them. The doors of these towers will be cleverly effaced and in their place will flow an uninterrupted fountain of real milk, which will be avidly absorbed by the warm sand.[48]

Although this vision never came to fulfilment, hundreds of Surrealist Objects, infinitely varied and always subversive of conventional reality, were produced over the next decade, Dalí himself making, and theorizing about, a wide range of such artefacts. In the spring of 1932 he told J.V. Foix that a 'very complete' exhibition of Surrealist Objects was about to be held in Paris (it was postponed), insisting that, when genuine, such objects were totally free of conscious intervention on the part of the artist.[49] In September 1932 he published his elucubrations on 'edible objects',[50] and a month later informed Breton that he was working on 'liquid objects' and 'blind objects' and writing a piece on 'the cannibalism of objects' for Edward W. Titus, editor of the Paris-based English review *This Quarter*.[51] The May 1933 issue of *Le Surréalisme au Service de la Révolution* carried his suggestions for the creation of a new category, the 'Psycho-Atmospheric-Anamorphic Object', to be elaborated entirely in the dark (maybe this was the 'blind' variety).[52] Some of Dalí's objects were to make a tremendous impact both on the public and on his Surrealist colleagues, not least his *Retrospective Bust of a Woman* (1933) and *Aphrodisiac Dinner Jacket* (1936).

How to shock the French CP

In December 1931 Dalí published *Love and Memory* (*L'Amour et la mémoire*), termed 'poem' in the colophon although such a designation could be disputed. The text oscillates between clarity and opacity, as is so often the case with Dalí, and constitutes in essence a paean to Gala, to the change wrought on the painter's life by her appearance. To underline the depth of that change, Dalí contrasts the Muse with the woman who most occupied his sentiments before she took him by storm . . . his sister, Anna Maria:

> The image of my sister
> her anus red
> with bloody shit
> my prick
> semi-erect
> leaning elegantly
> against

an immense
lyre
colonial
and personal
the left testicle
half plunged
in a glass
of tepid milk
the glass of milk
placed
inside
a woman's shoe.

Four sections follow, each beginning with the line 'The image of my sister' and revealing other aspects of her intimate anatomy. Anna Maria appears here like some weird Surrealist Object. Then it is time for Gala:

Far from the image of my sister
Gala
her eyes resembling her anus
her anus resembling her knees
her knees resembling her ears
her breasts resembling the big lips of her genitals
the big lips of her genitals resembling her belly-button
her belly-button resembling the finger of her hand
the finger of her hand resembling her voice
her voice resembling the toe of her foot
the toe of her foot resembling the hair of her armpits
the hair of her armpits resembling her forehead
her forehead resembling her thighs
her thighs resembling her gums
her gums resembling her hair
her hair resembling her legs
her legs resembling her clitoris
her clitoris resembling her mirror
her mirror resembling her walk
her walk resembling her cedars.

The text offers a valuable insight into the qualities of temperament that Dalí appreciated in his Muse. The woman he loves 'integrally'

> gives me degrading notions
> of egoism
> of an absolute lack of pity
> of desirable cruelty

Such is the all-devouring intensity of Dalí's obsession with Gala, we are told, that the most atrocious torture of a best friend would now more readily stimulate an erection than feelings of sorrow. Breton's reaction to the text is not known but can easily be imagined, for he was deeply concerned when, on other occasions, Dalí expressed similar views in his presence.

Love and Memory shows to what an extent Dalí was involved with Anna Maria before the arrival of Gala, and suggests there was a strongly incestuous element in their relationship. Did she see a copy? It seems unlikely, unless, that is, Dalí took it upon himself, in an act of supreme cruelty, to send her one. If he did so, one can imagine that the impact was shattering.

The publication of *Love and Memory* coincided with the appearance of another provocative piece, 'Reverie', in the fourth issue of *Le Surréalisme au Service de la Révolution* (December 1931). Composed according to Dalí in Port Lligat on 17 October 1930, immediately after his habitual siesta, the text purports to document, with clinical detachment, a masturbatory fantasy sparked off by meditating on Böcklin's spine-chilling *The Isle of the Dead*, a picture that fascinated Dalí and which he intended to analyse in a projected book, *Surrealist Painting Throughout the Ages*. The fantasy, which begins at Hallowe'en and stretches over several days, fuses two settings important in Dalí's boyhood: the Pichots' mill-tower outside Figueres, where, as we saw, he spent a convalescent month in the summer of 1916; and the 'Font del Soc', the cypress-surrounded spring between Figueres and Vilabertran to which the family had enjoyed walking when Salvador was a child. As for the voluptuous, eleven-year-old Dulita, the reverie's object of desire, she is based on Julieta, Pepito Pichot's adopted daughter, whose erotic charms were recalled by Dalí in his diary in 1922, and later in the *Secret Life*.

With the scrupulous attention to detail that characterizes him, Dalí regales the reader with precise indications concerning each stage of his plan to sodomize Dulita on the floor of the tower's stable. For her initiation he engages the services of the girl's widowed mother, Matilde (masochism drives her to comply because she is in love with Dalí), and of an old prostitute, Gallo, who show her an album of pornographic postcards. Dalí being a buttocks-worshipper, Dulita is suitably endowed. Erections of varying degrees of tumescence come and go as the fantasy proceeds, with Dalí constantly at his penis ('mobilizing' it, putting it away, taking it out again); and, as penetration is about to be achieved at last, after six dense pages, Dulita, surprise surprise, turns into Gala.[53]

Perhaps the most interesting thing about 'Reverie' is the obsessive quality of the fantasy, whose 'most microscopic details and nuances' the text itself acknowledges: for orgasm to occur every aspect must be organized with faultless precision; if not there can be no ejaculation.

'Reverie' was obsessive, certainly. It was also shocking, and not least to the mind of orthodox Communists. On 3 February 1932, Aragon, Unik, Sadoul and Maxime Alexandre, the only Surrealists in the French Communist Party at the time, were summoned to the Party's HQ at 120, Rue Lafayette to answer for the publication of the peccant text. 'All you want is to complicate the simple, healthy relations between men and women,' an official pontificated, as Aragon reported to Breton. The exhortation to abjure Surrealism was greeted with 'a tumultuous refusal', according to Alexandre.[54]

It is clear that Aragon, whatever he may have said on that occasion, had by then developed serious misgivings about Dalí. According to André Thirion, who knew him well, Aragon had returned from Kharkov in November 1930 with the conviction that Freud was a counter-revolutionary, and had quite lost his previous sense of humour. Dalí's deification of Freud and flaunting of his inner life increasingly irritated Aragon during 1931; and Thirion had had to spend a lot of time and energy convincing him not only that the Catalan was vital to Surrealism but that he should be allowed his head, provided always that he was not permitted to become excessively engulfing. The Party's strictures concerning 'Reverie', therefore, did not fall on deaf ears.[55]

At the beginning of March 1932 Breton published *The Poverty of Poetry* (*Misère de la poésie*), an impassioned and closely reasoned defence of Aragon's rabidly Communist and anti-imperialist poem 'Red Front', published in January, which had offended the French army to such an extent that the author was in danger of being imprisoned for five years on the charge of encouraging military disobedience and murder.[56] But if Breton deprecated the French political establishment, which he proclaimed 'pro-Fascist', he equally deplored the campaign currently being waged against both Trotskyism and Surrealism by the Communist Party. On 9 February 1932 a diatribe in *L'Humanité* had referred scornfully to the Surrealists' 'revolutionaryism', branding it as 'merely verbal'.[57] Breton was outraged. In a hard-hitting footnote he now expressed scorn for the Communists' sexual puritanism and for their rejection of Freud's 'magnificent discoveries'. They had been incapable, he wrote, of seeing beyond the 'manifest content' of Dalí's 'Reverie', which personally he found 'very beautiful'.[58]

When *The Poverty of Poetry* appeared Dalí was in Catalunya. From there he wrote to Breton, commenting with scorn on the ludicrous popularity of Soviet films, with their naive idealism, among the Barcelona bourgeoisie. More importantly, he enclosed a copy of his replies to the questionnaire on desire then being circulated by a group of Yugoslav Surrealists.[59] The questions touched on Dalí's deepest convictions. His answers were published the following June in the Belgrade Surrealist journal *Nadrealizam Danas i Ovde* ('Surrealism Today and Here'):[60]

1. What importance do you attach to man's desires and most immediate needs, and, in particular, to your own desires and needs?

I attach a very great importance to man's desires and the greatest importance to my own desires.

2. Do you think your desires and needs can be in conflict with your vocation and your obligations (in the widest sense of these terms)? If you do, state what these needs, desires and obligations are. How do you resolve this conflict theoretically and how in practical situations?

I can't conceive of my vocation (!) or obligations as being separate from my desires, because my vocation and my obligations are the realization of my desires.

3. Have you any secret desires, either the kind generally considered reprehensible, immoral or base, or those which you yourself find vile, infamous, revolting? If you have, what do you do about this? Do you struggle against them, or do you satisfy them in your imagination? Or even in reality? What role do you allow to your will power in such a case? And to your conscience?

I haven't the slightest problem in making public my most shameful desires, which doesn't mean that I've yet achieved this fully, despite my very considerable exhibitionist tendencies. I have hidden desires, hidden from myself since I am constantly discovering new ones. I believe that our secret desires represent our true potential, and also that true culture of the spirit can only reside in our desires. No desire is reprehensible, the only fault is to repress them. All my desires are 'vile, infamous, revolting', etc. . . . I give great importance to the will, pushing it to the limit of 'paranoiac delirium' in the service of the realization of my desires.

4. Have you any elevated ideals? What do you do to put them into practice? What are the desires you find the most noble?

I have no so-called elevated ideals. The ones I hold most noble are those that I consider 'the most human, that's to say the most perverse'.

5. Do you think the word 'desire' is justified in all those cases where it is habitually used? Do you think that perhaps we should distinguish between different needs habitually termed desires? Do you think, for example, that there's an essential difference between sensorial needs (the need to listen to music)? What importance and what role do you attach to each?

　　The term 'desire' seems to me justifiable in all cases with libido potential, that is to say in all habitual cases. No fundamental difference (see 'sublimation').

6. Do you think, on the other hand, that certain distinctions are incorrectly established, that they should be suppressed and the notion made more precise? Do you consider, for example, that passion or ambition are different from desire?

　　Same as for all the concepts in general.

7. What role do you attribute to parents and teachers of the young in relation to desire? What dangers do you see in poor methods of education, if they exist, and what is the use of good ones in such a case? What is your opinion of the educational methods currently in use, or which have been used in different countries and periods, concerning the febrile desires of youth?

　　To awaken as many desires as possible; to strengthen the pleasure principle (man's most legitimate aspiration) against the reality principle. The consequence of the opposite method (the strengthening of the reality principle against the pleasure principle) is moral degradation. Sade: the only perfect educator for the febrile desires of youth.[61]

Dalí's replies go to the heart of Surrealism's convictions about human nature and of its rejection of Christian morality (considered as a monstrous aberration whose unconfessed purpose is to enslave). True to his fanatical temperament, and now encouraged by a partner who for years had been living out her desires as fully as possible, Dalí was determined to put shame behind him once and for all. But it would not prove so easy.

Meanwhile the presence of Gala, who never seems to have been tempted to abandon him, or to have doubted that Dalí would eventually prosper, was the mainstay in the midst of great uncertainty. From Julien Levy we know that, where Dalí's work was concerned, she was already behaving 'like a tiger defending a cub'. Levy, who thought of himself as someone motivated by enthusiasm rather than cupidity, was always to find Gala hard going.[62]

A fortnight after receiving Dalí's letter, and while controversy in Paris raged about Aragon's recent defection from the Surrealist movement, Breton, accompanied by his lover of the moment, the painter Valentine Hugo, made a lightning visit to Dalí and Gala in Port Lligat before moving on to see Éluard in the Var at Grimaud. Years later, Valentine Hugo recalled that Breton had found Port Lligat decrepit and been annoyed by the flies. But such inconveniences did not prevent him from contributing to a *cadavre exquis*, which they sent to the Surrealist poet and essayist Marco Ristic in Belgrade. A few days later Crevel arrived. Dalí as usual kept his friend J.V. Foix abreast of events, telling him that it was his intention to turn Port Lligat into 'a Surrealist centre' and that he was planning to publish a popularizing book on the movement. Foix did his duty and spread the good news in *La Publicitat*.[63]

Sebastià Gasch, whose dislike of Surrealism was unabated, now chose to publish a tirade against the movement. And to do so in *La Publicitat*, which Dalí, thanks to Foix, had come to see as his preserve. The Surrealists' Communism, Gasch sneered, was 'a solemn farce', since they published luxury editions of their effusions for the delectation of the rich and the snobs. What about the workers? As for Dalí's painting, it had deteriorated to the level of 'a Mantegna in decomposition'.[64] Dalí was livid and dashed off a vitriolic letter that began 'Imbecilic Gasch':

> The fact that it's some time since you abandoned your idiotic avant-garde articles for the most abject and stupid journalism that has ever existed in the world only serves to corroborate the opinion I've always had of your failed and insignificant person, that is, that you're a miserable oaf. The unprecedented article in '*La publi*' reveals a *total* ignorance and lack of understanding and moreover shows me what you think of Surrealism, which in itself would be sufficient for me to tell you that I consider you the ultimate bastard. I must warn you that if you continue to occupy yourself with these matters (surely the music hall is enough to entertain you) you'll be punished in a few days when I go to Barcelona.[65]

Although the threatened castigation was not carried out, the friendship, reflected in hundreds of letters written during the heroic days of *L'Amic de les Arts* (and still withheld from publication), had come to a brusque conclusion.[66]

By 11 May 1932 Dalí was back in Paris where his second exhibition at Pierre Colle opened on the twenty-sixth of the month, running until 17 June.[67] The catalogue, which was introduced by Éluard's poem 'Salvador Dalí', lists twenty-seven works in all, fifteen of them unknown or untraceable today, including one entitled *The Youth of William Tell* which presumably would tell us more about the place of this myth in Dalí's work at the time.

The Old Age of William Tell (owned by Charles de Noailles) was the first work listed in the catalogue, its primacy indicating the extent to which Dalí's father was still on the painter's mind. Surrealist Objects were much in evidence, two in their own right (*Hypnagogic Clock* and *Clock Based on the Decomposition of Bodies*), others being represented in the paintings themselves: *Anthropomorphic Object Indicating the Loss of Memory, Wrapped Object and Hypnagogic Object, Systematized Delirious Objects* and *Surrealist Objects Indicative of Instantaneous Memory.*

XXII

Hallucination: Six Images of Lenin on a Piano (1931) made the biggest hit with the public (Dalí said later that the phosphorescent haloes surrounding Lenin's head as it sprouts from the white keys had come to him as he was dropping off to sleep).[68] The Chinese-ink drawing *Paranoiac Metamorphosis of Gala's Face*, however, strikes one today as a much more original work. It shows Gala at her most vulnerable, a far cry from the cruel harpy portrayed by Max Ernst. Of all Dalí's paintings and drawings featuring Gala, this is surely the most subtle. Amidst the objects (most of them erotic) making up the two metamorphoses of the Muse's head, one cannot fail to notice the inkwell and pen: a clear indication that, if Dalí's father continued to obsess him, he was never far from Gala's thoughts, either.

Dalí, Paranoiac Metamorphosis of Gala's Face, *1932. Indian ink, 29 x 21 cm. Gala at her most vulnerable. The inkwell and pen suggest that the opposition of Dalí's notary father was never far from his thoughts at this time.*

Coinciding with the Colle exhibition, the Belgrade Surrealists published the enquiry on desire to which Dalí, Éluard, Breton and Crevel had contributed, and also a tiny fragment of Dalí's 'Surrealist novel', *Long Live Surrealism!* The previous February Dalí had told Foix about the latter, announcing that its characters were Gala, Dulita (of 'Reverie' fame), André Breton, Marlene Dietrich, René Crevel, Buster Keaton, Kaerguiski (?) and diverse Surrealist Objects. None of these appear in the Belgrade fragment, which has more the air of an essay on Surrealism than of a novel. Dalí announced the imminent publication of the work that summer, but it never appeared. Nor has the manuscript come to light. Santos Torroella has suggested that some of its episodes may have been incorporated into the more fanciful passages of the Secret Life but, there is no proof of this.[69]

Babaouo

Since the spring of 1930 Dalí and Gala had been living at 7, Rue Becquerel, just below the Sacré-Coeur. Now, just in advance of Gala and Éluard's divorce, granted on 15 July 1932,[70] they moved across town to a modest studio at 7, Rue Gauguet, a quiet cul-de-sac, not far from the Parc Montsouris, that backs on to another called Villa Seurat, then famous for its colony of painters and writers. The 'modern functionalist building' that housed the studio was an example of 'auto-punitive architecture', Dalí wrote, 'the architecture of poor people—and we were poor'. But soon Gala made it shipshape:

> So, not being able to have Louis XIV bureaus, we decided to live with immense windows and chromium tables with a lot of glass and mirrors. Gala had the gift of making everything 'shine', and the moment she entered a place everything began furiously to sparkle. This almost monastic rigidity, meanwhile, excited my thirst for luxury even more. I felt like a cypress growing in a bathtub.[71]

The move coincided with the publication of Dalí's Babaouo. It's a Surrealist Film. Thus the cover. The title-page read: 'Babaouo, an unpublished filmscript, preceded by a synopsis of a critical history of the cinema and followed by William Tell, a Portuguese ballet'. Dalí wrote in 1978 that, when Babaouo appeared, people assumed that the eponymous protagonist was himself.[72] The assumption was justified in the case both of the filmscript and of the ballet (which we are explicitly told is 'extracted' from the film), for each is shot through with autobiographical references as well as with borrowings from Dalí's paintings of the moment (soft watches, fried eggs on a plate 'without the plate', cyclists with stones on their heads and so forth). The woman who in amorous despair summons Babaouo to the Château de Portugal at the beginning of the film (whose action is set in 1934 'during a civil war in no matter what European country') is called Matilde Ibáñez, a girl Dalí had known in Barcelona (Matilde is also the name of Dulita's mother in 'Reverie', as we have seen).[73] The reference to the transformation of certain rooms at the former 'Chambre Agricole' at Figueres looks like a recondite nod in the direction of Dalí's first teacher, Esteban Trayter, whose apartment was in the block that gave way to the building in question. The landscape described in the ballet is unmistakably that of Cape Creus, with its mica-schist rocks, and the old woman and her two fishermen sons, both of them eccentric to a degree, remind us immediately of Lídia and her unfortunate offspring (who ended up in a mental asylum). As well as this there are constant allusions in both works to *Un Chien andalou* and *L'Age d'or*. The orchestra interrupted in its attempts to perform the overture to *Tannhäuser* on the Metro station platform, for example, reminds us of the lovers' frustrated attempts to consummate their passion in the second film (to the accompaniment of the climax of *Tristan and Isolde*); the crowd passing unconcernedly amongst the impassive musicians, or rushing through them to their train, brings to mind the scene, also in *L'Age d'or*, of the cart that rumbles through the drawing room, ignored by the guests; the tango *Renacimiento* ('Rebirth'), that plays throughout, calls up the two in *Un Chien andalou*; the strange noise that greets Babaouo as he arrives at the Château de Portugal, and turns out to be the sea crashing on the beach, alludes, surely, to the insistent drums that beat during the Château de Seligny sequence at the end of *L'Age d'or*. And so on. One gets the impression that Dalí wanted to underline the fact that his contribution to both films had been as fundamental as Buñuel's (a point he makes in the synopsis of the history of the cinema at the front of the volume); and it seems that he already suspected that Buñuel, who had distanced himself from Breton's group in 1932,[74] was trying to play down the importance of that contribution. This suspicion was to grow over the next two years.

If Dalí made any concerted efforts to have *Babaouo* filmed, these have not come to light. The script had potential, there are some memorable scenes (the ghost town viewed from the fourth floor of the empty theatre, for example), arresting sound effects, and even a remarkable sequence that suddenly switches from black and white to colour. Had Dalí known a rich backer, something might have been made of it. But there was no such backer forthcoming, Charles de Noailles, the best bet, having withdrawn from the scene after the social embarrassment caused by *L'Age d'or*.

Babaouo was the second in what was to be a long line of frustrated film projects. As for *William Tell*, the 'Portuguese ballet', Dalí told Noailles that he had read it to Leonide Massine and that, contrary to his expectations, the latter had expressed his desire to put it on. But this project came to nothing either.[75]

Once Dalí had collected his first copies of *Babaouo* (the colophon states that printing was completed on 12 July 1932), he and Gala set off for Spain, J.V. Foix reporting in *La Publicitat* on 28 July that the painter had just arrived in Port Lligat and planned to stay there for three months. Dalí and Gala were visited again shortly afterwards by René Crevel, with Breton and Valentine Hugo in hot pursuit. Breton had just finished *The Communicating Vessels* (*Les Vases communicants*) while staying with Éluard at Castellane, and appears to have been in good spirits this time (despite the flies), expressing appreciation of *Babaouo*. Buñuel also received an invitation to Port Lligat, but was unable to take it up. He told Noailles that Dalí had sent him *Babaouo*. Certain passages seemed to him 'amusing', and the theoretical part 'pretty bizarre'.[76]

After Breton and Valentine Hugo left, Dalí spent a few days in Barcelona, accompanied by Crevel. There he saw Foix (who had announced the publication of *Babaouo* in his column on 2 September, providing a Catalan translation of the prologue),[77] Zdenko Reich (a dissident Yugoslav Surrealist) and his old friend Jaume Miravitlles, who was no less depressed than Dalí by the current behaviour and tactics of the Communists. Dalí wrote to Breton at the beginning of October to tell him that he was more and more convinced of the idiocy of the party bureaucrats who repeated in a stereotyped way the 'abstract and incomprehensible' orders reaching them from Moscow: the Third International was becoming totally distanced from life, from what was really happening in the world. A good example of such distancing, he felt, was the naively idealistic Russian film about the re-education of delinquent children, *Le Chemin de la vie* (1931), which to Dalí's chagrin was about to be shown in Barcelona to, of all people, the members of the Catholic Youth Organization. Dalí told Breton that his main reason for visiting Barcelona was to try and get two Surrealist magazines off the ground: one inspired by the Paris-based *This Quarter* (which had recently published a special Surrealism issue), the other by Breton's *The Communicating Vessels*, some extracts of which in *Le Surréalisme au Service de la Révolution* had greatly impressed him. Neither venture was destined to succeed. The Barcelona press was showing some interest in Surrealism, Dalí told Breton, and there was a chance that a new theatre group called 'Anticipations' might produce a Surrealist play and take it to Madrid (which it didn't). As for his own work, he was broadening the scope of his Surrealist Objects, having devised both a 'liquid' and a 'blind' variety. He would be taking back new pictures to Paris, part of a novel and, above all, a compelling desire to be as useful as possible to Surrealism.[78]

Foix received a fuller account of Dalí's 'blind objects' at about the same time, reproducing the artist's letter in *La Publicitat* with some ironic observations.[79] Dalí also sent him a copy of the Surrealist issue of *This Quarter*, which contained translations of several of his 'poems' and a long theoretical text, 'The Object as Revealed in Surrealist Experiment'.[80] As usual, Dalí was determined to extract the maximum benefits from his friend's commanding position on one of the Catalan capital's leading newspapers. As for Paris, it seems that by this time he had already made the acquaintance there of an enterprising woman whose influence on the course of his life was to be significant.

Americans in Paris

Caresse and Harry Crosby were a rich young American couple with literary aspirations who had joined the post-World War I rush to Paris in the early 1920s. By 1927, the year in which they founded their Black Sun Press, the Crosbys were figures of prominence on the Anglo-Saxon expatriate scene in the French capital. Caresse (a pet-name: she had been born a more banal Mary Peabody, in 1892) told her side of the story engagingly in *The Passionate Years* (1955), a book much less well known than Hemingway's *A Moveable Feast* but containing an account of the Paris of the Roaring Twenties every bit as entertaining. The Crosbys, as the title of Caresse's memoirs suggests, lived life to the full. They were handsome, sexually liberated, creative and hugely generous with their money, a steady supply of which was always available thanks to Harry's family connection with the Morgan and Company Bank. Caresse looked like one of the Kodak beauties in Dalí's paintings of the mid-twenties: she had a friendly, Griskin bust (maybe this was why she was impelled to invent the brassière), was leggy when legs were all the rage, exuded energy, and thought of herself as The Girl Who Never Said No. One of the men to whom she didn't say no was Lorca's friend, Manuel Angeles Ortiz, the young Andalusian painter who had taken Dalí to meet Picasso in 1926. Ortiz, who apparently conned Caresse into believing that he was a 'blue-blooded Spanish gypsy', did an excellent drawing of her.[81] As for Harry, his RAF-style good looks, his wealth, daredevil attitude to life, racing cars (he even had a Bugatti) and his intensely romantic poetry ensured that he was always a hit with the ladies. So, too, did his rebelliousness. Why did he prefer to live outside America? 'Because I do not wish to devote myself to perpetual hypocrisy . . . because I love flagons of wine . . . because I am an enemy of society and here I can hunt with other enemies of society . . . because I am not coprophagous . . .'[82]

Today the Black Sun Press is part of the mythology of 1920s Paris, and its publications have become collectors' pieces that get snapped up as rapidly as they appear in the catalogues, not least the couple's edition of part of James Joyce's *Work in Progress*, the negotiations for which are amusingly recalled in *The Passionate Years*.[83]

The Crosby hospitality was proverbial, especially that provided at the old mill they had discovered in 1927 near Senlis, just north of Paris. It stood in the grounds of the Château de Ermenonville, a property owned by their friend Count Armand de la Rochefoucauld, one of the richest and most sought-after young men in Europe. The mill had belonged to Jean-Jacques Rousseau when he was in love with the Duchess of Montmorency, and Giuseppe Cagliostro, the alchemist, wrote Caresse later, 'had worked his magic formulae beside the Moulin stream'. The place boasted a tower and ten bedrooms. It was the ideal hideaway. Harry, true to fashion, bought it on the spot, and Caresse renamed it Le Moulin du Soleil in deference to his cult of sun worship. But Harry was only destined to enjoy the Moulin for two summers. In December 1929 he and a girlfriend committed joint suicide in New York, with no explanations given.[84]

Caresse, deeply wounded but undaunted, continued to provide lavish hospitality over the following years at the Moulin du Soleil—'Lucullan feasts' she called them later. Among the regulars were D.H. Lawrence, Hart Crane, André Breton, René Crevel, Max Ernst, the bevy of American, English and Irish writers associated with the review *Transition* and Julien Levy, who used to arrive armed with his 16mm Bell and Howell. 'This collection of attractive women and talented men brought to mind,' wrote Levy, 'in the luxurious setting of the *moulin*, such a gathering as Marie Antoinette might have assembled at Le Hameau. So, too, the intricate feuding and flirting everywhere sparking up and spluttering out.'[85]

In the *Secret Life* Dalí states that it was René Crevel who introduced him and Gala to Caresse, taking them to lunch one summer's day (almost certainly in 1932) at her Paris apartment. Dalí would have us believe that on that occasion everything in the room was white except the tablecloth and the china: the food, the drink (milk), the curtains, the telephone, the rug, Caresse's clothes, her earrings, shoes and bracelets.[86] Crosby denies all of this in her memoirs, but whatever the truth of the matter they all got on wonderfully. Caresse became one of the couple's best friends in Paris and before long they were spending weekends at the Moulin du Soleil. By now Dalí was accustomed to frequenting the salons of the Parisian aristocracy, where little by little he felt less timid (although some recourse to alcohol was still necessary),[87] but this was different:

> We ate in the horse-stable, filled with tiger skins and stuffed parrots. There was a sensational library on the second floor, and also an enormous quantity of champagne cooling, with sprigs of mint, in all the corners, and many friends, a mixture of Surrealists and society people who came there because they sensed that it was in this Moulin du Soleil that 'things were happening'. At this period the phonograph never stopped sighing Cole Porter's 'Night and Day', and for the first time in my life I thumbed through *The New Yorker* and *Town and Country*. Each image that came from America I would sniff, so to speak, with the voluptuousness with which one welcomes the first whiffs of the inaugural fragrance of a sensational meal of which one is about to partake.[88]

Caresse encouraged Dalí to think about exhibiting in New York, reinforcing the pressure already being exerted by Julien Levy, Pierre Colle and Alfred Barr. She was sure he would be successful. Initially the painter resisted the prospect of crossing the Atlantic, which terrified him almost as much as it had done Lorca a few years earlier. But little by little the conviction grew that in New York, where Levy's Surrealist show in January 1932 had been such a success, he could not only make a hit but, even more important, money.

The Zodiac

Money at the time was a tremendous problem. Despite Dalí's growing notoriety, he and Gala were still struggling; the contract with Pierre Colle was ending, and the dealer was not financially strong enough to renew it; the market for Dalís was still very limited; and the couple's meagre savings had fallen to a low ebb.[89]

Relief, however, was at hand. There are rival claims as to who devised the formula. The painter's aristocratic admirer, Prince Jean-Louis Faucigny-Lucinge, stated years afterwards that one day Gala, after confiding to him that she and Dalí were finding the going very difficult, proposed a solution to prevent Salvador 'from having to commercialize himself'. This was that twelve affluent art lovers, one for each month of the year, should be persuaded to make an annual payment to the artist in return for a painting of their choice. They would draw lots for their month. 'Like that,' said Gala, 'we'd have no more difficulty and Dalí could work quietly.' Faucigny-Lucinge agreed to participate and to find other members, and thus was born the Zodiac.[90] The French-American writer Julien Green, however, has always maintained that it was his sister Anne who thought up the idea after Dalí (not Gala) had begged her to help, dragging her into his bedroom and, to Anne's surprise, locking the door behind him. 'Anne, we've no money,' he said sadly. According to Green, the idea of the Zodiac came to his sensitive sister in a flash. But there seems no way of being sure which version, Green's or Faucigny-Lucinge's, is the more accurate.[91]

While Anne Green had known Dalí for two years, her brother met him for the first time on 24 November 1932, when Christian Bérard, their painter friend, took them to see the Catalan's third exhibition at Pierre Colle's, held between 22 November and the afternoon of their visit. Eleven works were on show: *Unfinished Portrait of Gala*, *The Birth of Liquid Desires*, *The Liquid-Archaeological Situation of Lenin (Transformed Dream)*, *The Cannibal's Nostalgia (Instantaneous Image)*, *Fried Eggs on a Plate without the Plate*, *William Tell Has Died (Hallucinatory Presentiment)*, *House for an Erotomaniac*, *Surrealist*

Architecture, Sentimental Memory, The Rose Complex (*drawing*) and *Study* (*Birth of Liquid Desires*).[92]

The Greens loved the exhibition, and a few days later, on 28 November, visited Dalí and Gala at their Rue Gauguet studio. The fact that they arrived too early, and apparently disturbed the couple's siesta, did not spoil the afternoon: Gala and Dalí were charming. 'Gala is perhaps thirty. A grave and handsome face,' Green wrote in his diary that evening, the entry showing once again how much younger Gala looked than her years (she was now thirty-nine). As for Dalí's paintings, 'I lose myself in the contemplation of this marvellous world in which one is drawn back into the furthest of one's childhood dreams. The impression produced by this extraordinary universe is strange but *possible*; it seems somehow *to propagate silence*, it develops in the midst of silence like a plant in a flood of light.' The Greens bought two paintings, and the writer thought his 'as beautiful as one of those huge blue and black butterflies that one puts under glass'. He did not record its title in his diary, but later wrote that it was called *The Persistence of Twilight*. Today its location is unknown.[93]

The visit to Rue Gauguet marked the beginning of a friendship between Dalí and Green that was to last untarnished, according to the latter, for fifty-seven years. As for the Zodiac, it got under way quickly, Dalí writing on 26 December 1932 to tell Charles de Noailles, who had agreed to join the club, that the other eleven members had been found much more rapidly than he had expected. Dalí listed them from one to eleven in what may not necessarily have been the chronological order of their incorporation: Caresse Crosby, the architect Emilio Terry, Julien and Anne Green, the Marquesa Margaret ('Toto') Cuevas de Vera (granddaughter of John D. Rockefeller and wife of the Chilean art patron Jorge de Piedrablanca de Guana, Marqués de Cuevas de Vera),[94] the illustrator André Durst ('I've met him, he's genuinely interested in my things'), the Comtesse Anna Laetitia de Pecci-Blunt, René Laporte ('publisher of Breton's *Les Vases communicants*, etc.'), Prince Faucigny-Lucinge, Félix Rolo ('I don't know him, it was Boris Kochno who introduced us') and Julien Green's close friend, the diplomat Robert de Saint-Jean. In the same letter Dalí informed Noailles that, in the first draw, Anne Green, acting for the Vicomte in his absence, had picked out January 1933, the first month of the Save Dalí operation.[95]

February had fallen to Julien Green, who went again to Dalí's apartment to pick up his picture:

> I am given the choice between a large painting with an admirable landscape of rocks as a
> background, but with the foreground taken up by a sort of naked and whiskered Russian

general, his head sorrowfully bent to show the shells and pearls that pepper his skull, and a small picture in wonderful shades of gray and lilac, plus two drawings. I choose the small painting. Dalí talks to me about Crevel, who is ill but 'estoical'. He enlarges greatly on the beauty of his own painting, carefully explains the meaning of my picture which he calls 'Geological Transformation' and which represents a horse turning into rock in the midst of a desert. He is going to Spain and speaks with terror of the customs formalities and the thousand petty annoyances of a trip by *ferrocarril*, for he is a little like a child who is scared by life.[96]

Green does not comment that in the background of the painting, better known by its French title, *Le Devenir géologique*, we see a male figure holding a small boy by the hand. The degree to which this motif recurs in the paintings of 1932 and 1933 indicates the extent to which Dalí was continuing to brood on his rejection by his father.[97]

The Zodiac proved a great success. Looking back to 1933, Julien Green wrote that the paintings thus acquired were displayed to such effect on the 'most scrutinized walls in Paris' that, within a year, Dalí was famous.[98] Something of an exaggeration, perhaps, but it is certainly true that the arrangement gave the artist, now at the height of his powers, a full year's financial security just when he needed it—security in which to paint and to publicize himself and his wares. He devoted himself to these tasks with the immense energy that characterized him all his life.

Maldoror and Millet's *Angelus*

On 28 January 1933 Dalí wrote to Charles de Noailles, holding back until the end of the letter the 'big news' that he was going a sign a contract that afternoon with Albert Skira. The commission: forty engravings to illustrate Lautréamont's *The Songs of Maldoror*. Skira was a young Swiss art publisher who had set up in Paris in 1928, operating from a small office at 25, Rue de la Boëtie, next door to Picasso, who would shout messages to him from his sixth-floor atelier through a child's trumpet.[99] By 1933 Skira had an international reputation. As Dalí reminded Noailles, he had recently brought out a marvellous edition of Ovid's *Metamorphoses*, illustrated by Picasso, and another of the poetry of Mallarmé done by Henri Matisse. Dalí was exultant to be in such company, not least because he had twelve months in which to complete the work.[100] In 1948 Skira stated that it was René Crevel who persuaded him to engage Dalí to illustrate *Maldoror*.[101] This seems to give the lie to Dalí's claim that the commission was the result of Picasso's intervention.[102]

The contract duly signed, Dalí and Gala hurried back in February to Port Lligat. Two days after their arrival Gala wrote to Skira asking him to send the copper plates stored in their apartment because Dalí wanted to start work straightaway. Dalí added a footnote: he had already begun the drawings, and approved of what he had achieved so far. He was bursting with ideas, he said, and elated about 'their' book. He and Gala were guzzling 'phenomenal' sea urchins. To make their happiness complete, would Skira please lodge to their account the *petits sous* he owed them?[103]

On 10 March 1933 Dalí had still not received the plates (or money) and was becoming impatient.[104] Soon afterwards the former arrived and Gala was able to tell Skira that Dalí had immediately begun to engrave.[105] Then Dalí himself wrote. He was working all day from five in the morning, he said, and was very satisfied with the results so far. He wanted the publisher to send more copper plates and to ensure that next month's payment arrived on time, for he and Gala were 'beginning to be broke'. They must, therefore, have been making deep inroads into the money supplied by the Zodiac, spending it perhaps on new improvements to the house.[106]

During March and April, then, Dalí was engraving in Port Lligat on the copper plates forwarded by Skira, using whatever ability he had developed with Juan Núñez in Figueres. How much he achieved before returning to Paris we do not know. Nor is it clear how the work progressed during the rest of the year. Rainer Michael Mason's brilliant investigations have demonstrated conclusively, however, that at some stage during 1933 Dalí's drawings were engraved by other hands, as had been the case with his frontispiece for *The Visible Woman* (1930) and his illustrations (one each) for Breton and Éluard's *Immaculate Conception* (1930), René Char's *Artine* (1930) and Breton's *The Revolver with White Hair* (1932). The *Maldoror* plates were prepared at the workshop of Roger Lacourière, Skira's engraver in Paris, by the procedure of heliogravure for which this establishment was celebrated. Despite the title page of Skira's *Maldoror*, therefore, which specified that the illustrations were 'original etchings' (*eaux-fortes*) by Dalí, they were not original in the terms of the definition laid down by the Chambre Syndicale de l'Estampe, du Dessin et du Tableau of Paris in 1937 ('Qualifying as original etchings, prints and lithographs are proofs pulled in black or colours from one or several plates completely conceived and executed by hand by the same artist, whatever technique may be employed and excluding any mechanical or photomechanical procedure'). Mason makes the point that, even if Dalí touched up the plates prepared by another hand, this still would not make them original etchings, and reports that, anyway, nobody seems to have seen him working on the plates in Lacourière's workshop.[107]

If Dalí was prepared to state that it was Picasso who suggested to Skira that he commision him for *Maldoror*, he also put it about that he and Picasso had done a joint etching at this time. 'Dalí is the only painter with whom Picasso wanted to collaborate,' the artist said in an interview in 1977. 'Now it's been proved, because they've just found an engraving which we produced in tandem. I did some fried eggs; I passed it to him and he added a chair; he gave it back to me and I drew an ironing board; and so on . . .'[108] A graphite proof of the work in question is in the Musée Picasso in Paris, attributed to Dalí and his great rival.[109] But, again, Mason has demonstrated that, without the knowledge of the older artist, Dalinian additions were made to a previous Picasso print (*Trois Baigneuses II*) and then a new engraving of their 'collaboration' was run off. Who was responsible for this demonstration of Dalí's obsession with Picasso and of his desire to be considered his friend and peer? Mason suggests that both Dalí and Paul Éluard were involved, and that the work was executed in the workshop of Roger Lacourière.[110] The resultant engraving was a confidence trick, and so too, strictly, were the 'original etchings' for *Maldoror*. Dangerous precedents had been set, and they would be followed by far greater abuses later in Dalí's life.

Dalí's illustrations for *The Songs of Maldoror* relate much more closely to his personal obsessions than to Lautréamont's text, and not least to his obsession with Jean-François Millet's *Angelus* (1857–9), that perennially popular rendering of a couple of peasants entoning their 'Hail Mary!' as the sun goes down over the fields around them.

XVII

As a child at the de la Salle school in Figueres, Dalí had been deeply moved by a reproduction of *The Angelus* that hung in the passageway outside the classroom, the painting producing in him 'an obscure anguish' so poignant that the memory of the two motionless silhouettes pursued him for several years 'with the constant uneasiness provoked by their continual and ambiguous presence'. Twilight and the *Angelus* became intimately associated in Dalí's mind. Then the conscious memory of the painting subsided, only returning in 1929 when he saw another reproduction of the work and was 'violently seized by the same uneasiness and the original emotional upset'.[111]

As a result of this recovered memory, the 'two motionless silhouettes' of the *Angelus* were introduced that same year into *Imperial Monument to the Child-Woman*, Dalí's first important pictorial tribute to Gala. Then, in June 1932, such a powerful 'delirious image' of the *Angelus* apparently presented itself to him that he was compelled to explore it not only in numerous paintings and drawings but in a long essay, *Paranoiac-Critical Interpretation of the Obsessive Image in Millet's 'Angelus'*.[112] Dalí told Foix in February 1933, at the time of the *Maldoror* commission, that the essay was almost finished and would appear in a volume containing some thirty 'photographic documents'. It was an 'anticipation', he said, of his book *Surrealist Painting Through the Ages*, an ambitious project frequently announced by the artist but never published and probably never finished.[113] The imminent publication of *A Paranoiac-Critical Interpretation of the Obsessive Image in Millet's 'Angelus'* was advertised in the sixth and last issue of *Le Surréalisme au Service de la Révolution* (15 May 1933). But, for reasons never explained, it did not appear. What *did* appear, in the first issue of Albert Skira's lavishly illustrated magazine *Minotaure*, which came out a month later, was the essay's 'prologue'. Entitled 'New General Considerations on the Mechanism of the Paranoiac Phenomenon from the Surrealist Point of View', it was accompanied by photographs of *The Angelus* and of other works by Millet.

The prologue acknowledges Dalí's appreciation of Jacques Lacan's thesis *De la Psychose paranoïaque dans ses rapports avec la personnalité*, published in 1932. The book had not only stimulated further Dalí's investigations into paranoia but had acted as a confirmation to him that these were on the right lines. There is no proof that Lacan and Dalí had seen each other again after their first meeting, but it cannot have been been fortuituous that, in *Minotaure*, Dalí's piece was followed immediately by one by the psychiatrist.[114] In the minds of those who were alert to the evolution of Surrealism, Lacan and Dalí were now closely associated.

As for the manuscript of the unpublished essay, left behind in 1940, when the Germans invaded France, it surfaced twenty years later. Dalí issued it without revision in 1963, adding only a new prologue about his recent investigations and a scattering of marginal comments. Its definitive title was *The Tragic Myth of Millet's 'Angelus'. A Paranoiac-Critical Interpretation.*[115]

The essay is undoubtedly Dalí's most original contribution to art criticism. It is also deeply revealing of his inner conflicts in the early 1930s. Refining on the technique of pseudo self-analysis employed in the controversial 'Reverie', and with Freud's *Leonardo da Vinci and a Memory of his Childhood* very much in mind, Dalí attempts to get to the root of the fascination exerted over him from childhood by Millet's seemingly banal painting. The only explanation for the huge popularity of the picture, he argues, in tune with Freudian dream theory, is that its *manifest* content masks a much more significant *latent* one. And that latent content, he concludes, relates to oedipal anxiety: to the male child's desire for and simultaneous fear of the mother. Observe, asks Dalí, that in the painting the husband is of slighter build than his wife (who, to judge from her stout profile, may well be pregnant); his eyes are cast down because he is praying, certainly, but he has a suspiciously ashamed look, has he not? Why? Because his hat is hiding an erection. The fork stuck into the earth is an obvious allusion to intercourse, as well as to swallowing. And the wheelbarrow? Does it not symbolize a hesitant, *trundling* sexuality? In fact, does the man not look more like a son than a husband? Like a son who desires his mother?

The essay recruits memories of stories read to Dalí as a child (tales populated with exotic flora and fauna set in Tertian twilight) and of places visited in those early years: a hill with fossils outside Figueres, the rocks of Creus (with their weird transformations), a damp meadow near Port Lligat inhabited by frogs, grasshoppers and . . . praying mantises. When, probably in Madrid, Dalí read about the praying mantis in Fabre's *The Life of Insects* (a book beloved of Buñuel), he had been astonished to discover not only that the female kills her mate after copulation but sometimes does so *during the act*. Is not the woman in the *Angelus* standing in a posture akin to that of the mantis, is she not about to pounce? The suspicion becomes conviction: the Angelus scene is 'the maternal variant of the immense and atrocious myth of Saturn, Abraham, the Eternal Father with Jesus Christ and of William Tell devouring their own children'.[116]

Dalí explains that he suffers from an oedipal fixation 'of extremely important and determining character'. That we knew already. But the next revelation comes as a shock, for he now claims that his mother made him terrified of sex when he was a child 'by sucking, by devouring' his penis. Dalí concedes that this might be a 'false memory', rather than the recollection of a true historical event, but, either way, he now wants us to believe that it was his mother who caused his impotence,[117] an impotence so tenacious that only Gala has been capable of alleviating it, 'the resources of her love surpassing in vital intuition the most subtle advances of psychoanalytic treatment'.[118] No mention now of Dalí Cusí, of the book on venereal disease placed on the family piano: Dalí is reaching back further in time, back, virtually, to the breast. He never seems to have repeated publicly the charge that it was his mother who rendered him unvirile, but the accusation is expressed here with such vigour that it is difficult to believe that he made it lightly.

Since Dalí had decided that the *Angelus* reflected his deepest fears and frustrations, it is not surprising that the theme appeared compulsively in dozens of his paintings and drawings. The majority of these were done between 1933 and 1934, but the *Angelus* was to surface sporadically in his work for the rest of his life.

Of the paintings, *Meditation on the Harp* (1932–4) perhaps constitutes the strongest statement. Here the male figure is in a state of manifest erection in response to the naked female, plump to a degree, whose arms encircle his neck. At their feet, his covered head placed close to the man's genitals, kneels a monstruous masked creature, whose brainphallus (sex in the head?) is propped up by a crutch. Perhaps the mask takes the place of the hands that cover faces in other paintings, hiding the shame provoked by witnessing sexual scenes. Dalí seems not to have 'explained' this picture, contrary to his normal practice, but its oedipal significance is surely clear enough.

The *Angelus* theme is a major constituent of the drawings Dalí supplied for Skira's

Maldoror, and this, the artist argued cleverly when the book was launched in 1934, was because in his view Millet's painting was the exact pictorial equivalent of Lautréamont's famous simile. The ploughed earth plays the part of the dissecting table; the fork plunged into it that of the scalpel; the man and woman those of the umbrella and sewing machine. The umbrella is a 'flagrant' male sex symbol (in its simulation of tumescence and detumescence), as Dalí had learnt from Freud, and the sewing machine as obviously represents the castrating female. With her needle the female 'empties' the male just as the mantis kills her lover, causing the penis-umbrella to subside. Conclusion: Millet's *Angelus*, like Lautreamont's adolescent, is 'as lovely as the fortuitous encounter on a dissecting table of a sewing-machine and an umbrella'. It was a brilliant thesis, argued with all the fanatical logic for which Dalí was becoming notorious.[119]

Dalí, Meditation on the Harp, *1932–4. Oil on canvas, 67 x 47 cm. One of Dalí's finest variations on Millet's* Angelus *(colour plate xvii).*

Five or six of the illustrations for *Maldoror* allude directly to the *Angelus*. Of the others, the most striking develop the theme of cannibalism that Dalí believes he has discovered in Millet's painting, proposing for our consideration the repeated image of a contorted body propped up by crutches and busily slicing off choice cuts of itself and holding a fork in readiness in the other hand. In another plate, a male figure is eating a child whose brain has been pierced by a sewing-machine. Everywhere, evocative of the butcher's shop, are soft, visceral forms accompanied by bones and cutlets. Inkwells abound, a reminder of Dalí Cusí's practice in Figueres and, contrasting with the horrors taking place in the foreground, we observe in six plates the distant presence of the father and child, hand-in-hand: a compulsive icon of more secure times.[120]

In the *Maldoror* illustrations we also find the presence of a slightly older Dalí, the same child who, in *The Spectre of Sex Appeal*, stares transfixed, hoop in hand, at the horrifying apparition that has materialized on the shore at Cape Creus. This picture, done in 1934 (not 1932 as has so often been stated) is today one of the treasures of Dalí's

Theatre-Museum in Figueres. Of tiny proportions (17 x 13 cm), the artist termed it an 'erotic bogie of the first order'.[121] Contemplating it in 1995, Nanita Kalaschnikoff, one of Dalí's closest friends, recalled the way the painter's voice would change at the slightest danger of sexual intimacy. 'Sexuality for him was always a monster and he never overcame the anxiety it produced in him,' she said. 'That was his tragedy.'[122]

Colle and Levy Again

Between 7 and 18 June 1933 a comprehensive Surrealist group show was held at the Pierre Colle Gallery, which featured sculptures, objects, paintings and drawings by twenty-two artists. The surprise was that the show included some works by Picasso, briefly attracted by Breton's movement at this time. Among Dalí's eight exhibits were two of his most successful Surrealist Objects, the early *Board of Demented Associations* and his recent *Retrospective Bust of a Woman*.[123]

XXI

The exhibition was immediately followed by Dalí's fourth (and last) show at the same gallery, which ran from 19 to 29 June. The catalogue was introduced by a convoluted and highly amusing open letter from Dalí to Breton in which, after providing a long list of his current obsessions (from Louis II, the mad boy-king of Bavaria, to *trompe l'oeil*), the artist proceeded to justify his current appreciation of Ernest Meissonier (1815–91), a painter who had fallen into almost complete disrepute but whose meticulously academic technique now seemed to him 'the most complex, intelligent and extra-pictorial medium for the forthcoming deliriums of irrational exactitude to which Surrealism seems to me to be immediately destined'. Dalí maintained that De Chirico, so admired by the Surrealists, had employed academic means to achieve his 'revolution of the anecdote'. So why should not he? He signed off by asking Breton to believe in his 'unconditional loyalty to Surrealism'.

Twenty-two paintings, ten drawings and two objects were listed in the catalogue. Of these, seven of the paintings and two of the drawings had been shown by Colle the previous November. Several of the works had been lent by members of the Zodiac or other friends (Julien Green, André Durst, 'Toto' Cuevas de Vera, Robert de Saint-Jean, Emilio Terry, Prince Jean-Louis de Faucigny-Lucinge, René Laporte and Comte Etienne de Beaumont). With one exception, the drawings and objects exhibited at Pierre Colle's are impossible to identify today, the same holding true for at least six of the paintings. Given that Dalí had recently been working on his essay on Millet, it comes as no surprise that the Angelus theme figured prominently in at least three of the works on show: *The Invisible, Fine and Middling Harp* (1932), *Meditation on the Harp*—the first two works listed—and *Gala and Millet's 'Angelus' Preceding the Imminent Arrival of the Conic Anamorphoses.*[124]

Writing in *Beaux-Arts*, the critic Georges Hilaire noticed Dalí's extreme attention to detail. The Catalan was a dreamer in search of total precision, sharp geometrical outlines. No mystery here, no ambiguity. Things in themselves, unexplained, starkly individual. Dalí was 'a paranoiac of geometrical temperament'. It was an apt definition.[125]

After the exhibition, Gala and Dalí returned for the summer to Port Lligat, where at the end of July we find the artist writing again to Breton—but this time privately. In his letter Dalí reasoned that, if the Object had now become a Surrealist speciality, so too should politics. By politics he meant the movement's attitude to Hitler (who had been accorded full powers a few months earlier, on 30 January 1933, and was now using these to crush all opposition). The Nazi phenomenon deserved serious and urgent consideration from a Surrealist point of view, Dalí said, not least because the Communists, who ought to be perceptive on the subject, were completely failing to grasp what was happening. He had been hearing them say constantly that Hitler's revolution was not important, meant nothing, would soon fizzle out. How could they be so blind! And the West be so idiotic, searching for compromise? It was the duty of Surrealism to clarify the subject of Hitler and to do so before Georges Bataille, rumoured to be preparing a panegyric of the Nazi leader, removed the ground from under their feet. So in the autumn, when they were all together once again in Paris, Dalí thought the Surrealists should publish a collective manifesto on the German question, all the more so since the movement had now been officially excluded from the Communist AEAR (Association des Écrivains et Artistes Révolutionnaires) which it had helped to found.[126]

This seems to be the first time that Dalí had alluded to Hitler in his correspondence with Breton. The letter gives no indication of admiration for the Führer, but it does hint at a certain fascination. Before long Breton would begin to feel that the painter's interest in Hitler's person was excessive.

On 13 September 1933 J.V. Foix announced in *La Publicitat* that Man Ray had arrived in Catalunya to take photographs of Cape Creus and of Barcelona's Art Nouveau architecture for a forthcoming article by Dalí in *Minotaure* ('On the Terrifying and Edible Beauty of Art Nouveau Architecture').[127] Elated by the discovery that Gaudí had visited Creus as an adolescent, Dalí was now convinced that his architecture was influenced by the cape's geological delirium. One of Man Ray's photographs shows a typical section of mica-schist with the characteristic alveoli which Dalí had reproduced in so many paintings and drawings, filling them with keys, ants and other symbolic presences. The artist gave the picture a witty caption in *Minotaure*: 'An attempt at geological Art

'Beauty will be edible or not at all'—Dalí's revamping of Breton's 'Beauty will be convulsive or not at all'. The photograph accompanied Dalí's celebrated article on Art Nouveau architecture in Minotaure. *The unidentified building is La Rotonda (1918), Barcelona, by Adolf Ruiz Casamitjana.*

Nouveau, botched like everything that comes straight from Nature without imagination'.[128]

By October, after visiting an exhibition in Barcelona of his admired Modest Urgell, painter of cemeteries, ruins and twilights,[129] Dalí was back in Paris, Gala presumably taking to Breton the 'at least' six pipes she said in September she had bought for him, an indication of the excellent relations existing between the couple and the Surrealist leader at this moment.[130] Installed again at their Rue Gauguet flat, they had lunch on 21 October with Julien Green, who recorded that Dalí talked about Freud 'like a Christian talks about the New Testament'. Green asked Dalí if his life had been simplified by reading the work of the Master. 'Everything had been made easier for him by the solution of conflicts,' Dalí replied. Green took this to mean that Freud's work had helped the painter to be a freer human being.[131]

Preparations were well under way by this time for Dalí's first exhibition in New York, to be held at Julien Levy's gallery at 602 Madison Avenue between 21 November and 8 December 1933. Levy continued to be on excellent terms with Pierre Colle, who acted on the artist's behalf and generously shipped out the paintings with no cash down, no guaranteed sales and freight expenses prepaid.[132] Twenty-six works went on show at Levy's, ten of them from the previous summer's exhibition mounted by Pierre Colle. That Dalí had worked intensely hard during the summer was obvious. Indeed, so unusually great was his production that Rafael Santos Torroella considers this one of his most astonishing bursts of effort ever, the more impressive if we take into account that at the same time he was also writing *Surrealist Painting Throughout the Ages.*[133]

It was the first time New Yorkers had been exposed not only to a substantial selection of Dalí's paintings but to his fanciful titles, hardly calculated to facilitate the understanding of the works. As for the Bosch listed at the end of the exhibition catalogue, one can only presume that its inclusion was intended to point to the link between Surrealism and earlier expressions of the same, or a similar, tendency in art.[134]

The public loved the show, finding it perplexing and disturbing, and according to Julien Levy it was a sell-out.[135] The reviews were good, too. Lewis Mumford, writing in *The New Yorker*, noted that Dalí's dreamscapes had a hard, precise quality quite unlike the sentimentality and vagueness with which dreams tended to be represented. He deemed them 'frozen nightmares'.[136] Dalí was elated by the notices, and quickly informed Foix.[137] It must have occurred to him that, if his paintings could do so well in New York without him, a personal visit was bound to be a great success.

Coinciding with the Julien Levy show, Dalí's old friend Josep Dalmau, who had been forced to close down his premises, organized an exhibition of the painter's work at the Galeria d'Art Catalònia in Barcelona (today the Casa del Libro, 3, Ronda de San Pere) which Dalí attended. It ran from 8 to 21 December 1933. On show were *The Birth of Liquid Desires*, *The Enigma of William Tell* (not to be confused with the much larger painting of the same name, featuring Lenin), photographs by Man Ray of six other key Dalí paintings, three drawings, a Surrealist Object and twenty-seven engravings, twenty-five of them being the first states of those done for Skira's edition of *The Songs of Maldoror*.[138]

The critic Magí A. Cassanyes, one of Dalí's friends from the *L'Amic de les Arts* days, was excited by the exhibition, particularly by *The Enigma of William Tell* and the *Maldoror* prints. The location of the former work, which according to Cassanyes was minute, is unknown today. Reproduced in the fifth issue of *Minotaure* (February 1934), where it accompanies Dalí's article 'The New Colours of Spectral Sex Appeal', the painting is a pendant to *The Spectre of Sex Appeal*. Here again is Dalí as a child, dressed in a sailor suit and holding his hoop. This time, however, a cutlet has been placed on his head and he is staring, not at a monstrous apparition on the beach but at a weird anthropomorphic materialization formed by clouds in the sky. Beside him sits his nurse, looking down all unawares, while to the latter's right two recumbent men, equally indifferent to the phenomenon taking place in the heavens, are deep in conversation. Cassanyes felt sure that the painting was another example of Dalí's courage in probing his anxieties.[139] As for the *Maldoror* etchings, he thought them 'sismographic documents' of such implacable honesty and power that only a man of the greatest moral and artistic integrity could be capable of executing them. And that man was Salvador Dalí. 'If, as we sincerely believe, dreams and unconfessable aspirations express the most real, pure and authentic part of ourselves,' wrote Cassanyes, 'it is hardly surprising that today, when

self-satisfied mediocrity is made aware more insistently each moment of its total futility, the highway to a new world of surprises, revelations and digressions that is
Surrealism alone merits our interest and attention.'[140]

Not everyone agreed, of course. The show's numerous visitors were attracted more by
the sensationalism associated with the artist's name, sneered the critic Just Cabot, than
by the intrinsic value of the work exhibited, which he considered mediocre. Dalí, for
Cabot, was the 'pseudo-genius of Figueres'.[141]

Dalí gave a lecture during his brief stay in Barcelona, reporting on its success to
Breton. In his reply the latter praised 'On the Terrifying and Edible Beauty of "Modern
Style" Architecture', which had just appeared in *Minotaure*, and informed Dalí that a
huge Surrealist exhibition was being planned for the Galerie de Paris, a villa situated
exactly opposite the entrance to the Grand Palais. For this, and for other reasons, he and
the rest of the group were awaiting the artist's return with mounting impatience.[142]

Breton did well to praise Dalí's article. One of the best he had produced to date, it was
the result of a fascination with Gaudí and Art Nouveau (which Dalí calls 'Modern Style')
that stretched back to the artist's childhood visits to Barcelona, where he had been
thrilled by the Parc Güell, with its crooked 'soft' columns, grottoes and dazzlingly
colourful mosaics. Later had come the impact of Gaudí's buildings in the Passeig de
Gràcia, particularly 'La Pedrera' (with its balconies of wrought iron expressing 'the
spume of the sea'), and, of course, his great unfinished church, the Sagrada Familia.

In the article Dalí recalls that in 1929, in *The Visible Woman*, he had been perhaps the
first painter of his generation to consider Art Nouveau architecture 'the most original
and extraordinary phenomenon in the history of art'. Since then he has come to the conclusion that Art Nouveau emanates from the world of dreams. In the flowing lines of a
single Art Nouveau window, he argues, we find Gothic metamorphosing into Hellenic,
Far Eastern and even Renaissance styles. Only dream language can match this.
Moreover, Art Nouveau, like the dream, expresses sexual desire. Dalí has heard people
comment, looking at Art Nouveau buildings, that 'you could eat them'. For him this puts
it in a nutshell. And, since if you love somebody you want to eat them, it follows that
Art Nouveau architecture is also intensely erotic. Dalí has found remarkable proof, in
the lamps presiding over the entrances to the Paris Métro, that Art Nouveau manifests
the urge to make a meal of the beloved: nobody has noticed that they are praying mantises! The accompanying illustration by the Hungarian photographer Brassaï (who had
met Dalí and Gala at Picasso's studio the previous year and had taken striking pictures
of them at their Rue Becquerel flat) forces one to agree this time with the justice of
Dalí's 'paranoiac-critical' insight.[143]

Dalí concluded by refining on Breton's famous pronouncement that 'Beauty will be convulsive or not at all.' 'The new Surrealist age of the "cannibalism of objects",' he proclaimed, 'equally justifies the following conclusion: Beauty will be *edible* or not at all.'

It was a remarkable *tour de force*, and Breton could not but be impressed. Nor was he the only one. In *La Nouvelle Revue Française*, the critic Jean Wahl had been struck by Dalí's contribution to this issue of *Minotaure*, which also contained his comments on painting to E. Tériade, a brief article on the phenomenon of ecstasy (accompanied by a collage of photographs taken by himself), a drawing (*The Horseman of Death*) and four engravings from Skira's forthcoming edition of *The Songs of Maldoror*. 'Dalí,' wrote Wahl,

> is a discoverer and a discovery, beyond any doubt one of the most authentic exponents of Surrealism. His comments to Tériade on objectivity and delirium, his pursuit of images capable of throwing us into ecstasy, his praise (in tune with Breton) of 'convulsive-ondulatory', 'terrifying and sublime' Art Nouveau, his idea of a dream space which should be the domain of the artist, his formula, so Baudelairian, that 'beauty is but the sum of the awareness of our perversions' . . . all of this is disturbing and exciting.

Such an accolade in such a publication was proof, if anyone now needed it, that by 1934 the Parisian literary and artistic establishment considered Dalí one of Surrealism's most authentic and original exponents.[144]

Gertrude Stein's Dalí

Gertrude Stein prided herself on being acquainted with everyone who was worth knowing in Paris, but so far had not met Dalí. Picasso, accordingly, announced that he would take him and Gala to see her. The couple arrived as planned—but Picasso did not turn up. Stein's recollections of the meeting, published in *Everybody's Autobiography* (1937), are not only amusing but contain some sharp insights into Dalí's personality. Stein had been to Spain and, as we have seen, knew and liked Picasso's great friend, Ramon Pichot, who had died in 1925. She had strong views on the country and its inhabitants. True Spaniards, for example, 'have no sense of time'; they are 'very brutal not brutal but callous to human emotions'; and, of course, they never listen: 'They do not hear what you say nor do they listen but they use for the thing they want to do what they are not hearing.' Dalí, certainly, was no listener but Stein did not mind, transfixed as she was by his moustache, 'the most beautiful moustache of any European and that moustache is Saracen there is no doubt about that and it is a most beautiful moustache there is no doubt about that'.[145]

Stein had been interested to learn that Dalí was the son of a notary, and her observations on the role played by these functionaries, so characteristic of life in France and Spain, are extremely perceptive. Moreover, she sensed that, where the arts are concerned, notaries' sons in both countries correspond more or less to ministers' in America and Britain, which is probably true: they are rebels. It appears from this account that Dalí himself told Stein about being thrown out by his father, and about the picture that had caused all the trouble, although it is possible that the source was Picasso, whom Dalí and Gala were seeing quite often at this time. At all events, Stein is understanding:

> He knew about Freud and he had the revolt of having a notary for his father and having his mother dead since he was a child. And so painting this picture with this motto was a natural thing and it made of him the most important of the painters who were Surrealists. Masson's wandering line had stopped wandering and he was lost just then, Miró had found out what he was to paint and he was continually painting the same thing, and so Dalí came and everybody knew about him.[146]

Stein might have mentioned that another and perhaps more important reason for Dalí's sudden impact was that the work of Yves Tanguy did not quite have the excitement that Surrealism required in 1929–30. Brassaï, who took the Parisian photographs for Dalí's *Minotaure* article on Art Nouveau, saw this clearly. Tanguy's 'desolate, dead planet beaches exercised a phantasmagorical appeal', but they lacked the 'convulsive beauty' that was then obsessing Breton and Éluard. Dalí, on the other hand, was 'the painter of dreams about whom they had long dreamt'. He could not fail to conquer.[147]

Nearly Another Expulsion

If Breton was still impressed by Dalí's art and valued him as a friend, he was becoming increasingly disturbed by his behaviour. On 23 January 1934 he wrote him a long letter. For years, he said, he had been trying to give him a fair hearing, even when some of his opinions were unacceptable (such as Dalí's claim that he preferred train accidents in which the third-class passengers suffered most). Dalí had justified himself by saying that he was the victim of a sexual perversion so peculiar to himself that the expression of such views could not therefore be dangerous. But Breton was not convinced. Dalí's opinions, he believed, had permanently damaged Surrealism. His 'anti-humanitarianism' particularly revolted the older man. How could he possibly say that his friends' mishaps delighted him? Breton had thought until recently that Dalí was reserving for his Surrealist companions the 'paradoxical and delirious' opinions inspired in him by Hitler. But the previous Thursday he had heard him publicly praise the Nazi government for its 'worst exactions'. Could he and Dalí now possibly be on the same side?

Breton had also been outraged to hear Dalí defend academic painting and deprecate 'modern art'. How could he adopt such a stance, demanding a return to Meissonier when modern art was being attacked violently in both Nazi Germany and Communist Russia? Dalí was now also arguing in favour of the 'profound reality of the family' and of the need for paternal authority. The latter, Breton concluded, explained his dangerous faith in Hitler. Breton was in no doubt: Dalí had become a reactionary. Surrealism implied above all a certain moral rigour, a certain concern for moral integrity. It could not and must not abandon its principles, its belief in the need for proletarian revolution. Dalí was now travelling in another direction.

There was the question of *The Enigma of William Tell*, too. Breton was appalled by this gigantic painting, which portrays Tell as a smiling Lenin with a grotesquely distorted and elongated naked buttock propped up by a crutch. He considered it academic and 'ultra-conscious', and believed that it adhered to Surrealism only by the merest thread. And what about Dalí's recent private showing of the painting at his studio? What had that to do with Surrealism? Breton had been among the guests and it had shocked him to see Dalí's concessions to 'society'. The painter wanted flattery. He wanted to be wanted. This was incompatible with the nature of Surrealism.

Then came the nub of the letter. Would Dalí be prepared to sign an assurance, to be published in the first issue of the new Surrealist review Breton was planning, in which he denied any appreciation of German Fascism? The text should also make it clear that there was no fundamental discrepancy between Dalí's views and the Surrealists' hopes for proletarian revolution. And would Dalí be good enough to renounce attacking systematically the artistic achievements of the last sixty or eighty years? Particularly now that German artists were being forced to leave their country? Breton ended by insisting that Dalí reply in writing, immediately and explicitly, to his questions. It depended on his answers whether they could remain together, something he, Breton, very much desired.[148]

Dalí sat down at once and, with Gala's help, wrote an eight-page reply, taking Breton's points one by one.

On the question of his alleged 'anti-humanitarianism', his position was foreseeable.

Yes, it was a fact that he experienced pleasure when mishaps occurred to his friends. In the case of close friends this pleasure was explicitly sexual, even giving him an erection. A sexual perversion, he admitted, but was it his fault? Moreover he was only following the dictates of Sade, his guide where morals were concerned (as he had made clear in his answers to the Yugoslav enquiry on desire).

Modern art? Dalí reminded Breton that he had already explained his position in the open letter to him printed in the catalogue for his last Pierre Colle exhibition, and which Breton had praised. Since then Dalí's opinions had not changed. Nevertheless, for the record, he now wanted to clarify that he was only talking about modern art produced outside the orbit of Surrealism. To be precise, he was in favour of Tanguy, Ernst, De Chirico, Magritte and so on and against artists such as Utrillo, Mondrian, Vlaminck, Kisling, Derain, Ozenfant, Chagall and Matisse. The former drew on the unconscious, the latter were 'intellectualist'. Gris, Braque and the experimental side of Cubism he excepted from his anathema and, of course, Picasso, 'a vital phenomenon very often surpassing the most ambitiously Surrealist previsions'. Dalí concluded this section of his long letter by insisting that only an academic technique (admittedly indefensible from an aesthetic point of view) was capable of reproducing the visions and images of the unconscious, of the 'new delirious world to which we are beginning to have access'. In short, Böcklin was more Surrealist than Matisse.

As for the charge of Hitlerism, few books would be consigned more readily to the flames by both Nazis and Communists than *The Visible Woman, Love and Memory* and the poem he had just written (not identified). Of this, Dalí said, Breton was well aware. The painter then revealed that he had written a 'vast study' on German racism which proved that Hitler was a nurse with particularly evil-smelling testicles and foreskin, compressed in the same way as the genitals of Napoleon. He was sure that such 'paranoiac-critical' considerations would not go down well in the Third Reich! Nor would his paintings fare any better than his writings in either Russia or National-Socialist Germany. Dalí denied point-blank that he was in favour of Hitler, but insisted on his right to interpret the phenomenon for himself, given the fact that the Communists were totally failing to do so. Hitlerism, he said, was shaking his intellectual convictions in the political sphere, and should do so for anyone not a prey to 'frenetic mysticism'. It was his duty to try and penetrate to the hidden causes of the phenomenon.

Dalí went on to say that, insofar as it was possible, he would always subordinate his personal ideas to the demands of Surrealist group activity. As for *The Enigma of William Tell*, what difference was there between exhibiting it in his own studio or at Pierre Colle's, where he would certainly have shown it had the gallery not shut down? With his work he always tried to disturb as many people as possible. *The Enigma of William Tell* was no exception, the more so since the protagonist was his father who wanted to eat him, while the piece of meat placed on the buttocks represented the paternal testicles. He might have added, as he did thirty years later, that he was the child the cannibalistic Tell was rocking in his arms and that, if the viewer looked closely, he would see that a tiny nut next to Tell's left foot was a cradle containing Gala and about to be crushed by the monster. Dalí Cusí in the guise of Tell is out to kill not only his son, therefore, but his partner, the threat being magnified by the enormous size of the figure's body, emphasized by the dimensions of the painting itself (201.9 x 146 cm). In 1974 the artist recalled that the painting reflected one of the 'most dangerous moments' in his life.[149]

In regard to the palinode required by Breton, Dalí was prepared to sign a collective Surrealist manifesto in this line provided it did not involve disowning anything he had written up to that moment. But no more. He ended by asking Breton to trust in his 'Surrealist unconditionality' and that he had the situation under control.[150]

Perhaps as an antidote to all this hassle, Dalí and Gala decided to get married. Moreover, Éluard had been urging Gala for a year to do so, warning her that if Dalí died she might be left with nothing, not least in view of the fact that his father had disinherited him and would probably seize all his paintings in Port Lligat.[151] The ceremony took place in the town hall of the fourteenth *arrondissement* on the morning of 30 January 1934. Éluard was not present—perhaps he would have found the occasion too painful. The witnesses were Yves Tanguy—which implies that the Dalís had very friendly relations with him at this time—and one André Gaston, described, like Tanguy, as an 'artiste-peintre'. He lived in the same building as the Dalís at 7, Rue Gauguet.[152]

Dalí's notion of 'having the situation under control' was different from Breton's, and he had another disagreeable surprise in store for the Surrealist leader. On 2 February 1934, the fiftieth anniversary exhibition of the Salon des Indépendants opened at the Grand Palais. The Surrealists had decided not to participate, but Dalí defied group discipline and sent, of all paintings, *The Enigma of William Tell* (along with an inoffensive drawing, *The Cannibalism of Objects*), telling Charles de Noailles that he hoped thereby to enable his work to reach a wide public.[153] The gesture was considered by Breton the last straw. On the opening day a resolution was passed by him, Victor Brauner, Ernst, Jacques Hérold, Georges Hugnet, Meret Oppenheim, Péret and Tanguy. It proposed that Dalí, guilty of 'several counter-revolutionary acts tending to the glorification of Hitlerian Fascism', be excluded from the Surrealist movement 'as a Fascist element' and combated by all possible means. It was also proposed that Pierre Yoyotte, accused of aid-ing and abetting Dalí in his 'counter-revolutionary activity', should be suspended until he revised his views.[154] Roger Caillois, who left before the meeting ended, proposed in writing that Dalí be ousted from the movement on the grounds that his views on racial conflict (which the painter maintained was essentially different from the class struggle) were incompatible with Surrrealism's adherence to the cause of the proletariat.[155] The angry conclave, led by Breton, then visited the exhibition with the intention of damaging the offensive painting. But they discovered to their chagrin that it hung so high on the wall that it was out of reach of their sticks.[156]

The following day the resolution to exclude Dalí was communicated to all the members of the group and a special meeting to discuss the case was convened for 5 February. Crevel, Éluard, Giacometti and Tzara, out of Paris at the time, were invited to give their opinions in writing.[157] As for Dalí himself, he received a curt letter from Breton, who upbraided him for not having attended the meetings held on 2 and 3 February, explained about the resolution and warned him to make sure that he was present on 5 February. When half of the letter was written, Breton received a *pneumatique* (express communication transmitted by pneumatic tube) from Dalí in which the latter apparently pleaded his cause with eloquence. But Breton was not to be moved, saying that, while he felt geniune admiration and affection for the painter, it was his most elementary duty to forgo his personal feelings at this moment in the interests of maintaining the revolutionary purity of the Surrealist movement. If Dalí did not act decisively to clarify his position to the satisfaction of the group, he would be regarded henceforth as the representative of a particularly dangerous deviation.[158]

No strictly contemporary account of the meeting on 5 February has come to light. Later ones, including Dalí's, conflict, and in several cases seem to incorporate anecdotal material from previous gatherings. The most detailed version, at all events, is Hugnet's, and it is broadly ratified by Marcel Jean's. Dalí, who had a cold and had come equipped with a thermometer and numerous layers of warm clothing, which he kept taking off and then putting on again, apparently turned the trial into little short of a farce. Even Breton found it hard to keep a straight face, there was outright laughter, and Dalí managed to talk himself out of trouble—for the time being.[159]

The extreme uneasiness that Dalí's attitude to Hitler was now producing in Breton is better understood when we take into account that France at this time was rife with political dissension and that, on 6 February 1934, the day after Dalí's 'trial', the Fascists provoked a riot in Paris in which twelve people were killed. Within a week a general strike had been called and Édouard Daladier, who had been prime minister for only a few days, was forced to resign. The Third Republic seemed to be floundering.[160]

Paul Éluard was also worried about Dalí's obsession with the Führer. He and Tzara had written to Breton complaining about the attacks to which the painter was being subjected within the group, he told Gala. But he had to admit that Dalí's 'Hitlerian-para-noiac attitude' would have 'almost unsurmountable consequences' if he persisted in it. *'It's absolutely necessary* for Dalí to find another subject of delirium,' he recommended.[161]

Having narrowly avoided expulsion from the movement, Dalí now returned to Port Lligat, where at the beginning of March he and Gala received a delightful, chatty communication from Breton. The latter was working on a new edition of *Surrealism and Painting*, and was surprised that Dalí (about to be included) had not sent the promised illustrations. Publication had had to be put off until the painter's return to Paris as a result, but Breton did not appear at all irritated. The fifth number of *Minotaure* was under way and he wanted Dalí to write something on ghosts, tailors' dummies and so forth. He thought it would be a good excuse for using the lovely photographs Man Ray had taken in Cadaqués, including those showing Dalí with a loaf of bread on his head. (Dalí complied, sending 'The New Colours of Sex Appeal'.) Breton then referred to his determination to reestablish efficient group action (always one of the principal tenets of Surrealism), and ended by expressing the fervent hope that Dalí and Gala would forget the recent 'difficulties', which he felt sure were merely transient. He wanted them to be assured of his deep affection. It was, for Breton, a very warm letter indeed, almost brotherly. Dalí replied with equal affability, blaming a maid for mislaying the photographs. After the storm, it seemed that the halcyon days had returned.[162]

The euphoria of the reconciliation continued to waft through their correspondence over the coming months. On 11 April, while Julien Levy was showing Dalí's *Maldoror* plates and drawings in New York,[163] the painter lectured on Surrealism at the Ateneu Enclicopèdic Popular in Barcelona, taking the opportunity, he told Breton, of setting the balance straight on the subject of his alleged conversion to Hitlerism. At the end of the lecture, he said, he had been heckled by a group of Communists, who succeeded briefly in swaying the audience against him, but had won the day. The only press report of the event that has come to light suggests, however, that Dalí did not succeed in convincing everyone present of his innocence. 'Dalí only just fell short of declaring himself a Nazi,' commented *La Publicitat*.[164]

By an extraordinary coincidence, Federico García Lorca disembarked in Barcelona on the morning of Dalí's lecture after a triumphant six months in Buenos Aires. An interview with the poet appeared a few days later on the front page of *La Publicitat*. Now hugely famous, Lorca expressed his dissatisfaction with the contemporary Spanish theatre and made it clear that he intended to do his best to revolutionize it.[165] He and Dalí did not meet in Barcelona (he left for Madrid the evening of his arrival), but we can be sure that the painter read the interview (he considered *La Publicitat* his newspaper in Barcelona)—and that he was impressed by his old friend's meteoric rise to international celebrity. A few days later he wrote him a postcard from Cadaqués:

> I'm sure we'd enjoy seeing each other again. Do you want to? You've passed through Barcelona, what a shame you didn't come to Cadaqués where I'm spending a few months! After 2 May I'm going to Paris for a month. I've a big project for an opera based on important characters: Sacher-Masoch, Louis II of Bavaria, Wagner [?], etc. I think you and I could do something together. If you came to see me we'd now agree much better on a lot of things. Gala's desperate to meet you.

Had Federico seen the latest issue of *Minotaure* (no. 3–4, published the previous December), Dalí went on? He wanted him to read his article on Art Nouveau architecture. Also Éluard's piece on picture postcards and Breton's *mise au point* on the subject of communication. The latter, Dalí assured Lorca, was very, very important. Signing off as 'Your Buddha' (as he had sometimes done in the Residencia de Estudiantes days), Dalí ordered him to write immediately. The poet could hardly have received a more pressing invitation to resume their relationship. But if he replied (and it is difficult to imagine that he did not) the letter has not been found.[166]

Dalí's discovery of Sacher-Masoch was inevitable, given his obsession with Sade and sexual deviations in general, and there are numerous allusions to the author of *Venus in Furs* in his drawings of the period. As for Louis II, the mad boy-king of Bavaria, protector of Wagner and founder of Bayreuth, he was fast becoming another of Dalí's obsessions, not least because of the erotic excesses imputed to him. Having just read that Lorca intended to revolutionize the Spanish theatre, Dalí, no doubt correctly, felt that a project involving such unconventional personages might appeal to the poet-dramatist-musician. But the desired collaboration never took place.

Exhibitions in Brussels, London, Paris

Dalí and Gala were back in Paris at the beginning of May, their minds for the moment on Brussels, where a Surrealist issue of the review *Documents 34* was about to appear, coinciding with an exhibition on *Minotaure* organized by Albert Skira. The issue was strongly anti-Fascist in tone (the deaths in Paris in February were to the forefront of the editors' minds), but this is not reflected in Dalí's text, 'The Latest Modes of Intellectual

Excitement for the Summer of 1934', notable only because it was apparently the first time the painter had referred to himself publicly in the third person, a practice soon to become habitual. 'If you wish to be as "well preserved anachronically" as possible and desirable,' he wrote, 'pay close attention to the ideas and systems of Salvador Dalí, some of which follow.' All the reader had to do was to engage in 'paranoiac-critical activity' as defined by its begetter ('a spontaneous method of "irrational knowledge" based on the critical and systematic objectivization of delirious associations and interpretations'), and which had already proved its use in *The Tragic Myth of Millet's Angelus*. One of Dalí's weaker efforts, the piece suggests that so much thinking about paranoia was beginning to tell on his relation to the world around him.[167]

Dalí travelled to Brussels for the *Minotaure* exhibition (12 May–3 June 1934), sending a card to Foix. Among his contributions were *The Great Masturbator* (which all his life he would refuse to sell), an unidentified painting of Gala by the sea, and a large drawing, *Cannibalism of Objects*. Breton lent *William Tell*.[168]

The Brussels show coincided with a 'Bores, Beaudin, Dalí' exhibition in London, which ran at the Zwemmer Gallery from 14 May to 2 June 1934. The exhibition catalogue listed five unidentified drawings by Dalí and an etching, *Fantasie*, from a 'signed edition of 100' not registered by Michler and Löpsinger in their standard work on Dalí's graphics. The catalogue explained that, since Dalí's etchings for *The Songs of Maldoror* had regrettably not arrived on time, they would be shown at a later date. It is almost certain that Dalí and Gala visited London for the show, staying with a new friend, Edward James, at his luxurious Wimpole Street residence.[169]

Edward James was a friend of Charles and Marie-Laure de Noailles, and it was through the latter that he had entered the world of ballet and music in Paris and begun to commission work from young composers such as Darius Milhaud, Poulenc and Henri Sauguet. He said later that he had become aware of Dalí when, staying with the Noailleses at Hyères, in 1932, he

Dalí with Gala and Edward James in Rome, 1930s.

saw his arresting portrait of Marie-Laure. When he and Dalí first met is not certain, although it seems that it was at Hyères in the summer of 1933 and that the encounter was followed by another that took place some weeks later at Mas Juny, the spectacular villa owned by the painter Josep Maria Sert at Palamós on the Costa Brava, eighty kilometres down the coast from Cadaqués. James was interested in Surrealism, and from the beginning had helped to finance Albert Skira's *Minotaure*.

Given Dalí's passionate admiration for aristocrats, particularly when rich, and equally fervent craving for patronage, Edward James must have seemed the answer to his most paranoid dreams. Born in 1907, three years after Dalí, James, godson of Edward VII, had inherited a fortune from his industrialist father on coming of age. He was handsome, sensitive, affable, eccentric, a brilliant raconteur with a love of poetry and art, and seemed destined for happiness and success. Yet behind the charming exterior of this diminutive and fastidiously dressed personage there was an emotionally deprived and deeply disturbed little boy who had been permanently wounded by the rejection of his bluestocking mother, Evelyn Forbes ('the most admired hostess of the Edwardian period'),[170] and who had suffered the usual English-style bullying at his prep school and then Eton before going up to Oxford. Towards the end of his life, in a poem aptly titled 'The Sum', he put it succinctly:

> Fate from her balance gave me wealth
> of farms and castles and field and hill . . .
> then, with these, in her bitter stealth
> she mixed in the blight of a sick weak will.
>
> To this starved rich child, there might belong
> not money only; that strains might come
> Fate added even the gift of song:
> yet love she gave not. That is my sum.[171]

When James divorced his wife, the ballerina Tilly Losch, in 1934, she said in court that he was homosexual. His biographers tend to agree, although, if gay, James did not flaunt it (as George Melly once put it, brilliantly imitating James's squeaky voice, 'Edward was and *wasn't* homosexual').[172] Indeed, James was very guarded about his private life. Dalí, always fascinated by sexual ambiguity, must have found the hidden side to his new friend as appealing as his wealth.[173] James was not yet Dalí's patron, but he was on the point of becoming so and it seems likely that it was he who had brought the artist to the attention of Zwemmer's.

It was the first time that Dalí's work had been seen in London. The young poet David Gascoyne, about to join the Surrealists in Paris, could hardly contain his enthusiasm. 'Salvador Dalí is the most important living literary painter,' he wrote in the *New English Weekly*.[174]

Meanwhile preparations were going ahead for the launch of Skira's edition of *The Songs of Maldoror*, which was held on 13 June at the Quatre Chemins bookshop (99, Boulevard Raspail). On show were the forty-two Dalí engravings included in the book and thirty related drawings. In the catalogue, as we have seen, Dalí went to some lengths to justify the allusions to Millet's *Angelus* featuring in so many of the works exhibited.

Pierre Colle's had closed, so for his end-of-season show Dalí switched this year to the nearby Jacques Bonjean Gallery at 3, Rue d'Argenson. The wide-ranging exhibition ran from 20 June to 13 July and received an appreciative review from Louis Chéronnet in *Art et Décoration*.[175] Introducing the catalogue was a brief text in which Dalí stated that the works on show constituted 'instantaneous handmade colour photographs of subconscious, Surrealist, extravagant, paranoiac, hypnagogic, extra-pictorial, phenomenal, super-abundant, super-fine, etc. images of Concrete Irrationality'. The insistence on photography chimed with Dalí's statements elsewhere at this time: Surrealist art, at any rate *his* Surrealist art, consisted in the meticulous, academic annotation of images welling up from the depths of the unconscious.

Forty-seven paintings and drawings were on exhibition, along with two sculptures, four Surrealist Objects and a selection of Dalí's illustrations for Skira's edition of *The Songs of Maldoror*. Of the paintings and drawings, seventeen proceeded from private collectors, mainly members of the Zodiac. The minute *The Spectre of Sex Appeal* was undoubtedly the finest work now shown for the first time, and *Atmospheric Skeleton Sodomizing a Grand Piano* (1934) the most calculated to stop viewers in their tracks. If Rafael Santos Torroella is right, the picture, set on the beach at Port Lligat, alludes to Lorca's attempts to bugger the painter and shows that, despite the advent of Gala, these were still very much on Salvador's mind. The painter, that is, continued to be racked by the anxiety that, despite his protestations to the contrary, he might after all be homosexual.[176]

Once the exhibition opened the Dalís returned to Port Lligat, where in August Gala heard from Éluard that he was going to marry Nusch the following day and was disturbed to find himself sunk in melancholy. Éluard still dreamt about Gala naked, was missing her more and more and was sure that one day they would be together again.[177]

But it was too late: all Gala's efforts were now directed towards assuring Dalí's fame and

I Ramón Pichot, *Cala Nans*, undated. Oil and cardboard, 36 x 48 cm. One of the Pichots that inspired Dalí to become an Impressionist.

II *Fair of the Holy Cross*, 1921. Gouache on card, 52 x 75 cm.

III *Bañistas de Es Llané*, 1923. Oil on cardboard, 72 x 103 cm. Dalí was a lifelong worshipper of the female posterior.

IV *Night-Walking Dreams*, 1922. Watercolour on paper, 51.5 x 24 cm. A late-night foray through downtown Madrid with Luis Buñuel and Maruja Mallo.

V *Still Life (Syphon and Bottle of Rum)*, 1924. Oil on canvas, 125 x 99 cm. One of the paintings given by Dalí to Lorca.

VI *Figure at a Window*, 1925. Oil on canvas, 103 x 75 cm. Anna Maria Dalí contemplates the bay of Cadaqués from a window of the family's summer house at Es Llané.

VII *Girl from Figueres*, 1926. Oil on canvas, 21 x 25 cm. The view from the balcony of the Dalís' second home in Figueres, at Carrer Monturiol 24. This was the painting Dalí showed Picasso on his first visit to Paris in April 1926.

VIII *Still Life (Invitation to Sleep)*, 1926. Oil on canvas, 100 x 100 cm. Dalí's celebration of Lorca's enactments of his own death (see photograph on p. 179).

IX *Composition with Three Figures (Neo-Cubist Academy)*, 1926. Oil on canvas 200 x 200 cm. One of Dalí's greatest paintings from the mid-1920s, not exhibited since 1927. The influence of Picasso is manifest (see photograph on p. 189). It develops the theme of Saint Sebastian that so fascinated Lorca and Dalí.

X *Gadget and Hand (Apparatus and Hand)*, 1927. Oil on panel, 62.2 x 47.6 cm. Arguably the red hand of the guilty masturbator, surrounded by the components of his fantasies.

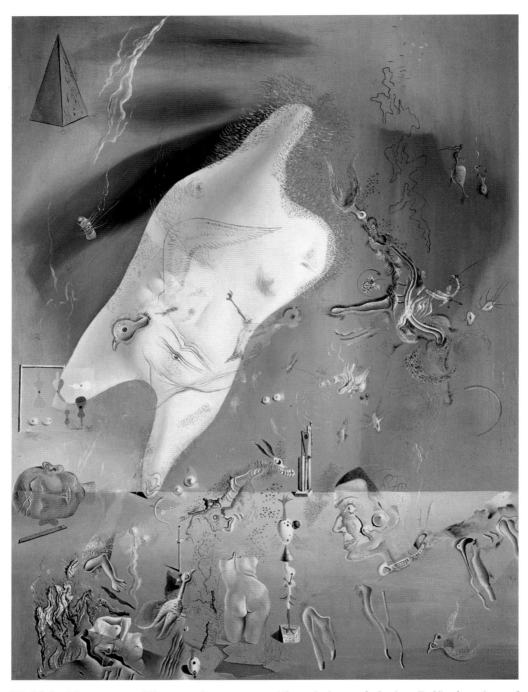

XI *Little Ashes*, 1927–8. Oil on panel, 64 x 48 cm. The painting anthologizes Dalí's obsessions of the moment.

XII *Dialogue on the Beach (Unsatisfied Desires)*, 1928. Oil, seashells and sand on cardboard. The painting they refused to show in Barcelona.

XIII *The First Days of Spring*, 1929. Oil and collage on panel, 49.5 x 64 cm. Dalí took this work to Paris in 1929. Robert Desnos, he said, was deeply impressed. It marks Dalí's full entrance into the Surrealist orbit.

XIV *The Great Masturbator*, 1929. Oil on canvas, 110 x 150 cm. The figure of the masturbator was inspired in part by a rock formation at Creus (see photograph on p. 71).

XV *The Lugubrious Game*, 1929. Oil and collage on cardboard, 44.4 x 30.3 cm. The title was suggested by Paul Éluard. This was the painting that first alerted Dalí's family to his change of direction in the summer of 1929, and which led the Surrealists to suspect that he was a coprophagist. It contains one of Dalí's first representations of the ashamed adolescent.

XVI *Illumined Pleasures*, 1929. Oil on panel, 24 x 34.5 cm. One of Dalí's most Freudian paintings. Indeed, the elderly gentleman helping the lady in distress seems to be Freud himself, borrowed from Ernst's *Pietà or Revolution by Night* (see photograph on p. 284).

XVII Jean-François Millet, *The Angelus*, 1857. One of Dalí's lifelong obsessions, the painting inspired his most original art criticism.

XVIII *The Profanation of the Host*, 1929. Oil on canvas, 100 x 73 cm. Dalí's variation on Paolo Uccello's work of the same title, this is probably his most sacrilegious painting.

XIX *Imperial Monument to the Child-Woman*, 1930. Oil on canvas, 140 x 80 cm. The Child-Woman is Gala, who appears here for the first time in Dalí's work.

XX *William Tell*, 1930. Oil and collage on canvas, 113 x 87 cm. One of Dalí's more shocking comments on his relationship with his father. The painting belonged to André Breton (see photograph on p. 320).

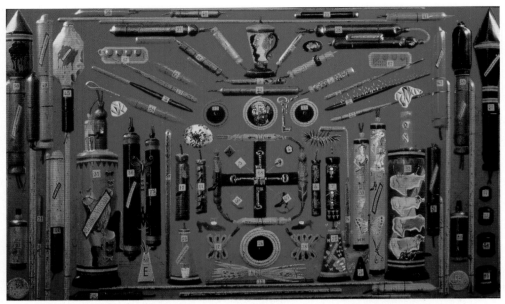

XXI *Board of Demented Associations (Fireworks)*, 1930–1. Oil on embossed tin, 40 x 65.5 cm. The dedication reads 'Painted for Paul Éluard by his friend Salvador Dalí'. Éluard, who enjoyed his erotica as much as Dalí, must have been impressed by this *tour de force*.

XXII *The Old Age of William Tell*, 1931. Oil on canvas, 98 x 140 cm. Action behind the sheet, in the presence of the ubiquitous lion. Dalí said the painting referred to his and Gala's repudiation by his father. There are allusions to Gala's operation, which Dalí feared might be fatal.

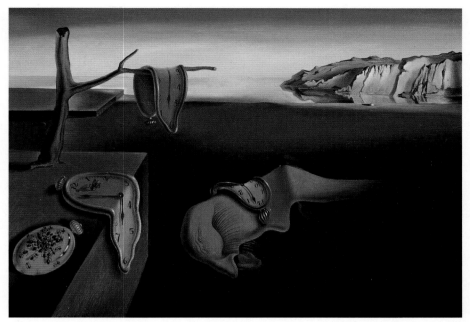

XXIII *The Persistence of Memory*, 1931. Oil on canvas, 24 x 33 cm. Thanks to the advent of the melting watch, perhaps Dalí's most famous painting.

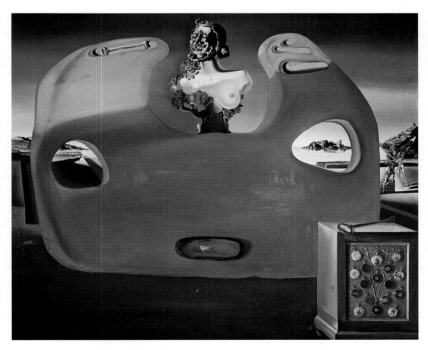

XXIV *Memory of the Child-Woman*, 1931. Oil on canvas, 99 x 119.3 cm. The painting perhaps suggests that Dalí's father, in the guise of William Tell (represented here as a bust), was not indifferent to the charms of Gala.

XXV *The Spectre of Sex Appeal*, 1932. Oil on canvas, 18 x 14 cm. Dalí at his miniaturist best in a tiny work expressive of his sexual anxieties.

XXVI *Soft Construction with Boiled Beans*, 1936. Oil on canvas, 100 x 99 cm. This great painting was later renamed, with fitting opportunism, *The Premonition of Civil War.*

XXVII *Outskirts of the Paranoiac-Critical Town*, 1936. Oil on panel, 46 x 66 cm. The painting belonged to Edward James. The 'paranoiac-critical town' is composed of elements deriving principally from Cadaqués and Palamós.

XXVIII *The Great Paranoiac*, 1936. Oil on canvas, 62 x 62 cm. The painting belonged to Edward James. Surely one of Dalí's finest double images.

XXIX *Metamorphosis of Narcissus*, 1936–7. Oil on canvas, 50.8 x 78.3 cm. This is the painting Dalí took to show Freud in London. It belonged formerly to Edward James.

XXX *The Endless Enigma*, 1938. Oil on canvas, 114.3 x 144 cm. The ever-present, brooding presence of Lorca.

XXXI *Galarina*, 1944–5. Oil on canvas, 64.1 x 50.2 cm. Perhaps Dalí's most honest appraisal of his Muse.

XXXII *Atomic and Uranian Melancholic Idyll*, 1945. Oil on canvas, 65 x 85 cm. The atom bomb was good news for Dalí's commercial art.

XXXIII *My Wife, Nude, Contemplating Her Own Body Transformed into Steps, the Three Vertebrae of a Column, Sky and Architecture,* 1945. Oil on wood, 61 x 52 cm. One of Dalí's finest paintings from the 1940s.

XXXIV *The Madonna of Port Lligat*, 1949 (first version). Oil on canvas, 49.5 x 38.3 cm. Dalí's atomic variation on the Assumption, with Gala as tutelary goddess of Port Lligat.

XXXV *Leda Atomica*, 1949. Oil on canvas, 61.1 x 45.3 cm. Gala-Leda rendered 'in accordance with the modern "nothing touches" theory of intra-atomic physics' (Dalí).

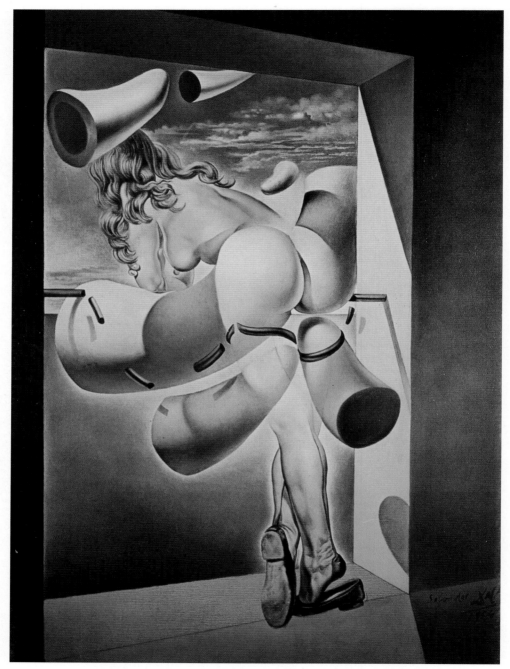

XXXVI *Young Virgin Auto-Sodomized by the Horns of her Own Chastity*, 1954. Oil on canvas, 40.5 x 30.5 cm. Dalí prided himself on being the world's greatest ever painter of the female posterior.

XXXVII *The Discovery of America by Christopher Columbus*, 1958–9. Oil on canvas, 410 x 284 cm. Dalí and Gala had every reason to be grateful to America, which had showered them with dollars. Here, as Columbus, the painter kneels on the shore, holding aloft a silver crucifix. Gala appears once more as Virgin Mary, on the banner.

XXXVIII *The Hallucinogenic Toreador*, 1969–70. Oil on canvas, 398.8 x 299.7 cm. Optical tricks galore and, yet again, the presence of Lorca.

their joint fortune. This meant, among other things, organizing the practical side of the painter's life and assuming a dazzling social role at his side in Paris, Barcelona and at Josep Maria Sert's villa in Palamós, where this summer the couple were again in attendance, perhaps accompanied by Edward James.[178] As regards big money, Gala must have felt convinced, by the summer of 1934, that it was to be made, if anywhere, in America, where Julien Levy was now preparing a new Dalí exhibition for the autumn. It was to be a show with a difference, for this time, Dalí informed Foix, he intended to be there in person.[179]

Foix continued to be Dalí's main ally in Barcelona, not least because the painter knew he could always count on free publicity in the aptly named, so far as he was concerned, *La Publicitat*. Dalí had one bone of contention, however: in August, when *L'Age d'or* was shown at a cinema club, the announcement in *La Publicitat* for the film had excluded his name as co-scriptwriter. Dalí's anger was an indication of how very seriously he took his involvement in the controversial film, which had now acquired mythical status. Dalí asked Foix to intervene, but since the advertisements had been inserted by the club, not the newspaper, there was little he could do. Was Buñuel in any way responsible for the suppression of Dalí's name? The painter suspected it. Back in Paris in the autumn his fears were confirmed when he discovered that his name had been removed from the credits of *Un Chien andalou*, then being shown again in Studio 28. A bitter letter was dashed off to Buñuel, whose reply, which has not come to light, failed to satisfy him. Dalí then wrote again, this time more angrily. And soon he began to think about revenge.[180]

Revolution in Barcelona

Since 1931 the Paris Surrealists, with Crevel to the fore, had been following the fortunes, and misfortunes, of the Second Spanish Republic with extreme interest and concern. The left-wing revolution they had hoped for had not taken place, to be sure, but nonetheless great progress had been made between 1931 and 1933 in dragging the country into the twentieth century. The fiercest battle had been fought in the field of primary and secondary education, which for centuries had been controlled by the Church. In 1931, out of a population of 25 million, 32.4 per cent of Spaniards were illiterate and it was estimated that 27,150 new schools were needed. In thirty years of monarchy, only 11,128 had been built; but by 1934 the Republic had created 13,570.[181]

The reforming zeal of the Republic, to no small degree shaped by the spirit emanating from the Free Teaching Institute and its offshoot, the Residencia de Estudiantes, was not limited to education. Among the controversial measures pushed through before the Right won the elections of 1933, were divorce, the secularization of cemeteries and hospitals, the reduction of the religious orders and the, admittedly timid, initiation of agrarian reform, vital to satisfy the aspirations of the landless peasants.[182]

It had not been easy going. No sooner was the Republic in place than the Catholic Church had begun its attacks on the new democracy and the disgruntled monarchists their conspiracy to bring it down. In the summer of 1932 a military rising against the Government had been suppressed without difficulty, but behind the scenes the plot continued. The conspirators were facilitated by the Republicans themselves, who in the autumn of 1933, rent by internal divisions, had failed to form a common front to fight the general elections. As a result the Right, spurred on by the advance of Fascism in Europe, won a resounding victory. Over the next two years much of the progressive legislation achieved in the previous two was to be undone, and land reform completely halted. The death penalty was restored; José María Gil Robles's Catholic Party, the largest right-wing group in the country, grew more militant by the day and sprouted a large, quasi-Fascist youth organization; while the Fascist party proper, the Falange Española, resorted increasingly to Hitlerian bully-boy tactics. The spectre of civil war was looming.[183]

The situation took a decisive turn for the worse in the autumn of 1934. On 1 October there was a cabinet reshuffle in which the Catholic Party obtained three vital ministries: Agriculture, Labour and Justice. The reaction of the Left was to assume that these appointments spelt the beginning of a Fascist takeover fashioned on that which had catapulted Hitler to power the previous year. The trade unions took immediate action, calling a revolutionary general strike for 4 October.

The strike was supported massively in the Basque provinces, the coal-mining region of Asturias, and Catalunya. In Barcelona the 'Catalan Republic within the Spanish Federal Republic' was proclaimed on 6 October. The daring and dangerous bid lasted for only ten hours before the rebellion was put down by the army, largely without bloodshed. The rising in Asturias fared better, and was not crushed until 15 October by units of the Spanish army in Africa, with considerable loss of life. Thousands of political prisoners now thronged Spain's gaols. It was a further step down the road to civil war.[184]

Dalí had arrived in Barcelona from Port Lligat a few days before the rising to attend an exhibition of his most recent paintings at the Llibreria Catalònia and give a lecture entitled 'The Surreal and Phenomenal Mystery of the Bedside Table'. The show ran from 2 to 4 October. It comprised only five works, all of miniature proportions: *The Weaning of Furniture-Nutrition, Goldfinch-Goldfinch* (later entitled *Cardinal Bird-Cardinal Bird*), *Mediumistic-Paranoiac Image, Materialization of Autumn* (. . . *At Seven it's Already Night*) and *Hypnagogic Image of Gala*.[185] Dalí was unable to give his lecture on 5 October, when the shutters came crashing down in central Barcelona and the Catalans took to the streets to defy the central Government. No such defiance could be expected from Dalí, however. If we can afford any credence to the highly colourful and witty account of these hours included in the *Secret Life*, he and Gala fled hell-for-leather to the French frontier on 6 October in a taxi driven by an anarchist, barely escaping with their lives. There is no mention in the book of Dalí's reunion with his old friend J.V. Foix in Barcelona the previous day, carefully documented by Santos Torroella; nor of the important interview granted to the art critic Just Cabot, the man who, a year earlier, had savaged his exhibition at the Llibreria Catalònia.[186]

Dalí read Cabot the lecture that circumstances had prevented him from delivering. More a Surrealist poem than a talk, it analysed that banal object, the bedside table, in terms of the different notions of space current from Euclid to Einstein. The demanding nature of the theme, Cabot reported, was duly relieved by the occasional irreverence and scatological allusion without which no Dalí talk would be complete. The artist, excited by his imminent trip to New York, told him that the time was ripe for the Americans to meet him face to face, and that he reckoned Surrealism was about to take off on the other side of the Atlantic. To assist the process, he was taking with him a film project: a revamping in cinematographic terms of the operatic project he had proposed to Lorca, and which starred Wagner, Sacher-Masoch and Louis II of Bavaria.

As regards what he was attempting to achieve in his Surrealist paintings, Dalí had never expressed himself so clearly in an interview. People were surprised, commented Cabot, by the almost 'calligraphic' detail of these works. Dalí explained:

> My ambition is to give the world of the imagination the same degree of objectivity and reality as the everyday world. What Surrealism revolutionizes above all is art's themes, and to express these I use the same means as always. It's the themes, derived from Freudianism, that are new. In this way, using the most habitual and traditional means, the images are more effective and convincing. Abstraction has led to decorativism, while my method goes back to the great sources of painting. I now look at the pictures of Vermeer, Leonardo, etc., and concentrate (as well as on their technique) on their enigmatic side, which we need to examine afresh, differently. In a word, we have to rewrite the history of painting.

Dalí explained that he was aware that the application of Freudian theory to art could lead to problems of misunderstanding. For instance, take that painting of his that had irresponsibly been interpreted as an insult to his family (the one of the Sacred Heart of Jesus bearing the inscription 'Sometimes I spit for pleasure on the portrait of my mother'). How could anyone still believe that it had been intended as an affront? 'I have always had the greatest love for my mother and father,' Dalí explained. 'In the case in question, all I wanted to demonstrate, in the most dramatic way possible, was the discrepancy, the traumatic rupture, existing between the conscious and the unconscious. That such a rupture exists is demonstrated by the frequent dream, reported time and again, in which we assassinate someone we love.'[187]

An Attempt at Family Reconciliation

Dalí was making energetic attempts at this time to persuade his father to accept him back into the bosom of the family, so it is significant that he raised the issue of the guilty picture while talking to Cabot. Although he had written to his father directly about the matter, his main hope was his supportive uncle, Rafael Dalí, who now sent a brief if impassioned letter to Figueres:

> My Dear Brother,
>
> I've received a registered letter from your son which I include. Don't lose it, and give it back to me when we meet. I, who never keep anything, have kept everything by your son since he was a child, and have drawings and paintings from when he was four, which shows that I was already totally certain that one day he'd be a famous artist. You and I are now only ten years away from our deaths. I'm certain that your son is genuinely repentant.
>
> It's up to you, and I expect you to tell me what to do. Given your exemplary life and your austerity, I won't hesitate to accept your decisions.[188]

That the painter had raised the matter again with Rafael Dalí before leaving Barcelona seems clear from Dalí Cusí's letter to his brother dated 17 October 1934 (the 'they' of the first paragraph refers, one assumes, to Dalí and Gala):

> I've received your letter. I'm grateful for your kind sentiments but have to tell you that they have taken advantage of your generosity.
>
> You have moved too quickly. You shouldn't have forgiven the boy[189] without the conditions which I imposed and which are:
>
> First: to make amends to the memory of his mother, so criminally insulted.
>
> Two: an interview with the boy in which you must be present since during it I'll make such serious charges that if the boy retains any rudiments of dignity he'll blush of necessity as he listens to them. Taking those charges as my basis I will impose conditions for the future.

Thus you consider the matter settled when it isn't. It seems that you can't understand how premature would be the telephone conversation you ask me for, no doubt because of your deep desire that there should be a reconciliation.

If you only realized who was going to be back in the family with your daughter and wife you'd tremble.

I can't put down on paper what I must tell you face to face.

I'll see you in Barcelona so that we can talk alone.

I've received a letter from the boy in Paris. As usual I refuse to reply because if there's going to be a reconciliation I want to settle things properly and weigh every full stop and comma.

Don't tell the boy anything about this letter nor about anything which in the future I may explain to you. I want him to hear it all directly from me if we succeed in having the interview at which you have to be present.

Dalí Cusí added a postscript: 'Keep this letter carefully among your papers. It could be that one day you may have to read it aloud in my presence.'[190]

Rafael Dalí was not one to give up easily. He continued to badger his brother, and shortly before the painter left for New York was able to inform him that they had spoken by telephone. The notary had promised to see them together when Salvador returned. Dalí was jubilant, interpreting his father's reaction, somewhat prematurely, as a 'reconciliation'.[191]

The events of October 1934, and his scare in Barcelona, seem to have convinced Dalí that civil war was a real possibility in Spain. It was a conviction many people found difficult to avoid at the time. Already, that May, Dalí had done preliminary drawings for an ambitious painting showing people tearing each other to pieces. Contrary to his claims in the *Secret Life*, though, the painting was not begun on Dalí's return to Paris that autumn but in early 1936, when the possibility of civil war in Spain had become a probability. The great work, one of Dalí's finest from this period, was first entitled *Soft Construction with Boiled Beans* and later renamed, with fitting opportunism, *The Premonition of Civil War*. It showed, he wrote, 'a vast human body breaking out into monstrous excrescences of arms and legs tearing at one another in a delirium of auto-strangulation'.[192]

Dalí does not mention in the *Secret Life* that, on 24 October 1934, a fortnight before he and Gala embarked for America, his first one-man show in London opened at the Zwemmer Gallery. It ran until 10 November and comprised sixteen paintings, twenty drawings (seventeen of them unidentified in the exhibition catalogue), sixteen plates from *The Songs of Maldoror* and the etching *Fantasie*, unknown today. Of the six-

XXVI

teen paintings listed in the catalogue, only two can be identified with any certainty: *Vegetable Metamorphosis* (acquired by Cecil Beaton) and *Fried Eggs on Plate without the Plate*.

The show made a modest mark, but no more. In the *Listener* Herbert Read found parallels between Dalí's inspiration and that of Hieronymous Bosch, whose *The Crowning with Thorns* had just been acquired by the National Gallery: both drew on the unconscious.[193] Douglas Goldring, in the *Studio*, was struck by the 'curious affinity' between Dalí and the Pre-Raphaelites, being reminded particularly of Holman Hunt's *Scapegoat* and *Flight into Egypt* and Millais's *Sir Isumbras at the Ford*. Dalí, like the Pre-Raphaelites, was 'a virtuoso in paint', the difference lying in his 'startling and revolutionary' subject-matter. 'There are not many shows in any year which I feel tempted to revisit,' Goldring ended his short note. 'This one, I must confess, had for me a peculiar fascination.'[194] Anthony Blunt was not so sure. Disturbed by Dalí's nightmare visions, he cautioned in the *Spectator* that many painters 'have condemned themselves to the second class by their refusal to take material reality as the foundation for their work'. For Blunt, Surrealist painting belonged more to the realm of 'psycho-sexual exposition' than to that of art, and he found Dalí's idiom so personal 'that even those to whom the matter is sympathetic will find satisfaction hard to obtain.'[195] Clive Bell apparently did not visit the exhibition, but he saw some Dalí drawings and paintings a few weeks later at Zwemmer's mid-winter show. He loathed them. 'These paintings are vulgar trash intended, I surmise, to take in the would-be smart and up to date, in which purpose they have succeeded,' he thundered in the *New Statesman and Nation*. Dalí's drawings were as sham as his paintings. His brushwork, neither 'nervous nor expressive', was 'merely tight'. There was nothing to be said for him:

> Every year in the summer exhibition of the Royal Academy there must be scores of pictures better drawn and better painted than these. As for the literary import, to which admirers seem to attach the greatest importance, I do not know what message may be conveyed by clapping on to a tightly drawn lamp post the tightly drawn genital organs of a female, but I do know that such pretty conceits will not turn a tenth-rate Meissonier into a fifth-rate one. No: if I must be bored with bad jokes and bad drawing give me *Punch*.[196]

The word Surrealism does not appear in Bell's review, the critic appearing utterly ignorant of its existence. It would not be long, however, before the movement began to acquire its adepts in England.

New York

On 7 November 1934 Dalí and Gala embarked for New York at Le Havre. With them on the *Champlain* was Caresse Crosby, making her thirtieth crossing.[197] The amiable inventor of the brassière had helped with the couple's travel arrangements, promising to deliver them safe and sound to Julien Levy. But she gets no credit for her efforts in the *Secret Life*, which gives the reader to understand that her presence on board was a mere coincidence.[198] The person who does get credit is Picasso who, according to Dalí, lent them money to cover their expenses in New York.[199] Was this true? The alleged gesture has never been substantiated, and, knowing Dalí's obsession with Picasso, may have been a mere invention, like their collaboration on an engraving.

Crosby's account of the preparations and the crossing itself is almost as funny as Dalí's, and probably more accurate. It had needed all her determination and skill at organization to get the artist to agree to travel, and when he did so he installed himself on the train hours in advance of its departure:

> In a third-class compartment next to the engine he sat like a hunter in covert, peering out from behind the canvases that were stacked around, above, below and in front of him. To each picture he had attached a string. These strings were tied either to his clothing or his fingers. He was very pale and very nervous. 'I am next to the engine,' he said, 'so that I'll get there quicker.'[200]

The Dalís spent most of the trip beneath deck, only appearing, muffled up to the eyes, when it was time to eat, or to partake with fearful intensity in safety drill. When the *Champlain* docked in New York at midday on 14 November,[201] Caresse Crosby arranged Dalí's first meeting with the reporters, accompanied these to the painter's cabin and acted as interpreter. It was Dalí's introduction to the New York press—and he loved it:

> Dalí was indeed a sight for newsmongering eyes, again his paintings were attached to him and he attached to them. 'They want to see some of your work,' I explained. 'These are the gentlemen of the Press and,' I hissed in French, 'they can take or leave you.' He got the idea at once, untangled himself from his harness and began stripping the paper from the largest and most unwieldy of the paintings. 'This is important,' I said, 'let me tell you a little about Surrealism.' I gave a brief lecture and when they asked Dalí which was his favourite picture he answered, 'The portrait of my wife.' 'Yes,' I agreed, 'you see he has

painted her with lamb chops on her shoulder.' 'Lamb chops?' they roared. That did it! The pencils began to move, the cameras to click.[202]

Caresse Crosby wrote that, next day, Gala and the lamb chops made a great impact 'in all the morning editions'. In fact they made their first appearance in the media only hours after the couple's arrival, the pun-given *New York Evening Journal* publishing a piece entitled 'Painter Here With "Chop" On Shoulder' and a photograph of Dalí and Gala under the heading 'FROM LAMB CHOPS TO ART'. With Caresse mediating, Dalí had tried to tell America what Surrealism was all about. The newsmen had not quite grasped the point, not even when Dalí gave an example: 'He would paint a piano and it might even look like a piano. But that wouldn't be his fault. What he would be striving for would be something really different, something dreamlike.' As the pencils scribbled excitedly, the showman in Dalí grasped immediately that big-hearted, somewhat naïve America was his oyster.

Some of the morning papers, if not all (as Crosby claimed), also included brief interviews with the painter, given during an improvised press conference in his hotel suite. The one appearing on the twenty-second page of the *New York Times* was fairly representative. 'SALVADOR DALI ARRIVES', it was headed. 'Surrealist Painter Brings 25 of His Pictures for Show Here', ran the subtitle. Dalí had told the reporter about his *modus operandi*:

> I do all my work subconsciously. I never use models or paint from life or landscapes. It is all imagination. That is, I see everything in a dream as I am working, and when I have finished a picture, I decide what the title is to be. Sometimes it takes a little time before I can figure out what I have painted. The scenes in my imagination all have Spain in the background—my own Catalonia or, perhaps, the south of Andalusia.

The reference to Andalusia could not be more unexpected, since at no time had Dalí ever done paintings inspired by the south of Spain, with the sole exception of the scenery for Lorca's *Mariana Pineda*, seven years earlier. Was his remark intended as a secret allusion to the poet the moment he set foot in New York? Perhaps it is not too fanciful to imagine that, arriving now in the great city for first time, Dalí remembered that five years earlier he had been preceded by Lorca, some of whose New York poems, deeply influenced as they were by Surrealism, he must undoubtedly have known.

Caresse Crosby underestimates the extent to which Dalí had prepared the ground for his arrival in New York. With Julien Levy he had even had prepared a broadsheet, 'New

York Salutes Me', which was distributed just before he disembarked. Headed (with a few words missing) by Breton's definition of Surrealism from the first *Manifesto* ('pure psychic automatism, by which means it is proposed to transcribe the real functioning of thought: dictates of thought in the absence of all control exercised by reason, beyond all control aesthetic or moral'), the document portrayed Dalí as the John the Baptist of Surrealism in the United States.[203]

The advance publicity for Dalí's exhibition at the Julien Levy Gallery was more than even he could have hoped for. A few days before the show opened he wrote to J.V. Foix in Barcelona, knowing that his friend would give due prominence in *La Publicitat* to whatever he told him. There had been 'long articles and interviews' the very first night of his arrival, he reported rapturously (exaggerating a bit). The Museum of Modern Art had already acquired a painting. He hoped to make a film. 'New York is a totally Böcklinian city,' he assured Foix, alluding to *The Isle of the Dead*. 'It's full of monumental tombs, cypresses, dogs and fossilized humidities.'[204]

Dalí's show at the Julien Levy Gallery opened on 21 November 1934 and ran until 10 December. Twenty-two works are listed in the exhibition catalogue, which was introduced by the same indications concerning 'handmade snap-shot photography in colour' with which Dalí had headed his Bonjean Gallery notes the previous summer. He had told the *New York Times* on arrival that all the exhibits had been executed 'in the last two months'. But this was quite untrue. Some ten had been shown at Bonjean's; *Myself at the Age of Ten when I was a Grasshopper Child* was from 1933 and had been seen at Dalí's first Levy exhibition; and the artist had also brought *Imperial Monument to the Child-Woman* (1929) and the unfinished *The Invisible Man*, begun the same year. Only a minority of the works had been done very recently, in fact, among them *The Weaning of Furniture-Nutrition*, which portrays the by-now recurrent figure of a nurse sitting on the beach at Port Lligat, but with the difference that this time a window has been cut out in the middle of her torso, allowing an unusual view of the sea.

New Yorkers loved the exhibition, Henry McBride of the *Sun* deeming it the city's most fashionable show of the moment, 'very controversial and very difficult'.[205] In the main the reviews were good, and the doyen of Manhattan's art critics, Edward Alden Jewell of the *New York Times* (nicknamed 'the Jewel of the Times' by Peggy Guggenheim),[206] expressed particular enthusiasm: Dalí was 'one of the greatest', a magnificent draughtsman who worked best in miniature.[207] The New York correspondent of the Barcelona newspaper *La Vanguardia*, Aurelio Pego, reported home on Dalí's huge success and noted that, since his first Levy exhibition, Americans had made great progress in their understanding of Surrealism. *The Persistence of Memory*, with its soft watches, was now famous throughout the country (thanks to having been exhibited at the Chicago World Fair), and only two months earlier the painter had received an 'honourable mention' at the annual exhibition of modern art held at the Carnegie Institute in Pittsburgh. There could be no doubt about it, Dalí, whatever the indifference in Barcelona, was 'the Parisian and Catalan ambassador of Surrealism' in America. Pego had been surprised to discover that the painter neither drank nor smoked, having assumed too hastily that the visions recorded in his works were the product of artificial stimulation. Dalí put the record straight. He painted his obsessions in order to remain sane. He needed no drugs to help him. His art was his therapy, and drugs might damage or destroy what he considered a 'privileged faculty'.[208]

Dalí dashed off a postcard to his uncle Anselm Domènech when the show ended to tell him it had been an 'unprecedented success'. Ten paintings had been sold, among them one to the Museum of Modern Art and two to the Hartford Athenaeum. He and Gala planned to return to Europe in a month, and Dalí was anxious to start painting again because he had arranged an exhibition in London for the following June.[209]

On 28 December 1934 André Breton received a letter from Dalí which interested him so much that he replied to it the same day, addressing Salvador as 'My Very Dear Friend'. Dalí's letter is unknown, but Breton's answer shows that the painter had assured him he was doing everything in his power to spread the good news of Surrealism in America. Dalí had been trying to persuade Breton to set up a specifically Surrealist platform on political issues. Breton now expressed his agreement, stressing that the differences between them had never been more than of method. The letter shows how sensitive Breton was at this moment to the divisions within Surrealism. Perhaps the policy of appeasement he had been employing over the last few years deserved criticism, he conceded, but it had been and still was essential to prevent the movement from falling apart. Take *Minotaure*: given that Surrealism no longer had its own periodical, it was absolutely necessary to retain the connection with Skira's publication, but as a result the current issue included such a reactionary as Paul Valéry alongside Surrealist texts!

Breton went on to complain that he and Dalí now rarely saw each other in Paris, and that when they did so they achieved nothing useful. When Dalí returned it was vital that he put aside the time necessary for them to set up a precise plan of action which they would pledge themselves to carry out scrupulously. In particular, they must organize the public sessions planned before the summer holidays and which had come to nothing, and revitalize the group's Surrealist experiments, currently languishing, to which Dalí had made such a positive contribution. Finally the forthcoming Surrealist exhibition, planned for the end of January 1935, must be both rigorous and brilliant. Breton then revealed that he had severe economic problems, having had to sell Julien Levy his last set of *La Révolution Surréaliste*. Would Dalí thank Levy for his letter and tell him he was sorry not to have replied but could not afford the postage! Breton ended by providing some information about Surrealist activity in Prague and a few smatterings of gossip about Paris. It is a touching communication that shows not only his liking for Dalí but his appreciation of the latter's dedication to the cause of Surrealism. He talks to him as a friend and as an equal.[210]

Dalí also wrote enthusiastically to Éluard to tell him about the huge success of his exhibition. He had been particularly struck by the coverage given to the show by the press 'with the biggest distribution in the world', from society publications such as *Vanity Fair* to the most popular newspapers. Concrete Irrationality was the order of the day, and whole pages had been devoted to Surrealism and even to Lautréamont! Dalí's experience in New York had convinced him that to get Surrealism through to the masses it was necessary to go for shock-tactics such as *trompe l'oeil*, capable of facilitating the objectivization of the Surrealist world 'in the most fetishistic and dramatic way'. He now believed that Surrealism needed to adopt an ideological position of extreme rigour in order to capitalize on the avid interest it was awakening internationally. This included the need for a political platform (as he had been urging Breton for some time) and the delineation of 'a new anti-mystical, materialist religion, based on the progress in scientific knowledge (particularly the new ideas about space, inaccessible not only to the Greeks but to Christianity), a religion which would fill the void of the imagination caused by the collapse of metaphysical ideas in our era'. Dalí ended by assuring Éluard that he was doing everything in his power to promote the ideals of Surrealism.[211]

To celebrate the success of the exhibition, a party in Dalí's honour was thrown on 10 December in the Casa de las Españas, the focal point of Spanish culture in New York. Dalí was introduced to the guests by Angel del Río, the professor of Spanish literature at Columbia University who five years earlier had seen much of Lorca during his visit to the city and had heard the poet's complaint about *Un Chien andalou*. Dalí had not been invited to speak, but given the great interest of those present in learning how he executed his Surrealist paintings, he improvised a short talk. As always these days he had recourse to Breton's definition of Surrealism in the first *Manifesto*, which he could rattle off by heart, and explained that his sole method of composition was to transcribe, without the intervention of reason or of aesthetic or moral considerations, the images thrown up by his subconscious. To paint in this way, he said, was for him a matter of life or death, 'a sort of curative system in order to free himself from the obsession that dominated him'. His work could be compared to that of someone 'communicating the feelings that produce a pessimistic view of life'.[212]

On at least three occasions during his stay Dalí gave a more elaborate version of this improvised lecture on Surrealism. On 18 December he was in attendance at the Wadsworth Athenaeum in Hartford, Connecticut, where, apparently for the first time, he enunciated the phrase that he was to repeat ad nauseam until almost his dying day: 'The only difference between me and a madman is that I am not mad.' The lecture, illustrated by slides, was preceded by a showing of *Un Chien andalou*.[213] On 7 January 1935 he was back at the Casa de las Españas, where he talked about the connections between Lautréamont and Freud and insisted that Surrealism aimed at the total moral revolution of the individual and the liberation of the instincts. Art was a mere tool with which to work towards this goal. Among the slides he projected were *Invisible Horse, Sleeping Woman, Lion, etc.* with its multiple, 'paranoiac' images, two pictures by Picasso, and Leonardo da Vinci's *Madonna and Child with Saint Anne*, the work analysed by Freud in the famous essay which had made such a deep impression on the painter.[214] Then, on 11 January 1935, he lectured at the Museum of Modern Art. This time the talk, given in French with a synopsis in English, was entitled 'Surrealist Paintings and Paranoiac Images' and was illustrated with slides of works by Ernst, Picasso and himself, as well as of some seventeenth-century engravings in which Dalí believed he had found Surrealist precedents. He repeated that he was a disciple of Freud and that in his paintings he merely transcribed the images thrown up by his subconscious. The justification for such a procedure seemed to him obvious:

> The subconscious has a symbolic language that is truly a universal language, for it does not depend on a special habitude [sic] or state of culture or intelligence, but speaks with the vocabulary of the great vital constants, sexual instinct, feeling of death, physical notion of the enigma of space—these vital constants are universally echoed in every human. To understand an *aesthetic* picture, training in appreciation is necessary, cultural and intellectual preparation. For Surrealism, the only requirement is a receptive and intuitive human being.

In case anyone missed the point, Dalí insisted that, just because he himself often failed to understand the images appearing in his work, this was not to say that these had no meaning. At all events his foremost duty as a Surrealist painter was to record, not to interpret.[215]

In mid-January Dalí reported to Foix (from the St Moritz on the Park Hotel) on the 'colossal' success of his exhibition at Levy's. He had sold twelve paintings 'at very high prices' and was 'convinced that the irrational and poetic tendencies of Surrealism could produce a genuine spiritual revolution here'. On 19 January he and Gala would be leaving on the *Ile de France*, and planned to rest for two months in Port Lligat to recover from the 'tremendous excitement of these two months'. Foix duly reproduced the contents of the letter in *La Publicitat*.[216]

Caresse Crosby and Joella Levy decided on impulse to give the Dalís a farewell party they would never forget, and invitations were hurried out for a 'Bal Onirique' at the Coq Rouge on 18 January 1935 to which guests were requested to come in the guise of their favourite recurrent dream.[217] Dalí helped Caresse in the production of a fittingly Surreal décor that included a bath tub full of water which, suspended over the stairway to the gallery, threatened at any moment to empty its contents onto the revellers, and the carcass of a huge cow from whose innards a gramophone relayed the latest French songs. The event caught the imagination of the press, a two-page headline in the *Sunday Mirror* running: 'Mad "Dream Betrayal" of New York Society at the Astounding Party to its Newest Idol. All-Time High in Gotham Smart Set's Traditional Pursuit of New Thrills, No Matter How Crazy, is the Latest Cock-Eyed Rage for Salvador Dalí, the "Super-Realist" Who Paints His Nightmares Which Critics Applaud While Mortals Grow Dizzy'. The account of the Dream Ball that followed was suitably witty:

> Society out-did itself trying to out-Dalí the painter. If you had looked into the Coq Rouge on the night of the party, you would have seen women in white shimmering gowns with green snakes emerging from their heads, a man with his cheeks apparently serving as a pincushion, a man in a tailcoat, but minus the trousers, a woman fully clothed in front but (at first glance) nude from the rear elevation, a woman giving birth to a doll from the top of her head, and other novelties equally startling.

The *Sunday Mirror* printed colour photographs of Dalí, Gala and Caresse Crosby, and a description of their get-ups. Dalí's head 'was neatly bandaged by yards and yards of hospital gauze', the paper reported. 'His stiff-bosomed shirt was cut out in the form of a showcase. Behind the glass of the showcase reposed a pink silk article, which is one of the foundation items of feminine attire. It is known as the brassiere.' No doubt Dalí's window-display was intended as an allusion, and perhaps a homage, to his hostess, Caresse Crosby. As for Crosby herself, she was dressed as the White Horse of Dream Desire, although the *Sunday Mirror* photograph shows her looking more like the White Rabbit. In another picture Gala is the woman 'giving birth to a doll from the top of her head'. It was a baby doll with outstretched arms and a lobster curling around its temples. Dalí said later that the child was being devoured by ants, but there is no sign of these in the photograph. He also forgot to mention the rest of Gala's apparel: a tightly-fitting sweater emphasizing her apparently naked breasts underneath and an ankle-length transparent skirt of red cellophane over a miniskirt that enabled her to show off her shapely legs to the best advantage. The *Sunday Mirror* man asked Gala to explain what the Dream Ball was all about. 'It was an experiment to see how far New Yorkers would respond to a chance to express their own dreams,' she is quoted as replying. 'Only a dozen or two actually succeeded in this expression. The others may think they are expressing themselves, but, really, they have betrayed themselves.' The remark was typical of Gala, who always kept the knife of her deadly tongue at the ready.

Caresse Crosby would like us to believe that 'every paper in town' covered the Dream Ball and printed pictures. This was by no means the case, but the wild event certainly enhanced Dalí's reputation (and opportunities for sales) in New York.[218]

A few hours later, on the morning of 19 January 1935, Dalí and Gala left as planned for Europe on board the *Ile de France*. When they got home they found that the Dream Ball was having an unexpected side effect. A few months previously, a man called Hauptmann had been convicted of kidnapping and murdering the baby of Charles Lindbergh, the aviator, and his wife Anne. The brutal details of the gory murder had greatly shocked American society. Might not Gala's head-dress have been a deliberately provocative allusion to the horrible event? According to Dalí no one in New York had considered any such association until the correspondent of the *Petit Parisien* sent a cable to his paper with the 'sensational news'. Either way the matter was soon forgotten.[219]

Dalí had now had his first taste of the good life in New York, and had begun to make big money, although exactly how big we do not know. Enough, certainly, to whet his appetite, and particularly Gala's, for much more. As well as this, he had not only established excellent relations with the press and grasped its potential for his nationwide promotion in the States, but had set up a deal with *American Weekly* for publishing illustrated articles on his 'Surrealist' impressions of New York, to appear during 1935. It must have seemed apparent to the couple, as they headed for Paris and Port Lligat, that international fame and financial success might now be only just around the corner.

An Uneasy Reconciliation

One of the first things Dalí did on returning to Europe was to take up his father's offer of a face-to-face discussion about a possible reconciliation. It took place in Figueres at the beginning of March 1935, in the presence of Rafael Dalí and his wife María Concepción. The latter wrote to her daughter Montserrat a few days afterwards about the 'very emotional' confrontation. 'The matter has not yet been completely settled,' she explained, 'since there are lots of loose ends to be tied up. Uncle Salvador's torn between his heart and his head because, despite the clarity of the latter, I'm convinced he's even more ruled by his kindly disposition.'[1] Montserrat Dalí heard the full details when her parents returned to Barcelona: the notary had shouted recriminations at his son, Salvador had burst into tears and finally father, son and uncle had collapsed into each other's arms, all weeping uncontrollably. It seems that Anna Maria had arrived home from an outing to Roses just in time to witness the grand finale of the tempestuous re-encounter.[2]

Immediately afterwards Rafael Dalí and his wife travelled down to Cadaqués with Salvador and Anna María, staying for a few days at Es Llané. Carnaval was in full swing and the weather brilliant, but a tremendous wind upset Rafael and perhaps reminded him of his father's madness and suicide. 'My native village would be a paradise if it weren't for the tramuntana,' he wrote to Montserrat. Rafael was desperately impatient to see Salvador's house, and had no sooner arrived at Es Llané than he walked around the headland to Port Lligat. He must have been impressed by the transformation wrought since 1930 on the fisherman's cottage Salvador had bought from Lidia's son, for with the acquisition of some adjoining properties the place was now growing into a

Chapter TEN

Dalí's house at Port Lligat, 1995.

labyrinth of narrow passageways, stairs and secret spaces that mirrored the sinuosities of Dalí's complex psyche.[3]

In the wake of the stormy session in Figueres, and thinking things over carefully, Dalí Cusí decided to revoke the will by which he had disinherited Salvador in January 1931. He accordingly drew up a new one, signed on 6 April 1935. The lion's share of the estate still went to Anna Maria, with adequate provision for 'la tieta'. Dalí's legal right to half of the fourth part of the estate (known as *la legítima*) was reinstated, but his father made him sign a document, attached to the will, in which he agreed that he had already received 25,000 pesetas over the years (about £30,000 today) and accepted that this sum should stand in lieu of his 'legitimate share'. To 'complement' the latter, and as 'a special favour', Dalí was to receive a token monthly income of 200 pesetas (about £220), the payment of which was entrusted to Anna Maria. The will shows that the painter had been accepted back into the bosom of the family, but that Dalí Cusí was determined to provide above all for his daughter. It was a cautious reconciliation, so far as the notary was concerned, but a reconciliaton none the less.[4] A year later, pleased at the way the relationship was developing, Dalí Cusí produced another will by which the painter was to receive an eighth part of the estate, tantamount to the full satisfaction of his *legítima*.[5] During the last fifteen years of his life the notary was to make no fewer than nine new wills. All of them continued to favour Anna Maria, whose well-being was understandably his principal preoccupation, while at the same time accommodating the legitimate rights of the prodigal son.[6]

The Death of Crevel

By the summer of 1935, eleven years after the appearance of Breton's first *Manifesto*, Surrealism was a force to be reckoned with in Europe. In March Breton and Éluard were received with open arms in Prague, where, the following month, the first *Bulletin International du Surréalisme* was published.[7] Then, in June, came the Second World Exhibition of Surrealism, held in Santa Cruz, Tenerife. Breton had hoped that Dalí would accompany the Paris group to the exotic island but, for reasons unknown, the artist failed to do so. Éluard, who was ill, did not attend either, while René Crevel only got as far as Madrid. Breton was outraged to discover that, under the right-wing government then in power in Spain, censorship was even more repressive than in France: he and Péret were prevented from showing *L'Age d'or*.[8]

The nineteen-year-old David Gascoyne had just arrived in Paris at this time to research a short book on Surrealism and, recommended by Éluard, had undertaken to translate Dalí's new essay, *The Conquest of the Irrational*. He worked on the text each morning for a week at the painter's studio in Rue Gauguet, and had the opportunity to talk to both Dalí and Gala. Gascoyne noticed Dalí's underlying timidity and was impressed by Gala, who was always fashionably dressed—he particularly remembered her Schiaparelli blouse with a newsprint design. One day Éluard came to lunch with Cécile.

> 'Do you know the most beautiful love poem I ever wrote?' he asked, and we all said no. He went to the bookcase and got a copy of *Nuits partagées*, 'Shared Nights', and read a page of this aloud at the table. It was rather extraordinary. Dalí sat there playing around with a piece of bread and Gala gave a smile of great gratification. I realized then that she had this sort of magnetic power for at least two men of genius.[9]

On 20 June 1935 Gascoyne arrived at the painter's studio to find an anguished Dalí charging out of the house. Something terrible had happened to Crevel, he said, and he was going to the hospital. When he returned it was to announce that the writer had committed suicide. Gascoyne, unaware of the friendship uniting Crevel, Gala and Dalí, witnessed great distress that afternoon at Rue Gauguet.[10]

Writing to Foix shortly afterwards, Dalí concluded that, while the immediate reason for Crevel's suicide was the certainty of further illness (he had incurable tuberculosis), his despair over the consistent refusal of the Communist Party to accommodate the postulates of Surrealism also played its part. Thanks particularly to Crevel's efforts, the Surrealists had been invited, begrudgingly, to the Writers' Congress for the Defence of Culture, which opened in Paris on 25 June. But the organizers had refused to allow Breton and the others to speak. 'The antagonism of our group towards the Communists has reached its peak with Crevel's suicide,' wrote Dalí.[11]

Crevel had turned on the gas tap after pinning to his jacket a card on which he had written one word: 'Disgust'. Near by was found a little attaché case full of manuscripts and correspondence. Among the papers was a long undated letter from Dalí in which he analysed a political text Crevel had submitted to him for comment. The letter shows that the two understood each other perfectly, and that they agreed about the stupidity of the official Communist line on Surrealism and about the 'dogmatic fossilization' currently immobilizing Marxist thought. Crevel, obsessed by the need to reconcile Surrealism and Marxism, thought that the desired entente might still be possible. But Dalí had lost hope. He had recently attended two meetings convened by Breton with the aim of redefining the Surrealists' political position. They had confirmed his scepticism about the Communists, he told Crevel. He now felt that war was not only inevitable but even necessary to clear up the mess (*la grande marmelade*): a new 'medieval-type historical period' was on the horizon, with its attendant neo-romanticism, racism (underlined) and all the 'vital realities' underestimated by Marxism and perceived only by the Surrealists. Fascism, that is. Dalí advised Crevel not to submit his text to Breton for the moment, and ended by asking him to reply with the frankness that had always characterized their relationship, and which he himself had just demonstrated in his comments. It seems likely that it was one of the last letters Crevel received before deciding to kill himself and, who knows, it may even have meant the final blow to his aspirations.[12]

With Edward James and Lorca

It was now almost time for the annual trip south to Port Lligat, but there were a few matters to settle first. At the beginning of July Dalí went to London to make arrangements for his next exhibition, and presumably stayed with Edward James in Wimpole Street. Then, back in Paris, he saw *The Conquest of the Irrational* through the press. Printing was finished on 20 July 1935 (1,200 copies in French, 1,000 in English for Julien Levy in New York), and soon afterwards Dalí set off for Catalunya with Gala.[13]

The Conquest of the Irrational, nineteen pages long in small format, is illustrated with a colour frontispiece of The *'Angelus' of Gala* and thirty-five black-and-white reproductions of Dalí's works. It attempts to establish the primacy, after Surrealism's initial stress on passive automatism, of Dalí's 'paranoiac-critical method'. To this end Dalí introduces the essay with the words of praise accorded the previous year by Breton: 'Dalí has endowed Surrealism with an instrument of primary importance, in particular the paranoiac-critical method, which has immediately shown itself capable of being applied equally to painting, poetry, the cinema, to the construction of typical Surrealist Objects, to fashion, to sculpture, to the history of art and even, if necessary, to all manner of exegesis.'

The title of the essay, like that of Dalí's 'method' itself, was a *trouvaille*, and put his current thinking in a nutshell: irrationality, yes, but instead of the unconscious being allowed to have its say untrammelled, it should now be harnessed and put to work. And there was work to be done because, in Dalí's opinion, people were hungry for the spiritual food that used to be supplied by Catholicism and could now only be provided by Surrealism or . . . National Socialism. Not that Dalí sides overtly with Nazism. But the hints are there in the evocation of his contemporaries who, 'systematically cretinized' by a host of social and ideological disorders, including 'affective paternal hungers of all kinds', 'seek in vain to bite into the doting and triumphal sweetness of the plump, atavistic, tender, militarist and territorial back of some hitlerian nurse'. Dalí's analysis of this alleged hunger recruits terms from the orbit of Fascism ('hunger for Empire', 'glorious conquests', 'territorial ambiance') and suggests that his deep need for reconciliation with his father, recently achieved, was related to his growing approval of Hitler.

Dalí, certainly, was now thinking about his own goals in quasi-Fascist terms of conquest: 'My whole ambition in the pictorial domain is to materialize the images of concrete irrationality with the most imperialist fury of precision.' To achieve this, *trompe l'oeil*, whatever other illusionistic tricks came to hand and, of course, 'the most discredited academicism', were all perfectly legitimate. Anything was acceptable when the main aim was to achieve 'the objective value, on the real plane, of the delirious unknown world of our irrational experiences'.

Breton must have been disturbed by the essay, both on account of its covert Fascism and of the evidence it provided of Dalí's growing megalomania. But no record of his reaction has come to light.

At the end of July the Dalís went down to see the Serts at Mas Juny, in Palamós, where they found Edward James already in attendance. Dalí was in one of his creative white heats, and, according to James, had begun to paint marvels.[14] But this year the fun and games had hardly begun before they ended in tragedy. Prince Alexis Mdivani, the brother of Sert's wife, Roussie, was staying at the villa with his lover Maud von Thyssen-Bornemiesu. On 1 August they left for Perpignan in his Rolls Royce. They never got there. Only a few miles from Mas Juny there was a spectacular crash and Mdivani died instantly (his mistress only received minor injuries).[15] After the harrowing funeral in Palamós most of the guests, including Edward James, dispersed, but Dalí and Gala stayed on for a few days. It was heart-rending to witness the grief of their dear friends, Dalí wrote on a postcard to James from Cadaqués. Dalí adored Roussie Sert, whose face, he wrote later, resembled that of the young girl in the portrait by Vermeer in the Hague.[16] To see her in such terrible distress was appalling, and he had found it difficult to get back to work. Nonetheless he was now immersed again in his and James's 'imaginary town'.[17]

The reference was to *Outskirts of the Paranoiac-Critical Town*, one of Dalí's finest and most complex paintings of this period, which James had undertaken to purchase. The picture was begun in Palamós just before the tragedy (Dalí later said that it was 'painted' there),[18] and contains two architectural elements taken from the town: the tall portico of the building on the left (reminiscent of De Chirico) echoes that of the Casino La Unión, and the cupola that crowns it is a stylized version of the dome that topped the imposing Art Nouveau mansion belonging to the Ribera family. Both buildings were demolished in the 1970s.[19] The painting, of modest dimensions (46 x 66 cm), is almost an anthology of the motifs currently obsessing Dalí, and contains a plethora of precise detail. At the right, a picture-postcard-style evocation of the Carrer del Call in Cadaqués shows that Dalí's village forms an integral part of the 'paranoiac-critical' town which a friendly Gala, proffering a bunch of black grapes, invites us to enter. But why did Dalí choose to represent Cadaqués by this particular street? Not, presumably, because, as its name shows, it was once the hub of the Jewish quarter (*call* means ghetto). Nor only because of its picturesqueness (Cadaqués has any number of charming corners and perspectives). A more likely reason is that, as Dalí well knew, his paranoiac grandfather Gal Dalí had lived only a few steps away. On top of the safe in the foreground lies a golden key, and in the keyhole we see the minute image of a child echoed by the figure lingering under the archway at the end of the street. Might the suggestion not be that Gal is the key, or one of the keys, to the understanding of Dalí's personality? It seems a reasonable hypothesis. Cadaqués, which according to Dalí boasts 'the greatest paranoiacs produced by the Mediterranean',[20] was the birthplace of the unhappy grandfather who, in a burst of madness, had killed himself in Barcelona. How could the painter ever forget that? Or not worry that he himself might have inherited a paranoid tendency from his ancestor?

The crumbling portico to the 'paranoiac-critical' town, held up by a crutch and containing a visual trick indebted to Magritte, is echoed by the tower behind with its bell

XXVII

in the shape of a girl. It seems that Dalí maintained that the tower evokes that of Vilabertran, the village a few kilometres outside Figueres which as an adolescent he had
often visited with his friends.[21] But it is difficult to see any similarity, for the tower in
question is Romanesque. As for the bell-girl, she was inspired by the campanile of Anna
Maria Dalí's convent school in Figueres, which, as is shown by *Girl from Figueres* (1926),
was visible from the family terrace. It had a classical pediment and round arch, although
no ball finial, and was destroyed during the civil war.

We have seen that Dalí explained on several occasions that as an adolescent his masturbatory fantasies were habitually set in three superimposed belfries: those of Sant Pere
in Figueres, Sant Narcís in Girona and a church in Delft painted by Vermeer (see p. 111
above). The belfry of Anna Maria's convent was a later addition to these, and it seems
fair to assume that the swinging girl-bell, so ubiquitous in the artist's work from 1935
onwards, represents Dalí as Masturbator. Years later Dalí was to make a gift of such a
bell to the little chapel of Sant Baldiri, which guards the entrance to the cemetery of
Cadaqués.[22]

In *Landscape with a Girl Skipping* (1936) the three towers appear explicitly. In the fore-

VII

Landscape with Girl Skipping, *1936. Oil triptych on canvas, 293 x 280 cm. The painting belonged
to Edward James. The image of the girl skipping, a reminiscence of Dalí's dead aunt Carolineta,
recurs dozens of times in his work.*

ground, as in *Outskirts of the Paranoiac-Critical Town* and so many other pictures and drawings done over the following years, a girl in a white dress runs skipping. Dalí told Antoni Pitxot that she represented his cousin (in fact aunt) Carolineta, who as we saw died in 1914 when Salvador was ten, occasioning grief in the family.[23] Carolineta is named explicitly in several pictures from 1933–4 onwards, notably in the two entitled *Apparition of my Cousin Carolineta on the Beach at Roses*. Always associated with summer, one is tempted to conclude that this relative, whom the young Dalí saw on his trips to Barcelona and who may have visited the family in Figueres, was one of the first women to arouse his sexual curiosity. On the evidence of these pictures and drawings, it seems likely that she became one of the actors in his masturbatory fantasies.

Many elements in *Outskirts of the Paranoiac-Critical Town* serve deliberately to confuse and disturb the viewer. Gala's bunch of grapes is echoed in the delineation of the horse's rear parts (not least in its testicles); the eye sockets of the skull on the table correspond to the spaces within the handles of the nearby amphora; the arcaded building is repeated in miniature on top of the cushion at bottom left; the keyhole of the drawer above this is equivalent to that of the safe at bottom right; the tiny bells relate to the figures on top of the arcaded building; and so on. If paranoia, in Dalí's conception, involves the 'delirious association' of images, there could be no better example than this of his determination to express the phenomenon in his art and, in the process, to induce in the viewer, if not a paranoiac delirium, at least a *dérèglement des sens*.

James and the Dalís were now on excellent terms and greatly enjoyed being together. From the moment of Mdivani's death they wrote to each other constantly (always in French, which James spoke very fluently) and soon dropped the 'vous'. After a visit to Salzburg, where he said the music had helped him to cope with the tragedy, James drove down to Florence, took a train to Naples and opened the house at Ravello which he had rented from Lord Grimthorpe. The Villa Cimbrone stood on the cliffs above the town and looked out over Amalfi and the Bay of Salerno. It was an ideal retreat, and soon James was urging the Dalís to visit him there in October. He was so impatient to see them again that he then decided he could not wait that long, and jumped on a train for Spain. They spent ten days together, half in Cadaqués and half in Barcelona.[24]

Edward James, ever on the move, ever impulsive and unpredictable! Thanks to his inability to stay for long in one place he was privileged to witness the re-encounter that autumn in Barcelona of Dalí and Lorca, who was then at the height of his success as Spain's most popular young poet and dramatist. Lorca was so elated by being with Dalí again that he did something most unusual for him: he let other people down. On the night of 28 September he was to have participated in a poetry and music recital given in his honour. The hall was full, the orchestra ready, the choir lined up; expectation was mounting . . . but Lorca's admirers waited in vain. The charismatic poet had gone down the coast to Tarragona with Dalí, with no explanations given.[25]

Lorca was in Barcelona for a season of his plays, and was the talk of the town. When the young journalist Josep Palau i Fabre, later an authority on Picasso, was granted an interview, the poet chattered on and on about the renewal of his friendship with Dalí. They were going to work together on a project, they would design the sets together . . . 'We are twin spirits,' he said. 'And here's the proof: seven years without seeing each other and yet we agree on everything as if we'd never stopped talking since then. Salvador Dalí is a genius, a genius.'[26] The poet's observation that he and Dalí were twin spirits calls up the drawing he had done of the painter in 1927, seeing him (if we can believe Dalí) as one of the Dioscuri, Castor and Pollux (see p. 202 above).[27]

Gala seems to have been as fascinated with Lorca as he was to meet the woman who had succeeded not only in seducing Dalí but in retaining him. According to the painter, in 1952, she was 'staggered by that total viscous and lyrical phenomenon', while Lorca, amazed, did nothing for three days but talk about her.[28] As for Edward James, he was beside himself with excitement, writing to Diane Abdy that he had met many of Dalí's friends in Barcelona but in particular García Lorca, who had read to them for one whole evening. He considered him a 'really great poet', perhaps the only one he had ever met.[29]

James's appearance and manner had amused Lorca. According to Dalí he was in Tyrolian get-up that day, with short trousers (Lederhosen, obviously) and a frilly lace shirt, and Lorca thought him 'a humming-bird dressed like a soldier from the time of Swift'.[30]

James invited Lorca to accompany him and the Dalís to Ravello, but the poet, given the pressure of his Barcelona season and other plans, was unable to accept. He and Dalí were never to meet again.

Years later, wittingly or unwittingly, Dalí produced a very inaccurate account of his last meeting with the 'greatest friend' of his youth, maintaining that it had taken place just before the Spanish Civil War. If he had insisted enough, he said, Lorca would have accompanied him and James to Italy—and escaped the fate that awaited him shortly afterwards in Granada. But this was rubbish, for it would be nine months before the civil war unleashed itself and destroyed the democracy with which Lorca had so closely identified.[31]

From Ravello and Rome Dalí sent enthusiastic postcards to Foix ('Italy's turning out to be more Surrealist than even the Pope'). It is difficult to believe that he failed to write to Lorca, too, after the renewal of their unique friendship, but no correspondence has come to light.[32] The visit to Italy was a great success. James told Edith Sitwell that he had become very attached to Dalí and Gala, and that in the last year the painter had made enormous strides and cast off many of the 'tiresome and unfortunate obsessions' that had damaged his work. He considered him now 'the most normal and happy man imaginable, no longer overwrought with nerves'.[33]

The Dalís, in turn, were delighted with James. Back at Rue Gauguet at the end of October, Dalí wrote to tell him that he was fascinated by his 'extraordinary poetic-critical spirit' and deeply pleased that they now understood each other so well. He assured James that he and Gala really loved him, and that his absence was leaving a hole in his back like the nurse's in *The Weaning of Furniture-Nutrition*.[34]

That November James invited the Dalís to London and introduced Salvador to the architect Hugh Casson, then busily at work on alterations to Monkton, a house by Edwin Lutyens near the Solent that James had intended for his wife. Now, after the divorce, he had decided to make it his personal retreat. Dalí's contribution to the revamped design was to propose that the outside walls be painted puce. They were. Dalí's suggestions for the Surreal interior, however, were considered too complex to be implemented.[35]

By this time James was so convinced of Dalí's genius that he had decided to become his patron. In March 1936 Dalí, then in Port Lligat and working at full stretch, needed 10,000 francs to buy a shack adjoining the house. James advanced 5,000 on his 'big painting' and got Lord Berners to put up the rest. What less could he do for his 'dearest friends', as he was now calling them?[36]

Dalí had met Lord Gerald Berners in Paris at the concerts given by the Princesse de Polignac, whose large drawing-room was decorated by Josep María Sert 'with tempests of embryo elephants'.[37] A composer and writer, Berners had been associated with the Ballets Russes. He enjoyed private means almost as lavish as those of James and was nominally attached to the British Embassy in Rome, driving around the city in such a spectacular Rolls Royce that Italians assumed he was the ambassador. He was notoriously gay, and at his house at Faringdon in Oxfordshire kept up a 'grand style' with his lover Robert Heber-Percy. It seems that Dalí took to him at once.[38]

The beginning of James's patronage coincided with the painter's last known communication to Lorca, which came in a postcard sent that March from Port Lligat. Dalí had seen the recent Barcelona revival of Lorca's play *Yerma*:

> My dear Federico,
>   What a pity you couldn't come to see us in Paris. What a time we would have had! We've

got to do things together again. *Yerma* is full of dark and Surrealist ideas. We're spending two months in Port Lligat to carry out an analysis and objectivity cure, and to eat these extravagant things that NOBODY knows: first-class stewed beans, superfine and smooth, fantastic to look at and the very mysteries of Eleusis where food is concerned. *Tell me what you're doing and what you plan to do.* We'll always be delighted to see you in our house. Do you remember that quaint structure of flesh and blood (but which seemed impossible) called Max Aub?

Gala sends her affection and I hug you.[39]

The Dalís stayed on in Cadaqués until the beginning of June, corresponding regularly with Edward James, now affectionately nicknamed 'Petitou'. They told him that they had been unable to buy the next-door shack after all and that, instead, a local man (Emilio Puignau) was adding a new storey to the existing building. Soon they would be able to put him up in due comfort.[40] The weather continued atrocious, so Dalí was sticking to his easel 'like the monkey in the painting by Teniers'. He was also writing an article on the Pre-Raphaelites for *Minotaure* and designing the magazine's next cover. Gala told James in May that Dalí was working in a frenzy surpassing anything she'd seen previously, and that he was pleased with the paintings he'd finished. His next exhibition would undoubtedly be his most complete and beautiful, with a great diversity of paintings. This was the show to be held at Alex, Reid and Lefevre in London that June. Dalí added a note: would James please lend them *Paranoiac Head* (which combined the double image of an African village discovered by Dalí on a postcard and a head by Picasso) for the forthcoming Surrealist Exhibition in London?[41] James complied. He now had a bee in his bonnet about decorating one of the rooms in Wimpole Street with rocks from Cap Creus. But his architect had told him that the house would fall down. What was he to do? Dalí offered to paint him a mural of Creus instead when he came to London in June: it would be less dangerous and more effective.[42]

Meanwhile a Surrealist Exhibition of Objects (not to be confused with an Exhibition of Surrealist Objects) was held between 22 and 29 May at the Charles Ratton Gallery in Paris. The fascinating show comprised Natural Objects, Natural Objects Interpreted, Natural Objects Incorporated (two objects by Max Ernst), Perturbed Objects, Found Objects, Found Objects Interpreted, American Objects, Oceanic Objects, Mathematical Objects, a Readymade and an Assisted Readymade by Marcel Duchamp, and, finally, Surrealist Objects proper: a wide-ranging selection of works by Arp, Bellmer, Breton, Jacqueline Breton, Serge Brignoni, Claude Cahun, Calder, Dalí (*Aphrodisiac Dinner Jacket* and *Monument to Kant*), Gala (*Staircase of Cupid and Psyche*), Oscar Domínguez, Duchamp,

Ernst, Angel Ferrant, Giacometti, S.W. Hayter, Georges Hugnet, Marcel Jean, Magritte, Léo Malet, Man Ray, Ramon Marinello, E.L.T. Mesens, Miró, Paul Nougé, Meret Oppenheim (the famous fur cup, saucer and spoons), W. Paalen, Roland Penrose, Picasso, Jean Scutenaire, Max Servais and Yves Tanguy. If ever it had been needed, here was definitive proof that the Surrealist Object had arrived.[43]

The Ratton exhibition, termed by Dalí in a letter to Foix 'the best collective Surrealist manifestation to date',[44] was accompanied by a special issue of Christian Zervos's *Cahiers d'Art*. It included Dalí's article 'All Honour to the Object!' and his comments on Gala's first known incursion into the world of art, *Staircase of Cupid and Psyche* (a model for a Surrealist apartment) and his own *Aphrodisiac Dinner Jacket*, by then one of the most popular Surrealist Objects in circulation. Dalí pointed out that the small glasses covering the jacket contained 'Pippermint' [sic], a green liqueur (crème de menthe) reputed to have strongly aphrodisiac properties. Between the lapels he had affixed a tiny brassière (in deference to Caresse Crosby?), with, underneath, the manufacturer's ad ('Diamond Dee Uplift'). Dalí considered that the jacket would be suitable for outings on evenings meteorologically calm but pregnant with human emotion, provided that the person wearing it were transported in a very powerful machine travelling very slowly (in order not to upset the liqueurs).

'All Honour to the Object!' contained lucubrations on the symbolism of the swastika and showed the growing hold that Fascism was now exerting on Dalí's thinking. In his 'paranoiac' conception, the swastika was an emblem signifying the fusion of Left and Right, the resolution of 'antagonistic movements'. To anyone versed in the Fascist propaganda of the time, it must have seemed clear that Dalí approved of National Socialism's claim to offer a new synthesis between the forces of revolution and reaction by harnessing them to the yoke of common action. Dalí's friend Ernesto Giménez Caballero had laid down the theoretical basis of Spanish Fascism in *Genius of Spain* (1932), a book the painter had almost certainly read by 1936—and perhaps even discussed with its author. In it Giménez Caballero unashamedly explained that Fascism was inseparable from imperialism, that the merging of the energies of Right and Left only made sense in the pursuance of an aim which, put crudely, was the conquest of the weak by the strong. All of this would have appealed to Dalí, as hell-bent on the conquest of international celebrity and self-aggrandizement as Hitler was on the physical conquest of Europe.

At the end of his article Dalí envisages the development of the Surrealist Object in terms that make him sound like the Führer of the movement: a new era is beginning and henceforth the Surrealist Object (thanks of course to Dalí) 'will succeed in imposing its paranoiac-critical hegemony'. Given Dalí's programme for world fame, which he had begun to elaborate at the age of sixteen, it was little wonder that Hitler fascinated him increasingly, not least because of the latter's small size, apparent banality and humble origins. 'All Honour to the Object!' shows how right Breton was to suspect Dalí's sympathy for the cause of the proletariat.

The London Surrealist Exhibition of 1936; the Alex, Reid and Lefevre Show

Surrealism was now making inroads in Britain, where artists such as James's friend Roland Penrose, 'the instigator and ambassador of Surrealism in Britain', Paul Nash, Henry Moore, Eileen Agar, John Banting, Humphrey Jennings, Julian Trevelyan, and later Conroy Maddox and Ithell Colquhoun, 'had all spent extensive periods in France and relied on constant communication with the continent'.[45] The British Surrealists lacked a leader with the intellectual stature and drive of André Breton (the arrival of E.L.T. Mesens from Belgium in 1938 was to make up partially for this deficiency). Nonetheless by 1935 their voice was beginning to be heard in a country far more puritanical than France, and where the 1920s, scarcely touched by the rebellious spirit of Dada, had been characterized, Roland Penrose recalled, 'by stultifying conservatism and insularity'.[46] Fascism was becoming increasingly virulent in Britain, as it was in France; many artists were searching for freer modes of expression; and Surrealism, with its impassioned commitment to society and its programme for personal liberation, seemed to offer hope for change. Moreover, Breton's 1924 *Manifesto* had paid homage to several British writers considered precursors of Surrealism, in particular William Blake, as David Gascoyne pointed out to potential adherents in his pioneer study *A Short Survey of Surrealism*, published in November 1935. Altogether, therefore, the announcement that a major Surrealist exhibition was to be held in London in the summer of 1936 seemed extremely timely. As Penrose put it, he and his friends hoped that the show would 'make clear to Londoners that there was a revelation awaiting. It could release them from the constipation of logic which conventional public-school mentality had brought upon them.'[47]

The International Surrealist Exhibition opened at the New Burlington Galleries (Burlington Gardens) on 11 June and ran until 4 July. The English organizing committee comprised Hugh Sykes Davies, David Gascoyne, Humphrey Jennings, Rupert Lee, Diana Brinton Lee, Henry Moore, Paul Nash, Roland Penrose and Herbert Read (who wrote a brief introduction to the catalogue). On the French side were ranged André

Breton, Paul Éluard, Georges Hugnet and Man Ray. E.L.T. Mesens was on duty for Belgium; Dalí, for Spain.

The exhibition was opened by André Breton in the presence of some two thousand people. It was an ambitious effort, certainly, with over four hundred paintings, drawings, sculptures and objects by sixty-eight artists, twenty-three of them British. In all, fourteen nationalities were represented. There was such huge public interest that at times the traffic in Bond Street ground to a complete halt, and it was calculated that some 20,000 people visited the show.[48]

The Dalís missed the opening ceremony, Gala writing to James to say they would be arriving on 21 June and going straight down to Faringdon with Lord Berners. It seems that James got in on the act and that, before Faringdon, there was a houseparty at Cecil Beaton's place, Ashcombe, in Wiltshire. After the fun was over the Dalís settled in at 35 Wimpole Street with James.[49]

Five lectures were given during the exhibition: Breton, 'Limits, not Frontiers, of Surrealism' (in French, 16 June); Herbert Read, 'Art and the Unconscious' (19 June); Éluard, 'Surrealist Poetry' (in French, 24 June); Hugh Sykes Davies, 'Biology and Surrealism' (26 June); and Dalí, 'Authentic Paranoiac Fantasies' (in French, 1 July). There was a public debate on Surrealism, notable for a paper by Herbert Read on the political position of the movement. Paul Éluard gave a recital of poems by Lautréamont, Baudelaire, Rimbaud, Cros, Jarry, Breton, Mesens, Péret, Picasso and himself (with David Gascoyne and others reading translations). Inside and outside the gallery passionate discussions took place about the movement now hitting London for the first time, and there was massive newspaper and magazine coverage.[50] The press, Herbert Read reported, had prepared 'an armoury of mockery, sneers and insults'.[51] And not only the conservative press. *The Daily Worker*, the British Communist Party's counterpart to *L'Humanité*, expressed deep scorn for the exhibition and its begetters. 'The general impression one gets is that here is a group of young people who just haven't got the guts to tackle anything seriously and attempt to justify themselves by an elaborate rationalization racket,' it preached the day after the opening. The CP's view was contested energetically by the Surrealists. As for the British Fascists, they threatened to break up the exhibition but, in the end, refrained.[52]

Dalí had contributed three paintings—*The Dream* (lent by Marie-Laure de Noailles), *Daybreak* (by Paul Éluard) and *Paranoiac Head* (by James)—an engraving, *Fantasy* (by the Zwemmer Gallery), a drawing, *The Horseman of Death* (by David Gascoyne), *Aphrodisiac Dinner Jacket* and four series of pencil studies for Skira's *Les Chants de Maldoror*.[53]

Faber and Faber had just brought out a tract by Breton, *What is Surrealism?*, edited and translated by David Gascoyne. It included Breton's review of Dalí's 1929 Goemans exhibition, his first in Paris, and Dalí was one of the four painters favoured with an illustration (his Surrealist Object *Retrospective Bust*). More important were Breton's remarks on Dalí's contribution to Surrealism contained in the eponymous main essay (a slightly revised version of his 1934 lecture of this title). A review of the movement's origins, aims and achievements to date, the essay was generous in its appreciation of Dalí, 'whose exceptional interior "boiling",' Breton wrote, 'has been for Surrealism, during the whole of this period, an invaluable ferment'. Dalí, for Breton, was not only a major Surrealist painter but one of the movement's most relevant theorists. It was praise indeed, and Dalí must have been delighted to see it in print in London, where he hoped for lucrative sales at his forthcoming exhibition at Alex, Reid and Lefevre's.[54]

Dalí's importance to the movement in other respects was stressed in Faber and Faber's *Surrealism*, edited (and combatively introduced) by Herbert Read, published shortly after the exhibition ended and soon in a second edition. Read had noted the painter's interest in the Pre-Raphaelites, and doubted if any Englishman could 'approach these artists with the freshness and freedom that Salvador Dalí, for example, brings to their revaluation'.[55] It seems clear from this remark that Read was aware of Dalí's article 'The Spectral Surrealism of the Pre-Raphaelite Eternal Female', published in the eighth issue of *Minotaure*. The article shows that Dalí was familiar with the Tate's Pre-Raphaelite collection, which doubtless he had visited with Edward James, and is notable for his claim to have discovered the earlier movement's 'flagrant Surrealism', a claim consistent, after all, with his championing of Art Nouveau since 1929.[56]

As for Georges Hugnet, who provided an anthology of Surrealist texts for the volume edited by Read, Dalí's poetry was 'so incredibly authentic that it makes one blink. It is a kind of complete confession in the course of which the poet describes his love, his deliriums and his obsessions. Free and violent, it adheres to the most direct mode of expression, the externalization of desires.' An excerpt from 'The Great Masturbator' was provided as supporting proof. A poem on masturbation, that horror of horrors, for the delectation of the English, albeit only the French-reading minority! No better text could have been adduced in support of Surrealism's belief in 'the fullest liberation of the impulses', of its determination to cast off the shackles of sexual repression and censorship.[57]

Where Dalí's promotion in Barcelona was concerned, J.V. Foix was still his most reliable ally. The painter lost no time, therefore, in informing him of the success of the Surrealist Exhibition. As for his own one-man exhibition that was about to open at Alex, Reid and Lefevre's, seven of the most important works had been sold in advance of the show. Dalí was elated. 'Surrealism is catching on wonderfully in London,' he told his friend, paraphrasing Herbert Read's words in the exhibition catalogue, 'for it's awakening the hidden atavisms latent in the English tradition of W. Blake, Lewis Carroll, Pre-Raphaelism, etc.' Soon afterwards *La Publicitat* carried Foix's report on the latest Surrealist news from London, with Dalí to the fore.[58] At Alex, Reid and Lefevre's Dalí exhibited twenty-nine paintings and eighteen drawings. The catalogue incorporated a page designed by the artist which indicated that the works on display comprised:

SNAPSHOTS IN COLOUR AND PROMPTED BY DREAMS

OBJECTIVE AND SUBJECTIVE PHANTOMS
DIURNAL FANTASIES
IMAGES IN HALF-SLEEP
OVERWHELMING OBJECTS
OBJECT-BEINGS
MORPHOLOGICAL SPECTRES
LILLIPUTIAN UNEASINESS
PARANOIAC ASSOCIATIONS
EXPERIMENTAL ONEIRISM
CAPRICES WITHIN THE WOMB
DRAWERS OF FLESH
MALLEABLE WATCHES
VERY HAIRY APARTMENTS
SUBCONSCIOUS IMAGES
IMAGES OF CONCRETE IRRATIONALITY[59]

Gala's confidence in the exhibition was fully justified, for it included many remarkable paintings, not least Edward James's *Suburbs* (more correctly, *Outskirts*) *of the Paranoiac-Critical Town*. Number five in the catalogue should have read *Soft Construction with Boiled Beans*, not 'Boiled Apricots' (one presumes the translator confused 'abricots' and 'haricots' which, knowing Dalí's chaotic orthography, he had probably spelt without an 'h'). The picture's origins, in May 1934, have already been discussed (p. 389 above). Undoubtedly it is one of Dalí's greatest works from this period, the supreme expression of the theme of cannibalism, autophagy and self-mutilation that had dominated so many tormented works over the previous four years. After the Spanish Civil War broke out in July 1936, Dalí began to allege that the work was prophetic, subtitling it *Premonition of Civil War*. But there is no evidence, contrary to what the painter wrote later, that the

XXV

new designation had occurred to him before the rebel Spanish generals rose against the Republic. Significantly, the subtitle figures neither in the Alex, Reid and Lefevre catalogue nor in the 15 June 1936 issue of *Minotaure*, where the painting was first reproduced.[60]

The Alex, Reid and Lefevre show, as Dalí had hoped, placed him at the very centre of the contemporary art scene in London. By lunchtime on the opening day he had sold ten paintings at 'well over an average price of 100 pounds apiece', according to a source quoted by the *Star*, and five drawings that fetched not less than £35 each.[61] On balance the reviews were appreciative. In *The Studio* an anonymous reviewer wrote that, of the newer figures associated with Surrealism, 'by far the most accomplished is Salvador Dalí, who paints like a Pre-Raphaelite gone queer in the head'. He noted that visitors to the gallery had been particularly pleased by the qualities in Dalí's work which it shared 'with that of eminently respectable figures like Holman Hunt'. But there were jibes, too, and irritated letters to editors. The taunt from the critic of the *Daily Telegraph* was fairly typical: 'These pictures from the subconscious reveal so skilled a craftsman that the artist's return to full consciousness may be awaited with interest'.[62]

But neither the Alex, Reid and Lefevre show nor Dalí's works in the International Surrealist Exhibition caught the public imagination so much as his lecture in Burlington Gardens on 1 July. Since the title of the talk was 'Authentic Paranoiac Fantasies', and its theme the benefits to be derived from immersion in the unconscious, Dalí decided to deliver his talk suitably attired. The *Star* reported:

> Mr Dalí and an audience of 300 turned up at the lecture, and Mr Dalí dressed for his part.
> He wore a diving suit, decorated like a Christmas tree.
> The diver's helmet had a motor car radiator on top.
> Plasticine hands were stuck on the bodice.
> Round his waist was a belt with a dagger.
> He carried a billiard cue and was escorted by two big dogs.
> To make the performance more mystifying he spoke in French, through loudspeakers.
> Half-way through his patter he began to get warm and asked somebody to take his helmet off.
> It had stuck and a spanner was no use, but the billiard cue came in handy as a can opener.
> Now and again the lanternist put the slides in sideways or upside down but nobody knew or minded. 'Surrealism is like that'.
> But if anybody thinks this crazy business is funny . . . pause: people buy these daft pictures. Who laughs last?
> Mr Dalí was asked why he wore the diving suit. 'To show that I was plunging down deeply into the human mind,' he replied.[63]

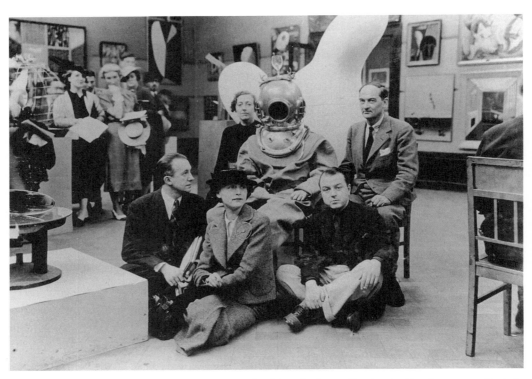

Dalí in diving suit about to give his lecture on plumbing the Surrealist depths, London, 1936. Seated on the floor, from left to right: Paul Éluard, Nusch Éluard and E.L.T. Mesens. On Dalí's right, Diana Lee; on his left, Rupert Lee.

Dalí later claimed that he had been on the point of asphyxiation when help arrived. According to one newspaper, it was Edward James ('the former husband of Miss Tilly Losch, the dancer, who was acting as the very charming chairman') who succeeded in removing the recalcitrant helmet.[64] David Gascoyne claimed that it had fallen to him to locate a spanner—no easy task in Bond Street.[65]

James would certainly have been keen to ensure Dalí's survival, for at this time he he was busily engaged in hammering out a contract which would give him full control of the artist's production for two years. On 20 June his lawyer in Paris, Robert Bernstein, had sent him a draft proposal of the document. It was couched in the form of James's acknowledgment of, and complete acceptance of, the terms set out in a putative letter from Dalí. In this, the artist agreed that all the pictures, watercolours and drawings he produced between 1 July 1936 and 1 July 1938 were to be the sole property of James and that he was strictly forbidden to sell or surrender to anyone else works executed during this period. The number and sizes of the works to be produced were to be specified, and the sums to be paid to Dalí by James every six months.

If Dalí failed to deliver the agreed number of works, the payments were to be reduced accordingly.[66]

John Lowe, James's biographer, has written that this draft contract, 'with the details agreed', was signed during the summer of 1936. But this was not the case. The definitive document giving James the rights to Dalí's total output was not signed until the end of the year and, as we shall see, only came into operation on 1 June 1937.[67]

What James did succeed in achieving this summer was a convoluted contract whereby Dalí sold him his painting *Geodesic Portrait of Gala*. Signed by Dalí and James's attorney in London on 31 July 1936, the agreement allowed the artist to retain the painting at his own risk until 30 July 1939. Dalí received 20,000 francs on signature, and a final 5,000 were to be paid to him when he handed over. It was a remarkably generous contract on the part of James. In the event, Dalí was to hang on to the painting for longer that the date stipulated in the contract. James was understandably furious. Today the work is in the Yokohama Museum of Art.[68]

The Death of Lorca

Dalí and Gala were staying with James in Wimpole Street when they heard that the long-awaited Fascist coup had taken place in Spain. James maintained in a letter to Dalí drafted two years later, and perhaps never sent, that at the time the painter had expressed the hope that the Republic would prevail, reacting enthusiastically each day as the news came in of Communist and Anarchist successes. According to James, Dalí had even ridiculed a friend of his, Yvonne de Casa Fuerte, because, as a Catholic, she was pro-Franco. In view of Dalí's growing sympathy for Fascism at this time, however, it is hard to credit the accuracy of James's recollection. Or perhaps it was that Dalí, indulging in his favourite game of subterfuge, had pretended to be Republican while he waited to see what happened.[69]

In August James joined the Dalís in Paris. He had devised a novel plan for helping the Republic. This was to raise money for the purchase of bombers by persuading the Spanish Government to lend him some of the El Grecos in the Prado. The pictures would be exhibited at Burlington House and the funds generated by the entrance fees remitted to the Spaniards. James approached Sir Kenneth Clark, then head of the National Gallery, and he seemed interested in the proposal.[70] James got Dalí to introduce him to Luis Buñuel, who at this time was working in a political, and partly secret, capacity for the Spanish Embassy in Paris. Buñuel recalls in his memoirs that he communicated James's offer to the Republic's Minister of Foreign Affairs, Alvarez del Vayo. The latter would have liked to accept (the government badly needed bombers), but he felt unable to do so: international opinion would be hostile to an exchange of war material for works from the Prado, no matter what guarantees were provided.[71]

In Paris, that September, Dalí heard that Lorca had been executed by the Fascists in his native Granada. At first the poet's friends found it impossible to believe the rumour, but little by little, as the rebels failed to demonstrate that he was still alive, and more details of the brutal repression of Granada became known, the terrible truth imposed itself. There is no contemporary account of Dalí's reaction to the news. In the *Secret Life*, by which time he was rewriting history, he recalled:

> At the very outbreak of the revolution my great friend, the poet of *la mala muerte*, Federico García Lorca, died before a firing squad in Granada, occupied by the Fascists. His death was exploited for propaganda purposes. This was ignoble, for they knew as well as I that Lorca was by essence the most a-political person on earth. Lorca did not die as a symbol of one or another political ideology, he died as a propitiatory victim of that total and integral phenomenon that was the revolutionary confusion in which the Civil War unfolded. For that matter, in the Civil War people killed one another not even for ideas, but for 'personal reasons', for reasons of personality; and like myself, Lorca had personality and to spare, and with it a better right than most Spaniards to be shot by Spaniards. Lorca's tragic sense of life was marked by the same tragic constant as that of the destiny of the whole Spanish people.[72]

Dalí may not have been aware of just how politically committed Lorca had proved himself to be in the turbulent months leading up to the war, pledging his support to the Popular Front, signing left-wing manifestos, going out of his way publicly to condemn Fascism and even stating, in a newspaper interview, that the Granada Right was not only 'the worst bourgeoisie in Spain' but was actively plotting against the government. Dalí was correct, however, in suspecting that elements of personal enmity had played their part in the poet's assassination.[73] One of the most charismatic Spaniards ever born, Lorca aroused intense envy as well as admiration (as Dalí well knew from the Madrid days). The artist claimed later that, when he heard the news of Lorca's death, he had exclaimed 'Olé!', using the term in its bullfighting sense of admiration for a brilliantly executed pass: Lorca, obsessed by death, had fulfilled his destiny to perfection. Faced with the loss of 'the best friend of his youth', Dalí could not but remember how, in the Residencia, the poet had tried to cope with his terror of dying by compulsively acting out his demise, burial and gradual decomposition, while his friends followed the ritual with fascination and horror.[74] Now that Lorca had been sacrificed, at the age of only thirty-eight, Dalí came to realize that something had snapped in his own life. Lorca was to accompany him closely for the rest of his days. When things went well, he would thank him for helping him; Lorca's voice, music and poetry would ring constantly in his ears and reverberate in both his paintings and literary work; and he would never fail to allude with pride to the 'Ode to Salvador Dalí', the full relevance of which only struck him after the poet's tragic disappearance. Truly it is as impossible to understand Dalí without taking into account his friendship with Lorca as it is to conceive of his life and work in the absence of Gala. Yet in the case of both relationships our knowledge is painfully deficient.

In the *Secret Life*, where he rationalizes his decision not to return to Spain and align himself politically, Dalí claims that the news of Lorca's death, and the 'suffocating atmosphere of partisanship' created in Paris by the Spanish war, determined him to set off on a trip to Mussolini's Italy.[75] His account of the visit is a tissue of inaccuracies: he did not spend 'a long season' that autumn with Edward James at the Villa Cimbrone,[76] and the visit to Lord Berners in Rome (and briefly to Sicily), when he painted *Impressions of Africa*, took place in 1938, not 1936. The only bit of historical truth in these amusing pages is that he and Gala spent some time in the Dolomites (where they waited in vain for James to join them), staying at the Hotel Tre Croci in Cortina d'Ampezzo. From there Dalí wrote to Breton to tell him that the mountains were stimulating him mentally to such an extent that he could not sleep and kept wanting to burst out laughing. Another reason for his excitement, he added, was the forthcoming exhibition in New York. This was Fantastic Art, Dada and Surrealism, organized by Alfred Barr and scheduled to open at the Museum of Modern Art in December, coinciding with Dalí's third show at Julien Levy's. 'On vous aime,' Dalí ended the brief and inconsequential missive.[77]

By 5 October 1936, after moving on from Cortina d'Ampezzo to Florence,[78] the artist and Gala were back in Paris. The ninth issue of *Minotaure* had just appeared and included a colour reproduction, and detail, of *Soft Construction with Boiled Beans*, now strategically renamed *Spain. Premonition of Civil War*. Dalí, Gala told James, was furiously preparing work for his forthcoming exhibition in New York. Would 'Petitou' please lend them *Paranoiac Face, The Automobile of Death* and *City of Drawers* for the MOMA exhibition? A few days later Dalí begged James also to send *Autumn Cannibalism* and *Child Looking at the Moon*. James compromised, sending *Paranoiac Face* and *City of Drawers*.

Just before Dalí and Gala boarded ship for New York the painter received a pained letter from Breton, dated 22 November 1936, in which he complained about Dalí's failure to return a book and the typescript of an article by Gilbert Lély (presumably both on Sade) and the copy he had lent him of Jarry's *Ubu Enchained*. Breton listed other failures by Dalí to keep his word, and reminded him of the many favours he had done him, not least correcting his texts for publication (habitually written, he was too polite to say, in orthographically abominable French). Surely Dalí could be more considerate? The letter was not unfriendly, though. Breton simply felt let down, and ended by saying that between them there should be no place for irrationality.[79]

With Julien Levy in New York

On 7 December 1936 Dalí and Gala arrived in New York on board the *Normandie*, pride of the French line. The timing of their visit, as of Dalí's exhibition, had been planned carefully by the ever-alert Julien Levy to coincide with the opening of Barr's Fantastic Art, Dada, Surrealism show at the Museum of Modern Art. Levy was confident that Dalí was about to hit the jackpot in New York. He had seen him and Gala at their Rue Gauguet studio the previous summer and been struck by the change in the painter, a change that augured well for the autumn. 'Dalí was no longer the half-timid, half-malicious foreigner, but now expensive and elegant and quite formidable,' he recalled in *Memoir of an Art Gallery*. Levy had met Edward James for the first time on that occasion, and been dismayed to find that he was acquiring 'all' Dalí's best work. But they had got on well and James had promised to lend pictures for Dalí's New York show. He kept his word.[80]

Julien Levy had seen to it that Caresse Crosby's Black Sun Press, now based in Manhattan, brought out his beautifully produced book, *Surrealism*, on time for the Barr and Dalí shows. It meant further publicity for Dalí (as well as for Levy). So too did the appearance of the New York edition of Faber and Faber's book of the same title, edited by Herbert Read, which was doing so well in London. Clearly, this was to be New York's Great Surrealist Season, with Dalí as main player.

Fantastic Art, Dada, Surrealism opened on 9 December 1936 and was a huge success with public and critics alike. As Barr explained in the exhibition catalogue (reprinted in a much embellished and expanded version in July 1937), this was the second in a series of shows 'planned to present in an objective and historical manner the principal movements of modern art' (the first, Cubism and Abstract Art, had been held the previous spring). The exhibition, which ran until 17 January 1937 and attracted massive crowds, included six works by Dalí: *Illumined Pleasures* (1929), *The Font* (1930), the by now famous *The Persistence of Memory* (1931), *Puzzle of Autumn* (1935) and the two works sent by Edward James, both done in 1936: *Paranoiac Face* and the ink drawing *City of Drawers*.

Barr had commissioned Georges Hugnet to write two historically oriented articles on

Dada and Surrealism for the exhibition catalogue. Dalí had executed a suitably erotic frontispiece for Hugnet's *Onan* in 1931, and seems to have been on good terms with the young writer, who had been accepted into the Surrealist ranks at about the same time as himself. He could have expected, therefore, an appreciative account of his contribution to the movement. In the event it was particularly glowing:

> At the same time as Breton in his *Second Surrealist Manifesto* proceeds toward an evaluation of the Surrealist spirit, a new painter assumes a rôle of capital importance. The poetic, pictorial and critical contributions of Salvador Dalí turned Surrealist research in a particular direction and gave a strong impulse to experiments which had been approached till then only in the most tentative fashion. His work is like an immense carnivorous flower blooming in the Surrealist sun. Moved by the lyrical expression of certain works of Ernst and Tanguy rather than won over by their plastic processes, and carrying to their extreme conclusions certain statements of the *First Manifesto*, he gives full rein to dreams and hallucinations which he represents in the most faithful and meticulous way. He asserts his taste for chromolithographs, the most colored, the most complete, and the least accidental imitation of nature. He disdains all experiments with surfaces and all the familiar clichés of the painter's craft. He puts his 'manner', his pictorial talent directly at the service of delirium. The *trompe l'oeil* is his way out. He creates a feverish world in which rôles are played by simulations, physical illnesses, nervous conditions, sexual phenomena, inhibitions. Without inconsistency his range extends from collage to chromo, from ready-made objects to perfect illusions, from De Chirico and Picasso to Millet and Meissonier—and all by the method of paranoiac association. His experiments, though remarkably fruitful, could not be successfully vulgarized. His conception of the purpose of painting accounts for his anti-artistic tendency, his delight in double images, and his desire to make his paintings like 'handmade snapshots'. His method of subjective criticism, his interpretation of the most familiar works of art as recurrent obsessions, his acceptance of every aberration both in his paintings and in his writings, and his respect for dreams in their integrity no matter how contradictory, are all essential contributions to Surealist documentation.[81]

Dalí, while he must have been pleased with this appraisal, was unhappy with the drift of Hugnet's preface. He told Breton that in his view the text was deficient from an ideological, and even from an historical, point of view. Dada (which had received twenty pages to Surrealism's eighteen!) should have been given 'three historical lines, as if it were something really distant'. A gullible press and an ignorant public were being seriously misled, and to make matters worse Hugnet had not afforded due prominence to Surrealism's current position vis-à-vis 'the irrational', that is, to its desire to harness the energies of the unconscious rather than record passively its functioning (as in the first phase of Surrealism). Breton himself should have done the preface.[82]

On 10 December, the day after the opening of Fantastic Art, Dada, Surrealism, came the private view of Dalí's exhibition at Levy's; and on 14 December, the eve of the public opening, the artist received the ultimate accolade when a photograph of him by Man Ray appeared on the front cover of *Time*. 'SURREALIST SALVADOR DALÍ. A blazing pine tree, an Archbishop, a giraffe and a cloud of feathers went out the window', read the caption. *Time* had referred a year earlier to Dalí's collaboration on *L'Age d'or* (without mentioning Buñuel), and Dalí must have been pleased by this new allusion to the by now legendary film, which had been shown 'behind locked doors' in Manhattan in 1932.[83] In its inside pages *Time* reviewed the MOMA exhibition and provided a detailed and appreciative synopsis of Dalí's career to date. 'Surrealism', it wrote, 'would never have attracted its present attention in the U.S. were it not for a handsome 32–year-old Catalan with a soft voice and a clipped cin-

At work on The Secret Life of Salvador Dalí, *1940, at Coresse Crosby's Hampton Manor, Virginia.*

emactor's moustache, Salvador Dalí.' This was true. The magazine added, with evident approval, that Dalí had 'a faculty for publicity that should turn any circus press agent green with envy'. If Breton saw this issue of *Time* he must have been pained.[84]

Dalí, who as yet spoke no English, was unaware of how widely read *Time* was. Suddenly he found that he could not cross the street without being recognized and asked to sign autographs. It was one thing to be known in Figueres. But in Fifth Avenue! 'Fame,' he recalled, 'was as intoxicating to me as a spring morning.'[85]

Julien Levy and Dalí had devised a spectacular 'Souvenir-Catalogue' (printed in Paris) for the artist's third individual exhibition in New York. The cover displayed a woman with furry shoulders, an open drawer for a face and pendulous naked breasts from beneath which two strips, affixed by studs inserted into the nipples, could be pulled down to reveal miniature reproductions of some of the works on show. 'A treasure trove of little accordioned reproductions restrained by snaps,' Edward Alden Jewell termed the novel device in the *New York Times*.[86] Above the woman's left shoulder was a print-ed list of the exhibits' characteristics copied word for word from the catalogue of Dalí's show the previous summer at Alex, Reid and Lefevre's in London. To the right, the public was informed, in Dalinian calligraphy, that the artist rendered 'the invisible straight from nature'. There were three further indications: 'Disturbing images', 'The epidermas [sic] of orchestras' and 'Saliva Sofas'. On show at Levy's were twenty paintings, twelve drawings (not identified in the catalogue) and the popular *Aphrodisiac Dinner Jacket*.[87]

The show was a triumph. Having joked about the risqué catalogue, Edward Alden Jewell went on: 'On the craft side, Dalí has outdone himself. In all seriousness, he can paint like an angel. I do not think he has ever painted as well as he is painting now.'[88] This was probably true: Edward James's support had enabled Dalí to produce outstand-ing work. So much so that *Art News*, unaware of this special relationship, was positive-ly bemused. 'It seems extraordinary,' the review commented, 'that Salvador Dalí can continue to produce such pictures with such energy and such wild joy.'[89]

The painting that attracted most attention at the exhibition was *Soft Construction with Boiled Beans*, now subtitled *Premonition of Civil War*, which one critic considered not only Dalí's masterpiece but 'the incontestable masterpiece of surrealism to date'.[90] Dalí's recently painted *Autumn Cannibalism* was a further reminder of the Spanish war—a war in which many idealistic Americans were soon to lose their lives. 'These Iberian beings devouring each other in the autumn,' Dalí commented later, 'express the pathos of civil war considered (by me) as a phenomenon of natural history, as distinct from Picasso, who considered it a political one.'[91]

Picasso, always perceived as the great rival! Dalí's remark, though retrospective, pin-points the differences between his and Picasso's attitude to the Spanish war. One looks in vain for any statement by Dalí supporting the Republic or condemning the infamous Non-Intervention Pact signed by the British and French Governments while Germany and Italy were supplying aircraft and other equipment to Franco. Dalí observed 'the phenom-enon of natural history' from afar; and since at this stage of the war nobody could foresee its outcome, decided to keep his mouth shut, in public at least, presumably thinking that as a result he would be able to return home no matter which side won. Nothing could be more unlike this sit-on-the-fence attitude than the passionate indignation and concern for justice registered day after day in his adolescent diaries of twenty years earlier.

Bonwit Teller's, the famous department store in Fifth Avenue, had commissioned Surrealist windows from a series of artists to coincide with the opening of the Fantastic Art, Dada, Surrealism exhibition at the MOMA. It was Dalí's display that caught the public imagination, however, the crowd standing six-deep in the street to gape at his inventions. His theme was 'She was a Surrealist Woman, She was Like a Figure in a Dream', 'the most coherent title,' a reporter quipped, 'ever tacked on a Dalí composition to date'. Against a backdrop of papier-mâché clouds reclined a female, black-gowned dummy with a head of red roses: the Surrealist Woman in person. Long red arms reached for her from fissures in crumbling walls, or offered her gifts, but none quite succeeded in touching her. On a small table beside her was the bright red lobster-telephone that Dalí had designed for Edward James. 'We had thought that by this time everyone knew about Surrealism,' wrote the same reporter, 'Salvador Dalí, its arch-exponent, being a born publicist who makes even a Harry Reichenbach look like an amateur.' Harry Reichenbach was a raffish theatrical press agent well known in New York for his publicity stunts.[92]

Julien Levy, too, was a good publicist. His timely book *Surrealism* included an excellent anthology of the movement's texts, printed on paper of different colours, and a fine selection of black-and-white reproductions. The introduction was enthusiastic, and Levy made no effort to hide his deep admiration for André Breton. Nor for Dalí, who, as both writer and artist, received more coverage than any other member of the group: seven reproductions (*The Weaning of Furniture-Nutrition, Illumined Pleasures, The Persistence of Memory, Outskirts of the Paranoiac-Critical Town, The Accommodations of Desire, Aphrodisiac Dinner Jacket, Finis*) and a series of texts that included excerpts from *Babaouo*, 'The Putrescent Ass', *Love and Memory* and 'an announcement', as Levy explained, 'written euphonically by Dalí to be read aloud upon his first visit to New York':

SURREALISM

> aye av ei horror uv joks
> Surrealism is not ei jok
> Surrealism is ei strangue poizun
> Surrealism is zi mosst vaiolent and daingeros
> toxin for dsi imagineichon zad has so far
> bin invented in dsi domein ouve art
> Surrealism is irrezisteible and terifai-ingli
> conteichios
> Biuer! Ai bring ou Surrealism
> Aulredi meni pipoul in Nui York jave bin infectid
> bai zi laifquiving and marvelos sors of Surrealism[93]

Levy's commentary shows that he knew hardly anything about Dalí's pre-Paris period, and that the artist had been telling him some tall stories about his childhood. 'As a boy he walked to school across the vast morbid plains of Catalonia,' we are assured, 'the bleached bones of the dead asses to right and left, always beside him his terror, his father, and always within him that frantic, repressed energy, equal to the energy of madness.' Dalí had never had to walk more than a few yards to school. As for the vast morbid plains of Catalunya, littered with the skeletons of asses, they sound more like the Sahara than the lush meadows of the Upper Empordà. But the allusion to Dalí's fearful father rings true enough.[94]

At the end of December Dalí and Gala spent a week in Quebec to escape from what the painter, in a letter to Breton, termed 'the uninterrupted agitation' of New York. The success of the Fantastic Art, Dada, Surrealism show was proving even greater than that of the previous summer's Surrealist exhibition in London, Dalí told Breton. As for his own exhibition, it was faring well, and he was going to give some lectures in which he would strive to present Surrealism in the clearest possible light. The word Surrealist was now all the rage in New York. People were saying things like 'this colour is more Surrealist than that'. Did Breton have any news of Stalin? It was ages since Dalí had heard anything about him. 'I'm doing my best for our activity,' he finished.[95]

Dalí was certainly doing the best for himself—and for Gala. To this end he now entered into a special agreement with Edward James, who had arrived in New York to take part in the Surrealist high jinks. On 21 December 1936 the two signed the definitive contract by which James was to purchase all of Dalí's work between June 1937 and June 1938. Dalí was obliged to produce not fewer than twelve large pictures of approximately 550 square inches in size, eighteen smaller pictures of approximately 120 square inches and sixty drawings of the same size as the letter. In return he was to receive the sum of £2,400 paid in monthly instalments of £200. Penalty clauses were included to cover any failure on Dalí's part to honour the contract, and provisions were made for currency fluctuations. It was a great deal of money, and for a year was to give the Dalís an economic stability they had never enjoyed previously, not even in the balmy days of the Zodiac.[96]

The New Marxism

Dalí had come to the conclusion by this time that Karl Marx was out and the Marx Brothers were in. He had been enjoying the latter's antics for years, and particularly admired 'the biological, hysterical and cannibalistic frenzy' of *Animal Crackers*.[97] In his opinion the most Surrealist of the brothers was Harpo, whom he had met briefly the previous summer in Paris, and he now sent him a Dalinian present for Christmas: a harp with barbed-wire strings. It was probably accompanied by a message announcing his imminent arrival in Hollywood. Harpo replied with a photograph: it showed him with his fingers bandaged. He told Dalí that he would delighted to be 'smeared' by him if he went west, and declared himself a great admirer of *The Persistence of Memory*.[98]

Dalí arrived in Hollywood with Gala at the end of January 1937 and was soon visiting Harpo, with whom he had probably already decided he wanted to make a film. He discovered that Harpo's eyes shone with 'the same spectral light to be observed in Picasso's' and that, like Dalí, he admired Watteau.[99] They got on like a house on fire, and the *Los Angeles Examiner* photographed Dalí drawing the actor at his barbed-wire instrument. He had a lobster on his head. Dalí raised the subject of their collaborating on a film, and it seems that Harpo expressed some initial interest.[100]

From Hollywood Dalí told Edward James that, as well as meeting Harpo, he and Gala had seen lots of desert and any number of platinum blondes.[101] To Breton he reported that that he was in contact with 'the three American Surrealists' (the Marx Brothers), Cecil B. de Mille and Walt Disney. He felt he had considerably intoxicated them all and that there were genuine possibilities for Surrealism in the cinema. He ended by assuring Breton, as he had done in earlier communications, that he was doing all he could for the Surrealist cause.[102]

When Dalí and Gala returned to Europe in March the projected film with Harpo was much on the painter's mind. From the Arlberg-Wintersporthotel in Zürs, where the couple spent a month relaxing in the snow, he drafted a letter in which he told Harpo that he was about to start on the screenplay for a short film in which Harpo would be the sole protagonist. He was absolutely determined to work with him, he said, now that he had discovered they understood each other so perfectly and had such similar imaginations. The scenery would be extraordinary. Perhaps Cole Porter could do the music. They would enjoy themselves hugely while at the same time revolutionizing the cinema![103]

The script has only recently come to light. It concerns a Spanish businessman with the unlikely name of Jimmy who lives in the United States. He is unhappy with his girlfriend Linda. One night he meets and falls in love with 'a beautiful Surrealist woman' who is never seen face-to-face by the spectator. Their ineffable romance is intended as a Bretonian synthesis of dream and reality, but the script is banal beyond belief. It is also very self-indulgent. Dalí's sexual obsessions pervade it, and the artist is careful to give full billing to his personal icons, not least soft watches and lobster-telephones. A troop of cyclists with loaves of bread on their heads is lifted straight from *Babaouo*; the passing clouds reflected in the Surrealist Woman's mirror are a reminder of a scene in *L'Age d'or*; so too is the giraffe (but Dalí has gone one step better and set it on fire). Clearly Dalí was still trying to pick up from where he had left off with Buñuel.[104]

And still not succeeding. If Harpo responded positively to the script, or indeed even saw it, there is no record. Nor is there any of interest on the part of a producer. But this did not stop Dalí from proclaiming that he was going to make a film with the Marx Brothers. Dalí could never be accused of a lack of boastfulness, and he had an almost superhuman tenacity in the pursuit of his own interests.

Metamorphosis of Narcissus

At Zürs, as well as working on his film script, Dalí embarked on a new experiment: the composition, in French, of a 'paranoaic' poem, *The Myth of Narcissus*, to be concurrently illustrated, 'word by word', in a painting.[105] The latter, for which Dalí did at least two studies,[106] was finished in mid-June 1937, and soon afterwards both it and the poem were definitively titled *Metamorphosis of Narcissus*. The poem was published by Editions Surréalistes that summer with a colour reproduction of the painting as frontispiece. Two colour details of the work were also included for good measure. The black-and-white cover photograph, by Cecil Beaton, showed Gala sitting in front of Dalí's *Couple with their Heads in the Clouds*. An English version of the text, by Francis Scarpe, was brought out at the same time by Julien Levy in New York, following the practice of simultaneous publication in France and America established by *The Conquest of the Irrational*. Both editions were dedicated to Paul Éluard. For his epigraph, Dalí quoted yet again the words with which Breton had praised his 'paranoiac-critical method' in 1934.

The subtitle of the poem explained that the latter constituted a 'way of visually observing the course of the metamorphosis of Narcissus' and claimed that it was the first time that both a painting and a poem had been obtained 'entirely through the integral application of the paranoiac-critical method'. The claim should not be taken too seriously, but the picture certainly deserves our scrutiny.

XXIX

Dalí's interest in the Narcissus myth may have been stimulated by Albert Skira's edition of Ovid's *Metamorphoses*, illustrated by Picasso. Given his own, Narcissus-style self-absorption it was hardly surprising that he considered the myth of great personal relevance. In this he was assisted by Freud's *Three Essays on Sexuality* and, particularly, 'Psycho-Analytic Notes on an Autobiographical Account of a Case of Paranoia'. In the latter Freud uses the term 'narcissism' (defined in *The Interpretation of Dreams* as 'the unbounded self-love of children')[107] to designate 'a stage in the development of the libido which it passes through on the way from auto-erotism to object-love', stressing that it is a moment when fixations can easily be established and neuroses and paranoia take firm hold.[108] Dalí must have been been struck to discover that Freud interprets paranoia as a defence against homosexuality. Since the painter now claimed to be not only the Great Masturbator but the Great Paranoiac, featured in the painting of this title done the previous year, he must have been aware that, to be consistent, he should have claimed fear of homosexuality, real or imagined, as an important factor in his personality. But, as Santos Torroella has pointed out in his penetrating analysis of *Metamorphosis of Narcissus*, Dalí was never prepared, or able, to take this step.[109]

XXVIII

Dalí said that *The Great Paranoiac* had been conceived after a discussion with Josep María Sert about Arcimboldo, and that the protagonist's face is fashioned on 'Empordà countryfolk, the greatest paranoiacs of all'.[110] The remarkable work suggests strongly that Dalí was now convinced that the intense feelings of shame which had always troubled him were paranoid in character. The leitmotif of the person hiding his head in shame had first appeared in Dalí's work in 1929, and between then and 1936 had recurred in more than thirty paintings and drawings. In *The Great Paranoiac* it attains its most eloquent expression. Almost all the characters in the picture are burying their heads in their hands or refusing to look, particularly the seated female whose buttocks form the nose of the protagonist. Brushing against this buttocks-nose is the shapely bottom of Gala: presumably Dalí is hinting once again that his shame-imbued erotic fantasies are centred on this part of the body. The double figuration employed in the delineation of the head of the Great Paranoiac is as successful as any achieved by the painter, and is perhaps even more striking in the repetition of the motif in the left background, where the back of the head merges into an anguished group of people all hiding their faces or running away.

As the eye scans the details of the painting, one is struck by the male couple among the rocks just behind the Great Paranoiac's head, one of whom has an unexpected red blob on his head, as if Dalí wanted us to look closely. This figure, who is ordering an ashamed male to leave (like God expelling Adam from the Garden of Eden), has the indubitable look of Dalí's father. Clearly he continued to be a major problem.

Given Dalí's fear of homosexuality, now fused with his fear of paranoia, it comes as no surprise to find allusions to Lorca in the poem *Metamorphosis of Narcissus* and, by extension, in the picture of the same name. One section of the text contains an explicit acknowledgement that the poet is on Dalí's mind as he writes. He apostrophizes Narcissus:

> Narcissus, you are losing your body,
> carried away and confounded by the millenary
> reflection of your disappearance

> your body stricken dead
> falls to the topaz precipice with yellow wreckage
> of love,
> your white body, swallowed up,
> follows the slope of the savagely mineral torrent
> of the black precious stones with pungent perfumes,
> your body . . .
> down to the unglazed mouths of the night
> on the edge of which
> there sparkles already
> all the red silverware
> of dawns with veins broken in 'the wharves of
> blood'.

A footnote by Dalí indicates that the expression 'the wharves of blood' is from Lorca, but does not identify the source. The image, imperfectly rendered by Francis Scarpe, would be better translated 'landing stage of the blood'. It comes in the poem 'Blind Panorama of New York' ('Panorama ciego de Nueva York'), not published until four years after Lorca's death but which presumably he had recited to Dalí when they met for the last time in Barcelona in 1935 (unless, that is, he sent him a copy). The passage in which the image occurs is worth quoting not only for the direct borrowing by Dalí, and the explicit homage that it implies to Lorca, but because it shows that the poet's New York *manner* influenced him powerfully, at least in *Metamorphosis of Narcissus*. Lorca is expressing the almost ineffable oppression that New York exerted on his spirit when he arrived there in 1929:

> It's a capsule of air where the whole world hurts us,
> it's a tiny space throbbing in the crazy unison of light,
> it's an indefinable ladder where clouds and roses forget
> the Chinese hubbub pounding along the landing stage of the blood.
> Many times I've got lost
> looking for the burn that maintains things alive
> and all I've found is sailors sprawled over the railings
> and little creatures of the sky buried under the snow.[111]

Almost ten years earlier, when Lorca published his *Gypsy Ballads*, Dalí had criticized what he considered the poem's old-hat Andalusian localism. This did not prevent the painter from hinting now in *Metamorphosis of Narcissus* at one of Lorca's most moving poems in that collection. The allusion comes when Dalí evokes the dancers in the background of the painting, whom he terms 'the heterosexual group'. The males comprise a Hindi, a Catalan and a German; the females an Englishwoman, a Russian, a Swede, an American and:

> the great sombre Andalusian
> robust with glands and olive-green from anguish.

This must be Soledad Montoya, the protagonist of Lorca's 'Ballad of Black Anguish', whom we find searching desperately, like so many of Lorca's characters, for a love denied to her. Her presence here is yet another indication of how much Lorca, a year after his assassination, was haunting Dalí.

Santos Torroella is correct, surely, in seeing the full sense of Dalí's poem, and henceforth of the painting, in the appearance of Gala at the end.[112] Immersed in self-absorption; in danger, when Lorca was alive, of succumbing to homosexual tendencies, and perhaps still in danger of doing so; his sexual activity reduced to the fantasy world of masturbation, as symbolized by the monumental, fossilized hand into which Narcissus is transformed in the painting: Dalí has been offered the chance of survival, if not cure, by the epiphany of the Muse who came into his life at Cadaqués in the summer of 1929. In this respect it is significant that the scene is set at Cape Creus, the low hills of whose hinterland are unmistakable in the background, for it was here that the couple had discovered their love. Gala does not appear directly in the painting, but is symbolized by the narcissus that bursts from the head of the despairing self-contemplative, now changed into an egg:

> When this head splits open,
> when this head crackles,
> when this head explodes,
> it will be the flower,
> the new Narcissus,
> Gala—
> my narcissus.

For José Pierre, *Metamorphosis of Narcissus*, despite Dalí's claim that it was the first picture executed 'entirely through the integral application of the paranoiac-critical method', falls very far short of such a pretension. The double image had been at the core of Dalí's 'paranoiac' aesthetic since the early 1930s, but here it is entirely lacking, the image, rather than 'double', being simply 'dédoublée' ('unfurled'), that is, 'just the opposite'. Pierre is in no doubt that the painting indicates the beginning of a decline in Dalí's commitment to his own 'method', and hence to Surrealism in the sense that Breton understood it. That this was so is borne out by his production over the next three years.[113]

As Dalí worked on *Metamorphosis of Narcissus*, poem and painting, he was in constant contact with Edward James, who not only paid for the colour photograph of the picture for the poem's frontispiece, then an expensive process, but footed the hefty printer's bill as well.[114] Was James in love with Dalí the man as well as with his art? The painter never intimates in his published work that he and his patron had a homosexual relationship, even of the mildest kind, yet James's papers suggest that at times they came close to intimacy. In a note, perhaps from 1936, he records that Gala was perfectly aware of how 'close' he and Dalí were and accepted the arrangement as 'workable', even though one night, in a hotel at Modena, she had staged a jealous scene. On that occasion, James recalled or perhaps fantasized, Dalí had come to his room in tears, wearing only the top of his pyjamas, saying he couldn't stand Gala nagging him about Lorca and James any longer. James came to the conclusion that Gala's tantrums were calculated mainly to squeeze placatory money and gifts out of him. The ploy never failed to succeed. Once Dalí had spent all night with him at the Ritz in Paris and returned home, with James in tow, to face a Gala threatening to leave him and push off to Portugal. But James had in his pocket a marvellous Christmas present for the irate muse: a case of stringed cabochon sapphires, rubies and emeralds in a gold setting. Portugal was forgotten and soon Gala was happily making scrambled eggs in the kitchen.[115] On another occasion James wrote perceptively about Dalí:

> His real interests were instinctively far more homosexual than heterosexual; Gala tried to believe that she had cured him of his homosexuality, but she knew in her heart that she had not really at all. She had, however, managed to keep it 'sublimated' (if you can call it that) by channelling it into erotic drawings and some obscene pictures which are owned by private collectors who buy pornography . . . as for Dalí's sex life with his wife, far from being jealous of her sexual infidelities, he actually facilitated them; one day he confessed to me; 'Je laisse Gala prendre des amants quand elle veut. Actuellement [sic] je l'encourage et je l'aide, parce que cela m'excite.'[116]

None of this suggests that there was anything overtly sexual between James and Dalí. James's biographers seem to agree that the Englishman was as sexually inhibited with men as he was with women; as for the Catalan, being touched or caressed, unless it was by Gala, threw him into an absolute panic. So one must conclude that, whatever attraction existed between the two men, it did not find a physical outlet.

At the end of June 1937 Dalí asked James for permission to exhibit at his forthcoming summer show in Paris the paintings he had finished since the first of the month, the date on which their contract came into operation. James agreed. The exhibition ran from 6 to 30 July at Renou et Colle (140, Faubourg Saint-Honoré) and included *Metamorphosis of Narcissus, Geodesic Portrait of Gala, Giraffes on Fire, Portrait of Harpo Marx, Frenetic Love, Meissonier, Invention of Monsters, Epidermis of Piano, Face of Mae West Which Can Serve as a Surrealist Apartment, Drawings for the Cinema* (for Dalí's project with the Marx Brothers) and other drawings.[117]

James suspected that among the latter were some done after 1 June, and reminded Dalí in August that, when he visited him in Paris on 29 May, five large drawings that appeared in the show had not even been started. They could hardly have been executed in two days! He also complained that Dalí had dashed off a great number of drawings in the weeks before the contract came into operation—Dalí had admitted this in a letter—thereby flooding the market and reducing the value of *his* works. James was to continue to have endless contractual problems with Dalí, but he put up with the situation because his liking for the painter, and for Gala, was quite genuine. So, of course, was his great admiration for Dalí's ability. Had this not been so, he would never have invested so much money in him. James sincerely believed that by having a regular, and generous, salary, Dalí would produce much better work than would otherwise have been possible. Their contract, he wrote, was the best means of enabling the artist to produce pictures which, not having been painted in too much haste, would make an important mark on the history of painting. In this he was undoubtedly right.[118]

Was Dalí asked to contribute to the Spanish Pavilion at the Paris International Exhibition of the Arts and Techniques of Modern Life, which opened at the beginning of May 1937? It seems likely, although no documentation has come to light. His absence, certainly, was glaring, given the fact that the emphasis of the Pavilion, symbolized by Picasso's *Guernica*, was on helping Republican Spain in its struggle against Franco and on condemning the Non-Intervention Pact. Had Dalí wished or cared, there is no question that he would have been included. His abstention, therefore, was a clear indication that he was not prepared to support the Republic, and contained more than a hint of where his true sympathies lay. What Dalí did do, breaking Surrealist group discipline once again, was to send eight paintings to the exhibition Origins and Development of

Independent International Art, held at the Jeu de Paume from 30 July to 31 October and repudiated by Breton for its 'biased' selection of artists.[119]

At the end of August, just before Dalí and Gala set off on a trip to Austria, Hungary and Italy, the painter wrote to Edward James from Paris to tell him he had signed a contract with Léonide Massine for a ballet, *Tristan Fou*. His great friend, the couturier Elsa Schiaparelli, was to do the costumes. Dalí assured James, who had recently been ill, that the drawings would of course belong to him in accordance with the provisions of their contract, and told him he had ordered another Schiaparelli dress for Gala on his account. Hadn't James said he was going to give her a present? James was not to forget this cheek. The letter throws some light on the problems currently besetting *Minotaure* (from which James had withdrawn his financial backing). The new editorial committee was composed of Breton, Pierre Mabille, Maurice Heine, Éluard and Duchamp. Dalí had not been consulted. The exclusion, he surmised, was because of his close friendship with James. He hoped that, despite all, he would be asked to collaborate. In the event he was—but not for long.[120]

Paris and Rome

As the civil war raged on in Spain there could be no question of Dalí's returning to Catalunya where, he must have felt, anything might happen to him . . . interrogation at the frontier, arrest, injury, even death. News may already have reached him of assassinations in Cadaqués, of anarchist excesses throughout the region, of denunciations, summary executions, of a pervasive terror. Perhaps it was known that he had done nothing to help the Republic. Altogether there was no option but to wait until the hostilities ended, when, no matter who won, he would probably be able to talk himself out of any difficulties that might arise. Meanwhile there was Edward James's Villa Cimbrone in Rapallo. Dalí and Gala arrived there in September 1937 via Saint-Moritz and Nice. Éluard, generously, was pleased to hear from Gala that Dalí had enjoyed the latter resort: generously because Nice was one of the places in which he had been happiest with her. As for James, it seems that he was still talking about buying a bomber for the Republicans in exchange for a loan of paintings from the Prado.[121]

By October the Dalís were back in Paris and moved into a sumptuous appartment at 88, Rue de l'Université, in the seventh *arrondissement* near the Invalides, where a huge stuffed polar bear given by Edward James greeted callers in the hall. Here they were visited by Rosa Maria Salleras, whom Dalí had wanted to 'buy' years before as a child in Cadaqués, promising to be her 'guardian angel'. Rosa Maria and her family were in exile in Sète, and she had written asking Salvador to find her work in Paris. Dalí had immediately seen to everything. He met her at the station, he and Gala found her a respectable small hotel (*nobody* was ever allowed to stay with the Dalís) and, as for the job, she did a brief spell with Dalí's friend Coco Chanel before being more permanently installed at the Museum of Ethnography. Rosa Maria, then twenty-five, saw a lot of the Dalís in Paris, ate with them on Sundays and was able to appreciate their high standard of living. Gala was good to her, buying her dresses and taking her on shopping expeditions. The young woman witnessed at first hand Dalí's efforts to help his own family. He sent them money via the Spanish Embassy, and when Rosa Maria returned to Catalunya at the end of the war she took a huge suitcase full of clothes for them. It appears that Anna Maria Dalí was jealous of Rosa Maria, and that she had written to Salvador asking him to find work for her, too, in Paris. But Dalí refused, saying that it was her duty to look after their father and stepmother.[122]

Meanwhile, on 17 January 1938, a unique Surrealist group exhibition opened at the Galerie des Beaux Arts (140, Faubourg Saint-Honoré), with Dalí as one of the 'technical advisers'. The owner, Georges Wildenstein, had given the Surrealists *carte blanche* to devise whatever décor they chose, and Marcel Duchamp was detailed to transform the spacious premises into a setting in which the works exhibited would be completely 'at home'. In the lobby the visitors were greeted by Dalí's *Rainy Taxi* (a replica of which today graces the entrance to the painter's Theatre-Museum in Figueres). Marcel Jean remembered it as 'an old crock inside which an ingenious system of tubing produced a violent downpour that soaked two mannequins, one, with a shark's head, in the driver's seat, the other, a bedraggled blonde in evening dress, seated in the rear among heads of lettuce and chicory over which enormous Burgundy snails were drawing their slimy trails, exhilarated by the deluge'. After the lobby came *Surrealist Street*, a long wide passage flanked by twenty or so alluring female wax models in various stages of undress, some highly suggestive, by Man Ray, Ernst, Duchamp, Miró and a group of younger Surrealists. Dalí's model had a toucan's head and an egg between her breasts, and was adorned with small spoons. Also on show were his *The Great Masturbator* and *Giraffe in Flames*. The street signs were redolent of Surrealist associations, and mixed the real and the invented (Rue Vivienne, where Lautréamont had lived, the Passage des Panoramas and Rue de la Glacière being cheek by jowl with the fictitious Rue de Tous les Diables and Rue aux Lèvres). The passage led into the gallery's central hall, transformed by Duchamp into a vast leaf-strewn grotto, or subterranean glade, with a pool of water-lilies fringed with reeds. At the centre of the hall stood a glowing brazier (symbol of the Surrealist brotherhood), there were four enormous beds around the edges (representing love), and the ceiling was composed of hundreds of bags of coal. Objects lit up in the darkness and then disappeared, and graphic works were exhibited on revolving doors. The public were given torches with which to see individual works and to make their own discoveries (the experiment was later discontinued when the torches began to 'disappear').[123]

The big event of the opening night was a dance performed around the pool by the ballerina Hélène Vanel attired as a witch from *Macbeth*, her midnight entrance and Surrealist choreography having been planned by Dalí. Breton, 'who knew nothing about music or dancing', had been resistant to the scene, but eventually gave in. Vanel danced that night, according to Dalí, 'with Dionysian fervour', throwing the unsuspecting guests into a frenzy.[124]

'The entire press spoke of the event,' recalled Marcel Jean. 'With a very few exceptions, it was an outcry of indignation: sneers, insults, recriminations, expressions of disgust. Naturally, the general public packed the Galerie des Beaux Arts throughout the run of the exhibition.'[125] Dalí commented later that much of the work on show had been 'pretty poor', with little that would have moved an Edgar Allan Poe, a Baudelaire or a Nietzsche. It had certainly been fun, although André Breton had proved yet again that he was a puritan, insisting that some of the more overtly erotic details of the models lining *Surrealist Street* be suppressed.[126]

To complement the Surrealist show the Beaux-Arts Gallery brought out a *Short Dictionary of Surrealism* (*Dictionnaire abrégé du surréalisme*), compiled anonymously by Breton and Éluard. Perhaps Breton thought that, having provided the word 'Surrealism' with a mock-serious dictionary-style definition in 1924, it would now be useful and entertaining to attempt this for the whole range of Surrealist activity. Members of the movement since its early days, with their several achievements; a wide range of quotations from Surrealist texts (with Breton himself predominating); reproductions of works by Surrealism's leading exponents: the slim volume was as masterly in its concision as it was ironic in its mode of expression. Dalí was well represented with reproductions and quotations from his theoretical works and, in an unattributed self-definition, termed 'Prince of Catalan intelligence, colossally rich'.[127] His description of Gala was also appropriated: 'Violent and sterilized woman'. There were other Dalí entries: 'Anachronism', 'Crutch', 'Ecstasy', 'Phantom', 'Modern Style', 'Paranoia', 'Aphrodisiac Telephone' and 'Aphrodisiac Dinner Jacket'. A photograph of the artist sketching Harpo was included, also one of him as a 'Being-Object' disguised as Millet's *Angelus* (with an 'incipient erection', he later indicated).[128] The section of reproductions was introduced by a still from *L'Age d'or* showing the mumbling bishops at Cape Creus. All in all Dalí came out of it very well: despite their qualms about his politics, the authors clearly considered him one of the leading members of the movement.

After the exhibition Dalí and Gala visited Rome with Edward James and stayed for two months with Lord Gerald Berners in his luxurious mansion overlooking the Forum. There was a brief visit to Sicily, where the artist found 'mingled reminiscences of Catalonia and of Africa' (perhaps he was surprised by the proximity of Tunisia) and began his painting *Impressions of Africa*. It was baptized thus in deference to Raymond Roussel's book of the same title, one of Dalí's favourites—among other reasons because the author had never set foot in Africa. Dalí wrote from Taormina to tell James he was pleased with the picture and working 'in a fury'. He hoped to finish it back in Rome at Berners's house.[129]

The painting shows Dalí at work on a canvas hidden from us. Since he is gesticulating, one presumes that the subject is a person, most probably Gala. Behind him there is a jumble of double images: the eyes of the woman's face (if Gala's, a poor likeness) are the gaps in an arcade, the outline of a shadowy priest is repeated on the head of a donkey, the entrance to a cave doubles as a tree, the lower branches of an umbrella pine are also a bird of prey. The sea and cliffs beyond are more reminiscent of the Empordà than of Africa, as is the group of peasants and fishermen on the right. In the distance, behind the painter, recurs the motif that since 1929 had appeared obsessively in at least fifty paintings and drawings: the father figure holding a little child by the hand.[130]

If Dalí's father was never far from his mind, nor were his two father figures: Picasso and Freud. Dalí was forever boasting that he and Picasso were friends, which was hardly the case. Now he was determined to fulfil what was perhaps his deepest urge of all: to meet the genius who had taught him that the true hero is the son who rebels against his father and defeats him. It was as though the painter felt that, until he had been in the presence of Freud, seen him face to face, listened to him, been heard by him, *been noticed by him*, he would never be free of Salvador Dalí Cusí, the notary of Figueres.

With Freud in Primrose Hill

On 11 March 1938 the Germans invaded Austria and a week later it was announced in Paris that Sigmund Freud was under arrest. Breton lost no time in publicly expressing his outrage, hardly diminished when it transpired that the Nazis were merely keeping Freud under close watch.[131] On 4 June Freud, his wife and daughter Anna fled from Vienna, where he had lived for seventy-nine years. They passed quickly through Paris and on 6 June arrived at their destination, London, where the warmth of their reception greatly comforted them.[132] Dalí, who had apparently made several fruitless attempts over the years to see Freud in Vienna,[133] now asked Edward James for the address of Stefan Zweig, which he had mislaid. Zweig, a close friend of Freud, and like him Jewish, was also in exile in London and greatly admired Dalí's work. The two had certainly met, although no documentation has come to light. Dalí felt sure that through Zweig he could reach his idol.[134] He was not mistaken. Zweig wrote three successive, and increasingly persuasive, letters on his behalf to the ailing professor, informing James of his progress. The signs being propitious, James summoned Dalí to London.

Zweig told Freud that in his opinion Dalí was 'the only painter of genius of our epoch, and the only one who will survive'. It was as though Zweig had never heard of Picasso. Dalí, moreover, was 'the most faithful and most grateful disciple of your ideas among the artists'. The third and last letter shows that Dalí had by then arrived in London: 'For years it has been the desire of this real genius to meet you. He says that he owes to you more in his art than to anybody else. And so we are coming tomorrow to see you, he and his wife'. Zweig went on:

> He would like to take the opportunity, during our discussion, to make a short portrait of you, if possible. The real portraits he always does from memory, and from his inner 'Gestaltung'. As a kind of legitimization, we are going to show you his last picture, in the possession of Mr Edward James. I think that since the old masters nobody has ever found colours like these, and in the details, however symbolical they may appear, I see a perfection compared with which all the paintings of our time seem to pale. The picture is called *Narcissus* and may have been painted under your influence.
>
> This is meant as an excuse, because we are going to form a little caravan. But I think that a man like you should see once an artist who has been influenced by you as nobody else, and whom to know and to esteem I have always regarded as a privilege. He is only here for two days from Paris (he is a Catalan), and he will not disturb our conversation. I am happy to let you know this probably greatest of your adepts. I hope you will find these high-sounding expressions not unfitting. The picture may perhaps surprise you at first sight, but I cannot imagine that it should fail to disclose to you the worth of this artist.

Zweig then added an afterthought: 'Salvador Dalí would have liked, of course, to show you his pictures in an exhibition. We know, however, that you only reluctantly go out, if ever, and therefore will bring his last, and as it seems to me, his most beautiful picture to your home.'[135]

The visit to Freud's provisional lodgings at 39 Elsworthy Road, Primrose Hill, took place on 19 July 1938. Edward James (who hoped that Freud would accept him for analysis) accompanied Dalí and Zweig. There is no indication that Gala was present. Since Dalí knew no German and as yet hardly any English, we must assume that whatever words he and Freud exchanged were in French. It is highly unlikely, on the face of it, that any genuine conversation took place between them, particularly since Dalí spent most of his time sketching the Master.

Six years earlier, when Breton sent Freud a copy of his *The Communicating Vessels*, the latter had confessed his ignorance of Surrealism and its aims, giving as his excuse his lack of knowledge of the world of contemporary art.[136] The letter Freud wrote to Zweig the day after Dalí's visit shows that since 1932 he had hardly progressed in his understanding of the movement. Acceding to Dalí's request, Freud had not only looked carefully at *Metamorphosis of Narcissus* but had made some comments on it to the assembled company:

> I have to thank you indeed for the introduction of our visitor of yesterday. Until now I was inclined to regard the Surrealists—who seem to have adopted me as their patron saint— as 100 per cent fools (or let's rather say, as with alcohol, 95 per cent). This young Spaniard, with his ingenuous fanatical eyes, and his undoubtedly technically perfect mastership, has suggested to me a different estimate. In fact, it would be very interesting to explore analytically the growth of a picture like this. From a critical point of view, one might still say, that Art by its definition would refuse enlarging its scope so widely, unless the quantitative relation of unconscious material and pre-conscious elaboration should be kept within certain limits. In any case these are serious problems from the psychological point of view.[137]

If the visit had pleased Freud, the excitable Edward James could hardly contain himself. The following day he wrote to Christoper Sykes:

> Dr Sigmund Freud, aged 82, is adorable. He is full of sparkle though a little baffled at moments by having newly become a bit deaf. He talked to me for a long while, during which Dalí sketched him hastily but accurately into a drawing book. Salvador was looking so inspired, his eyes were so blazing with excitement while he sketched the inventor of psychoanalysis, that the old man whispered in German . . . 'That boy looks like a fanatic. Small wonder that they have civil war in Spain if they look like that.'[138]

It is almost certain that before Dalí left London Zweig communicated to him the contents of this letter. Perhaps he even supplied him with a written translation of the original German. There is no question, at all events, that what Dalí thought Freud had said about *Metamorphosis of Narcissus* strongly influenced his perception not just of the painting but of Surrealism. As for Freud's remark about his fanaticism, he was to rejoice in it for the rest of his life.

Unfortunately we do not have Dalí's contemporary account of the visit to Freud. The first known reference comes in a letter to Breton at the beginning of 1939. It gives a version of Freud's words that Dalí was to repeat endlessly thereafter: 'He remarked (I showed him one of my pictures) that "in the paintings of the Old Masters one immediately tends to look for the unconscious whereas, when one looks at a Surrealist painting, one immediately has the urge to look for the conscious".' Freud's observation deserved to give rise to a 'pretty lively debate', Dalí felt, and he had written a little article on the subject which he promised to show Breton (the 'little article' is unknown).[139]

Dalí's drawing of Freud was strongly conditioned by his intuition of some time earlier that the doctor's head resembled a snail's. Whatever the accuracy of the insight, the sketch is that of a very tired and sick old man who had not long to live (in fact, only a year). Zweig succeeded in preventing Freud from seeing it, feeling it might have come as a terrible shock.[140]

Dalí claimed some years later that the 'lesson of classic tradition' of Freud's old age had borne in on him 'how many things were at last ended in Europe with the imminent end of his life', and repeated what he had told Breton: Freud, after contemplating *Metamorphosis of Narcissus*, had said 'in classic painting I look for the sub-conscious—in a Surrealist painting, for the conscious'. This Dalí now alleged to have immediately interpreted 'as a death sentence on Surrealism as a doctrine, as a sect, as an "ism", while at the same time confirming the movement's validity as 'a state of the spirit'.[141]

The meeting, however Dalí cared to interpret its significance later, was undoubtedly one of the most important experiences of his life. Having followed Freud's teaching since his student days, he had now not only met him in person but, as Freud's thankyou letter to Zweig showed, impressed him. The disciple could feel profoundly satisfied, and afterwards would never miss an opportunity to proclaim that the founder of psychoanalysis had been forced, as a result of their encounter, to reconsider his view of Surrealism.

After the visit to London the Dalís stayed briefly in Florence before settling down, that September, at Coco Chanel's villa La Pausa, in Roquebrune, Cap Martin, where for four months the painter frenetically produced work for his forthcoming exhibition in New York. He was worried about the situation in Europe, where at Munich, Britain and France had indulged in the dangerous game of attempting to appease an increasingly aggressive Hitler. Gala's cards were predicting war, although 'not yet', and the inmates of La Pausa lived with their ears glued to the radio.

The guests included, to Dalí's delight, the poet Pierre Reverdy, one of Chanel's closest friends. Editor of the avant-garde review *Nord-Sud* in 1917–18 and much admired by the early Surrealists, Reverdy's definition of the poetic image, which became famous, had been quoted approvingly by Breton in his first *Manifesto*, where Dalí must have read it: 'The image is a pure creation of the spirit. It does not arise from a comparison but from the coming together of two realities more or less distant . . .' Since then Reverdy had become a Catholic, but an independent-minded one. In the *Secret Life* Dalí records that at Roquebrune the poet's 'terribly elemental and biological Catholicism' struck him forcibly: 'He was "massive", anti-intellectual, and the opposite of myself in everything, and provided me a magnificent occasion to strengthen my ideas. We fought dialectically like two Catholic cocks, and we called this "examining the question".'[142]

Dalí was then painting *The Enigma of Hitler*, a work inspired, he tells us, by dreams occurring at the time of the Munich Agreement (29 September 1938), although it may have been begun earlier. The picture inaugurated a series of gloomy canvases alluding to the inevitability of war and to the breakdown of dialogue between the Great Powers, symbolized by a decayed telephone, its cord snapped, which in this instance hangs over a plate containing a portrait of Hitler. The setting is Dalí's familiar beach scene, and the glassy stillness of the grey sea suggests an impending storm. 'This picture appeared to me to be charged with a prophetic value, as announcing the medieval period which was going to spread its shadow over Europe,' Dalí commented. 'Chamberlain's umbrella appeared in this painting in a sinister aspect, identified with the bat, and affected me as extremely anguishing at the very time I was painting it.'[143]

As well as preparing work for his New York exhibition, Dalí sketched out during these months the structure of the book of memoirs that was to become the *Secret Life*. Also, taking advantage of the fact that the Ballets Russes were based in nearby Monte Carlo, he began work with Massine on the production of *Tristan Fou*, which Edward James had promised to stage in London. The ballet was soon renamed *Venusberg* and, not long after that, definitively baptized *Bacchanale*.[144]

The ballet was the end-result of the opera project on which Dalí had invited Lorca to join him in 1934, and whose protagonist was Louis II, the mad king of Bavaria. By 1938, Louis had become another of Dalí's obsessions, not least because he had discovered that the young king, protector of Wagner and founder of Bayreuth, was such a passionate admirer of the composer that in his deliriums he believed he was Lohengrin or some other Wagnerian hero. In *Bacchanale*, which Dalí proudly subtitled 'The First Paranoiac Ballet', Louis, standing in for the eponymous hero of *Tannhäuser*, acts out the Venusberg scene of the opera, the supporting cast including Leda and the Swan, Leopold von Sacher-Masoch and Louis's Irish lover (an actress who performed under the stage name of Lola Montes). The programme notes Dalí later wrote for the ballet are interesting for their comments on his admiration for Wagner. As a man from the Empordà, he explained, his feet were well rooted in the plain; nonetheless he had always been fascinated by mountains (no doubt he had the Canigó in mind). Wagner seemed to him the 'greatest mountain', so it was natural that Venusberg should have been 'the peak' of his 'first theatrical ascent'. Dalí added that the ballet was also intended as a tribute to psychoanalysis and to Freud. The script is unknown.[145]

That Lorca continued to be on Dalí's mind as he worked on *Bacchanale* is confirmed   *XXX*
by a painting done during these months at La Pausa, *The Great One-Eyed Cretin* (or *Moron*), soon re-named *The Endless Enigma*. Like two other works executed the same year, *Invisible Afghan Hound with the Apparition on the Beach of the Face of García Lorca in the Form of a Bowl of Fruit with Three Figs* and *Apparition of a Face and a Bowl of Fruit on a Beach*,[146] the painting, remarkable for its intricate assemblage of multiple images (reminiscent of *Invisible Sleeping Woman, Horse, Lion, etc.*, done eight years earlier), presents

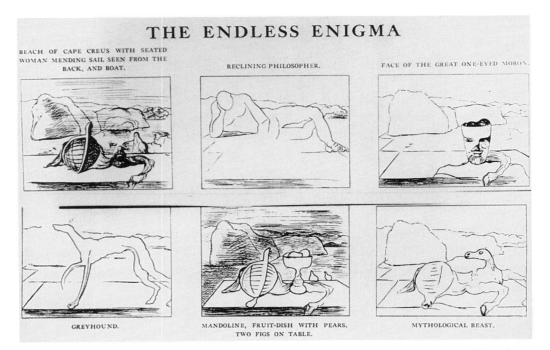

Dalí's catalogue 'disentanglement' of the multiple images in The Endless Enigma, *1938 (see colour plate XXX).*

a 'materialization' of the poet's head on the shore at Cape Creus, whose cliffs are mirrored in a *calma blanca*.

For the catalogue of his forthcoming exhibition in New York Dalí prepared a sketch disentangling the complicated network of images that overlap in the painting. He did not explain, however, that the Great One-Eyed Cretin in question was his dead friend. That the picture concerns Dalí's relationship with Lorca is confirmed by the upper part of Gala's head, inserted half-way up the right-hand side of the picture as if excluded from what is happening on the beach. Her eyes have the baleful glare of the Medusa, and in the opinion of Santos Torroella are reading Dalí's innermost feelings for his murdered friend, feelings with which the painter is still not at ease . . . which is perhaps why Lorca has to be downgraded to the level of Moron.[147]

At the beginning of January 1939 Dalí wrote to Breton from La Pausa, the letter showing that there had been no contact between them since the Surrealist leader returned from a protracted visit to South America the previous August. Having told Breton briefly about his visit to Freud, he explained that he had been working for months on the refinement of his 'paranoiac-critical method' and that he was trying to get a new review called *Paranoiakinesis* off the ground. He felt that his researches into paranoia had made considerable progress, and looked forward to informing Breton more fully about them when he returned to Paris at the end of the month. Dalí clearly still felt himself to be an integral part of the Surrealist movement, and wanted to come to an agreement with Breton about the tactics to be employed during his forthcoming visit to America. It was vital, he said, that action there should not be allowed to fizzle out, given the current receptivity of Americans to Surrealist ideas.

Dalí then went on to comment on the manifesto published in Mexico by Breton and Trotsky the previous July, *For an Independent Revolutionary Art* (*Pour un art révolutionnaire indépendant*), and on the recent foundation of the resultant International Federation of Independent Revolutionary Art (FIARI), of which Breton was Secretary General. Dalí retained his scepticism, he wrote, about all attempts by the Surrealists at what he termed 'compulsive organization', a scepticism he had shown earlier in connection with the Association of Revolutionary Writers and Artists (AEAR) and similar initiatives. He ended his letter by saying he had just re-read Breton's *Mad Love*, which he admired more than ever.[148]

Breton replied immediately on FIARI notepaper. The letter, which began 'My dear Salvador Dalí', was polite but distant. The cordiality had gone. He would like to hear more about the painter's visit to Freud, he said, and regretted that Dalí was in the habit of informing him from a distance of his thoughts and projects but hardly ever followed up such communications with a visit. He believed that this lack of contact was extremely negative for the health of Surrealism. Common action should be undertaken not only in America but here in Europe, and he had frequently asked Dalí to remember this—unsuccessfully.[149]

When Dalí returned to Paris he made good his promise to visit Breton, who was shocked to hear him express racist views. Whether Breton repudiated him there and then is not clear, but in 'The Latest Tendencies in Surrealist Painting', published the following May in the last issue of *Minotaure*, he was to state that all his ties with Dalí had been severed from that moment:

> In February 1939 Dalí said (I have this from Dalí himself and I've taken the trouble to make sure that no humour was involved) that all the present trouble in the world is racial in origin, and that the best solution, agreed on by all the white races, is to reduce all the dark races to slavery. I do not know what doors such a declaration can open for the author in Italy and America, the countries between which he now oscillates, but I know which they'll close. After this I cannot see how, in independent-minded circles, his message could be taken seriously.[150]

Dalí left for New York shortly after the meeting with Breton in February. But not before holding a private view of the works about to be exhibited in America. The invitation to the opulent premises at 88, Rue de l'Université indicated that guests would be able to see, among other paintings and objects, *The Great One-Eyed Cretin*, *The Long Siphon* and *Imperial Violets*; it was surmounted by a tiny, stroboscopic photograph of a crown (symbol of Dalí's imperial aspirations) formed by a drop of milk exploding as it hits a white-hot sheet of iron.[151]

America Again

Dalí's stay in New York got off to a rip-roaring start with the blaze of publicity generated by the Bonwit Teller episode. The Fifth Avenue department store, remembering his successful efforts on their behalf in 1936, had now commissioned two window displays from him to promote its new spring fabrics. Dalí decided to illustrate the 'Narcissus complex', one window showing this in a day-time context, the other in a nocturnal. Day was represented by an old-fashioned bath tub lined with black Persian lamb and filled with water on whose surface floated narcissi. From the water there emerged three wax hands holding mirrors. Into the bath was about to step a 1890s-vintage wax mannequin, picked up in a second-hand shop and now wearing a negligee made of green feathers. It had bright red hair and was covered in dust and cobwebs. Night was a bed over which hung a canopy composed of a buffalo's head with a bloody pigeon in its jaws. The bed stood on four buffalo legs. On the black satin sheets rested another wax mannequin apparently undisturbed by the live coals that burnt beneath her. Dalí hoped that 'this manifesto of elementary poetry right out in the street' would stop pedestrians in their tracks and provide them with 'an authentic Dalinian vision' to offset all the spurious 'decorativism', allegedly Surrealist, which by then was rampant in New York.[152]

He was not disappointed. When the display went on show on the morning of 16 March 1939, it soon drew crowds. The management sent spies into the street to report on the reactions of the multitude. These were mixed, but there seemed to be a consensus on one point: the dummy with the see-through negligee was decidedly titillating. By noon, without consulting Dalí, a seated mannequin had been substituted for the sleeping one, and in place of the dummy in the green negligee stood 'a streamlined model' in a tailored suit. When 'The Surrealissimo' (as *Time* had now nicknamed Dalí) arrived on the scene that evening to admire his work, he was horrified. 'I took friends to see the window,' he told the *New York Post*, 'and there was this shocking modernistic figure substituted for my lovely old figure, in the center of the design. It ruined all meaning.' Dalí demanded that the curtain be lowered. The management told him that to do so would ruin the store's reputation. He replied that to leave it up would ruin his. 'So I dashed into the window to disarrange it, so that my name, signed in the window, should not be dishonored. I was never so surprised as when that bath tub just shot through the window when I pushed it and I was thereafter most confused.'[153]

Dalí was catapulted through the broken plate glass window with the bath tub and arrived on the sidewalk outside miraculously unscathed. The crowd was 'delighted' by the performance.[154] A few seconds later he was apprehended by the law and escorted to the police station at 51st Street East. There Edward James intervened, strings were pulled, and the magistrate on duty, Louis B. Brodsky, was understanding. While Dalí's reaction had certainly been excessive, he said, an artist had a right to defend the integrity of his work. Dalí received a suspended sentence for disorderly conduct, and the bill for the damage was his only punishment. The episode made a dramatic story and the painter was delighted with the vast amount of free press coverage it spawned in both the States and Europe, coverage which included photographs of the broken window and of the arrest. Dalí was also delighted with the few hours he had spent in a genuine New York cell, which must have reminded him of his term of imprisonment in Figueres and Girona in 1924. He exploited the incident to the utmost, and later deemed it 'the most magical and effective action' of his entire life, alleging that he had received hundreds of letters from American artists praising his energetic gesture.[155]

The Bonwit Teller incident was a magnificent curtain-raiser to Dalí's exhibition at Julien Levy's, which opened two days later and ran until 18 April. The catalogue, which included Dalí's schematic breakdown of the images in *The Endless Enigma*, listed twenty-one paintings and five drawings but omitted some unspecified 'objects'.[156]

The catalogue was introduced by a text, 'Dalí, Dalí!', in which the artist insisted that the paranoaic image is 'consubstantial with the human phenomenon of sight' and traced it back to prehistory. To the caveman who, in the irregularities of the walls of his primitive dwelling, has a vision of 'the precise silhouette, the truculent profile, of his nutritive and magical obsessions, the hallucinating contours of the veritable prey of his imagination, these animals which he engraves merely by accentuating or retracing certain of the "stimulating" irregularities'. Aristophanes in *The Clouds*; Leonardo da Vinci in his *Treatise on Painting*; Bracelli and Arcimboldo; Freud in *Leonardo de Vinci and a Memory of his Childhood*: these had laid 'the epistological and philosophical cornerstone of the majestic edifice of imminent "paranoiac painting"'. Dalí also claimed that his obsession with the double image, reaching back ten years, had left its mark on Surrealism and, to a lesser degree, Neo-Romanticism. Only in his recently completed *The Endless Enigma*, however, had he embarked on a 'systematic investigation' of the 'paranoiac phenomenon'. Clearly, the message was, his public could expect more from him in this direction.

The catalogue included an anthology of appreciative words about Dalí from the famous. Picasso, first in the list, was quoted as saying: 'Dalí eats up the miles. His imagination effects [sic] me like an outboard motor continually running.' Breton's vindication of Dalí's 'critical-paranoiac method' was hauled out yet again. Stefan Zweig's encomium, although Dalí did not say so, was lifted from one of the letters in which the writer had striven to persuade Freud to see the painter. James Thrall Soby made a particularly grand gesture. 'Only Dalí,' he said, 'has gone on to something new in art, while the others have for the most part been pale reflections of Picasso's genius.'[157]

Life reported the day before the show ended that no exhibition in New York had been so popular since Whistler's *Mother* was shown in 1934. Open-mouthed, the crowds had stood transfixed in front of *Debris of a Motorcar Giving Birth to a Blind Horse* and *The Great One-Eyed Cretin*. A fortnight after the inauguration, *Life* revealed, Dalí ('one of the richest young painters in the world') had sold twenty-one works to private collectors for more than $25,000. Only two had failed to go: *The Enigma of Hitler* (at $1,750) and, surprisingly in view of the fact that Dalí promoted it as the *clou* of the show, *The Endless Enigma* (at $3,000).[158]

Dalí was discovering as never before that success breeds success. Before his triumphant exhibition closed on 18 April another unique opportunity for self-promotion
and financial gain presented itself. This was a lucrative commission to design a
Surrealist pavilion for the Amusement Area of the New York World's Fair, scheduled to
open in early June. Julien Levy had been involved in the project from the outset, and
come to the conclusion that it would get nowhere unless linked to Dalí's name. At this
point Edward James stepped in to form a corporation and put up half the money.

Dalí's draft contract was dated 10 April 1939, and it was understood from the outset
that he would have to work at breakneck speed.[159] The venture had first been called,
unbelievably, *Bottoms of the Sea*, but Dalí soon renamed it *Dream of Venus*. His plan envisaged a palace of fake coral with an inner L-shaped pool made of transparent plate glass.
Here would be performed a spectacle intended to represent the workings of the unconscious, with soft watches, 'women-pianos', a divan in the shape of Greta Garbo's lips and
'splendid female underwater swimmers' whose submarine gyrations would be choreo-
graphed to express the inner secrets of the dream. Also included was the inevitable
'rainy taxi', occupied this time by Christoper Columbus.[160]

Dalí soon ran into trouble with the Fair's organizers and the pavilion's co-investors
(a rubber company in Chicago), who were annoyed by his determination to erect a large
statue of Botticelli's *Venus* topped by a fish's head outside the building. The rubber com-
pany's director wrote an irate telegram to his agent, William Morris: 'OUR SHOW IS
SIXTY PERCENT AN UNDERWATER MERMAID SHOW AND FORTY PER-
CENT A SURREALIST SHOW SO WHY SHOULD FRONT BE ALL SURREAL-
IST AND NOT PUBLICIZE THE MOST IMPORTANT PART OF OUR SHOW . . .
MEN'S PASSION TO SPEND A QUARTER WILL NOT BE AROUSED BY A GIRL
WITH A FISH'S HEAD BUT BY A SUGGESTIVE MERMAID PRESENTATION
ON THE FRONT OF THE BUILDING . . . DALI'S FRONT MAY STOP THEM
FOR A FEW SECONDS WHILE THEY SHAKE THEIR HEADS THEN WALK ON
BUT WE WANT THEM TO STOP AND COME IN.'[161]

Row succeeded row, with mounting tension on both sides, modifications of the original design and bitter recriminations.[162] The final product, like the Bonwit Teller window,
was a caricature of Dalí's original conception. He and Gala embarked for Europe on the
Champlain before the Fair opened on 6 June, leaving Edward James to hold the baby. On
21 June James drafted a long cable to the Dalís: the preview had been a disaster; the
water in the pool was dirty; bits of the décor had broken off; nothing but vermouth and
whisky had been available for the journalists; so far the only press coverage had been an
appreciative article in the *Herald Tribune*, despite the fact that they had paid for public-

ity;[163] and to make matters even worse Julien Levy, dead drunk, had told the reporters that Dalí left before the opening because of a 'subconscious prompting', not because he had to resume his work with the Ballets Russes. James decided not to send the telegram, thinking it might upset Dalí too much, and wrote instead.[164]

Despite all these teething troubles, *Dream of Venus* was a considerable success. After a few days the press coverage picked up, focusing particularly on the show's liberal display of bare breasts.[165] 'It is the scantly clad, live and very normal-looking mermaids who cavort in these morbid surroundings that hold the attention of the crowd, which still likes its Dalí spelled "Dolly",' reported one newspaper.[166] The Fair's vast amusement zone, commented *Time* magazine, contained 'more public nudity than any place outside of Bali'. *Dream of Venus* was no exception, shrewdly combining Surrealism with sex and proving again that there was 'plenty of Broadway method in Dalí's madness':

> Upon a 36-foot, red-satin bed called 'The Ardent Couch' an unclad Venus lies dreaming. Of her four uninhibited dreams, the first—an underwater vision called 'Venus's Pre-natal Château Beneath the Water'—is the real crowd-catcher. A long glass tank is filled with such subaqueous décor as a fireplace, typewriters with funguslike rubber keys, rubber telephones, a man made of rubber ping-pong bats, a mummified cow, a supine rubber woman painted to resemble the keyboard of a piano. Whatever this may mean as art, the exhibitors did not dilly-Dalí over it. Into the tank they plunged living girls, nude to the waist and wearing little Gay Nineties girdles and fish-net stockings. Swimming, grimacing, doing the Suzy Q, milking the cow, playing the 'piano', these Lady Godivers [sic], seen at close range and a trifle water-magnified, should win more converts to Surrealism than a dozen high-brow exhibitions.[167]

Before leaving New York, an angry Dalí had written a brilliant tract entitled *Declaration of the Independence of the Imagination and the Rights of Man to his Own Madness*, hundreds of copies of which, according to Julien Levy, were dropped from a plane over New York City. In it Dalí deprecated the crass attitude of the World's Fair's organizers who had not allowed him to erect his statue of Botticelli's Venus with the head of a fish, and urged American artists to stand up and defend their rights against the sort of mediocrities capable of pontificating, literally, that 'a woman with the tail of a fish is possible; a woman with the head of a fish is impossible'. Dalí voiced the opinion (already formulated by him in the mid-1920s) that people at large intuitively understand far more about art than the '"middlemen of culture" who, with their lofty airs and superior quackings, come between the creator and the public'.

The tract showed that Dalí was still happy to present himself as a loyal disciple of

Breton. Not only was its tone similar to that employed by Breton himself in various texts but it quoted yet again, as if it were sacred writ, the definition of Surrrealism promulgated in the first *Manifesto*: 'Pure mental automatism, by means of which it is proposed to express, either in speech, in writing or in any other manner, the true functioning of thought. Dictation by thought without any rational, aesthetic or moral control.'[168]

Two Letters to Buñuel

Whatever his continuing protestations of loyalty to Breton at this time, Dalí was now swept up in such a frenzy of self-promotion that the Surrealist revolution was one of the last things on his mind. Moreover, the Spanish Civil War had just ended with the victory of Franco, and Dalí had decided that his sympathies lay fair and square with the Caudillo. No documents are more revealing of his thinking and obsessions at this time than two letters exchanged with Luis Buñuel during the preparations for the World's Fair.

Buñuel was then in Hollywood, where he had been sent by the Spanish Republican authorities in 1938 as adviser to films being made on the civil war. Even before Franco's victory in April 1939 he lost his job, and his overtures to Chaplin, René Clair and others about alternative work were proving unsuccessful. He was beginning to despair—and turned to Dalí.[169]

In his first letter (which has not been found) it seems that Buñuel did not mention his financial straits. What he did mention was a rumour he had heard to the effect that Dalí and Gala were going to divorce. Dalí replied from the St Moritz Hotel, strewing his letter with emphatic underlinings as was his habit:

> Dear Old Fellow,
>
> I'm pleased with the songs you tell me about in your letter. I'm going to answer you methodically. First, no question of a divorce from Gala, on the contrary our understanding is *absolute* and we've never been as happy together as we are now, but given that I spent four months in Chanel's house (with Gala) in Montecarlo, there will have been the usual 'ritual' society gossip.
>
> You already know that I don't believe there'll be a world war. Although we're experiencing some moments of 'objective danger', I'm convinced that before two months are up there'll be a sudden change (already prepared and decided). France and Italy will patch things up and once the 'axis' is broken Stalin will arrange things with Hitler so that the latter can gobble up the big juicy chop of the Ukraine. When this happens, with the Japanese imperialists automatically feeling threatened (by Russia-Germany), the conflict will break out precisely in the United States.

In two weeks I have to leave here for Montecarlo to see to my show, which will be put on in the Paris Opera in June, and then London. In principle I'm still interested in Hollywood but since my financial situation is improving each day, and there's no need for me to go there, *the cleverest thing for me to do* is to wait and to refuse all projects until the moment (inevitable, given the acceleration of my *prestige and popularity*) when they ask me to go as a *dictator*—with *as many dollars* for my film *as I fucking want*, and as quickly—it's the only basis for a contract that *I'll accept*, and this would be impossible if I accepted anything *provisionally*—do you get the point?

Your new position seems to me much more realistic than those *Marxist idealisms*. My advice as a friend, as the Dalí of the Toledo days, is to disinfect yourself of all those Marxist points of view, since Marxism, philosophically and from every point of view, is the most imbecilic theory of our civilization, it's totally false and Marx is probably the acme of abstraction and stupidity—it would be terrible for you to abandon political Marxism but to continue thinking as a Marxist in other spheres, since Marxism prevents us from understanding anything about the phenomena of our epoch—about a young and materially marvellous science such as 'morphology', the meeting of morphology and psychoanalysis (older but still beautiful, with one of the most melancholy and intelligent smiles in the world!).

Good day, write to me and if you come to New York let's see each other immediately, Dalí.

Dalí added a marginal note about the recently concluded civil war in Spain, referring to two of the Republic's outstanding leaders, the Socialist doctor Juan Negrín (the last Prime Minister) and the Communist hero La Pasionaria: 'The end of the Negríns and the Pasionarias has sickened me,' he wrote. 'Why didn't they just let themselves be killed? Or make peace two months before Tarragona fell? All this is the apotheosis of mediocrity, the same old mediocrity which never lets up.' Ordering Buñuel to turn the page, he went on:

Another thing: my individualism had grown stronger and each day I'm doing the things that enter my head with a furious intensity, so much so that it would now be impossible for me to collaborate with anybody else. Gala's the only person I listen to since she possesses an undeniable gift as a medium—objective CHANCE, paranoiac interpretation of fortuitous events in order to follow the thread of my frenetic-critical acts.

Good day, here the most incredible things are happening to me one after the other.

At the foot of the page and around the margins Dalí added some significant news and comments:

The Reds imprisoned my sister in Barcelona for twenty days! They tortured her, she went mad, she's in Cadaqués, they have to force-feed her, she shits in her bed, imagine the tragedy of my father from whom they stole everything, he has to live in a boarding house in Figueres, naturally I'm sending him dollars, he's turned into a fanatical worshipper of Franco, he considers him a demi-god, the 'glorious Caudillo' as he calls him in each of his delirious letters (they managed to keep all my things in the house in Cadaqués safe). The revolutionary effort was such a disaster that everyone prefers Franco. On this subject I'm receiving tremendous information. Life-long Catalanists, federal Republicans, bitter anti-clericals—they're all writing to me enthusiastically about the new regime.[170]

The letter constitutes the earliest documentation yet to come to light about Dalí's father's change of political heart as a result of the family's experience during the war.

Buñuel, no doubt heartened by Dalí's confirmation of the the buoyant state of his finances, now asked him for a loan. Dalí replied:

Dear Luis: I can't send you anything at all, and it's a decision taken after great hesitations and much reflection, which I'm now going to explain to you. This is the reason for my delay in answering you, since normally I hate making people wait for replies having to do with money—

Here is the outline of my attitude (tremendously abbreviated, but I know that you appreciate my sincerity in such matters).

For three years now I've been occupying myself passionately with all matters relating to 'objective chance'. Destiny—prophetic dreams—interpretation of the smallest events in daily life in order to act in consequence—chiromancy—astrology (very important—morphology applied to the immediate moment), etc. etc. All of this was inevitable given my almost inhuman sentiments of 'FRENETIC egoism', that is to say the need to control, as long as I live, and with the maximum intensity, every situation (Freud's pleasure principle).

All the predictions and experiences I've had recently counsel me not to lend you money—Before I got your letter its arrival had been foretold to me in various different ways, particularly by a female Swiss medium, one of the most important in New York at the moment, who guides me a lot (although it's I who decide whether I'm convinced or not). My present situation is as follows: the overcoming of my William Tell complex, that is to say, the end of hostilities with my father, the reconstruction of the ideal of The Family, sublimated in racial and biological factors, etc. etc. etc. As a result of this, I send everything I can to Cadaqués (everything I am able to do in this sense will contribute to my own triumphant self-construction). At the same time it's been predicted that I'll be assailed by all the myths of family inconformity, represented by my old friends.

Since PARACELSUS (he's very good!) and NOSTRADAMUS European thought has been in a state of phenomenal decay. What can a humanist doctor like Negrín contribute compared to the PAST, TO ISABEL THE CATHOLIC, consecrated hosts, melons, rosary beads, the truculent indigestions that precede bullfights, the drums of Calanda,* the *sardanas* danced on the beaches of the Empordà and all that—Negrín was leading us in the direction of a nauseating Socialist mediocrity that has been totally surpassed by the 'Falanges', by Spanish biological reality—If you knew the position of the stars you could never think there was going to be a war! How far you are from the truth!

To recapitulate—my life must now be *orientated towards Spain* and The Family. *Systematic destruction* of the *infantile* past represented by my Madrid friends, images which have no *real consistence.* Gala, the *unique reality* because she's incorporated in a *constructive* sense in my libido. It would be impossible for me to talk to you more FRANKLY.

Long live the *individuality* of the sharks (Marquis de Sade) who eat the weak—NIETSCHE [sic]—and the Empordà, realist-surrrealist.

What shit Marxism is, the last survival of Christian shit—Catholicism I respect *a lot,* it's SOLID.

Ask Noailles for money, he won't refuse you (Dalí guarantees it) and it'll be within tradition : 'STELLAR configuration'.

SPAIN IS *SERIOUS,* DESTINED FOR *'WORLD HEGEMONY'.* A SURREALIST 'ARRIBA ESPAÑA!'

Lack of imagination is the death of everything. STALIN—the most bestial of ANTI-IMAGINATIVE people.

Here I'm designing a Surrealist pavilion for the World's Fair with genuine explosive giraffes.

Good day from your friend DALI—1929.[171]

Did Dalí write 1929 deliberately for 1939? The possibility that the apparent slip was intentional is suggested by a devastating marginal afterthought: 'In the past our collaboration was bad for me. Remember that I had to make great efforts to have my name on *Un Chien andalou.'* Ten years had passed, almost to the day, since the screening of their first film. Now Dalí was on the up and up and Buñuel was down. What better opportunity for sweet revenge! Buñuel never forgot or forgave Dalí's refusal to help him. According to his son Juan Luis, he carried the letter in his wallet for years afterwards.[172]

The letter shows that no sooner had Franco won his war than Dalí was talking admiringly about José Antonio Primo de Rivera's Falangist Party, a Spanish variation on Italian Fascism founded in 1933. The handsome and charismatic Primo de Rivera had been executed by the Republicans at the beginning of the war, aged thirty-three, and

*Buñuel's home town in Aragon.

Franco had cunningly promoted his mythification while at the same time harnessing the energies of the Falange for his own purposes. 'Arriba España!', 'Long Live Spain!', was the Falange's slogan; theirs, too, was the ludicrous notion that Spain was destined for 'world hegemony'. Dalí was clearly under the influence of Falangist propaganda, the chief generator of which was his old friend Ernesto Giménez Caballero, and thinking about a triumphant return to the Spain now ruled by Franco. Buñuel must have been sickened not only by Dalí's refusal to help him but by his embracing of a political ideology that was anathema to Surrealism.

André Breton, too, was disgusted with Dalí. When the artist arrived back in Paris in June he was confronted with Breton's article 'The Latest Tendencies in Surrealist Painting' in the current issue of *Minotaure*. As well as reporting Dalí's outrageous suggestion for the solution of the 'racial problem', Breton wrote that his influence on new painters was now in 'very rapid decline' in France. Vitiated by 'profound, authentic monotony', his work was being supplanted in importance by that of Yves Tanguy. And how could it be otherwise, Breton asked, given Dalí's obsessive desire to please, which involved the need constantly to outdo himself in the propagation of his paradoxes?:

> By dint of wishing to over-refine on his paranoiac method, we observe that he is beginning to indulge in a game of amusement akin to the *crossword puzzle*. If, on the contrary, Tanguy's star continues to rise, it is because he retains his ideals intact, because his nature prevents him from indulging in any manner of compromise.[173]

In view of Dalí's significant debt to Tanguy, and of the fact that to some extent he felt himself his rival, these words must have made their mark. So, too, must have Breton's assertion that the new Surrealist painters (Domínguez, Paalen, Brauner, Matta, etc.) were more attracted by the automatism of the first *Manifesto* than by the control of unconscious impulses now advocated by Dalí. Later, covertly glossing the article, Dalí claimed that on arriving back in Paris he had been dismayed to find that, in his absence, Surrealism had retreated to an outdated concern with automatism, denying the advances achieved by his 'method'.[174] But that method had never truly been a method. It worked, if at all, only for him—and that was its intention. The return to automatism was inevitable because it was Surrealism's most genuine contribution to the liberation of the psyche. But to admit that would, for Dalí, have been to admit that he was wrong. And Dalí, so far we know, never in his life made such an admission.

Breton's *Minotaure* article amounted to Dalí's definitive expulsion from the Surrealist movement. We do not know if the painter protested, or if the two men met at this time, or communicated by some other means, but it seems that there was no further contact of any kind.

Dalí reacted to his expulsion with the defiance he had shown in 1926 when ejected from the Royal Academy School of San Fernando, and when his father threw him out of the family home in 1929. From now on he would go it alone and, bringing all his proven gifts for self-publicity to bear, propagate the myth that he, Salvador Dalí, and he alone, was the only true Surrealist. In America, where Breton was known to only a tiny minority but Dalí was already famous, he can have foreseen no difficulty in persuading a gullible public of the truth of this proposition. Given the clouds of war gathering in Europe, Dalí was now more convinced than ever that his future, and his fortune, lay on the other side of the Atlantic.

War and Flight

Dalí had returned to Europe to supervise the Ballets Russes production of *Bacchanale*, now scheduled to open at Covent Garden, not Paris, in mid-September. At the beginning of August he and Gala went to rest in the Grand Hôtel at Font Romeu, a spa in the French Pyrenees not far from the Spanish frontier at Puigcerdà. From there Gala replied to Edward James's letter about the sad fate of *Dream of Venus*. Unlike the latter, *Bacchanale* was shaping up wonderfully, she said, with Dalí feverishly at work on the final details, ably supported by Prince Chernady. She hoped that they could stay with him in Wimpole Street for the première.[175] But the London production never took place. On 1 September Hitler invaded Poland and Britain and France declared war on the Third Reich. The Ballets Russes switched their season to the Metropolitan Opera House in New York.

The Dalís returned post-haste to Paris. There they were telegraphed on 10 September by an Edward James in New York deeply anxious about the fate of his paintings, which the couple had stored with Tailleur et Fils, the carriers, at 91, Rue Cherche-Midi. Assuming that they would travel to New York for the première of *Bacchanale*, he instructed them to take the paintings with them, adding that he would pay for the freight.[176]

The Dalís had other things on their mind, however. After gathering together their most important belongings, and desperate to flee from Paris, they hurried down to the sea at Arcachon, near Bordeaux, where they rented a large house, the Villa Flambergé (131, Boulevard de la Plage). Dalí said later that he chose Arcachon because it was famous for its oysters, not far from gastronomy-intensive Bordeaux and close enough to the Spanish border to facilitate escape should that become necessary. Marcel Duchamp and the painter Léonor Fini had already sought refuge near by, and before long other artists and friends arrived, among them Coco Chanel.[177]

On 2 October Gala replied to James's telegram, which she had found 'curt and not very friendly'. She did not mention the pictures.[178] Dalí did, a few days later. It had been impossible to take them down to Arcachon, he said, but they *had* brought *Geodesic Portrait of Gala*. Dalí asked James to send him a spoof invitation to New York in his capacity as 'President' of *Dream of Venus* (which was still running). It would make it easier to get a visa. James complied at once.[179]

Léonor Fini, whom the Dalís knew from Paris, was good fun ('Quand c'est Fini, ça commence', quipped Paul Éluard[180]). She now proved to be useful as well, for she had a friend with a large American car that Gala quickly commandeered for trips into the countryside and comfortable transport to two excellent restaurants in Bordeaux, the Chapon Fin and the Château Trompette. Fini noted that Gala rarely smiled, and that when she did so it was to express derision.[181]

It seems that Gala went up to Paris a few times to see to the storage of their paintings, which she confided, like James's, to Tailleur et Fils. During one of these visits she sold Peggy Guggenheim *The Birth of Liquid Desires*. Other paintings Gala brought back with her and stored in a warehouse on the outskirts of Bordeaux.[182]

Meanwhile the Metropolitan Opera House's production of *Bacchanale* was encountering almost insuperable difficulties. Coco Chanel, who had worked for months at Roquebrune on the costumes requiring special care, refused to send them to America unless Dalí was there to supervise. But Gala was adamant that under no circumstances would the painter cross the Atlantic in wartime. Edward James tried to mediate as best he could. On 25 October he cabled Dalí to say that Madame Karinska, a well-known designer in New York, could make up the costumes using Dalí's photographs. Massine had said that if the ballet was not put on in November it would be a flop. Did Dalí want James to ensure that his designs were properly executed? He feared that the costumes would be begun before Dalí arrived and that therefore it would be preferable for him to supervise the work. James added that he would be happy to find some dwarfs for Venus's bed, since he knew several personally—and very charming ones, at that.[183] Dalí's reply on 28 October was so unfortunate that James never forgot it. He told him to stop 'meddling' in the 'sinister business' if he valued his friendship. Massine must be made to delay the première.[184] James's answer was equally tetchy. He thanked Dalí for his 'pretty rhetoric', said that nothing could be done to stop Massine, because he had all the rights, and insisted that, if he had tried to intervene, it was to protect Dalí's work and reputation. Hurt as he was, James maintained his offer of help. If Dalí wanted, he would send his man, Thomas, from Europe to New York with Chanel's costumes.[185]

Other pained communications ensued between the two, James eventually accepting Dalí's instructions to have nothing further to do with the production. He then fled from New York to the countryside to get away from the hassle. The notes and draft letters he wrote at the time show how deeply wounded he had been by Dalí's attitude. Had he not been a true friend to the painter? Had he ever let him down? How could he treat him like this? And so on. Little by little James was beginning to learn that gratitude was a sentiment unknown to Dalí.[186]

Meanwhile, Chanel had continued to refuse permission for her costumes to cross the Atlantic, and, with only four days to go to opening night on 9 November, substitutes had to be prepared at breakneck speed. As James foresaw, the première was little short of a fiasco, a frenzy of wild improvisation, although the audience did not seem to notice until there was a forty-minutes' delay between the first and second scenes. Many of Madame Karinska's costumes were unfinished, taxis rushed to and from her workshop while the show proceeded, some of the ballerinas never arrived and some of those who did appeared on stage wearing only full-length tights. Venus herself, played by Niní Theilade, wore a flesh-coloured body stocking that caused a sensation. But John Martin, critic of the *New York Times*, was not impressed. 'To take such a ballet as a serious piece of psychoanalysis or as an important work of art would be a grave mistake,' he judged.[187]

Dalí failed to register the mounting irritation contained in Edward James's communications, and at the end of the year told his long-suffering patron that he had undergone a radical change and was eliminating almost every trace of frivolity from his life. The only thing that counted now, he wrote, was to produce work that would impose itself by dint of 'a ferocious, implacable and dazzling rigour'. In four months he had been more productive than in four years. James should not forget that Picasso invented Cubism during the last war. 'At my already advanced age,' Dalí joked, 'it's now or never.' He then proceeded to rattle on about the failure of *Dream of Venus* and now *Bacchanale*, hinting that James had counselled him badly and asserting that he, Dalí, would never be so 'weak' again.

Dalí justified his new determination to be forceful by referring James to Lorca's view of him in the 'Ode to Salvador Dalí'. In the opening lines of the poem Lorca had mentioned the 'Impressionist mist' eschewed by the Cubists and, by extension, Dalí. The painter now tells James that 'the horrible mist' of confusion will be banished from his life. Then he explicitly quotes the line 'Alma higiénica, vives sobre mármoles nuevos' ('Hygienic soul, you live on new marbles'), seeing in it a call to a new classicism.[188] In a letter to another friend there was also an allusion to the ode. Dalí and Gala were living a truly inter-uterine existence in their villa, the painter reported, and he had undertaken some very serious things, with 'a great thirst for limits, for contours, for a desperate and perfect realism'. This phrase echoed Lorca's line 'Un deseo de formas y límites nos gana' ('a desire for forms and limits possesses us').[189] The borrowings, acknowledged or covert, are a further indication of the extent to which Lorca's great poem was now conditioning Dalí's perception of himself.

Over the following months James and the Dalís continued to nag at each other about *Dream of Venus* and *Bacchanale*. James told Dalí to bear in mind that he had lost between $25,000 and $30,000 in the former venture.[190] In March 1940 Dalí informed him that he had painted some genuine masterpieces ('you'll see!') and that he and Gala planned to travel to the States in the autumn. As for James's pictures with Tailleur et Fils, Dalí recommended him to have them shipped to America. This would be useful for him, too, since some of them could be exhibited at his next show in New York. Dalí was elated by the thought of returning to the States, where his *Declaration on the Rights of Man to His Own Madness* was now being reproduced even in the provincial press.[191]

As the Germans stepped up their pressure on France, James and Caresse Crosby became increasingly concerned about the Dalís' safety. Caresse had promised to publish Dalí's *Secret Life* with the Dial Press in New York (they must have talked about this during his last stay), and wanted to know how the manuscript was progressing. In May she wrote:

> I am counting on you and Gala visiting me at my country place in Bowling Green, Caroline County, Virginia. Your rooms are ready and waiting for you . . . it will be a tranquil place for you to work. I hear that you now have enough material together to start the book of memoirs that I am planning to bring out this fall. It is absolutely necessary that you be here during the summer months to work on this with me.[192]

If the Dalís needed any further encouragement to flee to America, it came on 14 June 1940 when the Germans occupied Paris, provoking a massive southbound exodus. The couple were panic-stricken, Leonor Fini recalled. Hitler did not now seem so quaint, his soft flesh so enticing. Salvador was drinking a lot and had made a bomb shelter in the garden. He even wondered if a suit of armour might prove useful.[193] When the Nazis reached Bordeaux the Dalís beat a hasty retreat to Spain, crossing the frontier just ahead of the invading troops, who raised the swastika at Hendaye on 28 June and were warmly welcomed by a representative of the Franco regime.[194] Among the belongings the painter left behind at Arcachon was the manuscript of *The Tragic Myth of Millet's 'Angelus'*, which was not recovered till years later.

While Gala, always the practical member of the partnership, went to Lisbon to make arrangements for their passage to New York, Dalí crossed Spain to see his family in Figueres. He found them shattered by their experience during the war, and received a detailed account of the sufferings of Anna Maria at the hands of the Communist-run SIM. (Military Intelligence Service). Figueres had been bombed by Franco, and the retreating Republicans had tried unsuccessfully to blow up the fort, causing a lot of damage in the process. Part of the town was in ruins.

Dalí made a lightning dash to Cadaqués and found Lidia, who had enjoyed her war, in fine fettle. Both Red and Fascist graffiti had been scratched on the walls of the house in Port Lligat, marking the fluctuations of the struggle. He then hurried on to Madrid, staying at the Hotel Palace, the scene of so much revelry with Buñuel and Lorca. While there, he saw two old acquaintances who were now leading Falangists, the writers Eugenio Montes (author of the rave review of *Un Chien andalou* in the *Gaceta Literaria* in 1929) and Rafael Sánchez Mazas, an authority on the Italian Renaissance. He also met another important Falangist, the poet and essayist Dionisio Ridruejo.[195]

These were days of extreme elation for the Franco regime, with the newspapers proclaiming daily that Spain's Nazi allies were on the point of crushing Britain. France's fall was regarded with great official satisfaction, and it was made clear to the nation that, with a victorious Hitler on the one hand and Mussolini on the other, Spain was about to participate in the creation of a new Europe, with imperialist expansion in Africa (and, naturally, the recovery of Gibraltar guaranteed).[196]

Dalí was predisposed to enjoy his return to Franco's Spain, as his letters to Buñuel had shown; and he was much affected by the enthusiasm of the Spanish Fascists he met in Madrid and the variety of euphoric rhetoric in which they indulged. The group, he wrote to Caresse Crosby at the end of July, was surely one of the most intelligent, inspired and original of the age! He prophesied that Spain was about to become the spiritual saviour of the world.[197] Dalí said later that 'illustrious members' of the Falange had invited him earnestly to join the party, but that he had declined.[198]

In the *Secret Life* Dalí was to write of finding the country, after three years of civil war, 'covered with ruins, nobly impoverished, with faith in its destiny revived, and with mourning engraved with a diamond in every heart'.[199] Dalí failed to point out that mourning was engraved particularly in the hearts of the ordinary people of Spain— mourning, despair and humiliation; and there was, of course, no mention of the mass executions of innocents that had begun when the war ended, and were still continuing.

As for Spain's 'revived faith in its destiny', this was just the the sort of Fascist mumbo-jumbo with which Montes, Sánchez Mazas, Ridruejo and the like were filling their newspaper columns in the summer of 1940.

Edward James had heard the rumour that Dalí had been arrested in Spain, and, recalling the fate of Lorca, was sick with anxiety. On 8 July he cabled Franklin D. Roosevelt, no less, and asked for an enquiry to be made. He was informed that, according to the American Embassy in Madrid, Dalí was staying at the Hotel Palace and was expected to leave on 17 July for Lisbon. By this date Gala had already put James's mind at ease: Dalí was safe in Madrid, waiting to get his visa. When the painter flew to Lisbon soon afterwards he cabled James to say that he had had a 'marvellous stay' in Spain—and to ask for $500. James, one imagines, complied by return.[200]

There was little press coverage for Dalí's brief return to Spain, but one or two snippets did appear. In the Barcelona weekly *Destino*, the writer Carlos Sentís sneered at the hordes of rich refugees passing through Madrid on the way to Lisbon, and noted that Dalí, 'a superman in that world', had been among them.[201] The same magazine reported that Dalí had been to the Prado, where apparently he said that he was now determined 'to rectify the orientation and manner of his painting'. Such, he may have given his listeners to believe, had been the impact of seeing the new order in Spain.[202]

Under dictator Oliveira Salazar, Lisbon was a hive of rumours and counter-rumours as more and more refugees arrived from Europe. Dalí recalls in the *Secret Life* that you never knew whom you would bump into next. Among those desperate to get away were friends such as Man Ray, Elsa Schiaparelli and Josep Maria Sert. René Clair and his wife had also arrived (and Julien Green would do so soon). There was no shortage of spies, either. They included the Duke of Windsor, who was secretly working for the Nazis (and for the recovery of his throne). He had just made a much-publicized visit to Spain and was now embarking for his new job as Governor General of the Bahamas, where the British government hoped he would be far enough away to desist from plotting.[203]

The Dalís managed to secure a passage on the *Excambion*, of the American Export Line, which set off for New York early in August. They were not to set foot in Europe again for eight years.[204]

The *Secret Life*

Dalí was now famous in New York and had more than taken the measure of the American sensational press. As he crossed the Atlantic for the third time he must have pondered carefully what he was going to say to the reporters on arrival. There could be no point in repeating more or less the antics of his previous disembarkations, that was clear. Giant loaves of bread or strategically placed cutlets had lost their shock value. Give them something new, something unexpected. So, as the *Excambion* nosed into its berth on 16 August 1940, Dalí, dressed immaculately in a pinstripe suit with a demure Gala at his side, knew exactly what he was going to tell the newspapermen—then and over the forthcoming months.[1]

He told them that the Surrealist movement was dead and that he, its greatest exponent, was about to initiate the return to classicism. He also told them that his forthcoming autobiography would chart his progress from Surrealist *enfant terrible* to saviour of modern art. Dalí knew from experience that, when he put his extravagance publicly in the service of his convictions of the moment, there was never any shortage of either potential converts or media coverage. He also knew that the vital thing now was to express the novel formulation with the maximum energy, and must have been gratified when, as he had calculated, the pencils scratched furiously and the cameras flashed.[2]

The Dalís put up at the St Regis, and ten days later travelled down as planned to stay with Caresse Crosby in Virginia.[3] After abandoning Paris in 1936, Crosby had scoured Caroline County in search of an American version of the Moulin du Soleil. She knew exactly what she wanted: an old plantation house with columns, lots of rooms for creative guests, a deer park, an avenue of elms and a pond. And, being Caresse, she found

Chapter ELEVEN

it. Hampton Manor stood in five hundred acres of mixed woodland and fields forty kilo-metres south of Fredericksburg and eight from Bowling Green. The latter was 'a tiny town', a Washington reporter discovered the following February, 'about the size of a couple of baseball diamonds put together'.[4] The mansion was very run-down when Crosby located it, but in every other respect it fitted the bill to perfection. For good measure it could boast historical associations, for it had been built in 1836 to designs by Thomas Jefferson, and as a result was something of a tourist attraction. By the time Dalí and Gala arrived the place had been tastefully refurbished and Caresse had not only married her third husband but was in the process of divorcing him.[5]

In his first letter home Dalí told Anna Maria:

> We've been installed for a few weeks now in this tranquil spot in the middle of an ancient forest. The house is extraordinarily comfortable, there's a huge library in which we make sensational discoveries with Gala, five servants (all black as anthracite), two horses for riding, a lake in which to bathe, 'et tout et tout'.

Dalí was impressed by the size of the estate, and told Anna Maria about the cabins inhabited by blacks who spent their time singing and doing 'little jobs'. They reminded him of the most lazy man in Cadaqués, Ramon de la Hermosa.

The main point of the letter was to inform the family that he was hard at work on his autobiography. Dalí felt sure that the book could be a commercial success, and asked Anna Maria to send him childhood photographs. Then came a confidence:

> You know as well as I do that my scandalously anarchic period is behind me. In my book what I want to do is to write about my family precisely in such a way as to eradicate once and for all any mistakes and misunderstanding there may have been between us. At any rate I'll send father the passage in which I talk about the family so that he can approve it or make suggestions.[6]

By his own admission, then, the reformed Dalí had his relations with his family very much in mind as he sat down to write the memoirs mapped out a few years earlier at Coco Chanel's residence in Monte Carlo. Clearly, he was going to be very selective in what he said about them.

As well as working strenuously on his book during this spell at Hampton Manor, Dalí produced four or five paintings for his next exhibition at Julien Levy's. Totally engrossed in what he was doing he hardly ever ventured out into the estate, let alone the surrounding countryside, which he told a reporter reminded him strongly of the Touraine.[7]

Anaïs Nin and Henry Miller were in occupation when the Dalís arrived. Nin did not think much of Gala, an opinion confirmed during subsequent visits, although she grew to like Dalí, and he her. Miller, who at this time was adding some material to the second part of *Tropic of Capricorn*, was amused by neither Dalí nor Gala, and told Nin that he considered the painter's work 'the Styx, the river of neurosis that doesn't flow'. Later, manic diarist Nin recalled her first breakfast with Dalí and the Muse:

> Both small in stature, they sat close together. Both were unremarkable in appearance, she all in moderate tones, a little faded, and he drawn with charcoal like a child's drawing of a Spaniard, any Spaniard, except for the incredible length of his mustache. They turned towards each other as if for protection, reassurance, not open, trusting or at ease.[8]

Gala soon made it clear that Dalí was the principal house guest, and that it was everyone else's duty to cater to his needs. She (and some of the other visitors) resented the fact that he and Nin talked to each other in Castilian, and when the latter prepared a Spanish dish, thinking it would make the couple feel at home, Gala said she disliked Spanish cooking. The extraordinary thing was that no one protested—at least at first. 'So we each fulfilled our appointed tasks. Mrs Dalí never raised her voice, never seduced or charmed. Quietly she assumed we were all there to serve Dalí, the great, indisputable genius.' But before long Gala was getting on everyone's nerves.[9]

In September 1940, with Caresse Crosby away, her estranged husband turned up with his girlfriend one night and, in a burst of rage, threatened to destroy Dalí's paintings. Dalí and Gala left hurriedly for Washington and then paid a brief visit to Edward James in Taos, New Mexico. There James introduced them to Frieda Lawrence whom Gala treated with disdain, remarking the following day (according to James): 'Poor Edward! What you've come to! Spending your time with left-overs!' James was deeply shocked. Moreover, he was still angry about Dalí's failure to honour fully the terms of their pre-war contract. The Dalís moved on to Hollywood, where it seems they saw James again, and a few months later returned to Hampton Manor to continue work on the *Secret Life*.[10]

The *Secret Life* was written in a convoluted French that stretched to the utmost the abilities of Dalí's translator, Haakon Chevalier, well known in America for his versions of French novels, when Caresse Crosby entrusted it to him the following summer.[11] By then a typescript had been made from a handwritten fair copy produced by Gala in her vital capacity as editor of Dalí's literary production, initiated in 1930 with *The Visible Woman*.[12] Chevalier's rendering reads wonderfully but tidies up Dalí's prose style so neatly that only when the French original has been published will it be possible to get the full flavour of the book.[13]

The *Secret Life* is a megalomaniac memoir written largely without recourse to documentation, and with the deliberate exclusion, or misrepresentation, of vital episodes or moments in Dalí's life. His virulent Marxism as an adolescent is never mentioned; the reasons for his father's repudiation in 1929 are not given (there is no mention of the offensive painting of the Sacred Heart); his reverence for Breton in the early 1930s,

Painting, unknown today, reproduced in The Secret Life of Salvador Dalí *with the commentary 'Mysterious mouth appearing in the back of my nurse'. The head is that of Lorca.*

attested in their correspondence, goes unacknowledged—indeed, Breton is hardly named; we are asked to believe that, within a year of joining the Surrealist ranks, Dalí had rejected automatism, had invented the slogan 'the conquest of the irrational' (in fact first formulated in 1935)[14] and had embarked on a covert programme to take control of the movement and redirect its energies;[15] Dalí claims all the credit for creating 'the fashion of Surrealist Objects', with no reference to their forerunners or to Breton's explicit instructions for their propagation;[16] he expresses scorn for the political commitment of the Surrealist movement when he himself shared it for a time ('personally, politics have never interested me,' he assures us, conveniently forgetting about his involvement in the Workers' and Peasants' Front);[17] the blame for the anti-clericalism of *L'Age d'or* is placed solely on Buñuel's shoulders, Dalí stating that by 1930, when the film was made, he was already 'dazzled and obsessed by the grandeur and the sumptuousness of Catholicism';[18] he asks us to admire his and Gala's stoical refusal to confess to their lack of means during their early years together, excising all reference to the Zodiac, set up explicitly in response to their request for help; Picasso is portrayed as a great friend;[19] as regards the Spanish Civil War, Dalí denies that Lorca, 'by essence the most a-political person on earth', could have been killed by the Fascists other than as a 'propitiatory victim' required by 'revolutionary confusion';[20] and so on. Betrayal follows betrayal: betrayal of former friends, betrayal of what Dalí himself had said, written or done, betrayal of truth, betrayal of the claim, made at the beginning of the book, that the work is an 'honest attempt at self-portraiture'.[21]

The driving purpose of the *Secret Life* is to present Dalí as a mixture of ambitious-child-made-good-at-thirty-seven ('Since my earliest childhood I have desperately striven to be at the "top"'),[22] prophet of war (both of the Spanish and the European), saviour of modern art (by rescuing painting from abstraction and reclaiming it for the 'eternal tradition' of the Renaissance)[23] and reborn Spanish Catholic (he even tells us that like a snake he has cast off his 'old skin').[24] A related purpose is to create the myth of Gala as preordained muse, mistress, psychotherapist and wife, adumbrated in childhood, glimpsed again in adolescence and finally incarnated on the beach at Cadaqués in 1929. There are other aims: to flatter America—envisaged, with the collapse of Europe into chaos, as the Promised Land; to establish the Empordà plain, Cadaqués and Port Lligat as the most important places in the world; to prepare the ground for Dalí's eventual return to Spain; and, of course, to increase his fame in the States and enhance his sales at a time when the art market was at a low ebb.

With all these ends in view, Dalí constructs a narrative fabric in which fact and fiction, truth and lies, are inextricably entwined, the issue being further complicated, where the early chapters are concerned, by the introduction of what he terms 'false childhood memories', memories that even include a few (admittedly blurred) intra-uterine 'recollections' inspired by Otto Rank's *The Traumatism of Birth*.

Within Dalí's chosen framework the chronology of his memoir is as indeterminate as that of the anonymous *My Secret Life*, the Victorian erotic epic purveyed as true history about which he may have heard in Paris and whose title perhaps suggested his own. The author affects to possess total recall of his early childhood, to the extent of being able to reproduce conversations, or the exact colours of a sunset, at the age of six, but the sequence of events evoked is often radically dislocated. As for the 1930s, episodes separated in some instances by four or five years are linked with blithe insouciance to give an impression of temporal continuity ('it was at about this period', 'not long afterwards', 'I began at about this period to appear', 'at about this time', 'at this period', etc.). Towards the end of the book the chronology of events becomes increasingly chaotic.

Perhaps the most striking aspect of Dalí's autobiography, however, is the author's claim, in its closing pages, to be seeking reconciliation with the Catholic Church. There is no acknowledgement in these pages to Dalí's acquaintance Ernesto Giménez Caballero, editor-owner of *La Gaceta Literaria* and the principal theorist of Spanish Fascism, but it is impossible not to sense the influence on them of the latter's book *Roma madre* ('Mother Rome'), published in Madrid in 1939 just after the civil war ended. Dalí may have seen Giménez Caballero when he passed through the capital in the summer of 1940 on his way to Lisbon, or perhaps one of the Falangists he says he talked to on that occasion may have brought the book to his attention. Whatever the truth of the matter, Dalí's exaltation of Rome, the Rome of the Vatican, of the Renaissance, of hierarchy and now of imperialism is almost indistinguishable from Giménez Caballero's, as is his new-found enthusiasm for the virtues of Spanish Catholicism.[25]

Dalí emerges from the *Secret Life* as a first-rate, and often very funny, storyteller, his opening sentence setting a mock-serious tone that is ably maintained throughout the book: 'At the age of six I wanted to be a cook.[26] At seven I wanted to be Napoleon. And my ambition has been growing steadily ever since.' Many passages remain vividly in the mind. His account of the mammoth 'two-day orgy' in Madrid that initiated him into the joys of going on a bender, for example; or that of the foundation in Paris of a Dalinian society devoted to causing international mass hysteria by the strategic placing in cities around the world of unexplained and ever more gigantic loaves of bread. His descriptions of Lídia of Cadaqués are witty, penetrating and even touching; and every so often he comes up with an apothegm almost worthy of Wilde ('The hair of the elegant woman must be healthy; it is the only thing about the elegant woman that must be healthy'; or 'Very rich people have always impressed me; very poor people, like the fishermen of Port Lligat, have likewise impressed me; average people, not at all').[27]

'The Last Scandal of Salvador Dalí'

In the midst of his work on the *Secret Life* Dalí staged his sixth (and final) exhibition at Julien Levy's gallery in New York, which ran from 22 April until 23 May 1941. The invitation card began: 'Salvador Dalí requests the pleasure of your company at his last scandal, the beginning of his classical painting'.[28] The lavish catalogue, acting as a curtain-raiser to the autobiography, was designed to substantiate this claim. The cover framed Dalí's *Soft Self-Portrait with Grilled Bacon* within a print of a Renaissance arch by Palladio adorned with mythological scenes inspired by ancient Rome. Below, the artist had affixed his name in copperplate lettering combined with geometrical embellishments suggestive of one of his new obsessions, the Golden Section. Inside came a preposterous piece of self-promotion, 'The Last Scandal of Salvador Dalí'. Attributed to 'Felipe Jacinto' (Dalí's second and third Christian names), its epigraph humorously established the tone of the piece: 'The two luckiest things that can happen to a contemporary painter are: first to be Spanish, and second to be named Dalí. Both have happened to me.' 'Felipe Jacinto' claimed to have met Dalí in Paris a week before the war broke out, and to have heard him expatiate brilliantly on the consequences of the hostilites about to be unleashed. The 'psychological epoch' was coming to an abrupt end, Dalí had informed him. Its place would be taken by a 'morphological era' characterized by a return to form, control and structure. 'Felipe Jacinto' is quite beside himself: 'Behold the luck, the grace and the miracle that in this year of Spiritual Sterility 1941 there can still exist a being such as Dalí, capable of continuing the conquest of the irrational merely by becoming classic and pursuing that research in *Divina Proportione* interrupted since the Renaissance.'

And so on. But how did it all work out in practice? A note in the catalogue indicated that the works were hung in 'antique frames', no doubt to indicate their classical essence,

Dalí, Daddy Longlegs of Evening—Hope!, *1940. Oil on canvas, 39.3 x 78.6 cm. The first painting Dalí executed at Caresse Crosby's. Its theme, perhaps, is that out of the turmoil of war would come a new order. A Fascist order?*

but the nineteen paintings on show revealed no marked break with what Dalí had been doing over the last few years, neither the fifteen or so executed in France before the couple fled from the Germans nor the handful done during their sojourn in Virginia.

At the end of March Dalí had shown a *Richmond Times-Dispatch* reporter the first painting he had produced since his arrival in America, *Araignée du soir, espoir*, soon afterwards renamed *Soft Violoncello, Spider, Great Masturbator*.[29] Today the picture is known, less satisfactorily, as *Daddy Longlegs of Evening—Hope!* The reporter felt flattered that Dalí, despite having hardly stepped outside Hampton Manor during his stay, had incorporated in the painting a fine example of Bowling Green entomology. The insect's presence, however, was more a reminiscence of Europe than a casual field observation in Virginia, for, as Dalí later recalled, a French superstition holds that a spider seen at evening is a sign of good luck.[30] Dalí told the reporter that the soft object being vomited by the cannon, alongside the horse, was an aeroplane, from whose wings victory was being born: airpower would decide the European war. It seems that the theme of the painting, consistent with Dalí's many statements about the imminent return to classicism, was that out of the turmoil of war (represented by the cannon borrowed from De Chirico) would come a new order.

Dalí apparently did not explain to the journalist that the central figure in the painting, whose neck merges into the figure of a limp female cello player draped over a branch like the soft watch in *The Persistence of Memory*, is the Great Masturbator (as the painting's new title was to indicate). The two inkpots placed on the female's midriff, suggestive of Dalí's father in his capacity as notary public, reinforce the suspicion that the scene alludes to Dalí's nostalgia for his homeland and to his early portrait of Lluís Pichot practising at Es Sortell. And the angel or Cupid in the left-hand bottom corner? He is hiding his face with one hand: an indication, perhaps, in view of so many earlier paintings referring to the subject, that compulsive masturbation is still for Dalí a motive of shame.

There is nothing in the painting's composition to suggest a radical departure in Dalí's work. In *Family of Marsupial Centaurs* (1940), however, one can see Dalí's attempt to back up theory with practice, the rigidly geometrical pattern of the picture, reminiscent of the 1926 *Figure on the Rocks*, being highlighted in the exhibition catalogue, where the reproduction of a study for the painting is provided. 'More design, more balance and precise technique,' Dalí commented to *The New Yorker*.[31] The exhibition also included three society portraits (a foretaste of one of the ways in which Dalí's energies were to be deployed over the next two years), some unspecified drawings (Ingres's dictum, 'Drawing is the integrity of art', first quoted by Dalí in his 1927 catalogue, resurfaces),

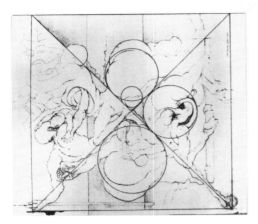

Dalí, sketch for Family of Marsupial Centaurs, *1940. Included in the catalogue to Dalí's 1941 exhibition at Julien Levy's, the point is to demonstrate that Dalí is now going classical.*

six jewels based on Dalí's designs and executed by the Duke di Verdura (who had paid a brief visit to the artist in Hampton Manor) and a crystal cup designed by Dalí and made by Steuben Glass. Finally, the catalogue reproduced a page of the manuscript of *The Secret Life of Salvador Dalí*, with an over-optimistic indication from the Dial Press that the book would appear that September, and some witty promotional additions by Dalí: 'Can one remember one's prenatal life? Explained in the book. Why are these horrible cats' tails grafted upon breasts? Explained in the book . . .'

Despite the publicity, despite Dalí's growing fame, despite the catalogue, despite the message of the return to classicism, despite Julian Levy's belief in the paintings done since the artist's arrival the previous August,[32] the exhibition was not a sell-out. 'In 1941 business was not only terrible, it was nonexistent,' Levy was to recall.[33]

The reviews were not outstanding, either, and few critics seemed prepared to believe in the sincerity of Dalí's conversion to classicism. 'Salvador Dalí has gone classical,' wrote Henry McBride in the *New York Sun*. 'Did you know that? So he says. But you'd never notice it. As far as you and I are concerned it's the same old Salvador.'[34] A particularly energetic broadside came in the June issue of the magazine *View* from the poet Nicholas Calas, a leading member of the group of Surrealist exiles in New York.[35] Calas had no hesitation in terming Dalí a renegade who had only changed sides in order to guarantee his personal survival. The rediscovery of Spain, Catholicism, penitence and classicism—it was all a ploy to please 'the masters of the counter-revolution'. Dalí, his own worst enemy, no longer knew what he was at; he resembled the peasant girl who thought that by adding a ribbon to her grandmother's antique bonnet she was at the height of style.[36] In the *Secret Life* Dalí expressed his gratitude to this article for providing him with his new identification papers as an 'Anti-Surrealist'.[37]

The Dalís spent the summer of 1941 at the luxurious Del Monte Lodge in Pebble Beach, California, which over the following years was to be their American Port Lligat, an illusion suggested by the vague similarity of the Pacific coastline to the Costa Brava, and by the Spanish placenames in which the area abounds: Monterey, Carmel, Buena

Vista, Santa Rita. The Del Monte Lodge management not only gave them VIP treatment but, pressurized by Gala ('Dalí is good for business'), charged them very little. Near by, at Carmel, a studio with a delightful garden was found for the painter, who was soon working his customary long hours.[38]

It may be that the Del Monte Lodge had been suggested as a retreat by Julien Levy, who that summer, in response to the disastrous slump in the New York market, had taken his Dalí exhibition on the road. The first destiny of this 'caravan of modern art' was Chicago, where the Dalí show ran at the Arts Club from 23 May to 14 June.[39] Then came San Francisco and finally Los Angeles, where the Dalzell Hatfield Galleries hung the Dalís between 10 September and 5 October 1941.[40]

On 2 September, at the Del Monte, Dalí and Gala staged a well-publicized 'Night in a Surrealist Forest', based (with no acknowledgement) on Caresse Crosby's 'Bal Onirique' of 1935 and on the weird décor of the Surrealist group show held at the Galerie des Beaux Arts three years later. Ostensibly the purpose of the occasion was to collect funds for exiled European artists in the United States, but in practice the aim was to establish Dalí and Gala as a socially desirable addition to West Coast society. Dalí's list of props for turning the hotel into a Surrealist Forest, which included animals from the local zoo, horrified the management. But the project went ahead. Clark Gable, Bob Hope, Bing Crosby and Ginger Rogers flew up from Hollywood. The Hitchcocks and a sprinkling of millionaires came from New York. A radiant Gala presided with Dalí over a long table piled with allegedly Surrealist bric-à-brac; the ceiling was hung with sacks to give the effect of a grotto; and Bob Hope got a shock when a live toad covered in sauce leapt at him from one of the dishes. Everyone enjoyed the party but, when it was all over, there was no money left in the kitty for the exiled European artists. Dalí and Gala had made their mark on California, however, and set off for Manhattan well satisfied with their effort.[41]

There they were interviewed at the St Regis by a reporter on *American Weekly*, who commented that Dalí had 'a flair for personal publicity that makes the late Barnum look like an amateur'. It was true—his instinct for publicity was unerring, both for arranging it himself and for taking advantage of it when it was served up with no charge by 'objective chance'. He showed *American Weekly* a seven-foot chair placed on the backs of four turtles (kindness towards animals was never one of Dalí's strong points). It was up there, close to the ceiling, that he got his best ideas. He demonstrated. Down below Gala explained that the 'perpetual motion' of the turtles stimulated the Master's creative power. The reporter thought they looked pretty dead. 'They are simply asleep, brooding in their own unconscious world,' snapped Gala. And money? Dalí's 'Surrealist portraits' were selling like hot cakes despite the war, Gala assured her, and there was no shortage of projects under way.[42]

It was true. That very evening the Ballets Russes de Monte Carlo's production of Dalí's *Labyrinth* opened at the Metropolitan Opera House. He had devised the ballet, which was based on the story of Theseus and Ariadne, in discussion with his friend the Marqués de Cuevas, patron of the Ballets Russes, and had designed the sets and costumes during the summer at Pebble Beach. The music was by Franz Schubert and the choreography by Massine, with whom Dalí had worked on *Bacchanale* in 1939. A reconstruction of one of Dalí's backdrops hangs today in the central hall of his Theatre-Museum in Figueres. It shows the torso of a bald giant standing up to his midriff in the sea in front of a Böcklinesque island. His skull is cracked, his head lowered, as if meditating, and a doorway—the entrance to the labyrinth—has been opened in his chest. One of the other backdrops was based on Botticelli's *The Birth of Venus*. Dalí appropriated the latter's foamcrested waves and transplanted the goddess to the sky, where her huge breasts and haunches doubled as clouds. The design was crude beyond description.[43]

Labyrinth was not a success with the critics. Nor did Dalí himself particularly like it. But it was talked about, and provided a useful curtain-raiser for the remarkable Miró–Dalí joint exhibition that was about to hit New York.[44]

The Museum of Modern Art Retrospective

In 1929 Dalí had told a journalist in Barcelona that his major aim at that time was international fame.[45] The MOMA retrospective, which opened on 18 November 1941, proved not only that twelve years later he had achieved his goal but that Americans were awed by the gift for self-promotion that had helped him to do so. 'The fame of Salvador Dalí has been an issue of particular controversy for more than a decade,' began the cautious foreword to the exhibition catalogue by Monroe Wheeler, the museum's Director of Exhibitions and Publications. 'Our opinion of him differs from that of the public as reflected in the press,' he added somewhat guardedly, 'and also, in some degree, from his own self-interpretation.' Aware that the subject-matter of Dalí's paintings could be considered shocking, or arbitrary, Wheeler justified the exhibition by presenting Dalí as an artist peculiarly fitted for expressing 'the tormented psyche of today', the psyche of 'a troubled epoch'. 'Is it not unreasonable for us to welcome revolutionary achievement in the sciences and then shudder at revolution in the realm of art?' he asked. 'Dalí's conduct may have been undignified, but the greater part of his art is a matter of dead earnest, for us no less than for him.'[46]

The MOMA had no such qualms about the Joan Miró half of the joint exhibition. 'Gaiety, sunshine, health—color, humor, rhythm: these are the notes which characterize the work of Joan Miro,' began the author of the monograph-catalogue, James Johnson Sweeney. 'Going from the Dalí section to the Mirós is like moving from some dark, solemn chamber—say, a room where clinical photographs are being studied—to the gaiety and light of a children's nursery,' mused Robert M. Coates in *The New Yorker*.[47] The purpose of the double exhibition, clearly, was to illustrate how Surrealism could accommodate both the dark and the light sides of human nature; or, as Edward Alden Jewell put it, to show 'how divergent may be the acting of two protagonists in one and the same play'—the play being Surrealism.[48]

The earliest painting in the Dalí retrospective was *The Basket of Bread* (1926): his Impressionist and Cubist phases were entirely unrepresented. Of the key works executed in 1929, two were on show—*Illumined Pleasures* and *The Accommodations of Desire*; from 1930, *The Font* and *The Feeling of Becoming*. Dalí's best-known painting in America, *The Persistence of Memory* (1931), which had recently been anonymously donated to the museum, was there, as was *Shades of Night Descending* from the same year. Other outstanding works exhibited included *Myself at the Age of Ten When I was a Grasshopper Child* (1933), *Gala and Millet's 'Angelus' Preceding the Imminent Arrival of the Conic Anamorphoses* (1933), *The Ghost of Vermeer of Delft, Which can Be Used as a Table* (1934), *Portrait of Gala* (1935)—which had also been given anonymously to the MOMA—*Soft Construction with Boiled Beans (Premonition of Civil War)*, here dated 1936, two important works lent by Edward James, *Sleep* (1937) and *Impressions of Africa* (1938), and another, *Imperial Violets* (1938), which he had donated to the MOMA, *Apparition of Face and Fruit-Dish on a Beach* (1938), and, from Dalí's private collection, *The Spectre of Sex Appeal* (1934), *Average Atmospherocephalic Bureaucrat in the Act of Milking a Cranial Harp* (1934), *Philosophy Illuminated by the Light of the Moon and the Setting Sun* (1939), *Two Pieces of Bread Expressing the Sentiment of Love* (1940) and *Old Age, Adolescence, Infancy* (1940). To the forty-two oils were added Dalí's design for the cover of the *Second Surrealist Manifesto* and sixteen drawings done between 1934 and 1940.

The fact that Edward James had lent two paintings recovered with difficulty from France suggests that, despite his anger about Dalí's failure to honour their pre-war contract, he had now more or less agreed to let bygones be bygones.

The reviews of the Dalí–Miró joint retrospective reveal that, whatever the individual preferences of the critics, Dalí stole the show. No one could deny his ability to disturb and fascinate the public. 'If Americans like to rebel they also like to be shocked,' commented Henry McBride, 'and Señor Dalí has shocked them more deeply and more often than any other artist of modern times.'[49] Robert M. Coates agreed, but felt that Dalí's shock tactics were now so old-hat that they had lost 'a good share of their intended impact'. He considered that there was 'a sense of shallowness' about most of the work, and that virtuosity was Dalí's severest handicap. Dalí was repeating himself. Coates was also unhappy that Dalí had succeeded in convincing America that he, and he alone, represented Surrealism. This was harming the appreciation of other Surrealist painters and their differing styles—Lurçat, Tanguy and Masson in France, for example, Peter Blume, Philip Evergood and James Guy in the United States; it also meant that people were finding it difficult to distinguish between 'surrealism in art and surrealism as an escapade of Dalí's, such as hanging pianos in trees or arranging peep shows at the World's Fair'.[50] Peyton Boswell Jr, in *Art Digest*, thought that Miró did not quite fit 'into the layman's conception of surrealism as popularized by its acknowledged leader', that is by Dalí. Miró's was 'the lighter motif, more decorative in the modern mode, and yet, withal, startling enough in his uniquely patterned symbols'. Dalí, on the other hand, was:

> 20,000 volts of uninhibited imagery. His is a diseased, sadistic, nihilistic art expression, but undeniably it has the hypnotic gift of exciting even those who are surfeited with the acres and acres of canvases done with the sole idea of mutilating virginal linen . . . Dalí's is a voice of his time. When times change and humans return to sanity, the vogue for his exquisitely painted and temptingly titled nightmares will change with them. While we wait, there can be little harm in escaping for a while from the strain of world-wide hysteria by shedding our worries in the presence of Dalí's incongruous juxtapositions of familiar objects.[51]

James Thrall Soby's essay for the exhibition catalogue contained the best account of Dalí's life and work to date, not least because he had had the advantage of reading the typescript of the *Secret Life* in advance of publication. This did not prevent him from making one or two glaring blunders, however: he called Picasso Dalí's 'fellow Catalan'; and, although he had never set foot in Catalunya, felt free to talk of 'the Catalan love of fantasy and sanctification of instinct'! Soby's observations on the influence on Dalí of De Chirico's deep perspective and of Giovanni Battista Bracelli's furniture-figures and double images were original and perceptive. He thought Dalí had contributed forcibly to the reinstatement of the anecdote in painting (which was true), and felt that his stand against abstract art was making its mark (which it was not). The 'indubitable fact', at all events, was that Dalí was the most famous of the younger artists then painting. Ten thousand copies of the handsome catalogue were printed (to eight thousand of Miró's), and it added greatly to Dalí's standing in America. When the retrospective ended in February 1942, three months after Pearl Harbor and America's entry into the war, it set off on a tour of eight cities throughout the United States: Northampton, Cleveland, Indianapolis, San Franciso, Williamsburg, Utica, Detroit and Omaha.[52] Many people, who only knew about Dalí from the popular press, were surprised to find that as well as a showman he was a remarkable painter. The tour was a great success and generated reams of newsprint. By the time it ended Dalí could have been justified in feeling that, at the age of thirty-eight, he had arrived. So much for the Royal Academy Special School in Madrid!

The *Secret Life* Hits America

In September 1942 Dalí launched a campaign to promote the *Secret Life*, which was about to appear simultaneously in New York and London. For the magazine *Click* he designed a lavish preview combining trick photography, snatches of commentary and drawings. We see Dalí writing at his 'symbolic table' (a headless naked girl lying on her back); a soft watch drapes the head of Gala; fried eggs standing in for severed breasts parade across one of the pages; and two ballerinas culled from Dalí's dreams of the previous night leap across his bed. Dalí is sporting his turned up moustache. He is dark, elegant and undeniably handsome.[53]

There were pre-publication excerpts, too. One of these Dalí hurried off to his sister from Los Angeles at the beginning of September, where he and Gala were installed at the Beverly Hills Hotel, haunt of famous movie stars such as Clark Gable. Unlike their father or stepmother, Anna Maria could read English, which she had begun to study at Barcelona University in 1935. Indeed, she even did occasional translations and soon entertained the hope that Salvador would allow her to prepare the Spanish-language version of his *Secret Life*, a hope dashed when the Argentinian edition appeared in 1944.[54] Dalí asked Anna Maria not to be upset by the Halley's Comet passage, in which he claims to have kicked her in the head when she was two and he six. Its purpose, he explained, was simply to portray him as a nasty child. Later on in the book, he assured her, all the family were treated very lovingly, 'wiping out completely any misunderstandings there may have been in our lives in the past'. In the same letter Dalí told her excitedly about the ultra-luxurious Cadillac he and Gala had just bought. They had travelled west in it and were now about to begin the return journey to New York. He had had the windows replaced with double coloured ones designed by himself, and Louis

XVI handles substituted for the standard fittings. His paintings were selling so well that he had tried to send them money, but the international situation made it absolutely impossible. Instead, he would do his best to transfer to them some funds he and Gala had left behind in Lisbon. He hoped that they would be able to return to Spain the following spring, and wanted her to write more often.[55]

Dalí may not have been feeling at home in the United States, but he was certainly having a whale of a time. To cap it all the *Secret Life* was an immediate hit when it appeared in October, and attracted dozens of reviews. Physically, the book was exquisite, thanks in no small measure to Caresse Crosby, who received due acknowledgement from the publisher, Burton C. Hoffman, on the back of the title page (this credit disappeared in later editions). Dalí's most famous painting in America, *The Persistence of Memory*, was reproduced in colour on the front of the jacket; on the back there was a charming sketch of a naked, girlish Gala astride a little boat with an eagle's head. The legend read 'Gala, celle qui avance' (Gala always refused to dwell on the past). The hard covers were of black cloth. In the centre of the front one there was a stuck-on ink drawing in which, against a pink background, an emaciated seated personage stretched the crucifix grasped in his right hand in the direction of two fighter planes that had been engaged in combat. One of them was nose-diving in flames. The message, in tune with the book's closing pages about Dalí's search for God, was that the world needed a resurgence of Catholic faith.[56]

Hundreds of drawings, photographs and reproductions illustrated the text, and praise for Dalí on the back flap included three quotations from the famous: 'Dalí's imagination reminds me of an outboard motor continally running' (Picasso); 'I have never seen a more complete example of a Spaniard. What a fanatic' (Freud); 'Dalí's book is a strange picture, madly humorous, aggressive, offensive, fanatically provoking, yet unwillingly beautiful. Look for the conscious: you will find an intelligence respectful of tradition, and a heart craving for faith' (André Maurois).

Among the many photographs of Dalí contained in the volume, that by Philippe Halsman, which shows the painter with the words SECRET LIFE etched on his forehead, is one of the most remarkable. The two had got on well, not least on account of their similarly zany sense of humour. Dalí was as impressed by Halsman's inventiveness as the photographer was by the Spaniard's non-stop flow of ideas, and their friendship was to lead to a sporadic collaboration lasting for decades.

The *Secret Life* received a mixed reception, as no doubt Dalí both intended and foresaw, but even the critics who hated it could not deny its originality or its daring. By and large the ignorance of Spain on the part of the reviewers, let alone of Catalunya, made it difficult for them to assess Dalí's account of his background. Hardly anyone seems to have grasped the book's humour. An exception was James Thurber, who came up with a witty piece called 'The Secret Life of James Thurber' in *The New Yorker*. 'What Salvie had that the rest of us kids didn't,' he wrote sardonically, 'was the perfect scenery, characters, and costumes for his desperate little rebellion against the clean, the conventional, and the comfortable.'[57] An anonymous commentator in *Time* also caught some of the humour: the autobiography was 'a wild jungle of fantasy, posturing, belly laughs, narcissist and sadist confessions', 'one of the most irresistible books of the year'.[58] Of the year? 'It is one of the most extraordinary books of the century,' opined another critic.[59] One reviewer sensed that the secret life proposed by Dalí had little to do with the real man (the book was 'perhaps the greatest feat of willed obscurantism of all time'),[60] and Malcolm Cowley, in *New Republic*, thought that a century later Dalí's *Secret Life* would provide 'evidence of the collapse of Western Europe'—and not in the military sense of the term.[61] Clifton Fadiman, of *The New Yorker*, considered it a 'grinning nightmare of a book'. Dalí was a bad boy, 'and if you think bad boys should not be permitted to write their memoirs, you had better not poke your nose into *The Secret Life*'.[62] Elsa Maxwell did poke her nose into it, and enjoyed the experience. 'Read this Baudelairian book, and give yourself a free ride through the mazes of the psychoneuroses,' she counselled.[63] Sol A. Davidson of *The Art Digest* thought the book schizophrenic and sadistic: it read like an account written by an inmate of a psychiatric hospital.[64]

Luis Buñuel had been working since 1941 in the film documentary department of the Museum of Modern Art, and was curious to see what Dalí had written in the *Secret Life* about him and their collaboration. The few marginal comments in his copy suggest that he did not think much of the book ('It's a lie!' he scribbled down twice). The passage in which Dalí argues that the anti-Catholicism of *L'Age d'or* was solely Buñuel's responsibility is not annotated; nonetheless it was this which apparently aroused the animus that forced Buñuel to resign from the MOMA the following June. Buñuel's political history was being examined by the Washington authorities at this time, and he could well have done without Dalí's twisted account of the making of *L'Age d'or*, presumably designed to ensure that Dalí at least had no trouble in the States.[65]

If Buñuel did not think much of the *Secret Life*, George Orwell despised it. Orwell's long review, 'Benefit of Clergy: Some Notes on Salvador Dalí', was by far the most interesting contemporary response to the book in England. In Orwell's view, Dalí was a disgusting human being whose pictorial work, outstanding for its immaculate draughtsmanship, had 'great value' as a symptom of the decadence of capitalist civilization. That the work was perverse there could be no doubt: 'The point is that you have here a direct, unmistakable assault on sanity and decency; and even—since some of Dalí's pictures would tend to poison the imagination like a pornographic postcard—on life itself.' The puritanical Orwell, constitutionally incapable of warming to Dalí, was obsessed by pornography (there is another reference to 'dirty' postcards in the review), and the *Secret Life* seemed to him 'simply a strip-tease act conducted in pink limelight'.

For Orwell, the two main characteristics of the book are its 'sexual perversity and its necrophilia', with coprophilia coming in a close third. Looking through its numerous illustrations, he is struck by the ubiquity of sexual objects and symbols, among them 'our old friend the high-heeled slipper' (as Dalí was happy to admit, this was one of the 'most active' fetishes in his life).[66] The crutches and cups of warm milk, Orwell allowed, were Dalí's own original contribution to the list of perversities, as was his penchant for rotting donkeys. As for Dalí's insistence that he was not homosexual, Orwell had his doubts. What about those 'pansified drawings of youths'? When Dalí was not doing specifically Surrealist work, Orwell noted, he tended to slip back into his Edwardian manner, that is, into compulsive pastiche of Art Nouveau. Perhaps, after all, this was the style that best expressed him. Orwell could not fail to be strongly offended by Dalí's attitude to the Spanish Civil War, given his own wartime experience in Catalunya, and notes that the painter 'astutely avoids taking sides', abandoning France 'like a rat' when the Germans invade the country, and hurrying away as fast as possible to America, with his conversion to Catholicism in his bag of tricks and 'moving at one hop and without a shadow of repentance from the fashionable *salons* of Paris to Abraham's bosom'. There is not a single reference to Dalí's sense of humour, surely one of the book's fundamental characteristics. And no appreciation whatsoever of his ability as a writer. The *Secret Life* 'is a book that stinks. If it were possible for a book to give a physical stink off its pages, this one would—a thought that might please Dalí.'

The irony was that Orwell's honest attempt to appraise the *Secret Life* came up against the ludicrous rigidity of British censorship at the time. 'Benefit of Clergy' made a sort of 'phantom appearance' in 1944 in the *Saturday Book*, which had already been printed when the publishers, Hutchinsons, decided to suppress the piece on the grounds of obscenity. The essay was painstakingly removed from each copy. Such was England fifty years ago.[67]

Reynolds and Eleanor Morse

When Dalí's MOMA retrospective went on the road and reached the Cleveland Museum of Art on 6 March 1942, Reynolds Morse, a twenty-eight-year-old businessman from Denver, Colorado, made a bee-line for the exhibition with his vivacious fiancée, Eleanor Reese. Morse, who had taken a first degree in geology before going on to the Harvard School of Business Administration, had seen some Dalí reproductions in Life in April 1939. They included *Sleep*, *The Enigma of Hitler* and *The Endless Enigma*; and they had fascinated him. He was predisposed, therefore, to enjoy the show, but it far exceeded his and his fiancée's expectations. 'We were just engaged to be married and discovered that we had one more thing in common, a consuming admiration for the painting of Dalí,' Eleanor Morse wrote forty years later. 'We were impressed by his superb draftsmanship. The nostalgia of his deep perspectives beguiled us. His unusual surrealist subject matter intrigued us. In short, we were enchanted by Dalí's art.' At the exhibition the Morses equipped themselves with a copy of James Thrall Soby's catalogue. It was to become their Dalí 'bible'.[68]

Over the following months the Morses' eccentric friend Charles Roseman acquired three Dalís at George Keller's Bignou Gallery in New York, bearing them back triumphantly to Cleveland: *Myself at the Age of Ten When I Was a Grasshopper Child* (exhibited at the MOMA but not on tour with the retrospective), *Paranoia* and *The Sublime Moment*. Goaded by his example, the Morses decided that they simply had to have a painting by Dalí—but it took them a year almost to the day.[69]

The painting they bought was *Araignée du soir, espoir*, the first work Dalí had executed at Caresse Crosby's in 1940. Dalí had renamed it *Soft Violincello, Spider, Great Masturbator*, as we have seen, but the Morses preferred the French original, which they rendered *Daddy Long-Legs of the Evening—Hope!* The picture was purchased over the phone from George Keller on 21 March 1943 after seeing the photograph of it in Dalí's *Secret Life*. It cost the couple $600. 'Before shipping the work,' Eleanor Morse recalled, 'Mr Keller phoned to ask if we also wanted the frame—an ornate black wooden carved frame "of the period" which Dalí himself had selected. Of course, we agreed.' When the bill arrived the Morses discovered to their dismay that the frame cost double the painting: $1,250.[70]

Soon afterwards the couple bought another Dalí, *The Archaeological Reminiscence of Millet's Angelus* (1935).[71] Then, on 8 April 1943, at the suggestion of George Keller, they wrote to the Dalís in New York requesting an interview. It was time to meet the great man in person. Gala replied, in French, suggesting that they get together either at the St Regis Hotel on 13 April or the following day at the opening of the exhibition of society portraits by Dalí at the Knoedler Gallery. The Morses opted for the former venue, and the historic encounter took place in the hotel's famous King Cole Bar, with its huge mural by Maxfield Parrish. It marked a turning-point in the lives of Eleanor and Reynolds Morse and also, to a certain extent, in that of the Dalís.[72]

The forthright Reynolds Morse asked Dalí on that first meeting why he and Gala had no children, hardly a tactful question with which to inaugurate the relationship:

> He said he had none because he was afraid how they might turn out. Then he elaborated with the story of one of Picasso's sons who was found running around the streets of Paris, half-crazed and naked except for a loin cloth on which a death's head was painted. 'If the son of a genius like Picasso was THAT crazy,' Dalí concluded, 'imagine what a son of mine would be like!'[73]

Before long the Morses bought directly from Gala the outstanding *Average Atmospherocephalic Bureaucrat in the Act of Milking a Cranial Harp* (1933). It cost them $800. Morse was hesitant about the price, but Charles Roseman reassured him: 'Why, Ren,' he exclaimed, 'the title alone is worth more than that!'[74] The acquisition was followed by that of the watercolour *The Madonna of the Birds* (1943). The Morses now had the bit between their teeth and within a few years would be well on the way to forming the world's most outstanding collection of Dalís.[75]

For Gala, financial success served as a potent aphrodisiac, and, as her and Dalí's fortunes soared, she was beginning to acquire a reputation for promiscuity. On 24 June 1943 she and Reynolds Morse had lunch together in New York. By this time the Morses had acquired some ten works by Dalí and were anxious to know if there was anything available after the Knoedler show. After lunch Gala took Morse to the St Regis and explained that she had a portfolio of erotic drawings by Dalí if he'd like to see them. She went into the bedroom to look for them and called him in. Morse was 'totally bowled over' by what he saw. It was like looking at Leonardo da Vinci's private notebooks. While he was examining them he heard Gala say that everyone wanted to make love to her. It took him a while to realize that she was propositioning him. He brushed her off as politely as he could and, having bought two drawings, hurried for the stairs. 'I got the fright of my life,' he laughed years later. 'She said Dalí wouldn't mind, that they led their own lives, that they were weren't a couple in the true sense of the word. She even suggested that, if I acquiesced, we could come to some relaxed financial arrangement for my purchases. I told her that I loved my wife and couldn't possibily be unfaithful to her. I think she was really hurt by my rejection. I was horrified. She could have been my mother!'[76] Eleanor Morse came to the conclusion that Gala was not only a snob but 'cruel, mean and hard-bitten', resulting probably from the fact that she was a Tartar. As a seller, Gala was greedy and did not really appreciate the finer details of the market. When someone protested that she was asking too much she would interpret it as disloyalty to 'the Dalinian cause', letting the Morses know her feelings, if they were present, 'by means of sly digs and snide remarks'. The couple were amazed that she had apparently completely suppressed her maternal feelings. She was always on the lookout for hidden motives, and seemed incapable of imagining that anyone could be honest or decent.[77]

One of the strengths of the Morses was that they were not ashamed to admit their ignorance. About Spain they knew little, and about Catalunya absolutely nothing. But they were prepared to learn, indeed they were desperately eager to do so. Dalí teased them, but they didn't mind—both had a good sense of humour. As they grew closer to him, and bought more of his work, their questioning became more insistent. At times it infuriated Dalí, who still spoke hardly any English. Also it irritated him that Eleanor, who knew some French (Reynolds had none), had difficulty in coping with his thick Catalan accent. But an entente cordiale was achieved, and during the eight years the Dalís spent in America the Morses saw them frequently, attended all the painter's vernissages and bought more works. Gradually, as patrons, they took the place of Edward James in the Dalís' life; although they did not command the Englishman's huge wealth, their support and passionate interest, as well as their money, were undoubtedly important to Dalí during the 1940s and, to a lesser extent, later on.

Dalí's view of human relations was basically that others were there to be used. If people wanted to be his friends, that was their business. But they could expect no reciprocity. Foremost among those to be used were, of course, the rich. In America Dalí soon realized that the best way to extract huge sums from these fortunates was to persuade them to let him paint their portraits. His 1943 Knoedler exhibition was a case in point. The faces of the moneyed sitters had been inserted into hackneyed Dalinian scenarios replete with props once original but now done to death, and the critics were not impressed. Nor were some of the clients. The wittiest demolition job on the show appeared in the *New York Sun*:

> There is no exhilaration in the portrayals. Nothing but plodding, plodding workmanship and an infinity of detail. So much for so much. Even the attempts to laugh off the money go for nothing. Our best-dressed lady, Mrs Harrison Williams, is shown in tatters and shoeless. All God's chillun's got shoes. All save Mrs Harrison Williams. It seems to be an extreme case. And it's not funny. The Princess Gourielli's face is carved upon a mountainside like the Gutzon Borglum monstrosities out west. It's not at all interesting. Mrs Dorothy Spreckles reposes above the waves on some kind of a sea urchin. And so on. One's sympathies are all with the artist. So much effort is worthy of better direction.[78]

Princess Gourielli was the cosmetics and beauty salon entrepreneur Helena Rubinstein, who, not content with her portrait, now commissioned Dalí to do three frescoes for the dining room of her Manhattan apartment. Dalí was fascinated by Rubinstein (whose title was fake), recalling their relationship years later in some of the most brilliant pages of the *Unspeakable Confessions*. In 1942 Rubinstein was worth a hundred million dollars, Dalí claimed, and 'plastered more than 50 percent of the feminine sex in a carapace of illusions that remade their faces as well as their souls'. With 'the character of an unyielding corset', she had devoted her life to being Number One, and this could not fail to impress Dalí, nor the brazen way she stole ideas from other people for her famous slogans (Dalí was careful not to talk too much when he was with her). Oddly enough, in some ways she was as unpractical as he: she could direct men and women around the world like a dictator, but did not know how to dial a telephone number. Deep within her immense apartment (she had had to buy the whole block because the owner wouldn't rent to Jews) she had a bedroom where 'she nestled like the minotaur in the heart of the labyrinth and waited for her prey in an immense transparent bed, the legs and incurved half-canopy of which were fluorescent'. Dalí and Rubinstein were two of a kind. He had never seen anyone bedecked in so many jewels, heard anyone talk so unashamedly about their wealth. Her monologues always came back to money, to how much she had made and how much more she was going to make. Money was her religion, her only criterion of success. Dalí felt that he could readily have made her his 'vestal virgin', for she inspired him to make even greater efforts to ensure his own rise to spectacular opulence.[79]

'Clédalism', the 'Key' to Dalí: *Hidden Faces*

Encouraged by the polemical reception and buoyant sales of the *Secret Life*, Dalí decided to write a novel in which to develop his views on the breakdown of the old order in Europe and the spiritual resurrection he claimed would follow. To this end, while the war raged on several fronts, he esconced himself in the autumn of 1943 on the Marquis de Cuevas's estate at Franconia, New Hampshire (set amongst the mountains not far from the Canadian border) and produced *Hidden Faces* in, he said, four months, 'writing fourteen hours a day'. Even Dalí was impressed by the achievement, concluding that he was probably 'the most hard-working artist of our times'.[80]

Haakon Chevalier, apprised by Dalí that he was beginning work on a novel, had visited him and Gala somewhat sceptically in New Hampshire. The translator of the *Secret Life* discovered to his amazement that, having finished the first, long chapter, the whole novel 'was sharp and clear' in Dalí's mind, with most of the scenes worked out in detail. Chevalier read the first chapter with growing admiration. 'I had known Dalí the painter and Dalí the solipsist; now I was learning to know Dalí the novelist.' Here was an artist with an international reputation 'wholly preoccupied now with problems of character, situation, dramatic intensity—concerned with how Balzac, Stendhal, Cervantes had handled a particular kind of problem'. It was astonishing. Dalí's mind was moving 'in a wholly different realm'. Not surprisingly, Chevalier agreed to translate the book when it was finished.[81]

In the 'Author's Foreword' to the novel, Dalí explained that one of the reasons that had compelled him to write *Hidden Faces* was the desire to complete the 'passional trilogy' of 'isms' inaugurated by the Marquis de Sade. 'Sadism' had led to 'Masochism', but 'the third term of the problem, that of synthesis and sublimation', was lacking. Dalí, accordingly, had invented it: Clédalism. The term derived, he explained, from the name of the aristocratic protagonist of the novel, Solange de Cléda. But this was putting the cart before the horse. Years later he told a friend that Clédalism was a system containing the 'key' (French 'clé') to Dalí—'Clé-Dalí'—and that Solange de Cléda was created to embody it.[82]

In the foreword to *Hidden Faces* Dalí continued:

> Sadism may be defined as pleasure experienced through pain inflicted on the object; Masochism, as pleasure experienced through pain submitted to by the object. Clédalism is pleasure and pain sublimated in an all-transcending identification with the object. Solange de Cléda re-establishes true normal passion: a profane Saint Teresa; Epicurus and Plato burning in a single flame of eternal feminine mysticism.[83]

Clédalism develops the theory of erotic self-denial or sublimation first formulated in 1927 in Dalí's *Saint Sebastian*, a theory to which he and Lorca had devoted much discussion, effort and ink.[84] That Solange de Cléda is, at least in part, a female version of Sebastian is suggested in Dalí's frontispiece for the novel, where the naked heroine is affixed, in the posture of the saint, to a cork-oak, heraldic device of the Grandsailles family whose scion, Count Hervé, is the male protagonist of the book. Despite Dalí's high claims for Solange de Cléda, who dies without having been allowed to consummate her passion for the merciless ex-politician Grandsailles (who has a lot in common with the adolescent Dalí of the *Secret Life* who imposes a rigid 'five-year plan' of abstention on his girlfriend), the novel appears to hinge less on 'eternal feminine mysticism' than on the theme of male impotence. While we are asked to believe that Grandsailles has had countless women, we are shown none of this in action; and at one point we actually find the count, who (like Gala) is sterile, assailed by what he calls 'the recurrence of my complex of impotence'.[85] Whatever the arguments adduced by the narrator in favour of the supremacy of denial over indulgence, it is impossible, reading this novel, not to be reminded of Dalí's brutally honest statements elsewhere about his sexual shortcomings ('I have never found an immense pleasure in orgasm. What counts is everything that precedes it, and less in acts than in the mind',[86] for example, or 'For me total orgasm is complete failure. As you know I always avoid physical contact. A little voyeurism, accompanied by masturbation, is quite enough').[87]

In his foreword to *Hidden Faces* Dalí informs his reader that beneath the surface of the fiction is to be found 'the continual and vigorous familiar presence of the essential myths of my own life and of my mythology'.[88] A further clue to the novel's theme comes on the title page, where, by way of epigraph, Dalí has affixed the first maxim of Descartes's *Cogitationes privatae*, 'Larvatus prodeo', 'I advance masked'. Since Dalí's adolescent diaries show that by the age of sixteen he already conceived of his life as essentially a masquerade, the Latin phrase invites us to search for the true face of the writer-artist among the hidden ones we are to meet in the novel.[89]

One of the most persistent of these faces is that of Federico García Lorca, whose largely undeclared presence pervades the book. In the author's foreword we are informed that in 1922 Lorca foretold a literary career for Dalí (in fact they first met a year later), suggesting that his future lay in the 'pure novel'. Dalí also recalls the project for a joint opera hatched with Lorca in 1927—a project he must now tackle alone—and in the prologue to the Spanish edition of the book there is an allusion to their visit to the ruins of Ampurias.[90] As well as this open acknowledgement of Dalí's relationship with the poet, Lorca's 'hidden face' peers at us from between the lines of the text almost with as much insistence as it does from the paintings in which Dalí evoked his dead friend. In particular, the 'Ode to Salvador Dalí' continues strongly to affect Dalí's perception of himself. In the poem Lorca notes Dalí's Apollonian refusal to become emotionally entangled, of his search for balance, equilibrium and serenity. Observing of a rose that it is 'tranquil and concentrated as a blind statue', the poet goes on to praise Dalí's determination to be, himself, like an impassive statue. In *Hidden Faces* we read that Veronica Stevens is 'quiet and concentrated as a blind statue', an enigmatic footnote explaining: 'Federico García Lorca, speaking of his friend.'[91] The quotation recurs later, again applied to Veronica Stevens.[92] Another line in the ode, celebrating Dalí and Lorca's common pursuit of artistic sobriety, reads: 'A desire for forms and limits takes hold of us' (*un deseo de formas y límites nos gana*). A pronouncement by John Randolph, alias Baba, the heroic aviator who has fought for the Republic during the Spanish Civil War but now sees the error of his ways, incorporates these words:

> 'No,' said Baba, 'I too believe once more in the ineradicable forces of tradition and aristocracy, and today I feel my revolutionary illusions of the Spanish war days like a distant germination that has already been harvested in my life. A fresh craving for contours and solidity begins to possess us, and when I fly it is no longer, as before, the proud revolt of the archangels who are out to win a chimerical paradise. On the contrary, I am urged by a desire to reconquer the earth, the earth, in its hardness, its nobility . . . renunciation . . . to recover the dignity of bare feet resting on the ground. I know now that man must look at heaven with humility. You see, this war is making me a Catholic.'[93]

Since the sentiments being voiced here by Baba are manifestly Dalí's, who at various points in the novel explicitly identifies with the narrator, the appropriation of the phrase from Lorca's ode is particularly poignant. It shows that, in Dalí's mind at the time, Lorca is urging him to return to the 'classical' serenity of his pre-Surrealist period. Lorca, that is, is envisaged as an accomplice in the process of Dalí's 'reformation'.

Other Lorca images, unacknowledged, float into the text. When Betka expresses her dislike of the colour green, for example, Dalí cannot refrain from making her say 'Green! how I detest you—green!', an amusing joke at the expense of one of Lorca's most famous lines, *Verde que te quiero verde* ('Green how I love you green'), from the 'Sleepwalking Ballad';[94] while the poet's dawn description in the 'Ballad of Black Anguish' (roosters pecking in search of the new day) is also borrowed to preside over the execution by the Nazis of Grandsaille's faithful notary, Pierre Girardin.[95]

As for Solange de Cléda, she not only incorporates one of the aspects of Lorca that most struck Dalí—his obsession with his death and putrefaction, enacted nightly at the Residencia de Estudiantes—but becomes a Dalinian reincarnation of Soledad Montoya, the protagonist of Lorca's 'Ballad of Black Anguish', whom Dalí had already evoked in 1937 in *Metamorphosis of Narcissus*. Like Lorca, Solange is given to pondering 'the minutest ceremonies' of her burial, the 'choking and pressures of the winding-sheet', the descent into the tomb and 'the horrible apparition of the first drops of the liquids, creams, balms and juices of her own decomposition'. And like Soledad Montoya, that crazed victim of frustrated passion, she receives a rebuke from the narrator: 'Solange de Cléda, what are you doing with your body? What are you doing with your spirit?' Clearly, 'Ballad of Black Anguish' had become part of Dalí's flesh and blood.[96]

Back in 1928, with Buñuel in sarcastic support, Dalí had claimed to despise the 'traditional' elements in Lorca's *Gypsy Ballads*, but we can see that by 1943 he had recanted (although, characteristically, he never admitted to this). Apart from the direct borrowings from Lorca's most famous book of poems, moreover, one senses throughout *Hidden Faces* the pressure of his Andalusian imagery on what Haakon Chevalier termed 'the lush jungle' of Dalí's prose.[97]

If the main purpose of *Hidden Faces* is to propound and explore Clédalism, also fundamental are Dalí's indictment of the old Europe, presented as torn apart by the political dissensions of Left and Right, and his predictions and canvassing for the new one that he wants us to believe will arise from its ashes. The action of the novel begins on 6 February 1934, the day of the Fascist riots in Paris (which, significantly, coincided with Breton's first attempt to oust Dalí from the Surrealist movement), leads us through the pre-war salons of aristocratic Paris (Dalí drawing on his first-hand experience), moves to Casablanca, then to the United States and concludes with the symbolic return of the exiled Grandsailles, in 1943, to Vichy France and his beloved estate in the 'illuminated plain', the Creux de Libreux.

The principal message of the novel is made explicit in the closing pages as Solange de Cléda, after fruitless years of waiting for the return of Grandsailles (trapped by a confusion of identities into marrying Veronica Stevens in America), prepares to die, alone as ever, on her neighbouring estate, while the seigneurial cork-oak forest, symbol of tradition, strength and perpetual resurgence, prepares to push forth its new shoots:

> In the plain of Creux de Libreux the persistent November rains were followed, after the mists and snows and sunny days of winter, by the March downpours. Beneath the Germans' yoke Europe was rediscovering the tradition of its ancient catholic unity through the community of suffering, and in Libreux the Middle Ages were being reborn with their springtime of superstitions.[98]

The narrator's depiction of the Parisian salon life he now scorns owes an evident debt to Radiguet's *Count Orgel's Ball*, read, as we saw, by Dalí during the 1920s (and warmly recommended by him to Lorca). Dalí must have been delighted to discover, on settling in Paris, that the Count and Countess of Orgel were modelled on Caresse Crosby's friends Étienne and Édith de Beaumont, whom he met, and there is little doubt that Hervé de Grandsailles owes something to that 'Diaghilev of the costume ball', as Beaumont has been termed.[99] Dalí's Barbara Stevens seems to have been modelled more on Radiguet's Hester Wayne (in turn drawn from Hoytie Wiborg, a handsome and rich American of lesbian tendencies) than, as has been alleged, on Daisy Fellowes, heiress to the Singer fortune.[100] The opium-smoking Cécile Goudreau is almost certainly based on Coco Chanel; the painter Christian Bérard appears under his own name; Alcan is a barely disguised anagram of Lacan (although the similarity between the two doctors goes no further); and there is a fleeting reference to Lorca's friend, the painter Manuel Angeles Ortiz. It would probably be unproductive to search for further parallels among Dalí and Gala's Parisian acquaintances.[101] Haakon Chevalier, for whom the basic theme of *Hidden Faces* is 'love-in-death: a treatment in modern dress of the old and perennial Tristan and Isolde myth', felt that in translating the book, which involved discussions with Dalí, he had learnt 'a good deal about the creative process'. He was convinced that Dalí's novelistic '*blitzkrieg* on the literary front' would be recognized as 'a remarkable achievement'.[102]

Hidden Faces was very widely reviewed when, with a foreword by Chevalier, it appeared in April 1944, but not everyone agreed with the latter's high rating of the book. Edmund Wilson was probably the most distinguished critic to tackle the novel. He thought it 'startling', but only because it was 'one of the most old-fashioned novels' that anyone had produced for years, 'a pot-pourri of the properties, the figures, and the attitudes of the later and gamier phases of French romantic writing'. This was true: no trace here of James Joyce or Gertrude Stein. Wilson's list of precedents included *Balzac* (*La Fille aux yeux d'or*), Villiers de l'Isle Adam and, of course, Huysmans. Surprisingly he forgot Lautréamont. He was bored by the 'uncontrollable tendency' of Dalí's characters to write each other long letters that read like burlesques of those in *Werther* or *La Nouvelle Heloïse*. And, alive to Dalí's 'perkily-moustachioed disdain' for 'Anarchists and Communists and all that they try to do', he judged him, on the basis of the novel, to be himself like 'some trashy old French royalist snob such as Barbey D'Aurevilly', another of his literary models. Wilson saw, rightly, that if Dalí has a penchant for John Randolph, the aviator and lapsed Spanish Republican, it is Count Henri de Grandsailles who seduces him. 'The war, from the author's point of view,' wrote Wilson, 'is being fought to save the honor of old France—betrayed by ignoble politicians—against the upstart and ill-bred Nazis.'

For all his hostility, Wilson was prepared to allow that Dalí was 'a very clever fellow' and that the book could 'afford entertainment'. And if the later part of the novel 'was more or less unadorned balderdash', the earlier included elements that gave it 'an illusion of brilliance'. Wilson liked the theory that Hitler was a heroic masochist, subconsciously working for his defeat and that of his people; and thought that the portrayal of the relationship between Grandsailles and the rural notary, Girardin, had a glimmer of satirical fire. But the final judgement was that, on the evidence of this novel, Dalí was 'no writer'. In making it, Wilson took into account Haakon Chevalier's excellence as a translator. Noticing the clumsinesses of some passages, Wilson sensed that Chevalier had become rather demoralized 'by his original's Hispanic French and orgies of loose-squandered verbiage'. In conclusion, he felt that Dalí's literary models had been bad ones and that it had been an error to stray away from his true métier as a painter. It was a dazzling but unfair, and incomplete, appraisal, for Wilson made no attempt to explain the book's theme, and least of all what Dalí meant, or might have meant, by Clédalism.[103]

No other critic did any better in this respect, and most of the reviews were superficial in the extreme. They also tended to be pretty puritanical: the United States was undergoing one of its periodical swings towards intolerance. One review suggested that, if all Frenchmen were like Grandsailles, it would be better not to send Americans to their deaths trying to liberate France from the Nazis;[104] another described the Count's entourage as 'a febrile scum of nymphomaniacs, dope addicts, lesbians, and other such unsavoury wastrels, along with a few peasants'.[105]

Dalí, whose grasp of English was still minimal, paid no heed to the adverse reviews. When he heard that a good one had appeared he would ask someone to translate it for him. One of these he quoted later with relish (without providing the source):

> His approach to life is a logical projection of the decadent movement which started with Poe, was translated into French with Baudelaire, evolved through Huysmans to be returned to the English speaking world via Aubrey Beardsley and the Yellow Book boys.
>
> The war has silenced most of the brilliant insanity of the Transition group; and James Joyce has reached his widest public through Thornton Wilder's dramas. But Dalí remains a psychopathic milestone in Man's roller-coaster descent into planetary pathology.[106]

Spurred by such encouragement, and remembering that his father had prophesied that he would be a better writer than a painter, Dalí now started to think about writing a novel based on the life and deeds of Lídia, his paranoiac friend in Cadaqués, who believed she was the protagonist of Eugenio d'Ors's book *The Well-Planted One*. In the summer of 1945 he wrote excitedly to his family from California to tell them the good news. The novel was to be called *The True Well-Planted One*, and all the details would be authentic. With one exception: the mine of rare minerals that Lídia's sons believed they had located at Cape Creus would turn out at the end of the book to exist in reality! Dalí considered that the novel would be 'fabulous', and that it could be very successful in Spain. But no more was heard of the project. It was the end of Dalí's career as a novelist.[107]

Dalí as Ad Man and Set Designer

Early in the 1940s it had begun to dawn on Dalí and Gala that there was money to be made by linking the painter's name to commercial products. One of the first ventures, in 1943, had been a commission from Elsa Schiaparelli to publicize her 'Shocking Radiance', four oils guaranteed to do wonders for women's bodies, faces, lips and eyelids. Dalí's sub-Botticellesque drawing showed a cherub pouring oil over the breasts of a naked, conch-borne Venus engaged in admiring her face in a mirror.[108] Soon he was being asked to publicize other products. His advertisement for Bryan Hosiery was a big hit. In it the foot of an elegant stockinged leg trod on a soft watch placed on top of a cracked plinth inhabited by a large black ant. Other jaded Dalinian clichés were in atten-dance: an endless beach, Creus-style cliffs, tiny figures in the distance, even a severed head lying in the sand. The announcement read: 'One of a series of illustrations by the eminent surrealist Salvador Dalí, inspired by the loveliness of Hosiery by Bryan.' Inspired, certainly, by the lust for easy money.[109] Next in line was a commission, in October 1944, to design a set of ties for the McCurrach Organization Inc. of Fifth Avenue. Dalí hauled out another selection of hackneyed props: lobsters, telephones, soft watches, ants. 'This collection of Dalí's work is refreshingly original,' ran the ad nonetheless, 'and the artist's genius keeps the ties in excellent taste.'[110]

Excellent taste was the last thing that concerned a painter whose aim, he often said later, was to cretinize the public. As the flow of commissions increased, Dalí began to prostitute himself more and more. For the new Leigh perfume, 'Desert Flowers', he exe-cuted three paintings, entitled *Trilogy of the Desert*, in which the old Surrealist clichés were commandeered once again. They were exhibited privately at Knoedler's on 30 October 1946. The art critics present were not impressed.[111]

Book illustrations provided another source of easy income—easy because in general they were not so much illustrations as more or less arbitrary variations on work done during the 1930s.[112] During the eight years Dalí spent in America he produced dozens of such 'illustrations' for, among other books, Maurice Sandoz's *Fantastic Memories* (1944) and *The Maze* (1945), *Macbeth* (1946), *Don Quixote* (1946), Montaigne's *Essays* (1947), Billy Rose's *Wine, Women and Words* (1948) and John A. Symond's translation of *The Autobiography of Benvenuto Cellini* (1948). In these, on the same repetitive beach or plain, the same props recur constantly: Carolineta dancing with her hoop; crutches, keys, the ants, inkwells, the father holding his infant by the hand, the child Dalí looking at the

Spectre of Sex Appeal and so on. Dalí is merely doing the same things over and over again.[113]

Dalí also dashed off numerous sets and costumes for ballets. Following on the heels of *Labyrinth*, he had begun the designs for a ballet based on *Romeo and Juliet.*[114] This may have been the project on which he worked with Anne Green, Julien's sister, and which included a scene with a troop of cyclists with stones on their heads.[115] The project came to nothing, but the cyclists (who had first appeared in 1929 in *Illumined Pleasures*, recurring three years later in *Babaouo*) ride again in Dalí's backdrop for the Ballet International's production, *Sentimental Colloquy*, which opened at New York's International Theatre on 30 October 1944. *Sentimental Colloquy* was inspired by Paul Verlaine's tiny poem of this name in the *Fêtes Galantes*, the music was by Paul Bowles and the choreography by André Eglevesky. Once again it was the ballet-mad Marqués de Cuevas who, drawing on the limitless finances of his Rothschild wife, had made the production possible, signing up Dalí for the sets and costumes.

In Dalí's backdrop the cyclists, some draped in wedding veils, others in shrouds, glide backwards and forwards past a grand piano whose interior is a pool with a gushing pipe (the piano can be read as an obvious allusion, along with the cyclists themselves, to *Un Chien andalou*). Paul Bowles recalled that his heart sank when he saw Dalí's set, which seemed to him quite inappropriate both to the spirit of Verlaine's poem and to the music he himself had composed for the ballet:

> There were men with yard-long beards riding bicycles at random across the stage, and there was a large mechanical tortoise encrusted with coloured lights . . . The Marquess had assured me repeatedly that this ballet would have none of the usual Dalí capers; it was to be the essence of Verlaine, nothing more. I had been royally duped.[116]

Dalí, however, was pleased with his work—and with a critique that appeared in the *New York Times* on 5 November 1944. The writer had been very impressed by Dalí's backdrop, and felt that in scenery design the painter had found his true métier:

> The fact becomes clear. Dalí needs a stage with greater urgency than he needs an art gallery. His surrealism (which, framed for the wall, has long since settled into formula), thrives in wide-open spaces. There its sophistication, no longer just a well-memorized *dernier cri*, acquires an effect of preciosity that is in a sense monumental.

Dalí quoted these words approvingly a few weeks later, but he must surely not have grasped their deeper significance, which was to state the obvious fact that his so-called Surrealist paintings had become merely repetitious, stereotyped.[117]

Two months later the Ballet International revived Dalí's *Bacchanale*, which now reverted to its earlier title, *Mad Tristan. The First Paranoiac Ballet Based on the Eternal Myth of Love unto Death*. It opened in New York on 15 December. Dalí's backdrops drew yet again on his stock-in-trade of clichés deriving from the 1930s: crutches, a wheelbarrow, Böcklin-style cypresses, flesh peeling back to reveal brickwork underneath, the cliffs of Creus in the background. Dalí took on the critic of the *New York Times*, John Martin, who had dared to accuse him of practising 'deliberate iconoclasm' in his designs, and for a few weeks the controversy raged. It meant more publicity.[118]

Finally, after this hectic succession of ballets, there came *The Café of Chinitas*, a 'flamenco show' based on an Andalusian folksong about a bullfighter that Lorca and his friend Encarnación López Júlvez, 'La Argentinita', the singer and dancer, had recorded for HMV in the 1930s. Dalí was asked to design the sets and costumes. His backdrop rang some changes on the well-tried metaphor assimilating guitars and women's bodies. The instrument had sprouted a gypsy girl's head and arms. The castanets she held in both palms were the nails of the Crucifixion pinning her to the wall. From her arms dripped blood— blood suggesting that of the assassinated poet. Dalí said that everyone loved it.[119]

Produced by the Ballet Théâtre, thanks again to the largesse of the Marqués de Cuevas, *The Café of Chinitas* opened in Detroit and then moved to the Metropolitan Opera House. Dalí was proud, he wrote, to have participated in this 'first homage' in America to his dead friend, and recalled that members of Lorca's family were present at the opening performance in New York.[120]

Not long after this Dalí wrote a letter home. He was elated by the signs that the war was coming to an end, and felt sure that soon he and Gala would be able to return in safety to Europe. He told his family about the portrait of Gala on which he had been working every day for six months. It was painted 'like a Vermeer', and everyone who saw it was 'deeply moved'. Dalí said later that *Galarina* had taken him 540 hours to complete, and that the title was indebted to Raphael's *La Fornarina*. The painting, today in Dalí's Theatre-Museum in Figueres, is certainly remarkable. It shows the Muse at her most wilful, domineering. Also, with her defiantly exposed left breast, at her most brazenly physical. Looking back in 1956 over the twelve years in which he had known her, Reynolds Morse wrote that he had never once seen Gala relax. Greedy, demanding, critical, she was 'part tiger, part martyr, part mother, part mistress and part banker, a curious and inaccessible mixture', and so 'single-purposed' in the pursuit of her and Dalí's interests that she had no real friends of her own. The picture tells it all.[121]

The *New York Times* reviewer of the *Sentimental Colloquy* had said correctly that Dalí's

'Surrealist' paintings were now executed according to a mere formula. That was also Edward James's view.[122] Dalí needed new subjects and new techniques if he was going to continue interesting the American public. The answer came when the Americans dropped Little Boy on Hiroshima.

'The atomic explosion of 6 August 1945 shook me seismically,' Dalí claims in the *Unspeakable Confessions*. 'Thenceforth, the atom was my favorite food for thought. Many of the landscapes painted in this period express the great fear inspired in me by the announcement of that explosion.'[123] In the wake of the bomb, Dalí, who since the 1920s had professed an interest in science, began to explore the potential for his painting of the world of protons and neutrons. Thus would be born his 'atomic period'.

Hitchcock and Disney

But first there was another film project. In September 1945 Dalí was in Hollywood to begin work with Alfred Hitchcock, who had commissioned him to design the nightmare sequences for his new psychological thriller, *Spellbound*, starring Gregory Peck and Ingrid Bergman. Why Dalí? David O. Selznick, the producer, thought at first that Hitchcock had signed up Dalí mainly for his publicity value. Hitchcock put him straight. In films dreams were habitually blurred, he said, which was a travesty. He wanted them vivid, sharply defined. Dalí, with his long perspectives, his black shadows and the solidity of his imagery was, he felt sure, the right man for the job. That was why he had invited him on board. If Hitchcock could have had his way, he would have shot the dream sequences in bright sunshine, not in the studio, thus forcing the cameraman to stop down and get 'a very hard image'.[124]

Dalí liked Hitchcock ('one of the rare personages I have met lately with some mystery') and settled down happily to work, a $4,000 fee having been agreed. He was pleased with his nightmarish scenario for the ballroom sequence: fifteen of 'the heaviest and most lavishly sculpted pianos possible' were to hang from the ceiling to create an impression of great weight and terror. But he had not allowed for the expense:

> I went to the Selznick studios to film the scene with the pianos. And I was stupefied at seeing neither the pianos nor the cut silhouettes which must represent the dancers. But right then someone pointed out to me some tiny pianos in miniature hanging from the ceiling and about 40 live dwarfs who according to the experts would give perfectly the effect of perspective I desired. I thought I was dreaming.

Neither Hitchcock nor Dalí liked the results. The scene was scrapped, and changes were made to the others without informing the painter. It was all a bit like what had happened to *Dream of Venus* a few years earlier, and Dalí was similarly disgruntled.[125]

Dalí's exhibition at Bignou, 'Recent Paintings by Salvador Dalí', followed hard on the heels of this minor setback and ran from 20 November to 29 December 1945. It comprised eleven oils, watercolours and drawings unspecified in the catalogue, and a selection of the illustrations for Sandoz's *The Maze*, *The Autobiography of Benvenuto Cellini* and *Don Quixote*. Dalí boasted in his catalogue notes that the works had been produced 'during nine consecutive months of strict seclusion'.[126] The paintings included *The Basket of Bread, My Wife, Nude, Contemplating Her Own Flesh Becoming Stairs, Three Vertebrae of a Column, Sky and Architecture, Atomica Melancholica, Apotheosis of Homer* (*Diurnal Dream of*

XXXII

Gala) and *Galarina*. The painting to attract most attention was *Atomic and Uranian Melancholic Idyll*, inspired by Hiroshima. Like *Apotheosis of Homer* (*Diurnal Dream of Gala*), it contained a selection of Dalinian clichés deriving from the 1930s (a melting watch, a key and a cylinder bristling with little rods) and had the appearance of a backdrop for a ballet on nuclear fission, with the presence of some baseball players to give it a genuinely American flavour.

My Wife, Nude, Contemplating Her Own Body Transformed into Steps, the Three Vertebrae of a Column, Sky and Architecture, on the other hand, was one of the finest, and most refreshingly original, paintings Dalí was to execute during his eight-year sojourn in the

XXXIII

United States. Three years later he reproduced it in colour in *50 Secrets of Magic Craftsmanship*, which suggests that for him it represented one of the purest expressions of the new classicism he was now propounding (symbolized by the Greek head affixed to the wall, reminiscent of the emblem of the Residencia de Estudiantes). The deep perspective of the painting, however, is in Dalí's best Surrealist manner, while both the design and the colouring of the pavilion into which Gala's body is transformed owe an unacknowledged debt to the fantastic pink constructions invented by Hieronymous Bosch in *The Garden of Delights*, which Dalí and Lorca had admired together in the Prado.

To mark the opening of the exhibition Dalí published the first issue of a spoof newspaper, the *Dali News*, a hilarious enterprise in which he was aided and abetted by his old friend from Figueres, Jaume Miravitlles, who had collaborated with him years earlier on the school magazine *Studium*. *Dali News* (a deliberate pun on the New York *Daily News*) was subtitled *Monarch of the Dailies*, and an adjoining, tongue-in-cheek indication explained that it incorporated the *Dali Mirror* (the *Daily Mirror* was the arch rival of the *Daily News*). Above the title was a crown and a scroll which read 'GALA FIRST'. Every line in the four-page publication referred to Dalí's deeds, projects and miracles. And, like any self-respecting newspaper, it carried ads. 'Do You Suffer "Periodic" Intellectual Misery?':

> Esthetic depression, fatigue, disgust of life, manic depression, congenital mediocrity, gelatinous Cretinism, diamond stones in the kidneys, impotence, frigidity?
> TAKE 'DALINAL', THE ARTIFICAL FIRE OF THE SPIRIT WHICH WILL STIMULATE YOU AGAIN.

The newsheet informed readers of the perfidy with which Hollywood had emasculated Dalí's ideas for *Spellbound*; assured them that the 'prediction' made in the *Secret Life* that the 'racial theory of National-Socialism' would be defeated was about to be proved correct (there was no such prediction in the book, far from it); and announced that Dalí was 'close to signing' a contract with Walt Disney 'to produce in direct collaboration a new animated film in a new medium never yet tried'. No more information about the film could be given for the moment, but American admirers of Dalí's soft watches need not worry: 'These will appear in the film, and thanks to the virtuosity of Disney, and for the first time, one will see how they move.'[127]

Just before the Bignou show opened, Dalí telegraphed the *San Francisco Chronicle* (in French) to give them a bit of hot news: his film with Disney was to be called *Destino* (in Spanish). It would be a perfect fusion of Technicolor photography and drawing. He would be arriving in Hollywood on 15 January to begin work.[128]

He did so, and got on well with Disney, who found him bursting with ideas. Disney ruled that the film should run for six minutes and be part of what was then called a 'package film'—one made up of a series of short episodes. Dalí was placed under the supervision of a young animator, John Hench, who recalled that Disney had decided to let the painter go ahead 'and see what would happen'.[129] In an interview with the magazine *Arts* that April, Dalí provided a résumé of the film's storyline. The opening sequence, although he did not say so, was based on his 1939 painting *Swans Reflecting Elephants*, one of his least successful efforts ever in the handling of the double image:

> First we see a very conventional garden scattered with statues and decorated in the middle with a fountain representing a swan. Then the garden disappears. The neck and the wings of the swan become the trunk and the ears of an elephant upside down. The elephant is transformed in turn into a pyramid on which there is engraved a head of Chronos towards which a young girl is walking. Suddenly the pyramid disappears and the long triangle it occupied on a canvas now shows the perspective of a road.

The girl pauses on the road, and a moment later we see her riding on the back of a huge elephant with spider's legs among all sorts of monsters. Then the landscape changes and again we see a pyramid, accompanied this time by a church floating over a pond encircled by two human hands out of which two cypresses sprout. Around the pond circulate naked forms riding bicycles. The naked forms end up disappearing in the pond.

At this moment a bell sounds a death-knell. The shadow of the bell fuses with the silhouette of the young girl and both begin to dance. The head of Chronos sculpted on the pyramid struggles free from the stone and also begins to dance, while at the same time trying to escape from a rain of monsters which falls from the sky all around. Chronos rips the monsters off his body and each time he does so a gaping hole opens in him.[130]

As one of Dalí's drawings for the film confirms, the sequence with the bell-girl was an attempt to animate the image of Dalí's 'cousin' Carolineta dancing with a hoop that had already appeared literally hundreds of times in his work.[131] Dalí told *Arts* that he had put 'everything' into the film, everything meaning his complete arsenal of Surrealist objects and hallucinations. The reporter sensed that it would be a long time before *Destino* was finished. Dalí told him that the film was worth the effort: it could initiate the public into the world of Surrealism better than painting or writing.[132]

Only one, fifteen-second experimental sequence of the film was shot. Years later John Hench ran it for Reynolds Morse, who thought it full of promise. The sequence showed 'a few precious seconds of a double image in which a ballet dancer in the form of a chalice is separated, carried on the backs of two turtles, who return to the center of the screen leaving the original image intact'.[133] According to another source, the ballerina's head 'was a baseball on the horizon'.[134]

Destino was yet another of Dalí's film projects that came to nothing. After a few months Disney 'changed his mind about the future success of package films' and scrapped the project.[135] Part of the deal had been that the studio would retain Dalí's original ink drawings and oils. Never exhibited, only a handful of these have been reproduced to date.[136]

There was an epilogue to *Destino*. Hench and Dalí had collaborated on a 'stereoscopic' snow-scene with two half-arches which the eye could merge so as to bring a human face into visibility. The experiment did not work until Hench made some adjustments to the snow. He persuaded *Vogue* to publish the finished result in its 1 December 1946, Christmas issue. 'True to form,' wrote Morse in his diary, Dalí pretended 'that the idea was wholly his and executed by himself.'[137]

Only eight or ten letters written by Dalí to his family during the American years have come to light, but there were undoubtedly many more. The ones we have show that he was determined to maintain good relations. There are constant offers of help and expressions of affection; and, to prove that he is doing well in the States, every so often he sends a packet of press clippings about his activities. Dalí could not easily admit to himself or to anyone else that *Destino* had fallen through. In the autumn of 1946 he informed his family that the project had been held up by film industry strikes in Hollywood (there was no hint that Disney had changed his mind) and that, as a result, he had had to postpone his return to Port Lligat.[138]

The Dalís had signed up with an agency so that they could see everything published about themselves the length and breadth of America. But their knowledge of English was still dismal and, according to Reynolds Morse, they were incapable of working out whether the items were favourable or otherwise. What most concerned them, anyway, was the length of the pieces, not their content.[139]

If Dalí's name was appearing everywhere at this time in the States, he was scarcely mentioned in the Spanish press between 1940 and the end of World War II. A significant breakthrough came in September 1946, however, with the appearance in the Barcelona magazine *Destino* (Dalí was struck by the coincidence) of a long and intelligent article entitled 'Salvador Dalí Seen from Cadaqués'. Signed 'Tristan', its author was the celebrated Catalan writer Josep Pla, an admirer of Dalí from the evening he had attended the painter's provocative lecture to the Ateneu Barcelonès in 1930. In 1943 Pla had referred in an article in the same magazine to Dalí's debt to his art teacher in Figueres, Juan Núñez Fernández,[140] but now, after a visit to the painter's father in Es Llané, he realized that a more detailed treatment was called for. Dalí Cusí had lent him his signed copy of the American edition of the *Secret Life*, and Pla thought the book extraordinary.

'I have the strong suspicion, I would almost say the conviction, that the moment has come to begin talking in this country about Salvador Dalí and his work seriously, with a crescendo of seriousness,' he began, going on to suggest that a miserably provincial 'conspiracy of silence' had been woven around Dalí's name in Spain. Dalí's talent was now recognized internationally, insisted Pla. He had made his mark on his epoch, and it was perverse, and useless, to deny it.

Pla then analysed the *Secret Life*, which he had 'read and re-read' in Cadaqués. He was convinced, he said, that the tenor of the writing was authentically Empordanese in its irony and in its mixture of mental freedom and 'biological timidity'. It could only have been written by 'a Catalan with the typical virtues and defects of the Empordà'. Dalí exemplified the furious individualism of the region, particularly intense in Cadaqués,

and like all the distinguished products of the Empordà (Pla included himself by implication) he was both doggedly local and 'frenetically cosmopolitan'. Moreover, Pla felt,
only the natives of the Empordà, accustomed to the brutal tramuntana wind and the
brilliant light it engenders, were equipped fully to understand Dalí. As for the painter's
skill as an international 'social strategist', Pla believed that it came from his mother's
side, from the Domènechs of Barcelona, more urbane, more sophisticated than the Dalís.
That skill, he thought, was simply prodigious.[141]

Pla's article had the effect of stimulating a new interest in Dalí in Barcelona and of
preparing the ground for his return. Dalí was delighted with it, and asked his family to
thank the writer on his behalf. He told them that he hoped to be back in Spain the following spring, and that the Museum of Modern Art in Madrid was planning to exhibit seven or eight pictures from his private collection. They would be 'the historical credentials of my spiritual activity during these five years of war'.[142] This information was
passed on by the family to *Destino*, which in November announced Dalí's imminent
return to Spain.[143] Then, in December, when Dalí Cusí retired from his *notaría* and was
given a send-off banquet in Figueres, *Destino* illustrated its report with the splendid pencil drawing Dalí had done of his father in 1926. The author of the piece, Manuel Brunet,
was a Barcelona writer, journalist and art critic who had settled in Figueres and become
friendly with the painter's family. Salvador Dalí Cusí was as typical a product of the
Empordà as his son, he wrote, and each evening at the club his 'glaucous' eyes were
those of 'a thundering Jupiter':

> The Dalís come originally from Llers, and this is perhaps the secret of the notary and the
> secret of the painter. Llers is a place of witches, say the people of the Empordà, a place of
> witches in every sense of the word. There's as much witchcraft in the composition and the
> finish of the deeds drawn up by Dalí the notary as there is in a picture by Dalí the artist.
> In both predominates that 'Dionysian fury' which may very well be a product of the tra-
> muntana, which blows in Llers with unheard-of violence.[144]

Dalí Cusí, Brunet reported, had a special stamp, reproduced by the magazine, which
he applied to legal documents. It bore the capital letters G and T, which stood for his
parents Gal and Teresa, and also for 'Gràcies i Torneu', 'Thanks and Please Come
Again'. As we saw, Gal had affixed the same initials to the horse-drawn bus he operated
between Cadaqués and Figueres in the days before he fled with his family to escape from
the tramuntana. Dalí Cusí must have known this, but he did not explain the circumstance to Brunet. Nor that his father had gone mad, despite having run from the dreaded wind, and had jumped to his death from a balcony in Barcelona.

Gala, Leda and the Virgin

'Gala, the only mythological woman of our time'
Dalí, *The Diary of a Genius*, p. 11

It was fifteen years since Dalí and Gala had met in Cadaqués. With her encourage-ment, support, practical sense and business acumen he was now one of the richest and most famous painters in the world. It was a remarkable joint achievement. Even Salvador Dalí Cusí was forced to concede that Gala's role had been vital. One day in the late 1940s he showed Roser Villar, the future painter, some press cuttings about his son's triumphs in America. 'Without Gala, Salvador would have ended up under a bridge in Paris,' he told the girl.[145]

Dalí himself was only too happy to admit his debt to Gala. In the early 1930s he had begun to sign his paintings 'Gala–Salvador Dalí', as if they were one person, and by the 1940s this practice had become habitual;[146] in the *Secret Life* the debt was made explicit again and again; by 1944 he had painted and drawn her dozens of times; the next step had come with the invention of 'Clédalism' in *Hidden Faces*.

If we knock off the initial 'C' of Clédalism we find ourselves looking at the word 'lédal-ism', in which 'léda' and 'Dalí' overlap. As he toyed initially with 'clé' ('key') and 'Dalí', it seems that the painter suddenly perceived this further significance, perhaps feeling that it was another instance of Surrealist 'objective chance'. In Greek mythology Leda, the daughter of Thestios, the king of Aetolia, was married to the king of Sparta, Tyndareus. Seduced by Zeus in the form of a swan, she bore the twins Castor and Pollux, the Dioscuri ('sons of Zeus'), and perhaps also the beautiful Helen (later of Troy). Since Gala's real name was Helen, it was an easy jump to the conclusion that Dalí and she were twin souls, and divine at that (in 1961 he signed a study for *The Battle of Tetuan* 'Pour Hélène, son dioscure, Dalí').[147] But Dalí went further and also identified Gala with Leda herself, since, for him, as well as soul-mate, she was a substitute for his dead mother. It is in this latter guise that she is mythified in *Leda Atomica*, the unfinished study for which *XXXV* was shown at Dalí's second exhibition at the Bignou Gallery, along with other recent works, between 25 November 1947 and 5 January 1948. Dalí commented then:

As far as I know—and I believe I do know—in *Leda Atomica* the sea is for the first time represented as not touching the earth; that is, one could easily put one's arm between the sea and the shore without getting wet. Therein resides, I believe, the imaginative quality which has determined the treatment of one of the most mysterious and eternal of those myths in which the 'human and the divine' have crystallized through animality.

Instead of the confusion of feathers and flesh to which we have been accustomed by the traditional iconography on this subject, with its insistence on the entanglement of the swan's neck and the arms of Leda, Dalí shows us the hierarchized libidinous emotion, suspended and as though hanging in mid-air, in accordance with the modern 'nothing touches' theory of intra-atomic physics.

Leda does not touch the swan; Leda does not touch the pedestal; the pedestal does not touch the base; the base does not touch the sea; the sea does not touch the shore. Herein resides, I believe, the separation of the elements earth and water, which is at the root of the creative mystery of animality.[148]

Leda Atomica, finished in 1949, 'exalted Gala,' Dalí said later, 'as goddess of my metaphysics'.[149] That Dalí put a huge amount of thought and work into the painting is borne out not just by the unfinished study exhibited at Bignou's, but by the detailed sketches, done in collaboration with the Romanian mathematician Prince Matila Ghika, in which the painting's proportions and layout are plotted with extreme precision.[150] But while it may be conceded that the finished work exalts Gala as goddess of Dalí's metaphysics, the impression of 'suspended space' is not satisfactorily achieved in Dalí's handling of the sea, which looks as if it is stuck to the earth by glue rather than levitating just above it. The swan, copied from a stuffed specimen, looks more like the model than the real thing.[151] Dalí's failure to render Gala's face is also striking. In the study the resemblance is minimal; in the finished painting only approximate. Dalí was never to match again the marvel of *Galarina*, and when he tried to embellish Gala's appearance, to smooth out the lines in her visage, to make her look younger than she was and, above all, pleasant, the result was invariably unsatisfactory.

Along with the study for *Leda Atomica*, the Bignou Gallery showed fourteen other recent oils, the 1926 *The Basket of Bread* ('re-exhibited by popular demand'), an etching, illustrations for *The Essays of Montaigne*, Billy Roses' *Pitching Horseshoes*, *Macbeth* and Dalí's forthcoming *50 Secrets of Magic Craftsmanship* and, as in the previous show, unspecified watercolours and drawings.[152]

Of the oils, *Dematerialization Near the Nose of Nero* (later also known as *The Separation of the Atom*) and *Intra-Atomic Equilibrium of a Swan's Feather*, both painted in 1947 before *Leda Atomica was completed*, were further experiments in the exploration of the new, 'nothing touches' atomic physics, a subject whose potential Dalí was now exploiting to the utmost.[153]

By the time Dalí began work on *Leda Atomica*, a related concept had begun to take shape. Port Lligat and Cadaqués were always to the forefront of his mind in America, as his work shows. He thought constantly about his return. One day it ocurred to him that Gala, as well as being Leda, was the tutelary deity of their home by the Mediterranean. Of course! She had encouraged him to buy the shack from Lídia, had given up the pleasures of Paris to be with him in his isolated retreat, had worked at his side to make the place habitable and to expand it, had imbued it with her presence, had helped him with sex. Who but she presided over the magic spot?

From tutelary deity to Madonna of Port Lligat was but a short step. Madonnas had begun to appear in Dalí's work in 1943,[154] but the first one specifically ascribed to Port Lligat, but not yet representing Gala, dates from 1946. Dalí used it for the frontispiece to *50 Secrets of Magic Craftsmanship*, where the caption reads 'Port Lligat Madonna, Help Me!'

Gala was more of a Magdalene than a Madonna, and, while she may have mothered Dalí, she certainly had not given much in the way of maternal affection to her daughter, Cécile. Nonetheless, for Dalí the idea of presenting her to the world as a Port Lligat version of the Virgin soon became increasingly irresistible. Another factor came to bear on this resolution. In the late 1940s the Assumption of Mary was being much discussed in the Church, and the deliberations were to lead to the proclamation of the dogma in 1950. Dalí, his antennae waving, sensed that he could make a connection between the Assumption and nuclear fission. The result would be *The Madonna of Port Lligat*.[155]

50 Secrets of Magic Craftsmanship

To coincide with the Bignou exhibition Dalí brought out the second issue of *Dali News*. James Thrall Soby felt that it had 'put people off a good deal' at the gallery, although personally, he told Reynolds Morse, he admired Dalí's insistence 'on the megalomania to which he is and for so long has been committed'.[156] *Dali News* was megalomaniac, certainly. It included the first chapter of the imminent *50 Secrets of Magic Craftsmanship* (loudly announced elsewhere in its four pages), proclaimed Dalí's alleged return to classicism with renewed vigour, pushed *Leda Atomica* and informed the public at large that the painter was now working on an opera in which everything, including the music, was to be his own creation (this never materialized). *Dali News* reproduced the painter's satirical *Portrait of Picasso* (1947) over the caption 'THE ANARCHIST'[157] and his own soft self-portrait over one reading 'DALI EL SALVADOR'. Clearly Dalí was as obsessed as ever by the older man. Among other snippets of Dalinian news the paper reported that, in 1947, more American cartoons had been devoted to *The Persistence of Memory* than to any other single subject (one of them, from *The New Yorker*, was reproduced). The painting was becoming more popular year by year—proof, in Dalí's view, that in it he had prophesied nuclear fission.[158]

Reynolds Morse, who had now been collecting Dalís for four years, felt that it was time to branch out as a Dalí authority. His first effort did not augur well. In a review published in a Cleveland newspaper he wrote: 'The new Salvador Dalí Show, just opened at the Bignou Gallery in New York, proves that Dalí is one of the great romantic painters of our age. Gone is the chaos of surrealism and the frenzy of Dalí's private madness. Instead we find a new romantic, a new classical role.' At the gallery the Morses had met for the first time someone who knew very much more about art, and about Dalí, than they did: Edward James. Declaring that Dalí's current work did not interest him, James had whisked them away to see a Leonora Carrington show at Pierre Matisse's. When they returned to the Bignou, Dalí was angry: he did not want the Morses to have anything to do with his former collector. 'The point should definitively be reiterated,' Morse wrote in his diary, 'that Dalí does not want to see his admirers become friendly with each other. In the Dalí Circus you are there to be used as a tool of the painter, to be manipulated exclusively by him and for his own benefit. Camaraderie among his aficionados is something neither the artist nor his wife like to see because it prevents them from complete domination of their courtiers.'

Beautifully produced by the Dial Press, Haakon Chevalier's translation of *50 Secrets of Magic Craftsmanship* appeared early in 1948. In its way it is a remarkable book, an ironic compendium of practical advice and whimsy, the jokes and the seriousness being combined in such a way that often it is difficult to known when Dalí wants us to believe him and when simply to burst out laughing. Despite this ambiguity, however, the book contains plenty of sensible hints about the craft of painting, from the mixing of pigments to the choice of brushes, and shows how much Dalí enjoys the materials and vocabulary of his profession (he positively revels in terms such as gum arabic, powdered pumice, rectified turpentine or aspic oil, while the names of the colours—Naples Yellow, Burnt Ochre, Ultramarine Blue, Veronese Green, Vandyke Brown—have the power almost to throw him into a state akin to ecstasy).

Some of the passages show Dalí at his wittiest and most scintillating, with his gift for anecdote and irreverent generalizations coming through strongly (he has also managed to slip in some erotic drawings). The description of the *ménage à trois* uniting Gala, him and Painting is hilarious, and his invention of the 'aranaeum' sticks in the mind as an astonishing example of his ingenuity (spiders, for Dalí, are the geometricians of Nature, and his 'aranaeum', if feasible, would enable us to recapture buried memories in a less haphazard way than Proust's *madeleines*). Dalí's insistence on the Return to Classicism, announced when he landed in New York eight years earlier, is maintained throughout, with much talk of monarchy (absolute, of course) and cupolas, symbols of imperialist aspirations. As regards Catholicism, Dalí confesses at the end of the book, just as he had done in the closing pages of the *Secret Life*, that he does not yet possess the faith, but implies that he is searching for it earnestly.

In February 1948 the Barcelona journalist Carlos Sentís, who had seen Dalí in New York, published a 'Letter to the Father of Salvador Dalí' in *Destino*. Announcing the painter's imminent return to Spain, Sentís informed Dalí Cusí that his son, who had not produced a single American landscape during his eight unbroken years in the United States, had just done a painting with a view of the Costa Brava. He was homesick, he wanted to talk to the fishermen of Port Lligat, see them stretch their nets on the beach. He could stay away no longer.[161]

It was true. Dalí could not live without Port Lligat. 'I am home only here; elsewhere I am camping out,' he was to say thirty years later.[162] After eight years in America Dalí still hardly spoke any English. Gala had done better: Dalí's business manager could not possibly manage without a working knowledge of the language, and she had applied herself to the task of acquiring it with her customary energy. How much money they had made, where it was kept and how administered, is a mystery. But that they had amassed a great deal of it, day by day, month by month, is certain. As certain as the fact that by 1948 Dalí was the most talked-about painter in America. Who could rival him? As for friends, Dalí always said he never needed them. For a friend he had Gala and that was enough. He preferred clients, and thanks to his genius for publicity and for selling his wares, there was never any shortage of these in America.

Early in July 1948, after their accumulated belongings had been packed into dozens of crates and prepared for shipment to Barcelona along with the Cadillac, the couple embarked for Le Havre. Dalí must have felt, given his loudly proclaimed return to orthodoxy, that he was in a strong position to be welcomed in Franco's Spain. And no doubt he had thought carefully about what he was going to say to the Spanish press after his long absence. Of one thing he must have been fully aware: in the conformist Spain that had emerged nine years earlier from a terrible civil war even Salvador Dalí Domènech, the Saviour of Modern Art, would have to watch his step.

The Return of the Prodigal Son

On 21 July 1948 Dalí and Gala landed at Le Havre and a week later arrived by train in Figueres, where they were met by their builder, Emilio Puignau, who brought them up to date about the improvements he had made to the house in Port Lligat during their long absence.[1] Then they hurried down to Cadaqués, moving in provisionally with Dalí's father, Anna Maria and his stepmother ('La Tieta') at Es Llané.

The Barcelona magazine *Destino*, which over the last few years had been following Dalí's career in America with interest, lost no time in sending a well-known Catalan writer and journalist, Ignacio Agustí, to interview the painter. He spent three days in Cadaqués, talking to Dalí, watching him with his family and noting his delight at being back in the landscape that meant most to him in the world. On its front cover *Destino* published a photograph of Dalí sitting with his father and proudly displaying the recently published *50 Secrets of Magic Craftsmanship*.[2]

For Anna Maria, with Gala under her father's roof, these were very difficult days indeed. She had no intention of ever forgiving her for causing such unhappiness to the family, and by this time was already at work on the book in which she planned to set the record straight. But for the moment she put on a brave face and held her peace.

Shortly afterwards Dalí wrote to his father from the Ritz in Barcelona. The letter, which shows that they had been together in Figueres as well as in Cadaqués, contained a remarkable revelation about Gala and revealed that Dalí now knew that Anna Maria was at work on her memoirs:

> First of all, thank you for your hospitality. In the few days spent at your side I found my affection for you growing as much as my admiration for your great personality. I'm sorry

Chapter TWELVE

Dalí's father with his second wife, Catalina ('La Tieta'), left, and Anna Maria at Es Llané in 1948, when the painter and Gala returned to Spain after their eight years in America.

that Anna Maria didn't show me her writings, since if they're like what you told me in Figueres they could turn into something really interesting in every sense, but as I told you my sister would need to devote one hour of her leisure every day to this, systematically, an hour which should be considered sacred in the house so that nobody interrupts her. Gala would be very interested to see these writings, since not only does she know a thousand times more than I do about literary matters but could show them to the publishers who are going to bring out her own autobiography (on which she's been working for *four consecutive years*) and which is already being pushed as a future best-seller in the United States. In other words, in Catalan, 'on with the job'. But above all I want to be shown what Anna Maria is writing, even if I only see a little of it. Lots of kisses for 'Tieta' and for all of you the affection of your son who loves you.[3]

Was it true that for four years Gala had been working on an autobiography and already had a publisher lined up? It is hard to believe that Dalí's revelation was a blatant lie designed merely to persuade Anna Maria to show them what she was preparing. But who were the publishers, and what became of the manuscript? No information has come to light on the subject. But it would not be surprising if Gala's papers existed and were to turn up some day for, when Dalí told his father that she knew 'a thousand times' more than he did about literary matters, he was not overstating the case. Gala had certainly read far more fiction than he had. And where relationships were concerned he could not match her experience. It would not be surprising if American publishers had pricked up their ears when they heard that Dalí's muse intended to tell her side of the story.

In Barcelona Dalí renewed contact with his uncles Anselm Domènech and Rafael Dalí and, particularly, with his lawyer cousin, Gonzalo Serraclara, whom he had not seen since his last exhibition at the Llibreria Catalònia in 1935. Gala liked Serraclara, and soon he was acting as their unofficial representative and legal adviser. When the Dalís were in Paris or New York it would be Serraclara who bore the brunt of Gala's constant requests, which mainly concerned additions to the house at Port Lligat.[4]

A great stir was created in Barcelona when the Dalís' brand-new Cadillac was unloaded in the port, Serraclara having been enlisted by Dalí's father to see to the customs formalities.[5] Gala, with the determination that characterized her, had learnt to drive well in America, and her diminutive size as she perched behind the wheel contrasted with the vehicle's huge dimensions. One day Dalí made her park directly at the door of his father's house in Figueres. In the early 1950s there were still very few cars in Spain, and those that were there tended to be modest. The citizens stood in awe in front of the gleaming monster. Dalí's gesture was presumably intended to demonstrate that he had fulfilled Freud's dictum that the true hero is the son who stands up to his father and defeats him. As for Salvador Dalí Cusí, he was by all accounts thrilled with the car and enjoyed being taken for trips in the countryside by Gala. Anna Maria's reaction to the Cadillac and what it represented is not recorded, but can easily be imagined.[6]

During these months Dalí went to considerable lengths to convince the Spanish authorities of his enthusiasm for General Franco and of his allegiance to the Catholic Church. On 1 September a Figueres weekly, *Ampurdán*, published an interview with him. In some recent declarations Dalí had insinuated his dissatisfaction with the 'silence' surrounding his return home: he felt he wasn't getting enough publicity. The interviewer wondered if this was perhaps because some people disapproved of his 'literary production'? The allusion, Dalí grasped immediately, was to the Argentinian edition of the *Secret Life*, which had been banned by the Franco régime. Dalí explained that in the book he did not attack religion, as some people thought, and that in this respect he had been 'misunderstood'. As for his erratic behaviour in the past, that was all over. 'Reason forces me to be Catholic,' he is quoted as saying. 'And just as many people have attained to religious truth via physics, I hope to attain to it via metaphysics and art. Believe me, this is one of my deepest urges.' The religious content of his current work, he continued, was of the purest Catholic orthodoxy. Where contemporary society was concerned, he claimed to see on all sides indications of spiritual rebirth, spearheaded by the Church of Rome. Catholicism was on the march in the United States, and Dalí expressed deep admiration for Cardinal Spellman, the tremendously influential prelate of New York. Since one of the clichés of Franco's régime was that the mission of Catholic Spain was to save the world from sin and degradation, it was not surprising that the journalist asked Dalí if he believed in the country's 'providential destinies'. 'Of course I do!' Dalí replied. 'And I hope you stress this in the interview, because I'm convinced that Spain, or better the Spanish-speaking nations, have a great common destiny. Spain will be an example for the world and a quarry for Catholicism.' It was more or less what Dalí had written to Buñuel in 1939—and equally ludicrous.[7]

Such declarations turned the stomachs of many people who had known Dalí in the 1920s and 1930s—and, particularly, of those who had fought to defend democracy during the civil war and were still suffering at the hands of a brutally repressive régime supported enthusiastically by the Catholic Church. But they greatly pleased his father. The erstwhile atheist, whose swing to Catholicism had prefigured Dalí's, took up his pen and wrote to the journal. He thanked the reporter for concentrating on his son's work and intentions and not on 'the anecdotes of his life, which lead to nothing and which, for that very reason, should not be published in the press'. Dalí's past excesses the father now chose to see as 'sicknesses natural to painters who seek to find for art the new paths leading to horizons that facilitate the better expression of the beautiful'. Dalí Cusí then proceeded to give the readers of *Ampurdán* a lecture about art. All the 'isms', and not least Surrealism, had failed because art was not improved by destroying what has gone before but by *incorporating* it: 'In place of automatism, technique; in place of destruction, construction; neither reaction nor revolution: rebirth, faith, tradition.' The injunction read like a Falangist pamphlet. 'These', he concluded, 'are the current tendencies of my son, adumbrated in the *Secret Life*. The return to grace, tradition, classicism: the only way to save not only art but also our civilization.' On the showing of this letter, relations between Dalí Cusí and his prodigal son could not have been better. But the storm was brewing.[8]

In the autumn Dalí wrote to the family from Barcelona. He had just seen the proofs, or perhaps an advance copy, of a book entitled *The Lie and the Truth of Salvador Dalí*, by a Catalan biologist called Oriol Anguera and was irritated:

> As I told you in my postcard from Palamós, the days we spent with you were full of marvellous Cadaqués atmosphere and we're very grateful for your kindness towards us. Here we

haven't stopped for a moment and everyone's been very pleasant, the only setback's a book that's been published without consulting me. Its provinciality and bad taste are shameful, since they've included whatever lay to hand, in an appalling mixture, but the worst of all is that they've reproduced several paintings, including some in colour, which are COMPLETE-LY FALSE and which I never painted, and they've even gone to the lengths of forging my signature! And that's not all, for with unforgivable indiscretion they've dared to reproduce an intimate letter of mine to Miravitlles! Montserrat ('he who doesn't commit evil doesn't think evil') handed over, for the purposes of reproduction, ALL Rafael's paintings executed when I was young and which are now, as a result, 'very badly catalogued' and impossible to reproduce later in the book Gudiol is preparing, which will be serious, well done and totally supervised by me.[9] All of this leads me to beg you not to lend for reproduction any painting of mine without consulting me first, since the value of these paintings could be severely undermined. All the collectors in every country in the world are now asking me for permission to reproduce their works of mine even though they own them—it's a question, apart from other considerations, of politeness. Only here do people take the liberty of reproducing my work (the moral ownership of which I can't lose) without even telling me!

Luckily I'm in time and the false paintings can still be suppressed.[10]

I know that other books are being prepared and I beg you to let me know if they ask you for anything. I'm going to say the same thing to Uncle Anselm and the others who have paintings from my adolescent period.

A big hug for all of you from your Dalí and Gala.[11]

Oriol Anguera's book showed that he had mixed feelings about Dalí, having read the Argentinian edition of the *Secret Life*, and he strongly disliked his obsession with sex and excrement, which he considered pseudo-Freudian ('I've even seen letters of his which end simply: *Shit, shit!*'). He also strongly objected to Surrealism, and Dalí may well have been infuriated by the ignorance of his comments on the movement and its adherents. But what did he expect? Freud's works were banned in Franco's Spain; sexual repression was the order of the day; and the painter's past was considered reprehensible. Dalí now realized that he needed to make an energetic effort if people were going to believe that he had really reformed.

The Madonna of Port Lligat and Other Theatricals

XXXIV   Dalí's first 'religious painting', designed to ingratiate himself with Church and State, was *The Madonna of Port Lligat*, about which he had begun to think in America. It was executed in the spring and summer of 1949. The composition of the small-scale painting (48.9 x 37.5 cm) derives clearly from the 'atomic' works done from 1945 onwards in the wake of Hiroshima, particularly *Leda Atomica* and *Dematerialization Near Nero's Nose*, but the colouring is pure Italian Renaissance.

The egg which hangs over the head of the Virgin, suspended by a thread from a venus-shell, Dalí borrowed from Piero della Francesca's *Madonna with the Duke of Urbino as Donor*, better known as the *Brera Madonna*, which he had reproduced the previous year in *50 Secrets of Magic Craftsmanship*. Piero's egg, he says there, was 'one of the greatest mysteries of the painting of the Renaissance'.[12] Later Dalí explained that, since the ancients considered the ellipse the most perfect form in nature, the egg was a very appropriate symbol for the Mother of God.[13] All the more so, it can be added, since it is also represents fecundity. Dalí had already placed an egg at the feet of Leda in *Leda Atomica* where, although broken, it casts the shadow of a regular ellipse.

XXXV

The face of Dalí's Madonna is recognizably Gala's, albeit considerably prettified. To use her as his model for the Mother of God seemed to some people the ultimate proof of the painter's cynicism; but once Dalí had decided to convert her into a Costa Brava version of Saint Mary of the Sea it would have been out of character for him to change his mind. In *The Madonna of Port Lligat* the representation of the Virgin, with the gap in her midriff, derives directly from *The Weaning of Furniture-Nutrition* (1934), which shows a nurse with a hole cut through her back seated on the beach in front of Dalí's house. What he did in *The Madonna of Port Lligat*, he explained later, was to 'sacralize' the earlier image.[14]

Dalí knew that to convince the world, and not just Spain, of his Catholic sincerity he would have to pull out all the stops. It was not enough merely to produce a 'nuclear' version of the Madonna and Child. Ever since the days of his collaboration with Buñuel, he had been trying to make a comeback in the film world. To no avail, if we except the dream sequences in *Spellbound*. Now, in July 1949, he announced that he had written a screenplay for a 'paranoiac film' entitled *The Wheelbarrow of Flesh*, which he was going to direct himself. 'Just as Rossellini represents neo-realism in Italy,' he told a Barcelona journalist, 'I'm going to attempt neo-mysticism in Spain.' Neo-mysticism? The journalist was nonplussed. Neo-mysticism, Dalí explained, was 'the incorporation, in realism in general, of the mystical tradition, which is the typical spiritual expression of Spain'. The film would demonstrate how primitive fetishism and delirious love can be transformed into religious feeling. But why a wheelbarrow? Dalí replied that wheelbarrows had obsessed him all his life and that he had painted them a thousand times. In his film a woman, 'traumatized by her involvement in a crime', seeks refuge in a wheelbarrow, which gradually acquires eighty-two symbolic meanings for her, no less, from coffin and marriage bed to chest-of-drawers and *prie-dieu*. In one of the scenes a troop of cyclists (yet again!), each of them with an umbrella, plummets into the sea from the cliffs of Cape Creus; in another an old woman with no hair, dressed in a bullfighter's 'suit of lights', shivers beside the pond at Vilabertran. *The Wheelbarrow of Flesh* was to occupy Dalí's thoughts for four or five years, but it never got beyond the talking and boasting stage.[15]

During his second summer back in Spain Dalí worked on the sets and costumes commissioned for three important productions scheduled to open the following November: Zorrilla's *Don Juan Tenorio* (Madrid), Strauss's *Salome* (London) and Shakespeare's *As You Like It* (Rome). He was particularly pleased with the *Don Juan* commission, which gave him a welcome opportunity to reassert himself in Madrid. Dalí got on famously with the eccentric director, Luis Escobar, and turned out designs which, if not to everyone's taste, created the desired expectation and then sensation. *Don Juan* opened on 1 November 1949. Outside the Teatro María Guerrero after the show, one critic wrote, the air reverberated with noisy discussion. The sets were 'monstruous, fabulous, crazy, divine, insulting, suggestive and incongruent'. The production made such an impression that it was revived the following year.[16]

Soon afterwards, on 11 November, Peter Brook's highly controversial version of *Salome* opened at Covent Garden. Brook, who greatly admired Dalí, had visited him in Port Lligat during the summer to pick up the designs, coming away full of excitement, and felt very let down when the painter failed to travel to London to help with the production (Brook had told Gala that unless Dalí was there it would be difficult to implement his ideas satisfactorily). Brook was experiencing what so many people had been through before him, such as Edward James: Dalí had no qualms about going back on his word. Nonetheless, Brook stood up for him when the critics tore into his much diluted designs, and complained, among other things, that Dalí's scenery represented 'a rocky canyon with a tent and a rough road', hardly apposite, and that one of the props looked like 'a Biblical cocktail cabinet'.[17] Brook explained in *The Observer* that he had chosen Dalí because he was the only artist he knew in the world 'whose natural style has both what one might call the erotic degeneracy of Strauss and the imagery of Wilde'. Some years later, recalling Dalí's defection, Brook mused: 'This kind of collaboration simply isn't good enough. Dalí should have carried through. Yet even when he does, he sometimes feels his thumb-print isn't as big as he wants it—and then he decides to do something dreadful to enlarge it. He's too difficult . . . And now it's too late, he's too old-hat.'[18]

Next it was the turn of Dalí's designs for *As You Like It*, which had been commissioned by Luchino Visconti. Dalí had conceived an ingenious single set, which brilliantly inventive lighting enabled to double successfully as Room in the Palace and Forest of Arden. Visconti was delighted.

Dalí and Gala travelled to Rome, but not just for the première on 26 November. The painter had become so pleased with *The Madonna of Port Lligat* that he felt it would be an excellent gambit to show it to the Pope and, in view of its unconventionality, to receive a pontifical *nihil obstat* for the much larger version he was planning.[19] If His Holiness approved of the painting, Dalí's Catholic orthodoxy could hardly be gainsaid, and his stock with the Franco régime would rise accordingly. He had therefore petitioned for an audience and, on 23 November 1949, he and Gala were ushered into the presence of Pius XII. Dalí had *The Madonna of Port Lligat* under his arm. The audience lasted for only ten minutes.[20]

At the time Dalí refused to divulge publicly the Pope's observations on his picture, fobbing off the reporters waiting outside with a few generalities about the need for modern art to be Christian.[21] Back in Port Lligat, however, he told Emilio Puignau that Pacelli had 'loved' the work; and a few months afterwards informed a journalist that he had received the general impression that the Holy Father was in favour of his continuing to paint in the same vein.[22]

Dalí explained later that one of the main reasons for visiting the Pope had been to raise the issue of his marriage to Gala. Since he had now returned to the fold, could they not be joined in holy matrimony? But even the Pope was powerless to help: Gala and Éluard had been married by the Church, their civil divorce was null from a Catholic viewpoint, and, above all, the poet was still alive.[23]

When André Breton heard of Dalí's visit to the Pope he was, predictably, disgusted. The news came just in time for him to add a footnote to the Dalí section of a new edition of his *Anthology of Black Humour*. 'It goes without saying,' Breton wrote, 'that the present account only applies to the first Dalí, who disappeared towards 1935 to give way to the personality better known as Avida Dollars, a painter of society portraits who has recently embraced the catholic faith and "the artistic ideal of the Renaissance", and who now benefits from the felicitations and encouragement of the pope.'[24]

Breton's anagram was a brilliant *trouvaille*, and soon became famous. Dalí was thrilled with it, put it to work and claimed that it made him even more money. He explained on one occasion, however, that it was *gold*, not banknotes, that he really craved. Ironically, the feminine adjective 'Avida' made the tag more applicable to Gala than to Dalí, by far the more avid of the two. Gala wanted and needed a lot of money, the more the better; and, while she could be mean about small things, where her own pleasures were concerned there were no limits. Moreover, she was becoming a compulsive gambler.

Visconti's *As You Like It* was a success, and the audiences packing the Eliseo theatre loved Dalí's ingenious set and the spindly legged elephants of one of the backdrops. There could be no doubt that Dalí's work had greatly contributed to the magic of the production, and the exhibition of his designs that ran concurrently at the Dell'Obelisco Gallery also attracted crowds.[25]

After their trip to Rome, Dalí and Gala left for Paris and then sailed to New York, where they arrived at the end of November.[26] Thus was inaugurated a rigid timetable that was to hold good for thirty years: spring, summer and autumn would be spent in Port Lligat (with occasional escapades to Barcelona, Madrid or Italy) and winter split between Paris and New York. Usually the Dalís would abandon Port Lligat in early December, returning in April or May. In Port Lligat Dalí would work from dawn to dusk, except on Sundays, taking only an hour or so for lunch and his habitual siesta; the early hours of summer evenings would be devoted to entertaining the increasing number of fans flocking to do homage to the Master. Paris (always the Hotel Meurice) and New York (always the St Regis Hotel) would be mainly for social life, business and promotion.

Almost every year during the first decade of this arrangement the labyrinth at Port Lligat would be enlarged or improved by Emilio Puignau during the couple's absences, growing, Dalí said, 'exactly like a real biological structure, by cellular budding'.[27] And as the house grew, so more help would be needed to run it. Servants were taken on, and a sturdy fourteen-year-old from Cadaqués, Arturo Caminada, was given the job of looking after the garden and the boat. He was to stay with the Dalís for thirty-seven years and to prove their most loyal retainer.

A Sister's View

In December 1949 Anna Maria Dalí, who was now forty, released her long-pent-up feelings in *Salvador Dalí Seen by his Sister*. Her father had written a few lines of introduction, prominently reproduced in facsimile, which suggested that relations with his son were once again strained:

> I would have been spared a lot of bitterness if I had foreseen that, as an old man, I would be able to read this book which reflects the history of our family with absolute fidelity. Sometimes I wonder if the hand of my dead wife did not guide that of our daughter throughout these pages. It must be so if they give me such great satisfaction.

Anna Maria's theme was that Surrealism in general, and Gala (never mentioned by name) in particular, had destroyed Salvador Dalí and his family. As she worked on the book the *Secret Life* had clearly been on the table beside her, and she was at pains to disprove the claims Dalí makes there for having been a monstruous, sadistic child. In Anna Maria's version of those early years, all is light and grace. Salvador had tantrums, certainly, and always insisted on getting his own way. But 'he made you love him despite his terrible temper'.[28] Which was not surprising since, like his father, he was decent at heart: 'Both faces had the same expression of intelligence and goodness, the fundamental basis of their exalted temperaments.'[29] As for Dalí's exhibitionism, it was pretty harmless, really: 'My brother was affable and cordial, with a great sense of humour. It was only when an abnormal desire to attract attention dominated him that he became capable of the most absurd things.'[30]

Anna Maria's moving pages on their mother's illness and death help us to understand the horror and incredulity with which the family learnt what Dalí had scribbled on the painting of the Sacred Heart of Jesus. How could he have done such a thing? He who had loved his mother? Since Anna Maria insists that Dalí was 'easily influenced', there could be no doubt about who was to blame: 'His need to draw attention to himself, working under the impulse of a nefarious influence, was the only explanation that we could find.'[31] The 'nefarious influence' was Gala and her Surrealist friends with their 'enflamed eyes'.[32]

Anna Maria's hatred of Surrealism as she understood it made it impossible for her to comprehend that it had helped Dalí to create his best work. But the book was also seriously flawed in its recounting of events before 1929. While the evocations of childhood Cadaqués were charming, the narrative was as chronologically confused and imprecise as that of the *Secret Life*, and very little documentation of any kind was adduced to substantiate it. All in all it was a brave but sadly insufficient and biased account of Dalí's relationship with his family in the days before Gala came into his and their lives.

Dalí and Gala were in New York when the book appeared. It took them by surprise. Dalí read the alternative view of himself with mounting fury and fired off letters to Spain complaining about Anna Maria's 'hypocrisy'. To his cousin Montserrat he wrote:

> You've seen the *total* hypocrisy of my sister. I believe that it's the family's duty to advise her to withdraw PUBLICLY all the manifest and chronological *falsehoods*, which *I'll point out to her*. If she does this, and '*asks me to forgive her*', I'm prepared to do so, given the advanced age of our father. Please tell Uncle Rafael, since he's always been the most human of them in all this.[33]

Dalí was no doubt thinking about the reconciliation with his father in 1935, which Rafael Dalí had engineered on his behalf. Gonzalo Serraclara received a more forceful communication:

> The 'hypocrisy' of my family, publishing the book without telling me, obliges me to take precautions and to recover *all the paintings* which are in my father's house. At the same time it obliges me to publish ALL THE TRUTH ABOUT THE FAMILY QUESTION, which out of *decency* I veiled in my *Secret Life*. At the same time I'm going to send you an auto-biographical note alluding to the matter for publication in the book being prepared by Gudiol. I now want everyone in Spain to know that I was thrown out and that I've achieved everything on my own initiative and with the UNIQUE and heroic abnegation of my sublime Gala. I'M NOT ASKING YOU TO INITIATE PROCEEDINGS, DON'T WORRY! BUT IF YOU DON'T REPEAT MY VERSION, which you know is the truth, the worse for you and specially for your conscience. Bon jour![34]

Dalí's 'autobiographical note' was printed on cards which he distributed widely:

> Memorandum
>
> I was expelled from my family in 1930 without a single cent to my name. I have achieved my entire world-wide success solely with the help of God, the light of the Empordà and the heroic daily abnegation of a sublime woman, my wife, Gala.
>
> Once famous, my family accepted a reconciliation, but my sister could not resist specu-lating materially, and pseudo-sentimentally, with my name, selling paintings of mine with-out my permission and publishing absolutely false accounts of verifiable facts of my life.
>
> For which reasons I feel it my duty to warn collectors and biographers.
>
> Salvador Dalí. New York. January 1950.[35]

Dalí suspected, perhaps correctly, that, if he used the postal service to write to his father, Anna Maria would intercept the correspondence. So he enlisted the services of a painter acquaintance in Cadaqués, Jaume Figueres:

> By now you'll have seen that the 'hypocrisy' of my family has reached its *zenith*. Please *take by hand* to my father the enclosed letter . . . since I suspect that otherwise he won't get it. Thanks! We'll be back at the beginning of May.[36]

It must be presumed that Figueres delivered the letter, and that in it Dalí bitterly reproached Anna Maria. There is no record of any further correspondence between father and son, and on 30 January 1950 Dalí Cusí made a new will in which he named Anna Maria his sole heir and signed over to her the house at Es Llané. In return she was to pay him a token annual stipend of 8,000 pesetas, a trifling amount, until his death. As for Salvador, he got 60,000 pesetas.[37]

In the midst of all this strife and fury Dalí was given a splendid opportunity for publicizing his new-found Catholic convictions. Early in 1950 a Paris-based Peace Commission, headed by Picasso and the 'Red Dean' of Canterbury, announced its desire to visit President Truman, the Secretary of State Acheson and several members of Congress. The aim: to persuade the Americans to take the initiative in ending the nuclear arms race with the Soviet Union. Dalí was invited to join the Reception Committee in New York. His reply, more a rejoinder, was published in March in the *New York Times*, just ahead of the State Department's refusal to grant a visa to the delegation. There could be no question of his having anything to do with such a committee, Dalí said, since violence and the doctrine of violence were at the basis of the materialist interpretation of history. As a painter, his sole aspiration was to paint better every day, combating in this way the lack of spirituality that was threatening to annihilate the 'artistic beauty' of the past and the present. The issue of the atomic bomb should be left to the United Nations; and all anti-materialists should attend to 'today's highest moral conscience', represented by the Pope and 'the other leaders who oppose spiritual and moral values to the materialism and violence of Marxist doctrine'.[38] The Spanish news agency, Efe, saw to it that the letter received massive publicity. It is not difficult to grasp why in Franco's Spain left-wing and progressive people were coming increasingly to loathe and resent Dalí.[39]

The painter gave an interview in New York at this time to *Destino*, the Barcelona weekly. It hinged on the subject of his Catholicism and his classicism. As he had done so often, Dalí misrepresented his initial relationship with André Breton, alleging that from the very beginning he had known that he was destined to displace him, above all because of the movement's 'total lack of spiritual content'. He recalled a brief meeting with Breton in New York after he had been expelled from the movement, and reflected gleefully: 'I, with my Mediterranean and passionate Surrealism, triumphed. He, the author of the First Manifesto, failed in the midst of complete indifference.' The comment gives us the measure of the person Dalí had become. To betray Breton was no longer enough, it was now necessary to ridicule him publicly for his lack of 'success'.

Dalí's main current aim, he went on, was 'to overcome the materialist and atheist elements in Surrealism and incorporate its sources of inspiration in Spanish mysticism, giving it a Christian and mystical content'. As for the *Madonna of Port Lligat*, he considered it the 'compendium' of his evolution as an artist and an earnest of his new classicism. That summer in Port Lligat he was going to begin his second, much larger version of the work. In it the Virgin would be surrounded by fishermen and the Child have an opening in its chest containing a piece of white bread in a basket, the 'vital and mystical nucleus' of the painting. Dalí had another major project lined up for the summer, he went on: a commision (from the Italian Government) to illustrate *The Divine Comedy*. He had been reading Dante's great work with passionate interest, he said, and had discovered that it reflected his own spiritual evolution. In his mind the work was already planned.[40] (Later Dalí was to say that he had never read *The Divine Comedy*, and would enjoy telling the story of a life-long student of the work whose dying words to his family were 'Dante bores the shit out of me!')[41]

Among his other achievements, Dalí was now the most famous Spaniard in America. It was natural, then, that when *Vogue* decided to publish an article on tourism in Spain he should be called in. 'To Spain, Guided by Dalí' appeared in the 15 May 1950 issue of the magazine. Dalí's itinerary for a fortnight's tour, illustrated by sketches, got off to a cracking start in Barcelona, where visitors were enjoined to see the Gaudí wonders (first rediscovered, of course, by Dalí himself) and the beautiful Gothic church of Santa María del Mar, gutted during the civil war. After a quick dash up the Costa Brava, and another back down to the sacred mountain of Montserrat, Dalí guided his readers to Madrid, recommending them to stay in the State paradors along the way. In Madrid, the Ritz was proposed—both for its excellence and for being next to the Prado. Dalí provided a shortlist of the museum's most notable treasures. They included Mantegna's *The Death of the Virgin*, 'the painting of all the paintings in the museum that most impressed García Lorca'; his own favourites, Raphael's *The Cardinal* and 'a little family scene by the same artist' (not identified); and *The Garden of Delights* ('the greatest and most Surrealistic picture that Hieronymous Bosch ever painted'). After Madrid came two days in Toledo (with disguised allusions to Buñuel and his Order), the Escorial ('which I consider the most beautiful place in the world') and Saint Teresa's Avila, followed by a breathless descent into Andalusia (which Dalí only knew from his month with Gala in Malaga in 1930).

The Dalís were back in Port Lligat that spring, and the painter went to work immediately on his new version of the *Madonna of Port Lligat*, for which Emilio Puignau, who was a talented draughtsman, prepared the canvas. In his head Dalí had already planned the picture down to the last detail, and showed Puignau some preparatory drawings. Referring to Velázquez and Delacroix, he told him that he now intended to paint large-scale works.[42]

The second *Madonna of Port Lligat* measures 144 x 96 cm and is as grey in colouring as the smaller study is vibrant. The Madonna's head is now that of an older Gala, and our attention is deflected from the Virgin by the superabundance of symbolic elements that attend her atomic 'lift-off' throne. It is a jumbled picture, with none of the grace of its predecessor, and the mood is strangely foreboding, as if Dalí were trying to give the feel of Port Lligat just before a storm.[43]

Was this perhaps because he knew his father had not long to live? It is tempting to think so. One day during the summer he heard that Dalí Cusí was seriously ill and hurried over to Cadaqués, accompanied by Emilio Puignau in case there should be a scene with Anna Maria. But she received them civilly enough. Dalí spent half an hour at his father's bedside. 'I think it's the end, son,' Puignau heard the old man say.[44]

So it proved, for Dalí Cusí had cancer of the prostate. He died a few months later, on 21 September 1950. Dalí visited the corpse, saying later that he had kissed his father on the lips, but despite his professed Catholicism he did not attend the funeral or the burial in the little cemetery of Sant Baldiri that overlooks the sea behind Port Lligat. Anna Maria was too upset to be present at the graveside, and Montserrat Dalí represented the family. A particularly violent tramuntana was raging and twice she was blown to the ground.[45]

Dalí was deeply upset by the loss of his father, the person who had most obsessed him during his life, and according to Puignau it revived his deep-rooted fears of illness and death.[46] His state of mind was presumably not improved by Dalí Cusí's last will, which was opened, in accordance with Spanish practice, a fortnight later. It had been drawn up on 31 May 1950. Since the house at Es Llané was already in Anna Maria's name by that date, the will referred only to the monies in Dalí Cusí's bank accounts and to his meagre investment portfolio, all of which went to his daughter. Dalí Cusí's second wife, Catalina ('La Tieta'), was not mentioned—it was assumed that Anna Maria would look after her. As for Salvador, instead of the 60,000 pesetas allotted in the previous will he now got 22,000, 'in total payment of his legitimate rights', with provision for an extra 10,000 in case a supplement to those rights should be considered apposite in law. In other words he had once again been virtually disinherited. There is no record of Dalí's reaction to the document, a copy of which was sent to him in October, but his rage can be imagined. He did not need the money but it appears that he and Gala, particularly Gala, thought they might have got a portion of the house at Es Llané. It was probably Dalí Cusí's last will that converted Gala's scorn for Anna Maria into hatred. From now on she would do everything in her power to ensure that Dalí never forgave his sister.[47]

The will did not solve the question of Dalí's belongings, particularly the paintings and drawings left behind in Figueres and Cadaqués when he was expelled from the family

in 1929. Dalí had always maintained that, despite his father's repudiation, these possessions were still his. He now raised the matter again with Anna Maria, reminding her in
a letter from the St Regis:

> Dear Sister:
>   The day our father died (may God have forgiven him) I pardoned you for all the inten
> tional chronological errors in your book, given that the documents of the period disprove
> them sufficiently. But I couldn't have imagined that after the pardon and the kiss we gave
> each other, you would continue maintaining in bad faith that the paintings which for sen
> timental reasons I had allowed you to keep in the house while Father was alive belonged
> to you. The *only* painting which I gave you is the portrait of you sewing . . .
>   I want you to acknowledge the truth, that's all. If not, the law, with irrefutable proofs
> and testimonies, will take care of the matter.
>   I want
>   (1) Your acknowledgement that the painting *Figure from Behind*, sold to Gudiol, was
> taken without my permission from my house, and the sale ordered by my father.
>   (2) An explanation about the second painting sold to Gudiol.
>   (3) A complete list of all the other paintings and drawings sold, with their prices and the
> places where you think they can be found now.
>   (4) A complete list of all the paintings and drawings given as presents, I remember one
> to [illegible] etc.
>   (5) The *unconditional* return of my works, of which I'll accept the ARBITRARY list you
> establish, with the undertaking not to sell the others without giving me first choice.
>   (6) The return of the magazines and the *Encyclopedia Espasa*, which my father always
> promised me.
>   If you do this I'll give the share of the inheritance that in law belongs to me to Tieta and
> drop all legal proceedings concerning the pictures.[48]

That Dalí believed that his family had removed works from his house in Port Lligat is
confirmed in a postcard he sent in December 1950 to Joaquim Cusí, the old friend of his
father who had bought some of his best early pictures, including the marvellous
Composition with Three Figures (Neo-Cubist Academy.) Dalí told Cusí that he had discovered twenty drawings in a New York museum proceeding from Port Lligat 'via Es
Llané'. 'Isn't it incredible,' he wrote, 'that still today all the obstacles to my career come
from the same place, my family.' One of the paintings sold by Anna Maria had just been
sold again in an auction. Dalí was livid. Whether these charges were justified, and
whether his family had really removed works from Port Lligat it now seems impossible
to establish.[49]

Gonzalo Serraclara acted on Dalí's behalf during the latter's absence, putting a lawyer in contact with the executors of Dalí Cusí's will and spelling out to him the painter's position vis-à-vis Anna Maria.[50] Emilio Puignau has written that Dalí and Anna Maria eventually reached an agreement on the question of the pictures, which were divided equally between them. Puignau collected Dalí's share, and, according to him, the painter was delighted to see the works again.[51]

Two years later there was a colourful sequel to these events. On 6 September 1952 the Figueres notary Evarist Vallès Llopart arrived in Port Lligat at siesta time for Dalí to sign a document relating to the agreement with Anna Maria. Dalí refused to see him but Vallès insisted. In a fury Dalí tore up the document and physically ejected the notary. As a public servant forcibly obstructed in the fulfilment of his duties, Vallès immediately initiated legal proceedings. Sick with apprehension at the vision of a year in prison, Dalí then enlisted the aid of a local potentate, Miguel Mateu, ex-mayor of Barcelona and a close friend of General Franco, who intervened with the minister of Justice in Madrid. Dalí's letters to Mateu are grovelling and sycophantic. Notwithstanding such an ally he was put on bail and required to present himself to the authorities twice a month during proceedings. Never can he have suffered such an indignity. Finally he was let off the hook after signing an apology to the College of Notaries. There was great satisfaction amongst the painter's adversaries that at last he had been taken down a peg or two. Eighteen years later he wondered if perhaps his 'lamentable act' had not been oedipal in character. Perhaps it was his own notary father whom, symbolically, he had booted out of his house in Port Lligat![52]

Nuclear Mysticism

On 19 October 1950, barely a month after his father's death, Dalí gave a lecture to the Barcelona Ateneu which marked the beginning of the most outrageous self-publicity campaign of his life. This was designed to prove not only that he had returned to the Catholic fold but that he was now a mystic. He chose the venue deliberately, for it was at the Ateneu, in 1930, that he had made his most aggressive profession of Surrealist faith, shocking many of its members in the process. 'Why I was Sacrilegious, why I am a Mystic' was widely advertised. The huge audience, hungry for Dalí's revelations, included representatives of the city's Franco establishment and a goodly sprinkling of ecclesiastics. He began by launching a furious attack on the writer Manuel Brunet, a native of Vic who had settled in Figueres and who, as we saw, wrote an appreciative article in *Destino* when Salvador Dalí Cusí retired as a notary in 1946. Brunet had become friendly with him and Anna Maria; and Dalí, although he did not say so in his lecture, suspected that he had helped the latter with her *Salvador Dalí Seen by his Sister*. Hence, partly, the animus. Dalí told the audience that Brunet had been a systematic enemy of his for years, always making a point of digging up examples of his 'sacrilegious' behaviour in the past. But Brunet was not alone: the world was full of mediocrities whose only purpose was to attempt to discredit those who were successful. Dalí had decided to name such beings, generically, *brunets*, and hoped that the word would enter the dictionaries (it did not).

In his 1930 lecture Dalí had greatly offended part of the Ateneu audience by expressing scorn for the recently deceased Catalan dramatist, Angel Guimerà. Now there was a similar reaction, particularly when Dalí listed the differences between him and Brunet, which ran from clothes, saliva, ties and intelligence to . . . bank accounts. The last jibe was considered lamentable, and rightly so, by many of those present.[53]

Dalí had brought with him from Port Lligat a large, two-pronged wooden fork, which he now brandished. It was, he said, the exact symbol of his philosophy and life. Left prong: the revolutionary and sacrilegious Dalí of 1923, inspired, in his struggle to realize himself as an artist, by 'all the ammoniacal angels of putrefaction'. Right prong: the mystical Dalí of 1950, the painter of *The Madonna of Port Lligat*, the antithesis of the other. Handle: symbol of Dalí's unity, his ecstasy. Unity and ecstasy? 'Ecstasy is the dialectic, the harmony, of opposites, of the two antithetical but absolutely authentic Dalís,' he hastened to explain. Without giving the audience time to digest such a *sui generis* definition, Dalí showed them a slide of *The Madonna of Port Lligat*, to the accompaniment of a 'theological poem' written, he said, while he was painting it. Then came some further observations on mysticism. The unity of the universe as revealed by Einstein sensationally reactualized, he said, 'the sublime mysticism of the Bible', and in 1950, for the first time in the history of science, physics was providing proof of the existence of God. The duty of the artist, now that Picasso (with his Dora Maar pictures) had rendered art incapable of greater ugliness, was to paint again like Raphael, to return to the great tradition of the Renaissance. It was the same message that Dalí had preached for eight years in America, with the mysticism added for good measure. Catholic mysticism, Dalí assured the Ateneu, was going to experience a flowering in the next fifty years, and Spanish painters must now produce religious paintings. It was the duty of the Spain of Valdés Leal, Velázquez and Zurbarán to take the lead in order to achieve, once again, 'the spiritual hegemony of our glorious imperialist tradition'.[54]

Of those present who had heard Dalí's 1930 lecture, Sebastià Gasch was probably the best equipped to query the sincerity of the painter's current profession of faith. He listened in awe as Dalí explained that he had always been instinctively religious. Gasch, who from the start had objected to what he considered the more immoral aspects of Surrealism (incurring Dalí's wrath as a result), could hardly believe his ears as the convert to Catholicism vehemently repudiated the ideas which in that very room he had sought with fanatical intensity to propagate.[55]

According to the now indispensable Emilio Puignau, who had driven Dalí down from Port Lligat (Gala had refused not only to go but also to allow them to use the Cadillac), the evening went off quite well. There were some whistles from the back, but the general feeling, despite the bad taste of Dalí's attack on Brunet, was of satisfaction. Such was the stifling atmosphere of Franco's Spain in 1950.[56]

From 27 November 1950 to 10 January 1951 the second version of *The Madonna of Port Lligat* was exhibited at the Carstairs Gallery in New York, where it served as excellent publicity on the other side of the Atlantic for the painter's return to the faith. Not all the critics were convinced of the sincerity of the work which, according to Reynolds Morse, aroused 'considerable skepticism'.[57]

Dalí was now planning *The Christ of Saint John of the Cross*, which, as its title acknowledges, owed an explicit debt to the remarkable drawing of the Crucifixion attributed to the saint in question, and which had been brought to Dalí's attention by a Carmelite monk, Father Bruno de Froissart.[58] In Beverly Hills Jack Warner had introduced Dalí to Russ Saunders, the acrobatic Hollywood stand-in, and arrangements had been made to photograph him tied to a wooden panel in the posture of Saint John of the Cross's crucified Christ. Back in Port Lligat in the spring of 1951, Dalí showed the enlargements, blown up to the size of his projected painting, to Emilio Puignau, and asked him to map out a scale drawing of the cross. Puignau was dumbfounded but, nonetheless, carried out Dalí's instructions as best he could. Dalí was delighted with the results and Puignau's drawing was transferred to the canvas.[59]

In Dalí's vast painting (205 x 116 cm), Christ hangs over the claustrophobic, island-enclosed bay of Port Lligat as it appears from the painter's terrace. The same scenario was to recur in dozens of drawings and paintings done in the 1950s, now animated by the Madonna, Christ and the local fishermen, as well as by an assemblage of angels. One of the latter, in *The Angel of Port Lligat* (1952), is Gala,[60] who appears again, in 1956, as *Saint Helen of Port Lligat*, sporting a crucifix, a book (not identified) and a tempting cleavage. Most of these works strike one as repetitive kitsch.[61]

Puignau was detailed over the next few years to do the hard mechanical work on other of Dalí's 'mystico-nuclear' paintings, such as *The Disintegration of the Persistence of Memory* (1952–4), *Assumpta Corpuscularia Lapislazulina* (1952–3) and *Nuclear Cross*

(1952). The latter proved particularly exacting, with its 950 cubes in perspective. Later, when reproductions were published, Dalí gave his talented assistant a copy with the dedication 'For Emilio Puignau, who did the cubes', but there was never any public acknowledgement of his contribution. When Puignau could no longer give up so much of his time to help the Master with the technical problems engendered by such works, two trainee architects from Figueres, Ferrer and Jacomet, were occasionally employed to do geometrical drawings and perspectives for Dalí.[62]

In April 1951 Dalí published his *Mystical Manifesto*, which developed directly out of the lecture he had delivered at the Ateneu Barcelonès. Published both in French and in Latin (presumably to lend it an appearance of proper spiritual seriousness), it proclaimed the arrival of what Dalí now termed his 'paranoiac-critical mysticism'. The manifesto starts from the assumption that modern art is decadent, and that such decadence 'comes from scepticism and lack of faith, a consequence of rationalism, positivism and also of dialectical and mechanistic materialism'. This being so, modern art needs to be saved—and who better to save it than the Catalan ex-Surrealist genius whose first name means 'Saviour'?

Dalí's 'paranoiac-critical mysticism', he explains, is principally based on the startling advances in modern science, above all on the 'metaphysical spirituality' of quantum mechanics and on the concept of form as the result of a constricting, inquisitorial process ('Freedom has no form. Every rose grows in a prison'). For Dalí the most beautiful buildings in the world are Bramante's minute church in Rome, the Tempietto di San Pietro in Montorio (1503), and Spain's massive Escorial, the work of Juan de Herrera (1557). Both are the products of 'ecstasy', he alleges, returning to the theme of his Ateneu lecture, and represent a model of classical perfection that modern artists are too ashamed to contemplate, preferring to seek their inspiration in pre-Renaissance barbarity: cave paintings, Cretan and Romanesque frescoes and those 'aberrations for the mentally deficient', African artefacts.

So, how is an artist to become 'mystical'? Dalí tells us that the candidate must subject his 'mystical reverie' (never defined) to a daily process of rigorous examination, in order to fashion for himself 'a dermo-skeletal soul (the bones outside, the finest of flesh inside) like that which Unamuno attributes to Castile, where the flesh of the soul can only grow towards the sky'. Hardly very practical advice, one might feel. The 'mystical ecstasy' to be obtained by this method, we are assured, is '"super-joyful", explosive, disintegrated, supersonic, ondulatory and corpuscular, ultragelatinous, for it is the aesthetic eruption of the highest paradisiacal happiness that mankind can achieve on earth'.

And what will the 'mystical artist' see in his ecstasy? Well, perhaps the 'golden, corpuscular' Immaculate Virgin of Port Lligat, as painted by Dalí; or, who knows, a child-angel on the beach at Roses (featured in *Myself at the Age of Six, When I Thought I was a Girl, Lifting with Extreme Care the Skin of the Sea to Observe a Dog Sleeping in the Shadow of the Water*, 1950); or he may even be vouchsafed an original vision of his own, uninfluenced by Dalinian images. But whatever the experience, the 'mystical artist' must render it in the style of the Renaissance, because the Renaissance has laid down, for all time, the rules for painting. To this end the trustworthy guides are Pythagoras, Heraclitus, Vitruvius, Luca Pacioli (whose treatise *On Divine Proportion* Dalí greatly admired) and Saint John of the Cross, 'the maximum exponent in poetry of the militant Spanish mysticism which Dalí is now resuscitating'.

Dalí's 'paranoiac-critical mysticism' had much more to do with nuclear physics and the theory of relativity than with mysticism as understood by the Church of Rome, despite Michel Tapié's claims in a leaflet, 'Concerning Dalinian Continuity', inserted into the *Mystical Manifesto*. Tapié used a well-tried ploy (which would be applied by others to the atheistic Luis Buñuel) to maintain that the marked 'sacrilegious obstination' of Dalí's Surrealist period was, in reality, 'a circumstantial form of acts [sic] of Faith, in a group that oscillated between sterile negation and materialistic sectarianism'.[63]

Intimations of incipient spirituality in the young Dalí, perverted by the wicked Surrealists! Prayer disguised as blasphemy! It was all too far-fetched, too ridiculous. Dalí, however, was delighted with Tapié's apology for his trajectory from materialism to alleged spirituality. In 1930 he had misled his audience at the Ateneu Barcelonès by claiming that when, on his painting of the Sacred Heart, he wrote 'Sometimes I spit for pleasure on the portrait of my mother', he was referring to his dream activity. Now he went a step further: 'It is possible, in dreams, to curse beings one worships in one's waking life. And to dream of having spat on one's mother. In several religions the act of spitting often has a sacred character.' When awake, therefore, he had never been tempted to spit on the portrait of his mother; when he had done so in sleep it had been a deeply religious gesture. As usual, Dalí never took responsibility for his harmful actions. He was always right, always justified in what he did.[64]

In August 1951, a few months after the appearance of the *Mystical Manifesto*, Dalí was questioned about his religious convictions by a nicely sceptical Barcelona journalist, Manuel del Arco. Was the painter really a Catholic? Yes, totally, and all the better for having become one after such a turbulent past.[65] Did he go to confession and take Holy Communion? Yes. Why had he been sacrilegious in his youth? Because he was seeking ecstasy by material means. Today all that had changed, Dalí added, and he was now seeking ecstasy 'by travelling along the road of perfection; by spiritual means'. Moreover, he believed in the resurrection of the flesh.[66] What about attendance at mass?

That was a 'nuisance', Dalí conceded, but he imposed it on himself in an attempt to achieve faith.[67] Was he going to end up as a monk? No, Dalí said, he had no aptitude for sanctity: 'You can be a mystic and stop being one; but you can't be holy and then not.'[68] That put it well. Mysticism for Dalí was yet another ego trip, and implied no obligations outside of itself. No piety. No charity. And, glaringly, no love either. In all Dalí's religious pleading the word love never once occurs. Moreover, if it was true in August 1951 that Dalí was attending mass and going to confession, this soon changed. There is no reference to the fulfilment of such duties in the sporadic diary Dalí began in 1952 and published twelve years later with the immodest title of *The Diary of a Genius*; and close associates of the painter have said that they never saw him go to mass.[69]

In September 1951, taking a brief holiday from 'nuclear mysticism', Dalí accompanied Gala to Venice to attend a sumptuous fancy dress ball thrown for the world's rich, famous and beautiful by the millionaire Carlos Béstegui. As the guests stepped out of their gondolas at the Labia Palace, restored for the occasion to its former opulence, they were gawped at by a multitude of incredulous Venetians. The Dalís appeared disguised as seven-metre-tall giants (the costumes had been designed by Gala and Christian Dior) and were much applauded, despite the stiff competition. Dalí remembered 'the ball of the century' with delectation. Everyone who was anyone was there, from Orson Welles to Lady Churchill. 'The city was in transports, and my success so great that, twenty years later, I still dream of it some nights,' Dalí recalls in *The Unspeakable Confessions*.[70]

But, in terms of propaganda, Dalí's success in Venice was nothing compared to that of the lecture 'Picasso and I', his third great self-promotional set piece of these months, which was delivered in Madrid's María Guerrero theatre on 11 November 1951. It made an enormous impact in Spain and abroad—so much so that it stood out in Dalí's memory as one of his greatest moments of all.

The María Guerrero, one of Spain's most venerable theatres, was filled to bursting point that evening. The *crème de la crème* of Madrid high society was in attendance, along with a variegated concourse of writers, journalists, artists and critics. Everyone knew that, where the 'Communist' Picasso, *bête noire* of the Franco régime was concerned, Dalí would have some explosive things to say. He did not disappoint his audience. The second paragraph of the talk became legendary overnight, and he himself was to go on quoting it for the rest of his life:

> As always, Spain has the honour of producing the greatest contrasts, this time in the persons of the two most antagonic artists of modern painting: Picasso and myself, your humble servant.

Picasso is Spanish; so am I. Picasso is a genius; so am I. Picasso is about 74; I'm about 48. Picasso is known in every country in the world; so am I. Picasso is a Communist; *nor am I.*

The lecture was, first and foremost, a paean to the genius of Spain. Dalí and Picasso were geniuses, of course, everyone knew that; but so too was Juan Gris, the Madrid-born inventor, with Picasso, of Cubism. How ludicrous that Cubism should be considered a French phenomenon, argued Dalí, when it was obvious that it derived from the intricate arabesques of the Alhambra, reborn by a quirk of atavism in the Andalusian brain of Malaga-born Pablo Picasso! And Gris? The 'Juan de Herrera of Cubism', as Dalí termed him, had given an ascetic twist to Picasso's 'Dionysian' cubism. All praise. But how come that Gris was unknown in his own country? Dalí had his provocative answer at the ready: it was all the fault of the *brunets*, the pathetic local critics. It was they who were responsible. All Spanish geniuses, Dalí went on, have to struggle against the indifference and mediocrity that characterizes their countrymen. What better example of this than Spain's glorious Caudillo? 'Before Franco,' he said, emphasizing his words, 'every politician and every new government only increased the confusion, the lies and the disorder of Spain. Franco broke violently with this false tradition, imposing clarity, truth and order in the country at a time when the world was experiencing its period of greatest anarchy. That seems to me highly original.' The eulogy provoked 'great applause' from a sector of the audience.[71]

The lecture became obscure when, quoting literally from the *Mystical Manifesto*, Dalí assumed a connection between 'ecstasy' and the morphology of 'inquisitorial form'. At this point the audience registered bemusement, although Dalí's conclusion, that the aim of Spanish painting must now be to fuse mysticism and realism, seemed to make more sense to them. At the end of his lecture Dalí read out the text of the telegram he had just sent to Picasso:

> The spirituality of Spain today is the maximum opponent of Russian materialism. You know that in Russia they're purging even music for political reasons. Here we believe in the total and Catholic liberty of the human soul. You know, therefore, that despite your current Communism we consider your anarchic genius an inseparable heritage of our spiritual empire, and your work a triumph of Spanish painting. God protect you.[72]

Among those who were shocked by Dalí's praise of Franco and his régime, and by his patronizing remarks on Picasso, was the young painter Antonio Saura. He loathed

Franco and what he represented, had been influenced by Surrealism and thought that Dalí stood for freedom. So he had gone along to hear him. But Dalí's performance filled him with disgust. 'Every statement he made was an offence to freedom,' he recalled, 'to the struggle against the régime that a handful of us were maintaining against all the odds.'[73]

The lecture was exactly what the Spanish Government wanted to hear, however, and Franco himself was by all accounts extremely pleased. He was beginning to see that Dalí could be useful at a time when his régime was under attack from the democratic world and was only just emerging from the ostracism imposed on it by the United Nations in 1946.

Also in the María Guerrero that evening was a young art critic, Rafael Santos Torroella, who had first met the painter when the Dalís arrived back from America in 1948. Santos Torroella, whose father was a customs official, had been born in the Catalan frontier town of Portbou in 1914 and was now working for Cobalt, the Barcelona publishers, where he had seen Oriol Anguera's book on Dalí through the press. Cobalt was originally to have brought out Anna Maria's *Salvador Dalí Seen by his Sister*, and Santos Torroella had got to know her and her father well as a result, even staying with them for a while at Es Llané. Although the book eventually went to another publisher, the friendship continued, and it was strengthened when Santos Torroella began work on an edition of Lorca's *Letters to his Friends*, which contained excerpts from the poet's correspondence with Anna Maria. The fact that Santos Torroella had himself met Lorca, and had heard him recite, served to enhance his relationship with the Dalí family, who remembered the poet with deep affection.[74]

Santos Torroella's first article on Dalí appeared just before the Picasso lecture, and his first book on the painter—more an essay—a few months later. The latter was carefully researched, sober yet enthusiastic, clear in its exposition and enriched by the critic's personal experience of the Empordà. Santos Torroella, while extremely appreciative of Dalí at his best, was fully alive to the flaws in his character, and dared to question the sincerity of the artist's alleged mysticism. He also pointed out how excessively, in his paintings, he quoted from his previous work. Santos Torroella sensed that Lorca and Dalí's friendship had been fundamental to both, and that it would reward careful investigation. The little book laid the basis on which Santos Torroella was patiently to build the corpus that today establishes him as a world authority on Dalí.[75]

The Spanish press, and the Spanish-speaking press worldwide, gave massive publicity to Dalí's lecture, which was also featured on Nodo, Spain's version of Pathé News. Not all the comment was favourable, and the hardline Franco daily, *Madrid*, expressed outrage that anyone could propose even the partial rehabilitation of Picasso, the 'defender, accomplice and protector of those who caused a million deaths in Spain'.[76]

A few months later the writer and journalist Miguel Utrillo, one of Dalí's main followers in Madrid, published a petulant little volume, *Salvador Dalí and his Enemies*, in which he not only sided with the painter against Manuel Brunet but claimed that the latter actually wrote Anna Maria Dalí's *Salvador Dalí Seen by his Sister*, 'a book which will be remembered only as an example of what can be achieved by an atrophied femininity'.[77] The charge was ludicrous and scurrilous. More usefully, Utrillo documented the tremendous polemical aftermath to Dalí's lecture, describing the banquet that was held in the painter's honour in the Palace Hotel. During it, Dalí's old friend, Eugenio Montes, had lamented the absence of the founder of the Falange, the Spanish Fascist party, José Antonio Primo de Rivera, executed by the Republicans at the beginning of the war. It fell to Spain, said Montes, to be 'the leader of Christianity, the leader of Humanity'. The Falange's nationalist rhetoric, partially adopted by Dalí, was ringing hollower by the day.[78]

That December the Alex, Reid and Lefevre gallery in London exhibited the second version of the *Madonna of Port Lligat* and *The Christ of Saint John of the Cross*, thereby affording the British public a chance to acquaint itself with the products of Dalí's new 'mysticism'. Reactions were mixed, particularly when it was announced that the Glasgow Art Gallery had purchased the latter work for a considerable sum.[79] When the show closed, and before embarking for New York, Dalí issued a statement entitled 'The Current Situation of Dalinian Painting'. 'I needed ten years to win my Surrealist battle,' he said. 'Now I need a year to win my *classical, realist and mystical battle*. Against me are ranged all the extreme left-wing intellectuals, of course. With me are the intuitive public, the new current of the epoch, the leading intelligences. I will win the battle for Spanish painting.' That Dalí had a gift for bravado no one could reasonably doubt.[80]

In America Dalí gave a series of lectures proclaiming the good news of what he was now terming 'nuclear mysticism', accompanied part of the way by Reynolds and Eleanor Morse. No one took the good news too seriously, a typical newspaper headline reading 'Crowd Likes Dalí, Cool to "Mysticism"'.[81] Along the circuit Dalí sent a ridiculous and well-publicized telegram of condolence to Queen Elizabeth on the death of her father: 'Do accept testimony of my profound emotion and also my hope and my belief that your reign will be a fulfilment of the new renaissance of the mystic values in the world'. Her Majesty's reply, if any, has not been recorded.[82]

'My present nuclear mysticism,' Dalí wrote in his diary in May 1952, 'is merely the fruit, inspired by the Holy Ghost, of the demoniacal and Surrealist experiments of the first part of my life.'[83] It made it all sound very straightforward. A few pages later Dalí envisaged 'nuclear mysticism' as a movement that was going to sweep the world, and in which the role of Spain would of course be essential. Other countries would contribute:

> America, because of the unheard-of progress of its technology, will produce the empirical (we might even call them the photographic or microphotographic) proofs of this new mysticism.
>
> The genius of the Jewish people will involuntarily give it its dynamic and anti-aesthetic possibilities, thanks to Freud and Einstein. France will play an essentially didactic role. She will probably draw up the constitutional form of 'nuclear mysticism' owing to her intellectual prowess. But, once again, it will be the mission of Spain to ennoble all by religious faith and beauty.[84]

Dalí cannot have believed a word of this, and after 1952 the entries in his diary referring to 'nuclear mysticism' diminish (as do the assertions about Spain's 'supreme and glorious mission' to renew her 'great classical tradition of realism and mysticism').[85] He continued to propound 'nuclear mysticism' for a few more years, however, albeit increasingly sporadically, mounting ferocious attacks on 'Socialist Realism' as he went, doing the word 'spiritual' to death and every so often directing a jibe at Picasso.[86]

So far as Picasso was concerned, Dalí simply did not exist. He refused to mention him in conversation, to discuss him, to hear his name and, above all, to contemplate replying to any of his provocations. During the 1950s Fleur Cowles, one of his earliest biographers, asked him 'if a blank piece of paper could be used to signify his reaction to Dalí'. Picasso, she wrote, 'declined even that method of acknowledging Dalí's existence'.

Dalí, Assumpta Corpuscularia Lapis-lazulina, *1952. Oil on canvas, 230 x 144 cm. Gala again as Virgin Mary.*

Such a refusal to rise to the bait was the worst punishment Picasso could have inflicted on his rival, as he was surely aware.[87]

In November 1952, while they made preparations for their annual migration to New York, the Dalís heard that Paul Éluard had died. He was only fifty-six. Dalí noted the poet's demise in his diary, with no particular emotion.[88] As for Gala, it apparently never crossed her mind to attend the funeral. It was a moving ceremony that afternoon in the Père Lachaise. Éluard's Communist friends were there in strength, with Picasso and Aragon to the fore, and they gave him a hero's send-off. His death meant that Gala and Dalí could now to be married by the Church. To facilitate this, Gala asked her daughter to obtain for her a copy of the marriage certificate showing that she and Éluard had had a Catholic wedding. It would be six years, however, before the Dalís were finally joined in holy matrimony.[89]

That December Dalí was back at the Carstairs Gallery in New York with six new 'religious' paintings: *Assumpta Corpuscularia Lapislazulina, Nature Morte Evangélique, Nuclear Cross, Gala Placidia, The Angel of Port Lligat* and *Corpuscular Persistence of Memory*. So far as Dalí was concerned, *Assumpta Corpuscularia Lapislazulina* was the most important of the six, and he concentrated on it in the exhibition catalogue. The painting, he said, was 'the opposite of the atomic bomb. Instead of the disintegration of matter, we have the integration, the reconstitution of the real and glorious body of the Virgin in the heavens.' Dalí maintained not only that he had produced a masterpiece, but a masterpiece that was the *summum* of all preceding experiments in modern art:

> This painting also justifies in itself every experimental effort in modern art, since I have succeeded in bringing these experiments to a classical end; experiments which would otherwise have remained sterile, since the majority of the great and courageous innovators are today returning to archaeological inspiration; and only a few impetuous young abstract painters continue with 'interesting plastic experiments' which, unfortunately, are destined to remain decorative art because of their means of purely graphical expression. There was Seurat with his Divisionism, who without knowing it, introduced nuclear physics; also Cubism; and especially the great Futurist genius, Boccioni, but he expresses himself in terms of speed, motor-cars and action. This is childish, and it is because of this lack of theological and philosophical meaning that all those efforts perished so soon.
>
> But all of them had foreseen a thing that was to be the *great, immeasurable and categorical innovation of our time—a new conception of matter.* That of NUCLEAR PHYSICS.[90]

Dalí was entitled to his own view of his work, but the fact is that *Assumpta Corpuscularia Lapislazulina* was simply another variation on the dance of protons and neutrons that he had first begun to exploit a few years earlier, and it was typical of him that, in view of the public success of his *Christ of Saint John of the Cross*, he had incorporated that celebrated image in the new painting. As for Gala's face at the pinnacle of the nuclear whirl, it at least has the advantage of showing her more or less as she was at the time, unlike the first *Madonna of Port Lligat*. 'If Nietzsche's Superman has not come into being, a Nietzschean superwoman exists in the Assumption,' Dalí commented a few years later on this painting. 'She rises to heaven pushed by anti-matter Angels.'[91]

Dalí's new-found spirituality did not prevent him from busying himself during 1954 with a three-act play in French alexandrines entitled *Erotic-Mystical Delirium*. Dalí prided himself on his productivity, but this work, which became *Martyr. Lyrical Tragedy in Three Acts*, was to occupy him for two decades and was never finished.[92] To judge from the fragments that have been published, it was a sorry affair.[93] Dalí, however, believed it to be something of a breakthrough in erotic drama. Set in Delft the year of Vermeer's birth, it had a cast of three: a nineteen-year-old-virgin (desperate for sex), a prince better at masturbation than copulation, and a Catholic confessor. In the early 1970s, Dalí was to fantasize about Catherine Deneuve, in the role of the virgin, reciting some of its more outrageous lines and blushing with shame as she did so.[94] The fragments show, if nothing else, that Dalí had the vocabulary of French eroticism at his fingertips (although he still couldn't spell). Significantly he was also working at this time on *The 120 Days of Sodom of the Divine Marquis in Reverse*, a project of which nothing further is known.[95]

The only person who seems to have teased Dalí about his 'atomic mysticism', or to have tried to do so, was Malcolm Muggeridge, when he interviewed the painter on the BBC TV programme *Panorama* in 1955. Dalí was in splendid fettle on that occasion, and produced a much more agile and entertaining English than Muggeridge had expected. 'Nothing is more gay than the collision and explosion of intra-atomic conflicts, of nuclear physics,' the painter explained, referring to his current works. 'Electrons and pi-mesons and atoms, everything jooomping and rooomping in a completely extraordinary eu-rhy-thmic feeling.' Muggeridge pretended to look amused. The exchange continued:

> Muggeridge: Now, all your wonderful jokes that we know about, taxi cabs with the rain inside and so on, you're going to go on with those jokes?
>
> Dalí: Eh, this correspond to le first period of my life. The moment of myself is very big interest in psychoanalysis, coming in London for meet le Docteur Freud. But now my only interest is about le tremendous progress of nuclear recherches and nuclear physics.

Muggeridge: And so really that represented a phase in your career, those jokes that we all knew about, and now you move on, and all your life will be to the rhythm of atomic explosions?

Dalí: Exactly, one new kind of, eh, atomic and nuclear mysticism.

Muggeridge: Well, thank you very much, that's a fascinating phrase, nuclear mysticism.[96]

As Dawn Ades has commented, referring to Dalí's painting *Anti-Protonic Assumption* (1956), Christian dogma, in the artist's 'nuclear mysticism', has become 'a form of superior science fiction'.[97]

Reynolds Morse's Dalí

Dalí's edition of Dante's *The Divine Comedy*, commissioned by the Italian government, had fallen through when the left-wing opposition, outraged that a pro-Franco artist had been signed up to illustrate one of Italy's greatest works, launched a parliamentary protest. The government of the day had had to climb down, and Dalí recovered his 102 watercolour illustrations.[98] In May 1954 he returned to Rome to mount an exhibition of these in the Sala della Aurora of the Palazzo Pallavicini, along with twenty-four other paintings and seventeen drawings from different periods of his production.[99] Dalí told a Spanish monarchist acquaintance that he felt an urge to be 're-born' in the Holy City. This he achieved by staging a press conference on 1 June in which he suddenly burst out of a 'metaphysical cube'. The cube had become another of his obsessions, thanks to reading the *Discourse on the Cubic Figure* by Juan de Herrera.[100]

Dalí was interviewed in Rome for a Spanish film magazine by his friend Miguel Utrillo, author of *Salvador Dalí and his Enemies.* He told him that soon he would begin shooting *The Wheelbarrow of Flesh* in Cadaqués and the surrounding countryside. He himself would direct, and Anna Magnani, he claimed, was going to play the lead. Among the other actors there would be a hundred swans, more than a hundred bearded men looking like Karl Marx, the fishermen of Port Lligat, and Dalí himself in the role of house painter. In his diary, Dalí described other scenes that he had added to the script over the years, and explained that five of the swans would be blown up by explosive charges inserted in their guts, their disintegration being followed by the camera in slow motion. It was another example of his persistent indifference to the suffering of animals. There seems to be no evidence that Anna Magnani was aware of the project for which she was billed. Anyway, as was the usual case with Dalí's attempts to take the film world by storm, it came to nothing.[101]

Reynolds and Eleanor Morse had travelled to Rome to help Dalí mount the exhibition in the Palazzo Pallavicini, which included six of their paintings. Morse was now president of his own firm, the Injectors Molding Supply Company, in Cleveland, and was continuing to build up his Dalí collection. 'I remember our thrill,' wrote Eleanor, 'when we saw posters announcing the exhibit with a blow-up of our picture *The Ghost of Vermeer* pasted up all over Rome.' One Sunday Gala took them on an expedition and pointed out the studio in which Dalí had worked at Lord Berners's mansion just off the Forum in 1938. The Morses then moved on ahead of the Dalís to make their first visit to the Empordà, putting up in the fly-infested Hotel Port Lligat on the hill behind the painter's labyrinthine house.[102]

The Morses were dazzled by Cadaqués and Port Lligat. They felt they were dreaming. Here was the epicentre of Dalí's world, the real-life source of the works that they had now been amassing for a decade. Looking back, Morse wrote somewhat proudly:

> Strange as it now seems, in 1954 Dalí's Surrealism was popularly supposed to represent only an imaginary dream world peopled by subconscious hallucinations. The idea that such a landscape as seen here actually existed and was a living part of Dalí's Surrealism had not yet penetrated to the effete world of modern art in Paris and New York.[103]

Almost sick with excitement the Morses explored the cliffs and coves of Cape Creus, the narrow streets of Cadaqués, the little roads of the Empordà plain, the immense beach at Roses. They walked up and down the Rambla in Figueres, sat in the pavement cafés and wondered in which house Dalí had lived with his family. They made a point of visiting Anna Maria Dalí at Es Llané. She showed them her collection and gave them her forceful views on Salvador and the horrible Gala. Then, when the Dalís returned from Rome, the Morses saw them in Port Lligat.[104]

During subsequent visits no place of Dalinian relevance was to be left unvisited or unphotographed by the Morses, from the rock metamorphoses of Creus, the Graeco-Roman remains of Ampurias, the mountain lake at Requeséns and the ruined fortress on top of the Montgri mountain (which marks the southern confines of Dalí's empire), to the dolmen behind Roses, the castle of Quermançó at the edge of the Empordà plain and the great Romanesque monastery of Sant Pere de Roda, perched on its eyrie above Port de la Selva with, to its left, the tiny ruined chapel of Santa Elena (Gala!) and, far above, the remains of the stronghold of Sant Salvador (Dalí!). Was Sant Salvador, as the Morses heard, really the Montsalvat of Wagner's *Parsifal*? That must be investigated! The shadow of the Pení mountain at sunset was observed, savoured and related to Dalí's paintings ('an undulating hem of twilight', Morse defined it nicely on one occasion);[105] the oranges, yellows and pale-greens of the lichens on the rocks at Creus duly noted; the local food and wine relished to the full, sea urchins included. The Morses' enthusiasm for 'Dalí-land', as Reynolds soon termed it, was inexhaustible.[106]

Two years later, in the summer of 1956, the couple were back in Cadaqués and Morse wrote there the first volume of his *A Dalí Journal*, trying to piece together the events of the last fourteen years and wishing he had begun to keep a diary earlier. By this time he and Eleanor had got to know some of the local inhabitants quite well. They found that, while Dalí was popular in Cadaqués, no one had a good word to say for Gala, who was rumoured, moreover, to have no hesitation in approaching the fishermen of Port Lligat when she wanted sex.[107]

Gradually the Morses got to know Anna Maria better, and bought some of the Dalís in her collection. Through her they met the Domènech side of the family in Barcelona, from whom they also bought. Morse recalled in 1993 that Dalí always resented their having made friends with his sister 'and considered it a hostile and anti-Gala gesture to mention her name'.[108]

After each trip to 'Dalí-land' the Morses would return to the States to continue, with renewed vigour, their campaign to convince the American public that Dalí was as great a genius as Picasso, if not a greater. The collecting, interrogating and badgering of Dalí, the effort to understand him and his work, combined with growing affection, gave rise to a series of monographs and opuscules by Reynolds Morse, beginning in 1954 with a small spiral-bound booklet on Dalinian associations in Cadaqués.

Given the fact that Reynolds Morse was to become Dalí's leading propagandist in the United States, it has to be said that his writings on the painter, which span forty years, have serious shortcomings. The most glaring is his profound ignorance about Surrealism, a movement which (along with Anna Maria Dalí) he considers 'nihilistic' and destructive.[109] Morse is under the impression that the Surrealists were a group of utterly incompetent Parisian mediocrities, beginning with André Breton ('Breton's slow and pedantic brain was soon eclipsed by Dalí's lightning intelligence,' he wrote in 1960).[110] These people, clearly, had nothing to give Dalí. Morse's comments on *Illumined Pleasure* make it quite clear: 'The most complex of Dalí's surrealist works, this little panel is the prime visual statement of all the irrational and Freudian sentiments which the movement's adherents were unable to express in their various manifestos, dictums and declarations.'[111] Discussing *The Lugubrious Game*, Morse goes further in the same direction: 'Dalí exposed Surrealism's erotic motivations by linking it to the basic realities. Here he routs any poetic illusions which might have given the surrealists refuge.

Dealt a death blow, they hastily expelled Dalí—too late, however, to save themselves from being eclipsed by the young painter from Barcelona.'[112]

In 1993, forty years after he first met Dalí at the St Regis, Morse's scorn for Surrealism was unimpaired. 'The fly,' he wrote in *Animal Crackers*, 'fascinated Dalí as it has no other painter, and always with reasons that went light years beyond Surrealism.'[113] And in the same place he made perhaps his most muddleheaded statement of all:

> Dalí's early attempts at a double image in his *Allegory of Sunset-Air* around 1930 are a fascinating metamorphosis. His works in this vein went totally unappreciated, and were clearly well over the heads of his Surrealist consorts. This was for only one reason. The transformation was the epitome of his Surrealism, but being SURREALISTS they totally missed Dalí's contribution both actual and potential to their wobbly movement, and one ill-timed for in the Great Depression of 1930 the world was in no mood for art without discernable [*sic*] reason to which one could cling in a global slump.[114]

Another major defect apparent in all Morse's writings on Dalí is his utterly unquestioning acceptance of the 'paranoiac-critical method', which, despite his determination to 'explain' Dalí to the American layman, he never seeks to elucidate. The so-called method is simply taken for granted. This lack is all the more glaring when we are asked to believe, for example, that early in 1929 it was 'actually functioning even though its literary definitions had not yet been spelled out'.[115] For Morse, in 1973, the unexplained 'method' is 'no longer just a literary conceit promulgated by a half-mad surrealist clown. Instead it has become a respectable method of stimulating ideas with bio-feedback along brain wave channels as well as a means of eliminating the dangerous hallucinogenic drugs.'[116] Once passing time enables a true perspective, moreover, 'Picasso's Cubism and Dalí's Paranoiac-Critical Method will turn out to be the two predominant influences in the [sic] 20th century art.' Not even Dalí ever made such a claim for his non-existent method.[117]

Then there is Morse's obsession with 'Dalinian Continuity', a term borrowed from Michel Tapié's 1957 study of the painter. 'Dalinian Continuity' means that Dalí repeats himself over and over again, but Morse never considers the possibility that such repetition is a flaw. On the contrary, he sees it a virtue. If a rose appears in two paintings separated by forty years, 'the importance of both these works is increased by Dalinian Continuity';[118] 'Dalinian iconography and Dalinian Continuity become inseparable as one traces the figure of the nurse sitting on the beach from work to work';[119] we can enjoy a 'superb example of Dalinian Continuity' by comparing the figure who indicates an ellipse in *William Tell* (1930) and the one pointing at the egg in *Geopoliticus Child Watching the Birth of the New Man* (1943); in *The Font* (1930) a 'white spot of holy light' over the grail [sic] is 'the same focal point that 28 years later reappears as a dot in [the] sail in *The Dream of Columbus*, thus reaffirming the inexorable principle that unifies so much of Dalí's oeuvre: Dalinian Continuity!'[120] In his attempt to prove that Dalí is Picasso's peer, Morse takes much comfort from 'Dalinian Continuity'. 'All of Dalí's art is linked into a single metaphysical unit by the phenomenon of Dalinian Continuity,' he assures us, 'yet in all Picasso's giant catalog there is nothing even remotely resembling the re-use of certain symbols that link Dalí's works of various periods into a concatenous manifestation.'[121]

In his seminal *Dada and Surrealism* (1968) William Rubin concluded that Morse wrote more as an apologist for Dalí's later work than as an art critic or historian capable of risking value judgements. The assessment was not unfair.[122] Reynolds Morse's monumental *A Dalí Journal*, however, is a major achievement. When published, hopefully without too many cuts (Morse can be hard on Dalí's entourage), the diary will prove to be our most detailed and reliable source for the day-to-day practicalities and impracticalities, the grandeur and the misery, of Dalí's life over four decades. 'Today,' Morse wrote in 1993, 'this Dalí Journal had turned me into a kind of mini-Boswell to Dalí's Johnson as my mother once prophesied many years ago.' Mrs Morse knew her son. The journal is of priceless value and Morse's true talent, beyond a doubt, is that of Dalinian chronicler.[123]

The Rhinoceros and DNA

It was probably early in 1950 that Emmanuel Looten, a little-known Flemish poet, had made Dalí the unexpected and 'gelatinous' gift of a rhinoceros horn. 'This horn will save my life!' Dalí exclaimed to Gala, without quite knowing why.[124] Dalí had never before had the opportunity of inspecting a rhinoceros horn. Now he actually owned one. It had to be significant! The rhinoceros was added to his list of obsessive icons in two paintings done the same year: the second version of *The Madonna of Port Lligat* and *Rhinoceros in Disintegration*.[125] Then, on 5 July 1952, Dalí felt that his spontaneous prediction to Gala on receiving the gift was coming true when suddenly he perceived that the painting of Christ on which he was then working was made up of . . . rhino horns! There could be no doubt about it. 'You should have seen me fall to my knees in my studio, like a real madman,' he wrote in his diary. Now that the revelation had burst upon him, he began to perceive rhinoceros horns in all his paintings, even in the ones done years earlier. How could he have failed to notice their presence before? He saw them out of doors, too—among the micaschist metamorphoses of Cape Creus and, particularly, in a projection on top of the Great Masturbator rock at Cullaró. It was clear that he must now exploit rhino horns fully, making up for lost time.[126]

XXXVI   One of Dalí's first efforts in the new genre was *Young Virgin Auto-Sodomized by the Horns of her Own Chastity* (1954). Based on a photograph he had seen in a sex magazine,[127] it was bought, fittingly, by the Playboy Collection (Los Angeles), for of all Dalí's paintings in praise of the female bottom it is the most blatantly erotic. Dalí, tongue in cheek, had no difficulty in denying the phallic nature of the picture's horns. 'The rhinoceros horn is derived from the unicorn, the symbol of chastity,' he told Reynolds Morse. 'Paradoxically this painting which has an erotic appearance is the most chaste of all.'[128]

Rhino horns appeared in another painting done this year, *Dalí Naked Contemplating Five Regular Bodies Metamorphosed into Corpuscles in Which Suddenly Appears Leonardo's Leda Chromosomized by the Face of Gala.* The horns were accompanied by an element making its first appearance in Dalí's work and soon to become another new icon: the DNA molecule. As someone with a paranoid grandfather who had committed suicide, Dalí could hardly fail to be interested in the transmission of hereditary factors, and DNA really excited him. It had been identified in 1930, but it was only with Francis Crick and James Dewey Watson's model of the double helix structure of the molecule, published in 1953, that it caught the popular imagination—and Dalí's, as this painting shows.

The setting is a stylized Cape Creus. A 'hyperrealist' Dalí kneels on the shore with his left leg underwater and his genitals somewhat ludicrously hidden by a suspended sea urchin. Beside him, on the seabed, sleeps the same dog that had appeared in two works done in 1950. Gala's head (which does not look like her head at all) is formed of a whirl of molecules and rhinoceros horns surrounded by coloured molecules.[129] Reynolds Morse was about to buy the painting when Dalí introduced the coloured molecules, which presumably he had planned from the outset. The collector was horrified. He felt the balls added confusion and detracted 'from the impact of the great little work with Dalí kneeling there in the nude':

> I felt this was a truly super-work until the artist decided 'to crap it up'. I used those words to Dalí in declining to buy this final version, and while he pretended not to understand my bold and impetuous position, I stood my ground. At the end Gala got into the act. She said her price for the work was set so high because Dalí had spent so many

hours suffering as he kneeled in front of a mirror in the nude trying to capture his own pose.[130]

At about the time that the DNA molecules began to pullulate in his work Dalí decided that Vermeer's *The Lacemaker* was also composed of rhinos' horns, surprising the staff at the Louvre with the 'copy' they allowed him to do from the original, in which the picture became an explosion of cones. Dalí commented darkly at a later date: 'These horns being the only ones in the animal kingdom constructed in accordance with a perfect logarithmic spiral, as in this painting, it is this very logarithmic perfection that guided Vermeer's hand in painting *The Lacemaker*.'[131]

Dalí's new-found rhinomania led to a film project to take the place of *The Wheelbarrow of Flesh*. It was called *The Prodigious History of the Lacemaker and the Rhinoceros*, and to work with him Dalí used a twenty-eight-year-old French photographer from Nevers whom he had met recently in Paris, Robert Descharnes. Several scenes of the film were shot between 1954 and 1961, one of them at Vincennes Zoo (where a reluctant rhinoceros was encouraged unsuccessfully to charge a reproduction of *The Lacemaker*), but it was never finished. Over these years Robert Descharnes increasingly gained the confidence of Dalí and Gala, took more than 18,000 pictures of the couple and began to study the painter's life and work. Years later he was to become the Dalís' last secretary.[132]

Dalí made sure that he obtained the maximum publicity for his rhinomania. On 17 December 1955 he arrrived at the Sorbonne in an open Rolls Royce filled with cauliflowers to deliver a lecture entitled 'Phenomenological Aspects of the Paranoiac-Critical Method'. It was one of the most brilliant performances of his career, and the students loved his closely argued thesis that cauliflowers, sunflowers and rhino backsides share a common morphology based on logarithmic spirals.[133] One of those present praised Dalí's ability as a debunker. 'We badly need superior entertainers to enable us to laugh at our familiar gods,' wrote Alain Jouffroy.[134]

Dalí said later how amused he had been, as a result of his further investigations, to learn that the rhino takes its time over copulation—an hour and half to be precise. He had also discovered that (like himself) the beast has a marked anal fixation and is given to studying its stools. Over the next few years Dalí got up to other rhino antics, was photographed by Philippe Halsman deep in conversation with one of the creatures and even thought of launching a review with Albert Skira called . . . *Rhinocéros*.[135]

New Players

The mid-fifties saw the arrival on the Dalinian scene of three people who, in different ways, were to play significant roles in the painter's life.

The first was Isidor Bea, a forty-five-year-old scenery designer from Torres del Segre, in the province of Lleida. Bea had studied art and scenography in Barcelona, and after the civil war (which he never liked to talk about) worked for the stage designer Francesc Pou before setting up his own studio with two associates. He was employed by all the leading Barcelona theatres and acquired a considerable reputation. In the summer of 1955 he received an unexpected commission: to paint a ceiling in Palamós based on a small picture by Salvador Dalí. When Dalí was invited to view the result he was greatly impressed, the more so when they told him that it had only taken Bea one day, and he asked to be introduced.

Bea was just the person that Dalí needed at a time when he was planning a series of large-scale paintings, for, as a scenographer, he was used to laying out theatrical backdrops and had an unerring eye for perspective. Moreover he was affable, discreet, totally reliable and highly industrious. So Dalí determined to engage him. There was some initial haggling by Gala, but an agreement was reached. It was the beginning of a collaboration that was to last for thirty years. Soon Bea was helping Dalí to map out his giant *The Last Supper*. To make the task easier, a special pulley was installed in Port Lligat which enabled the canvas to be raised and lowered through a crack in the floor to the eye-level height that Dalí required. Thanks to Bea, the painting, which measured 167 x 295 cm, was finished before the Dalís returned to New York that autumn.[136]

'I'm a painter from birth but a stage painter,' Bea said shortly before his death:

> In Barcelona they taught us classical painting, you know, all the tricks, the basic rules for different styles and, of course, perspective. Particularly perspective, and the technique of how to blow up a small picture into a huge one. For me this became a purely mechanical matter. Quite straightforward. It wasn't easy for me at first to adapt to Señor Dalí, though—he had a very strong personality, a very contradictory personality. But we were soon getting along well. When he was with me he was always perfectly normal, but the moment a journalist arrived he would begin to put on a show.

Bea soon realized that Dalí and Gala functioned like a limited company. 'It had taken them a long time to achieve success, and having done so they weren't going to give anything away to anyone else. That's the way they were. They took me on as an assistant and by God I worked hard. I was a sort of robot imbued with the spirit of Dalí.' The first summer Bea lived at the nearby Hotel Port Lligat, but then Dalí did up a shack for him next door. He was expected to slave, like Dalí, from dawn to dusk, and the painter only grudgingly allowed him Sundays off when Bea insisted that he was a practising Catholic and was obliged to go to mass and to rest.[137]

By the time Bea began to work for Dalí the painter had met Peter Moore, who later became his secretary. Moore was born in London in 1919. His father, John Moore, an Irishman from Cork, was a tunnel engineer with Vickers Armstrong, and worked on the Continent. His mother was Liverpool Irish. When Moore was young the family alternated between Ostend and Nice. An only child, he got on well with his father, who was

Dalí with Reynolds Morse and Peter Moore at the opening of the former's Dalí museum in Cleveland, March 1971.

something of a character, and would always be grateful to him for insisting that he become fluent in French. 'If you acquire perfect French you'll be two people, and you'll earn twice as much,' he used to say. Moore took him at his word but went one better: by the age of ten he not only spoke French like a native but excellent Italian, thanks to an Italian maid who worked for them in Nice, and some Flemish.

When he was fourteen, and attending a private school in Nice, Peter Moore lost both his parents in a car crash. Since his father and mother had no brothers or sisters, the orphan was looked after by a guardian, Mr Watkins. And when, in 1938, aged almost twenty, he joined the British army's Royal Corps of Signals, he found his second home. He loved it. 'The army made me self-reliant, tough. I owe everything to the army. Without the war I'd probably have spent my life working in an Irish pub.' With his parents dead, no relatives, no fiancée and no ties, Signalman Moore was free to devote his energies fully to the army.

He did so with great success. His totally fluent French (he could easily pass himself off as a Frenchman) was of particular interest to the Signals Corps, and in no time, with the coming of the war, he was a corporal. In 1940 he went to Cherbourg with the British Expeditionary Force and was made a lance sergeant. Then, in 1942, came the landing in Algiers, where Moore was commissioned as a second lieutenant. Soon afterwards he was enlisted in Psychological Warfare, 'a strange outfit half civilian, half military, Britain's answer to the Germans' Propagandastaffe. It was the political wing of the army. The whole thing was very complicated because in Britain, of course, the army's not meant to meddle in politics.' Moore's boss was Duff Cooper, the Minister of Information. He claims to have been involved in secret, and often dangerous, missions about which he prefers not to talk, and was surprised when one of Dalí's biographers discovered years later that at one point he worked for the top-secret 61st Teleprint Operating Unit.[138]

In the course of his work in Psychological Warfare Moore sometimes reported directly to Winston Churchill, and seems to have been appreciated by the warlord for, when he was discharged in 1946, Churchill put in a good word for him with Sir Alexander Korda, the head of London Films, an organization that was in part a front for espionage activities in Europe. Korda interviewed him in London, telling him that 'they' had spoken very highly of him, and offered him the job of heading London Films International in Rome, with a salary of £150 a week (astronomical in those days), plus a house and a car. Moore accepted on the spot and thus was launched into the world of films, running the organization, he says, 'along military lines'.

Moore's discharge notification from the War Office, dated 1 November 1946, informed him that, under the terms of Army Order 128 of 1945, he was to be granted the honorary rank of captain, a notification to this effect appearing in the *London Gazette* (supplement) dated 22 November 1946. From this moment Moore would always style himself Captain, confident that a reminder to the world that he was a British military man of some distinction would increase his chances of entrepreneurial success. In this he was almost certainly right, the effect being enhanced by an upper-crust accent so redolent of the army that no one could ever have suspected that his father was an Irishman with a marked brogue.

In 1955 Korda was making *Richard III* with Laurence Olivier in the lead role, and decided to commission Dalí to do a portrait of the actor for publicity purposes. The painting was executed that May in London, where Dalí stayed at Claridges. Dalí demanded his £10,000 fee in Italian money, which was difficult because of exchange controls, and Korda said that he should talk to his man in Rome. Peter Moore had never heard of Dalí, and was lunching with Orson Welles the day the painter introduced himself. When he handed over the money, Dalí said he had a request. Korda had told him

Dalí painting Laurence Olivier during the shooting of Richard III, *1955.*

that Moore could get him privately to the Pope. Would he be so kind? At the time Moore was supervising the installation of a French closed-circuit TV system in the Vatican and had got to know the Pope (who was intrigued by television) quite well. It was easy to arrange the meeting. In 1949 Dalí had been granted only ten minutes. Now he talked with the off-duty Pacelli for two hours. The following day he expressed surprise that the 'audience' had not been reported in the *Osservatore Romano.* Moore recalls: 'I said to him, "Do you think that every time the Pope talks to his cook or his electrician it gets into the papers? If you want an official audience, do it through the Spanish Embassy!"'[139]

Man of the world, raconteur, buccaneer and bon viveur, the dapper Peter Moore impressed Dalí, not least on account of his military background.

The other person who entered Dalí's life at this time was a woman. In February 1955 Dalí and Gala attended the annual charity ball given by the Knickerbockers in New York. It was a very select affair: to get invited you had to be either rich, famous or beautiful. Many of the guests were all three. During the evening Dalí suddenly found himself staring across the room at a stunning blonde in a red evening gown. She had the tall, stately, curvaceous body that Spaniards call *escultural*, 'sculptural'. Unable to take his eyes off the vision, he finally got to his feet and made his way across the room. 'I am Dalí,' he said. 'I want to see you every day for the rest of my life. Who are you?'

The woman in red's reply left him speechless—a rare condition for the Dalí that few people could now have suspected of having any problems with timidity. For it turned out that not only was she Spanish (a possibility that had not crossed Dalí's mind), with the exotic name of Nanita Kalaschnikoff, but that she had been born in the Puerta del Sol, only a few paces from the San Fernando Royal Academy and Special School in the centre of Madrid. And there was something even more amazing. Nanita revealed that she was the daughter of a hugely famous, and wealthy, writer of semi-pornographic novels, José María Carretero, whose books had sold in their tens of thousands in the 1920s and 1930s and were read by Dalí, behind his father's back, when he was in his teens.

Carretero, who had died in 1951, was from Montilla, in Andalusia, and wrote under the pseudonym of El Caballero Audaz, 'The Man who Dares'. And daring he certainly was, in his life as well as in his writing. A giant by Spanish standards (he measured well over six feet), he was already a celebrity in both Spain and South America by the time Dalí arrived in Madrid in 1922, and enjoyed a great, and deserved, reputation for womanizing, duelling and practical jokes. It is said that when he entered a room swirling his Madrid cape, the ladies almost swooned and their partners paled with anxiety. Carretero was also well known for his interviews with famous personalities in the Madrid press. In his memoirs, Luis Buñuel calls him 'a novelist of the lowest kind',[140] but this did not prevent the film director from drawing without acknowledgement on one of his books, *La bien pagada* ('The Well-Paid Woman'), in *Belle de jour*.[141]

Dalí simply could not believe that Nanita Kalaschnikoff was the daughter of a writer whose stories had given him sexual kicks as a schoolboy. In one of them, he once recalled, the woman's body, when penetrated, 'made a noise like a watermelon being opened with a fork. And I said to myself: "If I have to open a hole in a watermelon with this little thing of mine I'll never be able to do it!"'[142]

Nanita's father had wanted to call her Ambarina because of her pale skin and blonde hair, but the ecclesiastical authorities had refused. So The Man who Dares had named her María Fernanda, after his lover at the time, the actress María Fernanda Ladrón de Guevara ('Nanita' was a diminutive of Fernanda).

In 1931, at the advent of the Spanish Republic, Nanita's father, a passionate monarchist and anti-democrat, had decided that he could not live in the Spain from which Alfonso XIII had just gone into exile. Moreover he thought he had killed a celebrated aristocrat, the Conde de los Andes, in a recent duel (his thirteenth to date). So he took himself and his family hastily to Paris. Nanita was then seven. She was put into a French school and soon spoke the language fluently. Meanwhile, Carretero and his wife had separated: she found it impossible to put up with his constant infidelities.

As a beautiful teenager, Nanita Carretero caught the eye of a French artist called Jean-Gabriel Domergue who, having failed commercially as a landscape painter, was now turning his hand to the world of fashion. Nanita began to model for him, featured in many of his paintings and thus was launched into the world of haute couture, art and good living through which she was to sail happily for the rest of her life. Fêted, adulated, adored, pursued, she soon became aware, as she once said, of the justice of the French dictum 'le destin c'est dans l'anatomie' ('anatomy is destiny'). 'One of my teachers at the Institut was Simone de Beauvoir,' she recalled. 'I often thought I'd like to be a writer, but I was made to feel so special because of my looks that I was never left alone.'[143]

When Nanita Carretero met Dalí at the Knickerbockers' ball she had been married for ten years to Michel Kalaschnikoff, an amiable Russian educated in England who worked for Winston's, the jewellers, in New York, and was the mother of three daughters. She did not warm to Dalí at the ball ('I thought he was just a crazy Spaniard acting the fool') but nonetheless he was Dalí, so she agreed to see him the following day. The second meeting went better. Dalí was soon crazy about Nanita, and almost every afternoon until he left for Europe a few months later he would pick her up at work (Lilly Daché's popular cosmetics establishment on Fifty-Sixth Street). Because of her regal bearing (accentuated by a majestic nose) Dalí soon nicknamed Nanita 'Louis XIV' or, simply, 'Le Roi'. Her husband put up with it all goodhumouredly.

Gala, surprised by what was happening, soon decided that the beautiful newcomer posed a threat to her relationship with Dalí and suspected that Nanita was getting tired of her husband. But this was not the case. Gala was also jealous to start with because, given their years in Madrid, Nanita and Dalí shared a whole area of experience from which she was barred. The two exulted in each other's company, certainly, chattering non-stop about Spain and singing snatches of their favourite Spanish operettas together (they both knew all the words by heart). They were delighted to discover, morover, that their eyes were almost exactly the same colour, greyish-green. 'Dalí called it a symbiosis, and we always joked about the coincidence together,' Nanita recalled. Another coincidence was that they had both had to put up with difficult fathers.[144]

Dalí was struck by the fact that Nanita, although born in Madrid, felt herself to be deeply Andalusian, having spent her childhood holidays at her father's home in Montilla. He often talked to her about Lorca, whom he had failed signally to visit in

Granada despite the poet's constant invitations, telling her he was the greatest friend of his youth, and together they would recite lines from his poems. Whenever Dalí sold a painting, he said, he would raise his eyes to heaven and thank Federico, whom he felt sure had just put in a good word for him. There can be no doubt that Dalí grew to love Nanita Kalaschnikoff, insofar as he was capable of loving anyone, nor that she soon became vital to his well-being. Nanita, too, came to feel deep affection for the 'real' Dalí, the private man, the engaging person hiding under the onion-layers of disguise. The relationship was never overtly sexual but it contained a degree of erotic complicity that the painter failed to achieve with Gala. Nanita was not only immensely likeable and sociable but sexually uninhibited. And she had no qualms about posing naked for Dalí. 'She played an important part, she was the woman Dalí would really have liked to marry,' Peter Moore has said emphatically. 'And of course, unlike Gala, she was active, she participated in his little games, which Gala always refused to do.'[145]

The Albarettos

In April 1956, while returning to Europe on the SS *America*, Dalí dashed off a tiny opuscule in French entitled *Les cocus du vieil art moderne* (*The Cuckolds of Old Modern Art*), a compendium of the ideas developed in his lectures and pamphlets of the previous six years. The thesis was that all modern painting, or almost all, was rubbish, and that only an art capable of expressing the discovery of the 'discontinuity of matter' was now valid. Dalí's art, that is. The text was published later in the year in Paris, fleshed out with the 1933 Gaudí-championing article which Dalí considered one of his major contributions to criticism, 'On the Terrifying and Edible Beauty of "Modern Style" Architecture'. After a short spell in Paris the Dalís returned to Spain where, on 16 June, the painter had his first interview with General Franco. The meeting took place at El Pardo, the dictator's official residence outside Madrid, and went off well. No doubt Dalí thanked Franco effusively for the decree protecting Port Lligat and its surroundings from tourist development that had been issued by the government a few years earlier. Then, having ingratiated himself with the Caudillo, he hurried home to begin his usual summer stint of hard work.[146]

It so happened that at this time two doctors from Turin, Giuseppe and Mara Albaretto, were holidaying in Llansà, just around the corner from Cadaqués. There they got to know the art critic Rafael Santos Torroella and his wife Maite, who by now were frequent visitors to Dalí's house. When the Albarettos discovered that the couple knew the painter, and were about to go and see him, they begged to be taken along. It was love

Dalí with Maite and Rafael Santos Torroella, Port Lligat, 1954.

at first sight, at least where the Albarettos were concerned, and they bought a drawing there and then. Dalí took to their little daughter, Cristiana (and she to him), and invited them back the following day. Thus began an adventure that almost exactly paralleled that on which Reynolds and Eleanor Morse had embarked in 1943. The Santos Torroellas saw it happen before their eyes: within months the Turin doctors had become Dalí collectors. Over the following years Dalí began to treat them as his 'Italian family'.[147]

The Albarettos' money proceeded mainly, it seems, from Mara, whose father was a rich industrialist from Imperia. Or did it? Giuseppe Albaretto's first vocation had been for the priesthood. Educated by the Salesians, one day he had seen a film about missionaries and decided he wanted to follow their example and save souls. But he was an only son, his parents did not want to lose him and finally the Order persuaded him that his calling would be better professed 'in the world'. So he took a degree in dentistry, and practised for two years. But this was not his vocation either. Then he became financial adviser to the Salesians, involving himself particularly in the Order's educational publishing sector. There he made money.[148]

Giuseppe Albaretto, fiery, sentimental and generous, was every Anglo-Saxon's idea of the archetypal Italian, and as passionate about his Catholicism as he was about everything else. Not to be taken in by Dalí's 'nuclear mysticism', he decided to put his frustrated vocation as a missionary in the service of winning the Maestro's soul for God. As for Gala, he considered her lost to the Church. Mara was cast in a quieter mould than her husband, although she could stand up for herself when the occasion demanded it. Soon the Albarettos were in close attendance upon the Dalís, wherever they happened to be in Europe. 'When we first met Dalí he had no dealer looking after the promotion and sale of his work,' Mara Albaretto has recalled, 'and the truth is that he was far better known in America than in Europe. We were lucky to meet him when we did. There was simply no serious competition and his work was really very reasonably priced.'[149]

Behind Dalí's back, and particularly Gala's, the Albarettos became friends of Anna Maria Dalí, as the Morses had done, and bought several of the paintings and drawings by Salvador in her collection at their father's death. 'Anna Maria always needed money,' Mara Albaretto remembers. As a rule the transactions were handled by the Sala Gaspard in Barcelona, 'because Anna Maria didn't want to be seen to be selling'.[150] Among the Albarettos' major purchases from her were the 1926 *Still Life (Invitation to Sleep)*, featuring Lorca's head, and a charming portrait of Anna Maria herself, from 1925.[151]

VIII

More Giant Paintings

In November 1956, as the Catalan autumn began to turn chilly, the Dalís followed their migratory instinct and set off on their annual jaunt to New York. As usual, Dalí had organized a full programme for his brief stop-over in Paris. This year it included further work on his and Robert Descharnes's film *The Prodigious History of the Lacemaker and the Rhinoceros*, and some publicity stunts connected with the fifteen lithographs commissioned by Joseph Forêt for his edition of *Don Quixote*. For these Dalí employed a mixed technique that included filling an egg with ink and breaking it over the stones, scratching the latter with two rhino horns dipped in ink, and firing nails at the stones from a blunderbuss. The latter invention he termed Bulletism, and there is a photograph of Max Ernst looking on with some apprehension while Dalí takes aim.[152]

A fortnight later Dalí was in New York. There *The Last Supper* was in the news because it had been bought by the millionaire Chester Dale, perhaps the leading collector of French Impressionists in America. For Dale, Salvador Dalí meant a major departure. In 1954 he had been so 'bowled over' by *Corpus Hypercubus* that he had acquired it for the Metropolitan Museum of Art.[153] Now he donated *The Last Supper* to the National Gallery of Art in Washington. There, in November 1956, the huge canvas was scrutinized by Paul Tillich. The distinguished theologian thought the work sentimental and trite, and was quoted as saying that Jesus looked like a 'very good athlete on an American baseball team'. The painting was to cause embarrassment to a series of curators at the museum, and eventually was moved to an inconspicuous position in the collection. According to Sherman Lee, one-time head of the Cleveland Museum of Art, it was 'the most overrated individual work' in an American museum.[154] As for Dalí's view of the painting, he told Alain Bosquet in 1965 that more postcards of it were sold than of all the works by Leonardo Da Vinci and Raphael put together. This proved that his 'strategy' had triumphed, since his purpose in works such as this was to demonstrate that he was capable of painting the most popular pictures in the world.[155]

Dalí had now begun another giant painting, *Saint James the Great* (400 x 300 cm), representing the apostle and patron saint of Spain whose shrine at Santiago de Compostela was the goal of one of medieval Europe's most famous pilgrimages. Today in the Beaverbrook Art Gallery in Fredericton, Canada, the painting, which was finished in 1957, shows a naked Saint James rising from the sea on a horse apparently propelled by atomic power to help the Spanish Christians in their struggle against the invading Moors. The steed is surely the most disproportioned and ungainly ever painted by Dalí, while the athletic Christ soaring upwards with outstretched arms towards the dome of Heaven (carefully mapped out by Isidor Bea) is a piece of the merest kitsch.

Saint James the Great was followed by *The Discovery of America by Christopher Columbus* (1958–9), which had been commissioned by Huntington Hartford, heir to the A & P grocery empire, perhaps because the art gallery he was building in New York City was situated at 2, Columbus Circle. Uppermost in Dalí's mind while he painted it was the approaching tercentenary, in 1960, of the death of Velázquez. The standards that fill the right side of the vast work (410 x 284 cm) echo the twenty-eight lances in *The Surrender of Breda*, and Dalí said that the hole in the centre of the upper sail of Columbus's ship was a reference to that of the key in Velázquez's painting—the key to Breda that is handed by Justinus of Nassau, the Flemish leader, to the Spanish conquerors.[156]

Dalí was convinced, or convinced himself that he was convinced, that Columbus was not only a Catalan but from Girona.[157] There are allusions to Girona in the canvas, therefore, the town being symbolized by its patron, Saint Narcissus, who can be seen at the bottom left of the work. The presence of the cliffs of Creus in the upper left-hand corner could be similarly justified (if Dalí needed any such justification). Isidor Bea, seen from behind, was the model for the saint, an acknowledgement, no doubt, of the vital

XXXVII

part he was now playing in the production of this and other similarly large-scale canvases.[158]

Since the Spaniards took Catholicism to the New World, the theme of the 'Discovery' enabled Dalí to include yet another portrait of Gala in the role of the Virgin Mary, this time figuring on a banner as the Immaculate Conception. Dalí also quoted once more *The Christ of Saint John of the Cross*, and he himself is the balding and moustachioed personage who kneels on the shore holding aloft a heavy silver crucifix. Dalí and Gala had every reason to be grateful to America, of course. It had showered them with dollars, and, with commissions like this, was continuing to do so. As Dalí worked on the painting he must surely have remembered that, despite opening up the New World, Columbus had died in poverty. Dalí had said many times, and would continue to do so, that *he* had no intention of ending up the same way.

The previous summer in Port Lligat, Reynolds Morse had had the 'temerity' to object that the sea urchin in the foreground of the picture surrounded by rings was too ponderous and should be left out. Dalí was extremely irritated by the remark. There could be no question of removing it! 'In "le Columbus" myself is paint one very klar record of somesing que is no appen yet . . . If you is no like-ee "le Columbus" is only necessary que you is wait and see. Sue-dently-you is realize she is becoming le most important verk of me life!'[159] What had not 'appen' yet? When the painting went on show Dalí explained that the pear shape of the ringed urchin alluded to the earth as seen from the American spaceship Explorer, and symbolized 'nuclear science'.[160] Some years later he went further and boasted that the urchin heralded the launching of the first satellite two years afterwards.[161] Eleanor Morse decided in 1971 that Dalí had taken literally John Kennedy's promise that America would land a man on the moon within a decade, and that the sea urchin was an advance celebration of the great event that was to occur on 21 June 1969. But, even if she was right, this does not make the painting prophetic, merely opportunistic.[162]

The Heavenly Twins

One other noteworthy personage was making his mark on Dalí's life by this time, the psychoanalyst and student of mythology Pierre Roumeguère. Between 1954 and 1958 Dalí had frequent conversations in Paris with this man, whom he later called his 'favourite psychiatrist'.[163] The conversations were recorded onto a machine (but never published). Whether they began on the initiative of Roumeguère or of Dalí is not clear, although the doctor's written observations on his 'patient', as he referred to Dalí in inverted commas on one occasion,[164] reveal such an unconditional reverence for the man and the artist that one suspects the proposal may have come from him. The earliest of these observations are contained in a short paper, 'Dalinian Mysticism in the Light of the History of Religions', which shows Roumeguère's fervent admiration for the *Secret Life*, which he terms 'an incomparable document and an authentic gold mine, certainly, for the devotees of humour, for psychiatrists and also for psychologists and aesthetes who feel an interest in understanding the mechanisms of artistic creation . . . a portentous human document from every point of view, comparable in scientific importance to that of President Schreiber, the celebrated mystical paranoiac that we are told about by Freud'.[165]

On 5 June 1958 Roumeguère read Dalí the thesis in which he argued that he and Gala were the reincarnation of the myth of the Dioscuri, Castor and Pollux, 'born of one of the divine eggs of Leda'[166] (with Gala in the role of the mortal Castor, taking over that of the first Salvador, and Dalí in that of the immortal Pollux). Dalí described the occasion a few years later to Alain Bosquet:

> For the first time in my life I experienced, with incomparable shudders, the absolute truth about myself: a pschoanalytic thesis had revealed the drama that was at the very basis of the tragic structure of my personality. It was a question of the unavoidable presence, in the depths of my being, of my dead brother, who was so hugely loved by my parents that when I was born they gave me his name, Salvador. The shock was terrible, like that of a revelation. It explains, moreover, the terrors that assailed me every time I entered my parents' bedroom and saw the photograph of my dead brother: a very beautiful child, bedecked in delicate lace, whose picture had been so prettified that, by way of contrast, I would spend the whole night imagining this ideal brother in a state of total putrefaction. I could go to sleep only by thinking about my own death and accepting that I was in a coffin, finally at rest. Thanks to Pierre Roumeguère, I have been able to prove that an archetypal myth like that of Castor and Pollux has for me a sense of visceral reality.[167]

Roumeguère's subsequent writings on Dalí show that, where the death of the first Salvador was concerned, he had swallowed whole the inaccurate version provided in the *Secret Life*, and no doubt repeated to him verbally by Dalí. He accepts uncritically that the first Salvador died of meningitis at the age of seven, three and a half years before the birth of the future painter, when in fact he died nine months before the birth of Salvador II at the age of twenty-two months; that the two were mirror images, the first Salvador being 'the double and identical twin of the other'; and that the parents had committed an unconscious crime in giving Salvador the same name as his dead brother.[168] He even invents a maternal voice which warned Dalí that, if he didn't wrap himself up well in a muffler, he'd catch cold and die of meningitis like his brother.[169] It is clear, moreover, that despite four years of conversations, Dalí had not told the psychoanalyst about the suicide of his grandfather, Gal, nor of his fears that he might have inherited a paranoid tendency. Roumeguère's conclusion is surely grotesque: 'Dalí remained truly identified with a real dead twin; he scarcely lived, at the most he survived, on the verge of madness toward which he lucidly felt himself wending his way during the beautiful summer of 1929 in Cadaques.'[170]

Then, of course, came Gala, the therapeutic miracle, to rescue Dalí from the internalized ghost of his dead brother, to heal his 'psychosis' (Roumeguère's word).[171] Before the French doctor appeared, Dalí had already decided that he and Gala were the heavenly twins, as *Leda Atomica* and his comments on the picture demonstrate. He didn't need Roumeguère to tell him this. But the confirmation carried tremendous weight for him, coming as it did from a 'learned man'.[172] Roumeguère's thesis about the first Salvador dovetailed into the scheme perfectly. Gala had taken the place of Castor, cast out the spectre and restored harmony. She was Dalí's 'exact replica', as the first Salvador had been; his 'living female twin'.[173]

It was all very neat and tidy—and very flawed. Roumeguère claimed that the revelation of the 'secret' came as a great liberation to Dalí, and that for several years, in a state of 'jubilant exultation', he told everyone about it.[174] The last was true, certainly: Dalí told *everyone*. As regards his liberation, however, we can be more sceptical. Roumeguère's main achievement, arguably, was to furnish Dalí with a convincing diagnosis of his aberrant behaviour before he met Gala, behaviour for which he need now take even less responsibility than he had done before. After all, how could Dalí be held to blame if he wasn't yet himself, but, rather, a nebulous, insubstantial version of his dead brother— the brother whose death was symbolized by Velázquez's *Christ*, a reproduction of which hung on the wall of the parental bedroom alongside a photograph of the first Salvador? It could be maintained that, far from helping to liberate Dalí, Roumeguère's 'revelation' only served to strengthen the walls of his mental prison.

On the wave of enthusiasm provoked by Roumeguère's 'discovery', Dalí decided that, six years after the death of Paul Éluard, it was now time for him and Gala to be married by the Church. The ceremony took place on 8 August 1958, in the strictest intimacy (presumably because the intensely private Gala insisted), at the mountain sanctuary of Our Lady of the Angels, not far from Girona at Sant Martí Vell. Gala and Dalí drove first to Girona (with Gala at the wheel), where three chaplains climbed aboard the Cadillac and some adversaries scribbled 'Picasso is better than Dalí' on the windows. At the sanctuary the group was awaited by Francesc Vilà i Torrent, parish priest of Fornells de la Selva, who officiated. There were no photographers, no reporters. It was something of a miracle. The following day Dalí's friend, the Figueres photographer Meli, took an official picture of the couple in their wedding-day finery.[175]

Dalí's industry in promoting himself and his produce continued unabated as the decade moved to a close, each winter exhibition in New York being the occasion for the latest novelty. In December 1958 the catalogue to his show at the Carstairs Gallery contained an 'Anti-Matter Manifesto' in which he proclaimed that he had finally abandoned his exploration of the unconscious. Anti-matter and only anti-matter now concerned him! This was also the gist of *The Cuckolds of Old New Art*, the American publication of which was timed to coincide with the show. One of the paintings at Carstairs was *The Sistine Madonna* (also known as *Ear with Madonna*), which had been inspired by a photograph of John XXIII.[176] Seen close up, Dalí explained, it looked like an abstract picture; seen from six feet it became Raphael's *Sistine Madonna*; and from forty-five it metamorphozed into the ear of an angel. It was painted, he explained, 'with anti-matter: therefore with pure energy'. It was painted, certainly, with hundreds of dots. But did it amount to more than yet another Dalinian visual trick? As her eye roved over it and the other exhibits, and was assailed by flurries of pi-mesons and protons, the French critic Margaret Breuning had her doubts.[177]

Now that Dalí had married Gala it was clearly time for another papal audience. Moreover Dalí approved of John XXIII, not only because of his interesting ears but on account of his plans for the Ecumenical Council. The audience took place on 2 May 1959 in an appropriate blaze of publicity. Dalí told the Pope about the commission he had received to design a cathedral for the Arizona desert. In tune with the times he had plumped for an 'ecumenical' one that would 'float' thirty centimetres above the ground on a cushion of tar. The building would be in the shape of a pear since in the Middle Ages, Dalí explained, the fruit symbolized the Resurrection and the moral unity of the world that were now to be represented by the forthcoming Ecumenical Council. Pope John's response to the chimerical project is not known.[178]

That same summer Dalí came up with some more novel ideas when he was commissioned to supply three illustrations and the cover for Joseph Forêt's one-copy edition of *The Apocalypse of Saint John*, billed as the most expensive book in the world. They included exploding a nail-bomb against a copper plate and the flattening by a steamroller of a Singer sewing machine onto another. All these operations were, of course, carried out in the full view of the media. And they were beginning to get on a lot of people's nerves.[179]

The year ended with Dalí's presentation in Paris of the prototype of his newest invention, the Ovocipède, a revolutionary mode of personal transport which consisted of a transparent plastic sphere, 1 metre 40 centimetres in diameter, that was propelled by the mere pressure on the floor of the driver's foot. The advantage of the contraption was that it not only got you from place to place but did so while giving you the feeling that you had returned to the womb. The stunt had been arranged by Forêt to promote *The Apocalypse of Saint John*. Dalí arrived dressed as a spaceman, and Josephine Baker and Martine Carol were in attendance later for added publicity. That Dalí could maintain his Buster Keaton straight face on occasions such as this is difficult to credit, but he did. He was by now such a consummate showman that he could go through with the most ludicrous performances without batting an eyelid. Shame, at least in its external manifestations, had been severely put to rout.[180]

The Captain Takes the Helm

Ever since George Keller of the Bignou Gallery had retired in 1948, Gala had been handling Dalí's sales by herself, strictly on a cash basis. But as Dalí's fame continued to grow and the commissions to multiply, it was becoming increasingly difficult to cope. Clearly the Dalís needed a professional business manager. But who? As 1959 drew to a close Dalí decided to contact Peter Moore.

Sir Alexander Korda had died in January 1956 and with him London Films. It took Moore four years to wind up the Italian part of the operation. Lord Bernstein offered him a job in television, but he turned it down on realizing that he would be expected to take a course in Manchester. Peter Moore did not wish to go back to school. During these years he never lost touch completely with Dalí and, in early 1960, the painter sent him a first-class TWA ticket and summoned him to New York, where he explained that he wanted him to become his business manager and 'military adviser'. 'Dalí said that every South American banana republic had a military adviser and that, since he was much more important than they were, he deserved one too,' Moore laughs.[1] The terms were that he would not receive a salary for running Dalí's affairs but take a 10 per cent commission on all the deals he generated. These were to include everything except the sale of original paintings and drawings, which were Gala's preserve: sculpture, ties, shirts, shoes, perfumes, aeroplane decoration, jigsaw puzzles and anything else Moore could think up.[2]

Peter Moore immediately accepted the offer, and claims that that first weekend he did business for Dalí worth $500,000: 'I thought to myself, my God, I'm sitting on a pile of gold. And so it turned out to be.' Moore has an impressive gift of the gab inherited from

Chapter THIRTEEN

his Irish father, and the sum quoted may be an exaggeration. Or it may not. He says he was surprised to discover that both Gala and Dalí were strongly anti-semitic, and that they had alienated the New York Jewish dealers. In Moore's view that was very foolish indeed. The dealers had ganged up against Dalí, and his paintings were not fetching the prices they deserved. Moore decided he would soon put that right. Before long he conceived of his mission as 'amplifying' Dalí's talent—and multiplying the Master's income proportionately.[3]

Reynolds Morse, somewhat anti-semitic himself, had also noted Dalí's problems with New York's Jewish dealers. But he ascribed them to a different cause. Writing in 1973 he reflected that during the past two decades 'such factors as predominance of powerful Jewish money and personalities in many sectors of the arts could not be mentioned'. That predominance had resulted, in Morse's view, 'in a prolonged discrimination against Dalí as a Catholic in favour of Picasso, who kept religion off his easel'. The charge was ludicrous. If New York's Jewish dealers did not want to hear of Dalí, it was because he had offended them by his anti-semitic remarks, not because he professed to be a Roman Catholic. What did they care about his religion?[*]

Peter Moore soon formed a very poor opinion of Gala's handling of the sale of Dalí's paintings and drawings. She was a 'lousy dealer' who habitually sold to the wrong people at the wrong price, he writes in his unpublished memoir, *Soft Watches and Hard Times*. She was ripped off time and again, with disastrous results.[5]

The arrangement the Dalís made with the captain encouraged him to find more and more ways in which to earn his 10 per cent commission. What Moore hit on above all was the multiples market, which was beginning to boom in the early 1960s 'under the pressure', wrote Reynolds Morse in 1971, 'of an immense demand for works by a few of the most famous artists which far exceeded the supply'. At this time, according to Morse, 'a promoter persuaded Dalí to sign a haughty declaration that a common reproduction, when blessed with his signature, should become transposed in value to that of an original etching or lithograph just because the artistic content was the same'. Presumably the promoter in question was Peter Moore. What the declaration meant in practice was that Dalí was prepared to facilitate an original watercolour for reproduction by whatever method the publisher chose but without himself intervening. A limited edition would then be run off and Dalí would sign each copy. If these reproductions were then sold as 'original works', as often happened, it was fraud. Either way the door had been opened to deceit on a massive scale.[6]

It was the beginning of the slippery slope down which Dalí's reputation as a serious artist was to slide with alarming rapidity, and with his consent, as the decade progressed. The process was fuelled by Gala's greed: all that counted was cash in the hand, up front, and as much as possible. In the 1940s Dalí had earned good money producing rubbishy ads for the likes of Bryan Hosiery. Now, twenty years later and much more famous, he was in a position to make a fortune thanks not only to his on-going commercial advertising, from Jack Winters sportswear to Lanvin chocolates, but, particularly, to the new reproduction technology.

The Dalís habitually insisted on cash deals and no questions asked, taking huge risks in their blatant scorn for the laws of the United States, France and Spain, between which countries they moved constantly. Perhaps Gala used the eyes that penetrated walls to demolish the resistences of customs officers as she stalked through the 'nothing to declare' areas of the three countries, carrying huge wads of foreign currency in her bags. Reynolds Morse was party to this practice, knowing that, if he did not pay in banknotes, he would not get his pictures. 'Rest assured,' he tells us, recalling a payment made in 1965, '$100,000 in pesetas was a heavy bundle which I helped Gala stuff into her luggage!'[7]

Since the Dalís had little in the way of professional ethics, they tended to corrupt everyone they dealt with. Moreover this was part of Dalí's programme, as he stated over and over again: to cretinize the world. If people allowed themselves to be ensnared, that was their fault.

Peter Moore claims that during his first seven years with Dalí his 10 per cent commission brought him in $230,000 tax free per annum, and $1,000,000 during the next five as the multiples market soared. By his own account he ended up as a millionaire many times over thanks to his handling of the Dalís' affairs and to his related dealings.[8]

In February 1960, just as Peter Moore was getting into his stride as Dalí's 'military adviser', *The Discovery of America by Christopher Columbus* was shown privately at French and Company's in New York, pending the opening of Huntington Hartford's Gallery of Modern Art. By March it had been seen by more than seven hundred visitors. The critics were not impressed by the gigantic canvas. One museum director thought that it set painting back a hundred years, and the general feeling was that it represented yet one more Dalinian exercise in High Kitsch. Huntington Hartford, however, was pleased: the work exceeded his 'greatest expectations'.[9]

XXXVII

One of the first publishing deals which Moore handled was Joseph Forêt's edition of *The Divine Comedy*, with wood engravings of the 101 watercolour illustrations which Dalí had recovered from the Italian government. Dalí, however, brags in *The Diary of a Genius* that it was he himself who persuaded Forêt to pay him double the money he had received from the Italians.[10] The illustrations were exhibited at the Palais Galliera when the book was published in May 1960. Dalí enjoyed the vernissage and the adulation he thought he perceived all around him: 'It is a very pleasant sensation, this admiration, as it flows over me in magic waves, again and again making nonsense of abstract art, which is dying of envy.'[11]

Back in Port Lligat that spring and summer, Dalí got to work on his next giant canvas, *The Ecumenical Council* (400 x 300 cm), with Isidor Bea slaving away at his side as usual. John XXIII had announced the Council on 24 January 1959, only a few months after becoming Pope. Dalí, always with an eye to the main chance and these days thoroughly determined to be topical, must have seen that the forthcoming conclave was an excellent subject for another huge picture. Into the canvas he inserted a portrait of Gala directly copied from the 1956 *Saint Helen of Port Lligat*, cleavage included. And he himself is there in the lower left-hand corner from which, in the guise of Velázquez at his easel in *Las Meninas*, he stares at us almost challengingly. At the top of the picture, hiding his face with an outstretched arm, is God the Father, depicted as a naked male figure with no penis or testicles framed within a classical arch or portico. (He has testicles in Dalí's study for the painting, *The Trinity*. Perhaps they were scrapped to avoid giving offence to potential buyers.)[12] If God's head is invisible, those of the two figures representing the Son and the Holy Ghost are there for us to behold and must surely be among the most unattractive in any of Dalí's so-called religious works. The best thing in the painting, perhaps, is the scene showing the rocks at Creus reflected in one of the cape's innumerable coves.[13]

The Ecumenical Council, finished in December 1960, was Dalí's last full-scale 'religious' work and, arguably, one of the worst paintings he had done in the genre. That same month an International Exhibition of Surrealism was organized at the D'Arcy Galleries in New York by André Breton, Marcel Duchamp, Édouard Jaguer and José Pierre. To Breton's horror, Dalí managed to persuade Duchamp, the only organizer of the foursome in New York, to allow him to hang his *Sistine Madonna* (or *Ear with Madonna*). Breton and his friends in Paris immediately published a tract protesting. Entitled 'We Don't Ear it That Way', it reproduced Gala's head from Dalí's *Assumpta Corpuscularia Lapislazulina*. In a witty take-off of Marcel Duchamp's famous caricature of the *Mona Lisa* she is wearing Dalí's moustache, and beneath her hands clasped in prayer has been affixed Duchamp's caption 'L.H.O.O.Q.' ('Elle a chaud au cul', i.e. 'She's feeling randy') with the addition, in brackets, 'as always'. The tract pointed out that Dalí had been expelled from the Surrealist movement more than twenty years earlier; and that since then the Surrealists had never been able to see him as other than 'the ex-apologist of Hitler, the Fascist, clerical and racist painter and the friend of Franco, who opened Spain as a drilling field for the worst bar-

barism ever known'.[14] Reynolds Morse and others have tended to see Breton's attitude to the post-Surrealist Dalí as merely a matter of sour grapes, of jealousy, even, because Dalí had 'succeeded' where he, the movement's founder, had 'failed'. Nothing could be further from the truth. It was a question of disgust and moral outrage.

A Dalí Museum in Figueres

On 8 November 1960, before setting off on their annual trip to Paris and New York, Dalí and Gala made joint wills. They appointed each other sole heirs. After their deaths their personal effects were to be divided equally between Cécile Éluard and Gala's sister, Lídia; all their paintings, drawings and other 'artistic creations' were to go to the Prado; and their real estate to the Fine Arts Department of the Ministry of Education in Madrid. There was no reference to Figueres, to Cadaqués or to Catalunya.[15]

A month earlier Figueres had got a new mayor, Ramon Guardiola Rovira, a lawyer and teacher from Girona who had been living in the town since 1951.[16] Guardiola was energetic, intelligent and interested in the arts. He felt it was disgraceful that the Empordà Museum in Figueres, inaugurated in 1945, did not possess a single Dalí. Nor, indeed, did any other local institution. Guardiola decided that it was his duty, as mayor, to remedy the situation.[17]

When the Dalís returned to Port Lligat the following May, Guardiola hurried down to see them. He suggested that a special room should be devoted to the painter in the Empordà Museum and that, in return, the painter should contribute some works since, in Guardiola's view, the town and the painter were mutually in debt. Soon afterwards the photographer 'Meli' (Melitón Casals Casas), whom Dalí greatly appreciated, visited Guardiola with a message from the Master. Dalí, he told him, had other plans. He wanted, not a room in the Empordà Museum, but a whole museum to himself.[18]

Guardiola returned immediately to Port Lligat, where Dalí told him that he not only wanted his own museum in Figueres but had chosen the site for it: the Teatro Principal, which had been burnt at the end of the civil war in 1939 when a contingent of Franco's Moorish soldiers bivouacked inside and carelessly set the place alight. If Figueres restored the building according to his instructions, Dalí said, he would endow it with works. Dalí had already planned in his mind, moreover, how he would launch the project. A bullfight was going to be held in his honour in Figueres that August. It would be a splendid occasion on which to announce to the media that Salvador Dalí Domènech, the Saviour of Modern Art, was to have a museum in his home town.

Guardiola was delighted. A committee was formed, and within days the operation was under way.[19]

The choice of the ruined Teatro Principal was an inspired one from every point of view, as Dalí must have realized the more he thought about it. He himself said later that the original idea had been suggested to him by the Caryatids Room at the Palazzo Reale in Milan, gutted during the war, to which his *Divine Comedy* exhibition had moved from Rome in 1954.[20] Finished in 1850, the Teatro Principal in Figueres was on the lavish scale that befitted a garrison town. From the outset the leading opera companies performing at the Liceu, in Barcelona, had come here on tour, as well as the many *zarzuela* and theatrical groups that were constantly on the move throughout Spain. When Dalí was a child it was the only theatre in Figueres, and it was here that he saw his first plays and other shows. Not only that, in the theatre's foyer, now a heap of blackened stones, he had first exhibited his work: in 1918 with the older painters Bonaterra and Montoriol; then, by himself, in 1919. For Dalí, who by the time he was sixteen already thought of himself as an actor in the farce of life, to have a museum that had previously been a theatre must have seemed not only deeply metaphorical but a matter of destiny. Even the Moors' intervention may have seemed providential to Dalí, always happy as we know to claim Islamic origins, for if the soldiers had not burned the theatre down unintentionally it would not have been available for his greatest project to date.

On 12 August 1961 the bullfight and other celebrations in honour of Dalí went off brilliantly. He made a ceremonial entry into the bullring in his Cadillac convertible, circling the plaza to the applause of the crowd (one of the giants' costumes from the Béstegui ball in 1951 had been placed in the limousine for extra effect). The three bullfighters performed well, particularly the famous Paco Camino, and a plaster bull stuffed with fireworks was exploded at the end of the *fiesta*, to the amusement of the crowd. Only one thing went wrong. Dalí had been assured that, according to his wishes, a helicopter would appear unannounced to carry off the last bull and drop it in the Bay of Roses as an offering to Neptune. But a strong tramuntana prevented it from taking off.

That evening, after the unveiling of a plaque on the façade of the house where Dalí was born in Carrer Monturiol and a multitudinous reception in the Town Hall, came the culminating moment of the day when, amidst the charred ruins of the Teatro Principal, Dalí announced the creation of his museum. The site was predestined, he told the crowd, since here he had held his first exhibition. But nothing must be changed, since every centimetre of the place's filthy walls was in itself an abstract painting! It would be the only Surrealist museum in the world. And it would contain no originals! Dalí would install huge photographs of all his works in the windows, covered in plastic to resist the elements. Visitors would not be disappointed: photographs of paintings were better than the real thing! Those interested in Dalí's work would have to come to Figueres, because it would be the only place in the world where the whole corpus of his production could be viewed. And, when not studying the photographs, they would be able to watch, through large windows, the activity in the fish market which was located just behind the building.

Despite the smiles and the applause, the worthy councillors of Figueres must have wondered what they had let themselves in for. A museum with no roof, no original work and, for exhibits, hundreds of photographs of Dalí's paintings and drawings! It hardly sounded like a great tourist attraction, or a centre for Dalinian studies. This was also the view in Madrid, and although Dalí had given the media to understand that the Government's Fine Arts Department would be involved in the project, there was no official representation from that body present.[21]

Dalí soon realized that the building would have to be completely reconstructed, not left open to the rain and the tramuntana as he had first thought, and that, if official finance was to be obtained for 'the only Surrealist museum in the world', it would need to contain a substantial corpus of original work. In the event ten years were to pass before work began, and then only because of the almost superhuman tenacity of Ramon Guardiola. During the 1960s the museum would be constantly on Dalí's mind, and his plans for it modified again and again. But of one thing he was sure. This was to be a Theatre-Museum, in accordance with its origins. A place, not just of exhibits, but where things happened, where people's perceptions were challenged and, hopefully, modified.

Dalí had announced on 12 August that within a week he would be in Venice, where, as the unofficial ambassador of Figueres, he promised to plant a fig tree, symbol of the town (whose name means 'fig trees'). Dalí's reason for going to Venice was the première, in the La Fenice theatre, of a spectacle he had devised in collaboration with Maurice Béjart. The programme consisted of a comic operetta, *The Spanish Lady and the Roman Cavalier*, adapted by the composer Giulio Confalieri from Alessandro Scarlatti's *Scipio in Spain*, followed by *Gala*, described on the poster as 'a new ballet by Pierre Rhallys and Maurice Béjart', with scenery by Dalí. Ludmilla Tcherina was the star dancer. Isidor Bea had prepared the five backdrops from Dalí's designs. They measured nine by seven metres, and he felt later that he was not given due credit for his contribution.[22]

Peter Moore, who travelled to Venice with the Dalís, was impressed by Bea's skill and soon realized how dependent the painter had become on him. Bea would prepare Dalí's canvasses, and put on the first and second coatings. Then he would work out the perspectives. Dalí's 'atomic' paintings, with objects floating in space, were largely plotted by Bea. And Moore discovered that he was also very good at clouds, which would be considerably advanced before Dalí 'finished' them.[23]

Maurice Béjart had not found it any easier to collaborate with Dalí than had Peter Brook in 1949. He had consulted the painter about the production in Barcelona and Port Lligat, but in Venice found to his dismay that Gala was keeping him locked up in his room until he finished two paintings commissioned by rich Americans.[24]

On the opening night, 22 August 1961, Dalí sat in a box above the orchestra dressed as a gondolier, with a red Catalan *barretina* on his head. As the audience waited for the show to start he began splashing paint on a canvas, which he then tore open to release a dozen homing pigeons. The terrified birds flapped in disarray around the theatre 'looking wildly for their cote', according to the review in *Time*.

Dalí may have thought the scene amusing, but it was yet another example of his indifference to the tribulations of animals. Over the years he would cover frogs and octupi in ink to see what sort of drawings they produced; he enjoyed throwing cats into the swimming pool in Port Lligat, and boasted of having forced nutshells onto the front paws of one to see it hobbling around; guests were regaled with an oft-repeated account of how to cook a turkey alive without killing it; and frightened sheep were once herded into a vernissage. Reynolds Morse commented on the latter exploit: 'We felt the stunt was in bad taste, but the sadistic artist loved it, especially since it had cost his client a bundle of money.'[25]

When the curtain rose on *The Spanish Lady and the Roman Cavalier*, it revealed, reported *Time*, a 'ghostly painted image of Dalí, mustache tips rising to eyebrows, eyes piercing the audience'. As this faded away, the heroine came on, 'her two-yard-long tresses supported by a red crutch'. From her bosom she extracted for her suitor, what else, 'a pie-sized Dalían watch'. The backdrop showed a large violin walking on spindly legs. One of its arms was stretched in the direction of a piano from which milk was gushing. On stage there was a blind man sitting watching television, a beef carcass hung above the singers' heads with a trumpet fixed over its rear (was it hoped that it would fart?), and eight actors dropped armfuls of china as a rousing accompaniment to the orchestra. *Time* went on:

> Through all this interference, Mezzo Soprano Fiorenza Cossotto and Bass Lorenzo Alvary—the opera's entire singing cast—struggled to tell Scarlatti's simple allegory of an aging Roman centurion's efforts to win a Catalan coquette long after the decline of the Roman Empire had doomed to failure any such suit. The singers struggled against impossible odds. Three more curtain-size Dalían tableaux fell, each full of the usual Dalían symbols; butterflies, breasts, limp watches and legions of crutches.[26]

The Spanish Lady and the Roman Cavalier having run its course, Dalí came out from the wings in the interval, wearing his *barretina*, and stopped mid-stage in front of the curtain. He bent down as if to peer through a keyhole, made a cabbalistic sign and went off again. Nobody understood what it was all about.[27]

Then came *Gala*, which was also set to music by Scarlatti. The ballet began in the dark with a figure pushing a wheelchair in which sat a cripple flashing a light. Then on came other cripples who, discarding their crutches, got to work plunging wire frames into seven barrels filled with a special liquid for making 'weird geometric bubbles'. When Ludmilla Tcherina appeared in the role of the Woman (Gala), 'she launched', wrote *Time*, 'into some of the most erotic dancing since Minsky, in a black leotard so tight that she seemed more nude than nude'. The point had to be made, one assumes, that Dalí's Gala was a very sexy lady. In the ballet's climax, Tcherina 'emerged as the Supreme Mother, in a black and white gown with flesh-colored breasts. Her nourishing power was symbolized by a cascade of "milk"—liquid carbon dioxide from beneath the rafters.'[28] Not surprisingly, the *Figaro Littéraire's* reporter felt that the whole thing was a mere parody of Surrealism. But this did not prevent it from being revived in Brussels and Paris the following year.[29]

The Battle of Tetuan

In 1860 the Spaniards had conquered the North African city of Tetuan from the Moroccans. Proud of the Catalan contribution to the victory, the Barcelona County Council comissioned some paintings of this and related events from Marià Fortuny (1838–74), a painter called by Dalí in the *Secret Life* 'one of the most skilful beings in the world'.[30] Fortuny's unfinished *The Battle of Tetuan* was begun in 1862, and since 1920 the giant canvas (300 x 972 cm) has been housed in Barcelona's Museum of Modern Art.[31] In 1962 Dalí decided to paint an ironic gloss on the picture to coincide with the centenary of its execution. His *The Battle of Tetuan* portrays himself and a radiant Gala at the head of a Moroccan charge (copied, apparently, from a photograph in *Life*),[32] and seems to suggest that, despite the sword brandished with a grand flourish by the arm of Prim, the Spanish general, at the top right of the picture, the infidel is about to prevail. One is reminded forcibly of Dalí's diary entry back in 1921 when, commenting on news of the African war, he wrote 'I consider myself completely Moorish' (see p. 83 above).

Dalí's revamping of Fortuny is set in a landscape more Empordanese than Moroccan (as was the case with his 1938 *Impressions of Africa*), and the promontory on the skyline is reminiscent of Cape Norfeu, between Cadaqués and Roses. In the shack at the centre, too, there seems to be an allusion to the *barraca* in Port Lligat that Dalí bought from Lídia in 1930. More than a homage to Fortuny, then, the painting looks like yet another affirmation of the triumphant progress through life of the 'divine twins', Salvador Dalí and Gala Diakanoff; and it is significant that Dalí dedicated one of the work's preparatory studies 'To Gala, from her Dioscurus'.[33]

On 15 October 1962 the two paintings were exhibited side by side in the Sala Tinell, in Barcelona. Dalí had said publicly that his canvas was the product of indigestion, and that he had aimed at producing the most kitsch work imaginable. Rafael Santos Torroella, who had now been following Dalí closely for ten years, dared to agree. The painting was a mess, a hotch-potch of disparate elements, self-quotations included, the product of very bad indigestion indeed! It revealed Dalí as a virtuoso, in the pejorative sense of the term, and, like so much of his work, lacked that 'profound and mysterious emotion' that characterizes true art. Dalí, who could never take criticism lying down, dashed off an irritated rejoinder to the newspaper.[34]

The Battle of Tetuan, whatever Santos Torroella thought of it, appealed to Huntington Hartford (who had already purchased *The Discovery of America*) when Dalí sprang a special viewing of the work on him in New York. The millionaire bought it for his Gallery of Modern Art.[35]

The autumn of 1962 was also marked by the publication of Robert Descharnes's book *Dalí de Gala* ('Gala's Dalí'), entitled *The World of Salvador Dalí* in the English and American editions. According to Descharnes, in 1960 he and Dalí had simultaneously thought of doing a book together. The result was the first luxuriously produced work on Dalí. Along with Descharnes's observations, it included colour reproductions of a representative selection of Dalí paintings, with tape-recorded comments by the painter (not always very illuminating) and photographs of Dalí, Gala and Port Lligat by Descharnes.

It was nine years since Descharnes had first met Dalí. Their film project had fallen through, as Dalí's film projects tended to do, but the Frenchman had continued to frequent the couple. Descharnes had an inquisitive mind and was gradually building up a considerable fund of background knowledge about Dalí, but he was far too prepared to take Dalí at his word. In particular, he had swallowed uncritically the painter's version of the death of his brother (twenty years after the publication of the *Secret Life* we are still being told that the first Salvador was seven when he died), and accepted Roumeguère's Castor and Pollux thesis as if it were gospel truth. Nor was Descharnes much of an art critic. Referring to Dalí's comments on the colour reproductions he writes: 'They are not explanations of the paintings, which are products of Dalí's subconscious, and whose meanings even he cannot explain in any rational way.' But only a small percentage of the works illustrated could in any sense be considered products of subconscious automatism, and all of them were capable of being 'explained'. The strength of the book lay in Descharnes's photographic documentation, some of it brilliant, which took the reader inside the labyrinth of Port Lligat and revealed the links between much of Dalí's work and the landscape that inspired it. Descharnes's colour photographs of the bay of Port Lligat and the rocks and cliffs of Creus were particularly arresting.

Dalí and Gala were pleased with the book. Marie-Laure de Noailles threw a party to celebrate its publication, and on 10 December 1962 Dalí signed copies in La Hune, the famous bookshop on the Boulevard Saint-Germain, using a novel procedure for such occasions. With his right forearm wired up to a system registering his heartbeats, each 'oscillogramme' signature expressed a personal response to the dedicatee. One has to give Dalí credit for endless inventiveness, not least when it was a question of selling his wares to the best advantage.[36]

DNA, Perpignan Station and Continental Drift

Since 1953 Dalí, apparently convinced that DNA held the key to life (in its role of transmitter of the genetic code 'to each living cell'),[37] had continued to incorporate representations of the molecule in his paintings, in much the same way as he had done earlier with Great Masturbators, crutches, sacred hosts and the like. Towards the end of 1962 he began a painting with the impossible title of *Galacidalacideoxyribonucleicacid* (his longest single title in one word, as he proclaimed proudly). The starting point of this giant canvas (305 x 345 cm) was the flood that ravaged the district of El Vallès, near Barcelona, that September, causing the deaths of hundreds of poor immigrants living in the dry bed of the River Llobregat.

The painting, subtitled *Homage to Crick and Watson*, was first shown in New York at Knoedler's in November 1963, along with nine other recent works which revealed, according to one critic, how well informed Dalí was about contemporary life, from prostitution in high places to pop music (the latter reference was to his painting *Twist in the Studio of Velázquez*).[38] Newspaper cuttings of the Nobel Prize winners Crick and Watson were featured on the cover of the exhibition catalogue above a Dalinian version of the DNA model, and *Galacidalacideoxyribonucleicacid* was purchased by the New England Merchants National Bank of Boston, according to the press, for $150,000.[39]

The painting, executed in the swirling style of *The Ecumenical Council*, shows Gala in the centre foreground looking out over El Vallès and its river. The shadowy figure at the top left, holding a tablet with the picture's title, is, Dalí said, the prophet Isaiah. God presides over the scene in a crudely painted double-image cloud (reminiscent of Dalí's rendering of Venus in one of his backdrops for *Labyrinth*). Inside His head we glimpse the figures of Christ and the Madonna. God's right arm is reaching down to encircle and bear heavenwards the body of the Son (from whose pierced left side issues a trickle of blood). When Christ's inverted head suddenly becomes visible as one studies the painting one has the same feeling of discovery as with the rabbit's in the 1929 *The Lugubrious Game*: Dalí is still specializing in optical tricks, in the unexpected revelation that things are not only what they seem to be.

'You feel the heaviness of the body and of the sacrifice, don't you?' Dalí said to the writer Carlton Lake as they looked at the picture together. Lake had been asked by a friend at the bank that had bought the picture to find out what the work was all about. 'That's what I want to stand out—God taking Christ up to heaven,' Dalí added.[40] Beside the body of Christ Dalí has inserted his version of Crick and Watson's model of the 'stick-and-ball' structure of the spiral DNA molecule, the intention being, he told Lake, to express 'the upwards movement of Christ in the arm of God'.[41]

Lake wondered about the cubes formed of Arab riflemen apparently shooting each other on the right of the picture. After explaining about his own Arab origins, and the importance of the Moorish contribution to the civilization of Spain and the world, Dalí replied that here the Arabs, contrary to the DNA spirals, 'represent a kind of destruction, like minerals in the process of annihilating themselves'. It seems that he had in mind the Algerian war.[42]

Dalí, like his father before him, felt compelled to have clear, 'conclusive' ideas on every subject with which to crush all possible verbal opposition. To a mind such as his, dialogue was unthinkable, the purpose of conversation being to talk 'at' (or 'against') others but never 'with' them. Speech existed in order to convince, not to be convinced; and part of the fun, as Dalí saw it, lay in forcing upon other people propositions in which he himself only believed for the purposes of the game. To cretinize others was so satisfying. This had been the case with his professed 'nuclear mysticism', it was now the case with DNA and it was about to become the case with Perpignan station.

By 1963 Perpignan station and Dalí were old friends. The nearest major French railway station to Port Lligat, it was his and Gala's departure point each autumn, after months of hard work, for the delights of Paris, 'its gastronomical feasts, its erotic celebrations'.[43] Usually they only checked in their luggage and Dalí's paintings here, continuing to Paris in the Cadillac. But sometimes they too boarded the train. Either way the station was their farewell to Spain. Perpignan was a frontier, not only between France and Catalunya, but between Dalí's private and public worlds. Here, after months of isolation, he was invariably recognized by people who did not know him personally. 'It's Dalí! Look, it's Dalí!' It was an indication of how famous he was, and of how successful he was going to be yet again in Paris and New York as the season got under way.

But there was more to Perpignan railway station than that. Over the years Dalí had begun to notice that he always got brilliant ideas in the vicinity of the town, an 'acceleration of intelligence'.[44] The ideas would begin to impinge at Le Boulou, on the border, and would become so intense as he approached the station that, Dalí claimed, a 'mental ejaculation' would occur. This would continue while Gala saw to the luggage. Then, as they set off, the excitement would begin to diminish, and by the time they reached Lyon it had quite faded. There simply had to be an explanation for the phenomenon.[45]

On 19 September 1963 Perpignan station provided Dalí with a specially intense experience which he described in *Diary of a Genius*:

> I had a kind of cosmogonic ecstasy stronger than the previous ones. I had an exact vision of the constitution of the Universe. The Universe, which is one of the most limited things that exist, turned out to be more or less similar in its structure to Perpignan railway station, with the only difference that in the place of the ticket office there was the enigmatic sculpture the engraving of which had been tantalizing me for days.[46]

The engraving in question, which Dalí reproduces, is indeed enigmatic. Probably eighteenth-century, it shows a sculpture of a boy in classical garb seen from three different sides. He seems to be pulling the urn which, placed on a plinth, has sprouted two fingers. What relationship Dalí's subconscious perceived between the sculpture and Perpignan station it is difficult to imagine.[47]

There were more revelations to come in Perpignan railway station. It was here, Dalí claimed, that on 17 November 1964 he discovered the possibility of painting in the third dimension 'by pressing into the surface of an oil painting microscopic patterns in the form of parabolic lenses like those of the eyes of flies'. This in order to produce 'the stereoscopic phenomenon of moiré, for which my friend Dr Oster has found the equation, resulting in a new illusionist and paralyzing realism'. Flies' eyes, that is, were helping Dalí towards greater achievements in the field of optical illusions.[48]

Dalí is never trustworthy where dates are concerned, so it was probably in 1965, not 1966 as he says, that he discovered that the standard metre, 'the measurement of the earth', had been established by Pierre Méchain just north of Perpignan on a straight line twelve kilometres long between Vernet and Salses. Here was further evidence of the uniqueness of the area. Dalí was elated:

> I then took a taxi and went slowly around the station, inspecting it as if it were some eso-teric monument of which I had to find the meanings. The setting sun was ablaze and the flood of its light created flames on the façades and especially the central skylight of the sta-tion that seemed to become the centre of an atomic explosion. About the station I could see a radiating aura in a perfect circle: the metal trolley cables of the streetcars that ringed the edifice and gave it a crown of glinting light. My penis sprang to attention with joy and ecstasy: I had seized truth, I was living it. Everything became overpoweringly evident. The center of the universe was there before me.[49]

Dalí being Dalí, his new vision of the universe demanded pictorial expression. *The Station of Perpignan* (295 x 406 cm), executed in 1965, was exhibited that December at Knoedler's. Dalí's invitation to the vernissage, couched in dubious English, expressed the view that the work was his 'best painting to-date'. It showed:

> Gala looking at Dalí in a state of anti-gravitation in the work of art 'Pop-op-yes-Pompier' in which one can contemplate the two 'anguishing' characters from Millet's Angelus in a state of atavic hibernation standing out of a sky which can suddenly burst into a gigantic Maltese cross right in the heart of the Perpignan railway station where the whole Universe must begin to converge.[50]

The work was a technical *tour de force*, undoubtedly, and once again Isidor Bea's skills in handling perspective had clearly been brought to bear. But why the return of Millet's 'anguishing couple'? In 1963 Dalí had published the recovered manuscript of *The Tragic Myth of Millet's Angelus*, left behind in Arcachon in 1940, and the critical response had been encouraging.[51] This probably explains the presence of the couple in the painting, to the accompaniment of wheelbarrows and numerous bags of potatoes. In the right-hand panel of Dalí's imagined mural in Perpignan station, a male figure is about to pen-etrate a female who is bending over one of these bags. *Dar por saco* ('stick it into the sack') used to be a common alternative for the current Spanish expression *dar por culo*, 'to sodomize', and it seems clear that Dalí was playing with this concept here.

The final explanation of Perpignan's mysterious aura came not long afterwards when Dalí decided that millions of years ago a great cataclysm had taken place in the Bay of Biscay, cleaving the continents asunder. Thanks to Perpignan, that 'sacred place' at the centre of the universe, Europe had stood firm. Otherwise, said Dalí, we would all have been in Australia co-existing with kangaroos—and nothing could have been more unpleasant than that.[52]

Perpignan station was to be a great Dalinian standby for the rest of his life, and, like his set phrases 'the only difference between Dalí and a madman is that Dalí is not mad', or 'Picasso is . . . a Communist, nor am I', it would be hauled out again and again in lectures, broadcasts, TV appearances and articles. Particularly the bit about the kangaroos, which rarely failed to raise a laugh.

Gala and William

In August 1962 Gala the Muse, the Virgin of Port Lligat, had reached the age of sixty-eight. Obsessed with growing ugly, she had been dyeing her hair for years (soon there would be a wig) and was beginning to think about her first facelift and youth injections. With each passing year, and each new wrinkle, her hunger for young men seemed to increase. Moreover, with Peter Moore now pushing up the price of Dalí's wares, virtually unlimited funds were available for the running of her liaisons. She needed them. 'Gala's boys cost a fortune,' Mara Albaretto has said, adding that some of the money she and her husband handed over to her for Dalí's commissions was spent on her lovers without the painter's knowledge.[53]

Not all Gala's toyboys were simply there for the money, or the promise of a film career, or the hopes of becoming a champion racing driver; not all were like a youth called Eric Samon, who arranged for Gala's car to be stolen by accomplices while he was dining with her in a restaurant.[54] Some of them, on the contrary, seem to have been genuinely fascinated by her as a woman, and to have cared for her. Such was William Rotlein, a twenty-two-year-old drug addict Gala stumbled across one day in New York. Amazed by what she perceived as a striking resemblance to the Dalí she had known as a young man, she took him back to the St Regis, cleaned him up, got him a fancy suit, weaned him temporarily off drugs—and turned up with him soon afterwards in Spain.[55]

Rotlein brought out Gala's successfully suppressed maternal instincts as well as appealing to her sexually, and by the time she introduced him to the Albarettos in 1963 she was giving all the signs of being passionately in love. Gala, who loved travelling (Dalí hated it increasingly), had driven with William to Italy in the Cadillac, arriving in Turin after a spell gambling in Monte Carlo. Mara Albaretto, who by now knew Gala well, quickly perceived that William was different from her other young lovers. There was no doubt that the couple were not only copulating but deeply involved in each other. One day, intrigued, she quizzed William. Until they arrived in Italy, he said, they had not done much, just a little kissing. But in Verona (where Gala habitually made her boys swear eternal love at the tomb of Romeo and Juliet) a miracle had happened. And now they were doing everything! Gala, said William, was fantastic in bed. As for Gala, she confided to Mara that William was the most proficient performer she had ever known—with the exception of Paul Éluard. In this respect, she made clear, Dalí was a complete non-starter.[56]

Mara Albaretto preserves many letters from Gala in which she refers to William. This following is typical (Gala and Dalí had just arrived in Madrid):

> My dear friend, dear Mara,
> I haven't had any news either from you or from William and I'm worried. Please phone me or send a telegram at once. We arrived today and will be here for about a week—then in Port Lligat for a few days. But, please, give me news of yourselves and William and everything that's going on in connection with him. I kiss you tenderly, your Gala.

The draft of a telegram to Gala from William, written in block capitals, is even more eloquent:

> MY DEAR GALA,
> I DON'T UNDERSTAND ANYTHING STOP I LOVE YOU STOP I DON'T USE DRUGS STOP I DON'T DRINK STOP I'M COMPLETELY LOST STOP I LOVE YOU STOP I'M CRAZY STOP PLEASE WIRE ME OR TELEPHONE ME IMMEDIATELY STOP I NEED YOU STOP I LOVE YOU—I'M SICK STOP EVERYTHING IS GOOD WITH ME AND YOU STOP THE REASON I DIDN'T WRITE TO YOU OR WIRE BEFORE IS BECAUSE I'M CRAZY STOP I LOVE YOU STOP DON'T LEAVE ME STOP I DON'T WANT TO GO AWAY—I WAIT HERE FOR YOU STOP WILL

By 1964 Dalí was apparently convinced that Gala was going to leave him for William. Normally, when she went off with her boys, he was happy to be alone for a week, even a fortnight, without her controlling presence. But then he would get bored and begin to miss her. Now it was not boredom, however, but fear of abandonment. Mara Albaretto preserves a pathetic letter from Dalí to Gala in which he begs her to return to him. It begins 'My dear Olivette I need you badly, please come home quickly.' Gala did not respond to the call, and Dalí was so distraught that he found it almost impossible to work.[57]

Gala's passion for William began to wane after the Albarettos persuaded Fellini to take some time off from filming *Giulietta degli Spiriti* in 1965 to give him a screen test.

When Rotlein failed miserably to come up to scratch, the praying mantis decided that it was time to eliminate the latest male in her collection. But the affair lingered on a little longer. Nothing about it seems to have appeared in the heavily censored Spanish press, but in Italy only swift action by the Albarettos, who bought off the photographers, prevented a sensational article from appearing in a glossy magazine. Some of the suppressed pictures show Gala and William emerging together from a restaurant in Rome and trying to avoid the paparazzi.

Peter Moore, disturbed by the effect that Gala's infatuation with William was having on Dalí, felt relief when, in 1966, the Muse instructed him to put Rotlein on a plane to New York with a one-way ticket. Before this happened the Albarettos appropriated Gala and William's correspondence, in case the latter should decide to sell it to the sensationalist press. It seems that William died not long afterwards of an overdose.[58]

William Rotlein was a down-and-out in New York when picked up by Gala. He reminded her of Dalí as a young man. Their affair upset the painter, who thought Gala was going to abandon him. Here they leave a Roman restaurant in 1966. Dalí's collector friends the Albarettos bought off the photographer to avoid scandal.

The episode was typical of Gala's manner of living and loving. Only by having a constant succession of boys could she dispel her terror of growing old. And no sooner did she begin to tire of one than she used her astonishing sex appeal, her charm, her power and her money to acquire another.

A prime witness to the lengths to which Gala was prepared to go to remain young and sexually vigorous during her declining years was a thirty-eight-year-old doctor who arrived in Cadaqués in 1960 and stayed for a lifetime. For over a decade Manuel Vergara saw the Dalís regularly when they were in Port Lligat, and he was expected to drop whatever he was doing at any time, day or night, to alleviate their slightest discomfitures. These were constant, for both were obsessed about their health and would contact him for the merest cold—at a flat rate of 1,000 pesetas per annum! How this arrangement was tacitly arrived at Vergara does not know to this day, and, if he hoped for payment by kind—a drawing, say, or even a small painting—all that ever materialized was an illustrated dedication in a book. A jovial, outspoken, no-nonsense man, the doctor never failed to be amazed by Gala's vitality and sexual appetite, nor by her domineering personality. Whatever she wanted she went for with complete determination. As for Dalí, he was terrified of everything. Vergara was also Anna Maria Dalí's doctor and therefore in a position to compare brother and sister. There could be no doubt that both of them were 'very special' indeed in their idiosyncrasies, and very similar.[59]

Gala's nymphomania, of which everyone in Cadaqués was only too well aware, encouraged Dalí to surround himself with beautiful people, mainly androgynous in aspect, in order to give the impression that he, too, was sexually active. But Dalí wasn't fucking anybody. He was still, and always would be, the shame-bound Great Masturbator.

Shame-bound? Few people could have suspected it by the mid-sixties as Dalí continued to dazzle the world with his public performances, and Peter Moore continued to make him richer and richer. Moreover the media interviewers almost always failed to ask Dalí the right questions about his sexuality, despite the erotic obsessions evident everywhere in his work. An exception to the rule was the French writer and journalist Alain Bosquet, whose little book *Conversations with Salvador Dalí* was published in 1966. In the course of these wide-ranging talks, tape-recorded in Paris in the autumn of 1965 just before Dalí and Gala set off on their annual jaunt to New York, Bosquet suddenly asked Dalí if he had ever known shame. 'Very much so,' replied Dalí:

> As a child I was very timid, particularly in the presence of society people, of people whose social class was higher than mine. I used to blush terribly when I had to take my hat off to them. During my first visits to Marie-Laure de Noailles I was always terrified of committing a faux pas. That's all changed now: it's me who intimidates others![60]

It was a pity that Bosquet did not push this line of enquiry further, instead of veering off in quite a different direction. Had he done so, and done so with sensitivity, he might have discovered that behind the exhibitionistic exterior Dalí was still the morbidly timid little boy who lost face the moment he suddenly felt exposed. To intimidate others, moreover, to make others feel small, is a defensive ploy well documented clinically. No fame in the world could have freed Dalí from his neurosis, only a readjustment of his whole personality. And that readjustment was never on the cards.

Some Commissions for the Albarettos

When the freak flood hit Barcelona's hinterland in September 1962, Dalí had done another oil, *The Christ of El Vallès*, to complement *Galacidalacidesoxyribononucleicacid*. The painting shows a gaunt Christ hanging in the clouds above the flooded landscape, and was bought by Mara and Giuseppe Albaretto. This purchase led on to a series of commissions from the couple for watercolour illustrations that were to keep Dalí occupied on and off for several years. The first, in 1963, was for an edition of the Bible: one hundred illustrations. Giuseppe Albaretto, ever the potential priest, has claimed that the reason for commissioning these was to lead the painter to God. 'Dalí's soul was in danger because his wife was a witch,' Albaretto said in 1995. 'He was completely dominated by her. So I did everything I could to persuade him to meditate on the Catholic religion.' In order to find subjects for the illustrations, Dalí had no option but to read the Bible carefully, or at least parts of it, mainly the Old Testament. Albaretto holds that the process 'transformed' him, but the illustrations are conventional and one raises a sceptical eyebrow.[61]

While he was working on the Bible, Dalí announced that he was going to illustrate

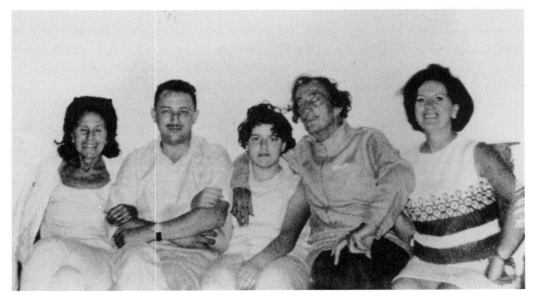

Dalí and Gala with the Albarettos, the painter's 'Italian family'.

The Arabian Nights. Beppe Albaretto was not enthusiastic: he knew his man and feared that he would produce erotic works. Dalí insisted, however, and Albaretto agreed to commission the work. Gala forbade Dalí to look at a copy of the book in case it should impede his spontaneity, and these hundred illustrations, mainly watercolours, somewhat in the line of Gustave Moreau, are among the most colourful and spontaneous works he ever produced. As Giuseppe Albaretto had feared, they exude eroticism. What more pleasing scenario for the imagination of Dalí the voyeur and atavistic Arab than a Moorish harem? His visions are notable, as might have been expected, for their insistence on female posteriors. Mara Albaretto, who has made the observation that 90 per cent of Dalí's representations of women show them from behind, recalls that Dalí did these illustrations with far more gusto than those for the Bible. So much for her husband's proselytizing.[62]

Dalí also greatly enjoyed doing the hundred illustrations for the Albarettos' projected edition of the *Odyssey* (1966–70), which was not surprising in view of his passionate identification with the Mediterranean and its myths. The paintings are not great art, but they have a freshness lacking in so much of Dalí's work at the time, and are mercifully free of the repetitive clichés with which he was then cluttering his commercial work. Isidor Bea played a hand in them, as Giuseppe Albaretto freely acknowledges, and saw to the mechanical bits that bored Dalí.

The other illustrations done for the Albarettos included forty-six for *Don Quixote* (1964–8). They are pretty conventional, but one is interesting in that Dalí has fused a view of the bay of Port Lligat with another of Cadaqués, as if to form an ideal synthesis of the two places dearest to his heart. As for the illustrations for *Hamlet* (1967), that Dalí is short on ideas can be appreciated from the proliferation of old props (including soft watches).

Carlton Lake's Dalí

The day after meeting Dalí at Knoedler's in November 1963, Carlton Lake had accepted the painter's invitation to attend his habitual Sunday evening gathering at the St Regis (held before the Dalís went out for dinner with a few chosen friends). There, in the King Cole Bar, Dalí had introduced him to Carlos Alemany, the Argentinian jeweller, the Paris publisher Joseph Forêt (then trying unsuccessfully to stir up American interest in his one-copy edition of *The Apocalypse of Saint John*, on which Dalí had collaborated), and Albert Field.

Field, a Manhattan schoolteacher, had seen his first Dalís twenty-two years earlier at the 1941 MOMA exhibition, and been profoundly impressed by their combination of technical mastery, drawing skill and power to disturb. Dalí himself had also impressed him, and had given him an autograph. Within days, perhaps hours, Field had decided to limit his art interests exclusively to Dalí, and soon, inspired by James Thrall Soby's excellent exhibition catalogue, had embarked on a tentative card index of the painter's works. He had found his vocation.

In 1948, when Dalí and Gala returned to Spain, Field had undertaken the first of many trips to Europe, where he devoted himself with obsessive energy to tracking down paintings and drawings by Dalí and people who knew him or had had dealings with him. Like the Morses, he was a frequent visitor to Port Lligat and enjoyed scouring the Empordà in search of Dalinian references. The card index grew apace.

Before long, Field had acquired one of Dalí's earliest paintings, *Landscape* (see above, p. 81), and the minuscule *Portrait of Gala* (1931) which had belonged to Paul Éluard. Then, in 1954, Dalí had named him his 'official cataloguer', no doubt amazed at the American's continuing industry, which included going to endless pains to sort out the chaos caused by the blithe insouciance with which, over the years, the artist had frequently changed the titles of his works, or had dated them inaccurately.

By 1963, when Lake met him, Field was a seasoned habitué of Dalí's Sunday court at the King Cole Bar and enjoyed his privileged status as a friend and collabortor of the painter. Lake noticed that he spoke in a 'precise, meticulous manner'. Referring to his projected 'complete catalogue' of Dalí's oeuvre, Field observed wryly, 'I expect it will be a long job.' It was. *The Official Catalog of the Graphic Works of Salvador Dalí* would not appear until 1996, and that left the paintings and drawings still to be dealt with.[63]

Carlton Lake had been the Paris art critic of the *Christian Science Monitor* for many years and spoke fluent French. He was highly intelligent, a perceptive judge of character, knowledgeable about modern art and an excellent writer with an ironic sense of humour. Dalí pricked up his ears when Lake told him that he was preparing a book on Picasso in collaboration with the latter's ex-lover, the painter Françoise Gilot. He might have pricked them up even more if Lake had told him that, overnight, he had decided he might also write something on *him*. Lake's first idea was a long article, which then became a book. That he carried a hidden tape recorder is indicated not only by his detailed transcription of Dalí's dazzling monologue the following morning on the 17th floor of the St Regis but by all the conversations that were to make up the bulk of *In Quest of Dalí*. On the back cover of the paperback edition the publisher included a revealing excerpt from a review. 'The direct conversation approach,' it ran, 'suggests a tape recorder was used so that the Camembert succulence of Dalí's thought might come through with full flavour.' Considerations of ethics aside, Lake's method not only made it a straightforward book to write but was a guarantee of absolute accuracy. The result was a milestone in the annals of Dalí biography, Dalí *pris au vif* as he never had been before.

At their first session in the St Regis, Dalí gave Lake a long lecture on what he liked to term *art pompier*, the academic, 'old-fashioned' nineteenth-century painting represented by Bouguereau, Meissonier and Gustave Moreau which he was now championing as a reaction against abstract art. Every year when Dalí issued forth from Port Lligat to remind the world of his existence he would arrive in Paris with a new bee in his bonnet. This year it was Meissonier and narrative painting. People were craving for substance in art, Dalí argued, and at least Pop Art gave them something they could look at. But Pop Art was tawdry. There was nostalgia for objects, solid, well-made things. Society was sick of painters without *métier*. Dalí told Lake that he was doing a painting 'based on the scientific principle of moiré', a material that he considered had great potential for his work. For 'an extension of *trompe l'oeil*', asked Lake pertinently? Yes, that was it. Dalí as always was into optical tricks, into deceiving the eye of the beholder. He was also at work on a large painting based on the dollar sign (*The Apotheosis of the Dollar*) since 'after Madame Dalí that is what I love the most, because I am a mystic'. And mystics, as surely Mr Lake knew, had often been alchemists in the Middle Ages, alchemists who devoted their efforts to the transmutation of base metals into gold. It was gold Dalí loved, not banknotes. As for the dollar sign, the great precursor was, *of course*, Velázquez, whose brushstrokes were invariably composed of two vertical lines and a curved line. That is, of dollars.[64]

In painting *The Apotheosis of the Dollar*, Dalí clearly had Breton's inspired anagram, 'Avida Dollars', in mind. And, as the anagram had done, he considered that the picture greatly increased his cash flow. After he finished it, he said later, 'my business deals went even better. So far as my celebrity, my bank balance and the influence of my art and ideas were concerned, I was one of the Kings of the World.'[65]

Carlton Lake's transcription shows Dalí at his most brilliant, dogmatic, provocative and seemingly logical, a formidable dialectical opponent against whom only the most daring would ever take arms. Not surprisingly, by the time Lake returned to Paris a few weeks later to continue working on Picasso, he had definitely decided to write a book on the latter's younger rival.[66] Five months later, in May 1964, just after the painter's sixtieth birthday, Lake reestablished contact with Dalí at the Meurice and for a solid ten days was in constant attendance on him, the tape recorder ensuring that not a word was lost.

The moment was propitious. To start with, a huge retrospective Surrealist exhibition, organized by Patrick Waldberg and opposed by André Breton, had opened on 13 April at the Galerie Charpentier. Dalí was represented by, among other works, the crucial *The Lugubrious Game*. Then, Dalí's 'paranoiac-critical' analysis of Millet's *Angelus*, published a few months earlier, was still being talked about. And now, in a few days, he would be bringing out his megalomaniacal *The Diary of a Genius*. As a result of these and other activities Dalí was more in the news than ever and the Meurice was positively seething with hangers on, photographers, journalists, television crews, model girls, publishers and art dealers, all marshalled with suave aplomb by Peter Moore and, from time to time, scowled or roared at by Gala in one of her terrifying imitations of a Siberian lion. Moore, 'a short, thin man in his forties with wavy, brown hair and a small mustache', was sporting, the first time Lake saw him, 'a tight-fitting dark-gray suit with a red boutonniere and leading an ocelot with a jeweled collar'. The 'military adviser' comes across in these pages as the perfect gentleman, but there is no indication that Lake ever talked to him.[67]

Nor did he converse with 'Louis XIV', the 'middle-aged statuesque blonde whose hair was ornately arranged in an eighteenth-century manner' who accompanied them one afternoon to a party in Montmartre. Another member of the group assured Lake that she was a 'very special friend of Dalí'. Had he struck up an acquaintance with her and discovered that she was Nanita Kalaschnikoff, the second woman in Dalí's life, the book would have acquired a new dimension. But Lake was in a hurry and could not be expected to sort out in eight days who was who in the painter's court at the Meurice. The composition of Dalís' entourage in Paris and New York was constantly shifting, like a kaleidoscope. New members arrived, with or without invitation, received an apt nickname and were all the rage for a few weeks. Then they would disappear, perhaps never to resurface. Or sometimes they would return a few years later, transformed. At the Meurice Lake met the Turtle, the Baroness and Mademoiselle Ginesta, who had the most erotic tongue in Paris (Ginesta was Dalí's generic name for girls of Pre-Raphaelite cast). But, alas, Nefertiti failed to show up.

Robert Descharnes, self-confident in the wake of his *The World of Dalí*, now clearly occupied a place of special relevance in the Dalí setup. He told Lake that he was organizing an exhibition of Dalí's work in Tokyo for the autumn. Dalí and Gala didn't want to fly to Japan—they were afraid of flying—and it would take too long by boat. 'So,' said Descharnes, 'it's all mine from start to finish. It hasn't been easy rounding up all those pictures, either.' The exhibition went off as scheduled, moving from Tokyo to Nagoya and Kyoto, and Descharnes's experience in putting it together was to stand him in good stead later on.[68]

The scope of *In Quest of Dalí* is narrow but the depth is considerable and no other published account brings us so close to the workings of Dalí's mind and to the incredible energy he packed into every minute of his day. His life-style is so manic that Lake makes one feel exhausted. Is it a circus, with Dalí as ring-master? A non-stop, one-man variety show? All this and more. When the action moves from the Meurice to some other Parisian location, an afternoon disco, say, in Montmartre, the convertible Cadillac with the New York plates is ready at the door to convey the inner circle thence in suitable style. The lesser fry must follow as best they can. Dalí emerges as the supreme egoist, utterly indifferent to the sufferings or embarrassment of others. But his saving grace is that he can be extremely witty and is always full of ideas.

Before Dalí and Gala returned to Spain in mid-May 1964 Lake told the painter that he was going to write a book about him: a long magazine article would not do the job properly. Dalí seemed pleased.[69] But first Lake got back to Picasso. His and Gilot's book was published that November and became famous overnight. Picasso tried to have it seized, there was pressure from the French Communist Party, manifestos against the book were signed by numerous Picasso supporters and Lake became *persona non grata* in many art circles. In the spring of 1965 Lake saw Dalí again in New York and received a full frontal attack for the book. What right had he and that 'concierge' Gilot got to throw mud at the Genius? Moreover, the book was full of nonentities. Lake soon realized that most of Dalí's pique was a result of the fact that his name did not appear once. Gilot, in fact, had never heard Picasso mention Dalí—and she had an elephantine memory. Every time the subject of the Lake–Gilot book arose, Dalí would refer to Brassaï's on Picasso. Now, there was a real book! The reason, of course, was that it was the only one in which Picasso showed any awareness of Dalí.

Dalí was also irritated because in the American edition of *The Diary of a Genius* his appendix on farting had been suppressed. It was the fault of the Protestants. In Catholic countries you can fart to your bowels' content, the proof being that even in Franco's Spain the book was not touched by the censor. But not in America. Dalí, a great farter himself, was outraged.

When Lake saw Dalí again at the Meurice that spring he was growing tired of the painter's boasting and megalomania and anyway he knew that the material for most of the book was already in the can. One day the painter pulled out a photograph showing 'a slender male model of about twenty with dark wavy hair and, beside him, Dalí wearing a heavily brocaded jacket and a curly black wig'. The model was going to play the young Dalí in a film. 'One of the handsomest boys I've ever seen. Everyone thinks so. Even Fellini,' explained Dalí. A few days later Lake saw Gala in the company of the boy in the photograph. Apparently no one told him that he was William Rotlein. Nor does Lake seem to have suspected that he was Gala's lover.[70]

Lake was now beginning to see behind Dalí's mask. On one occasion he raised the question of the books that had been written about him so far, saying that he himself thought them pretty superficial. 'Oh, they're all very bad,' Dalí replied. 'Fleur Cowles's book is a disaster. The work of a secretary. And Morse's book is nothing. Nothing.' The latter reference was presumably to Morse's *Dalí. A Study of his Life and Work* (1958), published a year before Cowles's biography. 'What about *The Secret Life of Salvador Dalí?* Lake then asked slyly. Dalí was caught off guard:

> He looked surprised. 'But I did that,' he said.
>
> Maybe so, I said, but however theatrical it might be in spots, it was not awfully convincing: all those exceedingly detailed and highly imaginative accounts of 'critical' episodes of childhood and adolescence that could only be taken—to put it politely—as overextended metaphors. I said I wanted to see him just the way he was—without the literary window dressing.
>
> His face reddened, then he nodded. 'That interests me,' he said. 'That's why I talk to you as frankly as I do.'[71]

Dalí put on the spot for once! The sudden blush of shame! There are other moments in the book where Lake notices a similar reaction when Dalí is momentarily crossed or challenged. He suddenly feels exposed, caught out—and the reaction is an incipient blush.[72] Lake also noticed something else. A fabulous six-foot Swedish model with infinitely long legs was among the company at the Meurice during his eight days with Dalí. Nobody could take their eyes off her, or them. Dalí wanted the girl to perform naked in one of his stunts, but Yvonne had her misgivings. 'What about my breasts?' she asked. '"Ah!" Dalí simultaneously raised his eyebrows and lowered his eyelids. '"They absolutely *must* be seen."'[73] This momentary closing of the eyes noted by Lake was very typical of Dalí when he felt suddenly discomfited, as can be seen in some of his television appearances. It was a gesture calculated to stave off embarrassment, sudden panic. On the evidence of Lake's book, Dalí was still in thrall to feelings of shame, despite the appearances to the contrary; and it was not surprising that the author concluded, agreeing with one of the most pleasant members of Dalí's entourage at that time, a young woman called Marina Lussato, that the painter's basic problem was a crushing sexual neurosis.

The grand finale of Lake's book is a description of the major Dalí retrospective that opened at Huntington Hartford's Gallery of Modern Art on 18 December 1965 and ran until 28 February 1966. A BBC TV crew was covering the run-up to the show, and the film forms a fascinating pendant to Lake's account of Dalí in late 1966. The painter-show-man found it difficult to cope with the film's presenter, the playwright Jane Arden, who noted that, despite Dalí's interest in mathematics and higher physics, the people he frequented were intellectually 'of a very low level indeed'. Arden was not only as attractive as most of the women who graced Dalí's court, she was much more intelligent. An uneasy Dalí brushed aside most of her questions, got into a tremendous rage when she pressed him too hard, told her he needed no one but himself and Gala, and produced his most stereotyped monologues ('Dalí love le money because Dalí is one mystic, he transmute everysing into gold', 'In reality is not interested at all in painting and literature, ees exclusively interested in cybernetics, quantum physics and biology'). Arden was not impressed by Dalí's hangers-on, nor by the fatuous session in which Dalí signed copies of *The Diary of a Genius* while Peter Moore hovered about with an ocelot draped around his shoulders. Moore explained to camera how much Dalí appreciated having in his service a person who had been in Psychological Warfare and had specialized in 'softening, you might say, the mind of the enemy, making them feel that they'd lost the war'. According to Moore, when Dalí needed him for anything he would say 'Bring in Psychological Warfare'. In these images Moore, then forty-seven, comes across as a charming but rather infantile adventurer who cannot really believe his good luck in being Dalí's right-hand man. This is certainly not a person likely to restrain Dalí's lust, or his own, for easy money, nor to have too many qualms about dealing with dishonest publishers. And indeed, to his credit, Moore, who thirty years later retains intact his boyish charm and *joie de vivre* but is altogether more sensible, has never tried to deny it.[74]

The Huntington Hartford retrospective was on the large scale, the bulk of the works coming from the Morse and Edward James collections, with important items from Dalí and Gala's. The exhibition catalogue listed 170 paintings; 59 drawings, gouaches and watercolours; 10 prints; and 18 collages, objets d'art and sculptures. The most important paintings done over the last fifteen years included *The Christ of Saint John* (all the way from Glasgow), *The Apotheosis of the Dollar* and, of course, the museum's own pride and joy, *The Discovery of America*. But none of these could match the marvel of the tiny *The Spectre of Sex-Appeal* from 1934, which appeared to Carlton Lake 'more monumental than most of the more grandiose canvases I saw on all sides'.[75]

Visitors were required to take the lift to the fifth floor of the museum and to work their way down through the eleven galleries housing the exhibition. Lake made the trip three times, on three successive days. He felt he understood Dalí better as a result, disliking his work with the exception of the great Surrealist period from 1929 to the mid-1930s. On all sides he found Dalí repeating himself. For example, Voltaire's double-image head (which had first appeared in 1940) was everywhere; it seemed that Dalí just could not leave it alone.

Trompe l'oeil had been original in 1935, but to find Dalí still working it to death in 1965 seemed to Lake pathetic. Throughout the exhibition you felt that Dalí was merely concerned with impressing: there was no warmth. As he went around the show, a phrase floated into Lake's mind. It came from the text in which the sportswear purveyor Jack Winters, who had commissioned Dalí to do his advertising, assured his potential clients that the painter's 'astute manipulation of all schools of art has assuredly captivated the world'. That was it, *manipulation*. Dalí had been telling Lake insistently since he first met him at Knoedler's that true art must represent faithfully what the artist sees in the external world. Yet he twisted everything for his own purposes, represented nothing as it was, could not leave things to be themselves. Dalí was a victim of 'the straightjacketing requirements of his compulsive *trompe l'oeil* routines', and all values were scrapped 'in the interest of making each major picture a newsworthily exhibitionistic Dalí anthology'. There was a glaring discrepancy between what Dalí said he cared about and what he did. Why? Because he simply had to show off. And also because he had nothing to say. Lake felt there was 'a total absence of emotional content' in the paintings. 'One could only assume that Dalí didn't feel a thing—and therefore we don't.'

Lake did not fail to notice what no other critic dared to suggest: the 'full gamut of narcissistic and invert outcroppings' apparent in the works displayed. He found them first in *The Font* (1930), where 'one idealized nude male figure is down on his knees in front of another, the standing one reaching out with a protesting hand and covering his eyes with his right'; then in *Meditation on the Harp* (1932–3) and *Memory of the Child-Woman* (1931); in *Cardinal! Cardinal!* (1934), he points out, Gala's breasts are bare, stressing her femininity, yet her skimpy shorts 'bulge at the front in a most extraordinary way for a woman'. It was *Two Adolescents* (1954), however, that not surprisingly most disturbed Lake, in which the reclining youth's genitals

XXIV

are elaborately laid out for inspection, the penis pink and glistening, each pubic hair lovingly delineated. The boy's mouth is open and his teeth have been touched with brighter accents of white so that they catch the light, as in theatrical photography or Italian calendar art of candy-box buckeye. At right a dark-haired faceless boy of similar taste, style, and equipment stands like a fashion mannequin, his left hand on his shoulder and his left leg drawn back, the toe daintily pointing into the ground.[76]

Dalí, Two Adolescents, *1954. Oil on canvas, 86.4 x 110 cm. Surely one of Dalí's sleaziest and most homoerotic paintings.*

Lake judged, correctly, that these pictures revealed an obsession with fellatio. What most grated, however, was 'the obtrusive makeup man's technique: the highlights and glints. It was the Hard Sell made flesh.'[77]

As for Dalí's *Homage to Meissonier*, it was 'so successfully sloppy an effort that without Dalí's signature it could only have crashed the gate at the Gallery of Modern Art'. In this work, which after all, given Dalí's proselytizing on behalf of Meissonier, should at least have been dignified, he 'seemed to be parodying all the dribble, squirt, and swab of the kind of modern art he and his host [Huntington Hartford] detest. There was no doubt—Dalí the painter was no match for Dalí the showman.'

On his last trip downstairs, Lake had a final look at *The Apotheosis of the Dollar*. 'It was so overcrowded and diffuse,' he writes, 'so deliberately and gratuitously confusing, that I suddenly saw it as the perfect pictorial symbol of our inflationary age. At least in this respect, I thought, Dalí was right up to the times, a sort of High Priest of Showmanship as the ultimate Fine Art.' Lake concluded that Dalí's post-Surrealist paintings could not stand by themselves, they needed 'the dynamic context of his ceaselessly invented daily life to take meaningful shape'. Dalí's quandary was that he had 'played out his historical role as painter but could not bear the thought that he no longer mattered'. So he carried on producing what he knew was rubbish. Lake ended his book: '"My painting is the least important thing about me," Dalí had told me more than once. As I had often observed before, there was always a grain of truth in whatever Dalí said, no matter *how* preposterous his statements might sound at first. That one, I decided, was no exception.'[78]

By and large the critics expressed opinions similar to Lake's (although they failed to notice, or at least to mention, the 'invert outcroppings' that had so forcibly impinged on him). The reaction of the *New York Times* was fairly typical: the good works on display were swamped beneath 'the dozens of polished absurdities that have for so long been Dalí's substitute for the talent he killed by abuse'.[79]

Such a review in such a place must have shaken Reynolds Morse, if not Dalí, who declared that he had 'never been presented better'.[80] The exhibition meant a great deal to Morse, not least for the publicity it gave to his collection. According to one press report, this was worth $2 million and was 'the most valuable shipment of paintings ever to arrive in New York by van'.[81] On 19 December, at 'An Evening with Salvador Dalí' held in the museum, Morse gave a talk on the Master, thereby becoming, he wrote later, 'the only collector-critic in the world to give a lecture on the works of a senior living painter with the artist himself present in the audience'. The programme included a screening of *Un Chien andalou*.[82]

Morse's 'Homage to Dalí', or at least the version of the talk reproduced in a later edition of the exhibition catalogue, was naive beyond belief. The main aim of the piece was to establish that the post-Surrealist Dalí was not only every bit as good as the Surrealist one, but better. Another was to demonstrate (yet again) that Dalí was a total genius. We are told that 'single-handedly Dalí has done more to stem the overwhelming tides of 20th century nihilism than anyone else in the world'; that in the *Secret Life* the painter 'lucidly explains his obsessions in a style which ranks Dalí with Proust and Joyce'; and that, when Dalí told him he had seen an angel in Port Lligat, Morse 'neither joked nor doubted him. How far other people lag behind in realization of Dalí's genius one cannot guess.' Morse's piece also reveals that despite Dalí's heroic, single-handed stand against nihilism, widely syndicated photographs had recently been published showing him apparently inserting a paint brush into a pig's anus at a seedy nightclub. As regards Dalí's commercial activities, Morse thought them highly laudable ('It is merely to his credit that he has made himself a very rich man by astute application of his dynamism to an incredibly vast number of projects'). And if, thanks to Dalí, Morse had come to believe in angels in Port Lligat, he now also accepted that Dalí was an outstanding inventor. For 'who else but a Dalí could have conceived a method of photographing the substance of thought through the nerve endings in the human eye?' Only Dalí, certainly, Dalí the genius who as well as his other gifts to humanity 'has made the good taste of the aristocrat palatable to the common man'. As for Gala, to whom Morse dedicated the 'foreword' to his 'Homage to Dalí', she had sacrificed all for the painter, to such an extent that 'her own great poetic qualities' had perforce been 'masked by her role as financier-in-chief of the Dalí entreprises'. 'Today Gala's greatest credit,' we are earnestly assured, 'is the barrier of inscrutability and selflessness behind which Dalí's neuroses have been nurtured and developed to the point of salability.'[83]

Morse could not refrain, naturally, from attacking the art critics; nor from trying to take Picasso down a peg or two. And every so often we get a big word for effect: 'It was clear that Dalí was approaching an almost ferine crisis in his life'; 'In fact, some of his greatest proprioceptive paintings date from the maverick years of 1934–1939.'

Dalí continued to worry about Lake and Gilot's Picasso revelations, and eventually decided that, whatever he might have said to Lake about his having a free hand in his book, he wanted to see the manuscript before publication. When Lake refused, Dalí threatened him with 'obscene penalties'.[84] How Dalí reacted to the book, which appeared in 1969, is not recorded, although it is not difficult to imagine. Morse thought Lake's treatment of his subject 'shallow', and compared the book unfavourably with Roland Penrose's biography of Picasso. Lake, wrote Morse, saw Dalí 'as some sort of aimless Pied Piper surrounded by a horde of quidnuncs and sycophants as he wanders around New York and Paris, while Penrose's devotion to Picasso gives new depth to his art and life.'[85] The comparison was unfair, since the aims of the two books were very different. Moreover, if Lake's Dalí is a Pied Piper, he is certainly not aimless. On the contrary, he has an aim and a ruthless one: his own aggrandizement, his fun and his publicity, and it does not matter at whose expense, Reynolds Morse's included.

Tuna Fishing (Homage to Meissonier); Louis Pauwels

Just outside Roses there is a cove called L'Almadrava. The word, Arabic in origin, designates a place where tuna fish are captured and slain. The most famous almadraba in Spain was at Zahara de los Atunes, near Algeciras, and Cervantes immortalized it in his 'exemplary novel' *Rinconete y Cortadillo*. That at Roses, which survived until just into the twentieth century, was less famous nationally than its Andalusian counterpart (not many bluefins reached so far north) but, where the Empordà was concerned, it constituted a local wonder.

Dalí wrote in 1967 that his knowledge of the almadraba came from his father, who, with 'a narrative gift worthy of Homer', had conjured up for him a vision of the blue sea turning red with blood amidst the frenzy of churning tunas and their slaughterers. To accompany his account, the notary had shown him a print of tuna fishing done by an unidentified Swedish painter.[1] Later Dalí told Reynolds Morse that, as a child, he had seen the bloody carnage with his own eyes, but this seems unlikely in view of his earlier statement.[2] What is certain is that the Roses almadraba and the memory of the anonymous Swedish print were the starting point of the huge canvas *Tuna Fishing* (304 x 404 cm) that Dalí began in the summer of 1966 and finished the following season.

Tuna Fishing was a lurid *tour de force*, and was recognized as such when Dalí first exhibited it in Paris in November 1967 as the protagonist of a 'Homage to Meissonier' (the painting's subtitle) in the Meurice. In the catalogue (which included a preliminary drawing for the naked girl in the painting which brazenly over-emphasized her buttocks)[3] Dalí wrote that the canvas was his most ambitious to date. The immediate stimulus had been reading in Teilhard de Chardin that the universe was finite and limited,

Chapter
FOURTEEN

not the endless space that people so often imagined, and that it was this circumstance that made energy possible. The cosmos converged in a single point and, so far as Dalí was concerned, for the moment it was converging in this painting in which he had attempted to concentrate its 'terrifying energy', exemplified in both the killers and the victims of the bloody fray.[4]

Tuna Fishing was bought by Paul Ricard, of *pastis* fame, who, the story says, arrived at Port Lligat in his yacht to look at some watercolours and found himself agreeing to pay $280,000 for the monster canvas. Not long afterwards it was stolen, which Dalí enjoyed since the theft generated massive publicity. Then it was recovered unscathed: apparently the thief had simply wanted to prove himself capable of absconding with such a huge painting under his arm, as it were.[5]

While Dalí worked on *Tuna Fishing* during the summers of 1966 and 1967 he was visited by the French writer Louis Pauwels, whom he had known for some fifteen years. Pauwels had never been in Port Lligat before and was much impressed by Cape Creus: Dalí, he now realized, could only be fully understood if one took into account this extraordinary landscape that had shaped his thinking. Pauwels tape-recorded his conversations with Dalí and used them for a book of Dalinian monologues, *The Passions According to Dalí*, which was published in March 1968. The book, which includes some comments by Dalí on the text, does not have the authenticity of Carlton Lake's, since Pauwels, as he himself explains in his preface, had put into 'plain language' what was certainly not plain in the original, so that the phrases are short, pithy and coherent in a way that Dalí's written sentences never were. The book, then, is not a transcript of what Dalí actually said but a reworking of his comments and pronouncements ('It is the inner Dalí seen by me,' Pauwels explained elsewhere).[6] Nonetheless it provides useful insights and reveals Dalí as a person convinced that his total and 'viscerally prophetic' personality is what counts, not just his painting. This he had already told Alain Bosquet: 'A picture's nothing compared with the magic which constantly irradiates from my person.'[7] Pauwels's Dalí insists that he is 'a man who has a vision of the world and a cosmogony and who is inhabited by a genius capable of glimpsing the total structure of things'. He is 'the only imperialist, classical painter' in the world and, 'botched or not', his pictures incorporate and order the greatest possible number of elements deriving from his knowledge and sensibility. Clearly this was how Dalí really did choose to see himself.[8]

The book confirms how intensely Catalan Dalí felt himself to be, whatever he may have said on occasions about his 'Spanishness'. 'My geniuses are Catalan, my own genius comes from Catalunya, country of gold and ascesis,' he assures us.[9] Other Spaniards consider Catalans the country's meanies (the Scotsmen of Spain), as is shown by thousands

of jokes on the subject, and it is a fact that Catalunya is the only part of Spain where people do not buy rounds of drinks, for example, and the fact that there are more savings
banks in Catalunya than in all the rest of Spain has already been alluded to. Referring
to his own unwillingness to part with his money, Dalí always ascribed it to the fact that
he was a Catalan.

On Dalí's insistence Pauwels included, in an appendix, a tongue-in-cheek passage
about Catalunya written by Francesc Pujols, a little-known Catalan philosopher much
admired by the painter. Dalí often paraphrased the passage at dinner parties, when the
guests would double up with laughter. Part of it went thus:

> We'll probably never witness it ourselves, because we'll already be dead and buried, but it
> is certain that those who come after us will see the kings of the Earth prostrating them-
> selves before Catalunya. And it will be then that the reader of this book (if any copies of it
> survive, that is) will realize that I was right all along. When one beholds the Catalans, it
> will be like looking at the blood of truth; when one shakes hands with them, it will be like
> shaking hands with truth.
>
> Many Catalans will weep then from pure joy; people will have to dry their tears with
> handkerchiefs. And because they're Catalans, all their expenses, wherever they go, will be
> paid for them. There'll be so many of them that people won't have room to put them all
> up in their homes, so they'll lodge them in hotels, which is the very best present you can
> make to a Catalan when he's travelling.
>
> In the last analysis, and when you think about it, it'll be better to be a Catalan than a
> millionaire. And since appearances are deceitful, even if a Catalan is as ignorant as an ass,
> foreigners will assume he's a learned man, in possession of the truth. When Catalunya's
> the queen and mistress of the world, our reputation will be such, and the admiration we
> inspire so limitless, that lots of Catalans won't dare to say where they come from and will
> disguise themselves as foreigners.

One of the virtues of both Pujols and Dalí was that they were what Spaniards call
cachondos: ironic, mickey-taking, never quite serious. Dalí greatly enjoyed the ambigui-
ties involved in being both Spanish and Catalan and he extracted the maximum fun from
such a happy circumstance, irritating many Catalan nationalists in the process.

The latter were also appalled by Dalí's monarchism, which comes through very
strongly in Pauwels's book. In 1947 Franco had promulgated a Law of Succession which
defined Spain as a monarchy and provided that the dictator's successor be styled King.
It contained no reference to the restoration of the Bourbon monarchy, however, and if
Franco had produced a son it might, in theory, have fallen to him to take over the reins.

About one thing only the Caudillo was determined: that the legitimate heir to the throne, Don Juan de Borbón y Battenberg, son of Alfonso XIII (who had died in Rome in 1941), would never be king. In 1949 Don Juan's son, Juan Carlos, had travelled to Spain to begin his schooling under Franco's tutelage. Franco grew very fond of the boy and by 1966 it was generally assumed that he would name him his successor. Certainly Dalí assumed that he would, and he was proved right in 1969.

Dalí also assumed, as Pauwels's book shows, that the coming monarchy would be absolute, not constitutional, and more medieval than modern, with Divine Right included as a matter of course. It seemed inconceivable to Dalí, as it did to many of Franco's other admirers, that the coming of the monarchy could mean a return to democracy. Monarchy fitted in perfectly with the notions of heredity Dalí had been working out since the discovery of DNA. Indeed, so far as he was concerned, Crick and Watson had 'legitimized' hereditary monarchy as the ideal system for ordering human affairs. It was a matter of pure biology.[10]

Dalí, then, was a fervent monarchist. And since the cupola, as he told everyone at this time, is the symbol of monarchy, it followed that his museum in Figueres had to be covered with a dome (not left open to the elements, as he had originally propounded). In American magazines Dalí had seen the geodesic structures designed by Buckminster Fuller, and been much impressed. It was something like that that he wanted for Figueres. But Fuller was not available. When Dalí heard that a brilliant young Spanish architect called Emilio Pérez Piñero specialized in similar articulated structures, he contacted him. They understood one another immediately and Piñero was commissioned to design the 'monarchic covering' for the Theatre-Museum. But it would be several years before it was installed. Today his transparent, articulated dome is one of the most familiar landmarks in Figueres.

Amanda Lear

Some six years before this, Dalí had begun to frequent Le Carrousel in Paris, perhaps the most famous drag club in the world. There he had been fascinated by one of the cabaret's leading stars, April Ashley, a devastating English transvestite whose real name was Georges Jamieson. According to Ashley, the painter went to see her perform every night for six weeks, showered her with presents, and wanted to paint her naked as 'Hermaphroditos'. But she was not impressed, declined the offer and, in her own words, 'turned him over to Alain'.[11]

Alain was Alain Tap, who performed at Le Carrousel under the stage name of Peki d'Oslo. In her splendidly frank autobiography, *April Ashley's Odyssey*, Ashley recalls that Tap, whose Franco-Oriental family lived in Provence, told her that he was an art student and showed her some postcards he had painted in order to survive in Paris. 'I said, "But, my dear, these are lovely—you must stay as you are, you must develop your talent, you mustn't waste yourself in cabaret."'[12]

Tap, who was also a talented polyglot, stayed on at Le Carrousel, and in her book Ashley includes a photograph of the two of them eating spaghetti in Milan while on tour in 1959. Tap, meanwhile, had confided to her that he was determined to have a sex-change operation. So was Ashley, who submitted himself to the agonizing operation in Casablanca in May 1960, aged twenty-five. Tap was among those who saw him off at Orly.

By the time Alain Tap, alias Peki d'Oslo, turned up in Chelsea in 1965, after a spell at the Chez Nous Club in Berlin, he too had had his 'Operation Pussycat', as he called it, but only after, according to Ashley, 'terrible hesitations'. The two had kept in touch by letter and telephone since the Carrousel days, and Ashley is amusing on the now transsexual Peki's arrival in London, where she was

Alain Tap, alias Peki d'Oslo but not yet Amanda Lear (left), with April Ashley in Milan, 1959, on tour with the Paris transvestite club Le Carrousel.

engaged for a 'whip 'n' leather' act at Raymond's Revue Bar in Soho. At this time her main ambition, Ashley recalls, was to be the proud possessor of a British passport. This she achieved by marrying a Scotsman called Mr Lear, chosen at random in a bar and given fifty pounds for going through with the ceremony at the Chelsea Register Office. Now Mrs Amanda Lear, no less, Peki, who apparently never saw her husband again, immediately applied for the cherished document with the dark blue cover that was to proclaim her status as a British citizen. 'To her Eurasian beauty and mystery was now added a voguish sense of style,' Ashley continues. 'She became one of Ozzie Clark's favourite models and gravitated towards the pop-music world, especially towards Brian Jones of the Rolling Stones.' Soon they began to lose contact, Amanda only telephoning when she needed an address—or was depressed (which was often). Finally, as Lear struck deep into the heart of the pop world, having affairs with David Bowie and Bryan Ferry on the way, Ashley heard from her no more. She came to the conclusion that Amanda was deeply uneasy about her sexual identity, that she was one of those trans-sexuals who was terrified of being found out. 'She had the bone structure but lacked the nerve. Even when she became the Disco Queen of Europe you could hear it in her voice—a moose at bay.'[13]

April Ashley's account of Amanda's marriage is no invention, as anyone can find out simply by telephoning Chelsea Register Office. The wedding took place on 11 December 1965. The certificate states that the groom was Morgan Paul Lear, a twenty-year-old student of architecture. The bride's name is given as Amanda Tap, described as a fashion model, aged twenty-six, daughter of André Tap, a retired captain in the French army.[14]

There is no reference in Amanda Lear's book to her meeting with Dalí at Le Carrousel, and she situates their first encounter in 1965 at the Castell restaurant in Paris. The following summer, although she does not mention this either, she saw him in Barcelona. Amanda was then performing (still as Peki d'Oslo) at the New York, a nightclub in the Carrer dels Escudellers, where, using her long legs and husky voice to advantage, she enthused audiences with a stunning take-off of Marlene Dietrich (who had been a frequent visitor to the Carrousel, according to April Ashley). Amanda stayed at the Mesón Castilla, just off the top of the Rambla, producing her French passport and registering under her true name of Alain Tap.[15] She was spotted at the New

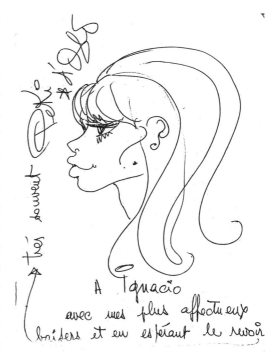

Peki d'Oslo improvised this self-portrait in Barcelona c. 1966. Today Amanda Lear denies point blank that she was ever Peki d'Oslo.

York by some of Dalí's friends, among them Sue Guinness and a young Barcelona art dealer, Ignacio de Lassaletta. Unaware that Dalí already knew Amanda, they urged him to go and see her. He did so, and soon afterwards she turned up in Cadaqués. In Lassaletta's autograph book she left a charming souvenir of their meeting.[16]

A proud Dalí with Amanda Lear.

Today Amanda Lear flatly denies having ever been Peki d'Oslo or that she once knew a young Spaniard called Ignacio de Lassaletta.[17] Since, unlike April Ashley, she has chosen not to publicize her transsexuality or to acknowledge her previous incarnations, it may seem indelicate to insist upon them. The justification for doing so is that Lear's published account of her relations with Dalí is fundamentally flawed by her failure to come clean about her identity. Moreover there can be no doubt whatsoever that the fascination she aroused in Dalí was related to the fact that he knew she was boy turned girl. 'Amanda's transsexuality was part of her attraction for Dalí,' Nanita Kalaschnikoff, who knew and liked Lear, has insisted. 'He

Dalí with Amanda Lear (to his right), Nanita Kalaschnikoff (first left), the Myers twins and other beautiful friends at the Lido, Paris.

loved collecting oddities.'[18] Dalí, for his part, enjoyed surprising people with the revelation of Amanda's sexual history. Years later he showed Luis Romero, one of his biographers, a photograph of Lear in a magazine. 'Do you like her?' he asked. 'Not bad,' replied Romero. Dalí burst out laughing and exclaimed: 'Well, she's a man!' Romero was understandably nonplussed. So, too, were many of the people who saw Amanda naked in Dalí's phallic swimming pool or in his studio, and who could not believe that the gorgeous creature had not always been a woman. Isidor Bea was one of those for whom there could be no doubt about it—and he saw her day in, day out.[19]

It is clear that Dalí soon developed a genuine affection for Amanda. She was not only stunning to look at, but intelligent, quick on the uptake, a fast learner and, as April Ashley rightly points out, a very gifted linguist. She cared about art and wanted to know more. She asked questions, and Dalí, like Scott Fitzgerald with Zelda, delighted as much in his new role as teacher as he did in being seen in public with such a spectacular protégée. His appearances with her made him feel good, manly—he could pretend that he was her lover—and for years, as Amanda progressed from model and Mary Quant girl to singer and 'Disco Queen of Europe', he revelled in her sporadic company (it was always sporadic) and in showing her off. Amanda, hell bent on pushing her career—she was almost as ambitious as Dalí himself—was only too happy to comply: given Dalí's immense fame there could be no better publicity than to be considered his lover, particularly in Franco's repressed Spain ('Love Story in Cadaqués', the headline of one magazine article ran).[20] But there was more to it than this. Amanda needed a father figure as well as somebody to help her to be famous, and Dalí, thirty-five years older than she, fitted the bill to perfection. They were well matched.

Dalí soon became aware that Lear was keeping notes of their conversations. 'Be careful what you say to Amanda, it's all going into her diary,' he said one day to Peter Moore.[21] Nanita Kalaschnikoff remembers that after an evening's fun and talk Dalí would joke 'Right, Amanda's got enough material now for tonight's homework, let's go.'[22] These jottings laid the basis for *Le Dalí d'Amanda* (1984), a hotchpotch of fact and fiction almost as untrustworthy as Dalí's *Secret Life*. Amanda claims in the book that she is the only child of a mother of Russo-Mongol extraction, which is possible (hence her oriental looks), and of an English father, which is eyewash. The book does not provide her parents' names or any details of their lives, other than to say they were divorced; we are left in the dark as to where Amanda was born, or when; there are no details of her childhood; and no reference to her sex-change. All we are told is that, when she met Dalí in 1965, the year of her father's death, she was studying in London at an unspecified art school where she fell under the spell of Surrealism. Subsequently she denied that the art school in question was in London: the ghost writer got it wrong—it was the Beaux Arts in Paris. And so on.[23]

Lear claims that, the night she first met Dalí and his entourage in Paris, the company included John and Dennis Myers (two handsome English twins who had settled in Cadaqués), Nanita Kalaschnikoff and Dado Ruspoli, an Italian prince reputed to have one of the largest penises in Europe. Like Kalaschnikoff ten years earlier in New York, Lear says she did not take to Dalí at her first encounter: she thought him brash and ludicrous. But the following day, after attending his Court of Miracles, as she calls it, at the Hotel Meurice (held each afternoon from five to eight), she began to change her mind. Soon, as Nanita had been in Manhattan, she was hooked. One day Dalí radioed her from the liner taking him to New York. 'To be called from the middle of the ocean was precisely the sort of madness calculated to impress a young English girl,' Amanda comments tongue-in-cheek. A young English girl indeed![24]

Lear's account of Dalí's *modus vivendi* in Paris is well observed and informative. She soon noticed, for example, that Dalí's suite in the Meurice was always adorned with sprays of heavily perfumed spikenard. Why? The artist explained: when you press the smooth white flowers between your fingers, they exude a fluid that resembles sperm. Dalí immediately told her that he was impotent. She noticed his obsession with gossip, particularly about the aristocracy and royalty: he wanted to know all the details of the private lives of the famous, and, where his own court was concerned, who was doing exactly what to whom and how often. He explained to her that for him the ideal being was the hermaphrodite, which was why he apportioned female names to the male members of his pretty entourage and vice-versa, thus leading the uninitiated to assume that all the courtiers were transvestites. Lear discovered that the court used a special sexual argot invented by Dalí: *limousine* meant penis, for example, and *machine à coudre* (sewing machine) copulation.

And Gala, who was now in her early seventies? She seems to have found Amanda intolerable to start with, her youth, height (1.76m—5ft 9in) and glamour highlighting cruelly her own decline. In the Fundació Gala–Salvador Dalí archives in Figueres there are dozens of group photographs in which Gala and Amanda appear together. In many of them Gala has cut out not only her own face but that of her rival: the sight of both had become intolerable to her. Gradually, however, she grew to accept Amanda, and even to treat her with a degree of deference. Obsessed as she was with her own love affairs, it made sense that in her absences Dalí should be accompanied by someone whom he really appreciated but who caused no threat to the stability of their lives. So she acquiesced.

Amanda Lear's book is chronologically chaotic, a pot pourri of undated episodes often widely separated in time but run together in the interests of narrative fluidity (it is said that her friend Roger Peyrefitte acted as ghost writer). This is Tout Paris and Tout Londres with a vengeance. Famous names zigzag back and forth, like bats on a summer's evening, and, with the exception of Dalí and Gala, there is no character delineation. Sewn loosely into the folds of the narrative, however, are some priceless jewels. Thanks to Lear we know, for example, that, if by the 1960s Dalí was jealous of Buñuel, he nonetheless enjoyed showing visitors to Port Lligat a worn copy of *Un Chien andalou* (fleshing out the bill of fare with shorts by Chaplin, Harry Langdon and Buster Keaton). Arturo Caminada would work the old projector. Lear confirms that Dalí was quite musical, and much given to humming, or singing, Catalan folksongs; that he knew the *sardana* repertory backwards (much as he had sometimes claimed to despise it); and that he had a string of Catalan proverbs at his beck and call. One of his favourites was *prometre no fa povre*, roughly 'promises cost nothing', which Dalí considered a neat formulation of Catalan tightfistedness—that allegedly national characteristic he said he was happy to exemplify. Among the other telling details we find Dalí's unfailing determination to cretinize those around him; his habit of wearing filthy sweatshirts, which he hated to change; his conviction that his sister Anna Maria had become a lesbian; his superstitiousness; and his truly pathetic obsession with Picasso, revealed in the ludicrous boast that he and the older painter used to frequent Barcelona brothels together when Dalí was young, and that the two, again together, often visited Juan Gris in Paris (impossible because Gris died in 1927 before Dalí settled down in the French capital). We learn that the servant Rosa was always hiding away Dalí's collection of pornography and dildos; that he loved to recite from Zorrilla's *Don Juan*, learnt by heart at the Residencia de Estudiantes; and that his favourite pantomime as a child was Cinderella.

May 1968 proved an important month for Dalí, and Amanda was there to take part in the fun. First, Louis Pauwels's book was published, then a luxury illustrated volume, *Dalí de Draeger*, which quickly went through five or six editions and made so much money for Dalí, the publisher (Charles Draeger) and Peter Moore that the Captain still chortles when he remembers it. Dalí showed Amanda off to his heart's content these days, and she sat beside him (he was on a throne) throughout the Draeger launch. The gossip columns responded accordingly. Amanda was the most fabulous new addition to Dalí's entourage, his 'new love'.[25]

True to form, when the French students' rebellion broke, Dalí had to get involved, dashing off a manifesto entitled *My Cultural Revolution*, dated 18 May 1968, which was printed at breakneck speed and distributed in the faculties. The drift, as might have been expected, was that the only true opposition to bourgeois values lay in a return to tradi-tion, to an 'aristocracy of the spirit', to be achieved by the application of his paranoiac-critical method, 'singularly well suited, it seems to me, to the happily irrational nature of the events that are currently taking place'. Among his more concrete suggestions was to turn the UNESCO, that 'seat of super boredom', into a brothel to be styled the Ministry of Public Cretinization. Instrumental in rushing *My Cultural Revolution* into print was the effervescent Pierre Argillet, who had begun to publish Dalí graphics in the early 1960s. Argillet, a fervent admirer of André Breton, had tried to persuade him in 1965 to accept a reconciliation with Dalí, pleading that he take into account what the painter had written about him in *Diary of a Genius*: 'Whatever you may think of Breton, above all he is a man of integrity and as rigid as a cross of Saint Andrew.'[26] Breton, who still owned—and admired—*William Tell*, had thought about it—and decided that no such reconciliation was possible. According to Argillet, his decision mortified Dalí. A year later Breton was dead.[27]

Having issued *My Cultural Revolution* Dalí decided he did not like the mood of Paris, so he and Gala 'fled' (the word is Amanda Lear's) to Spain in their new blue Cadillac.[28]

Amanda Lear witnessed the incorporation in Dalí's entourage of a twenty-year-old Colombian called Carlos Lozano who had worked with the Living Theater in California. In April 1969 Lozano landed up in Paris and within days had been taken by the actor Pierre Clementi to one of Dalí's celebrated 'high teas' at the Meurice. Dalí, by Lozano's account, was so besotted with him that he virtually ignored the other guests and hang-ers-on. This was understandable, for the new arrival could have been mistaken for a hippy version of an Aztec boy god. Slim and dark-skinned, with pitch-black long hair, flashing teeth, an infectious laugh and an easy charm, the deity wore psychodelic colours, used exotic perfumes and liked to leave his midriff bare. Not surprisingly, the Spanish ambassador thought he was a girl and kissed his hand. Dalí asked Lozano to return the following day and was soon treating him as one of his very special protégés.[29]

Dalí arranged for Lozano to be given a part in *Hair*, which was then running suc-cessfully in Paris,[30] and one night he and Gala took Amanda Lear to see him in the show. She was not as impressed with Carlos as Dalí was (but nor was she as turned off as Gala, who positively loathed him at first). Over the next few days Lear was able to observe Carlos at close quarters in the Meurice, and felt that there was not much more to him than his gaudy outfits and his posturing. But this was unfair. He had a mind too—and a sensitivity.[31]

Carlos Lozano was amazed by Dalí and his court, and could hardly believe his good fortune. Dinners in the most expensive restaurants, Dalí's astonishing conversation,

visits to museums and art galleries, and, of course, the photographers and the glamour—it was different from anything he had experienced before, even in California. Like
Amanda and like Louis Pauwels, he soon discovered that Dalí's preference, where physical beauty was concerned, was for 'androgynous, angelic types' and particularly for
boys who looked as much like girls as possible ('To see a prick stand up on a very sup-
ple, almost feminine body delights my eyes,' Dalí told Pauwels,[32] while Peter Moore,
who knew as much as anyone about Dalí's sexual preferences, has commented that 'Dalí
wanted a boy with tits').[33] Lozano also discovered that Dalí was a rampant voyeur, and
that he hated being touched by anyone—man, woman or child. Lozano's attempts to
communicate with the Master via body language were a flop: Dalí 'shied away'. As for
Dalí's own attempts to touch, 'he sort of clawed at you when he wanted something'.
Lozano, himself unconcernedly gay, felt sure that Dalí's inclinations were fundamentally homosexual. Clearly he had a huge resistance to acknowledging them, let alone
acting on them. But that he preferred the male body to the female there could be no
doubt.[34]

At first Lozano was surprised, but not shocked, by Dalí's exclusive dependence on
masturbation, which he was quite prepared to practise openly during the erotic games
he enjoyed orchestrating for his voyeuristic amusement. Soon Lozano himself was participating in these sessions, and was even detailed to find suitably androgynous youths
to join the ranks. 'Having been procured myself, I became a procurer,' he laughed years
later.[35] Dalí's 'orgies' were not really orgiastic in the Dionysian sense, because he
planned them down to the last detail and constantly intervened to tell the actors what
to do, what to stop doing (he enjoyed interrupting them when they were just on the
point of orgasm, for example) or how to do whatever they were doing a bit better. He
was the all-powerful master of ceremonies in an erotic ceremony, and nobody knew what
stage directions were coming next. Sometimes these involved heterosexual sodomy, and
Dalí told Louis Pauwels about a girl who had gone through it recently screaming 'I'm
doing it for the Divine! Only for the Divine Dalí!'[36]

Normally the ordeals were less exacting. Robert Whitaker, an Australian photographer who got to know Dalí quite well in the late 1960s, was present when, at Port Lligat,
the artist invited pretty girls to pose naked in his inner sanctum and, while pretending
to draw them, proceeded to masturbate behind his easel. When Whitaker's pretty wife
Susie turned up in 1972, 'the first thing Dalí did was to throw her a vibrator and ask her
if she masturbated'. Those who took part in Dalí's libidinous evenings tend to be a little coy about them today, but Carlos Lozano is a refreshing exception. It did not take
him long to discover that Dalí had a complex about the size of his penis, nor that his

greatest pleasure was persuading boys to drop their trousers and masturbate while he looked on (or masturbated himself).[37]

Carlos Lozano made another discovery. It was that Dalí not only constantly stuffed himself with vitamin pills but that he had recourse to anti-depressants. According to Lozano, the painter continued to take the latter during the twelve years or so that he frequented him. The revelation is of great importance and shows that, while Dalí may have convinced the world that he had lost his inhibitions, his subconscious was not to be tricked. Dalí now never took alcohol. This was no doubt wise for a person whose whole life was geared to vigilance, to not being caught out, to the deployment of his intelligence at the highest level. Alcohol, though, as Dalí well knew from his experience in Madrid in the 1920s, and later in Paris, has the advantage of providing temporary release from timidity, self-consciousness and similar states. Here was a quandary. Perhaps anti-depressants (we do not know exactly what pills these were) helped to alleviate Dalí's feelings of shame without at the same jeopardizing the self-control that he held so essential to his survival.[38]

Amanda Lear's book, which was reprinted almost word for word in 1994 with a new title and no acknowledgement of its former appearance,[39] can be read as a metaphor of the world of confusion, ambiguity and zaniness that Dalí deliberately created around him. In this respect one episode particularly stands out: Lear's account of Dalí's proposal that he and she be united by the Church in a 'spiritual marriage'. To this end, we are asked to believe, a hermit was consulted at the sanctuary of Rocacorba, a wooded mountain standing at almost a thousand metres above sea level inland from Girona. If today it is only possible to reach the top of this eminence in a four-wheel-drive, such is the appalling condition of the unsurfaced road that begins at Pujarnol, nine kilometres from the sanctuary, one can imagine the difficulties that would have been experienced by Arturo Caminada in the early 1970s at the wheel of the low-slung Cadillac. Lear says that, when the car could proceed no further, she and Dalí made the final ascent on donkey-back and on foot. Not surprisingly they were exhausted when they arrived at the sanctuary. The wise man had a long, regulation hermit's beard. Dalí was pleased: the 'spiritual marriage' was a possibility, but they would have to consult a certain monk at the monastery of Sant Pere de Roda. Lear provides no further information. Did the episode really take place as described? Did a donkey really transport Dalí and Amanda up the last haul to the sanctuary, and then down again? We shall probably never know whether the whole thing was a brilliant invention by Amanda Lear or if it had some basis in reality.[40]

By 1970 Amanda had become a habitual summer visitor to Cadaqués, accompanying

Dalí to bullfights in Barcelona and social gatherings up and down the Costa Brava. Wherever the couple appeared together they were gawped at by locals and tourists alike, and their liaison made just the sort of copy needed by the gossip columns. The Girona newspaper *Los Sitios* had such a column. Its author, Enric Sabater Bonay, was from the town of Corçà, in Lower Empordà, where his father was a car mechanic. Born on 20 November 1936, four months after the civil war began, Sabater was intensely ambitious and a man of many parts. He was a good footballer (at seventeen he had played for the Girona junior team), a competent photographer and a skilled pilot. A period in Switzerland had stimulated an innate gift for languages. When he returned to Catalunya he had a variety of jobs: radio station chauffeur, employee in a travel agency, public relations man at the Ampuriabrava tourist development near Roses. Sabater was charming, darkly handsome and successful with women. Above all, he had a Catalan flair for making money.[41]

Sabater's gossip column in *Los Sitios* gave him access to famous people holidaying on the Costa Brava, and their life-style whetted his determination to make the big time. Since Dalí was near at hand, it would obviously have been foolish not to cultivate him. The first meeting took place in 1968, when Dalí gave Sabater an interview for *Los Sitios*. They got on well and soon Sabater was a regular visitor to Port Lligat, accepted not only by Dalí and Gala but by Peter Moore, who, he says, was charming to him in the early days. Moore can hardly have expected that before long Sabater would begin to push him out.[42]

Gérard Dou and the New Stereoscopy

Gérard Dou (1613–75), the Dutch portrait and genre painter, a pupil of the young Rembrandt and contemporary of Vermeer, was one of the masters featured in the Gowans's Art Books collection that had been Dalí's pride as a boy. These scenes of domestic life, often candle-lit, have charm, and one can see why they were so popular in Dou's lifetime.

In the spring of 1969 a Dou exhibition was held at the Petit Palais in Paris and Dalí went along with Amanda Lear. There Lear was struck by a painting in which a golden ewer gave the appearance of standing out in relief. From Lear's description it seems possible that the work was *Maidservant at Window*, in which Dou cleverly captures the light on the jar.[43] Dalí was impressed and went to see if he could find a reproduction in a second-hand bookshop he frequented on the Rue Mont-Tabor. They bought a book on Dou but it did not contain the picture in question. It did, however, spring a surprise.

Lear noted not only that there were two versions of many of the paintings but that they were slightly different. Dalí checked and saw that she was right. Maybe it was done deliberately? Maybe Dou intended them to be looked at side by side? Maybe he was after a 3-D effect? Thanks to Amanda, a new bee was now buzzing loudly in Dalí's bonnet. In Port Lligat, as he reminded her, he had a pair of anaglyphs, coloured spectacles (one lens red the other blue) which were popular at the beginning of the century and allowed the viewer to see a photographic image in 3-D. As a result of her insight, Dalí told Amanda, he would now try to invent a system enabling him to apply the same principle to painting. Dalí does not seem to have mentioned the 'magic theatre' of his teacher Trayter on this occasion, but it is difficult to doubt that he remembered it as he began to toy with the possibility of experimenting with the third dimension.[44]

Not long afterwards Dalí told Luis Romero that he was convinced that Dou was 'the first stereoscopic painter' and that his pairs of almost identical pictures were made to be viewed through optical devices still not documented. It was no coincidence, in Dalí's view, that Dou's contemporary, the scientist Cornelius Van Drebbel, who died at Leyden in 1636, had invented a gadget considered the first microscope. Clearly, Leyden was a centre of optical research. From the point of view of Dalinian logic, it all made perfect sense.[45]

Whether Dou had really been involved in stereoscopic painting is not substantiated and, on the face of it, seems highly unlikely. But that did not matter. Dalí had found yet another *trompe l'oeil* variation to toy with, and would apply himself to it in earnest over the next few years. Some of the results, not particularly interesting, are on show at the Theatre-Museum in Figueres.

Delighted with Amanda's discovery, Dalí rewarded her by taking her to the Spring Fair in Seville. They travelled down in the Cadillac (Gala had already left), stopping at Lyon and Avignon to eat in the best restaurants. As Amanda tells it, she would snooze on his shoulder as the car sped south and wake up to find Dalí looking at her and caressing her hair. He was trying to work out what she was dreaming about, he said. In Seville they were joined by Nanita Kalaschnikoff, and a snatch of newsreel shows Dalí revelling in the limelight as, flanked by the two beauties in an open horse-drawn carriage, he is questioned by a reporter. Also in Seville for the revelries was Ricardo Sicre, a from-rags-to-riches adventurer who had given Dalí English classes in New York, and whose yacht *The Rampager* was one of the most luxurious in the Mediterranean. Nanita Kalaschnikoff found Sicre repellent and could never understand his fascination for Dalí. According to Kalaschnikoff, what Dalí enjoyed most in Seville was visiting the Hospital de la Caridad to see the tomb of Miguel de Mañara, popularly believed to have been the prototype of Tirso de Molina's Don Juan. At the entrance to the building is the site Mañara chose for his tomb (he was buried inside despite his wishes). The epitaph, on which he wanted everyone to walk, reads 'Here lie the bones and the ashes of the most evil man who ever lived. Pray to God for him.' Dalí loved that, and even more the famous painting by Juan Valdés Leal that had inspired the scene of the bishops at the beginning of *L'Age d'or*, and which until now he only knew in reproduction: the spine-chilling *Finis Gloriae Mundi* (1672), popularly known in the Residencia de Estudiantes as *The Rotting Bishop*.[46]

The Hallucinogenic Toreador

Dalí, unlike Picasso, was not a true *aficionado*, but every so often he would go to a bull-fight. Having worked hard to establish himself in the foreign mind as Spain's greatest painter, he could hardly not patronize the country's 'national fiesta'. Moreover bullfights had the added advantage of free publicity, particularly when organized by himself, as had been the case in Figueres in 1961, when the helicopter had failed to turn up to add the final flourish. The Morses attended at least four corridas with the Dalís. 'Gala liked the attention of the matadors who left their hats with her,' Reynolds wrote, 'while Dalí loved the whispered adulation of the crowd around him.' Adulation is hardly the right word, though. Dalí was never adulated in Spain, but he was famous. And famous people naturally get stared at at bullfights, particularly when they sit in the front row of the best seats.[47]

Dalí must have scorned those who deem bullfighting a cruel sport. It is not a sport. Bullfighting is the survival of a Mediterranean fertility ritual with roots deep in antiquity. It is a sacrifice. And, as is more obvious, it is about courage. There is some cruelty involved, certainly, by the *picador*, and when the *torero* botches his work, but it is not intentional.

Since the early nineteenth century the bullfight has been a staple of Spanish art and literature, from Goya to Picasso. Dalí could not ignore this fact nor, as a painter, remain aloof. Moreover, Lorca's great 'Lament for the Death of a Bullfighter', written in 1934 when his friend Ignacio Sánchez Mejías died after being gored, was a poem Dalí had interiorized almost as fully as 'Ode to Salvador Dalí'. He was haunted particularly by the stark contrast of sun and shadow in Lorca's exclamation of grief

¡Oh blanco muro de España!
¡Oh negro toro de pena!

literally, 'Oh white wall of Spain! Oh black bull of anguish!', on one occasion thinking of his Port Lligat patio in terms of such chiaroscuro.[48] It was not entirely surprising, then, that when the news of Lorca's assassination reached Dalí, he reacted with a bullfighting 'Olé!': Lorca, like Sánchez Mejías, had been unable to escape his fate and had died facing the adversary.[49]

In retrospect, it seems inevitable that eventually Dalí should have felt the need to devote a great canvas to the theme of the corrida, and with Lorca as one of its strands.

Dalí saw a face in Venus's midriff and thus was born The Hallucinogenic Toreador, *1969–70 (colour plate XXXVIII).*

The starting point came early in 1968 when one day in a New York artists' suppliers he found himself staring fixedly at the label on a box of pencils. Suddenly in the Venus de Milo's torso, as it bent around the edge of the box, he saw the face of a bullfighter. It was a ready-made double-image.[50] Reynolds Morse considers the revelation 'paranoiac-critical', but it hardly seems necessary to call on paranoia. We know that Dalí always tended 'to see pictures in the stains on walls', as Leonardo Da Vinci had recommended; this time he saw a face, a sad face, in the torso of the Venus de Milo, just as he once had perceived Picasso's in a photograph of an African village.[51]

The central motif of *The Hallucinogenic Toreador,* which Dalí began to paint in Port Lligat in the spring of 1969 after working on so many preparatory sketches, is the double image he had perceived in the pecil-box label. The canvas measured 398.8 x 299.7 cm, almost exactly the same size as *Saint James the Great, The Discovery of America* and *The Ecumenical Council.*

XXXVIII

The writer Luis Romero, who lived part of the year in Cadaqués, had first met Dalí in 1951 at the time of the *Mystical Manifesto* (which didn't convince him) and since then had been frequenting the painter regularly.[52] He had been planning a book on Dalí for some years but the lavish *Dalí de Draeger* had set the project back. Now Dalí came up with another suggestion: why not write a book about him based on the great new painting on which he was now embarking and which he intended to be 'an anthology of all his work'? Dalí thought that, since the canvas measured twelve square metres, Romero should divide his study into twelve parts. Romero agreed, and the contract was signed. It was to be six years, though, before the invaluable *Todo Dalí en un rostro* (*All Dalí in One Face*) was published.[53]

Thanks particularly to Romero, but also to the photographer Melitón Casals ('Meli') and to Reynolds Morse, the making of *The Hallucinogenic Toreador*, which took fifteen months, is well documented. Almost every component in Dalí's pictorial 'anthology' has been analysed and classified, from the Cubist chair in the bottom left-hand corner (taken from Juan Gris's *Still-Life on a Chair*, 1917), the gaudily coloured 'atomic particles' indicating the fatal swordthrust in the bull's neck, Henri Matisse's indiscrete fly button at Venus's midriff, the teardrop in the bullfighter's eye ('premonitory', Dalí termed it, because the *torero* knows he is going to die)[54] and the female tourist on the lilo in a cove at Creus (a reference to the scandalous takeover of the rocky seafront at Tudela by the Club Meditéranée) to the 'invisible' dog at bottom centre (copied from a famous experimental photograph of a Dalmatian by R.C. James),[55] the praying woman from Millet's *Angelus* (seen as a shadow on Venus), the flies of Girona, the source photograph of the dead or dying bull and the recovery of the child Dalí from the 1934 *The Spectre of Sex-Appeal.*

Reynolds Morse saw the whole painting, naturally, as a supreme and dazzling example of Dalinian Continuity. Take the button:

> This is seen just above the shadowed leg of the Venus that transforms itself into the toreador's necktie. The progression back to the hole in the upper sail of the *Columbus*, to the hole in the 1927 work *Apparatus and Hand* and finally to the doorway at the rear of *Las Meninas* provides the links with tradition so often omitted from 'modern' art. If Dalí's painting does indeed represent a kind of 20th century renaissance, it is also an adventure in space, time and the intelligent use of the great wisdom of his precursors.

Despite Dalinian Continuity, Morse rejected the possibility that the dog at bottom-centre could have anything to do with *Un Chien andalou*. A great mistake, for Dalí himself scribbled on a piece of paper while Romero worked on his book: 'The Andalusian Dog, visitor to Perona Cove' (Cala Perona, pronounced locally 'Prona', is on the northernmost point of Cape Creus).[56] Since for Dalí and Buñuel the 'Andalusian Dog' of the film was Lorca, and since Lorca had visited Creus with Dalí, the reference to the poet seems clear, particularly in view of the many other elements in the canvas alluding to him and the 'Lament for the Death of the Bullfighter'.

Dalí told Romero that the bullfighter was a composite figure fusing his dead brother and a group of departed friends: Pierre Batcheff (star of *Un Chien andalou*), Prince Alex Mdivani, René Crevel and Lorca.[57] It is just possible that the bullfighter's unusual green tie is an allusion to Lorca's famous line 'Green how I love you green' ('Sleepwalking Ballad'), while the rose in his lapel may refer to the central role of the flower in the 'Ode to Salvador Dalí'. Here the testimony of Carlos Lozano is interesting. When Dalí returned to Port Lligat in the spring of 1969 to begin work on the painting, Lozano sent him an affectionate postcard from Paris with a red rose. When he visited the studio that summer he was surprised and delighted to find that Dalí had incorporated the flower. 'Dalí was like that, he would use anything that lay to hand,' he recalled. 'He would suddenly see the latent potential of something that was lying there and he would use it. He was so creative in that way that I felt myself being completely taken over, and it went on for years.'[58]

The arches of the bullring at the top of the canvas, executed in the manner of De Chirico, are reminiscent of a Roman arena (Spanish bullrings almost always have neo-Moorish arches). This detail makes one think immediately of Lorca's 'Lament', in which the dead Ignacio, whose head is gilded 'by the breeze of Roman Andalusia', is imagined climbing the moonlit steps of the arena in search of the dawn, of his 'sure profile', of his handsome body. But there is no dawn, no profile, no body. Only the spilt blood on the sand, which Lorca implores the moon to cover with its white jasmine light. At the very centre of Dalí's arcade is an arch which, unlike all the others, casts no shadow. Flanked by two angels it is the doorway, surely, through which the soul of his bullfighter, and by extension of Ignacio and Lorca himself, ascend heavenwards.

The Lorca association is heightened by the fact that there is a crescent moon in the painting, placed half-way up on the left. Romero has pointed out that Dalí's world is almost exclusively sunlit, and that the moon rarely appears in his work.[59] This is true. Lorca on the other hand is essentially a lunar poet and was thought of as such by Dalí. The moon's presence here is surely another sign that Dalí has the 'Lament' in mind and that Lorca is the hidden protagonist of the painting.

Gala is there, too, appearing like a ghost on the steps of the ring and being saluted by Dalí who, as he explained in a preliminary sketch, 'has become a young bullfighter dreaming of offering Gala the bull of his Cultural Revolution'.[60] It is one of the ugliest representations of the Muse ever done by Dalí, and her expression contrasts brutally with that of the bullfighter, wistful and noble. Was this intentional on Dalí's part? One cannot rule out the possibility. Relations between Gala and Dalí had become deeply strained during her affair with William Rotlein, and were not going to improve.

Reynolds Morse bought *The Hallucinogenic Toreador* in 1970, before it was finished. It was the last painting he acquired from Dalí. After that, as the artist produced less and less good work, the Morses' purchases would be limited to a few Dalinian 'objects'. It was the end of almost thirty years' collecting.[61]

Gala's Castle and Dalí's Museum

The versatile Enric Sabater was now proving useful to Dalí in more ways than just as a photographer and a journalist. One of his most important early services was to help the painter find the castle that for years he had been promising to Gala for her summer quarters. The ideal property had to be far enough away from Port Lligat to enable Gala to feel genuinely independent, but not so far as to render physical communication too difficult. To assist the search Sabater's pilot's licence came in handy, and he began to scan the region, taking aerial pictures of possible sites. One day in 1969 he flew over a crumbling medieval mansion with a walled garden in the Lower Empordà village of Púbol, not far from his native Corçà, and thought it looked an interesting possibility. Dalí was working in the studio when Sabater arrived with the enlargements. 'Dalí left everything and started to say "Gala, Gala, Gala, Gala!"', recalls Sabater, whose English is fluent but sometimes ungrammatical. 'Right away he was in love already, just to see one photograph, I never understood that.'[62]

Negotiations to buy Púbol got under way immediately and Giuseppe Albaretto remembered with pride that the wad of $100 notes he had just handed over to Gala for Dalí's illustrations to the *Odyssey* served for the down payment. 'We've used them to buy Púbol,' Emilio Puignau told him excitedly.[63] From the moment Púbol was bought Gala made it clear to Puignau that the place had to be ready when she and Dalí returned to Spain the following summer. She would brook no delays. He had 'carte blanche' and could take whatever decisions were necessary in her absence, but the refurbished mansion must be finished on time. It was an almost impossible task, but Puignau was an experienced builder and, after his modifications to Port Lligat, knew his clients backwards. He promised that he would do his best.

For seven months Puignau marshalled teams of masons and decorators and tried to remain patient as letter upon demanding letter arrived from Gala. By May 1970, when the Dalís returned, the ruin had been transformed, or almost. Only the finishing touches remained, and the choice of furniture.[64] The Dalís were delighted with Puignau's

efforts and threw a small 'family' party to inaugurate Gala's retreat. The French photographer Marc Lacroix was on hand to record the event; Gala, he recalls, was as excited as a little girl when she took possession of her domain.[65] A local couple, Joaquim and
Dolors Xicot, were engaged as caretakers, and once Gala moved in the following summer Dolors would double as cook.[66]

For ten years Púbol was to be Gala's love nest, a secret place behind high walls to
which Dalí, as he enjoyed boasting, was only allowed access on the Muse's written invitation. The true history of the periods Gala spent there during the decade will never be
known. The lips of Joaquim and Dolors Xicot are sealed, the boys who came and went
have left no record (although there are photographs of some of them) and there was no
visitors' book. Although Dalí made a personal contribution to the décor of Púbol, painting the ceiling of the great hall and providing some rather tawdry *trompe l'oeil* effects
and what most people would consider an insufferably kitsch swimming-pool in the garden, most of his energies at this time were devoted to getting the Madrid authorities to
take charge of operations at the Theatre-Museum in Figueres. They had been dragging
their feet, there were endless problems about finance, and ministerial changes had made
everything more difficult. On 10 October 1968 Dalí had been granted a second audience
with General Franco and had explained the project in detail to him. It appears that the
now ageing Caudillo expressed interest and said that Dalí 'would convert Figueres into
a Mecca of Contemporary Art'. Dalí had not expected him to come up with a phrase like
that, and expressed his gratitude.[67] That same day Peter Moore, convinced that Madrid
was deliberately stalling, offered to arrange private finance for the museum—and to run
it. In conjunction with the photographer 'Meli' and Luis Durán Camps, the proprietor
of the famous Hotel Durán—Dalí's HQ in Figueres, just off the Rambla—Moore had
elaborated a plan to install a restaurant in the building and to lend his own Dalí collection. But he was told firmly by mayor Ramon Guardiola that for the moment the intentions of the Housing Ministry in Madrid, which had taken the project on board, seemed
to him honourable. The Captain's services were not required.[68]

Two years later there was still no progress and Dalí was becoming irritated. On 1
April 1970, April Fool's Day, he gave a press conference in the Musée Gustave Moreau
in Paris to announce the creation of his museum. Why on April Fool's Day? Because,
Dalí explained, he always did the opposite of other people and what he had to say today
was no joking matter. And the Musée Moreau? First because it was one of the museums
Dalí most admired in the world and which he always recommended his friends to visit,
and secondly because he considered Moreau 'the most glorious of erotic and scatological painters', a painter-alchemist who, like himself, converted base materials into gold.[69]

He said he had bought a castle for Gala; that he had suggested to the President of the Republic that France create a museum of Surrealism; that his going rate for a minute of publicity was now $10,000; and that (as he had told Carlton Lake a few years earlier) he was studying the possibilities of having himself hibernated. Dalí was at his most brilliant and provocative, and Carlos Lozano, attired that afternoon like a figure straight out of one of Moreau's paintings, remembers it as a 'field day'. Quizzed about the Theatre-Museum, and what works he was going to donate, Dalí answered that he would give more than Picasso had to his museum in Barcelona. Picasso, as always, was much on his mind.[70]

Finally, at a cabinet meeting held on 26 June 1970 in the castle at Perelada that belonged to Dalí's ally, the millionaire Miguel Mateu, the decision to go ahead with the museum was given the green light.[71] Work would begin on 13 October 1970 and, now that the project had at last become a reality, Dalí got down to some serious thinking about its structure, contents and general running. It was to be four years before the museum was ready.

Enric Sabater was now covering Dalí and his entourage regularly in his local newspaper column in *Los Sitios*. On 14 June he reported that Dalí had just donated to the Theatre-Museum the painting *Cadaqués Still Life With Soft Guitar*, better known as *Still Life by Moonlight* (1926). Dalí explained that the work reflected his relationship with Lorca and made what was apparently his first public statement ever about the fusion of his and the poet's heads in the paintings of the 1920s. 'The painting has the peculiarity of also being the portrait of a friend of ours,' he told Sabater, 'but the *shadow* of the bust is the *shadow* that corresponds to my own shadow, that is to say that it is to some extent the shadow of a self-portrait.' In the same interview Dalí told him that, since he had no children, his entire estate would go to his museum in Figueres. This meant in practice that he must already have been thinking about changing his will.[72]

In July, a few weeks later, Sabater first met Amanda Lear, who accompanied Dalí and Gala to a party in S'Agaró. Sabater took a lot of photographs, some of which illustrated his report in *Los Sitios*, and a few days later he showed them to Dalí and Amanda in Port Lligat. They liked them, and both Dalí and Amanda encouraged Sabater to take more. Little by little Sabater was becoming indispensable.[73]

During these early years of their relationship, Sabater spent many hours with Dalí in his studio and was amazed by the painter's capacity for hard work. Dalí was always at his easel by seven in the morning, and worked until lunchtime. Then came a siesta, then another work session. Only in the evenings, for a few hours, would he relax. The pattern was invariable—with one exception. When Gala was about to go away on a jaunt with one of her lovers to Italy, her usual destination, Dalí would phone Amanda or Nanita Kalaschnikoff, who would arrive a few days later and stay for a week or two. Then and only then would Dalí give himself a break.[74]

If Amanda Lear soon had her doubts about Sabater, as her book shows, he had none too high an opinion of her. She was pleasant, attractive, he recalled in 1996, but merely a plaything Dalí flew in when Gala was off in the summer with her latest boyfriend. In the house and in Cadaqués generally she was nicknamed 'La Pisseuse', because when she went out with Dalí she was forever asking for a few pesetas to go to the loo. According to Sabater, she was paid $60 an hour to pose for Dalí, and he claims he still has some of the receipts.[75]

Sabater's appraisal of Amanda's role is unjustly scornful. When Dalí was commissioned to design the special December 1971 issue of the French edition of *Vogue*, he dedicated it to Gala and made her and Púbol the protagonists of the show. But he also drew heavily on Amanda, who appeared in several photographs by Robert Descharnes and David Bailey. Amanda was not just a hired model, she was much more important than that.

Amanda Lear posing in Port Lligat for Roger Freeing Angelica, *1970–4.*

Amanda had never seen Dalí so happy as when she visited him in Port Lligat in the summer of 1972: the museum was going ahead well, and he was thrilled with the architect Emilio Piñero's plans for the geodesic dome to cover the old theatre; Gala was happily ensconced in Púbol and off his back; and Dalí was confident that, on Franco's death, there would be a smooth transition to the monarchy of Juan Carlos. Ever since Amanda first met Dalí he had been telling her that he was a monarchist. Now he was going to have a real king to whom he could do homage! Isidor Bea had been ill and was convalescing in Barcelona, so Amanda replaced him a little in the studio.[76]

One day Gala invited Dalí and Amanda to Púbol. The atmosphere was rather tense and Gala made a point of not showing them her private apartments. Amanda thought the place somewhat spartan. Gala rejoined that Port Lligat was too baroque, too 'surchargé'. That awful swimming pool full of hippies! 'You have the taste of a provincial bumpkin from Figueres,' she snapped at Dalí. As they left, Dalí said, perhaps jocularly, 'Come home soon, Galuschka, I'm missing you. "Baby come back to me."' 'Never, I'm too happy here,' Gala replied. 'Stay with your Amanda!'[77]

In May 1973, when London Weekend Television arrived in Spain to make a programme on Dalí, Russell Harty, the genial presenter of *Aquarius*, was allowed to show a glimpse of Gala in Púbol, the Muse appearing for a few seconds at a window of her medieval love nest. Dalí told Harty how happy it made him, as a masochist, only to be allowed access to the castle on the reception of a written invitation.

Dalí's thoughts at this time, Harty discovered, were centred on his Theatre-Museum in Figueres. The Master showed him round. 'All my ambition is reconstruct here my early adolescent period in Figueres and Cadaqués and Figueres,' he told the camera emphatically. 'All my early remembrance and erotic events happen exactly in this place, and, for this, this is the more legitimate place for that my museum exist.' Harty went up on the scaffold to see Dalí do some work on the ceiling, and, noticing that he was painting a crutch, enquired about its significance:

Dalí: This is only one man carry one crutch for one flag.
Harty: You like crutches a lot.
Dalí: Yes, because it is one symbol of impotency.
Harty: Impotency?
Dalí: Yes, all le great people who realize sensational achievements is impotent. Napoleon, everybody. Le people who is not impotent make childs, embrions, and no more. But imme-

diately que le sex work with extreme difficulty, you create fantastic music, architecture and invasions, imperial invasions.

Harty: Right.

Since Dalí obviously included himself in the band of those for whom sex worked with extreme difficulty, Harty's bland 'Right', which put an end to the exchange, must stand as one of the all-time bungled reactions in the history of television interviewing. Britain in 1973 could have taken whatever answer Dalí chose to give to a pointed question about his impotence, but Harty fluffed it. Perhaps because, after a few manic days with Dalí, he was so exhausted mentally that his reflexes were no longer functioning at their normal speed.[78]

The Blank Sheets Scandal

In the early 1960s, excited by the possibilities for making easy money provided by the multiples market, Dalí had adopted the dubious procedure of appending an original signature to reproductions of his work done by other hands. It was so much easier than producing genuine engravings or lithographs!

Around 1965 Dalí then took a step fraught with danger: he began to sign blank sheets of lithographic paper. In *Soft Watches and Hard Times* Peter Moore states that it all began when one of Dalí's French publishers (Pierre Argillet, according to a note by Reynolds Morse) persuaded him to sign some blank paper so that he could put the prints on sale even if the painter did not turn up in Paris as planned to sign them. Argillet paid Dalí an extra ten dollars per signature, according to Moore, and, since Dalí was capable of signing as many as a thousand sheets in an hour, this meant that he could earn money at a phenomenal rate simply by putting his name on a piece of paper. 'In the first instance,' writes Moore, 'Dalí signed 10,000 sheets and this gave us $100,000. It was all in hundred dollar bills. "This will pay our expenses in America," Dalí announced proudly.'[79]

Signing blank sheets became second nature to Dalí, and sometimes, when he returned to the St Regis after dinner, he would ask Moore to let him spend a few hours dispatching more 'against the possibility that we won't be here again for a year'.[80]

In his unpublished memoir Moore accepts no responsibility whatsoever for Dalí's behaviour in this matter, and there is no indication that he sought to restrain Dalí's greed. After all, he got a 10 per cent commission. But not always. Such was Dalí's meanness that eventually he began to sign blank sheets stealthily without the knowledge of his 'military adviser' in order to avoid having to pay him. The cunning Moore soon realized what was happening, however, and intervened.[81]

The situation got out of hand before long as more and more demand for Dalí prints built up. According to Moore the pre-signed paper was stored in most cases with a reliable publisher. But, of course, there were always some unscrupulous operators 'who held on to piles of blank paper'. The result, according to Moore, was that 'as far apart as Barcelona, Paris and New York there are thousands of blank sheets of Arches and Japan paper bearing the authentic signature of Salvador Dalí. This paper is stored in dark warehouses; it will be used for reprints of Dalí editions. Sometimes this is done with the approval of the artist and sometimes without his knowledge.'[82]

Luis Romero has stated that what Dalí liked best of all was *signing*—blank paper, prints, books, whatever. 'More, more, more . . .', he would say, gesticulating excitedly. According to Romero, Dalí never cared how many prints were run off, whether the plates were destroyed after printing, what happened to them. All he wanted was to sign more and more copies—and to rake in more and more money.[83]

The blank sheets situation was to become chaotic before Moore left Dalí's service in 1974. That year the French customs stopped a small lorry entering the country from Andorra and discovered that it was carrying 40,000 blank lithographic sheets signed by Salvador Dalí. The sheets were in the name of one Jean Lavigne, a Paris art publisher then living in Palm Beach, Florida. Lavigne argued that no breach of law was involved in the importation of such sheets into France, and the consignment was allowed to continue to Paris. It proceeded, presumably, from Port Lligat.[84]

Emilio Puignau knew more about the painter's daily routine in Port Lligat than probably anyone else. He was deeply disturbed by what he now saw:

> Since I was a first-hand witness to their relationship I can vouch that Mr Moore's attitude to Dalí was always very correct. However there was one matter that was much discussed, repeated and even criticized. I refer to the signing of hundreds of leaves or sheets to be used for reproductions of Dalí's work.
>
> In his shack in the little street outside there were several boxes of these sheets, a table and Dalí sitting at it. I remember well those whole days that Dalí would spend signing in a totally automatic manner: a man placed a sheet on the table, Dalí would sign, and while he took it away someone else would put another in its place; and so on again and again as if it were a printing shop.
>
> I couldn't fathom that Dalí would submit to such a tiresome, and, particularly, boring chore which had nothing whatsoever to do with his art. I told him, once only, that I couldn't understand what it was all about, and I dared to say to him: 'If you sign so many blank

sheets they'll be able to print any imitation they want on them, anything that looks like Dalí.' His reply was: 'I've already been paid what they offered for the work. So what they do with them's no concern of mine.'

In truth, Dalí was an *Avida Dollars*.

As for the money 'the captain' made out of it, only he knows, although he can always say to those who followed him 'let he who's free of sin throw the first stone'.[85]

Moore made no secret of the fact that on Dalí's behalf he marketed blank sheets bearing the painter's signature. But how many? On 22 October 1981, by which time the issue was an international scandal, he was to state that, with the express authorization of Dalí, he had sold 15,000 pre-signed blank sheets to Gilbert Hamon; 3,500 to Klaus Cotta; 9,500 to Carlos Galofre; 7,500 to Jacques Carpentier. A total of 37,500. He swore that no blank paper remained in his possession. His statement was countersigned by Gala.[86]

None of these men were noted for their strict ethics, as Lee Catterall (whom Peter Moore refused to see)[87] demonstrates in *The Great Dalí Art Fraud and Other Deceptions*. Hamon, a Paris-based graphics dealer born in 1924 in Algiers, was mainly a wholesaler who sold reproduction rights to publishers and who later confessed in court to his forgeries;[88] Klaus Cotta imported television programmes and films into Spain via Barcelona;[89] Carlos Galofre ran a gallery next to the Picasso Museum in Barcelona and at one time specialized in selling prints with fake Dalí signatures;[90] while Jacques Carpentier, another Paris art publisher, was an associate of Hamon.[91] Elsewhere Moore spoke of a further consignment of 22,000 blank sheets signed by Dalí that, after a period in storage in Geneva, went to Galofre, Hamon and another shady dealer, Pierre Marcand, whose activities are well documented by Catterall.[92]

After Gala's death, Reynolds Morse recalled that, when told that Hamon was a crook, she had exclaimed: 'They are ALL crooks! Who cares! They pay us cash, so what difference does it make? Dalí painted the work. He can sell the rights to anyone he wishes, and as many times as he wants.' Morse was in no doubt that the corruption began with Gala and Dalí themselves.[93]

Moore has written that, during his term of office, which lasted until 1974, 'not one case of fraud took place', and that his successor, Enric Sabater, holds 'the key to the riddle'.[94] What is clear, however, is that the whole, pre-signed blank sheets operation got under way during Moore's tenancy and that, given the publishers involved, there could have been no certainty on Moore's or Dalí's part that the sheets would be handled honestly. Dalí did not care, of course, as he himself said: he had been paid up front. And while Moore looked on he began to destroy in this way his own reputation as an artist.

The growing hold Enric Sabater was exerting over Dalí and Gala by the early 1960s was observed uneasily by the painter's 'domestic administrator' in Cadaqués, Emilio Puignau.[95] According to Peter Moore, Dalí now wanted Sabater to be there in the morn-

ings and him in the afternoons but, realizing that such an arrangement was not feasible, decided that the Catalan would have to go. Moore begged Dalí not to throw him out.[96] Gala, however, was determined that Sabater should take over, and said to Moore: 'He'll take a 5 per cent commission instead of your 10 per cent, he's better looking than you are, he's younger than you are, he's more intelligent than you are *and* he speaks Catalan.' Moore says he replied 'That's the man you're looking for! It's a good idea!' Moore had made a fortune out of Dalí and was already thinking of quitting. Moreover he was not well. He decided to go quietly when the right moment came. One day he was approached by the painter's cousin, Gonzalo Serraclara, who told him that Sabater had twice been accused of theft. Dalí should be informed. Moore thought it was better for Dalí to find out for himself,

Enric Sabater (who succeeded Captain Peter Moore as Dalí's secretary) in 1996.

but apparently passed on the rumour. 'Dalí replied that he liked thieves,' he said.[97]

Neither Moore nor Sabater are strong on dates but it seems clear that by 1972 Sabater was already doing some business for the Dalís, and for himself, overlapping with Moore. The Captain was on the way out, but it would still take a few years.

Du Barry and Jesus Christ Superstar

Another wheeler-dealer had entered the Dalís' lives by this time. Jean-Claude Du Barry was a handsome, friendly and amusing Gascon who claimed to descend from the

Comtesse Du Barry, the mistress of Louis XV. He ran a modelling agency in Barcelona and by his own account first met Dalí in 1968 in the hall of the Hotel Ritz. Soon afterwards Du Barry began to supply the couple with beautiful young 'Saint Sebastians' and 'Ginestas' to satisfy their demanding needs: overtly physical in the case of Gala, artistic and voyeuristic in that of Dalí.[98]

Du Barry's friends, including Dalí, often called him 'Vérité' ('Truth'), and he was pleased by this recognition of his forthrightness (Gascons are said to be good at speaking their minds).[99] He claimed, moreover, that like all Gascons he was loyal to his friends.[99] According to Amanda Lear, Du Barry amused Dalí by his provincial French accent, his smutty stories and his generally libidinous ways.[100] As for Gala, she was flattered by his attentions. 'A Jean-Claude, mon bonissime ami', reads the dedication in one of Paul Éluard's books she gave him from her private collection.[101] Luis Romero, who coincided with Du Barry several times in the Barcelona Ritz and in Port Lligat, noticed that the models who accompanied him were always spectacular.[102] 'After a year I understood what kind of girl Dalí wanted,' Du Barry once said. 'Above all, he wanted perfectly beautiful girls, tall and blonde with long legs and very regular features.'[103] Grateful for his services, Dalí called Du Barry his 'officier de culs'.[104]

By 1973 Gala no longer needed pretty boys supplied by Du Barry because, after a prolonged affair with a French student from Aix en Provence called Michel Pastore, who

A happy Gala with Michel Pastore, known familiarly as Pastoret ('Little Shepherd'), one of her favourites before she met Jeff Fenholt.

spent protracted periods in Púbol,[105] she had met the last great love of her life. This was Jeff Fenholt, of *Jesus Christ Superstar* fame. He had long auburn hair and, according to Amanda Lear, 'Gala found him handsome and admired his talent.' Enric Sabater was once invited to his home for Thanksgiving. After dinner Fenholt gave him a framed picture of Jesus. 'Take it Enrique, this is me', he apparently said.[106]

Gala and Fenholt were soon seeing each other regularly, and for seven years he was to be a frequent summer visitor to Púbol, where to encourage him in his career Gala installed a grand piano and electronic equipment. He liked to practise his guitar by night, and made so much din that other guests were unable to sleep. One afternoon, not long after Gala met Jeff, Amanda Lear was in Port Lligat with Dalí when the two arrived. Dalí kissed Jeff and recommended him not to cut off his long hair. Jeff said little, seemed arrogant and, virtually ignoring Gala, stared fixedly with his black eyes at Amanda (later he would try to go to bed with her but Amanda says she never told Gala).[107]

The affair cost Gala a fortune and she not only bought a house for Fenholt on Long Island valued at $1.25 million but gave him Dalí paintings.[108] Gala once showed Reynolds Morse a telegram she had just received from Fenholt. It read 'Must have $38,000 or will die.' Morse refused to take the money to him, as Gala requested. Let her smuggle black money through the customs herself if she wanted, that was her lookout. But he was not going to be involved.[109]

When Dalí discovered the extent of Gala's outlay on Fenholt he was apparently enraged, and there is little doubt that her enduring infatuation with the actor was one of the factors that led to the painter's gradual decline during the late 1970s and early 1980s.

Fenholt later became a TV preacher in California and denied that there had ever been anything sexual in his relationship with Gala. Like Dalí, she was merely a friend. How could he possibly ever have gone to bed with an old woman with skin cancer? It was unthinkable.[110]

The Inauguration of the Theatre-Museum

In 1971, inspired by the work of Nobel Prize winner Dennis Gabor, Dalí had begun to experiment in holograms, Gabor himself providing some advice. In 1972, at Knoedler's, Dalí had exhibited three holographic compositions and some other results of his visual researches. They were written off in *Time* by no less a critic than Robert Hughes, for whom the artist, now merely repeating himself, had 'simply used a new medium to transmit his old mannerisms'.[111] Hughes's criticism was fair enough—Dalí was still basically into optical illusions—and there was no implication that the painter was not genuinely interested in holograms. He was as interested as he had been a few years earlier in rhinoceroses or DNA, and as he continued to be in stereoscopy. Holograms were, simply, the newest, 3-D obsessions of an artist who had always claimed to be excited by the latest scientific breakthroughs.

Knoedler's was now Dalí's main exhibition base in New York. In 1973 he issued from the gallery a statement about the importance of his work in holograms (one day, he claimed, it would be acknowledged in the history of art),[112] and, between 6 March and 6 April 1974 he held another show there. The Morses, who had their misgivings about the direction of Dalí's latest work, were on hand to help him close down the exhibition. They sensed that Dalí and the 'hot tempered' Peter Moore, that 'astute Irish adventurer', were about to part company. Soon afterwards, once Morse had gone around New York with a huge wad of dollars paying off Gala's outstanding bills, he and his wife accompanied Dalí and her to Cannes on board the SS *France*, which was making its last crossing. Gala spent an hour impatiently waiting for Jeff Fenholt to come and see her off, but Jesus Christ Superstar did not turn up. During the crossing Morse and Dalí devised a book about the role of animals in the painter's work, Dalí insisting that they use the title *Animal Crackers*. Morse found Moore intolerable during the voyage and felt sure that Dalí's aide was 'bitterly jealous' of their closeness to the artist. Morse had his own reasons for being angry with Moore. In the first place, the 'military adviser' was spreading the story that he and Dalí had met by chance while having a pee in the urinals at the St Regis. Then there was the issue of *The Discovery of America*, which still rankled. Huntington Hartford's Museum of Modern Art had not gone well, and by 1970 he had closed it and was selling off some of the paintings. *The Discovery of America* was put up for auction on 10 March 1971. In his *Dalí Journal* Morse records that he and Moore were to have bought the painting jointly, but that Moore, a 'psychotic and a liar', pushed off leaving him 'holding the baby'.[113] Moore's story is different. According to him, the estimated price of the painting was $27,000, which he considered ludicrously low. Had he not just sold six lithographs to a Mrs Lucas for $50,000? She would go beserk if the huge painting fetched so little! So Moore roped in some friends to compete for the picture and push the price up to $100,000. The gambit worked and Reynolds Morse, who had hoped to buy the painting for the estimated $27,000 was furious. He paid up nonetheless—and then complained bitterly to Dalí. 'It was ridiculous,' Moore recalls. 'I'd just made his collection worth a fortune. He was a bloody millionaire and all he could do was complain!'[114] Moore, in fact, was not in the least jealous of the couple's relationship with Dalí and felt nothing but scorn for Reynolds Morse, whom he considered boorish, ignorant and loud-mouthed. The two men were utterly incompatible.[115]

When Dalí landed in Cannes on 30 April 1974 he must have been pleased to discover that the bookshops were prominently displaying André Parinaud's recently published *Comment on devient Dalí* (issued in English with the title *The Unspeakable Confessions of Salvador Dalí*). 'How to Get Rid of One's Father', 'How to Become Erotic While Remaining Chaste', 'How Not to Be a Catalan', 'How to Become a Super-Snob', 'How to Make Love to Gala'—such chapter headings set the tone of the book. Parinaud's introduction showed that he had tacked together Dalí's comments from a wide variety of sources, and should have made the wary reader launch into the book with some scepticism. The author had tried to follow Dalí's ideas through 'his writings, his memories, the testimony of his intimates and friends', and was pleased with the results: 'Conversations, taped interviews, surveys, all the techniques of analysis have been used in order to situate the Dalinian statements in their proper contexts and frames of reference.' What 'all the techniques of analysis' were was not clarified, nor were the different sources that Parinaud had tapped identified in the text. The result was chaos, but this did not stop the critics from admiring the book—or future biographers from relying on it far too heavily. Dalí himself was presumably indifferent to considerations of authenticity. Parinaud had status (his book on Breton was well known) and *Comment on devient Dalí* was excellent publicity.

Dalí's Theatre-Museum in Figueres was much on his mind at this time, and from Cannes he telephoned Ramon Guardiola with instructions.[116] On 2 May, when he arrived in Figueres and donated to the museum one of his most treasured possessions, *The Basket of Bread*, Guardiola (no longer mayor but still closely associated with the project) knew that the battle was won.[117] It was now thirteen years since he had assumed the responsibility of turning Dalí's dream into reality. He had had to cut through swathe upon swathe of red tape, and there had been constant setbacks; but his efforts were about to have their reward. It was just a question of putting the last touches to the statutes of the Fundación and of finalizing the composition of the Board. On 20 May Dalí, who had just turned seventy, drove with Guardiola and Gonzalo Serraclara to Madrid, where he had interviews with Franco, Prince Juan Carlos and other authorities, all with the purpose of ensuring that the museum opened as planned that September.[118]

Guardiola realized during the trip to Madrid that Dalí was worried about his prostate. Every year he had had a check-up in the States and was told that all was in order. But now he needed to urinate twice during the night and felt sure that something was wrong.[119] The moment he got home he went to Barcelona and consulted Dr Antonio

Puigvert, one of Spain's leading hernia and prostate specialists. Puigvert diagnosed a hernia, not a prostate problem, and operated on 3 June. All went well and Dalí was able to return to Port Lligat on the 17th. He seemed to be in good spirits but there are indications that he was more shaken by the operation than he was prepared to let on.[120]

Before the operation Dalí and Gala had taken the precaution of making radically new joint wills in which, after provision for Cécile Éluard and Gala's sister Lídia, all their artistic possessions were now to go, not to the Prado, as in 1960, but, under the aegis of the National Heritage (Patrimonio Nacional), to the Theatre-Museum in Figueres.[121]

On 27 September the statutes of the 'Dalí Theatre-Museum Public Services Foundation' were passed by the Figueres Town Council. The following day saw the official opening of the building, although it was not yet entirely finished.[122] The invitation card had been designed by Dalí and showed a fanciful view of the building seen from the square outside. Piñero's cupola was surmounted by a ball and cross (never placed there in reality), and flames seemed to be issuing from the dome in every direction. In the very centre of the ground floor was a doorway with a figure in outline: anyone knowing Dalí's work would have recognized yet another double allusion to Raphael's *The Marriage of the Virgin* and to *Las Meninas*. The invitation was from 'Gala and Salvador Dalí and, in their name, the Honourable Town Council of Figueres'.[123]

Figueres was packed to bursting for the great occasion, with a liberal sprinkling of gaudily attired hippies in attendance. There were television cameras everywhere. Majorettes and dancers and musicians and an elephant performed in the streets, and not even the tremendous tramuntana that was blowing succeeded in dampening the high spirits of the crowd waiting to see Dalí and his Muse arrive in the open Cadillac. After the official ceremony in the Town Hall, in which the Minister of Housing handed over the building to the Town Council and Dalí was given the Gold Medal of Figueres, the couple walked the few metres to the Theatre-Museum, where more than a thousand guests were getting impatient because everything was running late.

Eighty years old and showing it, despite the facelifts and the black wig, Gala was carrying a bunch of sweet-smelling spikenard, and looked somewhat dazed as she entered the building with Dalí.[124] With them was Amanda Lear, stunning in the light-chestnut muslin dress Dalí had bought her specially for the occasion. Gala had flown Jeff Fenholt over from New York. As they pushed their way towards the entrance to the Theatre-Museum, Jesus Christ Superstar got left behind in the crush. 'Jeff! Jeff!' Amanda heard Gala scream frantically. 'Don't worry, he'll catch us up,' Dalí assured her. No sooner safely inside Jeff kept disappearing, which was hardly surprising in view of the array of fabulous young women assembled that evening under Emilio Piñero's articulated dome.

Before long, seething with jealousy, Gala grabbed him and whisked him back to Púbol.

Some of Amanda Lear's collages were on show, and according to her were much admired, while Dalí's unfinished painting *Roger Freeing Angelica*, which celebrated her angular form, dominated the great hall. Amanda felt proud to be beside Dalí in his moment of glory, just as she felt proud to have participated in a small way in the different phases of the museum's development.[125]

Reactions to the museum were mixed, but the general feeling was that it lacked work of substance, whatever Dalí's claims about it being a Theatre of Memory designed to stir the subconscious of the visitor and lead him or her to inner and unexpected discoveries. Dalí once told Reynolds Morse (whose own Dalí museum had opened in Cleveland in 1971) that he intended placing a 'vomitorium' outside so that people on leaving would be able to throw up at their ease. This was not quite the reaction of the critics to the Theatre-Museum, but it was certainly felt that, for the moment—with a few exceptions such as *The Spectre of Sex-Appeal*—the museum offered stones for bread.[126]

Probably the most disappointed person that evening in the Theatre-Museum was Ramon Guardiola. He considered that Dalí should have been accompanied not only by the local and Madrid authorities but by artists, writers and intellectuals of international standing, none of whom were to be seen. The occasion had been designed mainly to satisfy the interests and perspectives of the politicians, not to honour Dalí's expressed desire that the Theatre-Museum should be one of Europe's 'spiritual centres'. In Guardiola's opinion the inauguration had been shoddy and badly organized. If he had been in charge no doubt things would have gone better.[127]

Antoni Pitxot; *To Be God*

In 1972 a person had come into Dalí's life who was to assume great importance in the painter's last years. This was Antonio Pichot Soler, the son of the cellist Ricard Pichot Gironés, whom in 1920 Dalí had painted practising at Es Sortell, in Cadaqués. Antonio was born in Figueres in 1924, just across the square from the Dalís, and inherited the artistic temperament, as well as the striking looks, of his remarkable family. Like his older brother Ramon, he had decided early in life to be a painter. In this both of them followed consciously in the footsteps of their uncle, Ramon Pichot Gironés, the great friend of Picasso, whose late Impressionist paintings had inspired Dalí during his momentous stay at the Molí de la Torre in 1916.

Antonio Pichot was largely brought up in San Sebastian, in the north of Spain, where, by a surprising coincidence, his art teacher was Juan Núñez Fernández, the master who had taught Dalí in Figueres and whom he considered one of the most vital influences on his development as an artist. In 1964, after marrying Leocadia Pla, Pichot returned to the Empordà. As he became immersed in local life and culture, he decided to adopt the Catalan rendering of his Christian name and surname.

Antoni Pitxot had been aware of Dalí from his childhood, visiting him on several occasions with his family before the civil war. But it was not until 1972, when one day Dalí arrived at his studio in Cadaqués with Amanda Lear, that their friendship began. Dalí knew Antoni's brother, Ramon, but was not particularly interested in his painting. When he heard that Antoni was more original, and made paintings from the stones of Cadaqués, he wanted to see his work. Hence the visit to Es Sortell. Dalí liked what he saw and invited Antoni to help him in the Theatre-Museum. Before long Pitxot was making a weekly trip to Figueres.[128]

Dalí was charmed to be able to help the career of a nephew of his beloved Pepito Pichot, so, when he conceived the idea of exhibiting Catalan artists in the first-floor rooms of the museum, Pitxot was his first choice. Soon Pitxot's work was to become a permanent (and unexplained) feature of the museum, causing surprise to visitors and some resentment among other local painters. Pitxot helped Dalí with further developments to the building and by 1977 was a key figure in Dalí's entourage.[129]

In 1972, the same year that he met Pitxot, Dalí had begun work on an 'opera-poem', with himself in the role of protagonist, entitled *To Be God* (*Être Dieu*). The Catalan novelist Manuel Vázquez Montalbán was commissioned to produce the libretto, and the composer Igor Wakhévitch the music. Most of Dalí's operatic, film and ballet projects had fallen through, but this one fared somewhat better and in 1974 was recorded in Paris, although it would be ten years before it was issued (as a compact disc).[130] The theme of this megalomaniacal work is that Dalí is almost God—but not quite. After all, if he *were* God, as the Choir reminds us throughout, he would not be Dalí, and that would not do at all. Moreover, Gala is there to remind him that he is human, appearing at the end of the work to stretch towards him a 'redemptive hand'.

Among the work's strands there is a strongly anti-democratic element, and in one of his monologues Dalí passionately defends José Antonio Primo de Rivera, the founder of the Falange, and scorns electoral systems which enable 'cretins' to vote. The praise of absolute monarchy confirms that Dalí was now worried about the ageing General Franco's succession, although there is no direct allusion to the political situation in Spain.

A good deal of improvisation was involved during the recording sessions. The libretto is in French, but Catalan and Spanish break through frequently, with an occasional nod in the direction of English. No other recording captures the rich inflections of Dalí's speaking voice so well as this one, and listening to him singing snatches of bawdy Catalan folksongs, or reciting his favourite childhood tongue twister (taught to him by his maternal grandmother, Maria Anna Ferrés), one is made aware of the charm and humour that mitigated the painter's obsessive egoism. Despite such saving graces, one hearing of the work, which runs for over two hours, will be more than enough for most people. And it seems unlikely that, without Dalí to help it along, his 'opera-poem' will ever be performed.

The Departure of Peter Moore

With Gala insisting that she wanted Enric Sabater to take over completely from Peter Moore, and Dalí only putting up feeble opposition, the 'military adviser' knew that sooner or later, and probably sooner, she would get her own way. So he decided to quit. It was 1974.

There were other good reasons for going. Moore had made his money, a lot of it, and he had a tumour that needed urgent attention. 'When I left Dalí he had $32,000,000 in the bank,' he said in May 1993, adding that on one occasion Dalí had asked him how much that was in pesetas! At a conservative estimate, this meant that Moore had netted three million dollars for himself.[131] He had made a lot of enemies in the process. One of them was Robert Descharnes, or, as Moore liked to call him, 'Robert Sans Charme'. For the French photographer Moore felt nothing but scorn. One day Moore's wife, Catherine Perrot, the young Swiss woman he had married in 1971, gave tea to Descharnes's two sons. 'Where's the thief? Where are all the girls?' asked one of them. Moore returned shortly afterwards, heard what had been said, and, when Descharnes came to pick up the boys, kicked him down the stairs. This, at least, is his version of the episode.[132]

One of Moore's last deals before he left the Dalís was a contract by which the painter was to produce seventy-eight tarot card illustrations for a James Bond film. When Dalí procrastinated, and the producer backed out, an American publisher called Lyle Stuart came on the scene. Dalí again failed to produce, Stuart took legal action and $300,000 were frozen in the painter's First National City bank account. A settlement was negotiated whereby, between 1976 and 1977, Dalí was to sign 17,500 sheets of blank paper for the tarot illustrations. In fact he signed three thousand more than was necessary, and these were sold off to Leon Amiel, the art books and prints publisher. What they were used for is anybody's guess, and presumably Dalí did not care.[133]

Like Moore, Enric Sabater, who now took over, was never paid a salary, and worked on a commission basis. A 5 per cent commission, as Peter Moore claims? Sabater is indignant: 'I was born here, I am a Catalan, I don't think a Catalan could accept less than an Englishman! I got more than 10 per cent because Mr Moore was doing only the contracts for etchings, and contracts for TV shows, that sort of thing, but never for oil paintings, never.'[134]

Peter Moore had always been careful to separate his business and private lives. 'I made a pact with Dalí from the start,' he recalls. 'Pas de familiarité, pas de déjeuners, pas de dîners . . .' So he did not even invite him to his wedding with Catherine Perrot in 1971. Dalí was astonished by this, took to Catherine, and a year later did something totally out of character: he not only gave her a wedding present, the painting *The Triple Image* (1939), but signed it for her. Dalí had told Moore time and again how he enjoyed spreading confusion around him and cretinizing people. But he never tried it with his 'military adviser' for whom, beyond any doubt, he entertained a healthy respect.[135]

Dalí with Peter and Catherine Moore, 1975–6.

Enric Sabater made no such division between his life and the Dalís. 'The fact is,' he said in 1996, 'that through no particular merit of my own I lived with them, lunched and dined with them and travelled with them almost every day for about twelve years.' Since both Dalí and Sabater were Empordanese, they not only conversed in local Catalan but shared a similar background. This was important. And with Gala there was no communication problem either, since Sabater had a good command of French.[136] In a few years Sabater was well into the multi-millionaire category, driving a Maserati and running an empire that spanned four continents. The fact is that as a businessman and wheeler-dealer he made Peter Moore look like a novice.

Today Peter Moore looks back somewhat wistfully at the years he spent with Dalí, and wishes that he had paid more attention to what the Master said (unlike Reynolds Morse, Moore was no diary keeper). 'I never really knew Dalí because I wasn't that interested!' he says. 'I never tried to make my life a Dalí life. The only thing I did, when I got into Dalí's life, I made money. I certainly enjoyed my connection with Dalí, of course, but I didn't take it too seriously. After all, I used to eat and sleep at Churchill's house and I didn't even take *him* seriously! I often asked myself how long it could last. I made more money with Dalí than the President of the United States!'[137]

That Moore behaved well towards the Dalís is confirmed by Nanita Kalaschnikoff. 'Peter Moore loved Dalí,' she has said. 'Sure, he had his failings and was a bit of an adventurer, but he loved Dalí and never cheated him. And he was a gentleman. If he had stayed on, Dalí would have been looked after. It was a tragedy that he went.'[138]

Moore never pretended to understand much about art, but knew what he liked. By the time he left Dalí he had acquired several works, not only by Dalí himself but by other artists. These were to form the basis of the Dalí museum he opened in Cadaqués in 1978 in the Hotel Miramar, where Gala and Éluard had stayed in 1929. It has been said that Dalí was jealous of Moore's museum in Cadaqués, feeling that it had been set up in opposition to his own Theatre-Museum in Figueres. This is nonsense. Dalí visited it, approved, and told Moore that he feared that with the museum he would lose all the money he had made being his 'military adviser'.[139]

But Moore did not lose all his money in the venture, he was far too smart for that. As regards the means by which he had earned it, he insists today that these were legitimate: he was a good businessman, certainly, but not dishonest. And the blank sheets? He denies vehemently that he trafficked with these before or after he left the painter. But given the life-style of the Master and his determination to corrupt those around him, anyone working as his business manager was almost bound to lower his ethical standards: the huge amount of money involved made it virtually impossible to retain one's full integrity. In Moore's favour it could be argued that his presence and good manners had a certain civilizing influence on Dalí and his entourage. What came next, at all events, would be much worse.

Shocks to the System

On 27 September 1975 an ailing General Franco executed the last of his innumerable victims, five alleged terrorists of whom three reputedly belonged to the Basque organization ETA. He did so in the face of worldwide criticism; and several pleas for clemency from Pope Paul VI received particular publicity in view of the régime's professed Catholicism.

The Spanish Government reacted energetically against the foreign protests, and pro-Franco demonstrations were imposed throughout the country on 1 October (with severe penalties for the workers who did not take part). The largest was held in Madrid's Plaza de Oriente, where busloads of participants driven in from the surrounding towns and even the provinces swelled the huge crowd. *Le Monde* estimated that two hundred thousand people crammed the plaza, although the authorities claimed a million.[1] Anti-European banners were much in evidence, as were blue Falangist shirts and Fascist salutes. The chant 'Franco! Franco! Franco!' burst insistently from tens of thousands of throats until the diminutive dictator appeared on a balcony of the palace, accompanied by a 'rigid and impassive' Prince Juan Carlos de Borbón, his chosen successor. Wearing dark shades, the Caudillo gave a seven-minute speech in a tiny trickle of a voice hardly audible because of the deficient loudspeaker system. He was called back seven times, weeping with emotion. That evening Spaniards saw the demonstration on television and heard Franco ascribe the foreign protests to a sinister Marxist-Masonic plot, promise that the army and the forces of law and order would do their duty, and affirm that, clearly, Spaniards were once again becoming something important in the world.[2]

Chapter FIFTEEN

There had been some nasty incidents during the day. Three policemen were shot in Madrid, and foreigners, including journalists, were spat at, threatened and ridiculed.[3] The situation in the Basque country was particularly tense. The workers went on strike in Guipúzcoa and Vizcaya, and in San Sebastián the police prevented the celebration of a requiem mass for the executed men, going out of their way to increase their unpopularity in the process. One French journalist judged the situation 'pre-revolutionary'.[4]

The Spanish opponents of the dictatorship were heartened by the international reaction. Mexico called for Spain's expulsion from the United Nations. Amnesty International accused the Spanish police of 'massive and systematic use of torture'. The French trades unions organized a 'Day of Action and Boycott Against Spain', and engineered a massive electricity power cut in Paris. In support, Air France suspended its flights to Madrid and Barcelona, the Senate and National Assembly adjourned and an angry crowd gathered outside the Spanish Embassy. In England, the ground staff at Heathrow voted to boycott Iberia Airlines; there was a moment's silence in the Italian Senate; Finland and Austria recalled their ambassadors for discussion; and the EEC Commission advised breaking off deliberations with Spain about the country's entry into the Common Market.[5]

Agence France-Presse asked Dalí for his opinion of the executions and their aftermath. He replied that, in his opinion, the Madrid rally and the foreign protests were 'the biggest present that could have been made to our Generalissimo Franco', and went on:

> The success he's had today, with a crowd of more than two million people acclaiming him the greatest hero of Spain (the entire Spanish people supporting him), could never have happened if there hadn't been these incidents. The hostility of the other countries has made him thirty years younger in a second. He's a wonderful person. This guarantees that the coming monarchy will be totally successful. We'll see then that Spain is a country where, in a few months, there'll be no more terrorism because they're going to be liquidated like rats. Three times more executions are needed. But there've been enough for the moment.

Dalí proceeded to reel off his well-known view of liberty: 'Personally I'm against freedom. I'm for the Holy Inquisition. Freedom is shit, and that's why all countries fail when there's an excess of freedom. Lenin said so: "Freedom is no use for anything."'[6]

The following morning, Thursday 2 October, Dalí toned down his previous statement somewhat. He now explained that he was against all forms of terrorism and, in principle, all death penalties. But, since the latter existed in some countries, 'It's not for me,' he said, 'to meddle in how the law is applied.' As regards the future of Spain, it would be an error to introduce a democratic system. 'Like all Spaniards I am looking forward to the reign of Prince Juan Carlos, the future king of Spain.' To absolute monarchy, in other words.[7]

Dalí's remarks provoked another outcry, and film director Alexander Jodorowsky, who had hoped to sign him up to play the Emperor of the Galaxy in the film version of Frank Herbert's novel *Dune*, announced that he had changed his mind. 'I would be ashamed to use now in my work a man who in his masochistic exhibitionism demands the ignoble death of human beings', Jodorowsky put it.[8]

The protests caused by the executions, and by Dalí's comments, went largely unreported in Franco's censored press, but they were profusely disseminated by the Spanish-language radio stations operating in Europe, not least the BBC World Service (which had a large following in Spain). Dalí realized that this time he had gone too far; and when abusive graffiti were scrawled on the walls of his house in Port Lligat, stones thrown at the windows and death threats began to arrive by telegram and letter, he decided to quit the country without delay.[9]

He was encouraged to do so by Enric Sabater, now fully in charge of Dalí's affairs, who had recently acquired a private detective's licence and a gun. It has often been said that the weapon terrified Dalí and gave Sabater increased power over him. This was Amanda Lear's view, certainly: Sabater encouraged Dalí's fears in order to cast himself in the role of protector.[10] Today Sabater denies all of this vehemently and claims that the gun was Dalí's idea. Over the following years he was occasionally to draw it, notably when a lunatic Dutchman broke into the house and threatened the servants, but he never pulled the trigger.[11]

The Dalís flew from Barcelona to Geneva, accompanied by Sabater and Amanda Lear. Dalí was apprehensive about his first trip by air, so Amanda gave him Valium to calm him down. As a result he loved the flight and announced that henceforth he was going to travel by plane. Then, on 10 October, the Dalís and Sabater flew to New York, settling in once again at the St Regis.[12] There they found that everyone knew about the artist's comments on the executions, which had been widely reported in the American press. Dalí's attorney, Arnold Grant, was deeply concerned about the situation. 'Best known as the husband of Bess Myerson, former Miss America', Grant was particularly worried that the scandal might affect the prices of Dalí's work (an anxiety all the more understandable in view of the fact that the Dalís paid him in art work, not cash).[13] Sabater explained to Reynolds Morse that he and the Dalís had gone first to Geneva. Why? Morse suspected, probably correctly, that Gala (now eighty-one) had left Spain with a thick and illegal wad of banknotes, as was her wont, to be lodged to a Swiss account.[14]

Dalí now began to tell America that he had not expressed approval of the executions, or called for further ones. Yes, he was in favour of the Inquisition; yes, he hated liberty and supported Franco; but he was against the death penalty (the wrong man might be killed) and against abortion (you might be depriving the world of a genius, perhaps even of another Dalí)[15] Few people believed the disavowal, least of all the exiled Spanish Republicans in New York who were eagerly awaiting Franco's death so that they could return in good conscience to the fatherland. Eugenio Granell, a younger-generation Surrealist painter from Galicia and a friend of Breton, was a case in point. Dalí, he said, 'was absolutely despised by all serious intellectuals and artists'; and the general feeling among the anti-Franco community in New York was that he had changed 'from a genius in the 30s to a clown today'.[16]

Convinced that 'the Communists' and the Basque terrorist organization, ETA, were thirsty for revenge, the frightened artist's dependence on the gun-toting Sabater grew apace, and during these months he rarely showed his face in public. Reynolds Morse thought Dalí looked shattered. Sabater was 'playing the Communist threats to the hilt', he concluded, and the affair was affecting Dalí 'more than anything we have seen during the last 32 years'. Morse found that Dalí was following Franco's decline anxiously and that he 'seems to age in proportion as does the Generalissimo'.[17]

It was now clear, moreover, that Franco was seriously ill, and that, despite the dictator's provision for his monarchist succession, Spain might well be on the verge of another period of turmoil, perhaps even of a new civil war. Dalí, who despite his 'conversion' to Catholicism in the 1950s had rarely set foot in a church, now began to pay a daily visit to Saint Patrick's Cathedral, not far from the St Regis, to pray for the Caudillo's recovery, where Sabater was amazed to see him crossing himself and kneeling. Every day an anxious call would be put through to Franco's residence in Madrid to enquire about his health. And when the news came on 20 November that he had died, Dalí almost collapsed. Probably he feared that if the monarchy failed and the Left gained power, he might never be able to return home.[18]

Luckily for Dalí, and for Spain, the ably advised King Juan Carlos de Borbón proved a winner, piloting the dangerous course from dictatorship to full constitutional monarchy with consummate skill. The 'Transition', as it is known in Spain, was to culminate in the 1978 constitution, which enshrined the concept of national reconciliation, provided for democratic monarchy and demoted the Catholic Church from its previous position as the State's established religion.

The three years leading up to the promulgation of the constitution were fraught with tension and peril, and there was a strong possibility that the disgruntled Francoists, furious that Juan Carlos had broken his vows to the dictator, might stage a military coup and set the clock back. Dr Manuel Vergara, Dalí's doctor in Cadaqués, was struck by his decline when he saw him again. 'Franco's death terrified Dalí,' he remembered in 1996. 'So did Sabater's gun. He was in a state of constant fear. I tried to chivvy him along, "Come on, Salvador, for Christ's sake, there's nothing wrong with you, be a man", that sort of thing. He'd buck up for a day and then it would start all over again.'[19]

The year 1975 saw not only Franco's death and the beginning of a new democratic Spain, but a major change in the running of Dalí and Gala's professional life. It was brought about mainly by the nervous breakdown of their attorney, Arnold Grant, who was forced to retire. Grant's place was taken by an ambitious and clever young laywer from Wisconsin called Michael Ward Stout, who had met Dalí at a cocktail reception given by the painter in the St Regis. Stout was an admirer of Motherwell and Rauschenberg, and the introduction to Dalí took place somewhat against his will: Dalí's art did not appeal to him, nor his public performances, and the painter was known among Stout's friends in the visual arts as 'this sort of sell-out, this commercial former genius who basically was involved only in his own exploitation of his abilities to market himself'. The evening turned out well, nonetheless. Dalí found the thirty-two-year-old Stout fascinating (his chubby face and prematurely bald head reminded him of his father), and he was particularly interested when he learnt that he specialized in copyright law. Stout became the Dalís' lawyer in New York, and was soon working for them on an international footing. One of his first, and easiest, tasks was to sort out a business problem for Gala.[20]

Stout was to grow to appreciate Dalí, if not his art. But he never accepted drawings or anything else in lieu of fees, as Arnold Grant had done. Like any New York lawyer worth his salt, he charged by the hour (some accounts say by the quarter-hour), no matter what services he provided. Gala, resistent at first, eventually accepted this system, although she never failed to quibble over the bills.[21]

In New York Stout soon met not only Enric Sabater but Peter Moore. He saw at once that they were very different personalities. Moore, he felt, with his flamboyant and charming persona, had been good for the Dalís in the 1960s. But as the Dalís entered the 1970s and became increasingly dependent, Moore was not so useful. 'Enrique was much better in his first years at getting the table at the restaurant, getting the limousine in the rain, getting the aeroplane arranged.' He was also very clever at business. In Stout's opinion, though, Dalí did *not* need Sabater's gun: Dalí was in a continuous state of agitation, and although Sabater tried hard to protect him, his style of protection made Dalí even more frightened.[22]

It did not take Stout long to discover that the Dalís' affairs were in chaos, not least their tax situation. At that time Dalí claimed to be a United States permanent resident, and he and his wife were carriers of the 'green card'.[23] The Dalís had always paid some tax in the United States, but it had never corresponded to the reality of the artist's huge income, most of which was received in cash. For years Gala had been moving currency around illegally—and was doing so increasingly. Shortly after Stout took over, the Internal Revenue Service pounced and began a criminal investigation into the couple's tax situation (it seems that they had been alerted by the fact that the Dalís had sacked their long-standing accountant, Harry Bach, known to be an honest man).[24] An investigation by the IRS was a very serious matter indeed, and to handle it Stout retained a prominent firm of lawyers specializing only in 'the most sophisticated international tax problems'. After lengthy and intricate negotiations it proved possible for the Dalís' 1976–7 affairs to be settled to the satisfaction of the federal authorities, who had somehow been convinced that the couple should now be classified as 'non-resident aliens'. But from then on the IRS was never to relax its vigilance.[25]

Michael Stout's position within the Dalí entourage became much more complicated and ambivalent when he began to act in a professional capacity for Sabater as well as for Dalí. He claimed later that he had tried to avoid such a situation, but that both men had insisted on retaining him. This dual allegiance was to prove one of the key features in the tangle that characterized Dalí's declining years, with the empire-building Sabater at the centre of the web.[26]

One of the first major operations engineered by Stout was the setting up of a Spanish limited company for Dalí, Sabater and Sabater's wife. It went under the name of Dasa Ediciones ('Da' for Dalí, 'sa' for Sabater) and was registered in Girona on 31 May 1976.[27] Stout also participated in the creation of an off-shore company for Sabater (and perhaps Dalí) in tax-free Curaçao. It was called Dalart Naamloze Vernootschap (Dalart Ltd) and specialized in the sale of jewels and other objects designed by Dalí as well as in the reproduction rights to his work.[28]

Meanwhile, as Spain continued its progress in the direction of full democracy, Dalí was made aware on several occasions of the hostility felt towards him by many of his fellow Catalans. He was deeply disturbed when in February 1976 a bomb was discovered under his habitual seat in the Via Veneto Restaurant in Barcelona (Dalí was in New York at the time),[29] and no less so when, a few months later, he was not allowed to participate in an exhibition held in Girona to honour the writer and historian Carles Rahola, who had been executed by the Fascists in 1939.[30]

Dalí kept a low profile in Spain at this time, waiting for the situation to improve. The gradual consolidation of the monarchy sustained him, and as the stock of Juan Carlos and Queen Sofía rose he lost no opportunity to express his devotion to the royal couple, coming to see the King as Defender of Dalí and himself as potential court painter. His trust was justified, for, protocol apart, both Juan Carlos and Sofía felt some affection for Dalí and were to visit him informally on several occasions over the following years.

Spain's democratic process was not without serious obstacles. The ultra-conservative and neo-Fascist forces in the country were appalled by the changes that were taking place, and on 24 January 1977 an assassination squad murdered five left-wing lawyers in Madrid. Half a million people took to the streets in protest. In March 1977 Franco's State-controlled trades unions were abolished. Then, on 9 April, Easter Saturday, with most of the army on leave, the government legalized the Communist Party. The worst fears of the extreme Right had been confirmed. The military establishment was outraged (some of its sectors, true to Spanish tradition, were already planning a *coup d'état*), and several Cabinet ministers resigned. It was one of the most dangerous moments in the transition to democracy. Dalí kept a close and extremely apprehensive eye on what was happening. But he was careful not to open his mouth.[31]

His state of mind did not improve when, in June 1977, he found that he was again having difficulty urinating. Always anxious about developing cancer of the prostate, the illness that had killed his father, Dalí, panic-stricken, telephoned Antonio Puigvert, the Barcelona surgeon who had operated on his hernia in 1974. Puigvert sensibly refused to travel specially to New York (he knew his man) but sent an assistant to help prepare Dalí for the flight to Spain. The TWA staff were very co-operative, and curtained off four back seats so that the Master could have privacy. Sabater recalls: 'Every hour during the interminable flight I had to help Dalí to the lavatory, take his trousers down, empty the container the doctor had fixed up, put it back. I can never forget that flight. It was an inferno. It seemed to go on forever.'[32]

When Dalí arrived in Barcelona Doctor Puigvert noticed that there was something odd about him. Suddenly it dawned on him: he was drugged. It transpired that Dalí had been taking ten or more pills a day, prescribed independently by different doctors for a variety of real or imaginary complaints. Perhaps they included the anti-depressants that Carlos Lozano had seen Dalí swallow. Puigvert had Dalí detoxified. He then operated on his prostate. There were no complications. The artist was vastly relieved and henceforth was to call Puigvert his 'Angel of the Pee-Pee'. But the painting Dalí had promised him in payment was never handed over. So much for Dalinian gratitude.[33]

After a few weeks' rest Dalí was allowed home. He looked very shaken as he left the clinic, but when the writer Josep Pla saw him that July in Port Lligat he deemed him 'magnificent, healthy, extremely animated'.[34] Pla was a fellow *empordaneso* (although from Lower rather than Upper Empordà), had been a fan of Dalí's since before the war, and had written the best book on Cadaqués. Dalí admired Pla, insofar as he admired any contemporary. And when the writer proposed a book on him, putting the emphasis on his local roots, with some illustrations by the artist, Dalí accepted. Entitled *Salvador Dalí. Museum Works*, Pla's text was to be published by Dasa Ediciones, Sabater's imprint, in 1981.

While Dalí recuperated in Port Lligat, the Musée Goya in the French town of Castres (Tarn) held a summer exhibition of his eighty drypoint reworkings of Goya's *Caprichos*, executed (at Peter Moore's suggestion) between 1973 and early 1977 on heliogravures specially prepared in Paris.[35] These coloured adaptations have a certain interest, even charm. Drawing on his experiments as a schoolboy, when he would convert the illustrations in his textbooks into new creations, Dalí used Goya's powerful etchings as a vehicle for his secret obsessions. Developing the slightest sexual or scatological hint in the originals, and substituting his own captions for Goya's (with one or two exceptions), the works are peppered with crutches, soft watches, ejaculating penises (even a hanged man's), vaginas, delectable female bottoms and Great Masturbators (including an airborne variety). One of the most interesting variations is Number 8. Goya's plate shows an apparently dead young woman in an elegant dress being carried off by two sinister, hooded figures over the caption 'They took her away'. There is a suggestion of rape or violence. The caption reminded Dalí of the opening lines of Lorca's most famous ballad, 'The Faithless Wife', which begins 'And so I took her to the river/thinking she was a virgin/but she had a husband'. The copulation scene recounted by Lorca's gypsy is unique in Spanish poetry for the verve and richness of its imagery, and Dalí must have known the poem by heart. The new caption borrows Lorca's words 'to the river thinking she was a virgin', and into the space behind Goya's group Dalí has introduced a grotesque male monster which is contemplating the brutal scene in the foreground. It has a vast but noticeably flaccid penis. A crude allusion to both Dalí and Lorca's heterosexual impotence? The plate, at all events, is yet another indication of the continuing hold exerted over Dalí by Lorca and his work.[36]

Although by the end of the summer of 1977 Dalí had recovered from his prostate operation, he was in poor shape generally as he crossed the barrier of his seventy-third birthday. Gala, despite the fact that she was ten years older, was faring better. Dr Manuel Vergara had now been looking after her for seventeen years, and was amazed at her determination to go on living life to the full. This meant, above all, Jeff Fenholt. Jesus Christ Superstar's visits to Púbol had become less frequent, so Gala's main aim now, as well as staying eternally young, was to spend as much time as possible in New York.[37]

Dalí and Gala's life-style had for years required a constant flow of ready cash. While Dalí would now do almost anything for money up front, graphics continued to be his main source of income. Sabater was only too happy to let him have his way. The current rate by 1979 for a single reproduction, Morse noted in his diary, was $100,000, Sabater retaining the original and the rights to other editions of the same work for himself. Thanks to this arrangement he was growing richer and richer.[38]

In an attempt to reduce the Dalís' tax bill, or to enable them to avoid taxes altogether, Sabater arranged during 1977 for the couple to become resident in Monaco. It was a foolish mistake. The Dalís never stayed the requisite time in the principality, and the ploy only caused more problems for them later on when they sought to regularize their position in Spain.[39]

According to Morse, by this time Dalí had forced Sabater to purchase from Peter Moore the lease on the building in front of the Theatre-Museum in Figueres. Moore had hoped to sell a line of Dalí 'crap' there, but now the place was going to the man responsible for producing the crap, Enric Sabater. In the shop Sabater was planning to merchandise Dasa Edicioness' reproductions of Dalí work. Reynolds Morse was appalled: Dalí's partnership with his own business manager had introduced 'a whole new and even more questionable ball game, no matter how it is painted'. Meanwhile Gala was splashing out huge sums of money on Jeff Fenholt. 'Here is the stuff real fiction is made of,' wrote Morse in his diary. 'A Catalan gangster made incredibly rich by exploiting the world's most famous painter! A Catalan peasant watching a 90 some year old Russian woman lavish more cash in a single dollop on a young protégé-lover than he ever thought he would see in a life just a decade ago!' A bust of the protégé-lover soon adorned the 'oval room' at Port Lligat where, according to Morse, it was positively worshipped by the declining Gala.[40]

The Pompidou Retrospective

On 9 May 1979, two days before his seventy-fifth birthday, Dalí entered the Académie des Beaux-Arts of the Institut de France, to which he had been elected as an associate member a year earlier. He had had a special uniform made for the occasion, suitably Napoleonic in inspiration, and an enormous Toledo sword of gold whose hilt, designed by Dalí, featured Leda's swan surmounting the head of Gala (the sword was paid for by a group of friends and admirers).

On the eve of the investiture a reception was held at the Meurice. Dalí and Nanita Kalaschnikoff entertained the company by singing and dancing passages from *Pharaoh's Court*, their favourite *zarzuela*. Amanda Lear flew in for the party, and, once the photographs had been taken, flew out again.[41] Dalí had drawn up a ludicrous guest list of famous names for the ceremony in the Institut de France. None of them attended. Even Reynolds Morse stayed away. But not Eleanor. She went first to the Meurice to help Dalí get ready, and watched Nanita Kalaschnikoff cutting and combing his hair. Only Nanita, she mused, could look after Dalí when Gala died.[42]

The title of Dalí's rambling investiture speech was *Gala, Velázquez and the Golden Fleece*; what its theme was nobody was quite sure. Improvising from notes, Dalí ranged from Velázquez and DNA to Descartes, Leibniz, the mathematician René Thom, Perpignan station and the American hyperrealist, Richard Estes, whose work he glossed enthusiastically. Yet again Dalí praised academic painting, arguing that it was preparing the way for a new classical art. He made a remark about pubic hair as Golden Fleece which part of the audience thought inappropriate, and insisted, recruiting his 'friend' Michel de Montaigne in support, that it was the artist's duty to render the local universal. He ended with a rousing 'Long live Perpignan station and Figueres!' The press reviews were mixed. One of Dalí's fellow academicians, Michel Déon, hoped that he would now discard some of his more ridiculous 'clowneries'. He had been born with all the talent any artist could desire; why, therefore, the constant tomfoolery? Déon recognized that, alas, it was much too late to expect Dalí to change now, for the artist had raised mystification to the level of a dogma.[43]

In the wake of his investiture Dalí told a Spanish reporter, Antonio Olano, that his 'art was pure shit', a remark which Reynolds Morse considered more offensive than his comments on the Basque executions. Dalí was presumably casting himself in the role of alchemist, the transmuter of base metals into gold. But whatever the intention his words led to widespread criticism and scorn in Spain, as he no doubt discovered when he arrived home a few days later.[44]

He also found that there was trouble brewing in Figueres, where on 15 June the first democratic town council voted to give back its original name to the Plaça Gala–Salvador Dalí, so named under Franco, which is situated in front of the museum. The decision was revoked under national and international pressure, but it seems likely that Dalí never forgave this particular slap in the face.[45]

Back in Port Lligat, elated by his Beaux-Arts investiture, Dalí finished the painting *In Search of the Fourth Dimension*, begun the previous year and perhaps his last work of some importance. Despite the presence of threadbare Dalinian clichés—the melting watch, the loaf of bread on someone's head—the painting shows that Dalí was still master of his technique.[46]

To celebrate Dalí's seventy-fifth birthday and elevation to the French Academy of Fine Arts, Spanish Television made three programmes on his life and work. Structured around a long interview with Paloma Chamorro filmed during two successive days at the St Regis before Dalí travelled to Paris, they deliberately avoided contentious issues such as the blank sheets scandal, and anti-Dalí opinions were excluded. Most of Chamorro's questions to the Master centred on familiar ground and, as a result, elicited stock answers. But there were some memorable moments: his rendering of a song from *Pharaoh's Court*, his request for a young girl with a pure voice to recite Quevedo's famous sonnet on the virtues of the anus and, perhaps particularly, his response to a word-association test thrown at him by Chamorro during the first day's filming.

To Chamorro's 'Marcel Duchamp' Dalí had replied without hesitation 'Whale!' Why whale? He had pondered on this during the night. Next day Chamorro asked him about the stereoscopic painting on which he was at work, *Dalí's Hand Withdrawing a Golden Fleece in the Shape of a Cloud to Show Gala the Dawn, Completely Naked, Far, Far Off Behind the Sun*. The two panels, inspired by Claude Lorrain's *The Port of Ostia* in the Prado, were beside them as they talked, visible to the viewer. Did Dalí understand their irrational elements? All he knew, he replied, was that, if he had decided to paint the dawn behind the sun, it had something to do with the name Claude Lorrain. Then, remembering the 'whale' of the previous day, he suddenly had an association to an incident in Venice when preparations were going ahead at the Teatro La Fenice, in 1961, for the production of his ballet *Gala*. Onassis had promised to obtain a whale on whose back Dalí would effect a triumphal entry into the city, he said. This had proved impossible, but nevertheless a whale *did* appear at the première, the audience distinguishing its form in a piece of rumpled scenery that Dalí had ordered to be rolled up and stored almost out of sight above the stage! Dalí had gone to have a look and was staggered to find that the piece of scenery really did look like a whale. He now told Chamorro that, having recalled that incident, he felt sure that before long he would discover what it was about Claude Lorrain's name that had inspired him to produce a stereoscopic work based on *The Port of Ostia*. The sequence provides an unusual insight into the working of Dalí's mind and is proof that, whatever he may have said to the contrary, free association still fascinated him.

The programmes are also interesting for the opportunity they provide for close-up observation of Dalí's facial tics in the presence of a TV camera. When he is about to say something intended to be shocking, or daring, he habitually closes his eyes momentarily: a defence mechanism, presumably (Carlton Lake had noticed something similar a few years earlier). And when he has had his say, his eyes often flick to see who's watching, like a child searching for approval. One gets the impression, once again, that Dalí could be easily thrown by an unexpected question, and that most of the performance had been carefully prepared to prevent this from happening.[47]

Having made Dalí an 'immortal', the French now went one step better and honoured him with by far his most comprehensive retrospective to date. Held at the Centre Georges Pompidou and assembled from a wide variety of sources, it ran from 18 December 1979 until April 1980 and attracted almost a million visitors before moving on to the Tate in London.[48] The organizers had not respected Dalí's wishes for the layout of the exhibition, originally to have been held in the Grand Palais.[49] The artist had wanted the works to cover the walls of a single huge gallery, 'like in the "salons" of the last century, so as to be able to take in the whole of Dalí in one glance'.[50] Nothing could have been more different from Dalí's conception than the chaotic tangle of pictures crowding the fifth floor of the Pompidou.

Dalí and Gala arrived in Paris a few days before the opening, and made straight for the exhibition where, according to Reynolds Morse, the artist said 'I never realized I had had the time to paint so much.'[51] The Pompidou's ground floor had been transformed into a 'Kermesse Héroïque', a sort of hotch-potch of Dalinian symbols with Parisian additions. From the ceiling hung an assortment of imitation *butifarra* sausages of gigantic dimensions. They represented, somewhat arbitrarily, Catalunya, and also, no doubt, Dalí's obsession with the soft and edible. A Maigret-style Citroën (La France?) was suspended over a thirty-two metre spoon inspired by the ones featured in Dalí's *Agnostic Symbol* (1932) and other works. Water flowed into the spoon from the car's radiator. There was a copy of an Art Nouveau entrance to the Paris Métro. And so on. Dalí said later that he didn't like the spoon.

On 17 December, the day of the official inauguration, there was a strike at the Pompidou and no one was allowed in, not even Dalí and Gala. Dalí does not seem to have been particularly offended, and according to one account even expressed his support for the picketers. Gala, though, was furious, and made a great scene in the Meurice later in the day, attacking Pontus Hulten, the exhibition commissar, for 'subjecting' Dalí to such an 'indignity'. A few days later the Dalís took off for New York.[52] It has often been repeated that, in anger, Dalí now appended the phrase that figures at the end of *La Vie publique de Salvador Dalí*, a companion volume to the exhibition catalogue which was published in April 1980 ('On this 18 December 1989 ends, until his next scandal, the public life of Salvador Dalí').[53] But the statement, which echoes that appearing on the first page of the volume ('Here begins the public life of Salvador Dalí'), was probably written months earlier.

The Pompidou exhibition centred on Dalí's Surrealist period and comprised 120 paintings, 200 drawings and more than 2,000 documents. It virtually ignored the last thirty-five years of his production and did not cover the crucial period from 1925 to 1930 in anything like enough detail. But it was extremely impressive.

Before flying in to see the show Reynolds Morse was visited in Cleveland on 6 March 1980 by Michael Stout. They talked for ten hours about Dalí's situation. Stout was now not just Dalí's lawyer but increasingly, given Sabater's ever more frequent absences, his 'nursemaid'. Dalí had few true friends apart from Nanita Kalaschnikoff, Stout told Morse, and was reduced to 'his transvestites, seedy models and his $3,000 Sunday dinners at Trader Vic's with his queers and odd costumed freaks, paid companions and other free-loaders, all vacuous in the extreme, but hungry'.[54]

Morse was astonished by the amount and quality of the works on display at the Pompidou. Some of the best items proceeded from Dalí and Gala's collections, and had been prised by Sabater out of depositories in New York and Paris. As for the Edward James loans, they were 'the supreme products of Dalí's last truly peak years of creativity before the Bonwit Teller window episode turned him into a professional stunt man by accident'. Morse had reservations about the few later works on show. In his view they revealed all too obviously the hand of Isidor Bea—and possibly of others. Morse reflected on the fact that Dalí had succeeded in making himself world famous while holding back much of his best work. 'No other painter has been thus kept in the limelight on less concrete artistic evidence than Salvador Dalí. It is, in a way, a mark of his genius.'[55]

The Pompidou's exhibition catalogue, conceived and edited by Daniel Abadie, was bound in cloth based on a 'torn dress' design Dalí had done for Elsa Schiaparelli in the 1930s. The first part, *Salvador Dalí*, included among the reproductions an anthology of texts by Dalí and half a dozen essays on his work. The most important of these, by José Pierre, analysed in considerable depth, on the basis of their correspondence, the artist's relationship with Breton. The second part, *The Public Life of Salvador Dalí*, was an ambitious attempt to establish the ascertainable facts of the artist's trajectory and ceaseless activity (as distinct from his 'secret' life, as the title makes clear), and included many original documents and photographs never before published as well as a bibliography with almost 2,500 entries. The research that lay behind the exhibition and catalogue was remarkable, and the latter remains a key source of information on Dalí's life and work.

Morse had now grown not only to dislike Sabater, 'the oily, obsequious groom become master', but positively to distrust him, seeing signs of his machinations on all sides. If Moore had been bad, Sabater was much, much worse. Morse suspected that some of the works extracted from the vaults would get 'lost' somewhere along the line between the Pompidou and the Tate; and that, since they figured in no inventory, the secretary could never be brought to task. Morse himself had refused to lend works for the exhibition, yet found that some of them were reproduced in the catalogue without any credit. Others were being merchandised without his permission as posters. He felt he was being unfairly castigated for his lack of co-operation.[56]

Robert Descharnes, who had collaborated actively in the preparation of the exhibition,[57] contributing an essay to the catalogue, confided to Morse his deep concern about the extent of Dalí's dependence on Sabater. As they strolled around the exhibition he suggested that they set up a body to support Dalí in these critical moments. Morse was enthusiastic, and proposed different categories of membership. The Committee to Save Dalí soon became a reality. According to its headed notepaper, the members were Arturo Caminada, Benjamín Castillo (a Figueres friend of the painter), Robert Descharnes, Nanita Kalaschnikoff, Eleanor and Reynolds Morse, Antoni Pitxot and Gonzalo Serraclara. 'The Committee of Friends to Save Dalí', we read at the bottom of the page, 'is an international, non-profit organization chartered solely to preserve the physical well-being and the artistic welfare of Salvador Dalí.'[58]

Bad Times

In February 1980, while the crowds continued to flock to the Dalí retrospective at the Pompidou, Dalí and Gala had a heavy bout of flu at the St Regis and were at a very low ebb emotionally and physically, particularly Dalí. 'Although he had had two operations,' writes Albert Field, 'he had never had a long illness and became depressed that he did not recover. To calm him, Gala gave him Valium and other sedatives without medical supervision. His fears were to some extent relieved, but the drugs made him lethargic in the mornings.' This tiredness became 'a fresh source of unease', and, still without medical supervision, Gala began to dose Dalí with 'unknown quantities of one or more types of amphetamine'. According to Field, this irregular dosage of 'uppers' and 'downers' caused Dalí 'irreversible neural damage' and was the cause of the uncontrollable trembling of his hand which, since it prevented him from working, now obsessed him.[59]

Given the frequent absences of Enric Sabater, more and more occupied with his expanding business empire, the couple were now making heavy demands on Michael Stout, who, with a strike on at the hotel, was somewhat dismayed to find himself doubling as butler.[60] Luckily for the lawyer, and the Dalís, the ever-helpful Nanita Kalaschnikoff was also to hand. She needed urgently to return to Spain, but Dalí kept on insisting that she stay in New York until he was fully recovered. He would begin to weep, clutch Nanita's hands and beg her not to abandon him: 'If you leave me I'm going to fall very sick,' he would insist. 'Don't go!' Finally Louis XIV had no option but to fly home, promising to join the Dalís the moment they arrived in Europe.[61]

Not long afterwards she received a call from the painter. Could he and Gala not convalesce with her at her house in Torremolinos? Nanita said that there simply wasn't room. Would it not be a far better idea to go to the Incosol clinic (a health farm for the rich) just down the road in Marbella? She had friends who had stayed there and it had a high reputation. She would visit them every day and they would have the advantage of first-class medical care. Dalí and Gala agreed that it seemed an excellent idea.[62]

On 20 March, accompanied by Sabater, the Dalís flew to Spain in an Iberia Airlines DC 8, with the artist recumbent in a separate compartment. Nanita Kalaschnikoff went to see him immediately at the Incosol. She was deeply shocked by his appearance: 'When I left him in New York he was looking all right, but three weeks later he was a wreck. Skin and bones. It was that monster Sabater's fault.'[63] Incosol was hermetically sealed off from the dozens of journalists who now arrived on the scene, but a leak from the clinic confirmed Kalaschnikoff's impression: Dalí could hardly walk and was deeply depressed. But was his lamentable condition really Sabater's fault? Not his alone, certainly, for it transpired that Gala had been improving on the doctors' prescriptions by administering pills and potions to Dalí from her private medicine chest. Her 'treatment' included excessive doses of Valium.[64]

The Dalís occupied a whole suite at the Incosol and Sabater another. Every day cost a fortune. They remained until mid-April, when they were flown in a private plane to Girona, where Arturo Caminada was waiting with the Cadillac to drive them to Port Lligat.[65] A few days later the couple were visited by Michael Stout, who reported to the Morses by telephone on 26 April. In Port Lligat he had been told that he could not see Dalí, but had pushed his way into the house past armed guards. Stout was in an impossible position as both Dalí and Sabater's lawyer, and incapable, Morse felt, of grasping the extent to which the secretary had undermined Dalí's confidence. Morse himself was in no such doubt: Sabater's actions had reduced the artist to 'a trembling mass of jelly';

the secretary was never seen without his automatic pistol tucked into his belt; and he had arranged for Dalí's phone to be tapped. Both Dalí and Gala confided to Stout that they were worried about Sabater's business ventures. Yet Gala, with her constant demands for ready money, was as much to blame as Sabater for the situation that had built up.[66]

Stout's account of the Dalís' condition so alarmed Morse that a fortnight later he flew back to Spain for a meeting on 16 May with him and Robert Descharnes at the Motel del Ampurdán in Figueres: The Committee to Save Dalí had started to take action. The Committee did not include Peter Moore, considered too unreliable to be involved in the 'rescue operation'.[67] Before visiting Port Lligat the threesome saw Sabater, who as usual was carrying his gun. He seemed friendly enough, but Morse now distrusted him total-ly. In his view Dalí had gradually been forced to admit 'that Sabater has really been working the greatest con game ever on the greatest con man in art'.[68] But if Reynolds Morse now thought that Dalí was the greatest con man in art, what price all those hec-toring attempts to establish that the painter's post-Surrealist work equalled or sur-passed what he had achieved earlier?

After the meeting at the Hotel Ampurdán, Morse tried to see Dalí but was refused by 'the steely old Russian female curmudgeonly Gala', who in his presence rounded on one of the servants and demanded if she'd been sleeping with Arturo Caminada. The girl burst into tears, mortified. Arturo had stormed out of the house earlier when Gala was abusing Dalí, unable to stand it. Gala told Morse that 'he had left', but of course Dalí's most loyal servant of all was back a few hours later. Morse had never disliked Gala so much, and left without seeing Dalí. He wrote in his diary: 'Had I an end of the world choice to make at this moment of whom to save, it most certainly would have been Arturo, not his master or mistress.'[69]

The following day Dalí was examined by a neurologist from Barcelona, Manuel Subirana. He thought Dalí's problems psychological, not physical, but, according to Morse, 'could not get anything of medical value from a man who had spent his whole life professionally lying'.[70]

Meanwhile Morse and Stout had been trying to persuade Sabater voluntarily to leave Dalí's service, in his own as well as the painter's best interests. 'I said nobody would per-secute him if he simply took it and ran,' Morse wrote in his diary on 16 May. 'After all, he had taken on the enormous task of seeing the master through his critical transition-al years from the peak of his greatness to the onset of senililty and a nervous break-down.' In the end Sabater seemed to agree, and undertook to deliver Dalí immediately to Dr Puigvert's clinic in Barcelona for a complete check-up. Twice that night Morse asked God to divert 'the evil force of Gala' from Dalí. The Muse, now eighty-six, had resolutely turned Witch, and was deeply resentful that Dalí's neuroses were preventing her from living her life to the full. 'How many people realize just how terrible she is at heart as they gaze on her sublime visage in such works as *The Madonna of Port Lligat?*' mused Morse.[71]

Is it possible that Gala, in plying Dalí with a mixture of pills from her private medicine chest, was in fact now attempting to poison him? It is a suspicion that cannot be entirely ruled out.

Despite the fact that he had never been paid for operating on Dalí's hernia and prostate, Dr Puigvert, apprised by Morse, visited the painter in Port Lligat and persuaded him to enter his clinic. On 21 May 1980, the day Dalí was moved to Barcelona, another discussion, this time with momentous consequences, took place between Morse, Stout and Descharnes. The venue was the square outside the city's ancient cathedral, at siesta-time:

> Stout said he could not possibly give any more time to nurse-maiding the Dalís. I said that I was not about to attempt to become their guardian either. And that left no one but Robert Descharnes or Antoni Pitxot. We pleaded with Robert to undertake the thankless task. He said that Dalí had already cost him a small fortune. We said he should be well paid for the time he devoted to Dalí, and that he could afford to hire a lawyer to protect Dalí's rights. If he paid the lawyer $100,000 a year and took $100,000 for himself, there would still be several million left for Dalí and Gala. Robert was reluctant to attempt the job, but with the vacuum of Sabater's leaving, who else was there to do it? I felt it was a fateful sort of decision, and possibly not the best because Robert is not a good businessman nor is he capable of making a decision when it is necessary. He is timorous and will procrastinate endlessly, niggling over details—anything to keep from having to reach a firm decision. Both Stout and I had reservations about asking a Frenchman to step into the breach, but there were simply no Spanish or Catalan candidates capable of beginning to understand their countryman.[72]

And so it was decided that, when the moment was ripe, Robert Descharnes should take over from Enric Sabater. As with Moore and Sabater, however, the Dalís would refuse to pay their new secretary a salary, their stubbornness in this respect leading to further chaos in their affairs and, in Morse's view, to further corruption.[73]

The same hectic day that Dalí entered the Puigvert clinic, Morse, Descharnes and Stout consulted some Barcelona lawyers about his and Gala's legal situation in Spain. One of them, Ventura Garcés, said that the couple could not possibly continue without fixed residence, and that the Monaco ploy would only work if they stayed there for four months every year. Ventura Garcés insisted that somebody should be empowered to act on their behalf in Spain, not least in fiscal matters. It was a miracle that Gala, accustomed to carrying huge sums of black money through the customs, had escaped detection.[74]

In the Puigvert clinic Dalí was examined by Joan Obiols, Professor of Psychiatry at Barcelona University, and the neurologist Luis Barraquer. Also present was Manuel Subirana, who had seen Dalí a few days earlier in Port Lligat. The conclusion, once again, was that the painter's problems were in the main psychological, Subirana feeling that he was suffering from 'a depressive state of the melancholic variety'. Dalí received, therefore, 'an intense anti-depressive treatment'. It seemed to work quite well. As for Dr Puigvert himself, he said not long afterwards that for ten years Dalí had been slowly developing arteriosclerosis.[75]

Morse insisted on visiting Dalí in the clinic. When he entered room 417 Dalí was peeping out of the lavatory, with nothing on below the waist. Arturo and the nurse helped him to hobble back to the bedroom, where he sat in a chair, trembling, gasping for breath and hardly able to speak. Morse caught the words 'No family! I do not want to see anybody in my family! No Gonzalo! No Serraclara! My family hates me!' Morse was appalled by Dalí's physical condition. His arms and legs were fearfully thin and he seemed to have shrunk four or five inches in height. His right arm 'would sort of shake from shoulder to wrist'. Dalí muttered that Gala was going to leave him soon for Jeff Fenholt, and that he himself was about to die. Sabater was there throughout, eavesdropping when he was not attending to the telephone calls from reporters clamouring insistently for news about Dalí's condition. Sabater, in Morse's view, 'was clearly basking in his position as sole spokesman for the world's most famous living painter'.[76]

Reynolds Morse was never to see Dalí again. On 26 May, back in Cleveland, he wrote to update Peter Moore on the situation, given that he and the others had been unable to see him in Cadaqués. He told Moore that, in their opinion, there was only one way to help the couple. This was to make 'an amiable agreement' with them for their own protection:

> We proved pretty well that under Gala's untender care and Sabater's terroristic methods Dalí has been reduced to a shell of his former self. We are concerned that Sabater's income from Dalí has been more than 6 times that of his master, and that he is abusing the expense accounts they pay him to the tune of about $100,000 a year. Sabater's mismanagement of things Dalinian is appalling, and runs from failure to invite anyone from Figueres to

Pompidou to shenanigans with books being published by Pompidou on which Dalí gets no royalty. There are really two things to neutralize: Sabater and Jeff Fenholt. If we can do this, there is some hope that a trust can be set up and the affairs of the Dalís put into some kind of order so that they can live comfortably where and how they wish. The most serious omission of Sabater as manager was in his total failure to file for the amnesty offered by the tax people of the Spanish Government. The Dalís should be Spanish residents, but Sabater duped them into thinking Monaco was an out, when it is not, for tax purposes. A will should also be made that is valid in all the countries where they do business. All this can be done easily except for the fact that poor Gala is really senile, unable to tell the truth and worst of all totally friendless. And with Dalí in a state of total exhaustion, there is really nothing mere friends can do. I think it was very wise under the circumstances that you stayed out of the mess, as we were able, treating with the enemy, not only to get Dalí into the clinic in Barcelona, but also to see him. At this remove I do not have a way or a reason to activate a plan to action until some real crisis occurs, but Stout laid the groundwork for a plan to protect Dalí. His whole world has simply collapsed around him under Sabater's total incompetence and gross mismanagement of things Dalinian. Poor Sabater is a sick man, cannot tell the truth, and is in this thing way over his depth. And since the private world of Dalí is the topic of public gossip, and even the fish-woman in Cadaqués knows the last news before it happens, I do not think there is any need to try to disguise the facts of this essentially tragic case. The main thing now is to find the appropriate time to get to the Dalís, help them with their terribly complex tax matters, set up a trust, get the Spanish amnesty matter extended on the grounds of their senility and Sabater's neglect, stop the awful drain on their resources of the money poured down the Fenholt sump, etc. Descharnes would act as secretary for a year and this would help.[77]

The concluding reference to Robert Descharnes catches the eye. Clearly, following the discussion in Barcelona, he had now agreed to act as Dalí's secretary. But it would not prove easy to persuade the Dalís to dispense with the services of Enric Sabater.

The entry in Morse's diary for 21 May 1981, on which his letter to Peter Moore was based, shows that he was in no doubt about Gala's part in Sabater's rise to multi-millionaire status:

We all felt that Gala has made Sabater rich by her one-payment policy. In the past few years, she would set the price on a watercolour to be lithographed by a client. Sabater would then pay her the cash, getting it from the client, then he would sell the rights to reproduction to the work in the customer's own country to him, while retaining the original work for himself. Then when they went to another stand in another country, Sabater would again sell the right to reproduction for THAT country to still another client, so that he made 500,000 to Dalí's 100,000, and ended up with the only thing of real value at all: the original watercolour. Pretty smart, eh?[78]

Dalí enjoyed talking to Joan Obiols, the psychiatrist, by all accounts a likeable and intelligent man. When the artist was allowed home to Port Lligat in June, Obiols saw him there once a week. But then something grotesque happened. On 17 July, while chatting to Gala with a whisky in his hand, the doctor suddenly dropped dead from a heart attack. Gala was hysterical, and summoned Antoni Pitxot. When he arrived he found her screaming. Dalí was in another part of the labyrinth and unaware of what had happened. According to Dr Puigvert, who hurried up from Barcelona, Dalí was never told the truth about Obiols's failure to return.[79]

Obiols's place was taken by another psychiatrist, Ramón Vidal Teixidor, whom Dalí knew from the Puigvert clinic. Vidal broke his leg during his first visit to Port Lligat, and it must have seemed that Dalí was now a positive danger to the psychiatric profession.[80]

One of the most persistent Spanish journalists covering the Dalí case at this time was the correspondent of *El País* in Barcelona, Alfons Quinta. In early September Quinta published an ironic report on Dalí's financial situation that filled two pages of Spain's most important and influential newspaper. He had investigated Sabater's rise to multimillionaire status, and calculated that in five years he had amassed something in excess of a thousand million pesetas (about five million pounds). Quinta provided details of Sabater's companies and properties, explained how for tax evasion purposes he had arranged for the Dalís to be legally, if not *de facto*, resident in Monaco, and drew attention to the chaos reigning at the Theatre-Museum in Figueres, whose contents were still so tawdry that many tourists left in disgust, feeling that they had been cheated. Quinta made one serious error, however: he greatly underestimated the quantity and importance of the works in Dalí and Gala's private collections, not yet installed in the museum. A few months later the Madrid weekly, *Cambio-16*, published an inventory of seventy of them. Their value was incalculable.[81]

Shortly afterwards Quinta reported on Dalí's tax situation in Spain. Since 1978 Dalí had made no tax declarations, of either property or income, maintaining that as a Monaco resident he was under no obligation to do so and that, anyway, his earnings were generated solely outside Spain. The Inland Revenue authorities knew that the latter was untrue. Under the much more stringent tax laws that came into operation in 1980, Spaniards resident abroad were required to make an annual declaration of their property in Spain. And, if they spent more than six continuous months in the country, which Dalí had just done, they were also required to declare their earnings. On both counts Dalí was now obliged to put in a tax return. His failure to do so, presumably counselled by Sabater, was to condition future negotiations with the Government concerning his estate.[82]

A considerable campaign was now building up against Sabater in the international as well as the Spanish press. He was accused not only of making a fortune at the expense of Dalí and Gala, but of preventing the painter's friends from visiting him. All of which charges he consistently denied. One of the main thorns in Sabater's flesh was James M. Markham, the Madrid correspondent of the *New York Times*, who relayed much of the information being published on Dalí in Spain. Telling his readers on 12 October 1980 that Sabater was now a millionaire 'many times over', Markham provided details of his several off-shore companies. One of his two luxury residences on the Costa Brava had closed-circuit television, an all-year climatized swimming pool and even a lobster pond. Among the other trappings were a yacht, two cars, and lavish summer parties 'featuring Arab oil sheikhs and show business personalities'.[83]

Dalí now decided that, after seven months' absence from the public stage, it was time to make a comeback. And where better to hold an international press conference than in his own Theatre-Museum? It took place on the afternoon of 24 October 1980 and was attended by more than a hundred Spanish and foreign journalists. While a bronzed Sabater marshalled the reporters and gave orders, Dalí's entry was deliberately delayed to provoke the maximum anticipation. Finally he emerged to the strains of *Tristan and Isolde*, followed by Gala, who distributed branches of spikenard to the photographers. Dalí had aged beyond belief and looked exhausted, a grotesque parody of the man who had been interviewed by Paloma Chamorro the previous year. His opening words, 'Here I am!', intentionally echoed those spoken by Josep Tarradellas, president of the Catalan government in exile, when he returned in triumph to Barcelona after the death of Franco. The painter then banged the table three times with his cane and kissed Gala. He was wearing his famous leopardskin overcoat (no ecologist, Dalí) and, on his head, a red Catalan *barretina*. Gala sat beside him looking like the retired madame of an old-world Parisian brothel, her cracked face daubed with makeup, her lips a shocking red, her wig held in place by her habitual Minnie Mouse velvet bow. Dalí assured the gathering that he was now working three hours a day. 'Can you see how my hand is shaking?' he asked, raising his right arm. Suddenly the shaking stopped. 'It's not shaking now!' he muttered. He went on to explain, in a feeble voice, that he'd been close to death but was no longer frightened of dying because he had discovered to his relief that God was tiny. This discovery had convinced him to relinquish the idea of being hibernated. The French journalists, more confident and brash than their Spanish counterparts, were peculiarly obsequious that rainy afternoon in Figueres. Most of their questions were fatuous. Dalí answered laconically, in an indiscriminate mixture of French, Catalan and Spanish. There was only the occasional flicker of the old fire—but he proved that he could still recite complicated Catalan tongue-twisters without faltering.

The *pièce de résistance* of the afternoon was the unveiling of Gala's latest gift to the Theatre-Museum, a recent painting by Dalí called *The Happy Horse*. It showed a carcass disintegrating in the Empordanese countryside. But *was* it a horse, asked a French journalist? Might it not be a mule? 'I'm not sure if you can see that it's a horse,' Dalí replied. 'But you can certainly see that it's rotten.' Dalí then unveiled his most recent project: the model of a giant sculpture of a horse that, with the aid of cybernetics, he was planning to execute in Romania. No one was impressed. A few minutes later Dalí and Gala were borne away by Sabater in the blue Cadillac with the Monaco numberplate.[84]

The Spanish authorities had hoped that the Pompidou exhibition could move to Madrid and Barcelona after its spell at the Tate in London (14 May–29 June 1980). When this proved impossible they decided to organize a major home-grown Dalí retrospective in Spain. They would show the French! To this end a preliminary agreement was drawn up in Port Lligat on 22 November 1980. Dalí and Gala undertook to lend enough original works from their private collections to form the nucleus of the exhibition, and the inauguration in Madrid was set over-ambitiously for November 1981. But soon it was to be postponed until 1982—and finally to 1983.[85]

For several months now the Dalís had been working on drafts of new joint wills, Sabater claiming later that he had been instrumental in persuading them to do this during their last stay in New York.[86] On 12 December 1980 the finished documents were signed in the presence of Ramon Coll, the notary of Llançà, a small resort on the other side of Cape Creus, just beyond Port de la Selva. The new wills provided that on their deaths half the couple's art collection was to go to the Spanish State and half to the 'Catalan People through its regional Government [Generalitat] or whatever other institution should represent it', and urged the beneficiaries to ensure that the works would be seen in museums enabling them to be enjoyed by 'all the peoples of Spain without exception'. Legal provisions were included for settling any squabbles that might arise between the legatees over the admittedly complex apportionment of the works. The two wills differed in a few marginal respects: Gala's made a brutal attempt to exclude her daughter Cécile, alleging that she had already inherited 'more than sufficiently' at the death of Paul Éluard (an exclusion that was to prove impossible under Spanish law), while Dalí's added two clauses not figuring in his wife's. The first read: 'I recommend the Catalan Government particularly to bear in mind the affection I have always professed towards my museum in Figueres.' Given Dalí's obsession with his museum, this made perfect sense. But the second clause was extremely odd. Dalí, it said, 'declares categorically that he has never had, nor does now, a secretary or person of his confidence'. What did this mean? Arguably, with Sabater out of the room, Dalí wished to get across to the notary, and down on paper, that he now had serious doubts about Sabater's integrity. It is also likely that by this time Sabater had already announced his intention to leave the painter's service at the end of the year. Clearly, at all events, Dalí was much disturbed.[87]

Having made their wills, Dalí and Gala prepared to hurry away to Paris for Christmas. Sabater insisted, however, that first they accompany him to Geneva, apparently to arrange for those works of theirs exhibited at the Pompidou and the Tate to be stored in the city's free port so as to avoid any future problems about moving them to Spain. It seems that there was also a pre-Christmas trip to Monte Carlo to see to the formalities of renouncing Monégasque nationality, necessary so that the Dalís could now apply for full legal and fiscal residence in Spain (Sabater had told the Spanish authorities in September about the forthcoming change in the couple's status).[88]

In Paris Dalí and Gala occupied their usual suite at the Meurice. Agence France-Presse reported that, despite his illness, the painter had not lost his vitality. His horse sculpture was now to be thirty-five kilometres long, and Dalí showed the journalist his latest work, which was contained in a large black box. Called *The Burning of the School of Athens*, it was further proof that Dalí's lifelong fascination with stereoscopy and other optical tricks was as keen as ever. This time the trick consisted in fusing two paintings by Raphael, *The School of Athens* and *The Burning of the Borgo*, so that the flames of the second engulfed the philosophers discoursing in the first. Dalí said that the work expressed his concept of black holes. If a year previously he had left Paris insisting that 'painting should be stereoscopic or not at all' (a gloss on Breton's 'Beauty should be convulsive or not at all'), now the condition was that it should be cybernetic.[89]

The broadly optimistic picture of Dalí's condition conveyed by the French agency was contradicted in *Elle* this same January by Dr Pierre Roumeguère, who it seems had visited the painter. 'The truth is that Dalí has lost his will to live,' he said. 'What we're seeing is a suicide. Simply because Gala no longer looks after him. She's eighty-six, she's only got two or three hours of lucidity left each day, and she uses them to think about Jeff.' Dalí, he said, was dying like an abandoned baby. The diagnosis may not have been too far short of the mark.[90]

At about this time Gala telephoned Emilio Puignau. She told him that she and Dalí would not be staying much longer in Paris, enquired after Port Lligat and said that Dalí was very unwell. Puignau was worried and betook himself to Paris. He found Gala in consternation: Dalí didn't want anyone to see him, he wasn't walking well, couldn't co-ordinate his ideas; he was panic-stricken and often flew into terrible tempers; the doctors were unable to find out what was the matter with him. Gala herself was depressed and physically declining. When Puignau went upstairs to see Dalí he couldn't believe his eyes: his appearance and expression were unlike anything he had witnessed previously. He threw himself into Puignau's arms. 'I'm finished, I'm in despair!' he exclaimed. 'You probably know already, they've robbed me of everything!'[91]

It sounded paranoid—and it sounded like the newspaper reports of Grandfather Gal's ravings before he committed suicide in 1886. Sabater had certainly made a lot of money out of his connection with the Dalís, but to say that he, or the other dealers involved, had robbed him of everything was a gross exaggeration. Enric Sabater, either way, had resigned as the Dalís' secretary and dealer on 31 December 1980. But he agreed to stay on with them for the time being as their friend and collaborator, and was still installed at the Meurice.[92] In February he told a reporter laconically: 'Señor Dalí's character is very difficult, even insufferable. Not always, of course. He can also be pleasant and charming. Certainly, to be with him as much as I have you need to be from the Empordà and to be a bit touched by the tramuntana.' 'Dalí is a great masochist,' he ended.[93]

Sabater Takes His Leave

Gala was now frantically doing Dalí business on her own account with Jean-Claude Du Barry, the amiable Gascon who for ten years had supplied the couple with a steady stream of beautiful young people to enliven their evenings at Port Lligat and Púbol. Impressed by Du Barry's acumen, the Dalís had allowed him to set up some lucrative deals for them behind Sabater's back in the summer of 1980. Now they wanted more of the same.[94]

Early in 1981 Du Barry prepared many irregular contracts at Gala's instigation for the exploitation of Dalí's work, bringing back to the Meurice shady dealers who had been associated with Dalí years earlier. 'I started to call Dalí's old clients, people Sabater had completely cut off,' Du Barry said the following November, 'and told them, "If you want to do business with Dalí, call me."' They did want to do business, and Du Barry soon arranged contracts worth $1.3 million, earning handsome commissions for himself in the process.[95] 'The situation this created was utterly chaotic,' Michael Stout recalled.[96] The Gascon's term of office was brief, however, for coming up fast behind, and about to overtake him, was Robert Descharnes. Early in October 1980, sensing the forthcoming breakdown with Sabater and on the advice of Antoni Pitxot, Dalí had telephoned Descharnes in Paris to ask for his help.[97] Descharnes had acted quickly, establishing contact on Dalí's behalf with the French artists' royalties agency, Spadem (Société de la Propriété Artistique et des Dessins et Modèles). So it was that when Dalí arrived in Paris that Christmas he met a top Spadem representative, Jean-Paul Oberthur, and decided, or was persuaded, to engage the agency to handle his royalties. An agreement was signed on 6 January 1981 and on 27 February a letter with Dalí's signature brought the new arrangement to the attention of those 'friends, collectors, museums, publishers and other beneficiaries' with reproduction rights in his work. They were asked to provide Spadem with all the details of their contracts. Reynolds Morse was outraged: the Spadem contract was a mess and the letter so undiplomatically phrased that it was an insult to all those who received it.[98]

Both Descharnes and Sabater were present when Dalí signed up with Spadem. Sabater expressed his willingness to collaborate with the agency and to send a full list of all the activities he had undertaken on behalf of Dalí, with copies of the contracts. But he failed to keep his promise.[99] Spadem took the graphics rights on board first; then the totality of Dalí's art copyright. But soon the agency began to flounder, and five years later it was to go out of business in circumstances apparently still not fully clarified.[100]

During these months at the Meurice Dalí was seriously worried about his right hand, which was shaking worse than ever. In early February he was seen by Dr François Lhermitte, a world authority on Parkinson's disease, who disagreed with the diagnosis of Parkinson's made by other practitioners.[101] A week later, on 17 February 1981, Dalí broke into Sabater's Meurice suite at dawn crying for help. He had a black eye. Sabater went with him and found Gala lying on the bedroom floor. She was clearly in pain but, stoically, did not complain. It transpired that Dalí had yanked her out of her bed in a fit of rage. A doctor diagnosed two broken ribs and quite nasty bruises on Gala's arms and one of her legs. She was taken in an ambulance to the American Hospital in Neuilly. That she and Dalí had had a violent argument there was no doubt, perhaps provoked by Gala's determination to return to New York to see Jeff Fenholt and by Dalí's commensurate terror that her astronomical outlay on her love life would reduce them before long to poverty. The Albarettos had witnessed a similar scene with a livid Dalí screaming 'You've wasted a fortune on your boys, but I've spent hardly anything on Amanda!'[102]

On 13 March 1981, Alfons Quinta of *El País* published a detailed report on the chaotic state of the Dalí graphics market and on the blank sheets issue. Now that Dalí could no longer sign his name satisfactorily, he and his associates had devised, of all things, a thumb stamp! Contracts had already been signed by this procedure, notably with Gilbert Hamon, 'the largest graphics distributor in Paris'. Quinta revealed that, while Dalí continued to be paid large sums in cash up front for the exploitation of his jewellery and small sculpture designs, the dealers, notably one Isidro Clot Fuentes, were earning a thousand times more than he was. Clot Fuentes, Quinta insinuated, was in cahoots with Sabater, whose commercial empire now 'spanned the world'. No doubt this report was read with interest by the Spanish authorities.[103]

On 18 March the Dalís' now stormy relationship with Sabater came to an end when the painter issued a communiqué to Agence France-Presse: 'I declare that for several years, and above all since my sickness, my confidence has been abused in many ways, my will was not respected. That is why I am doing everything to clarify this situation, and Gala and I are once again resuming our freedom.' He had not named Sabater directly— but the ex-secretary took the hint. Two days later he left the Meurice in high dudgeon. According to James Markham, the hotel 'briefly impounded a Daimler-Benz that Sabater left in its garage against payment of outstanding bills'.[104]

Back in Spain a few hours later Sabater denied hotly that he had ever deceived Dalí, and insisted that the painter had rectified his statement to Agence France-Presse, telling the Spanish news agency Efe that he had had no one in particular in mind in his criticisms. As for his own business dealings on Dalí's behalf, they had ended in March 1980. The contracts signed since then had nothing to do with him. His friendship with the Dalís was intact.[105]

Sabater never saw the Dalís again, however, and Robert Descharnes now took over as the painter's secretary. All the evidence suggests that Dalí was vastly relieved by the change. Descharnes was to claim that it was he who convinced Dalí to return to Spain as soon as possible, and this was probably true. Through Dalí's Paris lawyer, Jacques Verdeuil, contact had been established with the Spanish authorities, and by June 1981 an influential Madrid lawyer, Miguel Domenech Martinez, had been engaged to begin work on Dalí and Gala's complicated tax and residence situation.[106]

Domenech was the ideal man for the job. Brother-in-law of the Prime Minister, Leopoldo Calvo Sotelo, vice-president of the ruling UCD centre party and a man of great charm, he knew all the right people and, through Calvo Sotelo, had the ear of the Crown, a vital matter where Dalí was concerned. In Paris Domenech assured Dalí and Gala that everything would be done to facilitate their return to Spain and that the King and Queen had expressed their personal interest in their welfare. So too had the Government. The news must have greatly pleased the Dalís.[107]

Gala was determined to make for New York when she recovered from her battering at the hands of Dalí. But for once she did not get her way, and neither she nor the painter were ever again to set foot in America.[108]

The Death of Gala

On 6 July 1981 Dalí and Gala flew from Paris to Perpignan in a hired plane, accompanied by Robert Descharnes. Arturo Caminada was waiting with the Cadillac and soon the company were speeding southwards down the motorway. It was to be the last time they crossed the frontier into Spain. Dalí had returned home for good.[109]

Dalí was so heartened by being back in Port Lligat, free of Sabater, that three days after his arrival he painted *The Exterminating Angel.* The angel's sword, he told journalists, contained an allusion to the line 'until my sword is resplendent' by the avant-garde Catalan poet Salvat-Papasseit, whom he had greatly admired in the 1920s. What Dalí meant was that he did not intend to return to public life until he was fully recovered.[110]

Operation 'Make Dalí Feel Wanted' was now under way in earnest. First he was visited by Jordi Pujol, the Catalan Prime Minister. Then, on 15 August, came King Juan Carlos and Queen Sofía. The photographs published the following day showed that Dalí was in lamentable physical shape, and a rumour circulated that Gala had recently wounded him in the head with her shoe.[111] The visit acted as a powerful tonic, however, and threw the painter into an ecstasy of royalist fervour. 'I've always been an anarchist and a monarchist', he explained. 'I'm a monarchist because monarchy means order, that the anarchy of the people, of those of us below, is protected by the order above. Monarchy means perfect order.'[112]

Dalí's main concern at this time, the reporters found, was for his Theatre-Museum in Figueres, which had become the most popular museum in Spain after the Prado and was drawing over two thousand visitors a day. As regards art, Dalí's views were as dogmatic as ever: he insisted that he had been the first painter to apply the discoveries of cybernetics to his work, and that masterpieces could no longer be created without recourse to computer science.[113]

Every autumn, for decades, Dalí and Gala had packed their bags and left Port Lligat for Paris and then New York, happy in the knowledge that they would return in the spring. But this was no longer possible and they now prepared to spend their first ever winter in Port Lligat. The place is depressing out of season: depressing when the rain falls on the black rocks, depressing when the cold tramuntana roars down from the north and keeps the inhabitants of Cadaqués indoors for days on end. Gala and Dalí were old and sick and bickered constantly. They must have thought often about death. It was, truly, the winter of their discontent.

In a long report published that November in the *New York Times Magazine*, James Markham reviewed Dalí's situation. Basically it had improved, and, 'against all the odds', the artist was making a comeback. The main reason for his recovery, in Markham's opinion, was the departure of Sabater, who in five years had risen 'from a sycophant in the Dalí entourage to a Rasputin figure who, dominating the artist, had made himself into a multimillionaire many times over'. Sabater's fall, Markham felt, was 'in a sense the story of Dalí's tentative rebirth', while the advent of Robert Descharnes meant a 'soothing presence' in Dalí's life, a vital factor in the 'mellow' mood now pervading Port Lligat. It was unfair, though, to blame Sabater for all the ills that had befallen Dalí, since, as Markham himself admitted, the centre of the corruption was the artist himself. Dalí had started to sign blank sheets long before Sabater took over the running of his affairs.[114]

A further sign that Dalí was now being cajoled by Madrid came in January 1982 when King Juan Carlos awarded him the State's highest decoration, the Grand Cross of the Order of Charles III. Dalí was delighted.[115]

Meanwhile Gala had had serious gall-bladder trouble and was rushed to the Platón Clinic in Barcelona where, on 30 December, Dr Ignacio Orsolà operated. She recovered satisfactorily but on 24 February 1982, back at Port Lligat, she had another setback, falling on the stairs (some people said pushed by Dalí) and hurting her leg; then, two days later, she slipped in the bath and one of her femurs snapped like a brittle reed. She was taken in great pain to a private clinic in Figueres where the doctors decided that the necessary operation would have to be carried out in Barcelona. Gala was admitted once more to the Platón.[116]

The operation took place on 2 March 1982, with Doctor Orsolà again in charge. Although the surgeons expressed initial satisfaction, serious complications soon arose: acute skin irritation and horrible sores. Gala could have died at any moment but once again she pulled through.[117] Dalí visited her at the time of her operation but did not see her again until she returned to Port Lligat at the end of April. Meanwhile, on 20 March, he received Catalunya's most prized award, the Gold Medal of the Catalan Government.[118]

Back home, Gala would eat nothing, her eyes were no longer concentrated into the penetrating stare celebrated by Éluard, and often she raved. When asked why she refused to eat she would reply: 'Why bother?' She had never made a habit of ringing Nanita Kalaschnikoff, but now she called her constantly to tell her how unwell, how unhappy she and Dalí were.[119]

In the middle of May the parish priest from La Pera, Joaquim Goy, was summoned to administer the last rites. Benjamí Artigas, the village's mayor, drove him to Port Lligat. Among those present were Descharnes, Domenech, Pitxot, Dalí's cousin Gonzalo Serraclara and the painter himself. Gala hardly reacted and did not speak a word, but both the priest and Dr Vergara had the impression that there was some fight in her yet.[120]

Forced to accept that Gala was dying, Dalí now instructed Emilio Puignau to prepare a tomb for both of them in the crypt at Púbol. For both of them? Puignau was surprised: he had always assumed, naïvely perhaps, that the painter would ask to be buried in the cemetery of Sant Baldiri, near to his father. Benjamí Artigas had no difficulty in obtaining the necessary special permission from the authorities: Dalí was Dalí.[121]

Cécile Éluard, informed by the media that her mother was dying, made one last attempt to see her, travelling to Port Lligat in early June. Both Dalí and Gala refused to allow her into their presence. Cécile returned disconsolately to Paris. It was the ultimate cruelty.[122] It seems that at about this time Amanda Lear received a telephone call from Gala. She was ill and in despair, she said, and coughing badly. As for Dalí, he refused to eat. What would happen to him when she was gone? She begged Amanda to look after him.[123]

Gala died at around 6 a.m. on 10 June 1982. In attendance were Dr Vergara, Dr José María Cos (of the Puigvert Foundation), Arturo Caminada and Robert Descharnes.[124] Antoni Pitxot had left some three hours earlier. Dalí had asked him if he thought Gala was going to die. 'I think so,' Pitxot says he replied. Dalí had become pensive, and asked Pitxot and Dr Vergara to place a screen between his bed and Gala's so that he could be alone with his thoughts.[125]

Gala had made it clear not only that she wished to be buried in Púbol but that, if possible, she wanted to die there, the latter request being confided to paper.[126] This posed a problem. If it were announced that the death had taken place in Port Lligat, a judge would have to see the body before it could be moved. There would be delays, kilometres of red tape. Dalí's entourage decided to move the corpse secretly, therefore. This way both her wishes could be respected, in appearance at any rate. It fell to Dr Vergara to arrange the illegal operation. He telephoned his colleague in Corçà, Carles Pongilupi Pagés. 'Gala is dead. Will you sign the papers saying she died in Púbol?' Pongilupi agreed. Gala was propped upright in the back of the Cadillac, as if still alive, and wrapped in a blanket. Then, at about eleven in the morning, Arturo Caminada drove her on her last ride to Púbol. A nurse travelled beside the corpse so that, if the car was stopped for any reason by the police, they could explain that they had been rushing Señora Dalí to hospital and that she had just died.[127]

But the Cadillac was not stopped. Shortly afterwards Arturo rang Nanita Kalaschnikoff to tell her that Gala was dead and that he had driven her body to Púbol. 'It's the first time ever that the Señora travelled with me in the back seat and not the front,' he said sadly.[128]

Dalí's spokesmen told the media that Gala had been taken to Púbol in an 'irreversible coma', and that she had expired shortly after her arrival.[129] The death certificate stated that Elena Diakanoff Devulina died from 'heart failure' in the castle of Púbol at 2.15 p.m. on 10 June 1982.[130] It seems that in his first draft Dr Pongilupi Pagés had written 'senile arteriosclerosis', but that Dalí, who apparently was consulted, objected to this formulation. The doctor had been accompanied to the town hall of La Pera by Miguel Domenech, who is described in the death certificate as the 'representative' of the deceased.[131] Since Gala had died officially in Púbol, no toll for her was rung from the bell of the little church of Sant Baldiri that stands just above Port Lligat next to the cemetery. It was a brutally unpoetic irony.[132]

Having deposited the corpse in Púbol, Caminada drove back to Port Lligat. Then he drove Dalí and Antoni Pitxot to the village. The Cadillac drew up once more at the entrance to Gala's castle at around 7.30 p.m. According to one report, Dalí, a tiny hunched figure in the back of the vast car, had with him his picture *The Three Glorious Enigmas of Gala* and a favourite photograph of Gala with King Juan Carlos and Queen Sofía: he wanted both to be on display in Púbol.[133] Meanwhile Robert Descharnes and Miguel Domenech had arrived. The castle was cordoned off from the gathering crowd by the civil guard and the local police. There was a brief press conference at 8.30 p.m. in which Domenech stated that Dalí was very upset but was retaining his dignity and lucidity. Gala's burial would take place the following afternoon.[134]

Next morning, 11 June, *El País* questioned the veracity of the official statement concerning the place of Gala's death. 'It seems beyond doubt that Gala was already dead when the Cadillac left the painter's residence in Port Lligat,' it wrote, 'and that the journey was carried out to avoid the red tape involved in moving corpses.'[135] Despite the illegality of the operation, soon common knowledge, no official investigation was ever undertaken: the law had been broken but the State could not afford to offend Dalí—and turned a blind eye.

Gala was embalmed by a team of Barcelona doctors. According to Antoni Pitxot, the instructions had been issued by Dalí: he wanted the body of his muse to resist the ravages of time for as long as possible.[136] She was then laid out in her coffin in her beloved red Dior dress. She had told Mara Albaretto, and presumably Dalí, that it was to be her shroud.[137]

The funeral service in the crypt, conducted by Joaquim Goy, began at around 6 p.m. on 11 June and lasted for half an hour. Dalí did not go down, and begged Antoni Pitxot to stay with him in Gala's room, where, in order not to think about what was happening below, he discussed trivial matters.[138] The service was attended by Robert Descharnes, Miguel Domenech, Arturo Caminada, Emilio Puignau, Dr José María Cos, the housekeepers Joaquim and Dolors Xicot and a few other servants.[139] The only member of the family authorized by Dalí to be present was his cousin Gonzalo Serraclara. To her outrage, not even Montserrat Dalí, of whom the painter had been so fond, was allowed in.[140]

According to Serraclara, Dalí visited the tomb a few hours after the inhumation. The painter not only seemed unmoved but made a point of saying to him, 'Look, I'm not crying.' Serraclara attributed this attitude to the fact that for months Dalí and Gala had been fighting and that, for the painter, her death came as a release. But what Dalí was really thinking at this moment we cannot know.[141]

A few days later, moved by a powerful impulse, Dalí struggled down into the crypt alone in the early hours of the morning. There the nurses found him trembling with terror and persuaded him to return to his room. Dalí told Pitxot later about the horror of his visit to the tomb: he had stumbled over the mortuary debris left by the masons and fallen to his knees. The visit left such an indelible impression that he never repeated it.[142]

There was widespread relief in Spain that Gala had died before Dalí. Had it been the other way round, many people felt, she might have gone abroad and disinherited a country for which she had never expressed great affection (although she was pleased with the attentions of the King and Queen). On 12 June 1982 it was revealed that, according to a deed signed by Dalí and Gala on 11 November 1977, Gala's famous private collection was to go on her death to Dalí for his lifetime, after which it would pass to the Theatre-Museum in Figueres.[143] The will which she made in 1980 modified this: if Dalí outlived Gala, her paintings were to be split equally at his death between the Spanish State and Catalunya. It seemed a very fair apportionment.[144]

Gala's daughter, Cécile, was shocked to find that her mother had attempted to disinherit her totally. Perfectly aware, however, that under Spanish law a child cannot be entirely excluded from its parent's will, she immediately initiated legal proceedings. An agreement mitigating Gala's last cruelty would eventually be reached with the Spanish Government.[145]

With Gala dead, the Government and the Crown redoubled their attentions to the artist. The first great surprise was a telephone call from the Royal House informing Dalí that King Juan Carlos had decided to create him Marquis of Púbol. All his life Dalí had revered the aristocracy; now he was to be part of it! The title was not entirely to his satisfaction, however, and he succeeded in having it extended to Marquis of Dalí and Púbol. The announcement of the change in his social status came on 20 July 1982.[146]

Another gesture followed immediately on 27 July: the purchase by the Government, for a hundred million pesetas (about half a million pounds at today's rate), of two leading works chosen personally by the artist: *Cenicitas* (*Little Ashes*) and *Harlequin*. By agreement with Dalí, the money was placed in his bank account in Figueres for the running of the Púbol domestic establishment, the payment of medical bills and so forth. According to Miguel Domenech, Dalí, terrified of being out of ready cash, was deeply grateful for the transaction. In return he donated to the State *The Three Glorious Enigmas of Gala* (1982), his last large-scale tribute to his wife.[147]

Final Work in Púbol

'If Gala were to disappear, no one could take her place. It's a total impossibility. I'd be completely alone,' Dalí had said in 1966, adding on a more positive note: 'If Gala died, it would be terribly difficult to come to terms with it. I don't know how I'd manage. But I would. I'd even continue to enjoy life because my love of life is stronger than everything.'[1] Now that it had happened, Dalí began to go to pieces. 'Whatever their differences, whatever the rows, they were vital to each other,' Mara Albaretto has commented. 'Gala was the mainstay, the will-power. And now she was gone. Dalí felt like a child abandoned by his mother. He stopped eating. It was a cry for help.'[2]

Dalí's attendants told reporters that, once the artist had assimilated the shock of Gala's death, he planned to return home and start painting again.[3] It seems that he did indeed envisage this, but trouble arose with the domestic staff that had been brought from Port Lligat, who dared to ask for some badly needed holidays and, in a fury, Dalí dismissed them. Arturo Caminada's wife, Paquita, was engaged instead. And then one day Dalí announced that he was going to remain in Púbol.[4]

He never again set foot in Port Lligat. Two former friends of his, the art critic Rafael Santos Torroella and Dalí's biographer, Luis Romero, have stated publicly that from this point onwards Port Lligat was not only abandoned but virtually sacked. 'Inside were a multitude of works of all kinds, drawings or sketches, manuscripts, innumerable documents, photographs, objects and works of art by other people, intimate things and goodness knows what else. Did someone install himself there?' wrote Romero guardedly in 1984.[5] 'Nobody made an inventory of what was in the house and others appropriated it,' he insisted five years later, adding in an enigmatic footnote:

Chapter SIXTEEN

It is incomprehensible that before entering the house that had been abandoned by its owner, and searching it prior to taking to France various cases with unspecified contents—as has been stated in the press—with the pretext that they were documents or works that needed to be photographed, no detailed inventory was drawn up in the presence of the authorities or of persons of proven integrity. It was stated that the cases crossed the frontier. Did their contents return? Who can prove it?[6]

That Romero was referring to Robert Descharnes there could be no doubt. Interviewed by the BBC in 1994, Rafael Santos Torroella was more explicit: Descharnes and his family occupied Dalí's house during the summer of 1982, and he was seen to remove several boxes. When queried by a neighbour, Descharnes replied that Dalí had given him permission to take documents to Paris to be photographed. 'Why did you not tell him that we have better light here than in Paris for taking pictures?' was the neighbour's rejoinder. Santos Torroella is convinced that the documents were not returned to Spain in their entirety.[7]

An entry in Reynolds Morse's diary confirms the misgivings of Luis Romero and Rafael Santos Torroella: 'Descharnes continues to appear two-faced and dangerous, and certainly not the simpering, bookish "nice fellow" he seems on the surface. He now has totally discredited Eleanor and myself with Dalí while denying it. He has spent two weeks in Dalí's house without any witnesses, while the locals kept tabs on his comings and goings with suitcases full of material "borrowed" from Port Lligat.'[8]

Given this situation, Santos Torroella attempted to have the house sealed and guarded. The judge in La Bisbal seemed favourable but said that a member of Dalí's family would have to make a statement. The following day Santos Torroella returned with Dalí's cousin, Gonzalo Serraclara, who, like him, was scandalized by what was happening in Port Lligat. Again, the judge was well disposed. But next day, when Santos Torroella and Serraclara returned, he refused to see them. They concluded that pressure had been brought to bear from Púbol.[9]

This was probably the case. Shortly before his death in 1950, Dalí's father had made Gonzalo Serraclara swear that, when Gala died, he would do his utmost to bring about a reconciliation between his son and Anna Maria. When Serraclara tried to do this, Dalí had flown into a ferocious temper, said he was meddling, and told him to leave. Antoni Pitxot has recalled that it was an extremely unpleasant incident. Arguably Dalí was infuriated when he heard that Serraclara, abetted by Santos Torroella, was now trying to have the house at Port Lligat sealed.[10]

Dalí's anger was understandable for, as Reynolds Morse's unpublished diary seems to establish, Descharnes had Dalí's permission to photograph in Paris the documents necessary for his forthcoming book, of monumental dimensions, *Salvador Dalí. L'Oeuvre et l'homme*, the publication of which was scheduled to coincide with Dalí's eightieth birthday in 1984. Morse, however, had his misgivings about Descharnes's motives: 'Still, he spread a great deal of doubt about what he was really up to, which those of us on the inside well knew was building up his "archives" to shore against his own ruin exactly as Moore and Sabater had done before him.'[11]

To the discredit of the Catalan authorities, Port Lligat was never put under guard. Other people entered it in 1982 and later, and their extractions were to give rise to a black market in Dalí documents that continues to this day. Always famous for smuggling and contraband, Cadaqués was living up to its reputation.

With Gala dead and his health declining, Dalí decided that he wanted to remain permanently in Spain. Since the previous autumn, his lawyer in Madrid, Miguel Domenech, had been working in close contact with the government on the artist's tax and residence situation. No doubt relieved that Gala had died first, the authorities were only too willing to co-operate: the successful resolution of Dalí's affairs was in everyone's interests.

On 9 August 1982 Dalí granted Domenech and Descharnes power of attorney to carry out in the USA whatever actions were necessary 'to draw up a detailed inventory of the totality of the effects, rights, monies, shares, pictures, paintings or anything else' belonging to him or Gala. To this end Domenech and Descharnes were empowered to examine 'investment accounts, current or credit accounts, safes, banks, premises, public or private establishments, or warehouses where such goods might be stored, signing whatever requests, petitions or private or public documents might be necessary'. The property was to be administered in whatever ways the attorneys judged convenient. Finally, the attorneys were obliged to keep a strict and legal record of the actions carried out on Dalí's behalf.[12]

In New York, Domenech stated later, the Dalís' account at the Fifth Avenue branch of the City Bank was found to hold some $1,200,000 in 1981–2. There was also an unspecified amount in the Chase Manhattan. As for Europe, an account in the Pictet Bank in Geneva held a further $3,000,000 and there was a much smaller sum in the Hispano-Americano Bank in Figueres.[13]

Dalí now made a new will in which he left his entire estate to the Spanish nation, 'with the fervent request to conserve, divulge and protect his works of art'. Catalunya, which under the terms of the previous will was to have shared the estate equally with Madrid, was not mentioned; nor was the Theatre-Museum in Figueres. Had pressure been brought to bear on Dalí to alter the will, perhaps by Miguel Domenech? The latter denies this. The artist, he claims, decided to effect the changes without any prompting, full of gratitude to the King and Queen for the consideration they had shown him. Presumably relief that the government was being accommodating about his tax situation also played a major part.[14]

The document was signed at Púbol on 20 September 1982 before the notary public of La Bisbal, José María Foncillas Casaus. The witnesses were Joaquim Xicot (Dalí's caretaker) and a Púbol villager, Narcís Vila Vila. It is unlikely that either had any understanding of the gravity of the occasion—which is why, in the opinion of the local mayor, Benjamí Artigas, they were chosen. But chosen by whom? Presumably, Artigas believes, by Dalí himself in consultation with Miguel Domenech.[15] The latter was not present that afternoon. Nor were Antoni Pitxot and Robert Descharnes. Pitxot had been trying to persuade Dalí for some time to bequeath the Port Lligat and Púbol properties to his foundation in Figueres, but such insinuations had always been greeted with silence. When Dalí told him on 23 September that he had made a new will, Pitxot wondered what changes had been effected. But the artist proffered no details.[16]

Two months later, in November 1982, the Socialists, led by Felipe González, won a landslide victory in the general elections. Miguel Domenech was brother-in-law not only of the Centre Party ex-Prime Minister, Leopoldo Calvo Sotelo, but of the new Socialist Minister of External Affairs, Fernando Morán. He was also a close friend of the incoming Minister of Culture, Javier Solana. These circumstances guaranteed that from the outset there was top-level communication between Dalí's advisers and the government headed by Felipe González.

The investigations into Dalí's financial and fiscal situation progressed slowly, and the painter only became fully resident in Spain for tax purposes in 1985. He was never to fill in a tax return, however. The Socialists proved as 'understanding' of Dalí as had been their centre-party predecessors, and Domenech admitted, after the painter's death, that it had been decided 'not to trouble Dalí in these last years of his life'.[17]

In the autumn of 1982 Dalí was not only thinking about his will but about Luis Buñuel, with whom he had long been trying to reestablish relations. On 6 November he sent him a telegram in Mexico: 'DEAR BUÑUEL EVERY TEN YEARS I SEND YOU A LETTER WITH WHICH YOU DISAGREE BUT I INSIST, TONIGHT I'VE THOUGHT UP A FILM WHICH WE COULD MAKE IN TEN DAYS NOT ABOUT THE DEMON OF PHILOSOPHY BUT ABOUT OUR OWN 'LITTLE DEMON'. IF YOU WISH, COME AND SEE ME IN PÚBOL. I EMBRACE YOU. DALÍ.' Dalí forgot to include his full address and immediately telegraphed again. Buñuel then did something unheard of: he decided to reply. He almost certainly knew that Gala had died and perhaps he felt that the time had come to make a minimal ges-ture of reconciliation. Among the papers preserved in the Buñuel archive in Madrid there is a manuscript draft of his telegram: 'I RECEIVED YOUR TWO CABLES, GREAT IDEA FOR FILM LITTLE DEMON BUT I WITHDREW FROM THE CINEMA FIVE YEARS AGO AND NEVER GO OUT NOW. A PITY. EMBRACES.' According to Antoni Pitxot, Dalí was much affected by Buñuel's message.[18]

It may have been this same November that Dalí telephoned the Spanish film director and photographer Luis Revenga and asked for his help. They had met two years earlier when Revenga was making a documentary about Picasso, and had got on well. Now Dalí wanted him to video the ending of his projected film with Buñuel so that he could send it to the latter in Mexico. Revenga hurried with a camera to Púbol, where, looking like a galvanized corpse, Dalí gave a wildly emotive rendering of a Catalan folksong, 'The Merchant's Daughter', with arms flailing and bulging eyes:

La filla del marxant	The merchant's daughter,
diuen que és la més bella	they say she's the prettiest,
no és la més bella, no,	but she's not the prettiest, no,
que altres n'hi ha sens ella . . .	there are others without her . . .

Having finished his performance Dalí collapsed, exhausted, into a chair. At this point, horrified by his appearance, Antoni Pitxot, who was now in almost daily attendance on the painter, interposed himself between Dalí and the camera. There was no further film-ing.[19]

The projected film derived to some extent from the frustrated *Babaouo* of 1932. It was to open and finish in a Metro station beset by an underground snow storm. A person-age half dwarf, half 'little demon', would gesticulate to himself while singing 'The Merchant's Daughter' over and over again. Trains would come and go, their wheels brushed by snowflakes.[20]

When Dalí refused to lend him money in 1939, Buñuel had sworn not to collaborate with the painter again. He never went back on this decision and died in Mexico on 29 July 1983, nine months after Dalí's pathetic last attempt to get in touch. As Buñuel had so often reminded him, quoting the Spanish proverb, 'Water that's passed the mill can't move the wheel.'

Dalí was now a physical shambles and was finding it increasingly difficult to control his trembling right hand. He was incapable of the fine detail that had characterized his best painting, and could only dab on the oils with a thick brush. Elda Ferrer, one of the

nurses enlisted at Púbol in 1983, was instructed at her interview for the job to tell journalists, if asked, that Dalí was still working. She thought this condition fair enough. But
when she saw Dalí she changed her mind: he desperately wanted to paint but simply
could not hold the brush.[21] On another occasion, Ferrer recalled that Dalí hardly spoke,
sobbed constantly and would spend hours making animal noises. He had hallucinations
and thought he was a snail. 'In two years,' she related, 'I only understood one coherent
phrase: "My friend Lorca".'[22] No worse fate could have befallen a man for whom performance was everything. He had lost his looks dramatically, so he could no longer show
off in public; he had lost his wonderful voice; and he had lost his ability to paint.

Dalí's last oils show his horror of death, and reaffirm his allegiance to Velázquez and
to Michelangelo. They also show the intervention of other hands. Bea admitted after
Dalí's death that he had helped, but refused stubbornly to provide details of his contribution.[23]

In 1982 Dalí executed two *pietàs*. The backdrop to one is a *calma blanca* at Port Lligat,
and through the holes that are the Virgin's breasts (Dalí is still into optical tricks) there
are miniature scenes of rocks and sea.[24] The other was inspired by Michelangelo's sculpture, the *Pietà di Palestrina*, and by comparison is a horribly crude daub.[25] Several of the
last works show that *Las Meninas* continued to haunt Dalí's imagination. In one of them,
Velázquez Dying Behind the Window, on the Left, from which a Spoon Emerges (1982), the
dwarf buffoon Sebastián de Porras, festooned with fried eggs, sits forlornly in the patio
of the Escorial; in another his place is taken by the Infanta Margarita.[26] The fried eggs
are not the only well-tried Dalinian motifs that populate these jaded works. Crutches
abound; the 'little sticks' (*bastoncillos*) that first began to hover over elongated cylindrical forms in 1926 reappear in two canvases; and there are several variations on the lac-
erated body of Saint Sebastian.

The most interesting of the last paintings is *We'll Arrive Later, Round about Five* or *The
Removal Van* (1983), which Dalí discussed in detail with Pitxot and the young art critic
Ignacio Gómez de Liaño. Done with broad strokes, it shows us the interior of a removal
van seen as if we were peering into it from the driver's seat. As he studied it, Gómez de
Liaño remembered André Breton's recommendation: 'Don't forget to make felicitous
wills: as for me, I demand that they take me to the cemetery in a removal van.' The
painting would seem to confirm that Dalí's thoughts were now never far from death.[27]

According to Robert Descharnes, Dalí's last painting was *The Swallow's Tail*, done in
May 1983. It is hard to envisage how by that date Dalí could have executed on his own
the lines occupying the centre of the canvas, let alone those of the cello's sound-holes or
the detail of the instrument itself in the top left-hand corner of the work. Antoni Pitxot

has insisted, however, that on occasion, when for a few moments Dalí's hand stopped trembling, he was still capable of painting steadily, and that this picture is a case in point. Pitxot was present part of the time while Dalí worked on it, and admits that Bea probably helped him with some of the mechanical details.[28]

At all events *The Swallow's Tail* was 'finished' too late to be included in the Dalí retrospective that opened in Madrid's Museo Español de Arte Contemporáneo (MEAC) on 15 April 1983. A huge banner hanging from the top of the building proclaimed that the show (Spain's answer to Pompidou) was entitled *400 Works by Salvador Dalí from 1914 to 1983*. At the express desire of Dalí, it was the King's son, Prince Felipe, who did the honours at the official inauguration. Dalí himself was too depressed to travel to Madrid, and sent a message in which he praised the royal family and, in the worst possible taste, attacked his own, proclaiming that they had been the 'major obstacle' to his artistic career. It was exactly what he had said in 1950 in the vicious memorandum circulated when Anna Maria published her book.[29] Such was Dalí's seething resentment at this time that in August he made sure that Anna Maria would get nothing from his estate by signing a document explaining why she had been excluded from his will. It was witnessed, in the presence of the notary of La Bisbal, by Antoni Pitxot, Arturo Caminada and Robert Descharnes.[30]

In their introduction to the catalogue, the curators, Robert Descharnes and Ana Beristain, pointed out that many of the pre-1929 works on show had never been exhibited. They were proof that, before Dalí arrived in France 'he had already incorporated the personal code that was to change so many aspects of Parisian Surrealism'.[31] This was a valid observation, but the critics were quick to see that, while the exhibition was much stronger than the Pompidou as far as Dalí's early production was concerned, the decade beginning in 1929 was so inadequately represented as to make the retrospective lamentably uneven.[32]

It was true that very few of Dalí's finest Surrealist canvases were on show. *The Great Paranoiac* was an exception; so too was *The Great Masturbator*, which proved a huge success with the crowds. But not even these could compensate for the absence of such marvellous paintings as *The First Days of Spring*, *The Lugubrious Game*, *Illumined Pleasures*, *Outskirts of the Paranoiac-Critical Town* or *Autumn Cannibalism*.

The lavish two-volume exhibition catalogue had been knocked together with great carelessness and was no match for the Pompidou volumes in either the matter of factual accuracy, the transcription of documents or the range and quality of the essays included. For Rafael Santos Torroella, in fact, it was little short of a national disgrace, and the person he held principally responsible was Robert Descharnes. Santos Torroella concluded that the Frenchman's pretensions to scholarly integrity had been thrown to the winds when he became Dalí's secretary after Sabater left.[33]

The exhibition attracted some 250,000 visitors before it ended on 29 May and moved on to the Pedralbes Palace in Barcelona, where its opening on 10 June was timed to coincide to the day with the first anniversary of Gala's death. Dalí stayed put in Púbol, ordered a bunch of spikenards to be placed on Gala's tomb—and refused to talk about her. Antoni Pitxot told the press that several specialists had been seeing Dalí recently, but that there was no crisis: they were merely routine check-ups. Meanwhile the walls of the garden were being raised to prevent the curious from being able to see inside, and as a warning to potential visitors. When Edward James turned up that August assuming that he could see Dalí, he was not allowed in. Robert Descharnes wrote to apologize in October, saying that Arturo Caminada had failed to transmit his name correctly to Dalí. He himself had arrived three days later and had tried to contact James, but it was too late: he had already left his hotel in Girona. Dalí, wrote Descharnes, was sad when he realized what had happened. Now, in October, he was in the midst of a tremendous depression. Would James do the painter the honour of joining the Honorary Board of the new Fundació Gala–Salvador Dalí?[34]

Descharnes had missed James because his own visits to Púbol were sporadic. Once or twice a month he would fly down from Paris, spend a week or so in the 'castle', and then fly back. Miguel Domenech's visits were also erratic. The day-to-day grind of looking after the cantankerous old man was left to Arturo Caminada and his wife, the Xicots, a bevy of nurses and doctors and, increasingly, Antoni Pitxot, who drove up from Cadaqués several times a week to keep Dalí company. They talked together in Catalan, and given Pitxot's family background and his own profession as an artist, there was never any shortage of conversation. As Dalí's speech became increasingly difficult to understand, only Pitxot was able to match Caminada in deciphering what he was saying.

Caminada was no literary man, so it fell to Pitxot to copy down a text dictated by Dalí on 31 October 1983: 'The Most Important Discovery of My Paranoiac-Critical Method: Perpignan Station'. For that innocent-looking station now to have surpassed Millet's *Angelus* in paranoiac-critical significance for Dalí was a sign that his brain, if not the rest of his body, was still working efficiently.[35]

Another sign was the huge interest he took in the extension to his Theatre-Museum. Once part of the medieval fortifications of Figueres, the Torre Gorgot adjoined the museum and had been purchased jointly by the town council and the Catalan regional government. Fascinated by towers from his youth, Dalí was delighted with the new acquisition and renamed it Torre Galatea, in honour of the dead Muse, proclaiming that he would make it a building 'unique in the world'. Perhaps, in lending it Gala's name, he recalled that in the early days of Surrealism, before he met her, she had been known as 'Tour', an acknowledgement of her mystery. The Torre Galatea, Dalí now told the world, would represent 'all enigmas'.[36]

The Fundació Gala–Salvador Dalí was formally constituted on 23 December 1983 before the notary public of La Bisbal, José María Foncillas Casaus, who a year earlier had presided over the signature of Dalí's new will. In the preamble to the document, Dalí explained that it had always been his desire that as many of his works as possible should be in Spain, where they could be visited and studied; and that it had always been his intention to convert Figueres, his birthplace, into 'a cultural and museum mecca of Spain and the world' (which was more or less what Franco had suggested to him). The first step had been the creation of the Dalí Theatre-Museum Foundation. 'But now,' Dalí continued, 'I wish to achieve the pinnacle and sublimation of my desires with the creation of a Foundation whose resonance and projection, transcending the boundaries of the Fatherland, will be the fountain of the infinite cultural benefits which, lovingly, I want for Spain, Catalunya, the Empordà and for my dear City of Figueres.' Before entering into details, Dalí explained that the new Fundació Gala–Salvador Dalí, unlike its predecessor, was to be a private institution.[37]

A few days later Dalí requested an initially somewhat bemused Figueres town council to consider the advisibility of dissolving the former foundation and integrating its functions in the new one, promising that if it did so numerous advantages would accrue to the Theatre-Museum: not only the donation of all the works Dalí had deposited in the original foundation and of the 621 he had just given to the new one, but of many more. The town council decided that they liked Dalí's vision of Figueres as a mecca of art, and expressed unanimous agreement. The King and Queen accepted the invitation to be honorary patrons. The Committee of Honour proposed by Dalí included, along with Edward James, Raymond Barre (the French ex-president), Julien Green, the Spanish biologist and Nobel Prize winner Severo Ochoa, the mathematician René Thom and the Catalan ex-president, Josep Tarradellas. Among those invited to join the board were, in the first place, Antoni Pitxot, Miguel Domenech and Robert Descharnes (already being referred to in the press as 'the troika'), Dalí's amiable cousin, Gonzalo Serraclara, the ex-mayor of Figueres Ramon Guardiola (without whom the Theatre-Museum would never have become a reality) and representatives of the Catalan autonomous parliament, the Madrid Government and other public bodies.

The Fundació Gala–Salvador Dalí was officially inaugurated in Figueres on 27 March

1984, and presented with pomp and ceremony in Madrid the following day. Dalí had dictated a zany message to the King and Queen: 'Your Majesties: Spain is a bleeding thorn; the King, a sublime crown of Spain. Santa Teresa and Nietsche believed that all work, in order to be universal, had to be inscribed in blood. Our blood and that of Gala.'[38]

Looking after Dalí at this time was a nightmare, as is shown by the notes entered in the daily register by Carme Barris, one of the nurses. Meals were a constant battle: as a rule, Dalí would refuse to eat, pushing the plates away furiously like a child, even those specially prepared for him by one of the best restaurants in the region, the Motel del Ampurdán in Figueres (and collected every day by Arturo Caminada in the Cadillac). He treated the nurses appallingly, often spitting at them, and refused to co-operate with the doctors. On 2 April 1984 Carme Barris wrote: 'Dalí woke at midnight, very worked up, and asked for a pill; when we took it to him he spat it out. Finally he agreed to take half a pill provided that the doctor took the other half.'[39]

The so-called troika *outside Gala's 'castle' at Púbol: From left to right: Miguel Domenech, Antoni Pitxot and Robert Descharnes.*

As he approached his eightieth birthday on 11 May 1984 the depression from which Dalí was suffering increased. So out of sorts was he that he even refused to greet the members of the new Foundation's Committee of Honour, whom he himself had chosen, when they went to Púbol.[40] On his birthday itself messages of congratulation arrived from around the world, but they did little to lift his gloom. Indeed, they probably deepened it. A young journalist with *Abc*, Blanca Berasátegui, was allowed in to see Dalí briefly. She got the impression that he was being looked after extremely well and that the rumours that were beginning to circulate about his being shut up against his will were rubbish. Dalí simply wanted to be left alone with his thoughts. She discovered that he was reading René Thom's *Paraboles et catastrophes* and, significantly, Ramon Guardiola's excellent monograph on the Theatre-Museum in Figueres, which had just been published. Robert Descharnes was in ebullient mood: his huge monograph *Dalí. L'Oeuvre et l'homme* was about to appear, he told Berasatágui, and he felt sure that, with 1,200 reproductions and much new material, it was going to be the most important work ever published on the genius.[41]

Descharnes had benefited from privileged access to Dalí and Dalí's archive (not least to the album of press cuttings put together by the painter's father, which saved him a lot of trouble). But it must be said that such access did not compensate for his ignorance about (and apparent indifference to) Spanish culture in general and Catalan culture in particular, apparent throughout the book. Nor did it save him from making some major mistakes where Dalí's life and work were concerned, as Rafael Santos Torroella demonstrated in three devastating, and prominent, reviews of the French and Spanish editions of the book. They castigated not only the Frenchman but his Barcelona publisher, Tusquets, for stating on the book's jacket that Descharnes was 'commonly considered as the best authority on Dalí's work'. Santos Torroella quoted an observation on Dalí's infantile sexuality that made the 'best authority' look ridiculous. 'From the masturbation expressed in several canvases to auto-sodomy,' Descharnes had written, 'his childhood is strongly present'. Auto-sodomy? Santos Torroella had never dreamt that the Dalí of tender years was capable of such unheard-of sexual acrobatics.[42]

The hostilities had begun with an open letter in which Santos Torroella criticized Descharnes for the chaotic catalogue of a recent Dalí exhibition in Ferrara, the first staged under the aegis of the new Fundació Gala–Salvador Dalí. The three reviews added fuel to the fire, and established the eminent critic and Dalí scholar as Descharnes's principal adversary in Spain. They also ensured that henceforth Santos Torroella was *persona non grata* at the Foundation.[43]

Despite Dalí's depression, there were days this summer when he would suddenly brighten. On one of them he announced that he wanted to organize an exhibition in honour of his teacher at Figueres Institute, Juan Núñez Fernández, the person to whom he said his career owed most. It was a generous impulse—but nothing more came of the project.[44]

The publication of Robert Descharnes's lavishly illustrated monograph greatly increased the already rampant scepticism in Spain concerning the authenticity of the artist's last paintings, several of which were reproduced. For an old friend of Dalí, the Catalan painter J.J. Tharrats, now excluded from Púbol, the works were not only bad but unlike anything he had done previously. Indeed, they could not rightly be considered Dalís at all.[45] Robert Descharnes rejected the allegation: all his life Dalí had used different techniques, and if his physical state in old age had made a stylistic change necessary, no one had any right to question the authenticity of the resultant works.[46]

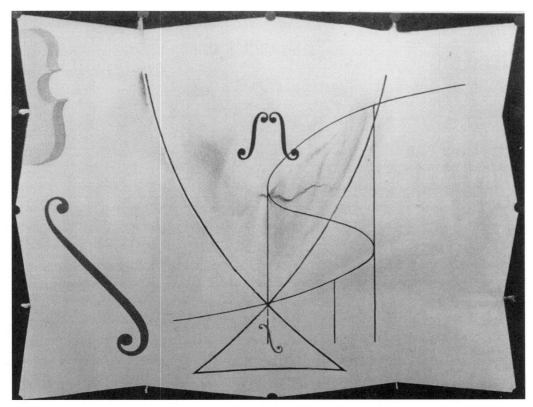

The Swallow's Tail, *1983. Oil on canvas. 73 x 92.2 cm. Dalí's last painting almost certainly shows the hand of his assistant, Isidor Bea.*

Descharnes did not explain how an artist with a violently shaking right arm could have executed a work of such pure precision as *The Swallow's Tail*, according to him Dalí's last painting. Over the following years the scepticism was to mount, particularly when the Fundació Gala–Salvador Dalí began to claim that between July 1982 and the middle of 1983 Dalí had produced as many as a hundred or so works.[47] The publisher Eduard Fornés, a Dalí specialist, accepted that the painter, perhaps for therapeutic reasons, had participated to some extent in their elaboration. But the intervention of other hands was undeniable, and it was incorrect, therefore, 'to say that during the last stage of his life Dalí was capable of producing such a voluminous and important body of work as they want to make us believe'.[48] Luis Romero was of the same opinion. 'They were bad, they didn't look like anything he'd painted before,' he said. 'Moreover, if when Dalí was well and optimistic it sometimes took him months to finish a painting, how could he possibly have painted a hundred works when he was almost always ill and useless? I don't believe it.'[49]

Only a tiny percentage of the alleged one hundred paintings have been exhibited since 1984 and the rest have never been made available to researchers. The scepticism of Luis Romero, Tharrats, Fornés and other Dalí authorities seems perfectly justified.

Fire in the Night

Dalí had always feared death and now, increasingly, he feared the night. He was finding it difficult to sleep, and would lie for hours awake in the darkness, propped up on pillows, alone with his thoughts. Alone . . . but in theory there was company within immediate reach. To the right sleeve of the smock which he now insisted on wearing over his pyjamas, Dalí's attendants had affixed a cable ending in a pear-shaped bell-push. The moment he felt he needed something, or wanted to annoy the nurse on duty just a few rooms away, or to talk to somebody, he would press the bell-push insistently. So insistently, in fact, that the ringing of the bell had maddened a succession of nurses who, despite their abnormally high salaries, had come and gone with understandable velocity, unable to stand the noise, the artist's tempers, his screaming, his spitting, his soiling his bed or his attempts to scratch their faces. Often, when the bell rang in the middle of the night, Dalí just wanted to be reassured that the nurse on duty was there. It seems likely that the latter sometimes ignored the bell and left the old man to his own devices, exhausted by his demands. According to Arturo Caminada, sometimes the apparatus was disconnected in order to stop the bell from ringing and, when Dalí discovered what was happening, he would insist that it be linked up again; finally, said Caminada, the maddening bell (which made it impossible for anyone to relax in the castle by day or by night) had been replaced by a special lamp which, activated by the bell-push, flashed in the nurses' room.[50] There were always two nurses in the castle at any one time, one on duty and the other resting, or sleeping, before taking over. The only condition was that one of them should always be fully responsible for looking after the painter.[51]

Just before dawn on Thursday 30 August 1984 Dalí's bed began to smoulder. The room was poorly ventilated and it was some time before flames appeared, perhaps half an hour. As the room filled with smoke and the bed grew hotter, Dalí became aware of what was happening. He must have pumped the bell-push in a frenzy but it was no longer working. He must have tried to shout. But no one came to his assistance. He threw himself out of bed, choking, and began to crawl towards the door to the passage. Then, at the foot of the bed, he collapsed.[52]

Carme Fábregas was the nurse in charge that night. As part of her normal routine she went to the bedroom to check that everything was in order. She found smoke issuing from under the door and rushed to warn the policeman on duty, Fortunato Golpe Bañuls. Then she shouted down to Descharnes from a window giving on to the inner courtyard.[53] Golpe Bañuls sprinted to Dalí's room and opened the door, to be greeted by a black cloud of belching smoke. He managed to reach the bed but found that Dalí wasn't in it. Then Descharnes arrived. There were now flames. Wrapped in wet towels the pair located Dalí on the floor, semi-conscious, and dragged him to safety.[54]

While this was happening the other nurse in the house, Carme Barris, who had been sleeping,[55] summoned the firemen and doctors from Girona. Descharnes and Golpe Bañuls, helped by her and Carme Fábregas, carried Dalí to the library, where he screamed at Fábregas: 'Bitch! Criminal! Assassin! I called you and you didn't come!' Despite the insults she gave Dalí mouth-to-mouth respiration while Barris applied a heart massage. Meanwhile, Golpe Bañols alerted the Civil Guard post at the nearby village of Flaçà.[56]

There was danger that the whole castle might go on fire, so Dalí was placed in Carme Fábregas's car and driven by her a few hundred metres away while they awaited the arrival of the firemen. Whether Dalí continued to insult her is not on record, but it seems likely given the situation.[57] When the firemen arrived it took them more than twenty minutes to put out the fire, which was quenched shortly after 7 a.m. Dalí's bedroom was almost completely destroyed.[58]

According to Emilio Puignau, who drove from Cadaqués the moment he heard what had happened, the first thing Dalí said to him was: 'Ah, you've come. It was my fault.' Puignau concluded that Dalí's constant use of the bell-push had provoked a short-circuit. The heat had been so intense that the silver frame of one of the pictures in his bedroom had almost melted.[59]

Dalí's injuries, first and second degree burns to his right leg, were not considered serious by the local practitioners who initially examined and treated him. Pitxot and Descharnes were interviewed by Spanish Television. Pitxot, normally very relaxed to camera, was visibly nervous: 'There was a little fire this morning in . . . in our friend Dalí's rooms,' he said with a forced smile, 'and even the firemen had to come! But we're all very pleased to be . . . to be able . . . able to say, well, that . . . that everything's all right, that Dalí is relatively well, he's bet . . . he's resting at the moment, he's had a fright.'[60]

Everything was far from all right. Twenty-four hours after the fire, on the advice of Dalí's habitual doctor, Juan García San Miguel, who had arrived at Púbol a few hours later, and of Dr José Visa Miracle, a specialist in burns summoned from Barcelona, it was decided to transfer the painter to the Pilar Clinic in the Catalan capital.[61] Dalí was adamant that he would only go to Barcelona on one condition: that first they take him to see his Theatre-Museum in Figueres. It was probably madness to give in to this request, since it meant adding an extra sixty-five kilometres to the journey to the clinic and losing perhaps three hours of vital time. But the 'troika', fully aware of how essential the Museum and its progress were to Dalí's well-being, allowed him, rightly or wrongly, to have his way.[62] Accompanied by Antoni Pitxot and a nurse, Dalí was driven by Arturo in the Cadillac to Figueres and carried into the museum on a stretcher. It was about 10 p.m. on 31 August 1984, almost forty hours after the fire.

Among those waiting for Dalí at the Theatre-Museum were the photographer Melitón Casals ('Meli'), the mayor of Figueres, Marià Lorca, and ex-mayor Ramon Guardiola. Lorca had the impression that Dalí was saying goodbye. The artist inspected the work done since his last visit, particularly Gala's yellow boat on its pillar, and declared the Torre Galatea finished. Then, at around 10.45 p.m., he started off for Barcelona in an ambulance. It was midnight before he arrived at the Pilar Clinic.[63]

As Dalí entered the Pilar he was heard to mutter over and over the words 'martyr, martyr'. The nurses thought that he meant that he was being martyrized. It seems, however, that he was expressing his anxiety that the manuscript of his erotic drama *Martyr*, which he always kept by him in Púbol, might have gone up in the flames. Happily this was not the case.[64]

An official medical report issued the following day stated that Dalí's burns, located in his right leg, buttocks and perineum, affected 18 per cent of his body. Referring to the painter's manifest state of malnutrition (he weighed only forty kilograms), Miguel Domenech told reporters how immensely difficult it had been over the last few years to persuade Dalí to eat.[65]

On 4 September Anna Maria Dalí insisted on visiting her brother in the clinic. It was over thirty years since the two had met, and probably she was the last person the artist wanted to see coming through the door of room 401. That he shouted at her to go away there is no doubt, and he may well have added 'you old lesbian!', as has been claimed, and tried to hit her. Dalí was so affected by the visit that a few weeks later he signed a legal document in which he set out the reasons for his rejection of his family. As for Anna Maria, she gave the press a more rosy account of her visit.[66]

Dalí's condition was now 'stable', according to his doctors. Then, on 5 September, they announced that there would have to be a long and difficult skin-grafting operation otherwise the artist's chances of survival were nil, given the certainty of infection. They admitted that it would be a high-risk intervention.[67] On 6 September Dalí stated before a notary public, and in the presence of the media, that he agreed to the operation. His relatives also gave their approval.[68] The operation began at 9 a.m. on 7 September, and lasted for more than six hours. The surgeons were optimistic: provided the skin grafts took, it seemed that Dalí would pull through. Over the next two days there was some fever, accompanied by respiratory problems. But Dalí battled on.[69]

As more information became available about the fire, it was widely felt that Dalí's entourage had been grossly negligent. Rafael Santos Torroella asked publicly for a judicial enquiry into what had happened, and for a broader investigation into the control being exercised over the ailing artist by Descharnes, Pitxot and Domenech.[70] Some journalists went so far as to suggest that Dalí had been 'kidnapped' by his collaborators, who were preventing him from seeing his relatives and friends. The 'troika', offended by these charges, responded by saying that once Dalí's health improved they would defend themselves in law against their accusers. Xavier Corberó, a young sculptor friend of Dalí's, stood up for the three men. He was confident, he said, that if Dalí had ever asked to see him, Antoni Pitxot would have telephoned him immediately. But Dalí was old and decrepit, he didn't want to be seen by his friends in such a lamentable state, he who had always shone in public. In his place Corberó would feel exactly the same way. It is hard not to agree with this analysis of the situation.[71]

On 7 September, the day of the operation, an official inquiry was opened by the judge of La Bisbal, José Isidro Rey Huidobro, to elucidate how the fire had occurred and what responsibilities, if any, should be imputed. Today the thick file can be perused in the offices of the town's magistrate's court.[72]

The day before the inquiry began, the judge was visited by Dalí's cousin, Gonzalo Serraclara, who was accompanied by Rafael Santos Torroella. Without accusing anyone in particular, Serraclara told the judge that he and other members of Dalí's family felt that the fire was the result of negligence on the part of the artist's attendants, and that, moreover, there were irregularities in the handling of his affairs.[73] Over the next few days and weeks the judge questioned Descharnes, Domenech and Pitxot, the nurses Carme Fábregas and Carme Barris, the doctors who had seen Dalí, Arturo Caminada, the gardener, the fire brigade men, the policeman Golpe Bañuls and, finally, Dalí himself.

Several statements made it clear that the electrical system with which Dalí had been provided for summoning the nurses was not only antiquated but extremely dangerous. Caminada told the judge that, while Dalí at first used the button only to call the nurses, it gradually became a plaything. He even used it when there were people with him, and subjected it to such abuse that it burnt out and had to be replaced. Then the same thing had happened again. As a result, Caminada had made sure that there were always

replacements to hand. All those around Dalí knew about this situation, Caminada insisted. He told the judge that he had warned Dalí that he might set himself alight and that
he should change the system, but that the painter had stubbornly refused to listen to
him.[74]

On this stubbornness all those questioned were agreed: Dalí could not be overriden.
Antoni Pitxot said that the artist went beserk when he did not get his own way. As for
the delay in getting Dalí to the clinic, Pitxot insisted that the painter was adamant that
he would only agree to being taken to Barcelona if he was first allowed to visit his museum in Figueres. For Pitxot, such a decision was 'heroic'.[75]

Dalí himself stated that, when the fire began, he had been using the bell-push contin-
uously, trying unsuccessfully to attract attention. In his opinion it was this intense use
of the push that had set the bed alight. In his last declaration to the judge, he exonerated his attendants of all responsibility for what had happened.[76]

The judge did not ask Carme Fábregas, the nurse, if she had seen the flashing light
and failed to respond, and it is impossible to know the facts of the matter. In her declaration she stated that Dalí could be extremely difficult, and that often he would
scream at those around him, calling them 'sons of bitches' (*fills de put*) and robbers.
On such occasions Arturo Caminada would sometimes burst into tears.[77] Fábregas
said later on the radio that, had Dalí been her father, she would have seen to it that
he was taken immediately to hospital after he was burnt, adding that in her own
house she would never have allowed such an antiquated electrical system.[78] Elda
Ferrer, who had left Dalí's service by the time the fire occurred, recalled that she too
had frequently pointed out that the installation was very dangerous, but that nobody
had listened.[79]

Dr García San Miguel, who had been looking after Dalí since May 1983, was asked
for his opinion of the painter's general condition. He replied that in his view Dalí was
not suffering from any particular physical illness. From a psychiatric standpoint, however, he had 'a psychopathological personality with very marked depressive traits'. As
for Dalí's trembling hands, San Miguel explained that the Parkinson's disease hypothesis had soon been abandoned: the trembling was the result above all of old age, and
became worse when Dalí was excited. Arteriosclerosis? Yes, but only moderate: more or
less what one would expect in a person of Dalí's age.

San Miguel confirmed that, given Dalí's extreme stubbornness, his attendants habitually gave him what he wanted in the line of medicaments, with the sole exception of
LSD, 'which he asked for to inspire images for his painting'. Dalí had always made a
point of denying publicly that he took drugs, but San Miguel's declaration suggests that

he was not averse to the occasional experiment. So far as San Miguel was concerned, Dalí was quite lucid. But it had to be admitted that he had a personality that expressed itself in 'aggressive acts, insults and a tendency towards hiding and darkness'.[80]

The judicial authorities in Girona, capital of the province, decided to carry out a full parallel investigation into 'the whole Dalí situation'. A professor of Legal Medicine from Seville, Luis Frontela, was entrusted with the task. His report was not completed until February 1985. Frontela concluded, as had the La Bisbal judge, that the fire had been caused by a deficient electrical installation and by Dalí's excessive use of the bell-push. Oddly enough, he attached no blame to Dalí's attendants for not having insisted on renovating the antiquated system. In view of Frontela's findings, the case was closed.[81]

Yet that there had been negligence seems clear enough. Given the danger that Dalí might ignite himself, a fire extinguisher at least should have been installed. But this was not done. As regards the replacement of the electrical system, a variation along the lines of a baby alarm, for example, could easily have been installed, giving Dalí a microphone instead of a bell-push. But there is no indication whatsoever in the La Bisbal file that anyone devoted any thinking to the subject. For this the 'troika' must surely take its share of the blame.

Dalí remained in the Pilar Clinic until 17 October 1984 when, with cameras flashing and journalists thronging the surroundings, Arturo Caminada arrived with the Cadillac to drive him to Figueres.

Interview in the Torre Galatea

According to Robert Descharnes, just before the fire Dalí told him that he would like to spend spring and autumn in Port Lligat, winter in the Torre Galatea and summer in Púbol.[82] It was natural enough, therefore, that since winter was now approaching he should have been installed in the extension to his Theatre-Museum, where preparations to accommodate him had gone ahead at breakneck speed while he was in the Pilar.

The Torre Galatea was to be Dalí's final abode. Despite his previous plans he would never again set foot in Púbol, let alone Port Lligat. The last five years of his life were to be swathed in a secrecy even more enveloping than that which had prevailed during his two years in Gala's castle. Occasionally he would issue a communiqué prepared for him by his aides, or announce that he was writing a poem. But the days of the television interviews in which he had revelled for decades were finished for ever. Moreover, his physical appearance, already revolting, was made worse when the doctors, in despair because he refused to eat, equipped him with a grotesque nasal-gastric tube leading directly to his stomach. The piece of apparatus made his speech even more incoherent and his throat painfully dry.

Dalí's mind, however, remained clear, and at this late point in the narrative I may perhaps be forgiven for adding my personal testimony. For several years I had been trying to obtain an interview with Dalí, to no avail. Enric Sabater had allowed me to be present at the Maestro's press conference in the Theatre-Museum on 24 October 1980, but I had not been able to talk personally to the painter. A few months later, when I telephoned Port Lligat in the hope of being granted an interview, Gala invited me to meet Dalí a few weeks later at the Meurice, but this had proved impossible. Then I gave up. When the first volume of my biography of Lorca was published in 1985, however, I sent Dalí a copy, later telephoning Antoni Pitxot to enquire if he had received it. Pitxot was extremely courteous and expressed his appreciation of the book, in which I had treated Dalí's relationship with Lorca at considerable length. He said he would try to persuade the painter to receive me.

Dalí poses in front of his photograph of José Antonio Primo de Rivera, founder of Falange Española, the Spanish Fascist Party, Port Lligat, 1974.

There was silence for several months and then, on 15 January 1986, Pitxot telephoned me from the Torre Galatea to say that Dalí had just told him that he wanted to see me immediately. 'If you don't come today he may change his mind,' Pitxot warned. At six that evening, after catching a plane from Madrid to Barcelona and dashing up the motorway in a hired car, I was being ushered by Pitxot through a succession of labyrinthine anterooms into the hall where the painter was to receive me.

At the end of the imposing chamber, garbed from head to foot in a white silk robe set off by a gold chain and topped by his famous red Catalan hat, or *barretina*, sat the man who as a child had enjoyed dressing up as a king. It was an awesome sight. And an awesome experience to approach the phantasmagorical figure down what appeared to be an interminably long red carpet.

Dalí's physical appearance was truly appalling. The handsome face had caved in, the slavering mouth hung open, and from his nose issued a clutter of plastic tubes. After a shaking hand had grasped mine, Pitxot sat to one side of the throne while I took my place on the other, placing the tape-recorder on the table beside us. Fixing me with watery, sea-blue eyes terrible in their intensity, Dalí began to speak fast in an almost unintelligible mumble of Spanish and Catalan made even more difficult to follow by the feverish drumming of his right hand on the arm of his chair.

Once my ear became acclimatized to Dalí's voice, I realized, with Pitxot's help, that he was telling me how much Federico García Lorca had loved him. The poet's love for him had been intensely physical, he said. No question of mere affection. Dalí had tried to return the passion but was unable to. Instead Lorca had made love in Dalí's presence, as we saw earlier, to the skinny but powerfully seductive Margarita Manso. He went on to recall the poet's obsession with death and his famous, stage-by-stage enactments of his death, burial and putrefaction in Granada. Gala was hardly mentioned: it was Lorca who was on Dalí's mind. I came away with the clear impression that Dalí's friendship with the poet was perceived by him as one of the fundamental experiences in his life.

I also left with the impression that very few people indeed, perhaps only Antoni Pitxot and Arturo Caminada, could possibly make out Dalí's speech. The tape-recording is proof that by 1986, given Dalí's enormous difficulty in articulating clearly and his life-long tendency to monologue, it was now impossible for anyone to have a satisfactory conversation with the painter.[83]

Demart Pro Arte BV

Dalí's copyright had been handled since January 1981 by the Société de la Propriété Artistique et des Dessins et Modèles in Paris (Spadem). In view of changes in French law introduced in 1985, and no doubt also because Spadem was doing badly, Dalí's advisers, particularly Robert Descharnes, persuaded him to sever his connection with the organization and confide his copyright to a new company specifically set up for the purpose.

Thus was born Demart Pro Arte BV, based in Amsterdam, with Descharnes as managing director. A year later, on 13 June 1986, Dalí assigned his copyright to Demart until 11 May 2004, the hundredth anniversary of his birth. The contract was prepared by Miguel Domenech, who has said that at the time Dalí, he and Pitxot were under 'tremendous pressure' from a now power-hungry Descharnes. According to Domenech, he drew up the contract as slowly and painstakingly as possible in order to gain time and ensure that the document contained sufficient checks and controls to curb the Frenchman's ambitions: validity subject to approval by the competent Spanish administrations, annual audit, penalty clauses for failure to respect the spirit of Dalí's will and so forth.[84]

Given the wide-ranging consequences that would inevitably be engendered by the contract, which gave a foreign company the right to administer Dalí's royalties for eighteen years, it must appear inconceivable that a notary public was not summoned to witness the signatures and to testify that Dalí was *compos mentis* when he appended his shaky one to the document alongside that of Descharnes.[85] The presence of such a notary was not required by Spanish law, but it would have lent a proper seriousness to the occasion; while the affidavit in which, more than a year later, Miguel Domenech and the French lawyer Jacques Sinard attested that the signatures of Descharnes and Dalí were authentic was hardly a compensation.[86]

Even when he was well, Dalí had never shown any interest in contracts, or any understanding of their small print. What he wanted was cash up front. It is difficult to believe, therefore, that despite Domenech's attempts to explain the contract to him, he could have grasped its exact nature or its potential consequences. The painter, moreover, was in very poor physical condition at this time. A month later, when the doctors found that his heart was not pumping adequately, a pacemaker was hurriedly installed.[87]

Neither Miguel Domenech nor Antoni Pitxot were present in the Torre Galatea when the Demart contract was signed on 13 June 1986. Pitxot hinted ten years later that Descharnes had deliberately arranged matters so that he would be absent that day.[88]

Not only did the Socialist Government not pester Dalí about his chaotic tax situation, it gave its *nihil obstat* to the Demart contract once the company's Spanish lawyer, José Briones, had submitted to the Inland Revenue, in September 1986, a list of Dalí's assets in Spain and abroad.[89] In February 1987 Dalí received a letter from the current Minister of Economy and Finance, Carlos Solchaga. 'Dear Maestro,' it began, 'I am pleased to be able to confirm the authorization regularizing the situation of the assets you built up abroad before returning to Spain. Also the authorization of the provisional cession of your copyright to the Dutch society Demart Pro Arte BV.'[90] Commenting on this letter, the Catalan publisher Eduard Fornés has written: 'It is difficult to fathom how a Spanish Minister of Finance authorized a foreign company to handle the painter's rights, thereby renouncing a heritage that should have been admininistered by the Dalí Foundation.' Difficult indeed.[91]

On 6 October 1987 Demart issued a communiqué announcing that the company had become operative. Robert Descharnes, the managing director, was 'an authority of world reputation', as well as being the Fundació Gala–Salvador Dalí 'delegate for national and international relations'. It made him sound just like the right man for the job.[92]

But not everyone thought so. In a letter to Jordi Pujol, the Catalan premier, the following year, Jean-Paul Oberthur, the former head of Spadem, set out his misgivings about Demart. If the company was above board, he asked, why was it based in Amsterdam and not in Spain, preferably in the Fundació Gala–Salvador Dalí? Why did it need an office in Geneva? Was the reason to avoid or to reduce taxation? Why had the contract signed by Dalí and Descharnes not been witnessed by a notary? Moreover, was it not a fact that the rights granted to Demart by Dalí were in conflict with clause four of the foundation's statutes, which established that its purpose was 'to promote, encourage, divulge, enhance, protect and defend in the territory of the Spanish State and in that of other States, the artistic, cultural and intellectual production of Salvador Dalí'? Was it really credible that Dalí could have wished his own foundation to lose some of its rights and attributions? Given that the Catalan autonomous government was represented on the board of the foundation, why had these questions not been raised publicly? Oberthur's letter was extremely courteous in its pinpointing of such basic questions. But so far as is known, he never received a reply from Jordi Pujol.[93]

Reynolds Morse was a good businessman, and felt sure that Descharnes was not.[94] Descharnes was to argue that almost all the company's income during these years went on the legal expenses incurred fighting Dalí forgers around the world. On one occasion, the Fundació Gala–Salvador Dalí agreed to accept in lieu of royalties a consignment of second-rate Dalí lithographs issued by Demart. These were then marketed. 'They're swindling people,' exclaimed Rafael Santos Torroella on television, 'putting out works by Dalí to which Dalí has contributed not so much as a nail-scratch. In any part of the world this would be considered dishonesty. And the organization responsible for the dishonesty, not only here but worldwide, is a company called Demart. And, as I've already said in a Madrid newspaper, I simply cannot understand how they've allowed this to be set up with the agreement of the Spanish authorities.'[95]

After Dalí's death Descharnes's running of Demart Pro Arte BV, as well as his eminently intractable personality, would lead to endless problems with the Fundació Gala–Salvador Dalí and the Spanish Government. Finally, in 1995, the Ministry of Culture issued a decree transferring Dalí's copyright to the Foundation, the decision being ratified by the Spanish High Court in March 1997 after an initially successful appeal by Descharnes.[96]

Death

On 27 November 1988 Dalí was admitted to Figueres Hospital on the advice of his doctor, Juan García San Miguel. The painter had a touch of flu which was being aggravated by lung and heart complications. He needed to be under close observation. The head of the hospital, Dr Carles Ponsatí, said that if all went well Dalí should be back at the Torre Galatea within a week.[97]

All did not go well, and the following afternoon the doctors decided to transfer Dalí immediately to the Quirón Clinic in Barcelona. He was driven there in an intensive care ambulance so large that it could not park at the door to the clinic. Consequently Dalí was subjected to public scrutiny as he was carried for several metres along the street on a stretcher. The reporters were ready with their cameras to capture the pathetic sight. A medical report issued that midnight stated that Dalí was suffering from a 'severe cardio-respiratory insufficiency, caused by infection, and pulmonary thrombo-embolism'. The doctors considered that the painter's recovery would be, at best, 'very difficult'. Dalí, meanwhile, had demanded that a TV set be installed in his room. According to a member of his entourage, 'the cunning old fellow wants it so that he can follow what they're saying about his health'.[98]

There was plenty to follow. The news bulletins on all the nation's TV and radio channels referred to Dalí constantly at this time; mobile units blocked the accesses reserved for ambulances; the newspapers touched up their dossiers on the painter's life and work; and there was a stream of visits from political and other notables—so many that the clinic had to impose restrictions. Among them was the head of the Catalan Government, Jordi Pujol, and the Socialist mayor of Barcelona, Pasqual Maragall (who for years had been waiting in vain for Dalí to make him a member of his foundation so that the painter's relation with the Catalan capital could be clarified). 'His eyes are shining and observing with great vitality', said Antoni Pitxot. 'It's a sign that he wants to continue living.'[99]

Apparently Dalí did want to continue living—and soon the doctors were reporting an improvement. He also wanted to see the King, who happened to be on a private visit to Barcelona at the time. Nagged by the painter, the foundation prepared at breakneck speed two luxury copies of four texts, written between 1985 and 1988, that Dalí was anxious to present to the monarch: 'The Alchemy of my Love', in praise of Queen Sofía, 'Elegies to Gala', 'Ode to the Monarchy' and a paean to the King and Queen entitled 'Laureada'.[100]

Don Juan Carlos complied with Dalí's wishes. The visit took place on 5 December and the new inmate of room 655, who that morning had been transferred from the intensive care unit, was propped up in bed for the occasion. A few minutes before the King arrived Dalí asked Arturo Caminada to clean up his moustache, which was looking a bit messy. Greatly excited, he gave Don Juan Carlos two copies of his book of poems and promised him that soon he would begin painting again. That, at least, was how Antoni Pitxot interpreted the painter's incoherent mumblings, which the King, as the television report showed clearly, found it impossible to decipher. At one point during the ten-minute visit Dalí grasped the King's hands. When he left, Don Juan Carlos said that he had found the painter 'very well taking into account his serious state'. Perhaps he knew that Dalí would be watching on television.[101]

Meanwhile, in Turin, Giuseppe and Mara Albaretto had been making some polemical declarations, blaming the 'troika' for what they considered 'the shameful speculation' in Dalí's works and pointing out that, contrary to current belief, Dalí and Gala had grown positively to hate each other in the last years of their relationship.[102] Interviewed by a Spanish magazine, Albaretto expressed the view that the Spanish State should intervene immediately to protect Dalí from the three 'guardian angels' who he believed were preventing the painter's true friends from gaining access to him.[103]

The improvement in Dalí's condition seemed to be continuing. 'He's no longer watching television or listening to the radio,' commented the mayor of Figueres, Marià Lorca. 'This means that he's beginning to feel much better.'[104] Dalí was listening to music if not to the radio, particularly to a recording made by the orchestra at Maxim's of Toselli's *Serenata* and *Les Millions d'Arlequin*. 'Put on the Maxim's,' he would order his attendants. He also requested tangos and *cuplés* from his youth.[105]

On 14 December Dalí was allowed to leave the Quirón and return to the Torre Galatea. But almost immediately there was another scare when, on 22 December, he was admitted to Figueres Hospital after suffering 'a light gastric haemorrhage'. It was only a brief setback, however, and on Christmas Day Dalí was installed once again in his tower.[106]

Then, in the early hours of Wednesday 18 January 1989, he was readmitted to Figueres Hospital with a serious cardiac insufficiency complicated by pneumonia. All that day and the following his condition seemed to remain stable. According to Robert Descharnes, who gave an interview on Spanish radio on the evening of 19 January, Dalí was perfectly lucid and had asked to hear the Maxim's recording. Marià Lorca had returned hurriedly from abroad. After visiting Dalí he was pessimistic. 'I've never seen the painter worse,' he said.[107]

As for Arturo Caminada, he was so convinced that Dalí was now dying that that night he telephoned Joaquim and Dolors Xicot in Púbol and told them to start making preparations for the burial in the crypt. The Xicots and the mayor of La Pera, Benjamí Artigas, went to work with a will: a technician was called from La Bisbal to get the heating going and Artigas marshalled a team of men to clean up the surroundings of the castle. The moment Púbol had been waiting for had arrived, and there was no time to lose.[108]

On 20 January the parish priest, Narcís Costabella, administered the last rites. 'Dalí was greatly comforted on receiving the sacraments,' he said. 'You could see it from the look in his eyes.'[109] While Dalí's life ebbed away, and the offices of the Figueres weekly, *Empordà*, were transformed into the *ad hoc* HQ of the international press, two women who had been important in the painter's life tried in vain to reach his bedside: his adolescent girlfriend, Carme Roget, the victim of 'the five-year plan', and Dalí's favourite cousin, Montserrat. 'I'll never know if he didn't want to see me or if they didn't allow him to see me,' said the latter. As for his sister Anna Maria, a fractured femur made it impossible for her to leave Cadaqués: perhaps it was for the best, since she knew that she too would almost certainly have been denied admission, given Dalí's consistent refusal to see her over the years.[110]

At midday on Saturday 21 January, with Dalí's death now imminent, Mayor Marià Lorca gave a press conference. Beside him sat Robert Descharnes, Miguel Domenech and the Figueres town councillor responsible for culture, Francesc Calvet. Lorca made a sensational announcement. On 1 December, he said, Dalí had called him to his bedside in the Quirón Clinic in Barcelona and, ordering everyone else out of the room, had told him that he wanted to be buried under the dome of the Theatre-Museum, not in Púbol beside Gala. Dalí had instructed him not to divulge his last wish to anyone. On leaving the room he had disobeyed the artist's orders for the first time in his life and immediately informed Pitxot and Domenech, who were outside. 'I didn't tell Descharnes because he was in Paris,' Lorca added. But presumably he telephoned Dalí's secretary immediately afterwards. Lorca told *La Vanguardia* that he had also informed the Catalan Prime Minister, Jordi Pujol.[111]

Dalí's last wish, Lorca informed the press, was going to be respected, and preparations for the burial in the Theatre-Museum were going ahead. Descharnes, Domenech and the councillor for Culture nodded their heads in agreement, but said nothing. Lorca went on to allege that from the moment Dalí left the Quirón and was installed in the Torre Galatea he had hoped to persuade the painter to express in written form his desire to be buried in Figueres, but that the propitious moment had never arisen.[112] There was a notable absence at the press conference. Lorca explained that Antoni Pitxot 'had had to go out' but was in 'total agreement' with the decision to bury Dalí in the museum.[113]

Robert Descharnes told *El País* that until very recently he had heard Dalí repeat his desire to be buried beside Gala in Púbol 'with his face covered', a desire specified in a document signed in the presence of a notary. However, Dalí being Dalí, a last-minute change of heart was not inconsistent. After all, the painter felt completely identified with his Theatre-Museum in Figueres.[114]

The document to which Descharnes referred has not been published and there is no record of it in the La Bisbal notary. Mayor Artigas of La Pera, however, claims that he has such a document in his possession and will produce it when the right occasion presents itself.[115]

Dalí's explicit request that his face should be covered when he died is of extraordinary interest. The Great Exhibitionist was so ashamed of his physical appearance in his declining years that he had refused to look in the mirror, and wanted none of his old friends to see him. Now it transpired that he had made legal provisions for his face to be covered at his death. It reminds one of *Hidden Faces*, of the mask with which the aviator John Randolph shielded the horror of his disfigured face from the world.

Three years later Robert Descharnes changed his tune somewhat, writing that he had been very dissatisfied by the decision to inter Dalí in Figueres. Not only had Dalí told him 'an infinity of times' that he wanted to be buried in Púbol beside his Muse, he had even planned an elaborate mausoleum for them in the crypt based on the 'Tomb of the Carmelites' in Nantes Cathedral. Given this insistence, Descharnes wrote, it was he and Arturo Caminada who had persuaded Dalí in the last few years of his life to dictate a document in which he asked explicitly to be buried beside Gala. Descharnes, therefore, did not believe that Dalí had changed his mind. 'The town of Figueres, full of impatience, wanted to hold on to its genius,' he wrote. In other words, it had stolen the body. But if Descharnes's dissatisfaction was transmitted to Lorca, Pitxot and Domenech during the weeks leading up to Dalí's death, it never reached the ears of the press. Nor did he express it clearly immediately afterwards.[116]

Before Gala's death the painter had made Antoni Pitxot promise that they would not inter him in the same cemetery as his father in Cadaqués, but take him to Figueres graveyard instead.[117] After Gala died he had mentioned to Pitxot a few times that he would like to be buried in his museum, this notwithstanding his usual insistence that he wanted to be at Gala's side in Púbol.[118] Dalí's change of heart came as no great surprise to Pitxot, therefore. 'Dalí's last desire to be buried under his cupola in Figueres seems to me marvellous,' he told reporters. 'The more I think about it the more certain I am that Dalí was telling us his desire, and that he wanted to be at the centre of his museum in Figueres, which he loved so much.'[119] In 1995 Antoni Pitxot confirmed that he was in a nearby room when Marià Lorca emerged with the news that Dalí wanted to be buried in his Theatre-Museum. 'We asked Dalí if he wanted to ratify his decision before a notary public,' Pitxot recalled, 'but he said no, that it was enough to have informed the mayor.'[120] In view of the fact that Dalí's speech was now so indistinct that apparently not even Caminada could understand what he was saying, it would have been prudent of Pitxot and Marià Lorca immediately to have repeated on oath before a notary what Dalí had just told them. By failing to do so they set the scene for speculation that continues to this day.

Dalí, Marià Lorca revealed cautiously at a later date, had told him on the same occasion that he wished to make some changes to his will—but what changes the ex-mayor has refused to disclose. Did Dalí want to modify the clause in which he left everything to the Spanish State, with no explicit reference to Catalunya? Perhaps. A notary public, José Gómez de la Serna, who knew Dalí well and had witnessed two of his wills, was put on permanent call in case the painter decided to see him. But, according to Dalí's entourage, he never expressed such a desire.[121]

The person most affected by the change of plans for Dalí's burial was undoubtedly Arturo Caminada, who felt he had been grossly betrayed by Lorca, Pitxot, Descharnes and Domenech. Caminada maintained later that the Master's deepest desire, to be with Gala, had been deliberately frustrated at the last moment by the Figueres authorities. He was convinced that, if Dalí had really changed his mind, he and not the 'troika' would have been the first to know. The reason he had not been told of the new arrangement, he felt sure, was that the foursome knew he would immediately protest publicly, and perhaps even tackle Dalí himself.[122]

The inhabitants of Púbol heard about the changed plans for Dalí's burial on the radio. Mayor Artigas was not informed officially. Nobody in the village believed that Dalí, if he had changed his mind, would have confided in the mayor of Figueres. Artigas had recourse to football imagery: it had been 'foul play' by Lorca, and an unfair goal had been scored against Púbol. 'Señor Dalí would have told Arturo first, or Señor Pitxot,' Dolors Xicot insisted. She and her husband Joaquim are as convinced today as ever they were that Figueres, in the person of Mayor Lorca, stole the artist's corpse.[123]

The announcement of the plans for Dalí's burial full-stage under his cupola made a great media story: Dalí, the born actor, the great exhibitionist, would continue to enjoy in death the theatrical limelight in which he had striven so consistently and successfully to bathe himself while alive. When the Theatre-Museum opened, Dalí had proclaimed with customary bombast: 'I want it to be the spiritual centre of Europe. From today the spiritual centre of Europe is situated in the perpendicular centre of the cupola of the museum.' Now that he had apparently decided to rest for ever at the heart of 'the spiritual centre of Europe', it all seemed to make sense.[124]

Figueres was humming with rumours and debate. Why had the 'troika' not insisted that he ratify his desire to be buried in his Theatre-Museum before a notary public? Surely, despite what Lorca had said, Dalí must have had moments of lucidity between 1 December and January during which his last wishes could have been legally validated? Was it not possible that the mayor, thinking of the economic benefits to Figueres, had in fact suggested to Dalí that he might *prefer* to be buried in his Theatre-Museum, choosing to interpret his consequent mumble, or gesture, as his consent? And so on.

As for Dalí's closest friends and associates over several decades, there was no consensus. Gonzalo Serraclara believed that Dalí was incapable of having decided not to be with Gala. Peter Moore is even more forthright: 'He didn't change his mind, they changed his mind, he had no mind when he changed his mind.'[125] Other friends were convinced that over the years, and particularly over the last five when he lived in the Torre Galatea, Dalí's museum had become more important to him than Púbol: the change of mind was consistent with his desire to identify himself fully, at the end, with his home town. They also suspected that Dalí's tense relationship with Gala in the last years had played its part. Rafael Santos Torroella, for example, told one journalist: 'Dalí invented the myth of Gala. Perhaps he didn't love her; she was his protection against his father. Their relations were always tempestuous. He'd said that he wanted to be buried in Púbol with his face covered, but the change he dictated at the last moment was Dalinian.'[126] Talking to another reporter, the same critic recalled that Dalí had termed himself 'the king of the cuckolds'. It made sense, therefore, that the painter should have wanted to be buried in his museum, since Gala had reserved Púbol exclusively for her erotic activities with other partners.[127] 'With his passion for god-kings, for the world of the Pharaohs, it was natural that like them he should have wanted to be buried with his playthings and to travel with them through eternity,' someone else commented.[128] 'He and Gala were always at loggerheads in the last years,' Nanita Kalaschnikoff mused in 1995, 'and Púbol meant nothing to him, it was just a place for Gala and her boyfriends. Dalí was always obsessed by his childhood, by Figueres and Cadaqués. Above all he loved his museum, and I'm convinced that he wanted to be buried there. It was his centre, his dream, and he knew that if he was buried there it would have more visitors and people would think constantly about him.'[129] Reynolds Morse shared the view that, after the constant fighting of the last years with Gala, it was natural that Dalí had opted finally for his Theatre-Museum.[130]

While the controversy raged about his last resting place, Dalí died at 10.15 a.m. on Monday 23 January 1989 in the presence of Miguel Domenech, Marià Lorca and Arturo Caminada. Until the end he had continued to mumble 'I want to go home' and had listened to his favourite music. On his bedside table were physicist Erwin Schrödinger's *What is Life?* and his well-worn copy of Raymond Roussel's *Impressions of Africa*, one of his favourite books.[131] The cause of death, according to the official medical bulletin, was 'cardiac insufficiency, associated with pneumonia, progressing irreversibly to severe respiratory insufficiency and cardio-respiratory failure'.[132]

A few days earlier Caminada had accurately predicted the date of the Master's demise. 'Dalí will die next Monday,' he said, 'because it's the day the moon begins to wane.'[133] Arturo had arrived at the hospital at 8 a.m. 'I took him by the hand, it was very hot, and he looked at me with those wonderful eyes of his. Then he shut them,' he said. 'I continued holding his hand. Then a strange warmth invaded his body and he opened his eyes again, but this time to look at death, not at me.' 'He and Gala were my family,' Caminada added with profound sadness. 'Now I need to rest.'[134]

The painter's body was taken almost immediately to the Torre Galatea and laid on his bed. That night, while arrangements for the burial went feverishly ahead, Dalí was embalmed, as Gala had been six years earlier. The doctor in charge, under the impression that Dalí had suffered from arteriosclerosis, thought that the arteries might not stand the pressure of the more than seven litres of formalin that needed to be injected. To his surprise he found them in perfectly good shape. Should the pacemaker be left in? It was decided that, given Dalí's interest in the advances of science and technology, the gadget which had made his heart perform better should be allowed to stay put.[135]

Burial

Dalí was shrouded in a simple tunic of beige silk on which some local nuns had embroidered a large gold crown (a reminder of the painter's recently acquired noble status) and a 'D'. Miguel Domenech explained that the tunic had no special significance, Dalí having worn similar garbs when he was alive.[136]

Dalí's death was now, of course, making the international news headlines. Figueres was crowded with reporters, and messages of condolence were reaching the Spanish authorities from all over the world. A 'capilla ardiente', or funeral chapel, was installed in one of the halls of the Torre Galatea, and opened to the public at 8 a.m. on 25 January. The

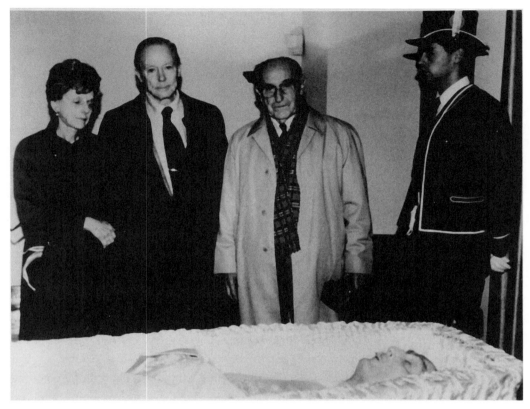

Faithful to the end. Reynolds and Eleanor Morse, Dalí's greatest collectors and most long-standing friends, grieve by his coffin accompanied by the photographer Meli Casals.

pressmen were allowed in two hours before. At the head of the open coffin was a mauve curtain against which hung the processional cross of the town of Figueres. The embalmer, Dr Narcís Bardalet, was pleased with his work, telling reporters that he had aimed at giving the impression that the painter was asleep, and that, with luck, the mummy should last for at least two hundred years. Certainly Dalí looked wonderful, if rather pale. His face showed hardly a wrinkle, his expression was serene, and the tips of his neatly trimmed moustache were turned confidently upwards. His hands were crossed over his stomach. The right one was hidden, and only three fingers of the left showed through the white shroud; the nails were decidedly grubby. Arturo Caminada thought Dalí looked 'very nice', but insisted that the Master would not have wanted to be exposed to public scrutiny. Dalí, he explained, had said that he did not want photographers or flowers, and that it was his wish that in death his face be covered. None of this had been respected. Next day the papers reported that some 15,000 citizens had filed through the room to get a last glimpse of Figueres's most famous and extravagant son.[137]

Meanwhile dissension was rife in the bosom of the Fundación. It had been agreed that no photographs of the corpse were to be allowed before it was embalmed, but now it was rumoured that Robert Descharnes had disregarded the ruling and taken an exclusive picture that he was about to sell to *Paris-Match*. To one reporter Descharnes refused to say whether he was guilty or not, replying with a cryptic: 'Why shouldn't I take a photograph of a friend and keep it?'[138] To another he denied point blank that he had taken a picture. During these hours Descharnes's officiousness and meddling got on many people's nerves. He behaved as if he were the only person with authority to take decisions on Dalí's behalf. The fact that he was French made matters worse, and there were chauvinistic rumblings in the air, not least concerning his handling of Dalí's copyright. There was a widespread feeling that the heirs to Dalí's estate, still thought to be jointly the central and Catalan administrations, would annul the Demart contract on the basis of non-fulfilment; Miguel Domenech told journalists that such action was quite feasible.[139]

The improvised chapel was closed at 3 p.m. on 26 January. Arturo Caminada took a last look at Dalí and, weeping bitterly, covered his face with a lace cloth.[140] The lid of the coffin was then screwed down. At 4.35 p.m. the funeral procession, headed by the Minister of Culture, Jorge Semprún, the Catalan Prime Minister, Jordi Pujol, and some lesser political notabilities, emerged from the Torre Galatea. It was raining and the square was crowded to bursting point. Everywhere there were reporters and television cameras. Behind the coffin, which was carried on the shoulders of four Theatre-Museum retainers wearing the resplendent uniform designed by the artist, walked the tiny, frail figure of his cousin Montserrat Dalí, wrapped in a fur coat. There was not far to go— just across the square to the church of Sant Pere, where Dalí had been baptized.

The Domènech side of the family had not been invited to the funeral, either by gross oversight or by intention, and when they arrived at the church they were refused admission. There was a tense scene, and eventually they were let in. Felipe Domènech Vilanova, Dalí's cousin, complained bitterly immediately afterwards in a letter to *La Vanguardia*, and today the family's blood still rises when they remember how they were snubbed that afternoon in Figueres, and how, for years, all their attempts to see Dalí had been frustrated. Their scorn for Robert Descharnes and Miguel Domenech, who had apparently refused to acknowledge their presence after the ceremony, is unlimited.[141]

The burial service was officiated in Catalan by Narcís Costabella, who a few days earlier had administered the last rites. A few words in Spanish and French were added at the end. If anyone expected this to be a Surrealist occasion they were greatly mistaken: it was a grimly serious affair and the brief sermon contained not the slightest hint of humour as the priest glossed the contribution of 'our brother Salvador' to the world of art. The only persons on the front benches who showed any overt emotion were Jordi Pujol, who could be seen padding his eyes from time to time, and Antoni Pitxot. Hidden among the crowd behind, however, and not scrutinized by the television cameras, were several close friends of Dalí who found this a powerfully emotive occasion. Nanita Kalaschnikoff had come from Marbella and was accompanied by a French friend of Dalí's, Miette, and by Carlos Lozano, who was horrified by the quantity of 'grey men' present who had never known Dalí. Reynolds and Eleanor Morse, damp-eyed, felt that they had been treated with an appalling lack of respect by Dalí's entourage. Peter and Cathy Moore were there, too, and the Albarettos, and Michael Stout. As for the absences, Enric Sabater was nowhere in sight (Stout was quoted as saying that he had been too cowardly to show his face),[142] nor Amanda Lear, nor Pierre Argillet who, infuriated by Robert Descharnes's refusal to see him a few hours earlier, had stormed back to his château outside Paris, where, on Midsummer Night, he was to stage an astonishing Surrealist extravaganza in celebration of Dalí's life and work. But the most notable absence was Anna Maria Dalí, who had stayed at home alleging that her fractured femur made it impossible for her to be present. She announced that she would hold a mass in Cadaqués in memory of her brother to which only his true friends would be invited.

The artist's wish that there should be no flowers was respected. The video of the funeral, however, shows that once the grave had been sealed a tiny sprig of herbs was placed, almost surreptitiously, on the tombstone. They were camomiles, which grow in profusion in Port Lligat.[143]

A few days later, in declarations to *La Vanguardia*, Enric Sabater explained that he had stayed away from the funeral not out of cowardice but out of respect for Dalí. The painter would have disliked the ceremony laid on by the Fundación, he said, and Arturo Caminada was the only person who had respected the Master's wish not to be scrutinized in death. Sabater would be attending the mass organized by Anna Maria Dalí in Cadaqués, 'because I consider it's the one Señor Dalí would have liked best, since his family and friends will be there, without people who want to appear in the media'.[144]

Sabater attended the mass in Cadaqués, as he had promised, on 30 January. He told a reporter that he was going to write a book about his relations with Dalí, and that it would set numerous cats among the pigeons. Then he vanished. It would be six years before he was heard of again and the book, if written, has still not appeared.[145]

Even before Dalí died there was more interest in the contents of his will than in the medical bulletins reporting his condition. Spanish law prescribes that a fortnight must pass before wills can be read, but two popular Spanish weeklies, *Cambio 16* and the titillating *Interviú*, gained access to the document beforehand (how has never been revealed). 'DALÍ DISINHERITS CATALUNYA' proclaimed the front cover of *Cambio 16* on the morning of Monday 30 January. Full details of the will were given inside.[146] Hurt pride and fury were the reaction in Barcelona and Figueres, while satisfaction prevailed in Madrid: the capital was about to acquire an excellent collection of prime Dalís (it only had four works), and without having to pay a peseta for them. The news could not have been better. In Catalunya tempers quickly boiled over. Max Cahner, the Culture Minister, called the central Government 'an occupation force' that had stolen Catalunya's rightful property, and Jordi Pujol, the Catalan premier, said 'We know we have been cheated but we don't know by whom.'[147]

Catalans are good negotiators, adept at compromise. When the contents of the will were officially announced, they set up an independent inquiry to see what could be done,[148] and Jorge Semprún, the enlightened Minister of Culture in Felipe González's cabinet, made every effort to be conciliatory. The compromise agreement inevitably favoured Madrid, however, which got the lion's share of the best works, including *The Great Masturbator*. The Catalans could never be convinced that Dalí's new will had not been devised by Madrid to disinherit them. In 1994, Jordi Pujol said on television: 'We were cheated and we know by whom.' He went on to implicate Miguel Domenech and the Centre Government led by his brother-in-law, Leopoldo Calvo Sotelo. In the seven years that passed before Dalí died, said Pujol, Domenech had never once so much as hinted to him that there had been any alteration to the 1980 will which, it was common knowledge, split the legacy equally between Madrid and Catalunya.[149]

Dalí's will not only left nothing specifically to Catalunya, it left nothing to any of the people who had been closest to him, or who had served him most faithfully or whom he had particularly liked. Arturo Caminada fitted better than anyone else into all these categories—and received not a peseta, despite the rumour, published in the press, according to which Dalí had provided for him.[150] Years earlier Peter Moore had given Caminada a little car, thinking that it was unfair that Dalí's most faithful servant should still have to bicycle to and from Cadaqués. 'Why are you giving him a car when I'm going to make him rich?' Dalí had said, adding that he was going to look after him in his will.[151]

Arturo could not believe that, after almost forty years with Dalí, he had been excluded from the legacy. Emilio Puignau accompanied him to La Bisbal, where the notary, Foncillas, showed them the will. They went through it clause by clause. There could be no doubt. Nothing. Back in the car, shattered, Caminada said to Puignau: 'Señor Dalí never loved anyone.' As a sop, he was taken on by the Fundació Gala–Salvador Dalí to look after the empty house in Port Lligat. But it was no consolation. He died less than two years later, on 14 December 1990, aged only fifty-seven. During those two years he kept his dignity and refused to be interviewed by journalists—he who knew more secrets about the Dalís' domestic life than any other person. Caminada is buried in Cadaqués cemetery and his death is attributed by the local people to a broken heart.[152]

Anna Maria, too, must have been hurt that Dalí had made no final gesture of reconciliation in his will. It was widely thought in Figueres that she would contest it but she never did. After the mass she held for her brother in Cadaqués she retired into her house at Es Llané and died a year later. She had waited until the last moment before telling Dr Vergara about the cancer in her breast. 'What have you done, Anna Maria?' he said to her, aghast. 'After the operation she refused to eat, as had Salvador, and let herself waste away little by little. They both died of what I call the Dalí Syndrome. The Dalís were a bit paranoid, fear lurked deep down inside them. Suddenly, just like that, they would give up.'[153]

Two thirds of this book are devoted to one third of Dalí's life. Such a structure was not imposed artificially, but shaped itself irresistibly as my research progressed. Dalí's work, after he moved to America in 1940, grows increasingly hackneyed and repetitious, whatever some people may have thought at the time. To chronicle it rigorously would have been extremely tedious not only for me but for the reader. The story had to be told, of course, but the urge to compress became imperative. Will future biographers revert the balance and seek to find much of interest in Dalí's later production and life? I doubt it. But, of course, I may be wrong.

Dalí liked to think of himself, or at least to project himself, as the complete, all-round genius. 'Spiritually I am the greatest genius of our age, the authentic genius of modern times', he informs us confidently in the introduction to *Journal d'un génie* (1964). Four years later, talking to Louis Pauwels, he apparently defined himself as 'a man who has a vision of the world and a cosmogony and who is inhabited by a genius capable of glimpsing the total structure of things'. Dalí did not pretend consistently to be a genius as a painter, however. In 1979 he said on Spanish TV 'I'm a very bad painter for the reason that I'm too intelligent to be a good painter. To be a good painter you've got to be a bit stupid'. He then added that he was 'much better as a writer'.

Dalí was not a total genius. His much-proclaimed understanding of scientific advances was, as he himself admitted on occasion, tenuous. His mysticism, 'nuclear' or otherwise, was little more than a confidence trick. His writing is often tangled and confused, even after having been tidied up by André Breton, Haakon Chevalier and Gala. He was not a poet and he knew it. His outlandish contentions about Perpignan Station and the sundering of the continents, if witty at the time, now seem pathetic. He had a sense of humour, certainly; he was an engaging raconteur; he often told good jokes and frequently invented brilliant quips (Mondrian: 'Piet? Niet!'). But the stories, jokes and quips were done to death as he repeated them over and over again, at dinner parties, on the radio, on television, in magazine interviews ('Picasso is . . . a Communist. Me neither', 'The only difference between Dalí and a madman is that DALÍ IS NOT MAD'—

how tiresome they become). Several observers noticed that Dalí tended to surround himself with intellectually mediocre people. It was true. Such hangers-on afforded no opposition. Their function was to look dazzling and to be dazzled. And never to challenge the man behind the exhibitionist's mask. No true intellectual would have stood for Dalí's antics, his ranting. And Ramón Guardiola need not have been surprised that the attendance of distinguished artists and writers at the opening of the Theatre-Museum was negligible.

Behind the Dalinian mask, I have argued, there hid a person for whom shame was a major problem. Perhaps I have not pleaded my case sufficiently, or with sufficient skill. Shame is arguably the least-known human emotion since it hides even from itself (Helen Merrell Lynd's 'double shame'). An ashamed person cannot admit publicly to being ashamed. How, then, to plumb his or her depths? That shame is a major component in Dalí's character is, I believe, made more explicit in the *Secret Life* than he may have realized, or intended, and there are further indications in *Hidden Faces*, with its significant title. But it is the paintings and drawings that provide the most convincing evidence, from *Le Jeu lugubre* onwards. There Dalí brings shame into the open, where it can be scrutinized. No other painter in the history of art has done this, and it may yet transpire that in depicting shame, and forcing us to contemplate its sources and its agonies, Dalí made one of his most important contributions to civilization.

Dalí maintained his mask tenaciously for a lifetime—or almost—and in doing so was often ruthlessly insensitive to the demands of common decency and honesty. His pose meant being prepared to twist the truth when necessary, and sometimes to betray people who believed they were his friends. It meant falsifying his debt to Breton and Surrealism, or denying that he had contributed to the anti-clerical content of *L'Age d'or*, or pretending to be a Catholic mystic. It meant prostituting his talent. It meant being a party to fraud.

'Señor Dalí loved nobody', Arturo Caminada commented desolately when he realized that after a lifetime's service he had not been left a single peseta in the painter's will. A person who loves nobody is impossible to love. Dalí was admired, lionized, adulated; cossetted by the rich and the aristocratic, even by the royals; but, constitutionally unable to express tenderness, he received little in return. As he lay in the Torre Galatea, waiting for the end, plugged with tubes, did he recall his father's omen that he would die alone, in poverty and without friends? According to Miguel Domenech, his lawyer, Dalí needed constant reassurance in the last years that he was not bankrupt.

And Gala? Reynolds Morse has written that it was she who built Dalí 'into the giant he became'. There is truth in this, certainly. She helped to assuage his sexual anxieties, for a time at least, and her courage, practical know-how and driving ambition were vital in launching him on the path to success, and in keeping him there. Had she not come into his life exactly when she did, the story would surely have been very different. The trouble is that Gala remains an enigma, despite the three books published on her to date. If the autobiography on which, in 1949, Dalí claimed she had been working for four years were to come to light we would presumably learn more about her, perhaps a lot more. The same would in all likelihood hold for the diary which Amanda Lear says Gala kept (in Russian). But so far there is no trace of either potential treasure trove. The destruction of Gala's letters to Éluard (with the fortunate exception of the early ones) does not help matters, nor the fact that, for over fifty years, she stubbornly refused to talk to reporters about her relationship with Dalí. It is sad to think that we may never know more than we do at the moment about that secretive woman.

So, at the end of the day, what is the balance now that Dalí the performer is dead, the clowning and the tomfoolery over, the tables in Paris and New York no longer in a roar? It is surely clear that, where Dalí's painting is concerned, the works executed between 1926 and approximately 1938 are his magnificent and crowning achievement, his real claim to our admiration and, yes, to our gratitude. As for the writing, there stand out a handful of pieces on art theory, the essay on Millet's *Angelus* and, particularly, *The Secret Life of Salvador Dalí*. All achieved before Dalí was forty.

And all achieved under the influence of Surrealism, which began to exert itself three years before the appearance of Gala and before Dalí met Breton. In retrospect it can be seen that Surrealism, with its desire to plumb, liberate and express the depths of the psyche as well as to *épater le bourgeois*, was exactly the powerful stimulus the young Dalí needed. His obsession with, and gift for, minute detail had prepared him to be the Meissonier of dreams; and Surrealism's programme of moral subversion was bound to appeal profoundly to a person who already loathed Church and State and was convinced with Freud that the true hero is the son who opposes his father and defeats him. Defeating Salvador Dalí Cusí was an undertaking of epic proportions, certainly.

Dalí was at his best when sharing the common ideals of the Surrealists, living their programme with strict adherence to the letter, as well as the spirit, of the Bretonian Law, and contributing energetically to their group activities and to their determination to change the world. The Surrealist experience curbed his egotism, inspired him to his most generous efforts and, briefly, made him more open to other people and to their needs.

During his twelve years or so within the Surrealist orbit, Dalí created images of horror, mental unbalance and sexual alienation unlike anything being produced by other artists. His key scenario of the nightmare beach, with its eerie juxtaposition of assorted flotsam and jetsam, see-through rocks, stark shadows and sharp contours, its deep perspectives, its aridity and its anguished human presences—all painted in laborious detail—is one of our age's most unforgettable and disturbing icons, as Hitchcock was quick to perceive. Surely it will continue to haunt mankind.

The scenario is a homage, too, to the landscape of the Upper Empordá that Dalí admired fanatically from childhood and with which he will always be associated: Cadaqués, Port Lligat and the mineral wilderness of Cape Creus, that weird theatre of optical illusions which taught him that something can be something else, and where, one springtime day in 1925, he, Anna Maria and Lorca had munched their sandwiches beneath The Eagle.

Dalí could never forget Lorca, whose presence pervades his work and whose ghost was with him till the end. Perhaps, after all, his greatest tragedy was the failure to cherish the poet sufficiently before it was too late.

NOTES

Abbreviations

AA: *L'Amic de les Arts, Sitges.*

AMD: Anna Maria Dalí, *Salvador Dalí visto por su hermana*, Barcelona, Juventud, 2nd ed., 1949.

BMDS: Buñuel, *Mon Dernier Soupir*, Paris, Robert Laffont, 1982.

CI: Dalí, *Confesiones inconfesables*, Barcelona, Bruguera, 1975.

DG: Dalí, *The Diary of a Genius*, translated by Richard Howard, London, Hutchinson, 1990.

DOH: Robert Descharnes, *Dalí. La obra y el hombre*, Barcelona, Tusquets/Edita, 1984.

EJF: Edward James Foundation, West Dean, Chichester.

GL: *La Gaceta Literaria*, Madrid.

LRS: *La Révolution Surréaliste*, Paris.

LSASDLR: *Le Surréalisme au Service de la Révolution*, Paris.

MDJ: Reynolds Morse, *A Dalí Journal.* Unpublished diary, Salvador Dalí Museum, Saint Petersburg, Florida.

MEAC: *400 obras de Salvador Dalí de 1914 a 1983*, 2 vols., Madrid, Ministry of Culture, 1983.

SDFGL: Rafael Santos Torroella (ed.), *Salvador Dalí escribe a Federico García Lorca [1925–1936], Poesía. Revista ilustrada de información poética*, Madrid, nos. 27–28, April 1987.

SL: Dalí, *The Secret Life of Salvador Dalí*, London, Vision Press, 3rd ed., 1968.

SVBLD: Agustín Sánchez Vidal, *Buñuel, Lorca, Dalí. El enigma sin fin*, Barcelona, Planeta, 1988.

UC: Dalí, *The Unspeakable Confessions of Salvador Dalí*, London, Quartet Books, 1977.

UD: Màrius Carol et al., *El último Dalí*, Madrid, El País, 1985.

VPSD: *La Vie publique de Salvador Dalí*, Paris, Centre Pompidou, 1975.

One: Catalunya

1   Beya i Martí, *passim.*

2   The vellum-bound books containing the Llers parish records were kept, when I consulted them, in the priest's residence ('casa parroquial') of the new town. Mosén Pere Travesa, the parish priest in 1993, informed me that the earlier records were lost during one of Spain's many conflicts with France.

3   Arxiu Històric de Girona, Protocolos notariales de Figueres, vol. 16, 12 April 1558; same archive, Protocolos de Figueres, vol. 571. I am indebted to the historian Don Antonio Egea for generously bringing these documents to my attention.

4   *SL*, p. 40, n. 1.

5   Lake, p. 21; Byron, p. 186, for Dalí Mamí.

6   Lear, *Le Dalí d'Amanda*, p. 180.

7   *SL*, p. 320.

8   Dalí in Descharnes, *The World of Salvador Dalí*, p. 171. For other references see *DG*, p.111 ('my atavistic and Arab urges') and p. 127, note ('my pre-natal Arab atavisms').

9   Lake, p. 21.

10 *SL*, pp. 227–8.

11 Gouvernat de Tunis telephone book, 1996, p. 402; consultations at the Algerian Embassy, Madrid, 1996; I am grateful to my friends Bernabé and Cecilia López García for exploring the Moroccan telephone guide on my behalf.

12 *Diccionari de la llengua catalana*, Barcelona, Enciclopèdia Catalana, S.A., 1982.

13 For Dalí as 'Saviour' of modern art, see *SL*, pp. 4, 89; *UC*, pp. 185, 217, 240, 255; *DG*, pp. 34, 177–8; *Manifiesto místico*, p. 192; for Dalí and 'delit', see *UC*, pp. 16, 145, 202, 227, *DG*, p. 85, Dalí and Pauwels, p. 124 and Lear, *L'Amant-Dalí*, p. 204.

14 *Llibre de Nupcias de la Iglesia Parroquial de Santa Julia y Sta Basilissa de la Vila de Llers.*

15 I have been unable to trace Pere Dalí Raguer's birth in the Llers parish records. His death certificate states that he died on 17 February 1830 at the age of

45 or—the writing is unclear—48 (*Llibre 3° de obits 1814–1854*, f. 103 v.).

16 My thanks to Don Joan Vives, a native of Llers, who showed me around the remains of the town and pointed out the Dalí landmarks. For useful information on the history and fate of Llers, see Beya i Martí, *Al terraprim de l'Alt Empordà. Llers.*

17 *Llibre de babtismes de la Parroquial Igla de Cadaqués, Bisbat de Gerona, que comensa lo dia quatre Janer del Any 1801, y fineix dia 25 Juliol de 1825*, 24 January 1804, f. 23 v.

18 *Libro de Desposorios de la parroquia de Cadaqués*, Book 3, f. 238. The marriage took place on 1 July 1817.

19 For example, the document referred to in the following note.

20 *Llibre de babtismes de la Parroquial Igla de Cadaqués, Bisbat de Gerona, que comensa lo dia quatre Janer del Any 1801, y fineix dia 25 Juliol de 1825*, f. 139. Salvador Manuel Sebastià Dalí Cruanyas was baptized on 19 January 1822.

21 *Libro de Desposorios de la parroquia de Cadaqués*, Book 3, f. 341 v. The marriage took place on 12 July 1843.

22 Birth certificate of Gal Josep Salvador Dalí, Josep Viñas's grandson, *Libro 7° de bautismos*, 1825–1851, 2 July 1849, f. 188 v.

23 Pla, *Obres de museu*, p. 61.

24 Rahola i Trèmols, p. 9; Pla, *Cadaqués*, pp. 11–12.

25 Ferrer, *Cadaqués des de l'arxiu*, p. 17.

26 Pla, *Cadaqués*, pp. 80–1.

27 Ferrer, *Cadaqués des de l'arxiu*, pp. 16, 33.

28 *Ibid.*, p. 43.

29 Cadaqués parish records, *Libro 7° de bautismos, 1825–1851*, 30 March 1846.

30 *Ibid.*, 2 July 1849, f. 188.

31 I am grateful to Don Gonzalo Serraclara for supplying me with the date of birth of his grandmother, Catalina Berta; Teresa Cusí Marcó was born in Roses on 13 July 1841 (*Empordà*, Figueres, 18 July 1995, p. 31).

32 Aniceta Francisca Ana died on 8 September 1872. Cadaqués parish records, *Libro de óbitos . . .*, Book 5, f. 60.

33 Salvador Dalí Cusí was baptized on 3 November 1872. Cadaqués parish records, *Libro IX de bautismos de la Iglesia Parroquial de Cadaqués, Años 1867–1884*, f. 89.

34 Rafael Dalí Cusí was baptized on 1 February 1874. The document states that his parents were united 'only by a civil marriage'. As for previous note, f. 105 v.

35 Cadaqués parish records, *Libro 5° de Desposorios . . .*, f. 55 and verso. The religious ceremony took place on 25 March 1874.

36 Conversation with Doña Montserrat Dalí, Barcelona, 26 November 1992.

37 Dalí, *Un diari: 1919–1920*, pp. 131–2.

38 Land Registry Office ('Registro de la Propiedad'), Roses, property number 651 (Cadaqués).

39 Conversation with the painter Doña Roser Villar, Figueres, 28 June 1996.

40 This colourful piece of information about the Civil Guard was supplied by Don Luis Durán, Hotel Durán, Figueres, January 1993.

41 Díaz i Romañach, pp. 12–13.

42 Teixidor Elies, p. 166.

43 Gabriel García Márquez, *Doce cuentos peregrinos*, Madrid, Mondadori, 1992.

44 Lomas, p. 34; Romero and Ruiz, p. 73.

45 Quoted by Teixidor Elies, p. 496.

46 Conversations on the subject of Gal with Doña Montserrat Dalí, Barcelona, 1991–2.

47 The information in this paragraph derives mainly from Hughes, *Barcelona*, 1992, pp. 325–37. For the quotation, *ibid*, p. 332.

48 A copy of Salvador Dalí Cusí's *bachillerato* record is included in his file at Barcelona University.

49 A copy of Rafael Dalí Cusí's *bachillerato* record is included in his file at Barcelona University.

50 Conversations with Doña Montserrat Dalí, Barcelona, 1992–3.

51 Details in Gonzalo Serraclara, *La nueva inquisición.*

52 Conversations with Doña Montserrat Dalí, Barcelona, 1992–3.

53 Gibson, '¿Un paranoico en la familia?'

54 *Ibid.*; Registre Civil de Barcelona, 1886, no. 899.

55 Conversation with Doña Montserrat Dalí, Barcelona, 26 November 1992.

56 Don Gonzalo Serraclara has assured me that, despite their close friendship, Dalí never raised the question of Gal with him. Nor, Doña Montserrat Dalí told me, did he ever discuss it with her.

57 Dalí and Pauwels, p. 24.

58 Tape-recorded conversation with Doña Montserrat Dalí, Barcelona, 26 November 1992.

59 For Oller's admission that the novel is a *roman à clef*, see the introduction by Carmen Arnau to the edition cited in the bibliography, I, p. 7.

60 Salvador Dalí Cusí's file at Barcelona University.

61 Rafael Dalí Cusí's file at Barcelona University.

62 Maria del Angels Vayreda, 'Com és Salvador Dalí?', p. 13.

63 *La Vanguardia*, Barcelona, 14 December 1896, p. 1.

64 This account of the brothers' personalities derives principally from my many conversations with Doña Montserrat Dalí and from the recollections of Josep Pla in 'Salvador Dalí, una notícia' (in *Homenots*), *Obres de museu* and, sporadically, other works.

65 Tape-recorded conversations with Doña Montserrat Dalí, Barcelona, 1991–2.

66   Salvador Dalí's file at Barcelona University.

67   Letter from Salvador Dalí Cusí to his mother and the Serraclara family dated 6 November 1911. I am grateful to Doña Montserrat Dalí for a copy of this biographically invaluable document in which Don Salvador insists that his father Gal, at his death, left sufficient sums for his family's upkeep and the education of his sons.

68   For this account I follow Hughes, *Barcelona*, pp. 421–2.

69   *La Vanguardia*, Barcelona, 14 December 1896, p. 1.

70   Hurtado, p. 32.

71   Telephone conversation with Don Antoni Pitxot (in Cadaqués), July 1993.

72   Josep Pichot's file at Barcelona University.

73   Conversations with Don Antoni Pitxot, 1993; Pla, *Vida de Manolo*, pp. 75–6; Pla, 'Cadaqués', p. 98.

74   Montero Alonso, pp. 10–11, 49–50, 96.

75   In the wedding certificate of her son Ricardo in 1919 it is stated that Antonia Gironés, deceased, was a native of Figueres (Registro Civil, Figueres, Section 2, Book 43, f. 118). This has been confirmed by Don Antoni Pitxot in our many conversations.

76   The 1900 census ('padrón de habitantes') for Figueres records that in that year Josep Pichot Gironés and Angeleta Gironés Bofill were already staying in the town at Calle Barceloneta, 4. The document gives their dates of birth, 1869 and 1871 respectively.

77   Conversations with Don Antoni Pitxot, Cadaqués, 1993. Anna Maria Dalí also maintained this view energetically (see Joan Guillamet, *Vent de tramuntana*, p. 114).

78   Doña Montserrat Dalí assured me that, if her Uncle Salvador always wanted to return to Cadaqués, her father, like Gal, swore never again to live in the place on account of the tramuntana. Perhaps he, too, feared the wind's effects on his emotions. In 1935 Rafael revisited Cadaqués and wrote to his daughter: 'My village would be a paradise if it weren't for the tramuntana' (archive of Montserrat Dalí's daughter, Doña Eulalia Maria Bas i Dalí, Barcelona).

79   The date of Salvador Dalí Cusí's incorporation in the Collegi de Notaris, Barcelona, has been kindly supplied by this body; the rest of the information concerning his appointment is contained in his file at the Ministry of Justice in Madrid.

80   *El Regional* can be consulted in the Fages de Climent Municipal Library, Figueres.

81   Felipa's marriage certificate (Parish of Santos Justo y Pastor, Barcelona) states that she was baptized in the parish of San Jaime on 26 April 1874. For the information about the lovers' meeting I am indebted to Don Gonzalo Serraclara, Barcelona, 26 May 1993.

82   He died on 6 October 1887. Copy of death certifi-cate kindly supplied by the Barcelona Diocesan Archive. My thanks to the archivist, Father Leandre Niqui Puigvert, and the director, Father Josep Maria Martí Bonet.

83   *AMD*, pp. 36, 86–7.

84   *Ibid.*, p. 86.

85   This, certainly, is the view of the Domènech family today. Conversation with Don Felipe Domènech Vilanova and his son, Don Felipe Domènech Biosca. Conversation with these, Barcelona, 24 October 1993.

86   Conversations with Don Felipe Domènech Biosca, Barcelona, 1993; *AMD*, p. 36.

87   Conversation with Don Felipe Domènech Biosca, Barcelona, September 1993.

88   *Ibid.*

89   *Ibid.*; *AMD*, p. 36.

90   Copy of marriage certificate kindly supplied by the Barcelona Diocesan Archive (see note 82).

Two: Early Days (1904–16)

1   Details from Romero and Ruiz, p. 20.

2   *Ibid.*, p. 76; Teixidor Elies, p. 295.

3   For an account of the 'Sport', see Teixidor Elies, pp. 57–62.

4   Birth certificate of the first Salvador Dalí, repro-duced by Rojas, pp. [298–9].

5   Death certificate of the first Salvador Dalí, repro-duced by Rojas, pp. [300–1].

6   'Crónica local', *El Regional*, Figueres, 9 August 1903, no. 893; burial records in Figueres Town Hall.

7   Reynolds Morse, quoted in *Surrealism in the Tate Gallery Collection* (catalogue); A. Reynolds Morse, 'The Dalí Adventure', p. 212.

8   Birth certificate reproduced by Rojas, pp. [302–3].

9   I am grateful to my friend Víctor Fernández for supplying me with a copy of the baptism certificate.

10   *SL*, p. 2.

11   *UC*, p. 241.

12   The painting is reproduced in *DOH*, p. 361.

13   In her biography of Dalí, Meryle Secrest has stated that both his parents, though perhaps particu-larly Don Salvador, were 'absolutely convinced that their dead son had been reborn', and made it their business to implant this notion on 'the pliant young mind' (p. 21). It must be said that there is not a shred of evidence to support this, on the face of it, ludicrous contention. Secrest asserts that, in calling the new baby after his dead brother, the Dalís were both flying in the face of local convention and laying some sort of curse on the child's head. 'In that part of Spain it is not customary to name a son after his father and even less

customary to name a baby after a dead child,' she assures us, adding: 'In fact, it is looked on with superstitious disfavour, in the conviction that the name will transmit to the second the fate of the first' (*ibid.*). None of this is accurate. In Catalunya, as in the rest of Spain, sons quite often receive their father's first name and, while it may not be common for a baby to be given the name of its dead predecessor, no necessary superstition is attached to the practice, particularly if the name in question is traditional in the family. In the event of there having been such qualms, it is surely inconceivable that the Dalís would have proceeded as they did. Secrest states that Felipa Domènech was 'vehemently opposed to the repetitious christening', believing that her second son 'had been placed in peril of his life' (*ibid.*). We are given no source for such an asseveration. Had Felipa's objections been so passionate, it is difficult to see how even Don Salvador Cusí, with his forceful personality, could have had his way.

14   *AMD*, pp. 9–22, *passim*.
15   Dalí, 'Ninots', quoted by Anna Maria Dalí, *Noves imatges de Salvador Dalí*, p. 75.
16   *AMD*, p. 12.
17   Maria Anna Ferrés and her daughter Catalina first appear in the town register ('padrón de habitantes') for 1911, f. 177, where it is stated that they have been living at Monturiol, 20, for a year (Arxiu Històric Municipal, Figueres Town Hall).
18   'Padrón de habitantes', Figueres Town Hall, 1906, f. 109.
19   Anna Maria Dalí, *Noves imatges de Salvador Dalí*, pp. 34, 40.
20   Lear, *Le Dalí d'Amanda*, p. 183.
21   *SL*, pp. 5–6; the date of Ursula Matas's birth is given as 12 June 1890 in the Figueres Town Hall's 'padrón de habitantes' for 1906, f. 109; the 1911 list, f. 176, no longer registers the Matas family at Monturiol, 20.
22   *AMD*, pp. 11–12.
23   *SL*, p. 48.
24   *Ibid.*, p. 67.
25   *AMD*, pp. 19–20.
26   *SL*, pp. 67, 234–6, 347. Anna Maria Dalí also remembers that Llúcia used to tell Salvador stories (*AMD*, p. 36).
27   Reproduced in colour in *MEAC*, I, no. 11, p. 20. For Llúcia, see Jiménez and Playà, 'Dalí vist des de l'Empordà—X. Llúcia Gispert de Montcanut', *Hora Nova*, Figueres, supplement to no. 361, May 1984, p. 39.
28   *AMD*, p. 9, for the words; the song is also mentioned by Dalí, *SL*, p. 67.
29   *AMD*, pp. 12–14.
30   *Ibid.*, p. 16.

31   Conversation with Doña Nanita Kalaschnikoff, Marbella, 13 September 1995; Lear, *Le Dalí d'Amanda*, p. 159; see also *DG*, p. 203.
32   *UC*, p. 32; Bernils i Mach, *Figueres*, p. 77; *AMD*, p. 35.
33   *SL*, pp. 11–12. The comet was seen on the night of 20 May 1910. According to *La Veu de l'Empordà*, 22 May 1910, it was not visible from Figueres owing to a rain storm.
34   *UC*, p. 28.
35   *SL*, p. 1; *UC*, p. 28.
36   *SL*, pp. 36–7.
37   *Ibid.*, p. 36.
38   *Ibid.*, p. 36; Don Pere Buxeda, owner of a magnificent collection of old photographs of Figueres, has one showing part of Trayter's collection of Romanesque pieces; for the information concerning Darwin, Lafayettes and Trayter's bad temper, I am indebted to my friend Doña Maria Asunción Trayter Sabater, the teacher's granddaughter (Figueres, October 1993).
39   'The Truth of the Myth of William Tell. The Whole Truth about my Expulsion from the Surrealist Group', p. 179. Dalí repeats this paragraph almost word for word in *DG*, p. 20.
40   When Dalí's comments on her father were reproduced in an article in *La Vanguardia*, his daughter, María Trayter Colls, like her father a dedicated teacher, wrote angrily to the newspaper (15 April 1972) insisting that he had never been an atheist and that many former pupils, still alive, could attest to this.
41   Conversation with Doña Maria Asunción Trayter Sabater, Figueres, October 1993.
42   For Don Salvador's atheism and free-thinking, see, as well as the source identified in n. 39, *SL*, p. 36; *DG*, p. 20.
43   *SL*, pp. 36–7.
44   *Ibid.*, pp. 40–1.
45   *Ibid.*, p. 41.
46   Special thanks are due to my friend Doña Maria Trayter Sabater, who helped me to track down the stereoscope, now in the possession of Don Enrique Orio Trayter of Barcelona. The latter kindly showed me the instrument and allowed me to operate it.
47   *SL*, p. 41.
48   *Ibid.*, p. 47.
49   *Ibid.*, pp. 43, 45.
50   *Ibid.*, p. 51.
51   Lynd, for example, lays great stress on this aspect of shame. See pp. 24, 33, 50, 64, etc.
52   *Ibid.*, pp. 52, 53.
53   *Ibid.*, p. 67.
54   *SL*, p. 47.
55   *Ibid.*, p. 61.
56   Romero, *Dedálico Dalí*, p. 10.

57   Conversation with Don Gonzalo Serraclara de la Pompa, Barcelona, 9 May 1992. Señor Serraclara refused to allow me to read this correspondence, which comprises some fifty letters, assuring me that he himself intended to publish it. He died in 1996 without having done so.

58   Caption to a photograph of these trees included in Plate IV of *SL*, opposite p. 87.

59   *AMD*, p. 16.

60   *Ibid.*, pp. 16–17; there is what seems to be a reference to the same incident in *SL*, p. 2.

61   Conversation with Don Gonzalo Serraclara, Barcelona, 26 May 1993.

62   *SL*, p. 11.

63   *Ibid.*, p. 13.

64   Telephone conversation with Don Antoni Pitxot, who was born in this house, 28 August 1993; Anna Maria Dalí also described it as a paradise to Joan Guillamet, quoted by Gómez de Liaño, 'En la casa del arte', p. 26.

65   For the miscarriages my source is Doña Paz Jiménez Encina, the daughter of Lluís Pichot, Madrid, 20 August 1983.

66   *SL*, p. 77, note.

67   Palau i Fabre, p. 60. Don Antoni Pitxot has confirmed this information in our numerous conversations.

68   The details of the purchase are in the register of the Land Property Office, Roses, property no. 1236 (Cadaqués), where it is stated to have been made in 1908. It is possible, however, that the acqustion was effected earlier (at that time, the authorities in Roses have assured me, registration commonly took place some years after the actual sale). According to Palau, whose information proceeded from the Pichots, the original house was built in 1899 to designs by Miquel Utrillo. It has not been possible to corroborate this date, but since we know that Pepito Pichot only settled in Figueres in 1900 it seems unlikely.

69   Palau i Fabre, p. 60; conversations with Don Antoni Pitxot, Cadaqués, 1993 and 1994.

70   Stein, *The Autobiography of Alice B. Toklas*, p. 30.

71   Richardson, *A Life of Picasso*, I, *passim*. A splendid photograph of Germaine Gargallo, *c.* 1900, is reproduced by Richardson at p. 162.

72   Reproduced in colour, *MEAC*, I, p. 24; *DOH*, p. 29.

73   My thanks to Don Antoni Pitxot, with whom I pored over this photograph in his house at Cadaqués in 1993 and who has provided me, over the years, with detailed information about his family.

74   Palau i Fabre, pp. 60–1.

75   The information concerning the stable proceeds from the woman who cooked for the Dalís in those early days, and has been transmitted to me by her son-

in-law, Miquel Figueres, ex-mayor of Cadaqués. Doña Rosa Maria Salleras has confirmed in our conversations that her father's house and Don Salvador Dalí's were both rented, and then bought, from Pepito Pitchot.

76   Conversations with Doña Rosa Maria Salleras, Cadaqués, 1993.

77   *SL*, p. 304.

78   Dalí and Pauwels, pp. 232–3 (1968 edn); Bofarull i Terrades, p. 57.

79   *UC*, p. 130.

80   *SL*, p. 304; Dalí in Descharnes, *The World of Salvador Dalí*, p. 49.

81   Conversation with Doña Paz Jiménez Encina, Madrid, 20 August 1983; Anna Maria Dalí, *Noves imatges de Salvador Dalí*, p. 24. Lluís Marquina Pichot was born on 25 May 1904.

82   Conversations with Don Antoni Pitxot, Cadaqués, 1993.

83   For Picasso's visit to Cadaqués in 1910 I have used the special 'Picasso a Cadaqués' issue of the Barcelona art journal *Negre + gris*, no. 10, Autumn 1985. See also Tharrats, 'Picasso entre nosaltres', in *Cent anys de pintura a Cadaqués*, pp. 59–70. For the Empordanese phrase, see Daudet, 1 March 1970, p. 47.

84   Bernils i Mach, *Els Fossos, 75 anys d'història*, p. 7–15.

85   *Ibid.*, pp. 15–20, 27–51; Jiménez and Playà, 'El collegi La Salle'; conversation with Doña Montserrat Dalí, Barcelona, November 1992.

86   According to Don Joan Vives, who entered 'Els Fossos' shortly after Dalí left, pupils heard talking Catalan in the playground were made to carry round a small stone called 'La Parleuse', 'The Chatterer' (conversation with Don Joan Vives, Figueres, 25 January 1993).

87   Jiménez and Playà, 'El collegi La Salle'.

88   My thanks to the then principal, Brother Domingo Bóveda, who kindly furnished me with a photocopy of the document concerning Dalí's time at 'Els Fossos', discovered in Béziers on the occasion of the 75th anniversary of the Figueres school.

89   Dalí, 'El sentit comú d'un germà de Sant Joan Baptista de La Salle'; Dalí, *50 Secrets of Magic Craftsmanship*, p. 108.

90   *SL*, pp. 63–4.

91   I am grateful to Brother Leoncio Gascón for his highly informative guided tour of the establishment in 1993.

92   *SL*, p. 64 and note.

93   The advertisement appeared on 6 July 1912, the last on 17 August following.

94   *AMD*, p. 22. The house is still standing, having been saved from demolition in the 1950s by the inter-

cession of Señora Abadal, the wife of the developer, who was devoted to a statue of Saint William housed in an *hornacina*, or niche, at one of its corners. Almost pressing against the balcony beloved of Anna Maria a large block was erected. Señor Abadal drastically narrowed the projecting balcony of the Matas' apartment beneath to accommodate the new building, and the stone balaustrades that had aroused Salvador's envy were lost.

95 *SL*, pp. 70–1.

96 For informing me that there were no other children in the house, I am grateful to the house's present owners, Señor and Señora Carbó; for the present of the cape, crown and sceptre, and Dalí's passion for disguise, *SL*, pp. 69–70; for being 'at the top', *ibid.*, p. 72.

97 *SL*, p. 71. The reference is to the painting entitled *La Source*, reproduced on p. 41 of the Ingres volume (no. 47).

98 Anna Maria Dalí, *Noves imatges de Salvador Dalí*, pp. 74–5. This 'forest', perhaps called 'La Forêt' in deference to Watteau, was presumably the wood on the outskirts of Figueres. Maybe it was the wood that became the municipal 'Parc-Bosc' of Figueres thanks to the generosity of Pepito Pichot and two other local worthies, Joaquín Cusí Fortunet and Marian Pujulá Vidal. The Brothers in question are almost certainly the Marists, whose school Dalí attended concurrently with the Instituto.

99 In order of publication the volumes were: Rubens, Van Dyck, Rembrandt, Raphael, Reynolds, Teniers the Younger, The Masterpieces of the Early Flemish Painters, Titian, Hals, Murillo, Wouwerman, Velázquez, Holbein, Veronese, Raeburn, Del Sarto, Correggio, Bronzino, Watteau, Botticelli, Fra Angelico, Tintoretto, Poussin, Perugino, Michelangelo, Goya, Dürer, Gainsborough, Lotto, Luini, Greuze, Carpaccio and Giorgione, Hogarth, Giotto, Moretto, Romney, Orcagna, Gérard Dou, Boucher, Constable, a volume comprising Massaccio, Uccello, Veneziano and Castagno, Jan Steen, Claude, Morland, Lippi, De Hooch and Vermeer, Ingres, Hoppner, Gozzoli, Metsu, Nattier, Lawrence.

100 The burial records of Teresa Cusí were kindly shown to me by her granddaughter, Doña Montserrat Dalí, owner of the tomb (and now inhumed in it herself).

101 *AMD*, p. 31.

102 Review by 'Puvis' of the exhibition in *Empordà Federal*, Figueres, no. 113 (17 May 1913), p. 2. The painting was inherited by Anna Maria Dalí at her father's death.

103 Rodrigo, *Lorca-Dalí. Una amistad traicionada*, pp. 47–8.

104 *SL*, p. 132.

105 Gibson, *Federico García Lorca*, p. 88.

106 Conversation with Doña Rosa Maria Salleras, Cadaqués, 1993.

107 Albert Field's painting is reproduced in colour in Romero, *Psicodálico Dalí*, p. 10, where, following *VPSD* (no. 344, p. 5), it is dated 1910. *MEAC* more prudently dates it 'towards 1914' (I, p. 16). Captain Peter Moore's painting, on exhibition in the Perrot-Moore Museum in Cadaqués, is reproduced in colour in *La Collection Salvador Dalí du Musée Perrot-Moore, Cadaqués* (see Bibliography, Section 1), no. 1. The other four paintings are reproduced in colour in *MEAC*, I, nos 2–5, pp. 16–17. No. 2, entitled *Paisaje*, is a view of the Empordà plain from, it appears to me, the top of the Molí de la Torre, the property outside Figueres belonging to Maria Pichot.

108 Reproduced in Descharnes and Néret, I, p. 12.

109 Conversation with Captain Peter Moore, Cadaqués, 1993.

110 Playà i Maset, *Dalí de l'Empordà*, p. 40.

111 *SL*, p. 66.

112 Death certificate drawn up 23 December 1914, Registre Civil de Barcelona, Llotja district, no. 1078; Dalí's account to Edward James is in *EJF*; the paintings are *Apparition of my Cousin Carolineta on the Beach at Rosas (Fluid Presentiment)*, executed in 1933, and *Apparition of my Cousin Carolineta on the Beach at Rosas* (1934).

113 Daudet, (8 March 1971), p. 30.

114 Conversation with Doña Nanita Kalaschnikoff, Marbella, 15 September 1995; Dalí had told the same story to the journalist Lluís Permanyer in 1978, asking him not to reproduce the details in his interview for *Playboy* ('El pincel erótico de Dalí') so as not to offend his sister Anna Maria. On that occasion, however, he situated the episode in 1929, saying that it happened five days after he finished painting *The Lugubrious Game*, which on the face of it seems unlikely. My thanks to Señor Permanyer for sending me a copy of the tape-recording of his conversation with Dalí.

115 Conversation with Doña Rosa Maria Salleras, Cadaqués, 1995; *CI*, p. 31.

116 Tixier's visit was fully reported in *Alt Empordà*, Figueres, 27 April, 4 and 11 May 1912.

117 Miravitlles, 'Dalí i l'aritmètica', p. 32.

118 The date of the entrance test, 2 June 1916, is provided on the second page of Dalí's *bachillerato* certificate, preserved at the Figueres Instituto. Dalí recalls the experience of the entrance examination in *Songs of When I was Twelve* (1922), an unpublished manuscript preserved at the Fundació Gala–Salvador Dalí, Figueres.

Three: Adolescence and Vocation (1916–22)

1 Documents in the Land Registry Office, Figueres, Estate no. 695. Maria Pichot extended her interest in the property in 1914. Many thanks to Don Josep Maria Juan Rosa, who accompanied me to the Molí de la Torre and made enquiries on my behalf concerning the present owners.

2 *Empordà Federal*, Figueres, 17 January 1914, p. 3.

3 *Les cançons dels dotze anys. Versus em prosa i em color*, notebook dated 1922.

4 Telephone conversation with Don Antoni Pitxot (in Figueres), 24 January 1997.

5 *SL*, p. 81.

6 See note 3.

7 Reproduced in *MEAC*, II, p. 16; Descharnes and Néret, I, p. 13.

8 *SL*, pp. 82–5; conversation with Don Antoni Pitxot, Cadaqués, 1995.

9 The manuscript, preserved in the Museu Joan Abelló, Mollet del Vallès (Barcelona), contains sixteen pages and was first published in 1966, by Víctor Fernández (see Bibliography, Section 5).

10 In 1924 the Marist Brothers moved to the village of Portós, twenty kilometres south of Figueres. The school closed down during the civil war and never re-opened. No archives seem to have survived. Alfons Romero and Joan Ruiz, *Figueres*, p. 34, for dates.

11 Dalí's *bachillerato* progress-sheet in his file at the Faculty of Fine Arts, Universidad Complutense, Madrid.

12 Details taken from Montserrat Vayreda and Ramon Reig in Juan Núñez Fernández catalogue (see Bibliography, Section 3).

13 *Catálogo General de la calcografía nacional*, Madrid, Real Academia de Bellas Artes, 1987, nos. 5,778 and 5,779.

14 Alfons Romero and Joan Ruiz, *Figueres*, p. 34.

15 A photograph of the diploma is provided by Morse, *Pablo Picasso, Salvador Dalí. A Preliminary Study in their Similarities and Contrasts*, p. 8.

16 *AMD*, pp. 51–2.

17 *SL*, p. 140.

18 Daudet, 8 March 1970, p. 33.

19 I am very grateful to my friend Alicia Viñas, director of the Museu de l'Empordà, for providing me with photographs of the Prado loan collection and with information about its arrival in Figueres.

20 Obituary notice reproduced in catalogue *Joan Núñez Fernández* (see Bibliography, Section 3), pp. [31–2].

21 Vallès i Rovira, I, p. 35; conversations in Figueres with Doña Alicia Viñas, 1994.

22 *SL*, pp. 45–6.

23 Dalí, *Un diari: 1919–1920*, pp. 71–2.

24 Leonardo da Vinci, *Leonardo on Painting*, pp. 201–2.

25 Dalí, 'Dalí by Dalí'.

26 A varied selection of these drawings is included in the Perrot-Moore catalogue, *Dalí à Perpignan* (see Bibliography, Section 1). Others are reproduced in *DOH*, p. 15, and Romero, *Todo Dalí en un rostro*, p. 13. Dalí himself later reproduced the parrot-nose in *50 Secrets of Magic Craftsmanship*.

27 Copy of Dalí's *bachillerato* progress-sheet in his file at the Faculty of Fine Arts, Universidad Complutense, Madrid.

28 Dalí, *Un diari: 1919–1920*, *passim*.

29 Miravitlles, 'Dalí i l'aritmètica', p. 32; 'Una vida con Dalí', p. 5.

30 *SL*, p. 15.

31 *DG*, p. 107.

32 *SL*, p. 66.

33 *Ibid.*, pp. 14–15.

34 I am extremely grateful to Michael Lambert, the authority on locusts, for helping me to identify the species in question, both on the basis of its representation in Dalí's work and on distribution factors.

35 Dalí, '. . . l'alliberament dels dits . . .', p. 6.

36 *SL*, p. 129.

37 Interview with Doña Rosa Maria Salleras, Cadaqués, 1993.

38 Jiménez and Playà Maset, 'Dalí des de l'Empordà. Jaume Miravitlles'. Other witnesses to Dalí's locust phobia are mentioned by Rojas, p. 94, note 10.

39 See, for example, the recollections of the eccentric mathematician Alexandre Deulofeu, whose father had a chemist's shop across the road from the Dalís (Deulofeu, p. 24). Rojas, p. 94, note 10, mentions other witnesses.

40 Dalí, *Un diari: 1919–1920*, p. 139.

41 *SL*, pp. 129–31.

42 Teixidor Elies, pp. 189–96; Romero and Ruiz, pp. 16–17, 72–3.

43 *Empordà Federal*, Figueres, 1 June 1918.

44 Dalí, *Ninots. Ensatjos sobre pintura*, 1922, reproduced by Anna Maria Dalí, *Noves imatges de Salvador Dalí*, pp. 27–8.

45 R. Girald Casadesús, 'L'exposició d'artistes empordanesos'.

46 Jiménez and Playà Maset, 'Dalí vist des de l'Empordà-XIII. Jaume Miravitlles', *Hora Nova*, Figueres, no. 370 (10 July 1984), p. 13; Miravitlles, 'Una vida con Dalí'.

47 Guillamet, '"Studium", la revista del jove Dalí'.

48 'Puvis', 'Notes d'art. L'exposició de la Societat de Concerts', *Empordà Federal*, Figueres, no. 415, 11 January 1919.

49 Reproduced in *DOH*, p. 18.

50 Dalí, *Ninots. Ensatjos sobre pintura*, quoted by Anna Maria Dalí, *Noves imatges de Salvador Dalí*, p. 28.

51 *Ibid.*, p. 27.

52 *DOH*, p. 26.

53 Anna Maria Dalí, *Noves imatges de Salvador Dalí*, p. 14.

54 *Studium*, Figueres, no. 2 (1 February 1919), p. 4.

55 *Ibid.*, no. 6 (1 June 1919), p. 5.

56 *AMD*, p. 65.

57 Lear, *L'Amant-Dalí*, p. 92.

58 *SL*, p. 140; Dalí, 'Le Mythe de Guillaume Tell', p. 21.

59 *Ibid.*, p. 22.

60 *SL*, pp. 140–2.

61 Dalí mentions in *SL* (p. 48) that his father won a medal for Esperanto. In 1904 Dalí Cusí published an article on the subject in the journal *Espero de katalanujo* (*Empordà*, Figueres, 31 October 1995, p. 44); and a note published in *La Veu de l'Empordà* in September 1913, 'Figueres pro esperanto', mentions that the notary, at that time head of the Casino Menestral, was a confirmed *esperantista*.

62 Volumes 2, 3, 9, 10 and 11 of the diary, edited by Fèlix Fanés, have been published under the title *Un diari: 1919–1920. Les meves impressions i records intims*, Barcelona, Edicions 62, 1994. Referred to in earlier notes in this chapter and henceforth as *Un diari: 1919–1920*.

63 Dalí, *Un diari: 1919–1920*, p. 135.

64 *Ibid.*, pp. 57–8.

65 Dalí, *Ninots. Ensatjos sobre pintura*, quoted by Anna Maria Dalí, *Noves imatges de Salvador Dalí*, pp. 28–9.

66 Dalí, *Un diari: 1919–1920, passim*.

67 *Ibid.*, pp. 97, 104.

68 *Ibid.*, p. 27.

69 *Ibid.*, p. 37.

70 *Ibid.*, p. 38.

71 *Ibid.*, p. 46.

72 *Ibid.*, p. 50.

73 *Ibid.*, pp. 36–8.

74 *Ibid.*, pp. 100, 137–8.

75 *Ibid.* p. 55.

76 *L'hora*, Barcelona, no. 38 (25 September 1931), p. 7; Miravitlles, *El ritme de la revolució*, pp. 13–14.

77 There is a good reproduction of the portrait in *MEAC*, I, p. 27; *DOH*, p. 26, supplies a colour photograph of the ceramic jar. Jiménez and Playà Maset ('Dalí vist des de l'Empordà', VII) state that six photographs have been preserved of the murals, painted jars and plates with which Dalí decorated the premises.

78 *Empordà Federal*, Figueres, 28 September 1912, p. 3, 6 April 1918, p. 3.

79 Giralt-Miracle, p. 45.

80 Oliver Belmás, p. 291; Giralt-Miracle, p. 45; Ghiraldo, pp. 201–5. *El futurisme*, given as a lecture to the Barcelona Ateneu in 1904, was published as a *plaquette* in 1905. The cover is reproduced in AC. *Las vanguardias en Cataluña* (see Bibliography, Section 3), p.44.

81 *Empordà Federal*, Figueres, 7 June 1919.

82 Miravitlles, 'Una vida con Dalí', p. 5.

83 *DG*, p. 20; for Alomar's friendship with Don Salvador Dalí, see *AMD*, p. 53.

84 The row between the notary and Alomar is remembered in the Pichot family (conversation with Don Antoni Pitxot, Cadaqués, 1995); Alomar's slighting reference to Dalí was published in *Mirador*, Barcelona, 22 May 1929, and pasted by Salvador Dalí Cusí into his album of cuttings, preserved in the Fundació Gala–Salvador Dalí.

85 Dalí, *Un diari: 1919–1920*, p.105.

86 Dalí, *Tardes d'estiu*, p. 23.

87 Jiménez and Playà Maset, 'Dalí vist des de l'Empordà—X. L'amistat amb Ramon Reig', *Hora Nova*, Figueres, supplement to no. 361, May 1984, p. 39.

88 For Núñez's painting *El Lago de Vilabertrán*, see the colour reproduction in the catalogue *Juan Fernández Núñez* (see Bibliography, Section 3), no. 50. *Vilabertran Bell-Tower* is reproduced by Descharnes and Néret in *Salvador Dalí*, I, p. 22; *The Lake of Vilabertran*, in *DOH*, p. 22.

89 Lear, *L'Amant-Dalí*, p. 222.

90 Dalí, *Un diari: 1919–1920*, pp. 127–8.

91 Teixidor Elies, pp. 34–6.

92 Dalí, *Un diari: 1919–1920*, p. 85.

93 Dalí, *Diario de un genio*, p. 57.

94 Dalí, *Un diari: 1919–1920*, pp. 135, 154, 172.

95 *SL*, p. 124.

96 Josep Clara, p. 53.

97 *SL*, p. 122.

98 *Ibid.*, p. 125.

99 Dalí, *Un diari: 1919–1920*, p. 66.

100 *Ibid.*, p. 98; see also *SL*, p. 139.

101 For the British medical establishment's view of masturbation in the nineteenth century, Acton's *The Functions and Disorders of the Reproductive Organs* (see Bibliography, Section 6) makes horrifying reading; for the medical profession's assumptions concerning the causal relation between masturbation and homosexuality, see Jerez Farrán's article in progress, 'García Lorca y *El paseo de Buster Keaton*'.

102 Dalí and Pauwels, pp. 51–3.

103 The remark by Doña Nanita Kalashnikoff was made while looking for the first time at *Girl in Figueres* with the author and Don Antoni Pitxot, Museu-Teatre Dalí, Figueres, 5 August 1995. Dalí also com-

ments on the belfry scenario in Permanyer, 'El pincel erótico de Dalí', p. 162.

104 Miravitlles, 'Notes a l'entorn de l'art d'avanguarda', p. 321.

105 Dalí, *Un diari: 1919–1920*, pp. 48–9.

106 Dalí, *Comment on devient Dalí*, p. 89, my translation.

107 Conversation with Don Carlos Lozano, Cadaqués, 29 June 1996.

108 Lynd, p. 136.

109 Permanyer, 'El pincel erótico de Dalí', p. 161.

110 *Ibid.*; Dalí also told Luis Romero about these pictures and the horror of the female genitals they induced in him (*Dedálico Dalí*, p. 57).

111 Dalí, *Un diari: 1919–1920*, pp. 26, 28–30, 42, 48, 49, 59, 72–3, 74, 88–9, 92, 93, 99, 124–5, 141–2, 161.

112 *Ibid.*, p. 125.

113 Interview with Doña Carme Roget, Figueres, 23 September 1993, accompanied by her niece, Doña Alicia Viñas, head of the Museu de l'Empordà, Figueres. In *SL*, p. 142, Dalí, who never mentions Carme by name in the book, contradicts himself and says that their mutual *coup de foudre* occurred at an extra-mural evening philosophy course given by one of the younger teachers at the Instituto. In my long conversation with Doña Carme, she explained that she never attended such a course but that for a while she agreed to go to the Instituto to help with the translation of a Spanish book into French, a language she knew well thanks to attending a school run by French nuns. She thought that it might have been then that she first became aware of Dalí.

114 Dalí, *Un diari: 1919–1920*, p. 144.

115 *Ibid.*, *passim*; the manuscript page recording Dalí's fantasy about America is dated 23 January 1920 and is in the collection of Don Pere Vehí, Cadaqués.

116 Dalí, *Un diari: 1919–1920*, p. 104.

117 *Ibid.*, pp. 106–8.

118 This letter, and another in similar tone dated 28 September 1920 in Figueres, are preserved at the Arxiu Històric Comarcal, Figueres, and were first published, in Spanish translation, by Albert Arbós (see Bibliography, Section 6).

119 The letter was first published by Arbós, p. 46, in Spanish translation, and, like that quoted previously, is preserved at the Arxiu Històric Comarcal, Figueres.

120 Dalí, *Un diari: 1919–1920*, pp. 141–2; with her habitual carelessness, Anna Maria Dalí, *Noves imatges de Salvador Dalí*, pp. 12–13, ascribes this evocation to 1917.

121 The letter was first published in Spanish translation by Albert Arbós, p. 46. I am extremely grateful to Don Eduard Fornés for supplying me with a copy of the Catalan original.

122 Conversation with Doña Carme Roget, Figueres, 23 September 1993.

123 *SL*, p. 145.

124 Conversation with Doña Carme Roget, Figueres, 23 September 1993.

125 Dalí, *Un diari: 1919–1920*, p. 48.

126 Fèlix Fanés, note 259 to Dalí, *Un diari: 1919–1920*, pp. 217–18.

127 Dalí, *Un diari: 1919–1920*, p. 121.

128 List of paintings drawn up by Dalí in *Ninots. Ensatjos sobre pintura* (1922), quoted by Anna Maria Dalí, *Noves imatges de Salvador Dalí*, pp. 29–30.

129 I am grateful to Don Antoni Pitxot for passing on to me his Uncle Pepito's phrase about the demise of Impressionism, which he heard from the mouth of Dalí himself when the latter made him a gift of the book in question. The title page reads: *Boccioni, futurista. Pittura, scultura, futuriste (dinamismo plastico), con 51 reproduzioni quadri sculture di Boccioni-Carrà-Russolo-Balla-Severini-Soffici, Edizioni Futuriste di 'Poesia'*, Milan, Corzo Venezia, 61, 1914.

130 Undated letter to Gasch reproduced in the latter's *L'expansió de l'art català al món*, p. 146.

131 Santos Torroella, *La trágica vida de Salvador Dalí*, p. 44.

132 Vallés i Rovira, *Diccionari de l'Alt Empordà*, p. 329; Dalí, *Un diari: 1919–1920*, *passim*. Subias became Art Commissary of the Catalan Government under the Republic. It was he who initiated the proceedings to make the great Benedictine monastery of Sant Pere de Roda a national monument.

133 Joan Subias, 'Cartells. A Salvador Dalí Domènech', *Alt Empordà*, Figueres, 2 May 1921, p. 1. For some reproductions of work by Nogués, see *El noucentisme. Un projecte de modernitat* (catalogue), pp. 129–30, 142–3, 183–5, 294–8, 327. For the critics, see Fèlix Fanés's note 365, p. 231 to Dalí, *Un diari: 1919–1920*; Dalí's disclaimer comes in his *Ninots. Ensatjos sobre pintura* (1922).

134 Vallés i Rovira, *Diccionari de l'Alt Empordà*, pp. 223–4; Teixidor Elies, pp. 165–7, 498–500.

135 Miravitlles, 'Encuentros en mi vida, Dalí y Buñuel'. According to 'Met', it was Dalí who introduced him to the poetry of Salvat-Papasseit, which they got to know by heart.

136 *Alt Empordà*, Figueres, 'La pàgina literaria', 17 January 1920.

137 The designs are reproduced in the catalogue *Dalí en los fondos de la Fundació Gala–Salvador Dalí* (see Bibliography, Section 1). They comprise covers for Maurici's translation of Léon-Paul Fargue's *Per la música. Poemes* (p. 145), and for Maurici's books of poems *Estrelles caigudes* (p. 146) and *Poemes amb ocells* (p. 147).

138 Catalogue *Miró, Dalmau, Gasch* (see Bibliography, Section 3), pp. 49–51; Borràs, *Picabia*, pp. 171–2.

139 *AC. Las vanguardias en Catalunya* (catalogue, see Bibliography, Section 3), pp. 156–7. The cover of the Dalmau catalogue is reproduced in *Miró, Dalmau, Gasch* (catalogue, see Bibliography, Section 3), p. 51.

140 Vidal i Oliveras, p. 51.

141 Dalí, *Un diari: 1919–1920*, p. 144; some of the illustrations are reproduced in *AC. Las vanguardias en Catalunya* (catalogue, see Bibliography, Section 3), pp. 156–7.

142 Dalí, unpublished ten-page diary, October 1921, Fundació Gala–Salvador Dalí, Figueres.

143 Conversation with Doña Carme Roget, Figueres, 23 September 1993 (see note 113); details of the grave supplied to me by Doña Montserrat Dalí, Barcelona, 1993; obituaries in *Alt Empordà*, Figueres, 12 February 1921 and *La Veu de l'Empordà*, Figueres, same day; death certificate of Felipa Domènech, Registre Civil, Barcelona. Dalí noted in his diary for 22 October 1920 that his mother was unwell: a first hint, perhaps, of the impending tragedy (*Un diari: 1919–1920*, p. 147).

144 Conversations with Doña Montserrat Dalí, Barcelona, 1993.

145 *SL*, p. 153.

146 Pepito Pichot died on 5 July 1921. An obituary appeared in *Empordà Federal*, Figueres, on 9 July, and an appreciative article on the dead man in the same paper on 16 July.

147 Dalí's unpublished ten-page diary for October 1921. Fundació Gala–Salvador Dalí, Figueres.

148 Dalí, *Un diari: 1919–1920*, p. 153.

149 As for note 142.

150 *L'hora*, Barcelona, no. 38 (25 September 1931), p. 7.

151 'Jak', 'De la Rússia dels soviets. Un museu de pintura impressionista a Moscou', *Renovació Social*, Figueres, no. 1, 26 December 1921. Reproduced in *L'alliberament dels dits. Obra catalana completa*, pp. 7–8. The only copy of this periodical is preserved at the Biblioteca Municipal Carles Fages de Climent, Figueres, and bears the manuscript signature of one of the group's leaders, Martí Vilanova.

152 'C' [Carlos Costa], 'De arte. En las "Galeries Dalmau"', *La Tribuna*, Barcelona, p. 1.

153 See, for example, Eusebio Corominas, 'Arte y Letras. Salon Parés. Galeries Dalmau', in *El Diluvio*, Barcelona, 21 January 1922, p. 17.

154 'Exposició d'obres d'art organitzada par l'Associació catalana d'estudiants', Catalunya gráfica, Barcelona, 10 February 1922, no pagination; Rafael Santos Torroella, *Salvador Dalí i el Saló de Tardor*, p. 6, n. 3.

155 *Empordà Federal*, Figueres, no. 574, 21 January 1922, p. 3.

156 *Empordà Federal*, Figueres, no. 597, 1 July 1922. The portrait of Torres is reproduced in colour by *MEAC*, II, p. 25. Those of Miravitlles, in black and white, by Jiménez and Playà Maset, 'Dalí, el fútbol i la Unió Esportiva Figueres', pp. 78 and 79.

157 See, for example, *Empordà Federal*, Figueres, 6 May 1922, p. 1: 'He will be the painter-poet of our sea, which in the inlets near Cape Creus and in the Costa Brava acquires such intense tonalities that only someone with great technical ability ...'

158 Dalí, *Ninots. Ensatjos sobre pintura*, Museo Abelló, Mollet del Vallès (Barcelona).

159 Reflections at the end of the unpublished notebook *Les cançons dels dotze anys* (*Songs of When I was Twelve*) (1922), Fundació Gala–Salvador Dalí, Figueres.

160 Quoted by Fèlix Fanés in his edition of Dalí, *Un diari: 1919–1920*, p. 194, n. 97; Andrea is mentioned by name on p. 165.

Four: The Madrid Years (1922–6)

1 The best account in English of the Free Teaching Institution is that given by J.B. Trend in *The Origins of Modern Spain*; the standard work in Spanish is Jiménez-Landi, *La Institución Libre de Enseñanza y su ambiente. Los orígenes*.

2 García de Valdeavellano, pp. 13–15; Jiménez Fraud (1971), pp. 435–6.

3 Pritchett, p. 129.

4 Crispin, p. 41.

5 *Ibid.*, pp. 40–1.

6 For the lack of wine, *BMDS*, pp. 78–9.

7 Trend, *A Picture of Modern Spain*, p. 36.

8 *AMD*, pp. 82–3.

9 Glendinning, p. 522.

10 Eugenio d'Ors, 'Las obras y los días', *El Día Gráfico*, Barcelona, 19 October 1924, p. 6 (in Spanish, 'una farsa desarticulada, blanducha y fofa').

11 There is a copy of this document in Dalí's file at the Faculty of Fine Arts, Madrid University (Universidad Complutense).

12 *SL*, pp. 156–9.

13 The letter is in the Museu Joan Abelló, Mollet del Vallès (Barcelona). Published by Fernández Puertas, 'Les cartes de Salvador Dalí al seu oncle Anselm Domènech al Museu Abelló'.

14 Dalí, 'Poesia de l'útil standarditzat', p. 176.

15 Rodrigo, *Lorca-Dalí. Una amistad traicionada*, pp. 18–21.

16 The document is in Dalí's file at the Faculty of

Fine Arts, Madrid University (Universidad Complutense).

17 *SL*, p. 159.

18 *Ibid.*, pp. 175–6.

19 Conversation with Don José Bello, Madrid, 14 October 1992.

20 Moreiro, 'Dalí en el centro de los recuerdos', p. 21.

21 *Ibid.*

22 Conversations with Don José Bello, Madrid, 1978–93.

23 *BMDS*, p. 61.

24 *Ibid.*, p. 64; Santos Torroella, *Dalí residente*, p. 28.

25 *BMDS*, pp. 62–4.

26 *Ibid.*, p. 78.

27 In a letter to his Figueres friend Juan Xirau quoted by Rodrigo, *Lorca-Dalí. Una amistad traicionada*, p. 26.

28 Videla, pp. 1–88, *passim*; *BMDS*, pp. 71–2.

29 Quoted by Rodrigo, *Lorca-Dalí. Una amistad traicionada*, p. 25.

30 Gómez de la Serna, *Greguerías. Selección 1940–1952*. In the original Spanish: 'Conferencia: la más larga despedida que se conoce'; 'Aquella mujer me miró como a un taxi desocupado'; 'El arco iris es la cinta que se pone la Naturaleza después de haberse lavado la cabeza'.

31 Candamo, p. 79.

32 *BMDS*, p. 72.

33 Dalí's presence in Pombo is attested by a Barradas sketch reproduced by Ramón Gómez de la Serna in his *Sagrada cripta*, p. 253.

34 Santos Torroella, *Dalí residente*, pp. 30–1.

35 The details of Barradas's life are conflated from the Barradas/Torres García and Rafael Barradas catalogues listed in Section 3 of the Bibliography.

36 Santos Torroella, *Dalí residente*, p. 31.

37 Several of these works are in the Estalella collection in Madrid, and are reproduced in black and white in the catalogue *Ramón Estalella y su tiempo* (see Bibliography, Section 3), pp. 77–9, and in the catalogue *Salvador Dalí: The Early Years* (Section 1), pp. 98–9. *Cabaret Scene* (François Petit Collection, Paris) is reproduced in colour in the catalogue *Salvador Dalí: the Early Years*, p. 100, as is another Madrid scene, also in colour, at p. 98. *The First Days of Autumn* (private coll.), set in Figueres, is reproduced in colour by Santos Torroella, *Dalí residente*, p. 29.

38 *The First Days of Spring*, in the Estalella collection in Madrid, is reproduced in colour in Santos Torroella, *Dalí residente*, p. 29.

39 Death certificate of Maria Anna Ferrés in the Registro Civil, Figueres.

40 *AMD*, p. 89.

41 The documents concerning the dispensation are preserved in the Diocesan Archive at Girona. I am extremely grateful to Don Leandre Niqui Puigvert, keeper of the Episcopal Archive in Barcelona, for directing me to the Girona ecclesiastical authorities. Without his help I would have despaired of ever discovering where and when the couple married. I am also grateful to Don Leandre for the search which resulted in the location of the marriage certificate.

42 Conversation with Doña Montserrat Dalí, Barcelona, 1992. The anecdote has been confirmed to me in a letter from her daughter, Doña Eulalia Maria Bas i Dalí, Barcelona, 28 October 1993.

43 Etherington-Smith, p. 42.

44 Conversations with Doña Montserrat Dalí, Barcelona, 1993.

45 Wedding certificate, see note 41.

46 'Hostes selectes', *Empordà Federal*, Figueres, no. 623 (30 December 1922), p. 3.

47 *SL*, p. 151.

48 See, for example, M. A. Cassanyes, 'Sobre l'exposició Picàbia i la conferéncia de Breton', *La Publicitat*, Barcelona, 22 November 1922, p. 3.

49 Breton, *Oeuvres complètes*, I, pp. 291–308.

50 Borràs, *Picabia*, pp. 236–7, describes the exhibition and identifies the paintings on show, reproducing several of them.

51 Breton's preface, like the lecture, was later included in *Les Pas perdus*. See *Oeuvres complètes*, I, pp. 280–3.

52 Moreno Villa, *Vida en claro*, p. 107.

53 Gasch, *L'expansió de l'art catalá al món*, p. 145.

54 *SL*, p. 176.

55 *Ibid.*, p. 203.

56 Conversation with Don José Bello, Madrid, 19 October 1994.

57 Alberti, *Imagen Primera de La arboleda perdida*, pp. 19–20.

58 *Dalí in New York*, produced and directed by Jack Bond, 1966 (see Bibliography, Section 7).

59 Dalí, 'En el cuarto numeru 3 de la Residencia d'Estudians. Cunciliambuls d'un grup d'avanguardia'.

60 Stein, *The Autobiography of Alice B. Toklas*, p. 209.

61 Rodrigo, *Lorca-Dalí. Una amistad traicionada*, p. 21.

62 Moreiro, p. 19.

63 *SL*, pp. 164–5.

64 *Ibid.*, p. 165.

65 A short account of the King's visit appeared on 4 March 1923 in *Abc*, Madrid ('El monarca pronuncia un interesante discurso con motivo de la inauguración de una biblioteca', p. 15). The report contains no reference to Dalí.

66 *BMDS*, pp. 85–9.

67 Conversation with Doña María Luisa González, Madrid, 8 April 1982.

68 Alberti, *La arboleda perdida*, p. 222; *SVBLD*, pp. 79–80.

69　Dalí, '. . . sempre, per damunt de la música, Harry Langdon'.

70　Letter in private collection of Don Pere Vehi, Cadaqués.

71　*SL*, pp. 186–7; conversations with Don José Bello, Madrid, 1994–5; *BMDS*, p. 78; for the Charleston lessons, *SDFGL*, p. 44.

72　*SL*, p. 187.

73　Lear, *Le Dalí d'Amanda*, p. 165; Dalí on the programme 'Imágenes', 6 June 1979 (see Bibliography, Section 7).

74　Dalí, 'Skeets arbitraris. De la fira'.

75　Santos Torroella, 'The Madrid Years', p. 84.

76　Dalí's academic progress-sheet preserved in his file at the Faculty of Fine Arts, Madrid University (Universidad Complutense). Reproduced in *VPSD*, document no. 371, p. 15, and *MEAC*, II, p. 171.

77　Document preserved in Dalí's file; see n. 76.

78　Francisco Alcántara, 'La vida artística. Las oposiciones a cátedra de Pintura al Aire Libre de la Escuela de San Fernando', *El Sol*, Madrid, 10 October 1923, p. 4.

79　Account and statement in the *Heraldo de Madrid*, 18 October 1923, p. 5; another account in *El Sol*, Madrid, 18 October 1923, p. 8.

80　The *Heraldo de Madrid* (report referred to in the previous note), reads: 'A group of students from the School of Fine Arts protests, on behalf of their companions, against the decision of the jury entrusted with making an appointment to the Chair of Open-Air Painting. The students maintain that the jury has not made a sensible decision, since it has declared vacant a position for which there was a suitable candidate.'

81　Dalí's letter to Rigol was first published, in Spanish translation, by Rodrigo, *Lorca-Dalí. Una amistad traicionada*, pp. 32–6. I am grateful to Don Rafael Santos Torroella for a photocopy of the original document, in Catalan. Rafael Calatayud's file at the Faculty of Fine Arts, Madrid University (Universidad Complutense), confirms that he was rusticated in 1923–4 but, unlike Dalí's, it contains no further information on the matter.

82　The document is reproduced in *DOH*, p. 35.

83　Moreiro, p. 19.

84　Salvador Dalí Cusí's commentaries on his son's definitive expulsion from the Special School, in his album of cuttings (Fundació Gala–Salvador Dalí, Figueres), pp. 144–50.

85　Unpublished document preserved in Dalí's file at the Faculty of Fine Arts, Madrid University (Universidad Complutense).

86　*Ibid.* In *AMD*, p. 96, Anna Maria Dalí states that it was the notary's second wife, Catalina Domènech, who arrived in Madrid to investigate what had happened. It is difficult to believe that 'La Tieta' would

have been capable of interrogating 'students, teachers and employees' and adequately assessing their opinons. Perhaps she accompanied her husband to Madrid.

87　*SL*, pp. 196–8.

88　Dalí, *Comment on devient Dalí*, p. 68; *AMD*, p. 100; for information on the etching, Michler and Löpsinger, p. 126, no. 1.

89　The first reference to Dalí's attendance at the 'Academia Libre', which was situated in the Pasaje de la Alhambra (no longer existing), comes in Rodrigo, *Lorca-Dalí. Una amistad traicionada*, p. 36, where no source is provided. From Rodrigo it has been taken by other writers, including the habitually cautious Rafael Santos Torroella (*Dalí residente*, pp. 39, 55, 74, n. 1).

90　Dalí, *Un diari: 1919–1920*, p. 137.

91　Rivas Cherif, p. 7.

92　*Abc*, Madrid, 16 May 1924, pp. 10–11.

93　*Diario de Gerona*, 22 May 1924, quoted by Clara, p. 53; *El Día Gráfico*, Barcelona, 25 May 1924.

94　*Justicia Social*, Barcelona, 31 May 1924; *El Autonomista*, Girona, 13 June 1924. No collection of these publications seems to have survived. The items in question are included in Salvador Dalí Cusí's album of clippings about his son (Fundació Gala–Salvador Dalí, Figueres), as is one that appeared in *La Veu de l'Empordà*, Figueres, 14 June 1924.

95　'Empresonaments', *Justicia Social*, Barcelona, 14 June 1924 (see previous note); *La Veu de l'Empordà*, Figueres, 14 June 1924 (see previous note); Clara, p. 53.

96　Clara, p. 53.

97　Salvador Dalí Cusí gave his side of what happened in an interview with *Empordà Federal*, Figueres, 2 June 1923.

98　Salvador Dalí [Cusí], 'Al Sr. Procurador de la República Española, Fiscal del Tribunal Supremo', *Empordà Federal*, Figueres, 9 May 1931; *SL*, p. 124.

99　*SL*, p. 198; Arco, p. 54.

100　The document is in Dalí's file at the Faculty of Fine Arts, Madrid University (Universidad Complutense).

101　The photograph is reproduced in *Poesía. Número monográfico dedicado a la Residencia de Estudiantes* (see Bibliography, Section 6 under *Poesía*), pp. 80–1, and *¡Buñuel! La mirada del siglo* (catalogue, see Bibliography, Section 3), p. 298; for the performances of *Don Juan Tenorio* in the Residencia, *SVBLD*, pp. 86–91.

102　Antonio Marichalar, review of Eugenio d'Ors's *El nuevo glosario: Los diálogos de la pasión meditabunda* in *Revista de Occidente*, Madrid, I, no. 4 (October 1923), p. 126.

103　Ruiz-Castillo Basala, pp. 108–9.

104 It was reviewed in *La Voz*, Madrid, on 10 June 1922.

105 Valenciano Gayá, *El doctor Lafora y su época*.

106 *BMDS*, p. 282.

107 Moreno Villa, *Vida en claro*, p. 111.

108 James Strachey in Editor's Note to Freud, *Three Essays on Sexuality* (Standard Edition), p. 126.

109 The book is dated 1923 but there is no colophon. Gonzalo Lafora, reviewing it in the *Revista de Occidente*, Madrid, VI, no. 16 (October 1924), pp. 161–5, says (p. 161) that it appeared 'a few months' ago.

110 *SL*, p. 167, note.

111 Most of Dalí's library remained in his family home when his father disowned him in 1929 and was never returned. Today Anna Maria Dalí's heir retains the following volumes: *Totem y tabú, Introduccion al psicoanalisis, Psicopatología de la vida cotidiana, El porvenir de las religiones, Interpretación de los sueños* and *Psicología de la vida erótica*.

112 I am grateful to my friend Pere Vehí of Cadaqués for furnishing me with details of Dalí's annotations.

113 Breton, *Oeuvres complètes*, I, p. 1332.

114 Vela, 'El suprarealismo'.

115 For the basic facts about Ducasse's life the best source is the chronology to the volume Lautréamont, Germain Nouveau, *Oeuvres complètes*, Paris, Gallimard ('Bibliothèque de la Pléiade'), 1970, pp. 4–12.

116 *Ibid.*, p. 1354.

117 *Ibid.*

118 Breton, *Oeuvres complètes*, I, pp. 300–1.

119 Breton, *Conversations. The Autobiography of Surrealism [Entretiens]*, p. 31.

120 The extract appeared in *Prometeo*, Madrid, no. 9 (July 1909), pp. 69–78. The Biblioteca Nueva edition is undated. It has not yet been possible to establish with certainty the year of publication. The book had certainly appeared by 1924, being listed in an extract from the publisher's catalogue printed at the end of Pirandello's novel *The Late Mathias Pascal*, issued that year in the same collection. Bibliographical allusions in Ramón Gómez de la Serna's prologue suggest that the latter was written in 1920. I have found no review of the book in the Spanish press of the time.

121 Lorca read *Los raros* in the 1908 edition published by Maucci, Barcelona. For the reference to Lautréamont in *Impressions and Landscapes*, see García Lorca, *Obras completas*, III, pp. 43–5.

122 Letter to the author from Don José Bello, Madrid, 17 March 1996.

123 *SL*, pp. 202–3.

124 The letter is reproduced in Gibson, *Federico García Lorca*, I, p. 401.

125 Rodrigo, *Lorca-Dalí. Una amistad traicionada*, p. 39.

126 Playà i Masset, *Dalí de l'Empordà*, pp. 15–16.

127 *AMD*, p. 107.

128 Jardí, pp. 306–9.

129 Dalí and Pauwels, p. 24.

130 *SL*, pp. 265–6.

131 The photograph is preserved at the Fundació Gala–Salvador Dalí, Figueres.

132 Manuscript in Fundación Federico García Lorca, Madrid.

133 *AMD*, p. 102.

134 *Ibid.*, pp. 101–3.

135 García Lorca, *Epistolario*, I, p. 121.

136 *AMD*, pp. 103–4.

137 Aragon, p. 25.

138 *BMDS*, p. 76.

139 The manifesto was published in the review *Alfar*, La Coruña, no. 51 (July 1925), p. 68, and has been reprinted by Brihuega, *Manifiestos, proclamas*, etc., pp. 114–18.

140 *Abc*, Madrid, 29 May 1925. The photograph is reproduced in *SDFGL*, p. 129, and *DOH*, p. 35.

141 Moreno Villa, 'Nuevos artistas', p. 80.

142 *MEAC*, II, p. 173.

143 Moreno Villa, 'La jerga profesional'.

144 Santos Torroella, *Dalí. Epoca de Madrid*, and 'Salvador Dalí en la primera exposición de la Sociedad de Artistas Ibéricos'.

145 Santos Torroella, 'The Madrid Years', p. 85.

146 The article with Lorca's comment is included in Salvador Dalí Cusí's album of cuttings (Fundació Gala–Salvador Dalí, Figueres). The item appeared in *Buen Humor*, Madrid, 21 June 1925. The previous issue of the magazine, 28 June, reproduced *Bather*, the subject of which is Dalí's Figueres friend Juan Xirau with whom he collaborated on *Studium*.

147 The painting is reproduced, with a detailed commentary, by Santos Torroella in *Dalí. Época de Madrid*, pp. 28–34.

148 Moreno Villa, 'La exposición de 'Artistas Ibéricos'.

149 Manuel Abril, in *Heraldo de Madrid*, 16 June 1925, p. 3.

150 Jean Cassou, 'Lettres espagnoles', *Mercure de France*, Paris, no. 655 (1 October 1925), pp. 233–4.

151 There are numerous press clippings in Salvador Dalí Cusí's album (Fundació Gala–Salvador Dalí, Figueres).

152 The letter is included in Salvador Dalí Cusí's album of cuttings (see previous note).

153 Dalí's progress-sheet in his file at the Faculty of Fine Arts, Madrid University (Universidad Complutense).

154 *SDFGL*, p. 16.

155 Alberti, *La arboleda perdida*, p. 176.

156 Letter from Salvador Dalí Cusí to Manuel Menéndez, secretary of the Special School (11 September 1925), preserved in Dalí's file in the Faculty of Fine Arts, Madrid University (Universidad Complutense).

157 *SDFGL*, p. 19.

158 *UC*, p. 56; the catalogue is reproduced in *SDFGL*, p. 122.

159 *UC*, p. 56.

160 'Celui qui ne voudra mettre à contribution aucun autre esprit que le sien même se trouvera bientôt réduit à la plus misérable de toutes les imitations, c'est-à-dire à celle de ses propres ouvrages'; 'Le dessin est la probité de l'art'; 'Les belles formes, ce sont des plans droits avec des rondeurs. Les belles formes sont celles qui ont de la fermeté et de la plénitude, où les détails ne compromettent pas l'aspect des grandes masses.'

161 *SDFGL*, pp. 24, 122, note 2 to letter IX.

162 Extracts from some of the reviews are reproduced in *AMD*, pp. 117-20.

163 *SL*, p. 205.

164 *Ibid.*, pp. 154-6.

165 The telegram is included in Salvador Dalí Cusí's album of clippings (Fundació Gala-Salvador Dalí, Figueres). It reads: 'A hug for your picture of Venus. Federico.'

166 Cipriano Rivas Cherif, 'Divagaciones de un aprendiz de cicerone. "Venus y un marinero"', *Heraldo de Madrid*, 21 January 1926.

167 Letter from Buñuel to Lorca (2 February 1926). Fundación Federico García Lorca, Madrid.

168 *SDFGL*, p. 36.

169 The letters are reproduced by Santos Torroella, *La miel es más dulce que la sangre*, pp. 239-40.

170 *SDFGL*, p. 127, col. 3, n. 1; Rodrigo, *Memoria de Granada*, p. 223.

171 *SL*, p. 206.

172 *SL*, p. 206; it may be that Dalí arrived with the letter from Lorca to Ángeles Ortiz in his pocket (Rodrigo, *Memoria de Granada*, p. 223).

173 Fernández Puertas, 'Anselm Domènech, l'oncle de Salvador Dalí Domènech', pp. 74-6.

174 *SL*, p. 206.

175 *Ibid.*

176 *SL*, p. 206.

177 Zervos, 'Oeuvres récentes de Picasso', includes two photographs showing the works assembled in corners of the artist's studio.

178 Alley, p. 13.

179 There is no reference to the visit in Brassaï's *Conversations avec Picasso*, where Picasso says that he first saw paintings by Dalí in Barcelona later that year.

180 *AMD*, pp. 120-1.

181 *SDFGL*, pp. 32, 124-6.

182 Rodrigo, *Memoria de Granada*, p. 223.

183 Miró, *Ceci est la couleur de mes rêves. Entretien avec Georges Raillard*, Paris, Editions du Seuil, 1977. Not seen. Quoted by Rosa Maria Malet in documents made available to RTE (Spanish Television) for a projected series on Surrealism by Juan Caño and Ian Gibson.

184 James Johnson Sweeney, 'Joan Miró: Comment and Interview', *Partisan Review*, New York, vol. 15, no. 2, February 1948. Not seen. Quoted by Rosa Maria Malet in the documents mentioned in n. 184.

185 Minguet Batllori, p. 65.

186 Breton, *Le Surréalisme et la peinture*, p. 70.

187 *LRS*, no. 6 (1 March 1926), announcement inside front cover.

188 Penrose, *Miró*, p. 44. The gallery's artists were listed in an advertisement published inside the front cover of *LRS*, no. 7 (15 June 1926).

189 Penrose, *Miró*, p. 44.

190 Conversation with Doña María Luisa González, Madrid, 28 November 1991; *BMDS*, p. 226.

191 Anna Maria Dalí, *Noves imatges de Salvador Dalí*, p. 116; *SDFGL*, p. 34.

192 Postmark on card of Cadaqués sent by Salvador and Anna Maria to Lorca (Santos Torroella, *Dalí residente*, p. 40 and note).

193 Fernández Puertas, 'Anselm Domènech, l'oncle de Salvador Dalí Domènech', p. 76.

194 *SDFGL*, pp. 16, 20, 32.

195 García Lorca, *Obras completas*, I, pp. 953-7.

196 Jean Cassou, 'Lettres Espagnoles', *Mercure de France*, Paris, no. 673 (1 July 1926), pp. 235-6.

197 Bosquet, p. 56. In the original French: 'Mais je me sentais fort flatté au point de vue du prestige. C'est que, au fond de moi-même, je me disais qu'il était un très grand poète et que je lui devais un petit peu du trou de c— du Divin Dalí! Il a fini par s'emparer d'une jeune fille, et c'est elle qui m'a remplacé dans le sacrifice. N'ayant pas obtenu que je mette mon c— à sa disposition, il m'a juré que le sacrifice obtenu de la jeune fille se trouvait compensé para son sacrifice à lui: c'était la première fois qu'il couchait avec une femme.'

198 Gibson, 'Con Dalí y Lorca en Figueres', p. 11.

199 Ontañón and Moreiro, p. 122.

200 Margarita Manso's file is preserved, like Dalí's, in the archives of the Faculty of Fine Arts, Madrid University (Universidad Complutense).

201 Conversation with Doña Maruja Mallo, Madrid, 15 May 1979.

202 *Ibid.*

203 *SDFGL*, p. 36.

204 *Ibid.*, p. 57.

205 *Ibid.*, p. 88.

206 García Lorca, *Obras completas*, I, p. 441.

207 *Ibid.*, p. 421. Cf. *SL*, p. 243: 'The month of September held over us the "dying silver" garlic-clove of the incipient crescent moon.'

208 Dalí's progress-sheet in his file at the Faculty of Fine Arts, Madrid University (Universidad Complutense).

209 Report by the San Fernando Disciplinary Committee in Dalí's file at the Faculty of Fine Arts, Madrid University (Universidad Complutense).

210 Salvador Dalí Cusí's seven pages of comments on his son's expulsion, dated 20 November 1926, in his album of clippings (Fundació Gala–Salvador Dalí, Figueres), pp. 144–50.

211 Document in Dalí's file at the Faculty of Fine Arts, Madrid University (Universidad Complutense).

212 *SL*, pp. 16–17.

213 Rodrigo, *Lorca-Dalí. Una amistad traicionada*, p. 85.

214 Copy of typewritten document entitled 'Junta de profesores, reunidos en consejo de disciplina el día 23 de junio de 1926, a las siete de la tarde', in Dalí's file at the Faculty of Fine Arts, Madrid University (Universidad Complutense).

215 The letter is preserved in the Fundación Federico García Lorca, Madrid.

216 Salvador Dalí Cusí's album of clippings (Fundació Gala–Salvador Dalí, Figueres), pp. 144–50.

217 *SL*, p. 204.

218 Dalí, *Un diari: 1919–1920*, p. 85.

219 Pedro Rodríguez, 'Dalí vuelve a casa. "Soy el primer distribuidor, a escala mundial, del libro *Camino* . . .'", *Los Sitios*, Girona, 12 July 1970.

Five: Saint Sebastian and the Great Masturbator
(1926–7)

1 Fernandéz Almagro, 'Por Cataluña'.

2 Santos Torroella, 'The Madrid Years', p. 84.

3 *DG*, p. 81.

4 *Ibid.*; Dalí, *Comment on devient Dalí*, p. 16.

5 Malanga, no pagination.

6 The painting is now in the possession of Doña Josefina Cusí, Joaquim Cusí Fortunet's daughter. My efforts to see it have proved hopeless, despite the intervention of several people close to Doña Josefina, a millionairess now in her nineties.

7 Santos Torroella, 'The Madrid Years', p. 88.

8 García Lorca, *Epistolario*, I, p. 167.

9 Beurdeley, p. 84.

10 Savinio, *Nueva enciclopedia*, p. 369.

11 Freud, *Introductory Lectures on Psycho-Analaysis*, Standard Edition, XV, p. 154.

12 *SDFGL*, p. 44.

13 *Ibid.*, p. 42. The Salisach house was next door to the Dalí's at the other end of Es Llané beach. 'Papini' is presumably the prolific writer Giovanni Papini (1881–1956), notable for his ideological volte-faces.

14 Santos Torroella was the first to point out this connection. See *La miel es más dulce que la sangre*, p. 224.

15 *On Classic Ground. Picasso, Léger, de Chirico and the New Classicism 1910–1930* (catalogue, see Bibliography, Section 3), p. 219.

16 Santos Torroella, *La miel es más dulce que la sangre*, p. 110.

17 Reproduced in *DOH*, p. 49; *MEAC*, II, p. 59.

18 Anna Maria Dalí, *Noves imatges de Salvador Dalí*, p. 94.

19 In the Salvador Dali Museum, Florida. Reproduced in *Salvador Dalí. The Early Years* (see Bibliography, Section 1), p. 128.

20 Santos Torroella, 'The Madrid Years', p. 89.

21 *Ibid.*

22 The photograph is preserved in the Fundación Federico García Lorca, Madrid.

23 Oil on copper, dimensions unknown, private collection (Carles Noguer Cusí, Barcelona), reproduced in black and white in Descharnes, *DOH*, p. 56, where it is dated 1925, and in *Salvador Dalí. The Early Years* (catalogue, see Bibliography, Section 1), p. 136, dated 1926 (which seems less likely). For an account of Dalí's participation in the Autumn Salon, see Santos Torroella, *Salvador Dalí i el saló de Tardor*.

24 The painting is in the Salvador Dali Museum, Florida, and is reproduced in colour in *Salvador Dalí. The Early Years* (catalogue, see Bibliography, Section 1), p. 128; *The Salvador Dali Museum Collection* (catalogue, see Bibliography, Section 1), no. 24 (where it is entitled *Femme Couchée*); *DOH*, p. 67; etc.

25 For colour reproductions of *Still Life by Moonlight*, see *DOH*, p. 69, and *Salvador Dalí. The Early Years* (see Bibliography, Section 1), p. 164; for *Barcelona Mannequin*, see *DOH*, p. 68, and *Salvador Dalí. The Early Years* (see above), p. 161.

26 Gasch, *L'expansió de l'art català al món*, pp. 139–40.

27 Gasch, 'De galeria en galeria', *AA*, no. 2 (May 1926), p. 5.

28 Gasch, 'Les exposicions', *AA*, no. 14 (31 May 1927), p. 40.

29 Gasch, 'De galeria en galeria', *AA*, no. 8 (November 1926), p. 4.

30 *Ibid.*, p. 6.

31 Gasch, 'Salvador Dalí', *La Gaseta de les Arts*, Barcelona, no. 60 (1 November 1926), reprinted in Gasch, *Escrits d'art i d'avantguarda (1925–1938)*, pp. 67–70.

32 Gasch, *L'expansió de l'art català al món*, p. 142.

33 *Ibid.*, pp. 143–4.

34 M.A. Cassanyes, 'L'espai en les pintures de Salvador Dalí', p. 30.

35 *SDFGL*, p. 46.

36 J.V. Foix, 'Presentació de Salvador Dalí'.

37 A black and white photograph of the painting, here entitled *Women Lying on the Sand*, is provided in *DOH*, p. 67.

38 Gasch, 'Salvador Dalí', *AA*, no. 11 (28 February 1927), pp. 16–17.

39 For Tanguy's discovery of De Chirico, see Biro and Passeron, p. 396; José Pierre, 'Le Peintre surréaliste par excellence', p. 43; Jean, p. 162; for Breton's discovery of the same painting, Pierre, *ibid.*

40 Reproduced in *DOH*, p. 76.

41 Santos Torroella, *La miel es más dulce que la sangre*, p. [107], caption: 'The solitary head is that of García Lorca'.

42 Buñuel, 'Recuerdos literarios del Bajo Aragón', in Buñuel, *Obra literaria* (edited by Sánchez Vidal), p. 241; for José Bello's memories of dead donkeys, see *SVBLD*, pp. 26–8.

43 Bataille, 'Le Jeu lugubre'.

44 Dalí, *Le Mythe tragique de l'Angélus de Millet*, p. 101, n. 1.

45 Miró, 'Je rêve d'un grand atelier'.

46 *UC*, p. 58.

47 *Ibid.*

48 *SDFGL*, p. 48.

49 *Ibid.*, p. 52.

50 The 'painted mouths of tailors' dummies' is a reference to Lorca's poem 'Árbol de canción', dedicated to Anna Maria Dalí and included in *Canciones* (*Obras completas*, I, p. 335).

51 *SDFGL*, pp. 58–60.

52 Rafael Moragas, 'Durante un ensayo, en el Goya, de "Mariana Pineda", cambiamos impresiones con el poeta García Lorca y el pintor Salvador Dalí', *La Noche*, Barcelona, 23 June 1927, p. 3.

53 Gibson, *Federico García Lorca. A Life*, I, p. 480.

54 *Ibid.*, pp. 479–82.

55 Gasch, 'F.G. Lorca', *AA*, no. 15 (30 June 1927), p. 50.

56 García Lorca, *Cartas a sus amigos*, edited by Sebastià Gasch, pp. 8–11.

57 The drawing is reproduced in colour in García Lorca, *Dibujos* (see Bibliography, Section 3), no. 112, p. 152.

58 The comment was made to Robert Descharnes, *The World of Salvador Dalí*, p. 21; the drawing is reproduced in colour in García Lorca, *Dibujos* (see Bibliography, Section 3), no. 114, p. 153, and in Romero, *Todo Dalí en un rostro*, no. 277, p. 220.

59 García Lorca, *Cartas a sus amigos*, edited by Sebastià Gasch, p. 10.

60 Montanyà, 'Superrealisme', *AA*, no. 10 (31 January 1927), pp. 3–4.

61 Montanyà, 'Panorama', *AA*, no. 16 (31 July 1927), p. 55.

62 Gasch, 'Intermezzo càustic', *AA*, no. 15 (30 June 1927), p. 50.

63 'Informaciones artísticas', *ibid.*

64 'Informacions literàries', *ibid.*, p. 48.

65 *SDFGL*, p. 46. There is a later use of the term at p. 93.

66 The subtitle, 'Irony', and opening paragraph are taken almost word for word from Alberto Savinio, '"Anadioménon". Principi di valutazione dell'Arte contemporanea', *Valori Plastici*, Rome, I, nos. 4–5, 1919.

67 The reference is perhaps to *Girl at the Window* (1925).

68 In fact it is Savinio, *loc. cit.*, who has said it, not the narrator: 'In fondo, non è che una ragione de nudità—per conseguenze di morale.'

69 In Catalan, as in Spanish, *contar* means both count and recount.

70 The reference to the broken capital and the black-and-white marble flagstones suggests that Dalí has in mind Mantegna's exquisite *Saint Sebastian* in the Royal Museum, Vienna. The same artist's *Saint Sebastian* in the Louvre, featuring a much less attractive saint, may have been seen by Dalí when he visited Paris in March 1926.

71 Dalí had admired Patinir's 'poisonous metallic blue' in the Prado (*SL*, p. 191).

72 Dalí seems to have got the date wrong. The painting was executed in 1918.

73 'Dinah' ('is there anything finer?') was one of the great hits of the American quartet, The Revellers, mentioned elsewhere by the narrator.

74 American film star and director (1880–1940).

75 The Polish Cubist painter Louis Marcoussis (1878–1941), who lived in Paris.

76 American film star (1890–1963) whose moustache Dalí much admired.

77 In English in the original.

78 The reference seems to be to Marinetti's *Il tattilismo*, published in 1921.

79 This two-sentence paragraph was not included in the *L'Amic de les Arts* text but appeared in the translation published by Lorca (in *Gallo*, Granada, 1928), from where I have taken it. The reference to the mouths of tailors' dummies reminds one immediately of what Dalí had written to Lorca about his book of poems *Canciones*: 'I read your "orange and lemon" and can't sense the painted mouths of tailors' dummies.'

80 *SL*, p. 207.

81 García Lorca, *Cartas a sus amigos*, edited by Sebastià

Gasch, p. 32, reproduced in García Lorca, *Epistolario*, II, p. 69.

82 *AA*, no. 17 (31 August 1927), p. 73.

83 The letter, in the Biblioteca de Catalunya, Barcelona, was first reproduced by Fernández Puertas, 'Una carta obligada'.

84 I am extremely grateful to Professor Dawn Ades for providing me with a photocopy of the catalogue. For the record, the paintings on exhibition were:

  1. *La Lueur ressemblante.*
  2. *Premier Message.*
  3. *Second Message.* (Coll. Louis Aragon)
  4. *Troisième Message.*
  5. *Leur Ventre blanc m'avait frappé.*
  6. *Bélomancie.*
  7. *Mort guettant sa famille.*
  8. *Une Couleur, une fleur, une personne présente.* (Coll. Roland Tual)
  9. *Vite! Vite!* (Coll. Mme J.T.)
  10. *Elberfeld.* (Coll. Paul Éluard)
  11. *Je Suis venu comme j'avais promis. Adieu.* (Coll. Janine Kahn)
  12. *L'Anneau d'invisibilité.* (Coll. Nancy Cunard)
  13. *Essai sur les erreurs populaires.*
  14. *Argent potable.*
  15. *Fumier à gauche, violettes à droite.*
  16. *Finissez ce que j'ai commencé.*
  17. *Un Grand Tableau qui représente un paysage.*
  18. *Il Faisait ce qu'il voulait.* (Coll. André Breton)
  19. *Tous ces détails étaient exacts.*
  20. *Extinction des lumières inutiles.*
  21. *Le 4 juin je ne vois plus.*
  22. *Maman, Papa est blessé.*
  23. *Je m'en vais, venez-vous?*

José Pierre states as a fact, without any evidence or arguing his case, that Dalí saw the exhibition catalogue (*Yves Tanguy*, Centre Georges Pompidou, Paris, p. 53). The same author provides details of the three pictures reproduced in the catalogue (*ibid.*, p. 61, n. 26). The cover of the catalogue and the page listing the works exhibited are reproduced in the German edition of the catalogue, p. 67 (see Bibliography, Section 3). The Pompidou edition of the catalogue reproduces Breton's preface to the 1927 exhibition (pp. 92–3).

85 Ades, p. 45.

86 Pierre, p. 53.

87 *Ibid.*

88 Secrest, p. 87.

89 *SL*, opposite p. 375.

90 *SVBLD*, p. 116.

91 Santos Torroella, *Dalí residente*, pp. 176–7.

92 Romero, Todo *Dalí en un rostro*, p. 172, no. 213.

93 *SL*, p. 298; from Eugenio D'Ors we know that Lídia was already using the phrase when he met her in 1911 (*La verdadera historia de Lídia de Cadaqués*, p. 34).

94 Santos Torroella, *La miel es más dulce que la sangre*, p. 74; *SL*, p. 221.

95 García Lorca, *Obras completas*, I, p. 531.

96 Santos Torroella, *La miel es más dulce que la sangre*, p. 75, n. 9.

97 See, for example, his comments on the subject in Permanyer, 'El pincel erótico de Dalí'.

98 Moorhouse, p. 32.

99 *SVBLD*, p. 158.

100 *SVBLD*, p. 159. The name of the village, whose etymology has nothing to do with 'disgusting', was later changed to Valderrubio.

101 *SVBLD*, p. 162.

Six: Towards Surrealism (1927–8)

1 Combalía, *El descubrimiento de Miró*, p. 83, n. 84. Gasch referred to the letter in 'Les fantaisies d'un reporter', p. 108.

2 Massot and Playà, 'Sis anys de correspondència entre Miró i Dalí', p. 36.

3 Gasch, 'Les fantaisies d'un reporter', p. 108.

4 Cf. the ending of Gasch's article on Miró, published in the *Gaseta de les Arts*, Barcelona, no. 39, 15 December 1925: 'To conclude, it should be underlined that the work of Joan Miró represents, within modern painting, the most original and important effort since Picasso. This affirmation may seem gratuitous to a lot of people. But it is not my affirmation. Miró had the great good fortune to hear it from the lips of the Malaga artist himself.'

5 *SDFGL*, p. 67.

6 Santos Torroella, *Salvador Dalí i el saló de Tardor*, pp. 32–3, n. 21.

7 Dalí, 'La fotografia pura creació de l'esperit'.

8 Ades, 'Morphologies of Desire', p. 142.

9 For the dates, Santos Torroella, *Dalí residente*, p. 193, n. 8; *AA*, no. 17 (31 August 1927), p. 73.

10 Gasch, 'Max Ernst'.

11 Gasch, 'Cop d'ull sobre l'evolució de l'art modern', p. 93.

12 Gasch, 'Del cubismo al surrealismo', *GL*, no. 20 (15 October 1927), p. 5. The original Catalan version of this article (*La Nova Revista*, Barcelona, no. 7, July 1927) does not have the phrase about immorality.

13 Gasch, 'L'exposició colectiva de la Sala Parés', *AA*, no. 19 (31 October 1927), p. 95.

14 Gasch, 'Comentaris. Al marge d'un article de Rafael Benet', *AA*, no. 22 (29 February 1928), pp. 166–7. It became increasingly clear that Gasch's main objections to Surrealism were its aggressive rejection

of God and its sexual explicitness. See, particularly, his article 'André Breton: le Surréalisme et la peinture', *La Veu de Catalunya*, Barcelona, 15 April 1928, reproduced in Gasch, *Escrits d'art i d'avantguarda (1925–1938)*, pp. 101–5, where we read: 'I accept the healthy, poetic part of Surrealism. But I reject, categorically, its sickly sadistic component, its pederasty, its constant filth, all the stench of drugs and brothels exhaled by literary Surrealism.'

15 Dalí, 'Els meus quadros del saló de Tardor'.

16 Massip, 'Dalí hoy'.

17 For Gasch, 'Del cubismo al superrealismo', *GL*, no. 20 (15 October 1927), p. 5, Foix is 'the Catalan Surrealist poet'; for Montanyà, 'Un "nou" poeta català' [Sebastià Sànchez-Juan], *GL*, no. 22 (15 November 1927), p. 3, he is 'the Catalan Surrealist (a Surrealist with the noblest of aesthetic preoccupations)'.

18 *SDFGL*, p. 66.

19 *SVBLD*, p. 165.

20 Dalí, 'Film artístico, film antiartístico'.

21 *Dalí joven. 1918–1930* (catalogue, see Bibliography, Section 1), p. 33.

22 *Ibid.*

23 *Ibid.*, pp. 29–30, 32.

24 *AA*, 29 February 1928, p. 164.

25 Quoted in *SVBLD*, pp. 166–7.

26 *SDFGL*, pp. 80–1.

27 The extracts appeared in *LRS*, no. 4 (15 July 1925), pp. 26–30; no. 6 (1 March 1926), pp. 30–2; no. 7 (15 June 1926), pp. 3–5; nos. 9–10 (1 October 1927), pp. 36–43.

28 'Today, 12 February 1928, at midnight, the boy has finished his military service', Salvador Dalí Cusí's album, Fundació Gala–Salvador Dalí, Figueres. See Bibliography for publication details of 'Nous límits de la pintura'.

29 Breton, *Le Surréalisme et la peinture*, pp. 47–8.

30 Dalí, 'Nous límits de la pintura' [first part], p. 167.

31 *Ibid.*

32 Dalí, 'Realidad y sobrerrealidad'.

33 *SDFGL*, pp. 89–90.

34 Breton, 'Le surréalisme et la peinture', *LRS*, nos 9–10 (1 October 1927), p. 41: 'It was in this way that Max Ernst began to enquire into the substance of objects, to give it every freedom for choosing, once again, their shadow, their attitude and their form'; *Le Surréalisme et la peinture*, p. 30. Cf. Dalí in 'Nous límits de la pintura': 'The highly complex and disturbing process of the instant in which these objects without sight begin to walk, or believe it is convenient to modify the course of the projection of their shadow' (part 2, p. 186).

35 *SDFGL*, p. 90; the same example occurs in 'Realidad y sobrerrealidad'.

36 Dalí, 'Nous límits de la pintura' [third part], p. 195.

37 According to Breton, *Oeuvres complètes*, I, p. liv, printing of *Le Surréalisme et la peinture* was completed on 11 February 1928.

38 Santos Torroella, *'Los putrefactos' de Dalí y Lorca*, p. 95.

39 In May 1928 Gasch reviewed the book testily in 'André Breton. "Le Surréalisme et la peinture"'.

40 Sánchez Vidal, *SVBLD*, p. 164.

41 Gasch, *L'expansió de l'art català al mon*, p. 150.

42 The Bernat Metxe Foundation was set up in the 1920s to promote the translation into Catalan of the Latin and Greek classics.

43 Gasch, *L'expansió de l'art català al món*, p. 150. Gasch omits the name of Aurea, given in a letter by him to Dalí included in Salvador Dalí Cusí's album of cuttings in the Fundació Gala–Salvador Dalí, Figueres.

44 *Ibid.*

45 Letter to Dalí from Gasch, December 1927.

46 Gasch, *L'expansió de l'art català al món*, p.152.

47 *Ibid.*, p. 153.

48 *AA*, 30 April 1928, p. 181.

49 The *sardana*, Catalunya's national dance, is as much a symbol of the Principality as the Virgen of Montserrat: sacrosanct.

50 Dalí, 'Per al "meeting" de Sitges'.

51 *La Veu de l'Empordà*, Figueres, 26 May 1928, pp. 5–6.

52 *Ibid.*, p. 6; a full account also appeared in *Sol Ixent*, Cadaqués, 2 June 1928, pp. 8, 10.

53 *SL*, p. 19.

54 Descharnes, *Dalí*, p. 64.

55 Ades, *Dalí*, p. 60.

56 Santos Torroella, *Salvador Dalí i el saló de Tardor*, p. 11.

57 Both works are illustrated in *DOH*, p. 75.

58 Ricardo Baeza, 'Los *Romances gitanos* de Federico García Lorca', *El Sol*, Madrid, 29 July 1928, p. 2.

59 García Lorca, *Obras completas*, III, p. 977.

60 Dalí, 'Realidad y sobrerrealidad'.

61 A reference to the fine poet Pedro Salinas, a friend of Lorca's.

62 *SDFGL*, pp. 88–94.

63 García Lorca, *Epistolario*, II, p. 113.

64 Santos Torroella, *Salvador Dalí i el saló de Tardor*, p. 17, n. 15.

65 It seems likely that this is the painting in the Salvador Dali Museum Collection in Florida, reproduced in colour in the museum catalogue at no. 31 (see Bibliography, Section 1).

66 Santos Torroella, *Salvador Dalí i el saló de Tardor*, p. 12.

67 *Ibid.*, pp. 13–14.

68 *Ibid.*, p. 15.
69 *Ibid.*, p. 20.
70 *Ibid.*, pp. 18–19.
71 'Les exposicions d'art. El Saló de Tardor. A dar-rera hora, Salvador Dalí retira els seus quadros del Saló', *La Nau*, Barcelona, 6 October 1928. The com-mittee's note was also printed in *La Publicitat*, Barcelona, 6 October 1928, p. 5 ('Una obra de Salvador Dalí es retirada del Saló de Tardor').
72 Santos Torroella, *Salvador Dalí i el saló de Tardor*, pp. 20–1.
73 *La Publicitat*, Barcelona, 17 October 1928, p. 4.
74 *Ibid.*, pp. 4–5.
75 *Ibid.*, pp. 4–5; *ibid.*, 24 October 1928, p. 6.
76 Pla in *La Veu de Catalunya* quoted by Gasch, *L'expansió de l'art català al món*, p. 153.
77 Santos Torroella, *Salvador Dalí i el saló de Tardor*, p. 24.
78 *Ibid.*, pp. 25–7.
79 *Ibid.*, pp. 27–9.
80 *Ibid.*, pp. 29–30.
81 *Ibid.*, pp. 32–4.
82 Francisco Madrid, 'El escándalo del 'Salón de Otoño' de Barcelona. Salvador Dalí, pintor de van-guardia, dice que todos los artistas actuales están putrefactos', *Estampa*, Madrid, 6 November 1928, p. [8].

Seven: Into the Surrealist Vortex (1929)

1 *SVBLD*, p. 186.
2 *Ibid.*
3 *BMDS*, pp. 124–5.
4 Sánchez Vidal, 'The Andalusian Beasts', p. 193.
5 *SL*, pp. 205–6; similar version in the later *UC*, pp. 76–7.
6 Lear, *L'Amant-Dalí*, p. 190; Aub, pp. 547–8.
7 *SVBLD*, p. 184.
8 Letter from Buñuel to Dalí, 24 June 1929. Museu Joan Abelló, Mollet del Vallès (Barcelona). In 1934, eight years before the publication of the *Secret Life*, furious that his name had disappeared from the credits of both *Un Chien andalou* and *L'Age d'or*, Dalí wrote to Buñuel: 'Without me these films wouldn't have hap-pened, remember your avant-garde projects and Gómez de la Serna, exactly at the time when I was writing the first draft of the *Chien* in which the *Surrealist film* was invented for the first time.' The indignation has a convincing ring (letter from Dalí to Buñuel quoted in *SVBLD*, pp. 248–9). The testimony of Dalí's friend Jaume Miravitlles, who took part in the film, is also relevant. According to him, if the execu-tion of *Un Chien andalou* was undeniably Buñuel's, the original idea was as undoubtedly Dalí's: he was its 'mother'. Buñuel, wrote Miravitlles, had confirmed this to him in a letter (Miravitlles, 'Dalí y Buñuel', 8 July 1977, and *Més gent que he conegut*, p. 160).
9 Letter from Buñuel to Pepín Bello (Paris, 10 February 1929), reproduced in *SVBLD*, pp. 189–91. Prof. Sánchez Vidal has confirmed to me in writing that Buñuel wrote 'La marista', not 'El marista' (letter to the author, 20 December 1995).
10 J. Puig Pujades, 'Un film a Figueres. Una idea de Salvador Dalí i Lluís Buñuel', *La Veu de l'Empordà*, Figueres, 2 February 1929, reproduced by Rafael Santos Torroella, *Dalí residente*, pp. 237–40.
11 Buñuel interviewed by José de la Colina and Tomás Pérez Turrent in *Contracampo*, Madrid, no. 16 (October–November 1980), pp. 33–4. The interview is reprinted in *Buñuel por Buñuel*, by the same authors, pp. 23–6.
12 *LRS*, no. 12 (15 December 1929), p. 34.
13 Rodrigo, *Lorca-Dalí. Una amistad traicionada*, pp. 214–15, reproduces the following account of Buñuel's system, given to her decades after the event by Anna Maria Dalí and hence not necessarily trustworthy. It seems that what Anna Maria is recalling here is how Buñuel used to polish the draft of the previous session with the painter: 'Luis was very methodical and really enjoyed his work. Every day, after lunch, he would install himself in the little sitting room with his type-writer, his packet of "Lucky Strike" cigarettes and his "White Label" whisky. He was completely absorbed in his work, writing on his machine until it seemed to him that he had managed to express plastically a scene or idea. Then he would pause, smoke another cigarette and drink a sip of whisky with *genuine pleasure*. He would call Salvador to comment on what he'd just written; they'd spend a while talking about it, and after another cigarette, to digest the discussion, he would start working again on the typewriter.'
14 Letter quoted in *SVBLD*, p. 203.
15 Bataille, 'Le "Jeu lugubre"'.
16 Reproduced in *DOH*, p. 47.
17 Dalí, 'La meva amiga i la platja', in 'Dues proses': 'My girlfriend likes the sleepy morbidities of lavabos and the sweetnesses of the finest scalpel-blades on the curved pupils, dilated by the extraction of the cataract.'
18 Aranda, p. 85, n. 2.
19 Santiago Ontañón to Max Aub, in Aub, p. 320.
20 In 'To Spain, Guided by Dalí', p. 94, Dalí says that *The Death of the Virgin* was the painting in the Prado that most impressed Lorca, who said that it was paint-ed 'with the light of an eclipse'.
21 Aranda, p. 85, n. 2; *BMDS*, p. 125.
22 For severed hands and eyes in European art, see

the catalogue *¿Buñuel! Auge des Jahrhunderts* (Bibliography, Section 3). Sánchez Vidal, *El mundo de Buñuel*, p. 69, reproduces Magritte's *Le Musée d'une nuit* (1927), the severed hand in which is very similar indeed to that in *Un Chien andalou*. The same authority has drawn our attention to a poem by Buñuel and Dalí's admired Benjamin Péret, 'Les Odeurs de l'amour', included in *Le Grand Jeu* (1928), in which the eye/razor connection is made explicit: 'S'il est un plaisir/c'est bien celui de faire l'amour/le corps entouré de ficelles/les yeux clos par des lames de rasoir' (Péret, *Oeuvres complètes*, I, p. 167).

23 Bataille, 'Le "Jeu lugubre"'.

24 Buñuel, 'Recuerdos literarios del Bajo Aragón', in *Obra literaria* (ed. Sánchez Vidal), p. 241; for Pepín Bello, see *SVBLD*, pp. 27–8.

25 Telephone conversation with Don Agustín Sánchez Vidal (in Zaragoza), 3 May 1995.

26 Freud, *Standard Edition*, vol. 5, p. 398, n. 1; *La interpretación de los sueños*, Madrid, Biblioteca Nueva, 1923, vol. 2, p. 113.

27 Buñuel, 'Notes on the Making of *Un Chien andalou*', p. 153.

28 The friend was Angel del Río. For Lorca's outburst, see Buñuel, *Obra literaria* (ed. Sánchez Vidal), p. 32, and *BMDS*, p. 193.

29 Buñuel, *Obra literaria* (ed. Sánchez Vidal), p. 32.

30 Aranda, pp. 65–6, note.

31 Aub, p. 59.

32 Durgnat, p. 23.

33 García Lorca, *Obras completas*, II, pp. 277–80. The piece was dated 'July 1925' on first publication in *Gallo*, Granada, no. 2 (April 1928), pp. 19–20.

34 *SDFGL*, p. 32.

35 Aub, p. 105.

36 For an interesting exploration of the homosexual content of Lorca's *Buster Keaton's Outing* I am grateful to Carlos Jerez-Farrán for sending me his article in progress: 'García Lorca y El paseo de Buster Keaton'.

37 *LRS*, no. 12 (15 December 1929), p. 35.

38 Gibson, 'Con Dalí y Lorca en Figueres'.

39 *BMDS*, p. 22.

40 *UC*, p. 76.

41 See note 10.

42 'Buñuel y Dalí en el Cineclub', *GL*, 1 February 1929, p. 6.

43 *SVBLD*, pp. 189–91.

44 'Un número violento de "L'Amic de les Arts"', *GL*, 1 February 1929, p. 7.

45 Letter from Buñuel to Dalí dated 22 March 1929. Collection of Don Pere Vehí, Cadaqués.

46 Miravitlles, 'Notes a l'entorn de l'art d'avanguarda. Miró-Dalí-Domingo', p. 321.

47 *LRS*, no. 8 (1 December 1926), p. 13.

48 *BMDS*, p. 123.

49 First published in *SVBLD*, pp. 193–8.

50 *BMDS*, p. 133.

51 Printing of the novel was finished on 25 May 1928 (Breton, *Oeuvres complètes*, I, p. liv).

52 Dalí, 'La dada fotográfica'.

53 *BMDS*, pp. 123–4.

54 Ce sont nos pères Messieurs nos pères/Qui trouvent que nous ne leur ressemblons pas/Honnêtes gens qui/Eux ne se sont jamais fait sucer qu'en dehors du foyer conjugal . . .

55 The home of Joan Miró, near Tarragona.

56 'Revistas', *GL*, 1 April 1929, p. 7; the rumour was confirmed by the well-informed Barcelona review, *Mirador*, whose Paris correspondent, Domenec de Bellmunt, reported on 18 April 1929 that Dalí had arrived to set up the ultimate avantgarde magazine.

57 Quoted in *Poesía. Revista ilustrada de información poética*, Madrid, nos 18 and 19 (1983), monographical issue devoted to the Residencia de Estudiantes, p. 124.

58 Proof that the painting was sold to the Duquesa de Lerma comes in Don Salvador Dalí Cusí's album of cuttings in the Fundació Gala–Salvador Dalí, Figueres, where a letter to Dalí from the Residencia de Estudiantes, dated 4 May 1929, states that *La miel es más dulce que la sangre* was purchased by the duchess for 700 pesetas (vol. II, f. 38). It has frequently been asserted that the painting was subsequently acquired by Coco Chanel, but there is no documentary evidence to support this. Doña Ana Beristain, of the Queen Sofía Art Centre, Madrid, curator of the exhibition *Salvador Dalí. The Early Years*, assured me in 1994 that the Duquesa de Lerma's family has no knowledge of the whereabouts of the work.

59 The painting is reproduced in *MEAC*, II, p. 79.

60 A. García y Bellido, 'Los nuevos pintores españoles. La exposición del Botánico', *GL*, no. 56 (1 April 1929), p. 1; a letter contained in Don Salvador Dalí Cusí's album of cuttings in the Fundació Gala–Salvador Dalí, Figueres, reveals that the painting was sold to the Duchess for 1,000 pesetas.

61 Antonio Méndez Casal, 'Crítica de arte. Comentarios del actual momento', *Blanco y Negro*, Madrid, 7 April 1929.

62 Collection of Don Pere Vehí, Cadaqués.

63 *SVBLD*, p. 203.

64 *BMDS*, p. 109.

65 *SL*, p. 212.

66 Declarations by Denise Tual in BBC Arena's programme *The Life and Times of Don Luis Buñuel*, 1984 (details in Bibliography, Section 7).

67 *SL*, p. 216.

68 'Chronique', *Documents*, Paris, no. 4, September

1929, p. 216; *SL*, p. 213.

69 Pere Artigas, 'Un film d'en Dalí', *Mirador*, Barcelona, I, no. 17 (23 May 1929), p. 6.

70 *SL*, p. 206.

71 *BMDS*, pp. 126–7.

72 Dalí, *Comment on devient Dalí*, p. 138, my translation.

73 Maxime Alexandre, *Mémoires d'un surréaliste* (Paris, La Jeune Parque, 1968), p. 181, quoted by Gateau, *Paul Éluard et le peinture surréaliste*, p. 156.

74 Fernández and Kobuz, p. 82.

75 Sadoul, *Rencontres*, p. 138; an earlier text by Sadoul reveals that he is hopelessly confused between the première of *Un Chien andalou* at the Studio des Ursulines in June 1929 and the film's subsequent commercial run at Studio 28, which began that October (Sadoul, preface to Buñuel's *Viridiana*, pp. 12–13, see Sadoul, Bibliography).

76 *SL*, p. 216.

77 *Ibid.*, p. 213.

78 *UC*, p. 82.

79 Lubar, p. 13.

80 See the useful 'Index of Symbols' in Freud, *Standard Edition*, XXIV, pp. 173–6.

81 *UC*, pp. 131–2, 150; Dalí and Pauwels, pp. 32–3.

82 *SL*, p. 219.

83 Moorhouse, p. 35.

84 *Ibid.*

85 Morla Lynch, p. 310.

86 Francisco Lucientes, '¡Hurra a la vanguardia! El ruidoso "jazz" artístico del Botánico', *Heraldo de Madrid*, 22 March 1929.

87 *SL*, p. 209.

88 *Ibid.*

89 Sylvester, *Magritte*, pp. 120–1.

90 Dalí, 'Documental-Paris-1929', *La Publicitat*, Barcelona, 23 May 1929.

91 Salvador Dalí Cusí's second, unbound book of cuttings at the Fundació Gala–Salvador Dalí, Figueres, f. 39.

92 Sylvester, *Magritte*, p. 181.

93 Dalí, 'Documental-Paris-1929', 7 May 1929.

94 *SL*, p. 217.

95 Éluard, *Lettres à Gala*, pp. 57–76; Gateau, *Paul Éluard, ou Le frère voyant*, pp. 163–4.

96 *SL*, p. 217.

97 *Ibid.*, p. 217; *Sol Ixent*, Cadaqués, no. 144, 15 June 1929, p. 10.

98 *SL*, pp. 214–17.

99 *Ibid.*, p. 213.

100 Volume 2 (unbound) of Don Salvador Dalí's collection of cuttings, f. 40. The physician was Dr Charles Brzezicki, at 88bis, Avenue Parmentier, Paris XIe.

101 The invitation to the première is reproduced by García Buñuel, *Recordando a Luis Buñuel*, p. 80.

102 Louis Chavance, 'Les Influences de "L'Age d'or"', *La Revue du Cinéma*, Paris, no. 19 (1 February 1931), p. 48.

103 *BMDS*, p. 128.

104 'Un Chien andalou', *D'ací i d'allà*, Barcelona, August 1929, p. 273.

105 André Delons, 'Un Chien andalou. Film de Buñuel', *Variétés*, Brussels, 15 July 1929, p. 22.

106 J. Bernard Brunius, '"Un Chien andalou". Film par Louis Buñuel', *Cahiers d'Art*, Paris, no. 5, 1929, pp. 230–1.

107 *Le Merle*, Paris, 28 June 1929, quoted by Murcia, p. 121.

108 *SL*, p. 212.

109 Montes, '"Un Chien andalou"'.

110 *SL*, p. 212.

111 Museu Joan Abelló, Mollet del Vallès (Barcelona).

112 Bouhours and Schoeller, p. 32.

113 *BMDS*, p. 138.

114 Bouhours and Schoeller, p. 31.

115 *Ibid.*

116 Aub, p. 62; see also *BMDS*, pp. 138–9.

117 Etherington-Smith, p. 124; Bouhours and Schoeller, pp. 32–3.

118 Bouhours and Schoeller, p. 32.

119 O.B. [Oswell Blakeston], 'Paris Shorts and Longs', *Close Up*, London, August 1929, pp. 143–4.

120 Gold and Fitzdale, p. 279.

121 *Ibid.*, p. 284, note.

122 Lord, p. 110.

123 *Ibid.*

124 Count Jean-Louis Faucigny-Lucinge interviewed by Patrick Mimouni in his programme for French TV, *Charles et Marie-Laure de Noailles*, 1990.

125 *Ibid.*

126 Aub, p. 336, interview with Charles de Noailles.

127 *BMDS*, p. 138.

128 Dalí, 'Documental-Paris-1929', 28 June 1929, p. 1.

129 *SL*, p. 219.

130 *Ibid.*, pp. 219–20.

131 *Ibid.*, p. 221.

132 Moorhouse, p. 38.

133 Bataille, 'Le "Jeu lugubre"'.

134 Ades, *Dalí*, p. 73.

135 Santos Torroella, *Dalí residente*, pp. 229–30.

136 Gowans's Art Books, no. 47, *The Masterpieces of Ingres*, London and Glasgow, Gowans and Gray, 1913, p. 43.

137 *SVBLD*, pp. 189–91.

138 Moorhouse, p. 38.

139 *Ibid.*

140 Ades, *Dalí*, p. 75.

141 *Ibid.*

142 *Ibid.*, p. 76.

143 *Ibid.*

144 Bataille, 'Le "Jeu lugubre"'.

145 *VPSD*, p. 150.

146 Swinburne, *Atalanta* (1865).

147 *AMD*, p. 141.

148 Sylvester, p. 181.

149 *Sol Ixent*, Cadaqués, 15 August 1929, p. 10.

150 Thirion, p. 192.

151 *UC*, p. 90.

152 Éluard, *Lettres à Gala*, p. 103.

153 *SL*, p. 229.

154 Paul Lorenz, editor of *Plaisirs de Paris*, to Eleanor and Reynolds Morse, as recounted to me by Mrs Eleanor Morse in St Petersburg, Florida, 16 July 1996.

155 Permanyer, 'El pincel erótico de Dalí', p. 163; see also Dalí and Pauwels, p. 266: 'A woman's face, to be erotic, must be acceptably disagreeable.'

156 The phrase comes in *Au Défaut du silence* (1925). See Éluard, *Oeuvres complètes*, I, p. 165.

157 Conversation with Doña María Luisa González, Madrid, 2 November 1991.

158 Conversation with Doña Nanita Kalaschnikoff, Marbella, summer 1996.

159 Navarro Arisa, p. 19.

160 Doña Nanita Kalaschnikoff insists that Dalí always said Gala's mother was Jewish (interviews with Doña Nanita Kalaschnikoff, 1994–5). Mme Cécile Éluard, in my interview with her, Paris, 25 February 1995, denied the allegation hotly. If anyone in the family was Jewish, she said, it was Antonina's man friend.

161 Vieuille, pp. 17–18.

162 Conversation with Mme Cécile Éluard, Paris, 25 February 1995.

163 McGirk, p. 12.

164 Vieuille, p. 11.

165 McGirk, pp. 12–13.

166 Gala's sister Lídia in McGirk, pp. 14–15.

167 McGirk, pp. 13–14.

168 *Ibid.*, p. 19.

169 Éluard, *Lettres à Gala*, p. 374.

170 *Ibid.*, pp. 373, 379–80, 382, 384–5, 386, 387–9, 391, 393.

171 *Ibid.*, p. 387.

172 *Ibid.*, p. 389.

173 *Ibid.*, p. 392.

174 *Ibid.*, p. 391.

175 *Ibid.*, pp. 392–3.

176 McGirk, p. 37. The confidence was made to Henri Pastoureau.

177 There is an excellent colour reproduction of the painting in Gimferrer, *Max Ernst o la dissolució de la identitat*, plate 45.

178 Vieuille, pp. 60–1; *LRS*, no. 5 (15 October 1925),

p. 28. It seems that the painting was destroyed by the Nazis (Vieuille, p. 61).

179 A selection of these drawings was reproduced in *Pleine Marge*, Paris, no. 6 (December 1987), pp. 33–7. For Gala 'la Gale', conversation with David Gascoyne, Isle of Wight, 1994.

180 See for example, those appearing in Valette's *Éluard, Livre d'identité*.

181 Gateau, *Paul Éluard, ou Le frère voyant*, pp. 166–7.

182 McGirk, p. 105.

183 Éluard, *Lettres à Gala*, p. 316.

184 Patrick Waldberg, *Max Ernst chez Paul Éluard*, quoted by Vieuille, p. 58; for 'the Tower', see Vieuille, pp. 61–2.

185 Éluard, *Lettres à Gala*, p. 72.

186 Lear, *Le Dalí d'Amanda*, p. 249.

187 Éluard, *Lettres à Gala*, p. 60.

188 *Ibid.*, p. 64.

189 *Ibid.*, p. 62.

190 *Ibid.*, p. 67.

191 *Ibid.*, pp. 60, 97.

192 *Ibid.*, p. 77; Gateau, *Paul Éluard, ou Le frère voyant*, p. 167.

193 *SL*, pp. 227–34.

194 McGirk, pp. 1–2. No source provided.

195 *SL*, p. 233.

196 *BMDS*, p. 116; Aub, p. 63.

197 Aub, pp. 63–4.

198 *SL*, p. 230.

199 Aub, p. 63.

200 Gateau, *Paul Éluard et la peinture surréaliste*, p. 157.

201 Sylvester, *Magritte*, pp. 181–2. The painting is reproduced in colour at p. 183.

202 Santos Torroella, 'El extraño caso de "El tiempo amenazador"'.

203 Sylvester, *Magritte*, p. 181.

204 *SL*, p. 231.

205 *Ibid.*, p. 230.

206 Dalí, *Le Mythe tragique de l'Angélus de Millet*, p. 100, n. 1.

207 Éluard, *Lettres à Gala*, pp. 86–90.

208 Aub, p. 64; *BMDS*, p. 116.

209 Conversation with Mme Cécile Éluard, Paris, 25 February 1995; Quiñonero, 'Cécile Éluard'.

210 Manuscript of *SL*, Fundació Gala–Salvador Dalí, p. 212.

211 *SL*, pp. 243–5.

212 Romero, *Dedálico Dalí*, p. 56.

213 The first will, dated 5 August 1926, was signed in Figueres in the presence of the notary Salvador Candal y Costa; the second, also in Figueres, in that of the notary Martín Mestres y Borrella. Both are preserved in the 'archivo notarial' of Figueres. My thanks to the then Minister of Culture, Doña Carmen

Alborch, for allowing me to consult these and other family wills, and to the notary responsible for the archive, Don Raimundo Fortuny i Marqués. Also to my good friend, the notary Don José Gómez de la Serna, whose detailed commentaries on the wills have been of immense help to me.

214 *SL*, p. 248; Éluard, *Lettres à Gala*, p. 89.

215 *SL*, pp. 248–9.

216 Descharnes, *Dalí*, p. 68.

217 Permanyer, 'El pincel erótico de Dalí'.

218 *SL*, p. 242.

219 My translation from *Comment on devient Dalí*, p. 113: 'Des gueules de lions traduisent mon effroi devant la révélation de la possession d'un sexe de femme qui va aboutir à la révélation de mon impuissance. Je me préparais au choc en retour de ma honte.'

220 Moorhouse, p. 40.

221 Descharnes, *Dalí*, p. 68.

222 The painting is reproduced in *DOH*, p. 95.

223 For a brilliant discussion of this painting, see Gee (Bibliography, Section 6). Some years earlier Dalí could have seen a reproduction in *LRS*, no. 4 (July 1925), p. [133]. Dawn Ades, *Dalí*, p. 69, reminds us that Éluard also had Chiricos. But it was Ernst's picture that 'seems above all to have cast its spell over Dalí'.

224 Rubin, *Dada, Surrealism, and their Heritage*, p. 113.

225 See Janis, 'Painting as a Key to Psychoanalysis'.

226 Ades, *Dalí*, p. 80.

227 Dalí, *Le Mythe tragique de l'Angélus . . .* , p. 57.

228 Descharnes, *The World of Salvador Dalí*, p. 154. For other references to the pebbles of Confitera, *ibid.*, pp. 52, 54, 56, 62, 63, 132, 160.

229 A good reproduction is included in *Salvador Dalí. The Early Years* (see Bibliography, Section 1), p. 182.

230 For Mauclaire and Studio 28, Bouhours and Schoeller, p. 31, n. 2; a copy of Studio 28's programme giving details of the films scheduled was included in the exhibition *¿Buñuel! La mirada del siglo*, Madrid, 1996.

231 Dalí, 'Un Chien andalou', in *Mirador*, Barcelona, no. 39 (24 October 1929), p. 6; a long quotation from Dalí's article was reproduced in *GL*, 1 November 1929, p. 5, with the announcement that the film would soon be seen in Madrid.

232 Gasch, 'Les obres recents de Salvador Dalí'. See also *La Nau*, Barcelona, 30 October 1929; A.F., 'L'argument de "Un chien andalou"', *La Publicitat*, Barcelona, 30 October 1929; *La Noche*, Barcelona, 30 October 1929 (Guillermo Díaz Plaja); Joan Margarit, 'Entorn d'*Un Chien andalou*', *Mirador*, Barcelona, 21 November 1929, p. 6.

233 *SL*, p. 249.

234 The first reference to the title *La Bête andalouse*

comes in a letter from Buñuel to Charles de Noailles dated 15 March 1930 (Bouhours and Schoeller, p. 63).

235 Bouhours and Schoeller, p. 118, n. 1.

236 Conversations with Doña María Luisa González, Madrid, 1994.

237 *BMDS*, p. 268. The edition in question must have been that published in Berlin in 1904 by the sexologist Iwan Bloch under the pseudonym Eugen Dühren. Only 180 copies were issued. The imprint was false: *Paris, Club des Bibliophiles* (Sade, *Les 120 Journées de Sodome*, p. 21).

238 *BMDS*, pp. 268–70.

239 In *SL*, p. 254, Dalí says the paintings were sold for between 6,000 and 12,000 francs.

240 The reunion is not described in *SL*; a few details are provided in *UC*, p. 99.

241 Dalí, 'No veo nada, nada en torno del paisaje. Poema'. The cutting is not included, perhaps significantly, in Don Salvador Dalí Cusí's album.

242 Dalí, 'Posiciò moral del surrealismo'; Del Arco, pp. 65–6.

243 André Breton's preface, entitled 'Stériliser Dalí', is reproduced in *Salvador Dalí* (Pompidou catalogue), pp. 124–5.

244 E. Tériade, 'Les Expositions', in *L'Intransigeant*, Paris, 25 November 1929. Cutting included in Don Salvador Dalí's album. Quoted in *VPSD*, p. 22.

245 'Le Rapin', *Comoedia*, Paris, 2 December 1929.

246 Flouquet, 'Salvador Dalí. Galerie Goemans, 49 rue de Seine', *Monde*, Paris, 30 November 1929; 'Les lletres. Meridians', *La Publicitat*, Barcelona, 6 December 1929, p. 5.

247 *SL*, p. 251.

248 *Ibid.*

249 'Crónica local' in *El Eco de Sitges*, no. 2268 (24 November 1919), p. 3. The same information was contained a few days later in the *Gaseta de Sitges*, no. 22 (1 December 1929), p. 5 ('Cap de la vila').

250 *SL*, pp. 251–2.

251 *UC*, p. 99.

252 *BMDS*, pp. 139–40.

253 *AMD*, p. 142.

254 Eugenio d'Ors, 'El juego lúgubre y el doble juego', *GL*, 15 December 1929, p. 3. Anna Maria Dalí believed that d'Ors also published the article in the Barcelona *La Vanguardia* (Aub, p. 539), but this was not the case. It does seem likely, however, that it appeared somewhere else before being published in *La Gaceta Literaria*.

255 Santos Torroella, 'La trágica vida de Dalí', p. 3.

256 *SDFGL*, p. 95.

257 Bouhours and Schoeller, p. 37.

258 *Ibid.*, p. 40; the presence of the two friends in Cadaqués was duly noted by *Sol Ixent*, the local fort-

nightly paper, on 15 December.

259 *SL*, p. 253.

260 Bouhours and Schoeller, p. 40; for Buñuel's presence in Madrid, 'Boletín del Cineclub', *GL*, 15 December 1929, p. 5, and Alberti, *La arboleda perdida*, p. 283.

261 *SL*, p. 254.

Eight: Paris, Gala and *L'Age d'or* (1929–30)

1 Bouhours and Schoeller, p. 44.

2 The screenplay had appeared first in *La Revue du Cinéma*, Paris, no. 5 (15 November 1929), pp. 2–16, in circumstances that Buñuel recalls in *BMDS*, pp. 130–2. The translation from the Spanish, ascribed to Maxime Zvoinski, tallies almost word for word with that published in *LRS*.

3 *LRS*, no. 12 (15 December 1929), p. 34.

4 Breton, *Entretiens*, Paris, Gallimard, 1952, p. 159, quoted by Pierre, 'Breton et Dalí', p. 132.

5 Breton, *Second Manifeste du surréalisme*, *Oeuvres complètes*, I, p. 793.

6 *Ibid.*, p. 791.

7 The frontispiece is reproduced in *Salvador Dalí* (Pompidou catalogue), p. 133. For publication details of the *Second Manifeste* in book form, see Breton, *Oeuvres complètes*, I, p. lxii.

8 A Surrealist game with folded paper consisting in the making of phrases or drawings by several people, each of whom is unaware of the preceding contribution. The example which gave its name to the game was the phrase 'Le cadavre—exquis—boira—le vin—nouveau'. 'The exquisite—corpse—will drink—the new—wine'.

9 Dalí's filmscript is on permanent loan to the Scottish National Gallery of Modern Art, Edinburgh. It has been published by Dawn Ades (see Bibliography, Section 6).

10 *SL*, p. 257.

11 Éluard, *Lettres à Gala*, pp. 90–1; there is a photograph of the hotel in *VPSD*, p. 23.

12 Éluard, *Lettres à Gala*, pp. 91–2. Postmarked 16 January 1930.

13 *SL*, p. 263; *UC*, pp. 99–101.

14 The drawing is reproduced in *SL*, p. 263; *BMDS*, p. 227.

15 *SL*, pp. 262–4.

16 *Ibid.*, p. 264.

17 Bouhours and Schoeller, pp. 48–9.

18 *SL*, pp. 267–8.

19 The letter is in the Noailles archive at the Musée National d'Art Moderne (Centre Pompidou), Paris.

20 Bouhours and Schoeller, pp. 59–60.

21 A photograph of the letter is printed in *VPSD*, p. 23.

22 The letters are preserved in the Filmoteca Nacional, Madrid, and were first transcribed and published, with accompanying photocopies, in *SVBLD*, pp. 237–44. Buñuel's half of the correspondence is unknown.

23 Bouhours and Schoeller, p. 60.

24 Sánchez Vidal, 'The Andalusian Beasts', p. 197.

25 The allusion is to Lubitsch's film *Lady Windermere's Fan* (1925), reviewed by Buñuel in *GL*, 1 April 1927.

26 Filmoteca Nacional, Madrid, documents R. 305 and R. 307; a photocopy of R. 305 is reproduced in *SVBLD*, p. 238.

27 Filmoteca Nacional, Madrid, document R. 306; a photocopy of the document is reproduced in *SVBLD*, p. 239.

28 Filmoteca Nacional, Madrid, document R. 308.

29 'Tellement longtemps que je t'attendais. Quelle joie! Quelle joie d'avoir assassiné nos enfants!' 'Mon amour!' (six times). My transcription from the sound track. It appears that the six-fold exclamation in off was spoken by Paul Éluard. For the full text of the shooting script, see Buñuel in bibliography.

30 *BMDS*, p. 140.

31 *SVBLD*, p. 246.

32 Bouhours and Schoeller, pp. 59–60.

33 *Ibid.*, p. 177.

34 Von Maur, p. 196.

35 For the date of departure, Éluard, *Lettres à Gala*, p. 421, n. 3 to letter 71.

36 *SL*, p. 268.

37 Land Registry Office, Roses, property (*finca*) number 1714, vol. 1157, f. 101.

38 *Ibid.*, f. 102. This document shows that the deeds of the purchase were signed in Figueres on 20 August 1930 in the presence of the notary public Francisco Lovaco y de Ledesma.

39 Miravitlles, *Contra la cultura burguesa*, p. 55.

40 There seems to be a word missing in the phrase 'parallelament als procediments'. The general sense suggests 'demoralizing'.

41 This whole paragraph is a gloss on a passage in Freud's *Totem and Taboo*, Standard Edition, vol. XIII, p. 60; Spanish edition, *Obras completas*, vol. VIII (1923), pp. 91–3.

42 The text has 'familiars'. It looks like a misprint, but for what?

43 Dalí is here venting the scorn for the Catalan dramatist that Gasch and Montanyà had made him restrain when the three were preparing the final draft of *The Anti-Art Manifesto in* 1927.

44 What he actually wrote, as we have seen, was

'Parfois je crache par plaisir sur le portrait de ma mère', 'Sometimes I spit for pleasure on the portrait of my mother'.

45 *Invisible Sleeping Woman, Horse, Lion, etc.* A photograph of the drawing, irreparably damaged soon afterwards, is published in *DOH*, p. 100.

46 Dalí would later prefer the term 'hypnagogic images'.

47 The text was printed in *Hélix*, Vilafranca de Penedés, no. 10 (March 1930), pp. 4–6 and is reproduced in facsimile by Molas, pp. 364–8. The manuscript, which would help us to clear up the doubtful readings, is unknown.

48 Miravitlles, *Contra la cultura burguesa*, p. 55.

49 Gasch, *L'expansió de l'art català al món*, p. 156.

50 *La Publicitat*, Barcelona, 23 March 1930, p. 8. I have found no reference to the lecture in *La Vanguardia, La Noche* or *El Día Gráfico*.

51 *SL*, p. 321.

52 *Ibid.*, p. 308.

53 Dalí, 'La Chèvre sanitaire', dated 13 August 1930 and included in *La Femme visible*.

54 In 'about 1933', according to Ades, p. 121.

55 Dalí to Paloma Chamorro in 1979 on the Spanish TV programme *Imágenes* (see Bibliography, Section 7).

56 *DG*, p. 195.

57 Ades, *Dalí*, p. 122.

58 Freud, *Standard Edition*, vol. xvi, p. 308.

59 Roudinesco, pp. 56–7.

60 *SL*, pp. 17–18. Dalí is under the impression that Lacan contacted him after reading his 'prologue' to the *Angelus* essay in *Minotaure* in 1933, but Roudinesco's account of their earlier meeting is much more convincing.

61 Roudinesco, p. 85.

62 Permanyer, 'Cuando Dalí no era divino ni arcángelico'.

63 *Dalí joven* (see Bibliography, Section 1), pp. 39–40.

64 Bouhours and Schoeller, pp. 66, 177.

65 *Salvador Dalí. The Early Years* (see Bibliography, Section 1), p. 44.

66 Bouhours and Schoeller, p. 66.

67 *Sol Ixent*, Cadaqués, no. 164 (5 May 1930), p. 6.

68 Jealously guarded by Anna Maria Dalí for decades in a biscuit tin, the film is now at the Filmoteca de Catalunya, Barcelona.

69 Descharnes, *The World of Salvador Dalí*, p. 156; *DOH*, p. 92.

70 Éluard, *Lettres à Gala*, pp. 99–100.

71 *SL*, p. 272.

72 Entitled 'Homenaje a Góngora', it is dated 1927 and is very similar to others done that summer when Lorca was in Cadaqués.

73 *SL*, p. 272.

74 Éluard, *Lettres à Gala*, pp. 99–104.

75 *SL*, pp. 272–3; *La Unión Mercantil*, Malaga, 15 April 1930, 'Notas de sociedad', p. 15.

76 Lacuey, p. 125.

77 Tomás García, *Y todo fue distinto*; telephone conversation with Don Tomás García, 16 May 1995; *SL*, p. 275.

78 *SL*, p. 274.

79 Cano, *Los cuadernos de Adrián Dale*, pp. 70–1.

80 Tomás García, pp. [9–10].

81 Sánchez Rodríguez, pp. 166–7.

82 *Ibid.*, p. 170.

83 Altolaguirre 'Gala y Dalí, en Torremolinos'.

84 Cano, *Los cuadernos de Adrián Dale*, pp. 70–1.

85 Carmona, p. [11].

86 Aleixandre was in Malaga at the time, his departure being noted in *La Unión Mercantil* on 10 May, 1930, p. 12.

87 Carmona, pp. [6–7]; Cano, *Los cuadernos de Adrián Dale*, pp. 69–70.

88 *SL*, p. 276; Carmona, pp. [10–11]; Cano, *Los cuadernos de Adrián Dale*, p. 69.

89 Santos Torroella, '"Las rosas sangrantes" y la imposible descendencia de Dalí'; *The Bleeding Roses* is reproduced in *DOH*, p. 107.

90 Éluard, *Lettres à Gala*, pp. 99–113.

91 *La Unión Mercantil*, Malaga, 22 May 1930, 'Notas de sociedad', p. 12.

92 Giménez Caballero, '¡¡Dalí!! ¡Querido Dalí!'. The original of the film is in the Filmoteca Nacional, Madrid.

93 Moreiro, p. 21.

94 Natalía Jiménez de Cossío, in *Poesía. Revista ilustrada de información poética*, Madrid, nos 18–19, 1983, p. 120.

95 Aranda, p. 104.

96 See Sánchez Vidal, 'De *L'Age d'or* à la ruée vers l'or', pp. 19–21.

97 *BMDS*, p. 140.

98 *VPSD*, p. 23.

99 Bouhours and Schoeller, p. 74.

100 *Ibid.*, p. 80.

101 Éluard, *Lettres à Gala*, p. 115.

102 *Ibid.*, pp. 116–17 and n. 3 (p. 426).

103 *Ibid.*, p. 116.

104 *Ibid.*, pp. 117–18.

105 *Ibid.*, p. 120.

106 *Ibid.*, pp. 425–6, n. 13; Char, p. lxvii.

107 Santos Torroella reproduces the photograph in *Salvador Dalí, corresponsal de J.V. Foix*, p. [49].

108 Dalí, 'La Chèvre sanitaire', in *La Femme visible*, pp. [21–34].

109 Dalí, 'Intellectuals castillans et catalans—Expositions—Arrestation d'un exhibitionniste dans le

métro'.

110 Éluard, *Lettres à Gala*, pp. 123–4.

111 Bouhours and Schoeller, p. 83.

112 *BMDS*, p. 142.

113 Bouhours and Schoeller, pp. 82–4.

114 Jean Cocteau, 'La Vie d'un poète', *Le Figaro*, Paris, 9 November 1930, p. 6.

115 Bouhours and Schoeller, p. 82; 'Notas del puerto', *La Prensa*, New York, 3 November 1930, p. 8; letter from Juan Vicéns to León Sánchez Cuesta, Paris, 29 October 1928 (Sánchez Cuesta archive, Residencia de Estudiantes, Madrid). The latter shows that Buñuel was accompanied on the crossing by the Spanish humourist Antonio de Lara ('Tono') and his wife, Leonor.

116 Buñuel, *Obra literaria* (ed. Sanchez Vidal), p. 32, and *BMDS*, p. 193.

117 Conversation with Don Rafael Alberti, Madrid, 4 October 1980.

118 The catalogue is reproduced in *Salvador Dalí. The Early Years* (see Bibliography, Section 1), p. 47.

119 Dalí's manuscript of the programme notes is among the Noailles papers preserved in the Musée National d'Art Moderne (Centre Pompidou), Paris, and is reproduced by Bouhours and Schoeller, pp. 84, 86–7. For the text, see *Salvador Dalí* (Pompidou catalogue), p. 100.

120 The words 'with Buñuel' were added, according to Bouhours, by André Breton. See Sánchez Vidal, 'The Andalusian Beasts', p. 200.

121 Dalí's footnote: 'Majorcans: inhabitants of the island of Majorca (Spain)'.

122 Dalí's footnote: 'In this film we also see, among other things, a blind man being mistreated, a dog being battered, a son being killed almost gratuitously by his father, an old woman being slapped in the face, etc.'

123 This account is compiled from the four-page pamphlet 'L'Affaire de *L'Age d'or*' (reproduced in *Salvador Dalí*, Pompidou catalogue, p. 115, and, in facsimile, in García Buñuel, between pp. 80 and 81) and from Dalí's letter to Noailles written the following day (see note 125). The audience's protest note is reproduced by Bouhours and Schoeller, p. 103.

124 Jean-Placide Mauclaire, the medical student who founded Studio 28 in 1928.

125 Bouhours and Schoeller, pp. 92–4.

126 *La Revue du Cinéma*, Paris, supplement to no. 8, 1 March 1930. For film censorship in Paris at the time, see Georges Altman, 'La Censure contre le cinéma', *ibid*., no. 19 (1 February 1931), pp. 36–7.

127 Cuttings reproduced by Bouhours and Schoeller, p. [174].

128 *Ibid.*, p. [176].

129 Jean-Paul Dreyfus, '*L'Age d'or*, par Louis Buñuel, scénario de Louis Buñuel et Salvador Dalí', *La Revue du Cinéma*, Paris, no. 17, 1 December 1930, pp. 55–6.

130 Leon Moussinac, 'Notre point de vue. *L'Age d'or*', *L'Humanité*, Paris, 7 December 1930, p. 2.

131 Louis Chavance, 'Les Influences de *L'Age d'or*', *La Revue du Cinéma*, Paris, no. 19 (1 February 1931), pp. 48–50.

132 Bouhours and Schoeller, p. 94.

133 Details from 'L'Affaire de *L'Age d'or*' (see n. 123 above). For Chiappe, see Andrews, p. 78.

134 Cuttings reproduced in Bouhours and Schoeller, p. [175].

135 Bouhours and Schoeller, p. 105; *BMDS*, p. 142.

136 The full text of the programme is reprinted in *Salvador Dalí* (Pompidou catalogue), pp. 110–14. It is signed by Maxime Alexandre, Aragon, Breton, René Char, René Crevel, Dalí, Éluard, Péret, Sadoul, Thirion, Tristan Tzara, Pierre Unik and Albert Valentin.

137 *BMDS*, pp. 296–7.

138 'Protesta surrealista contra Luis Buñuel', *Abc*, Madrid, 10 December 1930.

139 E.G.C. [Ernesto Giménez Caballero], 'El escándalo de *L'Age d'or* en Paris. Palabras con Salvador Dalí'.

140 For the illustrations, see *VPSD*, p. 24; for the blurb, Breton, *Oeuvres complètes*, I, p. 1632.

141 Éluard, *Oeuvres complètes*, II, pp. 827–8.

142 The will was signed in the presence of the Figueres notary Francisco Lovaco y de Ledesma, and is preserved in the Notarial Archive of the town. My thanks to the present notary Don Raimundo Fortuny i Marqués for providing me with a copy.

143 *André Breton. La Beauté convulsive* (see Bibliography, Section 3), p. 195; Lenier, p. xv.

144 The two sketches are reproduced in colour in the Stuttgart catalogue *Salvador Dalí, 1904–1989* (see Bibliography, Section 1), pp. 84–5. Details of the project in Thirion, pp. 267–8.

Nine: The Great Breakthrough (1931–5)

1 Jackson, pp. 30–4.

2 *Au Feu!* is reproduced by Nadeau, *Histoire du surréalisme. Documents surréalistes*, pp. 184–6.

3 I am grateful to the Museo Nacional Centro de Arte Reina Sofía, Madrid, for providing me with a photocopy of the catalogue, an extract from which is reproduced in *VPSD*, p. 26.

4 *SL*, p. 317.

5 *Ibid.*

6 Moorhouse, p. 20.

7   *UC*, p. 72; Permanyer, 'El pincel erótico de Dalí'; Romero, *Dedálico Dalí*, p. 57.

8   *UC*, p. 24.

9   I am grateful to Peter Tush, Curator of Education at the Salvador Dali Museum, St Petersburg, Florida, for supplying me with a transcription of these legends and other close-up details of the painting. 'Chienalie' might conceivably mean 'dog on the bed', an allusion to the scene in *Un Chien andalou* where the protagonist suddenly materializes on the bed. 'Chanasie' could just possibly refer to the 'Assyrian dog' in Lorca's chilling poem 'Paisaje con dos tumbas y un perro asirio' ('Landscape with Two Tombs and an Assyrian Dog'), written in New York and perhaps sent to the painter.

10   *SL*, p. 308.

11   Santos Torroella, 'Giménez Caballero y Dalí', p. 55; Dalí, *Un diari: 1919–1920*, p. 98.

12   Santos Torroella, 'Giménez Caballero y Dalí', p. 56; Giménez Caballero, *Yo, inspector de alcantarillas*, p. 70.

13   The painting is reproduced in Gowans's Art Books no. 41 (*Masterpieces of Masaccio* ['sic']), pp. 13–15, so Dalí may have been familiar with it from his childhood; it is also reproduced in *LRS*, no. 8 (December 1926), p. [276]), where he very likely saw it.

14   Ernst, 'Danger de pollution', *LSASDLR*, no. 3 (December 1931), pp. 22–5.

15   See, for example, *The Font*, 1930 (Morse Catalogue, no. 36); the frontispiece to *La Femme Visible*, 1930 (*DOH*, p. 105); the frontispiece to the *Second Surrealist Manifesto*, 1930 (Dalí, Stuttgart catalogue, p. 80); *Dessin érotique*, 1931 (*Salvador Dalí*, Pompidou catalogue, p. 168, no. 98); *Paul-Gala*, drawing, 1932 (Stuttgart catalogue, p. 86).

16   Levy, *Memoir of an Art Gallery, passim*.

17   *Ibid*., pp. 70–1; *SL*, p. 318.

18   Levy, *Memoir of an Art Gallery*, p. 72.

19   *Art News*, New York, 16 January 1932.

20   Levy, *Memoir of an Art Gallery*, pp. 76–83.

21   *Ibid*., p. 72.

22   *SL*, p. 326.

23   [Ernesto Giménez Caballero], 'Robinson habla de arte, teatro', *GL*, no. 112 (15 August 1931), p. 10.

24   Crevel, *Lettres de désir et de souffrance*, pp. 325–6, 329; Éluard, *Lettres à Gala*, p. 145.

25   Buot, p. 301.

26   Crevel, *Lettres de désir et de souffrance*, pp. 330–2; 'Benvinguda', *Empordà Federal*, Figueres, 15 August 1931.

27   Buot, pp. 302–3.

28   Thirion, p. 207.

29   *DOH*, p. 108.

30   Secrest, p. 131.

31   Buot, p. 305.

32   *Ibid*.

33   Guzmán, p. 411.

34   'A la recerca d'una nova moral', *L'hora. Setmanari d'avançada*, Barcelona, no. 38 (25 September 1931), p. 7.

35   The synopsis of the lecture published in *LSAS-DLR*, no. 3 (December 1931), pp. 35–6, differs considerably from that given in *L'hora* (see previous note) and seems to have been a highly revised version of what he said; for Crevel's account, *Lettres de désir et de souffrance*, p. 334.

36   See previous note. José Ortega y Gasset and Dr Gregorio Marañón were two of the leading Republican intellectuals of the day.

37   Miravitlles, *Contra la cultura burguesa*, p. 30.

38   Biro and Passeron, p. 306.

39   *LRS*, no. 1 (1 December 1924), p. 1.

40   Breton, 'Introduction au discours sur le peu de réalité', *Oeuvres complètes*, II, p. 277.

41   *LRS*, no. 11 (15 March 1928), p. 8.

42   Dalí, 'Revista de tendències anti-artistiques'.

43   Thirion, p. 295.

44   *LSASDLR*, no. 3 (December 1931), p. 22.

45   *Ibid*., p. 36.

46   An excellent colour photograph of this, one of the most disturbing Surrealist Objects ever produced, is printed in *André Breton. La Beauté convulsive* (see Bibliography, Section 3), p. 284.

47   *Ibid*., p. 286 (black and white).

48   Dalí, 'Objets surréalistes'.

49   Santos Torroella (ed.), *Salvador Dalí corrsponsal de J.V. Foix*, pp. 62–5.

50   Dalí, 'The Object as Revealed in Surrealist Experiment'.

51   Letter postmarked Cadaqués 3 October 1932. Fonds Breton, Bibliothèque Littéraire Jacques Doucet, Paris.

52   Dalí, 'Objets psycho-atmosphériques-anamophiques'.

53   *LSASDLR*, no. 4 (December 1931), pp. 31–6.

54   Éluard, *Lettres à Gala*, letter 126 and n. 1, p. 436 for quote from Alexandre's *Mémoires d'un surréaliste*; Breton, II, p. 23, note, and *Conversations: the Autobiography of Surrealism*, p. 131.

55   Thirion, p. 315.

56   'Tandis qu'Aymas-Maurras sont libres . . . Louis Aragon inculpé de "provocation au meurtre" pour un poème exaltant la lutte du prolétariat parisien', *L'Humanité*, Paris, 17 January 1932, p. 3.

57   'L'inculpation d'Aragon', *L'Humanité*, Paris, 9 February 1932, p. 2.

58   Breton, *Oeuvres complètes*, II, p. 23. Dalí's account of 'The Aragon Affair', not entirely accurate, is given in *UC*, p. 118.

59   Letter postmarked Cadaqués 5 March 1932. Fonds

Breton, Bibliothèque Littéraire Jacques Doucet, Paris.

60 See Aleksic, *Dalí: inédits de Belgrade*.

61 *Ibid.*, pp. 55–60.

62 Levy, *Memoir of an Art Gallery*, p. 73.

63 Santos Torroella (ed.), *Salvador Dalí corrsponsal de J. V. Foix*, pp. 58–61; for Valentine Hugo's recollection, Romero, *Dédalico Dalí*, p. 70 and note; the 'cadavre exquis' is reproduced by Aleksic, frontispiece.

64 Gasch, 'L'esperit nou', *La Publicitat*, Barcelona, 15 April 1932.

65 Gasch, *L'expansió del català al mon*, p. 156.

66 The late Doña Caritat Gasch, the critic's widow, refused to allow the present writer to see the letters from Dalí to her husband. Those from Gasch to Dalí seem to have disappeared, only a handful of them being preserved among Dalí's papers at the Fundació Gala–Salvador Dalí, Figueres.

67 *La Publicitat*, Barcelona; see Santos Torroella (ed.), *Salvador Dalí corresponsal de J.V. Foix*, p. 64, n. 1.

68 Dalí, *Le Mythe tragique de l'Angélus de Millet*, p. 101.

69 The fragment has been published by Aleksic, pp. 41–52; Santos Torroella (ed.), *Salvador Dalí corresponsal de J.V. Foix*, pp. 85–6.

70 Éluard, *Lettres à Gala*, letter 148, n. 1, p. 444; *SL*, p. 324.

71 'Prière d'insérer' to the 1978 edition of the filmscript (Barcelona, Editorial Labor), p. 10.

72 Lear, *Le Dalí d'Amanda*, p. 54.

73 *Dictionnaire abrégé du surréalisme*, p. 5.

74 Ades, *Dalí*, p. 202.

75 Éluard, *Lettres à Gala*, letter 145, n. 5, p. 443; Santos Torroella (ed.), *Salvador Dalí corresponsal de J.V. Foix*, p. 74, n. 1; Bouhours and Schoeller, p. 158. *André Breton. La Beauté convulsive* (Bibliography, Section 3), p. 205.

76 Santos Torroella (ed.), *Salvador Dalí corresponsal de J.V. Foix*, p. 69, n. 5.

77 Letter postmarked Cadaqués, 3 October 1932. Fonds Breton, Bibliothèque Littéraire Jacques Doucet, Paris.

78 Santos Torroella (ed.), *Salvador Dalí corresponsal de J.V. Foix*, pp. 78–81.

79 Éluard, *Lettres à Gala*, letter 145, n. 6, p. 443; the article is reproduced in French translation in *Salvador Dalí* (Pompidou catalogue), pp. 215–20.

80 Crosby, p. 136; the illustration is reproduced in *Devour The Fire: The Selected Poems of Harry Crosby*, introduction by Sy M. Kahn (Berkeley, Twowindows Press, 1983), p.vii.

81 *In Transition: A Paris Anthology*, London, Secker and Warburg, 1990, p. 223.

82 Crosby, pp. 191–7.

83 *Ibid.*, pp. 174–7. For more information on the Crosbys see Conover and Wolff in the Bibliography.

84 Levy, *Memoir of an Art Gallery*, p. 131.

85 *SL*, p. 326.

86 See, for example, *SL*, pp. 249–50, 320.

87 *Ibid.*, p. 327.

88 *Ibid.*

89 Faucigny-Lucinge interviewed in the BBC 'Arena' programme *Dalí*, 1986 (see Bibliography, Section 7).

90 Green, 'Los años mágicos', pp. 8–9.

91 Green, *Oeuvres complètes*, IV, p. 207; Anne Green's previous acquaintance with Dalí is recorded in Green, 'Los años mágicos', p. 8; for details of this little-known Dalí exhibition at Pierre Colle, see Santos Torroella (ed.), *Salvador Dalí corresponsal de J.V. Foix*, p. 87.

92 Green, *Oeuvres complètes*, IV, p. 209; Green, 'Los años mágicos', p. 8.

93 Éluard, *Lettres à Gala*, p. 433, n. 1.

94 *VPSD*, p. 32.

95 Green, *Oeuvres complètes*, IV, pp. 226–7; English translation, *Diary 1928–1957* (London, Collins Harvill, 1975), p. 35, quoted by Etherington-Smith, p. 194.

96 The painting is reproduced in *DOH*, p. 143.

97 Green, 'Los años mágicos', p. 9.

98 Information on sleeve of the facsimile reprint of Skira's review *Minotaure*, vol. II (see Bibliography, Section 8).

99 *VPSD*, p. 32.

100 Skira, *Vingt Ans d'activité*, p. 67.

101 *DG*, p. 31.

102 Undated letter in Skira Archives, Geneva, quoted by Mason, p. 27.

103 Telegram from Dalí to Skira, *ibid.*

104 *Ibid.*

105 Undated letter, *ibid.*

106 Mason, pp. 8–10, 62–3; Michler and Löpsinger, p. 128.

107 Porcel, p. 204.

108 It is reproduced by Mason, p. 51.

109 Mason, pp. 50–6.

110 *SL*, p. 64 and note.

111 Dalí, *Le Mythe tragique de l'Angélus de Millet*, p. 17.

112 Santos Torroella (ed.), *Salvador Dalí corresponsal de J.V. Foix*, p. 91.

113 Lacan, 'Le Problème du style et la conception psychiatrique des formes paranoïaques de l'expérience'.

114 Dalí, *Le Mythe tragique de l'Angélus de Millet*, p. 17.

115 *Ibid.*, p. 89.

116 *Ibid.*, p. 57.

117 *Ibid.*, p. 51.

118 Dalí's catalogue notes to the exhibition held to launch Skira's edition of *The Songs of Maldoror*, reproduced in *Salvador Dalí* (Pompidou catalogue), pp. 331–2, and incorporated as an appendix to *Le Mythe*

tragique de l'Angélus de Millet, pp. 93–7.

119 For the full series of Dalí's *Maldoror* illustrations, the best reproductions are provided by *Salvador Dalí* (Pompidou catalogue), pp. 335–9, and Michler and Löpsinger, pp. 128–34.

120 Caption to the reproduction of the picture in Plate VI.

121 Conversation with Doña Nanita Kalaschnikoff, Figueres, August 1995.

122 *VPSD*, pp. 34–5.

123 I am very grateful to the Salvador Dali Museum in Florida for supplying me with a photocopy of the catalogue. Dalí's open letter to Breton is reproduced in *Salvador Dalí* (Pompidou catalogue), pp. 178–80.

124 Georges Hilaire in *Beaux-Arts*, Paris, 30 June 1933, quoted in *VPSD*, pp. 34–6.

125 Letter postmarked Cadaqués, 29 July 1933. Fonds Breton, Bibliothèque Littéraire Jacques Doucet, Paris.

126 Santos Torroella (ed.), *Salvador Dalí corresponsal de J.V. Foix*, p. 108, n. 2.

127 Dalí, 'De la Beauté terrifiante et comestible de l'architecture "modern" style', p. 69.

128 M.A. Cassanyes, 'El pintor Modest Urgell', *La Publicitat*, Barcelona, 8 October 1933, reprinted in Spanish by Santos Torroella in *Salvador Dalí corresponsal de J.V. Foix*, pp.179–80.

129 Fonds Breton, Bibliothèque Littéraire Jacques Doucet, Paris.

130 Green, *Oeuvres complètes*, IV, p. 267.

131 Levy, *Memoir of an Art Gallery*, p. 75.

132 Santos Torroella (ed.), *Salvador Dalí corresponsal de J.V. Foix*, p. 118, n. 4.

133 The exhibition catalogue lists the following works (I have marked those previously shown at Colle's with an asterisk):

1. *Cannibal Nostalgia (Instantaneous Image)**
2. *Coiffure Distressed by Persistent Fair Weather**
3. *Instantaneous Presence of a Hypnogogical Atmospherocephalic Slipper and of a Cranial Mouth**
4. *Myself At the Age of Ten When I Was the Grasshopper Child**
5. *Atavisms at Twilight (Obsessional Phenomenon)**
6. *An Average Atmospherxocephalic Bureaucrat in the Attitude of Milking a Cranial Harp**
7. *Surrealist Architecture**
8. *The Photographic-Atmospheric Brain**
9. *Gala and the Angelus of Millet Immediately Preceding the Coming of the 'Anamorphous* [sic] *Cones'**
10. *The Invisible Man*
11. *The Enigma of William Tell*
12. *The Angelus of the Afternoon*
13. *Enigmatic Portrait of Gala*
14. *Sentimental Souvenir** (lent by Emilio Terry)
15. *Convalescence of a Cleptomaniac*
16. *Remorse*
17. *Surrealist Effect*
18. *Necessary Haemorrhage*
19. *The Prolonged Day*
20. *Diurnal Illusions*
21. *Heterosexual Life*
22. *In Memory of a Young Child*
23. *The Sensation of Speed*
24. *The Font*
25. *Surrealist Landscape* (lent by Mrs Harry Crosby)
26. *Temptation of Saint Anthony*, by Hieronymous Bosch (Flemish 1460–1518)

134 Levy, Memoir of an Art Gallery, p. 75.

135 Lewis Mumford quoted in *MEAC*, II, p. 100.

136 Santos Torroella (ed.), *Salvador Dalí corresponsal de J.V. Foix*, p. 117.

137 The catalogue is reproduced in *ibid.*, p. [50].

138 Cassanyes had already expressed his appreciation of *The Enigma of William Tell* in the article referred to in n. 128.

139 M.A. Cassanyes, 'Dalí o l'antiqualitat', *La Publicitat*, Barcelona, 22 December 1933. Reprinted in Spanish by Santos Torroella, *Salvador Dalí corresponsal de J.V. Foix*, pp.177–9.

140 J.C. [Just Cabot], 'Una exposició i un llibre', *Mirador*, Barcelona, no. 257 (4 January 1934), p. 7.

141 Undated letter from Breton to Dalí, National Gallery of Scotland, Edinburgh.

142 Brassaï, pp. 41–2.

143 *Nouvelle Revue Française*, Paris, no. 246 (1 March 1934), p. 565, quoted in Éluard, *Lettres à Gala*, letter 190, n. 3, p. 460.

144 Stein, *Everybody's Autobiography*, pp. 11–12.

145 *Ibid.*, pp. 17–18.

146 Brassaï, p. 44.

147 Fonds Breton, Bibliothèque Littéraire Jacques Doucet, Paris.

148 Dalí, 'L'énigme de Salvador Dalí', in *XXe Siècle*, December 1974, quoted in *Salvador Dalí* (Pompidou catalogue), p. 162.

149 Letter dated 25 January 1934, National Gallery of Scotland, Edinburgh.

150 Éluard, *Lettres à Gala*, p. 191.

151 Copy of the marriage certificate supplied by the Parquet de Tribunal de Grande Instance de Paris, 10 December 1996. I am extremely grateful to my friends Eutimio Martín, Antonio Portunet and Gérard Dufour for the immense trouble to which they went in order to convince the French authorities to release a copy of this document.

152 *VPSD*, p. 37.

153 *Ibid.*, p. 255.

154 Letter from Breton to Dalí, 3 February 1934. National Gallery of Scotland, Edinburgh.

155 Hugnet, *Pleins et déliés*, pp. 256–7.

156 Éluard, *Lettres à Gala*, p. 459, n. 1.

157 Letter from Breton to Dalí, 3 February 1934, National Gallery of Scotland, Edinburgh.

158 Jean, pp. 220–3; Éluard, *Lettres à Gala*, nn. 1 and 3 to letter 198, pp. 459–60; Hugnet, *Pleins et déliés*, pp. 25–7.

159 *Cronica del Siglo xx* (Barcelona, Plaza y Janés, 1986), p. 469; 'France', *Encyclopedia Britannica* (1957), IX, p. 638.

160 Éluard, *Lettres à Gala*, pp. 229–30.

161 National Gallery of Scotland, Edinburgh for the Breton letter; Fonds Breton, Bibliothèque Littéraire Jacques Doucet, Paris, for Dalí's reply.

162 *VPSD*, p. 37; Levy, *Memoir of an Art Gallery*, p. 299.

163 Dalí's letter to Breton, postmarked Cadaqués, 17 April 1934, is in the Fonds Breton, Bibliothèque Littéraire Jacques Doucet, Paris; *La Publicitat*, Barcelona, 14 April 1934, p. 2.

164 Joan Tomàs, 'El poeta García Lorca i l'escenògraf Manuel Fontanals venen de fer una revolució a Buenos Aires', *La Publicitat*, Barcelona, 13 April 1934, pp. 1, 6.

165 It has not been possible to see the original of this text, transcribed, without indication of source, by Rodrigo, *Lorca–Dalí. Una amistad traicionada*, p. 225.

166 *Documents 34*, Brussels, June 1934, pp. 33–5.

167 Santos Torroella (ed.), *Salvador Dalí corresponsal de J.V. Foix*, p. 131; Éluard, *Lettres à Gala*, p. 240.

168 I am extremely grateful to the Victoria and Albert Museum for a photocopy of the exhibition catalogue, the only one I was able to locate. For the likelihood that Dalí stayed with James, see Etherington-Smith, p. 211.

169 Purser, p. 6.

170 Quoted by Purser, p. 199.

171 George Melly to the author in the back of a Parisian taxi, 1 August 1995.

172 Lowe, *passim*.

173 Secrest, p. 164.

174 Quoted in *VPSD*, p. 39.

175 Santos Torroella, *La miel es más dulce que la sangre*, pp. 195–219.

176 Éluard, *Lettres à Gala*, pp. 247–8.

177 *José María Sert* (see Bibliography, Section 3), p. 61; Etherington-Smith, pp. 212–13.

178 Santos Torroella (ed.), *Salvador Dalí corresponsal de J.V. Foix*, p. 133.

179 *Ibid.*, pp. 131–2; Dalí's letters to Buñuel were first published in *SVBLD*, pp. 247–50.

180 Pérez Galán, *passim*.

181 Jackson, p. 30.

182 *Ibid.*, p. 175; Preston, pp. 184–8.

183 Jackson, pp. 148–68. For the background to the October rising, see also the comprehensive chapter 'The Bienio Negro', in Brenan, pp. 265–97.

184 Santos Torroella (ed.), *Salvador Dalí corresponsal de J.V. Foix*, p. 138, n. 5, and Appendix F, pp. 195–200.

185 *SL*, pp. 355–6; Santos Torroella (ed.), *Salvador Dalí corresponsal de J.V. Foix*, pp. [56], 140, 216.

186 J.C. [Just Cabot], 'Abans d'anar a Nova York. Una estona amb Dalí', *Mirador*, Barcelona, 18 October 1934, reproduced by Santos Torroella (ed.), *Salvador Dalí corresponsal de J.V. Foix*, pp. 215–18.

187 I am grateful to Doña Montserrat Dalí's daughter, Eulalia, for providing me with a photocopy of this letter.

188 It is interesting to note that Dalí Cusí was still referring to his son as 'the boy' (*noi*), despite the fact that the painter was then thirty.

189 See n. 185.

190 Postcard from Dalí to Anselm Domènech, postmarked New York 13 December 1934. Museu Abelló, Mollet del Vallès (Barcelona). Published, with some mistakes of transcription, by Fernández Puertas, 'Les Cartes de Salvador Dalí al seu oncle Anselm Domènech al Museu Abelló', p. 70.

191 For the preliminary drawings, *Salvador Dalí* (Pompidou catalogue), p. 304. On some of these drawings the exact date, Sunday 6 May 1934, can be read without difficulty. For Dalí's inaccurate account of events in Barcelona and the genesis of the painting, *SL*, pp. 357–8.

192 Read, 'Bosch and Dalí'.

193 Douglas Goldring, 'Artists and Pictures', *The Studio*, London, January 1935, p. 36.

194 Anthony Blunt, 'The Beaver and the Silk-worm', *The Spectator*, London, 2 November 1934.

195 Clive Bell, 'The Zwemmer Gallery', *New Statesman and Nation*, London, 22 December 1934, p. 938.

196 For the date of the boat's departure from Le Havre, see *La Prensa*, New York, 14 November 1934 ('Vapores que llegan', last page) and *New York Times*, 14 November 1934, p. 41. For its arrival in New York, *ibid.*, and *New York Times*, 15 November, p. 22.

197 *SL*, p. 329.

198 *UC*, p. 177.

199 Crosby, p. 329.

200 'Vapores que llegan', *La Prensa*, New York, 14 November 1934.

201 Crosby, p. 331.

202 *VPSD*, p. 41.

203 Santos Torroella (ed.), *Salvador Dalí corresponsal de J.V. Foix*, p. 139.

204 Henry McBride in the *Sun*, quoted by *VPSD*, p. 40. Original not seen. The translation is mine.

205 Levy, *Memoir of an Art Gallery*, p. 99.

206 Quoted in *VPSD*, p. 40. Original not seen. The translation is mine.

207 Aurelio Pego, 'Un pintor catalán en Nueva York', *La Vanguardia*, Barcelona, 22 January 1935, p. 9.

208 Fernández Puertas, 'Les cartes de Salvador Dalí al seu oncle Anselm Domènech', p. 70.

209 National Gallery of Scotland, Edinburgh.

210 Undated letter in Fonds Paul Éluard, Musée de Saint-Denis, Saint-Denis, quoted in *Salvador Dalí* (Pompidou catalogue) p. 300.

211 *La Prensa*, New York, 12 December 1934, pp. 4 and 6.

212 '"Not a Madman!"—Dalí', *Art Digest*, New York, 1 January 1935, p. 1.

213 A synopsis of Dalí's talk is given in *La Prensa*, New York, 9 January 1935, p. 4.

214 'Salvador Dalí dio en el Museo de Arte Moderno otra de sus conferencias', *La Prensa*, New York, 14 January 1935, p. 4; 'Dalí Proclaims Surrealism a Paranoiac Art', *Art Digest*, New York, 1 February 1935, p. 10; *VPSD*, p. 43; the quotation is taken from Levy, *Surrealism*, p. 7.

215 Santos Torroella (ed.), *Salvador Dalí corresponsal de J.V. Foix*, p. 143.

216 The invitation is reproduced in *VPSD*, p. 43.

217 *Sunday Mirror*, New York, 24 February 1935, pp. 10–11, reproduced in *VPSD*, pp. 42–3; *SL*, pp. 337–8; Crosby, pp. 331–2.

218 *SL*, p. 338.

Ten: The Consolidation of Fame (1935–40)

1 Letter dated Cadaqués 5 March 1935, private archive of Montserrat Dalí's daughter, Doña Eulalia Maria Bas i Dalí, Barcelona, to whom my warmest thanks.

2 Conversation with Doña Montserrat Dalí, Barcelona, 28 February 1992, in the presence of her daughter, Eulalia, and of Don Rafael and Doña Maite Santos Torroella; Anna Maria had given her side of the story some years previously to Santos Torroella, who recounted it on the same occasion.

3 Private archive of Doña Eulalia Bas i Dalí, Barcelona; the postcard from Rafael Dalí to his daughter, in the same archive, is dated 7 March 1935.

4 The will and the attached document were signed in the presence of the Figueres notary, Jesús Solís de Ecénarro. I am grateful to the Spanish Ministry of Culture for allowing me to obtain copies of these documents from the Notarial Archive, Figueres, and to the notary in charge, Don Raimundo Fortuny i Marqués, for his disinterested collaboration.

5 The will is dated 10 September 1936. Notarial Archive, Figueres. See previous note.

6 The wills are dated 12 May 1937; 19 November 1937; 17 July 1942; 20 December 1944; 17 October, 1947; 6 November 1948; 17 July 1949; 30 January 1950; 31 May 1950. Notarial Archive, Figueres. See n. 4.

7 Card to Dalí and Gala postmarked Prague, 30 March 1935, from Breton, his wife Jacqueline and Paul Éluard. Fonds Breton, Bibliothèque Littéraire Jacques Doucet, Paris; Éluard, *Lettres à Gala*, letter 206, n. 8, p. 466.

8 Éluard, *Lettres à Gala*, letter 207, n. 2, p. 467; Breton, 'Le Château étoilé', *Minotaure*, Paris, no. 8 (15 June 1936), p. 29.

9 Conversation with David Gascoyne, Isle of Wight, 22 March 1994.

10 *Ibid.*; also, Gascoyne, 'A propos du suicide de René Crevel'.

11 Santos Torroella (ed.), *Salvador Dalí corresponsal de J.V. Foix*, pp. 147–9.

12 The case and its contents are preserved in the Bibliothèque Littéraire Jacques Doucet, Paris, B'-111–12. I am grateful to M. François Chapon, ex-curator of the library, for bringing it to my attention.

13 For the trip to London, see the card to Anselm Domènech postmarked 5 July 1935. Biblioteca de Catalunya, Barcelona (according to Lowe, p. 124, James sailed for Barcelona on 21 July 1935); the details of print runs are supplied on p. [6] of the *plaquette*.

14 Letter from Edward James to Diane Abdy, 20 October 1935. EJF.

15 *La Publicitat*, Barcelona, 2, 3, 4 August 1935; *Crónica*, Barcelona, 11 August 1935.

16 *SL*, p. 343.

17 EJF.

18 In *Dalí* (Museum Boijmans-Van Beuningen, Rotterdam, catalogue, see Bibliography, Section 1), no. 49.

19 There are photographs showing these buildings in the *Palamós* 1995 *Festa Major* booklet.

20 Dalí and Pauwels, p. 24.

21 In *Dalí* (Museum Boijmans-Van Beuningen, Rotterdam, catalogue, see Bibliography, Section 1), no. 49.

22 For the donation of the bell, conversation with Don Antoni Pitxot, Figueres, 5 August 1995; Dalí also commented on the masturbatory belfry scenario to Permanyer, 'El pincel erótico de Dalí', p. 162.

23 Conversation with Don Antoni Pitxot, Figueres, 5 August 1995.

24 Edward James to Diane Abdy, 20 October 1935. EJF.

25 *L'Humanitat*, Barcelona, 1 October 1935, p. 1.

26 García Lorca, *Obras completas*, III, p. 661.

27 The drawing and Dalí's comments are repro-

duced by Descharnes, *The World of Salvador Dalí*, p. 21.

28 Dalí, 'Les Morts et moi'.

29 Letter from James to Diane Abdy dated 20 October 1935. EJF.

30 Dalí, 'Les Morts et moi'.

31 Dalí, 'Les Morts et moi', revamped in *Diary of a Genius*, pp. 81–5.

32 Santos Torroella (ed.), *Salvador Dalí corresponsal de J.V. Foix*, pp. 150–3.

33 Quoted by Lowe, pp. 125–6.

34 EJF.

35 Lowe, pp. 126–7.

36 EJF.

37 *SL*, p. 340.

38 Cossaert, p. 218.

39 *SDFGL*, p. 97. The writer Max Aub (1903–72) later compiled a book, *Conversaciones con Buñuel*, which contains important information on Dalí.

40 Undated letter from Dalí to Edward James. EJF.

41 Letter from Gala to Edward James, postmarked Cadaqués, 11 May 1936. EJF.

42 Correspondence between the Dalís and James. EJF.

43 I am grateful to the National Gallery of Scotland for supplying me with a photocopy of the exhibition catalogue, which is included in David Gascoyne's book of cuttings.

44 Santos Torroella (ed.), *Salvador Dalí corresponsal de J.V. Foix*, p. 155.

45 Buck, introduction to catalogue *The Surrealist Spirit in Britain*.

46 *Ibid.*

47 Penrose, *Scrapbook: 1900–1981*, London, Thames and Hudson, 1981, quoted by Etherington-Smith, p. 245.

48 The fourth issue of the *International Surrealist Bulletin* (London, Curwen Press, September 1936) gives a succinct account of events.

49 Letter from Gala and Dalí to James, EJF.; for details of the house parties, Etherington-Smith, pp. 244–5, no source provided.

50 See n. 48.

51 Read, *Surrealism*, p. 19.

52 *International Surrealist Bulletin*, see note 48; for the Fascist threat to the exhibition, see Louisa Buck, introduction to *The Surrealist Spirit in Britain* (catalogue, see Bibliography, section 3).

53 Exhibition catalogue, pp. 16–17.

54 Breton, *What is Surrealism?* (1936), p. 82.

55 Read, *Surrealism*, p. 59.

56 Dalí, 'Le Surréalisme spectral de l'Eternel Féminin préraphaélite'.

57 Read, *Surrealism*, pp. 240–2.

58 Santos Torroella (ed.), *Salvador Dalí corresponsal de J.V. Foix*, pp. 155–8 and 220–1.

59 The titles of the drawings allegedly containing such a wide variety of attractions were not provided in the catalogue. The paintings were listed as:

  1. *Mid-Day?* 1936.

  2. *Apparition of the Town of Delft*. 1936.

  3. *Spectre of Sex-appeal*. 1936.

  4. *The Fossil Automobile of Cape Creus*. 1936.

  5. *Soft Construction with Boiled Apricots*. 1936.

  6. *Diurnal Melancholy*. 1936.

  7. *City of Drawers*. 1936.

  8. and 9. *A Couple with their Heads Full of Clouds*. 1936.

  10. *'Geodesical' Portrait of Gala*. 1936.

  11. *Portrait of Gala with Two Lamb Chops in Equilibrium upon her Shoulder*. 1934.

  12. *The Invisible Man*. 1929–33.

  13. *Head of Gala with Hair Giving Birth to an Olive Branch*. 1934.

  14. *Morphological Echo*. 1936.

  15. *Sun-Table*. 1936.

  16. *Average Atmospheric-Cephalic Bureaucrat Milking a 'Cranial Harp'*. 1934.

  17. *Skull with its Lyric Appendage*. 1934.

  18. *Anthropomorphism, Extra Flat*. 1936.

  19. *Forgotten Horizon*. 1936.

  20. *Hypnagogical Image of Gala*. 1934.

  21. *Imperial Monument to the Child-Woman*. 1934.

  22. *The Weaning of Furniture-Nutrition*. 1935. (Lent by Mrs Jocelyn Walker, London.)

  23. *Interior Court of the 'Island of the Dead.'* 1935. (Lent by Mr Peter Watson, London.)

  24. *Fountain of Böcklin*. 1934. (Lent by Prince J.L. Faucigny Lucinge, Paris.)

  25. *Fine, Middle-Sized, Invisible Harp*. 1934. (Lent by Le Vicomte de Noailles, Paris.)

  26. *Suburbs of the Paranoiac-Critical Town*. 1935. (Lent by Mr Edward James, London.)

  27. *White Calm*. 1935. (Lent by Mr Edward James, London.)

  28. *Portrait of Emilio Terry*. 1934. (Lent by Mr Emilio Terry, Paris.)

  29. *Vegetable Metamorphosis*. 1935. (Lent by Mr Cecil Beaton, London.)

60 *SL*, pp. 357–8; see also Dalí's later claim along the same lines in Descharnes, *Dalí de Gala* (Lausanne, Edita, 1962), quoted in Descharnes, *DOH*, p. 189.

61 'Reali$m in Surrealism. Modernists are not Priceless Asses', *Star*, London, 2 July 1936.

62 *The Studio*, London, no. 112, September 1936, quoted by Etherington-Smith, p. 247; for the rapid sale of twelve paintings, *Standard*, London, 25 June 1936 (Secrest, p. 165); T.W. Earp, *Daily Telegraph*, London, 1 July 1936, quoted by Secrest, p. 165.

63 'Reali\$m in Surrealism. Modernists are not Priceless Asses', *Star*, London, 2 July 1936.

64 'Surrealist in Diving Suit. Helmet Gets Stuck', *Daily Mail*, London, 2 July 1936.

65 Conversation with David Gascoyne, Isle of Wight, 22 March 1994.

66 EJF.

67 Lowe, p. 133.

68 The contract is in EJF.

69 Undated letter quoted by Etherington-Smith, pp. 249–50; Dalí claims in *SL*, pp. 357–8, that he was dining in the Savoy when news of the rising came; Puignau, p. 20, says that the couple were in Port Lligat when they heard the news, and that they beat a hasty retreat to Paris, but this cannot have been the case.

70 EJF.

71 *BMDS*, pp. 202–3.

72 *SL*, p. 361.

73 See Gibson, The Assassination of García Lorca.

74 Dalí, 'Les Morts et moi'.

75 *SL*, p. 361.

76 Lowe, p. 133.

77 *SL*, pp. 361–8; Lowe, p. 133; Dalí's letter to Breton, Fonds Breton, Bibliothèque Littéraire Jacques Doucet, Paris.

78 Letters from Gala to Edward James. EJF.

79 Fonds Breton, Bibliothèque Littéraire Jacques Doucet, Paris.

80 Levy, *Memoir of an Art Gallery*, p. 173.

81 Hugnet, 'In the Light of Surrealism', *Fantastic Art, Dada, Surrealism* (catalogue, see Bibliography section 3), pp. 45–6.

82 Fonds Breton, Bibliothèque Littéraire Jacques Doucet, Paris. Envelope postmarked Quebec, 28 December 1936. The letter is on notepaper headed Canadian Pacific Hotels, Château Frontenac, Québec.

83 'Frozen Nightmares', *Time*, New York, 26 November 1934, pp. 44–5.

84 'Marvelous and Fantastic', *Time*, New York, 12 December 1934.

85 *UC*, p. 183.

86 E.A.J. [Edward Alden Jewell], 'The New Dalís Again', *New York Times*, 20 December 1936.

87 The paintings with asterisks were lent by Edward James:

    1. *The Moment of Transition.*

    2. *The Great Dreamer of Dalí.*

    3. *Three Young Surrealist Women Holding in their Arms the Skins of an Orchestra.*

    4. *Autumnal Cannibalism.**

    5. *Necrophilic Spring.*

    6. *The Negress from Harlem en Voyage in Catalonia Looks at Herself in Invisible Mirror.*

    7. *The Man with the Head of Blue Hortensias.*

    8. *A Chemist Lifting with Precaution the Cuticle of a Grand Piano.*

    9. *Feminine Head which has the Form of a Battle.*

    10. *The Bread on the Head, and the Prodigal with the Father.*

    11. *A Trombone and A Sofa Fashioned out of Saliva.*

    12. *Suburbs of the 'Paranoiac-Critical' Afternoon (on the Outskirts of European History).**

    13. *A Couple with their Heads Full of Clouds.**

    14. *Spectre of Vermeer's Chair.*

    15. *Mid-day? 1936.*

    16. *Soft Construction with Boiled Beans. 1936. (Premonition of Civil War.)*

    17. *Diurnal Melancholy. 1936.* (Private coll., London.)

    18. *'Geodesical' Portrait of Gala. 1936.* (Coll. Gala Dalí.)

    19. *Sun-table. 1936.**

    20. *Dream Puts her Hand on a Man's Shoulder.*

88 E.A.J. [Edward Alden Jewell], 'The New Dalís Again', *New York Times*, 20 December 1936.

89 *Art News*, New York, 2 January 1937, quoted in *VPSD*, p. 60.

90 'The Battle of the Surrealists', *New York Sun*, 19 December 1936.

91 Dalí in Descharnes, *Dalí de Gala* (1962), quoted in *DOH*, p. 223.

92 'Fifth Ave. Crowd Stops to View Dalí Window', *New York Weekly Telegraph*, 26 December 1936.

93 Levy, *Surrealism*, p. 160.

94 *Ibid.*, p. 23.

95 Fonds Breton, Bibliothèque Littéraire Jacques Doucet, Paris.

96 The conformed copy of this document is preserved in EJF.

97 Dalí, 'Surrealism in Hollywood'.

98 *DOH*, p. 158.

99 Dalí, 'Surrealism in Hollywood'.

100 The drawing is reproduced in *Salvador Dalí* (Pompidou catalogue), p. 358; the photograph in *DOH*, p. 158.

101 Letter from Dalí to Edward James postmarked 19 February 1937. The Dalís were staying at The Garden of Allah, 8159 Sunset boulevard, Hollywood. EJF.

102 Fonds Breton, Bibliothèque Littéraire Jacques Doucet, Paris.

103 EJF. It appears that Dalí gave the draft to Edward James for translation into English. It is not known if it was ever sent to Harpo.

104 The typescript of the scenario, apparently bought from Mme Cécile Éluard, is in the Musée National d'Art Moderne (Centre Georges Pompidou), Paris.

105 Dalí to Éluard in Éluard, *Lettres à Gala*, pp. 476–7, n. 2.

106 Reproduced in *Salvador Dalí* (Pompidou cata-

logue), pp. 286 and 288.

107 Freud, *Obras completas*, IV, p. 255, n. 1.

108 *Ibid.*, XII, p. 60.

109 Santos Torroella, *La miel es más dulce que la sangre*, p. 153.

110 Dalí in *Dalí*, Museum Boymans–van Beuningen, Rotterdam, catalogue (see Bibliography, Section 1), no. 50.

111 García Lorca, 'Panorama ciego de Nueva York', *Obras completas*, I, p. 483:

Es una cápsula de aire donde nos duele todo el mundo,
es un pequeño espacio vivo al loco unisón de la luz,
es una escala indefinible donde las nubes y rosas olvidan
el griterío chino que bulle por el desembarcadero de la sangre.
Yo muchas veces me he perdido
para buscar la quemadura que mantiene despiertas las cosas
y solo he encontrado marineros echados sobre las barandillas
y pequeñas criaturas del cielo enterradas bajo la nieve.

112 Santos Torroella, *La miel es más dulce que la sangre*, p. 149.

113 Pierre, 'Breton et Dalí', p. 140.

114 Documentation in EJF.

115 EJF. Document quoted by Etherington-Smith, pp. 258–60.

116 *Ibid.*, p. 260.

117 Invitation reproduced in *Salvador Dalí* (Pompidou catalogue), p. 62. My efforts to locate the exhibition catalogue have proved fruitless. According to Mme Evelyne Pomey, who was in charge of documentation for the Pompidou Dalí exhibition, it appears that perhaps no such catalogue was in fact printed (communication from Mme Nathalie Schoeller, Pompidou Centre, 11 April 1996).

118 Letter from Dalí to James, spring 1937, EJF; copy of letter from Edward James to Dalí dated 31 August 1937, EJF.

119 For Breton's criticism of the exhibition, see *Éluard, Lettres à Gala*, letter 234, n. 3, p. 479.

120 Letter from Dalí to Edward James. EJF.

121 Lowe, p. 139; Éluard, *Lettres à Gala*, pp. 282–3.

122 Conversations with Doña Rosa Maria Salleras, Cadaqués, 1994–6.

123 Jean, pp. 280–6.

124 *Ibid.*; *UC*, pp. 189–93.

125 Jean, p. 282.

126 *UC*, pp. 190–1.

127 The definition appeared in Dalí's 'Les Pantoufles de Picasso' (1935).

128 Dalí, *El mito trágico del 'Angelus' de Millet* (Tusquets edition), p. 10.

129 Letter from Dalí to James, EJF; *SL*, p. 363.

130 For colour reproductions see Moorhouse, p. 90, and *DOH*, p. 241; Romero, *Todo Dalí en un rostro*, p. 203, provides a useful detail of the group of double images; letter from Dalí to James, EJF.

131 *Cahiers* G.L.M., Paris, no. 7, 1938, p. 4.

132 Jones, pp. 642–3.

133 *SL*, p. 23.

134 Dalí to Edward James, EJF.

135 Cowles, pp. 291–3.

136 *LSASDLR*, no. 5 (13 May 1933), pp. 10–11, reproduced in the second edition of *Les Vases Communicants*, see Breton, *Oeuvres complètes*, pp. 210–13.

137 Cowles, p. 294. The translation, by Richard Friedenthal, looks somewhat defective. I have not been able to see the original.

138 Quoted in Lowe, p. 144, except for Freud's comment, added by Etherington-Smith, p. 279, in her transcription of the letter, the original of which I have been unable to see.

139 Fonds Breton, Bibliothèque Littéraire Jacques Doucet, Paris. Quoted by Pierre, p. 137.

140 *SL*, p. 23; Cowles, p. 293; Zweig, p. 325.

141 *SL*, pp. 397–8.

142 *Ibid.*, p. 371.

143 *Ibid.* The painting is reproduced in *DOH*, p. 221.

144 Etherington-Smith, p. 282.

145 'The Geological Foundations of Venusberg', quoted in *DOH*, p. 227.

146 Both paintings are reproduced in *DOH*, p. 238.

147 Santos Torroella, 'El Reina Sofía se equivoca con Dalí', p. 38.

148 Fonds Breton, Bibliothèque Littéraire Jacques Doucet, Paris.

149 Breton papers, National Gallery of Scotland, Edinburgh.

150 Breton, 'The Most Recent Tendencies in Surrealist Painting', p. 17.

151 The invitation is reproduced in *VPSD*, p. 73; Dalí's indications about the stroboscopic photograph in *50 Secrets of Magic Craftsmanship*, p. 171.

152 *New York Post* (see following note).

153 'Surrealist Dalí Explains Fury for his Art; Never Meant to Smash 5th Ave. Window. Couldn't Bear Sight of Expurgated Version of his Work', *New York Post*, 17 March 1939; see also 'Dalí's Display', *Time*, New York, 27 March 1939; *SL*, pp. 371–2.

154 *New York Post* (see previous note).

155 *Paris-Soir*, 18 March 1939, quoted in Éluard, *Lettres à Gala*, note 1 to letter 249, pp. 483–4; *Daily News*, New York, 17 March 1939, quoted in *VPSD*, p. 74; *Time*, New York, 27 March 1939; *SL*, pp. 371–6; Dalí, *Carta abierta a Salvador Dalí*, p. 31; Dalí,

Declaration of the Independence of the Imagination and the Rights of Man to His Own Madness (see note 166).

156 The exhibition catalogue lists the following works:

Paintings

1. *Debris of an Automobile Giving Birth to a Blind Horse Biting a Telephone.*
2. *Gala.*
3. *The Enigma of Hitler.*
4. *Telephone in a Dish with Three Grilled Sardines.*
5. *The Abyss of Reflection.*
6. *Spain.*
7. *Imperial Violets.*
8. *Women-horses.*
9. *Mad Tristan.*
10. *Endless Enigma:*
Mandoline, Fruit-Dish with Pears, Two Figs on Table.
Mythological Beast.
Face of the Great One-Eyed Moron.
Greyhound.
Reclining Philosopher.
Beach of Cape Creus with Seated Woman Mending Sail Seen from the Back, and Boat.
11. *Enchanted Beach with Three Fluid Graces.*
12. *Apparition of Face and Fruit-Dish on a Beach.*
13. *Melancholic Eccentricity.*
14. *Psychoanalysis and Morphology Meet.*
15. *The Image Disappears.*
16. *The Transparent Simulacrum of the Feigned Image.*
17. *Saint Jerome.*
18. *Evening Palisades.*
19. *Sleep.*
20. *Palladio's Corridor of Dramatic Disguise.*
21. *The Sublime Moment.*

Drawings

22. *Portrait of Gala.*
23. *Portrait of Doctor Freud.*
24. *Portrait of Walking Female Figure.*
25. *Imaginary Portrait of Lautréamont.*
26. *Portrait of Harpo Marx.*

157 *Ibid.*
158 *Life*, New York, 18 April 1939, quoted in *VPSD*, p. 75.
159 EJF.
160 There is a draft outline of *Dream of Venus*, in Dalí's hand in EJF. It is written in French.
161 EJF.
162 Memorandum by Edward James. EJF.
163 'Throngs Dazed By a Glimpse of World of Dalí. Exhibit at Fair Has Diving Girls Milk a Frustrated Cow as Giraffe Explodes', *Herald Tribune*, New York, 16 June 1939.
164 The draft telegram and a copy of the letter, dated 21 June 1939, are in EJF. For Dalí's account, see *SL*, pp. 376–7; *VPSD*, pp. 76–83, reproduces numerous

photographs of the preparations for *Dreams of Venus*.
165 There are three boxes of press cuttings in EJF.
166 Norman Siegel, 'Dalí and "Dollies" Make the "Dream of Venus" an Out-Standing Fair Exhibit', *Press*, Cleveland, 18 July 1939.
167 'World's Fairs. Pay As You Enter', *Time Magazine*, Chicago, 26 June 1939.
168 The full text of the *Declaration* is provided by Levy, *Memoir of an Art Gallery*, pp. 219–22; the cover, showing Botticelli's Venus with the head of a fish, is reproduced in *VPSD*, p. 84.
169 *SVBLD*, pp. 283–4.
170 Luis Buñuel Archive, Ministry of Culture, Madrid.
171 *Ibid.*
172 Conversation with Don Juan Luis Buñuel, Madrid, 1995.
173 Breton, 'Des tendances les plus récentes de la peinture surréaliste', p. 17.
174 *SL*, p. 378.
175 Letter from Gala to Edward James, 5 August 1939. EJF.
176 EJF.
177 *SL*, pp. 381–4.
178 EJF.
179 *Ibid.*
180 Levy, *Memoir of an Art Gallery*, p. 168.
181 Fini's written testimony in Vieuille, p. 181; Secrest, p. 175.
182 Etherington-Smith, p. 293.
183 EJF.
184 *Ibid.*
185 *Ibid.*
186 *Ibid.*
187 Lowe, p. 149; Etherington-Smith, p. 295.
188 EJF.
189 *VPSD*, p. 88.
190 EJF.
191 *Ibid.*
192 Conovan, p. 73.
193 Vieuille, p. 181; Secrest, p. 175.
194 'La bandera del Reich ondea en la frontera francoespañola', *Pueblo*, Madrid, 28 June 1940, p. 2.
195 *SL*, pp. 384–90.
196 See Rodríguez-Puértolas, pp. 347–8.
197 Etherington-Smith, p. 305.
198 Bosquet, *Dalí desnudado*, p. 13.
199 *SL*, p. 384.
200 EJF.
201 Carlos Sentís, 'Castillos en España y el fácil neo-americanismo', *Destino*, Barcelona, 17 August 1940, pp. 1–2.
202 'Secretos a voces', *ibid.*, 24 August 1940, p. 11.
203 *SL*, p. 391.

204 *VPSD*, p. 88.

Eleven: America (1940–8)

1 Photograph of the couple's arrival, in *New York Post*, 16 August 1940, reproduced in *DOH*, p. 231.
2 *New York Post*, 16 August 1940.
3 Etherington-Smith, p. 307.
4 John White, 'A Day with Dalí. Or—The Cow in the Library', *Times Herald*, Washington, 23 February 1941, reproduced in *DOH*, p. 260.
5 *Ibid.*; Crosby, p. 337.
6 Unpublished letter in Don Pere Vehí Collection, Cadaqués.
7 Parke Rouse Jr, 'Spiders—That's What Fascinates Dalí Most About Virginia', *Richmond Time-Dispatch*, 6 April 1941.
8 *The Diary of Anaïs Nin. 1939–1944*, pp. 39–40.
9 *Ibid.*, p. 40.
10 Etherington-Smith, p. 311; Lowe, pp. 185–6.
11 For Chevalier's difficulties with the text, see *SL*, p. 74, note.
12 This fair copy is preserved in the Fundació Gala–Salvador Dalí, Figueres. It is written on notepaper bearing the heading Beverly Hills Hotel and Bungalows, Beverly Hills, California ('11 acres of sunshine for 12 months of playtime in the heart of residential Los Angeles'). The typescript has ms corrections by Gala.
13 The manuscript and fair copies are preserved in the Fundació Gala–Salvador Dalí, Figueres.
14 *SL*, p. 223.
15 *Ibid.*, pp. 223, 250.
16 *Ibid.*, p. 312.
17 *Ibid.*, p. 339.
18 *Ibid.*, p. 252.
19 *Ibid.*, p. 339.
20 *Ibid.*, p. 361.
21 *Ibid.*, p. 11.
22 *Ibid.*, p. 72.
23 *Ibid.*, p. 250.
24 *Ibid.*, p. 393.
25 It seems likely that Dalí may also have known Giménez Caballero's *La nueva catolicidad*, of 1933 (see Bibliography).
26 *SL*, p. 1. The original French of the manuscript shows that he has in mind a female cook (*cuisinière*), not the male variety (Fundació Gala–Salvador Dalí, Figueres).
27 *SL*, pp. 193, 339.
28 Reproduced in *VPSD*, p. 89.
29 *SL*, plate XIV.
30 Morse, *Dalí. A Study of his Life and Work*, p. 51.

31 Quoted by Etherington-Smith, p. 315.
32 Edward James—Julien Levy correspondence, quoted by Etherington-Smith, p. 314.
33 Levy, *Memoir of an Art Gallery*, p. 255.
34 Henry McBride, 'The Classic Dalí. Not so Very Different From Dalí the Surrealist', *New York Sun*, 26 April 1941.
35 Sawin, pp. 151–2.
36 Nicholas Calas, 'Anti-surrealist Dalí: I Say his Flies are Ersatz', *View*, New York, June 1941.
37 *SL*, p. 207, note.
38 Photographs of the Carmel studio in Morse, 'Romantic Ampurdán', p. 209.
39 Morse, *Dalí. A Study of his Life and Work*, p. 56.
40 Levy, *Memoir of an Art Gallery*, p. 255; *DOH*, p. 258; 'Dalí Out West', *Art Digest*, New York, 1 October 1941, p. 9; 'Dalí in California', *ibid.*, 1 November 1941, p. 22.
41 Etherington-Smith, pp. 317–20; a snatch of film of the occasion was included in the BBC 'Arena' programme *Dalí* (see Bibliography, Section 7).
42 Inez Robb, 'Dalí's Daffy Day', *American Weekly*, New York, 8 October 1941.
43 *VPSD*, pp. 94–5; *DOH*, pp. 258, 276; Descharnes and Néret, *Dalí*, I, pp. 343–5.
44 'Richard Wagner Reported Killed', *Dalí News*, New York, 20 November 1945, p. 1, reproduced in *VPSD*, p. 116.
45 Madrid, Francisco, 'El escándalo del "Salón de Otoño"'.
46 Soby, *Salvador Dalí. Paintings, Drawings, Prints*, p. 7.
47 Robert M. Coates, 'The Art Galleries. Had Any Good Dreams Lately?', *The New Yorker*, 29 November 1941.
48 Sweeney, p. 13; Edward Alden Jewell, 'Melange. From the Antipodes to Surrealism', *New York Times*, 23 November 1941.
49 Henry McBride, 'Dalí and Miro', *New York Sun*, 21 November 1941.
50 Robert M. Coates, 'The Art Galleries. Had Any Good Dreams Lately?', *The New Yorker*, 29 November 1941.
51 'Peyton Boswell Comments: Mr Dalí Goes to Town', *Art Digest*, New York, 1 December 1941.
52 Morse, *Dalí. A Study of his Life and Work*, p. 57.
53 'The Secret Life of Dalí by Dalí', *Click*, New York, September 1942, reproduced in *VPSD*, p. 103.
54 Anna Maria Dalí published a translation of Maurice Baring's short story 'The Flute of Chiang Luang' in *Destino*, Barcelona, no. 429, 6 October 1945; letter from Salvador Dalí to Anna Maria in the private collection of Don Pere Vehí, Cadaqués.
55 Unpublished letter in the collection of Don Pere

Vehí, Cadaqués.

56 The drawing is reproduced in colour in Fornés, *Dalí y los libros*, p. 40.

57 *The New Yorker*, 27 February 1943, quoted by Secrest, p. 183.

58 'Not so Secret Life', *Time*, New York, 28 December 1942, pp. 30–1.

59 Benjamin De Casseres, in a cutting included in the album of reviews of the *Secret Life* compiled by Gala and preserved in the Fundació Gala–Salvador Dalí, Figueres.

60 *Nation*, New York, 6 February 1943.

61 Quoted by Etherington-Smith, p. 326.

62 *Ibid.*

63 'Elsa Maxwell's Party Line', *Dallas Texas Herald*, 24 January 1943.

64 Quoted in *VPSD*, p. 104.

65 *SVBLD*, p. 365; Buñuel's copy of the *Secret Life* is in the Buñuel Archive, Ministry of Culture, Madrid.

66 *SL*, plate VI.

67 Orwell, 'Benefit of Clergy', p. 195.

68 Reynolds Morse, *The Dalí Adventure*, p. [iii]; Eleanor Morse, 'My View', p. xxv; *MDJ*, vol. I; conversations with Mr and Mrs Reynolds Morse, Spain and Florida, 1995–6.

69 Written communication with Mrs Eleanor Morse, 31 May 1996; in *MDJ*, vol. I.

70 Written communication from Mrs Eleanor Morse, 31 May 1996; see also Eleanor Morse, 'My View', p. xxv. Reynolds Morse, 'Reminiscences and Reassessments', p. iii, says the painting cost $1,200 and the frame $1,850.

71 Written communication from Mrs Eleanor Morse, 31 May 1996.

72 Copy of Gala's letter kindly supplied by Mrs Morse.

73 Reynolds Morse, *The Dalí Adventure*, p. [iii].

74 Written communication from Mrs Morse, 31 May 1996.

75 Eleanor Morse, 'My View', p. xxv; *MDJ*, vol. I.

76 *MDJ*, vol. I, pp. 421–3; conversation with Mr Reynolds Morse, Salvador Dali Museum, St. Petersburg, Florida, 16 July 1996.

77 *MDJ*, vol. I.

78 *New York Sun*, 16 April 1943.

79 *UC*, pp. 204–9.

80 Chevalier, 'Translator's Foreword' to *Hidden Faces*; Dalí, 'Author's Foreword' to the novel.

81 Chevalier, 'Salvador Dalí as Writer'.

82 The friend was Carlos Lozano. Conversation with Señor Lozano, Cadaqués, 6 August 1995.

83 Dalí, *Hidden Faces*, p. 12.

84 *SDFGL*, p. 127, note 7.

85 *Ibid.*, p. 148.

86 Dalí and Pauwels, p. 241.

87 Permanyer, 'El pincel erótico de Dalí', p. 164.

88 Dalí, *Hidden Faces*, p. 13.

89 In 1972 Dalí attended an 'intimate dinner' given by Guy de Rothschild in Paris for 150 guests, who were asked to wear headpieces. Dalí refused. 'My head is my mask,' he explained (Carol *et al.*, *El último Dalí*, p. 44).

90 Dalí, *Rostros ocultos*, p. 10.

91 Dalí, *Hidden Faces*, p. 76.

92 *Ibid.*, p. 242.

93 *Ibid.*, p. 212.

94 *Ibid.*, p. 105.

95 *Ibid.*, p. 295.

96 *Ibid.*, p. 179.

97 Chevalier, 'Translator's Foreword' to *Hidden Faces*, p. 8.

98 Dalí, *Hidden Faces*, p. 337.

99 Gold and Fitzdale, p. 238. See also pp. 233, 238–9.

100 *Ibid.*, p. 233; Etherington-Smith, p. 334.

101 According to Secrest, p. 184, Bettina Bergery believed that Solange de Cléda 'was a mixture of Roussy Sert and herself'. This was as ridiculous as to hold that Gala 'came into the plot in a minor way as a young student of the Latin Quarter'. For Etherington-Smith, p. 333, Solange de Cléda is a combination of Bettina Bergery, Caresse Crosby and Marie-Laure de Noailles. One can see no evidence for this blanket assertion either.

102 Chevalier, 'Salvador Dalí as Writer'.

103 Edmund Wilson, 'Salvador Dalí as a Novelist'.

104 Harrison Smith, 'Salvador Dalí in Your Bathtub', *Saturday Review*, New York, 24 June 1944.

105 'Dalí's Love-in-Death', *Newsweek*, New York, 12 June 1944.

106 *The Dalí News*, New York, 20 November 1945, p. 3, reproduced in *VPSD*, p. 118.

107 Unpublished letter in the collection of Don Pere Vehí, Cadaqués.

108 *VPSD*, p. 105.

109 *Ibid.*, p. 106.

110 *Ibid.*

111 '3 New Dalí Paintings "Interpret" Perfume', *New York Times*, 31 October 1946; *VPSD*, p. 121.

112 For a discrepant view, at least where Dalí's illustrations for Sandoz's *Fantastic Memories* were concerned, see Thomas Sugrue, 'In a Fortunate Collaboration', *New York Herald Tribune Weekly Book Review*, 31 December 1944.

113 The illustrations for Sandoz's *Fantastic Memories* are reproduced in *VPSD*, pp. 107–11; for his *The Maze*, *ibid.*, pp. 114–15; three of the *Macbeth* illustrations, *ibid.*, p. 122; the cover of *Rose, Wine, Women and Words*, *ibid.*, p. 123.

114 Some of these designs are reproduced in *DOH*,

pp. 272–3; see also Descharnes and Néret, *Dalí*, I, pp. 352–3.

115 Green, 'Los años mágicos'.

116 Paul Bowles, *Without Stopping* (London, Hamish Hamilton, 1972), p. 252. Not seen, quoted by Etherington-Smith, p. 346.

117 'Richard Wagner Reported Killed', *Dalí News*, New York, 20 November 1945, reproduced in *VPSD*, p. 117.

118 *VPSD*, p. 113; *DOH*, pp. 274–5; Descharnes and Néret, *Dalí*, I pp. 368–71; Dalí on the controversy in *Dalí News*, New York, 20 November 1945, p. 2, reproduced in VSPD, p. 117.

119 *VPSD*, p. 114; Descharnes and Néret, *Dalí*, pp. 362–3; Dalí in *Dalí News*, New York, 20 November 1945, p. 1, reproduced in *VPSD*, p. 117.

120 Facsimile reproduction of a note by Dalí included in *Les Morts et moi* (Editorial Mediterrània, Barcelona, edn).

121 *MDJ*, I, 1942–56; reproduced in *DOH*, p. 297.

122 Lowe, p. 186.

123 *UC*, p. 216.

124 *Dalí*, BBC 'Arena', 1986 (see Bibliography, Section 7).

125 'Movies. Spellbound', *Dalí News*, New York, 20 November 1945, reproduced in *VPSD*, p. 117.

126 Fundació Gala–Salvador Dalí, Figueres.

127 *VPSD*, pp. 116–19.

128 Alfred Frankenstein, 'Dalí "Stops Experimenting"—But He's Still Enigmatic', *San Francisco Chronicle*, 19 November 1945.

129 Etherington-Smith, p. 356.

130 A. Frankenstein in *Arts*, Paris, 14 April 1946, quoted in *VPSD*, p. 120.

131 The drawing is reproduced, along with others for the film, in *DOH*, pp. 310–11.

132 See n. 129 above.

133 Morse, 'A Walt Disney Interlude', *MDJ*.

134 Etherington-Smith, p. 357.

135 *Ibid.*

136 *DOH*, pp. 309–11; Descharnes and Néret, *Dalí*, I, p. 393.

137 *MDJ*, vol. II; the cover of *Vogue* is reproduced by Descharnes and Néret, *Dalí*, I, p. 395.

138 Letters in private collection of Don Pere Vehí, Cadaqués.

139 Conversation with Mr Reynolds Morse, Florida, 15 July 1996.

140 Josep Pla, 'Calendario sin fechas', *Destino*, Barcelona, 29 May 1943, p. 8.

141 Tristán, 'Salvador Dalí desde Cadaqués'.

142 Unpublished letter in the private collection of Don Pere Vehí, Cadaqués.

143 'Salvador Dalí', *Destino*, Barcelona, 9 November 1946, p. 14.

144 Manuel Brunet, 'Despedida al notario'.

145 Conversation with Doña Roser Villar, Figueres, 28 June 1996.

146 Dalí signed *The Persistence of Memory* 'Olive Salvador Dalí 1931', see *DOH*, p. 114; perhaps the first painting signed 'Gala–Salvador Dalí' was *Encuentro de la ilusión y el momento detenido. Huevos fritos presentados en una cuchara* (1932, reproduced in *DOH*, p. 127).

147 Detail of dedication in Descharnes, *The World of Salvador Dalí*, p. 199.

148 'The Dalí Exhibition at the Bignou Gallery. Notes for the Study "Leda atomica"', *Dalí News*, New York, 25 November 1947, p. 2, reproduced in *VPSD*, p. 125.

149 *UC*, p. 218.

150 *Dalí. Arquitectura* (catalogue, see Bibliography, Section 1), pp. 152–3; Descharnes and Néret, *Dalí*, II, pp. 551–2.

151 Morse, *Animal Crackers*, p. 229.

152 Fundació Gala–Salvador Dalí, Figueres.

153 Reproduced in *DOH*, pp. 306–7.

154 Descharnes and Néret, *Dalí*, I, p. 362.

155 Descharnes, *The World of Salvador Dalí*, p. 182.

156 Etherington-Smith, p. 355.

157 Reproduced in *DOH*, p. 308.

158 The issue is reproduced in full in *VPSD*, pp. 124–7.

159 Press cutting reproduced in Morse, *The Dalí Adventure*, no pagination.

160 *MDJ*, vol. I.

161 Carlos Sentís, 'Carta al padre de Salvador Dalí', *Destino*, 28 February 1948.

162 *UC*, p. 131.

Twelve: A Renegade Surrealist in Franco's Spain
(1948–59)

1 Puignau, pp. 29–30.

2 Agustí, 'Bienvenida a Salvador Dalí'.

3 Undated letter in the private collection of Don Pere Vehí, Cadaqués.

4 Many of Gala's letters to Gonzalo Serraclara are in the Biblioteca de Catalunya, Barcelona, and proceed from the collection of Eduard Fornés.

5 Gonzalo Serraclara in the video made by Giuseppe and Mara Albaretto in early 1989.

6 For the parking of the Cadillac, conversation with Don Joan Vives, Figueres, 25 January 1993.

7 Miguel Alabrús, 'Extraordinarias declaraciones de Salvador Dalí', *Ampurdán*, Figueres, 1 September 1948.

8 'Una carta del padre del pintor Dalí', *Ampurdán*,

Figueres, 15 September 1948.

9   The reference is to Dalí's cousin, Montserrat Dalí, the daughter of his uncle Rafael. The art critic José Gudiol, later Montserrat's lover, never produced his book on Dalí.

10   The false paintings were suppressed, as well as Dalí's letter to Miravitlles.

11   Undated letter in the private collection of Don Pere Vehí, Cadaqués.

12   Dalí, *50 Secrets of Magic Craftsmanship*, p. 170.

13   Arco, pp. 37–8.

14   Descharnes, *The World of Salvador Dalí*, p. 175.

15   Arco, pp. 17–19.

16   Juan Luca de Tena, quoted by *Crónica de Madrid*, Barcelona, Plaza y Janés, p. 460.

17   'Art in Three Mediums', *The Sphere*, London, 19 November 1949, p. 287.

18   Cowles, pp. 197–202.

19   Morse, *Dalí. A Study of his Life and Work*, p. 62.

20   Arco, p. 122.

21   Massip, p. 3.

22   Puignau, p. 32; Arco, p. 79.

23   Arco, p. 78; *DG*, pp. 151–2.

24   Breton, *Oeuvres complètes*, II, p. 1152.

25   Photographs in *VPSD*, pp. 128–9. The designs were reproduced in the Folio Society's edition of *As You Like It*, introduced by Peter Brook, London, 1953.

26   *VPSD*, p. 131.

27   Descharnes, *The World of Salvador Dalí*, p. 26.

28   *AMD*, p. 16.

29   *Ibid.*, p. 38.

30   *Ibid.*, p. 50.

31   *Ibid.*, p. 138.

32   *Ibid.*, p. 136.

33   Eduard Fornés papers, Biblioteca de Catalunya, Barcelona.

34   *Ibid.*

35   Reproduced in *VPSD*, p. 132.

36   Eduard Fornés papers, Biblioteca de Catalunya, Barcelona.

37   Will signed in Figueres in the presence of the notary Raimundo Negre Balet. I am grateful to the notary Don Raimundo Fortuny i Marqués, of Figueres, for supplying me with a copy of the document.

38   Massip, p. 3.

39   See, for example, *Abc*, Madrid, 24 March 1950.

40   Massip, p. 5.

41   *UC*, p. 250.

42   Puignau, pp. 38–9.

43   Reproduced in *DOH*, p. 325.

44   Puignau, pp. 41–2.

45   Salvador Dalí Cusí's death certificate states that he died from 'generalized carcinomatosis' (Registre

Civil, Cadaqués); the information concerning Dalí's visit to his dead father proceeds from Doña Emilia Pomés, whose mother was the Dalís' housekeeper in Cadaqués; conversation with Doña Montserrat Dalí, Barcelona, 1 May 1992.

46   Puignau, p. 42.

47   Dalí Cusí's last will was signed, like the previous one, in the presence of the Figueres notary Raimundo Negre Balet. I am grateful once again to the notary Don Raimundo Fortuny i Marqués, of Figueres, for supplying me with a copy of it. According to an inscription at the end of the document, a copy was made for Dalí on 14 October 1950; for Dalí and Gala's hopes for inheriting part of the house, my source is the Albaretto family (conversation with Drs Giuseppe and Mara Albaretto, Turin, 24 October 1995).

48   Eduard Fornés papers, Biblioteca de Catalunya, Barcelona.

49   Unpublished postcard with postmark New York, 15 December 1950. Private collection of Don Pere Vehí, Cadaqués.

50   Letter from Gonzalo Serraclara to Dalí (4 December 1951) in Biblioteca de Catalunya, Barcelona.

51   Puignau, pp. 43–5.

52   Documents in Arxiu Històric, Girona (Department de Culture, Generalitat de Catalunya); for the intervention by Miguel Mateu, and Dalí's correspondence with the latter, file at the Castell de Perelada, Girona (my thanks to the librarian, Doña Inés Padrosa Gorgot); for Dalí's contemporary account, *DG*, pp. 66–70; Puignau, pp. 47–50; for the oedipal aspect, Daudet, 'Mágico Dalí', 1 March 1970, p. 46.

53   Arco, pp. 26, 92.

54   Dalí, 'Porque fui sacrílego, porque soy místico', typescript, dated Barcelona, 30 October 1930, in Biblioteca de Catalunya, Barcelona.

55   Gasch, *L'expansió de l'art catalá al món*, p. 163.

56   Puignau, pp. 53–6.

57   Morse, *Dalí. His Life and his Work*, p. 63.

58   *DOH*, p. 333; illustration, *ibid.*

59   Puignau, pp. 59–62; *DOH*, p. 318.

60   *Dalí* (Salvador Dali Museum, St. Petersburg, Florida, see Bibliography, Section 1), nos 79–80.

61   *Ibid.*, no. 86.

62   Puignau, pp. 62–4. A colour photograph of the *Nuclear Cross* with Dalí's dedication is included.

63   Reproduced in *VPSD*, p. 134.

64   Descharnes, *The World of Salvador Dalí*, p. 18.

65   Arco, pp. 61, 114.

66   *Ibid.*, p. 22.

67   *Ibid.*, p. 77.

68   *Ibid.*, p. 24.

69   Captain Peter Moore, Dalí's secretary in the

1960s and early 1970s, is adamant that Dalí never attended mass (conversations with Captain Moore, Cadaqués, 1995–6). So is Doña Nanita Kalaschnikoff, one of his few really close friends (conversations with Señora Kalaschnikoff, Paris and Marbella, 1994–5).

70   *UC*, p. 271. Pictures of the Dalís' costume in *VPSD*, p. 135.

71   The 'complete text' of the lecture printed by Utrillo, pp. 25–33, contains indications of the audience's responses throughout.

72   Utrillo, p. 37.

73   Antonio Saura, 'La playa desierta de Salvador Dalí', *El País*, Madrid, 9 October 1983, pp. 36–7.

74   Conversations with Don Rafael Santos Torroella, Barcelona, Cadaqués and Madrid, 1990–6; Jiménez and Playà, 'Dalí vist des de l'Empordà', no. VIII.

75   Santos Torroella, 'Con Salvador Dalí en Portlligat', *Correo Literario*, Barcelona, 1 September 1951, reproduced in Santos Torroella, *La trágica vida de Salvador Dalí*, pp. 21–7; Santos Torroella, *Salvador Dalí*, Madrid, Afrodisio Aguado, 1952. For the exhibition, held at the Sociedad de Amigos del Arte, see the latter, pp. 57–8.

76   *Madrid*, quoted by Utrillo, p. 50.

77   Utrillo, pp. 15, 19–20, 101.

78   *Ibid.*, p. 70.

79   Etherington-Smith, p. 384.

80   For the Alex, Reid Lefevre exhibition, *MEAC*, II, p. 128; for Dalí's statement, Santos Torroella, *Salvador Dalí*, p. 56.

81   Utrillo, p. 47.

82   *Ibid.*, p. 55.

83   *DG*, p. 32.

84   *Ibid.*, pp. 34–5.

85   *Ibid.*, p. 34.

86   Dalí, 'Authenticité et mensonge', *Arts*, 1 May 1952, quoted in *VPSD*, p. 136.

87   Cowles, p. 264, n. 1.

88   *DG*, p. 71.

89   Conversation with Mme Cécile Boaretto, Paris, 25 February 1995.

90   Catalogue in collection of Don Pere Vehí, Cadaqués.

91   Descharnes, *The World of Salvador Dalí*, p. 182.

92   *DG*, p. 123.

93   Dalí, *Martir. Tragédie-Lirique [sic] en III Actes*, published by Ignacio Gómez de Liaño (see Bibliography, Section 5).

94   Lear, *L'Amant-Dalí*, pp. 62–3.

95   *DG*, p. 123.

96   BBC TV *Panorama*, 4 May 1955.

97   Ades, p. 175.

98   *UC*, p. 166.

99   *MDJ*, vol. I; *VPSD*, p. 139; *MEAC*, II, p. 130;

three of the illustrations for *The Divine Comedy* are reproduced in *DOH*, pp. 330–1, and another four in Descharnes and Néret, *Salvador Dalí*, II, p. 449.

100 Juan Cortés Cavanillas, 'Salvador Dalí, el disparate genial', *Ideal*, Granada, 23 June 1983.

101 Miguel Utrillo, 'Dalí hará cine', *Cine Mundo*, Madrid, 5 June 1954; *DG*, pp. 92–3.

102 *MDJ*, vol. I; Eleanor Morse, 'My View', pp. xxvii–xxviii; Morse, *Animal Crackers*, p. 3.

103 Morse, *Dalí. A Panorama of his Art*, p. 159.

104 Conversation with Mr and Mrs Reynolds Morse, Madrid, Ritz Hotel, 23 October 1993.

105 Morse, *Dalí. A Panorama of his Art*, p. 127.

106 Reynolds Morse, 'Romantic Ampurdan', in Dalí. *A Panorama of his Art*, pp. 205–14; Eleanor Morse, 'My View', pp. xxvii–xxix; *MDJ*, Vol. I.

107 *MDJ*, vol. I.

108 Morse, *Animal Crackers*, p. 95.

109 Morse, *A Dalí Primer*, p. 31.

110 Morse, *A New Introduction to Salvador Dalí*, p. 22.

111 Morse, *Dalí. A Study of his Life and Work*, p. 25.

112 *Ibid.*, p. 24.

113 Morse, *Animal Crackers*, p. 115.

114 *Ibid.*, pp. 135–6.

115 *UD*, p. 170.

116 *Ibid.*, p. 203.

117 Morse, *Salvador Dalí, Pablo Picasso*, p. 24.

118 Morse, *Dalí. A Panorama of his Art*, p. 137.

119 *Ibid.*, p. 164.

120 *Ibid.*, p. 150.

121 Morse, *Salvador Dalí, Pablo Picasso*, p. 24.

122 Rubin, *Dada and Surrealism*, p. 220.

123 Morse, *Animal Crackers*, p. viii.

124 *DG*, p. 46.

125 Descharnes and Néret, II, no. 965, p. 437.

126 *DG*, pp. 46–7, 52; for the horn on top of the Great Masturbator rock, see Morse, *Dalí. A Panorama of his Art*, p. 193.

127 Descharnes and Néret, II, p. 480.

128 Morse, *Dalí. His Life and His Work*, pp. 78–82.

129 Reproduced in *DOH*, p. 338.

130 Morse, *Animal Crackers*, p. 72.

131 Descharnes, *The World of Salvador Dalí*, p. 54. The painting is reproduced at p. 55, and in *DOH*, p. 348.

132 Robert Descharnes was born at Nevers on 1 January 1926 (Juzgado de Instrucción de La Bisbal, Girona. Diligencias Previas núm. 1875, Año 1984, folio 25); *DOH*, p. 323; back flap of same for the number of photographs.

133 The text of the lecture is supplied by *VPSD*, pp. 144–5.

134 *Ibid.*, p. 146.

135 Dalí and Pauwels, p. 248; for Halsman's pho-

tographs of Dalí with rhinos, see catalogue *Dalí fotògraf*, *Dalí en els seus fotògrafs* (Bibliography, Section 1), pp. 52-3.

136 Carol, 'El escenógrafo de Portlligat'.

137 Tape-recorded conversation with Don Isidor Bea, Cadaqués, 10 August 1995.

138 Secrest, p. 205.

139 These paragraphs are the result of dozens of hours' conversation with Captain and Mrs Peter Moore in Cadaqués, Madrid and by telephone between 1991 and 1996. I am deeply grateful to Captain Moore for facilitating so much information and documentation concerning his life and his relationship with Salvador Dalí, including photocopies of his birth certificate, army demob papers and private correspondence. Without his collaboration this book would have been very much the poorer.

140 *BMDS*, p. 72.

141 Conversation with Doña Nanita Kalaschnikoff, Marbella, 14 September 1995.

142 Permanyer, 'El pincel erótico de Dalí'.

143 Conversation with Doña Nanita Kalaschnikoff, Marbella, 14 September 1995.

144 *Ibid.*

145 Conversation with Captain Peter Moore, Cadaqués, 1 December 1993.

146 Photograph of Dalí with Franco, *VPSD*, p. 136; the decree was issued on 9 October 1953 (Playà, *Dalí de l'Empordà*, p. 32).

147 Conversations with Don Rafael Santos Torroella and his wife Maite, Barcelona and Cadaqués, 1995-6; conversations with Drs Guiseppe and Mara Albaretto, Turin, 1995.

148 Conversation with Drs Mara and Giuseppe Albaretto, London, 2 March 1994.

149 *Ibid.*

150 *Ibid.*

151 The portrait of Anna Maria is reproduced in *Salvador Dalí. La vita è sogno* (catalogue, see Bibliography, Section 1).

152 *VPSD*, pp. 147-8.

153 Secrest, p. 214.

154 *Ibid.*, p. 216.

155 Bosquet, *Dalí desnudado*, p. 17.

156 Morse, *Salvador Dalí. A Panorama of his Art*, pp. 194-5. Descharnes, *The World of Dalí*, p. 68.

157 Descharnes, *The World of Dalí*, p. 68.

158 Tape-recorded conversation with Don Isidor Bea, Cadaqués, 10 August 1995.

159 Morse, *Salvador Dalí. A Panorama of his Art*, p. 195.

160 *VPSD*, p. 156.

161 Descharnes, *The World of Salvador Dalí*, p. 70.

162 *Ibid.*

163 Roumeguère, 'Canibalismo y estética'; *UC*, p. 242.

164 Roumeguère, 'Canibalismo y estética'.

165 Roumeguère, 'La mística dalíniana ante la historia de las religiones', pp. 277-8.

166 *DG*, p. 181.

167 Bosquet, *Dalí desnudado*, pp. 39-40.

168 Roumeguère, 'The Cosmic Dalí'.

169 *Ibid.*, p. v.

170 *Ibid.*, p. vii.

171 *Ibid.*, p. vi.

172 Bosquet, *Dalí desnudado*, p. 40.

173 Roumeguère, 'The Cosmic Dalí', pp. vii-viii.

174 Roumeguère, 'Canabalismo y estética'.

175 Playà i Maset, *Dalí de l'Empordà*, pp. 23-4.

176 *DOH*, p. 355.

177 *VPSD*, p. 151; the painting is reproduced in *DOH*, p. 355.

178 VSPD, p. 151.

179 *Ibid.*, p. 152; for the cover, *DOH*, p. 357.

180 *VPSD*, p. 153; *DOH*, p. 321.

Thirteen: The 'Amplification' of Talents (1960-6)

1 Conversations with Captain Peter Moore, Cadaqués, 1995-96.

2 Captain Peter Moore interviewed in *Dalí*, BBC TV 'Arena', 1986 (see Bibliography, Section 7).

3 Filmed conversation with Captain Peter Moore, Cadaqués, 6 August 1995; telephone conversation with him (in Cadaqués), 26 August 1996.

4 Morse, *Salvador Dalí, Pablo Picasso*, p. 36.

5 Reynolds Morse's copy of the typescript of *Soft Watches and Hard Times*, Salvador Dali Museum, St Petersburg, Florida.

6 'Up-dating' to Morse's *A New Introduction to Salvador Dalí*, pp. 13-14.

7 Morse, *Animal Crackers*, p. 197. The painting was *The Ecumenical Council*.

8 Conversation with Captain Peter Moore, Cadaqués, 27 October 1995.

9 Morse, *Salvador Dalí. A Panorama of his Art*, p. 194; Secrest, p. 215.

10 *UC*, p. 166.

11 *DG*, p. 189.

12 Reproduced in black and white by Morse, *Dalí. A Panorama of his Art*, p. 197.

13 Reproduced in *DOH*, p. 361; Descharnes and Néret, II, p. 530.

14 Tract reproduced in *VPSD*, p. 157.

15 Wills made before the notary Raimundo Negre Balet, Figueres. I am grateful to the notary Don Raimundo Fortuny i Marqués, Figueres, for supplying a copy of these.

16 Vallès i Rovira, I, p. 158.
17 Guardiola, p. 13.
18 *Ibid.*
19 *Ibid.*, p. 14.
20 Romero, *Todo Dalí en un rostro*, p. 254.
21 The account of the day's proceedings is taken from Guardiola, pp. 62–79; Playà, *Dalí de l'Empordà*, pp. 26–8.
22 Copy of the poster in the Salvador Dali Museum, St Petersburg, Florida; conversation with Don Isidor Bea, Cadaqués, 10 August 1995.
23 Moore, *Soft Watches and Hard Times*, pp. 53–4.
24 Etherington-Smith, p. 409.
25 'Dalí v Scarlatti', *Time*, New York, 1 September 1961; Morse, *Animal Crackers*, pp. 35, 45, 46, 183, 211, 238. See also *DG*, p. 147, for hints on how to make a farmyard goose suffer.
26 'Dalí v Scarlatti', *Time*, New York, 1 September 1961.
27 *Ibid.*
28 *Ibid.*
29 Etherington-Smith, p. 159; *VPSD*, p. 158; *ibid.*, p. 59, for a photograph of Ludmilla Tcherina dancing in the ballet.
30 *SL*, p. 149, note.
31 *Catàleg de pintura segles XIX a XX. Fons del Museu d'Art Modern*, Ajuntament de Barcelona, 1987, I, p. 406.
32 Morse, *Animal Crackers*, p. 142.
33 The painting is reproduced in *DOH*, p. 363; the painting and some studies by Descharnes and Néret, II, pp. 538–41.
34 Santos Torroella, 'Arte y no arte de Salvador Dalí en su homenaje a Fortuny'.
35 Secrest, p. 195.
36 *VPSD*, p. 160.
37 *UC*, p. 153.
38 Vivien Raynor in *Arts*, Paris, January 1964, quoted in *VPSD*, p. 161.
39 The catalogue's cover is reproduced in *VPSD*, p. 161.
40 Lake, p. 29.
41 *Ibid.*
42 *Ibid.*, p. 21.
43 *UC*, p. 156.
44 Dalí and Pauwels, p. 214.
45 *DG*, p. 214.
46 *Ibid.*
47 *DG*, p. 234.
48 Dalí, 'Résumé of History and the History of Painting'.
49 *UC*, p. 157.
50 *VPSD*, p. 165.
51 *Ibid.*, p. 161.

52 *UC*, p. 262.
53 Conversation with Dr Mara Albaretto, Turin, 25 October 1995.
54 *Ibid.*
55 The date of Gala and Rotlein's meeting is given as 1963 by McGirk, p. 127, but no source is provided.
56 Conversation with Dr Mara Albaretto, Turin, 23 October 1995.
57 *Ibid.*
58 Conversations with Drs Giuseppe and Mara Albaretto, Turin, 23–24 October 1995; with Captain Peter Moore, Cadaqués, 1994. The substance of the Albarettos' version, as told to me, was published a few years earlier in *La Vanguardia*, Barcelona, 29 January 1989, p. 43.
59 Conversation with Dr Manuel Vergara, Cadaqués, 6 August 1996.
60 Bosquet, *Dalí desnudado*, pp. 86–7.
61 Conversation with Dr Giuseppe Albaretto, Turin, 25 October 1995.
62 Conversation with Dr Mara Albaretto, Turin, 25 October 1995, while watching slides of the series.
63 Lake, pp. 30–40; Field, untitled article in *MEAC*, II, pp. 18–21; Field, *The Official Catalog of the Graphic Works of Salvador Dalí*, pp. 7–8.
64 *Ibid.*, pp. 41–2.
65 *Dalí à Perpignan* (catalogue, see Bibliography, Section 1), commentary to illustration 89.
66 Lake, p. 75.
67 *Ibid.*, p. 229.
68 *Ibid.*, p. 81; *VPSD*, pp. 200–1.
69 Lake, p. 182.
70 *Ibid.*, pp. 223, 263.
71 *Ibid.*, p. 202.
72 *Ibid.*, p. 239.
73 *Ibid.*, p. 163.
74 *Dalí in New York* (see Bibliography, Section 7).
75 Lake, p. 300.
76 *Ibid.*, p. 301.
77 *Ibid.*, p. 302.
78 *Ibid.*, p. 305.
79 Quoted by Secrest, p. 215.
80 Secrest, p. 215.
81 Morse, *The Dalí Adventure*, photograph no. 56.
82 *Ibid.*, caption to illustration 61, which reproduces the programme.
83 Morse, 'Homage to Dalí', in catalogue *Salvador Dalí 1910–1965* (see Bibliography, Section 1).
84 Secrest, p. 215.
85 Morse, *Salvador Dalí, Pablo Picasso*, p. 24.

Fourteen: Amanda Lear and Other Extravagances
(1966–75)

1 Excerpt from the 'Hommage à Meissonier' catalogue in Descharnes and Néret, II, p. 567.
2 Morse, *Animal Crackers*, p. 237.
3 Fornés, *Dalí y los libros*, p. 67; Descharnes and Néret, II, p. 567.
4 Excerpt from the 'Hommage à Meissonier' catalogue in Descharnes and Néret, II, p. 567.
5 Secrest, p. 195.
6 In *Les Nouvelles Littéraires*, quoted in *VPSD*, p. 167.
7 Dalí and Pauwels, p. 108; Bosquet, *Dalí desnudado*, p. 26.
8 Dalí and Pauwels, p. 108.
9 *Ibid.*, p. 125.
10 *Ibid.*, p. 182.
11 Telephone conversation with April Ashley (in San Diego, California), 10 March 1997; Fallowell and Ashley, *passim*.
12 Fallowell and Ashley, *passim*.
13 *Ibid.*, pp. 178–80, 240–1.
14 Copy of the 'Entry of Marriage' certificate supplied to me by Chelsea Register Office.
15 Conversation with the present head of the hotel, Señora Quinto, and Señora Angels Torres, who both remember Amanda Lear well; for Dietrich at Le Carrousel, telephone conversation with April Ashley (in San Diego, California), 10 March 1997.
16 Conversations with Don Ignacio de Lassaletta, Barcelona, July and August 1996, and Sue Guinness (Lady Moyne), Cadaqués, 7 August 1996.
17 Conversation with Amanda Lear, St. Rémy de Provence, 2 July 1996.
18 Conversation with Doña Nanita Kalaschnikoff, Marbella, 23 July 1995.
19 *Tiempo*, Madrid, special supplement on Dalí's death, 23 January 1989, p. 8; conversation with Don Isidor Bea, Cadaqués, 10 August 1995.
20 'Love Story en Cadaqués', *Turismo y Vida*, Madrid, October 1971.
21 Telephone conversation with Captain Peter Moore (in Cadaqués), 10 August 1993.
22 Telephone conversation with Doña Nanita Kalaschnikoff (in Marbella), 8 May 1996.
23 Conversation with Amanda Lear, St. Rémy de Provence, 2 July 1996.
24 Lear, *Le Dalí d'Amanda*, p. 29.
25 *Ibid.*, p. 85; *VPSD*, p. 168.
26 *DG*, p. 85.
27 Argillet, 'Dalí–Breton'.
28 Lear, *Le Dalí d'Amanda*, p. 87.
29 Conversation with Don Carlos Lozano, Cadaqués, 29 June 1996.

30 *Ibid.*
31 Lear, *Le Dalí d'Amanda*, pp. 140–3.
32 Dalí and Pauwels, p. 239.
33 Conversation with Captain Peter Moore, Cadaqués, 26 October 1993.
34 Conversation with Don Carlos Lozano, Cadaqués, 29 June 1996.
35 *Ibid.*
36 Dalí and Pauwels, pp. 160–1.
37 Telephone conversation with Robert Whitaker, 17 March 1997; Clifford Thurlow, *Sex, Surrealism, Dalí . . . and Me. The Memoirs of Carlos Lozano*, unpublished autobiography.
38 *Ibid.*
39 Lear, *L'Amant-Dalí. Ma Vie avec Salvador Dalí*, Paris, Michel Lafon, 1994.
40 Lear, *Le Dalí d'Amanda*, pp. 207–8.
41 Carol, *Dalí. El final oculto de un exhibicionista*, p. 110; conversation with Don Enric Sabater, Calella de Palafrugell, 30 June 1996.
42 Conversation with Don Enric Sabater, Calella de Palafrugell, 30 June 1996.
43 *Gowans's Art Books*, no. 38 (1910), p. 37.
44 Lear, *Le Dalí d'Amanda*, pp. 194–5; on anaglyphs and their further connotation at the Residencia de Estudiantes, see *SVBLD*, pp. 72–4.
45 Romero, *Todo Dalí en un rostro*, p. 160.
46 Conversation with Doña Nanita Kalaschnikoff, Granada, 7 June 1996.
47 Morse, *Animal Crackers*, p. 32.
48 *DG*, p. 181.
49 For an account of the circumstances of Sánchez Mejías's death, see my biography *Federico García Lorca. A Life*, pp. 387–91.
50 Morse, *Salvador Dalí. A Panorama of his Art*, pp. 198, 202.
51 *Ibid.*, p. 198.
52 Romero, *Todo Dalí en un rostro*, pp. 145, 311, note 15.
53 Romero, *Torero allucinogen*, p. 5.
54 Romero, *Todo Dalí en un rostro*, p. 189.
55 Reproduced by Morse, *Salvador Dalí. A Panorama of his Art*, p. 200.
56 Conversation with Mr Reynolds Morse, Florida, 15 July 1966; Romero, *Todo Dalí en un rostro*, p. 93.
57 Romero, *Todo Dalí en un rostro*, pp. 171–82.
58 Conversation with Don Carlos Lozano, Cadaqués, 29 June 1996.
59 Romero, *Todo Dalí en un rostro*, p. 225.
60 *Ibid.*, p. 217.
61 *MDJ*, 15 May 1979.
62 Conversation with Don Enric Sabater, Calella de Palafrugell, 30 June 1996.
63 Conversation with Drs Mara and Giuseppe Alba-

retto, Turin, 23 October 1995.

64 Puignau, p. 112.

65 Conversation with M. Marc Lacroix, Perpignan, June 1996.

66 Puignau, pp. 112–14.

67 Guardiola, p. 131.

68 Guardiola, p. 131; 'I wrote a proposition to the then mayor Guardiola offering to rent the old theatre with Mr Durán as a Restaurant–Museum showing my collection of Dalís. The rest is history. The Town Council then decided to advance some funds and clean the rubble after which Franco's boys moved in' (Captain Peter Moore in a written communication to the author); telephone conversation with Luis Durán Camps's son, my friend Luis Durán, the current owner of the hotel, 19 January 1997.

69 Dalí and Pauwels, pp. 132–3.

70 Guardiola, pp. 151–2.

71 *Ibid.*, p. 157.

72 Enric Sabater, 'Este será el primer cuadro que Dalí donará a su museo', *Los Sitios*, Girona, 14 June 1970, p. 7.

73 *Los Sitios*, Girona, 14 July 1970, p. 8; Lear, *Le Dalí d'Amanda*, pp. 156, 164.

74 Conversation with Don Enric Sabater, Calella de Palafrugell, 30 June 1996.

75 *Ibid.*

76 Lear, *Le Dalí d'Amanda*, pp. 201–3.

77 *Ibid.*, pp. 205–6.

78 *Hullo Dalí* (see Bibliography, Section 7).

79 Moore, *Soft Watches and Hard Times*, p. 152. The note by Morse is in his copy of the typescript, preserved in the Salvador Dali Museum, St Petersburg, Florida.

80 *Ibid.*

81 *Ibid.*, pp. 152–3.

82 *Ibid.*, p. 153.

83 Luis Romero in the Spanish TV programme *El enigma Dalí* (see Bibliography, Section 7).

84 Alfons Quinta, 'Dalí ha firmado papeles en blanco que facilitan la reproducción incontrolada de su obra', *El País*, Madrid, 13 March 1981, pp. 1, 28–9.

85 Puignau, pp. 255–6.

86 Document shown on the Spanish TV programme *Pintar después de morir* ('*Documentos TV*') in 1989 (see Bibliography, Section 7).

87 Catterall, p. 4.

88 *Ibid.*, pp. 60–1; Field, *The Official Catalog*, p. 247.

89 Catterall, pp. 60–1.

90 *Ibid.*, p. 273.

91 *Ibid.*, pp. 61, 183.

92 Carol, p. 120; Catterall, *passim*.

93 *MDJ*, vol. 12.

94 Captain Peter Moore's written answer to one of my questions.

95 Puignau, pp. 156–7.

96 Conversation with Captain Peter Moore, Cadaqués, 7 August 1996.

97 Telephone conversation with Captain Peter Moore (in Cadaqués), 1 December 1993; conversation with him in Cadaqués, 7 August 1996.

98 Màrius Carol, 'Jean Claude du Barry. "Los franceses no hemos sabido reivindicar a Salvador Dalí para Francia"', *La Vanguardia*, Barcelona, 27 January 1989, p. 43; Puignau, p. 127.

99 *UD*, pp. 105–8; Màrius Carol, 'Jean Claude du Barry. "Los franceses no hemos sabido reivindicar a Salvador Dalí para Francia"', *La Vanguardia*, Barcelona, 27 January 1989, p. 43.

100 Lear, *Le Dalí d'Amanda*, p. 175.

101 Bona, p. 383.

102 Romero, *Dedálico Dalí*, p. 269.

103 Secrest, p. 203.

104 *UD*, p. 104.

105 *Ibid.*, pp. 98, 103.

106 McGirk, pp. 140–1.

107 Lear, *Le Dalí d'Amanda*, pp. 248–9, 277.

108 McGirk, p. 145.

109 *MDJ*, 19 May 1980.

110 Letter to the Salvador Dali Museum, St Petersburg, Florida, from Fenholt's lawyer, D. John Hendrickson, protesting about an allusion to the actor's relationship with Gala published in the 'Exhibition Notes' to the museum's show of photographs 'Galuchka. Dalí's Russian Muse'.

111 Etherington-Smith, pp. 435–6; *VPSD*, p. 178.

112 'Statement by Salvador Dalí, 3 April 1978, at Knoedler Galleries'. I am grateful to my friend Frank Hunter for a copy of this document.

113 *MDJ*, vol. 11.

114 Telephone conversation with Captain Peter Moore (in Cadaqués), 26 August 1996.

115 Morse, *Animal Crackers*, pp. viii–ix; conversations with Captain Peter Moore, Cadaqués, 1995–6.

116 Guardiola, p. 247.

117 *Ibid.*

118 *Ibid.*, pp. 247–52.

119 *Ibid.*, p. 252.

120 *Ibid.*, pp. 254–6.

121 Wills sworn in Cadaqués before José Gómez de la Serna, the notary of Llançà, on 1 June 1974. I am grateful to Don Luis Ignacio Fernández Posada for supplying me with copies of these documents.

122 The text of the statutes is given by Fornés, pp. 11–30.

123 The invitation is reproduced by Romero, *Todo Dalí en un rostro*, p. 262.

124 Romero, *Aquel Dalí*, pp. 176–9, includes some

photographs of the event by Josep Postius.

125 Lear, *L'Amant-Dalí*, pp. 242–3.
126 *MDJ*, 18 March 1979.
127 Guardiola, pp. 283–4.
128 Telephone conversation with Don Antoni Pitxot (in Cadaqués), 18 January 1997; see also Lear, *L'Amant-Dalí*, p. 250.
129 Conversation with Don Enric Sabater, Calella de Palafrugell, 30 July 1996.
130 Dalí, *Être Dieu*, 'Opera-poema', produced by Distribucions d'art surrealista, Barcelona. DCD-50001-3.
131 Conversation with Captain Peter Moore, Cadaqués, 9 May 1993.
132 *Ibid.*
133 Catterall, pp. 45–7; 'Demandado en USA. Una editorial reclama a Dalí la entrega de 78 gouaches', *Diario de Barcelona*, 30 January 1975.
134 Conversation with Don Enric Sabater, Calella de Palafrugell, 30 June 1996.
135 Conversation with Captain and Mrs Moore, Cadaqués, 7 March 1994.
136 *Ibid.*
137 Telephone conversation with Captain Peter Moore (in Cadaqués), 25 November 1993.
138 Conversation with Doña Nanita Kalaschnikoff, Marbella, 11 January 1995.
139 Conversation with Captain Peter Moore, Cadaqués, 9 November 1991.

Fifteen: The Decline (1975–82)

1 *Le Monde*, Paris, 3 October 1975, p. 2.
2 *Le Figaro*, Paris, 2 October 1975, pp. 1, 3; *Le Monde*, Paris, 2 October 1975, p. 1.
3 *Le Monde*, Paris, 2 October 1975, pp. 1–3, 3 October 1975, p. 2.
4 *Ibid.*, 2 October 1975, p. 2.
5 *Ibid.*, 2 October 1975, pp. 1–3 'La campaña extranjera. La "Jornada de Protesta" causa perturbaciones en los transportes y en el suministro de electricidad de París', *La Vanguardia*, Barcelona, 3 October 1975, p. 24.
6 'Salvador Dalí: Franco est un être merveilleux', *Le Monde*, Paris, 3 October 1975, p. 2. Also consulted: 'Salvador Dalí: "Franco est merveilleux"', *Le Figaro*, Paris, 2 October 1975, p. 3; *La Vanguardia*, Barcelona, 3 October 1975, p. 24; 'Dalí: Bring Back The Inquisition', *New York Post*, 2 October 1975.
7 *Le Monde*, Paris, 3 October 1975; 'La campaña extranjera. La "Jornada de Protesta" causa perturbaciones en los transportes y en el suministro de electricidad de París', *La Vanguardia*, Barcelona, 3 October 1975, p. 24.
8 'Dalí Speaks his Mind and Loses his Job', *San Francisco Examiner*, 10 October 1975.
9 'La casa de Dalí, apedreada', *Tele-Express*, Barcelona, 4 October 1975, p. 5 (not seen); Sandra Lee Stuart, 'Dalí Denies he Called for Liquidations', *Times Advertiser*, Trenton, NJ, 12 October 1975.
10 Lear, *Le Dalí d'Amanda*, p. 262.
11 Conversation with Don Enric Sabater, Calella de Palafrugell, 30 June 1996.
12 Lear, *L'Amant-Dalí*. pp. 285–7.
13 For the quotation, Catterall, p. 46; *MDJ*, October 1975.
14 For the date of Dalí's arrival in New York, *New York Times*, 11 October 1975; *MDJ*.
15 *New York Times*, 11 October 1975.
16 Sandra Lee Stuart, 'Dalí Denies he Called for Liquidations', *Times Advertiser*, Trenton, NJ, 12 October 1975.
17 *MDJ*, October 1975.
18 *Ibid.*, 28 October 1979, 22 May 1980, etc.; *UD*, pp. 48–9.
19 Conversation with Dr Manuel Vergara, Cadaqués, 6 August 1996.
20 Conversation with Michael Stout, New York, 11 July 1996.
21 *Ibid.*
22 *Ibid.*
23 *Ibid.*
24 Alfons Quinta, 'La compleja y tortuosa situación financiera de Dalí', *El País*, Madrid, 4 September 1980, p. 23.
25 Conversation with Michael Stout, New York, 11 July 1996.
26 *MDJ*, 27 October 1979, 14 March 1980, etc.
27 Alfons Quinta, 'La compleja y tortuosa situación financiera de Dalí', *El País*, Madrid, 4 September 1980, p. 22.
28 *Ibid.*
29 *MDJ*, 15 September 1981.
30 Playà, *Dalí de l'Empordà*, pp. 30–1.
31 Gibson, *Fire in the Blood. The New Spain*, p. 52.
32 Conversation with Don Enric Sabater, Calella de Palafrugell, 30 June 1996.
33 Vila-San-Juan, pp. 228–30.
34 Pla, *Obres de museu*, p. 181.
35 Michler and Löpsinger, p. 252; telephone conversation with Captain Peter Moore (in Cadaqués), 30 August 1996.
36 *Les Caprices de Goya de Salvador Dalí*, Hamburg, Galerie Levy, 1977.
37 Conversation with Dr Manuel Vergara, Cadaqués, 6 August 1996.
38 *MDJ*, 27 October 1979.

39 Carol, p. 114.

40 *MDJ*, 8, 22 March 1980.

41 Antonio D. Olano, 'Salvador Dalí "Mi pintura es una m . . . "', *La Gaceta Ilustrada*, Madrid, 20 May 1979, pp. 100–2.

42 *MDJ*, 14 May 1979.

43 Dalí commented on his speech in that morning's *Figaro*, see *VPSD*, p. 194, which includes some brief extracts from the speech itself; for photographs of the occasion, *ibid.*, p. 195. A fuller extract from the speech is given in *DOH*, p. 420.

44 *MDJ*, 20 May 1979; Antonio D. Olano, 'Salvador Dalí "Mi pintura es una m . . . "', *La Gaceta Ilustrada*, Madrid, 20 May 1979, pp. 100–2.

45 Playà, *Dalí de l'Empordà*, p. 31.

46 Gómez de Liaño, *Dalí*, p. 32.

47 The three programmes, written, directed and presented by Paloma Chamorro, were shown on 'Imágenes', RTE, Madrid, on 30 May, 6 June and 13 June 1979.

48 *The Guardian Weekly*, 15 October 1995, p. 33, commenting on the Cézanne exhibition, says that the Dalí retrospective in the Pompidou was seen by 840,000 people.

49 *MDJ*, 21 March 1980.

50 *DOH*, p. 419.

51 *MDJ*, 22 March 1980.

52 Alvaro Martínez-Novillo, 'El largo proyecto de una exposición antológica', *El País*, Madrid, 'Artes', 9 April 1983, p. 2; according to Reynolds Morse, *MDJ*, 22 March 1980, an increasingly paranoid Gala considered Hulten and Daniel Abadie 'dirty Communists' and believed they had deliberately provoked the strike.

53 Màrius Carol, 'Las otras muertes de Salvador Dalí', *La Vanguardia*, Barcelona, 24 January 1989, p. 50; Romero, *Dedálico Dalí*, p. 261.

54 *MDJ*, 8 March 1980.

55 *Ibid.*, 19–22 March 1980.

56 *Ibid.*

57 *Salvador Dalí* (Pompidou catalogue), p. 3.

58 *MDJ*, 22 March 1980; a sheet of the notepaper is included by Reynolds Morse in his copy of Peter Moore's unpublished *Hard Times and Soft Watches*, Salvador Dali Museum archive, St Petersburg, Florida.

59 Field, *The Official Catalog*, p. 227.

60 Conversation with Michael Stout, New York, 11 July 1996.

61 Secrest, pp. 240–1; conversation with Doña Nanita Kalaschnikoff, Cadaqués, 25 August 1995.

62 Telephone conversation with Doña Nanita Kalaschnikoff (in Paris), 4 September 1996.

63 Telephone conversation with Doña Nanita Kalaschnikoff (in Marbella), 10 January 1995.

64 Conversation with Albert Field, New York, 11 July 1996.

65 *UD*, pp. 53–6.

66 *MDJ*, 26 April 1980.

67 Manuscript note by Reynolds Morse in his copy of Moore's unpublished *Hard Times and Soft Watches*, Salvador Dali Museum archive, St Petersburg, Florida.

68 *MDJ*, 13 May 1980.

69 *Ibid.*, 16 May 1980.

70 *Ibid.*, 18 May 1980.

71 *Ibid.*

72 *Ibid.*, 21 May 1980.

73 *Ibid.*, 30 October 1983.

74 *Ibid.*, 23 May 1980.

75 James Markham, *New York Times*, 12 October 1980; *UD*, p. 56.

76 *MDJ*, 22 May 1980.

77 Captain Peter Moore's personal archive, Cadaqués.

78 *MDJ*, 21 May 1980, 11.45 p.m.

79 Vila-San-Juan, p. 232.

80 *UD*, pp. 56–7; Secrest, p. 241; conversation with Don Antoni Pitxot, Figueres, 29 June 1996.

81 Alfons Quinta, 'La compleja y tortuosa situación financiera de Salvador Dalí', *El País*, 4 September 1980, pp. 22–3; Albert Arbós, 'Los tesoros ocultos de Dalí', *Cambio 16*, Madrid, 23 March 1981.

82 Alfons Quinta, 'Salvador Dalí no ha efectuado declaración de renta o patrimonio a la Hacienda española', *El País*, Madrid, 18 September 1980, p. 27.

83 James Markham, *New York Times*, 12 October 1980.

84 This account is based on the notes I took at the press conference, the first time that I had seen Dalí and Gala in person. Given the huge number of journalists present, the event was widely covered in the Spanish and international press.

85 'Retrasos de una exposición', *El País*, Madrid, 14 January 1981, p. 20: Alvaro Martínez-Novillo, 'El largo proyecto de una exposición antológica', *ibid.*, 9 April 1983, p. 2.

86 Spanish TV programme *El enigma Dalí* (see Bibliography, Section 7).

87 The text of Gala's will is in Fornés, *Les contradiccions del cas Dalí*, pp. 137–9. I am grateful to Señor Fornés for supplying me with a copy of Dalí's. For the date on which Sabater left the Dalís' service, see the interview with him in *El País*, Madrid, 29 January 1989, p. 56.

88 *UD*, p. 61; Romero, *Dedálico Dalí*, p. 268; 'Dalí y Gala anularán su residencia en Mónaco', *La Vanguardia*, Barcelona, 14 September 1980, p. 5.

89 'Dalí proyecta en París un gigantesco homenaje al filósofo Spinoza', *El País*, Madrid, 14 January 1981, p. 20.

90 *Elle*, Paris, 26 January 1981, quoted by Bona, p. 416; 'Dalí, abandonado por Gala, se deja morir de amor', *Noticiero Universal*, Barcelona, 28 January 1981.

91 Puignau, pp. 163–4.

92 *El País*, Madrid, 29 January 1989, p. 56.

93 Albert Arbós, 'Los tesoros ocultos de Dalí, *Cambio 16*, Madrid, 23 March 1981.

94 *UD*, pp. 105–8; Secrest, p. 242.

95 James Markham, 'Dalí Untangles his Life', *The New York Times Magazine*, 22 November 1981.

96 Conversation with Michael Stout, New York, 11 July 1996.

97 *UD*, p. 61.

98 Documents reproduced by Fornés, *Les contradiccions del cas Dalí*, pp. 177–81; *MDJ*, 3 April 1981.

99 Francisco Mora, 'Enrique Sabater: "'Desde noviembre hasta aquí han abusado de Dalí"', *Correo Catalán*, Barcelona, 21 March 1981; *UD*, pp. 61–2.

100 Romero, *Dedálico Dalí*, pp. 269–70; Fornés, *Les contradiccions del cas Dalí*, p. 186.

101 *UD*, p. 62.

102 *Ibid.*, pp. 62–3; Romero, *Dedálico Dalí*, pp. 268–9; conversation with Doctors Mara and Giuseppe Albaretto, Turin, 24 October 1995.

103 Alfons Quinta, 'Dalí ha firmado papeles en blanco que facilitan la reproducción incontrolada de su obra', *El País*, Madrid, 13 March 1981, pp. 1, 28–9.

104 James Markham, 'Dalí Untangles his Life', *The New York Times Magazine*, 22 November 1981. According to one source, Sabater handed in his written resignation on 12 March 1981, whereupon Gala spat in his face (Carol, p. 131).

105 Francisco Mora, 'Enrique Sabater: "'Desde noviembre hasta aquí han abusado de Dalí"', *Correo Catalán*, Barcelona, 21 March 1981.

106 Robert Descharnes, interviewed by Josep Playà in *La Vanguardia*, Barcelona, 30 September 1994; Carol, *Dalí. El final oculto de un exhibicionista*, pp. 133–4; tape-recorded conversation with Don Miguel Domenech, Madrid, 19 February 1997.

107 Tape-recorded conversation with Don Miguel Domenech, Madrid, 19 February 1997.

108 Robert Descharnes, interviewed by Josep Playà in *La Vanguardia*, Barcelona, 30 September 1994.

109 Romero, *Dedálico Dalí*, p. 270.

110 *El País*, Madrid, 27 August 1981, p. 17; there is a black-and-white photograph of Dalí and Gala with the painting in *DOH*, p. 421.

111 *UD*, p. 77.

112 *El País*, Madrid, 27 August 1981, p. 17.

113 *Ibid.*

114 James Markham, 'Dalí Untangles his Life', *The New York Times Magazine*, 22 November 1981.

115 *DOH*, pp. 419, 424.

116 *UD*, p. 79.

117 *Ibid.*, pp. 79–80.

118 *Ibid.*, p. 80; photograph of the occasion in *DOH* p. 422.

119 Conversation with Doña Nanita Kalaschnikoff, Marbella, 30 May 1996.

120 *UD*, p. 81.

121 *Ibid.*, pp. 80–1; Puignau, p. 173.

122 Conversation with Mme Cécile Éluard, Paris, 25 February, 1995; Puignau, p. 174.

123 Lear, *Le Dalí d'Amanda*, pp. 285–6.

124 *UD*, p. 82; Descharnes, 'La solitaria de Púbol'.

125 Telephone conversation with Don Antoni Pitxot (in Cadaqués), 30 August 1995; conversation with Dr Manuel Vergara, Cadaqués, 6 August 1996.

126 For Gala's desire to be buried in Púbol, conversation with Don Antoni Pitxot, Cadaqués, 30 August 1995, and with Doctors Mara and Giuseppe Albaretto, Turin, 23 October 1995; for her wish to die there, Robert Descharnes to *La Vanguardia*, Barcelona, 22 January 1989, p. 58.

127 Conversation with Dr Manuel Vergara, Cadaqués, 6 August 1996.

128 Telephone conversation with Doña Nanita Kalaschnikoff (in Marbella), 29 August 1995.

129 *La Vanguardia*, Barcelona, 11 June 1995, p. 6.

130 Copy of Gala Dalí's death certificate kindly supplied by the town hall of La Pera (Girona).

131 *UD*, pp. 82–3.

132 Telephone conversation with Captain Peter Moore (in Cadaqués), 25 August 1995.

133 *El Periódico*, Barcelona, 12 June 1982, p. 18.

134 *Ibid.*, 11 June 1992, p. 6.

135 *El País*, Madrid, 11 June 1982, p. 32.

136 Telephone conversation with Don Antoni Pitxot (in Cadaqués), 30 August 1995; *La Vanguardia*, Barcelona, 12 June 1982, p. 18.

137 *Ibid.*, p. 25, says she was laid out in a white tunic, but this was incorrect.

138 Telephone conversation with Don Antoni Pitxot (in Cadaqués), 30 August 1995.

139 *UD*, p. 84.

140 Conversation with Don Gonzalo Serraclara, Barcelona, 26 May 1993; conversation with Doña Montserrat Dalí, Barcelona, 10 June 1992.

141 Conversation with Don Gonzalo Serraclara, Barcelona, 26 May 1993.

142 Telephone conversation with Don Antoni Pitxot (in Cadaqués), 30 August 1995.

143 *El Periódico*, Barcelona, 12 June 1982, p. 17.

144 Gala Dalí's will is reproduced by Fornés, *Les contradiccions del cas Dalí*, pp. 137–9.

145 *Ibid.*, p. 135.

146 *UD*, pp. 170–1.

147 *Ibid.*, p. 171; conversation with Don Miguel Domenech, Madrid, 19 February 1997; for the date of the government's purchase, the source is a deed signed by Dalí and preserved at the *notaría* of La Bisbal (Girona).

Sixteen: The Fall (1982–9)

1 Dalí and Pauwels, pp. 62–3.
2 Conversation with Dr Mara Albaretto, Turin, 25 October 1995.
3 *La Vanguardia*, Barcelona, 12 June 1995, p. 25.
4 Puignau, p. 176.
5 Romero, *Aquel Dalí*, p. 35.
6 Romero, *Dedálico Dalí*, p. 62.
7 Conversation with Don Rafael Santos Torroella, Port Lligat, 5 June 1994.
8 *MDJ*, vol. 12, 9 January 1984.
9 Conversation with Don Gonzalo Serraclara, Barcelona, 26 May 1993.
10 Conversation with Don Gonzalo Serraclara, Barcelona, 26 May 1993; conversation with Don Antoni Pitxot, Cadaqués, 5 August 1995; Gonzalo Serraclara to *El País*, Madrid, 4 September 1984, p. 20.
11 *MDJ*, 13 October 1983.
12 Notaría de La Bisbal (Girona). I am indebted to the notary Don José María Martínez Palmer for supplying me with a copy of this document.
13 Miguel Domenech interviewed on Spanish TV programme *El enigma Dalí* (see Bibliography, Section 7).
14 The will is reproduced by Fornés, *Les contradiccions del cas Dalí*, pp. 221–2; tape-recorded interview with Don Miguel Domenech, Madrid, 19 February 1997.
15 Jesús Conte, 'Com Dalí va desheretar Catalunya', *Set Dies*, Barcelona, 12 October 1990; telephone conversation with Don Benjamí Artigas (in La Pera), 29 October 1996.
16 Carol, p. 189.
17 Miguel Domenech interviewed on Spanish TV programme *El enigma* Dalí (see Bibliography, Section 7).
18 Dalí's telegrams and the draft of Buñuel's reply are in the Luis Buñuel Archive, Ministry of Education and Science, Madrid; Antoni Pitxot, prologue to Carol, p. 10.
19 *UD*, pp. 13–15; I am deeply grateful to Don Luis Revenga for showing me the video, Madrid, 25 September 1996. There is a problem about the date of the filming. According to Antoni Pitxot it took place on 7 November 1982 (Carol, p. 9); Señor Revenga situates it at the beginning of 1983.
20 Antoni Pitxot, prologue to Carol, pp. 9–10; con-

versation with Don Luis Revenga, Madrid, 25 September 1996.
21 Elda Ferrer interviewed on the Spanish TV programme *El enigma Dalí*, 1989 (see Bibliography, Section 7).
22 Secrest, p. 17.
23 Spanish TV programme *Pintar después de morir*, 1989 (see Bibliography, Section 7).
24 Reproduced in *DOH*, p. 431.
25 Reproduced in *DOH*, p. 435.
26 Reproduced in *DOH*, p. 432–3.
27 Gómez de Liaño, 'Llegaremos más tarde, hacia las cinco . . .'; the painting is reproduced in *DOH*, p. 436.
28 Descharnes, *DOH*, p. 439. Telephone conversation with Don Antoni Pitxot (in Cadaqués), 18 June 1987.
29 *El País*, Madrid, 15 April 1983, p. 27.
30 The document was signed before the notary of La Bisbal, José María Foncillas Casaus, on 31 August 1983.
31 *MEAC*, I, p. 15.
32 See, for example, F. Calvo Serraller, *El País*, Madrid, 18 April 1983, p. 35.
33 Santos Torroella, 'La ceremonia dalíniana de la confusión'.
34 *El País*, Madrid, 11 June 1983, p. 29; Purser, p. 183; letter from Robert Descharnes to Edward James, 11 October 1983, EJF.
35 Text reproduced in *DOH* p. 423.
36 *DOH*, p. 423.
37 I am deeply grateful to the current notary, Don José María Martínez Palmer, for sending me a photocopy of this document.
38 Dalí's letter (28 December 1983) to Marià Lorca, mayor of Figueres, informing him of the change, and the mayor's favourable reply, are printed in Fornés, *Les contradiccions del cas Dalí*, pp. 66–9; *ibid.*, pp. 70–84, for other documents concerning the new foundation; for the inauguration itself, and Dalí's message for the Madrid presentation, *El País*, Madrid, 29 March 1984, p. 26, and Romero, *Dedálico Dalí*, p. 283. 'Spain is a bleeding thorn': Dalí insisted in proclaiming that the etymology of the word España was Latin *espina* (thorn, spine). In fact it appears that the word derives from an Iberian root meaning 'plentiful in rabbits'.
39 Carol, pp. 144, 148–9; for the long list of doctors who attended Dalí, *ibid.*, pp. 149–50.
40 Romero, *Dedálico Dalí*, p. 283.
41 Berasátegui, 'En Púbol con el genio escondido'.
42 Santos Torroella, 'Descharnes y el estilo "cárcel de papel"'.
43 Santos Torroella, *ibid.*, and 'Dalí fue un modélico alumno de Instituto', 'La ceremonia dalíniana de la confusión' and 'Carta abierta a monsieur Robert

Descharnes. La exposición de Salvador Dalí en Ferrara'.
44 Nuria Munárriz, 'Dalí, el voluntario escondido de Púbol', *Diario 16*, Seville edition, 'Cuadernos del Mediodía', 1 June 1984, p. 20.
45 J.J. Tharrats interviewed on the Spanish TV programme *Todos los hombres de Dalí*, 1984 (see Bibliography, Section 7).
46 *Ibid.*
47 Berasátegui, p. vi.
48 Eduard Fornés interviewed on the Spanish TV programme *Pintar después de morir*, 1989 (see Bibliography, Section 7).
49 Luis Romero interviewed on Spanish TV programme *El enigma Dalí* (see Bibliography, Section 7).
50 *UD*, pp. 209–11; Caminada's testimony at the enquiry, 12 September 1984, Juzgado de Instrucción de La Bisbal, Diligencias previas no. 1875 Año 1984, Registro General No. 1879/84. Sobre: INCENDIO en el castillo de Púbol, resultando lesionado SALVADOR DALÍ en Púbol.
51 'Relación de personas relaciondas de alguna forma con Salvador Dalí en el castillo de Púbol', list included in Juzgado de Instrucción de La Bisbal, Diligencias previas no. 1875 Año 1984, Registro General No. 1879/84. Sobre: INCENDIO en el castillo de Púbol, resultando lesionado SALVADOR DALÍ en Púbol, f. 40.
52 *UD*, pp. 211–12.
53 *Ibid.*, p. 212.
54 *Ibid.*, pp. 212–13.
55 'Relación de personas relacionadas de alguna forma con Salvador Dalí en el castillo de Púbol', see note 50.
56 *UD*, p. 213.
57 *Ibid.*
58 *Ibid.*, p. 214.
59 Puignau, p. 182.
60 Clip included in the Spanish TV programme *El enigma Dalí* (see Bibliography, Section 7).
61 *El País*, Madrid, 1 September 1984.
62 Miguel Domenech in declarations to *El País*, Madrid, 5 September 1984.
63 *Ibid.*, 1 September 1984; *UD*, p. 216.
64 Ignacio Gómez de Liaño, introduction to his edition of Dalí, *Martyr. Tragédie Lyrique en III Actes* (see Bibliography, Section 5), p. 13.
65 *El País*, Madrid, 2 September 1984, p. 24.
66 *Ibid.*, 6 September 1984, p. 21; 28 June 1985, p. 37; for Anna Maria Dalí's visit to the clinic and account to the press, *UD*, pp. 219–20.
67 The document is reproduced by Fornés, *Les contradiccions del cas Dalí*, p. 147. See also *El País*, Madrid, 6 September 1984, p. 21.
68 The notarial document is published by Fornés,

Les contradiccions del cas Dalí, pp. 148–51.
69 *UD*, pp. 218–19.
70 *El País*, Madrid, 4 September 1984, p. 20.
71 *Ibid.*, 9 September 1984, p. 35.
72 Juzgado de Instrucción de La Bisbal, Diligencias previas no. 1875 Año 1984, Registro General No. 1879/84. Sobre: INCENDIO en el castillo de Púbol, resultando lesionado SALVADOR DALÍ en Púbol.
73 *Ibid.*, f. 20.
74 *Ibid.*, ff. 65, 82.
75 *Ibid.*, f. 61 v.
76 *Ibid.*, ff. 80, 117.
77 *Ibid.*, f. 62.
78 *El País*, Madrid, 8 September 1984, p. 21.
79 Elda Ferrer interviewed on Spanish TV programme *El enigma Dalí* (see Bibliography, Section 7).
80 Juzgado de Instrucción de La Bisbal, Diligencias previas no. 1875 Año 1984, Registro General No. 1879/84. Sobre: INCENDIO en el castillo de Púbol, resultando lesionado SALVADOR DALÍ en Púbol, ff. 54–5.
81 *El País*, Madrid, 7 September 1984, p. 22; 1 February 1985; 12 February 1985; Fornés, *Les contradiccions del cas Dalí*, p. 145.
82 Descharnes, 'La solitaria de Púbol'.
83 My interview with Dalí was published in *El País*, Madrid, 26 January 1986.
84 Tape-recorded conversation with Don Miguel Domenech, Madrid, 19 February 1997.
85 The contract is reproduced by Fornés, *Les contradiccions del cas Dalí*, pp. 186–92.
86 Reproduced by Fornés, *ibid.*, pp. 193–4.
87 *El País*, Madrid, 14 July 1986, p. 25; *Ya*, Madrid, 15 July 1986, p. 33.
88 Conversation with Don Antoni Pitxot, Torre del Molí, Figueres, 29 June 1996.
89 Jesús Conte, 'El Estado quiere arrebatar a Descharnes el negocio de Dalí', *Cambio 16*, Madrid, no. 899, 20 February 1989, pp. 30–1.
90 The letter, with this paragraph highlighted, was shown on the Spanish TV programme *El enigma Dalí* (see Bibliography, Section 7).
91 Fornés, *Les contradiccions del cas Dalí*, p. 177.
92 The document is reproduced by Fornés, *ibid.*, pp. 195–6.
93 Letter reproduced by Fornés, *ibid.*, pp. 209–16.
94 *MDJ*, 29 August 1981.
95 Descharnes in the Spanish TV programme *Pintar después de morir*, 1989 (see Bibliography, Section 7).
96 See *La Vanguardia*, Barcelona, 14 March 1997; *Abc*, Madrid, same date, p. 59.
97 *Abc*, Madrid, 28 November 1988, p. 39; *El País*, Madrid, 29 November 1988, p. 43.

98   *El País*, Madrid, 29 November 1988, p. 38; *Diario 16*, Madrid, 29 November 1988, p.31.

99   *El País*, Madrid, 30 November 1988, p. 40.

100   *Empordà*, Figueres, 25 January 1989, p. 19.

101   *Abc*, Madrid, 6 December 1988, p. 43; *Diario 16*, Madrid, 6 December 1988, p. 27. A clip from the television report is included in the programme *El enigma Dalí* (see Bibliography, Section 7).

102   *Diario 16*, Madrid, 6 December 1988, p. 27.

103   *Interviú*, Madrid, no. 660 (3–9 January 1988), pp. 86–90.

104   *Diario 16*, Madrid, 6 December 1988, p. 27.

105   Conversation with Don Antoni Pitxot, Cadaqués, 5 August 1995.

106   *El País*, Madrid, 24 December 1988, p. 28, 26 December, p. 38; *Diario 16*, Madrid, 26 December 1988, p. 34.

107   *El País*, Madrid, 20 January 1989, p. 32.

108   *El Periódico*, Barcelona, 24 January 1989, p. 4; *El País*, Madrid, 27 January 1989, p. 36; Sr and Sra Xicot have confirmed to me that it was Arturo Caminada who telephoned them, Púbol, 20 October 1995.

109   *El País*, Madrid, 24 January 1989, p. 24.

110   Conversation with Doña Carme Roget, Figueres, 23 September 1993; *El País*, Madrid, 24 January 1989, p. 24.

111   'Salvador Dalí sigue muy grave y ya se preparan sus funerales', *El Periódico*, Barcelona, 22 January 1989; 'Dalí desea ser enterrado en su museo de Figueres, bajo la cúpula geodésica', *La Vanguardia*, Barcelona, 22 January 1989, p. 89; Carol, pp. 11–12.

112   'Salvador Dalí sigue muy grave y ya se preparan sus funerales', *El Periódico*, Barcelona, 22 January 1989.

113   *Ibid.*; James Markham, 'Dalí's Gift to Spain: No Homage to Catalonia', *New York Times*, 12 February 1989, reports that Dalí's instructions to Lorca were given on 1 December 1988; according to *Diario 16*, Madrid, 22 January 1989, p. 9, Pitxot 'was unable to arrive on time'. A year after Dalí's death Lorca told *El País*, Madrid (21 January 1990, p. 26): 'I entered the room. There was a nurse there and some other people. Dalí made signs for them all to leave and beckoned me to his side and said "I want to be buried under the dome of the Museum." I asked him to repeat it because it was difficult to understand him, although for those of us who'd been with him it was easier. Then I repeated his words and said to him: "Señor Dalí, is it this that you're telling me?" He nodded and added: "Don't tell anyone." Pitxot was there when I went out and I told him. I think it's the only time that I didn't obey Dalí. We also told Domenech.'

114   *El País*, Madrid, 23 January 1989, p. 26.

115   Conversation with Don Benjamí Artigas, Púbol, 30 June 1996.

116   Descharnes, 'La solitaria de Púbol'.

117   Conversations with Don Antoni Pitxot, Cadaqués, 1996–7.

118   Carol, p. 183.

119   *La Vanguardia*, Barcelona, 25 January 1989, p. 39.

120   Conversation with Don Antoni Pitxot, Figueres, 5 August 1995.

121   *Ibid.*

122   Conversations with the ex-mayor of Cadaqués, Don Isidre Escofet, a close friend of Caminada, Cadaqués, 21 October 1995.

123   *Cambio 16*, Madrid, 30 January 1989, p. 17; *El País*, Madrid, 27 January 1989, p. 36; *La Vanguardia*, Barcelona, 25 January 1989, p. 39; conversation with Sr and Sra Xicot, Púbol, 20 October 1995; for mayor Artigas's *ex abrupto*, see also Descharnes, 'La solitaria de Púbol'.

124   Playà, *Dalí de l'Empordà*, p. 34.

125   Conversation with Captain Peter Moore, Cadaqués, 7 August 1996.

126   *Diario 16*, Madrid, 24 January 1989, p. 37.

127   *El Periódico*, Barcelona, 24 January 1989, p. 3.

128   *La Vanguardia*, Barcelona, 24 January 1989, p. 45.

129   Conversation with Doña Nanita Kalaschnikoff, Cadaqués, 6 August 1995.

130   *La Vanguardia*, Barcelona, 26 January 1995, p. 45.

131   *Ibid.*, 23 January 1989, p. 46.

132   *Abc*, Madrid, 24 January 1989, p. 29.

133   *El Periódico*, Barcelona, 24 January 1989, p. 4.

134   *El País*, Madrid, 24 January 1989, p. 24.

135   Carol, p. 182.

136   *Abc*, Madrid, special Dalí supplement, 24 January 1989, p. i.

137   *El País*, Madrid, 25 January 1989, p. 31; *Diario 16*, Madrid, 25 January 1989, p. 27; *La Vanguardia*, Barcelona, 25 January 1989, p. 39; Spanish TV coverage.

138   *El País*, Madrid, 25 January 1989, p. 31; *Abc*, Madrid, 25 January 1989, p. 53.

139   *Ibid.*; Màrius Carol, 'Todo apunta a que Descharnes dejará de gestionar los derechos de la obra de Dalí', *La Vanguardia*, Barcelona, 25 January 1989, p. 38.

140   A video clip of this moving moment is included in the Spanish TV programme *El enigma Dalí* (see Bibliography, Section 7).

141   Letter from Felipe Domènech, *La Vanguardia*, Barcelona, 29 January 1989, p. 7; telephone conversation with Don Felipe Domènech Biosca, the latter's son (in Barcelona), 30 September 1996.

142   Màrius Carol, 'Retrato de grupo, con ausencia de Sabater', *La Vanguardia*, Barcelona, 26 January 1989, p. 43.

143   Telephone conversation with Doña Nanita

Kalaschnikoff (in Paris), 29 August 1995.

144 Màrius Carol, 'El ex secretario Enrique Sabater afirma que asistirá al funeral que Cadaqués dedicará a Dalí', *La Vanguardia*, Barcelona, 28 January 1989, p. 40.

145 *La Vanguardia*, Barcelona, 31 January 1989, p. 50.

146 Jesús Conte, 'Dalí nombra heredero universal de sus bienes al Estado español', *Cambio 16*, Madrid, no. 287 (6 February 1989), pp. 3–16. The issue, rushed through at great speed, appeared six days in advance of the publication date printed on its cover (telephone conversation with Don Jesús Conte, in Barcelona, 22 October 1996).

147 *El País*, Madrid, 4 February 1989, p. 32.

148 *Tribuna*, Madrid, 16 March 1992.

149 Jordi Pujol on the Spanish TV programme *El enigma Dalí* (see Bibliography, Section 7). In two non-committal letters written to the Catalan authorities in 1986, Domenech said that, according to Dalí's public statements, he had formally willed his estate to Spain and Catalunya (Fornés, *Les contradiccions del cas Dalí*, p. 217).

150 'El testamento hace referencia al mayordomo', *La Vanguardia*, Barcelona, 27 January 1989, p. 43.

151 Telephone conversation with Captain Peter Moore (in Cadaqués), 25 November 1993.

152 *Ibid.*; *La Vanguardia*, Barcelona, 27 January 1989, p. 43; date of Caminada's death kindly supplied by Cadaqués Town Hall.

153 Conversation with Dr Manuel Vergara, Cadaqués, 6 August 1996.

BIBLIOGRAPHY

I Dalí exhibition catalogues (arranged in chronological order)

New York: Museum of Modern Art. *Salvador Dalí. Paintings, Drawings, Prints.* 19 November 1941–11 January 1942. Catalogue by James Thrall Soby.
New York: Gallery of Modern Art. *Salvador Dalí. His Art. 1910–1965.* 18 December 1965–28 February 1966.
Rotterdam: Museum Boymans–van Beuningen. *Dalí.* 21 November 1970–10 January 1971.
Paris: Centre Georges Pompidou, Musée National d'Art Moderne. *Salvador Dalí. Rétrospective. 1920–1980.* 18 December 1979–21 April 1980. Catalogue by Daniel Abadie. A companion volume, *La Vie publique de Salvador Dalí*, was issued in April 1980.
London: Tate Gallery. *Salvador Dalí.* 14 May–29 June 1980. Catalogue by Simon Wilson.
Perpignan: Palais des Rois de Majorque. *Dalí à Perpignan. La Collection Salvador Dalí de Musée Perrot-Moore, Cadaqués.* August–September 1982.
Madrid: Museo Español de Arte Contemporáneo (MEAC). *400 obras de Salvador Dalí de 1914 a 1983,* two volumes. 15 April–29 May 1983. The exhibition moved from Madrid to the Palau Reial de Pedralbes in Barcelona. Published jointly by the Ministry of Culture, Madrid, and the Generalitat de Catalunya, Barcelona. Castilian and Catalan versions. Introduction by Ana Beristain and Robert Descharnes.
Barcelona: Centre Cultural de la Caixa de Pensions. *Dalí fotògraf, Dalí en els seus fotògrafs.* June–July 1983.
Stuttgart: Staatsgalerie, and Zurich, Kunsthaus. *Salvador Dalí. 1904–1989.* 13 May–23 July 1989 and 18 August–22 October 1989 respectively. Catalogue by Karin von Maur. Stuttgart, Verlag Gerd Hatje, 1989.
Clermont-Ferrand: *Musée Bargoin. Dalí. 1989–1990.* Catalogue by Pierre Argillet.
Dalí, The Salvador Dali Museum Collection, St Petersburg, Florida. Foreword by A. Reynolds Morse, introduction by Robert S. Lubar, 1991. Permanent exhibition.
Frankfurt: Schirn Kunsthalle. *Picasso–Miró–Dalí und der Beginn der spanischen Moderne 1900–1936.* 6 September–10 November 1991.
Valencia: IVAM, Centre Julio González. 3 December 1992–7 February 1993. *Dalí verdadero/grabado falso. La obra impresa 1930–1934.* Catalogue by Rainer Michael Mason.
Seville: Fundación Fondo de Cultura de Sevilla. *Dalí en los fondos de la Fundació Gala–Salvador Dalí.* 27 April–4 July 1993.
Teatre-Museu Dalí, Figueres, text by J. L. Giménez-Frontín, Barcelona, Tusquets/Electa, 1994. Permanent exhibition.
London: Hayward Gallery (South Bank Centre). *Salvador Dalí. The Early Years.* 3 March–30 May 1994.
Madrid: Museo Nacional Centro de Arte Reina Sofía. *Dalí joven (1918–1930).* 18 October 1994–16 January 1995.
Barcelona: La Pedrera, Barcelona, Fundació Gala–Salvador Dalí and Fundación Caixa de Catalunya. *Dalí Arquitectura.* 19 June–25 August 1996.
Cadaqués: Museu de Cadaqués. *Salvador Dalí. Antològica sobre paper, 1916–1980.* July 1996.
Turin: Palazzo Bricherasio. *Salvador Dalí. La vita e sogno.* November 1996–March 1997.

2 Catalogues Raisonnés

Field, Albert, *The Official Catalog of the Graphic Works of Salvador Dalí,* New York, The Salvador Dalí Archives, 1996.
Michler, Ralf and Lutz W. Löpsinger (eds), *Salvador Dalí. Catalogue Raisonné of Etchings and Mixed-Media Prints, 1924–1980.* Foreword by Robert Descharnes, Munich, Prestel-Verlag, 1994.

3 Other exhibition catalogues (in alphabetical order of surnames or exhibition titles)

AC. Las vanguardias en Catalunya, 1906–1939. Protagonistas, tendencias, acontecimientos, Barcelona, La

Pedrera, 1992.

Barradas/Torres-García, Madrid, Galería Guillermo de Osma, 1991.

Rafael Barradas, Madrid, Galería Jorge Mara, 1992.

André Breton. La Beauté convulsive, Paris, Centre Georges Pompidou, 1991.

André Breton y el surrealismo, Madrid, Museo Nacional Centro de Arte Reina Sofía, 1991.

¿Buñuel! Auge des Jahrhunderts, text by Yasha David, Bonn, Kunst-und Ausstellungshalle der Bundesrepublik Deutschland, 1994.

¿Buñuel! La mirada del siglo, edited by Yasha David, Museo Nacional Centro de Arte Reina Sofía, 1996.

Cubismo, Madrid, Galería Multitud, 1975.

Los Cuerpos perdidos. Fotografía y surrealistas, Madrid, Fundación 'La Caixa', 1995.

Dada y constructivismo, Madrid, Centro de Arte Reina Sofía, 1989.

Dada, Surrealism and their Heritage, by William Rubin, New York, The Museum of Modern Art, 1968.

Dada and Surrealism Reviewed, by Dawn Ades, with an introduction by David Sylvester and a supplementary essay by Elizabeth Cowling, London, Arts Council of Great Britain, 1978.

Max Ernst. A Retrospective, London, Tate Gallery in association with Prestel, 1991.

Max Ernst. Obra gráfica y libros ilustrados (Colección Lufthansa), introduction by Werner Spiers, Barcelona, Lufthansa Promoción Cultural, 1992.

Ramón Estalella y su tiempo, Madrid, Centro Cultural del Conde Duque, 1990.

Fantastic Art, Dada, Surrealism, edited by Alfred H. Barr Jr, essays by Georges Hugnet, New York, The Museum of Modern Art, third edition, 1947.

Federico García Lorca. Dibujos, edited by Mario Hernández, Madrid, Museo Español de Arte Contemporáneo, 1986.

La Femme et le surréalisme, Lausanne, Musée cantonal des Beaux-Arts, 1987.

Futurismo, 1909–1919. Exhibition of Italian Futurism, Newcastle-upon-Tyne, Northern Arts and the Scottish Arts Council, 1972.

Literatura y compromiso político en los años treinta, Valencia, Diputación Provincial, 1984.

The Magic Mirror. Dada and Surrealism from a Private Collection, by Elizabeth Cowling, Edinburgh, Scottish National Gallery of Modern Art, 1988.

Magritte, Madrid, Fundación Juan March, 1989.

Miró en las colecciones del Estado, Madrid, Centro de Arte Reina Sofía, 1987.

Miró, Dalmau, Gasch. L'aventura per l'art modern, 1918–1937, Barcelona, Centre d'Art Santa Mònica, 1993.

José Moreno Villa [1887–1955], edición de Juan Pérez

de Ayala, Madrid, Ministerio de Cultura, 1987.

El noucentisme. Un projecte de modernitat, Barcelona, Centre de Cultura Contemporània, 1994.

Juan Núñez Fernández (1877–1963), Figueres, Museu de l'Empordà, 1987.

On Classic Ground. Picasso, Léger, de Chirico and the New Classicism, 1919–1930, by Elizabeth Cowling and Jennifer Mundy, London, Tate Gallery, 1990.

Orígenes de la vanguardia española: 1920–1936, Madrid, Galería Multitud, 1974.

Pabellón Español Exposición Internacional de París 1937, Madrid, Centro de Arte Reina Sofía, 1987.

Benjamín Palencia y el Arte Nuevo, Obras 1919–1936, Barcelona, Centre Cultural Bancaixa/Ministerio de Cultura, 1994.

Picasso/Miró/Dalí. Évocations d'Espagne, Charleroi, Palais des Beaux Arts, 1985.

Picasso, 1905–1906. De la época rosa a los ocres de Gósol, Barcelona, Ajuntament de Barcelona, 1992.

Los Pichot. Una dinastía de artistas, Madrid, Centro Cultural del Conde Duque, 1992.

Regards sur Minotaure. La revue à tête de bête, Geneva, Musée d'art et d'histoire, 1987.

José María Sert (1874–1945), Madrid, Ministerio de Cultura, 1987.

La Sociedad de Artistas Ibéricos y el arte español de 1925, Madrid, Museo Nacional Centro de Arte Reina Sofía, 1995.

El surrealismo en España, Madrid, Galería Multitud, 1975.

Surrealism in the Tate Gallery Collection, London, 1988.

Surrealisme a Catalunya, 1924–1936. De 'L'Amic de les Arts' al Logicofobisme, Barcelona, Generalitat de Catalunya, 1988.

El surrealismo en España, Madrid, Museo Nacional Centro de Arte Reina Sofía, 1994.

El surrealismo entre el viejo y el nuevo mundo, Las Palmas de Gran Canaria, Centro Atlántico de Arte Moderno, 1989.

The Surrealist Spirit in Great Britain, written and researched by Louisa Buck, London, Whitford and Hughes, 1988.

Yves Tanguy. Rétrospective 1925–1955, Paris, Centre Georges Pompidou, 1982. Introduction by José Pierre.

Yves Tanguy. Retrospektive 1925–1955, Baden-Baden, Staatliche Kunsthalle Baden-Baden, 1983.

Treinta artistas españoles de la Escuela de París, Madrid, Centro Cultural del Conde Duque, 1984.

Modest Urgell 1839–1919, Madrid, Fundación 'La Caixa', 1992.

La vanguardia en Cataluña, 1906–1939, Barcelona, Fundación Caixa de Catalunya, 1992.

Ver a Miró. La irradiación de Miró en el arte español, Madrid, Fundación 'La Caixa', 1993.

4 Correspondence (in chronological order
of publication)

Santos Torroella, Rafael (ed.), *Salvador Dalí, corresponsal de J.V. Foix, 1932–1936*, Barcelona, Editorial Mediterrània, 1986.
–*Salvador Dalí escribe a Federico García Lorca [1925–1936]*, *Poesía. Revista ilustrada de información poética*, Madrid, nos. 27–28, April 1987.
–'Las cartas de Salvador Dalí a José Bello Lasierra', *Abc*, Madrid, literary supplement, 14 November 1987, pp. ix–xv.
–*Dalí residente*, Madrid, Publicaciones de la Residencia de Estudiantes, 1992.
Bouhours, Jean-Michel and Nathalie Schoeller (eds), *L'Age d'or. Correspondance Luis Buñuel–Charles de Noailles. Lettres et documents (1929–1976)*, Les Cahiers du Musée National d'Art Moderne, Hors-Série/ Archives, Paris, 1993.
Fanés, Fèlix, 'Joan Miró escribe a Salvador Dalí. El breve encuentro de los artistas catalanes en Figueres y su ambivalente relación posterior', *El País*, Madrid, supplement *Babelia*, 25–26 December 1993, pp. 6, 11.
Massot, Josep and Josep Playà, 'Six anys de correspondència entre Miró i Dalí', *Revista de Girona*, Girona, no. 164 (May–June 1994), pp. 36–41.
Fernández Puertas, Víctor, 'Las cartas de Salvador Dalí al seu oncle Anselm Domènech al Museu Abelló', *Revista de Catalunya*, Barcelona, no. 104 (February 1996), pp. 57–73.

5 Works by Dalí referred to (in chronological order)

'Los grandes maestros de la pintura.' *Studium*, Figueres: 'Goya', no. 1 (1 January 1919), p. 1; 'El Greco', no. 2 (1 February 1919), p. 3; 'Leonardo da Vinci', no. 4 (1 April 1919), p. 3; 'Miguel Angel', no. 5 (1 May 1919), p. 3; 'Velázquez', no. 6 (1 June 1919, p. 3.
'Capvespre' [poem], *Studium*, Figueres, no. 2 (1 February 1919), p. 5.
'Divagacions. Cuan els sorolls s'adorman' [poem], *ibid.*, no. 6 (1 June 1919), p.3.
Un diari: 1919–1920. Les meves impressions i records íntims, edited by Fèlix Fanés, Fundación Gala–Salvador Dalí, Edicions 62, Barcelona, 1994.
A Dalí Journal. 1920. Translation by Joaquim Cortada i Perez of Book 6 of Dalí's diary 'Impressions and Private Memoirs', privately printed by Stratford Press in a limited edition for The Reynolds Morse Foundation, Cleveland, 1962.
Tardes d'estiu. Sixteen-page fragment of novel, Museu Joan Abelló, Mollet del Vallès (Barcelona). 1920? Published by Victor Fernández in a limited edition of

600 copies, *Cave Canis*, Barcelona, 1996.
Unpublished ten-page diary, October 1921, Fundació Gala–Salvador Dalí, Figueres.
['Jak', *pseud.*] 'De la Rússia dels Soviets. Un museu de pintura impressionista a Moscou', *Renovació* Social, Figueres, any I, núm. 1, 26 December 1921.
Ninots. Ensatjos sobre pintura. Catalec dels cuadrus em notes. (1922). Sixteen-page unpublished manuscript (incomplete), Museo Abelló, Mollet del Vallés (Barcelona).
Les cançons dels dotze anys. Versus em prosa i em color (1922), unpublished manuscript, Fundació Gala–Salvador Dalí, Figueres.
En el cuartel numeru 3 de la Residencia d'Estudians. Cunciliambuls d'un grup d'avanguardia, two pages of manuscript, 1923?, Museu Joan Abelló, Mollet del Vallès (Barcelona).
'Skeets [sic] arbitraris. De la fira', *Empordà Federal*, Figueres, núm. 646 (26 May 1923), p. 2.
'Sant Sebastià', *L'Amic de les Arts*, Sitges, no. 16 (31 July 1927), pp. 52–4.
'Reflexions. El sentit comú d'un germá de Sant Joan Baptista de la Salle', *ibid.*, no. 17 (31 August 1927), p. 69.
'Federico García Lorca: exposició de dibuixos colorits. (Galeries Dalmau)', *La nova revista*, Barcelona, Vol. III, no. 9 (September 1927), pp. 84–5.
'La fotografia pura creació de l'esperit', *L'Amic de les Arts*, Sitges, no. 18 (30 September 1927), pp. 90–1.
'Els meus quadros en el Saló de Tardor', *ibid.*, Sitges, no. 19 (31 October 1927), additional sheet.
'Dues proses. Le meva amiga i la platja. Nadal a Brusselles (conte antic)', *ibid.*, no. 20 (30 November 1927), p. 104.
'Nous límits de la pintura', *ibid.*, no. 22 (29 February 1928), pp. 167–8; no. 24 (30 April 1928), pp. 185–6; no. 25 (31 May 1928), pp. 195–6.
'Poesia de l'útil standarditzat', *ibid.*, no. 23 (31 March 1928), pp. 176–7.
'Per al "meeting" de Sitges', *ibid.*, no. 25 (31 May 1928), pp. 194–5.
'Poema de les cosetes', *ibid.*, no. 27 (31 August 1928), p. 211.
'Realidad y sobrerrealidad', *La Gaceta Literaria*, Madrid, 15 October 1928, p. 7.
'La dada fotogràfica', *La Gaseta de les Arts*, Barcelona, Año II, no. 6 (February 1929), pp. 40–2.
'. . . sempre, per damunt de la música, Harry Langdon', *L'Amic de les Arts*, Sitges, no. 31 (31 March 1929), p. 3.
'. . . L'alliberament dels dits . . .', *ibid.*, pp. 6–7.
'Revista de tendències anti-artístiques', *ibid.*, p. 10.
'Documental-París-1929', *La Publicitat*, Barcelona, 26 April 1929, p. 1; 28 April 1929, p. 1; 23 May 1929, p. 1; 7 June 1929, p. 1; 16 June 1929, p. 6; 28 June 1929, p. 1.

'No veo nada, nada en torno del paisaje. Poema', *La Gaceta Literaria*, Madrid, no. 61 (1 July 1929), p. 6.

Un Chien andalou (with Luis Buñuel), *Revue du Cinéma*, Paris, no. 5 (15 November 1929), pp. 2–16, and *La Révolution Surréaliste*, Paris, no. 12 (15 December 1929), pp. 34–7. English translation in Buñuel and Dalí, *Un Chien andalou* (London, Faber and Faber, 1994), pp. 1–11.

'"Un Chien andalou"', *Mirador*, Barcelona, no. 39 (24 October 1929) p. 6.

L'Age d'or, with Luis Buñuel, 1929–30, shooting script published in *L'Avant-Scène du Cinéma*, Paris, June 1963, pp. 28–50.

'Porqué fui sacrílego. Porque soy místico', 1930. Typescript with ms corrections, Biblioteca de Catalunya, Barcelona.

La Femme Visible. Paris, Editions Surréalistes, 1930.

Unpublished scenario for a documentary on Surrealism (1930?), published by Dawn Ades in *Studio International. Journal of the Creative Arts and Design*, London, vol. 195, no. 993/4, 1982, pp. 62–77.

'Posició moral del surrealisme', *Hélix*, Vilafranca del Penedès, no. 10 (March 1930), pp. 4–6; reproduced in facsimile by Molas, *La literatura catalana d'avantguarda* (see below, Section 6), pp. 364–8.

'L'Ane pourri', *Le Surréalisme au Service de la Révolution*, Paris, no. 1 (July 1930), pp. 9–12.

'Intellectuaels castillans et catalans-Expositions-Arrestation d'un exhibitioniste dans le métro', *Le Surréalisme au Service de la Révolution*, Paris, no. 2 (October 1930), pp. 7–9.

L'Amour et la mémoire, Paris, Editions Surréalistes, 1931.

'Objets surréalistes', *Le Surréalisme au Service de la Révolution*, Paris, no. 3 (December 1931), pp. 16–17.

'Rêverie', *ibid.*, no. 4 (December 1931), pp. 31–6.

'Vive le surréalisme! Roman surréaliste (extrait)', *Nadrealizam danas o ovde*, Belgrade, June 1932, p. 17, reproduced by Branko Aleksic, *Dalí: inédits de Belgrade* (see below, Section 6), pp. 43–52.

'Réponse' to enquiry on desire, *Nadrealizam danas o ovde*, Belgrade, (see above), p. 31, reproduced by Branko Aleksic, (see above), pp. 55–61.

Babaouo. C'est un film surréaliste (cover). Title page: *Babaouo. Scénario inédit. Précedé d'un abrégé d'une histoire critique du cinéma et suivi de Guillaume Tell, ballet portugais*. Paris, Editions del Cahiers Libres, 1932. [Colophon says printing finished 12 July 1932.]

'The Object as Revealed in Surrealist Experiment', *This Quarter*, Surrealist Number, Paris, September 1932, pp. 197–207.

Le Mythe tragique de l'Angélus de Millet. Interprétation 'paranoïaque-critique' [1932–5?]. Paris, Jean-Jacques Pauvert, 1963.

'Objets psycho-atmosphériques-anamorphiques', *Le Surréalisme au Service de la Révolution*, Paris, no. 5 (15 May 1933), pp. 45–8.

'Notes–Communications', *ibid.*, no. 6 (15 May 1933), pp. 40–1.

'Interprétation paranoïaque-critique de l'image obsédante. "L'Angélus" de Millet'. Prologue. Nouvelles considérations générales sur le mécanisme du phénomène paranoïaque du point de vue surréaliste', *Minotaure*, Paris no. 1 (1 June 1933), pp. 65–7.

'Cher Breton: l'exposition des mes peintures . . . ', open letter to Breton introducing exhibition catalogue for Dalí's show at Pierre Colle, Paris, 19–29 June 1933. Dated by Dalí 12 June 1933. Reproduced in *Salvador Dalí* (Pompidou catalogue, see above, Section 1), pp. 178–80.

'De la Beauté terrifiante et comestible de l'architecture "modern" style', *Minotaure*, Paris, nos 3–4 (December 1933), pp. 69–76.

'Le Phénomène de l'extase', *ibid.*, pp. 76–7.

'Les Nouvelles Couleurs du sex appeal spectral', *Le Surréalisme au Service de la Révolution*, Paris, no. 5 (May 1934), pp. 20–2.

'"L'Angélus" de Millet', preface to exhibition catalogue for the launch of Dalí's edition of *Les Chants de Maldoror* at the Quatre Chemins Bookshop, Paris, 13–25 June 1934. Reproduced in *Salvador Dalí* (Pompidou catalogue, see above, Section 1), pp. 331–9.

'New York Salutes Me', broadsheet, New York, November 1934. Reproduced in *La Vie publique de Salvador Dalí*, catalogue (see section 1, above), p. 41.

'Honneur à l'objet!', *Cahiers d'Art*, Paris, nos. 1–2, 1935, pp. 33–6.

'Analyse de "L'Escalier de l'Amour et Psyché"', *ibid.*, p. 37.

'Analyse du veston aphrodisiaque de Salvador Dalí', *ibid.*

'Les Pantoufles de Picasso', *ibid.*, nos. 7–10, 1935, pp. 208–12.

'Crazy Movie Scenario by M. Dalí, the Super-Realist', *American Weekly*, New York, 7 July 1935.

La Conquête de l'irrationnel, Paris, Editions Surréalistes, 1935, and simultaneously, in English translation, by Julien Levy, New York.

'Le Surréalisme spectral de l'Eternel Féminin préraphaélite', *Minotaure*, Paris, no. 8 (15 June 1936), pp. 46–9.

'I Defy Aragon', *Art Front*, New York, March 1937.

'Surrealism in Hollywood', *Harper's Bazaar*, New York, June 1937, pp. 68, 132.

Métamorphose de Narcisse, Paris, Editions Surréalistes, 1937, and simultaneously, in English translation, by Julien Levy, New York.

'Declaration of the Independence of the Imagination

and the Rights of Man to his Own Madness', New York, 1939. The full text of the tract is reproduced in Levy, *Memoir of an Art Gallery* (see below, Section 6), pp. 219–22.

'Les Idées lumineuses. "Nous ne mangeons pas de cette lumière-là"', *Cahiers d'art*, Paris, no. 1–2 (1940), pp. 24–5.

The Secret Life of Salvador Dalí, New York, Dial Press, 1942.

Hidden Faces, translated by Haakon Chevalier, London, Nicholson and Watson, 1947; Spanish edition, *Rostros ocultos*, Barcelona, Planeta, 1974.

50 Secrets of Magic Craftsmanship, New York, Dial Press, 1948.

'To Spain, Guided by Dalí', *Vogue*, New York, 15 May 1950, pp. 54–5, 57, 94.

'Por qué fui sacrílego. Por qué soy mistico', lecture given in the Ateneu Barcelonés. Four typewritten pages dated 30 October 1950, with manuscript corrections, perhaps by Gala. Biblioteca de Catalunya, Barcelona.

Manifeste mystique, Paris, Robert J. Godet, 1951; reproduced in *Salvador Dalí* (Pompidou catalogue, see above, Section 1), pp. 372–4.

'Picasso y yo', lecture given in the María Guerrero Theatre, Madrid, 11 November 1951. Published in facsimile in *Mundo hispánico*, Madrid, no. 46 (1952), pp. 37–42. The most readily available modern edition is in Dalí, *¿Por qué se ataca a La Gioconda?*, pp. 228–32.

'Le Mythe de Guillaume Tell. Toute la vérité sur mon expulsion du groupe surréaliste', *La Table Ronde*, Paris, no. 55 (July 1952), pp. 21–38. 'The Myth of William Tell (The Whole Truth about my Expulsion from the Surrealist Group)', translated by Eleanor Morse and included in Dalí, *The Tragic Myth of Millet's Angelus*, The Salvador Dali Museum, St Petersburg, Florida, pp. 177–207.

'Les Morts et moi', *La Parisienne*, Paris, no. 17, May 1954, pp. 52–3. Facsimile edition of the manuscript, Barcelona, Editorial Mediterrània, 1991.

Martyr. Tragédie lyrique en III actes, 1954? Only the first act is known. Published by Ignacio Gómez de Liaño in *El Paseante*, Madrid, no. 5, 1987.

With Philippe Halsman, *Dalí's Moustache* (1954), Paris, Flammarion, 1994.

'Aspects phénoménologiques de la méthode para-noïaque-critique', lecture given at the Sorbonne, 17 December 1955, reproduced in *La Vie publique de Salvador Dalí* (exhibition catalogue, see above, Section 1), pp. 144–5.

Les cocus du vieil art moderne, Paris, Fasquelle, 1956.

Journal d'un génie, Paris, Editions de la Table Ronde, 1964; English edition, *The Diary of a Genius*, London, Hutchinson, 1966; Spanish edition, *Diario de un genio*, Barcelona, Tusquets, 1983.

'Résumé of History and of the History of Painting', *Salvador Dalí 1910–1965* (exhibition catalogue, see above, Section 1), pp. 13–15.

Lettre ouverte à Salvador Dalí, Paris, Albin Michel, 1966; Spanish edition, *Carta abierta a Salvador Dalí*, Buenos Aires, Ultramar, 1976.

Ma Révolution culturelle, tract, Paris, 18 May 1968.

Dalí par Dalí, preface by Dr. Roumeguère, Paris, Draeger, 1970; references are to the American edition, *Dalí by Dalí*, translated by Eleanor Morse, New York, Harry Abrams, 1972.

Oui, Paris, Éditions Denoël, 1971.

Comment on devient Dalí, Les aveux inavouables de Salvador Dalí, récit présenté par André Parinaud, Paris, Robert Laffont, 1973; Spanish edition, *Confesiones inconfesables, recogidas por André Parinaud*, Barcelona, Bruguera, 1973; American edition, *The Unspeakable Confessions of Salvador Dalí, to André Parinaud*, translated from the French by Harold J. Salemson, New York, William Morrow, 1976.

Les Caprices de Goya de Salvador Dalí, Hamburg, Galerie Levy, 1977.

¿Por qué se ataca a La Gioconda?, Madrid, Siruela, 1994. The best edition of Dalí's articles and poems in Spanish.

L'alliberament dels dits. Obra catalana completa. Presentació i edició de Fèlix Fanés, Barcelona, Quaderns Crema, 1995.

6 Books and principal articles

Abadie, Daniel, 'Les obsessions déguisées de Salvador Dalí', in *Salvador Dalí* (Pompidou catalogue, see above, Section 1), pp. 11–15.

Acton, William, *The Functions and Disorders of the Reproductive Organs*, London, Churchill, 5th edn, 1871.

Ades, Dawn, *Dalí*, London, Thames and Hudson, 'World of Art', 1982, reprinted 1990.

–Introduction to Dalí's unpublished film scenario for documentary on Surrealism, *Studio International. Journal of the Creative Arts and Design*, London, vol. 195, no. 993/4, 1982, p. 62.

–'Morphologies of Desire', in *Salvador Dalí: The Early Years* (catalogue, 1994, see above), pp. 129–60.

Agustí, Ignacio, 'Bienvenida a Salvador Dalí', *Destino*, Barcelona, 14 August 1948, pp. 3–5.

Alberti, Rafael, *Imagen primera de La arboleda perdida. Libros I y II de memorias*, Buenos Aires, Losada, 1945.

Aleksic, Branko, *Dalí: inédits de Belgrade* (1932), Paris, Change International/Equivalences, 1987.

Alexandrian, Sarane, *L'Aventure en soi. Autobiographie*, Paris, Mercure de France, 1990.

Alley, Ronald, *Picasso: 'The Three Dancers'*, London,

The Tate Gallery ('Tate Modern Masterpieces'), 1986.

Altolaguirre, Manuel, 'Gala y Dalí, en Torremolinos', *Diario 16*, 'Culturas', 1 September 1985, p. ii.

Andrews, Wayne, *The Surrealist Parade*, New York, New Directions, 1990.

Apollinaire, *Oeuvres Poétiques*, Paris, Gallimard ('Pléiade'), 1959.

–*Oeuvres en prose complètes*, Paris, Gallimard ('Pléiade'), two vols, 1991, 1993 respectively.

Aragon, Louis, 'Fragments d'une conférence', *La Révolution Surréaliste*, Paris, no. 4 (15 July 1925), pp. 23–5.

Aranda, J. Francisco, *Luis Buñuel. Biografía crítica*, Barcelona, Lumen, 2nd edn, 1975.

Arbós, Albert, 'Aquellos amores de Dalí y Pla', *Cambio 16*, Madrid, no. 542 (19 April 1982), pp. 44–51.

Arco, Manuel del, *Dalí al desnudo*, Barcelona, José Janés, 1952.

Argillet, Pierre, 'Dalí-Breton', in catalogue *Dalí*, Musée Bargoin, Clermont-Ferrand, 1989–1990, not paginated.

–'Les Hippies', *ibid.*

Aub, Max, *Conversaciones con Buñuel, seguidas de 45 entrevistas con familiares, amigos y colaboradores del cineasta aragonés*, prologue by Federico Alvarez, Madrid, Aguilar, 1985.

Bataille, Georges, 'Le "Jeu lugubre"', *Documents*, Paris, no. 7, December 1929, pp. 369–72. Reproduced in *Salvador Dalí* (Pompidou catalogue), pp. 150–3 (see above, Section 1).

Berasátegui, Blanca, 'En Púbol, con el genio escondido', *Abc*, Madrid, 'Sábado Cultural', 12 May 1984, pp. vi–viii.

Bernils i Mach, Josep Maria, *Els Fossos, 75 anys d'història, 1909–1984*, Figueres, 1984.

–'Dalí, a la presó', *El Perdrís. Revista cultural de 'L'Empordà'*, Figueres, no. 4, 12 June 1987.

–*Figueres*, Figueres, Editorial Empordà, 3rd edn, 1994.

Beurdeley, Cecile, *L'Amour bleu*, translated from the French by Michael Taylor, Rizzoli, New York, 1978.

Beya i Martí, Pere, *Al terraprim de l'Alt Empordà. Llers. El passat, en la vida local*, Figueres, privately printed, 1992.

Biro, Adam and René Passeron (eds), *Dictionnaire général du surréalisme et de ses environs*, Fribourg, Office du Livre, 1982.

Bockriss, Victor, 'A Dalírious Evening', *Exposure*, Los Angeles, October 1990, pp. 60–3.

Bofarull i Terrades, Manuel, *Origen dels noms geogràfics de Catalunya*, Barcelona, Editorial Millà, 1991.

Bona, Dominique, *Gala*, Paris, Flammarion, 1995.

Bonet Correa, Antonio (ed.), *El surrealismo*, Madrid, Universidad Menéndez Pelayo and Cátedra, 1983.

Borràs, Maria Lluïsa, *Picabia*, Barcelona, Polígrafa, 1985.

Bosquet, Alain, *Entretiens avec Salvador Dalí*, Paris, Pierre Belfond, 1966.

–*Dalí desnudado*, Buenos Aires, Paidos, 1967.

–'Les Peintres du rêve', *Magazine Littéraire*, Paris, no. 213 (December 1984), pp. 58–60.

Bouhours, Jean-Michel and Nathalie Schoeller (eds), *L'Age d'or. Correspondance Luis Buñuel–Charles de Noailles. Lettres et documents*, Paris, Centre Georges Pompidou, 'Les Cahiers du Musée National d'Art Moderne', 1993.

Brassaï, *Conversations avec Picasso*, Paris, Gallimard, 1964.

Brenan, Gerald, *The Spanish Labyrinth. An Account of the Social and Political Background of the Spanish Civil War*, Cambridge University Press, 1960.

Breton, André, 'Des tendances les plus récentes de la peinture surréaliste', *Minotaure*, Paris, nos. 12–13 (May 1930), pp. 16–21.

–*What is Surrealism?*, translated by David Gascoyne, London, Faber and Faber ('Criterion Miscellany No. 43'), 1936.

–[Anonymous, with Paul Éluard], *Dictionnaire abrégé du surréalisme*, Paris, Galerie des Beaux-Arts, 1938. Facsimile reprint, Paris, José Corti, 1980.

–*Le Surréalisme et la peinture, nouvelle édition revue et corrigée 1928–1965*, Paris, Gallimard, 1965, reprinted 1979.

–*Oeuvres complètes*, Paris, Gallimard ('Pléiade'), two vols, 1988 and 1992 respectively.

–*What is Surrealism? Selected Writing*, edited by Franklin Rosemont, London, Pluto Press, 1989.

–*Conversations. The Autobiography of Surrealism*, with André Parinaud and others, translated and with an introduction by Mark Polizzotti, New York, Paragon House, 1993. This is a translation of *Entretiens*, originally published in 1952.

Brihuega, Jaime, *Manifiestos, proclamas, panfletos y textos doctrinales. (Las vanguardias artísticas en España, 1910–1931)*, Madrid, Cátedra, 1982.

Brunet, Manuel, 'Picasso en Barcelona. Una conversación con el gran pintor', *Heraldo de Madrid*, 12 October 1926, p. 4.

–M.B. [Manuel Brunet], 'Despedida al notario don Salvador Dalí y Cusí', *Destino*, Barcelona, no. 491 (14 December 1946), p. 7.

Bullejos, José, *España en la Segunda República*, Madrid, Ediciones Júcar, 1979.

Buñuel, Luis, 'Notes on the Making of *Un Chien andalou*', in *Art in Cinema*, edited by Frank Stauffacher, San Francisco Museum of Art, 1947. Translated by Grace L. McCann Morley. Reprinted by Arno Press, Inc., 1968.

–*Mon Dernier Soupir*, Paris, Robert Laffont, 1982.

–*Obra literaria*, introduction and notes by Agustín

Sánchez Vidal, Zaragoza, Ediciones de Heraldo de Aragón, 1982.

Buot, François, *René Crevel. Biographie*, Paris, Grasset, 1991.

Buxeda, Pere, *L'Ahir de Figueres*, Figueres, 1992.

Byron, William, *Cervantes. A Biography*, New York, Doubleday, 1978.

Calvo Serraller, Francisco, 'Salvador Dalí y la vanguardia artística española de los años veinte', in catalogue *400 obras de Salvador Dalí de 1914 a 1983*, 1983 (see above, Section 1), II, pp. 9–15.

–'El vaivén artístico de una dinastía', in catalogue *Los Pichot. Une dinastía de artistas*, 1992 (see above, Section 3), pp. 49–71.

Cano, José Luis, *Los cuadernos de Adrián Dale (memorias y relecturas)*, Madrid, Orígenes, 1991.

Carmona, Darío, 'Anecdotario de Darío Carmona. (Apuntes de una conversación de Darío Carmona con José María Amado)', introduction to the facsimile edition of the Malaga review *Litoral*, Frankfurt, Detlev Avvermann and Madrid, Turner, 1975.

Carol, Màrius, *Dalí. El final oculto de un exhibicionista*, Barcelona, Plaza y Janés, 1990.

–'El escenógrafo de Portlligat. Muere Isidoro Bea, el hombre que durante treinta años colaboró con Dalí', *La Vanguardia*, Barcelona, 'Revista', 19 March 1996, p. 2.

Carol, Màrius, Juan José Navarro Arisa and Jordi Busquets, *El último Dalí*, El País, Madrid, 1985.

Cassanyes, M.A., 'L'espai en les pintures de Salvador Dalí', *L'Amic de les Arts*, Sitges, no. 13 (30 April 1927), pp. 30–1.

Catterall, Lee, *The Great Dalí Art Fraud and Other Deceptions*, New Jersey, Barricade Books Inc., 1992.

Cernuda, Luis, 'Gómez de la Serna y la generación poética de 1925', in *Estudios sobre poesía española contemporánea*, Madrid, Guadarrama, 1957.

Chadwick, Whitney, *Women Artists and the Surrealist Movement*, London, Thames and Hudson, 1991.

Chevalier, Haakon, 'Salvador Dalí as Writer. Surrealism Takes to the Typewriter', *Saturday Review*, New York, 15 April 1944.

Clara, Josep, 'Salvador Dalí, empresonat per la dictadura de Primo de Rivera', *Revista de Girona*, no. 162 (January–February 1993), pp. 52–5.

Combalía, Victoria, *El descubrimiento de Miró. Miró y sus críticos, 1918–1929*, Barcelona, Destino, 1990.

–'Los años 20–30. El impacto del primer Miró', in *Ver a Miró* (see above, Section 3), pp. 20–43.

Comfort, Alex, *The Anxiety Makers*, New York, Delta, 1970.

Conover, Anne, *Caresse Crosby. From Black Sun to Roccasinibalda*, Santa Barbara, Capra Press, 1989.

Cossart, Michael de, *The Food of Love. Princesse Edmonde de Polignac (1865–1943) and her Salon*, London, Hamish Hamilton, 1978.

Cowles, Fleur, *The Case of Salvador Dalí*, London, Heinemann, 1959.

Crevel, René, *Dalí ou l'anti-obscurantisme*, Paris, Editions Surréalistes, 1931.

–*Lettres de désir et de souffrance*. Préface de Julien Green. Présentation et annotation par Éric le Bouvier, Paris, Fayard, 1996.

Crispin, John, *Oxford y Cambridge en Madrid. La Residencia de Estudiantes, 1910–1936, y su entorno cultural*, Santander, La Isla de los Ratones, 1981.

Crosby, Caresse, *The Passionate Years*, London, Alvin Redman, 1955.

Dalí, Anna Maria, *Salvador Dalí visto por su hermana*, Barcelona, Juventud, 1949.

–*Noves imatges de Salvador Dalí*, prologue by Jaume Maurici, Barcelona, Columna, 1988.

Daudet, Elvira, 'Mágico Dalí', *Abc*, Madrid, Sunday supplement, 1 March 1970, pp. 41–7, 8 March 1971, pp. 28–33.

Descharnes, Robert, *The World of Salvador Dalí*, New York and Evanston, Harper and Row, 1962.

–*Dalí*, translated by Eleanor R. Morse, London, Thames and Hudson, 1985.

–*Dalí. La obra y el hombre*, Barcelona, Tusquets/Edita, 1984 (trans. as *Salvador Dalí. The Work, the Man*, New York, Harry Abrams, 1984).

–'La solitaria de Púbol', *Abc*, Madrid, 12 June 1992, p. 64.

Descharnes, Robert and Gilles Néret, *Salvador Dalí, 1904–1989. L'Oeuvre peint*, Cologne, Benedikt Taschen, 2 vols, 1993.

Deulofeu, Alexandre, 'El complex dalínià', *Revista de Girona*, no. 68 (third trimester, 1974), pp. 23–6.

Díaz i Romañach, Narciso, *Roses, una vila amb història*, Roses, Ajuntament, 1991.

Domènech [Ferrés], Anselm, *La llibreria Verdaguer i el renaixement català*, Barcelona, 1933.

Drummond, Phillip, 'Surrealism and *Un Chien andalou*', in Luis Buñuel and Salvador Dalí, *Un Chien andalou*, London, Faber and Faber, 1994, pp. v–xxiii.

Ducasse, Isidore, *see* Lautréamont, Comte de.

Durgnat, Raymond, *Luis Buñuel*, Berkeley, University of California Press, 1967, revised and enlarged edition 1977.

Egea Codina, Antoni, *Llers. Els homes i els fets*, off-print from *Annals de l'Institut d'Estudis Empordanesos*, Figueres, 1979–80.

'Eleanora' [Adelina Bello Lasierra], *Novísimo testamento*, Madrid, Editorial Barlovento, 1988.

Éluard, Paul, *Lettres à Gala (1924–1948)*, edited by Pierre Dreyfus, preface by Jean-Claude Carrière, Paris, Gallimard, 1984.

–*Oeuvres complètes*, Paris, Gallimard ('Pléiade'), two vols, 1968.

Erben, Walter, *Joan Miró, 1893–1983. Mensch und Werk*, Cologne, Benedikt Taschen Verlag, 1988.

Ernst, Jimmy, *A Not-So-Still Life. A Memoir*, New York, St Martin's/Marek, 1984.

Ernst, Max, *Écritures*, Paris, Gallimard, 1970.

Fallowell, Duncan and April Ashley, *April Ashley's Odyssey*, London, Jonathan Cape, 1982; London, Arena Books, 1983.

Fanés, Fèlix, 'Retrato del artista adolescente. El amor, los amigos, la política y la pintura vistos con el desparpajo y la inteligencia de un estudiante de 15 años', Madrid, *Babelia* (supplement to *El País*), no. 68 (30 January 1993), pp. 7–8.

Fernández, Jean and Patrick Kobuz, 'Conversación con Louis Aragon', *Poesía*, Madrid, Ministerio de Cultura, no. 9 (Autumn 1980), pp. 81–90.

Fernández Almagro, Melchor, 'Por Cataluña', *La Epoca*, Madrid, 17 July 1926, p. 1.

Fernández Puertas, Víctor, 'Anna Maria Dalí vista pel seu germà', *Hora Nova*, Figueres, 8–14, 15–21, 22–8 August 1995.

–'Una carta obligada', *ibid.*, 29 August–4 September 1995, p. 19.

–'Anselm Domènech, l'oncle de Salvador Dalí Domènech', *Revista de Catalunya*, Barcelona, no. 97, 1995, pp. 61–81.

–'Las cartas de Salvador Dalí al seu oncle Anselm Domènech al Museu Abelló', *Revista de Catalunya*, Barcelona, no. 104 (February 1996), pp. 57–73.

Ferrer, Firmo, *Cadaqués des de l'arxiu*, Barcelona, Montagud Editores, 1991.

Ferrerós, Joan, 'L'Institut i la ciutat', appended to the facsimile edition of *Studium*, Figueres, Edicions Federals, 1993, pp. 49–54.

Field, Albert, untitled article on his relationship with Dalí, MEAC, II, pp. 18–21.

Foix, J.V., 'Presentació de Salvador Dalí', *L'Amic de les Arts*, Sitges, no. 10 (31 January 1927), p. 3.

Fornés, Eduard, *Dalí y los libros*, Barcelona, Mediterrània, 1985.

–*Les contradiccions del cas Dalí*, Barcelona, Llibres de l'Avui, 1989.

Freud, Sigmund, *Psicopatología de la vida cotidiana (olvidos, equivocaciones, torpezas, supersticiones y errores)*, translated from the German by Luis López-Ballesteros y de Torres, Madrid, Biblioteca Nueva, 1922.

–*Una teoría sexual y otros ensayos. Una teoría sexual. Cinco conferencias sobre psicoanálisis. Introducción al estudio de los sueños. Más allá del principio del placer*, translated from the German by Luis López-Ballesteros y de Torres, Madrid, Biblioteca Nueva, 1922.

–*La interpretación de los sueños*, translated from the German by Luis López-Ballesteros y de Torres, Madrid, Biblioteca Nueva, 1923.

–*The Standard Edition of the Complete Psychological Works*, translated by James Strachey, in collaboration with Anna Freud, London, The Hogarth Press, 24 vols, 1966–1974.

G. de Candamo, Luis, 'Estalella en su paisaje cultural', in *Ramón Estalella y su tiempo*, Madrid, Centro Cultural del Conde Duque, 1990, pp. 69–83.

García, Tomás, *Y todo fue distinto*, edición de Angel Caffarena, Malaga, Publicaciones de la Librería Antigua El Guadalhorce, 1990.

García Buñuel, Pedro Christian, *Recordando a Luis Buñuel*, Zaragoza, Excma. Diputación Provincial/Excmo. Ayuntamiento, 1985.

García Gallego, Jesús, *La recepción del surrealismo en España (1924–1931) (La crítica de las revistas literarias en castellano y catalán)*, Granada, Antonio Ubago, 1984.

–*Bibliografía y crítica del surrealismo y la generación del veintisiete*, Malaga, Centro Cultural de la Generación del 27, 1989.

García Lorca, Federico, *Cartas a sus amigos*, edited by Sebastià Gasch, Barcelona, Cobalto, 1950.

–*Epistolario*, edited by Christopher Maurer, Alianza, Madrid, 1983, two volumes.

–*Obras completas*, Madrid, Aguilar, 22nd edn, 3 vols, 1986.

García Márquez, Gabriel, 'Tramontana', in *Doce cuentos peregrinos*, Madrid, Mondadori, 1992, pp. 177–86.

García de Valdeavellano, Luis, 'Un educador humanista: Alberto Jiménez Fraud y la Residencia de Estudiantes', introduction to Alberto Jiménez Fraud, *La Residencia de Estudiantes. Viaje a Maquiavelo*, Barcelona, Ariel, 1972.

Garriga Camps, Pere, 'El jove Dalí de la "Pairal"' (1), *Empordà*, Figueres, 3 February 1993, p. 25.

–'El joven Dalí de la "Pairal"' (2), *ibid.*, 10 February 1993, p. 25.

Gasch, Sebastià, 'Max Ernst', *L'Amic de les Arts*, Sitges, no. 7 (October 1926), p. 7.

–'Cop d'ull sobre l'evolució de l'art modern', *L'Amic de les Arts*, Sitges, no. 18 (30 September 1927), pp. 91–3.

–'Les fantaisies d'un reporter', *L'Amic de les Arts*, Sitges, no. 20 (30 November 1927), pp. 108–9.

–'André Breton. "Le Surréalisme et la peinture"', *La Veu de Catalunya*, Barcelona, 15 May 1928. Reproduced in *Escrits d'art* (see below), pp. 101–5.

–'Belleza y realidad', *La Gaceta Literaria*, Madrid, no. 49 (1 January 1929), p. 4.

–'Les obres recents de Salvador Dalí', *La Publicitat*, Barcelona, 16 November 1929, p. 5. Reproduced in *Escrits d'art* (see below), pp. 116–23.

–'Salvador Dalí', in *L'expansió de l'art català al món*,

Barcelona, privately printed, 1953, pp. 139–63.

–*Escrits d'art i d'avantguarda (1925–1938)*, Barcelona, Edicions del Mall, 1987.

Gascoyne, David, *A Short History of Surrealism*, London, Cobden-Sanderson, 1935.

–'A propos du suicide de René Crevel', *Europe*, René Crevel special issue, Paris, nos. 79–80 (November–December 1985), pp. 90–4.

–*Collected Journals, 1936–42*, London, Skoob Books Publishing, 1991.

Gateau, Jean-Charles, *Paul Éluard et la peinture surréaliste*, Geneva, Droz, 1962.

–*Paul Éluard, ou Le frère voyant*, Paris, Laffont, 1988.

Gee, Malcolm, *Ernst, 'Pietà or Revolution by Night'*, London, The Tate Gallery ('Tate Modern Masterpieces'), 1986.

Gérard, Max, *Dalí de Draeger*, Paris, Le Soleil Noir, 1968; references are to the Spanish edition, Barcelona, Blume, 9th edn, 1980.

–*Dalí . . . Dalí . . . Dalí . . .* , preface by Dr. Roumegère, Paris, Draeger, 1974; references are to the Spanish edition, Barcelona, Blume, 1985.

Ghiraldo, Alberto, *El archivo de Rubén Darío*, Buenes Aires, Losada, 1945.

Gibson, Ian, 'Con Dalí y Lorca en Figueres', *El País*, Madrid, 26 January 1986, Sunday supplement, pp. 10–11.

–*Federico García Lorca. A Life*, London, Faber and Faber, 1989.

–*Fire in the Blood. The New Spain*, London, Faber and Faber/BBC Books, 1992.

–'¿Un paranoico en la familia? El extraño caso del abuelo paterno de Salvador Dalí, un "infeliz demente" que se suicidó en Barcelona en 1886', *El País*, Madrid, supplement *Babelia*, 10 April 1993, pp. 2–3.

–'Salvador Dalí: the Catalan Background', in catalogue *Salvador Dalí: The Early Years* (see above, Section 1), pp. 49–64.

Giménez Caballero, Ernesto, *Yo, inspector de alcantarillas (Epiplasmas)*, Madrid, Biblioteca Nueva, 1928.

–'El escándalo de L'Age d'or en París. Palabras con Salvador Dalí', *La Gaceta Literaria*, Madrid, no. 96 (15 December 1930), p. 3.

–'Robinsón habla de arte, teatro. Salvador Dalí. Teatro de Bali', *ibid.*, no. 112 (15 August 1931), p. 10.

–'El comunismo español y madame Éluard', *ibid.*, no. 117 (1 November 1931), p. 6.

–*La nueva catolicidad. Teoría general sobre el Fascismo en Europa; en España*, Madrid, 'La Gaceta Literaria', 2nd edn, 1933.

–*Roma madre*, Madrid, Ediciones 'Jerarquía', 1939.

–*Memorias de un dictador*, Barcelona, Planeta, 1979.

–'¡¡Dalí!! ¡Querido Dalí! Gala te ha devorado ya medio cráneo', *Diario 16*, Madrid, 26 February 1981,

supplement, p. x.

Gimferrer, Pere, *Max Ernst o la dissolució de la identitat*, Barcelona, Ediciones Polígrafa, 1975.

–*Giorgio de Chirico*, Barcelona, Ediciones Polígrafa, 1988.

Giralt Casadesús, R., 'L'exposició d'artistes empordanesos', *Alt Empordà*. Figueres, 'Fulla artística', no. vi (June 1918), p. 1.

Giralt-Miracle, Daniel, 'Caminos de las vanguardias. Recorrido de una exposición', in AC. *Las vanguardias en Catalunya* (see above, Section 3), pp. 60–117.

Glendinning, Nigel, 'The Visual Arts in Spain', in P. E. Russell (ed.), *A Companion to Spanish Studies*, London, Methuen, 1973, pp. 473–542.

Gold, Arthur and Robert Fitzdale, *Misia. The Life of Misia Sert*, London, Macmillan, 1980.

Gómez de la Serna, Ramón, *La sagrada cripta de Pombo*. (Tomo II°, aunque independiente del 1°, pudiendo leerse el II° sin contar con el 1°) [1924], facsimile edition, Editorial Trieste, Madrid, 1986.

–*Ismos* [1930], Madrid, Guadarrama ('Punto Omega'), 1975.

–*Greguerías. Selección 1940–1952*, Madrid, Espasa-Calpe, 1952.

–*Dalí*, 'Epilogue' by Baltasar Porcel, Madrid, Espasa-Calpe, 1977.

Gómez de Liaño, Ignacio, 'Le théâtre Dalí de la mémoire', in catalogue *La Vie publique de Salvador Dalí*, 1980 (see Section 1, above), pp. 182–5.

–*Dalí*, Barcelona, Ediciones Polígrafa, 1982.

–'". . . Llegaremos más tarde, hacia las cinco". Dalí visto por Pitxot', in catalogue *400 obras de Salvador Dalí de 1914 a 1983*, 1983 (see above, Section 1), I, pp. 254–7.

–'Odisea Dalí', *ibid.*, II, pp. 21–43.

–'En la casa del arte', in catalogue *Los Pichot, una dinastía de artistas*, 1992 (see above, Section 3), pp. 15–45.

Green, Julian, *Oeuvres complètes*, Paris, Gallimard ('Pléiade'), vol. IV, 1975.

–'Los años mágicos', *Blanco y Negro*, Madrid, 26 February 1989, pp. 8–10.

–*La Fin d'un monde. Juin 1940*, Paris, Éditions du Seuil, 1992.

Guardiola Rovira, Ramon, *Dalí y su museo. La obra que no quiso Bellas Artes*, Figueres, Editora Empordanesa, 1984.

Guillamet, Jaume, '"Studium", la revista del jove Dalí', introduction to the facsimile edition of *Studium*, Edicions Federals, Figueres, 1993, pp. 5–11.

Guillamet, Joan, *Vent de tramuntana, gent de tramuntana*, Barcelona, Editorial Joventut, 1992.

Guzmán, Eduardo de, 1930. *Historia política de un año decisivo*, Madrid, Ediciones Tebas, 1973.

Halsman, Philippe, with Salvador Dalí, *Dalí's Moustache. A Photographic Interview* (1954), Paris, Flammarion, 2nd edn, 1994.

Hernández, Mario, 'García Lorca y Salvador Dalí: del ruiseñor lírico a los burros podridos (Poética y epistolario)', in Laura Dolfi (ed.), *L'impossibile/possibile di Federico García Lorca*, Naples, Edizioni Scientifiche Italiane, 1989, pp. 267–319.

Hernández, Patricio, *Emilio Prados: la memoria del olvido*, Zaragoza, Prensas Universitarias, 2 vols, 1988.

Hughes, Robert, *Barcelona*, New York, Knopf, 1992.

Hugnet, Georges, introduction to *Petite Anthologie poétique du Surréalisme* [edited anonymously by Éluard and Breton], Paris, Éditions Jeanne Bucher, 1934, pp. 7–42.

–*Pleins et déliés. Témoignages et souvenirs, 1926–1972*, La Chapelle-sur-Loire, Guy Authier Éditeur, 1972.

Hurtado, Amadeu, *Quaranta anys d'advocat. Història del meu temps, 1894–1930*, Barcelona, Edicions Ariel, 2nd edn, 1969.

Jackson, Gabriel, *The Spanish Republic and the Civil War*, New Jersey, Princetown University Press, 1965.

James, Edward, *Swans Reflecting Elephants. My Early Years*, edited by George Melly, London, Weidenfeld and Nicolson, 1982.

Janis, Harriet, 'Painting as a Key to Psychoanalysis', *Art and Architecture*, New York, February 1946.

Jardí, Enric, *Eugeni d'Ors*, Barcelona, Aymà, 1967.

Jean, Marcel, with the collaboration of Arpad Mezei, *The History of Surrealist Painting*, translated from the French by Simon Watson Taylor, London, Weidenfeld and Nicolson, 1960.

Jiménez, Xavier and J. Playà i Maset, 'Dalí vist des de l'Empordà', series of fifteen articles published from January to December 1984 in *Hora Nova*, Figueres. Those on which the book draws are listed in order of appearance, as follows: 'Joan Butchacas', no. 348 (24–30 January), p. 9; 'Pere Garriga Camps', no. 353 (28 February–5 March), p. 8; no. 354 (6–12 March), p. 6; no. 356 (20–26 March), p. 8; 'L'amistat amb Ramon Reig' and 'Llúcia Gispert de Montcanut', no. 361 ('Fires de Santa Creu' supplement, May), p. 39; 'El collegi La Salle', no. 365 (29 May–4 June), p. 6; 'Jaume Miravitlles', no. 370 (4–10 July), p. 13.

–'Dalí, el fútbol i la Unió Esportiva Figueres', *Revista de Girona*, Girona, June 1986, pp. 75–82.

Jiménez Fraud, Alberto, *Historia de la universidad española*, Madrid, Alianza, 1971.

Jiménez-Landi, Antonio, *La Institución Libre de Ensenanza y su ambiente. Los orígenes*, Madrid, Taurus, 1973.

Jones, Ernest, *Sigmund Freud*, edited and abridged by Lionel Trilling and Steven Marcus, Harmondsworth, Penguin Books, 1974.

Kaufman, Gershen, *The Psychology of Shame. Theory and Treatment of Shame-Based Syndromes*, London, Routledge, 1993.

Lacan, Jacques, 'Le Problème du style et la conception psychiatrique des formes paranöiaques de l'expérience', *Minotaure*, Paris, no. 1 (1 June 1933), pp. 68–9.

–'Motifs du crime paranoïaque. Le Crime des soeurs Papin', *ibid.*, nos. 3–4 (15 December 1933), pp. 25–8.

–*De la psychose paranoïaque dans ses rapports avec la personnalité*, Paris, Editions du Seuil, 1975.

Lacuey, J., *Torremolinos*, Torremolinos, Batan, 1990.

Lake, Carlton, *In Quest of Dalí* [1969], New York, Paragon House, 1990.

Larraz, Emmanuel, *Le Cinéma espagnol des origines à nos jours*. Preface by Luis García Berlanga, Paris, Les Editions du Cerf, 1986.

Lautréamont, Comte de, pseud. (Isidore Ducasse), *Los cantos de Maldoror par el conde de Lautréamont*. Translation by Julio Gómez de la Serna. Prologue by Ramón Gómez de la Serna, Madrid, Biblioteca Nueva, no date [1921?].

–*Les Chants de Maldoror. Lettres. Poésies I et II*, Paris, Gallimard, 1973.

Lear, Amanda, *Le Dalí d'Amanda*, Paris, Favre, 1984; reprinted, with the addition of two new final pages, as *L'Amant-Dalí. Ma Vie avec Salvador Dalí*, Paris, Michel Lafon, 1994. All references are to the latter edition.

Leiner, Jacqueline, 'Les Chevaliers du Graal au service de Marx', introduction to facsimile edition of *Le Surréalisme au service de la Révolution* (see below, Section 8).

Leonardo da Vinci, *Leonardo on Painting*. Edited by Martin Kemp, New Haven and London, Yale University Press, 1989.

Levy, Julien, *Surrealism*, New York, The Black Sun Press, 1936.

–*Memoir of an Art Gallery*, New York, G. P. Putnam's, 1977.

Lomas, John (ed.), *O'Shea's Guide to Spain and Portugal*, Edinburgh, Adam and Charles Black, 7th edn, 1885.

Lowe, John, *Edward James. A Surrealist Life*, London, Collins, 1991.

Lynd, Helen Merrell, *On Shame and the Search for Identity*, New York, Harcourt, Brace and World, 1958.

Madrid, Francisco, 'El escándalo del "Salón de Otoño" de Barcelona. Salvador Dalí, pintor de vanguardia, dice que todos los artistas actuales están putrefactos', *Estampa*, Madrid, no. 45, 6 November 1928, p. [9].

Malanga, Gerard, 'Explosion of the Swan. Salvador Dalí on Federico García Lorca' [interview with Dalí], *Sparrow 35*, Black Sparrow Press, Santa Rosa, California, August 1975.

Martínez Nadal, Rafael, *Federico García Lorca. Mi penúltimo libro sobre el hombre y el poeta*, Madrid, Editorial Casariego, 1992.

Mason, Rainer Michael, *Dalí verdadero/grabado falso. La obra impresa 1930–1934* (see above, Section 1).

Massip, José María, 'Dalí hoy', *Destino*, Barcelona, no. 660 (1 April 1950), pp. 1, 4–5.

Maur, Karen von, 'Breton et Dalí, à la lumière d'une correspondance inédite', in catalogue *André Breton. La Beauté convulsive*, Paris, Centre Georges Pompidou, 1991 (see above, Section 1), pp. 196–202.

McGirk, Tim, *Wicked Lady: Salvador Dalí's Muse*, London, Hutchinson, 1989.

Minguet Batllori, Joan M., 'Joan Miró en el arte español. Una aproximación cronológica (1918–1983)', in *Ver a Miró* (see above, Section 3), pp. 63–83.

Miravitlles, Jaume, 'Notes a l'entorn de l'art d'avantguarda. Miró-Dalí-Domingo', *La Nova Revista*, Barcelona, no. 24 (December 1928), pp. 318–23.

–*Contra la cultura burguesa*, Barcelona, Edicions 'L'hora', 1931.

–*El ritme de la Revolució*, Barcelona, Edicions 'Documents', 1933.

–'Encuentros en mi vida. Dalí y Buñuel', *Tele/eXpres*, Barcelona, 1 July 1977, p. 2, and 8 July 1977, p. 2.

–'Dalí i l'aritmètica', *Revista de Girona*, Girona, no. 68 (third trimester, 1974), pp. 31–5.

–*Gent que he conegut*, Barcelona, Destino, 1980.

–*Més gent que he conegut*, Barcelona, Destino, 1981.

–'He visto llorar a Gala', *La Vanguardia*, Barcelona, 11 June 1982, p. 6.

–'Una vida con Dalí', in catalogue *400 obras de Salvador Dalí de 1914 a 1983*, 1983 (see above, Section 1), II, pp. 5–9.

Miró, Joan, 'Je rêve d'un grand atelier', *XXe Siècle*, Paris, no. 2 (May–June 1938), pp. 25–8.

Molas, Joaquim, *La literatura catalana d'avantguarda, 1916–1938. Selecció, edició i estudi*, Barcelona, Antoni Bosch, 1983.

Molina, César Antonio, *La revista 'Alfar' y la prensa literaria de la época (1920–1930)*, La Coruña, Ediciones Nos, 1984.

Montero Alonso, José, *Vida de Eduardo Marquina*, Madrid, Editora Nacional, 1965.

Montes, Eugenio, '"Un chien andalou" (Film de Luis Buñuel y Salvador Dalí, estrenado en "Le Studio des Ursulines", Paris)', *La Gaceta Literaria*, Madrid, no. 60 (15 June 1929), p. 1.

Moore, Peter, *Hard Times and Soft Watches*, unpublished memoir.

Moorhouse, Alan, *Dalí*, Wigston (Leicester), Magna Books, 1990.

Moreiro, José María, 'Dalí, en el centro de los recuerdos', *El País Semanal*, Madrid, 23 October 1983, pp. 15–21.

Morelli, Gabriele (ed.), *Trent'anni di avanguardia spagnola. Da Ramón Gómez de la Serna a Juan-Eduardo Cirlot*, Milan, Edizioni Universitarie Jaca, 1987.

Moreno Villa, José, 'Nuevos artistas. Primera exposición de la Sociedad de Artistas Ibéricos', *Revista de Occidente*, Madrid, III, no. xxv (July–August–September 1925), pp. 80–91.

–'La jerga profesional', *El Sol*, Madrid, 12 June 1925, p. 5.

–'La Exposición de "Artistas Ibéricos"', *La Noche*, Barcelona, 12 June 1925, p. 4.

–*Vida en claro*, Mexico, El Colegio de México, 1944.

Morla Lynch, Carlos, *En España con Federico García Lorca*, Madrid, Aguilar, 1958.

Morris, C.B., *Surrealism and Spain. 1920–1936*, Cambridge: Cambridge University Press, 1972.

–*This Loving Darkness. The Cinema and Spanish Writers, 1920–1936*, Oxford: Oxford University Press, 1980.

Morse, Eleanor, 'My View', in Reynolds Morse, *Salvador Dalí . . . A Panorama of his Art* (see below), pp. xxv–xxxvi.

Morse, A. Reynolds, *Dalí. A Study of his Life and Work, with a Special Appreciation by Michel Tapié*, Greenwich, Connecticut, New York Graphic Society, 1958.

–*A New Introduction to Salvador Dalí*, Beachwood, Cleveland, The Reynolds Morse Foundation, 1960. 'Updating supplement', *The Decade 1971–1961* (sic), Beachwood, Cleveland, The Salvador Dali Museum, 1971.

–*A Dalí Primer*, Cleveland, The Reynolds Morse Foundation, 1970.

–*The Draftsmanship of Salvador Dalí*, Cleveland, The Salvador Dali Museum, 1970.

–*Salvador Dalí, Pablo Picasso. A Preliminary Study in their Similarities and Contrasts*, Cleveland, The Salvador Dali Museum, 1973.

–(with Eleanor R. Morse), *The Dalí Adventure. 1943–1973*, Cleveland, The Salvador Dali Museum (1973), expanded edition 1974.

–'Reminiscences and Reassessments', in above, pp. iii–xxiv.

–'Romantic Ampurdan', in above, pp. 205–14.

Murcia, Claude, *Luis Buñuel. Un Chien andalou, L'Age d'or*, Luis Buñuel. Étude critique. Paris, Nathan, 'Synopsis', 1994.

Nadeau, Maurice, *Histoire du surréalisme. II. Documents surréalistes*, Paris, Aux Éditions du Seuil, 1948.

–*The History of Surrealism*, introduction by Roger Shattuck, New York, Collier Books, 1967.

Navarro Arisa, J.J., 'Gala Dalí. Los secretos de una musa', *El País Semanal*, Madrid, no. 182 (14 August 1994), pp. 10–19.

Naville, *Le Temps du surréel. L'Espérance mathématique. Tome I*, Paris, Galilée, 1977.

Nin, Anaïs, *The Diary of Anaïs Nin. Volume Three. 1939–1944*. Edited and with a preface by Gunther

Stuhlmann, New York, Harcourt Brace, 1969.

Olano, Antonio D., *Dalí, secreto*, Barcelona, Círculo de Lectores, 1975.

Oliver Belmás, Antonio, *Este otro Rubén Darío*, Barcelona, Editorial Aedos, 1960.

Oller, Narcís, *La febre d'or* [1890–2], Barcelona, Edicions 62, two vols, 1993.

Ontañón, Santiago and José María Moreiro, *Unos pocos amigos verdaderos*, prologue by Rafael Alberti, Madrid, Fundación Banco Exterior, 1988.

Oriol Anguera, A., *Mentira y verdad de Salvador Dalí*, Barcelona, Cobalto, 1948.

d'Ors, Eugenio, 'El juego lúgubre y el doble juego', *La Gaceta Literaria*, Madrid, no. 72 (15 December 1929), p. 3.

–*La verdadera historia de Lídia de Cadaqués*, illustrations and jacket by Salvador Dalí, Barcelona, José Janés, 1954.

–*La ben plantada, seguida de Galeria de Noucentistes*, prologue by Enric Jardí, Barcelona, Editorial Selecta, 8th edn, 1980.

Orwell, George, 'Benefit of Clergy: Some Notes on Salvador Dalí' [1944], in *The Collected Essays, Journalism and Letters of George Orwell*, vol. III, Harmondsworth, Penguin Books, 1971, pp. 185–95.

Palau i Fabre, Josep, *Picasso i els seus amics catalans*, Barcelona, Aedos, 1971.

Pastoureau, Henri, 'Soirées chez Gala en 1933 et 1934', *Pleine Marge. Cahiers de Littérature, d'arts plastiques et de critique*, Paris, no. 6 (December 1987), pp. 39–43.

Pauwels, Louis and Salvador Dalí, *Les Passions selon Dalí*, Paris, Denoël, 1968.

–*The Passions According to Dalí*, translated by Eleanor Morse, The Salvador Dali Museum, St Petersburg, Florida, 1985.

Pella y Forgas, *Historia del Ampurdán. Estudio de la civilización en las comarcas del noreste de Cataluña*, Barcelona, Luis Tasso y Serra, 1883. Facsimile reprint, Olot, Aubert Impressor, 2nd edn, 1980.

Penrose, Roland, *Picasso: His Life and Work*, London, Gollanz, 1958.

–*80 años de surrealismo, 1900–1981*, Barcelona, Ediciones Polígrafa, 1981.

–*Miró*, London, Thames and Hudson, 'World of Art', 1988.

Péret, Benjamin, *Oeuvres complètes*, five vols, Paris, Association des amis de Benjamin Péret, Eric Losfeld and Librairie José Corti, 1969–89.

Pérez Galán, Mariano, *La enseñanza en la Segunda República Española*, Madrid, Cuadernos para el Diálogo, 2nd edn, 1977.

Pérez Turrent, Tomás and José de la Colina, *Buñuel por Buñuel*, Madrid, Plot, 1993.

Permanyer, Lluís, 'Salvador Dalí, a través del cuestionario "Marcel Proust"', *Destino*, Barcelona, 6 April 1962.

–'Cuando Dalí no era divino ni arcangélico', *La Vanguardia*, Barcelona, 7, 12 April and 5, 6 May 1972.

–'El pincel erótico de Dalí. Reportaje por Lluís Permanyer', *Playboy*, Barcelona, no. 3 (January 1979), pp. 73–4, 160–4.

Pierre, José, 'Breton et Dalí', in Pompidou catalogue, 1979 (see above, Section 1), pp. 131–40.

–'Le Peintre surréaliste par excellence', in catalogue *Yves Tanguy*, Centre Georges Pompidou, Paris, 1982 (see above, Section 1), pp. 42–61.

Piers, Gerhart and Milton B. Singer, *Shame and Guilt. A Psychoanalytic and a Cultural Study*, New York, W.W. Norton, 1971.

Pla, Josep, *Vida de Manolo contada per ell mateix* [1927], in *Tres artistes*, Barcelona, Destino, *Obra completa*, vol. XIV, 2nd edn, 1981, pp. 7–297.

–*Costa Brava. Guía general y verídica*, prologue by Alberto Puig, Barcelona, Destino, 1941.

–[Under pseudonym 'Tristán'], 'Salvador Dalí visto desde Cadaqués', *Destino*, Barcelona, 28 September 1946, pp. 3–5.

–and Salvador Dalí, *Obres de museu*, Figueres, Dasa Ediciones, S.A., 1981.

–'Salvador Dalí (una noticia)', in *Homenots. Quarta sèrie*, Barcelona, Destino, *Obra completa*, vol. XXIX, 2nd edn, 1985, pp. 159–201.

–'Cadaqués', in *Un petit món del Pirineu*, Barcelona, Destino, *Obra completa*, vol. XXVII, 2nd edn, 1981, pp. 7–212.

–'Pa i Raïm' and 'Contraban', in *Contraban i altres narracions*, Barcelona, Edicions 62, 1992.

Playà i Maset, Josep, *Dalí de l'Empordà*, Barcelona, Editorial Labor, 'Terra Nostra', 1992.

–and Victor Fernández, 'Buñuel escribe a Dalí. Dos cartas inéditas del cineasta aclaran aspectos de "Un chien andalou" y de las pugnas intelectuales de los años 20', *La Vanguardia*, Barcelona, 'Cultura y espectáculos', 1 April 1966, p. 25.

Poesía, Madrid, no. 18–19 (1983), número monográfico dedicado a la Residencia de Estudiantes (1910–1936) con motivo de cumplirse el centenario del nacimiento de su director, Alberto Jiménez Fraud (1883–1964) y en el que se da cuenta de su vida y de las actividades que en aquélla se desarrollaron.

Porcel, Baltasar, 'Con Salvador Dalí en su Teatro-Museo bajo la sombra místico-aurífera y el eco de Ramón Gómez de la Serna', 'epilogue' to Gómez de la Serna, *Dalí* (see above), pp. 196–212.

Pritchett, V.S., *Midnight Oil*, Harmondsworth, Penguin Books, 1974.

Puccini, Dario, 'La "Oda a Salvador Dalí" nella storia

poetica de Lorca', in *Il segno del presente. Studi di letteratura spagnola*, Turin, Edizioni dell'Orso, 1992, pp. 89–108.

Puignau, Emili, *Vivencias con Salvador Dalí*. Prologue by Luis Romero, Barcelona, Editorial Juventud, 1995.

Purser, Philip, *Poeted. The Final Quest of Edward James*, London, Quartet Books, 1991.

'Puvis', 'Notes d'art. L'exposició de la Societat de Concerts', *Empordà Federal*, Figueres, no. 414 (11 January 1919), p. 3.

Quiñonero, Juan Pedro, 'Cécile Éluard. El surrealismo llama a la memoria', *Blanco y negro*, Madrid, 20 March 1988, pp. 62–6.

Rahola i Escofet, Gaietà and Josep Rahola i Sastre, *La marina mercant de Cadaqués*, Girona, Editorial Dalmau Carles, Pla, S.A., 1976.

Rahola y Tremols, Federico, *Antiguas comunidades de pescadores de Cabo de Creus*, Barcelona, Imprenta de la Casa Provincial de Caridad, 1904.

Read, Herbert, 'Bosch and Dalí', *The Listener*, London, 14 December 1934.

–(ed.), *Surrealism*. With an introduction by the Editor, and contributions by André Breton, Hugh Sykes Davies, Paul Éluard, and George Hugnet, London, Faber and Faber, 2nd impression, 1937.

Revenga, Luis, 'Imágenes de un enigma: Dalí', in catalogue *400 obras de Salvador Dalí de 1914 a 1983*, 1983 (see above, Section 1), II, pp. 50–61.

Rey, Henri-François, *Dalí en su laberinto. Ensayo comentado por Dalí*, Barcelona, Editorial Euros, 1975.

Richardson, John, *A Life of Picasso. Volume I: 1881–1906*, London, Jonathan Cape, 1991.

–*A Life of Picasso. Volume II: 1907–1917*, London, Jonathan Cape, 1996.

Rivas Cherif, Cipriano, 'El caso de Salvador Dalí', *España*, Madrid, no. 413 (14 March 1924), pp. 6–7.

Rodrigo, Antonina, *García Lorca en Cataluña*, Barcelona, Planeta, 1975.

–*Lorca–Dalí. Una amistad traicionada*, Barcelona, Planeta, 1981.

–*Memoria de Granada: Manuel Angeles Ortiz y Federico García Lorca*, Barcelona, Plaza y Janés, 1984; 2nd edn, Fuente Vaqueros (Granada), Casa–Museo Federico García Lorca, 1984.

–*García Lorca, el amigo de Cataluña*, Barcelona, Edhasa, 1984.

Rodríguez Puértolas, Julio, *Literatura fascista española. I. Historia*, Madrid, Akal, 1986.

Rojas, Carlos, *El mundo mítico y mágico de Salvador Dalí*, Barcelona, Plaza y Janés, 1985.

Romero, Alfons and Joan Ruiz, *Figueres*, Girona, *Quaderns de la Revista de Girona*, no. 34, 1992.

Romero, Luis, *Todo Dalí en un rostro*, Barcelona, Editorial Blume, 1975.

–*Aquel Dalí*, photographs by Josep Postius, Barcelona, Argos Vergara, 1984.

–*Dedálico Dalí*, Barcelona, Ediciones B, 1989.

–*Torero allucinogen*, Barcelona, Editorial Mediterrània, 1990.

–*Psicodálico Dalí*, Barcelona, Editorial Mediterrània, 1991.

Roudinesco, Elisabeth, *Jacques Lacan. Esquisse d'une vie, histoire d'un système de pensée*, Paris, Fayard, 1993.

Roumeguère, Pierre, 'La mística dalíniana ante la historia de las religiones', in Dalí, *Diario de un genio* (Barcelona, Tusquets, 1983), pp. 275–8.

–'The Cosmic Dalí. The "Royal Way" of Access to the Dalinian Universe', preface to *Dalí by Dalí* (see *Dalí par Dalí* above, Section 5), pp. iii–ix.

–'Canibalismo y estética. Del canibalismo paranoico de la gastro-estética hacia una Estética Biológica. La oralidad, vía imperial de acceso al universo dalíniano', preface to Max Gérard, *Dalí . . . Dalí . . . Dalí* (see above).

Rubin, William S., *Dada and Surrealist Art*, New York, Harry N. Abrams, [1968].

Rucar de Buñuel, Jeanne, with Marisol Martín del Campo, *Memorias de una mujer sin piano*, Madrid, Alianza, 1990.

Ruiz-Castillo Basala, José, *El apasionante mundo del libro. Memorias de un editor*, Madrid, Biblioteca Nueva, 1979.

Sade, Marquis de, *Les 120 Journées de Sodome*, preface by Jean-François Revel, Paris, Jean-Jacques Pauvert, 1972.

Sadoul, Georges, *Rencontres (I) Chroniques et entretiens*, Paris, Denoël, 1984.

–Preface to Buñuel, *Viridiana. Scénario et dialogues. Variantes. Dossier historique et critique*, Paris, Pierre Lherminier Éditeur, 'Filméditions', 1984.

Sahuquillo, Angel, *Federico García Lorca y la cultura de la homosexualidad masculina. Lorca, Dalí, Cernuda, Gil-Albert, Prados y la voz silenciada del amor homosexual*, Alicante, Instituto de Cultura 'Juan Gil-Albert' and Diputación de Alicante, 1991.

Sánchez Rodríguez, Alfredo, '1930: Salvador Dalí, a Torremolinos. Come e perché fallisce il progetto di pubblicare a Malaga una rivista del surrealismo spagnolo', in Gabriele Morelli, (ed.), *Trent'anni di avanguardia spagnola* (see above), pp. 165–77.

Sánchez Vidal, Agustín, (ed.), *Luis Buñuel. Obra literaria*, Zaragoza, Ediciones de Heraldo de Aragón, 1982.

–*Luis Buñuel. Obra cinematográfica*, Madrid, Ediciones J.C., 1984.

–*Buñuel, Lorca, Dalí: el enigma sin fin*, Barcelona, Planeta, 1988.

–'La nefasta influencia del García', in Laura Dolfi (ed.), *L'Imposible/posible di Federico García Lorca*, Napoli, Edizione Scientifiche Italiane, 1989, pp. 219–28.

–*El mundo de Luis Buñuel*, Zaragoza, Caja de Ahorros de la Inmaculada, 1993.

–'The Andalusian Beasts', in catalogue *Salvador Dalí: The Early Years* (see above), pp. 193–207.

Santos Torroella, Rafael, *Salvador Dalí*, Madrid, Afrodisio Aguado, 1952.

–'Arte y no arte de Salvador Dalí en su homenaje a Fortuny', *Noticiero Universal*, Barcelona, 17 October 1962. Dalí's rejoinder, 'Dalí no digiere a Dalí', and Santos Torroella's reply, *ibid.*, 24 October 1962. Reproduced in Santos Torroella, *La trágica vida de Salvador Dalí* (see below), pp. 51–8.

–*La miel es más dulce que la sangre. Las épocas lorquiana y freudiana de Salvador Dalí*, Barcelona, Planeta, 1984.

–'Carta abierta a monsieur Robert Descharnes. La exposición de Salvador Dalí en Ferrara', *La Vanguardia*, Barcelona, 2 September 1984, p. 30.

–'Descharnes y el estilo "cárcel de papel"', *ibid.*, Barcelona, 27 September 1984, p. 38.

–'Nuevas puntualizaciones al libro de Robert Descharnes. Dalí fue un modélico alumno de instituto', *ibid.*, 25 October 1984.

–'La ceremonia dalíniana de la confusión', *ibid.*, 6 June 1985, p. 33.

–*Salvador Dalí i el saló de Tardor. Un episodi de la vida artística barcelonina el 1928*, Barcelona, Reial Acadèmia Catalana de Belles Arts de Sant Jordi, 1985.

–'"Las rosas sangrantes" y la imposible descendencia de Dalí', *Abc*, Madrid, 26 November 1987.

–'Giménez Caballero y Dalí: influencias recíprocas y un tema compartido', *Anthropos. Revista de documentación científica de la cultura*, Barcelona, no. 84 (1988), pp. 53–6.

–'Barradas y el *clownismo*. Con Dalí y García Lorca al fondo', en *Barradas*, catálogo, Madrid, Galería Jorge Mara, 1992, pp. 25–33.

–'El extraño caso de "El tiempo amenazador"', *Abc*, Madrid, supplement 'Abc de las artes', 14 August 1992, pp. 32–3.

–*Dalí, residente*, Madrid, Publicaciones de la Residencia de Estudiantes, Consejo de Investigaciones Científicas, 1992.

–'El Reina Sofía se equivoca con Dalí', *Abc*, Madrid, supplement 'Abc de las artes', 2 October 1992, pp. 36–8.

–'La trágica vida de Dalí', *Diario 16*, Madrid, supplement 'Culturas', 25 September 1993, pp. 2–4.

–'The Madrid Years', in *Salvador Dalí: The Early Years*, catalogue (see above, Section 1), pp. 81–9.

–'*Los putrefactos*' de Dalí y Lorca. Historia y antología de un libro que no pudo ser*, Madrid, Residencia de Estudiantes, 1995.

–*Dalí. Época de Madrid. Catálogo razonado*, Madrid, Residencia de Estudiantes, 1994.

–'Salvador Dalí en la primera exposición de la Sociedad de Artistas Ibéricos. Catalogación razonada', in catalogue *La Sociedad de Artistas Ibéricos y el arte español de 1925* (see above, Section 3, pp. 59–66.

–*La trágica vida de Salvador Dalí*, Barcelona, Parsifal, 1995.

Savinio, Alberto, *Nueva enciclopedia*, translated by Jesús Pardo, Barcelona, Seix Barral, 1983.

Sawin, Martica, *Surrealism in Exile and the Beginning of the New York School*, Cambridge, Massachusetts, MIT Press, 1995.

Secrest, Meryle, *Salvador Dalí*, New York, E.P. Dutton, 1986.

Serraclara, Gonzalo, *La nueva inquisición. Proceso del diputado Serraclara y sucesos ocurridos en Barcelona el día 25 setiembre de 1869*, Barcelona, Librería de I. López, 1870.

Shattuck, Roger, *The Banquet Years. The Origins of the Avant Garde in France. 1885 to World War I*, New York, Vintage Books, revised edition, 1968.

Skira, Albert, *Vingt ans d'activité*, Paris, Skira, 1948.

Soby, James, 'Salvador Dalí', in catalogue *Salvador Dalí. Paintings, Drawings, Prints*, New York, Museum of Modern Art, 1941.

Stein, Gertrude, *The Autobiography of Alice B. Toklas* [1933]. London, Penguin Books, 1966.

–*Everybody's Autobiography* [1937], London, Virago, 1985.

Sylvester, David, *Magritte*, London, Thames and Hudson in association with the Menil Foundation, 1992.

Teixidor Elies, P., *Figueres anecdòtica segle XX*, Figueres, patrocinat per l'Excm. Ajuntament', 1978. 'Pòrtic' by Montserrat Vayreda i Trullol.

Terry, Arthur, *Catalan Literature*, London, Ernest Benn, 1972.

Tharrats, Joan Josep, *Cent anys de pintura a Cadaqués*, Barcelona, Ediciones del Cotal, 1981.

–(ed.), *Picasso a Cadaqués*, special issue of *Negre + gris*, Barcelona, no. 10, Autumn 1985.

Thirion, André, *Révolutionnaires sans révolution*, Paris, Le Pré aux Clercs, 1988.

Torre, Guillermo de, *Hélices. Poemas*, Madrid, Editorial Mundo Latino, 1923.

–*Literaturas europeas de vanguardia*, Madrid, Caro Raggio, 1925.

–*Historia de las literaturas de vanguardia*, Madrid, Ediciones Guadarrama, 1965.

Trend, J. B., *A Picture of Modern Spain, Men and Music*, London, Constable, 1921.

–*The Origins of Modern Spain*, Cambridge University Press, 1935.

Ultra Violet, 'Dallying with Dalí', *Exposure*, Los Angeles, October 1990, pp. 56–9.

Utrillo, Miguel, *Salvador Dalí y sus enemigos*, Sitges–Barcelona, Ediciones Maspe, 1952.

Valdivielso Miquel, Emilio, *El drama oculto. Buñuel, Dalí, Falla, García Lorca y Sánchez Mejías*, Madrid, Ediciones de la Torre, 1992.

Valenciano Gayá, L., *El doctor Lafora y su época*, Madrid, Ediciones Morata, 1977.

Valette, Robert D., *Éluard, Livre d'idéntité*, Paris, Tchou, 1967.

Vallés i Rovira, Carles, *Diccionari de l'Alt Empordà* (Històric, geogràfic, biogràfic, gastronòmic, folkòric . . .), Girona, Carles Vallès Editor, 2 vols, 1984–5.

Vayreda, Maria dels Angels, 'Com és Salvador Dalí?', *Revista de Girona*, Fìgueres, no. 68 (1974), pp. 11–14.

Vela, Fernando, 'El suprarealismo', *Revista de Occidente*, Madrid, Vol. VI, no. xviii (December 1924), pp. 428–34.

Vidal i Oliveras, 'Josep Dalmau. El primer marxant de Joan Miró', in catalogue *Miró, Dalmau, Gasch* (see above, Section 3), pp. 49–74.

–*Josep Dalmau. L'aventura per l'art modern*, Manresa, Fundació Caixa de Manresa, 1988.

Videla, Gloria, *El ultraísmo. Estudios sobre movimientos poéticos de vanguardia en España*, Madrid, Editorial Gredos ('Biblioteca romànica hispánica'), 1963.

Vieuille, Chantal, *Gala*, Faver, Lausanne and Paris, 1988.

Vila-San-Juan, F., *Dr. Antonio Puigvert. Mi vida . . . y otras más*, Barcelona, Planeta, 1981.

Waldberg, Patrick, *Surrealism*, London, Thames and Hudson, 1965.

–'Salvador Dalí', in Museum Boymans–van Beuningen, Rotterdam, catalogue, pp. 34–7, 1970 (see Section 1, above).

Wilson, Edmund, 'Salvador Dalí as Novelist', *The New Yorker*, 1 July 1944.

Woolf, Geoffrey, *Black Sun. The Brief Transit and Violent Eclipse of Harry Crosby*, New York, Random House, 1976.

Zerbib, Mónica, 'Salvador Dalí: "Soy demasiado inteligente para dedicarme sólo a la pintura"', *El País*, 'Arte y Pensamiento', 30 July 1978, pp. i, vi.

Zervos, Christian, 'Oeuvres récentes de Picasso', *Cahiers d'Art*, Paris, no. 5 (June 1926), pp. 89–93.

–*Pablo Picasso*, Paris, Editions 'Cahiers d'Art', 1952, vols 5 and 7.

Zweig, Stefan, *El mundo de ayer*, Barcelona, Editorial Juventud, 1968.

7. Television programmes (consulted on video)

1955. Dalí interviewed by Malcolm Muggeridge, BBC, 'Panorama', 4 May 1955.

1966. *Dalí in New York*. BBC. Produced and directed by Jack Bond. Presenter, Jane Arden.

1973. *Hello Dalí!* London Weekend Television, 'Aquarius'. Produced and presented by Russell Harty; directed by Bruce Gowers; edited with introduction by Humphrey Burton.

1979. Three programmes on Dalí in *Imágenes*, RTE (Second Channel), Spain. Written, directed and presented by Paloma Chamorro. Produced by Jesús González. 30 May 1979, 6 June 1979, 13 June 1979.

1984. *La máscara se trasluce*. TVE, Spain, 'Informe Semanal', 30 June 1984.

1984. *The Life and Times of Don Luis Buñuel*. BBC, 'Arena'. Produced by Alan Yentob, directed by Anthony Wall.

1984. *Todos los hombres de Dalí*. TVE, Spain, 16 September 1984 ('El Dominical').

1986. *Dalí*. BBC 'Arena' in association with Demart, 1986. Produced by Adam Low.

1989. *Pintar después de morir*. TVE, Spain, 'Documentos TV', 25 September 1989.

1993. *El Enigma Dalí*. TVE, Spain, 1993. Scripted by Juan Manuel Sáenz, directed by Jordi Lladó. Not shown until 7 August 1994.

8 Facsimile editions of principal literary magazines referred to or quoted

L'Amic de les Arts, Sitges, 1926–9. Sabadell, Editorial Ausa, [1990].

La Gaceta Literaria, Madrid, 1927–32. Three vols, Vaduz/Liechtenstein, Topos Verlag, 1980.

Gallo. Revista de Granada, 1928. Granada, Editorial Comares, 1988.

Littérature, Paris, 1919–21. Paris, Jean-Michel Place, 1978.

Littérature, Paris, Nouvelle Série, 1922–4. Paris, Jean-Michel Place, 1978. *Minotaure*, Paris, 1933–9. Paris, Editions Albert Skira, no date.

Nord–Sud, Paris, 1917–18. Paris, Jean-Michel Place, 1980.

La Révolution Surréaliste, Paris, 1924–9. Paris, Jean-Michel Place, 1975.

Studium, Figueres, 1919. Figueres, Edicions Federals, 1989.

Le Surréalisme au Service de la Révolution, Paris, 1930–33. Paris, Jean-Michel Place, 1976.

391, Barcelona–New York–Zurich–Paris, 1917–24. Paris, Le Terrain Vague, 1960.

Troços [later *Trossos*], Barcelona, 1916–18. Barcelona, Leteradura, 1977.

Ultra, Madrid, 1921–2. Madrid, Visor, 1993.

Verso y prosa, Murcia, 1927–8. Murcia, CHYS, Galería de Arte, 1976.

Numbers in *italics* refer to illustrations.